FROMMER'S

BUDGET TRAVEL GUIDE

ENGLAND '92
ON $50 A DAY

W9-ASD-771

by Darwin Porter
Assisted by Danforth Prince

PRENTICE HALL TRAVEL

NEW YORK • LONDON • TORONTO • SYDNEY • TOKYO • SINGAPORE

FROMMER BOOKS

Published by Prentice Hall General Reference
A division of Simon & Schuster Inc.
15 Columbus Circle
New York, NY 10023

ISBN 0-13-334996-9
ISSN 1042-8399

Design by Robert Bull Design
Maps by Geografix Inc. of New York

Manufactured in the United States of America

FROMMER'S ENGLAND '92 ON $50 A Day
Editor-in-Chief: Marilyn Wood
Senior Editor: Judith de Rubini
Editors: Alice Fellows, Paige Hughes, Ted Stavrou
Assistant Editors: Peter Katucki, Lisa Renaud
Contributing Editors: Sara Hinsey, Eve Novick, Megan Rundlet

CONTENTS

LIST OF MAPS

INVITATION TO THE READERS

In researching this book, I have come across many wonderful establishments, the best of which I have included here. I am sure that many of you will also come across appealing hotels, inns, restaurants, guest houses, shops, and attractions. Please don't keep them to yourself. Share your experiences, especially if you want to comment on places that have been included in this edition that have changed for the worse. You can address your letters to:

Darwin Porter
Frommer's England on $50 a Day
Prentice Hall Travel
15 Columbus Circle
New York, NY 10023

A DISCLAIMER

Readers are advised that prices fluctuate in the course of time and travel information changes under the impact of the varied and volatile factors that affect the travel industry. Neither the author nor the publisher can be held responsible for the experiences of readers while traveling. Readers are invited to write to the publisher with ideas, comments, and suggestions for future editions.

SAFETY ADVISORY

Whenever you're traveling in an unfamiliar city or country, stay alert. Be aware of your immediate surroundings. Wear a moneybelt and keep a close eye on your possessions. Be particularly careful with cameras, purses, and wallets, all favorite targets of thieves and pickpockets.

CHAPTER 1

GETTING TO KNOW ENGLAND

Hundreds of millions of people around the world can trace their ancestry back to England, Scotland, or Wales. In ever-growing numbers they come to visit the land of their forebears.

What's the big attraction?

England is not a big country—it's almost exactly the same size as New York State—but 2,500 years of eventful history have left their mark on its rich texture. Today it has moved far from the prim-and-proper Puritanism of the mid-17th century, and is an exciting land of change and experiment.

Why go to England? Many of the greatest writers of the world have placed this little country at or near the top of the list of places to savor and explore in a lifetime. Some of the world's greatest Anglophiles have no ancestral link to England at all, but they are inspired and ensnared by its cultural, historical, and spiritual heritage. Traveling in England is like experiencing a living, illustrated history book. You can ponder the ancient mystery of Stonehenge, relive the days of Roman Britain when you walk through an excavated villa, and hear the linguistic influence of Celtic, Norse, and Norman as well as Anglo-Saxon in words and place names.

It's a formidable task to condense the best of England between the covers of a guide. The best—not only hotels, restaurants, pubs, and nightspots, but also cities, towns, and sightseeing attractions—doesn't have to be the most expensive. Hence, my ultimate aim, after familiarizing you with the life of merrie old England, is to stretch your buying power, to show you that you need not always pay top dollar for charm, top-grade comfort, and food.

A lot of attention is devoted to the tourist meccas of London, Stratford-upon-Avon and Oxford. But these ancient cities and towns do not come close to reflecting fully the complexity and diversity of the country. England defies a clear, logical, coherent plan of sightseeing. It's a patchwork quilt of treasures, with many of the most scenic items tucked away in remote corners—an Elizabethan country estate in Devon, a half-timbered thatched cottage by the sea in Dorset, a Regency manor in the Lake District.

Try to arrive with as few preconceptions about the English as possible; generalizing about their national character is fraught with hazards. Suffice it to say, they'll surprise you—particularly if you think of the English as a cold, snobbish, withdrawn people. A few visits to the haunts of Soho, or to a local pub for a "lager and lime," or even a look at the racy London tabloids, will cure you of stereotypes.

1. GEOGRAPHY, HISTORY & POLITICS

GEOGRAPHY

England is a part of the British Isles, which lie in the Atlantic, separated from the European continent by the Channel and the North Sea.

The name United Kingdom refers to the political entity of England, Wales, Scotland, and Northern Ireland. Only 50,327 square miles, roughly comparable in size to New York State, England has an amazing amount of rural land and natural wilderness (easily observed from an airplane) and an astonishing regional physical and cultural diversity. The Pennine mountain chain is the backbone of the island splitting the country in two with Lancashire on the west of the divide and Yorkshire on the east; other highland areas include the Cumbrian mountains (in the region better known as the Lake District) with the country's highest peak, Scafell Pike, at 3,210 feet. Several rivers empty into either the North Sea or the Irish Sea, like the Tyne at Newcastle and the Mersey at Liverpool, but the most famous of all is, of course, the 209-mile Thames, which empties into the Channel 20 miles downstream from London Bridge.

THE REGIONS IN BRIEF

The Cotswolds   A ridge of limestone hills about a 2-hour drive west of London, dotted with honey-colored stone villages with such names as Stow-on-the-Wold and Moreton-in-Marsh. The most visited is Broadway.

East Anglia   A region of fens and salt marshes, similar to the Netherlands, this is the name given to the semicircular bulge northeast of London composed of four very flat counties: Essex, Cambridge, Norfolk, and Suffolk. Primary attraction is Cambridge University, followed by the cathedral at Ely, the recreational boating centers on the Norfolk Broads and the landscape, made familiar by John Constable, which features also enchanting villages like Thaxted and Dedham.

East Midlands   Primarily an industrial area consisting of Derbyshire, Leicestershire, Lincolnshire, Northamptonshire, and Nottinghamshire, it also has much to interest the visitor including several great houses like Chatsworth in Derbyshire, the seat of the dukes of Devonshire; Sulgrave Manor, the ancestral home of George Washington; and Althorp House, the childhood home of the Princess of Wales, both in Northamptonshire. In Lincoln there's the old seaport town of Boston and the great cathedral at Lincoln, while Nottingham is famous for Robin Hood and Sherwood Forest.

The Midlands & Heart of England   The Midlands consists of the Potteries in Staffordshire with Birmingham as its industrial center. Neighboring Warwickshire and Worcestershire include Stratford-upon-Avon, Warwick, and Coventry. Herefordshire and Shropshire border the Welsh Marches.

Northwest England   From Liverpool to the Scottish border the Northwest includes the Lake District, where Shelley, Keats, Wordsworth, and Coleridge composed many of their great poems. Lake Windermere is the largest lake in England, but there are several others surrounded by magnificent peaks and hiking country. The region's most-visited cities are Chester, which has some fine medieval buildings, and Liverpool.

Hampshire & Wiltshire   These two counties southwest of London possess two of England's greatest cathedrals—Salisbury and Winchester. Stonehenge on the Wiltshire Downs is another compelling attraction.

The Southeast   Kent, Surrey, and the Sussexes are easily explored from London, and contain such major attractions as Brighton, Canterbury, and Dover, as

ENGLAND

SCOTLAND

Glasgow
Edinburgh

NORTH SEA

Newcastle upon Tyne
Sunderland

IRELAND

Dublin

Carlisle

Solway Firth

Middlesbrough

Scarborough

Isle of Man

Barrow

IRISH SEA

Blackpool
Preston
Bradford Leeds
York

Liverpool Bay
Liverpool
Manchester
Sheffield
Grimsby

Chester
Stoke-on-Trent
Lincoln

The Wash

St. George's Channel

Derby
Nottingham

WALES

Shrewsbury
Stafford
Leicester

Norwich

Wolverhampton
Walsall
Great Yarmouth

Birmingham
Coventry
Ely
Aldeburgh

Warwick
Northampton
Cambridge
Ipswich

Worcester
Stratford-upon-Avon
Bedford

Hereford
Cheltenham
Chipping Norton

Woodstock
Oxford
Hertford

Buckingham
Dedham

Swansea
Cardiff

LONDON
Benfleet
Rochester

Bristol
Bath
Camberley
Croydon
Canterbury

Bristol Channel
Guildford
Maidstone

Salisbury
Winchester
Royal
TunBridge
Wells
Dover

Exmoor Nat'l Park
Taunton
Southampton
Brighton

Exeter
Bournemouth
Portsmouth
Hastings
Eastbourne

Strait of Dover

Isle of Wight

Looe
Torbay
Weymouth Bay

Penzance
Plymouth

The Lizard Peninsula

E n g l i s h   C h a n n e l

FRANCE

IMPRESSIONS

Rule Britannia! rule the waves; Britons never will be slaves.
—JAMES THOMPSON, *MASQUE OF ALFRED*, 1740

---

well as such famous country homes and castles as Hever Castle and Leeds Castle. Rye and Winchelsea are two medieval seaport towns. The former attracted many famous folks, including Charles Lamb and Henry James.

The Southwest These four counties—Dorset, Somerset, Devon, and Cornwall—are the great vacation centers and retirement havens of England. Dorset, associated with Thomas Hardy, is a land of rolling downs, rocky headlands, well-kept villages, and rich farmlands. Somerset is associated with King Arthur and Camelot and such magical towns as Glastonbury. Devon has both Exmoor and Dartmoor and northern and southern coastlines with such famous resorts as Lyme Regis and such villages as Clovelly. In Cornwall you're never more than 20 miles from the rugged coastline, which ends at Land's End. Among the cities worth visiting in these counties are Bath, with its impressive Roman baths and Georgian architecture, Plymouth, departure point of the *Mayflower,* and Wells, site of a great cathedral.

The Thames Valley The Thames has influenced much of England's history and its banks are lined with such historical landmarks as Runnymede, where King John signed the *Magna Carta,* Windsor Castle, Eton, and Oxford, all within easy reach of London.

Yorkshire & Northumbria The first of these counties will be familiar to the readers of works by the Brontës (*Wuthering Heights* especially) and James Herriot. York with its immense cathedral is the most visited city. Northumbria consists of Northumberland, Cleveland, Durham, and Tyne and Wear (the area around Newcastle upon Tyne). Durham is famous for its Romanesque cathedral, while the whole area echoes with the ancient border battles between the Scots and the English. Hadrian's Wall is a definite highlight.

HISTORY

Britain was probably split off from the continent of Europe some eight millennia ago, by continental drift and other natural forces. Even after the split, some brave souls on the mainland made their way across the often turbulent Channel.

The earliest known inhabitants of the British Isles were the small, dark people known as Iberians (related to the early people of Spain, Portugal, and Sicily), also called Pre-Celts. These people are believed to have created Stonehenge before the massive invasions of iron-wielding, blond, often blue-eyed Celts around 500 B.C. The Iberians were driven back to the Scottish Highlands and Welsh mountains, where some of their descendants continue to live today.

In 54 B.C. Julius Caesar invaded. He wanted to eliminate a refuge for rebellious Gauls and also to investigate reports of precious metals, particularly tin. The Britons resisted, but lacking leadership and war experience they lost all of the southern part of the island to the Romans, from the Cheviot Hills in Scotland to the English Channel.

During almost four centuries of occupation, the Romans built roads, villas, towns, walls, and fortresses,

DATELINE

- **54 B.C.** Julius Caesar invades England.
- **43 A.D.** Romans conquer England.
- **410** Jutes, Angles, and Saxons form small kingdoms in England.
- **500–1066** Anglo-Saxon kingdoms fight off Viking warriors.
- **1066** William, duke of Normandy, invades England, defeats Harold at the Battle of Hastings.
- **1154** Henry II, first of the

(continues)

farmed the land, and introduced first their pagan religions and then Christianity. Agriculture and trade flourished.

After the withdrawal of Roman legions around A.D. 410, waves of Jutes, Angles, and Saxons flooded in, establishing themselves in small "kingdoms" throughout the formerly Roman colony. From the 8th through the 11th centuries, they contended with Danish raiders for control of the land.

In 1066 William the Conqueror invaded from Normandy and defeated and slew Harold, the last Anglo-Saxon king, at the Battle of Hastings. The Norman rulers were on the throne from 1066 to 1154, when the first of the Plantagenets, Henry II, was crowned. That line held power until 1399. A notable date here is 1215, when King John was forced by his nobles to sign the *Magna Carta* at Runnymede, guaranteeing certain rights to his subjects and the rule of law, beginning a process that led eventually to the development of parliamentary democracy.

In 1337 the Hundred Years' War began, impoverishing both England and France. A long period of civil strife ended at the battle of Bosworth Field with the victory of the first Tudor, Henry VII, who pacified the country and laid the foundations of a strong central monarchy. His work was continued by his son, Henry VIII, and his granddaughter Elizabeth I. Under the Tudors England moved rapidly out of the Middle Ages. The Church of England established its independence from Rome. The country's wealth increased and its power, especially naval power, too. The New Learning of the Renaissance that spread from Italy stimulated a cultural movement that culminated in the works of Spenser, Bacon, and Shakespeare. In 1588 the Spanish Armada was defeated and English power firmly established.

The Stuarts ascended the throne in 1603 and held it, except for the 17-year interlude of Oliver Cromwell's Protectorate, through a century of civil war and religious dissension. The Puritans and other Dissenters, many of whom were in Parliament, began agitating for more power, and in 1629 Charles I dissolved Parliament, determined to rule the kingdom without it. Civil War followed. From 1642 to 1649 the Cavaliers and Roundheads (the Royalists and Parliamentarians) fought until the Parliamentarians triumphed and Charles I was executed in 1649. Cromwell became Lord Protector in 1653, establishing England's first and only dictatorship, which lasted until Charles II was restored in 1660. It was the beginning of a dreadful decade that saw London decimated by the Great Plague and destroyed by the Great Fire. The last male Stuart, James II, who tried to return the country to Roman Catholicism, was deposed in the "Glorious Revolution" of 1688, and succeeded by his daughter Mary and her husband William of Orange, thus securing the Protestant succession which has continued to this day. These tolerant and levelheaded monarchs signed a Bill of Rights, establishing the principle that the monarch reigned by the will of Parliament, not by divine right from God.

When Queen Anne, last of the Stuarts, died childless a Protestant, George I of Hanover was invited to ascend the

DATELINE

Plantagenets, launches their rule (until 1399).

- **1215** King John signs the *Magna Carta* at Runnymede.

- **1337** Hundred Years' War between France and England begins.

- **1485** Battle of Bosworth Field ends War of Roses between the Houses of York and Lancaster. Henry VII launches Tudor dynasty.

- **1509** Henry VIII brings the Reformation to England and dissolves monasteries.

- **1558** The accession of Elizabeth I ushers in an era of exploration and a renaissance in science and learning.

- **1588** Spanish Armada defeated.

- **1603** James VI of Scotland becomes James I of England, uniting the crowns of England and Scotland.

- **1620** Pilgrims sail from Plymouth on *Mayflower* to found colony in the New World.

- **1629** Charles I dissolves Parliament, ruling alone.

- **1642–49** Civil War between Royalists and Parliamentarians. The Parliamentarians win.

- **1649** Charles I beheaded, and England is a republic.

(continues)

DATELINE

- **1653** Oliver Cromwell becomes Lord Protector.
- **1660** Charles II restored to the throne with limited power.
- **1665–66** Great Plague and Great Fire decimate London.
- **1688** James II, a Catholic, is deposed, and William and Mary come to the throne, signing a Bill of Rights.
- **1727** The first of the Hanoverians, George I, assumes the throne.
- **1756–63** In the Seven Years' War, Britain wins Canada from the French.
- **1775–83** Britain loses its American colonies.
- **1795–1815** The Napoleonic wars lead finally to the 1815 Battle of Waterloo and the defeat of Napoléon.
- **1837** Queen Victoria begins reign as Britain reaches the zenith of its empire.
- **1901** Victoria dies, and Edward VII becomes king.
- **1914–18** England enters World War I and emerges victorious on Allied side.
- **1936** Edward VIII abdicates throne to marry an American divorcée.
- **1939–45** Bri-

(continues)

throne in 1727, the first in this 110-year dynasty. Under the Hanoverians the British empire was extended: Canada was won from the French in the Seven Years' War (1756–63); British control over India was affirmed and expanded; Captain Cook claimed Australia and New Zealand for England. The American colonies, though, were lost and the British became embroiled in the Napoleonic Wars (1795–1815), achieving two of their greatest victories, Trafalgar by Admiral Lord Nelson and Waterloo by the Duke of Wellington.

Perhaps the single most important development from the mid- to late 18th century was the Industrial Revolution, which changed the lives of the laboring class, created a wealthy middle class, and changed England from a rural, agricultural society to an urban, industrial economy.

During the reign of Queen Victoria, which began in 1837, the first trade unions were formed, a public school system was developed, and the railroads were built. Benjamin Disraeli induced Parliament to declare Victoria Empress of India. When Edward VII succeeded to the throne in 1901, the country entered the 20th century at the height of its imperial power, while at home the advent of the motorcar and the telephone radically changed social life.

Edward's son, George V, ascended the throne in 1910, and led the nation through World War I. His oldest son, Edward VIII, abdicated before his coronation to marry the American divorcée, Wallis Simpson (he became the duke of Windsor). George VI became king.

Queen Elizabeth II came to the throne on the death of her father in 1952. Since then, Britain has joined the NATO alliance and the Common Market, albeit somewhat reluctantly.

In 1939, World War II was declared and Britain's inspiring leader Winston Churchill, son of an American mother, led the nation during its "finest hour." The Blitz, the Battle of Britain, the Dunkirk evacuation in 1940, and the D-Day invasion of German-occupied France are still remembered by many, and are recorded in many documentaries and books.

After World War II, when Labour came into power in 1945, the welfare state was established and the empire was dismantled. During the 50s and 60s power seesawed back and forth from Conservative to Labour until Margaret Thatcher was elected in 1979. Her popularity soared as the economy revived and was at its zenith during the Falklands War. Afterwards it declined, especially after the introduction of the poll tax. Eventually, the party forced her from the leadership and John Major replaced her as prime minister in 1990.

POLITICS

The United Kingdom of Great Britain and Northern Ireland comprises England, Wales, Scotland, and Northern Ireland. It is a constitutional monarchy, the present head of state being Queen Elizabeth II. The head of government, however, is the prime minister, selected by the majority party in Parliament and then requested by the queen to form a government, in other words, to take charge and name cabinet members to head the various branches of government.

Parliament consists of the House of Lords and the House of Commons. The government consists of the prime minister and the cabinet members (who must be members of Parliament). The sovereign is Commander-in-Chief, but is "above politics," playing a ceremonial role only. There are two main political parties, Conservative and Labour. The Conservatives, currently led by John Major, believe in free enterprise, private ownership, and membership in the European Community. Labour believes in public ownership of important industries, with a maximum support structure for the individual. The Liberals and the Social Democrat party have joined in an uneasy alliance to form the middle-of-the-road Social Democratic and Liberal party.

2. ENGLAND'S FAMOUS PEOPLE

Baden-Powell, Robert Stephenson Smyth (1st baron Baden-Powell) (1857–1941) A hero of the battle of Mafeking against the Boers, he is most famous for establishing, in 1908, the Boy Scouts. Two years later his sister, Agnes, established the Girl Guides (precursor to the Girl Scouts) in 1910.

Beardsley, Aubrey Vincent (1872–98) A master of art nouveau, his romantically evocative illustrations were rediscovered during the 1960s and 1970s. Two of his most famous commissions were illustrations for Alexander Pope's *The Rape of the Lock* and Oscar Wilde's *Salome*.

Beaton, Cecil (1904–80) One of the most famous English designers, and photographers of his era. Everyone (yes, everyone) who mattered in the 1940s, 50s, and 60s was photographed by him, including Wallis Warfield Simpson who designated him as the "official photographer" at her notorious wedding in France in 1936. American audiences knew him best for the sets he created for the New York City Ballet, and for the costumes he designed for the Broadway production of *My Fair Lady*.

Beecham, Sir Thomas (1879–1961) The most famous English conductor of his era, heir to a fortune his father had earned marketing a health remedy known as "Beecham's Pills," he was instrumental in introducing London audiences to Russian ballets, Richard Strauss's operas, and scores of musical works never before heard in England.

Besant, Annie (1847–1933) Popular opinion differed as to whether she was a harmless eccentric or a dangerous revolutionary. Co-editor (with Charles Bradlaugh) of the radical *National Reformer,* she was one of the best-known social reformers and occultists of her day. An advocate of both birth control and free speech, she promoted incendiary laborite and socialist causes.

Blake, William (1757–1827) Artist, illustrator, and mystical poet, he received critical acclaim for his illustrations of *The Book of Job,* Dante's *Divine*

DATELINE

tain stands alone against Hitler until America enters the war in 1941. Dunkirk is evacuated in 1940, as Blitz bombs rain down on London.

- **1945** Churchill is defeated; Labour Government introduces the Welfare State and dismantles Empire.
- **1952** Queen Elizabeth II comes to the throne.
- **1973** Britain joins the EC.
- **1979** Margaret Thatcher becomes prime minister.
- **1982** Britain, led by Thatcher, defeats Argentines in Falklands War.
- **1990** Thatcher is ousted. John Major appointed prime minister.
- **1991** Britain fights with Allies to defeat Iraq.

Comedy, and Milton's *Paradise Lost.* He is considered one of his era's most evocative catalysts of the exaltation of Spirituality through Art, using a complex religious symbolism which almost explodes from his illustrations and poetry.

Bligh, Capt. William (1754–1817) Sailor and sea captain, and inspiration for novels and film versions of *Mutiny on the Bounty.* When not inspiring rebellion at the hands of his sailors, being cast adrift into lifeboats in the midst of the Pacific Ocean, or acting as governor of New South Wales, Captain Bligh maintained a residence for almost 19 years in London's Lambeth Road.

Booth, Gen. William (1829–1912) Minister and social worker, he founded (in 1878) the Salvation Army in the East End of London. Much of his career was spent traveling to the United States, Australia, and India evangelizing the poor and sinful to the comforts and protection of basic Christian fellowship.

Britten, Benjamin (1st Lord) (1913–76) Son of a father who was a dentist and a mother who was an amateur musician, Britten became one of Britain's best-known composers with such works as *Billy Budd* and *Death in Venice.*

Brontë, Emily (1818–48) English novelist and poet, author of *Wuthering Heights,* and creator of Heathcliff as vividly depicted by Laurence Olivier in the film. Although Emily's novel in its day didn't sell as well as that of her sister's (Charlotte Brontë's *Jane Eyre*), *Wuthering Heights* is now listed among world masterpieces.

Brummel, George Bryan ("Beau") (1778–1840) Supreme arbiter of fashion in Regency England, and a fearsome (if foppish) wit, his whims, dress code, and values influenced the definition of social prestige in early 19th-century London. Inheriting a vast fortune in 1799, he was eventually ruined by gambling and by his many enemies. He died a pauper in a French asylum.

Byron, Lord George Noel Gordon (1788–1824) Romantic poet, Byron was born in London to ne'er-do-well parents, and inherited a title and a modest fortune from his titled uncle. After a brief and disastrous marriage to Annabella Milbanke in 1815, Byron left London in 1816 and never returned, dying of fever in Greece.

Cartland, Barbara (1899–) Queen of the romance novel 90-year-old Barbara Cartland has sold five hundred million books. She dictated many of them with a white Pekingese, Twi-Twi, lying at her feet as she stretched out on a gold upholstered couch.

Chippendale, Thomas (1718–79) The most famous cabinetmaker in English history. Original highboys, lowboys, tables, and chairs bearing his signature today command pricetags in the millions.

Churchill, Sir Winston (1874–1965) British statesman who became prime minister in 1940, led his beloved country during World War II rallying the people with his oratory when England stood alone against Hitler (1940–41). A prolific writer, he was knighted in 1953, the same year he received the Nobel Prize for literature. An Act of Congress in 1961 made him an honorary citizen of the United States.

Constable, John (1776–1837) Landscape artist whose works are considered the cream of dozens of English collections. His *View on the Stour* (1819) and his *Hay Wain* (1820) won Gold Medals at the Paris Salon of 1824 and now hang in London's National Gallery.

Coward, Noël (1899–1973) An international wit, and a captivating gossip, this London-born prodigy wrote and produced such famous plays as *Private Lives.*

IMPRESSIONS

England is a prison for men, a paradise for women, a purgatory for servants, a hell for horses.
—THOMAS FULLER, *HOLY STATE,* 1642 (QUOTED AS A PROVERB.)

His memorial stone, set into the floor of Westminster Abbey, is inscribed simply "a talent to amuse."

Disraeli, Benjamin (1st earl of Beaconsfield) (1804–81) In 1837, he was elected a member of Parliament, having already authored five novels. As Prime Minister of the Tory party, his greatest diplomatic victory was the securing of the Suez Canal for Britain in 1875, a route which cut the transit time to India almost in half.

Elgar, Sir Edward (1857–1934) Favorite composer of Victoria's son, King Edward VII, for whose coronation in 1902 he composed two of his *Pomp and Circumstance* marches. Many of his compositions reflected the power and majesty of the British Empire and are invariably played at commencement exercises today at universities around the English-speaking world.

Fleming, Ian Lancaster (1908–64) Son of a Member of Parliament, and descended from a prosperous family of bankers, Ian Fleming joined the staff of Reuters and, from Moscow, covered the trials of alleged British spies during the height of the Cold War. He wrote the first of the "007" books (*Casino Royale*) in two months. Naming his fictional hero (cool-headed, suave, dashing, oversexed, and rich) after the author (James Bond) of a standard ornithological reference to birdwatching in Britain, Ian Fleming started an international industry.

Garrick, David (1717–79) The most famous actor of his era, and honored for his craft with burial in the "Poet's Corner" of Westminster Abbey, he was the first important actor to interpret the characters of Shakespeare in a way that revitalized the interest of the British theatergoing public. His interpretations of Lear, Hamlet, and Macbeth (usually performed in the Drury Lane Theatre) were among the most famous ever portrayed.

Gibbons, Grinling (1680–1720) The most famous of the hundreds of brilliant wood-carvers employed by Sir Christopher Wren during the reconstruction of London after the Great Fire. The delicacy of Gibbon's designs have become legendary, especially of flowers, carved into wooden panels, so realistic that they seem to sway in the breeze.

Gladstone, William Ewart (1809–98) Liberal British politician, and endless source of fretfulness for his monarch, Victoria, with whom he served contemporaneously for four terms as prime minister. A superb orator, he dominated the British Liberal Party between 1868 and 1894.

Hardy, Thomas (1840–1928) Forever associated with Dorset, his beloved county, Hardy, poet and novelist, has been called "the last of the Victorians." After the moral and critical hostility aroused by *Jude the Obscure* and *Tess of the d'Urbervilles*, he turned to poetry and drama, never again producing another novel.

Hogarth, William (1697–1764) Painter and engraver, Hogarth's works satirized the social customs, hierarchies, and foibles of his era. His series of paintings, *The Rake's Progress*, and *Marriage à la Mode*, are considered among the greatest British artistic works.

Hoyle, Edmond (1672–1769) An expert on gaming, he was the author of *Hoyle's Games* (1746) which reached an avid audience of dilettantes and gamblers during the Regency period. Hoyle's authority on the rules of cards and gambling is the standard throughout the world.

IMPRESSIONS

Let not England forget her precedence of teaching nations how to live.
—JOHN MILTON, *THE DOCTRINE AND DISCIPLINE OF DIVORCE*, PREFACE, 1644

England is a good land, and a bad people. This is a French proverb.
—THOMAS FULLER, *THE HISTORY OF THE WORTHIES OF ENGLAND*, 1662

Keynes, John Maynard (1883–1946) Considered the most brilliant economist of the 20th century, largely because of *The Economic Consequences of the Peace (1919)*. He helped stimulate economic aid as a way of reviving the world economy after the Great Depression.

Langtry, Lillie (b. Emily Charlotte Le Brêton) (1852–1929) The greatest English beauty of her era, she rose to fame through the English stage and her discreet affairs with prominent men. Her greatest fame came as the publicly acknowledged mistress of the son of Queen Victoria (later king of England), Edward VII. Born on the Channel isle of Jersey (and known variously as "The Lily of Jersey" or "Jersey Lillie"), she reigned as one of the most famous arbiters of taste of her era from her town house near London's Cadogan Square.

Maugham, William Somerset (1874–1965) Author of novels, short stories, plays, and—later in his life—essays on writing. His most famous works include *Of Human Bondage, The Circle,* and *The Constant Wife.*

Milton, John (1608–74) This poet and prose writer, after losing his sight, composed what is considered the greatest epic poem in the English language, *Paradise Lost.* Other works include *Lycidas,* several dozen sonnets in the Italian style, and many different tracts supporting more liberal education and more realistic divorce laws.

Purcell, Henry (1659–95) Organist at Westminster Abbey from 1679 until shortly before his death, he is considered the greatest English composer prior to the late 19th century.

Queensberry, marquess of [John Sholto Douglas] (1844–1900) English aristocrat who formulated in 1865 the official rules of boxing and prize fighting. More famous, and far more notorious, was the libel suit brought against him by Oscar Wilde (which led to Wilde's eventual imprisonment for homosexuality).

Reynolds, Sir Joshua (1723–92) The most famous portrait painter in the history of English painting, Reynolds created works that included *The Strawberry Girl* and *Age of Innocence.*

Sullivan, Sir Arthur Seymour (1842–1900) Composer of comic operas, worked with librettist W. S. Gilbert. Enormously popular throughout the English-speaking world, Gilbert and Sullivan operettas included *The Mikado, Pirates of Penzance,* and *H.M.S. Pinafore.* In a distinctly different style, he also wrote one of the most famous hymns of the Anglican Church, "Onward, Christian Soldiers." His obituary in the *Times* read, "The death of Sir Arthur Sullivan . . . may be said without hyperbole, to have plunged the whole of the Empire in gloom . . ."

Waugh, Evelyn Arthur St. John (1903–66) This London-born author was a master of pessimistic and savage satire, often aimed at the pretensions of the English aristocracy, the institution of war, and the funeral business in America. Famous works include *Brideshead Revisited* and *The Loved One.*

Wesley, John (1703–91) After an involvement in a "romantic misunderstanding" during a brief sojourn in the American colony of Georgia, he returned to London where he experienced an evangelical conversion on May 24, 1738. Using London as his base, he traveled frequently, delivered as many as 40,000 sermons, established the Methodist branch of Protestantism, and wrote several works on grammar and history.

Woolf, Virginia (1882–1941) Novelist, essayist, and "literary priestess," she was the founder of the Hogarth Press, and at the center of the brilliant group of intellectuals who formed the Bloomsbury Group. Her novels, which rely on the stream of consciousness, were extremely innovative and include *To the Lighthouse, Jacob's Room,* and *Orlando.* She was a supreme essayist, too, as proved by *The Common Reader.* She died by drowning herself.

Wren, Sir Christopher (1632–1723) Known for his masterly plans to rebuild London after the Great Fire of 1666, he is the most famous architect and designer in English history. The appearance of London today (including the design of St. Paul's Cathedral, Buckingham Palace, Marlborough House, and dozens of London churches) is a direct result of his influence. He was buried in the crypt of what is generally believed to be his finest creation, St. Paul's Cathedral.

3. ART, ARCHITECTURE, LITERATURE & MUSIC

ART

Any discussion of English art in this book obviously has to be brief and omit much. There are many Pre-Roman and Roman remains to visit like Stonehenge, Avebury Circle, and Bath, to name only a few. Art from the medieval period consists mainly of religious objects—intricately wrought crosses, religious statuary, and illuminated manuscripts. Ornate tombs with sculptured effigies marked the resting places of the nobility and the princes of the church of the Middle Ages, and the cathedrals became art galleries of awesome beauty. Little has survived from this period.

During the later Gothic period glorious stained-glass windows, religious paintings, and other church-related art became the primary art forms, and much can be seen at such cathedrals as Salisbury, Winchester, and Canterbury. Inevitably, such ornamentation overflowed into secular life as well.

During the Renaissance the primary secular painting was portraiture, as executed by the great Hans Holbein the Younger, a Swiss-born artist who became court painter to Henry VIII. The great miniaturist Nicholas Hilliard and his pupil Isaac Oliver rendered similar service to Queen Elizabeth I. Among the outstanding painters of the Stuart period, neither Van Dyck nor Lely was English-born.

Native English painters came into their own by the 18th century. Among the great portrait artists of the period were Gainsborough and Reynolds, and they were supplemented by such remarkable social satirists as Hogarth, and such great landscape artists as Constable and Turner. The Royal Academy of Arts was formed in 1768 and it still flourishes in Piccadilly, though considered rather stuffy by many.

Among 19th-century English painters great names include the multitalented William Blake and Pre-Raphaelites Sir Edward Burne-Jones, Dante Gabriel Rossetti, and Augustus John. Many of their works can be seen in the Tate Gallery, along with such famous 20th-century painters as Ben Nicholson, Francis Bacon, and Graham Sutherland.

Early British sculpture was mostly commissioned by the Church. The religious conflicts of the 16th and 17th centuries temporarily ended the lavish ornamentation of churches, but in the late 17th and early 18th centuries, sculpture came back into vogue, producing such artists as Grinling Gibbons. In the 20th century sculpture became a serious competitor to painting in England when Henry Moore, Barbara Hepworth, Sir Jacob Epstein, and Kenneth Armitage all came to the fore.

ARCHITECTURE

The most stirring examples of early English architecture are the Pre-Celtic religious sites like Stonehenge; a few well-preserved Roman sites like Bath; a handful of Saxon churches; several Norman castles, the most famous being the White Tower at the Tower of London; and the great Romanesque cathedrals, like those at Durham, Norwich, and Ely.

In England the great Gothic period is usually divided into three periods spanning from the late 12th to the mid-16th century: Early English, Decorated, and Perpendicular, each more lavishly ornamented than the previous period. The finest example of the first is Salisbury Cathedral, closely followed by Wells and Lichfield cathedrals and the abbeys of Glastonbury and Fountains; of the second, the facades at Exeter cathedral and York Minster and the Angel Choir at Lincoln Cathedral; of the last, the great chapels at Eton, King's College, Cambridge, and St. George's at Windsor. Hampton Court Palace and Bath Abbey are outstanding examples of Tudor Gothic. Other fine examples of 15th- and 16th-century architecture include Penshurst Place in Kent and such timber-frame buildings as the Guildhall at Lavenham and the Feathers Inn in Ludlow, Shropshire.

The Renaissance came late to England and, rather than following the Italian manner, tended to imitate the more Mannerist approach found in Germany and the Low Countries, using Flemish gabling and brickwork. The wealthy wool and other merchants built lavish mansions like Longleat House in Wiltshire and Hardwick Hall in Derbyshire. The Jacobean period in the early 17th century produced highly decorative domestic architecture like that of Hatfield House in Hertfordshire. It was Inigo Jones (1573–1652) who brought the formal classicism of the Italian Renaissance to England and the results can be seen at the Banqueting Hall in Whitehall, and parts of Wilton House in Wiltshire.

This classicism continued through the 17th century leaving the baroque and rococo with only a foothold in England compared to the Continent. Sir Christopher Wren, undoubtedly the leading 17th-century English architect, helped rebuild much of London after the Great Fire in 1666. He built a new St. Paul's and rebuilt 53 churches—two of the most famous being St. Bride in Fleet Street and St. Mary-le-Bow. Other Wren masterpieces include the Royal Hospital at Greenwich, the Sheldonian Theatre in Oxford, and the library at Trinity College, Cambridge.

At the end of his life, Wren was eclipsed by such famous 18th-century architects as Sir John Vanbrugh (1664–1726), creator of Castle Howard and Blenheim Palace, and Sir Nicholas Hawksmoor (1661–1736). After 1720 the baroque influence declined and Palladianism took over, especially in domestic architecture. Great houses surrounded by parkland and natural landscapes dotted with classical sculptures and fountains like Holkham Hall were built by such architects as William Kent and Colen Campbell. Capability Brown was the foremost landscape artist of this period.

In the later 18th century a Classical Revival took place, led by such architects as Sir William Chambers and Robert Adam, whose Syon House near London and Kedleston Hall in Derbyshire are prime examples. The 18th century also saw the laying out of whole terraces and crescents like Royal Crescent in Bath designed by John Wood. Similar schemes can be seen in Cheltenham and Brighton.

In the 19th century the types of buildings changed as a result of the Industrial Revolution. Factories, railroad stations, concert halls, and theaters were added to the roster of churches and domestic buildings. All kinds of earlier styles were interpreted—Romanesque, Byzantine, Gothic—new materials were used like glass and iron, and the mode of building changed, with many of the internal decorative elements like moldings being mass produced. England produced some fine architecture in the late Georgian and Regency periods by such architects as John Nash and Sir John Soane. From 1840 on, the English exhibited a preference for Gothic and Gothic Revival, which can be seen clearly in the Houses of Parliament, the Law Courts in London, the Natural History Museum, and the most controversial of all, the Albert Memorial. A few architects at the end of the century, like Charles Rennie Mackintosh, rejected the over-decoration and heaviness of this Victorian style and sought greater simplicity.

The famous architects of the early 20th century include Sir Edwin Lutyens (1869–1944) who built country houses, commercial buildings like the Reuter Building in Fleet Street, and laid out such grand schemes as the Cenotaph in Whitehall. He is also associated, of course, with the grand designs of British Delhi. Modern architecture as we know it really began after World War II. Many early modern buildings were created by immigrants en route to the United States including Walter Gropius. Much of modern British architecture is blockish and dull with some relief provided by such figures as Sir Hugh Casson and Sir Basil Spence.

LITERATURE

The most outstanding figure of all in England's literary heritage is William Shakespeare (1564–1616), but if England had had no Shakespeare, its literature would still be among the richest in the world. From the Old English epic poem, *Beowulf*, to the works of the "angry young men" of the '50s, English literature is vast, and in this limited space we can only touch on the highlights.

The Old English poetry and historical prose found in such works as the

Anglo-Saxon Chronicle of Alfred the Great's time gave way in the 13th and 14th centuries to so-called Middle English (Old Anglo-Saxon English enriched by the Norman) of which the great master was Geoffrey Chaucer, author of the *Canterbury Tales,* a rollicking series of often bawdy tales. The literary highlight of the 15th century was *Le Morte d'Arthur,* Sir Thomas Malory's free-handed story about the legend of King Arthur and his court. Ballads were also popular storytelling devices in that century, a sort of continuation of the bardic epic tradition.

During the Tudor and Elizabethan era the literary stars were many—Sir Thomas More (*Utopia*), Edmund Spenser (*The Faerie Queen*), and Christopher Marlowe (*The Tragical History of Dr. Faustus*). Among poets the sonnet form adopted from an Italian verse model was popular and composed by such as Sir Philip Sidney and the greatest of them all, William Shakespeare.

The Elizabethan period was the golden era of the theater in England. London's first theater opened in 1576 in the Fields at Shoreditch, followed by the Curtain, and, in 1598, the most famous of all, the Globe, which belonged to Shakespeare and Marlowe.

The coming to the throne of the Stuarts ushered in the Jacobean period, when "rare Ben Jonson," who led the poets who met at the Mermaid Tavern in London, wrote some of his best satirical comedies, and John Donne ("never send to know for whom the bell tolls . . .") was at his finest. The translation of the Bible, known as the King James Version, was undertaken at this time under the auspices of James I, and it assumed its immortal place in literature.

By the mid-17th century, writers, like all English people, began to be divided in allegiance between the king and Parliament. The Cavalier poets, of whom Robert Herrick heads the list, wrote lyrical verse and backed the king. The literary giant of the mid-17th century was John Milton, a Pro-Parliamentarian and the author of *Paradise Lost,* who was considered even in his lifetime a genius. John Bunyan, a Baptist lay preacher also caught up in the Puritan cause, author of *Pilgrim's Progress,* the first prose work, was sent to prison after the restoration of the monarchy. After Charles II returned to the throne, theaters which had been closed by Cromwell were reopened, and literature took on a lighter, more lively tone, reflected in the plays of Sheridan and the diary of Samuel Pepys.

Throughout the 18th century, England's literary world was crowded with the output of geniuses and near-geniuses from the rising middle class. Among these were Daniel Defoe (*Robinson Crusoe* and *Moll Flanders*), Alexander Pope (*An Essay on Man*), Henry Fielding (*Tom Jones*), and a host of essayists and novelists. Most memorable in this period, however, is Samuel Johnson, whose *Dictionary of the English Language* made him the premier lexicographer and man of letters. His association with James Boswell from Scotland resulted in Johnson's becoming a major figure in literary annals, albeit through Boswell's writings. In Johnson's circle of close friends was another notable literary figure of the time, Oliver Goldsmith (*She Stoops to Conquer* and *The Vicar of Wakefield*).

To try to expound on the stars of the early 19th-century literary scene in England in limited space would be impossible, so I'll just mention several of the names known to everyone: William Blake, William Wordsworth, Samuel Taylor Coleridge, Lord Byron, John Keats, Percy Bysshe Shelley, Jane Austen, and Charles Lamb—but there are so many more. As you travel through the country, you will see birthplaces, residences, and burial places of many of these writers.

Now to the years that challenge a student of literature—the mid- and late-1800s when a broad literate middle-class public devoured the works of Charles Dickens, William Thackeray, the Brontë sisters, Matthew Arnold, Alfred Lord Tennyson, the Brownings, Lewis Carroll, George Eliot, George Meredith, Thomas Hardy, Algernon

---

IMPRESSIONS

Sir it is not so much to be lamented that Old England is lost, as that the Scotch have found it.
—SAMUEL JOHNSON, IN BOSWELL, *LIFE OF JOHNSON,* MAY, 1776

IMPRESSIONS

*America is a land whose center is nowhere; England one whose center is
everywhere. In America every town has its Chamber of Commerce; here every
shire has been the site of a poem.*
—JOHN UPDIKE, "LONDON LIFE," 1969

Charles Swinburne, and Oscar Wilde, with a little heavier reading from John Ruskin thrown in.

Straddling the turn of the century but usually considered literary figures of modern times—from the early 1900s, it's true—are such notables as Rudyard Kipling, H. G. Wells, John Galsworthy, W. Somerset Maugham, Walter de la Mare, and Sir Arthur Conan Doyle. Writers of the 20th century include Robert Graves, Stephen Spender, W. H. Auden, Virginia Woolf, D. H. Lawrence, Aldous Huxley, Kingsley Amis, Graham Greene, George Orwell, E. M. Forster, Antonia Fraser, Ted Hughes, William Golding, Muriel Spark, and—not to be forgotten—Winston Churchill.

I could go on and on and on—and I still might well leave out your favorite English writer. In fact, I'm sure someone will ask, "But what about Jonathan Swift? George Bernard Shaw? Sir Walter Scott? Robert Burns? Robert Louis Stevenson? Joseph Conrad? Dylan Thomas? Doris Lessing?" My only defense might be that these novelists and poets are not English born, though they have certainly made their mark in English literature. There's no question about it—the British Isles are rich in literary greats, and I've only reminded you of *some* of them.

MUSIC

From the time the English monks' choirs surpassed those of Germany and France in singing the Gregorian chant (brought to this country in 597 by St. Augustine of Canterbury, Pope Gregory's missionary), and were judged second only to the choirs of Rome, music has been heard throughout England. Polyphonic music developed after the simple chant, and sacred vocal music was early accompanied by the organ. The first organ at Winchester was installed in the 10th century. One of the earliest written compositions was the polyphonic piece (a round), "Summer Is Icumen In," with six parts.

Instruments commonly used in the Middle Ages, besides the organ found only in churches, were the fiddle, the lute, and the rebec, used in court circles for the entertainment of royalty and hangers-on. Plantagenet and Tudor monarchs had musicians at court, with Henry VIII in particular making himself known as a composer. He wrote sonnets for his lady loves and set them to music, the best known being "Greensleeves"; the British Museum contains some 34 manuscripts of Henry's compositions. So flourishing was music in England in the 16th century that Erasmus of Rotterdam reported after one of his visits: "They are so much occupied with music here that even the monks don't do anything else."

Music among the common people of the time may have been less polished but it was no less enthusiastic, as ditties and rounds were composed and heard in taverns and fields, the richness of the tunes compensating for the frequent vulgarity of the words. Some of the songs Shakespeare had his characters sing attest to the coarseness of the lyrics.

During the Tudor dynasty English cathedral music came into full flower and during these years also masques—the forerunners of the opera—were frequently performed. These combined instrumental and vocal music, dancing, satire, recitations, and elaborate scenic effects.

IMPRESSIONS

*There are ill friends to England, who strive to write a history of her nudities, and
expose, much less recommend her wicked part to posterity.*
—DANIEL DEFOE, *A TOUR THROUGH THE WHOLE ISLAND OF GREAT BRITAIN*, 1724-7

Under Cromwell's Commonwealth, musicians were persecuted in the 1600s but they came back into glory with the restoration of the Stuart monarchy: Henry Purcell wrote the first English opera, *Dido and Aeneas,* in 1689. In the 18th century, Italian opera became the rage, even as John Gay satirized such productions in *The Beggars' Opera* in 1728. Handel, who became an English subject, composed many operas and oratorios in London, including *Messiah,* and other musicians followed (sometimes haltingly) in his train.

England's outstanding 19th-century contribution to the musical repertoire were the uniquely English operettas of Gilbert and Sullivan.

Many great names in the 20th century music world are English: Sir Edward Elgar, Ralph Vaughan Williams, Sir William Walton, Benjamin Britten, to name just a few.

Paul McCartney and John Lennon of the Beatles began what has been called in America "the British invasion." Since the 1960s, English rock musicians have often dominated the American music scene. Individual vocalists such as Phil Collins, David Bowie, and Sting, and guitarists such as Eric Clapton have been leading forces in popular music. But the biggest musical influence from England has been the rock bands: The Rolling Stones, The Who, Pink Floyd, Genesis, The Sex Pistols, and XTC. British rock's influence on Western popular music and culture has been and still is tremendous.

4. LANGUAGE, RELIGION & FOLKLORE

LANGUAGE

Any visitor to England will surely experience communication problems.

The already mentioned William the Conqueror did more than transform London (or rather Westminster) into a royal capital. He and his nobles superimposed their Norman French on the country's original Anglo-Saxon language and thus originated English as it is spoken today. Both the richness and the maddening illogicality of our tongue are direct results of that concoction.

For an American it can be a minor shock to discover that the English in fact speak English. We Americans speak American. There are just enough differences between the two to result in crossed wires and occasional total communication breakdowns. For, although the British use words and phrases you think you understand, they often have quite different connotations from their U.S. equivalents.

When the British call someone "mean," they mean stingy. And "homely," meaning ugly or plain in America, becomes pleasant in England. "Calling" denotes a personal visit, not a phone call. But a person-to-person phone call is a "personal call." To "queue up" means to form a line, which they do at every bus stop. And whereas a "subway" is an underground pedestrian passage, the actual subway system is called "the Underground" or "the tube." The term "theatre" refers only to the live stage; movie theaters are "cinemas," and what's playing in them are "the pictures." And a "bomb," which suggests a disaster in America, means a success in England.

In a grocery store, canned goods become "tins," rutabagas become "swedes," eggplants become "aubergines," and endive is "chicory," while conversely chicory is "endive." Both cookies and crackers become "biscuits," which can be either "dry" or "sweet." That is, except graham crackers, which—unaccountably—are "digestives."

The going gets rougher when you're dealing with motor vehicles. When talking about the actual vehicle, very little means the same except for the word "car," unless you mean a truck, which is called a "lorry." In any case, gas is "petrol," the windshield is the "windscreen," and bumpers are "fenders." The trunk is the "boot" and what you do on the horn is "hoot."

Luckily most of us know that an English apartment is a "flat" and that an elevator is a "lift." And you don't rent a room or apartment, you "let" it. Although the ground floor is the ground floor, the second floor is the "first floor." And once you set up housekeeping, you don't vacuum, you "hoover."

Going clothes shopping? Then you should know that undershirts are called "vests" and undershorts are "pants" to the English, while long pants are called "trousers" and their cuffs are called "turn-ups." Panties are "knickers" and panty hose are "tights." Pullover sweaters can be called "jumpers" and little girls' jumpers are called "pinafores." If you are looking for diapers, ask for "nappies."

The education system offers such varied types of schools identified by an equally wide variety of terms that to explain them all to the general visitor would be too confusing. Briefly, however, the large English "public schools" (such as Eton) are similar to our large private prep schools (such as Andover). But the English also have other private, or "independent," schools on all levels. And all of the above charge tuition. In addition, there are "state schools," which we would call public schools. These include "primary schools" and secondary "comprehensive schools," "modern schools," and "grammar schools" that are equivalent to our junior and senior high schools.

In school and elsewhere, the letter Z is pronounced "zed," and zero is "nought." And if you want to buy an after-school treat, a Popsicle is called an "iced lolly."

Please note that none of the above terms—except the last—are slang. If you really want a challenge in that arena, you can always take on cockney. The cockneys are indigenous Londoners, although strictly speaking the label refers only to people born within the sound of the bells of St. Mary-le-Bow in Cheapside.

The exact derivation of the word "cockney" is lost in the mist of antiquity, but it's supposed to have meant an "odd fellow." And the oddest feature about this fellow is undoubtedly the rhyming slang he concocted over the centuries, based on the rhyme—or the rhyme of a rhyme—that goes with a particular word or phrase. So take my advice and don't try to delve further, unless you happen to be Professor Higgins—pardon me—'iggins.

RELIGION

England is very different from the United States in that Church and State are inextricably intertwined. This relationship between Church and State dates back to the Reformation when Henry VIII broke with Rome in 1534, proclaimed himself "Supreme Head of the Church of England," confiscated Catholic treasuries and lands, and dissolved hundreds of monasteries and convents. After the religious conflicts of the 17th century, which defeated the attempts of the Stuarts to return England to Rome, the Church of England was secured and the law stated that the sovereign must be a member of the Church of England and must swear to uphold its doctrines. Thus today the monarch, Queen Elizabeth II, is the titular head of the Church of England or Anglican Church while she reigns over a nation that grants freedom of worship to everyone. Britain is officially divided into two dioceses—Canterbury and York, the first the more powerful of the two. Besides these links between Church and State there are still others. The Church is not free to change either its doctrines or its form of worship, as originally defined in *The Book of Common Prayer* (compiled in 1549) without the specific assent of Parliament. Despite these legal and historical links, the Church of England is not fiscally subsidized by the State or by the Crown, but rather earns its income from its own capital, real estate, and communal contributions.

Although 60% of the population claim membership in the Church, only 8% of its baptised members attend on Easter Sunday. Contemporary Britain also contains a variety of Protestant and other sects: Baptists, Methodists, Quakers, Congregationalists, as well as Roman Catholics, Jews, and a growing number of Muslims and Hindus.

FOLKLORE

Although it's far too arcane to discuss here, England's history is rich in early myth and mystery, as anyone who has visited Stonehenge will have witnessed. The myth most often associated with England though is the Arthurian legend of Camelot, which

IMPRESSIONS

Pox on the modern phrase Great Britain, which is only to distinguish it from Little Britain, where old clothes and books are to be bought and sold.
—JONATHAN SWIFT, LETTER TO JOHN BARBER, AUGUST, 1738

---

originated in southwestern England and Wales. This story was published in literary form for the first time by Geoffrey of Monmouth in Norman France around 1135. It told of the birth of Arthur, his exploits with his knights of the Round Table, and the shattering of his idyllic kingdom by the adultery of Arthur's Queen Guinevere with his favorite knight Lancelot, and by Arthur's search for the Holy Grail. Some historians even trace within the Arthurian legend certain exploits that, historically, were achieved by a mixture of Viking, Saxon, and even Roman military leaders. Every era, it seems, has produced its own version of the Arthurian legend from the medieval and Tudor versions by Sir Thomas Malory and Edmund Spenser, through the Victorian versions by William Morris, Tennyson, and Swinburne to our very own 20th-century renderings by T. H. White and C. S. Lewis.

The other great legend that seems to have great resonance in England is the legend of Robin Hood and his merry men who stole from the rich and gave to the poor, and resisted the authority of the Sheriff of Nottingham—a role model that seems to underlie the British love of justice and the fervor with which they root for the underdog.

5. FOOD & DRINK

FOOD

The reputation that Britain had for years for its soggy cabbage and tasteless dishes which prompted British humorist George Mikes to write that "The Continentals have good food; the English have good table manners," is no longer deserved. Contemporary London boasts many very fine restaurants indeed, and they're also found throughout the country.

MEALS & DINING CUSTOMS

Mealtimes are much the same as in the United States. Britain is famous for its enormous **breakfasts** of bacon, egg, grilled tomato, and fried bread and although it has been replaced in some places by a continental variety, it can still be found at the finer hotels and other places. Kipper, which is the name given to a smoked herring, is also a popular breakfast dish. The finest come from the Isle of Man, Whitby, or Loch Fyne in Scotland. The herrings are split open and placed over oak chips and smoked slowly to produce a nice pale-brown smoked fish. **Lunch,** usually eaten between noon and 2 pm, is often taken at the pub, or else consists of a sandwich on the run. **Afternoon tea** is still enjoyed by many and it may consist of a simple cup of tea or a formal tea that starts with tiny crustless sandwiches filled with cucumber or watercress, proceeds through scones or crumpets with jam and possibly cream to cakes and tarts, all accompanied by a proper pot of tea. In London the tea at Browns is

IMPRESSIONS

Ideleness is the malus genus of our nation.
—ROBERT BURTON, *ANATOMIE OF MELANCHOLIE*, 1621

It is only in England that truth is made a basis of morality.
—FREYA STARK, *TRAVELLER'S PRELUDE*, 1950

quintessentially English, while the Ritz tea is an elaborate affair complete with orchestra and dancing. In the country teashops abound, and in Devon, Cornwall, and the West Country you'll find the best cream teas ever served, consisting of scones spread with jam and thick clotted Devonshire cream. A delicious treat indeed. It is a misconception to believe that "everything" stops for tea. People in Britain drink an average of four cups of tea a day, mainly at work. **Dinner** is usually enjoyed around 8 pm and may consist of traditional English dishes or any number of ethnic cuisines that are currently found in London. **Supper** is traditionally a late-night meal usually eaten after the theater.

THE CUISINE

You don't have to travel around England to sample regional English dishes—you'll find them on many a London menu—but it's fun to see the regions and taste their bounty. On any pub menu you're likely to encounter such dishes as Cornish pasty and shepherd's pie. The first is traditionally made from the Sunday-meal leftovers consisting of chopped potato, carrot, onion, and seasoning mixed together and put into a pastry envelope and taken originally by the West Country fishermen on Monday for lunch. The second is a deep dish of chopped cooked beef mixed with onions and seasoning and covered with a layer of mashed potatoes and served hot. Another version is cottage pie, which is minced beef covered with potatoes and also served hot. The most common pub meal, though, is the ploughman's lunch—a traditional farm worker's lunch—consisting of a good chunk of local cheese, a hunk of homemade crusty white or brown bread, some butter, and a pickled onion or two, all washed down with ale. You will now find such variations as pâté and chutney replacing the onions and cheese. Cheese is still, however, the most common ingredient. Or you might find Lancashire hot pot, a stew of mutton, potatoes, kidneys, and onions (sometimes carrots). This concoction was originally put into a deep dish and set on the edge of the stove to cook slowly while the workers spent the day at the local mill.

Among appetizers, which are called "starters" in England, the most typical is potted shrimps (small buttered shrimps preserved in a jar), prawn cocktail, or smoked salmon. You might also be served pâté, or even "fish pie" which is very light fish pâté. If you're an oyster lover try some of the famous Colchester oysters. Most menus will feature a variety of soups including cock-a-leekie (chicken soup flavored with leeks) and game soups that will often be flavored with sherry.

Among the best known and traditional of English dishes is, of course, roast beef and Yorkshire pudding. The pudding is made with a flour base and cooked under the joint, allowing the fat from the meat to drop onto it. The beef could easily be a large sirloin (rolled loin) which, so the story goes, was named by King James I (not Henry VIII as some claim) when he was a guest at Houghton Tower, Lancashire. "Arise, Sir Loin," he cried, as he knighted the joint with his dagger. Another dish that makes use of a batter similar to Yorkshire pudding is toad-in-the-hole, in which sausages are cooked in batter. Game, especially pheasant and grouse, is also a staple on British tables.

On the west coast, you'll find a not-to-be-missed delicacy, Morecambe Bay shrimp, and on any menu you'll find fresh seafood—cod, haddock, herring, plaice, and the aristocrat of flat fish, Dover sole. Cod and haddock are the most popular fish used in the making of that British tradition, fish-and-chips (chips, of course, are fried potatoes or french fries), which the true Briton covers with salt and vinegar.

The East End of London has quite a few interesting old dishes, among them tripe and onions. Dr. Johnson's favorite tavern, the Cheshire Cheese on Fleet Street (closed until 1993), still offers a beefsteak-kidney-mushroom-and-game pudding in a suet case in winter and a pastry case in summer. East Enders can still be seen on Sunday at the Jellied Eel stall by Petticoat Lane, eating eel or perhaps cockles (small clams), mussels, whelks, and winkles, all small shellfish eaten with a touch of vinegar. Eel-pie-and-mash shops can still be found in London purveying what is really a minced-beef pie topped with flaky pastry and served with mashed potatoes and a portion of jellied eel.

The British call desserts "sweets," or "pudding." Trifle is perhaps the most famous of English desserts—a sponge cake soaked in brandy or sherry, coated with fruit or jam, and topped with a cream custard. A "fool," such as gooseberry fool, is a light cream dessert whipped up from seasonal fruits. Regional sweets include such items as the northern "flitting" dumpling consisting of dates, walnuts, and syrup mixed with other ingredients and made into a pudding that can be sliced easily and carried along when one is "flitting" from one place to another. Similarly, "hurry pudding" or hasty pudding, a dish from Newcastle, is said to have been invented by those avoiding the bailiff. It consists of stale bread (some dried fruit and milk are added before it is put into the oven).

Cheese is traditionally served after dessert as a savory. There are many regional cheeses, the best known being Cheddar, a good, solid, mature cheese. Others are the semismooth-textured Caerphilly from a beautiful part of Wales, and Stilton, a blue-veined crumbly cheese, often enriched with a glass of port.

DRINK

Tea   Most of the English drink tea in the morning, and it's usually superior to the American tea bag in lukewarm water variety. It will usually come in a pot accompanied by milk and sugar.

Water & Soft Drinks   Tap water is safe to drink, but you will usually have to ask for water with your meal as it is not automatically served. Neither is ice. Popular brands of soda and soft drinks are available but you may want to try some of Schweppes bottled waters such as "bitter lemon."

Liquor, Beer & Wine   London pubs serve a variety of cocktails but their stock in trade is beer—brown beer or "bitter," blond beer or lager, and very dark beer, which is called "stout." The standard English draft beer is a) much stronger than American beer and b) is served "with the chill off" because it doesn't taste good cold. Lager is always chilled and stout can be served either way. One of the most significant changes in English drinking habits has been the popularity of wine bars, and you will find many to patronize, some turning into discos late at night.

Britain is not known for its wine, although it does produce some medium-sweet fruity white wines. Its cider, though, is famous and very potent in alcohol content contrast to the American variety.

Whisky (spelled without the "e") in England refers to scotch. Canadian and Irish whiskey are also available, but only the very best stocked bars have American bourbon and rye. While you're in England you may want to try the very English drink Pimm's, a mixture developed by James Pimm, owner of a popular London oyster house in the 1840s. Though it can be consumed on the rocks, it's usually served as a Pimm's Cup—a drink that will have any number and variety of ingredients depending on which part of the world (read Empire) you're in. Here just for fun is a typical recipe. Take a very tall glass filled with ice. Add a thin slice of lemon (or orange), add a cucumber spike (or a curl of cucumber rind) and 2 ounces of Pimm's liquor, then fill with a splash of either lemon or club soda, 7-Up, or Tom Collins' mix.

6. SPORTS & RECREATION

SPORTS

Football—called soccer in the United States—is the most popular British sport (having about 35 million devotees) and it is taken so seriously that it has led to widely publicized riots in which people have been killed. It's a fast game played by two teams of 11 for 90 minutes (two halves of 45 minutes each) who are allowed only to use their feet and their heads to move the ball and score goals by kicking it between two fixed goalposts.

Rugby, which supposedly originated at the famous public school in Warwickshire, is closer to American football insofar as both the ball and the goalposts are similarly shaped and the ball is thrown and kicked. In England it's primarily an upper-middle-class sport played at the private schools. Welsh rugby, though, is a more popular sport.

In summer, cricket and tennis are the prime sports. Cricket is "the most English of games" conducted in a polite and gracious manner by two teams of 11 wearing white flannels, who adhere to the umpire's judgments without demur. From this game came such English phrases as "a sticky wicket" and "it's not cricket." An inning is one turn at bat by each side. Games can last for 1 or 5 days as they do in The International Test Matches. Players bat in pairs from opposite ends of the pitch, a 22-yard-long patch of well-rolled and mowed grass at the center of the oval field that can be as big as a football field. The bowlers of the opposite team pitch the small hard ball with a straight arm so that the ball bounces in front of the batman, aiming to dislodge the wicket (an assemblage of three upright stumps with a "bail" slotted across the top of them). The intricacies of the game are many but the whole performance on a sunny weekend afternoon complete with picnic or afternoon tea is quintessentially English.

The fox hunt is also traditionally English. Men and women on horseback sporting so-called "pink coats" (actually blood red) race across the fields of England following a pack of hounds in pursuit of their elusive but badly outnumbered fox or hare. Brits are great animal lovers, and many citizens view this as a cruel sport and loudly protest against it.

Horse racing is a distinctly royal pastime. The "flat" racing season lasts from late March until November and the classic race is the Derby run at Epson Downs in early June. Steeplechasing, which involves jumping over fences and hedges, is more thrilling and certainly more dangerous than "flat" racing. The most famous steeplechase is the Grand National, held annually at Liverpool's Aintree.

RECREATION
BICYCLING

Bicycles are forbidden on most highways, trunk roads, and on what the English call "dual carriageways" (two-lane highways). In town, city, and country the bike is a great way to get around. If you're interested in a cycling holiday in England, contact the Cyclists' Touring Club, 69 Meadrow, Godalming, Surrey GU7 3HS (tel. 04868/7217). Membership is £18.50 ($34.25) a year.

BOATING

England is crisscrossed by historic canals and waterways, the most popular being the Norfolk Broads in East Anglia. You can also take canal and river cruises in Bath, York, Bristol, and Stratford-upon-Avon. For more information about boat-rentals contact the Association of Pleasure Craft Operators, 35A High Street, Newport, Shropshire, TF10 8JW (tel. 0952/813572).

CAMPING

Throughout England there are many campsites which can get very crowded in summer. For information, contact the Camping and Caravan Club Ltd., 11 Lower Grosvenor Place, London SW1W 0EY (tel. 071/828-1012).

GOLFING

Hundreds of excellent courses are found all over England. If you're an avid golfer consider buying *The Golf Course Guide to Great Britain and Ireland,* by Donald Steel (Collins, £5.95, or $11), available in British bookstores.

HIKING

Hiking, or "rambling," is one of the most popular British activities. In England and Wales alone there are some 100,000 miles, maybe more, of footpaths and trails—many historical, like the Pennine Way in Yorkshire. Contact the Ramblers Association,

1-5 Wandsworth Road, London SW8 2XX (tel. 071/582-6878), which publishes a bimonthly magazine and also lists B&B's near the trails.

TENNIS

This is a favorite summer game and all cities and towns have municipal courts. Ask at local tourist offices for information.

WATER SPORTS

England has many lakes and rivers, and locals do fish and swim in them, but always check locally with the tourist office about whether they are indeed safe. Better to use indoor municipal pools or hotel pools.

The best beaches in England are found on the Cornish coast but they are crowded in summer. Some visitors from hotter climes find the waters around Great Britain too cold for comfort.

7. RECOMMENDED BOOKS, FILMS & RECORDINGS

BOOKS

GENERAL & HISTORY

Both Anthony Sampson's *The New Anatomy of Britain* (Stein & Day) and *The Changing Anatomy of Britain* (Random House) provide insights into the social institutions and idiosyncrasies of English society.

Among historians the great writers are legion. Anything by Asa Briggs on the Victorians—*Victorian People,* for instance—will be entertaining and worth reading. The same is true of A. L. Rowse on the Tudor period, C. V. Wedgwood on the 17th century, J. H. Plumb on the 18th century, A. J. P. Taylor on the 20th century (*English History 1914–45*), and Christopher Iibbert on anything. The changes that ushered in the modern era at the turn of the century are charted in *The Strange Death of Liberal England* (1935) by George Dangerfield. Winston Churchill's *History of the English Speaking World* (Dodd Mead, 1956) is a tour de force in four volumes while his *The Gathering Storm* captures Europe and London on the brink of World War. The impact of the first and second world wars on English society has been well-examined by Arthur Marwick in his book *The Deluge.* The period between the wars is handled elegiacally by Robert Graves in his *Goodbye to All That* and also in *Children of the Sun,* by Martin Green (Basic Books, 1976) which portrays the "decadent" Twenties and the lives of such people as Randolph Churchill, Rupert Brooke, the Prince of Wales, and Christopher Isherwood.

In *A Writer's Britain* (Knopf, 1979), contemporary English author Margaret Drabble takes the reader on a tour of the sacred and haunted literary landscapes of England, places that inspired, Hardy and Woolf, Spenser and Marvell. It's well-illustrated, too. There are several other guides to literary landmarks available, including one by American Frank Morley.

Outsiders often paint more penetrating portraits than residents of any culture ever can. In England's case there are many who have expressed their views of the country at different periods. An early 18th-century portrait is provided by K. P. Moritz in his *Journeys of a German in England in 1782* (Holt, Rinehart & Winston, 1965), about his travels from London to the Midlands. Nathaniel Hawthorne recorded his impressions in *Our Old Home* (1863) as did Ralph Waldo Emerson in *English Traits* (1856). For a marvelous ironic portrait of mid-19th-century Victorian British morals, manners, and society, seek out *Taine's Notes on England* (1854). Henry James comments on turn-of-the-century England in his *English Hours.* In *A Passage to England* (St. Martins, 1959) Nirad Chaudhuri analyzes Britain and the British in a delightful, humorous book—a process continued today by such authors as Salman Rushdie, V. S. Naipaul, and Paul Theroux, among many. Among the more interesting portraits written by natives are Cobbet's *Rural Rides* (1830), depicting early 19th-century England; *In Search of England* (Methuen, 1927) by H. V. Morton; and *English Journey* by J. B. Priestley (Harper, 1934). For what's really going on behind that serene Suffolk village scene, read Ronald Blythe's *Akenfield: Portrait of an English Village* (1969).

And finally, *English Cooking* (W. H. Allen, 1960) by Rupert Croft-Cooke is a cookbook to be read. The recipes are incidental; the legend and lore substantial.

ART & ARCHITECTURE

For general reference, there's the huge multivolume *Oxford History of English Art* (Oxford University Press), and also the *Encyclopedia of British Art*, by David Bindman (Thames Hudson, 1988). *Painting in Britain 1530–1790* (Penguin, 1978) by Ellis Waterhouse covers British art from the Tudor miniaturists to Gainsborough, Reynolds, and Hogarth, while *English Art, 1870–1940* (Oxford University Press, 1979) by Dennis Farr covers the modern period.

On architecture, for sheer, amusing opinionated entertainment there's John Betjeman's *Ghastly Good Taste—the Rise and Fall of English Architecture* (1971). Betjeman is well-known for his British TV programs on buildings. *A History of English Architecture* by Peter Kidson, Peter Murray, and Paul Thompson (Penguin, 1979) covers the subject form Anglo-Saxon to modern times. Nikolaus Pevsner's *The Best Buildings of England: An Anthology* (Viking, 1987) and his *Outline of European Architecture* (Penguin, 1960) are both eloquent. *Architecture in Britain 1530–1830*, John Summerson (Penguin, 1971), concentrates on the great periods of Tudor, Georgian, and Regency architecture. Mark Girouard has written several books on British architecture including *The Victorian Country House* (Country Life, 1971) and *Life in the English Country House* (Yale University Press, 1978), a fascinating social/architectural history from the Middle Ages to the 20th century complete with handsome illustrations.

ABOUT LONDON

London Perceived by novelist and literary critic V. S. Pritchett is a witty portrait of the city—its history, art, literature, and life. Virginia Woolf's *The London Scene* brilliantly depicts the London of the '30s—a literary gem. *In Search of London* by H. V. Morton is filled with anecdotal history and still well worth reading even though it is nearly 40 years old.

In *London: The Biography of a City* popular historian Christopher Hibbert paints a very lively portrait. For some real 17th-century history, you can't beat *Diary of Samuel Pepys* or Daniel Defoe's *Tour Thro London about the Year 1725*.

Americans in London, by Brian N. Morton (William Morrow, 1986), is a street-by-street guide to the clubs, homes, and favorite pubs of more than 250 illustrious Americans—Mark Twain, Joseph Kennedy, Dwight Eisenhower, and Sylvia Plath—who made London a temporary home. The *Guide to Literary London* by George Williams (Batsford, 1988) charts a series of literary tours through London from Chelsea to Bloomsbury. *The Capital Companion* by Peter Gibson (Webb & Bower, 1985) contains more than 1,200 alphabetical entries, and is filled with facts and anecdotes about the streets of London and their inhabitants.

The Architect's Guide to London by Renzo Salvadori (Reed International, 1990) documents 100 landmark buildings with photographs and maps. *Nairn's London* by Ian Nairn (Penguin, 1988) is a stimulating, opinionated discourse on London's buildings. Donald Olsen's *The City as a Work of Art: London, Paris, and Vienna* (Yale University Press, 1986) is a well-illustrated text tracing the evolution of these great cities. *London One: The Cities of London and Westminster* and *London Two: South* (Penguin, 1984) are works of love by well-known architectural writers Bridget Cherry and Nikolaus Pevsner. David Piper's *The Artist's London* (Oxford University Press, 1982) does what the title suggests—captures the city that artists have portrayed.

In *Victorian and Edwardian London* (Batsford, 1969) John Betjeman expresses his great love of those eras and their great buildings.

FICTION & BIOGRAPHY

Among English writers are found some of the greatest exponents of mystery and suspense novels from which a reader can get a good feel for English life both urban and rural. Agatha Christie, P. D. James, and Dorothy Sayers are a few of the familiar names, but the great London character is, of course, Sherlock Holmes of Baker Street, created by Arthur Conan Doyle. Any of these writers will give pleasure and insight into your London experience.

England's literary heritage is so vast that it's hard to select particular titles but here are a few favorites. Master storyteller Charles Dickens re-creates Victorian London in such books as *Oliver Twist, David Copperfield,* and his earlier satirical *Sketches by Boz.*

Edwardian London and the '20s and '30s is captured wonderfully in any of Evelyn Waugh's social satires and comedies; any work from the Bloomsbury group will also prove enlightening, like Virginia Woolf's *Mrs. Dalloway,* which peers beneath the surface of the London scene. For a portrait of wartime London there's Elizabeth Bowen's *The Heat of the Day* (1949); for an American slant on England and London there's Henry James's *The Awkward Age.* Colin MacInnes's novels—*City of Spades* (1957), *Absolute Beginners* (1959), and *Love and Justice*—focus on more recent social problems. Among contemporaries Margaret Drabble and Iris Murdoch are both challenging. And there are so many more.

Among 18th-century figures, there's a great biography of Samuel Johnson by W. Jackson Bate. Among political biographies, it's hard to find better than Robert Blake's portrait of Benjamin Disraeli, prime minister and leader of the Conservative Party during the imperial Victorian era. Antonia Fraser has written several lively biographies of English monarchs and political figures including Charles II and Oliver Cromwell. Great biographies of all time include Lytton Strachey's *Queen Victoria,* along with his *Eminent Victorians.* Winston Churchill's *Autobiography* is also a great work of the English language. Richard Ellman's *Oscar Wilde* (Knopf, 1988) is a masterpiece revealing such Victorian era personalities as Lillie Langtry, Gilbert and Sullivan, and Henry James along the way. Quintessential English playwright Noël Coward and the London he inhabited along with the likes of Nancy Mitford, Cecil Beaton, John Gielgud, the Oliviers, Evelyn Waugh, and Rebecca West is captured in Cole Lesley's *Remembered Laughter* (Knopf, 1977). More recently *The Lives of John Lennon* by Albert Goldman (William Morrow, 1988) traces the life of this most famous of all '60s musicians.

FILMS

The British film industry used to be much more important than it is today, enjoying a golden era roughly from 1929 to 1939. The country's foremost director was Alfred Hitchcock, who made the first English talkie, *Blackmail,* in 1929. Other masterpieces followed, like *The Thirty-Nine Steps* (1935), *The Lady Vanishes* (1938), and *Jamaica Inn* (1939), all made before he left for Hollywood and even greater glory.

Another famous figure in English cinema was Hungarian Alexander Korda, who settled in London in 1933 and made such memorable movies as *The Private Life of Henry VIII,* starring Charles Laughton, and *The Private Life of Don Juan* (1934), the last film of Douglas Fairbanks.

In the '40s David Lean emerged as a major director making such films as *Blithe Spirit* (1944), an adaptation of Noël Coward's play and *Brief Encounter* (1945), which some feel is his paramount achievement.

After the war J. Arthur Rank formed the Rank Organization, which produced an array of films, among them Olivier's *Henry V* and *Hamlet,* which were acclaimed all over the world.

Carol Reed is remembered for the memorable *Odd Man Out* (1946), with a screenplay by Graham Greene, and *The Third Man* (1949), starring Orson Welles.

Many movies and British actors have portrayed the British scene. Among some of the great movies that you might want to see again are *Kind Hearts and Coronets* in which Alec Guinness played all the members of the family, *Lady Killers,* made in the '60s, *The Mouse That Roared* and *I'm All Right Jack,* both starring Peter Sellers. *Oliver Twist* with Alec Guinness as Fagin and *Great Expectations* are two real classics. In the '60s Tony Richardson established himself with such English hits as *A Taste of Honey* and *The Loneliness of the Long Distance Runner.* Another '60s movie depicting the intellectual British middle class was *Sunday Bloody Sunday* starring Glenda Jackson and Peter Finch. Ken Russell came on the scene at the same time with his lustrous *Women in Love.*

Among more recent film portraits of the British at home and abroad are *A Room with a View, Maurice,* both by Merchant and Ivory, *Educating Rita,* starring Michael Caine, and *Shirley Valentine* (1989) directed by Lewis Gilbert.

RECORDINGS
MEDIEVAL & RENAISSANCE MUSIC

For an English version of Gregorian chant seek out *A Feather on the Breath of God,* featuring compositions (written in 1098) of Saint Hildegard, performed by a group called Gothic Voices. Directed by Christopher Page, it was recorded in the Church of St. Jude on the Hill in Hampstead, London, and produced by the Musical Heritage Society, Ocean, New Jersey (MHS-4889).

The courtly music of the troubadours is reputed to have been performed with skill (at least during his youth) by the Renaissance monarch Henry VIII, and by dozens of other musicians who composed and performed sophisticated and sometimes coyly flirtatious songs for the distraction and amusement of their aristocratic guests. Good examples of the music performed at the court of Elizabeth I are the works of composer Thomas Morley (1557–1602), which have been recorded by the Deller Consort on such titles as *Now Is the Month of Maying: Madrigal Masterpieces.* (Vanguard BG 604).

For a taste of England's Renaissance Church music, best exemplified by English composer William Byrd (1540–1632), listen to his *Cantiones Sacrae: 1589* performed by the Choir of New College, Oxford, and recorded in the New College Chapel on London Records (London CRD 3408).

ORCHESTRAL & OPERATIC WORKS

Henry Purcell's *Dido and Aeneas* is widely available with different performers. For an example of Purcell's orchestral music for horns find *The Virtuoso Trumpet,* performed by trumpeter Maurice André, accompanied by the Academy of St. Martin-in-the-Fields, and conducted by Neville Marriner (RCA Red Seal CRL 3-1430).

John Gay's *The Beggar's Opera* (first performed in 1728) is available performed by Britain's National Philharmonic Orchestra and the London Opera Chorus on Polygram Records (London: LDR 72008).

Although the debate continues about whether or not George Frideric Handel (brought to the English court by the German-born monarch George I) should be classified as an English composer, certainly his *Water Music,* first performed on July 17, 1717, during a royal procession along the Thames, conjures up 18th-century London. There's a fine recording by the English Chamber Orchestra, conducted by Raymond Leppard (Phillips 6500-047).

The works of the beloved British team of Sir Arthur Sullivan (composer) and Sir W. S. Gilbert (librettist), are widely available. *The Mikado,* for example, performed by the Pro Arte Orchestra and the Glyndebourne Festival Chorus, and conducted by Sir Malcolm Sargent is available on Angel Records (3573 B/L).

The compositions of Sir Edward Elgar, are musical tributes to the splendor and pageantry of the British Empire. The favorite composer of Edward VII, for whom he wrote two coronation marches, Elgar's music can be heard on a recording of *The*

Pomp and Circumstance marches, performed by Britain's Philharmonia Orchestra, conducted by Andrew Davis (CBS Records/Masterworks IM 37755).

England's modern master, Ralph Vaughan Williams, has been widely recorded. The *Symphony No. 3 (Pastoral)*, performed by the London Symphony Orchestra (Chandos Records CHAN 8594), and *A Sea Symphony*, performed by the London Symphony Orchestra and Chorus with André Previn conducting, and Heather Harper, soprano, and John Shirley-Quirk, baritone, performing (RCA 6237-2RC) are both fine.

Benjamin Britten's *Ceremony of Carols* performed by the Choir of St. John's College, Cambridge (Argo Records ZRG 5440) and his *Variations for a String Orchestra*, performed by the London Philharmonic Orchestra, with Roger Best, viola (Chandos Records: CHAN 8514), are both fine examples of this preeminent British composer.

RECENT RELEASES

In the 1960s, record impresarios claimed that for a pop recording to be noticed by American audiences, its chances were greatly increased if it originated in Britain. The U.S. airwaves were flooded with music by British-based musical artists whose names later became household words around the world. Later, punk rock and an entirely new generation of musical artists emerged. Their numbers are legion, their tastes range from mildly provocative to deliberately outrageous, and no list could possibly include them all. Here follows, however, a representational and highly subjective selection of some of the most visible:

The Beatles' *Past Masters (Volumes I and II)* (Capitol CDP 7-900-432 and CDP 7-900-442), is a retrospective collection of this influential group. Equally important is the Beatles' milestone album, *Sergeant Pepper* (Capitol 2653), released in 1967, which is considered both a musical watershed and a sociological landmark that altered the perceptions of a generation.

The Rolling Stones' *Flashpoint* (Sony/CBS Records CK 47-456), is a textbook study of the spirit of rock and roll, with Eric Clapton performing as a guest ace on a track entitled "Little Red Rooster." Another Rolling Stone great is *Exile on Main Street* (Sony/CBS CGK 40489).

Liquidizer (SBK Records CDP-944-80), by Jesus Jones, a new and emerging British rock group, combines drums, bass guitar, keyboard, and vocal, meshing high-tech drumbeats with wild guitars. One of this album's tracks, "Right Here, Right Now," has become one of the biggest alternative-radio hits of the year.

The Stone Roses' *The Stone Roses* (Silvertone Records-RCA/BMG 1184-2-JX), exemplifies the newly reemerging British wave of psychedelia infused with a distinctive '90s touch.

Courtney Pine's *Journey to the Urge Within* (Antilles ANT-8700) features Afro-Caribbean jazz by a British artist influenced by Sonny Rollins and John Coltrane.

FOLK MUSIC

Flower of Scotland is by the Corries (BBC ZCD 844), a leading Scottish folk music group. The title song, appealing to Scottish pride, is now the unofficial national anthem of Scotland, and usually sung lustily by Scottish audiences at football (soccer) and tennis matches throughout Britain.

In the same folkloric vein is a celebration of Irish (and to a lesser degree, English) music compiled by the BBC, entitled *Bringing it All Back Home* (BBC CD844/REF 844). This is the recorded result of a $1.5-million study—funded partly by the BBC—which traced the musical lineage, through musical themes and 19th century immigration patterns, of American and Australian folk and blues music back to Irish, English, and Scottish roots. The recording includes tracks by such artists as Sinead O'Connor, The Everly Brothers, Kate Bush, Bob Dylan, Pete Seeger, The Waterboys, and Thin Lizzy, and is considered of major interest to sociologists, musical historians, and folk music fans.

Richard Thompson, who performs on *Amnesia* (Capitol C4-48845), has been reviewed as one of the most unusual and iconoclastic of modern British folk performers. His melodies include the guitar, the mandolin, and the hammer dulcimer. His lyrics showcase both political and social satire and soulfully nostalgic ballads.

The Pogues' *Rum, Sodomy, and the Lash* (Stiff Records 222701) was recorded by this half-English, half-Irish group, based in London. It's folk and rock music with a decidedly funky (sometimes shocking) twist.

On Benjamin Britten's *Song Cycles* (Chandos CHAN-8514), an unusual arrangement of folk songs and poems by mystic William Blake, is performed by baritone Benjamin Luxon and pianist David Willison.

PLANNING A TRIP TO ENGLAND

This chapter is devoted to the where, when, and how of your trip—the advance-planning issues required to get it together and take to the road.

After deciding where to go, most people have two fundamental questions: What will it cost? and how do I get there? This chapter will answer both these questions and also resolve other important issues such as when to go, what pretrip preparations are needed, where to obtain more information about the destination, and many more.

1. INFORMATION, ENTRY REQUIREMENTS & MONEY

SOURCES OF INFORMATION

Before you go, you can obtain information from the following British Tourist Offices in the United States. **Atlanta:** 2580 Cumberland Parkway, Atlanta, GA 30339-3909 (tel. 404/432-9635). **Chicago:** 625 North Michigan Avenue, Suite 1510, Chicago, IL 60611-1977 (tel. 312/787-0490). **Dallas:** Cedar Maple Plaza, 2305 Cedar Springs Road, Suite 210, Dallas, TX 75201 (tel. 214/720-4040). **Los Angeles:** World Trade Center, 350 South Figueroa Street, Suite 450, Los Angeles, CA 90071 (tel. 213/628-3525). **New York:** 40 West 57th Street, New York, NY 10019 (tel. 212/581-4700).

In **Canada,** information is available at 94 Cumberland Street, Suite 600, Toronto, ON M5R 3N3 (tel. 416/925-6326).

In **England** the British Tourist Authority has a British Travel Centre at Rex House, 4-12 Lower Regent Street, London S.W.1 (tel. 071/730-3400), providing information about the whole of Britain, a British Rail ticket office, a travel agency, a theater-ticket agency, hotel-booking service, a bookshop, and a souvenir shop, all under one roof. Hours are Monday to Friday 9am to 6:30pm and Saturday and Sunday 10am to 4pm, with extended hours on Saturday June through September. Telephone information is available Monday to Saturday.

For specific information about London sources of information, see Chapter 3. Outside London most major cities and towns have tourist offices (see "Essentials," under individual towns).

Detailed information on adjacent countries are available in London from the following agencies: the **Wales Tourist Board,** 34 Piccadilly W.1 (tel. 071/409-0969); the **Scottish Tourist Board,** 19 Cockspur Street, S.W.1 (tel. 071/930-8661); and the **Northern Ireland Tourist Board,** 11 Berkeley Street, W.1 (tel. 071/493-0601).

For general information always check newspapers and magazines. To find the latest articles published about England go to your library and ask for the *Reader's Guide to Periodical Literature* and look up England or the city of interest.

The State Department also publishes background bulletins. Write to the Superintendent of Documents, U.S. Government Printing Office, Washington DC 20402 (tel. 202/783-3238).

A good travel agent can also provide information, but make sure the agent is a member of the American Society of Travel Agents (ASTA) so that you can complain to the Consumer Affairs Department of the Society at P. O. Box 23922, Washington, DC 20006 if you receive poor service.

ENTRY REQUIREMENTS

DOCUMENTS

All U.S. citizens, Canadians, Australians, New Zealanders, and South Africans must have a passport with at least 2 months' remaining validity. No visa is required. The Immigration officer will also want proof of your intention to return to your point of origin (usually a round-trip ticket) and visible means of support while you're in Britain. If you are planning to fly from, say, the United States to the U.K. and then on to a country that requires a visa (India, for example), it's wise to secure the Indian visa before your arrival in Britain.

CUSTOMS

Visitors from overseas entering England may bring in 400 cigarettes and 1 quart of liquor. If you come from the European Community (EC, or Common Market) area, you're allowed 300 cigarettes and 1 quart of liquor, provided you bought and paid tax in that EC country. If you buy your allowance on a ship or plane, you may import only 200 cigarettes and 1 liter of liquor. There is no limit on money, film, or other items for your own use, except that all drugs other than medical supplies are illegal. Commercial goods such as video films and nonpersonal items will require posting a bond and will take a number of hours to clear Customs. Importing live birds or animals is forbidden and they will be destroyed.

U.S. citizens returning home who have been away for 48 hours or more are allowed to bring back, once every 30 days, $400 worth of merchandise duty free. You'll be charged a flat rate of 10% duty on the next $1,000 worth of purchases. Be sure to have your receipts handy. On gifts, the duty-free limit has been increased to $50.

MONEY

Before leaving home it is advisable to secure traveler's checks and a small amount of foreign currency to cover costs on arrival overseas. Also take along about $200 in cash.

CURRENCY/CASH

At the time of writing this book, the pound (£) was worth $1.85, but rates are volatile, and this ratio may have changed by the time you arrive in Britain. Each pound (called a quid by the natives) breaks down into 100 pence (p). There are £1 coins as well as banknotes, plus coins of 50p, 20p, 10p, 2p, and 1p.

For the best exchange rate, go to a bank, not to hotels or shops. Currency and traveler's checks (for which you'll receive a better rate than cash) can be changed at the airport and some travel agencies, such as American Express and Thomas Cook. Note the rates; it can sometimes pay to shop around.

THE CONVERSION TABLE

Pence	U.S.	Pounds	U.S.$
1	.02	1	1.85
2	.04	2	3.70
3	.06	3	5.55
4	.07	4	7.40
5	.09	5	6.75
10	.19	7.50*	13.88
25	.46	10	18.50
50	.93	15	27.75
75	1.39	20	37.00

*Note: You read £7.50 as 7 pound, 50 pence.

TRAVELER'S CHECKS

Traveler's Checks are the safest way to carry cash while traveling. Most banks will give you a better rate on traveler's checks than for cash. If you can, purchase them in pound denominations. The following are the major issuers of traveler's checks:

American Express (tel. toll free 800/221-7282 in the U.S. and Canada) charges a 1% commission. Checks are free to members of the American Automobile Association.

Bank of America (tel. toll free 800/227-3460 in the U.S. or 415/624-5400, collect, in Canada) issues checks in U.S. dollars for a 1% commission everywhere but California.

Citicorp (tel. toll free 800/645-6556 in the U.S. or 813/623-1709, collect, in Canada) issues checks in U.S. dollars, pounds, or German marks.

MasterCard International (tel. toll free 800/223-9920 in the U.S. or 212/974-5696, collect, in Canada) issues checks in about a dozen currencies.

Barclays Bank (tel. toll free 800/221-2426 in the U.S. and Canada) issues checks in both U.S. and Canadian dollars and British pounds.

Thomas Cook (tel. toll free in the U.S. 800/223-7373 or 212/974-5696, collect, in Canada) issues checks in U.S. or Canadian dollars or British pounds. It's affiliated with MasterCard.

Each of these agencies will refund your checks if they are lost or stolen, upon sufficient documentation or their serial numbers. When purchasing checks ask about refund hotlines; American Express and Bank of America have the greatest number of offices around the world.

CURRENCY EXCHANGE

Many hotels in London will simply not accept a dollar-denominated check, and if they do, they'll certainly charge for the conversion. In some cases they'll accept countersigned traveler's cheques, or a credit card, but if you're prepaying a deposit on hotel reservations, it's cheaper and easier to pay with a check drawn upon a London bank.

This can be arranged by a large commercial bank or by a specialist like Ruesch International, 1350 Eye Street, Washington, D.C., 20005 (tel. 202/408-1200 or toll free 800/424-2923), which performs a wide variety of conversion-related tasks, usually for only $2 U.S. per transaction.

If you need a check payable in sterling, call Ruesch's toll-free number, describe what you need, and note the transaction number given to you. Mail your dollar-denominated personal check (payable to Ruesch International) to their office in Washington, D.C. Upon receipt, the company will mail a check denominated in sterling for the financial equivalent, minus the $2 charge. The company also sells traveler's checks denominated in sterling, and can help you with many different kinds of wire transfers and conversion of VAT refund checks. They'll mail brochures and information packets upon request.

WHAT THINGS COST IN LONDON	U.S. $
Taxi from Victoria Station to a Paddington Hotel	11.75
Underground from Heathrow Airport to central London	3.50
Local telephone call	.20
Double room at the Ritz (deluxe)	345.00
Double room at Green Park (moderate)	195.00
Double room at Edward Lear (budget)	111.00
Lunch for one at Bombay Brasserie (moderate)	24.05
Lunch for one at Mandarin Kitchen (budget)	16.65
Dinner for one, without wine at Le Gavroche (deluxe)	112.00
Dinner for one, without wine at Langan's Brasserie (moderate)	37.00
Dinner for one, without wine at Porter's (budget)	15.00
Pint of beer	2.30
Coca-Cola in a café	1.40
Cup of coffee	1.30
Role of ASA 100 color film, 36 exposures	7.50
Admission to the British Museum	Free
Movie ticket	7.80
Inexpensive theater ticket	7.50

WHAT THINGS COST IN BATH	U.S. $
Taxi from the Bath Rail Station to a centrally located hotel	3.50
Local telephone call	.20
Double room at the Royal Crescent (deluxe)	323.75
Double room at Dukes Hotel (moderate)	175.75
Double room at Orchard House (budget)	111.00
Lunch for one at Woods (moderate)	17.60
Lunch for one at Pump Room (budget)	14.80
Dinner for one, without wine at Popjoys (deluxe)	46.25
Dinner for one, without wine at Tarts (moderate)	31.45
Dinner for one, without wine at Evans Fish Restaurant (budget)	17.60
Pint of beer	2.00

	U.S. $
Coca-Cola in a café	1.20
Cup of coffee	1.10
Role of ASA 100 color film, 36 exposures	7.00
Admission to American Museum	6.50
Movie ticket	6.70
Inexpensive theater ticket	7.50

2. WHEN TO GO — CLIMATE, HOLIDAYS & EVENTS

CLIMATE

British temperatures can range from 30° to 110° but they rarely drop below 35° or go above 78°. Evenings are cool even in summer. No Britisher will ever really advise you about the weather—it is far too uncertain. If you come here from a hot area, bring some warm clothes. If you're from cooler climes, you should be all right. Note that the British, who consider chilliness wholesome, like to keep the thermostats about 10° below the American comfort level. They are also hopelessly enamored of fireplaces, which warm little except whatever portion of your anatomy you turn toward them. Hotels have central heating, but are usually kept just above the goose-bump (in English, "goose pimple") margin.

London's Average Daytime Temperature & Rainfall

	Jan	Feb	Mar	Apr	May	June	July	Aug	Sept	Oct	Nov	Dec
Temp. °F	40	40	44	49	55	61	64	64	59	52	46	42
Rainfall	2.1	1.6	1.5	1.5	1.8	1.8	2.2	2.3	1.9	2.2	2.5	1.9

HOLIDAYS

Christmas Day, Boxing Day (December 26), New Year's Day, Good Friday, Easter Monday, May Day, and spring and summer bank holidays (the last Monday in May and August respectively) are observed.

ENGLAND CALENDAR OF EVENTS

For more information about these and other events contact the various tourist offices throughout England.

FEBRUARY

☐ **Jorvik Viking Festival.** A month-long celebration of this historic cathedral city's role as a Viking outpost. For more information, call 0904/64611.

IMPRESSIONS

The way to ensure summer in England is to have it framed and glazed in a comfortable room.
—HORACE WALPOLE, LETTER TO THE REV. WILLIAM COLE, MAY, 1774

MARCH

✪ **THE SHAKESPEARE SEASON** *The Royal Shakespeare Company at Stratford-upon-Avon begins its annual season, presenting a varied program of works by the Bard in his hometown.*
Where: Royal Shakespeare Theater, Waterside (tel. 0789/295623), in Stratford-upon-Avon. When: March–December. How: Tickets at box office or else through such agents as Keith Prowse (many locations) in London.

APRIL

☐ **Grand National Meeting.** This is the premier steeplechase event in England. Takes place over a 4-mile course at Aintree Racecourse, Aintree, outside Liverpool, Merseyside (tel. 051/523-2600).

☐ **Devizes to Westminster International Canoe Race.** A 125-mile race along the Avon and Kennet Canals and the River Thames. No tickets are needed. Call 0344/483232 for more information.

MAY

☐ **Chichester Festival Theatre Season.** Some of the best of classic and modern plays are presented at this West Sussex theater whose season extends from May to September. For tickets and information, call Chichester, West Sussex P019 4AP (tel. 0243/781312).

✪ **GLYNDEBOURNE FESTIVAL OPERA SEASON** *Ever since it was founded in 1934, this has been one of the premier opera presentations of Britain, with world-acclaimed stars.*
Where: Glyndebourne, Lewes, East Sussex BN8 5UU (tel. 0273/541111). When: May–Aug. How: Tickets are sold at various theater ticket offices in London, including Keith Prowse (at many London locations, check phone book).

☐ **The Royal Windsor Horse Show.** The country's major show-jumping presentation, attended by the queen herself. Mid-May (dates vary). Home Park, Windsor, Berkshire (tel. 0298/72272 for more information).

✪ **BATH INTERNATIONAL FESTIVAL** *One of Europe's most prestigious international festivals of music and the arts. As many as 1,000 performers appear.*
Where: At various venues in Bath, Avon. When: Mid-May to late June. How: Full details can be obtained from Bath Festival, 1 Pierrepont Place, Bath BA1 IJY (tel. 0225/462231).

JUNE

☐ **Derby Day.** Famous horse-racing event at Epsom Racecourse, Epsom, Surrey. For more details, contact United Racecourses Ltd., Racecourse Paddock, Epsom, Surrey KT18 5NJ (tel. 03727/26311).

☐ **Aldeburgh Festival of Music and the Arts.** Benjamin Britten, the late composer, lived near Aldeburgh and in 1948 launched this festival of music and the arts. Lasts from mid- to late June. For more information, write or call Aldeburgh Foundation, High Street, Aldeburgh, Suffolk LP15 5AX (tel. 0728/452935).

☐ **Royal Ascot.** A premier horse-racing event and stellar social event, attracting such guests as Queen Elizabeth and Prince Philip. Information is available from The Secretary, Grand Stand Office, Ascot Racecourse, Ascot, Berkshire SL5 7JN (tel. 0990/22211).

JULY

☐ **Henley Royal Regatta.** An international rowing competition and premier event on the English social calendar. Takes place at Henley-on-Thames in Oxfordshire in early July. For more information, call 0491/57253.

AUGUST

☐ **Cowes Week.** A yachting festival held in early August off the Isle of Wight (Hampshire). For details, call 0983/295744.

SEPTEMBER

☐ **Burghley Horse Trials.** This annual event is staged on the grounds of the largest Elizabethan house in England, Burghley House, at Stamford, Lincolnshire (tel. 0780/52131). Mid-September.

OCTOBER

☐ **Cheltenham Festival of Literature.** A Cotswold event featuring readings, book exhibitions, and theatrical performances—all in this famed spa town of Gloucestershire. From early to mid-October. Call 0242/521621 for more details.

NOVEMBER

☐ **London-to-Brighton Veteran Car Run.** Begins in London's Hyde Park and ends in the seaside resort of Brighton in East Sussex. Tickets aren't necessary. Early November. Call 0753/681736 for more details.

DECEMBER

☐ **Christmas observances.** Throughout England's villages, towns, and cities.

LONDON
CALENDAR OF EVENTS

JANUARY

☐ **London International Boat Show.** The largest boat show in Europe takes place at Earl's Court Exhibition Centre, Warwick Road. First 2 weeks in January.

☐ **The Charles I Commemoration.** Anniversary of the execution of King Charles I "in the name of freedom and democracy." Hundreds of cavaliers march through central London in 17th-century dress, and prayers are said at the Banqueting House in Whitehall. Last Sunday in January. Free.

☐ **The Chinese New Year.** The famous Lion Dancers in Soho perform free. Late January or early February (based on the lunar calendar), celebrated on the nearest Sunday.

FEBRUARY

⊘ **CRUFT'S DOG SHOW** *The English, they say, love their pets more than their offspring. Cruft's offers an opportunity to observe the nation's pet lovers crooning over the 8,000 dogs representing 100 breeds that strut their stuff. An emotionally charged event for the English.*
Where: *Earl's Court Exhibition Centre, Warwick Road (tel. 071/493-6651).* **When:** *1st weekend in February.* **How:** *Tickets can be purchased from Keith Prowse or at the door.*

APRIL–MAY

☐ **The Easter Parade.** Brightly colored floats and marching bands around **Battersea Park,** a full day of activities. Free.
☐ **The Chelsea Flower Show.** The best of British gardening, with displays of plants and flowers of all seasons, at the Chelsea Royal Hospital. Tickets are available abroad from overseas booking agents. Contact your local British Tourist Authority office to find out which agency is handling ticket sales this year, or write Chelsea Show Ticket Office, P.O. Box 1426, London W6 0LQ.

JUNE

☐ **Grosvenor House Antique fair,** Grosvenor House. A very prestigious antiques fair. 2nd week.

⊘ **TROOPING THE COLOUR** *The official birthday of the queen. Seated upon a horse for hours the queen inspects her regiments and takes their salute as they parade their colors before her. A quintessential British event watched by the populace religiously on TV. The pageantry and pomp is exquisite. Depending on the weather the young men under the Busbys have been known to pass out from the heat. They remain prostrate; nothing is allowed to mar the perfect regimentation of the day.*
Where: *Horse Guards' Parade.* **When:** *June 16.* **How:** *People sleep on the sidewalk to secure a prime view.*

⊘ **LAWN TENNIS CHAMPIONSHIPS** *Ever since the players in flannels and in bonnets took to the grass courts at Wimbledon in 1877, this tournament has drawn a socially prominent crowd. Although the courts are now crowded with all kinds of tennis fans, there's still an excited hush at the Centre Court and a certain thrill to being there. Savor the two or three strawberries and cream that are still part of the experience.*
Where: *Wimbledon, London.* **What:** *Last week in June and 1st week in July.* **How:** *Tickets obtainable through a lottery which opens January 1. Write to Lawn Tennis Association, Church Road, Wimbledon, London, SW19 5AE (tel. 081/946-2244).*

JULY

☐ **Royal Tournament.** The British armed forces put on dazzling displays of athletic and military skill—an event of "military pomp, show biz, and outright jingoism." For information contact the Royal Tournament Exhibition Centre, Warwick Road, London SW5 9TA (tel. 071/373-8141). 2½ weeks in mid-July.
☐ **City of London Festival.** An annual art festival throughout the city. Call 081/377-0540 for information.

AUGUST

☐ **African-Caribbean Street Fair.** Held for 2 days in the community of Notting Hill, this is one of the largest annual street festivals in Europe attracting over half a million people annually. Live reggae and soul music plus great Caribbean food. Late August. Free.

SEPTEMBER

✪ *Opening of Parliament* *Ever since the 17th century, when the English beheaded Charles I, the British monarch has been denied the right to enter the Commons. Instead, the monarch officially opens Parliament in the House of Lords, reading an official speech which is in fact written for her by the Government of the day. She rides from Buckingham Palace to Westminster in a royal coach accompanied by the Yeoman of the Guard and the Household Cavalry.*
  Where: Houses of Parliament. When: First Monday in September. How: Public Galleries are open on a first-come, first-served basis.

NOVEMBER

☐ **Guy Fawkes Night.** Commemorates the anniversary of the "Gunpowder Plot," an attempt to blow up King James I and his parliament. Huge organized bonfires are lit throughout the city and Guy Fawkes, the plot's most famous conspirator, is burned in effigy. Early November. Free.

✪ *The Lord Mayor's Procession and Show* *The queen has to ask permission to enter the City's square mile—a right that has been jealously guarded by the merchants of London from the 17th century to this very day. Suffice to say that the Lord Mayor is a powerful character and the procession from the Guildhall to the Royal Courts appropriately impressive.*
  Where: The City. When: 2nd week in November. How: You can watch the procession from the street: The banquet is by invitation only.

3. HEALTH, INSURANCE & OTHER CONCERNS

You will encounter few health problems traveling in England. The tap water is safe to drink, the milk is pasteurized, and health services good. Occasionally the change in diet may cause some minor diarrhea so you may want to take some anti-diarrhea medicine along.

Carry all your vital medicine in your carry-on luggage and bring enough prescribed medicines to sustain you during your stay. Bring along copies of your prescriptions that are written in the generic—not brand-name—form. If you need a doctor, your hotel can recommend one or you can contact your embassy or consulate. You can also obtain a list of English-speaking doctors before you leave from the **International Association for Medical Assistance to Travelers (IAMAT)** in the United States at 417 Center Street, Lewiston, NY 14092 (tel. 716/754-4883); in Canada at 40 Regal Road, Guelph, ON N1K 1B5 (tel. 519/836-0102).

If you suffer from a chronic illness, talk to your doctor before taking the trip. For such conditions as epilepsy, diabetes, or a heart condition, wear a **Medic Alert Identification Tag,** which will immediately alert any doctor to your condition and provide the number of Medic Alert's 24-hour hotline so that a foreign doctor can obtain medical records for you. For a lifetime membership, the cost is $30. Contact the Medic Alert Foundation, P. O. Box 1009, Turlock, CA 95381-1009 (tel. 800/432-5378).

INSURANCE

Before purchasing any additional insurance check your homeowner's, automobile, and medical insurance policies as well as the insurance provided by credit-card companies and auto and travel clubs. You may have adequate off-premises theft coverage or your credit card company may even provide cancellation coverage if the ticket is paid for with a credit card.

Remember, Medicare only covers U.S. citizens traveling in Mexico and Canada.

Also note that to submit any claim you must always have thorough documentation including all receipts, police reports, medical records, and the like.

If you are prepaying for your vacation or are taking a charter or any other flight that has cancellation penalties, look into cancellation insurance.

The following companies will provide further information:

Travel Guard International, 1145 Clark Street, Stevens Point, WI 54481 (tel. toll free 800/826-1300), which offers a comprehensive 7-day policy that covers basically everything, including lost luggage. It costs $52, including emergency assistance, accidental death, trip cancellation and interruption, medical coverage abroad, and lost luggage. There are restrictions, however, which you should understand before you accept the coverage.

Travel Insurance Pak, Travelers Insurance Co., 1 Tower Square, 15 NB, Hartford, CT 06183-5040 (tel. toll free 800/243-3174 or 203/277-2318), offers illness and accident coverage, costing from $10 for 6 to 10 days. For lost or damaged luggage, $500 worth of coverage costs $20 for 6 to 10 days. You can also get trip-cancellation insurance for $5.50.

Mutual of Omaha (Tele-Trip), 3201 Farnam Street, Omaha, NB 68131 (tel. toll free 800/228-9792 or 402/345-2400), charges $3 a day (with a 10-day minimum) for foreign medical coverage up to $50,000 which features global assistance and maintains a 24-hour "hotline." The company also offers trip-cancellation insurance, lost or stolen luggage coverage, the standard accident coverage, and other policies.

HealthCare Abroad (MEDEX), 243 Church Street NW, Suite 100D, Vienna, VA 22180 (tel. toll free 800/237-6615 or 703/255-9800) offers a policy, good for 10 to 90 days, costing $3 a day, including accident and sickness coverage to the tune of $100,000. Medical evacuation is also included, along with a $25,000 accidental death or dismemberment compensation. Trip cancellation and lost or stolen luggage can also be written into this policy at a nominal cost.

WorldCare Travel Assistance Association, 605 Market Street, Suite 1300, San Francisco, CA 94105 (tel. toll free 800/666-4993 or 415/541-4991), features a 9- to 15-day policy, costing $105, including trip cancellation, lost or stolen luggage, legal assistance, and medical coverage and evacuation.

Access America, 600 Third Avenue, P.O. Box 807, New York, NY 10163-0807 (tel. toll free 800/955-4002 or 212/949-5960), has a 24-hour "hotline" in case of an emergency, and offers medical coverage for 9 to 15 days costing $49 or $10,000. If you want medical plus trip cancellation, the charge is $89 for 9 to 15 days. A comprehensive package for $111 grants 9- to 15-day blanket coverage, including $50,000 worth of death benefits.

4. WHAT TO PACK

Always pack as light as possible. Sometimes it's hard to get a porter or a baggage cart in rail and air terminals. Also, airlines are increasingly strict about how much luggage you can bring, both carry-on and checked items. Checked baggage should not be more than 62 inches (width, plus length, plus height), or weigh more than 70 pounds. Carry-on luggage shouldn't be more than 45 inches (width, plus length, plus height) and must fit under your seat or in the bin above.

The most essential items of your English wardrobe are a good raincoat, a sweater or jersey, and, if possible, an umbrella.

Note also that conservative middle-age English people tend to dress up rather than down and that they dress very well indeed, particularly at theaters and concerts. Nobody will bar you for arriving in sports clothes, but you may feel awkward, so include at least one smart suit or dress in your luggage.

Better-class restaurants usually demand that men wear ties and that women not wear shorts or jogging clothing, but those are the only clothing rules enforced.

Pack clothes that "travel well" because you can't always get pressing done at hotels. Be prepared to wash such garments as underwear in your bathroom and hang it up to dry overnight.

The general rule of packing is to bring four of everything. For men, that means four pairs of socks, four pairs of slacks, four shirts, and four sets of underwear. At least two of these will always be either dirty or in the process of drying. Often you'll have to wrap semiwet clothes in a plastic bag as you head for your next destination. Women can follow the same rule.

Take at least one outfit for chilly weather and one outfit for warm weather. Even in the summer, you may experience suddenly chilly weather. Always take two pairs of walking shoes in case you get your shoes soaked and need that extra pair.

5. TIPS FOR THE DISABLED, SENIORS, SINGLES, FAMILIES & STUDENTS

FOR THE DISABLED

Before you go, there are many agencies that can provide advance planning information.

For example, contact **Travel Information Service,** Moss Rehabilitation Hospital, 12th Street and Tabor Road, Philadelphia, PA 19141 (tel. 215/456-9900). It charges $5 per package for its data, which will contain names and addresses of accessible hotels, restaurants, and attractions often based on firsthand reports of travelers who have been there.

You may also want to subscribe to *The Itinerary,* P.O. Box 2012, Bayonne, NJ 07002-2012 (tel. 201/858-3400), for $10 a year. This travel magazine, published bimonthly, is filled with news about travel aids for the disabled, special tours, information on accessibility, and other matters.

You can also obtain a copy of *Air Transportation of Handicapped Persons,* published by the U.S. Department of Transportation. It's free if you write to Free Advisory Circular No. AC12032, Distribution Unit, U.S. Department of Transportation, Publications Division, M-4332, Washington, DC 20590.

You may also want to consider joining a tour for disabled visitors. Names and addresses of such tour operators can be obtained by writing to the **Society for the Advancement of Travel for the Handicapped,** 347 Fifth Avenue, New York, NY 10016 (tel. 212/447-7284). Yearly membership dues in this society are $40 or $25 for senior citizens and students. Send a self-addressed stamped envelope.

The **Federation of the Handicapped,** 211 West 14th Street, New York, NY 10011 (tel. 212/206-4200) also operates summer tours for members, who pay a yearly fee of $4 (U.S.).

For the blind, the best information source is the **American Foundation for the Blind,** 15 West 16th Street, New York, NY 10011 (tel. 800/232-5463).

FOR SENIORS

Many senior discounts are available but note that some may require membership in a particular association.

For information before you go, write to *Travel Tips for Senior Citizens* (publication no. 8970), distributed for $1 by the Superintendent of Documents, U.S. Government Printing Office, Washington, D.C. 20402 (tel. 202/783-5238). Another booklet—and this one is distributed free—is called *101 Tips for the Mature Traveler,* available from Grand Circle Travel, 347 Congress Street, Suite 3A, Boston, MA 02210 (tel. 617/350-7500 or toll free 800/221-2610).

SAGA International Holidays runs all-inclusive tours for seniors, preferably for those 60 years old or older. Insurance is included in the net price of their tours. Contact SAGA International Holidays, 120 Boylston Street, Boston, MA 02116 (tel. 800/343-0273). Membership is $5 a year.

In the United States, the best organization to join is the **American Association of Retired Persons,** 1909 K Street, NW, Washington, DC 20049 (tel. 202/872-4700), which offers members discounts on car rentals, hotels, and airfares. AARP travel arrangements, featuring senior citizen discounts are handled by American Express. Call toll free 800/927-0111 for land arrangements, 800/745-4567 for cruises. Flights to and from various destinations are handled by both numbers.

Information is also available from the **National Council of Senior Citizens,** 1331 F Street, NW, Washington, DC 20004 (tel. 202/347-8800), which charges $12 per person to join (couples pay $16) for which you receive a monthly newsletter, part of which is devoted to travel tips. Reduced discounts on hotel and auto rentals are available.

Elderhostel, 75 Federal Street, Boston, MA 02110 (tel. 617/426-7788) offers an array of university-based summer educational programs for senior citizens throughout the world, including England and Scotland. Most courses last around 3 weeks and are remarkable values, considering that airfare, accommodations in student dormitories or modest inns, all meals, and tuition are included. Courses include field trips, involve no homework, are ungraded, and emphasize liberal arts.

Participants must be over 60, but each may take an under-60 companion. Meals consist of solid, no-frills fare typical of educational institutions worldwide. The program provides a safe and congenial environment for older single women, who make up some 67% of the enrollment.

FOR SINGLE TRAVELERS

Unfortunately for the 85 million single Americans the travel industry is far more geared to duos, and singles often wind up paying the penalty. It pays to travel with someone and one company that resolves this problem is **Travel Companion,** which matches single travelers with like-minded companions and is headed by Jens Jurgen, who charges between $36 and $66 for a 6-month listing in his well-publicized records. People seeking travel companions fill out forms stating their preferences and needs and receive a mini-listing of potential travel partners. Companions of the same or opposite sex can be requested. For an application and more information, contact Jens Jurgen, Travel Companion, P.O. Box P-833, Amityville, NY 11701 (tel. 516/454-0880).

FOR FAMILIES

Advance planning is the key to a successful overseas family vacation. If you have very small children you should discuss your vacation plans with your family doctor and take along such standard supplies as children's aspirin, a thermometer, Band-Aids, and the like.

On airlines, a special menu for children must be requested at least 24 hours in advance, but if baby food is required, bring your own and ask a flight attendant to warm it to the right temperature. Take along a "security blanket" for your child—a pacifier, a favorite toy or book, or, for older children, something to make them feel at home in different surroundings—a baseball cap, a favorite T-shirt, or some good luck charm.

Make advance arrangements for cribs, bottle warmers, and car seats if you're driving anywhere (in England small children aren't allowed to ride in the front seat).

Ask the hotel if it stocks baby food, and, if not, take some with you and plan to buy the rest in local supermarkets.

Draw up guidelines on bedtime, eating, keeping tidy, being in the sun, even shopping and spending—they'll make the vacation more enjoyable.

Baby-sitters can be found for you at most hotels, but you should always insist, if possible, that you secure a baby-sitter with at least a rudimentary knowledge of English. With the influx of foreign workers in English hotels, you can no longer be certain that all members on the staff speak English.

Family Travel Times is a newsletter about traveling with children. Subscribers to the newsletter, which costs $35 for 10 issues, can also call in with travel questions, but Monday through Friday only from 10am to noon eastern standard time. Contact TWYCH, which stands for Travel With Your Children, 80 Eighth Avenue, New York, NY 10011 (tel. 212/206-0688).

FOR STUDENTS

The largest travel service for students is CIEE (Council on International Educational Exchange), 205 East 42nd Street, New York, NY 10017 (tel. 212/661-1414) providing details about budget travel, study abroad, working permits, and insurance. It also sells a number of helpful publications, including the *Student Travel Catalogue* ($1) and issues to bona-fide students International Student Identity Cards for $10.

For real budget travelers it's worth joining IYHF (International Youth Hostel Federation). For information write AYH (American Youth Hostels), P.O. Box 37613, Washington, DC 20013-7613 (tel. 202/783-6161) Membership costs $25 annually except for under 18s who pay $10.

6. ALTERNATIVE/ADVENTURE TRAVEL

More and more seasoned travelers are looking for fresh, challenging vacation ideas. What follows is not meant to be an exhaustive list, only a place to start.

ADVENTURE/WILDERNESS

Outward Bound, 383 Field Point Road, Greenwich, CT 06830 (tel. 203/661-0797, or 800/243-8520 outside Connecticut), founded in 1941 by a German-English educator, Kurt Hahn, aims to help people "go beyond their self-imposed limits, to use the wilderness as a metaphor for personal growth and self-discovery." Courses last from 3 days to 3 months. A 3-month course will sometimes be accepted for college credit toward a degree. Outward Bound maintains 48 different schools and centers in wilderness areas throughout the world.

Wilderness Travel, Inc., 801 Allston Way, Berkeley, CA 94710 (tel. 415/548-0420 or 800/247-6700 outside California), specializes in mountain tours and bicycle tours, but also offers walking tours of Cornwall and the Cotswolds which combine vehicular transport with strategic walking sessions of no more than 3 hours at a time.

Country Cycling Tours, 140 West 83d Street, New York, NY 10024 (tel. 212/874-5151), has tours of the back roads of England and Ireland. Tours (costing from $1,699 to $1,899) include overnight accommodations in three-star hotels, breakfast, and most dinners, and last 10 to 13 days. Luggage precedes you in a van. Cyclists can bring their own bicycles or rent them on site.

The American company referred to as "the granddaddy of cycle tour operators" is **Vermont Bicycle Touring,** P.O. Box 711, Bristol, VT 05443 (tel. 802/453-4811). Tours range from 25 to 40 miles a day, and a van transports luggage. The tours allow flexibility for individual levels of cycling experience, but additional guidance, assistance, and services are always available. Most of this group's tours are in England.

For hiking, walking, and sightseeing tours, contact **Outdoor Bound,** 1A, 18 Stuyvesant Oval, New York, NY 10009 (tel. 212/505-1020). Tours last 1 to 2 weeks, and the hiking trips are designed for the average active person. In the Lake District, accommodations and gourmet meals are in a charming 17th-century country inn near Ambleside and Windermere. A minibus takes hikers and sightseers daily to trails and sightseeing points throughout the region. Experts lecture on the culture, nature, and history of the area. Depending on the tour and options, charges are $1,000 to $1,800 per person.

Boating holidays make sightseeing easy. You can either leave your luggage aboard as you spend the days exploring or you can take your boat right into the center of a city, as at Chester, Stratford-upon-Avon, Norwich, Cambridge, York, and Windsor.

Cruising areas include canals, the River Thames, Scottish and Irish lochs, and the fascinating Cambridgeshire rivers: Ouse, Cam, and Nene. You can choose between a skipper-yourself boat, equipped with food, comprehensive instructions, and suggested routes, or else a hotel boat, where you get good food, a helpful crew, and the companionship of fellow passengers. For information and reservations, contact **UK Waterway Holidays Ltd.,** Welton Hythe, Daventry, Northamptonshire NN11 5LG (tel. 0327/843773).

EDUCATIONAL/STUDY TRAVEL

University vacations, or UNIVAC, offers liberal-arts study programs usually lasting from 7 to 12 days, at Oxford and Cambridge. Courses combine lectures, excursions, and guided walking tours, without the pressures of exams or preparing papers. There are no formal academic requirements and all adults over 18 can attend, living in one of the colleges, eating in an elaborate dining hall or intimate Fellows' dining rooms.

For information contact UNIVAC, the International Building, 9602 N.W. 13th St., Miami, FL 33171 (tel. 305/591-1736, or 800/792-0100). In the United Kingdom, its headquarters is at 8 Beaufort Pl., Cambridge, England CB5 8AG; in summer, Brasenose College, Oxford, England OX1 4AJ, or Corpus Christi College, Cambridge, England CN2 1RH.

British Universities Summer Schools, University of Oxford, Department for Continuing Education, Rewley House, 1 Wellington Square, Oxford OX1 2JA, England, offers academic programs in literature and history in association with the universities of Birmingham (at its Stratford-upon-Avon center), London, and Oxford. These programs are designed for graduates, particularly teachers, for graduating seniors, and some undergraduates.

The **Institute of International Education,** the largest U.S. organization in the field of international higher education, administers a variety of postsecondary academic, training, and grant programs. It is best known for administering the USIA predoctoral Fulbright grants. For information write or visit the U.S. Student Programs Division of IIE, 809 United Nations Plaza (First Avenue at 45th Street), New York, NY 10017 (tel. 212/984-5330).

If you're interested in ecology write **Earthwatch,** Belsyre Court, 57 Woodstock Road, Oxford OX2 6HU, a nonprofit organization, that organizes scientific projects throughout the world, Europe included. Most expeditions are organized into 1- to 3-week paying-volunteer work teams which might be doing a variety of things from surveying glaciers in Switzerland to identifying birds and mammals in Majorca's wetlands.

Payments that volunteers make are considered tax-deductible contributions to a scientific project. The organization publishes a magazine six times a year, listing more than 130 unusual opportunities. No special skills are necessary. The U.S. headquarters is at P.O. Box 403N, 680, Mt. Auburn St. Watertown, MA (tel. 617/926-8200).

HOMESTAYS/HOME EXCHANGES

Homestays are an in ideal way to gain greater insight into the country. Write to any of the BTA offices asking for their publication listing dozens of agencies and services providing homestays. See the addresses listed above.

For home exchanges which can be fun and save money contact the following:

World Wide Exchange, 1344 Pacific Avenue, Suite 103, Santa Cruz, CA 95060 (tel. 408/425-0531), will list your home and also send you three booklets of listings.

Vacation Exchange Club, 12006 111th Avenue, Suite 12, Youngstown, AZ 85363 (tel. 602/972-2186), has many English listings, charges $24.70 to list your home in their spring and winter listings. Subscribers pay $16 for the listings only.

International Home Exchange Service, Box 190070, San Francisco, CA 94119 (tel. 415/435-3497), charges $35 for three directories annually. The fee includes a listing in one of them. Seniors get 20% off.

PROMOTING INTERNATIONAL UNDERSTANDING

The Friendship Force, 575 South Tower, 1 CNN Center, Atlanta, GA 30303 (tel. 404/522-9490), was founded in Atlanta, Georgia, under the leadership of former Pres. Jimmy Carter during his tenure as governor. It exists for the sole purpose of fostering and encouraging friendship among disparate peoples around the world.

Dozens of branch groups throughout North America meet regularly and arrange group tours which take advantage of low-cost group fares. Each participant is required to spend 2 weeks in the host country (primarily in Europe, but also throughout the world), including 1 full week as a guest in the home of a local family. In this way it is hoped meaningful friendships will develop between the host family and the participants. Most volunteers spend the second week traveling independently.

No particular study regime or work program is prescribed, but participants are asked to behave in a way that represents America well.

People to People International, 501 East Armour Boulevard, Kansas City, MO 64109 (tel. 816/531-4701), defines its purpose as the promotion of international understanding among individuals through educational and cultural exchanges. It was established by Pres. Dwight D. Eisenhower in the late 1950s and organizes 3- to 4-week adult professional exchanges around the world in many different specialized fields. There is also a summer 4-week high-school educational program. A collegiate summer study-abroad program offers courses by American professors for credit. Located throughout the United States and abroad, local chapters help provide homestay possibilities for members. Privileges include access to membership travel opportunities, newsletters, and a magazine. Costs are $25 annually for families, $15 for individuals, and $10 for students.

World Wide Christian Tours, P.O. Box 506, Elizabethtown, KY 42702 (tel. 502/769-5900 or toll free 800/732-7920), focuses on Christian travel. These trips include ecumenical tours of England and golf-related tours of Scotland. This organization will tailor-make tours for special-interest and church groups of from two to more than 200.

Servas, 11 John Street, New York, NY 10038 (tel. 212/267-0252). Servas (translated from the Esperanto, it means "to serve") is a nonprofit, nongovernmental, international, interfaith network of travelers and hosts whose goal is to help build world peace, goodwill, and understanding. Servas travelers are invited to share living space within a community, normally staying without charge for visits lasting a maximum of 2 days. Day visits as well as a single shared meal can also be arranged. Visitors pay a $45 annual fee, fill out an application, and are interviewed for suitability. They then receive a Servas directory listing the names and addresses of Servas hosts on six continents who welcome visitors into their homes.

For $5 **International Visitors Information Service,** 733 15th Street NW, Suite 300, Washington, DC 20005 (tel. 202/783-6540), will mail anyone a booklet listing opportunities for contact with local residents in foreign countries. Europe is heavily featured. Checks should be made out to Meridian House/IVIS.

After World War I, a work-camp program for youth was set up to promote "peace and understanding." Participants arrange their own travel and sometimes—depending on the camp—pay for bed and board. Registration fees range from $25 to

$70. For information contact **Volunteers for Peace,** 43 Tiffany Road, Belmont, VT 05730 (tel. 802/259-2759), which issues a work-camp directory covering 36 countries and costing $10.

OPERA TOURS

Dailey-Thorp, 315 West 57th Street, New York, NY 10019 (tel. 212/307-1555), is probably the best-regarded organizer of music and opera tours in America. Because of its "favored" relation with European box offices, it's often able to purchase blocks of otherwise unavailable tickets to such events as the Salzburg Festival, the Vienna, Milan, Paris, and London operas, or the Bayreuth Festival in Germany. Tours range from 7 to 21 days, including first-class or deluxe accommodations and meals in top-rated European restaurants. Dailey-Thorp also offers visits to operas in Eastern Europe and the regional operas of Italy.

7. GETTING THERE

BY PLANE

While the facts and figures below are as accurate as research can make them, the fast-moving economics of the airline industry, particularly since deregulation make them all very tentative. Always check for the very latest flight and fare information.

Airlines compete fiercely on the North America–London route, which is one of the most heavily traveled in the world, and offer a confusing barrage of options so that the best strategy for securing the lowest-priced fare is to shop around and above all remain as flexible about dates as possible. Keep calling the airlines or your travel agent because often as the departure date nears airlines will discount seats if the flight's not fully booked.

Other general rules to keep in mind are that fares are usually cheaper during the week (Monday through Thursday noon) and that there are also seasonal fare differences (peak, shoulder, and basic). Transatlantic, peak season is summer; basic is winter and shoulder is in between. Travel during Christmas and Easter weeks is usually more expensive than in the weeks just before or after those holidays.

In any season airlines offer regular first-class, business, and economy seating. Most airlines also offer discounted fares, like the Advance Purchase Excursion, which carry restrictions (some severe) usually including advance purchase, a minimum stay abroad, and cancellation or alteration penalties.

THE MAJOR AIRLINES

More airlines fly to Britain, it seems, than any other country outside of North America. **British Airways** (tel. toll free 800/247-9297), the national carrier, operates the most flights and also provides an added bonus—an advance preview of British manners, methods, and style. The airline serves at least 19 U.S. cities, and is the only non-U.S. carrier with its own terminal at New York's JFK.

American Airlines, (tel. toll free 800/433-7300) is the U.S. carrier with the most routes into London, totaling a dozen daily routes into London from seven U.S. cities, including three nonstops per day from New York's JFK to Heathrow, and at least one daily nonstop from Chicago, Dallas/Fort Worth, Los Angeles, Boston, Newark, and Miami. They also fly to Manchester from Chicago and New York.

Despite the sale to American Airlines of its best and most-traveled routes into London, **TWA** (tel. toll free 800/221-2000) is still a visible presence on the transatlantic routes, offering daily nonstop service to Heathrow from St. Louis and Chicago and daily nonstop service to Gatwick from Baltimore.

Delta (tel. toll free 800/241-4141), depending on the season, makes either one or two daily nonstop flights between Atlanta and Gatwick and a daily nonstop from Cincinnati to Gatwick.

Northwest Airlines (tel. toll free 800/225-2525) flies nonstop from both Minneapolis and Boston to Gatwick with good connections from Detroit to Gatwick through Boston.

Pan Am (tel. toll free 800/221-1600) recently sold the bulk of its transatlantic routes to United Airlines but it does fly daily nonstop to Gatwick from Miami.

United Airlines (tel. toll free 800/241-6522) offers daily nonstop service to Heathrow from New York's JFK, San Francisco, Washington, D.C.'s Dulles, and Miami International with additional routes possible in the future.

Air Canada (tel. toll free 800/776-3000) flies to London's Heathrow nonstop from both Calgary and Edmonton between three and seven times a week, depending on the season. From Canada's larger cities (Vancouver, Toronto, and Montreal) the airline flies to Heathrow nonstop every day of the week, summer and winter.

Long considered a no-frills alternative to Western Europe's larger airlines, **Virgin Atlantic Airways** (tel. toll free 800/862-8621) now offers services, amenities, and—in many cases, prices—comparable to those of most of the world's major carriers. Owned by the same people who own Virgin Atlantic Records and several of London's more unusual nightclubs, the airline flies to London's Gatwick from Newark, New Jersey, Boston, and Miami, and to London's Heathrow from New York's JFK and Los Angeles. Depending on their origin, flights leave between four and seven times a week.

BEST-FOR-THE-BUDGET FARES

APEX Generally, your cheapest option on a regular airline is to book an APEX fare. This is the most heavily used fare to London from North America on any airline, although its exact definition can vary widely even within the same airline. British Airways, for example, offers two types of APEX fares. The least expensive is a nonrefundable ticket which requires a 30-day advance purchase, and a minimum stay of 7 to 21 days. Depending on the season, midweek round-trip fares range from $598 to $878, weekend fares range from $658 to $938. British Airways, in conformity with all the other carriers, adds an additional $18 to the price of each round-trip ticket for government taxes.

A slightly more expensive APEX fare offered by British Airways allows you to change travel plans for a fee. Requiring a 21-day advance booking, and a minimum stay of between 7 days and 6 months, it allows cancellations or changes of prearranged flight dates for the payment of a $100 fee. From New York to Heathrow, fares range from $738 to $1,068 midweek, and from $798 to $1,128, plus tax, on weekends, depending on the season.

Special Promotional Fares British Airways is always introducing promotional fares like last year's $398 round-trip fare from New York to London, available from January to mid-March, or the Late Saver Fare, available 48 hours before departure from any of British Airways' departure points in North America.

These fares are cited only to give you an idea of what is likely to be available. Even though they may be discontinued, rest assured that others will come along to take their place.

Discounts Senior citizens (in this case, anyone over 60) receive special 10% discounts at BA through its much-appreciated "Privileged Traveler" program. They also qualify for less stringent restrictions on cancellation policies of APEX tickets. The discounts are granted to BA's inventory of tours, and intra-Britain air tickets as well. For information on joining this program (it requires mailing a $10 fee to BA and waiting for a membership card), contact one of the company's reservations staff. The $10 fee almost immediately pays for itself with the savings and added incentives. BA also offers youth fares to anyone aged 12 to 24.

OTHER GOOD-VALUE CHOICES

Bucket Shops In the '60s, mainstream airlines in Britain gave this insulting name to resellers of blocks of unsold tickets consigned to them by major transatlantic carriers; it might be more polite to refer to them as "consolidators." They act as clearing houses for blocks of tickets that airlines discount and consign during normally slow periods of air travel.

Tickets are usually priced 20% to 35% below the full fare. Terms of payment can vary—anything between last-minute and 45 days prior to departure. Tickets can be purchased through regular travel agents, who usually mark up the ticket 8% to 10%, maybe more, thereby greatly reducing your discount. A survey conducted of flyers who use consolidators voiced only one major complaint. Use of such a ticket doesn't qualify you for an advance seat assignment, and you are therefore likely to be assigned a "poor seat" on the plane at the last minute.

The survey revealed that most flyers estimated their savings at around $200 per ticket off the regular price. Nearly a third of the passengers reported savings of up to $300 off the regular price. But, and here is the hitch, many persons who booked consolidator tickets reported no savings at all, as the airlines will sometimes match the consolidator ticket by announcing a promotional fare. The situation is a bit tricky and calls for some careful investigation on your part to determine just how much you are saving.

Bucket shops abound from coast to coast. Here are some recommendations. Look also for their ads in your local newspaper's travel section. They're usually very small and a single column in width.

Maharaja Travels Inc., 393 Fifth Avenue, New York, NY 10016 (tel. 212/213-2020 or toll free 800/223-6862), has been around for some 20 years, offering tickets to 400 destinations worldwide, including London.

Access International, 101 West 31st Street, Suite 1104, New York, NY 10001 (tel. 212/465-0707 or toll free 800/825-3633), may be the country's biggest consolidator, specializing in discounted tickets to the capitals of Europe, including London.

Phoenix Travel, 280 Madison Avenue, New York, NY 10016 (tel. 212/689-9010), specializes in New York–to–London discounted fares, usually with no more than a 3-day advance purchase and no minimum stay.

Travel Avenue, 180 North Des Plaines, Chicago, IL 60661 (tel. toll free 800/333-3335), is a national agency whose headquarters are in Chicago. Its tickets are often cheaper than most shops in that it charges the customer only a $25 fee on international tickets, rather than taking the usual 10% commission from an airline. Travel Avenue rebates most of that back to the customer—hence, the lower fares.

Out West, you can try **Sunline Express Holidays, Inc.,** 607 Market Street, San Francisco, CA 94105 (tel. 415/541-7800 or toll free 800/877-2111); or **Euro-Asia, Inc.,** 4203 East Indian School Road, Suite 210, Phoenix, AZ 85018 (tel. 602/955-2742 or toll free 800/525-3876). Since dealing with unknown bucket shops might be a little risky, it's wise to call the Better Business Bureau in your area to see if complaints have been filed against the company from which you plan to purchase a fare.

Charter Flights   For reasons of economy (and never for convenience), some travelers opt for charter flights.

Strictly speaking, a charter flight occurs on an aircraft reserved months in advance for a one-time-only transit to some predetermined point. Before paying for a charter, check the restrictions on your ticket or contract. You may be asked to purchase a tour package and pay far in advance. You'll pay a stiff penalty (or forfeit the ticket entirely) if you cancel. Charters are sometimes canceled when the plane doesn't fill up. In some cases, the charter-ticket seller will offer you an insurance policy for your own legitimate cancellation (hospital confinement or death in the family, for example).

There is no way to predict whether a proposed flight to England will cost less on a charter or less in a bucket shop. You have to investigate at the time of your trip.

One company arranging charters is the **Council on International Educational Exchange (Council Travel),** 205 East 42nd Street, New York, NY 10017 (tel. 212/661-1450), the travel division of CIEE. It offers the budget traveler a full range of affordable services on travel, work, and study abroad. Council Travel operates 32 other offices nationwide and 11 offices abroad. The London office is at 28A Poland Street, London, W.1 (tel. 071/437-7767).

One of the biggest New York charter operators is **Travac,** 989 Sixth Avenue, New York, NY 10018 (tel. 212/563-3303 or toll free 800/TRAV-800), which operates charters from New York to London and other continental destinations such as Paris.

REBATORS

To confuse the situation even more, rebators also compete in the low-cost airfare market. These outfits pass along to the passenger part of their commission, although many of them assess a fee for their services. Most rebators offer discounts that range from 10% to 25% (but this could vary from place to place), plus a $20 handling charge. They are not the same as travel agents, although they sometimes offer similar services, including discounted land arrangements and car rentals.

Rebators include: **Travel Avenue,** 180 North Des Plaines, Chicago, IL 60661 (tel. 312/876-1116 or toll free 800/333-3335); **The Smart Traveller,** 3111 SW 27th Avenue, Miami, FL 33133 (tel. 305/448-3338 or toll free 800/226-3338 in Florida and Georgia only); and **Blitz Travel,** 8918 Manchester Road, St. Louis, MO 63144 (tel. 314/961-2700).

Standbys   A favorite of spontaneous travelers with absolutely no scheduled demands on their time, standby fares leave your departure to the whims of fortune, and the hopes that a last-minute seat will become available. Most airlines don't offer standbys, although some seats are available to London and to Vienna. These fares are generally offered from April to November only.

Virgin Atlantic Airways (tel. 800/862-8621) features both a day-of-departure and a day-prior-to-departure standby fare from New York to London.

GOING AS A COURIER

This cost-cutting technique may not be for everybody. You travel as a passenger and courier and for this service you'll secure a greatly discounted airfare or sometimes even a free ticket.

You're allowed one piece of carry-on luggage only; your baggage allowance is used

---

Ⓕ FROMMER'S SMART TRAVELER: AIRFARES

1. Take off-peak flights. That means not only autumn to spring departures, but Monday to Thursday for those midweek discounts.
2. Avoid any last-minute change of plans (if you can help it), and that way you'll also avoid penalties airlines impose for changes in itineraries.
3. Keep checking the airlines and their fares. Timing is everything. A recent spot check of one airline revealed that in just 7 days it had discounted a New York to London fare by $195.
4. Shop all airlines that fly to your destination.
5. Always ask for the lowest fare, not just a discount fare.
6. Ask about frequent-flyer programs to gain bonus miles when you book a flight.
7. Check "bucket shops" for last-minute discount fares that are even cheaper than their advertised slashed fares.
8. Ask about air/land packages. Land arrangements are often cheaper when booked with an air ticket.
9. Check "standby" fares offered by Virgin Atlantic Airways.
10. Fly free or at a heavy discount as a "courier."

by the courier firm to transport its cargo (which by the way, is perfectly legal). As a courier, you don't actually handle the merchandise you're "transporting" to Europe, you just carry a manifest to present to Customs.

Upon arrival, an employee of the courier service will reclaim the company's cargo. Incidentally, you fly alone, so don't plan to travel with anybody. (A friend may be able to arrange a flight as a courier on a consecutive day.) Most courier services operate from Los Angeles or New York, but some operate out of other cities, such as Chicago or Miami.

Courier services are often listed in the Yellow Pages or in advertisements in travel sections or newspapers.

For a start, check **Halbert Express,** 147-05 176th Street, Jamaica, NY 11434 (tel. 718/656-8189 from 10am to 3pm daily); or **Now Voyager,** 74 Varick Street, Suite 307, New York, NY 10013 (tel. 212/431-1616). Call daily from 11:30am to 6pm (at other times you'll get a recorded message announcing last-minute special round-trip fares).

BY SHIP

Cunard Line, 555 Fifth Avenue, New York, NY 10017 (tel. 212/880-7500 or toll free 800/221-4770), boasts as its flagship the *Queen Elizabeth 2,* quite accurately billed as "the most advanced ship of the age." It is the only ocean liner providing regular transatlantic service—18 sailings a year between July and December—which dock at such cities as New York, Baltimore, and Fort Lauderdale, before sailing to the European ports of Cherbourg, France; Cork, Ireland; and Southampton, England. Built along the Clyde River near Glasgow in the late 1960s, the *QE2* was radically modernized in 1987 at a cost of $152 million. On board, you'll find four swimming pools, a sauna, nightclubs, a balconied theater, cinema, chic boutiques (including the world's first seagoing branch of Harrods), five restaurants, paddle-tennis courts, and a children's playroom staffed with English nannies.

The life-style on the ship also includes an on-board branch of California's "Golden Door Spa at Sea;" a computer learning center with 12 IBM personal computers; seminars by trained professionals on astrology, cooking, art, fitness, and health; and a Festival of Life series that introduces you to such personalities as James Michener, Carly Simon, Dick Cavett, or Ben Kingsley.

Fares are extremely complicated, based on cabin standard and location and the season of sailing. In thrift/superthrift season—roughly defined as late autumn—sailings usually cost a minimum of $1,480 in transatlantic class and around $2,765 in first class. Prices go steeply uphill from there, eventually reaching a maximum of $9,640 for a suite in high season. These prices are per person, based on double occupancy. All passengers pay a $150 port tax, regardless of the class of cabin. Many different packages are promoted, most of which add on relatively inexpensive airfare from your home city to the port of departure, plus a return to your home city from London on British Airways.

BY FREIGHTER

For an offbeat, often less expensive alternative (note, though, that a budget accommodation aboard the *QE2* can cost less money), if you have time and an adventurous spirit, you can try to secure a cabin aboard a freighter. No freighter can carry more than 12 passengers because a full-time ship's doctor would be required. Your cabin will be adequate, but don't expect organized activities.

Most freighters dock at Le Havre, Rotterdam, or Bremerhaven, but a few make stops at such unlikely British ports as Felixstowe. The voyage takes from 7 to 12 days from the U.S. East Coast. Sometimes the final port will change during crossing, throwing prearranged itineraries into confusion, so you need to be flexible.

In summer, cabins are often booked as much as a year in advance. Space is more likely to be available in winter.

For more information, write to Ford's Freighter Travel Guide, 19448 Londelius Street, Northridge CA 91324 (tel. 818/701-7414).

Lykes Brothers Steamship Co., Lykes Center, 300 Poydras Street, New Orleans, LA 70130 (tel. 800/535-1861) is an American-registered company running four freighters, which travel every 6 days between New Orleans, Antwerp, and Bremerhaven. On the way back from Bremerhaven, vessels stop at Felixstowe, England, and at Le Havre, France, before crossing to Norfolk, Virginia, and Galveston, Texas, and finally, New Orleans. Six passengers only can be accommodated in the two double cabins and one suite on each vessel. Passengers dine with the officers and crew and mingle in the alcohol-free lounge. There is no entertainment of any kind.

BY TRAIN/BUS/CAR FROM THE CONTINENT

There is, of course, no way of reaching England overland from North America, but if you are going from the Continent, your Eurailpass will *not* be valid when you get there. BritRail, however, has its own pass if you plan to do extensive traveling in the British Isles.

If you're touring Britain and France, consider using the BritFrance Railpass, which includes Hovercraft round-trip Channel crossings. You may choose a total of any 5 days of unlimited rail travel during a 15-day consecutive period, or 10 days during a single month—on both the British and French rail networks. Adult first-class fares (any 5 days in 15) sell for $335; adult standard fares for $249. There is also a youth standard (ages 12 to 25), costing $199 for any 5 days in 15. Obtain the pass at FrenchRail, Inc. (tel. 800/848-7245) or at BritRail Travel International (tel. 212/599-5400).

The most popular rail crossing from the Continent is from Paris' Gare du Nord via Boulogne where you board a Hovercraft to Dover and to London. It takes 5½ hours.

If you plan to take a rented car across the Channel, check carefully with the rental company before you leave about license and insurance requirements. In a few years, the long-heralded "Chunnel," or tunnel-under-the-Channel between France and Britain, may alter this situation radically.

BY FERRY/HOVERCRAFT

The major carriers are Sealink, Townsend Throsen, and the P&O Channel Lines operating passenger and car-ferries between Calais or Boulogne, and Dover or Folkestone. Calais to Dover takes 90 minutes, and Boulogne to Folkestone takes 1 hour and 50 minutes. The fastest seaway to England—40 minutes—is via Hoverspeed's Hovercraft from Boulogne to Dover.

In summer, always make reservations as far in advance as possible for one of these crossings.

For Sealink information call 212/599-5400 in New York, 213/624-8787 in Los Angeles, 214/748-0860 in Dallas, 416/929-3334 in Toronto, and 604/683-6896 in Vancouver.

If you plan to take a rented car across the Channel, check carefully about license and insurance requirements with the rental company before you leave.

ORGANIZED TOURS

Some of Britain's best-valued and most imaginative tours are offered by British Airways (call 800/AIRWAYS for details). They offer 4-day/3-night, 7- and 10-day, and longer tours. Some are themed. They vary from super-structured and guided tours to ones that are designed for independent-minded visitors who need no more than discounted vouchers for a car rental and rooms at specific types of hotels.

Chicago-based **Abercrombie & Kent International,** books carefully organized 5- to 7-day tours using first-class rail transport. Each night is spent in four- or five-star hotels, often buildings classified as Stately Homes making these carriage-trade tours par excellence with tabs as high as $2,600 per person. For more information, contact Abercrombie & Kent International, Inc., 1520 Kensington Road, Oak Brook, IL 60521 (tel. 708/954-2944 or toll free 800/323-7308).

8. GETTING AROUND

BY PLANE

British Airways (tel. toll free 800/247-9297) flies to more than 20 cities outside London, including Manchester, Glasgow, and Edinburgh. British Airways telephone representatives within North America can give price and schedule information, and make reservations for flights, hotels, car rentals, and tours within the U.K. Ask about the British Airways Super Shuttle Saver fares, which can save you up to 50% on travel to certain key British cities. Trips must be reserved and ticketed 2 weeks in advance, and you can fly only during off-peak times. This usually (but not always) is restricted to anytime on weekends, or weekdays between 10am and 3:30pm, and any night flight after 7pm.

Other cost-conscious options include a 14-day round-trip APEX which must be reserved and paid for 14 days in advance, and travel completed within 3 months of departure.

British Airways' U.K. airpass allows travel in a continuous loop to between 3 and 12 cities on BA's domestic routes. Passengers must end their journey at the same point they began. If such a ticket is booked (say, London to Manchester to Glasgow to Aberdeen to the Shetland Islands, with an eventual return to London), each segment of any itinerary will cost (subject to change) between $65 and $85. This is considerably less (as much as 50% less) than if each segment were booked individually. The pass is available for travel to about a dozen of the most-visited cities and regions of Britain. It must be booked and paid for at least 7 days before departure from the United States, and all sectors of the itinerary must be booked simultaneously. Some changes are permitted in flight dates (but not in the cities visited) after the ticket is issued. Check with BA for full details and restrictions.

BY TRAIN

Eurailpass is not valid in Great Britain.

There are several special national passes for train travel outside London. For railroad information go to the British Rail/Sealink office, 4-12 Lower Regent Street, S.W.1. (tel. 071/928-5151) and at the British Rail Travel Centres in the main London railway stations—Waterloo, King's Cross, Euston, Victoria, and Paddington—where each deals mainly with its own region.

BRITRAIL PASS

This pass permits unlimited rail travel in England, Scotland, and Wales on all British Rail routes (it is not valid on ships between the U.K. and the Continent, the Channel Islands, or Ireland). An 8-day gold (first-class) pass costs $319; a silver (economy class) $209; a 15-day pass costs respectively $479, and $319; a 22-day pass costs $599 and $399; a 1-month pass $689 and $465. Kids 5 to 15 pay half fare; under 5s are free.

Youth passes (for ages 16 through 25), all silver, are $169 for 8 days, $255 for 15 days. If you choose to go first class, you will pay full adult fare.

BritRail also offers a Senior Citizen gold pass to people 60 and over. For 8 days, it's $289 in first class, $189 second; for 15 days, $429 first class, $289 second; for 22 days, $539 first, $359 second; and for 1 month, $619 first, $419 second.

Note: Prices for BritRail Passes are higher for Canadian travelers because of the different conversion rate for Canadian dollars.

BritRail passes cannot be obtained in Britain, but should be secured before leaving North America either through travel agents or by writing or visiting BritRail Travel International, 1500 Broadway, New York, NY 10036. Canadians can write to 94

Cumberland Street, Toronto, ON M5R 1A3; or 409 Granville Street, Vancouver BC V6C 1T2. BritRail passes do not have to be predated. Validate your pass at any British Rail station when you start your first rail journey.

BRITRAIL FLEXIPASS

The Flexipass lets you travel anywhere on British Rail, but it's available for 8 days or for 15 days only. The 8-day Flexipass can be used for any 4 (nonconsecutive) days and costs $269 in first class, $179 in economy. Seniors pay $239 (first class or $159 second class), and youths 16 through 25 pay $145 to travel economy class. The 15-day Flexipass can be used for any 8 (nonconsecutive) days of travel out of 15 and costs $379 first class; $255 economy. A senior pass is $339 (first class), $229 second class; the youth economy class is $199.

Flexipass must also be purchased from either your travel agent or from BritRail Travel International in the U.S. and Canada (see addresses above).

LONDON EXTRA

If you're planning to confine your itineraries to easy day-trips from London, London Extra may make better sense than a BritRail Pass. It allows unlimited travel to accessible destinations on British Rail's "Network SouthEast," which includes Oxford, Cambridge, Canterbury, Salisbury, and Portsmouth. Frequent trains—41 to Brighton alone—let you leave early in the morning and return to London in time for the theater or dinner.

A 3-day London Extra Pass costs in first-class $95 for adults; $48 for children; $75 for adults or $38 for children in second class. A 7-day London Extra Pass costs adults $170, children $85 in first class; $135 for adults in second class, $68 for children.

BRITAINSHRINKERS

From early April to the end of October, British Rail operates these discounted full-day escorted tours that include train transportation and sightseeing by bus during the day. You have a light lunch in a local pub, take some free time to shop or explore, and return in time for dinner or the theater. Rates include entrance fees and VAT.

The Britainshrinkers offer excellent value for the money and if you use a valid BritRail Pass or Flexipass, you can save up to 60% of the cost of each tour you take. For example, passholders can visit Bath and Stonehenge in 1 day for $66, Stratford-upon-Avon for $66, or Oxford and the Cotswolds for $62. Regular tour prices are $98 to Bath and Stonehenge, $98 to Stratford-upon-Avon, and $87 to Oxford and the Cotswolds.

BY BUS

In Britain a "coach" is usually a long-distance or touring bus; a "bus" is for local transportation.

The express motorcoach networks, operated by National and Scottish Citylink coaches, cover most of Britain linking cities and towns efficiently and frequently. Most places off the main route can be easily reached by stopping and switching to a local bus. Tickets are relatively cheap, often only half the rail fare and it's usually cheaper to purchase a return ticket rather than two one-way fares.

Victoria Coach Station, 172 Buckingham Palace Road, S.W.1 (tel. 071/730-0202), a block up from Victoria Station (railroad) in London, is the departure point for most buses including the large long-distance coach operators, National Express and Caledonian Express. Reservations should be made and tickets bought in advance if possible.

National Express and Caledonian Express offer the Britexpress Card which grants one-third off all adult tickets purchased on Britain's Express Coach network. The card is valid for any 30-day period throughout the year. You can travel when and where you like with a choice of around 1,500 destinations in England, Scotland, and Wales. The card costs £10 ($16.50).

National Express Rapides are luxurious long-distance coaches equipped with hostesses, light refreshments, reclining seats, toilets, and no-smoking areas. Details of all coach services can be obtained from 071/730-0202 from 8am to 10pm daily. The National Express ticket office at Victoria Coach Station is open from 6am to midnight daily. Ask about their Tourist Trail Pass, offering unlimited travel on their network throughout the United Kingdom (although service is most extensive in England and Wales). A 5-day pass costs £56 ($103.60); an 8-day pass, £78 ($144.30); a 15-day pass, £116 ($214.60); a 22-day pass, £138 ($140.55); and a 30-day pass, £160 ($296). The ticket bureau for Ireland and Europe is open daily from 7:30am to 10:30pm. You can arrange coach excursions here, as well as sightseeing tours, rail and ferry travel tickets, and even hotel accommodations.

The Credit Card Sales Department of Victoria Coach Station (tel. 071/730-3499) can make reservations and precharge tickets to anywhere within Britain on either National Express bus lines or the Scottish Citylink bus lines. Pick up your tickets at the counter as late as 30 minutes before your departure. Phone reservations and purchases are taken daily from 8am to 9pm; only MasterCard and VISA are accepted.

For journeys within a roughly 35-mile radius of London, including such major attractions as Windsor, Hampton Court, Chartwell, and Hatfield House, try the Green Line bus service. Go to the Green Line Enquiry office at Eccleston Bridge, Victoria, S.W.1 (off Buckingham Palace Road, or call 071/668-7261 for more information.

With a 1-day Golden Rover ticket, costing £9 ($16.65) for adults and £43.40 ($6.29) for children, you can visit the environs of London, including such places as Windsor Castle. The pass is valid for 1-day on almost all Green Line coaches and London Country buses Monday to Friday after 9am and all day Saturday and Sunday. The Three-Day Rover, costs £12.50 ($23.15) for adults and £8.40 ($15.54) for children.

For more information, write to Green Line Country Bus Lines, Lesbourne Road, Reigate, Surrey RH2 7LE (tel. 0737/222905). The Country Bus Lines routes circle London. They never go to the center of the capital, although they hook up with the routes of the red buses and the Green Line coaches that do.

BY CAR

Partly because of the huge number of visitors to the United Kingdom, the car-rental market is among the most competitive in Europe. Many companies offer discounts to clients who reserve cars in advance, usually 48 hours from offices in a renter's home country. When renting, always ask if the 17½% VAT, insurance, and collision damage waiver (CDW) are included. Check to see if you are covered by the credit card you use, thus avoiding the added coverage if possible. This can make a big difference in your bottomline costs.

Budget Rent-a-Car (tel. 800/472-3325 in the U.S.) has 15 offices throughout London, including one at each major airport and at Victoria Railway Station. The most central office is near Marble Arch, 89 Wigmore Street, London W1 (tel 071/723-8038). The lowest rates are granted to those who reserve their car at least 24 hours in advance from North America. A compact Ford Escort rents for £38 ($70.30) per day for 1- to 3-day rentals with VAT, personal accident insurance (PAI), and collision damage waiver (CDW) included. Discounts are granted for longer rentals.

At **Hertz** (tel. 800/654-3001 in the U.S.), whose main London office is at 35 Edgware Road, Marble Arch, London W1 (tel. 071/402-4242), a Ford Fiesta, with unlimited mileage, VAT, PAI, and CDW included costs £51 ($94.35) per day at Hertz's downtown London office (more at the airports). Discounts also for weekly rentals.

At **Avis** (tel. 800/331-2112), whose main downtown office is at 35 Headfort Place, London S.W.1 (tel. 071/245-9862), the cost of a Ford Fiesta is so expensive at £83 ($153) per day plus CDW of £7 ($12.95), plus VAT that most visitors opt for one of its more economical longer-term rates. Four-day rentals with reservations made at least two days in advance from the U.S., cost £112 ($207) plus VAT and CDW.

Also ask the airline you're flying about car rentals. British Airways (tel. 800/247-

9297 in the U.S.) offers inexpensive car rental arrangements (10 days through Avis for the regular price of five days) for clients who simultaneously book air passage from North America.

Though these airline promotions come and go, always ask about car rentals when you book your airline ticket.

DRIVING RULES & REQUIREMENTS

In England you drive on the left and pass on the right. Road signs are clear and the international symbols unmistakable.

To drive a car in Britain, you need your passport and your driver's license (no special British license is needed). The wise driver will secure a copy of the *British Highway Code,* available from almost any stationer or news agent.

A word of warning: Pedestrian crossings are marked by striped lines (zebra striping) on the road and flashing orange curbside lights. Drivers *must* stop and yield the right of way if a pedestrian has stepped out into the zebra zone to cross the street. Wearing seat belts is mandatory in the British Isles.

ROAD MAPS

The best road map, especially if you're trying to locate some obscure village in Britain, is the *The Ordnance Survey Motor Atlas of Great Britain,* revised annually and published by Temple Press. It's available at most book stores, including W. & G. Foyle Ltd., 113-119 Charing Cross Rd., London, W.C.2 (tel. 071/439-8501).

BREAKDOWNS

Membership in one of the two major auto clubs in England can be helpful: the Automobile Association at Fanum House, Basingstoke, Hampshire RG21 2EA (tel. 0256/20123) and the Royal Automobile Club at P.O. Box 700, Spectrum, Bond Street, Bristol, Avon BS99 1RB (tel. 0272/232340). You can secure membership in one of these clubs through the car rental agent. Upon joining, you'll be given a key to the roadside emergency telephone boxes. In London, for 24-hour breakdown service call 081/954-7373 for the AA, or 0923/335-55 for the RAC.

GASOLINE

Gasoline or "petrol" is sold by the liter, with 4.5 liters to an imperial gallon. Prices are much higher than Stateside and you'll probably have to serve yourself. In some remote areas, stations are few and far between, and many all over the country are closed on Sunday.

HITCHHIKING

Hitchhiking is legal and generally safe. However, getting into a car with any stranger anywhere in the world can be extremely dangerous, especially for solo travelers. Always excercise caution. In Great Britain, it is illegal to hitchhike on motorways. The cleaner and tidier you look, the better your chances for getting a ride. Have a board with your destination written on it to hold up for drivers to see.

9. SUGGESTED ITINERARIES

CITY HIGHLIGHTS

The cities or towns below are not ranked in order of importance.

1. London
2. Windsor
3. Oxford

4. Canterbury
5. Portsmouth
6. Winchester
7. Plymouth
8. Salisbury
9. Glastonbury
10. Bath
11. Broadway
12. Stratford-upon-Avon
13. Cambridge
14. Lincoln
15. York
16. Windermere
17. Liverpool

PLANNING YOUR ITINERARY
IF YOU HAVE 1 WEEK

Days 1–4: London (for specific suggestions see "Suggested Itineraries" in Chapter 6).
Day 5: Day-trip to Stratford-upon-Avon (try to see one of Shakespeare's plays performed).
Day 6: Day-trip to Windsor.
Day 7: Day-trip to Canterbury.

IF YOU HAVE 2 WEEKS

Spend the first week as outlined above.
Day 8: Head for the West Country, visiting Winchester where you can overnight.
Day 9: Visit Salisbury and nearby Stonehenge.
Day 10: Head southwest to the coast to Plymouth.
Day 11: Continue west to Looe.
Day 12: Head north to Glastonbury and then to Wells for the night.
Day 13: Travel to Bath for the night.
Day 14: Head west back to London.

IF YOU HAVE 3 WEEKS

Spend weeks 1 and 2 as outlined above.
Day 15: From London, head north into East Anglia, overnighting at Cambridge.
Day 16: Visit Ely Cathedral and continue to Boston for lunch, with an overnight in Lincoln.
Day 17: Drive northwest from Lincoln to York for the night.
Day 18–19: From York head across England on the A59 for lunch in Harrogate. Continue to the Lake District, with a 2-night stopover in Windermere. On Day 19 explore the lakes.
Day 20: Drive south to Liverpool and spend the night.
Day 21: Spend most of the day getting back to London, perhaps for a night at the theater, followed by a late supper in Soho.

10. ENJOYING ENGLAND ON A BUDGET

For years, especially in the postwar era and right up until the mid-1970's, England was considered an inexpensive country to visit, especially outside London. That is no longer true. Rampant inflation—plus the decline of the dollar—have made England, especially London, an expensive travel destination. Therefore, the budget traveler will have to work harder than ever to keep travel costs trimmed.

THE $50-A-DAY BUDGET

This daily budget covers the basic living costs of three meals a day and the price of a room. Naturally, the cost of sightseeing, transportation, shopping, and entertainment are extra, but in this section I'll discuss how to keep those expenses trimmed, too.

The $50-a-day budget breaks down roughly this way: $26 per person (based on double occupancy) for a room and a continental breakfast, $8 for lunch, and $16 for dinner. Of course, for those who can afford more, I've included many hotels and restaurants that are worth the extra bucks.

SAVING MONEY ON ACCOMMODATIONS

BEST BETS

Stay at One- and Two-Crown or "listed" Hotels The British Tourist Authority rates hotels in England based on crowns. An even better bet is a hotel designated only as "listed," which has no crowns, mainly because it doesn't have rooms offering a private bath, but it represents one of the cheapest ways to live in England.

Patronize Bed & Breakfasts For the budgeteer, this is virtually the only way to tour England and pay only a modest sum for lodgings. Throughout the country, B&B signs are posted. Usually this is a way housewives earn extra money if they have one, two, or three free rooms to rent. Prices are almost always modest, and, in lieu of a private bath, an English breakfast is included.

Overnight at Guesthouses These accommodations are slightly better than a typical B&B, and they usually have more rooms, often 4 to 15. Sometimes they'll have a TV or reading lounge, and many of them will serve you dinner if you make arrangements that morning.

Go Youth Hosteling There are more than 350 youth hostels in England, and they are an even better bet financially for those who don't mind shared facilities. Many of them have private rooms—usually double or family rooms—but the cheapest accommodations are in shared dormitory facilities. No age restriction is imposed. Complete information is available from YHA Headquarters, Travelyan House, 8 St. Stephen's Hill, St. Albans, Hertfordshire AL1 2DY (tel. 0727/55215).

OTHER MONEY SAVING STRATEGIES

1. Take advantage of off-season (November to March) discounts from 15% to 30%. Always ask; they won't be offered.
2. Stay in rooms with shared bath. Hallway or corridor baths are adequate.
3. Even in rooms with private plumbing, ask for a room with a shower instead of a bath, it's less expensive.
4. If there are three or more in your party, ask for an additional bed in your room. In a single, an extra bed usually costs 60% less than the maximum price for the room; in a double, 35% less.
5. In order to ensure securing a budget room, arrive early in the day then use the rest of the day for sightseeing, returning to your accommodation at night knowing you've got one at a price you probably don't mind paying.
6. Rent a furnished "flat" (apartment), house, or cottage. Even trailers are available for rent, but be prepared to stay a while—at least a week.
7. Stay in university housing, often available from mid-June until September 1, in cities and towns. Contact the British Universities Accommodation Consortium, P.O. Box 486, University Park, Nottingham NG7 2RD (tel. 0602/504571).

SAVING MONEY ON MEALS

1. Choose the set menu. The French call them table d'hôte, the English the set menu or fixed-price menu, but the result is the same: a major savings to you. It is estimated that in some restaurants if you order a set menu, it will cost 30% less than if you'd ordered the same dishes à la carte. Many of the best deals are available at lunch, although countless restaurants offer set dinners as well.
2. Patronize the pubs, especially at lunch. Pub lunches throughout England are the dining bargains of the country—everything washed down with some lager if you wish. But it's also possible to enjoy pub meals in the evening when you'll get some dishes that are served in the dining room for a fraction of the price.
3. Eat at cafeterias and fast-food places—you'll find them everywhere. The food won't be great, but it will be cheap.
4. Don't overtip. Service (10% to 15% plus 17½% VAT) is usually included in the price of your food item. Where the service has been included, it's customary to leave only some small change.

SAVING MONEY ON SIGHTSEEING

1. Join English Heritage, the public organization responsible for the preservation, conservation, and maintenance of historic buildings and monuments in England. Membership entitles you to free entry to all their 350 properties, including Stonehenge, Dover Castle, and Osborne House (Queen Victoria's Isle of Wight retreat). You'll also receive a guide to the properties, a map and events diary, and the quarterly *English Heritage Magazine.*

It costs £15 ($27.75) for adults or £30 ($55.50) for families. You can join at any property or contact English Heritage, Membership Department, P.O. Box 1BB, London, W1A 1BB (tel. 071/973-3400).
2. Patronize the many museums that charge no admission, including the British Museum.
3. Students and seniors should take advantage of special discounts granted with proof of age and/or identity. So it's worth securing some kind of ID (see "Tips for Students and Seniors," above). Domestic train fares in England are also reduced for students.
4. Families also can take advantage of special discounts which can cut admission costs considerably.

SAVING MONEY ON SHOPPING

1. The best buys in England are English crafts, woolen products (including tweeds, scarves, skirts, sweaters, and tartans), traditional Celtic jewelry, and such world-renowned pottery and china as Royal Doulton, Wedgwood, and Royal Worcester. You can also find excellent and high-quality posters, along with art prints, crafts, and art books in many of England's museums.
2. Price items that you think you might want to look for before you leave home so you'll know a bargain when you see one.
3. Patronize factory outlets. At these you can save as much as 50%, although the really prestigious names in china, such as Wedgwood or Royal Doulton, don't discount merchandise at their factory outlets so as to protect their retail distributors. You may want to purchase a copy of *Factory Shop Guides* (£2.75, or $5.10) by Rolf Stricker and Gillian Cutress, 34 Park Hill, London SW4 9PB.
4. Go for the London department store sales during the 2 weeks in January and 1 week in July. Many Europeans cross the English Channel just to take advantage of these sales. Look for the advertisements in local newspapers.
5. Check out the flea markets, or "street markets" which you'll find all over England, but especially in London. You may have to wade through a lot of junk, but you might find an attractive, reasonably priced souvenir. Try haggling—it does work.

6. Reclaim the 17½% Value Added Tax (VAT). See "Taxes" in "Fast Facts: England," below, for details.

7. Shop the duty-free before you leave home, but check the regular retail price of items that you're most likely to buy so that you don't pay more than you would in a discount store at home. Duty-free prices vary from one country to another.

SAVING MONEY ON SERVICES & OTHER TRANSACTIONS

1. Don't overtip. See "Fast Facts: England," below, for guidelines.

2. Always change your money at a bank, not at the hotel or a store. If you use a credit card, remember that you'll be billed at a later date and the rate of exchange from the date of transaction to the billing date may have changed adversely or favorably.

FAST FACTS: ENGLAND

For information on London, refer to "Fast Facts: London" in Chapter 3.

Business Hours Business hours with many, many exceptions are Mon–Fri 9am–5pm. The lunch break lasts an hour, but most offices stay open all day. In general, stores are open Mon–Sat 9am–5:30pm. In country towns, there is usually an early-closing day (often Wed or Thurs), when the shops close at 1pm. The day varies from town to town.

Camera/Film Film is readily available, especially in large cities. Processing takes about 24 hours although many places, particularly in London, will do it almost while you wait. There are few restrictions on the use of your camera, except where notices are posted, as in churches, theaters, and certain museums. If in doubt, ask.

Cigarettes Most U.S. brands are available in major towns. *Warning:* More and more places now ban smoking. Make sure you enter a "smoker" on the train or Underground, and only smoke on the upper decks of buses or in the smoking area of single-deckers, theaters, and other public places. Some restaurants restrict smoking, as do many bed-and-breakfasts.

Climate See "When to Go," above, in this chapter.

Crime See "Safety," below.

Currency See "Information, Entry Requirements & Money," above in this chapter.

Customs See "Information, Entry Requirements & Money," above in this chapter.

Dentists Outside London, ask the nearest sympathetic local resident—usually your hotelier—for information.

Doctors Hotels keep lists of local practitioners for whom you'll have to pay. Outside London, dial 100 and ask the operator for the local police, who will give you the name, address, and telephone number of a doctor in your area. Emergency treatment is free, but if you visit a doctor at his or her surgery (office) or if he or she makes a "house call" to your hotel, you will have to pay. It's wise to take out adequate medical/accident insurance coverage before you leave home.

Documents Required See "Information, Entry Requirements & Money," above in this chapter.

Driving Rules See "Getting Around," above, in this chapter.

Drug Laws Britain is becoming increasingly severe in enforcing anti-drug laws. Persons arrested for possession of even tiny quantities of marijuana have been deported, forced to pay stiff fines, or sentenced to jail for 2 to 7 years. Possession of "white powder" drugs such as heroin or cocaine carry even more stringent penalties.

Drugstores In Britain, they are called chemists. Every police station in the country has a list of emergency chemists. Dial "0" (zero) and ask the operator for the local police, who will give you the name of the nearest.

Electricity British current is 240 volts AC, 50 cycle, roughly twice the voltage of North American current, which is 115-120 volts AC, 60 cycle. American plugs don't fit British wall outlets. Always bring suitable converters and/or adapters (some but definitely not all hotels will supply them). Be warned that you will destroy your appliance (and possible start a fire as well) if you plug an American appliance directly into a European electrical outlet without a converter. Tape recorders, VCRs, and other devices with motors intended to revolve at a fixed number of r.p.m. probably won't work properly even with converters.

Embassies & Consulates See "Fast Facts: London" in Chapter 3.

Emergencies Dial 999 for police, fire, or ambulance. Give your name, address, and telephone number, and state the nature of the emergency. Misuse of the 999 service carries a heavy fine. Cardiac arrest, yes. Sprained ankle, no. Accident injury, yes. Dented fender, no.

Etiquette Be normal, be quiet. The British do not like hearing other people's conversations. In pubs you are not expected to buy a round of drinks unless someone has bought you a drink. Don't talk politics or religion in pubs.

Gasoline See "Getting Around," above in this chapter.

Hitchhiking See "Getting Around," above in this chapter.

Holidays See "When to Go," above in this chapter.

Information See "Information, Entry Requirements & Money," above in this chapter and individual city chapters.

Laundry/Dry Cleaning Most stores and most hotels need 2 days to do the job. London and most provincial towns have launderettes where you can wash and dry your own clothes, but there are no facilities for ironing. Many launderettes also have dry-cleaning machines. One-day dry-cleaning service is available.

Legal Aid The American Services section of the U.S. Consulate (see "Fast Facts: London" in Chapter 3) will give advice if you run into trouble abroad. They can advise you of your rights and even provide a list of attorneys (for which you'll have to pay if services are used). But they cannot interfere on your behalf in the legal processes of Great Britain. For questions about American citizens who are arrested abroad, including ways of getting money to them, telephone the Citizens Emergency Center of the Office of Special Consulate Services in Washington, D.C. (tel. 202/647-5225).

Liquor Laws 18 is the legal drinking age. Children under 16 aren't allowed in pubs, except in certain rooms, and then only when accompanied by a parent or guardian. Don't drink and drive. Penalties are stiff.

In England, pubs can open Mon–Sat 11am–11pm and Sun noon–3pm and 7–10:30 or 11pm. Restaurants are also allowed to serve liquor during these hours but only to people who are dining on the premises. The law allows 30 minutes for "drinking-up time." A meal, incidentally, is defined as "substantial refreshment." And, you have to eat and drink sitting down. In hotels, liquor may be served 11am–11pm to both residents and nonresidents; after 11pm, only residents, according to the law, may be served.

Lost Property Report the loss to the nearest police station. For London information, see "Fast Facts: London," in Chapter 3.

Mail Letters and parcels for you may, as a rule, be addressed to you at any post office except a town sub-office. The words "To Be Called For" or "Poste Restante" must appear in the address. When claiming your mail, always carry some sort of identification. Letters generally take 7 to 10 days to arrive from the U.S. Post Restante service is provided solely for the convenience of travelers, and it may not be used in the same town for more than 3 months. It can be redirected, upon request, for a 1-month period, or up to 3 months if so specified on the required application form. Post offices and subpost offices are centrally located and open Mon–Fri 9am–5:30pm, Sat 9:30am–noon; closed Sun. To send an airmail letter to North America costs 32p (60¢) and postcards require a 27p (50¢) stamp. British mail boxes are painted red and carry a royal coat-of-arms as a signature. All post offices will accept parcels for mailing providing they are properly and securely wrapped.

Newspapers *The Times* is the newspaper of record. *The Telegraph* is white-collar oriented, the *Daily Mail* less so, and the *Guardian* intellectual-liberal. The *International Herald-Tribune,* published in Paris, and an international edition of *USA Today* are available daily.

Pets It is illegal to bring in pets, except with veterinary documents, and then most are subject to 6 months in quarantine. Hotels have their own rules, but usually dogs are not allowed in restaurants or public rooms, and often not in bedrooms.

Police Dial 999 if the matter is serious. The British police have a helpful reputation and if the local police cannot help, they will know the address of the person who can. Losses, theft, and other criminal matters should be reported to the police immediately.

Radio/TV There are 24-hour radio channels operating throughout the United Kingdom, with mostly pop music and talk shows during the night. TV starts around 6am with breakfast TV and educational programs. Lighter entertainment begins around 4 or 5pm, after the children's programs, and continues until around midnight. There are now four television channels—two commercial and two BBC without commercials.

Religious Services Times of services are posted outside houses of worship. Almost every creed is catered to in London and other large cities, but in the smaller towns and villages you are likely to find only Anglican (Episcopalian), Roman Catholic, Baptist, and Nonconformist churches.

Rest Rooms The signs usually say "Public Toilets." Women pay 5p (8¢) to enter a stall. Men pay nothing. Hotel rest rooms are only grudgingly available to nonresidents. Garages (filling stations) also have facilities for customers only, and the key is often kept by the cash register.

Safety Stay alert. Be aware of your immediate surroundings. Don't sling your camera or purse over your shoulder; always lock your car and protect your valuables. Stay in well-lit areas and out of questionable neighborhoods. While Britain is a fairly safe country, every society has its criminals. It's your responsibility to be aware and alert even in the most heavily touristed areas, especially in London and other large cities.

Shoe Repairs Many of the large department stores in Britain have "Heel Bars" where repairs are done while you wait.

Taxes To encourage energy-saving, the British government levies a 25% tax on gasoline (petrol). There is also a national 17½% Value Added Tax (VAT) that is added to all hotel and restaurant bills, and will have been included in the price of many of the items you purchase. This can be refunded if you shop at stores that participate in the Retail Export Scheme (signs are posted in the window). When you make a purchase, show your passport and request a Retail Export Scheme form (Form VAT 407) and a stamped, preaddressed envelope. Show the VAT form and your sales receipt to British Customs when you leave the country. They may also ask to see the merchandise. After Customs has stamped it, mail the form back to the shop in the envelope provided *before you leave the country.* Your VAT refund will be mailed to you.

Here are three organizing tips to help you through the Customs procedures: Keep your VAT forms with your passport; pack your purchases in a carry-on bag so you will have them handy; and allow yourself enough time at your departure point to find a mailbox. See "Saving Money on Shopping," above in this chapter.

Telephone British TeleCom is radically improving its public pay-phone service but during the transition, you will encounter four types of pay phones. The old style (gray) requires 10p (20¢) coins. Don't call overseas from these. The newer blue-and-silver pushbutton model accepts coins of any denomination. Two other types of pay phone accept cards instead of coins. The Cardphone takes specially designed green cards, available from news agencies and post offices in five values—£1 ($1.65), £2 ($3.30), £4 ($6.60), £10 ($16.50), and £20 ($33)—and they are usable until the face value is exhausted. Finally, the Creditcall pay phone operates on credit cards—Access (MasterCard), VISA, American Express, and Diners Club—and is most common at airports and large railway stations.

Outside the major cities phone numbers consist of an exchange name plus telephone number. To reach the number, you will need to dial the digital code for the exchange (like the area code) plus the number. The digital code for the exchange is usually posted in the call box. If your code is not there, however, dial 100 for the operator, and ask for it. In major cities phone numbers consist of the exchange code and number. These local digits are all you need to dial if you are calling from within the same city. If you are calling from elsewhere, you will need to prefix them with the dialing code for the city. Again, you will find these codes on the call box information sheets. If you do not have the telephone number of the person you want to call, dial 192 or 142 for either London or elsewhere in the country. Give the operator the name of the town and then the person's name and address.

It is less expensive to dial international calls yourself. After you have inserted the coins, dial 010 (the international code), then the country code. For the United States, the code is 1, which is followed by the area code and the local number. If you're calling collect, or else need the assistance of an international operator, dial 155. Caller beware: Some hotels routinely add anywhere from 40% to 300% surcharges to local, national, and international phone calls, so make calls outside your hotel room at a post office or phone booth.

Telex & Fax   Both are common in offices and hotels. Refer to the Yellow Pages for telex bureaus or dial 100 and ask for Freefone Intelpost for information on fax.

Time   England uses Greenwich mean time, 5 hours ahead of the U.S. East Coast. British summer time (GMT + 1 hour) is in effect roughly from the end of March to the end of October.

Tipping   Cab Drivers: Add about 10% to 15% to the fare as shown on the meter. However, if the driver personally unloads or loads your luggage, add 25p (45¢) per bag.

Hotel Staff: Porters get 75p ($1.40) per bag even if you have only one small suitcase. The hall porter is tipped only for special services. Maids receive 75p ($1.40) per day. In top-ranking hotels the concierge will often submit a separate bill, showing charges for newspapers, and the like; if he or she has been particularly helpful, tip extra.

Hotels often add a service charge of 10% to 15% to most bills. In smaller B&Bs, the tip is not likely to be included. Therefore, tip for special services, such as the waiter who serves you breakfast. If several persons have served you in a B&B, many guests ask that 10% to 15% be added to the bill and divided among the staff.

Restaurant Staff: In both restaurants and nightclubs, a 15% service charge is added to the bill. To that, add another 3% to 5%, depending on the quality of the service. Waiters in deluxe restaurants and nightclubs are accustomed to the extra 5%, which means you'll end up tipping 20%. If that seems excessive, you must remember that the initial service charge reflected in the fixed price is distributed among all the help. Sommeliers (wine stewards) get about £1 ($1.65) per bottle of wine served. Tipping in pubs is not common, although in cocktail bars the waiter or barmaid usually gets about 75p. ($1.25) per round of drinks.

Services: Barbers and hairdressers expect 10% to 15%. Tour guides expect £2 ($3.70), although it's not mandatory. Gas station attendants are rarely tipped. Theater ushers also don't expect tips.

Weather   For London, call 071/246-8091; for Devon and Cornwall, 0392/8091; for the Midlands, 021/8091.

Yellow Pages   Throughout England, local phone books contain yellow pages at the back of the book. If you can't find what you are looking for, you may not be looking under the proper English equivalent. For example, instead of drugstore, try chemist or pharmacist.

CHAPTER 3
SETTLING INTO LONDON

This chapter aims to give you a quick orientation to the layout of this sprawling city, to tell you the best and cheapest ways to get around, and generally to answer any questions that any visitor would have while staying in London.

1. FROM A BUDGET TRAVELER'S POINT OF VIEW

BUDGET BESTS

Not only does London offer many of the world's "bests," but most of these attractions are either free, or priced well below comparable sights Stateside. Most of London's museums are free, as are the main sections of such major attractions as Westminster Abbey and the Houses of Parliament. The Changing of the Guard at Buckingham Palace is also free, along with the often-acerbic Speaker's Corner every Sunday in Hyde Park (see "More Attractions" in Chapter 6). Tickets to the London stage are typically half the price of those in New York, and cheap seats are regularly available to the opera, ballet, and symphony. Whether you're window-shopping in the West End or sightseeing in The City, the following pages will convince you that London is enjoyable on a budget.

WHAT'S WORTH PAYING FOR

In London, it's worth paying for a clean, decent hotel room (many of them in the budget category are rather unsavory and often not clean). It's better—at least for this city—to cut back on your food budget to get a good room for the night, one in which you can feel safe and secure.

So many of London's B&Bs are notoriously bad, and you may not feel comfortable in them which could cast a blight on your stay and affect your opinion of London.

2. ORIENTATION

London is a city that has never quite made up its mind about its own size. The "City of London" proper is merely 1 square mile of (very expensive) real estate around the Bank of England. All the gargantuan rest is made up of separate cities, towns, boroughs, and corporations, called Westminster, Chelsea, Hampstead, Kensington, Camden Town, and so forth, each with its own mayor and administration. Together, they add up to a mammoth metropolis—once the largest city on the globe, now dropped to 16th in a United Nations survey of population.

The millions of people loosely governed by the Greater London Council live spread out over 609 square miles of Greater London; luckily, only a minute fraction of this territory need concern us—the rest is suburbs. But the heart of this giant is perhaps the most fascinating area on earth. For about a century, one-quarter of the world was ruled from here, and with every step you take, you'll come across some sign of the tremendous influence this city has exerted over our thoughts and past actions—and still wields today.

ARRIVING
BY PLANE

Heathrow, in Hounslow, is one of the (if not the) busiest airports in the world. It is divided into four terminals. Most flights from North America, including those of Pan American and Trans World Airlines, arrive at Terminals 1 and 2. Terminal 3 is home to inter-European flights. Terminal 4, is the long-haul hub operation of British Airways, and also home to British Airways' Super Shuttle, linking London with Edinburgh, Glasgow, Belfast, and Manchester. And also the airline's long-haul hub.

For **flight information,** call Heathrow at 081/759-4321.

Many charter and some scheduled flights arrive at the smaller **Gatwick Airport** (tel. 0293/531299).

London City Airport, used mainly for STOL (short takeoff and landing) and commuter flights to and from the Continent, lies about 6 miles east of "The City" in the Royal Docklands. Among Airlines that use this terminal are Brymon Airlines, with routes to Lille, Strasbourg, and Nantes in France; Flex Air's flights to Rotterdam; London City Airways' (linked to Sabena) routes to Brussels; and UTA's flights to Paris.

For **flight information,** call London City Airport at 081/474-5555.

GETTING INTO TOWN

From **Heathrow:** It takes 50 minutes by **Underground** to travel the 15 miles from **Heathrow Central** to central London and costs £2.10 ($3.90). You can also take an **airbus,** which takes about an hour and costs £5 ($9.25) for adults and £3 ($5.55) for children. A taxi will cost more than £20 ($37).

From **Gatwick:** Gatwick lies 30 miles south of London. **Trains** leave for London every 15 minutes during the day, and every hour at night. There is also an express bus (Flightline Bus 777) from Gatwick to Victoria Station every half hour from 6:30am to 8pm and every hour from 8 to 11pm costing £6 ($11.10) per person. A taxi will cost £40 ($74) to £45 ($83.25), and you will have to negotiate a fare with the driver as the meter does not apply.

From **London City Airport:** There are no direct subway or rail links to central London (it's still too new). You can take a short taxi ride to the Plaistow station of the Underground's District Line, but most business passengers take a taxi into London costing £12 ($22.20) and up. It's cheaper to go by riverbus which leaves from the pier a short walk from the airline terminal, leaving every hour on the hour from 7am to 7pm Monday to Friday, and stopping at Swan Lake Pier (close to the financial district; tube: Monument) and, finally, at Charing Cross Pier (tube: Embankment). It costs £4 ($7.40) to Swan Lane Pier £5 ($9.25) to Charing Cross.

BY TRAIN

Most trains from Paris arrive at Victoria Station; trains from Amsterdam arrive at Liverpool Street Station; and trains from Edinburgh arrive at King's Cross Station. Each station is connected to the bus and Underground (subway) network and has phones, restaurants, pubs, luggage storage, and London Transport Information Centres.

TOURIST INFORMATION

The London Tourist Board's **Tourist Information Centre,** Victoria Station Forecourt, S.W.1 (tube: Victoria Station), can help you with almost anything of interest to a tourist in the U.K. capital, including tour and theater reservations. Open Mon. to Sat. from 8am to 7pm and Sun. from 8am to 4pm. The bookshop is open Monday to Saturday from 9am to 7pm and Sunday 9am to 4pm.

The tourist board also has offices at:

Harrods, 87-135 Brompton Road, Knightsbridge, S.W.3, in the basement. Open during store hours. **Tube:** Knightsbridge.

Selfridges, Oxford Street, W.1, basement services area, Duke Street entrance. Open during store hours. **Tube:** Bond Street.

Heathrow Airport Terminals 1, 2, and 3, Underground Concourse, open daily from 9am to 4:30pm.

Telephone inquiries may be made by calling 071/730-3488 Monday to Friday from 9am to 6pm. Written inquiries should be addressed to the Correspondence Assistant, Distribution Department, London Tourist Board and Convention Bureau, 26 Grosvenor Gardens, London SW1W ODU.

For riverboat information in London, phone 071/730-4812. For accommodations bookings (credit-card holders only), call 071/824-8844.

CITY LAYOUT

MAIN ARTERIES & STREETS

There is—fortunately—an immense difference between the sprawling vastness of Greater London and the pocket-size chunk north of the River Thames that might be called Tourist Territory.

Our London begins at **Chelsea,** on the north bank of the river, and stretches for roughly 5 miles north to **Hampstead.** Horizontally, its western boundary runs through **Kensington** while the eastern lies 5 miles away at **Tower Bridge.** Within this 5-by-5-mile square, you'll find all the hotels and restaurants and nearly all the sights.

The logical (although not geographical) center of this area is **Trafalgar Square,** which we'll therefore take as our orientation point.

This huge, thronged, fountain-splashed, pigeon-infested square was named after the battle in which Nelson destroyed the combined Franco-Spanish fleets and lost his own life. His statue tops the towering pillar in the center, the famous Nelson's Column.

If you stand facing the steps of the imposing **National Gallery,** you're looking northwest. That is the direction of **Piccadilly Circus**—the real core of tourist London—and the maze of streets that make up **Soho.** Farther north runs **Oxford Street,** London's gift to moderately priced shopping, and still farther northwest lies **Regent's Park** with the zoo.

At your back—that is, south—runs **Whitehall,** which houses or skirts nearly every British government building, from the Ministry of Defence to the official residence of the Prime Minister at **Downing Street.** In the same direction, a bit farther south, stand the **Houses of Parliament** and **Westminster Abbey.**

Flowing southwest from Trafalgar Square is the table-smooth **Mall,** flanked by magnificent parks and mansions and leading to **Buckingham Palace,** residence of the Queen. Farther in the same direction lie **Belgravia** and **Knightsbridge,** the city's plushest residential areas, and south of them lies **Chelsea,** with its chic flavor, plus **King's Road,** principally a boulevard for shopping.

Due west from where you're standing stretches the superb and distinctly high-priced shopping area bordered by **Regent Street** and **Piccadilly (Street,** as distinct from the **Circus).** Farther west lie the equally elegant shops and even more elegant homes of **Mayfair.** Then comes **Park Lane** and on the other side **Hyde Park,** the biggest park in London and one of the largest in the world.

Charing Cross Road is running north from Trafalgar Square, past **Leicester Square,** and intersecting with **Shaftesbury Avenue.** This is London's theaterland, boasting an astonishing number of live shows as well as first-run movie houses. A bit farther along, Charing Cross Road turns into a browser's paradise, lined with new and secondhand bookshops.

Finally it funnels into **St. Giles Circus.** This is where you enter **Bloomsbury,** site of the **University of London,** the **British Museum,** some of our best budget hotels, and erstwhile stamping ground of the famed "Bloomsbury Group," led by Virginia Woolf.

Northeast lies **Covent Garden,** known for its **Royal Opera House** and today a major shopping, restaurant, and café district. Covent Garden was London's first square, originally laid out by Inigo Jones as a residential piazza. In the 16th century the area became fashionable to live in and was soon to become one of the centers of London nightlife. The first theater was built on the present site in 1732. The existing opera house, one of the most beautiful theaters in Europe, was built in 1858 and is now the home of the Royal Opera and Royal Ballet, the leading international opera and ballet companies. However, until a few years ago the whole area was a thriving fruit and vegetable market, originally started by the nuns selling surplus stocks from their convent garden.

Follow the **Strand** eastward from Trafalgar Square, and you'll come into **Fleet Street.** Beginning in the 19th century, this corner of London became the most concentrated newspaper district in the world. But over the decades the newspapers folded or moved away. The last newspaper edition was published in Fleet Street in 1989.

Where the Strand becomes Fleet Street stands Temple Bar, and only here do you enter the actual City of London. Tradition requires that the monarch, when visiting the City, stop at Temple Bar until given leave to proceed by the Lord Mayor.

The city was the original walled settlement and is today what the locals mean when they refer to "The City." Its focal point and shrine is the **Bank of England** on **Threadneedle Street,** with the **Stock Exchange** next door and the **Royal Exchange** across the road.

The City is unique insofar as it retains its own separate police force (distinguished by a crest on their helmets) and Lord Mayor. Its 677 acres are jammed with cars and rushing clerks during the week and totally deserted on Sunday, because hardly a soul lives there. Its streets are winding, narrow, and fairly devoid of charm, but it has more bankers and stockbrokers per square inch than any other place on the globe. And in the midst of all the hustle rises **St. Paul's Cathedral,** a monument to beauty and tranquility.

At the far eastern fringe of The City looms the **Tower of London,** shrouded in legend, blood, and history, and permanently besieged by battalions of visitors.

And this, as far as we will be concerned, concludes the London circle.

FINDING AN ADDRESS

Now I'd like to be able to tell you that London's thoroughfares follow a recognizable pattern in which, with a little intelligence, even strangers can find their way around. Unfortunately they don't and you can't.

London's streets follow no pattern whatsoever, and both their naming and house numbering seem to have been perpetrated by a group of xenophobes with an equal grudge against postal carriers and foreigners.

So be warned that the use of logic and common sense will get you nowhere. Don't think, for instance, that **Southampton Row** is anywhere near **Southampton Street** and that either of these places has any connection with **Southampton Road.**

And this is only a mild sample. London is checkered with innumerable squares, mews, closes, and terraces, which jut into or cross or overlap or interrupt whatever street you're trying to follow, usually without the slightest warning. You may be walking along ruler-straight **Albany Street** and suddenly find yourself flanked by

Colosseum Terrace (with a different numbering system). Just keep on walking and after a couple of blocks you're right back on **Albany Street** (and the original house numbers) without having encountered the faintest reason for the sudden change in labels.

House numbers run in odds, evens, clockwise, or counterclockwise as the wind blows. *That is, when they exist at all, and frequently they don't.* Many establishments in London, such as Inn on the Park or Langan's Brasserie, *do not use street numbers.* This is even truer when you leave London and go to a provincial town. Even though a road might run for a mile, some buildings on the street will be numbered, others will say only "King's Road" or whatever, with no number, whereas a building right next door will be numbered. This is just one aspect that makes traveling around England maddening. Of course, you can always ask for a location to be pinpointed, as locals are generally glad to assist a bewildered foreigner.

Every so often you'll come upon a square that is called a square on the south side, a road on the north, a park on the east, and possibly a something-or-other close on the west side.

Your only chance is to consult a map, or better yet, the *London A to Z* or ask your way as you go along. Most of the time you'll probably end up doing both.

But there are a couple of consoling factors. One is the legibility of the street signs. The other is, as mentioned, the extraordinary helpfulness of the locals, who sometimes pass you from guide to guide like a bucket in a fire chain.

STREET MAPS

If you're going to explore London in any depth, you'll need a good and detailed street map with an index like the one published by *Falk*. They're available at most newsstands and nearly all bookstores. If you can't find one, go to **W. & G. Foyle Ltd.,** 113-119 Charing Cross Road, W.C.2 (tel. 071/439-8501).

2. GETTING AROUND

BY PUBLIC TRANSPORTATION

It's easy and inexpensive and made even more so by the Travel Information Centres in the Underground stations at King's Cross, Oxford Circus, St. James's Park, Liverpool Street Station, and Piccadilly Circus, in the British Rail stations at Euston and Victoria, and also in each of the terminals at Heathrow Airport.

These centers provide information and maps about bus and Underground services plus much other information. They also operate 24-hour telephone information service (tel. 071/222-1234).

Information is also available by writing **London Regional Transport,** Travel Information Service, 55 Broadway, London SW1H OBD.

DISCOUNT PASSES

Travelcards covering adjacent-zones are offered by **London Regional Transport** for use on bus, Underground, and British Rail services within Greater London. These can be purchased for a minimum of 7 days or for any period (including odd days) from a month to a year. For example, a Travelcard allowing travel in two zones for 1 week costs adults £10 ($18.50) and children £3.15 ($5.85).

To purchase a Travelcard, you need a **Photocard** (if you're 16 and over you can obtain it free if you take along a passport-type picture of yourself). Child-rate Photocards are issued only at main post offices in the London area, and besides a passport-size photograph, proof of age is required (for example, a passport or a birth certificate). Teenagers (14 or 15) are charged adult fares on all services unless in possession of one of the cards.

For shorter stays in London, you may want to consider the **One-Day Off-Peak**

Travelcard, usable on most bus, Underground, and British Rail services throughout Greater London after 9:30am Monday to Friday and at any time on weekends and bank holidays. Available at Underground ticket offices, bus garages, Travel Information Centres, and some newsstands, it costs, for two zones, £2.60 ($4.80) for adults, £1 ($1.85) for children 5 to 15.

BY UNDERGROUND [SUBWAY]

Known locally as "the tube," this is the fastest and easiest way to get from place to place. All Underground stations are clearly marked with a red circle and blue crossbar and accessible either by stairways, escalators, or huge elevators, depending on the depth. Some Underground stations have complete subterranean shopping arcades and several boast high-tech gadgets such as pushbutton information machines.

Compared to, for instance, its New York subway counterpart, the tube is a luxury cruiser. The stations are clean, ventilated, orderly, and fairly quiet. Above all, they're superbly signposted, and in such a well-calculated fashion that it takes a certain amount of talent to catch the wrong train.

You pick the station for which you're heading on the large diagram displayed on the wall, which has an alphabetical index to make it easy. You note the color of the line it happens to be on (Bakerloo is brown, Central is red, etc.). Then, by merely following the colored band, you can see at a glance whether and where you'll have to change and how many stops there are to your destination.

If you have British coins, you can get your ticket at one of the vending machines that make change. Otherwise, you buy it at the ticket office. You can transfer as many times as you like so long as you stay in the Underground. The flat fare for one trip within the central zone is 70p ($1.30). Trips from the central zone to destinations in the suburbs range from 60p ($1.10) to £3 ($5.55) in most cases.

Note: Be sure to keep your ticket; it must be presented when you get off. If you owe extra, you'll be asked to pay the difference by the attendant. And if you're out on the town and dependent on the Underground, watch your time carefully; many trains stop running at midnight (11:30pm on Sunday).

BY BUS

London has just two types of buses, which you can't possibly confuse: the **red** double-decked monsters that bully their way through the inner-city areas, and the **green** single-deckers that link the center with the outlying towns and villages.

The first thing you learn about London buses is that nobody just gets on them. You "queue up," that is, form a line single file at the bus stop. The English do it instinctively, even when there are only two of them. It's one of their eccentricities, and you will grow to appreciate it during rush hours.

The comparably priced bus system is almost as good as the Underground, and you have a better view. To find out about routes, pick up a free bus map at one of the London Transport Travel Information Centres listed above. It's not available by mail, you must go in person.

After you've queued up for the red double-decker bus and selected a seat downstairs or on the upper deck (the best seats are on top, where you'll see more of the city), a conductor will come by and you'll tell him your destination and pay the fare, receiving a ticket in return. Generally, fares which vary with the distance are 10p (20¢) to 20p (35¢) lower than the tube. If you want to be told when to get off, simply ask the conductor.

BY TAXI

London cabs are specially designed for their function, have a glass partition to prevent driver and passengers from bothering each other, and have the maneuverability of fighter planes. At first glance they seem oddly staid and upright, but you quickly learn to appreciate the headroom they provide and the uncanny U-turns they can execute.

LONDON UNDERGROUND

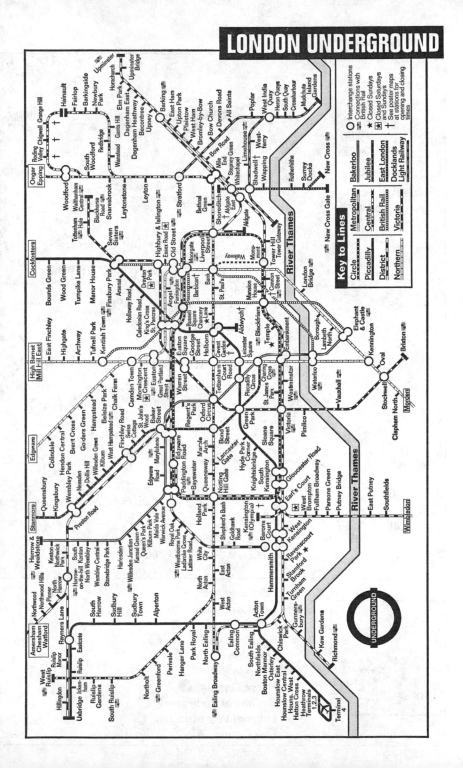

Key to Lines

Circle	Metropolitan	Bakerloo
Piccadilly	Central	Jubilee
District	British Rail	East London
Northern	Victoria	Docklands Light Railway

Interchange stations
Connections with British Rail
Closed Sundays
Closed Saturdays and Sundays
See poster maps at stations for opening and closing times

River Thames

UNDERGROUND

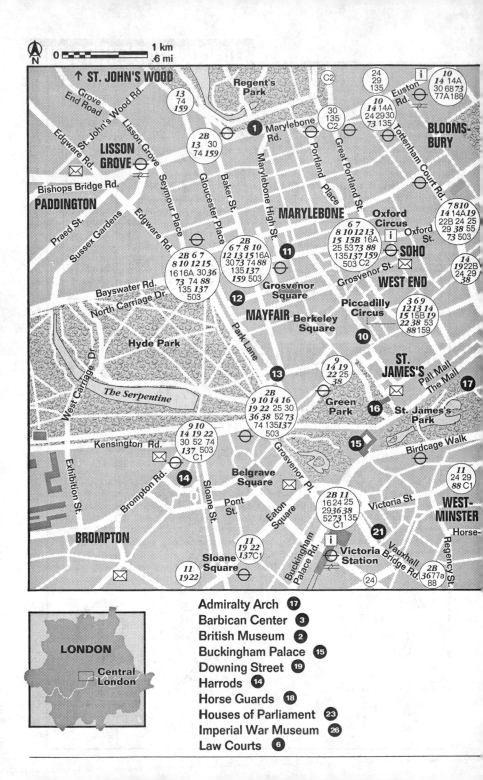

↑ ST. JOHN'S WOOD

Regent's Park

Grove End Road

Edgware Rd.

LISSON GROVE

PADDINGTON

Bishops Bridge Rd.

Praed St.

Sussex Gardens

Bayswater Rd.

North Carriage Dr.

West Carriage Dr.

Hyde Park

The Serpentine

Kensington Rd.

Exhibition St.

BROMPTON

Brompton Rd.

Sloane St.

Pont St.

Eaton Square

Belgrave Square

Sloane Square

Marylebone Rd.

Lisson Grove

Baker St.

Gloucester Place

Seymour Place

Edgware Rd.

Marylebone High St.

MARYLEBONE

Portland Place

Great Portland St.

Oxford Circus

Oxford St.

SOHO

WEST END

Grosvenor St.

MAYFAIR

Berkeley Square

Grosvenor Square

Park Lane

Piccadilly Circus

ST. JAMES'S

Pall Mall

The Mall

Green Park

St. James's Park

Birdcage Walk

BLOOMS-BURY

Tottenham Court Rd.

Euston Rd.

WEST-MINSTER

Victoria St.

Victoria Station

Grosvenor Pl.

Buckingham Palace Rd.

Vauxhall Bridge Rd.

Regency St.

Horse-

LONDON

Central London

Admiralty Arch ⑰
Barbican Center ③
British Museum ②
Buckingham Palace ⑮
Downing Street ⑲
Harrods ⑭
Horse Guards ⑱
Houses of Parliament ㉓
Imperial War Museum ㉖
Law Courts ⑥

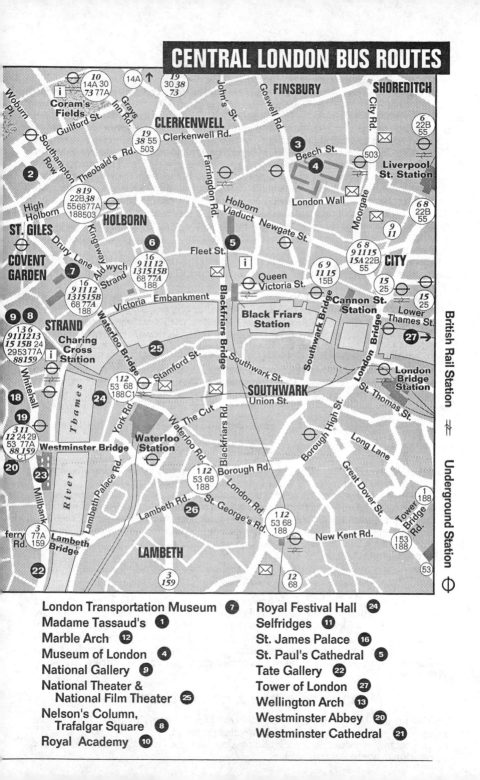

CENTRAL LONDON BUS ROUTES

London Transportation Museum 7
Madame Tassaud's 1
Marble Arch 12
Museum of London 4
National Gallery 9
National Theater &
   National Film Theater 25
Nelson's Column,
   Trafalgar Square 8
Royal Academy 10

Royal Festival Hall 24
Selfridges 11
St. James Palace 16
St. Paul's Cathedral 5
Tate Gallery 22
Tower of London 27
Wellington Arch 13
Westminster Abbey 20
Westminster Cathedral 21

They are, in fact, the best-designed taxis anywhere and moreover their drivers are polite, know their streets, and thank you for tips.

You can pick up a cab in London either by heading for a cab rank or by hailing one in the street (the taxi is free if the light on the roof is on). Or else you can call 071/253-5000, 071/272-0271, or 071/272-3030 for a radio cab. The minimum fare is £1 ($1.85) for the first 1,152 yards or 3 minutes and 49.5 seconds with increments of 20p (35¢) thereafter, based on a distance or time. Each additional passenger is charged 20p (35¢). From 8pm to midnight Monday to Friday and from 6am to 8pm on Saturday, after the £1 ($1.85) minimum, increments are 40p (75¢). From midnight to 6am Monday to Friday and between 8pm on the day before until 6am on the day after Sunday and public holidays, the meter clicks over at 60p ($1.10). From 8pm on December 24 to 6am on December 27 and from 8pm on December 31 to 6am on January 1, the flag still drops at £1 ($1.85) but increments are £2 ($3.70). Passengers are charged 10p (20¢) for each piece of luggage in the driver's compartment and any other item more than 2 feet long. All these tariffs include VAT. It's recommended that you tip 10% to 12% of the fare.

Be warned: If you call for a cab, the meter starts running when the taxi receives instructions from the dispatcher. So you could find £1 ($1.85) or more on the meter when it arrives.

If you have a complaint about the taxi service, or if you leave something in a cab, phone the **Public Carriage Office,** 15 Penton St., N.1 (tel. 071/278-1744). If it's a complaint, you'll need the cab number, displayed in the passenger compartment.

Cab sharing (for 2 to 5 persons) is now permitted in London. These taxis display a notice on yellow plastic, with the words "Shared Taxi" and operate at Heathrow Airport, main train stations, and some 200 taxi stands in London. The savings per person is as follows: Each of two riders sharing is charged 65% of the fare a lone passenger would be charged. Three persons pay 55%, four are charged 45%, and five (the seating capacity of all new London cabs) pay 40% of the single-passenger fare.

BY CAR

RENTALS

Car rentals are relatively expensive. Most companies will accept your U.S. driving license, provided you're over 21 and have held it for more than a year.

Many companies grant discounts to clients who reserve in advance, usually 48 hours, through the toll-free reservations offices in a renter's home country. Always ask if the price includes the 17½% VAT and the Collision Damage Waiver (CDW), and other insurance options. If not, ask what they will cost.

For addresses and toll-free numbers of specific firms operating out of London, refer to "Getting Around" in Chapter 2.

PARKING

It's expensive and difficult to find. Meter parking is available. You'll need the right change and also to watch out for the traffic wardens who issue tickets. Some zones are marked "permit holders only." Don't park there unless you have a permit as a local resident. Your vehicle will be towed if you do. A yellow line along the curb indicates "no parking"; a double yellow line signifies "no waiting." However, at night (meters indicate exact times) and on Sunday, you're allowed to park along a curb with a single yellow line.

DRIVING RULES & REQUIREMENTS

Driving around London is a tricky business even for the native motorist. It's a warren of one-way streets, and parking spots are at a premium.

In England, you drive on the left and pass on the right. Road signs are clear and the international symbols unmistakable.

A word of warning: Pedestrian crossings are marked by striped lines (zebra striping) on the road; flashing lights near the curb indicate that drivers must stop and yield the right of way if a pedestrian has stepped out into the zebra zone to cross the street.

Wearing seat belts is mandatory in the British Isles.

BY BICYCLE

You can rent bikes by the day or by the week from a number of outfits.

On Your Bike, 22 Dukes' Street Hill, London Bridge, S.E.1 (tel. 071/378-6669; tube: London Bridge) is open Monday to Friday from 9am to 6pm and on Saturday from 9:30am to 4:30pm, and has about 50 bikes for both men and women. The 10-speed sports bikes, with high seat and low-slung handlebars cost £6 ($11.10) per day or £25 ($46.25) a week, requiring a £40 ($74) deposit; 18-gear "mountain bikes" with straight handlebars and oversize gears cost £10 ($18.50) a day or £55 ($101.75) per week, requiring a deposit of £200 ($370). Deposits are payable by MasterCard or VISA.

ON FOOT

This is the best way to explore London, but be careful. Many Americans have accidents because they look the wrong way when crossing a street. Remember, cars drive on the left. Always look both ways before stepping off a curb. Unlike some countries, vehicles have the right-of-way in London over pedestrians.

 LONDON

American Express The main office is 6 Haymarket, S.W.1 (tel. 071/930-4411; tube: Piccadilly Circus). Full services are available Mon–Fri 9am–5pm and Sat 9am–noon. At other times—Sat noon–6pm and Sun 10am–4pm—only the foreign exchange bureau is open. The American Express office at the British Travel Center, 4-12 Lower Regent St., S.W.1 (tel. 071/839 2682; tube: Piccadilly Circus), is open Mon–Fri 9am–6:30pm, Sat–Sun 10am–4pm.

Area Code London has two area codes—071 and 081. The 071 area code is good for Central London within a 4-mile radius of Charing Cross (including the City of London, Knightsbridge, and Oxford Street, and as far south as Brixton) and 081 for outer London (including Heathrow Airport, Wimbledon, and Greenwich). Within London, you will need to dial the area code when calling from one of these sections of the city to the other, but not within a section.

Baby-sitters These are hard to find, but sometimes you can get your hotel to recommend someone, possibly a staff member. Expect to pay the cost of a taxi fare to and from your hotel. A number of organizations providing registered nurses and trained nannies as sitters advertise in the Yellow Pages.

Childminders, 67A Marylebone High St., W.1 (tel 071/935-9763) charges £3.75 ($6.95) per hour in the daytime, £2.65 ($4.90) per hour at night, depending on the day of the week. There is a 4-hour minimum and you must pay reasonable transportation costs. Tube: Regent's Park.

Universal Aunts, P.O. Box 304, London SW4 ONN (tel. 071/371-9766), established in 1921, provides many services, including child care, mother's helpers, proxy parents, and nannies. Interviews can be arranged in the Fulham-Chelsea area. You must call first for an appointment or a booking, and details will be supplied over the phone.

Business Hours Banks are usually open Mon–Fri 9:30am–3:30pm. Office business hours are Mon–Fri 9am–5pm. The lunch break lasts an hour, but most places stay open during that time. Pubs and bars are allowed to open Mon–Sat 11am–11pm, Sun noon–3pm and 7–10:30 or 11pm. Many pubs observe these extended hours; but some prefer to close during the late afternoon, 3–5:30pm. London stores generally open 9am–5:30pm, with a late Wed or Thurs night, until 7pm. Most central shops close Sat around 1pm.

Banks In general, banks in London provide the best exchange rates and you're likely to get a better rate for traveler's checks than for cash. There are branches of the main banks at London's airports, but they charge a small fee. There are also bureaux de change at the airports and around London that charge a fee for cashing traveler's checks and personal U.K. checks, and for changing foreign currency into sterling. Some travel agencies, such as American Express and Thomas Cook, also have currency exchange services.

Dentists For dental emergencies, call 24-hour Emergency Dental Service (tel. 071/752-0133) which will direct you to dentists located not only in London, but also throughout England.

Doctors In an emergency, contact Doctor's Call at 071/351-5312 which will direct you to a nearby doctor. Some hotels also have doctors on call. Ask at the reception desk. **Medical Express,** 117A Harley St., W.1 (tel. 071/499-1991) is a private British clinic of 20 different specialists. An initial consultation costs £50 ($92.50). For filling the British equivalent of a U.S. prescription, there is a surcharge of £20 ($37) on top of the cost of the medication. A British doctor must validate the U.S. prescription. Open Mon–Fri 9am–7pm, Sat 10am–5pm.

Drugstores One of the most centrally located chemists, keeping long hours, is **Bliss The Chemist,** 5 Marble Arch, W.1 (tel. 071/723-6116) which is open daily 9am–midnight. Tube: Marble Arch. Every London neighborhood has a branch of the ubiquitous **Boots,** the leading pharmacist of Britain.

Embassies & High Commissions The U.S. Embassy, 24 Grosvenor Sq., W.1 (tel. 071/499-9000). Hours in the passport office are Mon–Fri 8:30am–1pm. Tube: Bond Street.

The Canada High Commission is at Canada House, Trafalgar Square, W.1 (tel. 071/629-9492), open Mon–Fri 9am–5:30pm. Tube: Charing Cross.

The Australian High commission is at Australia House, The Strand, W.C.2 (tel. 071/397-4334), open Mon–Fri 9am–5:30pm. Tube: Charing Cross or Aldwych.

The New Zealand High Commission is at New Zealand House, Haymarket at Pall Mall, S.W.1 (tel. 071/930-8422). Tube: Charing Cross or Piccadilly Circus.

The Irish Embassy at 17 Grosvenor Square, S.W.1 (tel. 071/235-2171), is open Mon–Fri 9:30am–5pm. Tube: Hyde Park Corner.

Emergency Dial 999 for police, fire, or ambulance.

Eyeglasses Lost or broken? Try **Sterling Opticians** at Selfridges Department Store, 400 Oxford St., W.1 (tel. 071/629-1234, ext. 3889) where an eye exam costs £15 ($27.75), and the least expensive pair of eyeglasses with an uncomplicated prescription an additional £50 ($92.50). Contact lenses are also available on the same day in most cases. Multifocal lenses sometimes take 2 to 3 working days to complete, but simple prescriptions may be filled in 2 to 3 hours. It's always wise to take a copy of your eyeglass prescription with you when you travel. Open Mon–Sat 9am–6pm; on Thurs until 8pm.

Hairdressers/Barbers Hairdressers and hairstylists range from the grandly imperial refuge of English dowagers to punk-rock citadels of purple hair and chartreuse mascara. One of the most visible—and one of the best—is a branch of **Vidal Sassoon,** 11 Floral St., W.C.2 (tel. 071/240-6635), in Covent Garden. Unlike some other Sassoon outlets, this one caters to both men and women. A cut and blow dry costs from £25.75 ($48.10) for men and £30.25 ($55.95) for women. Open Mon–Fri 10am–7:30pm, Sat 8:45am–5:45pm. Tube: Covent Garden.

Hospitals The following offer emergency care in London 24 hours a day, with the first treatment free under the National Health Service: Royal Free Hospital, Pond St., N.W.3 (tel. 071/794-0500; tube: Belsize Park); University College Hospital, Gower St., W.C.1 (tel. 071/387-9300; tube: Euston Square). Many other London hospitals also have accident and emergency departments.

Hotlines Capital Helpline (tel. 071/388-7575) will answer almost any question you have about London. For a legal emergency, call Release 24 hours a day at

071/603-8654. The following are all 24-hour hotlines: the Lesbian and Gay Switchboard (tel. 071/837-7324); the Rape Crisis Line 071/837-1600; Samaritans, 46 Marshall St., W.1 (tel. 071/439-2224). Alcoholics Anonymous (tel. 071/352-3001) operates a hotline daily 10am–10pm.

Information   See "Information, Entry Requirements, and Money" in Chapter 2.

Laundry/Dry Cleaning   Danish Express Laundry, 16 Hinde St., W.1 (tel. 071/935-6306), open Mon–Fri 8:30am–5:30pm and Sat 9:30am–12:30pm, will clean, repair, or alter your clothes, even repair shoes. It's one of the best places in London for such service. Tube: Marble Arch.

Laundromats are plentiful. If you're staying in one of the B&B houses in the Bayswater area, try Lancaster Laundromat, 28 Craven Terrace, W.2 (tel. 071/723-5724) open Mon–Fri 8am–9pm, Sat 8am–8pm, Sun 9am–8pm. Tube: Lancaster Gate.

In the Bloomsbury area, try Red and White Laundries, 78 Marchmont St., W.C.1 (tel. 071/387-3667), open daily 7am–9pm. Tube: Russell Square.

Libraries   Two libraries that open their stacks to visitors are The Action Library, High St. W.3 (tel. 081/992-3295) and the Canning Town Library, Barking Rd., E.16 (tel. 071/476-2696).

Lost Property   First report the loss to the police and they will advise you where to apply for its return. Taxi drivers are required to hand over property left in their vehicles to the nearest police station. London Transport's Lost Property Office will try to assist personal callers only at their office at the Baker Street Underground station. For items lost on British Rail, report the loss as soon as possible to the station on the line where the loss occurred. For lost passports, credit cards, or money, report the loss and circumstances immediately to the nearest police station. For lost passports, you should subsequently go directly to your embassy or high commission. The address will be in the telephone book, or see "Embassies and High Commissions," above. For lost credit cards, also report to the appropriate organization; the same holds true for lost traveler's checks.

Luggage Storage/Lockers   Lockers can be rented at airports such as Heathrow or Gatwick and at all major rail stations, including Victoria Station. In addition, there are dozens of independently operated storage companies. The usual charge is £3 ($5.55) to £4 ($7.40) per week per item. Check the yellow pages for a convenient "luggage storage" establishment.

Mail   See "Fast Facts: England," Chapter 2, and refer to "Post Office," below.

Maps   See "Street Maps" earlier in this chapter.

Newspapers/Magazines   The *Times* is tops, then the *Telegraph,* the *Daily Mail,* and the *Guardian,* all London papers carrying the latest news. The *International Herald Tribune,* published in Paris, and an international edition of *USA Today,* beamed via satellite, are available daily. Copies of *Time* and *Newsweek* are also sold at most newsstands. Small magazines, such as *Time Out* and *City Limits,* contain the best cultural listings.

Photographic Needs   The **Flash Centre,** 54 Brunswick Centre, W.C.1 (tel. 071/837-6163), is considered the best professional photographic equipment supplier in London. You can purchase your film next door at Leeds Film and Hire, which has a wide-ranging stock. Kodachrome is accepted for 48-hour processing. Tube: Russell Square.

Police   In an emergency, dial 999 (no coin required). You can also go to one of the local police branches in central London, including New Scotland Yard, Broadway, S.W.1 (tel. 071/230-1212). Tube: St. James's Park.

Post Office   Post offices are subpost offices are centrally located and open Mon–Fri 9am–5:30pm, Sat 9:30am–noon. The Chief Post Office at King Edward St., EC1A 1AA (tel. 071/239-5047), near St. Paul's Cathedral, is open Monday–Fri 8:30am–6:30pm, closed Sat–Sun. Tube: St. Paul's. The Trafalgar Square Post Office, 24-28 William IV St., WC2N 4DL (tel. 071/239-5047), operates as three separate businesses: inland and international postal services and banking, open Mon–Sat 8am–8pm; philatelic postage stamp sales, open Mon–Fri 10am–7pm and Sat

10am–4:30pm; and the post shop, selling greeting cards and stationery, open Mon–Fri 9am–6:30pm and Sat 9:30am–5pm. Tube: Charing Cross. Other post offices and subpost offices are open Monday to Friday 9am–5:30pm and Sat 9am–12:30pm. Many subpost offices and some main post offices close for 1 hour at lunchtime.

Religious Services   Times of services are posted outside the various places of worship. Almost every creed is represented in London. The **Interdenominational American Church,** 79 Tottenham Court Rd., W.1 (tel. 071/580-2791) conducts a service Sunday 11am–noon. Tube: Goodge Street.

Secretarial Services   Chesham Executive Centre, 150 Regent St., W.1 (tel. 071/439-6288; tube: Piccadilly Circus), rents offices by the hour and has secretarial and stenographic services. They also accept walk-in business and will send fax messages, too. The cost of sending a 1-page fax from London to New York, for example, is £2.50 ($4.30), plus VAT and the cost of the phone call. That works out, in the case of a single page to New York, at around £5 ($9.25). Hours are Mon–Fri 9am–5:30pm and Sat 9am–noon.

Shoe Repair   Most of the major Underground stations, including the centrally located Piccadilly Circus, have "heel bars"— British for shoe repair centers. Mostly, these are for quickie jobs. For major repairs, go to one of the major department stores (see "Department Stores" under "Shopping A to Z", Chapter 7). Otherwise, patronize **Jeeves Snob Shop,** 7 Pont St., S.W.1 (tel. 071/235-1101).

Smoking   Most U.S. brands are available in London. Anti-smoking laws are tougher than ever. Smoking is forbidden in the Underground, in cars and on platforms. It is allowed only in the back of the upper level of double-decker buses, and is increasingly frowned upon in many other places.

Transit Information   For information in London, call 071/222-1234, 24 hours a day.

Weather   For information in London, call 071/246-8091.

4. NETWORKS & RESOURCES

FOR STUDENTS

Several organizations in London specialize in student discounts and youth fares. These include **STA Travel,** 74 Old Brompton Rd., S.W.7 (tel. 071/581-1022), which is open Monday to Friday from 9am to 5:30pm and on Saturday from 10am to 4pm. Tube: South Kensington.

Accommodations in university dormitories are available from early July to late September. These include **Imperial College,** 15 Princes Gardens, S.W.7 (tel. 071/589-5111, ext. 3600), near Royal Albert Hall and Hyde Park. The minimum stay is a week, which costs about £68 ($125.80) per person in a shared room without breakfast.

FOR GAY MEN & LESBIANS

The **Lesbian and Gay Switchboard** (tel. 071/837-7324), is open 24 hours a day, providing information about gay-related London activities, or else advice in general. There is also a **London Lesbian and Gay Centre,** 67-69 Cowcross St., E.1 (tel. 071/608-1471), which is open Monday to Thursday from noon to 11pm, on Friday and Saturday from noon to 2am, and Sunday noon to 11pm. Five floors contain a disco, bookstore, café, and bar. One floor is for women only. Tube: Farringdon. The **London Lesbian Line** (tel. 071/251-6911) is open Monday and Friday from 2 to 10pm and Tuesday through Thursday from 7 to 10pm.

FOR WOMEN

The **London Rape Crisis Centre,** P.O. Box 69, W.C.1 (tel. 071/837-1600) which operates 24 hours a day, offers additional services including medical and legal advice. It will even arrange for another woman to accompany you to a doctor, a clinic, or even the police station.

The leading feminist bookstore in London is **Silvermoon,** 68 Charing Cross Road, W.C.2 (tel. 071/836-7906) which stocks thousands of titles by and about women, plus tapes and records. Open Monday to Saturday from 10:30am to 6:30pm. Tube: Leicester Square.

LONDON: WHERE TO STAY

Since London is one of the gateway cities to Europe, some basic points about low-budget accommodations should be covered to avoid disappointing the first-timer abroad.

The majority of budget hotels aren't hotels at all (in the sense of having elevators, porters, and private baths). Rather, they are family-type guesthouses. Hundreds of these four- and five-story hotels dot the city. At first glance, they all look the same, but once inside you'll find widely varying degrees of cleanliness, service, and friendliness.

Most bed-and-breakfast hotels (B&Bs) serve an English breakfast, or at least a continental one, and rarely serve any other meal. Usually the rooms have sinks, innerspring mattresses, closet and dresser space, and a desk and armchair; the rooms on higher floors tend to be smaller. The bathroom may be a half flight down, two flights down, or on the same floor.

Ask what is included in the room rate, and in the case of a B&B, ask to see the room before accepting it. You'll probably be asked to pay in advance in B&B establishments. Incidentally, the designation of a private shower (or bath) on the tariff sheet presented to you doesn't always include a toilet.

A TRAVELER'S ADVISORY

If you're a first-time visitor to London and plan to seek low-cost lodgings, you should know that many of central London's B&B establishments and low-budget hotels are in very poor condition. In this chapter, you'll find a list of what I consider adequate B&B lodgings for London, but I present most without any particular enthusiasm. However, at the request of hundreds of readers who do not want to compromise a certain standard of living—that is, moderate comfort and a private bath—when traveling to London, I have also included a number of "big splurge" and in some cases "super splurge" hotels. But be warned: To get a decent room with a private bath in a moderately priced hotel, you may have to pay two to three times our room allowance.

For those who don't mind taking the tubes or trains, I've also included several B&B selections on the fringes of London, where establishments offer more reasonable tabs for quite good accommodations.

RESERVATIONS BY MAIL

Most hotels require at least a day's deposit before they will reserve a room for you. This can be accomplished either by an international money order or a personal check. Usually you can cancel a room reservation 1 week ahead of time and get a full refund. A few hotelkeepers will return your money 3 days before the reservation date. It's no trouble if you reserve well in advance, but if you cancel at the last minute, the hotel may keep your deposit. Many hotel owners operate on such a narrow margin of profit that they find just buying stamps for airmail replies too expensive. Therefore, you should enclose a prepaid International Reply Coupon.

VALUE ADDED TAX

Unless otherwise specified, rates quoted for the following hotels *include* Value Added Tax of 17½%.

PARKING

Naturally, budget hotels of London can't afford private underground garages. However, the staff is alert to directing you to the nearest public garages where daily charges range from £10 to £12 ($18.50 to $22.20) for the average vehicle.

1. LEICESTER SQUARE

Visitors flock to this area for its theaters, restaurants, and nightlife, but almost no one thinks of it as a hotel district. However, there is one closely guarded secret.

DOUBLES WITH BATH £62 [$114.70]

MANZI'S, 1-2 Leicester St., off Leicester Sq., London WC2H 7BL. Tel. 071/734-0224. Fax 071/437-4864. 16 rms (all with bath or shower). A/C TV TEL **Tube:** Leicester Square.
$ Rates (including English breakfast): £40–£47 ($74–$86.95) single; £62 ($114.70) double. AE, DC, MC, V.

The well-kept and comfortable bedrooms here are right above the oldest seafood restaurant in London (see Chapter 5). Guests climb a flight of steps and check in at a postage-stamp-size reception desk, right at the entrance to the busy restaurant. Unloading luggage might be a bit of a problem, but it's a great place to stay if you want to be right in the heart of London life. You'll save a lot on transportation.

2. BLOOMSBURY

Bloomsbury, a world within itself, lies northeast of Piccadilly Circus, beyond Soho. It is, among other things, the academic heart of London; you'll find the University of London, several other colleges, the British Museum, and many bookstores. Despite its student overtones, the section is fairly staid and quiet. Its reputation has been fanned by such writers as Virginia Woolf, who lived within its bounds (it figured in her novel *Jacob's Room*). The novelist and her husband, Leonard, were once the unofficial leaders of a group of artists and writers known as "the Bloomsbury group"—nicknamed "Bloomsberries"—which at times included Bertrand Russell.

The heart of Bloomsbury is **Russell Square,** and the streets jutting off from the square are lined with hotels and B&Bs. If you're searching for a hotel on foot, try the following itinerary: From the Russell Square Underground station (whose exit is on Bernard Street), walk first along Bernard Street. Then, 1 long block north of Bernard Street, try Coram Street, another hotel-lined block, and after that sample Tavistock Place, running 1 block north of Coram and parallel to it. North of Tavistock Place is Cartwright Gardens, which has a number of old converted town houses catering to overnight guests.

However, the Bernard Street-Coram Street-Tavistock Place hotels are the most likely Russell Square establishments to be booked in summer. You'll have a better chance on the other side of Russell Square (opposite Bernard Street), where you'll find

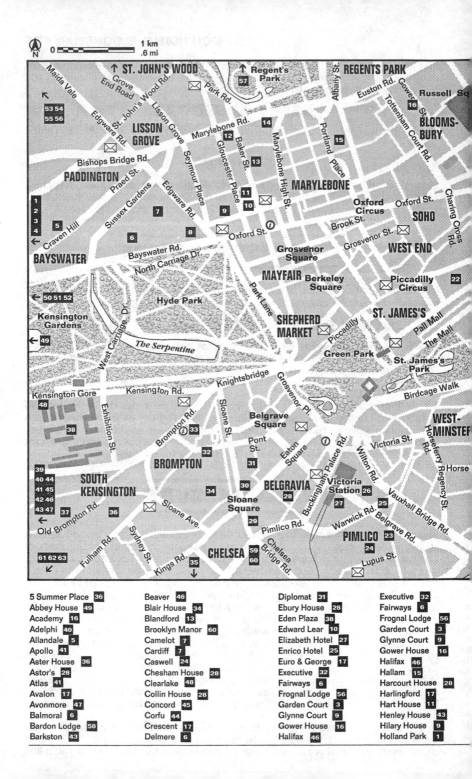

5 Summer Place 36	Beaver 46	Diplomat 31	Executive 32
Abbey House 49	Blair House 34	Ebury House 28	Fairways 6
Academy 16	Blandford 13	Eden Plaza 38	Frognal Lodge 56
Adelphi 40	Brooklyn Manor 60	Edward Lear 10	Garden Court 3
Allandale 5	Camelot 7	Elizabeth Hotel 27	Glynne Court 9
Apollo 41	Cardiff 7	Enrico Hotel 25	Gower House 16
Aster House 36	Caswell 24	Euro & George 17	Halifax 46
Astor's 28	Chesham House 28	Executive 32	Hallam 15
Atlas 41	Clearlake 48	Fairways 6	Harcourt House 28
Avalon 17	Collin House 28	Frognal Lodge 56	Harlingford 17
Avonmore 47	Concord 45	Garden Court 3	Hart House 11
Balmoral 6	Corfu 44	Glynne Court 9	Henley House 43
Bardon Lodge 58	Crescent 17	Gower House 16	Hilary House 9
Barkston 43	Delmere 6	Halifax 46	Holland Park 1

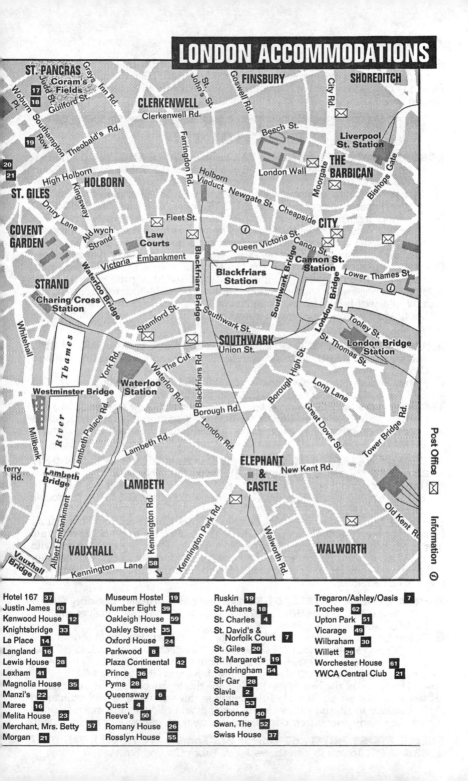

LONDON ACCOMMODATIONS

Hotel 167 **37**	Museum Hostel **19**	Ruskin **19**	Tregaron/Ashley/Oasis **7**
Justin James **63**	Number Eight **39**	St. Athans **18**	Trochee **62**
Kenwood House **12**	Oakleigh House **59**	St. Charles **4**	Upton Park **51**
Knightsbridge **33**	Oakley Street **35**	St. David's &	Vicarage **49**
La Place **14**	Oxford House **24**	Norfolk Court **7**	Wilbraham **30**
Langland **16**	Parkwood **8**	St. Giles **20**	Willett **29**
Lewis House **28**	Plaza Continental **42**	St. Margaret's **19**	Worchester House **61**
Lexham **41**	Prince **36**	Sandringham **54**	YWCA Central Club **21**
Magnolia House **35**	Pyms **28**	Sir Gar **28**	
Manzi's **22**	Queensway **6**	Slavia **2**	
Maree **16**	Quest **4**	Solana **53**	
Melita House **23**	Reeve's **50**	Sorbonne **40**	
Merchant, Mrs. Betty **57**	Romany House **26**	Swan, The **52**	
Morgan **21**	Rosslyn House **55**	Swiss House **37**	

Post Office ⊠ Information ⊙

the relatively high-priced hotels of Bloomsbury Street (lined with publishing houses) and those on the less expensive Gower Street, where you'll be at the midpoint of the University of London area. For instance, across from the Royal Academy of Dramatic Art, on Gower Street, you'll find a number of B&B houses.

DOUBLES WITHOUT BATH FOR LESS THAN £55 ($101.75)

ACADEMY HOTEL, 17-21 Gower St., London WC1E 6HG. Tel. 071/634-4115. Fax 071/636-3442. 32 rms (26 with bath). TV TEL **Tube:** Tottenham Court Road or Goodge Street.

$ Rates: £68 ($125.80) single without bath, £75 ($138.75) single with bath; £85 ($157.25) double without bath, £95 ($175.75) double with bath. AE, DC, MC, V.

Many of the original architectural details were preserved when these three 1776 Georgian row houses were joined. Substantially modernized and stylishly refurbished in 1987, the hotel is different from the usual chain hotel and is a good choice for travelers tired of paying four-star prices for two-star comforts. It is within walking distance of the theater section, Covent Garden, and other spots in the West End. Facilities include an elegant bar, library room, a secluded patio garden, and a restaurant serving French and Swiss food. The hotel offers 24-hour room service, and each of the well-furnished accommodations contains a radio and hot-beverage facilities. Most rooms have private showers and toilets, but public plumbing is adequate.

AVALON PRIVATE HOTEL, 46 Cartwright Gardens, London WC1H 9EL. Tel. 071/387-2366. 28 rms (5 with bath). TV **Tube:** Russell Square or King's Cross.

$ Rates (including an English breakfast): £30 ($55.50) single without bath; £42 ($77.70) double without bath, £50 ($92.50) double with shower. No credit cards.

The rooms in this brick Georgian town house have hot-beverage facilities, and a few have private baths or showers. Rooms are simple but comfortably furnished. Guests have use of a semiprivate, horseshoe-shaped garden across the street, where there's a tennis court.

CRESCENT HOTEL, 49-50 Cartwright Gardens, WC1H 9EL. Tel. 071/387-1515. 29 rms (8 with shower). TV **Tube:** Russell Square.

$ Rates (including English breakfast): £29 ($53.65) single without bath, £34 ($62.90) single with bath; £45 ($83.25) double without bath, £55 ($101.75) double with shower. MC, V.

Built in 1810, this could be what Mrs. Bessolo and Mrs. Cockle call your "home from home." The hotel overlooks a private square that is available to hotel guests, as are four tennis courts; rackets and balls are also available. There is a sitting room with color TV and a public telephone. All of the comfortably furnished bedrooms have hot and cold running water and hot-beverage facilities, and there are modern baths with showers on each floor.

EURO & GEORGE HOTELS, 51-53 Cartwright Gardens, London WC1H 9EL. Tel. 071/387-8666. Fax 071/383-5044. 74 rms (5 with bath or shower). TV TEL **Tube:** Russell Square.

$ Rates (including English breakfast): £29.50 ($54.60) single without shower, £42 ($72.70) single with shower; £43 ($79.55) double without shower, £52.50 ($97.10) double with shower; £52 ($96.20) triple without shower, £61 ($112.85) triple with shower; Children under 13 sharing room with parents £8 ($14.80). MC, V.

 This is one of the best of the B&Bs along this highly competitive and famous Georgian crescent. Several of the rooms in this well-run and well-maintained hotel are small, and all have a sink with hot and cold running water. Business clients often fill the rooms from Monday to Thursday, so reservations are important.

GOWER HOUSE HOTEL, 57 Gower St., London WC1E 6HJ. Tel. 071/636-4685. 16 rms (3 with shower). TV. **Tube:** Goodge Street.

$ Rates (including English breakfast): £25 ($46.25) single without bath, £28 ($51.80) single with bath; £34 ($62.90) double without bath, £39 ($72.15) double with bath; £16 ($29.60) per person in family room. MC, V.

A clean and suitable hotel, the Gower House is run by managers who cater to families. Some of the rooms have showers and toilets, but all have hot and cold running water. The family rooms are adequate for three to five persons, and there is a breakfast room and a TV lounge.

HARLINGFORD HOTEL, 61-63 Cartwright Gardens, London WC1H 9EL. Tel. 071/387-1551. Fax 071/387-4616. 44 rms (30 with shower). TV TEL **Tube:** Russell Square.

$ Rates (including English breakfast): £33 ($61.05) single without bath, £42 ($77.70) single with bath; £45 ($83.25) double without bath, £54 ($99.90) double with bath; £69 ($127.65) triple with bath; £80 ($148) quad with bath. MC, V.

This once-private 1820 town house is composed of three Georgian-era buildings connected via a bewildering array of staircases and meandering hallways. The hotel offers simple but comfortable bedrooms, and only breakfast is served. The overflow from Harlingford, on the corner of Marchmont Street in the heart of Bloomsbury, is siphoned into the Mabledon Court Hotel, on Mabledon Place (around the corner).

LANGLAND HOTEL, 29-31 Gower St., London WC1E 6HG. Tel. 071/ 636-5801. Fax 071/580-2227. 27 rms (6 with bath). **Tube:** Goodge Street, Russell Square, or Euston Station.

$ Rates (including English breakfast): £26 ($48.10) single without bath, £29 ($53.65) single with bath; £36 ($66.60) double without bath, £39 ($72.15) double with bath. MC, V.

Near the British Museum, this hotel has a 200-year-old facade of the yellow bricks known as "London stock." Bedrooms are simple but comfortable. Because of the traffic, the quieter rooms are in back. A three-course evening meal, if ordered in advance, costs £7 ($12.95).

MAREE HOTEL, 25-27 Gower St., London WC1E 6HG. Tel. 071/636-4868. 31 rms (none with shower). **Tube:** Goodge Street.

$ Rates (including continental breakfast): £22–£24 ($40.70–$44.40) single; £30–£35 ($55.50-$64.75) double. No credit cards.

This hotel, on a quiet street near the British Museum, lies within walking distance of the main West End shopping district, Piccadilly, and the major theaters. Behind a simple brick facade, it is a family-run place. Furnishings are in a simple modern style, clean but few frills. Many of the bedrooms overlook a rose garden at the rear of the hotel.

MORGAN HOTEL, 24 Bloomsbury St., London WC1B 3QJ. Tel. 071/ 636-3735. 21 rms (all with shower). TV TEL **Tube:** Russell Square or Tottenham Court Road.

$ Rates (including English breakfast): £40 ($74) single; £55 ($101.75) double. No credit cards.

In a row of similar buildings, this hotel is distinguished by its gold-tipped iron fence railings. Several of the rooms overlook the British Museum, and the whole establishment is very much part of the international scholastic scene of Bloomsbury. The lobby is a bit cramped, and the stairs rather steep, but the rooms are pleasant and the atmosphere congenial. The carpeted bedrooms in this completely refurbished hotel have big beds (by British standards), dressing tables with mirrors, ample wardrobe space, and central heating.

ST. GILES HOTEL, Bedford Ave., London WC1B 3AS. Tel. 071/636-8616. Fax 071/631-1036. 600 rms (all with shower). TV TEL **Tube:** Tottenham Court Road.

$ Rates: £47–51 ($86.95–$94.35) single; £73–80 ($135.05–$148) double. Breakfast £4.60 ($8.50) extra. AE, DC, MC, V.

At the Oxford Street end of Tottenham Court Road, this modern hotel opened in

1976 as the "Y" Hotel, which accounts for its large number of rooms. Its prices reflect its standard of comfort: Every bedroom has an outside window, in-house movies, a radio, comfortable furnishings, and wall-to-wall carpeting. A ground floor restaurant serves meals throughout the day.

ST. MARGARET'S HOTEL, 26 Bedford Place, London WC1B 5JH. Tel. 071/636-4177. 64 rms (6 with shower). TV TEL **Tube:** Holborn or Russell Square.

$ **Rates** (including English breakfast): £30.50 ($56.45) single without bath, £34.50 ($63.85) single with bath; £42.50 ($78.65) double without bath, £44.50 ($82.35) double with bath. No credit cards.

A quartet of Georgian town houses on historic Russell Square joins together to form this winning hotel of well-furnished bedrooms. For some four decades, it's been run with a certain flair by the Marazzi family, originally from Italy. Each bedroom is clean and comfortable, and all have hot and cold running water. Guests have the use of two lounges (one with TV).

YWCA CENTRAL CLUB, 16-22 Great Russell St., London WC1B 3LR. Tel. 071/636-7512. Fax 071/636-5278. 85 rms (none with bath). TV TEL **Tube:** Tottenham Court Road.

$ **Rates:** £30.10 ($55.70) single; £55.20 ($102.10) double; £16.50 ($30.55) triple or quad per person. Breakfast £3.50 ($6.45) extra. MC, V.

This large and attractive building was designed by Sir Edwin Lutyens, the famous architect. Even though called the YWCA, the club will rent to single men, but only if they book a single room. No two men can share a room, but women can bunk together. The club also rents to married men only if they share a room with their families. Reservations should be made by mail, enclosing an international money order in the amount of the first night's deposit. Rooms have hot and cold running water, and the public bathrooms are adequate. There are lounges, a writing room, TV room, swimming pool, and launderette. A coffee shop is open daily from 7am to 7pm.

3. VICTORIA

Directly south of Buckingham Palace is a section in Pimlico often referred to as Victoria, with its namesake, sprawling Victoria Station, as its center. Known as the "Gateway to the Continent," Victoria Station is where you get boat-trains to Dover and Folkestone for the trip across the Channel to France. The British Airways Terminal, the Green Line Coach Station, and the Victoria Coach Station are all just 5 minutes from Victoria Station. From the bus stations, you can hop aboard a Green Line Coach to the suburbs. In addition, an inexpensive bus tour of London departs from a point on Buckingham Palace Road just behind the Victoria Railroad Station.

Many of the hotels along Belgrave Road are now occupied by welfare recipients; you'll find the pickings better on the satellite streets jutting off Belgrave Road. Your best bet is to walk about Ebury Street, directly to the east of Victoria Station and Buckingham Palace Road. There you will find some of the best moderately priced lodgings in Central London.

DOUBLES WITHOUT BATH FOR LESS THAN £52 ($96.20)

ASTORS HOTEL, 110-112 Ebury St., London SW1W 9QU. Tel. 071/750-3811. Fax 071/823-6728. 22 rms (12 with bath). TV **Tube:** Victoria Station.

$ **Rates** (including English breakfast): £34 ($62.90) single; without bath, £41

($75.85) single with bath; £46 ($85.10) double without bath, £54 ($99.90) double with bath. MC, V.

This brick-fronted, Victorian house is in the popular Belgravia area of Ebury Street. Victoria main line and tube stations are a 5-minute walk away. The resident manager offers comfortably furnished rooms, each with hot and cold running water and tea-and coffee-making facilities.

CASWELL HOTEL, 25 Gloucester St., London SW1V 2DB. Tel. 071/834-6345. 20 rms (7 with bath). **Tube:** Victoria Station.
$ Rates (including English breakfast): £25 ($46.25) single without bath, £35 ($64.75) single with bath; £42 ($77.70) double without bath, £65 ($120.25) double with bath. No credit cards.

Built in 1850, this hotel contains four floors, a chintz-filled lobby, and understated but comfortable furnishings. Many visitors consider the calm and proximity to Victoria Station worth the lack of electronic comforts; the quiet derives from the location on a cul-de-sac with little traffic. Mr. and Mrs. Hare, the owners, serve breakfast daily from 8am to 9am.

CHESHAM HOUSE HOTEL, 64-66 Ebury St., London SW1 W9Q. Tel. 071/730-8513. Fax 071/730-3267. 23 rms (none with bath). TV **Tube:** Victoria Station.
$ Rates (including English breakfast): £29–£31 ($53.65–$57.35) single; £44–£46 ($81.40–$85.10) double. AE, DC, MC, V.

From looking at this stone facade flanked by a pair of old-fashioned carriage lamps, you would not guess that the interior is modern. Coffee is served continuously after 5pm every day, and breakfast is served in a functional basement room. The director, Maj. Eric J. Fletcher, rents the simple but comfortable rooms, which all have running water.

COLLIN HOUSE, 104 Ebury St., London SW1W 9QD. Tel. 071/730-8031. 13 rms (8 with bath). **Tube:** Victoria Station.
$ Rates (including English breakfast): £30 ($55.50) single without bath, £32 ($59.20) single with bath; £44 ($81.40) double without bath, £52 ($96.20) double with bath. No credit cards.

This good, clean B&B, in a privately owned mid-Victorian town house, is under the watchful eye of its resident proprietors, Mr. and Mrs. D. L. Thomas. Everything is well maintained, and all bedrooms have hot and cold running water, built-in wardrobes, and comfortable divan beds. There are several family rooms, and the main bus, rail, and Underground terminals are about a 5-minute walk from the hotel.

EBURY HOUSE, 102 Ebury St., London SW1W 9QD. Tel. 071/730-1350. 13 rms (none with bath). TV **Tube:** Victoria Station.
$ Rates (including English breakfast): £34 ($62.99) single; £42–£46 ($77.70–$85.10) double. No credit cards.

 Visitors arriving at this comfortable guesthouse are as likely to be greeted by Lola, the longtime manager, as by owners Marilyn and David Davies. All of the bedrooms contain hot and cold running water and hairdryers, and there is one full bath per floor and a pay phone on one of the stairwells. The pine-paneled breakfast room is the establishment's morning rendezvous point, where anyone wanting to discuss the weekend's rugby scores will find an avid connoisseur in David.

ELIZABETH HOTEL, 37 Eccleston Sq., London SW1V 1PB. Tel. 071/828-6812. Fax 071/821-9303. 38 rms (20 with bath or shower). **Tube:** Victoria Station.
$ Rates (including English breakfast): £30 ($55.50) single without bath, £46 ($85.10) single with bath; £46 ($85.10) double without bath, £68 ($125.80) double with bath; £58–£79 ($107.30–$146.15) for three with bath; £65–£87 ($120.25–$160.95) for four with bath. No credit cards.

An intimate, privately owned establishment, the Elizabeth Hotel overlooks the gardens of Eccleston Square, which was built by Thomas Cubitt, Queen Victoria's favorite builder, behind Victoria Station. This is an excellent place to stay; it's convenient to Belgravia and Westminster and is not far from Buckingham Palace. Each accommodation is individually decorated, and a Victorian atmosphere has been carefully preserved, as reflected in the furnishings, framed prints, and wallpaper.

ENRICO HOTEL, 77-79 Warwick Way, London SW1V 1QP. Tel. 071/834-9538. 26 rms (8 with bath or shower). **Tube:** Victoria Station.

$ **Rates** (including continental breakfast): £26 ($48.10) single without bath; £32 ($59.20) double without bath, £40 ($74) double with shower. No credit cards.

The Enrico is clean, and decorated in a functional "no frills" style. Bedrooms are often filled with a repeat clientele who know of its good value. Breakfast is served in a no-smoking room.

HARCOURT HOUSE, 50 Ebury St., London SW1W OLU. Tel. 071/730-2722. 10 rms (6 with bath or shower). TV **Tube:** Victoria Station.

$ **Rates** (including English breakfast): £40 ($74) single without bath, £42 ($77.70) single with bath; £44–£46 ($81.40–$85.10) double without bath, £52–£57 ($96.20–$105.45) double with bath. AE.

This pleasant hotel was originally built in the 1840s as a private house. Today, a confusing labyrinth of steep stairs leads to comfortably cozy bedrooms. Each bedroom has hot and cold running water. The major rail, tube, and coach stations are a 5-minute walk from the hotel.

LEWIS HOUSE HOTEL, 111 Ebury St., London SW1W 9QU. Tel. 071/730-2094. Fax 071/823-6728. 14 rms (5 with shower). TV **Tube:** Victoria Station.

$ **Rates** (including English breakfast): £30 ($55.50) single without bath; £45 ($83.25) double without bath, £48 ($88.80) double with bath; £65 ($120.25) triple with bath. MC, V.

From 1917 to 1930, this town house was the home of playwright Sir Noël Coward, and it was his parents who opened it to paying guests. During World War II, military leaders were housed here, each with a direct phone link to the Admiralty and the War Office. Today, this family-run hotel is managed by the Evans family. They have completely refurbished the establishment, adding more private showers in the bedrooms and restyling the breakfast room. It has pictures of Noël Coward adorning the walls, old play programs, Coward's old top hat, and other memorabilia of the Coward era.

MELITA HOUSE HOTEL, 33-35 Charlwood St., London SW1V 2DU. Tel. 071/828-0471. Fax 071/630-8905. 18 rms (8 with bath or shower). TV **Tube:** Victoria Station or Pimlico.

$ **Rates** (including English breakfast): £24 ($44.40) single without bath, £34 ($62.90) single with bath; £36 ($66.60) double without bath, £47 ($86.95) double with bath. No credit cards.

Originally built more than a century ago as a private house, the Melita House is on a residential street near Victoria Station. Bedrooms are comfortable in this family-run operation. To reach the hotel from the tube, head right off Belgrave Road, south of Warwick Way.

OXFORD HOUSE HOTEL, 92-94 Cambridge St., London SW1V 4QG. Tel. 071/834-6467. 18 rms (none with bath). **Tube:** Victoria Station.

$ **Rates** (including English breakfast): £26–28 ($48.10–$51.80) single; £35–£37 ($64.75–$68.45) double; £42–£45 ($77.70–$83.25) triple; £56–£60 ($103.60–$111) quad. Refundable key deposit of £5 ($9.25) required. No credit cards.

Set on a quiet one-way street (which taxi drivers have difficulty finding), only a few blocks from Victoria Station, this hotel is in a 150-year-old Victorian town house. It is owned and operated by an India-born interior designer, Y. A. Kader, and his Irish wife, Terry. Each room is decorated with flowery fabrics and coordinated bedspreads and carpets. Small, cramped, and relatively inconvenient single rooms lie on the fourth floor. The copious breakfast is served in a cozy cellar-level room.

PYMS HOTEL, 118 Ebury St., London SW1W 9QQ. Tel. 071/730-4986.
Fax 071/730-3267. 12 rms (2 with bath). TV **Tube:** Victoria Station.
$ Rates (including English breakfast): £40 ($74) single without bath; £52 ($96.20) double without bath, £67 ($123.95) double with bath. MC, V.

This "home from home" in Belgravia lies between Sloane Square and Victoria, just a 3-minute walk from the Victoria Station and its tube stop. The hotel enjoys a reputation for being "squeaky clean" and rents well-furnished rooms. There is a public phone, and a full English breakfast is served.

RUSKIN HOTEL, 23-24 Montague St., London WC1 5BN. Tel. 071/636-7388. Fax 071/323-1661. 33 rms (6 with shower). **Tube:** Holborn or Russell Square.
$ Rates (including English breakfast): £32 ($59.20) single without bath; £46 ($85.10) double without bath; £60 ($111) double with bath. AE, DC, MC, V.

Next to the British Museum, this is within walking distance of London's shopping district and major West End theaters. The hotel, listed as a building of historical interest, has retained many of its original architectural features. The centrally heated bedrooms, serviced by an elevator, have hot and cold running water, shaver points, intercoms, hot-beverage facilities, and electrical outlets.

ST. ATHANS HOTEL, 20 Tavistock Place, London WC1H 9RE. Tel. 071/837-9140. Fax 071/833-8352. 77 rms (none with bath). **Tube:** Russell Square.
$ Rates: (including English breakfast): £26–£35 ($48.10–$64.75) single; £36–£45 ($66.60–$83.25) double. AE, DC, MC, V.

These five interconnected buildings are linked by a labyrinth of staircases, fire doors, and not-quite-parallel hallways. The friendly, helpful owners, Mr. and Mrs. Hans Geyer, offer simple and functional bedrooms. St. Athans is not named after a saint but is a play on the phrase "Stay at Hans."

ROMANY HOUSE HOTEL, 35 Longmoore St., London SW1V LJQ. Tel. 071/834-5553. 10 rms (none with bath). **Tube:** Victoria Station.
$ Rates (including English breakfast): £22 ($40.70) single; £32 ($59.20) double. No credit cards.

This was established as a hotel in 1937 when a 500-year-old cottage was joined to a 200-year-old white-fronted Georgian town house. The name came out of a vision by a psychic. The owners, Mary and Peter Gulbitis, have owned the property for some 20 years and are honest about its shortcomings: "We don't want to sell it too lavishly, because we want people to know what they are getting," Mrs. Gulbitis explains. The place is old-fashioned but charming, and many visitors are repeats.

SIR GAR HOUSE, 131 Ebury St., London SW1W 9QU. Tel. 071/370-9378. Fax 071/823-6728. 11 rms (6 with bath). **Tube:** Victoria Station.
$ Rates (including English breakfast): £34 ($62.90) single without bath, £44 ($81.40) single with bath; £46 ($85.10) double without bath, £54 ($99.90) double with bath. MC, V.

A Victorian, brick-fronted town house on Ebury Street, 3 minutes' walk from Victoria Station, this is unusual for the area—the hotel has a walled-in, manicured garden for guests' use. The hotel offers comfortably furnished rooms, each with hot-beverage facilities and hot and cold running water.

4. KNIGHTSBRIDGE & BELGRAVIA

DOUBLES WITHOUT BATH FOR LESS THAN £57.50 ($106.50)

KNIGHTSBRIDGE

Several of the major department stores in London (including Harrods) are in this top residential and shopping district adjoining Belgravia. Just south of Hyde Park, Knightsbridge is close in character to Belgravia, and much of this section to the west of Sloane Street has 18th-century architecture and layout.

KNIGHTSBRIDGE HOTEL, 10 Beaufort Gardens, London SW3 1PT. Tel. 071/589-9271. Fax 071/823-9692. 20 rms (13 with bath). TV TEL **Tube:** Knightsbridge.

$ Rates (including continental breakfast): £38.50 ($71.25) single without bath, £44–£52.50 ($81.40–$97.10) single with bath or shower; £57.50 ($106.50) double without bath, £60–£85 ($111–$157.25) double with bath; £95 ($175.75) triple with bath. AE, DC, MC, V.

Sandwiched between the restaurants and fashionable boutiques of Beauchamp Place and Harrods, this place still retains the feeling of a traditional British hotel. On a tranquil, tree-lined square, free from traffic, the small, personally run hotel has a subdued Victorian charm. Units have radios and central heating, and there's a lounge with a color "telly" and a bar on the premises.

EXECUTIVE HOTEL, 57 Pont St., London SW1X OBD. Tel. 071/581-

Ⓕ FROMMER'S SMART TRAVELER: HOTELS

VALUE-CONSCIOUS TRAVELERS SHOULD TAKE ADVANTAGE OF THE FOLLOWING:

1. Reductions in rates for rooms without private bath. Usually a room with a shower is cheaper than a room with a private bath, and even cheaper is a room with a basin only.
2. You'll often pay at least 30% less than individual "rack" rates (off-the-street, independent bookings) if you book a package tour (or book land arrangements with your air ticket).
3. Sometimes on-the-spot bargaining can bring down the cost of a hotel room. There might be a business person's or schoolteacher's discount.
4. Reductions at some hotels if you pay cash instead of with a credit card.
5. Long-term discounts if you're planning to spend more than 1 week in London.

QUESTIONS TO ASK IF YOU'RE ON A BUDGET

1. Is there a garage? What's the charge?
2. Is there a surcharge on either local or long-distance calls? In some places, it might be an astonishing 40%. Make your calls at the nearest post office.
3. Does the hotel include service in the rates quoted, or will a service charge be added on at the end of your stay?
4. Is the 17½% Value Added Tax (VAT) included, or will it be added on later?
5. Is breakfast (continental or English), included in the rates?

2424. Fax 071/589-9456. 29 rms (all with bath or shower). TV TEL **Tube:** Knightsbridge.
$ Rates (including English breakfast): £54.95 ($101.65) single; £79.95 ($147.90) double or twin. VAT extra. AE, DC, MC, V.

★ Built in 1870 as a private house, this has been restored and is now one of the most appealing and convenient small hotels in the district. Part of its charm lies in its Adam-style frieze, which ascends and curves around the high ceilings and graceful stairway of the main entrance. Only a discreet metal plaque out front announces the establishment's status as a hotel; but once inside, you'll find comfortable, modern, unfrilly bedrooms—each with built-in furniture, a high ceiling, radio, in-house movies, a hospitality tray, ironing board/trouser press, and central heating. An elevator takes guests to one of the five upstairs floors. A cozy modern lounge is off the lobby, and the location, near the attractions of Knightsbridge, makes the Executive very, very central.

BELGRAVIA

Belgravia, south of Hyde Park, is the aristocratic quarter of London and challenges Mayfair for grandness. It's near Buckingham Palace Gardens and Brompton Road; the center is Belgrave Square, one of the more attractive plazas in London. A few townhouses once occupied by eminent Edwardians have been discreetly turned into moderately priced hotels—while others were built specifically to house guests.

DIPLOMAT HOTEL, 2 Chesham St., London SW1X 8DT. Tel. 071/235-1544. Fax 071/259-6153. 28 rms (all with bath). TV TEL **Tube:** Sloane Square.
$ Rates (including English breakfast buffet): £49.95 ($92.40) single; £74.95 ($138.65) double. Extra person £19.95 ($36.90). VAT extra. AE, DC, MC, V.

★ Part of a Diplomat Hotel's multifaced allure lies in its status as a small, reasonably priced hotel in an otherwise prohibitively expensive neighborhood filled with privately owned Victorian homes and high-rise first-class hotels. It was originally built by one of the neighborhood's most famous architects in the 19th century on a wedge-shaped street corner near the site of today's Belgravia Sheraton. You register at a desk framed by the sweep of a partially gilded circular staircase beneath the benign gaze of cherubs looking down from a "Regency-era chandelier."
Each of the comfortable bedrooms boasts a modern bath equipped with a hairdryer, among other necessities, a high ceiling, and well-chosen wallpaper in vibrant Victorian-inspired colors. The staff is very helpful, they even deliver morning newspapers.

5. CHELSEA

This fashionable district stretches along the Thames, south of Hyde Park, Brompton, and South Kensington. Beginning at Sloane Square, it runs westward toward the periphery of Earl's Court and West Brompton; its spinal cord is King's Road. Except for maybe Mayfair or Belgravia, Chelsea couldn't be more chic. Hence, the visitor seeking reasonably priced accommodations should follow Greeley's sage advice to go west. However, those who can afford a splurge may want to settle in here.

DOUBLES WITHOUT BATH FOR LESS THAN £65.95 [$122]

BLAIR HOUSE HOTEL, 34 Draycott Place, London, SW3 2SA. Tel. 071/581-2323. Fax 071/823-7752. 17 rms (10 with bath). TV TEL **Tube:** Sloane Square.

$ Rates (including continental breakfast): £38 ($70.30) single without bath, £60 ($111) single with bath; £55 ($101.75) double without bath, £70 ($129.50) double with bath. AE, DC, MC, V.

This hotel is a good, moderately priced choice for those who'd like to anchor deep in the heart of Chelsea. An old-fashioned building of architectural interest, it has been modified and completely refurnished, with every comfortable room sporting a radio and tea- or coffee-making equipment. Breakfast is the only meal served.

MAGNOLIA HOUSE, 104-105 Oakley St., London SW3 5NT. Tel. 071/ 352-0187. 24 rms (2 with bath). TV **Tube:** Sloane Square.

$ Rates (including continental breakfast): £22 ($40.70) single without bath, £25–£35 ($46.25–$64.75) single with shower (no toilet), £28–£35 ($51.80–$64.75) single with shower and toilet; £30 ($55.50) double without bath, £37–£44 ($68.45–$81.40) double with shower (no toilet), £40–£48 ($74–$88.80) double with bath. AE, MC, V.

From the outside, this clean, bright town house resembles a private residence; inside, it's decorated with contemporary furniture. Each of the comfortable rooms has hot and cold running water, and six contain showers but no toilets.

OAKLEY STREET HOTEL, 73 Oakley St., London SW3 5HF. Tel. 071/ 352-5599. 11 rms (none with bath). **Tube:** Sloane Station or bus no. 11 or 22 down King's Road.

$ Rates (including English breakfast): £18 ($33.30) single; £31 ($57.35) double; £10 ($18.50) per person in shared rooms. No credit cards.

A good budget choice, this hotel lies north of the Chelsea Embankment and can be reached by a 10-minute taxi from Victoria Station. You can have free tea and coffee whenever you want it, and the kitchen facilities include a refrigerator and a hotplate. Everything but food is provided for preparing your own meals. Some rooms are large enough for three or four beds, and these are rented at exceptionally low rates. Rooms are clean and attractively decorated. There is no hotel sign outside, as it is forbidden by a local ordinance.

WILBRAHAM HOTEL, 1-5 Wilbraham Place, off Sloane St., London SW1X 9AE. Tel. 071/730-8296. Fax 071/730-6815. 53 rms (40 with bath). TV TEL **Tube:** Sloane Square.

$ Rates: £36.50 ($67.55) single without bath, £51.50 ($95.25) single with bath; £62 ($114.70) double without bath, £85 ($157.25) double with bath. Breakfast £3 ($5.55) extra. No credit cards.

Wilbraham Hotel is as dyed-in-the-wool British as you can get. On a quiet little street, just a few hundred yards from busy Sloane Square, three Victorian town houses have been joined together as one hotel, where you can have simple meals at both lunch and dinnertime in an attractively old-fashioned bar/lounge. Bedrooms are traditionally furnished and well cared for.

WILLETT, 22 Sloane Gardens, Sloane Sq., London SW1W 8DJ. Tel. 071/824-8415. Fax 071/824-8415. 18 rms (15 with bath). TV TEL **Tube:** Sloane Square.

$ Rates (including English breakfast): £60.45 ($111.85) single without bath, £65.95 ($122) single with bath; £65.95 ($122) double without bath, £76.95 ($142.35) double with bath. VAT extra. AE, DC, MC, V.

A 19th-century town house opening onto gardens, Willett is one of the nuggets of Chelsea. It has many architectural flourishes, including a Dutch roof and bay windows. While retaining its traditional charm, the hotel has been fully renovated with new furnishings in all the well-equipped bedrooms and in the public lounge areas. The breakfast room is especially inviting, with plush red velvet chairs. In fact, the hotel has rapidly become a favorite address with many discriminating English people who like a town house address and who prefer being close to the restaurants, attractions, and shops of Chelsea.

6. KENSINGTON & SOUTH KENSINGTON

DOUBLES WITHOUT BATH FOR LESS THAN £54 [$99.90]

KENSINGTON

The Royal Borough (W.8) not only has great shopping (Kensington High Street), but it also contains a number of fine middle-class guesthouses, which are, for the most part, west of Kensington Gardens. The district is a convenient place to stay—plus it's close to Kensington Palace. The rows of houses along Kensington Palace Gardens once were inhabited by millionaires (yet Thackeray also lived here); today the houses are occupied in part by foreign ambassadors.

ABBEY HOUSE, 11 Vicarage Gate, London W8 4AG. Tel. 071/727-2594. 15 rms (none with bath). TV **Tube:** Kensington High Street.
$ Rates (including English breakfast): £26 ($48.10) single; £42 ($77.70) double; £52 ($96.20) triple. No credit cards.

Some hotel critics have rated this the best B&B in London. Thanks to renovations, this hotel, which was built in about 1860 on a typical Victorian square, is modern, though many of the original features have been retained. The spacious bedrooms have central heating, shaver points, vanity lights, and hot- and cold-water basins. The hotel offers shared baths, one to each two to four lodging units. The rooms are all refurbished annually. Considering how well run and maintained it is, it gets top marks for value in the area.

APOLLO HOTEL, 18-22 Lexham Gardens, London W8 5JU. Tel. 071/835-1133. Fax 071/370-4853. 59 rms (50 with bath). TV TEL **Tube:** Gloucester Road or Earl's Court.
$ Rates (including continental breakfast): £30 ($58.50) single without bath, £44 ($81.40) single with bath; £54 ($99.90) double with bath. AE, DC, MC, V.
The Apollo shares much in common with the also recommended Atlas. The same owner operates these Victorian buildings on a quiet residential street in Kensington, just off Cromwell Road. Both hotels have elevators servicing all floors, and guests of both hotels use the bar at the Atlas. The Apollo, however, has more rooms with baths (there are more showers in the Atlas).

ATLAS HOTEL, 24-30 Lexham Gardens, London W8 5JU. Tel. 071/835-1155. Fax 071/370-4853. 64 rms (45 with bath). TV TEL **Tube:** Gloucester Road.
$ Rates (including continental breakfast): £30 ($55.50) single without bath, £44 ($81.40) single with bath; £54 ($99.90) double with bath. AE, DC, MC, V.
In a Victorian building on a quiet residential street, just off Cromwell Road, this is a long-established hotel. Seventy percent of the rooms contain private baths, color TVs, and direct-dial phones, and elevators service all floors. Guests enjoy the use the bar.

AVONMORE HOTEL, 66 Avonmore Rd., London W14 8RS. Tel. 071/603-4296. Fax 071/603-4035. 9 rms (none with bath). MINIBAR TV TEL **Tube:** West Kensington. **Bus:** No. 9, 27, or 10.
$ Rates (including English breakfast): £33–£36 ($61.05–$66.60) single; £46–£50 ($85.10–$92.50) double. No credit cards.

This is easily accessible to West End theaters and shops yet it is located in a quiet neighborhood, only 2 minutes from the West Kensington station of the Underground's District Line. The Avonmore, a privately owned place, boasts wall-to-wall carpeting, radio alarms, and central heating in each room. There is a ratio of two rooms per clean, tiled bath. The owner, Margaret McKenzie, provides personal service, and her hotel is a winner of the National Award for the best private hotel in London.

CLEARLAKE HOTEL, 19 Prince of Wales Terrace, London W8 5PQ. Tel. 071/937-3274. 20 units (all with bath or shower). TV TEL **Tube:** Kensington High Street or Gloucester Road.
$ Rates: £25 ($46.25) single; £35–£65 ($64.75–$120.20) double; £130 ($240.50) apartment for four or more. AE, DC, MC, V.
This is a family hotel on a residential street facing Kensington Gardens. You can, of course, rent the comfortable single and double rooms, but the real finds here are the one-, two-, and three-room apartments with private baths and gas or electric kitchenettes. Some apartments also have a full-size kitchen and two bathrooms. The larger apartments can accommodate as many as eight, with plenty of closet space to go around.

HOTEL LEXHAM, 32-38 Lexham Gardens, London W8 5JU. Tel. 071/373-6471. Fax 071/244-7827. 66 rms (47 with bath or shower). TV TEL **Tube:** Gloucester Road.
$ Rates (including English breakfast): £32.50 ($60.15) single without bath, £44.50 ($82.35) single with bath; £41.50 ($76.80) double without bath, £64.50 ($119.35) double with bath. MC, V.
This owner-operated Victorian terrace hotel has an attractively quiet garden square with a wrought-iron fence out front. Of the comfortably furnished bedrooms, more than 70% contain private baths or showers. There are several large family rooms—and families with children receive a special welcome. All units contain electric shaver outlets and central heating. Guests have use of two well-appointed lounges and a restaurant, which overlooks a garden and serves breakfast along with moderately priced lunches and dinners.

VICARAGE PRIVATE HOTEL, 10 Vicarage Gate, London W8 4AG. Tel. 071/229-4030. 19 rms (none with bath). **Tube:** Kensington High Street and Notting Hill Gate.
$ Rates (including English breakfast): £27 ($49.95) single; £49 ($90.65) double. No credit cards.
The domain of Eileen and Martin Diviney, this has pleasant rooms with water basins and shaver outlets, and a good supply of public showers. Breakfast is individually prepared by Mrs. Diviney. Vicarage Gate is handy for boutiques and restaurants on Kensington Church Street, and a self-service laundry is nearby. If you bring a car into London, parking is likely to be a problem.

BROMPTON & SOUTH KENSINGTON

Brompton and South Kensington (S.W.7), south of Kensington Gardens and Hyde Park, are essentially residential areas, not as elegant as bordering Belgravia and Knightsbridge. The section is, however, rich in museums—in fact, it is often dubbed "museumland"—and it has a number of colleges and institutes, which draw large numbers of students.

ADELPHI HOTEL, 127-129 Cromwell Rd., London SW7 4DT. Tel. 071/373-7177. 54 rms (all with bath or shower). TV TEL **Tube:** Gloucester Road.
$ Rates (including English breakfast): £60 ($111) single; £75 ($138.75) double; £96 ($177.60) triple or quad. AE, DC, MC, V.
One of the best run hotels in the neighborhood, this rents comfortably furnished

bedrooms. The front parlor with a large bow window has been transformed into a stylish lounge with a bar, which serves hot snacks in the evening.

ASTER HOUSE, 3 Sumner Place, London SW7 3EE. Tel. 071/581-5888. Fax 071/584-4925. 12 rms (all with bath). MINIBAR TV TEL **Tube:** South Kensington.

$ Rates (including English breakfast): £50 ($92.50) single; £70–£89 ($129.50–$164.65) double. AE, DC, MC, V.

 The smallest hotel on this unusual street of hotels, the Aster has an early Victorian facade. Many consider it to be the best B&B in London. Rachel and Peter Carapiet are the owners, and their guests come from around the world, looking for the discreet no. 3, for which there is no hotel sign. Peter, an architect, has built L'Orangerie over the adjacent garage, adding a Machin Conservatory, which doubles as a breakfast room and lounge. All of the hotel's individually decorated rooms have central heating. Two of the attractive units are on the ground floor, one with a fireplace and a curtained four-poster bed—the rates for which are on the higher end of the scale. You can begin your day with a walk in the garden.

EDEN PLAZA, 68-69 Queen's Gate, London SW7 5TJ. Tel. 071/370-6111. Fax 071/370-0932. 65 rms (all with bath). TV TEL **Tube:** Gloucester Road.

$ Rates (including English breakfast): £59 ($109.15) single; £72–£79 ($133.20–$146.15) double; £89 ($164.65) triple. AE, DC, MC, V.

This modern, well-run hotel stands on a tree-lined boulevard. Windows are double glazed to cut down on the traffic noise, and the hotel's prices are reasonable for the neighborhood. It offers compact bedrooms equipped with all the necessary amenities, including hairdryers and radios. A cocktail bar makes a cozy rendezvous point, and a good restaurant on the premises serves full English breakfasts along with dinner nightly from 6:30 to 9pm; the menu includes a selection of British and continental dishes. The hotel has an elevator.

5 SUMNER PLACE, 5 Sumner Place, London SW7 3EE. Tel. 071/584-7586. Fax 071/823-9962. 14 rms (all with bath). MINIBAR TV TEL **Tube:** South Kensington.

$ Rates (including English breakfast): £65–£75 ($120.25–$138.75) single; £90–£95 ($166.50–$175.75) double. AE, DC, MC, V.

Next door to the Prince Hotel, this is a carefully restored Victorian terrace house built around 1850. Each of its bedrooms contains a radio, and some have a small refrigerator; the decor and furnishings are traditional. The hotel is served by an elevator, which delivers guests to a lovely, Victorian-style conservatory in the rear where breakfast is served.

NUMBER EIGHT, 8 Emperor's Gate, London SW7 4HH. Tel. 071/370-7516. Fax 071/373-3163. 15 rms (all with bath). MINIBAR TV TEL **Tube:** Gloucester Road.

$ Rates (including English breakfast): £65–£75 ($120.25–$138.75) single; £80–£90 ($148–$166.50) double. AE, DC, MC, V.

In a cul-de-sac in the museum district, this hotel offers warmth and elegance in a stately Victorian building. Personal service of a high standard is the keynote of Number Eight. The hotel is convenient for Knightsbridge and Kensington High Street shops, and the Earl's Court and Olympia exhibitions centers. Bedrooms in this small hotel are of individual decor, each one named after a county of England. All of the units have radios, hairdryers, and other modern amenities. A generous English buffet breakfast is served. There is a vending machine and room service.

PRINCE HOTEL, 6 Sumner Place, London SW7 3AB. Tel. 071/589-6488. Fax 071/589-5530. 30 rms (21 with bath). TV TEL **Tube:** South Kensington.

$ Rates (including English breakfast): £30 ($35.50) single without bath, £40 ($74) single with bath; £45 ($83.25) double without bath, £55 ($101.75) double with bath; £80 ($148) family room suitable for four. VAT extra. AE, DC, MC, V.

Ⓢ This early Victorian terrace house constructed around 1850 has been successfully converted into a hotel. Decorated and restored in a classic English style, it opens onto a conservatory and a garden in the rear. Bedrooms are individually decorated.

SORBONNE HOTEL, 39 Cromwell Rd., London SW7 2DH. Tel. 071/589-6636. Fax 071/581-1313. 20 rms (12 with bath or shower). TEL **Tube:** South Kensington.
$ **Rates** (including continental breakfast): £30 ($55.50) single without bath, £42 ($77.60) single with bath; £40 ($74) double without bath, £52 ($96.20) double with bath. MC, V.

Built in 1840, this gray-fronted Victorian town house was once the private residence of the aunt of Sir Winston Churchill. Nowadays, standing opposite the Museum of Natural History and near Harrods department store, it is an appealing hotel with pleasant rooms. Each unit has a radio and many rooms contain TVs.

---

7. EARL'S COURT & NOTTING HILL GATE

DOUBLES WITHOUT BATH FOR LESS THAN £58 ($107.30)

EARL'S COURT

Another popular hotel and rooming-house district is the area in and around Earl's Court, below Kensington, bordering the western half of Chelsea. A 15-minute tube ride from the Earl's Court station will take you into the heart of Piccadilly, via either the District or Piccadilly Lines. The area is convenient to both the West End Air Terminal and the exhibition halls. A young crowd is attracted to the district at night, principally to a number of pubs, wine bars, and coffeehouses. In summer, Australians stake out the cheap B&B houses.

BARKSTON HOTEL, 34-44 Barkston Gardens, London SW5 0EW. Tel. 071/373-7851. Fax 071/370-6570. 80 rms (all with bath). TV TEL **Tube:** Earl's Court.
$ **Rates:** £54 ($99.90) single; £72 ($133.20) double; £85 ($157.25) triple. Breakfast £4.50 ($8.35). AE, DC, MC, V.

Convenient to the Earl's Court tube stop with its direct link to Heathrow, this is also within easy access of the M4 motorway, going along Cromwell Road. On a historical note, the Barkston offered rooms for 5p (20¢) back in 1905, and, by the 1960s, was the first Trusthouse Forte property to open in London before that giant went on to found a hotel empire. Nowadays, it is privately owned, composed of six different buildings that were harmoniously connected. Each of its bedrooms is well maintained, with coffee-making equipment and a hairdryer. Some rooms are large family accommodations. The hotel also has its own restaurant; breakfast costs extra.

BEAVER HOTEL, 57-59 Philbeach Gardens, London SW5 9ED. Tel. 071/373-4553. Fax 071/373-555. 38 rms (20 with bath). TV TEL **Tube:** Earl's Court.
$ **Rates** (including English breakfast): £28 ($51.80) single without bath, £44 ($81.40) single with bath; £40 ($74) double without bath, £55 ($101.75) double with bath; £26 ($48.10) per person triple with bath. AE, MC, V. **Parking:** £2.50 ($4.65).

Built in the typical Victorian town-house fashion in 1887, this four-floor hotel offers rooms that are centrally heated and contain water basins and radios. A few rooms have three beds and are suitable for families with children. More than half of the units contain private bath and TV. A bar serves drinks and snacks in the evening.

CONCORD HOTEL, 155-157 Cromwell Rd., London SW5 0TQ. Tel. 071/370-4151. 40 rms (12 with bath or shower). TV TEL **Tube:** Earl's Court.
$ Rates (including continental breakfast): £30.50 ($56.45) single without bath, £39 ($72.15) single with bath; £44 ($81.4) double without bath, £61.50 ($113.80) double with bath. AE, MC, V.
Frankly, many of the hotels along Cromwell Road are disasters, but this one is suitable and a good value. The brick building has a garden and children's sandboxes out front. Inside, there's a sunken TV lounge with leather couches, and the modestly furnished guest rooms are clean and comfortable. The hotel is not licensed for alcohol but offers breakfast.

HALIFAX, 65 Philbeach Gardens, London SW5 9EE. Tel. 071/373-4153. 15 rms (4 with shower). **Tube:** Earl's Court.
$ Rates (including continental breakfast): £24 ($44.40) single without bath; £35 ($65.70) double without bath, £50 ($92.50) double with bath. AE, DC, MC, V.
This Victorian house has been brought up-to-date with such amenities as central heating. The hotel's bedrooms have hot and cold running water, radios, and intercom units; some accommodations contain private showers. Guests are given their own keys. The hotel opens onto a tree-lined crescent near the Earl's Court tube stop.

HENLEY HOUSE, 30 Barkston Gardens, London SW5 0EN. Tel. 071/370-4111. 20 rms (15 with bath). A/C MINIBAR TV TEL **Tube:** Earl's Court.
$ Rates (including continental breakfast): £32 ($59.20) single without bath, £40 ($74) single with bath; £43 ($79.55) double without bath, £51 ($94.35) double with bath. AE, MC, V.
This red-brick Victorian row house sits in front of a communal fenced-in garden that guests can enter by borrowing a key from the reception desk. With a bright contemporary decor, Henley House is a leader among B&Bs in the area (many of which are quite tacky). The guestrooms have matching curtains and wallpaper, and a cozy second-floor sitting room overlooks a rear courtyard.

HOTEL 167, 167 Old Brompton Rd., London SW5 0AN. Tel. 071/373-0672. Fax 071/373-3360. 19 rms (all with bath). MINIBAR TV TEL **Tube:** Gloucester Road.
$ Rates (including continental breakfast): £51–£60 ($94.35–$111) single; £64–£70 ($118.40–$129.50) double. MC, V.
One of the more fashionable guesthouses in the area, this is sheltered in a Victorian era, once-private town house, which, including the basement, has four floors of living space. Some of the bedrooms are in the basement, but they have big windows to illuminate them. The decor is stylish, with metallic and chrome touches and pinewood—sort of Scandinavian modern. Windows have venetian blinds and each accommodation contains a coffee machine.

HOTEL PLAZA CONTINENTAL, 9 Knaresborough Place, London SW5 0TP. Tel. 071/370-3246. Fax 071/373-9571. 20 rms (16 with bath or shower). TV TEL **Tube:** Earl's Court.
$ Rates (including continental breakfast): £32 ($59.20) single without bath, £40 ($74) single with bath; £57.50 ($106.40) double without bath, £73.60 ($136.15) double with bath. AE, MC, V.
This refurbished, well-maintained B&B hotel is in a simple Victorian row house. Privately owned and managed, it stands in a quiet section about a 2-minute walk from the tube stop. Each of the compact, tastefully furnished rooms has a radio and hot-beverage facilities, and the hotel has full central heating and an elevator.

SWISS HOUSE HOTEL, 171 Old Brompton Rd., London SW5 0AN. Tel. 071/373-2769. Fax 071/373-4983. 16 rms (10 with bath). TV TEL **Tube:** Gloucester Road.
$ Rates (including continental breakfast): £27.50 ($51.75) single without bath,

£39.60 ($73.25) single with bath; £41.80 ($77.35) double without bath, £49.50 ($92.45) double with bath. MC, V.

One of the more desirable B&Bs in the Earl's Court area, this hotel lies within a white, Victorian row house, festooned with flowers and vines, with a front porch portico. The rear windows overlook a charming communal garden. Its country-inspired bedrooms are individually designed; some have working fireplaces. There's a snack menu, including hot dishes, and all items can be served in the bedrooms. Traffic is heavy outside, but windows are double glazed.

NOTTING HILL GATE

Increasingly gaining in fashion and frequented by such persons as the Princess of Wales, Notting Hill Gate is bounded on the south by Bayswater Road, on the east by Gloucester Terrace, on the north by West Way, and on the west by the Shepherd's Bush ramp leading to the M40. It has many turn-of-the-century mansions and small houses on quiet, leafy streets.

HOLLAND PARK HOTEL, 6 Ladbroke Terrace, London W11 3PG. Tel. 071/792-0216. Fax 071/727-8166. 23 rms (17 with bath). TV TEL **Tube:** Notting Hill Gate.

$ **Rates** (including continental breakfast): £48 ($88.80) single without bath, £50 ($92.50) single with bath; £65 ($120.25) double with bath. No credit cards.

This white Victorian row house with a small, charming front garden stands on a tree-lined street; another garden is in the rear. Breakfast is served in the well-furnished and comfortable bedrooms, and a large, pleasant lounge is on the second floor.

SLAVIA HOTEL, 2 Pembridge Sq., London W2 4EW. Tel. 071/727-1316. Fax 071/229-0803. 31 rms (all with shower). TEL **Tube:** Notting Hill Gate.

$ **Rates** (including English breakfast): £34–£40 ($62.90–$74) single; £44–£55 ($81.40–$101.75) double. AE, DC, MC, V.

The Slavia Hotel is named for the owner's homeland, Yugoslavia, and sits across from the private gardens of Pembridge Square in a neighborhood popular with upwardly mobile young families. The Portobello Antique Market is just around the corner from the hotel. The simple but clean guest rooms have comfortable furniture, and the rustic, Yugoslav-inspired breakfast room is in the cellar.

8. ST. MARYLEBONE

The principally Georgian district of St. Marylebone (pronounced *Mar*-li-bone) is below Regent's Park, northwest of Piccadilly Circus, facing Mayfair to the south, and extending north of Marble Arch at Hyde Park. A number of simple but gracious town houses in this residential section have been converted into private hotels, and little discreet bed-and-breakfast signs appear in the windows. If you don't have a reservation, start at Edgware Road and walk past Seymour and Great Cumberland Place. Let the summer crowds fight it out in Bloomsbury.

DOUBLES WITHOUT BATH FOR LESS THAN £52 ($96.20)

BLANDFORD HOTEL, 80 Chiltern St., London W1M 1PS. Tel. 071/486-3103. Fax 071/487-2786. 33 rms (all with bath). TV TEL **Tube:** Baker Street.

$ **Rates** (including English breakfast): £56 ($103.60) single; £70 ($129.50) double; £87 ($160.95) triple. AE, DC, MC, V.

Located only a minute's walk from the tube, this hotel on the street of Sherlock Holmes fame is definitely one of London's better B&Bs for the price. Each room has a hairdryer and coffee-making equipment. Five rooms rented as triples are suitable for families. The hotel is family-run, and each guest gets personal attention.

EDWARD LEAR HOTEL, 28-30 Seymour St., London W1H 5WD. Tel. 071/402-5401. Fax 071/706-3766. 30 rms (12 with bath). TV TEL **Tube:** Marble Arch.

$ Rates (including English breakfast): £37.50 ($69.40) single without bath, £55 ($101.75) single with bath; £49.50 ($91.60) double without bath, £59.50 ($110.10) double with bath. MC, V.

 This popular hotel is made all the more desirable by the bouquets of fresh flowers set up around the public rooms. It's 1 city block from Marble Arch in a pair of brick town houses, both from 1780. The western house was the London home of the 19th-century artist and poet Edward Lear, whose illustrated limericks and original lithographs adorn the walls of one of the sitting rooms. Steep stairs lead to the cozy bedrooms, which are fairly small but have all the usual amenities, including radios and hot-beverage facilities. The owner, Peter Evans, is helpful.

GLYNNE COURT, 41 Great Cumberland Place, London W1H 7GH. Tel. 071/262-4344. Fax 071/724-2071. 15 rms (none with bath). TV TEL **Tube:** Marble Arch.

$ Rates (including continental breakfast): £37 ($68.45) single; £52 ($96.20) double. AE, DC, MC, V.

In the Marble Arch area of St. Marylebone, this B&B is considered one of the more desirable places to live. It's white with carriage lamps on each side of the front door and is run with a certain flair. There is one shared bath for each pair of units. The staff is attentive, and breakfast is carried to your room each morning.

HALLAM HOTEL, 12 Hallam St., Portland Place, London W1N 5LJ. Tel. 071/580-1166. Fax 071/323-4527. 23 rms (all with bath). TV TEL **Tube:** Oxford Circus.

$ Rates (including continental breakfast): £55 ($101.75) single; £75 ($138.75) double. AE, DC, MC, V.

 This heavily ornamented stone-and-brick Victorian house is one of the few on the street to escape bombing in World War II. Today it's the property of Earl Baker and his sons, Grant and David, who maintain it well. The bright breakfast room overlooks a pleasant patio, and there is also a bar for residents. An elevator leads to the simple but comfortable bedrooms, each with radio and 24-hour room service.

HART HOUSE HOTEL, 51 Gloucester Place, Portman Sq., London W1H 3PE. Tel. 071/935-2288. Fax 071/935-8516. 15 rms (9 with bath). TV TEL **Tube:** Marble Arch or Baker Street.

$ Rates (including English breakfast): £30 ($55.50) single without bath; £45 ($83.25) double without bath, £55 ($101.75) double with bath; £65 ($120.25) triple without bath, £75 ($138.75) triple with bath. AE, MC, V.

This well-preserved building is part of a group of Georgian mansions occupied by French nobility during the French Revolution. The hotel is in the heart of the West End and is convenient for shopping, theaters, and sightseeing. It is within a few minutes' walk of Oxford Street, Selfridges, Marble Arch, Hyde Park, Regent's Park, and the zoo, as well as Madame Tussaud's and the planetarium. All bedrooms have hot and cold running water and radios.

HILARY HOUSE, 54 Upper Berkeley St., London W1H 7PP. Tel. 071/723-0618. Fax 071/724-2905. 16 rms (13 with bath). TV TEL **Tube:** Marble Arch.

$ Rates (including English breakfast): £27 ($49.95) single without bath, £30 ($55.50) single with bath; £35 ($64.75) double without bath, £40 ($74) double with bath. AE, MC, V.[msp273]

Hilary House is a well-managed, clean, and comfortable B&B. The Sanchez family, the owners, have won respect from their guests, many of whom have adopted this hotel as their London home. Most bedrooms are large, and each is tastefully decorated. Breakfast is served in a basement-level room, and parents are welcome to bring their children.

**KENWOOD HOUSE HOTEL, 114 Gloucester Place, London W1H 3DB.
Tel. 071/935-3473.** Fax 071/224-0582. 16 rms (5 with bath). TV **Tube:** Baker
Street.

$ Rates (including English breakfast): £28 ($51.80) single without bath, £35
($64.75) single with bath; £35 ($64.75) double without bath, £48 ($88.80) double
with bath. AE, V.

In a 200-year-old Adam town house, this hotel is run by English-born Arline Woutersz
and her Dutch husband. The building's 18th-century front balcony and awning
mechanisms are said to be original. The house was a family home until 1942, when
the owner's two sons died in the war. Disheartened, the owner sold it to the British
Army, who used it to billet officers. Now converted into a small hotel, it is a preserved
historical monument.

**HOTEL LA PLACE, 17 Nottingham Place, London W1M 3FB. Tel. 071/
486-2323.** 24 rms (all with bath). MINIBAR TV TEL **Tube:** Baker Street.

$ Rates (including English breakfast): £50–£65 ($92.50–$120.20) single; £75–£85
($138.75–$157.25) double. DC, MC, V.

This former Victorian building with a red-brick facade, similar to many other
buildings on its street, is one of the finest B&B hotels in the area. The basement of this
little hotel contains the Greenery Restaurant, which serves lunch and dinner daily.
There's also a chic little wine bar. Bedrooms are clean and comfortable, with
traditional styling.

9. PADDINGTON & BAYSWATER

Another popular hotel area jammed with budget housing is **Paddington,** the section
around Paddington Station, just to the northwest of Kensington Gardens and Hyde
Park. **Bayswater,** slightly to the west of Hyde Park and to the north of Kensington
Gardens, is an unofficial district with a number of decently priced lodgings. Once this
area of London had a strong Russian influence, a memory that lives on in St.
Petersburg Place, considered by some the most charming street of Bayswater. Pick and
choose carefully among the B&Bs in Bayswater, however, because many are quite
scruffy. However, the area abounds in cheap restaurants, mostly ethnic.

Again, you'd be well advised to telephone ahead to see if rooms are available. If
you don't have a reservation, begin your trek by taking the Underground to either
Paddington or Edgware Road and walking to Sussex Gardens, which is a long avenue
flanked by bed-and-breakfast houses, many dreadfully run down—in fact, many of
the budget hotels in this area now deal mostly with homeless persons sent from the
local authorities. Postbreakfast hours, when guests have just checked out, is the best
time for finding a vacancy. If you're unable to find a room on Sussex Gardens, then try
the satellite Norfolk Square, which lies near Sussex Gardens (even closer to
Paddington Station).

Tube stops serving the Bayswater and Paddington areas are Paddington, Bayswater,
Queensway, Notting Hill Gate, and Ladbroke.

DOUBLES FOR LESS THAN £55 [$101.75]

**ALLANDALE, 3 Devonshire Terrace, London W2 3DN. Tel. 071/723-
7807.** 20 rms (18 with bath). TV **Tube:** Paddington.

$ Rates (including English breakfast): £28 ($51.80) single without bath, £30
($55.50) single with bath; £33 ($61.05) double without bath, £38 ($70.30) double
with bath. DC, MC, V.

Ignore all the other B&Bs on this street, near the Paddington Underground station,
and head for this one. Decorated with style, it is a bright and cheerful place, and its
owners keep it well maintained. Rooms are cozy but small, because of the addition of
private baths, and all are painted either green or pink.

BALMORAL HOTEL, 156 Sussex Gardens, London W2 1UD. Tel. 071/ 723-7445. 17 rms (3 with bath or shower). TV **Tube:** Paddington.
$ Rates (including English breakfast): £25 ($46.25) single without bath; £34 ($62.90) double without bath, £38 ($70.30) double with bath or shower. No credit cards.
The Balmoral, named after the famous Scottish retreat of Prince Albert and Queen Victoria, stands out on a street with many mediocre B&B choices. The hotel is a converted Victorian row house overlooking Sussex Gardens, and in summer, cheery flowerboxes decorate the windows. The comfortable rooms are simple but well kept and have hot-beverage equipment and hot and cold running water. The three more expensive family rooms have baths.

CAMELOT HOTEL, 45-47 Norfolk Sq., London W2 1RX. Tel. 071/723-9118. Fax 071/402-3412. 44 rms (40 with bath or shower). TV TEL **Tube:** Paddington.
$ Rates (including English breakfast): £32.50 ($60.15) single without bath, £46.50 ($83.05) single with bath; £55 ($101.75) double without bath, £62 ($114.70) double with bath. MC, V.
A former 1850 town house standing at the center of an old tree-filled square, this is only 2 minutes from Paddington Station. The hotel was recently refurbished and now has an elevator. The comfortable and well-furnished guest rooms have radios and complimentary beverage trays.

CARDIFF HOTEL, 5-9 Norfolk Sq., London W2 1RU. Tel. 071/723-9068. Fax 071/402-2342. 60 rms (55 with shower). TV **Tube:** Paddington.
$ Rates (including English breakfast): £27.50 ($50.90) single with shower (no toilet), £30 ($55.50) single with shower and toilet; £45 ($83.50) double with shower and toilet; £58 ($107.30) triple with shower and toilet. No credit cards.
One of the better values in this famous old London neighborhood, this hotel is on a tree-lined square and is named for the capital of Wales. Bedrooms are comfortably furnished; some are large enough to accommodate three. Breakfast is served in the hotel's sunny dining room.

DELMERE HOTEL, 130 Sussex Gardens, London W2 1UB. Tel. 071/706-3344. Fax 071/262-1863. 40 rms (all with bath or shower). TV TEL **Tube:** Paddington Station.
$ Rates (including continental breakfast): £68 ($125.80) single; £83 ($153.55) double. AE, DC, MC, V
One of the finer hotels in this section, the Delmere is in a stucco house, with a colonnade entrance, designed by Samuel Pepys Cockerell (Latrobe, who built the Capitol in Washington, was a pupil under Cockerell). In a neighborhood once frequented by Sir Alexander Fleming (the discoverer of penicillin) and the family of Sir Arthur Conan Doyle, you too can seek lodgings. All of the well-furnished bedrooms contain radios, hairdryers, and hot-beverage facilities. Close to Hyde Park and Oxford Street, the hotel has a residents' cocktail bar and a lounge with comfortable sofas and a welcoming fire in the winter. In the hotel's La Perla continental restaurant, a three-course dinner costs £9.75 ($18.05).

FAIRWAYS HOTEL, 186 Sussex Gardens, London W2 1TU. Tel. 071/ 723-4871. 17 rms (10 with bath). TV **Tube:** Paddington.
$ Rates (including English breakfast): £30 ($55.50) single without bath; £44 ($81.40) double without bath, £55 ($101.75) double with bath. MC, V.
Near Hyde Park, this black-and-white town house is easily recognized by its colonnaded front entrance with a wrought iron balustrade stretching across the front second-floor windows. Hot-beverage facilities are included in the bright, clean bedrooms. There is free parking for five cars.

GARDEN COURT HOTEL, 30-31 Kensington Gardens Sq., London W2 4BG. Tel. 071/229-2553. Fax 071/727-2749. 40 rms (13 with shower). TEL **Tube:** Bayswater.

$ Rates (including English breakfast): £25 ($46.25) single without bath, £37 ($68.45) single with bath; £37 ($68.45) double without bath, £49 ($90.65) double with bath. MC, V.
This hotel is situated opposite the iron fence that rings the gardens in the center of Kensington Gardens Square. Each of the economically furnished but well-kept bedrooms has a dresser, wardrobe, and hot and cold running water. There is a licensed bar downstairs.

PARKWOOD HOTEL, 4 Stanhope Place, London W2 2HB. Tel. 071/402-2241. Fax 071/402-1574. 18 rms (12 with bath). TV TEL **Tube:** Marble Arch.
$ Rates (including English breakfast): £40.50 ($74.95) single without bath, £52 ($96.20) single with bath; £54.50 ($100.85) double without bath, £65.50 ($121.20) double with bath. MC, V

 The Parkwood occupies one of the best locations for a good value hotel in London—near Oxford Street and Marble Arch on a fairly quiet street, just 50 yards from Hyde Park, in a section of London known as Connaught Village. The well-furnished bedrooms contain hot-beverage facilities and radios. The hotel prides itself on an excellent breakfast; in fact, the menu states if you're still hungry, you can have another meal free.

QUEENSWAY HOTEL, 149 Sussex Gardens, London W2 2RY. Tel. 071/723-7749. Fax 071/262-5707. 43 rms (all with bath or shower). TV TEL **Tube:** Paddington.
$ Rates (including English breakfast): £52–£56 ($96.20–$103.60) single; £62–£69 ($114.70–$127.65) double. AE, DC, MC, V.
One of the more attractive B&Bs in the Paddington area, this was renovated in 1989 and consists of two Victorian houses joined together. The prices reflect the higher status of this B&B. Most bedrooms are a soft pink, and each has a trouser press and hot-beverage facilities. Rooms vary in size; the more expensive doubles have Jacuzzis. There is a lovely reception room with the original mantelpiece and deep cove moldings.

ST. CHARLES HOTEL, 66 Queensborough Terrace, London W2 3SH. Tel. 071/221-0022. 35 rms (all with shower). **Tube:** Queensway.
$ Rates (including English breakfast): £22–£27 ($40.70–$49.95) single; £34–£38 ($62.90–$70.30) double. No credit cards.
Originally a private home, this is a stone's throw from Kensington Gardens on a street dotted with private houses and hotels. A few of the ornate plaster ceilings and much of the original oak paneling still remain. The modestly furnished bedrooms all contain private showers and hot and cold running water, although only four of them offer private toilets.

ST. DAVID'S AND NORFOLK COURT HOTELS, 16-20 Norfolk Sq., London W2 1RS. Tel. 071/723-4963. 50 rms (10 with shower). **Tube:** Paddington or Lancaster Gate.
$ Rates (including English breakfast): £20 ($37) single without bath, £25 ($46.25) single with bath; £36 ($66.60) double without bath, £42 ($77.70) double with bath. MC, V.
George Neokleous offers clean and comfortable bedrooms in two hotels that were joined together, a short distance from the tube stops. Only a few rooms are equipped with private showers. Guests have found the owner helpful and courteous.

TREGARON HOTEL/ASHLEY HOTEL/OASIS HOTEL, 13-17 Norfolk Sq., London W2 1RU. Tel. 071/723-9966. 52 rms (26 with bath). TV TEL **Tube:** Paddington.
$ Rates (including English breakfast): £21.80 ($40.35) single without bath; £40 ($74) double without bath, £46 ($85.10) double with bath. No credit cards.
Today this establishment is a combination of three mid-Victorian buildings, but since many repeat clients prefer to use the names they're used to, the hotel keeps three separate signs above each of the trio of front doors. You register, however, at 15

Norfolk Square for one of the small but comfortable bedrooms. Breakfast is served in the basement.

10. AIRPORT HOTELS

Most regularly scheduled planes will land at Heathrow, while charter flights are likely to go to Gatwick—which more and more is becoming the gateway to London. If you need to be near either airport, consider the following suggestions instead of the well-advertised and more expensive operations.

DOUBLES WITHOUT BATH FOR LESS THAN £47 [$86.95]

HEATHROW

THE SWAN, The Hythe, Staines, Middlesex TW18 3JB. Tel. 0784/ 452494. Fax 0784/461593. 11 rms (5 with bath). TV **Tube:** Heathrow, then taxi.
$ Rates (including English breakfast): £33 ($61.05) single without bath, £60 ($111) single with bath; £47 ($86.95) double without bath, £65 ($120.20) double with bath. AE, DC, MC, V. **Parking:** Free.
Dating back beyond the days of Samuel Pepys, this is on the south bank of the Thames, beside Staines Bridge, and is within easy access of Heathrow (15 minutes). Bedrooms have central heating and tea- or coffee-making facilities. The attractive old inn also has a reputation for good food ranging from bar snacks to traditional English "fayre." A three-course meal costs £11 ($19.35) in a gazebo-style dining room, featuring simple, wholesome cooking. Food is served daily from 12:30pm to 2pm and from 5:30 to 9:30pm, except on Saturday and Sunday, when the last orders go in at 10pm.

UPTON PARK GUEST HOUSE, 41 Upton Park, Slough, Berkshire SL1 2DA. Tel. 0753/28797. 11 rms (4 with bath). TV **Transportation:** Train to Slough Station.
$ Rates (including English breakfast): £25 ($46.25) single without bath, £27 ($49.95) single with bath; £44 ($81.40) double without bath, £48 ($88.80) double with bath. VAT extra. MC, V. **Parking:** Free.
The cab ride from Heathrow to this hotel is about 15 minutes. Jan and Pete Jones, who run the place, can arrange for a local cab to meet you if you preplan (and the local cab is cheaper than getting a cab at the airport). All rooms have central heating, hot and cold running water, and complimentary tea and coffee. There's also a pleasant bar.

GATWICK

Since this airport is 30 miles from central London, you may want to stay at a convenient perch nearby while waiting for the departure of your flight.

BROOKLYN MANOR HOTEL, Bonnetts Lane, Ifield, Crawley, West Sussex RH11 0NY. Tel. 0293/546-24. 11 rms (4 with shower).
$ Rates: £20 ($37) single without bath, £30 ($55.50) single with bath; £32 ($59.20) double without bath, £40 ($74) double with bath. Breakfast from £2 ($3.70) extra. AE, MC, V. **Parking:** Free.
The Brooklyn Manor is an old, well-cared-for Victorian house set on 5 acres of English countryside, and it's only 5 minutes from Gatwick. The hotel provides free

transportation to and from the airport—just call them when you arrive, and they'll come get you. Martin Davis rents rooms with full central heating and beverage-making facilities. Breakfast costs extra, and you can order a light snack in the evening.

In addition, a free courtesy service takes guests to and from a nearby restaurant, and there are two pubs within about a 10-minute walk, both of which serve inexpensive meals. The hotel does not have a bar, but it is licensed, so that you can have drinks served in the lounge if you wish.

OAKLEIGH HOUSE, West Park Rd., Copthorne, West Sussex RH10 3HG. Tel. 0341/712703. 5 rms (4 with bath). TV **Train:** Gatwick express from Victoria Station, then taxi.

$ **Rates** (including English breakfast): £25 ($46.25) single without bath; £36–£38 ($66.60–$70.30) double with bath; £65 ($120.25) family room for four. **Parking:** Free.

About 5 miles from Gatwick, this hotel offers comfortably furnished rooms, all with courtesy beverage trays. The hotel is a short drive from the Gatwick Airport Railway Station, from which an express train travels every 15 minutes to London's Victoria Station. Taxi service to and from Gatwick Airport costs about £5 ($9.25) per journey. The owners welcome senior citizens, children, and the disabled.

11. OTHER OPTIONS

STAYING WITH A FAMILY

Many agencies in Britain can arrange stays with a private family, either in London or in the country. This program is an intriguing way to involve yourself in the social life of a country and to see it from the inside. Plus, it's a bargain when compared to hotels. Some agencies limit themselves to teenagers; others welcome older travelers.

Ball Tourist Services, Staufenstrasse 6, D-4050 Mönchengladbach 1, Germany. (tel. 02161/34426; fax 02161/38898), will arrange for accommodations with selected families living in the southwest suburbs of London, including Streatham, Norbury, and Thornton Heath. Only 15 to 20 minutes by train to the center of London, the area is convenient for all sorts of recreational and sightseeing activities. Host-family accommodation is also available in Glasgow, Edinburgh, Canterbury, the

---

Ⓕ FROMMER'S COOL FOR KIDS
HOTELS

Clearlake Hotel (see p. 88) A family-run hotel on a street facing Kensington Gardens, this hotel offers several apartments with full-size kitchens and two bathrooms suitable for up to four or more.

Gower House Hotel (see p. 78) Families are especially welcome at this Bloomsbury hotel where several rooms are set aside for them. It's also within easy walking distance of the British Museum.

Euro & George Hotels (see p. 78) One of the best B&Bs, it's located on a famous crescent of London. Children under 13 sharing a room with their parents pay £8 ($14.80) a night.

Hotel Lexham (see p. 88) Families with children get a special welcome at this Victorian terrace hotel, lying in the South Kensington area. Several large family rooms are rented.

Isle of Wight, Cambridge, the Lake District, and other places. Accommodation with breakfast is from £25 ($46.25) daily. Prices include the booking fee. Bookings of 2 or more nights are preferred.

B&B IN PRIVATE HOMES

Susan Opperman and Rosemary Lumb run **Bed and Breakfast Nationwide,** Admirals House, Heckford Road, Great Bentley, Essex, CO7 8RS, an agency specializing in B&B accommodation in private homes all over Great Britain. Host homes range from small cottages to large manor houses, as well as working farms, and the prices vary accordingly. One thing you can be sure of is that owners have been specially selected for their wish to entertain visitors from overseas. You can vary your travel plans, perhaps spending a night in an Elizabethan manor, then the following night in a thatched cottage in the country, then on to a luxurious town house in the center of Edinburgh. Remember these are private homes, and hotel-type services are not available. You will, however, be assured of a warm welcome, a comfortable bed, a hearty breakfast, and a glimpse into British life. Write for a free brochure.

For bookings outside London call 0206/251540 or 0255/830227 or fax 0206/251805 seven days a week from 10am to 6pm. For London bookings call Julia Stebbing, **Stayaway Abroad** (tel. 071/586-2768; fax 071/586-6567). Send your requirements to Bed and Breakfast Nationwide or Stayaway Abroad, and let them handle all the reservations for you—or outside London you can make your own bookings, if you prefer. They are always happy to advise on suitable homes and locations for you. MasterCard and VISA credit cards are accepted by Bed and Breakfast Nationwide and by Stayaway Abroad.

YOUTH HOSTELS

In London youth hostels, reservations are imperative—and must be made months or even a year in advance. In one season alone, the youth hostels of London turned away 33,000 written applications with deposits! You must, of course, comply with each hostel's restrictions, such as a membership card and in many cases a curfew. A great number also limit the number of nights you can stay.

Britain is an ideal choice for those who want to take an adventure holiday; for information, contact the London office of the **Youth Hostels Association,** 14 Southampton Street, London WC2E 7HY (tel. 071/836-8541). The yearly membership is £7.80 ($14.45) for adults; hours are Monday to Saturday from 9:30am to 6pm. The nearest Tube station is Covent Garden. The activities are widely varied, ranging from underwater swimming off the coast of Devon, to canoeing on the River Wye, climbing, walking, and gliding.

In the United States, you can join **American Youth Hostels** (contact them at P.O. Box 37613, Washington, DC 20013-7613, or call 202/783-6161). Membership in AYH is honored at youth hostels in England as well as in more than 70 other countries. To join, mail a check for the yearly membership fee of $25 if you're between the ages of 18 and 54. If you are 17 or under, or 55 or older, you can obtain a youth or senior citizen membership at $10 and $15, respectively. A life membership costs $250 regardless of age. A family membership is available for $35 for 1 year for parent(s) and accompanying children, aged 17 and under. Parents can use a family membership without being accompanied by children, although children under 17 who arrive without their parents are required to have a junior membership of their own.

Astor Hostels is a group of student hostels for travelers from all over the world that attract a large American and Australian contingent. They mostly cater to the 18-to-30 age group, but also welcome more mature travelers. Hostels include:

CORFU HOTEL, 41 Longridge Rd., London SW5 9SD. Tel. 071/370-4942. Fax 071/589-1590. 65 beds (none with bath). **Tube:** Earl's Court.
$ Rates (including continental breakfast): £13.50 ($25) twin per person; £8.50–£9.50 ($15.75–$17.60) room for three and up per person. No credit cards.

Another member of the Astor Hostels, this has 13 rooms for six to eight guests, two dorms reserved for women only, and no singles. Cooking facilities, free videos, and satellite TV are included in the price. It is open 24 hours a day.

MUSEUM HOSTEL, 27 Montague St., London WC1B 5BN. Tel. 071/580-5360. Fax 071/589-1590. 94 rms (none with bath). **Tube:** Russell Square, Holborn, or Tottenham Court Road.

$ **Rates** (including continental breakfast): £18–£21 ($33.30–$38.85) single; £28–£32 ($51.80–$59.20) double; £9.50 ($17.60) quad per person; £8–£9.50 ($14.80–$17.60) dorm room with six to nine, per person. MC, V.

The hostel, opposite the British Museum, is open 24 hours a day. Rooms are spread across two buildings, and, except for the dorms, all have color TVs.

QUEST HOTEL, 45 Queensborough Terrace, London W2 3SY. Tel. 071/229-7782. Fax 071/589-1590. 80 beds (10 with bath). **Tube:** Queensway or Bayswater.

$ **Rates** (including continental breakfast): £14 ($25.90) twin per person; £8.50–£9.50 ($15.75–$17.60) room for four to six, per person. No credit cards.

Open 24 hours a day, this hostel has free cable TV, videos, and cooking facilities. Rooms are very simple but clean. There aren't any singles.

FOR WOMEN ONLY

REEVE'S PRIVATE HOTEL, 48 Shepherd's Bush Green, London W12 8PJ. Tel. 081/740-1158. Fax 081/740-5472. 8 rms (all with shower). TV TEL **Tube:** Shepherd's Bush.

$ **Rates** (including continental breakfast): £48–£60 ($88.80–$111) single; £66–£74 ($122.10–$136.90) double. MC, V.

This hotel caters to women: It offers room with extra security locks, double glazing on the windows, and a female staff. There is a bar and restaurant where only residents, many loyal repeat clientele, and their invited guests and outsiders who reserve in advance are welcomed. A sauna and limited off-street parking are available. The hotel offers a brunch on Sunday, and an upstairs women's bar on Friday, operating until midnight.

12. AWAY FROM THE CENTER

DOUBLES LESS THAN £55 ($101.75)

HAMPSTEAD

FROGNAL LODGE HOTEL, 14 Frognal Gardens, London NW3 6UX. Tel. 071/435-8238. Fax 071/794-0610. 17 rms (8 with bath). TV TEL **Tube:** Hampstead.

$ **Rates** (including English breakfast): £28 ($51.80) single without bath, £45 ($83.25) single with bath; £40 ($74) double without bath, £50 ($92.50) executive double with bath. VAT extra. MC, V.

In a completely refurbished, late 19th-century house, these are some of the finer accommodations in the area. Four rooms are "deluxe executive" doubles, which can take additional persons and can be rented as family rooms. One double—a "super executive deluxe suite"—can also be rented as a family room. Some of the rooms have private baths or showers; others must share facilities.

ROSSLYN HOUSE HOTEL, Rosslyn Hill, London NW3 1PH. Tel. 071/431-3873. Fax 071/433-1775. 20 rms (all with bath or shower). **Tube:** Belsize Park.

$ **Rates** (including continental breakfast): £29–£39 ($53.65–$72.15) single; £45–£59 ($83.25–$109.15) double. MC, V. **Parking:** Free.

This large Victorian house built in the 1880s still has many of its original features. Each of the comfortably furnished, tasteful bedrooms has coffee-making equipment. Breakfast is served in a large dining room, and there is also a public lounge and bar. The hotel lies at the junction of Rosslyn Hill and Pond Street within a few minutes' walk of the tube stop and the South End Green Bus Terminus. Parking is available.

SANDRINGHAM HOTEL, 3 Holford Rd., London NW3 1AD. Tel. 071/ 435-1569. Fax 071/431-5932. 19 rms (3 with bath). MINIBAR TEL **Tube:** Hampstead.

$ **Rates** (including English breakfast): £35 ($64.75) single without bath, £45 ($83.25) single with bath; £55 ($101.75) double without bath, £60 ($111) double with bath; £65 ($120.25) triple without bath, £71 ($131.35) triple with bath; £76 ($140.60) family room without bath, £83 ($153.55) family room with bath. No credit cards.

 This large Victorian house is on a residential street in one of the best parts of London. Coming out of the Hampstead tube station on Heath Street, turn right and walk up toward the hill. At the fourth right, you enter Hampstead Square, which leads to Holford Road. The hotel rents well-furnished bedrooms, each with hot and cold running water; the upper rooms have a view of Hampstead Heath and the heart of London. Breakfast is served in a pretty room that has a veiw of the well-kept garden.

BLACKHEATH

BARDON LODGE HOTEL, 15-17 Stratheden Rd., London SE3 7TH. Tel. 081/853-4051. Fax 081/858-7387. 39 rms (all with shower). **Bus:** No. 53.

$ **Rates** (including English breakfast): £46–£58 ($85.10–$107.30) single; £65–£75 ($120.25–$138.75) double. AE, MC, V. **Parking:** Free.

The Baron Lodge was a British Tourist Authority award-winner in 1987 and is composed of two grand, 1869 Victorian houses joined together and refurbished. It's located 5 miles from London's center, in a quiet residential area a short walk from Greenwich Park and the National Maritime Museum. From Greenwich Pier, a boat will take you to the Tower of London and Westminster. All of Barbara and Donald Nott's guest rooms have hot-beverage facilities, hairdryers, and trouser presses. The hotel also offers a restaurant that provides both set menus and à la carte offerings. A convenient bus line is nearby.

WIMBLEDON

JUSTIN JAMES HOTEL, 43 Worple Rd. (corner of Malcolm Rd.), Wimbledon, London SW19 4JA. Tel. 081/947-4271. 14 rms (12 with bath or shower). **Tube:** Wimbledon.

$ **Rates** (including English breakfast): £30 ($55.50) single without bath, £33–£35 ($61.05–$64.75) single with bath; £45 ($83.25) double without bath, £50–£55 ($92.50–$101.75) double with bath. No credit cards. **Parking:** Free.

The Justin James Hotel is located only about 30 minutes by train from Waterloo or Victoria stations (passengers coming from Victoria will have to change trains once).

TROCHEE HOTEL, 21 Malcolm Rd., London SW19 4AS. Tel. 081/946- 1579. Fax 081/785-4058. 37 rms (9 with bath). TV **Tube:** Wimbledon.

$ **Rates** (including English breakfast): £32 ($59.20) single without bath, £43 ($79.55) single with bath; £45 ($83.25) double without bath, £55 ($101.75) double with bath. MC, V.

A small private B&B hotel in southwest London, this comprises two buildings, one in a quiet cul-de-sac on Malcolm Road (with 19 rooms) and the other close by on Ridgway Place (with 18 rooms). Each room is comfortably furnished and has a hairdryer, a radio, and hot-beverage facilities. Many accommodations have private baths or showers. The hotel lies only 15 minutes from the tennis courts at Wimbledon, and it has a lounge, dining room, public phone, and car-parking facilities.

**WORCESTER HOUSE, 38 Alwyne Rd., Wimbledon, London SW19 7AE.
Tel. 081/946-1300.** Fax 081/785-4058. 9 rms (all with shower). TV TEL **Tube:**
Wimbledon.
$ **Rates** (including English breakfast): £45–£49.50 ($83.25–$91.60) single;
£58.50–£64 ($108.25–$118.40) double. DC, MC, V.
Built around 1910, this hotel has rooms with radios, hairdryers, and hot-beverage
facilities. It is a small B&B with a homelike atmosphere. It is only 10 minutes from the
tennis courts at Wimbledon.

HENDON

**SOLANA, 18 Golders Rise, Hendon, London NW4 2HR. Tel. 081/202-
5321.** 5 rms (none with bath). **Tube:** Hendon Central.
$ **Rates** (including English breakfast): £12 ($22.20) per person single or double;
family room £26 ($48.10). No credit cards.
This small, private B&B is in a clean, terraced house. Solana offers five bedrooms for
nonsmokers: one single, three twins, and one family room that sleeps four with twin
beds and a bunk for children. Most of the rooms have water basins. No infants,
please. Write to Mrs. L.M. Taylor.

HOLLOWAY

**MRS. BETTY MERCHANT, 562 Caledonian Rd., Holloway, London N7
9SD. Tel. 071/607-0930.** 3 rms (none with bath). **Tube:** Caledonian Road on
the Piccadilly Line. **Bus:** No. 17, 29, 43, or 271.
$ **Rates** (including English breakfast): £12 ($22.20) per adult; £10 ($18.50) per child
under 12. Two nights' stay required. No credit cards. **Parking:** Free on street.
This small, comfortable, private guesthouse has unrestricted on-street parking for
guests. The house has central heating, and the bedrooms include one single, one
double, and one family unit. Guests are asked to phone, not write, for reservations at
this popular B&B. Buses to the West End stop nearby.

LONDON: WHERE TO EAT

With the pressure of tourism and the influx of foreign chefs, London cuisine has improved considerably. Now a current wave of English-born, -bred, and -trained chefs are setting a superb standard of cookery, using high-quality ingredients. In addition, the introduction of espresso machines has made English coffee resemble—well, coffee.

There are some dishes—mostly connected with breakfast—at which the English have always excelled. The traditional morning repast of eggs and bacon or kippers (smoked herring) is a tasty starter, and locally brewed tea beats any American bag concoction. It's with the other meals that you have to use a little caution.

Mealtimes are much the same as in the United States. You can get lunch from about midday onward and dinner until about 11pm—until midnight in the Soho area. One difference is that few Londoners go out for a "business lunch"; they'll either have a sandwiches or snack in a pub. The once-hallowed custom of taking afternoon tea has been having a renaissance.

All restaurants and cafés in Britain are required to display the prices of the food and drink they offer in a place where the customer can see them before entering the eating area. If an establishment has an extensive à la carte menu, the prices of a representative selection of food and drink currently available must be displayed, as well as the table d'hôte menu if one is offered. Charges for service and any minimum charge or cover charge must also be made clear. The prices shown must be inclusive of VAT. Most—but not all—add a 10% to 15% service charge to your bill. You'll have to look at your check to make sure of that. If nothing has been added, leave a 12% to 15% tip.

What may astonish you is the profusion of international restaurants throughout the city. London offers a fantastic array of Italian, Indian, Chinese, French, German, Swiss, Greek, Russian, Jewish, and Middle Eastern dineries, which probably outnumber the native establishments. The majority of my selections are in the West End region, but only because this happens to be most convenient for visitors.

1. MAYFAIR & ST. JAMES'S

MEALS FOR LESS THAN £12 [$22.20]

MAYFAIR

Mayfair (W.1), bounded by Piccadilly, Hyde Park, and Oxford and Regent streets, is the elegant, fashionable section of London. Luxury hotels exist side by side with Georgian town houses and swank shops. Grosvenor Square (pronounced *Grov*-nor) is nicknamed "Little America" because it contains the American Embassy and a statue of Franklin D. Roosevelt. Berkeley (pronounced *Bark*ley) is the home of the English-Speaking Union. At least once you'll want to dip into this exclusive section, or perhaps you'll want to make repeated trips to Carnaby Street, which lies only 1 block from Regent Street.

BUBBLES, 41 N. Audley St., W.1. Tel. 071/491-3237.
    Cuisine: ENGLISH/CONTINENTAL/VEGETARIAN. **Reservations:** Recommended. **Tube:** Marble Arch.
    $ Prices: Appetizers £2.40–£6.30 ($4.45–$11.65); main courses £5.90–£14 ($10.90–$25.90); glass of wine from £1.60 ($2.95). MC, V.
    Open: Lunch Mon–Sat 11am–3pm; dinner Mon–Fri 5–11pm.

Bubbles is an interesting wine bar lying between Upper Brook Street and Oxford Street (in the vicinity of Selfridges). The owners attach equal importance to their food and their impressive wine list. Some selections of wine are sold by the glass, beginning at £1.60 ($2.95). On the ground floor guests can order fine wines, draft beer, and liquor, along with a limited but well-chosen selection of bar food, such as mussels marinara and meat and fish salads, including one made with honey-roasted ham. Downstairs is an à la carte restaurant serving both English and continental dishes, including a vegetarian selection. Begin, for example, with French onion soup, followed by roast rack of English lamb or perhaps roast duckling with a lemon and tarragon sauce.

CASPER'S BAR, GRILL, & TELEPHONE EXCHANGE, 6 Tenterden St., W.1. Tel. 071/493-7923.
    Cuisine: ANGLO/AMERICAN. **Reservations:** Not needed. **Tube:** Bond Street or Oxford Circus.
    $ Prices: Appetizers £2.50–£4 ($4.65–$7.40); main dishes £6.55–£9 ($12.10–$16.65); set menu £12.75 ($23.60); bar snacks £3–£4.50 ($5.55–$8.35). AE, DC, MC, V.
    Open: Lunch daily 11:30am–3pm; dinner daily 6pm–midnight.

Set within a cellar, this place has a re-created Victorian atmosphere with a hand-carved mahogany bar, burnished brass, Tiffany lamps, and stained glass. The restaurant is nestled just off the northwest corner of Hanover Square in the heart of Mayfair. It is the only establishment in London to place telephones on or beside each table in the bar so patrons can "ring up" anyone they choose. Bar lunches—served only in the bar—include such pub grub as chili, nachos, and fish-and-chips. In the restaurant section you can order cheeseburgers, ribs, grilled swordfish in a lemon-lime sauce, four kinds of chicken (including Cajun style or with apricots). There's usually jazz on Sunday from 1:30 to 3pm.

CHICAGO PIZZA FACTORY, 17 Hanover Sq., W.1. Tel. 071/629-2552.
    Cuisine: AMERICAN. **Reservations:** Recommended for lunch. **Tube:** Bond Street.
    $ Prices: Appetizers £2.50–£3.50 ($4.65–$6.45); main courses £4–£8 ($7.40–$14.80). No credit cards.
    Open: Mon–Sat 11:45am–11:30pm, Sun noon–3pm.

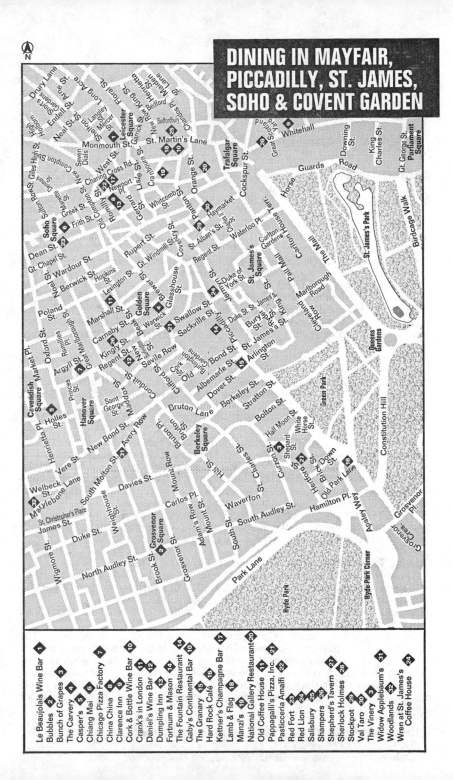

DINING IN MAYFAIR, PICCADILLY, ST. JAMES, SOHO & COVENT GARDEN

Le Beaujolais Wine Bar 1
Bubbles 2
Bunch of Grapes 3
The Carvery 4
Casper's 5
Chiang Mai 6
Chicago Pizza Factory 7
China China 8
Clarence Inn 9
Cork & Bottle Wine Bar 10
Crank's in London 11
Daniel's Wine Bar 12
Dumpling Inn 13
Fortnum & Mason 14
The Fountain Restaurant 15
Gaby's Continental Bar 16
The Granary 17
Hard Rock Café 18
Ketner's Champagne Bar 19
Lamb & Flag 20
Manzi's 21
National Gallery Restaurant 20
Old Coffee House 17
Pappagalli's Pizza, Inc. 21
Pasticceria Amalfi 22
Red Fort 23
Red Lion 26
Salisbury 25
Shampers 28
Shepherd's Tavern 27
Sherlock Holmes 28
Stockpot 29
Val Taro 30
The Vinery 3
Widow Applebaum's 31
Woodlands 32
Wren at St. James's Coffee House 24

The specialty here is deep-dish pizza covered with cheese, tomato, and a choice of sausage, pepperoni, mushrooms, green peppers, onions, and anchovies. This is one of the few places where a doggy bag is willingly provided, and there are smoking and no-smoking tables. The menu also includes stuffed mushrooms, garlic bread, salads, and homemade cheesecakes served with two forks. A video over the bar shows continuous American baseball or football, and the waitresses wear *Chicago Tribune* aprons. The Factory is just off Oxford Street in Hanover Square, opposite John Lewis and within easy reach of Regent Street.

CRANK'S IN LONDON, 8 Marshall St., W.1. Tel. 071/437-9431.

Cuisine: VEGETARIAN. **Reservations:** None. **Tube:** Oxford Circus.

$ Prices: Appetizers £1.55–£1.90 ($2.87–$3.50); main dishes £1.75–£3.25 ($3.25–$6). MC.

Open: Mon–Fri 8am–10:30pm, Sat 9am–10:30pm.

Located just off Carnaby Street, Crank's, the leader of London's natural-foods restaurants, makes vegetarian-health food dining a pleasure. The restaurant is decorated with natural wood, wicker-basket lamps, bare pine tables, and handmade ceramic bowls and plates. It's self-service: You carry your own tray to one of the tables on the raised level.

Stone-ground flour used for making bread and rolls. The uncooked vegetable salad is especially good and there's always a hot stew of savory vegetables (and secret seasonings), served in a hand-thrown stoneware pot with a salad. Homemade cakes, such as honey cake, gingerbread, and cheesecake, are featured and can be washed down with tiger's milk.

Bakery goods, nuts, and general health-food supplies are sold in an adjoining shop.

HARD ROCK CAFE, 150 Old Park Lane, W.1. Tel. 071/629-0382.

Cuisine: AMERICAN. **Reservations:** None. **Tube:** Green Park or Hyde Park Corner.

$ Prices: Appetizers £2.75–£6 ($5.10–$11.10); main dishes £4.50–£8 ($8.35–$14.80). No credit cards.

Open: Sun–Thurs noon–12:30am, Fri–Sat noon–1am.

This down-home American roadside diner serves good food at reasonable prices with pleasant service. Almost every night there is a line waiting to get in, as this is a popular place with young people. It is also the favorite of visiting rock stars, film stars, and tennis players from America. *People* magazine called it "the Smithsonian of rock 'n' roll."

The café gives generous portions, and the main dishes come with salad and fries. Specialties include various steaks. The dessert menu is tempting, including homemade apple pie and thick, cold shakes. They also have a good selection of beer.

SHAMPERS, 4 Kingly St., W.1. Tel. 071/437-1692.

Cuisine: CONTINENTAL. **Reservations:** Not needed. **Tube:** Oxford Circus.

$ Prices: Appetizers £2.65–£5.50 ($4.90–$10.20); main dishes £5–£11 ($9.25–$20.35); wine by the glass from £1.95 ($3.60). AE, DC, MC, V.

Open: Mon–Fri 11am–11pm, Sat 11am–3pm; hot food Mon–Sat noon–3pm, Mon–Fri 5–11pm.

The entire complex consists of a street level and a basement dining room. The basement is a restaurant, and the upstairs is a wine bar. In the restaurant you can order such main dishes as braised leg and breast of guinea fowl, but in the bar you can enjoy lighter meals designed to accompany the wine. Salads are especially popular, including tuna and pasta with a spicy tomato sauce, or chicken salad with a tarragon cream dressing. A platter of Irish mussels cooked in white wine seems to be everybody's favorite.

WIDOW APPLEBAUM'S DELI & BAGEL ACADEMY, 46 S. Molton St., W.1. Tel. 071/499-6710.

Cuisine: DELI. **Reservations:** Not needed. **Tube:** Bond Street.

$ Prices: Appetizers £1.40–$2 ($2.60–$3.70); main courses £3.50–£8.50 ($6.50–$15.75). No credit cards.
Open: Mon–Sat 8am–8pm (breakfast until 11am).
This is good for a before-theater meal, but avoid it during office lunch hours. Sandwiches, including roast beef and turkey, are topped with coleslaw and pickled cucumbers and are accompanied by potato salad. The pastrami is flown in fresh daily from New York. The restaurant also features a full English breakfast. South Molton Street is a pedestrian precinct, and tables are set outside in fair weather.

SHEPHERD MARKET
One of the curiosities of Mayfair is Shepherd Market, a tiny village of pubs, two-story inns, book and food stalls, and restaurants, all sandwiched between Mayfair grandness.

BUNCH OF GRAPES, 16 Shepherd Market, W.1. Tel. 071/629-4989.
Cuisine: ENGLISH. **Reservations:** None. **Tube:** Green Park.
$ Prices: Snacks from £1.50 ($2.80); lager from £1.60 ($2.95). No credit cards.
Open: Snack bar Mon–Sat 11am–3pm; pub Mon–Sat 11am–11pm, Sun noon–3pm and 7–10:30pm.
Dating from 1882, this pub has a fireplace, lace curtains, turn-of-the-century chandeliers, hunting trophies, and Staffordshire figurines. Join the locals and order "real ale." Hot and cold snacks and steak sandwiches are served during the busy lunch hours.

SHEPHERD'S TAVERN, 50 Hertford St., W.1. Tel. 071/499-3017.
Cuisine: BRITISH. **Reservations:** Recommended. **Tube:** Green Park.
$ Prices: Appetizers £2.95–£4.95 ($5.45–$9.15); main courses £8.95–£12.95 ($16.45–$23.95); three-course set lunch or dinner £14.95 ($27.65). AE, DC, MC, V.
Open: Lunch Mon–Sat noon–3pm; dinner Mon–Sat 6–11pm, Sun 7–10:30pm. Pub Mon–Fri 11am–11pm, Sat noon–3pm and 5:30–11pm, Sun noon–3pm and 7–10:30pm.
This tavern is a magnet, attracting a congenial mixture of patrons. There are many luxurious touches, including a collection of antique furniture. Chief among these is a sedan chair that once belonged to the son of George III, the duke of Cumberland. Many of the local habitués recall the tavern's association with the pilots of the Battle of Britain. Bar snacks and hot dishes include shepherd's pie or fish pie with vegetables. Upstairs, the owners operate a cozy restaurant, Georgian in style with cedar paneling, serving a classic British cuisine such as jugged venison or Oxford ham.

THE VINERY, 16 Shepherd Market. W.1. Tel. 071/409-7818.
Cuisine: ITALIAN. **Reservations:** Not needed. **Tube:** Green Park.
$ Prices: Appetizers £2.20–£3.75 ($4.05–$6.95); main courses £5–£10 ($9.25–$18.50). AE, MC, V.
Open: Lunch Mon–Fri noon–3pm Sat–Sun noon–3pm; dinner 6–11:30pm, Sat–Sun 7–10:30pm.
Upstairs from the Bunch of Grapes, this restaurant is operated by a different franchise and serves Italian meals. Begin with a pasta, or select such main dishes as swordfish, breast of duck in an orange and honey sauce, or veal Sorrentina.

ST. JAMES'S

St. James's (S.W.1), the beginning of Royal London, starts at Piccadilly Circus and moves southwest. It's frightfully convenient, as the English say, enclosing a number of locations, such as American Express on Haymarket and many of the leading department stores—it even encompasses Buckingham Palace. But don't be scared off: There are luncheon bargains available.

FORTNUM & MASON, 181 Piccadilly, W.1. Tel. 071/734-8040.
    Cuisine: ENGLISH. **Reservations:** Not needed. **Tube:** Piccadilly Circus or Green Park.
$ **Prices:** Fountain Restaurant breakfast £3.50–£6.50 ($6.50–$12.05); evening grill meal £12.50 ($23.15); Patio & Buttery Restaurant teas or snacks from £3.50 ($6.50); St. James Restaurant lunch from £14 ($25.90); full afternoon tea £6.50 ($12.05). AE, DC, MC, V.
    Open: Fountain Restaurant daily 9am–11pm; Patio & Buttery Restaurant daily 9am–5pm; St. James Restaurant Mon–Sat 9:30am–5pm.

⭐   Look first at the famous Fortnum and Mason clock outside, then enter the refined precincts of the world's most elegant grocery store (more about this in "Shopping A to Z" in Chapter 7). It's well known that this store has supplied "take-out" treasures to everybody from the Duke of Wellington to Florence Nightingale in the Crimea, even Mr. Stanley while he pursued Dr. Livingstone. Specialties include Welsh rarebit, steak-and-kidney pie, and liver and bacon in onion sauce.

    There are three places at which to dine: The **Fountain Restaurant,** which has its entrance on Jermyn Street, is famous for its extravagant ice-cream sundaes and attracts some of the après-theater crowd. The **Patio & Buttery Restaurant,** on the mezzanine, provides a cheerful atmosphere in which to meet friends over morning coffee, light lunches, or even cream teas. Finally, the **St. James Restaurant,** the most elegant of the three, is famous for its afternoon teas and specializes in English lunches, including a traditional roast beef with all the trimmings, carved from the trolley. A pianist performs between 3 and 5pm, and there is a choice of menus.

    Fortnum is also known for preparing superb picnic baskets, with prices beginning at £18.50 ($34.25).

RED LION, 2 Duke of York St., off Jermyn St., S.W.1. Tel. 071/930-2030.
    Cuisine: BRITISH. **Reservations:** Not needed. **Tube:** Piccadilly Circus.
$ **Prices:** Main courses £3.25 ($6); sandwiches £1.50 ($2.80). No credit cards.
    Open: Mon–Sat 11am–11pm; hot food Mon–Sat noon–2:30pm.
This is only a short walk from Piccadilly Circus and is near American Express on Haymarket. Ian Nairn compared its spirit to that of Edouard Manet's painting *A Bar at the Folies-Bergère* (see the collection at the Courtauld Institute Galleries). Everything is washed down with a pint of lager or cider in this refined little Victorian pub with posh turn-of-the-century decorations, including patterned glass and deep-mahogany curlicues. Food is more copious at lunch than in the evening—only sandwiches and "pasties" are offered at dinner.

2. PICCADILLY & LEICESTER SQUARE

MEALS FOR LESS THAN £16 [$29.60]

PICCADILLY CIRCUS

Garish, overneoned, crowded, but exciting, Piccadilly Circus keeps time with the heartbeat of this mighty city—it's comparable to Times Square in New York City. Here all walks of life converge, with the statue of Eros, named for love, in the center.

THE CARVERY, Regent Palace Hotel, Glasshouse St., W.1. Tel. 071/734-7000.
    Cuisine: ENGLISH. **Reservations:** Recommended. **Tube:** Piccadilly Circus.
$ **Prices:** All-you-can-eat meals £14.95 ($27.65); children under 14 £6 ($11.10). AE, DC, MC, V.

Open: Lunch daily noon–2:30pm; dinner Mon–Fri 5:15–9pm, Sat 5:15–9:30pm, Sun 6–9pm.

⑤ Who'd think that just 20 feet from Piccadilly Circus you could have all you can eat of these fabulous roasts? Yet that's the famous policy of this renowned all-you-can-eat establishment. There is a wide range of appetizers, and the buffet carving table offers prime rib with Yorkshire pudding, roast leg of Southdown lamb with mint sauce, and a roast leg of English pork with apple sauce. You carve the meat yourself, with carvers standing by to assist you. Then you serve yourself buttered peas, roast potatoes, new carrots, and gravy. In another area is cold food and assorted salads, whatever is in season. Desserts might include pineapple cake, or perhaps a strawberry mousse. Well-brewed coffee for "afters" is included in the price.

DANIEL'S WINE BAR (CAFE ROYAL), 68 Regent St., W.1. Tel. 071/437-9090, ext. 277.

Cuisine: BRITISH. **Reservations:** Not needed. **Tube:** Piccadilly Circus.
$ Prices: Appetizers £1.50–£3 ($2.80–$5.55); main courses £3–£5 ($5.55–$9.25). AE, DC, MC, V.
Open: Lunch Mon–Fri noon–2:30pm; wine bar Mon–Fri noon–3pm and 5:30–11pm.

This wine bar is an informal annex to the chillingly expensive Café Royal Grill, which dates from 1865. Both are accessible from the marble-floored lobby of a watering hole where the literary greats of 19th-century England trod. Designed in an opulent motif of art nouveau moldings, with lots of framed cartoons and illustrations, the wine bar has a resident pianist. Platters of food, such as beef Stroganoff, are served only at lunchtime, until 2:30pm; the rest of the day, until late into the night, only wine and drinks are served. A glass of wine costs from £1.70 ($3.15).

THE GRANARY, 39 Albemarle St., W.1. Tel. 071/493-2978.

Cuisine: ENGLISH. **Reservations:** Not needed. **Tube:** Green Park.
$ Prices: Appetizers all £3.20 ($5.90); main courses £6.50–£6.90 ($12.05–$12.75). No credit cards.
Open: Mon–Fri 11:30am–8pm, Sat noon–2:30pm.

⑤ This restaurant serves a variety of home-cooked dishes. A typical meal might include meat pie, vegetables, chocolate cake, a glass of wine, and coffee. Or, you might have roast pork in cider sauce, seafood pasta, or Lancashire hot pot. Desserts are tempting, especially the tipsy cake and the upside-down cake. All portions are large, and the menus are written on the blackboard.

PAPPAGALLI'S PIZZA, 7-9 Swallow St., W.1. Tel. 071/734-5182.

Cuisine: ITALIAN. **Reservations:** Required for dinner Thurs–Sat. **Tube:** Piccadilly Circus.
$ Prices: Appetizers £1.50–£2.50 ($2.80–$4.65); main courses £3.50–£6.50 ($6.50–$12.05). MC, V.
Open: Lunch Mon–Sat noon–3pm; dinner Mon–Sat 5:15–11pm; happy hour Mon–Sat 5:15–7pm.

In this old-time New York saloon decor, you can enjoy reasonably priced Italian fare in the heart of London. You can either select from an array of sauces and several pastas, or you can compose your own pizza from a selection of toppings. There is also a fresh salad bar—"Only one helping, please." Drink prices are reduced during happy hour.

WREN AT ST. JAMES'S COFFEE HOUSE WHOLEFOOD CAFE, 35 Jermyn St., S.W.1. Tel. 071/437-9419.

Cuisine: VEGETARIAN/WHOLEFOOD. **Reservations:** Not needed. **Tube:** Piccadilly Circus.
$ Prices: Appetizers £1–£1.95 ($1.85–$3.60); main courses £1.95–£2.80 ($3.60–$5.20). No credit cards.
Open: Mon–Sat 8am–7pm, Sun 10am–4pm.

S After visitors do brass rubbings at this enterprising church, they can visit the cheerful coffee shop with courtyard service in fair weather. There is always a fresh soup of the day, along with cold appetizers. The restaurant specializes in large potatoes baked in their "jackets," as the British say, and filled with a variety of stuffings, such as cheese and tuna. It's busy at lunchtime, when hot dishes are served. Teatime specialties include homemade cakes and large scones with cream and jam. No smoking is allowed.

LEICESTER SQUARE

Named for the second earl of Leicester, this 19th-century square has become the cinema center of London. It is a congested area of stores, theaters, cinemas, even churches, and there are some inexpensive restaurants and pubs in the little offshoot lanes and alleyways. Also, there's now a large paved pedestrian precinct rivaling Piccadilly Circus as a meeting place for travelers and locals. It's less dangerous than Piccadilly Circus for many reasons—particularly because there's no traffic.

CHINA CHINA, 38 Panton St., S.W.1. Tel. 071/925-2438.
   Cuisine: CHINESE. **Reservations:** Not needed. **Tube:** Piccadilly Circus.
$ Prices: Appetizers £1.75–£3.25 ($3.25–$6); main courses £6.50–£8 ($12.05–$14.80); set lunch £5.95 ($11); set dinner £8–£15 ($14.80–$27.75). AE, DC, MC, V.
   Open: Mon–Fri noon–3pm and 5:30–11:45pm, Sat noon–11:45pm.
China China serves Hong Kong, Cantonese, and Beijing dishes in the heart of the theater and cinema district, close to both Piccadilly Circus and Leicester Square. The extensive menu includes Cantonese fried steak, Peking duck, and sizzling chicken with chiles and black bean sauce.

CORK AND BOTTLE WINE BAR, 44-46 Cranbourn St., W.C.2. Tel. 071/734-7807.
   Cuisine: INTERNATIONAL. **Reservations:** Recommended. **Tube:** Leicester Square.
$ Prices: Appetizers £1.75–£4.75 ($3.25–$8.80); main courses £3–£7 ($5.55–$12.95); glass of wine from £1.95 ($3.60). AE, DC, MC, V.
   Open: Lunch Mon–Sat noon–3pm, Sun noon–2pm; dinner Mon–Sat 5:30–10:45pm, Sun 7–10:30pm.
Cork & Bottle is just off Leicester Square. The most successful dish is a raised cheese-and-ham pie that has a cream-cheesy filling, and a well-buttered crisp pastry—not your typical quiche. (In just 1 week the bar sold 500 portions of this alone.) The kitchen also offers a spicy chicken salad, smoked chicken with avocado and grape salad, tandoori chicken, and lamb in ale. The expanded wine list features an excellent selection of Beaujolais cru and wines from Alsace, as well as some 30 selections from "Down Under," 30 champagnes and a good selection of California labels.

MANZI'S, 1-2 Leicester St., off Leicester Sq., W.C.2. Tel. 071/734-0224.
   Cuisine: SEAFOOD. **Reservations:** Required for dinner. **Tube:** Leicester Square.
$ Prices: Appetizers £2.75–£6 ($5.10–$11.10); main courses £8–£15 ($14.80–$27.75). AE, DC, MC, V.
   Open: Lunch Mon–Sat noon–2:40pm; dinner Mon–Sat 5:30–11:15pm, Sun 6–10pm.
Manzi's is London's oldest seafood restaurant, where you can dine either in the simply decorated ground-floor restaurant or in the Cabin Room upstairs. Famous for its Whitstable and Colchester oysters among other specialties, it has a loyal patronage, drawn to its moderately priced fare and fresh ingredients. If you'd like something less expensive than their legendary oysters, I suggest a prawn cocktail, even fresh sardines.

If it's a luncheon stopover, you might happily settle for the crab salad. Main-course specialties include Dover sole and grilled turbot. Steaks are also available. The house has a good selection of wines and sherries.

SALISBURY, 90 St. Martin's Lane, W.C.2. Tel. 071/836-5863.
   Cuisine: BRITISH. **Reservations:** None. **Tube:** Leicester Square.
$ **Prices:** Buffet meal £3–£4.50 ($5.55–$8.35); beer from £1.40 ($2.60). No credit cards.
   Open: Mon–Sat 11am–11pm, Sun noon–3pm and 7–10:30pm.

⭐ Salisbury's glittering cut-glass mirrors reflect the faces of English stage stars (and hopefuls) sitting around the curved buffet-style bar. If you want a less prominent place to dine choose the old-fashioned wall banquette with its copper-topped tables and art nouveau decor. The light fixtures, veiled bronze girls in flowing robes holding up clusters of electric lights concealed in bronze roses, are appropriate. In the saloon, you'll see and hear the Oliviers of yesterday and tomorrow. But do not let this distract you from your food. The pub's specialty, an array of homemade pies set out on a buffet table with salads, is really good and inexpensive.

STOCKPOT, 40 Panton St., S.W.1. Tel. 071/839-5142.
   Cuisine: ENGLISH/CONTINENTAL. **Reservations:** Not needed. **Tube:** Piccadilly Circus.
$ **Prices:** Appetizers 65p–£1.20 ($1.20–$2.20); main courses £1.80–£4.85 ($3.35–$8.95). No credit cards.
   Open: Mon–Sat 8am–11:30pm, Sun noon–10pm.

 Penny for penny, I'd hazard a guess that this cozy little member of a popular chain offers one of the best dining bargains in London. Meals include a bowl of minestrone, spaghetti bolognese (the eternal favorite), a plate of braised lamb, and the apple crumble (or other desserts). Offering two levels of dining in a modern atmosphere, the Stockpot has a share-the-table policy during peak dining hours. The little restaurant lies off Haymarket, opposite the Comedy Theatre. Other branches are at 6 Basil Street, W.3, and at 98 King's Road, S.W.3.

3. SOHO

Soho (W.1) in a sense is a Jekyll and Hyde quarter. In the daytime, it's a paradise for the searcher of spices, continental foods, fruits, fish, and sausages, and has at least two street markets offering fruits and vegetables. But at night, it's a dazzle of strip joints, gay clubs, porno movies, and sex emporiums, all intermingled with international restaurants that offer good values. In fact, this section of crisscrossed narrow lanes and crooked streets is the site of many of the city's best foreign restaurants, and Gerrard Street has succeeded in becoming London's first Chinatown.

Soho starts impudently at Piccadilly Circus and spreads out ending at Oxford Street. One side borders the theater center on Shaftesbury Avenue. From Piccadilly Circus, walk northeast and you'll come to Soho, to the left of Shaftesbury. This jumbled section can also be approached from the Tottenham Court Road tube station: Walk south along Charing Cross Road, and Soho will be to your right.

MEALS FOR LESS THAN £11 [$20.35]

ANEMOS, 32 Charlotte St., W.1. Tel. 071/636-2289.
   Cuisine: GREEK/CYPRIOT. **Reservations:** Recommended. **Tube:** Goodge Street.
$ **Prices:** Appetizers £1.80–£3.50 ($3.35–$6.45); main courses £5–£7 ($9.25–$12.95); meze £10.95 ($20.35) per person. AE, DC, MC, V.

Open: Lunch Mon–Sat noon–3pm; dinner Mon–Sat 6–11:45pm.

Anemos, Greek for strong wind or tornado, is the place for breaking plates, dancing, and joining the waiters in a rip-roaring Greek song. There's even a magic show and a floor show with Greek dancing. Specialties include a typical Greek meal, called *meze*, with a variety of 12 to 14 different small dishes. A typical meal would be taramosalata, hummus, and kebabs, plus dessert, cheese, coffee, and wine.

LE BEAUJOLAIS WINE BAR, 25 Litchfield St., W.C.2. Tel. 071/836-2955.

    Cuisine: FRENCH. **Reservations:** None. **Tube:** Leicester Square.

$ **Prices:** Appetizers £1.85–£2 ($3.40–$3.70); main courses £4.50–£5 ($8.35–$9.25); glass of wine from £1.55 ($2.85) MC, V.

    Open: Food Mon–Sat noon–2:45pm and 5:30–10:30pm; bar Mon–Fri noon–11pm, Sat 5–11pm.

The wine bar here is open to everybody, but it is connected with a members-only club in a more formal restaurant. The wine bar food includes soups, pâtés, cheese plates, and platters of hot food which change daily, but might feature a dish of the day such as a classic coq au vin. Most wine vintages are French.

CHIANG MAI, 48 Frith St., W.1. Tel. 071/437-7444.

    Cuisine: THAI. **Reservations:** Required. **Tube:** Leicester Square.

$ **Prices:** Appetizers £3.95–£4.95 ($7.30–$9.15); main courses £4.95–£6.95 ($9.15–$2.85). MC, V.

    Open: Lunch daily noon–3pm; dinner daily 6–11:30pm.

In the center of Soho, this restaurant is named after the ancient northern capital of Thailand, a region known for its rich, spicy foods. Try their hot-and-sour dishes, their chili-laced specials, or one of their special vegetarian meals. The location is next door to Ronnie Scott's, the most famous jazz club in England.

DUMPLING INN, 15A Gerrard St., W.1. Tel. 071/437-2567.

    Cuisine: CHINESE. **Reservations:** Recommended. **Tube:** Piccadilly Circus.

$ **Prices:** Appetizers £2.50–£4 ($4.65–$7.40); main courses £3.50–£8 ($6.45–$14.80). AE, DC, MC, V.

    Open: Daily noon–midnight.

Despite its incongruous name, it is a cool and rather elegant eatery, serving a delectable brand of Peking Mandarin cuisine that dates back almost 3,000 years and owes some of its special piquancy to the inclusion of various Mongolian ingredients, such as hot pot.

    Regulars come here for the shark's-fin soup, the beef in oyster sauce, the seaweed and sesame-seed prawns on toast, duck with chili and black-bean sauce, and the fried sliced fish with sauce. Naturally, the specialty is dumplings, and you can make a meal from the dim sum list. Chinese tea is extra. Portions are not large, so you can order a good variety without fear of leftovers. Service is leisurely, so don't dine here before a theater date.

GABY'S CONTINENTAL BAR, 30 Charing Cross Rd., W.C.2. Tel. 071/836-4233.

    Cuisine: MIDDLE EASTERN/CONTINENTAL. **Reservations:** None. **Tube:** Leicester Square.

$ **Prices:** Appetizers £2–£3 ($3.70–$5.55); main courses £2.40–£6 ($4.45–$11.10). No credit cards.

    Open: Daily 9am–midnight.

Gaby's is a snack bar/restaurant, serving food all day long. It's a particularly good place for after theater, and the service is quick. Salt beef (corned beef to us) sandwiches are a featured selection, as are the hearty soups, such as bean and barley. Couscous royale with kebabs is the most expensive dish. Other Middle Eastern fare includes shashliks and a flavorful version of Egyptian broad beans known as *foulmadame*. The house also specializes in vegetarian dishes and salads. It is a fully licensed restaurant. A take-out window opens onto the sidewalk.

KETTNER'S CHAMPAGNE BAR, 29 Romilly St., W.1. Tel. 071/437-6437.
Cuisine: ITALIAN. **Reservations:** None. **Tube:** Piccadilly Circus.
$ Prices: Appetizers £2.50–£3.50 ($4.65–$6.50); main courses £4.50–£6.50 ($8.35–$12.05). AE, DC, MC, V.
Open: Mon–Sat 11am–3pm and 5:30–11pm, Sun 7–10:30pm.

Dating back to 1869, Kettner's was once patronized by King Edward VII, then Prince of Wales. Formerly a hotel, the place is huge, with dozens of rooms. Today it's the flagship restaurant of the Pizza Express chain; however, its service and food are far above the standard of a typical chain emporium. You can begin your evening in the champagne bar on the ground floor. Pizzas and burgers are standard fare, and you can also order pastas or selections from the charcoal grill. There's piano entertainment in the evening.

PASTICCERIA AMALFI, 31 Old Compton St., W.1. Tel. 071/437-7284.
Cuisine: ITALIAN. **Reservations:** Recommended. **Tube:** Leicester Square.
$ Prices: Appetizers £3–£4 ($5.55–$7.40); main courses £5.45–£10.45 ($10.10–$19.35). AE, DC, MC, V.
Open: Mon–Sat noon–11:15pm, Sun noon–10pm.

At this crowded, bargain-priced restaurant, Italian chefs prepare traditional dishes, including spaghetti, pizzas, veal in white wine, minestrone, and lasagne. If you have room for dessert, a pâtisserie makes excellent Italian pastries. Seating is on two levels.

OLD COFFEE HOUSE, 49 Beak St., W.1. Tel. 071/437-2196.
Cuisine: BRITISH. **Reservations:** None. **Tube:** Oxford Circus or Piccadilly Circus.
$ Prices: Main courses £2.50–£3.50 ($4.65–$6.45); beer from £1.65 ($3.05). No credit cards.
Open: Daily 11am–11pm; meals at lunchtime only daily noon–3pm.

Once honored as Soho pub of the year, this restaurant takes its name from the coffeehouse heyday of 1700s London. Coffee was called "the devil's brew" back then. But when most establishments switched to serving lager, or "demon drink," names were changed. The pub is heavily decorated with bric-a-brac, including old musical instruments and World War I recruiting posters. Have your drink at a long narrow bar, or else retreat to the restaurant upstairs where you can enjoy good pub food, such as steak-and-kidney pie, scampi and chips, or vegetarian dishes.

RED FORT, 77 Dean St., W.1. Tel. 071/437-2525.
Cuisine: INDIAN. **Reservations:** Required. **Tube:** Leicester Square or Tottenham Court Road.
$ Prices: Appetizers £2.50–£4.50 ($4.65–$8.35); main courses £5.50–£8.50 ($10.20–$15.75); Sun buffet £10.95 ($20.10). AE, DC, MC, V.
Open: Lunch daily noon–3pm; dinner daily 6–11pm.

Considered one of the finest Indian restaurants in London, the Red Fort offers superb meals. If you're on a tight budget, go for the help-yourself Sunday buffet, which has a spread of Mughlai delicacies. Try *masha*—that is, spicy beans stuffed into an onion and baked. Tandoori dishes sometimes feature quail, and Bangladeshi fish specialties as well as chicken and lamb curries tend to be succulently prepared. The waiters are helpful in explaining the menu.

VENUS KEBAB HOUSE, 2 Charlotte St., W.1. Tel. 071/636-4324.
Cuisine: GREEK. **Reservations:** Required in summer. **Tube:** Goodge Street or Tottenham Court Road.
$ Prices: Appetizers £1.80–£2.85 ($3.33–$5.25); main courses £4.60–£7.50 ($8.50–$13.90). MC, V.
Open: Lunch Mon–Sat noon–3pm; dinner Mon–Sat 5:30–11:30pm.

This corner restaurant is known for Greek specialties and good food in a low-price range. *Avgolemono*, the Greek national soup, is made with chicken stock, rice, egg, lemon, and spices. The standard specialties are *dolmades* (vine leaves stuffed with lamb, beef, rice, tomatoes, and spices) and moussaka, but the chef also prepares fish and vegetarian meals. In summer, the Venus has outdoor tables.

4. BLOOMSBURY & FITZROVIA

MEALS FOR LESS THAN £9 [$16.65]

BRITISH MUSEUM RESTAURANT, Great Russell St. W.C.1. Tel. 071/323-8599.
   Cuisine: ENGLISH. **Reservations:** None. **Tube:** Holborn or Tottenham Court Road.
$ Prices: Appetizers £1.85–£2.15 ($3.40–$4); main courses £4.50–£5.50 ($8.35–$10.20). No credit cards.
   Open: Mon–Sat 10:30am–4:15pm, Sun 2:30–5:15pm. **Closed:** Holidays.
This is obviously the best place for lunch if you're exploring the wonders of the world-renowned museum. The restaurant sits at lobby level in the East Wing. It is self-service and offers most presentable and reasonably priced fare. Fresh salads are made daily, and there's a good selection of fish and cold meat dishes. A few hot specials (there's always one for vegetarians) are also made fresh daily. Desserts include pastries and cakes.

MUSEUM TAVERN, 49 Great Russell St., W.C.1. Tel. 071/242-8987.
   Cuisine: ENGLISH. **Reservations:** None. **Tube:** Holborn or Tottenham Court Road.
$ Prices: Bar snacks £3–£4.75 ($5.55–$8.80); pint of lager £1.70 ($3.15). AE, DC, MC, V.
   Open: Mon–Sat 11am–11pm, Sun noon–10:30pm.
Opposite the British Museum, this turn-of-the-century pub has all the trappings: velvet, oak paneling, and cut glass. It's right in the center of the University of London area and is popular with writers, publishers, and researchers from the museum. Supposedly, Karl Marx wrote in the pub over a meal. Traditional English food is served, with steak-and-kidney pie, sausages cooked in English cider, and chef's specials on the hot-food menu. Cold food includes turkey-and-ham pie, ploughman's lunches, cheeses, salads, and quiches. Beverages offered are several English ales, cold lagers, cider, Guinness, wines, and spirits. Food and coffee are served all day; the pub gets crowded at lunchtime.

SPAGHETTI HOUSE, 15-17 Goodge St., W.1. Tel. 071/636-6582.
   Cuisine: ITALIAN. **Reservations:** Not needed. **Tube:** Goodge Street.

FROMMER'S SMART TRAVELER: RESTAURANTS

1. Enjoy lunch at some of London's great restaurants that offer a set luncheon at such reasonable prices that the kitchen actually loses money.
2. Select set luncheons or dinner when offered; it's at least a 30% savings off the à la carte menu.
3. Look for daily specials on the à la carte menu. They're invariably fresh, and often cheaper than regular à la carte listings.
4. Drink the house wine—it's a fraction of the price of bottled wine.
5. Watch the booze: Wine and liquor are expensive in London.

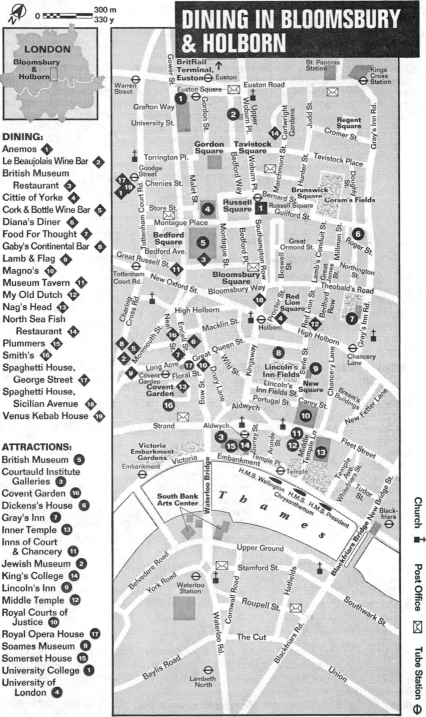

DINING IN BLOOMSBURY & HOLBORN

DINING:
Anemos **1**
Le Beaujolais Wine Bar **2**
British Museum
  Restaurant **3**
Cittie of Yorke **4**
Cork & Bottle Wine Bar **5**
Diana's Diner **6**
Food For Thought **7**
Gaby's Continental Bar **8**
Lamb & Flag **9**
Magno's **10**
Museum Tavern **11**
My Old Dutch **12**
Nag's Head **13**
North Sea Fish
  Restaurant **14**
Plummers **15**
Smith's **16**
Spaghetti House,
  George Street **17**
Spaghetti House,
  Sicilian Avenue **18**
Venus Kebab House **19**

ATTRACTIONS:
British Museum **5**
Courtauld Institute
  Galleries **3**
Covent Garden **16**
Dickens's House **6**
Gray's Inn **7**
Inner Temple **13**
Inns of Court
  & Chancery **11**
Jewish Museum **2**
King's College **14**
Lincoln's Inn **9**
Middle Temple **12**
Royal Courts of
  Justice **10**
Royal Opera House **17**
Soames Museum **8**
Somerset House **15**
University College **1**
University of
  London **4**

Church ✝

Post Office ✉

Tube Station ⊖

$ Prices: Appetizers £1.80–£4.65 ($3.35–$8.60); main courses £4.30–£8.20 ($7.95–$15.15). AE, DC, MC, V.
Open: Mon–Sat noon–11pm, Sun 5:30–10:30pm.
Chianti bottles enhance the inviting, Italian atmosphere on the four floors of this restaurant. The leader of a chain of spaghetti and pizza houses, this restaurant offers at least 10 different varieties of pasta and 10 different meat dishes made from veal, beef, or chicken. *Saltimbocca*, the classic veal and ham dish from Rome, is most popular. However, most of the culinary inspiration comes from north central Italy (Tuscany, Umbria, Emilia Romagna). For dessert, cassata siciliana is a good choice. The restaurant is across Tottenham Court Road in the vicinity of Russell Square.

5. STRAND, COVENT GARDEN & HOLBORN

MEALS FOR LESS THAN £11 [$20.35]
TRAFALGAR SQUARE & THE STRAND

Between Leicester Square and Westminster, Trafalgar Square is dominated by a monument honoring Lord Nelson, who died in the Battle of Trafalgar on October 21, 1805. Beginning at the square, the Strand, south of Covent Garden, runs east into Fleet Street. Londoners used to be able to walk along the Strand and see the Thames, but the river has receded. Although the wealthy built their homes here in the 17th century, today this area is in transition to something less grand—flanked as it is with theaters, shops, hotels, restaurants, and such landmarks as Somerset House.

CLARENCE INN, 53 Whitehall, S.W.1. Tel. 071/930-4808.
Cuisine: ENGLISH. **Reservations:** None. **Tube:** Charing Cross or Embankment.
$ Prices: Appetizers £1.50–£3 ($2.80–$5.55); main courses £5–£7 ($9.25–$12.95); bar snacks £3–£5 ($5.55–$9.25); lager £1.74 ($3.20). No credit cards.
Open: Pub Mon–Sat 11am–11pm, Sun noon–3pm and 7–10:30pm; restaurant daily noon–2:30pm.
Just down from Trafalgar Square, this 18th-century inn is the haunt of civil servants from the nearby ministry offices. They enjoy such lunchtime food as braised oxtail, Asian pork chops, and traditional shepherd's pie. There are always at least four hot dishes of the day, plus a range of cold dishes and salads. The pub is at street level, and bar snacks, such as ploughman's lunch and various meat pies, are served during pub opening hours. The more formal restaurant is upstairs, offering lunch daily. The decor includes blackened beams, a sawdust-strewn floor, church pews, and uncovered tables lit by flickering gaslights. On Monday through Thursday evenings, a strolling minstrel provides light music in the bar.

NATIONAL GALLERY RESTAURANT, Trafalgar Sq., W.C.2. Tel. 071/839-3321.
Cuisine: CONTINENTAL. **Reservations:** None. **Tube:** Charing Cross.
$ Prices: Appetizers £1.50–£2.50 ($2.80–$4.65); main courses £3.50–£6.50 ($6.45–$12.05). No credit cards.
Open: Mon–Sat 10am–5pm, Sun 2–5pm.
You can have lunch in this comfortable East Wing basement before or after you explore the gallery. Juicy quiches and flans are served, along with fresh, crisp salads. Hot daily specials may include chili with rice, coq au vin, or beef bourguignon. The hot food is served only from noon to 3pm; after that, pastries, sandwiches, tea, coffee, and buffet foods are available.

SHERLOCK HOLMES, 10 Northumberland St., W.C.1. Tel. 071/930-2644.

Cuisine: BRITISH. **Reservations:** Recommended for restaurant. **Tube:** Charing Cross.
$ Prices: Appetizers £2–£7 ($3.70–$12.95); main dishes £7.50–£18 ($13.90–$33.30); ground-floor snacks from £3 ($5.55). AE, DC, MC, V.
Open: Restaurant lunch Mon–Sat noon–2:15pm; dinner Mon–Sat 6–9:15pm; pub Mon–Sat 11:30am–11:30pm, Sun noon–3pm and 7–10:30pm.
A perennial favorite, this is the old gathering spot for "The Baker Street Irregulars," a once-mighty clan of mystery lovers who met here to honor the genius of Arthur Conan Doyle's most famous fictional character. The downstairs is mainly for drinking, with wine sold by the glass, although there's a good snack bar with cold meats, salads, and cheese. Upstairs you'll find a re-creation of the living room at 221B Baker Street and such Holmesiana as the cobra of *The Speckled Band* and the head of *The Hound of the Baskervilles.* Main dishes are reliable and include roast beef and Yorkshire pudding and chicken Sherlock Holmes with red wine and mushroom sauce. Desserts are selected from a trolley.

VAL TARO, 32 Orange St., W.C.2. Tel. 071/930-2939.
Cuisine: ITALIAN/CONTINENTAL. **Reservations:** Recommended. **Tube:** Leicester Square or Piccadilly Circus.
$ Prices: Appetizers £1.50–£5 ($2.80–$9.25); main courses £5.50–£12 ($10.20–$22.20). AE, DC, MC, V.
Open: Restaurant lunch Mon–Fri noon–3pm; dinner Mon–Sat 6–11pm. Bar lunch Mon–Fri noon–3pm; dinner Mon–Sat 5:30–11pm.
Popular as an after-theater dining spot, this restaurant offers an Italian menu that includes at least six superb veal dishes, grilled double filet of sole, excellent beefsteaks, and an array of pastas and antipasti. In the bar, you can order pasta or a salad to accompany your drink.

COVENT GARDEN

The flower, fruit, and "veg" market is long gone (since 1970), but memories of Professor Higgins and his "squashed cabbage leaf," Eliza Doolittle, linger on. Even without the market, Covent Garden is still associated with food, as it contains the liveliest group of restaurants, pubs, and cafés in London, outside Soho. This tradition of food dates from the time when the monks of Westminster Abbey dumped their surplus homegrown vegetables here. Charles II in 1670 granted the Earl of Bedford the right to "sell roots and herbs, whatsoever" in the district. The king's mistress, Nell Gwynne, once peddled oranges on Drury Lane. The restored marketplace with its glass and iron roofs has been called "a magnificent example of urban recycling."

DIANA'S DINER 39 Endell St., W.C.2. Tel. 071/240-0272.
Cuisine: INTERNATIONAL. **Reservations:** Recommended. **Tube:** Covent Garden.
$ Prices: Appetizers £1.50–£2.50 ($2.80–$4.65); main courses £3.50–£6 ($6.50–$11.10). No credit cards.
Open: Mon–Sat 7am–7pm, Sun 8am–2pm.
This busy, noisy place has no pretensions to elegance, but has a well-deserved reputation among local office workers for serving satisfying dishes at very reasonable prices. Photos of opera stars decorate the place, and patrons are likely to include such celebrities as Anthony Hopkins. Since the owners are Italian, the menu, naturally, offers many Italian dishes. But you can also get typical Cockney foods, such as "sausages and mash," and even Russian fare, such as chicken Kiev. Some vegetarian dishes are available, and the breakfast specials are popular. This unlicensed restaurant has no corkage charge, if you want to bring your own bottle of wine. Where's Diana? She's long gone elsewhere, but her name lives on at this place.

FOOD FOR THOUGHT, 31 Neal St., W.C.2. Tel. 071/836-0239.
Cuisine: VEGETARIAN. **Reservations:** Not needed. **Tube:** Covent Garden.
$ Prices: Appetizers £1–£1.70 ($1.85–$3.15); main courses £1.70–£3.50 ($3.15–$6.50). No credit cards.

Open: Breakfast Mon–Sat 8:30–11:30am; lunch Mon–Sat noon–3pm; dinner Mon–Sat 5–8pm.

⑤ Here you'll find some of the best and least expensive vegetarian food in the neighborhood. During the peak dining hours, it is likely to be crowded, so come after the rush. Food selections change twice a day, but they include good soups with whole-meal bread, freshly made salads, quiches, curries, and casseroles, with daily hot specials. All food is prepared from fresh, quality produce. The restaurant is ideally situated for the Covent Garden shopper or the pretheater diner: After leaving the tube at Covent Garden, stroll along Neal Street toward Shaftesbury Avenue; the restaurant is on the left in the second block. Take-out service is also provided.

LAMB & FLAG, 33 Rose St., off Garrick St., W.C.2. Tel. 071/497-9504.
   Cuisine: ENGLISH. **Reservations:** None. **Tube:** Covent Garden or Leicester Square.
 $ Prices: Bar snacks £1.50–£2.50 ($2.80–$4.65); lager from £1.70 ($3.15). No credit cards.
   Open: Food Mon–Sat noon–5pm, Sun noon–3pm; pub Mon–Sat 11am–11pm, Sun noon–3pm and 7–10pm.
Charles Dickens used to be a patron in this 300-year-old pub, once known as "The Bucket of Blood," and it is said that Dryden was roughed up here once because he'd satirized the mistress of Charles II. Today, all that history forms part of the legend and lore of this tiny, paneled pub, which lies in a cul-de-sac, on perhaps the smallest street in Covent Garden (you'll need a very detailed map to find it). Lager in good weather is often drunk outside. The upstairs room also absorbs the overflow. Come here for lunch and feast on one of several pâtés with French bread (washed down with real ale), or shepherd's pie, chili con carne, or one of the curry dishes.

MAGNO'S, 65A Long Acre, W.C.2. Tel. 071/836-6077.
   Cuisine: FRENCH. **Reservations:** Required. **Tube:** Covent Garden.
 $ Prices: Appetizers £2.50–£3.50 ($4.65–$6.50); main courses £5–£11 ($9.25–$20.35); set dinner 6–7pm £9.50 ($17.60) and 8–11:30pm £16.50 ($30.55). AE, DC, MC, V.
   Open: Lunch Mon–Fri noon–2:30pm; dinner Mon–Sat 6–11:30pm.
Magno's is convenient for before- and after-theater meals. Offering a selection of modern French cuisine, grills, and salads, it has an inviting atmosphere and good service. The fixed-price meal includes an appetizer, a main course, a glass of wine, and coffee.

NAG'S HEAD, 10 James St., W.C.2. Tel. 071/836-4678.
   Cuisine: ENGLISH. **Reservations:** None. **Tube:** Covent Garden.
 $ Prices: Sandwiches £2.25 ($4.15); salads £3.95 ($7.30); main dishes £5 ($9.25); pint of lager £1.68 ($3.10). No credit cards.
   Open: Lunch daily 11:30am–2:30pm; Pub daily 11am–11pm.
Nag's Head is one of the most famous Edwardian pubs of London. In days of yore, patrons had to make their way through lorries of fruit and flowers for a drink here. Elegantly dressed operagoers in the evening used to mix with Cockney cauliflower peddlers at the bar—and 300 years of British tradition happily faded away. With the moving of the market, all that has long ago changed, and the pub is patronized mainly by young people who seem to fill up all the tables every evening, including drinking space around the bar counter. Try a draft Guinness for a change of pace. Lunch is typical pub grub: sandwiches, salads, pork cooked in cider, and garlic prawns.

PLUMMERS RESTAURANT, 33 King St., W.C.2. Tel. 071/240-2534.
   Cuisine: ENGLISH/AMERICAN. **Reservations:** Recommended. **Tube:** Covent Garden.
 $ Prices: Appetizers £2.50–£4 ($4.65–$7.40); main courses £6.50–£9 ($12.05–$16.65). AE, DC, MC, V.
   Open: Lunch Mon–Fri 12:30–2:30pm; dinner Mon–Sat 6–11pm.

⭐ This is an informal place with enough room between the tables so that you don't have to listen to someone else's conversation. Appetizers include avocado vinaigrette or clam chowder. There is a wide selection of main dishes, including halibut and spinach in a parmesan cheese sauce, traditional steak-and-kidney pie, and vegetarian dishes, including vegetable casserole. There are Scottish beefburgers (100% meat) ranging from plain to Plummers Superburger topped with bacon, egg, and melted cheese. Desserts include ice cream and sorbet, plus apple and blackberry pie and cream. Coffee—as much as you can drink—finishes off the meal. A 12% service charge is added to all bills.

SMITH'S RESTAURANT, 25 Neal St., W.C.2. Tel. 071/379-0310.
   Cuisine: ENGLISH. **Reservations:** Recommended. **Tube:** Covent Garden.
$ Prices: Appetizers £3.50–£4.50 ($6.50–$8.35); main courses £5.95–£14.50 ($11–$26.65); two-course fixed-price dinner 6–8pm £10.50 ($19.45); three-course set dinner £12.75 ($23.60). AE, V.
   Open: Mon–Sat noon–midnight (last orders at 11:30pm).
Part of a converted old Covent Garden brewery, this restaurant uses high-quality ingredients. Try, for example, wild rabbit terrine with onion marmalade, black pudding with apple and cider compote, and English cheeses from Neal's Yard. The daily specials always include a vegetarian dish, and the menu reflects seasonal foods. The pretheater menu is a popular feature, as Smith's is adjacent to the Cambridge Theatre and is close to others.

HOLBORN

In "legal London," you can join barristers, solicitors, and law clerks for food and drink at the following recommendations.

CITTIE OF YORKE, 22-23 High Holborn, W.C.1. Tel. 071/242-7670.
   Cuisine: ENGLISH. **Reservations:** None. **Tube:** Holborn or Chancery Lane.
$ Prices: Appetizers £1.50–£2.50 ($2.80–$4.65); main courses £3.50–£6.50 ($6.45–$12.05); pint of lager £1.60 ($2.95). MC, V.
   Open: Mon–Fri 11am–11pm, Sat noon–3pm and 5:30–11pm.
The Cittie of Yorke stands near the Holborn Bars, the historic entrance to London marked by dragons holding the coat-of-arms of the city between their paws. A pub has stood on this site since 1430; the present one is named after a 16th-century hostelry, later called the Staple Inn (now across on the other side of High Holborn). The pub's principal hall is said to have the longest bar counter in England. The lunch menu has a choice of four different hot platters. Other fare includes burgers, goulash, and casseroles. Dinner is slightly more formal, and the menu includes ham steak, fresh fish, lasagne, and rumpsteak. Appetizers are served only at dinner.

MY OLD DUTCH, 131 High Holborn, W.C.1. Tel. 071/242-5200.
   Cuisine: DUTCH. **Reservations:** Not needed. **Tube:** Holborn.
$ Prices: Pancakes £2.50–£5.45 ($4.65–$10.10). AE, DC, MC, V.
   Open: Mon–Sat noon–11:45pm, Sun noon–10:30pm.
London's only Dutch restaurant, this cheerful place resembles a Dutch kitchen with scrubbed pine tables. The menu lists 105 different pancakes—all are enormous and are served on huge Delft plates. Fillings and garnishes include cheese, meats, and vegetables, as well as sweet fillings, such as Pandora's Pleasure (pear, ginger, and ice cream with crème de cacao sauce). Any one of these makes a good meal. Tea and coffee are available, or you can order wines and cocktails.

NORTH SEA FISH RESTAURANT, 7-8 Leigh St., W.C.1. Tel. 071/387-5892.
   Cuisine: FISH. **Reservations:** Recommended. **Tube:** Russell Square.
$ Prices: Fish platters £3.60–£8 ($6.65–$14.80). AE, DC, MC, V.
   Open: Lunch Mon–Sat noon–2:30pm; dinner Mon–Sat 5:30–10:30pm.
The fish served in this bright and clean restaurant is purchased fresh every day; the quality is high, and the prices are low. Fish is most often deep-fried in batter, but you

can also order it grilled. The menu is wisely limited. Students from the Bloomsbury area flock to the place.

SPAGHETTI HOUSE, 20 Sicilian Ave., W.C.1. Tel. 071/405-5215.
   Cuisine: ITALIAN. **Reservations:** Recommended Mon–Fri lunch. **Tube:** Holborn.
$ **Prices:** Appetizers £1.50–£2.50 ($2.80–$4.65); main courses £3.50–£6 ($6.50–$11.10). AE, DC, MC, V.
   Open: Mon–Thurs noon–11pm, Fri–Sat noon–11:30pm
This establishment was known for its pasta dishes long before pasta became "the thing" in London. The Italian-speaking waiters rush about, serving good, tasty, and reasonably priced food, with generous portions and a wide selection of moderately priced Italian wines. Children get a special welcome. In summer, you can dine on the terrace. It's a good value.

6. THE CITY

When the English talk about "The City" (E.C.2, E.C.3), they don't mean London. The City is the British version of Wall Street, and the buildings in this square mile are known all over the world: the Bank of England on Threadneedle Street, the Stock Exchange, and Lloyd's of London.
   Typical English food—shepherd's pie, mixed grills, roast beef—is dished up in dozens of the old pubs and wine bars of The City. Many of the establishments date back to Elizabethan days and have entertained literary celebrities. For the most part, I have selected the following recommendations not only because of their well-prepared and inexpensive food, but also because the buildings themselves have interest.

MEALS FOR LESS THAN £11 ($20.35)

BOW WINE VAULTS, 10 Bow Churchyard, E.C.4. Tel. 071/248-1121.
   Cuisine: ENGLISH. **Reservations:** Recommended. **Tube:** Bank or St. Paul's.
$ **Prices:** "The Restaurant" appetizers £3.50–£6.50 ($6.45–$12.05); main dishes £8–£11.50 ($14.80–$21.30); glass of wine from £2 ($3.70). AE, DC, MC, V.
   Open: Food Mon–Fri 11:30am–3pm; pub Mon–Fri 11:30am–8pm.
This firmly entrenched institution has existed since long before the current wine bar fad that began in the '70s. One of the most famous wine bars of London, it attracts cost-conscious diners and drinkers who head below ground to its steel and vaulted cellars. Menu choices in the cellar grill, as it's called, include such traditional fare as deep-fried Camembert, chicken Kiev, and a mixed grill, along with fish. More elegant meals are served in the street-level dining room, called "The Restaurant," such as mussels in cider sauce, English wild mushrooms in puff pastry, beef Wellington, and steak with brown-butter sauce. Adjacent to the restaurant is a cocktail bar, open from 11am to 8pm, that is popular with City employees after work.

GEORGE & VULTURE, 3 Castle Court, Cornhill, E.C.3. Tel. 071/626-9710.
   Cuisine: ENGLISH. **Reservations:** Accepted if you agree to arrive by 12:30pm.
   Tube: Bank.
$ **Prices:** Appetizers £2.50–£4 ($4.65–$7.40); main courses £5.50–£8.50 ($10.20–$15.75). MC, V.
   Open: Lunch Mon–Fri noon–2:30pm.
Dickens enthusiasts should seek out this olde Pickwickian hostelrie. Founded in 1660, the chophouse claims that it is "probably" the world's oldest tavern, and refers to an inn on this spot in 1175. The George & Vulture no longer puts up overnight guests (although Dickens used to spend the night), but its three floors are still used for serving

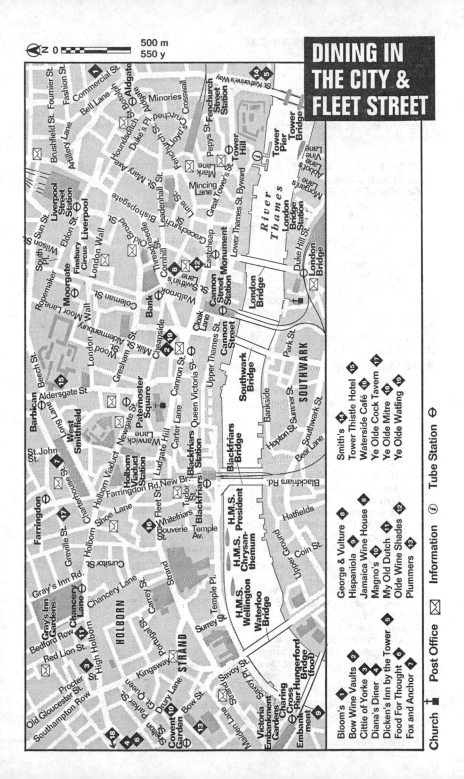

DINING IN THE CITY & FLEET STREET

N 0 | 500 m / 550 y

River Thames

SOUTHWARK

HOLBORN

STRAND

Bloom's 1
Bow Wine Vaults 2
Cittie of Yorke 3
Diana's Diner 4
Dicken's Inn by the Tower 5
Food For Thought 6
Fox and Anchor 7

George & Vulture 8
Hispaniola 9
Jamaica Wine House 8
Magno's 10
My Old Dutch 11
Olde Wine Shades 12
Plummers 13

Smith's 14
Tower Thistle Hotel 15
Waterside Café 16
Ye Olde Cock Tavern 17
Ye Olde Mitre 18
Ye Olde Watling 19

Church ✝   Post Office ⊠   Information ⓘ   Tube Station ⊖

English meals. Besides the daily specials, features include a mixed grill, a "loin chop, chump chop," or fried filets of Dover sole with tartar sauce. Potatoes and buttered cabbage are the standard vegetables, and the apple tart is always a reliable dessert. The system is to arrive and give your name, then retire to the Jamaica pub opposite for a drink. You are then "fetched" when your table is ready. After lunch, be sure to explore the nearby passageways, maze of shops, wine houses, pubs, and old buildings surrounding the tavern. By the way, the Pickwick Club meets in this pub.

JAMAICA WINE HOUSE, St. Michael's Alley, off Cornhill, E.C.3. Tel. 071/626-9496.
   Cuisine: ENGLISH. **Reservations:** None. **Tube:** Bank.
$ **Prices:** Bar snacks £1.50–£3.50 ($2.80–$6.45); lager £1.70–£2.60 ($3.15–$4.80). AE, MC, V.
   Open: Mon–Fri 11:30am–8pm; food served Mon–Fri 11:30am–3pm.
Hidden in a tangle of City alleyways, this is one of the first coffeehouses in England. In fact, the Jamaica Wine House is reputed to be the first coffeehouse in the Western world. Pepys used to visit it and even mentioned it in his *Diary*. The coffeehouse was destroyed in the Great Fire of 1666, rebuilt in 1674, and has remained, more or less, in its present form ever since. For years, London merchants and daring sea captains came here to lace deals with rum and coffee. Nowadays, the two-level house dispenses beer, ale, lager, and fine wines, including a variety of ports. An oak-paneled bar is at street level, whereas the basement bar is a cozier retreat. You can order light snacks, such as pork pie, stuffed baked potatoes with various fillings, and toasted sandwiches. The Bank of England is only a stone's throw away.

OLDE WINE SHADES, 6 Martin Lane, Cannon St., E.C.4. Tel. 071/626-6876.
   Cuisine: ENGLISH. **Reservations:** Not needed. **Tube:** Cannon Street.
$ **Prices:** Appetizers £1.80–£4.25 ($3.35–$7.85); main courses £4.80–£10 ($8.90–$18.50). MC, V.
   Open: Lunch Mon–Fri 11:30am–3pm. **Closed:** Bank holidays.
The oldest wine house in The City, dating from 1663, this was the only City tavern to survive the Great Fire of 1666, not to mention the blitz of 1940. Only 100 yards from the famous monument designed by Sir Christopher Wren to commemorate the Great Fire of 1666, the Olde Wine Shades used to attract Charles Dickens, among others. In the smoking room, the old oil paintings have darkened with age, and the 19th-century satirical political cartoons remain enigmatic to most of today's generation. Some of the finest European wines are served here, and port and sherry are drawn directly from an array of casks behind the counter. A candlelit bar and restaurant is found downstairs, but upstairs, along with your wine, you can order French bread with ham, Breton pâté, and sandwiches. Men must wear jackets and ties.

THE WATERSIDE CAFE, Level 5 of the Barbican Centre, Silk St., E.C.2. Tel. 071/638-4141.
   Cuisine: ENGLISH. **Reservations:** Not needed. **Tube:** Moorgate.
$ **Prices:** Appetizers £1.80–£2.50 ($3.35–$4.65); main courses £5–£7 ($9.25–$12.95). MC, V.
   Open: Daily noon–8pm.
This self-service cafeteria serves as a refreshment oasis for the entire Barbican community and is patronized also by students of the music school. It overlooks an artificial pond and landscaping. Many guests stop in only for a glass of wine, priced from £1.30 ($2.40), or else you can eat from a menu offering hot dishes, sandwiches, pastries, tea, or coffee. There are seats on the terrace in fair weather.

YE OLDE COCK TAVERN, 22 Fleet St., E.C.4. Tel. 071/353-8570.
   Cuisine: ENGLISH. **Reservations:** Recommended. **Tube:** Temple or Chancery Lane.
$ **Prices:** Appetizers £2.50–£4.50 ($4.65–$8.35); main courses £7–£12 ($12.95–$22.20). AE, DC, MC, V.

Open: Carvery lunch Mon–Fri noon–3pm; pub Mon–Fri 11:30am–2:30pm and 5–9:30pm.

Dating from 1549, this is one of the few buildings in London to have survived the Great Fire and boasts a long line of literary patrons. Charles Dickens used to frequent the pub, Samuel Pepys mentioned the pub in one of his diary entries, and Lord Tennyson referred to it in one of his poems—a copy of which is framed and proudly displayed near the entrance. Downstairs, you can order a pint as well as snack-bar food, steak-and-kidney pie, or a cold chicken-and-beef plate with salad. At the carvery upstairs, a meal includes all the roasts you can carve—beef, lamb, pork, or turkey.

YE OLDE WATLING, 29 Watling St., E.C.4. Tel. 071/248-6252.
   Cuisine: ENGLISH. **Reservations:** None. **Tube:** Mansion House.
   $ Prices: Main courses £5 ($9.25) each; beer from £1.65 ($3.05); bar snacks from £1.50 ($2.80). AE, MC, V.
   Open: Lunch Mon–Fri noon–2:30pm; pub Mon–Fri 11am–9pm.

Associated with Sir Christopher Wren, this was built after the Great Fire of London in 1666. On the ground level is a mellow pub, and an intimate restaurant is upstairs. The menu varies daily but always includes the choice of four hot dishes, such as beef-and-ale pie, steak-and-kidney pie, seafood Mornay, lasagne, chili con carne, and usually a vegetarian dish. All are served with two vegetables or a salad, rice, or potatoes.

7. WESTMINSTER & VICTORIA

Westminster (S.W.1), a large borough of London, includes Whitehall, the headquarters of many government offices. In fact, this section has been the seat of the British government since the days of Edward the Confessor. Dominated by the Houses of Parliament and Westminster Abbey, Parliament Square is the symbol of the soul of England. The sprawling area in and around Victoria Station (with many budget hotels and restaurants) is also a part of Westminster.

MEALS FOR LESS THAN £12.95 ($23.75)

THE ALBERT, 52 Victoria St., S.W.1. Tel. 071/222-5577.
   Cuisine: ENGLISH. **Reservations:** Not needed. **Tube:** Victoria.
   $ Prices: English breakfast £5 ($9.25); "gentleman's breakfast" £7 ($12.95); set Carvery menus £12.95 ($23.75). AE, DC, MC, V.
   Open: Breakfast Mon–Fri 8–10:30am; Sat 9–10:30pm; Carvery daily noon–9:30pm; pub Mon–Sat 11am–11pm, Sun noon–3pm and 7–10:30pm.

⑤ Once named "pub of the year," The Albert provides a real bit of Victorian England, and is visited both for its copious English breakfasts and its sumptuous roasts traditionally prepared and carved for you at its Carvery. It's so famous for its breakfasts that Princess Diana once chose it as the venue for her entire Kensington Palace staff who arrived en masse one morning. It is one of a handful of pubs which has bells controlled from the floor of the Houses of Parliament, notifying patrons when an important vote is coming up. At the Carvery you can return as often as you wish, sampling as many helpings of turkey, pork, beef, and other offerings as you want. Fish lovers and vegetarians can also find food here. Desserts are from the trolley, and the coffee is unlimited.

EBURY WINE BAR, 139 Ebury St., S.W.1. Tel. 071/730-5447.
   Cuisine: CONTINENTAL. **Reservations:** Recommended. **Tube:** Victoria Station or Sloane Square.
   $ Prices: Appetizers £2.50–£6.95 ($4.65–$12.85); main courses £6.95–£10.50 ($12.85–$19.40); wine by the glass £2 ($3.70). AE, DC, MC, V.

Open: Lunch Mon–Sat 11am–3pm, Sun noon–2:45pm; dinner Mon–Sat 5:30–11pm, Sun 6–10:30pm.

On one of London's most popular streets for budget hotels, this wine bar and bistro attracts a youthful clientele to its often crowded but atmospheric precincts. Wine is sold by the glass and by the bottle. The food is prepared fresh daily, and the *plat du jour* is always enticing—it may be traditional beef Wellington or perhaps grilled filet steaks.

GRANDMA LEE'S BAKERY AND RESTAURANT, 2 Bridge St., S.W.1. Tel. 071/839-1319.
Cuisine: SANDWICHES/INTERNATIONAL. **Reservations:** Not needed.
Tube: Westminster.
$ Prices: Appetizers £1.65–£2 ($3.05–$3.70); "granwiches" and sandwiches £3.75–£3.95 ($6.95–$7.30); breakfast £3.50 ($6.45). No credit cards.
Open: Daily 7am–9pm (breakfast until 11am).

This bright, cheerful place is across the street from the Houses of Parliament and Big Ben. Bread, buns, and rolls are freshly baked on the premises and later appear at the ground-floor service counter filled with your choice of an array of ingredients. Everything comes in a bun, including breakfast. Some sample meals include beef casserole with bread and chili with bread. "Granwiches" are prepared on thick sliced and freshly baked bread, and stuffed with about a dozen different fillings, including salmon, prawns in mayonnaise, and chicken filets.

METHUSELAH'S, 29 Victoria St., S.W.1. Tel. 071/222-0424.
Cuisine: FRENCH. **Reservations:** Required at lunch. **Tube:** Victoria Station.
$ Prices: Appetizers £2.75–£6 ($5.10–$11.10); main courses £4.25–£11 ($7.85–$20.35); wine by the glass from £3.50 ($6.45). AE, DC, MC, V.
Open: Lunch Mon–Fri 11:30am–3pm; dinner Mon–Fri 5:30–11pm.

Opposite New Scotland Yard, Methuselah's is popular with MPs from the House of Commons. The wine bar offers an excellent selection and also provides a sophisticated menu to back it up. The chef calls his food "bourgeois," and it shows a preference to Provence and Lyon. There is a ground-floor bar, along with two cellar buffet and wine bars, plus a more formal dining room, the Burgundy Room, on the mezzanine.

8. KNIGHTSBRIDGE & BELGRAVIA

MEALS FOR LESS THAN £15.95 [$29.50]
KNIGHTSBRIDGE

Adjoining Belgravia is Knightsbridge (S.W.1), another top residential, restaurant, and shopping section of London, just south of Hyde Park and to the west of Sloane Street. You'll find that much of the architecture and layout of this area is from the 18th century. Take the Piccadilly Line to Knightsbridge to patronize any of the following restaurants.

BILL BENTLEY'S, 31 Beauchamp Place, S.W.3. Tel. 071/589-5080.
Cuisine: ENGLISH. **Reservations:** Recommended. **Tube:** Knightsbridge.
$ Prices: Appetizers £2.50–£10 ($4.65–$18.50); main courses £7.50–£11 ($13.90–$20.35); glass of wine from £1.65 ($3.05). MC, V.
Open: Mon–Sat 11:30am–11pm.

Bill Bentley's stands right on this fashionable restaurant- and boutique-lined block. As the menu with its 19th-century male figures slurping oysters suggests, Bill Bentley's is really an oyster restaurant. The selection of first courses is superior to most restaurants in that it offers everything from giant prawns with Provence herbs to a shellfish bisque or Loch Fyne herring marinade. Meat dishes are fairly limited, but include succulent grilled sirloin steak. The fish is outstanding,

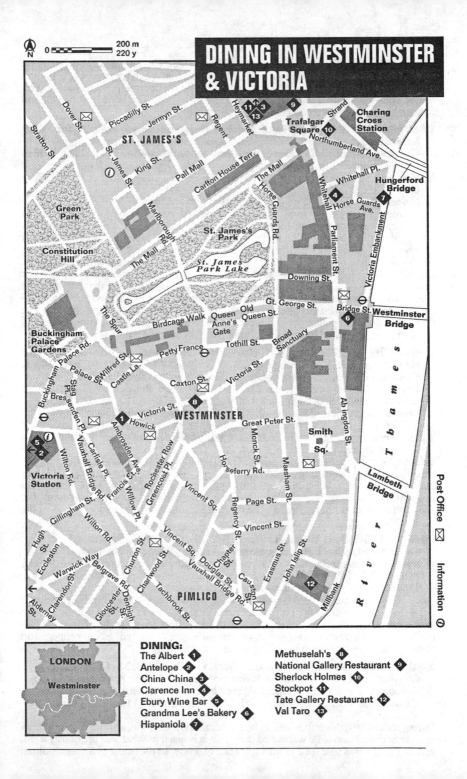

DINING IN WESTMINSTER & VICTORIA

0   200 m
     220 y

St. James's

Piccadilly St.
Dover St.
Jermyn St.
Heymarket
Stratton St.
Regent
St. James St.
King St.
Pall Mall
Carlton House Terr.
Marlborough Rd.
The Mall

Green Park

St. James's Park
St. James Park Lake

Constitution Hill

The Mall

The Spur

Buckingham Palace Gardens

Birdcage Walk
Queen Anne's Gate
Old Queen St.
Tothill St.
Broad Sanctuary
Gt. George St.
Bridge St.

Downing St.

Horse Guards Rd.
Whitehall
Horse Guards Ave.
Whitehall Pl.
Parliament St.
Victoria Embankment

Trafalgar Square
Strand
Northumberland Ave.
Charing Cross Station
Hungerford Bridge

Westminster Bridge

Buckingham Palace Rd.
Palace St.
Wilfred St.
Castle La.
Petty France
Caxton St.
Victoria St.

Stag Pl.
Bressenden Pl.
Bres
Vauxhall Bridge Rd.

Victoria Station

Wilton Rd.
Gillingham St.
Francis St.
Willow Pl.
Carlisle Pl.
Ambrosden Ave.
Rochester Row
Greencoat Pl.

Howick

Victoria St.
WESTMINSTER
Great Peter St.
Monck St.
Great Smith St.
Smith Sq.
Abingdon St.
Ab
Thames
River

Hugh St.
Eccleston
Warwick Way
Belgrave Rd.
Churton St.
Charlwood St.
Tachbrook St.
Clarendon St.
Gloucester St.
Denbigh St.
Alderney St.

Vincent Sq.
Chapter St.
Douglas St.
Vauxhall Bridge Rd.
Regency St.
Page St.
Vincent St.
Erasmus St.
Causton St.
John Islip St.
Millbank

Horseferry Rd.
Marsham St.

Lambeth Bridge

PIMLICO

Post Office   Information

LONDON
Westminster

DINING:

The Albert ● 1
Antelope ● 2
China China ● 3
Clarence Inn ● 4
Ebury Wine Bar ● 5
Grandma Lee's Bakery ● 6
Hispaniola ● 7

Methuselah's ● 8
National Gallery Restaurant ● 9
Sherlock Holmes ● 10
Stockpot ● 11
Tate Gallery Restaurant ● 12
Val Taro ● 13

especially the fish cakes, and, of course, Dover sole. The chef always prepares an assortment of fresh vegetables of the day, along with fine salads (try the watercress and orange), as well as a variety of desserts, mousses, and ice creams (perhaps you'd prefer to end your meal with a selection from the cheese board). The wine list is varied and reasonable, including a good selection of Bordeaux.

CHICAGO RIB SHACK, 1 Raphael St., Knightsbridge, S.W.7. Tel. 071/ 581-5595.
   Cuisine: AMERICAN. **Reservations:** Accepted Mon–Thurs only. **Tube:** Knightsbridge.
$ **Prices:** Side dishes £1.95–£3.75 ($3.60–$6.95); main courses £5.95–£8.95 ($11–$16.55). MC, V.
   Open: Mon–Sat 11:45am–11:45pm; Sun noon–11pm.
Real American barbecued foods cooked in imported smoking ovens and marinated in a barbecue sauce containing 15 secret ingredients are served in this restaurant, just 100 yards from Harrods. The menu also includes their famous onion loaf, which *Harper's & Queen* described as "either a Brobdingnagian French fried onion or the Illinois equivalent of an onion bhaji." Visitors are encouraged to eat with their fingers, and bibs and hot towels are provided. There are no appetizers, so many diners order from an array of side dishes instead. A video is suspended in the bar showing American sports games. There is an overwhelming number of Victorian architectural antiques that have been salvaged from demolished buildings all over the country. The 45-foot-long ornate mahogany and mirrored bar was once part of a Glasgow pub, and eight massive stained-glass windows came from a chapel in Lancashire.

GEORGIAN RESTAURANT, Harrods Department Store, 87-135 Brompton Rd., Knightsbridge, S.W.3. Tel. 071/730-1234, ext. 3467.
   Cuisine: ENGLISH. **Reservations:** Recommended. **Tube:** Knightsbridge.
$ **Prices:** Set two-course lunch £15.95 ($29.50); set three-course lunch £17.25 ($31.90); sandwiches and pastries at teatime £7.95 ($14.70). AE, DC, MC, V.
   Open: Lunch Mon–Sat noon–2:30pm; tea Mon–Sat 3:30–5:30pm.
Ⓢ Georgian Restaurant lies on the top floor of this fabled emporium, under elaborate ceilings and Belle Epoque skylights. It is one of the neighborhood's most appealing lunchtime restaurants. There is a sprawling buffet filled with cold meats and an array of fresh salads. Guests who want a hot meal can head for the carvery section where a uniformed crew of chefs dish out such offerings as Yorkshire pudding with roast beef, poultry, fish, and pork. First courses and desserts are brought to your table. Lunch and afternoon tea are served. One of the rooms, big enough for a ballroom, features a pianist, whose music trills among the crystals of the chandeliers.

LUBA'S BISTRO, 6 Yeomans Row, S.W.3. Tel. 071/589-2950.
   Cuisine: RUSSIAN. **Reservations:** Required. **Tube:** Knightsbridge.
$ **Prices:** Appetizers £2.45–£3.25 ($4.55–$6); main courses £5.75–£8.75 ($10.65–$16.20). MC, V.
   Open: Dinner Mon–Sat 6pm–midnight.
Ⓢ The moderately priced Russian food served here is good, and the chef believes in giving you enough of it. For openers, I suggest Luba's Russian borscht, or else *kapoostniak* (braised cabbage with prunes and sour cream). Main courses include beef Stroganoff, chicken Kiev, hussar's steak, stuffed green pepper, and shashlik. Bring your own wine; there is no corkage charge.

NAG'S HEAD, 53 Kinnerston St., S.W.1. Tel. 071/235-1135.
   Cuisine: ENGLISH. **Reservations:** Not needed. **Tube:** Knightsbridge.
$ **Prices:** Bar snacks £2.75 ($5.10); beer from £1.50 ($2.80). No credit cards.
   Open: Mon–Sat 11am–3pm and 5:30–11pm; Sun 11am–3pm and 5:30– 10:30pm.
Dating from 1780, this pub is said to be the smallest in London, although others claim that same distinction. The warm and cozy pub is housed in what was previously a jail, and in 1921, it was sold for £12 and 6p ($22.30). Here, in the midst of a cosmopolitan

clientele, you can enjoy real ale sausage (made with pork and ale), shepherd's pie, steak-and-mushroom pie, or even quiche. The pub is patronized by newspaper people, and musicians.

PASTA PREGO, 1A Beauchamp Place, S.W.3. Tel. 071/225-1064.
   Cuisine: ITALIAN. **Reservations:** Recommended. **Tube:** Knightsbridge.
$ **Prices:** Appetizers £1.50–£2 ($2.80–$3.70); main courses £4–£5 ($7.40–$9.25). AE, DC, MC, V.
   Open: Lunch daily noon–3pm; dinner daily 6–11pm.
Although this hole-in-the-wall Italian eatery is in one of the most expensive districts of London, you get good value and plenty of food. Tables are small and service is helpful. The pasta is fresh, including some whole-wheat versions. Begin with a selection of antipasti and follow with an order of cannelloni. Main dishes may include ravioli del mare (with seafood) or a delectable risotto. Desserts are excellent; try the chocolate mousse crumble. You can also order a moderately priced house wine to go with your meal.

THE WINDY CITY, 163 Knightsbridge, S.W.7. Tel. 071/589-7077.
   Cuisine: AMERICAN. **Reservations:** Required. **Tube:** Knightsbridge.
$ **Prices:** Appetizers £1.50–£3.25 ($2.80–$6); main courses £4.75–£10.50 ($8.80–$19.45). MC, V.
   Open: Mon–Sat 11:45am–11:45pm, Sun noon–10:30pm.
This big, bustling, spacious restaurant was part of the Chicago-inspired rage that long ago swept London. None of the offerings here approach world shattering cuisine statements, but people flock to the place for fun and familiar fare. Portions are generous, and the selections range from pizzas to pastas. Start with the honey-grilled chicken wings and go on to a grilled New York strip steak. Or, try the juicy Windy City burger, which remains the preferred selection. Many Harrods shoppers come here in the afternoon just for mixed cocktails.

BELGRAVIA

Belgravia (S.W.1), south of Hyde Park, is the so-called aristocratic quarter of London and challenges Mayfair for grandness. The locals include the top echelon in foreign embassies plus a rising new-money class—or at least young fashion models and actors. Belgravia is near Buckingham Palace Gardens (how elegant can your address be?) and Brompton Road, and its center is Belgrave Square. The nearest tube station is Hyde Park Corner.

ANTELOPE, 22 Eaton Terrace, S.W.1. Tel. 071/730-7781.
   Cuisine: ENGLISH. **Reservations:** Recommended for upstairs dining room.
   Tube: Sloane Square.
$ **Prices:** Appetizers £1.50–£2.50 ($2.80–$4.65); main courses £4.55–£6 ($8.40–$11.10). MC, V.
   Open: Lunch daily 11am–3pm; pub Mon–Sat 11am–11pm, Sun noon–3pm and 7:30–10:30pm.
Antelope, located on the fringe of Belgravia, at the gateway to Chelsea, caters to a hodgepodge of clients, aptly described as "people of all classes, colours, and creeds who repair for interesting discussion on a whole gamut of subjects, ranging from port to medieval, mid-European wicker-work, bed-bug traps, and for both mental and physical refreshment." It is also a base for English rugby aficionados (not to be confused with those who follow soccer).
   At lunchtime, the ground-floor bar provides hot and cold pub food, but in the evening only drinks are served. On the second floor (British first floor), food is served at lunch. It's principally English, with steak-and-kidney pie and jugged hare among the specialties. Steaks are also served. On Sunday a two-course carvery meal costs £7.50 ($13.90).

GRENADIER, 18 Wilton Row, S.W.1. Tel. 071/235-3074.
   Cuisine: ENGLISH. **Reservations:** Recommended. **Tube:** Hyde Park Corner.

$ Prices: Appetizers £2.95–£6.75 ($5.45–$12.50); main courses £8–£13.50 ($14.80–$25); beer from £1.40 ($2.60). AE, DC, MC, V.
Open: Lunch daily 11am–3pm; dinner daily 5:30–11pm.

An old-time pub on a cobblestone street, this is one of the special pubs of London—associated with the "Iron Duke." At the entrance to Wilton Row (in the vicinity of Belgrave Square), a special guard was once stationed to raise and lower a barrier for those arriving by carriage; the booth is still standing. A gentle ghost is said to haunt the premises, that of a Grenadier guard who was caught cheating at cards and died of the flogging given as punishment.

Today the pub is filled with a sophisticated crowd. English meals are served in front of fireplaces in two of the small rooms behind the front bar. A soup of the day might be followed by pork Grenadier, steak-kidney-and-mushroom pie, guinea fowl, or, in honor of the former patron, beef Wellington. Bar snacks are available during the same hours the restaurant serves. The Grenadier is known for its Bloody Marys, and it operates a Bloody Mary bar during lunchtime on Saturday and Sunday.

STAR TAVERN, 6 Belgrave Mews West, S.W.1. Tel. 071/235-3019.
Cuisine: ENGLISH. **Reservations:** None. **Tube:** Knightsbridge or Hyde Park.
$ Prices: Lunch pub snacks £1.20–£3.50 ($2.20–$6.45); dinner pub snacks £2.50–£5.20 ($4.65–$9.60). No credit cards.
Open: Lunch Mon–Fri 11:30am–3pm; dinner Mon–Fri 6:30–8:45pm. Pub Mon–Thurs 11:30am–3pm and 5–11pm, Fri 11:30am–11pm, Sat 11:30am–3pm and 6:30–11pm, Sun noon–3pm and 7–10:30pm.
Set in a Georgian mews, Star Tavern is one of the most colorful pubs in the West End, lying behind a picture-postcard-type facade. In winter it's one of the coziest havens around, with two fireplaces blazing. The attractive inside has Victorian walls and banquettes beneath 19th-century Victorian moldings. You can order such dishes as baby spring chicken, sirloin steak, or, perhaps, a vegetable quiche. There is no waitress service. Patrons place their orders at the bar.

9. CHELSEA & CHELSEA HARBOUR

MEALS FOR LESS THAN £12 [$22.20]
CHELSEA

Chelsea is comparable to the Left Bank of Paris or the more elegant parts of Greenwich Village. Here the diplomats and wealthy-chic, the stars of stage and screen, and successful sculptors and painters now live alongside a decreasing number of poor and struggling artists. Over the years, this area has been home to Oscar Wilde, Henry James, Whistler, and George Eliot, to name a few.

King's Road (S.W.3, named after Charles II) is the main street of Chelsea, lively both day and night. The district boasts some of the city's finest restaurants, but not the cheap ones. Still, you'll probably want to visit Chelsea, and the following recommendations offer good, reasonably priced meals. To get here, take the Circle or District Line to Sloane Square.

BLUSHES CAFE, 52 King's Rd., S.W.3. Tel. 071/589-6640.
Cuisine: INTERNATIONAL. **Reservations:** Not needed. **Tube:** Sloane Square.
$ Prices: Appetizers 95p–£4.95 ($1.55–$9.15); main courses £5.95–£13.95 ($11–$25.80); full English breakfast £5.50 ($10.20); beer from £2 ($3.70). AE, DC, MC, V.
Open: Mon–Sun 8:30am–midnight; breakfast Mon–Sat 8:30–11am, Sun 8:30am–1pm.
A face-lift put Blushes in the pink, through the efforts of proprietors Stephen Lynn and Geoffrey Thorpe. They bring a continental flavor to the establishment. All types

of food, from Italian to French to Mexican to Asian, are offered, including such specialties as seafood pasta and Cajun chicken breast.

CHARCO'S WINE BAR, 1 Bray Place, S.W.3. Tel. 071/584-0765.
  Cuisine: CONTINENTAL/BRITISH. **Reservations:** Required for restaurant.
  Tube: Sloane Square.
  $ Prices: Appetizers £2.50–£4.50 ($4.30–$8.35); main courses £5.75–£10.50 ($10.65–$19.45). AE, DC, MC, V.
  Open: Lunch daily noon–4pm; dinner Mon–Sat 5:30–11pm.
Charco's attracts those who enjoy its reasonably priced wines and inexpensive food. The establishment lies one block north of King's Road between two streets (Coulson Street and Bray Place), which run parallel to King's Road. The blackboard menu includes grilled burgers and steaks, grilled John Dory, and roast guinea fowl on a bed of tagliatelle and mushrooms. Charco's is divided into a street-level wine bar, where platters of food average £5 ($9.25), including gougeonettes of sole, fried chicken, prawns, or pork filet in phyllo pastry. The more formal dining is in the basement. Glasses of wine cost from £2.10 ($3.90).

THE CHELSEA KITCHEN, 98 King's Rd., S.W.3. Tel. 071/589-1330.
  Cuisine: INTERNATIONAL. **Reservations:** Recommended. **Tube:** Sloane Square.
  $ Prices: Appetizers 65p–£1.70 ($1.20–$3.15); main dishes £2.50–£3.70 ($4.65–$6.85); breakfast £1.20 ($2.20). No credit cards.
  Open: Mon–Sat 5am–11:45pm, Sun noon–11:45pm.
This place was established 35 years ago, with a stated goal of offering fast-moving, well-prepared food at the lowest reasonable prices. This policy has been so effective that the entire inventory is usually sold out each day, guaranteeing freshness. Menu items include leek and potato soup, chicken Kiev, chicken parmigiana, and steaks. The clientele includes a broad cross section of Chelsea artists, Sloane Rangers, "Lords and Ladies," and punk rockers—all having a good and cost-conscious time.

FRONT PAGE, Old Church St., S.W.3. Tel. 071/352-2908.
  Cuisine: CONTINENTAL. **Reservations:** Not needed. **Tube:** South Kensington.
  $ Prices: Appetizers £2.30–£3.60 ($4.25–$6.70); main courses £3.25–£5.70 ($6–$10.55). MC, V.
  Open: Pub daily 9am–3pm and 5:30–11pm; food daily noon–2:15pm and 7–10:15pm.
Favored by Chelsea yuppies who like its mellow atmosphere, this restaurant has a decor of wood paneling, wooden tables, and pews and benches. An open fire burns on cold nights. The pub is in an expensive residential section of Chelsea, and is a good, safe place to go for a drink. Lager costs from £1.60 ($2.95), or you can order bottled Budweiser. The blackboard lists the daily specials, which might include ratatouille au gratin or lamb curry, perhaps even mackerel with a kumquat sauce. The soup du jour is homemade.

HENRY J. BEAN'S (BUT HIS FRIENDS ALL CALL HIM HANK) BAR AND GRILL, 195-197 King's Rd., S.W.3. Tel. 071/352-9255.
  Cuisine: AMERICAN. **Reservations:** Not needed. **Tube:** Sloane Square.
  $ Prices: Appetizers £2.25–£3.50 ($4.15–$6.45); main courses £6–£8.50 ($11.10–$15.75). No credit cards.
  Open: Mon–Sat 11:45am–11pm, Sun noon–10pm.
This diner has brought renewed vitality to the restaurant scene in Chelsea. The decor is late 1950s, American saloon style, and the 250-foot garden is impossibly crowded on sunny days. Check the blackboard for Hank's daily specials, but know you can count on "chicken fried chicken," a smokehouse burger, nachos, and Henry J's own secret chili recipe. The restaurant is nearly opposite the fire station in Chelsea.

KING'S HEAD AND EIGHT BELLS, 50 Cheyne Walk, S.W.3. Tel. 071/353-1820.

Cuisine: ENGLISH. **Reservations:** Not needed. **Tube:** Sloane Square.
$ **Prices:** Appetizers £2–£4.50 ($3.70–$8.35); main courses £3.50–£8 ($6.45–$14.80). No credit cards.
Open: Mon–Sat 11am–11pm, Sun noon–3pm and 7–10:30pm.

In a fashionable residential district of London, this historic Thames-side pub is popular with stage and TV personalities, as well as writers. A short stroll in the neighborhood will take you to the former homes of Thomas Carlyle, Algernon Charles Swinburne, and George Eliot. The snack bar has been upgraded to Cordon Bleu standards at pub prices. The best English beers are served here, as well as a good selection of wines and liquors. A refrigerated display case holds cold dishes and salads offered at lunch, and there is also a modern hot table. The à la carte dinner menu usually includes seafood, including filet of plaice with prawns, tuna steak, or swordfish steak with mussels.

CHELSEA HARBOUR

BOATERS WINE BAR, Harbour Yard, Chelsea Harbour, S.W.10. Tel. 071/352-3687.

Cuisine: ENGLISH. **Reservations:** Not needed. **Transportation:** Riverbus from Charing Cross Mon–Fri or a Chelsea Harbour Hoppa Bus C3 from Earl's Court or Kensington High Street; on Sun, a taxi.
$ **Prices:** Main courses £1.50–£3.50 ($3.35–$6.45). AE, MC.
Open: Mon–Fri 11am–11pm, Sat 7pm–midnight, Sun noon–3pm.

Boaters occupies premises in one of London's new "villages," Chelsea Harbour. Well-heeled local flat dwellers who own the soaringly expensive apartments in this complex often come here to drink champagne by the bottle while munching from complimentary bowls of popcorn on the long wooden bar counter. Visitors from all over the world pour in as well, ordering, if not champagne, then wine and lager. No "hard spirits" are sold.

You can enjoy reasonably priced food during all opening hours. There are no specific appetizers, just main dishes. Cold food is served in the evening but you can order hot food at lunch. Most main dishes include such fare as Brie salad, chili con carne, and whole trout with almonds. An impressive wine list offers wine by the glass, costing from £1.95 ($3.60) for the house version.

DEAL'S RESTAURANT AND DINER, Harbour Yard, Chelsea Harbour, S.W.10. Tel. 071/376-3232.

Cuisine: INTERNATIONAL. **Reservations:** Recommended. **Transportation:** Chelsea Harbour Hoppa Bus C3 from Earl's Court or Kensington High Street Mon–Sat or riverbus from Charing Cross Mon–Fri; on Sun, a taxi.
$ **Prices:** Appetizers £2.50–£3.50 ($4.65–$6.45); main courses £8–£12 ($14.80–$22.20). AE, MC, V.
Open: Mon–Sat 11am–11pm, Sun noon–10pm.

After the Queen Mother arrived here on a barge to order a "Deals burger," the success of the place was assured. Deals is co-owned by Princess Margaret's son, Viscount Linley, and his friend, Lord Litchfield. The early 1900s atmosphere includes ceiling fans and bentwood banquettes. Some critics have characterized the food as "American diner" style, yet there are Asian variations on the theme—such as teriyaki burgers. You might try prawn curry, spare ribs, or even a vegetarian dish, and finish with New England apple pie.

FERRET & FIRKIN IN THE BALLOON UP THE CREEK, 114 Lots Rd., S.W.10. Tel. 071/352-4645.

Cuisine: ENGLISH. **Reservations:** Not needed. **Transportation:** Riverbus from Charing Cross Mon–Fri, or a Chelsea Harbour Hoppa Bus C3 from Earl's Court Mon–Sat. On Sun take a taxi.
$ **Prices:** Food plates from £2.50 ($4.65); lager from £1.60 ($2.95). No credit cards.
Open: Daily 11am–11pm.

Ferret & Firkin in the Balloon Up the Creek stands near Chelsea Harbour and is not the lowly pub it appears to be. Michael Caine, who owns an apartment at nearby Chelsea Harbour, might occasionally drop in for a drink, and the pub has been visited by Princess Margaret's son, Viscount Linley, who owns the nearby restaurant, Deals. Guests come to quaff Ferret ale, perhaps Dogbolter, which one pub critic called "aptly named." Some guests, often seen standing at the long bar counter, enjoy a mug of cider (more potent than you'd think). You can also enjoy pub food during the day—not only the traditional ploughman's lunch but salads and such fare as chili con carne and barbecued ribs. The pub offers evening entertainment, such as guitar and piano music.

10. KENSINGTON & SOUTH KENSINGTON

MEALS FOR LESS THAN £11.75 [$21.75]
KENSINGTON

Most smart shoppers in London patronize two busy streets: Kensington High, with its long string of specialty shops and department stores, and the abutting Kensington Church, with its antiques shops and boutiques.

BENEDICTS, 106 Kensington High St., W.8. Tel. 071/937-7580.
    Cuisine: IRISH/INTERNATIONAL. **Reservations:** Required. **Tube:** Kensington High Street.
$ Prices: Appetizers £1.95–£4.25 ($3.60–$7.85); main courses £4.95–£8.95 ($9.15–$16.55). AE, MC, V.
    Open: Lunch Mon–Sat noon–3pm; dinner Mon–Sat 5–10pm.
After you cross the street from the tube station, climb to the second floor and enter this transplanted Irish world. In a district filled with some high-priced restaurants, Benedicts keeps its tabs reasonable, with Irish and international meals. Along with a good selection of wines, you can order country pâté, perhaps wild Irish smoked salmon, then follow with steak-and-ale pie or hot Gaelic pepper steak laced with Irish whiskey.

MAGGIE JONES, 6 Old Court Place, off Kensington Church St., W.8. Tel. 071/937-6462.
    Cuisine: ENGLISH. **Reservations:** Required for dinner and weekends. **Tube:** High Street Kensington.
$ Prices: Appetizers £3.50–£5.50 ($6.45–$10.20); main courses £9.75–£10.75 ($18.05–$19.90); set lunch Mon–Sat £11.50 ($21.30); set lunch Sun £11.75 ($21.75). AE, DC, MC, V.
    Open: Lunch Mon–Sat 12:30–2:30pm, Sun 12:30–2:45pm; dinner Mon–Sat 7–11:30pm, Sun 7–11pm.
    A longtime favorite, this restaurant has dining on three levels (I prefer the basement). The furniture is plain pine, and the candles on the tables are stuck in bottles. The British fare includes grilled saddle of lamb with rosemary, baked mackerel with gooseberries, and Maggie's fish pie. Desserts, including a treacle tart, are called "puds."

TUMBLERS WINE BAR AND DINING ROOMS, 1 Kensington High St., W.8. Tel. 071/937-0393.
    Cuisine: ENGLISH. **Reservations:** Recommended. **Tube:** Kensington High Street.
$ Prices: Appetizers £1.75–£4.95 ($3.25–$9.15); main courses £5.50–£8.50 ($10.20–$15.75); fixed price dinner £9.50 ($17.60). AE, DC, MC, V.
    Open: Lunch Mon–Fri 11:30am–2:30pm; dinner Mon–Fri 5–10pm.
This restaurant occupies the white-tiled vaults of a bank from Victoria's day. Today,

guests come to drink and dine in a candlelit atmosphere decorated with copper jugs and pewter tankards. The kitchen promises "fine English food prepared and served in the proper manner." The small but adequate menu includes Tumblers homemade pies, such as chicken and chestnut with a flaky pastry top.

SOUTH KENSINGTON

When you've grown weary of exploring this district's many museums, try a feast in one of the following recommendations.

CHANTERELLE, 119 Old Brompton Rd., S.W.7. Tel. 071/373-5522.
    Cuisine: ENGLISH/CONTINENTAL. **Reservations:** Recommended. **Tube:** South Kensington or Gloucester Road.
$ **Prices:** Appetizers £2.50–£4 ($4.65–$7.40); main courses £6.50–£10 ($12.05–$18.50); set lunch £8.50 ($15.75); set dinner £15.50 ($28.70). AE, DC, MC, V.
    Open: Lunch daily noon–2:30pm; dinner daily 7–11:30pm.

⭐ While this used to be a part of the South Kensington Public Library, today you'll find highly original cookery served in a setting of wood paneling. Main courses at dinner are likely to include filets of sole stuffed with scallops and served with a champagne sauce, roast saddle of hare, and filet of veal sauteed in sage. Wines are limited but well selected.

DAQUISE, 20 Thurloe St., S.W.7. Tel. 071/589-6117.
    Cuisine: POLISH/CONTINENTAL. **Reservations:** Recommended. **Tube:** South Kensington.
$ **Prices:** Appetizers £1.80–£3.50 ($3.35–$6.45); main courses £3.80–£7.80 ($14.45). No credit cards.
    Open: Daily 10am–11:30pm.

Established during World War II, this restaurant immediately became a focal point of Polish culture in London, attracting a network of refugees who used it as a center to locate missing persons and organize a tattered but heroic resistance to Hitler. Today, almost all the staff speaks Polish and keeps alive nationalistic memories amid an old-fashioned decor with framed oil paintings decorating the walls. You might begin with borscht or marinated herring with potato salad, then follow with stuffed cabbage or beef à la Warsaw, perhaps steak à la Daquise.

GILBERT'S, 2 Exhibition Rd., S.W.7. Tel. 071/589-8946.
    Cuisine: ENGLISH/FRENCH. **Reservations:** Recommended. **Tube:** South Kensington.
$ **Prices:** Appetizers £3–£4.50 ($5.55–$8.35); main courses £8–£12 ($14.80–$22.20); set lunch £10 ($18.50); set dinner £13 ($24.05). AE, MC, V.
    Open: Lunch Tues–Fri 12:30–2pm; dinner Mon–Sat 7–10:15pm.

⭐ A small restaurant that opened in 1988, Gilbert's changes its menu every 2 weeks; the food is based on the fresh ingredients of the season. Virtually everything is prepared on the premises, including fudge with coffee and homemade rolls at dinner. The cuisine might be called "new English," for much of it is adaptations of French dishes. The menu is normally limited to five choices per course, and there are often specials. At dinner, there is a two- or three-course fixed-price meal, which includes bread, vegetables, and coffee, but not service. The wine list also changes frequently.

PHOENICIA, 11 Abingdon Rd., W.8. Tel. 071/937-0120.
    Cuisine: LEBANESE. **Reservations:** Required. **Tube:** High Street Kensington.
$ **Prices:** Appetizers £2.15–£4.30 ($4–$7.95); main courses £5.85–£7.65 ($10.80–$14.15); buffet lunch £8.95 ($16.56); set dinner £12.70–£23.30 ($23.50–$43.10). AE, DC, MC, V.
    Open: Daily 12:15–11:45pm.

Highly regarded both for the quality of its Lebanese cuisine and its moderate prices, this establishment offers outstanding food in both its presentation and its freshness. For the best value, go for lunch when you can enjoy a buffet of more than a dozen *meze* (appetizers), which are presented in little pottery dishes. The chef prepares two or three home-cooked dishes daily, including chicken in garlic sauce or stuffed lamb with vegetables.

At night, prices go up but you still get good value. Many begin their meal with the apéritif arak, similar to ouzo. Other appetizers include such classic Middle Eastern dishes as hummus or stuffed vine leaves. *Fatayer,* the "Lebanese pizza," is coated with onion, pine nuts, and spinach. Various charcoal grilled dishes are also offered. Minced lamb, spicy and well flavored, is the eternal favorite.

VICTORIA AND ALBERT MUSEUM RESTAURANT, Henry Cole Wing, Cromwell Rd., S.W.7. Tel. 071/581-2159.
  Cuisine: ENGLISH. **Reservations:** Not needed. **Tube:** South Kensington.
$ **Prices:** Appetizers £1.80–£2.20 ($3.35–$4.05); main courses £4.80–£5.75 ($8.90–$10.65). AE, V.
  Open: Mon–Sat 10am–5pm, Sun 2:30pm–5pm.
You'll find this to be a grade above your typical museum restaurant, and it's a remarkably good value. On very busy days, the line in the cafeteria will move slowly. The menu changes daily, but is likely to offer a good soup followed by many crisp salads, seafood, and fish and meat dishes. The pastries and cakes make terrific desserts, and an interesting selection of wines are for sale.

11. FULHAM

MEALS FOR LESS THAN £5 [$6.75]

EEL PIE AND MASH SHOP, 140 Wandsworth Bridge Rd., S.W.6. Tel. 071/731-1232.
  Cuisine: COCKNEY. **Reservations:** Not needed. **Tube:** Fulham Broadway or Parsons Green. **Bus:** No. 28 or 295.
$ **Prices:** Appetizers £1.25–£2 ($2.30–$3.70); main courses £2.50–£3.50 ($4.65–$6.45). No credit cards.
  Open: Tues–Wed 11:45am–6pm, Thurs–Fri 11:45am–8pm, Sat 11:45am–5pm.
A typical Cockney delight, this is outside of the East End and is therefore more accessible to visitors. You can feast on jellied or stewed eels with mashed potatoes, succulent homemade beef pie and mashed potatoes, or "bangers and mash" (sausages and mashed potatoes). Served in simple, pristine surroundings, it is something different, and you'll be sure to see some local color—this sort of food is still much loved by Londoners.

12. EARL'S COURT & NOTTING HILL GATE

MEALS FOR LESS THAN £12 [$22.20]
EARL'S COURT

KRAMPS CREPERIE & CAFE BAR, 6-9 Kenway Rd., S.W.5. Tel. 071/244-8759.

Cuisine: FRENCH. **Reservations:** Not needed. **Tube:** Earl's Court.
$ **Prices:** Appetizers £1.90–£3.20 ($3.50–$5.90); main courses £3.40–£4.95 ($6.30–$9.15). MC, V.
Open: Daily noon–11pm.

In an area filled with many B&Bs, this café is fully licensed and has a rustic French atmosphere. The music is mainly jazz at night, and the restaurant has a spacious, relaxed atmosphere. Kramps stuffs its crêpes with all sorts of fresh goodies, ranging from the least expensive (ham, cheese, and egg) to the most expensive (seafood). The dessert crêpes are excellently prepared, and some are stuffed with pineapple and banana.

NOTTING HILL GATE

When you're weary of wandering up and down Portobello Road, which since the late 1940s has become the major source of antiques in London and is the site of the famed street market, you may want to dine at one of the following. *Note:* Kensington Park Road runs parallel to Portobello.

GATE DINER, 184A Kensington Park Rd., W.11. Tel. 071/221-2649.
Cuisine: AMERICAN. **Reservations:** Recommended. **Tube:** Notting Hill Gate or Ladbroke Grove.
$ **Prices:** Appetizers £2.90–£3.60 ($5.35–$6.65); main courses £5.95–£12.20 ($11–$22.55). MC, V.
Open: Daily 11:30am–11:30pm.

A longtime favorite, this is a bit like an American saloon, with checkered tablecloths, movie posters, and old advertisements. If you're from the other side of the Atlantic, much of the fare is familiar: spareribs, steaks, fried chicken, big and juicy hamburgers, and bowls of chili. Salads are huge. Or try the fresh fish of the day or a vegetarian dish of the day. You can finish with a piece of creole pecan pie.

13. ST. MARYLEBONE, BAYSWATER & PADDINGTON

MEALS FOR LESS THAN £10 [$18.50]

ST. MARYLEBONE

This area has a fine cross section of the best of what London has to offer in culinary treats.

BAKER & OVEN, 10 Paddington St., W.1. Tel. 071/935-5072.
Cuisine: ENGLISH. **Reservations:** Required. **Tube:** Baker Street.
$ **Prices:** Appetizers £1.75–£4.75 ($3.25–$8.80); main courses £4.25–£12.50 ($7.85–$23.10). AE, DC, MC, V.
Open: Lunch Mon–Fri noon–3pm; dinner Mon–Sat 6–11pm. **Closed:** Bank holidays.

 Although this may be in an out-of-the-way neighborhood, it's still a big success. It's a little corner bakery with a sales shop converted into a tavern with a genuine pub atmosphere. The very English food often pleases the most critical; portions are large, tabs moderate. With a bit of luck, you'll be given a bare wooden table in one of the brick, cove-ceilinged nooks, the former ovens. Begin with the onion soup or the country pâté. Then I recommend roast Aylesbury duckling with

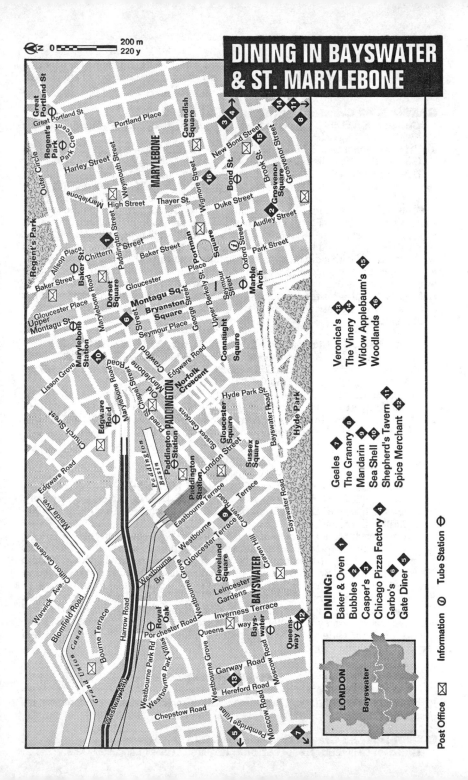

DINING IN BAYSWATER & ST. MARYLEBONE

0 `200 m` / `220 y`

MARYLEBONE

Regent's Park

Portland Place

Cavendish Square

New Bond Street

Bond St.

Harley Street

Marylebone High Street

Thayer St.

Duke Street

Audley Street

Park Street

Baker Street

Portman Square

Marble Arch

Chiltern Street

Dorset Square

Montagu Sq.

Bryanston Square

Oxford Street

Seymour Street

Connaught Square

Marylebone Road

Marylebone Station

Lisson Grove

Edgware Road

Norfolk Crescent

Hyde Park St.

Hyde Park

Paddington

Paddington Station

Sussex Gardens

Gloucester Square

Sussex Square

Bayswater Road

Eastbourne Terrace

Westbourne Terrace

Craven Road

Craven Terrace

BAYSWATER

Craven Hill

Cleveland Square

Leinster Gardens

Inverness Terrace

Queensway

Bourne Terrace

Bishop's Bridge Road

Westbourne Grove

Garway Road

Hereford Road

Chepstow Road

Pembridge Villas

Harrow Road

Maida Ave.

Clifton Gardens

Warwick Ave.

Blomfield Road

Grand Union Canal

Westway A40

DINING:

Baker & Oven **1**
Bubbles **2**
Casper's **3**
Chicago Pizza Factory **4**
Garbo's **6**
Gate Diner **5**
Geales **7**
The Granary **8**
Mandarin **9**
Sea Shell **10**
Shepherd's Tavern **11**
Spice Merchant **12**
Veronica's **13**
The Vinery **14**
Widow Applebaum's **15**
Woodlands **16**

Post Office ⊠   Information ⓘ   Tube Station ⊖

LONDON
Bayswater

stuffing and apple sauce, or jugged hare with red currant jelly. All main dishes include vegetables. For dessert, try the hot fruit pie and cream. The same prices are charged for both lunch and dinner.

GARBO'S, 42 Crawford St., W.1. Tel. 071/262-6582.
   Cuisine: SWEDISH. **Reservations:** Required. **Tube:** Baker Street, Edgware Road, or St. Marylebone.
$ **Prices:** Appetizers £1.65–£4.95 ($3.05–$9.15); main courses £3.50–£9.50 ($6.45–$17.60); buffet lunch £8 ($14.80). AE, DC, MC, V.
   Open: Lunch daily noon–3pm; dinner daily 6pm–midnight.

The most engaging and appealing Swedish restaurant in London, this place takes its theme from that country's most celebrated export, the elusive star herself. Lying south of Marylebone Road, it attracts patrons from the Swedish Embassy on Montagu Place. The best value—in fact, one of the finest lunchtime values in St. Marylebone—is the "mini-smörgåsbord." It may be called "mini," but it offers perfectly prepared hot and cold dishes and is most satisfying. For dinner, begin with *gravad lax* with a dill mustard sauce prepared in the old Viking manner, or else enjoy smoked eel or Swedish pea soup. Various meat courses are featured, including Swedish meatballs in a cream sauce or stuffed white cabbage with a beef and pork stuffing. Watch also for the specialties of the day, and finish with a dessert from the sweet trolley or else ask for crêpe Garbo, filled with ice cream and coated with a Melba sauce.

WOODLANDS, 77 Marylebone Lane, W.1. Tel. 071/486-3862.
   Cuisine: INDIAN. **Reservations:** Recommended. **Tube:** Bond Street.
$ **Prices:** Appetizers £1.75–£3.50 ($3.25–$6.45); main courses £3.25–£7.50 ($6–$13.90); set menus £8.50 ($15.75). AE, DC, MC, V.
   Open: Lunch Mon–Sat noon–3pm; dinner daily 5:30–10:45pm.
Woodlands offers the famous vegetarian cuisine from the south of India in the heart of London. It has several branches, of which the Marylebone Lane is the most central. Try *thalis* (a variety plate) or *dosas* (spicy vegetarian pancakes).

BAYSWATER

VERONICA'S, 3 Hereford Rd., W.2. Tel. 071/229-5079.
   Cuisine: ENGLISH. **Reservations:** Required. **Tube:** Bayswater or Queensway.
$ **Prices:** Appetizers £2.50–£5 ($4.65–$9.25); main courses £6.50–£10 ($6.95–$18.50). AE, DC, MC, V.
   Open: Lunch Mon–Fri noon–3pm; dinner Mon–Sat 7pm–midnight.

Called the "market leader in café salons," Veronica's offers some of the finest British cuisine in London at tabs you don't mind paying. In fact, it's like a celebration of British food, including some dishes based on recipes used in medieval times. However, each dish is given today's imaginative interpretation by Veronica Shaw, the owner. One month she'll focus on Scotland; another month, Victorian foods; yet another month, Wales. Many dishes are vegetarian, and everything tastes better when followed with one of the selections of British farmhouse cheeses, or else a "pudding." The restaurant is brightly and attractively decorated, and service is warm and ingratiating.

PADDINGTON

If you're staying in a B&B near Paddington Station and are seriously economizing, it's best to go Chinese.

MANDARIN, 33 Craven Rd., W.2. Tel. 071/723-8744.
   Cuisine: CHINESE. **Reservations:** Required. **Tube:** Lancaster Gate.

$ Prices: Appetizers £1.60–£5.95 ($2.95–$11); main courses £4–£6.20 ($7.40–$11.45); fixed-price dinner £9 ($16.65) per person for two. AE, DC, MC, V.
Open: Lunch daily noon–2:30pm; dinner daily 6pm–midnight.

A Bayswater budget favorite, this offers a wide selection of good Chinese dishes, including fragrant crispy duck, shredded beef (hot), grilled prawns Peking style, and a number of vegetable dishes, such as creamed Chinese cabbage. The place is informal, functional, and often lively. The bargain is the fixed-price dinner, although two must order it.

---

14. AWAY FROM THE CENTER

MEALS FOR LESS THAN £14.95 ($27.65)

EAST END

At least once, you may want to plunge into the colorful East End because a few of its restaurants stand out.

BLOOM'S, 90 Whitechapel St., E.1. Tel. 071/247-6001.
    Cuisine: KOSHER. **Reservations:** Recommended. **Tube:** Aldgate East.
$ Prices: Appetizers £2.50–£6 ($4.65–$11.10); main courses £6.50–£12 ($12.05–$22.20). AE, DC, MC, V.
    Open: Sun–Thurs 11:30am–10pm; Fri 11:30am–3pm (to 2pm in winter).

Overcrowded with frantic service, Bloom's continues to serve kosher delights supervised and inspected by a rabbi. Try a chicken blintz, borscht, boiled leg of fowl, or salt beef (corned, to us). Sunday lunch is the busiest meal. Only full-service dinner patrons are seated.

DICKENS INN BY THE TOWER, St. Katherine's Way, E.1. Tel. 071/488-2208.
    Cuisine: ENGLISH. **Reservations:** Recommended. **Tube:** Tower Hill.
$ Prices: Appetizers £3–£5.75 ($5.55–$10.80); main courses £10–£18 ($18.50–$33.30); snacks £4 ($7.40); hot dish of the day £5 ($9.25). AE, DC, MC, V.
    Open: Bar Mon–Sat 11am–11pm; Sun noon–3pm and 7–10:30pm; restaurant Mon–Sat noon–3pm and 6:30–10:30pm; Sun noon–3pm and 7–10pm.

Contained within a converted Victorian warehouse, this establishment draws its main decorative allure from the bricks and redwood timbers of the original 19th-century construction. It is deliberately devoid of carpets, curtains, or anything that might conceal its unusual antique trusses. Large windows overlook a sweeping Thames-side view of Tower Bridge. On the ground level the Tavern Room serves bar snacks and upstairs is a more formal dining room. In the bar, try freshly made salads, shepherd's pie, or smoked mackerel. The restaurant offers a choice of fresh seafood or traditional English meat dishes, such as roast lamb or roast beef with Yorkshire pudding.

YE OLDE MITRE, in Ely Court, off Ely Place, E.C.1. Tel. 071/405-4751.
    Cuisine: ENGLISH. **Reservations:** None. **Tube:** Farringdon.
$ Prices: Bar snacks 60p–£1.25 (85¢–$2.30). No credit cards.
    Open: Lunch Mon–Fri 11am–3pm; dinner Mon–Fri 5:30–11pm; pub Mon–Fri 11am–11pm.

Once frequented by Samuel Johnson, this hidden pub is on Ely Court, a narrow little entryway linking Ely Place, which leads off Charterhouse Street at Holborn Circus, and Hatton Garden, home of London's diamond trade. Another entrance is beside 8 Hatton Garden. The tavern was first built in 1546 by the Bishop of Ely for his servants. The sign hanging outside the present building bears a drawing of a bishop's miter, and the sign above the door bears the date. In good weather, you may be lucky enough to find a place to stand in the tiny courtyard between the pub and the Church of St. Etheldreda. Interesting relics in the pub include a preserved chunk of a cherry tree around which Queen Elizabeth I is said to have performed the maypole dance. A metal bar at the entrance of Ely Court was placed there to prevent horsemen from riding into this tiny space. English pub food such as steak and kidney pie is served.

PROSPECT OF WHITBY, 57 Wapping Wall, E.1. Tel. 071/481-1095.
   Cuisine: ENGLISH/FRENCH. **Reservations:** Required. **Tube:** Wapping.
$ **Prices:** Appetizers £2.95–£8.95 ($5.45–$16.55); main courses £11.25–£19.50 ($20.80–$36.10). AE, DC, MC, V.
   Open: Restaurant lunch Sun–Mon noon–2pm, dinner Mon–Sat 7–10pm; pub Mon–Sat 11:30am–3pm and 5:30–11pm, Sun noon–3pm and 7–10:30pm.

 One of London's oldest riverside pubs, this was originally founded in the Tudor days and was named after a coal barge that made weekly trips from Yorkshire to London. In a traditionally pubby atmosphere, the Prospect has a balcony overlooking the Thames, where "hanging judge" Jeffries used to enjoy his ale in the 18th century as he watched the executioner string up people he'd judged. The pub was also visited by Dickens, Whistler, and Turner. Come here for a tot, a noggin, or whatever it is you drink. Downstairs you can enjoy beer and snacks.

Or you can go upstairs to the Pepys Rooms, which honors the diarist, who may—just may—have visited the Prospect in rowdier days, when the seamy side of London dock life held sway here. You can enjoy such dishes as lemon chicken and homemade fish pies (with scallops, scampi, salmon, cod, and prawns).

To get here, take the Metropolitan Line to Wapping station. At Wapping High Street, turn right and head down the road along the river. Wapping Wall will be on your right, running parallel to the Thames. It's about a 5-minute walk.

TOWER THISTLE HOTEL, St. Katherine's Way, E.1. Tel. 071/481-2575.
   Cuisine: ENGLISH. **Reservations:** Not necessary. **Tube:** Tower Hill.
$ **Prices:** Set lunch £14.95 ($27.65); set dinner £15.95 ($29.50). AE, DC, MC, V.
   Open: Lunch Mon–Sat 12:15–2:30pm, Sun 12:15–3pm; dinner Mon–Fri and Sun 5:30–midnight, Sat 5pm–midnight.

In the carvery in this modern hotel built overlooking the Thames, you can enjoy all you want of some of the most tempting roasts in the Commonwealth. For example, you can select from a standing rib of prime beef with Yorkshire pudding, horseradish sauce, and the juice; or from tender roast pork with "crackling" accompanied by a spiced bread dressing and apple sauce. Perhaps you'll prefer a selection of cold meats and salads from the buffet table. No one counts—even if you go back for seconds or thirds. You can end the meal with a selection from the dessert trolley (especially recommended is the fresh fruit salad, ladled out with thick country cream poured over). You also receive a large cup of American-style coffee. Before or after dinner, you might want to visit the Thames Bar, which has a small balcony outside for drinks in summer.

HAMPSTEAD HEATH

This residential suburb of London, beloved by Keats and Hogarth, is a favorite excursion spot for Londoners on the weekend. The Old Bull and Bush, made famous by Florrie Forde's legendary song, is long gone. (The pub bearing that name today is modern.) However, there are pubs up here with authentic historical pedigrees. Take the Northern Line of the Underground to the Hampstead Heath station, N.W.3.

JACK STRAW'S CASTLE, North End Way, N.W.3. Tel. 071/435-8885.
   Cuisine: ENGLISH. **Reservations:** Not needed. **Tube:** Hampstead.
$ **Prices:** Appetizers £1–£2.50 ($1.85–$4.65); main courses £7.65–£11.65 ($14.15–$21.55). AE, DC, MC, V.
   Open: Carvery lunch Mon–Sun noon–2pm, dinner Mon–Sat 6–10pm, Sun 7–9:30pm; pub Mon–Fri 11am–3pm and 5:30–11pm, Sat 11am–11pm, Sun noon–2pm and 7–10:30pm.

This weather-board pub is on the summit of the heath, about 443 feet above sea level. The nearby Whitestone Pond was used in the war as an emergency water tank, and previously Shelley used to sail paper boats on the pond. The pub was rebuilt and enlarged in the 1960s on the site of the original. Jack Straw was one of the leaders of the peasants who revolted along with Wat Tyler in 1381 against what was, basically, a wage freeze.

The pub was created in Jack's old home, now a bustling place with a large L-shaped bar and quick-snack counter, where there are cold salads, meats, and pies, plus three hot dishes with vegetables served daily. You can eat in the bar or on the large patio overlooking part of the heath. After leaving the Underground station, the pub is a 5-minute walk up the hill.

MANNA, 4 Erskine Rd., N.W.3. Tel. 071/722-8028.
  Cuisine: VEGETARIAN. **Reservations:** Recommended for five or more. **Tube:** Chalk Farm.
  $ Prices: Appetizers £1.50–£2.50 ($2.80–$4.65); main courses £3.50–£6 ($6.45–$11.10). No credit cards.
  Open: Dinner daily 6:30pm–midnight (last orders at 11pm).
Established in 1968, this is one of the oldest vegetarian restaurants in Britain. The fine array of strictly vegetarian dishes will tempt even the most skeptical carnivore; daily specials are likely to include hot garlic mushrooms or lentil pâté, followed by such main dishes as stuffed pancakes or vegetable crumble. Desserts may be a lime mousse, chocolate and cashew tart, or meringues in brandy sauce. Manna's is fully licensed and has a non-smoking area. The location is within a short walk of the Chalk Farm tube station: Head down Adelaide Road and take the first left over the bridge to Regent's Park Road. Erskine Road is the first on the right.

SPANIARDS INN, Spaniards Lane, N.W.3. Tel. 081/455-3276.
  Cuisine: ENGLISH. **Reservations:** Not needed. **Tube:** Hampstead or Golders Green.
  $ Prices: Appetizers £1.50–£2.50 ($2.80–$4.65); main courses £3.50–£5 ($6.45–$9.25); beer from £1.10 ($2.05). No credit cards.
  Open: Meals Mon–Sat 11:30am–9:30pm, Sun noon–3pm and 7–9:30pm; pub Mon–Sat 11am–11pm, Sun noon–3pm and 7–10:30pm.
A Hampstead Heath landmark, this is opposite the old tollhouse, a bottleneck in the road where people had to pay a toll to enter the country park of the bishop of London. The pub, built in 1630, still contains some antique benches, open fireplaces, and cozy nooks in the rooms with their low, beamed ceilings and oak paneling. Old muskets on the walls are survivors of the time of the Gordon Riots of 1780, when a mob stopped in for drinks on their way to burn nearby Kenwood House, property of Lord Mansfield. The innkeeper served so many free drinks that when the Horse Guards arrived, they found many of the rioters *hors de combat* from too much libation and relieved the protesters of their weapons. Some notables who have patronized the pub are Byron, Shelley, Dickens, and Galsworthy, and even Keats may have quaffed a glass here. The pub serves traditional but above-average food, and in summer, customers can sit at tables on a garden terrace beside an aviary.

PIMLICO

TATE GALLERY RESTAURANT, Millbank, S.W.1. Tel. 071/834-6754.
  Cuisine: ENGLISH. **Reservations:** Required. 2 days in advance. **Tube:** Pimlico. **Bus:** No 88.
  $ Prices: Appetizers £2.50–£4.50 ($4.65–$8.35); main courses £8.95–£12.95 ($16.55–$24.05). V.
  Open: Lunch Mon–Sat noon–3pm.
Tate Gallery is particularly attractive to wine fanciers, offering what may be the best bargains for superior wines to be found anywhere in the country. It is especially strong on Bordeaux or burgundies. Management keeps the markup on wines ranging from 40% to about 65%, rather than the 100% to 200% added to the

wholesale price in other restaurants. In fact, the prices here are even lower than they are in most retail wine shops. Wines cost from £7 ($12.95) per bottle or £1.40 ($2.60) per glass. However, if you're looking for food (or in addition to) wine, the restaurant specializes in English cuisine. You can choose "umbles paste" (a pâté), "hindle wakes" (cold stuffed chicken and prunes), "pye with fruyt ryfshews" (fruit tart topped with meringue), or perhaps just one of "Joan Cromwell's grand sallets," made of raisins, almonds, cucumbers, olives, pickled beans, and shrimp, among other ingredients. Or you might prefer more customary dishes: steak, omelets, ham, roasts of beef and lamb, fish, and the traditional steak, kidney, and mushroom pie.

SOUTH OF THE THAMES

GOOSE AND FIRKIN, 47 Borough Rd., S.E.1. Tel. 071/403-3590.
　Cuisine: ENGLISH. **Reservations:** Required. **Tube:** Elephant and Castle.
$　**Prices:** Sandwiches from £1.70 ($3.15); small pies from £1.50 ($2.80); hot platters £3.15 ($5.85). No credit cards.
　Open: Mon–Fri 11am–3pm and 5–11pm, Sat noon–3pm and 6–11pm, Sun noon–3pm and 7–11pm.
Each day there is a different hot dish in this lovely old London pub. Or you can order extra large baps (bread buns) filled with your choice of meat and salad. The pub also brews its own beer in three special strengths: Goose, Borough Bitter, Dogbolter. Tuesday through Saturday a pianist plays all the old numbers in good old "knees up" style. Food and drink are served simultaneously during opening hours.

THE GEORGE, 77 Borough High St., S.E.1. Tel. 071/407-2056.
　Cuisine: ENGLISH. **Reservations:** Not needed. **Tube:** London Bridge.
$　**Prices:** Appetizers all £2.50 ($4.65); main courses £8.50–£9.50 ($15.75–$17.60); carvery meals £10 ($18.50); snacks from £1.50 ($2.80). AE, DC, MC, V.
　Open: Carvery lunch daily noon–2pm; dinner Mon–Sat 7–9pm; pub Mon–Fri 11:30am–11pm; Sat noon–3pm and 6–11pm; Sun noon–3pm and 7–10:30pm.
Across the bridge in Southwark, this National Trust property is the last of the old galleried coaching inns of London. The inn was known to Charles Dickens, and some claim that Shakespeare and his troupe performed in an old inn that stood on the same ground. The George today is essentially late 17th century. On the ground floor there are two bars and a wine bar where hot chili, sausages and mash, along with shepherd's pie and beans are served. There is a salad table, with some dozen different mixtures. A carvery is upstairs.

THE ROYAL FESTIVAL HALL RIVERSIDE CAFE, South Bank, S.E.1. Tel. 071/921-0810.
　Cuisine: CONTINENTAL. **Reservations:** Not needed. **Tube:** Embankment.
$　**Prices:** Café snacks from £2.50 ($4.65); Festival Buffet £6–£8 ($11.10–$14.80); salad bar only £4.25 ($7.85); Pasta Bar £4.25 ($7.85); Review Restaurant lunch from £15 ($27.75). AE, MC.
　Open: Café daily 10am–8pm. Coffee Lounge daily 10am–10pm. Buffet Bars lunch daily noon–2:30pm; dinner daily 5:30–10:30pm. Main bar daily 11am–10:30pm.
Here you can enjoy an inexpensive meal or snack in a relaxed setting on the banks of the Thames. It's worth the 5-minute walk from the nearest tube station to combine a meal with any of the activities at the Royal Festival Hall and the adjacent Jubilee Gardens. Free exhibitions and lunchtime concerts take place in the foyers, where there are a variety of places to eat and drink. The coffee lounge serves sandwiches, cakes, and pastries; the Festival Buffet has a large selection of cold meat, fish, and vegetable dishes served with a large self-service salad bar; the Salt Beef Bar offers freshly baked baguettes and salt (corned) beef carved to order; the pasta bar has a choice of pasta with six different sauces; the main bar is opposite the buffet; and the wine bar has a comprehensive range of wines from around the world. On Level 3, the Review Restaurant offers the best in international cuisine with a predominantly French flavor,

with lunchtime menus and special concert menus. As an additional treat, you'll have a stunning view of London's skyline overlooking the river.

ST. JOHNS WOOD

In northern London, this area began to develop in the mid-19th century as Gothic and Italianate houses were built in leafy, tree-filled gardens. The Victorians of the time considered a visit here like a trip to the country, but it has since been developed and is now one of the most sought-after residential areas of London. Incidentally, it was a favorite place for aristocrats to stash their mistresses, as exemplified by the old Clifton Hotel (see below). Many artists and writers were also drawn to the area, including George Eliot.

THE CLIFTON HOTEL, 96 Clifton Hill, N.W.8. Tel. 071/624-5233.
    Cuisine: ENGLISH. **Reservations:** Not needed. **Tube:** St. John's Wood or Maida Vale.
$ Prices: Appetizers £1.95–£6.95 ($3.60–$12.85); main courses £8–£11 ($14.80–$20.35). MC, V.
    Open: Pub Mon–Fri 11am–3pm and 5–11pm; Sat 11am–11pm; Sun noon–3pm and 7–10:30pm; food Mon–Fri noon–2:30pm and 7–9:30pm; Sat noon–3pm and 7–9:30pm, Sun noon–3pm.

One of the most charming pubs in the city, this stands in northern London in an expensive residential area. The Clifton is like a country pub, handsomely decorated with Victorian and Edwardian touches, and a working fireplace. Built in 1837, it was a hotel renowned for its fine ports and wines. Edward VII discovered it and used it as a place of retreat with his mistress, Lillie Langtry. Restored in 1984, the pub is better than ever. Look for the daily specials, such as beef-and-Guinness stew with dumplings, or order a steak sandwich, perhaps preceded by smoked mackerel pâté. Tables are placed outside in summer.

15. SPECIALTY DINING

FISH & CHIPS

With the wealth of restaurants in London, visitors are likely to miss the most English fare of all—fish-and-chips. True, the once ubiquitous fish-and-chips shops, also known as chippies, have become harder to find, and even those that remain are of such varying quality that it's difficult for a foreigner to be able to sample good chippie output.

    Proper shops offer a selection of such deep-fried fresh fish, found by the proprietor at the New Billingsgate Market, as plaice, cod, haddock, skate, and rockfish. This is served with french fries, with vinegar and salt on the table or counter. The purpose of the vinegar is to offset the grease in which the fish and potatoes have been fried. You can eat in the shop, usually at a communal table, or take your food outside.

GEALES, 2-4 Farmer St., W.8. Tel. 071/727-7969.
    Cuisine: FISH & CHIPS. **Reservations:** Not needed. **Tube:** Notting Hill Gate.
$ Prices: Appetizers 80p–£2.90 ($1.50–$5.35); main courses £4.50–£8 ($8.35–$14.80). MC, V.
    Open: Lunch Tues–Sat noon–3pm; dinner Tues–Sat 6–11pm.

If you're seeking some of the best fish-and-chips in London, this is worth the tube ride. The fish is bought fresh daily, and it's not greasy as it is in most London chippies. Cod, hake, and plaice are the featured mainstays. The corner restaurant is at the end of a mews street.

THE UPPER STREET FISH SHOP, 324 Upper St., N.1. Tel. 071/359-1401.

Cuisine: FISH & CHIPS. **Reservations:** Not needed. **Tube:** Angel.
$ **Prices:** Appetizers £1.50–£4.50 ($2.80–$8.35); main courses £4.75–£8.50 ($8.80–$15.75). No credit cards.
Open: Lunch Tues–Fri noon–2pm, Sat noon–3pm; dinner Mon–Sat 5:30–10pm.
My favorite shop is in Islington, near the Camden Passage antiques center. Your meal can include fish-and-chips, a drink, and perhaps a homey dessert, such as jam roly-poly. Cod and halibut (poached or fried) are the specialties.

SEA SHELL, 49-51 Lisson Grove, N.W.8. Tel. 071/723-8703.
Cuisine: FISH & CHIPS. **Reservations:** Not needed. **Tube:** Marylebone.
$ **Prices:** Appetizers £1.50–£4 ($2.80–$7.40); main courses £4.75–£8.50 ($8.80–$15.75). MC, V.
Open: Lunch Tues–Sat noon–2pm; dinner Tues–Sat 5:15–10:30pm.
This is one of the most popular places in London for fish-and-chips. The chips are more like Stateside french fries, and the fish is dipped in batter made with milk and egg and then fried in peanut oil. Other fish dishes, such as Dover sole are offered, and there's even a wine list. The restaurant has waitress service plus take-out service.

TEATIME

During the 18th century, the English from every class became enamoured of a caffeine-rich brew finding its way into London from faraway colonies. The great craftspeople of England designed furniture, porcelain, and silver services for the elaborate ritual, and the schedules of aristocrats became increasingly centered around teatime. Even Alexander Pope found it expedient to satirize teatime as something uniquely English.

The taking of tea is having a renaissance in the lives of the English. Viewed as a civilized pause in the day's activities, it is particularly appealing to people who didn't have time for lunch or who plan an early theater engagement. Some hotels feature orchestras and tea dancing in afternoon ceremonies, usually lasting from 3:30 to 6:30pm.

THE FOUNTAIN RESTAURANT, Fortnum & Mason, 181 Piccadilly W.1. Tel. 071/734-8040.
Cuisine: BRITISH. **Reservations:** None for tea. **Tube:** Piccadilly Circus.
$ **Prices:** Tea £4 ($7.40). AE, DC, MC, V.
Open: Mon–Sat 2:30–6pm.
The most famous place for afternoon tea is the world's most famous grocery store. You can enjoy sizeable pots of tea served with wafer-thin cucumber sandwiches, or, if you prefer, filled with caviar, followed by French pastries. For tea devotees, a visit here is part of the ritual of living in London. Of course, some people, instead of taking tea, prefer the sundaes, frappés, and sorbets—called "forbidden delights."

RICHOUX, opposite Harrods Department Store, 36 Brompton Rd., Knightsbridge, S.W.3. Tel. 071/584-8300.
Cuisine: ENGLISH. **Reservations:** Not needed. **Tube:** Knightsbridge.
$ **Prices:** Tea £5–£8 ($9.25–$14.80) per person; appetizers £2.50–£9 ($4.30–$16.65); main courses £7–£12 ($12.95–$22.20). AE, MC, V.
Open: Daily 9am–7pm.
Try the old-fashioned atmosphere of Richoux, where waitresses wear period dresses with frilly aprons. You can order four hot scones with strawberry jam and whipped cream, or choose from a selection of pâtisserie behind a display case. Of course, tea is obligatory; always specify lemon or cream, and one lump or two. Also, a full menu is served all day long: At least seven fresh salads are featured, and there are sandwiches, Welsh rarebit, burgers, and an array of freshly changing dishes such as lobster bisque, omelet with smoked haddock, and grilled trout. You can also order main meals, including such dishes as chicken Kiev, Dover sole, and steaks.

Richoux has two other branches: One is at the bottom of Bond Street, 172 Piccadilly W.1 (tel. 071/493-2204; tube: Green Park or Piccadilly Circus); and the other is at 41A South Audley Street, W.1 (tel. 071/629-5228; tube: Hyde Park).

They're both open Monday through Saturday from 8:30am to 11:30pm and Sunday from 10am to 11:30pm. The restaurants are licensed to serve alcohol only to diners.

HOTEL DINING

SPICE MERCHANT, Coburg Hotel, 129 Bayswater Rd., W.2. Tel. 071/221-2442.
   Cuisine: INDIAN. **Reservations:** Not needed. **Tube:** Queensway.
$ **Prices:** Appetizers £2.50–£6 ($4.65–$11.10); main courses £6–£10 ($11.10–$18.50); buffet lunch £13 ($24.05). AE, DC, MC, V.
   Open: Lunch daily 12:30–2:30pm; dinner daily 7–11:30pm.

 Spice Merchant is one of London's finest Indian restaurants, having made its debut in 1990. Part of the Coburg Hotel, it is decorated with artifacts of India. What makes this restaurant different from the hundreds of Indian restaurants that pepper London is its emphasis on very fresh ingredients. Dishes are individually prepared. Stewed dishes are cooked in their own juices, and the chef also barbecues meat and poultry to perfection.

DINING ON THE WATER

HISPANIOLA, Victoria Embankment, Charing Cross, W.C.2. Tel. 071/839-3011.
   Cuisine: ENGLISH. **Reservations:** Required. **Tube:** Embankment.
$ **Prices:** Set lunch £16.50 ($30.55); set dinner £20 ($37). Service extra. AE, DC, MC, V.
   Open: Lunch Mon–Fri, Sun noon–2pm; dinner Sun–Mon 6–10:30pm. Tues–Sat 7pm–midnight.
This large and luxurious air-conditioned ship offers a splendid view of the heart of London from Big Ben to St. Paul's, armchair comfort at the tables, and two cocktail bars. Meals are served on both the upper and lower decks, and at night the sparkling lights along the banks turn the entire area into a romantic setting. The menu offers many meat and vegetarian dishes, including roast quail with grapes and chestnuts, Barbary duck with lime and honey sauce, and Dover sole meunière.

MY FAIR LADY, 250 Camden High St., N.W.1. Tel. 071/485-4433 or 071/485-6210.
   Cuisine: ENGLISH. **Reservations:** Required. **Tube:** Camden Town.
$ **Prices:** Lunch trip £15.95 ($29.50); dinner trip £22.95 ($42.45). MC, V.
   Open: Dinner trip departs at 8pm Tue–Sat; lunch trip departs at 1pm Sun only.

 FROMMER'S COOL FOR KIDS
RESTAURANTS

Deal's Restaurant *(see p. 130)* Kids love to take the boat down to Chelsea Harbour, where they can enjoy food of North America, including "Dealsburgers." Reduced price children's portions are available.

Chicago Pizza Factory *(see p. 104)* If your kids are nostalgic for the food back home, they'll find it here at a place whose regular-size pizzas are big enough for two or three diners.

Spaghetti House *(see p. 114)* Kids love to be taken here where they get their fill of good-tasting pasta dishes—at least 10 different flavors and varieties. For dessert, the cassata siciliana is always a pleaser.

Traditionally decked out, this cruise-while-you-dine establishment, a motor-driven barge, noses through the Regent's Canal for 3 hours, crossing the zoo, Regent's Park, passing through Maida Hill tunnel until it reaches Robert Browning's Island at Little Venice, where a popular singer-guitarist joins you for the return journey. The menu, based on fresh seasonal ingredients, consists of traditional English fare, such as prime roast rib of beef, chicken suprême, and filet of beef.

DINING WITH A VIEW

THE ANCHOR BANKSIDE, 34 Park St., Southwark, S.E.1. Tel. 071/407-1577.
> **Cuisine:** ENGLISH. **Reservations:** Recommended. **Tube:** London Bridge.
> **$ Prices:** Appetizers £2.25–£6.40 ($4.15–$11.85); main courses £8.95–£17.95 ($16.55–$33.20). AE, DC, MC, V.
> **Open:** Lunch daily noon–2pm; dinner Mon–Sat 7–10pm, Sun 7–9pm.

Steeped in atmosphere, this stands near what used to be the infamous debtors' prison, Clink (hence, the expression—"thrown in the clink"). The original Anchor burned down in 1676 but was rebuilt, and the new one survived the bombing of World War II. Much of the present tavern, however, is aptly described by the management as "Elizabeth II." After getting off at the tube stop, you pass by Southwark Cathedral through a warehouse district that looks at night like Jack the Ripper country till you reach the riverside tavern. There's a viewing platform—especially popular during the day—right on the Thames. You'll find a number of bars named after the historical associations of the inn (Thrale Room, Dr. Johnson's Room, the Clink Bar, and the Boswell Bar). In addition, you can dine either upstairs or down in such "parlours" as the Globe Bar, the Chart Rooms, or the Georgian, pine-paneled Shakespeare Room. The food is good, and from May to October, there is an outdoor barbecue area.

CITY BARGE, 27 Strand-on-the-Green, Chiswick, W.4. Tel. 081/994-2148.
> **Cuisine:** ENGLISH. **Reservations:** Recommended. **Tube:** Hammersmith.
> **$ Prices:** Food platters £3–£4.75 ($5.55–$8.80); lager from £1.40 ($2.60). AE, MC, V.
> **Open:** Mon–Sat 11am–11pm; Sun noon–3pm and 7–10:30pm.

On a summer night, many Londoners head west for an outing and a pint of ale at this little country pub, which can be reached in 45 minutes from the center of London. It has the largest Thames side frontage of any London pub. Regulars often bypass the little tables set outside (in summer) to have their pints while sitting on the embankment wall under a willow tree and enjoying the boats chugging or gliding by. The kitchen serves only platters of food across the bar. A specialty is liver-and-bacon pie. During the 17th century, it was a preferred pub for Oliver Cromwell, who used a then secret passageway to make a hasty exit from his enemies, the Roundheads.

To get there, take the tube to Hammersmith, then change to bus no. 27 and get off at the beginning of Kew Bridge (during the day this can be combined with a visit to Kew Gardens). Then walk down a towpath (about a 5-minute jaunt), past moored boats and a row of little Regency, Queen Anne, Georgian, and Dutch houses, till you reach the pub. Or, you can go by boat from Westminster Pier to Kew Gardens, then visit the City Barge, and return to London by train.

BREAKFAST & SUNDAY BRUNCH

FOX AND ANCHOR, 115 Charterhouse St., E.C.1. Tel. 071/253-4838.
> **Cuisine:** ENGLISH. **Reservations:** Required. **Tube:** Farringdon or Barbican.
> **$ Prices:** "The full house" breakfast £7.50 ($13.90); steak breakfast £10.50 ($19.40). MC, V.
> **Open:** Breakfast Mon–Fri 6–10:30am; lunch Mon–Fri noon–2:15pm.

⭐ For a breakfast at its best, try this place that has been serving traders from the nearby famous Smithfield meat market since World War II.
Breakfasts are gargantuan, especially if you order "the full house," which

will have at least eight different items on your plate, including sausage, bacon, mushrooms, kidney, eggs, beans, black pudding, and a fried slice of bread, to mention just a few, along with unlimited tea or coffee, toast, and jam. Or perhaps you want a more substantial meal? Then you can have toast and jam, a filet steak with mushrooms, chips, tomatoes, and salad. Add a Black Velvet (champagne and Guinness) and the day is yours. Of course, in the modern British view, Guinness ruins champagne, but some people order it anyway—just to be traditional. More fashionable is a Buck's Fizz, with orange juice and champagne.

Butchers from the meat market, spotted with blood, still appear, as do nurses getting off their shift and clerks from The City who have been working at bookkeeping chores all night. Ale flows freely from 6 to 10:30am, since many of the drinkers are ending their night shifts.

GATE DINER, 184A Kensington Park Rd., W.11. Tel. 071/221-2649.
   Cuisine: ENGLISH/AMERICAN. **Reservations:** Recommended. **Tube:** Notting Hill Gate or Ladbroke Grove.
   $ Prices: Main brunch dishes £6.30–£7.60 ($11.65–$14.15). MC, V.
   Open: Brunch Sun 11:30am–4pm.
One of the best places in London for Sunday brunch is this American-style diner (see above). You can sample one of their special omelets, made with a choice of three fillings and served with home fries, or else you can order one of their many main dishes, including Scottish smoked salmon with cream cheese and bagels, or eggs Benedict. A "Mrs. Bellville" is a delectable dish of toasted muffins topped with Scottish smoked salmon, sour cream, and black caviar.

PICNIC FARE & WHERE TO FIND IT

Because of its "green lungs" (public parks), London is a great place for a picnic. All neighborhoods have a supermarket or a deli where you can purchase cold cuts, cheeses, and soft drinks to take away for a picnic.

However, if you'd like to follow an example—say, do as the queen of England might do if she were inviting guests for a picnic—then there is no better place than **Fortnum & Mason,** 181 Piccadilly, W.1. (tel. 071/734-8040), the world's most famous grocery store where you can find a wide array of food stuff. (See "The Parks of London" in Chapter 6 to decide where you'd like to enjoy your picnic.)

LONDON ATTRACTIONS

Dr. Johnson said, "When a man is tired of London, he is tired of life, for there is in London all that life can afford." In this chapter, we'll survey only a fraction of that life: ancient monuments, boutiques, Parliament debates, art galleries, Soho dives, museums, theaters, flea markets, and castles.

---

1. SUGGESTED ITINERARIES

IF YOU HAVE 1 DAY

Visit **Westminster Abbey, Big Ben,** and the **Houses of Parliament.** Then see **Poets' Corner** in the abbey, and the **changing of the guard.** Walk over to **10 Downing Street,** home of the prime minister. Have dinner at one of the restaurants in **Covent Garden.**

IF YOU HAVE 2 DAYS

Spend Day 1 as above. Spend Day 2 exploring the **British Museum,** considered the biggest and best in the world. Spend the afternoon visiting the **Tower of London** and seeing the collection of crown jewels.

IF YOU HAVE 3 DAYS

Spend Days 1 and 2 as above. On the third day visit the **National Gallery** in the morning. In the afternoon enjoy some time at **Madame Tussaud's Waxworks.**

IF YOU HAVE 5 DAYS

Spend Days 1 to 3 as above. On the morning of Day 4 head for **The City** to see Sir Christopher Wren's **St. Paul's Cathedral.** Take our walking tour of The City (see below) and visit the **Stock Exchange** and the **Guildhall.** In the late afternoon head down **King's Road** in **Chelsea** for some boutique hopping and have dinner at one of Chelsea's many restaurants.

On the fifth, explore the **Victoria and Albert Museum** in the morning, then head for the **Tate Gallery** for lunch. Spend the rest of the afternoon wandering through the gallery. Attend the theater that evening, or cram in as many West End shows as you can on the first 4 nights.

2. THE TOP ATTRACTIONS

London is not a city to visit hurriedly. It is so vast, so stocked with treasures that, on a cursory visit, a person will miss many of the highlights. For the traveler faced with an infinite number of important places to visit and a time clock running out, here are the top 10 sights of London. If you must, save the rest for "next time."

THE TOWER OF LONDON, Tower Hill, on the north bank of the Thames. Tel. 071/709-0765, ext 235.

⭐ This ancient fortress continues to pack 'em in because of its macabre associations with all the legendary figures who were imprisoned or executed here (or both). James Street once wrote, "there are more spooks to the square foot than in any other building in the whole of haunted Britain." Many consider the Tower to be the highlight of their sightseeing—so schedule plenty of time for it.

The fortress is actually a compound, in which the oldest and finest structure is the White Tower, begun by William the Conqueror. Here you can view the **Armouries,** the present collection that dates back to the reign of Henry VIII. A display of instruments of torture and execution will recall some of the most ghastly moments in the history of the Tower. At the Bloody Tower, the Little Princes (Edward V and the Duke of York) were allegedly murdered by their uncle, Richard III. Through Traitors' Gate passed such ill-fated, but romantic, figures as Robert Devereaux, a favorite of Elizabeth I, known as the second earl of Essex. At Tower Green, Anne Boleyn and Katharine Howard, two wives of Henry VIII, lost their lives. Lady Jane Grey, and her husband, Dudley, also were executed, along with such figures as Sir Thomas More.

To see the **Jewel House,** where the crown jewels are kept, go early as lines usually form by late morning. Ask one of the Yeoman Warders, the so-called Beefeaters in Tudor dress, to tell you how Colonel Blood almost made off with the crown and regalia in the late 17th century. Of the three English crowns, the Imperial State Crown is the most important—in fact, it's probably the most famous crown on earth. Made for Victoria for her coronation in 1838, it is today worn by Queen Elizabeth when she opens Parliament. Studded with some 3,000 jewels (principally diamonds), it contains the Black Prince's Ruby, worn by Henry V at Agincourt, the battle in 1415 when the English defeated the French. Don't miss the 530-carat Star of Africa, a cut diamond on the Royal Sceptre with Cross.

The Tower of London's evening ceremony, the **Ceremony of the Keys,** is the ceremonial locking up of the Tower for yet another day in its 900 years. Nothing stops the ceremony: During World War II, a bomb fell within the castle walls during the ceremony and nobody flinched—but the Tower was locked up 2 minutes late. The Beefeater will explain the significance of the ceremony. For free tickets, write to the Yeoman Clerk, Tower of London, London EC3N 4AB, and request a specific date, but also list alternative dates. At least 6 weeks' notice is required. All requests must be accompanied by a stamped, self-addressed envelope (British stamps only) or two International Reply Coupons. With ticket in hand, you'll be admitted by a Yeoman Warder around 9:35pm.

There are also six ravens, all registered as official Tower residents and each fed an exact 6 ounces of rations per day. According to a legend, London will stand as long as

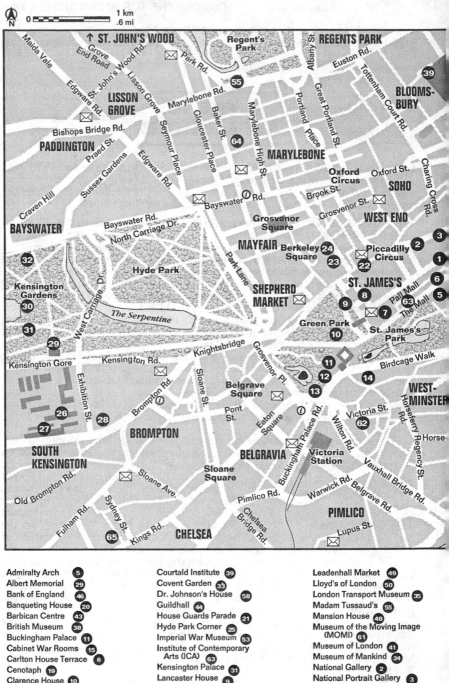

Admiralty Arch	**5**
Albert Memorial	**29**
Bank of England	**46**
Banqueting House	**20**
Barbican Centre	**43**
British Museum	**38**
Buckingham Palace	**11**
Cabinet War Rooms	**15**
Carlton House Terrace	**6**
Cenotaph	**19**
Clarence House	**10**

Courtald Institute	**39**
Covent Garden	**33**
Dr. Johnson's House	**58**
Guildhall	**44**
House Guards Parade	**21**
Hyde Park Corner	**25**
Imperial War Museum	**53**
Institute of Contemporary Arts (ICA)	**63**
Kensington Palace	**31**
Lancaster House	**9**

Leadenhall Market	**49**
Lloyd's of London	**50**
London Transport Museum	**35**
Madam Tussaud's	**55**
Mansion House	**48**
Museum of the Moving Image (MOMI)	**61**
Museum of London	**41**
Museum of Mankind	**24**
National Gallery	**2**
National Portrait Gallery	**3**

CENTRAL LONDON ATTRACTIONS

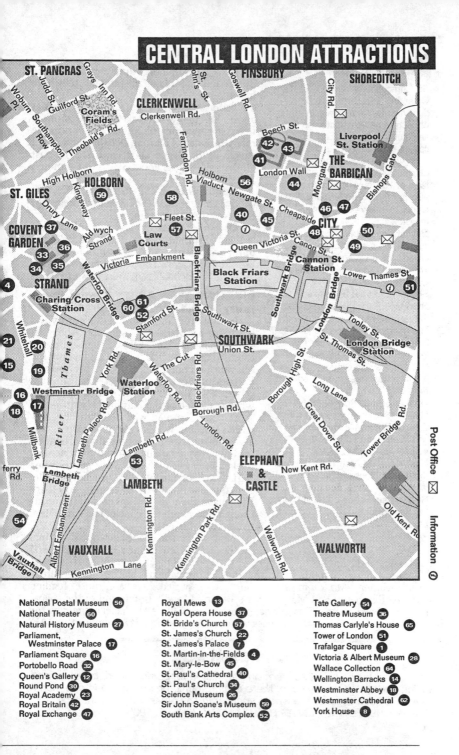

National Postal Museum 56	Royal Mews 13	Tate Gallery 54
National Theater 60	Royal Opera House 37	Theatre Museum 36
Natural History Museum 27	St. Bride's Church 57	Thomas Carlyle's House 65
Parliament, Westminster Palace 17	St. James's Church 22	Tower of London 51
	St. James's Palace 7	Trafalgar Square 1
Parliament Square 16	St. Martin-in-the-Fields 4	Victoria & Albert Museum 28
Portobello Road 32	St. Mary-le-Bow 45	Wallace Collection 64
Queen's Gallery 12	St. Paul's Cathedral 40	Wellington Barracks 14
Round Pond 30	St. Paul's Church 34	Westminster Abbey 18
Royal Academy 23	Science Museum 26	Westmnster Cathedral 62
Royal Britain 42	Sir John Soane's Museum 59	York House 8
Royal Exchange 47	South Bank Arts Complex 52	

❓ DID YOU KNOW ... ?

- Sir Christopher Wren's St. Paul's Cathedral is the fifth church dedicated to the patron saint of London to be constructed on the same spot—the first English cathedral built by one architect.
- A grocer's daughter from Lincolnshire, Margaret Thatcher, lived at 10 Downing Street, along with her millionaire husband, Denis, longer than any other prime minister.
- Covent Garden once had so many Turkish baths and brothels it was called "the great square of Venus."
- The famous May Fairs launched by Lord St. Albans in 1686 at Shepherd Market became so shocking for their bawdiness that they were eventually suppressed.
- The richest man in the world, the Sultan of Brunei, owns the landmark art deco Dorchester Hotel and issued orders to restore it until it was "the greatest hotel in the world."
- Franklin Delano Roosevelt (1882–1945) honeymooned with Eleanor at Brown's Hotel which had been launched by a manservant of Lord Byron.
- Nash's Marble Arch (1827), one of the most famous of London landmarks, was banned from Buckingham Palace because it was too narrow for the royal coaches to pass through.

those black, ominous birds remain in the Tower and so, to be on the safe side, they have had their wings clipped.

Tours are given by the Yeoman Warders at about 30-minute intervals and last about 1 hour, starting from the Middle Tower near the main entrance. The tour includes the Chapel Royal of St. Peter and Vincula. The last guided walk starts about 3:30pm in summer, 2:30pm in winter.

Admission: £5.50 ($10.20) adults, £3 ($5.55) children; £15 ($27.75) family ticket for five; free for children under 5. **Open:** Tower Nov–Feb Mon–Sat 9:30am–5pm; Mar–Oct Mon–Sat 9:30am–6pm, Sun 9:30am–6pm. **Closed:** Tower Dec 24–26, New Year's Day, Good Friday. **Tube:** Tower Hill. **Boat:** From Westminster Pier.

WESTMINSTER ABBEY, Broad Sanctuary, S.W.1. Tel. 071/222-7110.

Nearly every figure in English history has left his or her mark on Westminster Abbey. In 1065 the Saxon king, Edward the Confessor, founded the Benedictine abbey and rebuilt the old minster church on this spot, overlooking Parliament Square. The first English king crowned in the abbey was Harold in 1066, who was killed at the Battle of Hastings that same year. The man who defeated him, Edward's cousin, William the Conqueror, was also crowned at the abbey; the coronation tradition has continued to the present day, broken only twice by Edward V and Edward VIII. The essentially Early English Gothic structure existing today owes more to Henry III's plans than to any other sovereign, although many architects, including Wren, have made contributions.

Built on the site of the ancient lady chapel in the early 16th century, the **Henry VII** Chapel is one of the loveliest in Europe, with its fan vaulting, Knights of Bath banners, and Torrigiani-designed tomb of the king himself over which is placed a 15th-century Vivarini painting, *Madonna and Child*. Also buried here are those feuding half-sisters, Elizabeth I and Mary Tudor ("Bloody Mary"). In one end of the chapel you can stand on Cromwell's memorial stone and view the RAF chapel containing the Battle of Britain memorial stained-glass window, unveiled in 1947 to honor the RAF.

IMPRESSIONS

In the way of things to do, see, bet on, buy, listen to, participate in, travel far and near for, and spend money upon, there is more going on in England in one month than is advertised for the whole summer in any other country of Europe.
—JANET FLANNER, *LETTER FROM LONDON*, JUNE 11, 1938

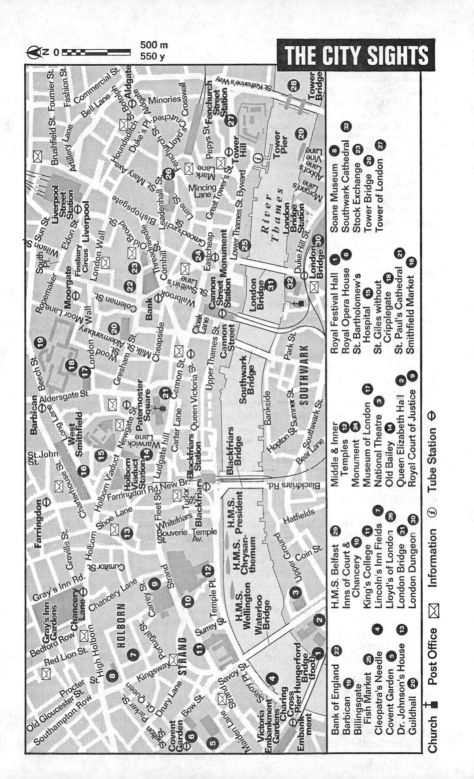

THE CITY SIGHTS

500 m
550 y

N

River Thames

SOUTHWARK

HOLBORN

STRAND

Bank of England ㉒
Barbican ⑲
Billingsgate
Fish Market ㉕
Cleopatra's Needle ⑤
Covent Garden ⑤
Dr. Johnson's House ⑳
Guildhall

H.M.S. Belfast ㉙
Inns of Court &
Chancery ⑩
King's College ⑪
Lincoln's Inn Fields ⑦
Lloyd's of London ㉖
London Bridge ㉛
London Dungeon ㉚

Middle & Inner
Temples ⑫
Monument ㉔
Museum of London ③
National Theatre ⑰
Old Bailey ⑭
Queen Elizabeth Hall ②
Royal Court of Justice ⑨

Royal Festival Hall ①
Royal Opera House ⑥
St. Bartholomew's
Hospital ⑮
St. Giles without
Cripplegate ⑱
St. Paul's Cathedral ㉑
Smithfield Market ⑯

Soane Museum ⑧
Southwark Cathedral ㉓
Stock Exchange ㉝
Tower Bridge ㉘
Tower of London ㉗

Church ✠   Post Office ⊠   Information ⓘ   Tube Station ⊖

You can also visit the most hallowed spot in the abbey, the shrine of Edward the Confessor (canonized in the 12th century). In the saint's chapel is the Coronation Chair, made at the command of Edward I in 1300 to contain the Stone of Scone. Scottish kings were once crowned on this stone (in 1950 the Scots stole it back, but it was later returned to its position in the abbey).

Another noted spot in the abbey is **Poets' Corner,** to the right of the entrance to the Royal Chapel, with monuments to Chaucer, Shakespeare, "O Rare Ben Johnson" (his name misspelled), Samuel Johnson, the Brontë sisters, Thackeray, Dickens, Tennyson, Kipling, even the American Longfellow. The most stylized monument is Sir Jacob Epstein's sculptured bust of William Blake. One of the more recent tablets commemorates the poet Dylan Thomas.

Statesmen and men of science—such as Disraeli, Newton, Charles Darwin—are also interred in the abbey or honored by monuments. Near the west door is the 1965 memorial to Sir Winston Churchill. In the vicinity of this memorial is the tomb of the Unknown Soldier, symbol of British dead in World War I. Some totally obscure personages are also buried in the abbey, including an abbey plumber.

Don't overlook the 13th-century **chapter house,** where Parliament used to meet. And even more fascinating are the treasures in the **museum** in the Norman undercroft (crypt), part of the monastic buildings erected between 1066 and 1100. The collection includes effigies—figures in wax, such as that of Nelson, and wood carvings of early English royalty. Along with the wax figures are ancient documents, old religious vestments (such as the cope worn at the coronation of Charles II), the sword of Henry V, and the famous Essex Ring that Elizabeth I is supposed to have given to her favorite earl.

Off the Cloisters, **College Garden** is the oldest garden in England, under cultivation for more than 900 years. Surrounded by high walls, flowering trees dot the lawns, and park benches provide comfort where you can hardly hear the roar of passing traffic.

The only time photography is allowed in the abbey is Wednesday evenings in the Royal Chapels. On Sunday the Royal Chapels are closed, but the rest of the church is open unless service is being conducted. For times of services, phone the Chapter Office (tel. 071/222-5152). Up to six super-tours of the abbey are conducted by the vergers Monday to Friday, beginning at 10am.

Admission: Royal Chapels, Royal Tombs, Coronation Chair, Henry VII Chapel, £2.60 ($4.80) adults, 60p ($1.10) children. Royal Chapels free Wed evenings.

Open: Mon–Fri 9:20am–4pm, Sat 9:30am–2pm and 3:45–5pm; Royal Chapels Wed 6–7:45pm. **Tube:** Westminster or St. James's Park.

HOUSES OF PARLIAMENT, Westminster Palace, Old Palace Yard, S.W.1. Tel. 071/219-472 for the House of Commons, or 071/219-3107 for the House of Lords.

These are the spiritual opposite of the Tower; they are the stronghold of Britain's democracy, the assemblies that effectively trimmed the sails of royal power. Both Houses (Commons and Lords) are in the formerly royal Palace of Westminster, the king's residence until Henry VIII moved to Whitehall.

The debates are often lively and controversial in the House of Commons (seats are at a premium during crises). The chances of getting into the House of Lords when it's in session are generally better than they are in the more popular House of Commons, where even the queen isn't allowed. The old guard of the palace informs me that the peerage speak their minds more freely and are less likely to adhere to party line than their counterparts in the Commons.

The present Houses of Parliament were built in 1840, but the Commons chamber was bombed and destroyed by the Luftwaffe in 1941. The 320-foot tower that houses Big Ben, however, remained standing and the "symbol of London" continues to strike its chimes. "Big Ben," incidentally, was named after Sir Benjamin Hall, a cabinet minister distinguished only by his long-windedness.

Except for the Strangers' Galleries, the two Houses of Parliament are presently closed to tourists. To be admitted to the Strangers' Galleries, you have to join a public queue outside the St. Stephen's entrance, and often there is considerable delay before the head of the public queue is admitted. You might speed matters up by applying at the American Embassy or the Canadian High Commission for a special pass, but this, too, is cumbersome. Besides, the embassy has only four tickets for daily distribution, so you might as well stand in line.

Admission: Free.

Open: House of Lords Mon–Thurs from about 3pm and on some Fridays (check by phone). House of Commons, open to the public Mon–Thurs from 4pm and Fri 9:30am–3pm. Join the "queue" at St. Stephen's entrance. Debates often continue into the night. **Tube:** Westminster.

THE BRITISH MUSEUM, Great Russell St., W.C.1. Tel. 071/636-1555.

The British Museum shelters one of the most comprehensive collections of art and artifacts in the world, including countless treasures of ancient and modern civilizations. To storm this bastion in a day is a formidable task, but there are riches to see even on a cursory first visit, among them the Asian collections (the finest assembly of Islamic pottery outside the Islamic world), the finest collection of Chinese porcelain in Europe, the best holdings of Indian sculpture outside India and Pakistan, and the Prehistoric and Romano-British collections, among many others. Basically, the overall storehouse splits into the national collections of antiquities; prints and drawings; coins, medals, and banknotes; and ethnography.

As you enter the front hall, head first to the Assyrian Transept on the ground floor, where you'll find the winged and human-headed bulls and lions that once guarded the gateways to the palaces of Assyrian kings. Nearby is the Black Obelisk of Shalmaneser III (858–824 B.C.), tribute from Jehu, King of Israel. From here, continue into the angular hall of Egyptian sculpture to see the Rosetta Stone, whose discovery led to the deciphering of the mysterious hieroglyphs, explained in a wall display behind the stone.

Also on the ground floor is the Duveen Gallery, housing the Elgin Marbles, consisting chiefly of sculptures from the Parthenon. The frieze shows a ceremonial procession that took place in Athens every four years. Of the 92 metopes from the Parthenon, 15 are housed today in the British Museum.

The classical sculpture galleries also holds a caryatid from the Erechtheum, a temple started in 421 B.C. and dedicated to Athena and Poseidon. Displayed here, too, are sculptures from the Mausoleum at Halicarnassus (one of the Seven Wonders of the Ancient World), built for Mausolus, ruler of Caria, who died around 350 B.C. Look also for the blue-and-white Portland Vase, considered the finest example of ancient cameo carving, which was made in the 1st century B.C. or A.D.

The Department of Medieval and Later Antiquities has its galleries on the first floor (second floor to Americans), reached by the main staircase. Of its exhibitions, the Sutton Hoo Anglo-Saxon ship burial, discovered in Suffolk, is, in the words of an expert, "the richest treasure ever dug from English soil," containing gold jewelry, armor, weapons, bronze bowls and caldrons, silverware, and the inevitable drinking horn of the Norse culture. No body was found, although the tomb is believed to be that of a king of East Anglia who died in the 7th century.

The featured attractions of the upper floor are the Egyptian Galleries, especially the mummies. Egyptian room 63 is extraordinary, looking like the props for *Cleopatra,* with its cosmetics, domestic utensils, toys, tools, and other work. Some items of Sumerian art, unearthed from the Royal Cemetery at Ur (southern Iraq), lie in a room beyond: a queen's bull-headed harp (oldest ever discovered); a queen's sledge (oldest known example of a land vehicle); and a figure of a he-goat on its hind legs, crafted about 2500 B.C. In the Iranian room rests "The Treasure of the Oxus," a hoard of riches, perhaps a temple deposit, ranging from the 6th to the 3rd century B.C., containing unique collections of goldsmith work, such as a nude youth, signet rings, a fish-shaped vase, and votive plaques.

If you want to know more about this treasure trove, I recommend M. L. Caygill's *Treasures of the British Museum,* which gives a detailed account of the major treasures and summaries of departmental collections.

Some of the treasures from the **British Library** (tel. 071/636-1544), one of the world's greatest libraries, are on display in the exhibition galleries in the east wing of the British Museum building. Western illuminated manuscripts are displayed in the Grenville Library. Notable exhibits are the Benedictional (in Latin) of St. Ethelwold, Bishop of Winchester (963–984), the Luttrell Psalter, and the Harley Golden Gospels of about 800.

In the Manuscript Salon are manuscripts of historical and literary interest. Items include two of the four surviving copies of King John's Magna Carta (1215) and the Lindisfarne Gospels (an outstanding example of the work of Northumbrian artists in the earliest period of English Christianity, written and illustrated about 698). Almost every major literary figure, such as Dickens, Austen, Charlotte Brontë, and Yeats, is represented in the English literature section. Also on display are historical autographs, including Nelson's last letter to Lady Hamilton and the journals of Captain Cook.

In the King's Library, where the library of King George III is housed, the history of the book is illustrated by notable specimens of early printing, including the Diamond Sutra of 868, the first dated example of printing, as well as the Gutenberg Bible, the first book ever printed from movable type, from 1455.

In the center of the gallery is an exhibition of fine, 16th-century bookbindings. Beneath Roubiliac's 1758 statue of Shakespeare is a case of documents relating to the Bard, including a mortgage bearing his signature and a copy of the First Folio of 1623. The library's unrivaled collection of philatelic items, including the 1840 Great British Penny Black and the rare 1847 post office issues of Mauritius, are also to be seen.

The library regularly mounts special temporary exhibitions, usually in the Crawford Room off the Manuscript Salon. The opening times of the British Library's exhibition galleries are the same as those of the museum and admission is free.

At Burlington Gardens, W.1 (tel. 071/437-2224), the **Museum of Mankind** houses the Ethnography Department of the British Museum, showing the art and culture of the indigenous peoples of many parts of the world. Hours are the same as at the main museum and admission is free. (The Café de Colombia within the Museum of Mankind closes a half hour before the museum itself.) Tube: Piccadilly.

Admission: Free.

Open: Mon–Sat 10am–5pm, Sun 2:30–6pm. (The galleries start to close 10 minutes earlier.) **Closed:** Jan 1, Good Friday, first Mon in May, Dec 24–26. **Tube:** Holborn or Tottenham Court Road.

MADAME TUSSAUD'S, Marylebone Rd., N.W.1. Tel. 071/935-6861.

In 1770, an exhibition of life-size wax figures was opened in Paris by Dr. Curtius. He was soon joined by his niece, Strasbourg-born Marie Tussaud, who learned the secret of making lifelike replicas of the famous and the infamous. During the French Revolution, the head of almost every distinguished victim of the guillotine was molded by Madame Tussaud or her uncle.

After the death of Curtius, Madame Tussaud inherited the exhibition, and in 1802 she left France for England. For 33 years she toured the United Kingdom with her exhibition, and in 1835 settled on Baker Street. The exhibition was such a success that it practically immortalized her in her day; she continued to make portraits until she was 81 (she died in 1850).

While some of the figures on display today come from molds taken by the incomparable Madame Tussaud, the exhibition also introduces new images of whoever is *au courant*. An enlarged Grand Hall continues to house years of royalty and old favorites, as well as many of today's heads of state and political leaders. In the Chamber of Horrors, you can have the vicarious thrill of walking through a Victorian London street where special effects include the shadow terror of Jack the Ripper. The instruments and victims of death penalties contrast with present-day criminals portrayed within the confines of prison. You are invited to mingle with the more current stars in the garden party, "meeting" Dudley Moore and Jane Seymour.

"Super Stars" offers latest technologies in sound, light, and special effects combined with new figures in a celebration of success in the fields of film and sports. A popular attraction—200 years of Tussaud's treasures—opened in 1990.

Admission: £5.60 ($10.35) adults, £3.85 ($7.20) children under 16.
Open: Mon–Fri 10am–5:30pm, Sat–Sun 9:30am–5:30pm. Doors open earlier in summer. **Closed:** Christmas Day. **Tube:** Regent's Park.

TATE GALLERY, beside the Thames on Millbank, S.W.1. Tel. 071/821-1313.

⭐ The Tate houses the best groupings of British paintings from the 16th century on, as well as England's finest collection of modern art, the works of British artists born after 1860, together with foreign art from the impressionists onward. The number of paintings is staggering. If time permits, schedule two visits—one to see the classic English works, the other to take in the modern collection. Since only a portion of the collections can be shown simultaneously, works on display vary from time to time. However, the following are almost invariably on view.

The first giant among English painters, William Hogarth (1697–1764), is well represented, particularly by his satirical *O the Roast Beef of Old England* (known as *Calais Gate*) and the ruby-eyed *Satan, Sin, and Death.*

Two other famous 18th-century British painters are Sir Joshua Reynolds (1723–92) and Thomas Gainsborough (1727–88). Reynolds, the portrait painter, shines brightest when he's painting himself (three self-portraits hang side by side). Works here by Gainsborough, noted for his portraits as well as his landscapes, include his *Wooded Landscape with Peasant Resting* and *Edward Richard Gardiner,* one of his most celebrated portraits, plus *Sir Benjamin Truman* and *Giovanna Baccelli* (1782), both recently acquired.

In the art of J. M. W. Turner (1775–1851), the Tate possesses its greatest collection of the works of a single artist. Most of the paintings and watercolors exhibited were willed to the nation by Turner. In 1987, a new wing at the Tate, called Clore Gallery, was opened so that the entire bequest of the artist can be seen. Of his paintings of stormy seas, none is more horrifying than *Shipwreck* (1805).

In a nation of landscape painters, John Constable (1776–1837) stands out. His finest works include *Flatford Mill,* a scene from his native East Anglia, and in a different mood, the stormy sketch for *Hadleigh Castle.* American-born Sir Jacob Epstein became one of England's greatest sculptors, and some of his bronzes are owned and occasionally displayed by the Tate. Augustus John, who painted everybody from G. B. Shaw to Tallulah Bankhead, is also represented with portraits and sketches.

The Tate has many major paintings from both the 19th and 20th centuries, including Wyndham Lewis's portraits of Edith Sitwell and of Ezra Pound, and Paul Nash's *Voyages of the Moon.* One of the best of the English artists of the 20th century, Sir Stanley Spencer (1891–1959) is best represented by his two versions of *Resurrection* and three remarkable self-portraits. But the drawings of William Blake (1757–1827) attract the most attention. Blake, of course, was the incomparable mystical poet and illustrator of such works as *The Book of Job, The Divine Comedy,* and *Paradise Lost.*

In the modern collections, the Tate contains Matisse's *L'Escargot* and *The Inattentive Reader,* along with works by Dali, Chagall, Modigliani, Munch, Ben Nicholson (large collection of his works), and Dubuffet. The different periods of Picasso bloom in *Woman in a Chemise* (1905), *Three Dancers* (1925), *Nude Woman in a Red Armchair* (1932), *Goat's Skull, Bottle, and Candle* (1952), and *Reclining Nude* (1968).

Truly remarkable is the room devoted to several enormous, somber, but rich abstract canvases by Mark Rothko, the group of paintings by Giacometti and sculptures by Giacometti (1901–66), and the paintings of two of England's best-known modern artists, Francis Bacon (especially gruesome, *Three Studies for Figures at the Base of a Crucifixion*) and Graham Sutherland (see his portrait of W. Somerset Maugham).

Rodin's world-famous *The Kiss* is on show as are sculptures by Henry Moore and Barbara Hepworth.

Downstairs is the internationally renowned restaurant (see Chapter 5), with murals by Rex Whistler, as well as a coffee shop.
Admission: Free, except special exhibitions.
Open: Mon–Sat 10am–5:50pm, Sun 2–5:50pm. **Tube:** Pimlico. **Bus:** No. 88 or 77A.

NATIONAL GALLERY, on north side of Trafalgar Square, W.C.2. Tel. 071/839-3321.

In an impressive neoclassic building, the National Gallery houses one of the most comprehensive collections of Western paintings, representing all the major schools from the 13th to the early 20th century. The largest part of the collection is devoted to the Italians, including the Sienese, Venetian, and Florentine masters.

Of the early Gothic works, the *Wilton Diptych* (French school, late 14th century) is the rarest treasure; it depicts Richard II being introduced to the Madonna and Child by John the Baptist and the Saxon king, Edward the Confessor.

A Florentine gem, a Virgin and grape-eating Bambino by Masaccio is displayed, as are works by Piero della Francesca, particularly *The Baptism*.

Matter and spirit meet in the haunting netherworld of the *Virgin of the Rocks,* a Leonardo da Vinci painting. Also shown are two other giants of the Renaissance—Michelangelo (represented by an unfinished painting, *The Entombment*), and Raphael (*The Ansidei Madonna,* among others).

Among the 16th-century Venetian masters, the most notable works include a rare *Adoration of the Kings* by Giorgione; *Bacchus and Ariadne* by Titian; *The Origin of the Milky Way* by Tintoretto, and *The Family of Darius Before Alexander* by Veronese.

Satellite rooms are filled with works by major Italian masters of the 15th century—such as Andrea Mantegna of Padua (*Agony in the Gardens*); his brother-in-law, Giovanni Bellini; and Botticelli (represented by *Mars and Venus, Adoration of the Magi,* and *Portrait of a Young Man*).

The painters of northern Europe are well represented. There is Jan van Eyck's portrait of G. Arnolfini and his bride, plus Pieter Brueghel the Elder's Bosch-influenced *Adoration.* The 17th-century pauper, Vermeer, is rich on canvas in a *Young Woman at a Virginal.* Fellow Delftite Pieter de Hooch comes on sublimely in a *Patio in a House in Delft.*

One of the big drawing cards of the National is its collection of Rembrandts. His *Self-Portrait at the Age of 34* shows him at the pinnacle of his life where his *Self-Portrait at the Age of 63* is more deeply moving and revealing. See also his *Portrait of Margaretha Trip, The Woman Taken in Adultery,* and the portrait of his mistress, Hendrickje Stoffels.

Part of the prolific output of Peter Paul Rubens can be seen, notably his *Peace and War,* the *Rape of the Sabine Women,* and *Samson and Delilah.*

Five of the greatest of the homegrown artists—Constable, Turner, Reynolds, Gainsborough, and Hogarth—have masterpieces here along with the three giants of Spanish painting: Velázquez, El Greco, and Goya.

Other rooms are devoted to early 19th-century French painters, such as Delacroix and Ingres; the later 19th-century French impressionists, such as Manet, Monet, Renoir, and Degas; and postimpressionists such as Cézanne, Seurat, and Van Gogh.
Admission: Free.
Open: Mon–Sat 10am–6pm, Sun 2–6pm. **Closed:** Jan 1, Good Friday, May Day, Dec 24–26. **Tube:** Charing Cross or Leicester Square.

KENSINGTON PALACE, The Board Walk, Kensington Gardens, W.8. Tel. 071/937-9561.

Home of the state apartments, some of which were used by Queen Victoria, the palace is located at the far western end of Kensington Gardens; the entrance is from The Board Walk. Acquired by William III (William of Orange) in 1689 and remodeled by Sir Christopher Wren, George II, who died in 1760, was the last king to use it as a royal residence.

The most interesting chamber is Queen Victoria's bedroom. In this room, on June 20, 1837, she was aroused from her sleep to learn that she had ascended the throne, following the death of her uncle, William IV. In the anteroom are memorabilia from Victoria's childhood—a dollhouse and a collection of her toys. As you wander through the apartments, be sure to admire the many fine paintings from the Royal Collection.

A special attraction is the Court Dress Collection, which shows restored rooms from the 19th century, including Queen Victoria's birthroom and a series of room settings with the appropriate court dress of the day, from 1760 to 1950. However, a more modern dress captures the attention of most visitors—the wedding dress worn by the Princess of Wales on July 29, 1981.

The palace gardens, originally the private park of royalty, adjoin Hyde Park and are also open to the public for daily strolls around Round Pond, near the heart of Kensington Gardens. Also in Kensington Gardens is the Albert Memorial, honoring Queen Victoria's consort. Facing Royal Albert Hall, the statue reflects the ostentation of the Victorian era.

Admission: £3.75 ($6.95) adults, £2.50 ($4.65) children.

Open: Mon–Sat 9am–5pm, Sun 1–5pm. **Tube:** Queensway or Bayswater on the north side of the gardens, or High Street Kensington on the south side. Then you'll have to walk a bit.

ST. PAUL'S CATHEDRAL, St. Paul's Churchyard, E.C.4. Tel. 071/248-2705.

During World War II, news footage in America showed the dome of St. Paul's Cathedral on fire due to the Nazi bombardment of London. That it survived at all is miraculous. But St. Paul's is accustomed to calamity, having been burned down three times and destroyed once by invading Norsemen. It was in the Great Fire of 1666 that the old St. Paul's was razed, making way for a new structure designed (after many mishaps and rejections) by Sir Christopher Wren.

The masterpiece of this great architect was erected between 1675 and 1710. Its classical dome dominates The City's square mile. Inside, the cathedral is laid out like a Latin cross, containing few art treasures (Grinling Gibbons's choir stalls are an exception) but many monuments, including one to the "Iron Duke" and a memorial chapel to American service personnel who lost their lives in World War II while stationed in the United Kingdom. Encircling the dome is the Whispering Gallery, where discretion in speech is advised. In the crypt lie not only Wren but also the Duke of Wellington and Lord Nelson. A fascinating Diocesan Treasury was opened in 1981.

Don't forget that you can climb to the very top of the dome for a spectacular 360-degree view of London.

St. Paul's is an Anglican cathedral with daily services held at 8am and 5pm. Sunday services are at 10:30 and 11:30am and 3:15pm.

Admission: Cathedral free; guided tours £5 ($9.25) adults, £2.50 ($4.65) children; ambulatory £1 ($1.85).

Open: Cathedral Mon–Sun 8am–6pm; crypt and galleries Mon–Fri 11am–4:15pm. **Tube:** St. Paul's.

VICTORIA AND ALBERT MUSEUM, Cromwell Rd., S.W.7. Tel. 071/589-6371.

Named after Queen Victoria and her husband, this fine museum is devoted to the applied art of many nations and periods. It's also one of the most difficult to explore, as many of the most important exhibits are so small that they can easily be overlooked.

The medieval holdings include many treasures, such as the Eltenberg Reliquary (Rhenish, second half of the 12th century). In the shape of a domed, copper-gilt church, it is enriched with champlevé enamel and set with walrus-ivory carvings of Christ and the Apostles. Other exhibits here include the Early English Gloucester Candlestick, the Byzantine Veroli Casket, with its ivory panels based on Greek plays, and the Syon Cope, a highly valued embroidery made in England in the early 14th century. The Gothic tapestries, including the Devonshire ones depicting hunting scenes, are displayed in another gallery. An area devoted to Islamic art contains the Ardabil carpet from 16th-century Persia (320 knots per square inch).

Renaissance art in Italy includes a Donatello marble relief, *The Ascension;* a small terra-cotta statue of the Madonna and Child by Antonio Rossellino; a marble group, *Samson and a Philistine,* by Giovanni Bologna; and a wax model of a slave by Michelangelo. The highlight of 16th-century art from the continent is the marble group *Neptune with Triton,* by Bernini. The cartoons by Raphael, which were conceived as designs for tapestries for the Sistine Chapel, are owned by the queen and can also be seen.

A most unusual, huge, and impressive exhibit is the Cast Courts, with life-size plaster models of ancient and medieval statuary and architecture, made from molds formed over the originals.

Of rooms devoted to English furniture and decorative art from the 16th to the mid-18th centuries, the most outstanding exhibit is the Bed of Ware, big enough for eight. In the galleries of portrait miniatures, two of the rarest ones are by Hans Holbein the Younger (one of Anne of Cleves, another of a Mrs. Pemberton). In the painting galleries are many works by Constable, including his *Flatford Mill,* a well-known scene from his native East Anglia. All paintings, prints, drawings, and photographs are in the new Henry Cole wing.

When you're ready for a break, a restaurant serves traditional English snacks and meals, and two museum shops sell gifts, posters, cards, and books.

Admission: Free, but donations of £3 ($5.55) suggested.
Open: Mon–Sat 10am–5pm, Sun 2:30–5:50pm. **Tube:** South Kensington.

3. MORE ATTRACTIONS

For those with more time to get acquainted with London, we'll continue our exploration of this sight-filled city.

ROYAL LONDON

From Trafalgar Square, stroll down the wide, tree-flanked avenue known as The Mall toward **Buckingham Palace,** the heart of Royal London, where English kings and queens have lived since the days of Victoria. Three parks—St. James's, Green, and the Buckingham Palace Gardens (private)—blanket the center of this area, where you'll find a memorial honoring Victoria. You can tell if Her Majesty is at home by whether the Royal Standard is flying on the flagstaff. You can't, of course, drop in for a visit, but you can peep through the railing into the front yard.

The palace was built as a red-brick country house for the notoriously rakish duke of Buckingham. In 1762, it was bought by King George III, who needed room for his 15 children. Since then, the building has been expanded, remodeled, faced with Portland stone, and bombed twice (during the Blitz). Today it stands 360 feet long in a 40-acre garden and contains 600 rooms.

London's most popular daily pageant, particularly with North American tourists, is the **Changing of the Queen's Guard** in the forecourt of Buckingham Palace. This ceremony is perhaps the finest example of military pageantry extant. The troops are from the Guards Division, Britain's elite equivalent of the United States Marines. The different regiments are distinguished by the plumes worn on the headdress: white for the Grenadiers, red for the Coldstreams, blue for the Irish, green and white for the Welsh. The Scots wear no plumes. **Tube:** St. James's Park or Green Park.

In the **Queen's Gallery,** S.W.1. (entrance on Buckingham Palace Road; tel. 071/930-4832), you can see a sampling of the royal family's art collection. Exhibitions change yearly, but the queen's collection contains an unsurpassed range

---

⭐ **FROMMER'S FAVORITE**
LONDON EXPERIENCES

Watching the Sun Set at Waterloo Bridge Waterloo Bridge, evoking memories of the Vivien Leigh/Robert Taylor film of the same name, is an ideal place to watch the sun set over Westminster.

Eating a Pub Lunch Take lunch in the bustling, overcrowded atmosphere of a London pub, vying for elbow space at the bar as you place your order for a roast beef sandwich and a mug of lager.

Enjoying a Traditional English Tea Nothing rounds out an afternoon quite like it—and nothing is more typically British. Try the Hotel Goring, dating from 1910, where you'll view the small garden, enjoy "finger" sandwiches, and sample a special Ceylon blend tea.

Brass Rubbing Re-create England's age of chivalry—all those costumed ladies and knights in armor—in medieval brasses. You can spend hours rubbing wax over paper taped over the brass to produce a picture to frame. One place to do this is the crypt of St. Martin-in-the-Fields in Trafalgar Square.

Spending a Night at a West End Theater In the theatrical capital of the world, this stage was for Shakespeare and Marlowe, but today it is also the stage for next year's Broadway hit.

---

of royal portraits, including the well-known profile of Henry V; the companion portraits of Elizabeth I as a girl and her brother, Edward VI; four fine Georgian pictures by Zoffany; two portraits of Queen Alexandra from Sandringham; plus paintings of Queen Elizabeth II and other members of the royal family. Admission to the gallery costs £2 ($3.70) for adults, £1 ($1.85) for children. It's open Tuesday to Saturday and bank holidays from 10am to 5pm, and Sunday from 2 to 5pm; closed Monday, except bank holidays. **Tube:** Green Park or St. James's.

You can get a close look at Queen Elizabeth's coronation carriage at the **Royal Mews,** on Buckingham Palace Road, S.W.1 (tel. 071/930-4832). Her Majesty's State Coach, built in 1761 to the designs of Sir William Chambers, is decorated with emblems and other paintings on the panels and doors executed by Cipriani. The coach, traditionally drawn by eight gray horses, was formerly used by sovereigns when they traveled to open Parliament in person and on other state occasions. Queen Elizabeth used it in 1953 for her coronation and in 1977 for her Silver Jubilee Procession.

You'll also see many other official carriages here, including the new Australian coach, Glass coach, and Scottish and Irish state coaches. The queen's carriage horses are also housed here. Admission costs £1.30 ($2.40) for adults, 70p ($1.20) for children. It is open Wednesday from October 1 to March 31 from noon to 4pm; Wednesday and Thursday from April 1 to July 11 from noon to 4pm, and Wednesday through Friday from July 17 to September 30 from noon to 4pm. **Tube:** Green Park or St. James's.

OFFICIAL LONDON

Whitehall, S.W.1, the seat of the British government, grew up on the grounds of Whitehall Palace and was turned into a royal residence by Henry VIII. Beginning at Trafalgar Square, Whitehall extends southward to Parliament Square (Houses of Parliament and Westminster Abbey, described earlier). Along it you'll find the Home Office, the Old Admiralty Building, and the Ministry of Defense.

Visitors today can see the **Cabinet War Rooms,** the bomb-proof bunker rooms, just as they were left by Winston Churchill and the British government at the end of World War II. The Imperial War Museum studied photographs to replace everything exactly as it had been, including notepads, files, and typewriters—right down to pencils and paper-clips. You can see the Map Room with its huge wall maps, the Atlantic map a mass of pinholes (each hole represents at least one convoy). Next door is Churchill's bedroom-cum-office, which has a bed and a desk with two BBC microphones on it for his broadcasts of those famous speeches that stirred the nation.

The Transatlantic Telephone Room, to give it its full title, is little more than a broom cupboard, but it had the Bell Telephone Company's special scrambler phone, called Sig-Saly, and it was where Churchill conferred with Roosevelt. The scrambler equipment was actually too large to house in the bunker, so it was placed in the basement of Selfridges Department Store on Oxford Street; the telephone was removed at the end of the war.

The entrance to the War Rooms (tel. 071/930-6961) is by Clive Steps at the end of King Charles Street, S.W.1, off Whitehall near Big Ben. Visitors receive a cassette-recorded guided tour, and charges are £3.50 ($6.45) for adults and £1.75 ($3.25) for children. The rooms are open daily from 10am to 6pm (last admission at 5:25pm); they're closed on New Year's Day, Christmas holidays, and state occasions (sometimes on short notice). **Tube:** Westminster.

To get to the **Cenotaph** (honoring the dead in two world wars), turn down Downing Street to the modest little town house at **No. 10,** flanked by two bobbies. Walpole was the first prime minister to live here: Churchill the most famous.

Nearby is the **Horse Guards Building,** Whitehall, S.W.1 (tel. 071/930-4466, ext. 2396), which is now the headquarters, Household Division and London District. There has been a guard change here since 1649, when the site was the entrance to the old Palace of Whitehall. Watch the Queen's Lifeguards ceremony at 11am (at 10am on Sunday), when 12 mounted troopers arrive from Knightsbridge Barracks. If you are at Hyde Park Corner at 10:30am, you can follow them. You can also see the hourly smaller change of the guard, when mounted troopers are changed. And at 4pm you can watch the evening inspection, when 10 unmounted troopers and 2 mounted troopers assemble in the courtyard. **Tube:** Westminster.

Across the street is Inigo Jones's **Banqueting House,** Palace of Whitehall, Horse Guards Avenue, S.W.1 (tel. 071/930-4179), site of the execution of Charles I. William and Mary accepted the crown of England here, but they preferred to live at Kensington Palace. The Banqueting House was part of Whitehall Palace, which burned to the ground in 1698, but the ceremonial hall escaped razing. Its most notable feature today is an allegorical ceiling painted by Peter Paul Rubens. Admission to the Banqueting House costs £2 ($3.70) for adults and £1.35 ($2.50) for children. Hours are Tuesday to Saturday from 10am to 5pm, Sunday from 2 to 5pm. **Tube:** Westminster.

Finally, you may want to stroll to Parliament Square for a view of **Big Ben,** the world's most famous timepiece. Big Ben is actually the name of the deepest and loudest bell, but it's become the common name for this clock tower on the Houses of Parliament. Opposite, in the gardens of Parliament Square, stands the statue of Churchill by Oscar Nemon. **Tube:** Westminster.

FINANCIAL LONDON

STOCK EXCHANGE, Visitors' Gallery Entrance, Old Broad St., E.C.2. Tel. 071/588-2355 (publicity department).

In terms of the number of stocks and shares listed, this is the largest stock exchange in the world. From the visitors' gallery, watch the dealers on the trading floor below while guides give talks and explain the functions and operations of the stock market. After each talk, there is a film on the financial world in the adjoining cinema. Reservations are required for the film. Admission is free. The Visitors' Gallery is open Monday to Friday 9:30am to 3:15pm. **Tube:** Bank.

LEGAL LONDON

The smallest borough in London, bustling **Holborn** (pronounced Hoburn) is often referred to as Legal London, the home of the city's barristers, solicitors, and law clerks. Holborn, which also houses the ancient Inns of Court—Gray's Inn, Lincoln's Inn, Middle Temple, and Inner Temple—was severely damaged in World War II. The razed buildings were replaced with modern offices, but the borough still retains pockets of its former days.

MIDDLE TEMPLE TUDOR HALL, Middle Temple Lane, E.C.4. Tel. 071/353-4355.

From the Victoria Embankment, Middle Temple Lane leads, between Middle and Inner Temple Gardens, to the area known as **The Temple,** named after the medieval order of the Knights Templar (originally formed by the Crusaders in Jerusalem in the 12th century). It was in the Inner Temple Gardens that Henry VI's barons are supposed to have picked the blooms of red and white roses and started the War of the Roses in 1430; today only members of the Temples and their guests are allowed to enter the gardens. But the Middle Temple contains a Tudor hall, completed in 1570, that is open to the public. It is believed that Shakespeare's troupe played *Twelfth Night* here in 1602. A table on view is said to have come from timber from Sir Francis Drake's *The Golden Hind.*

Admission: Free.
Open: Hall Mon–Fri 10am–noon and 3–4pm. **Tube:** Temple.

TEMPLE CHURCH, Middle Temple Lane, within the precincts of the Inner Temple, E.C.4.

One of three Norman "round churches" left in England, this was first completed in the 12th century—not surprisingly, it has been restored. Look for the knightly effigies and the Norman door, and take note of the circle of grotesque portrait heads, including a goat in a mortar board.

When you continue north on Middle Temple Lane to about where the Strand becomes Fleet Street going east, look for the memorial pillar called **Temple Bar,** which marks the boundary of the City.

Admission: Free.
Open: Mon–Fri 10am–4pm. **Tube:** Temple.

ROYAL COURTS OF JUSTICE, The Strand, W.C.2. Tel. 071/936-6000.

The Royal Courts of Justice stand north across the Strand. The building, completed in 1882 but designed in 13th-century style, was the home of such courts as admiralty, divorce, probate, chancery, appeals, and Queen's Bench. Leave the Royal Courts building by the rear door and you'll be on Carey Street, not far from New Square.

Admission: Free.
Open: Mon–Fri 10am–4pm. **Tube:** Temple.

LINCOLN'S INN, Carey St., W.C.2.

From Carey Street, you're in the vicinity of Lincoln's Inn, founded in the 14th century, whose chapel and gardens are well worth seeing. This ancient inn resembles colleges at Cambridge or Oxford and forms an important link in the architectural maze of London. The chapel was rebuilt around 1620 by Inigo Jones, and at one time Cromwell lived here.

To the west of the inn lies the late 17th-century square, one of the few such London areas still complete, called **Lincoln's Inn Fields.** Near the south of the fields on Kingsway is the **Old Curiosity Shop,** made famous by Charles Dickens.

Admission: Free.
Open: Chapel and gardens daily noon–2:30pm. **Tube:** Holborn.

STAPLE INN, High Holborn St., W.C.1.

If you proceed north on Chancery Lane to High Holborn, heading toward Gray's Inn, take a look at this old inn, near the Chancery Lane tube stop. This half-timbered edifice and eight other former Inns of Chancery are no longer in use in the legal world. Now lined with shops, it was built between 1545 and 1589 and has been rebuilt many times. Dr. Johnson moved here in 1759, the year *Rasselas* was published.

Tube: Chancery Lane.

GRAY'S INN, Gray's Inn Rd. (entrance on Theobald's Rd.), W.C.1.

Gray's Inn, north of High Holborn, is the fourth of the ancient Inns of Court still in operation. As you enter, you'll see a late-Georgian terrace lined with buildings that, like many of the other houses in the inns, are combined residences and offices. Gray's has been restored after being heavily damaged by World War II bombings. It contains a rebuilt Tudor Hall, but its greatest attraction is the tree-shaded lawn and handsome gardens, considered the best in the inns. The 17th-century atmosphere exists today only in the square. Francis Bacon, scientist and philosopher (1561–1626), was the most eminent tenant who resided here.

Admission: Free.

Tube: Chancery Lane.

OLD BAILEY (CENTRAL CRIMINAL COURT), on the corner of Old Bailey and Newgate St., E.C.4. Tel. 071/248-3277.

This courthouse replaced the infamous Newgate Prison, once the scene of public hangings and other forms of public "entertainment." Entry is strictly on a first-arrival basis, and guests queue up outside (where, incidentally, the final public execution took place in the 1860s). Courts 1 to 4, 17, and 18 are entered from Newgate Street, and the balance from Old Bailey (the street). To get here, travel east on Fleet Street, which becomes Ludgate Hill. Cross Ludgate Circus and turn left to the Old Bailey, a domed structure with the figure of Justice standing atop it.

Admission: Free. Children under 14 not admitted; ages 14–17 must be accompanied by responsible adult. No cameras or tape recorders allowed.

Open: Mon–Fri 10:20am–1pm and 1:50pm–4pm. **Tube:** Temple, Chancery Lane, or St. Paul's.

GUILDHALL, King St. in Cheapside, The City, E.C.2. Tel. 071/606-3030.

The present building was launched in 1411, but the Civic Hall of the Corporation of London has had a rough time, notably in the Great Fire of 1666 and the 1940 Blitz. The most famous tenants of the rebuilt Guildhall are Gog and Magog, two giants standing over 9 feet high. The present giants are third generation, because the original effigies burned in the London fire, and the next set were destroyed in 1940. Restoration has returned the Gothic grandeur to the hall, which is replete with a medieval porch entranceway; monuments to Wellington, Churchill, and Nelson; stained glass commemorating lord mayors and mayors; and shields honoring fishmongers, haberdashers, merchant tailors, ironmongers, and skinners—some of the major Livery Companies.

Admission: Free.

Open: Mon–Sat 2–4pm. **Tube:** Bank.

MUSEUMS

SIR JOHN SOANE'S MUSEUM, 13 Lincoln's Inn Fields, W.C.2. Tel. 071/405-2107.

This is the former home of Sir John Soane, an architect (1753–1837) who rebuilt the Bank of England (not the present structure, however). With his multilevels, fool-the-eye mirrors, flying arches, and domes, Soane was a master of perspective and a genius of interior space (his picture gallery, for example, is filled with three times the number of paintings a room of similar dimensions would be likely to hold). Don't miss William Hogarth's satirical series, *The Rake's Progress,* containing his much reproduced *Orgy,* and the satire on politics in the mid-18th century, *The Election.* Soane also filled his house with paintings (Watteau's *Les Noces,* Canaletto's large *Venetian Scene*) and classical sculpture. Finally, be sure to see the sarcophagus of Pharaoh Seti I, found in a burial chamber in the Valley of the Kings.

Admission: Free.
Open: Tues–Sat 10am–5pm. **Tour:** Sat 2:30pm. **Tube:** Chancery Lane or Holborn.

IMPERIAL WAR MUSEUM, Lambeth Rd., S.E.1. Tel. 071/735-8922.

Built around 1815, this large domed building, the former Bethlehem Royal Hospital for the Insane, or Bedlam, houses the museum's collections relating to the two world wars and other military operations involving the British and the Commonwealth since 1914. There are four floors of exhibitions, including the Large Exhibits Gallery, a vast area showing historical displays, two floors of art galleries, and a dramatic re-creation of London at war in the Blitz. You can see a Battle of Britain Spitfire, the rifle carried by Lawrence of Arabia, Hitler's political testament, as well as models, decorations, uniforms, photographs, and paintings. It's located just across the Thames.
Admission: £3 ($5.55) adults, £1.50 ($2.80) children.
Open: Mon–Sat 10am–6pm; Sun 2–5:50pm. **Tube:** Lambeth North or Elephant & Castle.

NATIONAL ARMY MUSEUM, Royal Hospital Rd., S.W.3. Tel. 071/730-0717.

Located in Chelsea, this museum traces the history of the British land forces, the Indian Army, and colonial land forces. Starting in 1485, the date of the formation of the Yeomen of the Guard, it also traces the saga of the forces of the East India Company beginning in 1602 and going up to Indian independence in 1947. The gory and glory is all here—everything from Florence Nightingale's lamp to the French Eagle captured in a cavalry charge at Waterloo, plus the staff cloak wrapped around the dying Wolfe at Québec. Naturally, there are the "cases of the heroes," mementos of such outstanding men as the dukes of Marlborough and Wellington. But the field soldier isn't neglected either: The Flanders to the Falklands gallery tells the soldier's story from the 1914–18 war through World War II and on to the conflict in the Falklands in 1982.
Admission: Free.
Open: Mon–Sat 10am–5:30pm, Sun 2–5:30pm. **Closed:** Jan 1, Good Friday, May bank holiday, Dec 24–26. **Tube:** Sloane Square.

APSLEY HOUSE, the Wellington Museum, 149 Piccadilly, Hyde Park Corner, W.1. Tel. 071/499-5676.

The former townhouse of the Iron Duke, the British general (1769–1852) who defeated Napoléon at the Battle of Waterloo and later became prime minister, was opened as a public museum in 1952. The building, designed by Robert Adam, was built in the late 18th century. In the vestibule, you'll find a colossal marble statue of Napoléon by Canova—ironic, to say the least; it was presented to the duke by King George IV.
In addition to the famous *Waterseller of Seville* by Velázquez, the Wellington collection includes Correggio's *Agony in the Garden,* Jan Steen's *The Egg Dance,* and Pieter de Hooch's *A Musical Party.* A large porcelain and china collection consists of a magnificent Sèvres porcelain Egyptian service originally made for Empress Joséphine and given by Louis XVIII to Wellington. Superb English silver and the extraordinary Portuguese centerpiece, a present from a grateful Portugal to its liberator, are also exhibited.
Admission: £2 ($3.70) adults, £1 ($1.85) children.
Open: Tues–Sun 11am–6pm. **Closed:** Jan 1, May Day, Dec 24–26. **Tube:** Hyde Park Corner.

MUSEUM OF LONDON, 150 London Wall, E.C.2. Tel. 071/600-3699.

In London's Barbican district near St. Paul's Cathedral, the Museum of London traces the history of London from prehistoric times to the present—through relics, costumes, maps, and models. Anglo-Saxons, Vikings, Normans—they're all here, arranged on two floors around a central courtyard. Exhibits are arranged so visitors can begin and end their chronological stroll through 250,000 years at the main entrance, and exhibits have quick labels for museum sprinters, more extensive ones for those who want to study, and still deeper details for scholars.

You'll see the death mask of Oliver Cromwell; the Great Fire of London in living color and sound; reconstructed Roman dining rooms; cell doors from Newgate Prison made famous by Charles Dickens; and an amazing shop counter with pre–World War II prices on the items. But the pièce de résistance is the lord mayor's coach, built in 1757 and weighing 3 tons. Still used each November in the Lord Mayor's Procession, this gilt-and-red, horse-drawn vehicle seems out of a fairy tale.

The museum, which opened in 1976, overlooks London's Roman and medieval walls and was built at a cost of some $18 million. It's an enriching experience for everybody. Free lectures on London's history are often given during lunch hours; ask at the entrance hall. You can reach the museum by going up to the elevated pedestrian precinct at the corner of London Wall and Aldersgate, 5 minutes from St. Paul's. There is also a restaurant, which overlooks a garden.

Admission: £3 ($5.55) for adults, £1.50 ($2.80) for children.
Open: Tues–Sat 10am–6pm, Sun 2–6pm. **Tube:** St. Paul's or Barbican.

LONDON'S TRANSPORT MUSEUM, The Piazza, Covent Garden, W.C.2. Tel. 071/379-6344.

Located in a restored Victorian building that used to house the flower market, horse buses, motorbuses, trams, trolleybuses, railway vehicles, models, maps, posters, photographs, and audiovisual displays illustrate the evolution of London's transport systems and how they have affected the growth of London. There are a number of unique working displays: You can put yourself in the driver's seat of a tube train, a tram, and a bus, and also operate full-size signaling equipment. The exhibits include a reconstruction of George Shillibeer's omnibus of 1829, a steam locomotive that ran on the world's first underground railway, and a coach from the first deep-level electric railway. The museum sells a variety of souvenirs (see "Shopping A to Z" in Chapter 7).

Admission: £2.50 ($4.80) adults, £1.20 ($2.20) children.
Open: Daily 10am–6pm (last admission at 5:15pm). **Closed:** Dec 24–26. **Tube:** Covent Garden, Leicester Square, or Charing Cross.

NATIONAL POSTAL MUSEUM, King Edward Building, King Edward St., E.C.1. Tel. 071/239-54200.

Actually part of the post office, this museum features permanent exhibitions of the stamps of Great Britain and the world. The special displays of stamps and postal history change every few months, according to certain themes.

Admission: Free.
Open: Mon–Thurs 10am–4:30pm, Fri 10am–4pm. **Tube:** St. Paul's or Barbican.

ROYAL AIR FORCE MUSEUM, Grahame Park Way, Hendon, N.W.9. Tel. 081/205-2266.

The Royal Force Museum, Britain's national museum of aviation containing one of the world's finest collections of historic aircraft, tells the story of flight through the display of more than 60 aircraft. The museum stands on 15 acres of the former airfield at Hendon in North London, and its main aircraft hall occupies two large hangars from World War I. The complex also includes a collection of famous bomber aircraft, including the Lancaster, Wellington, B17 Flying Fortress, Mosquito, and Vulcan.

In 1990, to celebrate the 50th anniversary of the Battle of Britain, the museum launched a major exhibition, the Battle of Britain Experience. Aircraft on display include the Spitfire, Hurricane, Gladiator, Blenheim, and Messerschmitt BF109. Features include cassette-tape tour guides and a flight simulator that allows visitors to experience flying an RAF Tornado.

The nearest British Rail station to the museum is Mill Hill Broadway. Access by road is via the A41, the A1, and the M2 Junction 4.

Admission: £4 ($7.40) adults, £2 ($3.70) children.
Open: Daily 10am–6pm. **Closed:** Jan 1 and Dec 24–26. **Tube:** Colindale.

SCIENCE MUSEUM, Exhibition Rd., S.W.7. Tel. 071/938-8000.

This museum traces the development of science and industry and their influence on everyday life. The collections are among the largest, most comprehensive, and most significant anywhere. On display is Stephenson's original Rocket, the tiny locomotive that beat all competitors in the Rainhill Trials and became the world's prototype railroad engine. You can also see Whittle's original jet engine and the Gloster aircraft, the first jet-powered British plane. A cavalcade of antique cars from the Stanley steam car to the yellow Rolls-Royce can be seen, side by side with carriages and vintage bicycles and motorcycles.

To help the visitor's understanding of science and technology, there are working models and video displays, including a hands-on gallery called Launch Pad. The East Hall welcomes visitors with an audiovisual slide show, and you can buy souvenirs at the shopping concourse.

Admission: £2.50 ($4.65) adults, £1 ($1.85) children ages 5–15.

Open: Mon–Sat 10am–6pm, Sun 11am–6pm. **Tube:** South Kensington. **Bus:** No. 14.

LINLEY SAMBOURNE HOUSE, 18 Stafford Terrace, W.8. Tel. 071/994-1019.

Step back into the days of Queen Victoria at this house, which has remained unchanged for more than a century. Part of a terrace built between 1868 and 1874, this is a five-story, Suffolk brick structure to which Linley Sambourne brought his bride (Sambourne was a draftsman who later became a cartoonist for *Punch*). The Sambourne family owned and occupied the house until 1980, when it was purchased by the Greater London Council and leased to the Victorian Society. From the moment you step into the entrance hall, you see a mixture of styles and clutter that typified Victorian decor, with a plush portière, a fireplace valance, stained glass in the backdoor, and a large set of antlers vying for attention.

Admission: £2 ($3.70) for adults; £1 ($1.85) children under 16.

Open: Mar–Oct Wed 10am–4pm, Sun 2–5pm. **Tube:** High Street Kensington.

JEWISH MUSEUM, Tavistock Sq., W.C.1. Tel. 071/388-4525.

In the precincts of the **Woburn House,** the major communal building for English Jewry, near Euston Station, you'll come across the hard-to-find Jewish Museum tucked away on a lovely square. Walk along Euston Road, and turn right onto Upper Woburn Place. When you reach Tavistock Square, turn right again, and there's the entrance. After you sign the guest book, you're guided up to the museum, a large salon filled with antiques relating to Jewish history.

Admission: Free.

Open: Apr–Sept Sun and Tues–Fri 10am–4pm. **Tube:** Euston, Russell Square, or Euston Square.

LONDON DESIGN MUSEUM, Butler's Wharf, Shad Thames, E.1. Tel. 071/403-6933.

The first museum in the world devoted to industrial design, this three-story building also houses a lecture theater, restaurant, bar, and library. Designs show the evolution of various items, such as the telephone exhibit, which ranges from one that might have been familiar to Alexander Graham Bell to a black Bakelite phone of the '30s and '40s. Computers allow you to "summon" biographies of famous designers, such as the Finnish designer Alvar Aalto. The museum constantly changes exhibitions. As you study the displays on each floor, notice the river view from the windows—you'll see Tower Bridge and the Tower of London.

Admission: £2.50 ($4.65), £1.50 ($2.80) children.

Open: Tues–Sun 11:30am–6:30pm. **Transportation:** Take the Design Museum boat from Tower Wharf (adjacent to Tower of London); the trip takes 3 minutes.

GALLERIES

NATIONAL PORTRAIT GALLERY, St. Martin's Place, W.C.2. Tel. 071/306-0055.

In a gallery of remarkable and unremarkable portraits, a few paintings tower over the rest, including Sir Joshua Reynolds's first portrait of Samuel Johnson ("a man of most dreadful appearance"), Nicholas Hilliard's miniature of Sir Walter Raleigh and a full-length Elizabeth I, along with the Holbein cartoon of Henry VIII (sketched for a family portrait that hung, before it was burned, in the Privy Chamber in Whitehall Palace). You'll also see a portrait of William Shakespeare (with gold earring, no less), which is claimed to be the most "authentic contemporary likeness" of its subject of any work yet known; a John Hayls portrait of Samuel Pepys; and even a portrait of Whistler. One of the most unusual pictures in the gallery—a group of the three Brontë sisters (Charlotte, Emily, Anne)—was painted by their brother, Branwell. An idealized portrait of Lord Byron by Thomas Phillips is here, as is a portrait of Aubrey Beardsley. For a finale, Princess Diana is on the Royal Landing.

The entrance to the museum is around the corner from the National Gallery on Trafalgar Square.

Admission: Free, except for special exhibitions.
Open: Mon–Fri 10am–5pm, Sat 10am–6pm, Sun 2–6pm. **Tube:** Charing Cross or Leicester Square.

WALLACE COLLECTION, Hertford House, Manchester Sq., W.1. Tel. 071/935-0687.

This outstanding collection of artworks bequeathed to the nation by Lady Wallace in 1897 is still displayed in the house of its founders, which is off Wigmore Street. There are important pictures by artists of all European schools, including Titian, Rubens, Van Dyck, Rembrandt, Hals, Velázquez, Murillo, Reynolds, Gainsborough, and Delacroix. Representing 18th-century France are paintings by Watteau, Boucher, and Fragonard, and sculpture, furniture, goldsmiths' work, and Sèvres porcelain. Also found are valuable collections of majolica and European and Asian arms and armor. Frans Hals's *Laughing Cavalier* is the most celebrated painting in the collection, but Pieter de Hooch's *A Boy Bringing Pomegranates* and Watteau's *The Music Party* are also well known. Other notable works include Canaletto's views of Venice (especially *Bacino di San Marco*), Rembrandt's *Titus*, Gainsborough's *Mrs. Robinson* (*Perdita*), and Boucher's portrait of the marquise de Pompadour.

Admission: Free.
Open: Mon–Sat 10am–5pm, Sun 2–5pm. **Closed:** Jan 1, Good Friday, first Mon in May, Dec 24–26. **Tube:** Bond Street.

COURTAULD INSTITUTE GALLERIES, Somerset House, the Strand, W.C.2. Tel. 071/873-2526.

The home of the University of London's art collection, the Courtauld is noted for its superb impressionist and postimpressionist works. It has eight works by Cézanne, including *A Man with a Pipe*. Other notables include Seurat's *La Poudreuse*, Van Gogh's self-portrait (with ear bandaged), a nude by Modigliani, Gauguin's *Day-Dreaming*, Monet's *Fall at Argenteuil*, Toulouse-Lautrec's delicious *Tête-à-Tête*, and Manet's *Bar at the Folies Bergère*. The galleries also feature classical works, including a *Virgin and Child* by Bernardino Luini, a Botticelli, a Giovanni Bellini, a Veronese, a triptych by the Master of Flemalle, works by Pieter Brueghel, Massys, Parmigianino, 32 oils by Rubens, oil sketches by Tiepolo, three landscapes by Kokoschka, and wonderful old-master drawings (especially Michelangelo and Rembrandt).

Admission: £3 ($5.55) adults, £1.50 ($2.80) children.
Open: Mon–Sat 10am–5pm, Sun 2–5pm. **Tube:** Charing Cross.

ROYAL ACADEMY OF ARTS, Piccadilly, W.1. Tel. 071/439-7438.

Founded in 1768, this is the oldest established society in Great Britain devoted solely to the fine arts. The academy is made up of a self-supporting, self-governing body of artists, who conduct art schools, hold exhibitions of the work of living artists, and organize loan exhibits of the arts of past and present periods. A summer exhibition, which has been held annually for 222 years, presents contemporary paintings, drawings, engravings, sculpture, and architecture. The academy occupies Burlington House, which was built in Piccadilly in the 1600s and is opposite Fortnum and Mason.

Admission: £1.50–£5 ($2.80–$9.25), depending on exhibition.
Open: Royal Academy Shop, restaurant, and exhibition hours daily 10am–6pm; framing workshop Mon–Fri 10am–5pm. **Tube:** Piccadilly Circus or Green Park. **Bus:** No. 9, 14, 19, 22, or 38.

HAYWARD GALLERY, South Bank Centre, S.E.1. Tel. 071/928-3144.
Opened by Queen Elizabeth II in 1968, this gallery presents a changing program of major exhibitions. The gallery forms part of the South Bank Centre, which also includes the Royal Festival Hall, the Queen Elizabeth Hall, the Purcell Room, the National Film Theatre, and the National Theatre. The gallery is closed between exhibitions, so check the listings before crossing the Thames. For recorded information, call 071/261-0127.
Admission: £4–£4.50 ($7–$8.35), depending on exhibition.
Open: Thurs–Mon 10am–6pm, Tues–Wed 10am–8pm, Sun 10am–6pm. **Tube:** Waterloo Station.

HAMPSTEAD & HIGHGATE

HAMPSTEAD HEATH

Located about 4 miles north of the center of London, Hampstead Heath consists of hundreds of acres of wild and unfenced royal parkland. The area is so elevated that on a clear day you can see St. Paul's Cathedral and even the hills of Kent south of the Thames. For years, Londoners have come here for kite-flying, sunning, fishing in the ponds, swimming, picnicking, and jogging. In good weather, it's also the site of big 1-day fairs. **Tube:** Hampstead Heath.

HAMPSTEAD VILLAGE

When the Underground came to this town in 1907, its attractions as a place to live became widely known, and writers, artists, architects, musicians, and scientists— some from The City—came to join earlier residents. Keats, D. H. Lawrence, Rabindranath Tagore, Shelley, and Robert Louis Stevenson all once lived here, and Kingsley Amis and John Le Carré still do.
The Regency and Georgian houses in this village are just 20 minutes by tube from Piccadilly Circus. There's a palatable mix of historic pubs, toy shops, and chic boutiques along Flask Walk, a pedestrian mall. The original village, on the side of a hill, still has old roads, alleys, steps, courts, and groves to be strolled through.

KEATS'S HOUSE, Wentworth Place, Keats Grove, Hampstead, N.W.3. Tel. 071/435-2062.
The famous romantic poet, John Keats lived here for only 2 years, but that was something like two-fifths of his creative life, because he died in Rome of tuberculosis at the age of 25 (1821). In Hampstead, Keats wrote some of his most celebrated odes—in praise of a Grecian urn and to the nightingale. His Regency house is well preserved and contains the manuscripts of his last sonnet ("Bright star, would I were steadfast as thou art"), and a portrait of him on his deathbed in a house on the Spanish Steps in Rome.
Admission: Free.
Open: Apr–Oct Mon–Fri 2–6pm, Sat 10am–1pm and 2–5pm, Sun 2–5pm; Nov–Mar Mon–Fri 1–5pm, Sat 10am–2pm, Sun 2–5pm. **Tube:** Belsize Park or Hampstead. **Bus:** No. 24 from Trafalgar Square.

KENWOOD (IVEAGH BEQUEST), Hampstead Lane, N.W.3. Tel. 081/348-1286.
Built as a gentleman's country home in the early 18th century, in 1754, Kenwood became the seat of Lord Mansfield and was enlarged and decorated by the famous

Scottish architect, Robert Adam from 1764. In 1927, Lord Iveagh donated it to the nation, along with his art collection. The rooms contain some fine neoclassical furniture, but the main attractions are the works by old masters and British artists. You can see paintings by Rembrandt (*Self-Portrait in Old Age*), Vermeer, Turner, Frans Hals, Gainsborough, Reynolds, Romney, Raeburn, Guardi, and Angelica Kauffmann, plus a portrait of the earl of Mansfield, Lord Chief Justice, who made Kenwood such an important home. A 19th-century family coach that comfortably carried 15 people stands in the Coach House, where there is also a cafeteria.

Admission: Free.

Open: Apr–Sept Mon–Sun 10am–6pm; Oct–Maundy Thursday 10am–4pm. **Closed:** Dec 24–25. **Tube:** Golders Green.

FENTON HOUSE, Windmill Hill, N.W.3. Tel. 081/435-3471.

This National Trust property is on the west side of Hampstead Grove, just a short distance north of Hampstead Village. You pass through beautiful wrought-iron gates to reach the red-brick house in a walled garden. Built in 1693, it is one of the earliest, largest, and finest houses in the Hampstead section. The original main staircase, some door frames, and chimney pieces remain intact. Paneled rooms contain furniture, pictures, English, German, and French porcelain from the 18th century, and the outstanding Benton-Fletcher collection of early keyboard musical instruments. Exhibits of these date from 1540 to 1805 and include a 17th-century Flemish harpsichord on loan from the queen mother, other harpsichords, spinets, square pianos, clavichords, and a virginal. Occasional concerts are held at the house.

Admission: £2.80 ($5.20); £1.40 ($2.60) children.

Open: Mar Sat–Sun 2–6pm; Apr–Oct Sat–Wed 11am–6pm. **Closed:** Good Friday. **Tube:** Hampstead.

THE FREUD MUSEUM, 20 Maresfield Gardens, N.W.3. Tel. 071/435-2002.

After he and his family left Nazi-occupied Vienna as refugees, Sigmund Freud lived, worked, and died in this spacious three-story red-brick house in northern London. On view are rooms containing original furniture, letters, photographs, paintings, and personal effects of Freud and his daughter, Anna. A focal point of the museum is the study and library, where you can see the famous couch and Freud's large collection of Egyptian, Roman, and Asian antiquities. The museum is developing as a research archive, educational resource, and cultural center, and temporary exhibitions and archive film programs are also on view.

Admission: £2 ($3.70) adults; children under 12 free.

Open: Wed–Sun noon–5pm. **Tube:** Finchley Road.

BURGH HOUSE, New End Sq., N.W.3. Tel. 071/431-0144.

A Queen Anne structure built in 1703 in the middle of the village, this was at one time the residence of the daughter and son-in-law of Rudyard Kipling, who often visited here. It is now used for local art exhibits, concerts, recitals, and talks and public meetings on many subjects, and the house is the home of several local societies, including the Hampstead Music Club and the Hampstead Scientific Society.

The Hampstead Museum, also in Burgh House, displays and illustrates the local history of the area. It has a good art collection, including a room devoted to the great artist, John Constable, who lived nearby for many years and was buried in the local parish church. There is also a bookstall, well stocked with souvenirs and postcards, plus a licensed buttery (tel. 071/431-2516) popular for lunch or tea (its prices are the lowest in Hampstead).

Admission: Free.

Open: Museum Wed–Sun noon–5pm; buttery Wed–Sun 11am–5:30pm. **Tube:** Hampstead.

HIGHGATE VILLAGE

A stone's throw east of Hampstead Heath, Highgate Village has a number of 16th- and 17th-century mansions, as well as small cottages, lining three sides of the now pondless Pond Square. Its most outstanding feature, however, is **Highgate Cemetery,** entered from Swain's Lane, N.6 (tel. 071/348-0808), an ideal setting for a collection of Victorian sculpture. Described as everything from "walled romantic rubble" to "an anthology of horror," the 37-acre burial ground attracts tombstone fanciers. Highgate's most famous grave is that of Karl Marx, who died in Hampstead in 1883; on the tomb is a huge bust of Marx, inscribed with his quotation, "Workers of the world, unite." *Note:* Don't go alone as muggings have been known to occur in this area. "Friends of Highgate" offers tours at various times (call number above). A £4 ($7.40) donation is required. **Tube:** Highgate or Archway.

THE PARKS OF LONDON

London's parks easily rate as the greatest "green lungs" of any large city. They are maintained with care and lavish artistry that puts their American equivalents to shame. Above all, they've been kept safe from land-hungry building firms and city councils. Maybe there's something to be said for inviolate "royal" property, after all. Because that's what most of London's parks are.

Largest of them—and one of the biggest in the world—is **Hyde Park,** W.2., once a favorite deer-hunting ground of Henry VIII. With the adjoining Kensington Gardens, it covers 636 acres of central London with velvety lawns interspersed with ponds, flowerbeds, and trees. Running through the width is a 41-acre lake known as the Serpentine. Rotten Row, a 1½-mile sand track, is reserved for horseback riding and on Sunday attracts some skilled equestrians.

Kensington Gardens, W.2, blending with Hyde Park, borders on the grounds of Kensington Palace. These gardens contain the celebrated statue of Peter Pan, with the bronze rabbits that toddlers are always trying to kidnap. The Albert Memorial is also here.

East of Hyde Park, across Piccadilly, stretch **Green Park** and **St. James's Park,** W.1, forming an almost unbroken chain of landscaped beauty. This is an ideal area for picnics, and you'll find it hard to believe that this was once a festering piece of swamp near the leper hospital. There is a romantic lake, stocked with a variety of ducks and pelicans, descendants of the pair that the Russian ambassador presented to Charles II in 1662.

Regent's Park, N.W.1, covers most of the district by that name, north of Baker Street and Marylebone Road. Designed by the 18th-century genius John Nash to surround a palace of the prince regent that never materialized, this is the most classically beautiful of London's parks. The core is a rose garden planted around a small lake alive with waterfowl and spanned by humped Japanese bridges. The open-air theater and the London Zoo are here, and, as in all the local parks, there are hundreds of deck chairs on the lawns in which to sunbathe.

MARBLE ARCH & SPEAKERS CORNER

At the northwest extremity of Mayfair, head for **Marble Arch,** an enormous *faux pas* that the English didn't try to hide but turned into a monument. Originally it was built by John Nash as the entrance to Buckingham Palace, until it was discovered that it was too small for carriages to pass through. If you see a crowd of people nearby who look as if they are plotting revolution, you might be right: In this part of Hyde Park (tube: Marble Arch) is **Speakers Corner,** where you will see English free speech in action. Everybody from terrorists to Orgone theorists mounts the soapbox to speak their minds. The speeches reach their most vehement pitch on Sunday, the best day to visit Marble Arch.

LANDMARK CHURCHES

St. Martin-in-the Fields, overlooking Trafalgar Square, W.C.2 (tel. 071/930-0089), is the Royal Parish Church, dear to the hearts of many English persons, especially the homeless. The present classically inspired church, with its famous steeple, dates from 1726, and James Gibbs, a pupil of Wren's, is listed as the architect.

The church goes back to the 11th century; among the congregation in years past was George I, who was actually a churchwarden, unique for an English sovereign. From St. Martin's vantage position in the theater district, it has drawn many actors to its door—none more notable than Nell Gwynne, the mistress of Charles II. On her death in 1687, she was buried in the crypt. Throughout the war, many Londoners rode out uneasy nights in the crypt, while Blitz bombs rained down overhead. One, in 1940, blasted out all the windows. Today the crypt contains a restaurant, a bookshop, and a gallery. **Tube:** Charing Cross.

St. Etheldreda's, Britain's oldest Roman Catholic church, lies on Ely Place, Clerkenwell, E.C.1 (tel. 071/405-1061), leading off Charterhouse Street at Holborn Circus. Built in 1251, it was mentioned by the Bard in both *Richard II* and *Richard III*. A survivor of the Great Fire of 1666, the church was built by and was the property of the diocese of Ely in the days when many bishops had their episcopal houses in London as well as in the actual cathedral cities in which they held their sees. Until this century, the landlord of Ye Olde Mitre public house near Ely Place had to obtain his license from the Justices of Cambridgeshire rather than in London, and even today the place is still a private road, with impressive iron gates and a lodge for the gatekeeper, all administered by six elected commissioners.

St. Etheldreda, whose name is sometimes shortened to St. Audrey, was a 7th-century king's daughter who left her husband and turned to religion, establishing an abbey on the Isle of Ely. The name St. Audrey is the source of the word *tawdry,* from cheap trinkets sold at the annual fair honoring the saint. St. Etheldreda's is made up of a crypt and an upper church. It has a distinguished musical tradition, with the 11am mass on Sunday sung in Latin. Other mass times are on Sunday at 9am and 6pm, Monday to Friday at 8am and 1pm, and Saturday at 8am. Lunches are served Monday to Friday from noon to 2pm in the Pantry, with a varied choice of hot and cold dishes. **Tube:** Farringdon or Chancery Lane.

ALONG THE THAMES

London's history and development is linked to this winding ribbon of water, which connects the city with the sea, from which London drew its wealth and power. For centuries, the river was London's main highway, and today there is a row of fascinating attractions lying on, across, and alongside the River Thames.

Some of the bridges that span the Thames are household words. **London Bridge,** which, contrary to the nursery rhyme, has never "fallen down," but was dismantled and shipped to the United States, ran from the Monument (a tall pillar commemorating the Great Fire of 1666) to Southwark Cathedral, parts of which date from 1207.

Its neighbor to the east is the still-standing **Tower Bridge,** E.1. (tel. 071/407-0922), one of the city's most celebrated landmarks and possibly the most photographed and painted bridge. Tower Bridge was built during 1886–94 with two towers 200 feet apart, joined by footbridges that provide glass-covered walkways for the public, who can enter the north tower, take the elevator to the walkway, cross the river to the south tower, and return to street level. From the bridge you can view St. Paul's, the Tower of London, and in the distance, a part of the Houses of Parliament.

You can also visit the main engine room with Victorian boilers and steam-pumping engines, which used to raise and lower the roadway across the river. Among the exhibitions that trace the history and operation of this unique bridge are models showing how the 1,000-ton arms of the bridge can be raised in 1½ minutes to allow ships to pass. Nowadays, electric power is used to raise the bridge, an occurrence that usually happens about once a day, more often in summer. You'll know if it is going to open when a bell sounds throughout the bridge and road traffic is stopped. Admission to exhibits is £2.50 ($4.65), £1 ($1.85) for children. It is open daily in summer from 10am to 6:30pm (to 4:45pm in winter). **Tube:** Tower Hill.

The piece of river between the site of the old London Bridge and the Tower Bridge marks the city end of the immense row of docks stretching 26 miles to the coast. Although most of them are no longer in use, they have long been known as the **Port of London.**

Particular note should be taken of the striking removal of pollution from the Thames in the past decades. The river, so polluted in the 1950s that no marine life could exist, can now lay claim to being "the cleanest metropolitan estuary in the world," with many varieties of fish, even salmon, living in these waters today.

THE THAMES FLOOD BARRIER

From time to time, the Thames estuary has brought tidal surges that have on occasion caused disastrous flooding at Woolwich, Hammersmith, Whitehall, Westminster, plus other areas within the river's flood reaches. The flooding has increased this century due to natural causes: the unstoppable rise of tide levels in the Thames; surge tides from the Atlantic; and the down-tilt of the country by some 12 inches a century.

All this led to the construction, beginning in 1975, of the Thames Flood Barrier with huge piers linking mammoth rising sector gates, smaller rising sector gates, and falling radial gates, all of which can make a solid steel wall about the height of a five-story building, which completely dams the waters of the Thames.

Since its official opening in 1984, the engineering spectacle has drawn increasing crowds, at a point in the river known as Woolwich Reach in east London, where the Thames is a straight stretch about ⅓ mile in width. **London Launches** (tel. 071/930-3373) offers trips to the barrier, operating from Westminster Pier. At the Barrier Centre, an audiovisual show depicts the need for the barrier and its operation, and there is also a souvenir shop, snack bar, and cafeteria. London Launches leave five times daily from Westminster Pier, with returns from Barrier Pier. Adults pay £4.50 ($8.35) round-trip or £2.80 ($5.20) one-way. Children under 14 are charged £2.50 ($4.65) round-trip or £1.50 ($2.80) one-way.

It's also possible to take the boat over and return by Underground; the tube stop is Charleton Station. Trains depart for central London every 30 minutes, and the ride takes 15 minutes.

The **Thames Barrier Visitors' Centre,** Unity Way, Woolwich, S.E.11 (tel. 081/854-1373), is open Monday to Friday from 10:30am to 5pm, Saturday and Sunday from 10:30am to 5:30pm. Admission is £2 ($3.70) for adults and £1.20 ($2.20) for children.

A FLOATING MUSEUM

HMS *Belfast*, Morgan's Lane, Tooley Street, S.E.1 (tel. 071/407-6434), Europe's largest historic warship, is permanently moored on the Thames, opposite the Tower of London. This World War II veteran was among the first to open fire against German fortifications on D Day and it also served during the Korean War. By exploring the ship from the bridge right down to the engine and boiler rooms, seven decks below, you discover how Royal Navy sailors lived and fought during the past 50 years. Visitors can explore the bridge, operations room, 6-inch gun turrets, living quarters, galley, and D Day exhibition. HMS *Belfast* is open daily from 10am to 5:30pm in summer and from 11am to 4pm in winter. Last boardings are 30 minutes before closing. Admission is £3.50 ($6.45) for adults, £1.75 ($3.25) for children. **Tube:** London Bridge or Tower Hill. A ferry runs daily in summer from Tower Pier (Tower of London) directly to the ship; in winter, it operates only on Saturday and Sunday.

LONDON DOCKLANDS

What was once 8 square miles of dilapidated property surrounded by water—some 55 miles of waterfront acreage within a sailor's cry of London's major attractions—has been reclaimed and restored.

Included in this complex are Wapping, the Isle of Dogs, the Surrey and Royal Docks, and more, all with Limehouse at its heart. Visit the **Exhibition Centre** on the Isle of Dogs to see what the Docklands past, present, and future include. Already the area has provided space for overflow from The City of London's square mile, and it looks as though the growth and development is more than promising. A shopping village at Tobacco Dock, a new home at Shadwell Basin for the Academy of St.

Martin-in-the-Fields Orchestra, and the London Arena (the largest self-contained sport and leisure complex in the country) at the tip of the Isle of Dogs are being joined by luxury condominiums, offices, hotels, museums, and theaters.

The former urban wasteland of deserted warehouses and derelict wharves can be visited by taking the **Docklands Light Railway** that links the Isle of Dogs and London Underground's Tower Hill station, via several new local stations. To see the whole complex, take the railway at the Tower Gateway near Tower Bridge for a short journey through Wapping and the Isle of Dogs. You can get off at Island Gardens and then cross through the 100-year-old Greenwich Tunnel under the Thames to see the attractions at Greenwich (see "Easy Excursions," below in this chapter). A regular water-bus service connects Greenwich with Charing Cross in a river voyage of about half an hour, and other tunnels are planned to link the Docklands with port points and motorways.

4. COOL FOR KIDS

The following attractions are fun places you can take youngsters. It's even possible that you'll enjoy them more than your kids. This isn't to say that the other sights listed in this chapter aren't fun for kids—at the British Museum, for example, I've watched group after group of kids stand absolutely spellbound in front of the Egyptian mummies, while their parents tug at them to trot along.

SIGHTS

THE LONDON DUNGEON, 28-34 Tooley St., S.E.1. Tel. 071/403-0606.

Set under the arches of London Bridge Station, the dungeon is a series of tableaux, more grizzly than Madame Tussaud's, that faithfully reproduces the ghoulish conditions of the Middle Ages. The rumble of trains overhead adds to the spine-chilling horror of the place. Bells toll, and there is constant melancholy chanting in the background. Dripping water and live rats (caged!) make for even more atmosphere. The heads of executed criminals were stuck on spikes for onlookers to observe through glasses hired for the occasion. The murder of Thomas Becket in Canterbury Cathedral is also depicted. Naturally, there's a burning at the stake, as well as a torture chamber with racking, branding, and fingernail extraction. The Great Fire of London is brought to crackling life by a computer-controlled spectacular that re-creates Pudding Lane, where the fire started.

Of course this experience may not be to every child's (or adult's) taste. If you survive, there is a souvenir shop selling certificates to testify that you have been through the works.

Admission: £5 ($9.25) adults, £3 ($5.85) children under 14.

Open: Apr–Sept daily 10am–5:30pm; Oct–Mar daily 10am–4:30pm. **Tube:** London Bridge.

NATURAL HISTORY MUSEUM, Cromwell Rd., S.W.7. Tel. 071/589-6323.

This is the home of the national collections of living and fossil plants, animals, minerals, rocks, and meteorites, with lots of magnificent specimens on display. Exciting exhibitions designed to encourage people of all ages to enjoy learning about modern natural history include "Human Biology—An Exhibition of Ourselves," "Dinosaurs and Their Living Relatives," "Man's Place in Evolution," "British Natural History," and "Discovering Mammals."

Admission: £3 ($5.55) adults, £1.50 ($2.80) children; family ticket (two adults and up to four children) £8 ($14.80).

Open: Mon–Sat 10am–6pm, Sun 11am–6pm. **Tube:** South Kensington.

BETHNAL GREEN MUSEUM OF CHILDHOOD, Cambridge Heath Rd., E.2. Tel. 081/980-3204.

Here you'll find displays of toys from the past century. The variety of dolls alone is staggering, and some are dressed in elaborate period costumes. Dollhouses range from simple cottages to miniature mansions, complete with fireplaces, grand pianos, carriages, furniture, kitchen utensils, and household pets. It might be wise to explain to your children beforehand that—no—none of this is for sale. In addition, the museum displays optical toys, toy theaters, marionettes, puppets, and an exhibit of soldiers and battle toys of both world wars. There is also a display of children's clothing and furniture.

Admission: Free.

Open: Mon–Thurs and Sat 10am–6pm, Sun 2:30–6pm. **Tube:** Bethnal Green.

LONDON TOY AND MODEL MUSEUM, 21-23 Craven Hill, W.2. Tel. 071/262-7905.

These two restored Victorian houses, off Bayswater Road, shelter one of the finest collections of commercially made toys and models on public display in Europe, with items by all the major toy and model manufacturers. The model and toy train collection is particularly comprehensive and traces the development of the miniature train from the inception of railways in the early 19th century. There are several garden railway systems, including a working child's train. The permanent collection details the rise of toys with the Industrial Revolution, and there is a fine display of dolls, teddy bears, and a quarter-scale child's model of a Cadillac sports roadster made in 1916. The museum also has a children's activity area, a café, and a large recreational garden area.

Admission: £2.70 ($5) adults, £1.20 ($2.20) children; free for children under 5.

Open: Tues–Sat 10am–5:30pm, Sun 11am–5:30pm. **Tube:** Lancaster Gate or Paddington.

ROCK CIRCUS, London Pavilion, 1 Piccadilly Circus, W.1. Tel. 071/734-7203.

Run by the Tussaud's Group of Madame Tussaud's waxworks, this tells the story of rock and pop music from the 1950s through the present day, using a combination of wax and "moving" bionic likenesses of all the big names in rock from the past four decades. The very young might not understand it, but others will love it. Visitors also get to hear famous songs from rock history. The highlight of the Rock Circus is a show using Audio Animatronic techniques, in which the Beatles, Elvis Presley, Madonna, Bruce Springsteen, and others, perform "live."

Admission: £5.75 ($10.65) adults, £3.85 ($7.10) children.

Open: Daily 10am–10pm. **Tube:** Piccadilly Circus.

ENTERTAINMENT

THE ARTS THEATRE, Great Newport St., W.C.2. Tel. 071/379-3280, or 071/836-3334 to book tickets at box office.

Situated in the heart of London's "Theatreland," the Unicorn, founded in 1947, is the only theater just for children. Adult actors present a season of plays for 4 to 12 year olds each year. Programs include specially commissioned plays, adaptations of old favorites, and high quality entertainment.

Prices: Tickets £3 ($5.55), £4 ($7.40), and £5 ($9.25), plus 10p (20¢) temporary membership just for show.

Performances: Sept–June Sat–Sun and school holidays 2:30pm. **Tube:** Leicester Square.

THE LITTLE ANGEL MARIONETTE THEATRE, 14 Dagmar Passage, Cross St., N.1. Tel. 071/226-1787.

Especially constructed for puppet shows, this theater has 200 to 300 performances each year. The theater is the focal point of a loosely formed group of some 20 professional puppeteers who present their own shows or help with performances of the resident company. The shows vary in range from *The Soldier's Tale*, using 8-foot-high figures, to *Wonder Island* and *Lancelot the Lion*, written especially for the humble glove puppet. Many of the plays, such as Hans Christian Andersen's *The Little Mermaid*, are performed with marionettes. You'll be enthralled with the exquisite lighting and skill with which the puppets are handled.

The theater is beautifully decorated and is well equipped. There is a coffee bar in the foyer and a workshop where the settings and costumes, as well as the puppets, are made. To find out what's playing and to reserve your seats, call the number above. Also, there are many special programs during the Christmas season.

Take the tube to Angel Station, and then walk up Upper Street to St. Mary's Church and down the footpath to the left of the church. Or go by car or taxi to Essex Road and then up to Dagmar Terrace.

Admission: Morning shows £3.50 ($6.45) adults, £2.50 ($4.65) children; afternoon shows £4 ($7.40) adults; £3 ($5.55) children.

Performances: Sat 11am, Sat–Sun 3pm. **Tube:** Angel Station.

OUTDOOR ATTRACTIONS

Battersea Park, S.W.11 (tel. 071/871-7530), is a vast patch of woodland, lakes, and lawns on the south bank of the Thames, opposite Chelsea Embankment between Albert Bridge and Chelsea Bridge. Formerly known as Battersea Fields, the present park was laid out in 1852–58 on an old dueling ground (the most famous duel fought here was between Lord Winchelsea and the Duke of Wellington in 1829). The park, which measures ¾ of a mile on each of its four sides, has a lake for boating, a deer field with fenced-in deer and wild birds, and tennis and football (soccer) fields. There's even a children's zoo, with an admission of 60p ($1.10), open from Easter to late September daily from 11am to 5pm.

The park's architectural highlight is a Peace Pagoda, built of stone and wood, that was donated in 1986 to the now-defunct Council of Greater London by an order of Japanese monks.

The park, open daily from 7:30am until dusk, is not well serviced by public transportation. The nearest **tube** is in Chelsea on the Right Bank (Sloane Square); from there, it's a 15-minute walk. If you prefer the **bus,** take no. 137 from the Sloane Square station, exiting at the first stop after the bus crosses the Thames.

One of the greatest zoos in the world, the **London Zoo,** Regent's Park, N.W.1. (tel. 071/722-3333), is more than a century and a half old. Run by the Zoological Society of London, this 36-acre garden houses some 8,000 animals, including some of the rarest species on earth. One of the most fascinating exhibits is the Snowdon Aviary. Separate houses are reserved for certain species: the insect house (incredible bird-eating spiders, a cross-sectioned ant colony), the reptile house (huge dragonlike monitor lizards and a fantastic 15-foot python), and other additions, such as the Sobell Pavilion for Apes and Monkeys and the Lion Terraces.

Designed for the largest collection of small mammals in the world, the Clore Pavilion has a basement called the Moonlight World, where special lighting effects simulate night time for nocturnal beasties, while rendering them clearly visible to onlookers.

Many spend an entire day here, watching the sea lions being fed, enjoying an animal ride in summer, and meeting the baby elephants on their walks. There are two fully licensed restaurants, one self-service and the other with waiters. Admission costs £5.20 ($9.60) for adults, £3.20 ($5.90) for children ages 4 to 15, and free for children under 4. The zoo is open daily from 9am from June through September, 10am from October through May to 6pm or dusk, whichever is earlier. Last entrance is half an hour before closing. Take the **tube** to Baker Street, then you can walk north through the park or take **bus** no. 21 or 742.

Hampstead Heath, the traditional playground of the Londoner, was dedicated "to the use of the public forever" by a special Act of Parliament in 1872. This 800-acre expanse of high heath entirely surrounded by London is a chain of continuous park, wood, and grassland that contains just about every known form of outdoor amusement. There are natural lakes for swimmers (who don't mind goosebumps), bridle paths for horseback riders, athletic tracks, hills for kite flying, and a special pond for model yachting. At the shore of Kenwood Lake, in the northern section, is a concert platform devoted to symphony performances on summer evenings. In the northeast corner, in Waterlow Park, ballets, operas, and comedies are staged at the Grass Theatre in June and July. **Tube:** Hampstead or Belsize Park.

5. SPECIAL-INTEREST SIGHTSEEING

FOR THE LITERARY ENTHUSIAST

See "More Attractions," above, for details on Keats's House.

SAMUEL JOHNSON'S HOUSE, 17 Gough Sq., E.C.4. Tel. 071/353-3745.

Dr. Johnson and his copyists compiled his famous dictionary in this Queen Anne house, where the lexicographer, poet, essayist, and fiction writer lived from 1748 to 1759. Although Johnson also lived at Staple Inn in Holborn and at a number of other houses, the Gough Square house is the only one of his residences remaining in London. The 17th-century building has been painstakingly restored, and it's well worth a visit. When you come out of the tube station, walk up New Bridge Street and turn left onto Fleet. Gough Square is a tiny, hidden square, north of Fleet.

Admission: £2 ($3.70) adults, £1.50 ($2.80) children.

Open: May–Sept Mon–Sat 11am–5:30pm; Oct–Apr Mon–Sat 11am–5pm. **Tube:** Blackfriars.

CARLYLE'S HOUSE, 24 Cheyne Row, S.W.3. Tel. 071/352-7087.

From 1834 to 1881, the author of *The French Revolution* and his letter-writing wife took up abode in this modest 1708 terraced house. Furnished essentially as it was in Carlyle's day, the house is located about three-quarters of a block from the Thames, near the Chelsea Embankment, along King's Road. The second floor contains the drawing room of Mrs. Carlyle, but the most interesting chamber is the not-so-soundproof "soundproof" study in the skylit attic. Filled with Carlyle memorabilia—his books, a letter from Disraeli, a writing chair, even his death mask—this is where the author labored over his *Frederick the Great* manuscript.

Admission: £2.20 ($4.05) adults, £1.10 ($2.05) children.

Open: Easter Sat–Oct Wed–Sun 11am–5pm. **Tube:** Sloane Square. **Bus:** No. 11, 19, 22, or 39.

DICKENS'S HOUSE, 48 Doughty St., W.C.1. Tel. 071/405-2127.

The great English novelist, born in 1812 in what is now Portsmouth, is known to have lived here from 1837 to 1839. Unlike some of the London town houses of famous men (Wellington, Soane), the Bloomsbury house is simple—the embodiment of middle-class restraint. The house contains an extensive library, including manuscripts and letters second in importance only to the Forster Collection in the Victoria and Albert Museum. Dickens's drawing room on the first floor has been reconstructed, as have the still room, wash house, and wine cellar in the basement.

Admission: £2 ($3.70) adults, £1.50 ($2.80) students; £1 ($1.85) children.

Open: Mon–Sat 10am–5pm. **Tube:** Russell Square.

FOR VISITING AMERICANS

Despite the historic fact that they fought two wars against each other, no two countries have stronger links than America and Britain.

In London mementos of this heritage are overwhelming. In front of the National Gallery you'll find a bronze **statue of George Washington** gazing at you over

Trafalgar Square. Visit **Westminster Abbey** and you'll see a memorial tablet to President Roosevelt, a bust of Longfellow in the Poets' Corner, and the graves of Edward Hyde (Hyde Park, New York, was named after him) and James Oglethorpe, who founded the state of Georgia.

Grosvenor Square, in the heart of the West End, is known as "Little America." Watched over by a statue of FDR, it contains the modern U.S. Embassy and the home of John Adams when he was minister to Britain.

Norfolk House, St. James Square, was General Eisenhower's headquarters during World War II, the spot from which he directed the Allies in the Normandy landing in 1944.

At 36 Craven Street, just off the Strand, stands **Benjamin Franklin's London residence.** And in **St. Sepulchre,** at Holborn Viaduct, is the grave of Capt. John Smith of Pocahontas fame—he who had been prevented from sailing on the *Mayflower* because the other passengers considered him an "undesirable character."

The most moving reminder of national links is the American Memorial Chapel at **St. Paul's Cathedral.** It commemorates the 28,000 U.S. service personnel who lost their lives while based in Britain during World War II. The Roll of Honor containing their names was handed over by General Eisenhower on the Fourth of July 1951, and the chapel—with the Roll encased in glass—has become an unofficial pilgrimage place for visiting Americans.

6. WALKING TOURS

The best way to discover London is on foot. This section is organized into a series of walking tours of some major attractions and districts. Your busy itinerary may not allow you to take all of the tours, but try to fit in as many as possible.

WALKING TOUR 1 —— Westminster/Whitehall

Start: The Entrance of the Tate Gallery.
Finish: Trafalgar Square.
Time: About 3 hours, excluding interior visits.
Best Time: Monday to Thursday, when Parliament is in session.
Worst Time: Evenings, or Sunday, when the district becomes almost deserted.

This tour will take you on a route parallel to the River Thames, past some of London's most visible symbols of both its democracy and its monarchs.

Begin your tour in front of the grand Palladian entrance to one of the finest art museums in the world:

1. ○ **The Tate Gallery.** Built in 1897 and donated to London by the scion of a sugar manufacturer, it is jammed with the works of virtually every great painter in British history. Return to browse the collections at your leisure, but for the moment, turn northward along the west bank of the Thames (the embankment here is known as Millbank), beside the river which made British history, with the Houses of Parliament looming skyward ahead of you. At the first left-hand turn after the first bridge you'll see (Lambeth Bridge), turn inland onto Dean Stanley Street, which in 1 block will arrive at the symmetrical elegance of:

2. **Smith Square,** whose centerpiece is St. John's Church. Designed with a highly personalized kind of neoclassicism by Thomas Archer in 1728, it was heavily damaged by bombs in 1941. Rebuilt (but not reconsecrated), it now serves as concert hall for some of the greatest musicians of the Western world.

Retrace your steps back to the Thames, turn left (northward) toward the Neo-Gothic regularity of the Houses of Parliament, and enter the verdant

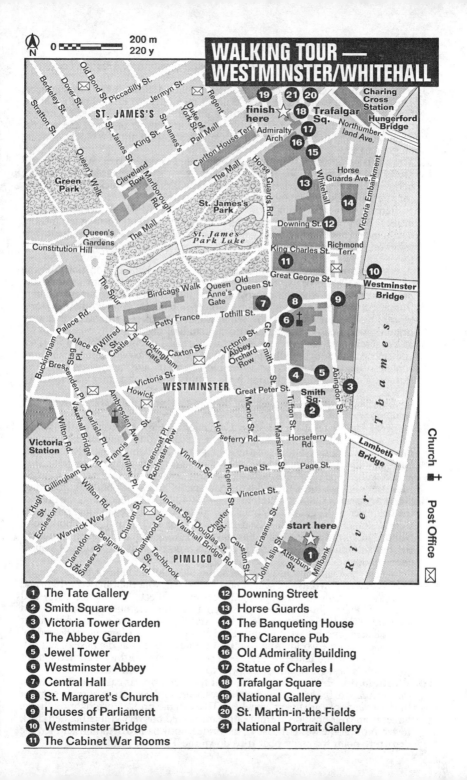

WALKING TOUR — WESTMINSTER/WHITEHALL

0 ⬛⬛⬛⬛ 200 m
220 y

N

1 The Tate Gallery
2 Smith Square
3 Victoria Tower Garden
4 The Abbey Garden
5 Jewel Tower
6 Westminster Abbey
7 Central Hall
8 St. Margaret's Church
9 Houses of Parliament
10 Westminster Bridge
11 The Cabinet War Rooms
12 Downing Street
13 Horse Guards
14 The Banqueting House
15 The Clarence Pub
16 Old Admirality Building
17 Statue of Charles I
18 Trafalgar Square
19 National Gallery
20 St. Martin-in-the-Fields
21 National Portrait Gallery

Church ✝

Post Office ✉

triangular-shaped park which prefaces its southern entrance. A tranquil oasis rich with sculpture, the:

3. Victoria Tower Garden contains a 1915 replica of Rodin's 1895 masterpiece, *The Burghers of Calais,* and A. G. Walker's monument to Emmeline Pankhurst, early 20th-century leader of the British suffragettes, who was frequently imprisoned for her actions and beliefs. Near the northern perimeter to the garden, detour inland by turning left on Great College Street for about a block, noticing on your right:

4. The Abbey Garden. Continuously cultivated over the past 900 years, and associated with nearby Westminster Abbey, it is the oldest garden in England, rich with lavender and ecclesiastical ruins. Even if the gate is locked, parts of this charming historic oddity are visible from the street.

Retrace your steps along Great College Street to Millbank (which on some maps at this point might be referred to as Abingdon Street), turning left (north), remaining on the opposite side of Millbank from the Houses of Parliament. The tower on your left, completed in 1366 by Edward III for the storage of treasure is the:

5. Jewel Tower. This is all that remains of the domestic portions of the once-mighty Palace of Westminster. It contains a small museum showing the dramas connected with the construction of the Houses of Parliament. Exiting from the Jewel Tower, continue north along Millbank (or Abingdon Street) for 2 blocks, passing on your left the semicircular apse of the rear side of one of Britain's most densely packed artistic and cultural highlights:

6. ✪ Westminster Abbey. The spiritual heart of London, completed in 1245, and steeped in enough tradition, sorrow, majesty, and blood to merit an entire volume of its own, this is one of the most majestic and most-visited sights in Europe. Turn left, skirting the building's northern flank, and enter via its western facade.

After your visit, exit by the same door you entered, and walk about a block west, across the square to the:

7. Central Hall, site of the Imperial Collection of Crown Jewels of the World. Most are replicas (the originals having a disconcerting habit of disappearing during wars and revolutions) of the state gems of Britain, France, Russia, Iran, Bavaria, and the Vatican, but the sight is nonetheless dazzling. After your visit, retrace your steps to Millbank (which at this point might be referred to as St. Margaret's Street), turn left, and notice the small Renaissance building known as:

8. St. Margaret's Church. Built between 1504 and 1523, it contains the body of the colonizer of Virginia, Sir Walter Raleigh (who was beheaded just outside its front entrance), and which served as the site for the marriages of both John Milton (1656) and Sir Winston Churchill (1908). Considered the parish church for the British House of Commons, it contains a noteworthy collection of stained glass windows.

When you exit from St. Margaret's, the Neo-Gothic bulk of the:

9. ✪ Houses of Parliament will almost overwhelm you. Built between 1840 and 1860 as the result of a competition won by architects Sir Charles Barry and Augustus Pugin (both of whom suffered several nervous breakdowns and eventual early deaths as a result of the overwork and stress it caused them), it covers 8 acres and has what might be the greatest volume of ornate stonework of any building in the world. Your tour of the interior begins at the base of Big Ben (its clock tower and tallest feature), near the building's northwest corner. One of Parliament's best views can be enjoyed from a position on the:

10. Westminster Bridge. Built in 1862 in the then-popular cast iron, and one of the most ornate bridges in London, it gives, from midway across its span, some of the best views of Parliament anywhere. To reach the bridge, turn right on Bridge Street from your position in front of the misnamed but very visible Big Ben clock tower. Note at the western base of the bridge, aptly named Westminster Pier, the departure point for many boat trips down the Thames.

Retrace your footsteps along Bridge Street, passing beside Big Ben, and take the second right-hand turn along the busy thoroughfare of Parliament Street. Take the first left along King Charles Street, where, on the left-hand side, you'll reach:

11. The Cabinet War Rooms, Clive Steps, King Charles Street. Set 17 feet underground to protect its occupants from Nazi air raids, this unpretentious handful of rooms was the meeting place for Churchill's cabinet during World War II, and the originating point of many of his most stirring speeches. A half dozen of the rooms are open for visitation.

Retrace your steps back to Parliament Street, turning left (north). Within 2 blocks, turn left at:

12. Downing Street. Though security precautions against terrorist activities might present you from passing too close, no. 10 along this street is the much-publicized official residence of the British Prime Minister, no. 11 the official residence of the Chancellor of the Exchequer, and no. 12 the office of the Chief Government Whip, the Member of Parliament responsible for maintaining discipline and cooperation among party members in Parliament's House of Commons.

Continue north along Parliament Street, which near Downing Street changes its name to Whitehall. At this point, either side of the street will be lined with the administrative soul of Britain, buildings which influence politics around the world, and whose grandiose architecture is suitably majestic. One of the most noteworthy of these is the:

13. Horse Guards, completed in 1760 and designed by William Kent. It is one of the most symmetrically imposing of the many buildings along Whitehall, and the venue of a ceremony (held Monday through Saturday at 11am, Sunday at 10am) known as the Mounting of the Guard (which is the first step of an equestrian ceremony which continues, every day at 11:30am, with the changing of the guard in front of Buckingham Palace).

Across the avenue rises one of London's most superlative examples of Palladian architecture:

14. The Banqueting Hall. Commissioned by James I, and designed by Inigo Jones in the early 1600s, it's considered one of the most aesthetically and mathematically perfect buildings in England. Containing a mural by Peter Paul Rubens, its facade was the backdrop for what might have been the most disturbing and unsettling execution in British history, the hanging of the English King Charles I by members of Parliament.

REFUELING STOP One of the most famous pubs of London, **15. The Clarence Pub,** at 53 Whitehall Street (tel. 071/930-4808), beloved of Parliamentarians from throughout England, was originally opened in the 18th century and has been cosseting the taste buds of government administrators ever since. With gaslights, oaken ceiling beams, antique farm implements dangling from the ceiling, and battered wooden tables ringed with churchlike pews, it contains at least a half dozen choices of real ale, and pub grub.

After your drinks, notice the building almost directly across Whitehall from the pub. The:

16. Old Admiralty Building, Spring Gardens, designed in 1725 by Sir Thomas Ripley, and strictly closed except for official business, it served for almost two centuries (until it was replaced by newer quarters between the wars) as the administrative headquarters of the British navy.

Continue walking north until you see what might be the finest and most emotive equestrian statue in London, the:

17. Statue of Charles I. Isolated on an island in the middle of a sea of speeding traffic, it commemorates one of the most tragic kings of British history and the beginning of:

18. **Trafalgar Square.** Centered around a soaring monument to the hero of the Battle of Trafalgar, Lord Nelson, who defeated Napoléon's navy off the coast of Spain in 1805, it is the single grandest plaza in London. Against the square's northern perimeter rises the grandly neoclassical bulk of the:

19. ✪ **National Gallery,** whose works cannot possibly be catalogued here, but which definitely merits a detailed tour of its own.

The church which flanks the eastern edge of Trafalgar Square is one of London's most famous, and the home of one of London's most famous chamber orchestras:

20. **St.-Martin-in-the-Fields.** Designed in the style of Sir Christopher Wren in 1726 by James Gibbs, it has a Corinthian portico and a steeple whose form has inspired the architects of many American churches. It was the christening place of English King Charles II, and the burial place of his infamous but fun-loving mistress, Nell Gwynne.

Finally, for an overview of the faces which altered the course of Britain and the world, walk to the right-hand (eastern) side of the National Gallery, where the greatest repository of portraits in Europe awaits your inspection at the:

21. **National Portrait Gallery,** 2 St. Martin's Place. They're all here—kings, cardinals, mistresses, playwrights, poets, coquettes, dilettantes, and names rich in historical connotations. Their assemblage into one gallery celebrates the subject of each painting rather than the artist who created it.

WALKING TOUR 2 —— The City

Start: The southern terminus of London Bridge.
Finish: St. Paul's Cathedral.
Time: About 3 hours.
Best Times: Weekday mornings, when the financial district is functioning but its churches are the most unvisited.
Worst Times: Weekends (unless you prefer the lack of traffic), when the district is almost deserted.

Encompassing only a small patch of urban real estate, this tour incorporates the densest concentration of historic and cultural monuments within Britain. The City is proud of its role as one of the financial capitals of the world.

Our tour begins on the southern edge of the Thames, directly to the west of one of the world's most famous bridges. Facing the Thames rises the bulk of:

1. **Southwark Cathedral.** When it was built in the 1200s, it was an outpost of the faraway diocese of Winchester. Deconsecrated after Henry VIII's Reformation, it later sheltered bakeries and colonies of pigs. Much of what you'll see is a result of a sorely needed 19th-century rebuilding, but a view of its Gothic interior, with its multiple commemorative plaques, gives an idea of the religious power of London's medieval church. After your visit, walk across the famous masonry of:

2. **London Bridge.** Originally designed by Henry de Colechurch under the patronage of Henry II in 1176, but replaced several times since, it's probably the most famous bridge in the world. Until as late as 1729, it was the only bridge across the Thames. During the Middle Ages, it was lined with shops and houses crowded close upon its edges, and served for centuries as the showplace for the severed heads—preserved in tar—of enemies of the British monarchs. (The most famous of these included the head of Sir Thomas More, the highly vocal lord chancellor of Canterbury.) From Southwark Cathedral, cross the bridge. At its northern end, notice the first street which descends to the right (east), Monument

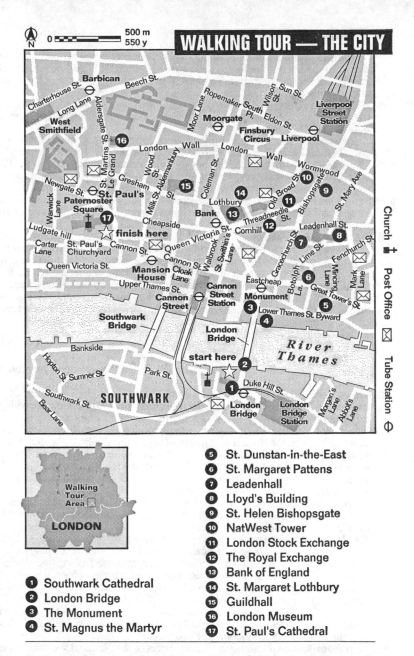

500 m / 550 y

WALKING TOUR — THE CITY

Charterhouse St. Barbican Beech St. Sun St. Wilson St. Ropemaker South Pl. Eldon St. Liverpool Street Station

Long Lane Aldersgate St. Moor Lane Moorgate Finsbury Circus Liverpool

West Smithfield St. Martins Le Grand London Wall London Wall Wormwood

Newgate St. Gresham St. St. Paul's Wood St. Milk St. Aldermanbury Coleman St. Old Broad St. Bishopsgate St. Mary Axe

Warwick Lane Paternoster Square Cheapside Lothbury Threadneedle St. Leadenhall St. Fenchurch St.

Ludgate hill finish here Bank Cornhill Gracechurch St. Lime St. Mincing Lane

Carter Lane St. Paul's Churchyard Cannon St. Queen Victoria St. Walbrook St. Swithin's Lane Botolph La. Great Tower's St. Mark Lane

Queen Victoria St. Mansion House Cloak Lane Eastcheap Monument Lower Thames St. Byward

Upper Thames St. Cannon Street Cannon Street Station

Southwark Bridge

Bankside Southwark Bridge Park St. London Bridge River Thames

Hopton St. Sumner St. start here Morgan's Lane Abbot's Lane

SOUTHWARK Southwark St. Duke Hill St. London Bridge London Bridge Station

Bear Lane

Church ✝ Post Office ⊠ Tube Station ⊕

Walking Tour Area
LONDON

❶ Southwark Cathedral
❷ London Bridge
❸ The Monument
❹ St. Magnus the Martyr

❺ St. Dunstan-in-the-East
❻ St. Margaret Pattens
❼ Leadenhall
❽ Lloyd's Building
❾ St. Helen Bishopsgate
❿ NatWest Tower
⓫ London Stock Exchange
⓬ The Royal Exchange
⓭ Bank of England
⓮ St. Margaret Lothbury
⓯ Guildhall
⓰ London Museum
⓱ St. Paul's Cathedral

Street. Detour down it a short distance to read the commemorative plaques attached to the:

3. Monument. Commemorating the Great Fire of 1666, this soaring Doric column is appropriately capped with a carved version of a flaming urn. The disaster which it memorializes erupted from a bakery in nearby Pudding Lane, raged for 4 days and nights, and destroyed 80% of the City. A cramped and foreboding set of stairs spirals up to the top's view over the cityscape so heavily influenced after the fire by architect Sir Christopher Wren.

Retrace your steps toward London Bridge, but before you actually step onto it, detour to the left (south, toward the river) at Monument Street's first intersection, Fish Hill Street. Set near the edge of the water, within its shadow of the bridge, is one of Wren's many churches:

4. St. Magnus Martyr. Completed in 1685 (with its tower added in 1705), it has a particularly magnificent interior which at one time was devoted to the neighborhood's many fishmongers.

After your visit, continue walking east along Lower Thames Street. At the corner of Idol Lane (the fifth narrow street on your left) turn left to see:

5. St. Dunstan-in-the-East, the bombed-out remains of another of Sir Wren's churches. Its unexpectedly verdant garden, the only part of the complex that regenerated itself after the Nazi blitz of World War II, offers a comforting oasis amid a sea of traffic and masonry. After your visit, continue walking northward. Where Idol Lane dead-ends at Great Tower Street, look straight ahead of you to the spire of:

6. St. Margaret Pattens, another of Wren's churches, this one in substantially better shape. Built between 1684 and 1689, it has much of its original 17th-century paneling and interior fittings, and a narrow and slender spire which later inspired, in one way or another, the form of many later churches.

After your visit, walk to the west side of the church, and take Rood Lane north 1 block to Fenchurch. Go left (west) for 2 blocks, then right on Gracechurch Street. Within a very short walk, on your right, you'll reach the Victorian arcades of one of the neighborhood's most densely packed shopping centers:

7. Leadenhall. Designed in 1881 by Horace Jones, it contains the accoutrements you'd need for either a picnic or a full gourmet dinner. Once you've finished browsing, return to Gracechurch Street, walk north about a block, then go right (east) on Leadenhall Street. Take the second right-hand (south) turn on Lime Street, where you can admire:

8. Lloyd's Building, the soaring and iconoclastically modern structure designed by Richard Rogers in 1986. This is the most recent home of a company which was originally founded in the 1680s as a marine insurance market. This is the most famous insurer in the world, with a hypermodern headquarters built atop the heart of the ancient Roman community (*Londinium*) whose builders launched London's destiny more than 2,000 years ago. Note that within just a few blocks of your position are headquartered the London Metal Exchange, The London Futures and Options Exchange, and hundreds of financial institutions whose clout is felt as far away as the Pacific Basin.

From Lime Street go back onto Leadenhall, turn left, then take the first right on Bishopsgate, then the second right-hand turn into an alleyway known as Great St. Helen's. Near its end, you'll find:

9. St. Helen Bishopsgate, the largest surviving medieval church in London. Begun in the 1400s, it was dedicated to St. Helen, the (according to legend) British mother of the Roman Emperor Constantine. Fashionable during the Elizabethan and Jacobean periods, the monuments, memorials, and grave markers within its interior are especially interesting. Exit back onto Bishopsgate, turning left (north). Two blocks later, turn left onto Wormwood Street. At the first left (Old Broad Street), go left. Towering above you—the most visible building on its street—rises the modern bulk of the tallest building in Britain, and the second-tallest building in Europe, the:

10. NatWest Tower. Housing the headquarters of the National Westminster Bank, it was designed in 1981 by Richard Seifert. As a permanent advertisement to aircraft passengers, its floor plan is shaped like the NatWest logo. Built upon massive concrete foundations above a terrain composed mostly of impervious clay, it was designed to sway gently in the wind. Unfortunately, there is no publicly accessible observation tower within the building so most visitors admire it from afar.

Continue south along Old Broad Street, noticing on your right the bulky headquarters of the:

11. London Stock Exchange. The center was built in the early 1960s to replace its outmoded original quarters. Its role has become much quieter (and somewhat redundant) since 1986, when the nature of most of The City's financial operations changed from a face-to-face agreement between brokers to a computerized clearing house conducted electronically.

Continue southwest along Old Broad Street until it merges with Threadneedle Street. Cross over Threadneedle Street, jog a few paces to your left, and head south along the narrow confines of Finch Lane. Cross the busy traffic of Cornhill (Finch Lane will change to Birchin Lane), then take the first left onto Castle Court.

REFUELING STOP Join the busy and milling crowd at the **12. George and Vulture,** at 3 Castle Court, E.C.3. (tel. 071/626-9710), for a cup of midmorning coffee, a simple meal, or an end-of-the-workday beer with the financial crowd. Originally established in the 1660s, it's one of the most authentically charming pubs in London.

After you tipple, explore the labyrinth of narrow alleyways which shelter you within an almost medieval maze from the district's weekday traffic. Head for the major boulevard (Cornhill) which lies a few steps north of your earlier refueling stop. There, near the junction of five major streets, rises:

13. The Royal Exchange. Designed by William Tite in the early 1840s, its imposing neoclassical pediment is inset with Richard Westmacott's sculpture of a victorious "Commerce." Launched by a partnership of merchants and financiers during the Elizabethan Age, its establishment was a direct attempt to lure European banking and trading functions from Antwerp (then the financial capital of northern Europe) to London. Separate markets and auction facilities for raw materials were conducted in frenzied trading here until 1982, when the building became the headquarters of the London International Financial Futures Exchange (LIFFE).

On the opposite side of Threadneedle Street rises the massive bulk of the:

14. Bank of England, originally established "for the Publick Good and Benefit of Our People" in a charter granted in 1694 by William and Mary. It is a treasure trove both of gold bullion, British banknotes, and historical archives. The only part of this massive building open to the public is the **Bank of England Museum,** whose entrance is on a narrow side street, Bartholomew Lane (tel. 071/601-4878). It's open Monday to Friday 10am to 5pm. Entrance is free.

From the Bank of England, walk northwest along Prince's Street to the intersection of Lothbury. From the northeast corner of the intersection rises:

15. St. Margaret Lothbury, another church designed and built by Sir Christopher Wren between 1686 and 1690. Filled with statues of frolicking cupids, elaborately carved screens, and a soaring eagle near the altar, it's worth a visit inside.

After you exit, cross Prince's Street and head west on Gresham Street. After traversing a handful of alleyways, you'll see on your right the gardens and the grandly historical facade of:

16. Guildhall. The power base for the Lord Mayor of London since the 12th century (and rebuilt, adapted, and enlarged many times since), it was the site of endless power negotiations throughout the Middle Ages between the English kings (headquartered outside the City of Westminster) and the guilds, associations, and brotherhoods of The City's merchants and financiers. Today, the rituals associated with the Lord Mayor are almost as elaborate as those of the monarchy itself. The medieval crypt of the Guildhall is the largest in London, and its east facade was rebuilt by Sir Christopher Wren after the Great Fire of 1666.

Continue walking westward on Gresham, and take the second right-hand turn onto Wood Street. Walk 2 blocks north to London Wall, go left for about a block, where you'll see the modern facade of:

17. The London Museum. Contained within new quarters built in 1975, it presents an assemblage of London memorabilia gathered from several earlier museums, as well as one of the best collections of period costumes. Built on top of the Western Gate of the ancient Roman colony of Londinium, it is especially strong on archeological remnants unearthed during centuries of London building. There are also tableaux portraying the Great Fire and Victorian prison cells.

After your visit, head south on Aldersgate, whose name changes to St. Martins-le-Grand. After you cross Newgate Street, you will begin to see the enormous and dignified dome of:

18. ✪ St. Paul's Cathedral, one of Europe's most famous and symbolic churches. Considered the masterpiece of Sir Christopher Wren, and the inspiration for the generation of Londoners who survived the firebombings of World War II, it was the scene of the state funerals of Nelson, Wellington, and Churchill, and the wedding celebration of Prince Charles. It is the only church in England built with a dome, the country's only church in the English Baroque style, and the first English cathedral to be designed and built by a single architect. Designated as the cathedral church for the sprawling diocese of London, its role as a church for Londoners contrasts distinctly with the national role of the Royal Church of Westminster Abbey.

WALKING TOUR 3 — St. James's

Start: The Admiralty Arch.
Finish: Buckingham Palace.
Time: About 2 hours, not including stops.
Best Time: Since this tour moves from east to west, the best time is before 3pm, after which the setting sun might glare into your eyes.
Worst Time: After dark.

Incorporating neighborhoods reserved almost since their original development for the British aristocracy, this walking tour includes many of the grandest sights of Britain's imperialistic 18th and 19th centuries.

Begin your tour near the southwest corner of Trafalgar Square, at the monumental eastern entrance of:

1. The Admiralty Arch. Commissioned by Queen Victoria's son, King Edward VII (who died before it was completed), it was designed in 1911 by Sir Aston Webb. Piercing its center are a quintet of arches faced with Portland Stone, whose assemblage marks the first (and widest) stage of a majestic processional route leading from Buckingham Palace eastward to St. Paul's Cathedral. The centermost of the five arches is opened only for ceremonial occasions, the two side arches are for vehicular traffic, and the two smallest arches are for pedestrians.

Pass beneath the arch and enter the wide panoramic thoroughfare which will eventually lead to Buckingham Palace. With your back to the Admiralty Arch, the wide and verdant expanse of:

2. The Mall will stretch out ahead of you. The only deliberately planned avenue in London, it was designed in 1910 as a memorial to the recently departed Queen Victoria by Sir Aston Webb. Lined with even rows of plane trees, it was originally the garden of the nearby palace of St. James's, and used for the aristocratic game of *paille maille* (a precursor of croquet) by the courtiers of Charles II. On Sunday, The Mall is often closed to traffic and becomes a pedestrian extension of the adjacent expanse of St. James's Park. The Mall's wide boundaries are a favorite exercise area for London's equestrians and their mounts. Immediately

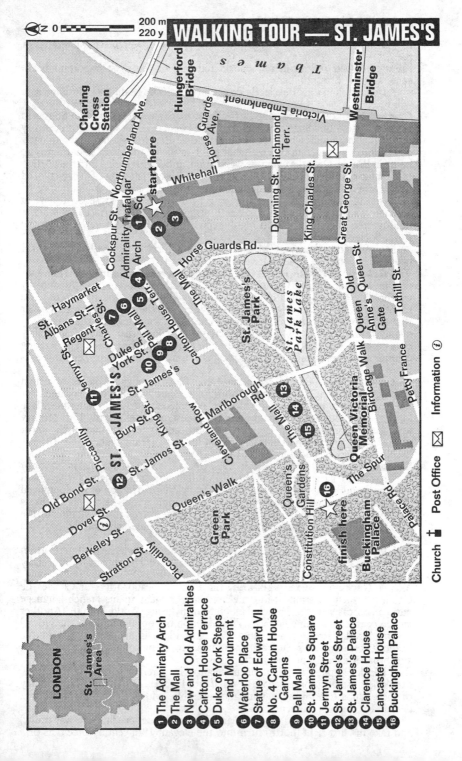

WALKING TOUR — ST. JAMES'S

Z 0 — 200 m / 220 y

start here

Thames

Charing Cross Station
Hungerford Bridge
Westminster Bridge
Horse Guards Ave.
Victoria Embankment
Whitehall
Downing St.
Richmond Terr.
King Charles St.
Great George St.
Northumberland Ave.
Cockspur St.
Admiralty Arch
Trafalgar Sq.
Horse Guards Rd.
The Mall
Carlton House Terr.
St. James's Park
St. James's Park Lake
Queen St.
Old Queen St.
Queen Anne's Gate
Tothill St.
Haymarket
St. Albans St.
Regent St.
Charles St.
Duke of York St.
Pall Mall
St. James's
Jermyn St.
Bury St.
King St.
St. James's St.
St. James St.
Cleveland Row
Marlborough Rd.
Birdcage Walk
Petty France
The Spur
Queen Victoria Memorial
The Mall
Queen's Gardens
Constitution Hill
finish here
Buckingham Palace
ST. JAMES'S
Old Bond St.
Piccadilly
Dover St.
Berkeley St.
Stratton St.
Queen's Walk
Green Park

Church ✚ Post Office ⊠ Information ⓘ

LONDON
St. James's Area

1. The Admiralty Arch
2. The Mall
3. New and Old Admiralties
4. Carlton House Terrace
5. Duke of York Steps and Monument
6. Waterloo Place
7. Statue of Edward VII
8. No. 4 Carlton House Gardens
9. Pall Mall
10. St. James's Square
11. Jermyn Street
12. St. James's Street
13. St. James's Palace
14. Clarence House
15. Lancaster House
16. Buckingham Palace

to your left (keeping your back to the Arch) are the interconnected buildings of the:

3. New and Old Admiralties, considered one of the most important nerve centers of the British military.

As you stroll in a southwesterly direction down The Mall, the right-hand side will reveal:

4. Carlton House Terrace, one of the most regal ensembles of town houses in London. These buildings replaced the once-palatial home of the 18th-century Prince Regent, a man who later became George III. He built (and subsequently demolished) at staggering expense what was considered the most beautiful private home in Britain. Only the columns were saved, and later recycled into the portico of Trafalgar Square's National Gallery. The subsequent row of ivory-colored neoclassical town houses was designed as one of Nash's last works before he died, much maligned, at the center of a financial scandal in 1835. Today, in addition to art galleries and cultural institutions, The Terrace houses the headquarters of one of the most highly reputed scientific bodies in the world, the Royal Society.

Midway along the length of Carlton House Terrace, its evenly symmetrical neoclassical expanse is pierced with:

5. The Duke of York Steps and **the Duke of York Monument,** built in honor of the second son of George III. The massive sculpture was funded by withholding 1 day's pay from every soldier within the British Empire. The resulting column was chiseled from pink granite, and the statue was created by Sir Richard Westmacott in 1834. Contemporary wits, knowing that the duke died owing massive debts to his angry creditors, joked that placing his effigy on a column was the only way to keep him away from their grasp. This soaring column and monument (the statue weighs 7 tons) dominates the square it prefaces:

6. Waterloo Place. Considered one of the most prestigious pieces of urban planning in London, it reeks with both aristocratic elegance and nostalgia for England's grand military victories over Napoléon. No. 107 Waterloo Place (designed in 1830 and considered one of the finest examples of early 19th-century neoclassical architecture in London) is the headquarters for one of the most distinguished gentlemen's clubs in Britain, the Athenaeum Club.

Notice, within Waterloo Place, the:

7. Statue of Edward VII, crafted in 1921 by Sir Bertram Mackennal in honor of the man who gave the world the Edwardian Age and much of the grand neighborhood to the northeast of Buckingham Palace. The son of the long-lived Victoria, he ascended the throne at the age of 60, only 9 years before his death. As if to balance the position of his statue, a statue dedicated to the victims of the Crimean War, part of which honors Florence Nightingale, stands at the opposite end of Waterloo Place.

History buffs will appreciate Carlton House Gardens, which runs into Carlton House Terrace's western end. Lovers of France and French history especially appreciate the plaques which identify the facade of:

8. No. 4 Carlton House Gardens, the London headquarters of Charles de Gaulle's French government-in-exile, and site of many of his French-language radio broadcasts to the French Underground during World War II. (Another facade of this same building faces The Mall, on the opposite side of the block.)

One of the streets intersecting Waterloo Place is an avenue rich in the headquarters of many exclusive private clubs. Not to be confused with the longer and broader expanse of The Mall, this is:

9. Pall Mall. Despite its variant pronunciation in different parts of the Empire, Londoners usually pronounce it *Pell-Mell* (not Paul Mawl). Membership in many of these clubs is both prestigious and desirable, with waiting lists of up to a decade for the best of them.

Walk west for a block along Pall Mall (beware of the speeding one-way traffic) and take the first right (north) turn into the elegant 18th-century precincts of:

10. St. James's Square. Laid out in the 1660s, it was built on land donated by the first earl of St. Albans, Henry Jermyn, a friend of the widow of Charles I and a friend of the future king Charles II. It was originally designed with very large private houses on all sides for noble families who wanted to live near the seat of royal power at nearby St. James's Palace. Buildings of special interest include no. 10 (Chatham House), private residence of three British prime ministers, the last of which was Queen Victoria's nemesis, William Gladstone. At no. 32, General Eisenhower and his subordinates planned the 1942 invasion of North Africa and the 1944 Allied invasion of Normandy. At no. 16, the announcement of the climactic defeat by Wellington of Napoléon's forces at Waterloo was delivered (along with the captured eagle-shaped symbols of Napoléon's army) by a bloodstained officer, Major Percy, to the British Regent.

Circumnavigate the square, eventually exiting at its northern edge via Duke of York Street. One block later, turn left onto:

11. Jermyn Street, one of the most prestigious shopping streets in London. Expensive and upscale the shops display a mixture of inviolable British tradition mingled with the perceived necessities for The Good Life.

REFUELING STOP At **12. Green's Champagne and Oyster Bar,** at 36 Duke Street, S.W.1 (tel. 071/930-4566) much about its facade and paneled decor might remind you of the many gentlemen's clubs you've already passed in the neighborhood. This one, however, welcomes nonmembers. There's a battered bar for the consumption of "spirits" and glasses of wine, platters of oysters, dollops of caviar, shrimp, or crabmeat (which you can eat at the bar or a table) and a wide variety of English-inspired appetizers and main courses.

Exit from Duke Street onto Jermyn Street, turn right (west) and continue to enjoy the shops. Two blocks later, turn left onto:

13. St. James's Street, with its share of private clubs, the most fashionable of which is, arguably, White's, at no. 37. (Its premises were designed in 1788 by James Wyatt.) Prince Charles celebrated his stag party here the night before his marriage to Lady (later, Princess) Diana. Past members included Evelyn Waugh (who received refuge here from his literary "hounds of modernity"). Even if you're recommended for membership (which is unlikely) the waiting list is 8 years.

At the bottom (southern end) of St. James's Street is:

14. ✪ St. James's Palace, one of the most historic buildings of London. Birthplace of many British monarchs, it served as the principal royal residence from 1698 (when Whitehall Palace burned down) until the ascent of Queen Victoria (who moved into Buckingham Palace) in 1837. Originally enlarged from a Tudor core built by Henry VIII for one of his ill-fated queens, it was altered by Sir Christopher Wren in 1703. The palace, rich in history and connotation, gave its name to the entire neighborhood you've just surveyed.

After your visit, walk southwest along Cleveland Row, then turn left (southeast) onto Stable Yard Row. On your left rises the side of:

15. Clarence House. Designed in 1829 by John Nash, it is the official London home of the queen mother. On the opposite side of Stable Yard Row rises the side of the very formal:

16. Lancaster House. Designed in 1827 by Benjamin Wyatt, it has, during its lifetime, been known variously as York House and Stafford House. Chopin performed his ballads and nocturnes for Queen Victoria here, and during the upsetting renunciation of his throne as a precondition to his marriage to Wallis Warfield Simpson, Edward VIII lived here during his tenure as the Prince of Wales. Heavily damaged by World War II bombings, it has been gracefully restored, furnished in the French Louis XV style, and now serves as a setting for State receptions and dinners.

Within a few steps, when you arrive at the multiple plane trees of The Mall, turn right for a vista of the front of:

17. ○ Buckingham Palace, the official London residence of every British monarch since Victoria. Its present occupant is the world's most famous woman, Queen Elizabeth II.

WALKING TOUR 4 — Chelsea

Start: Chelsea Embankment at the Battersea Bridge.
Finish: Chelsea's Old Town Hall, or any of the pubs nearby.
Time: 2 hours, not counting any stops.
Best Time: Anytime.

One of the most creative neighborhoods of London, home to some of the most prosperous residents of the capital, Chelsea is considered a complete, perfect, and attractively scaled "village within the city" in London. Residents have included Margaret Thatcher, Mick Jagger, Oscar Wilde, Thomas Carlyle, Turner, John Singer Sargent, Henry James, and Henry VIII.

Begin your tour above the massive masonry buttresses known as the Chelsea Embankment, at the northern terminus of the:

1. Battersea Bridge. Though not the most famous bridge in London, it will help you understand Chelsea's vital link to the Thames. Walk eastward through a historic neighborhood marred only by the roar of the riverside traffic. Across the water rises the district of Battersea, a rapidly gentrifying neighborhood.

The street which rambles beside the Thames is Cheyne Walk. Rich with Georgian and Victorian architecture (and containing some of the most expensive houses), it is considered an architectural treasure house. Although the bulk of your exploration along this street will be eastward, for the moment detour from the base of Battersea Bridge westward to number 119 Cheyne Walk:

2. Turner's House. Its tall and narrow premises sheltered England's greatest painter, J. M. W. Turner (1775–1851), during the last years of his life. His canvases are uniquely recognizable for the shimmering qualities of their colors. When he died in this house, his very appropriate final words were, "God is Light." Just to the east of Turner's House, at nos. 96–100 Cheyne Walk, is:

3. Lindsey House, a building considered one of Chelsea's most beautiful, completed in the 1670s. Built by the Swiss-born physician to two British kings (James I and Charles II), it became the British headquarters of the Moravian Church around 1750. Later divided and sold as four separate residences, it housed the American-born painter James Whistler (at no. 96 between 1866 and 1879). The gardens of no. 99 and no. 100 were designed by Britain's most celebrated Edwardian architect, Sir Edwin Lutyens (1869–1944).

At this point, retrace your steps eastward to Battersea Bridge and begin the eastward ramble along Cheyne Walk. Midway between the heavy traffic of Beaufort Street and the much quieter Danvers Street, you'll see:

4. Crosby Hall. There is no street number, but its original brick and stone construction (resembling a chapel) is prefaced with a modern wing of gray stone added in the 1950s. Originally built in the early 1400s, and owned successively by both King Richard III and Sir Thomas More, it was transported in the early 1900s stone by stone from Bishopsgate, partly under the financial incentive of American-born Nancy Astor. Today it provides apartments and dining facilities for the British Federation of University Women. Parts of its interior (which contain paintings by Holbein, a gracefully trussed roof, and some Jacobean furniture) are open, free, to the public daily except Sunday morning, from 10am to noon, and from 2:15 to 5pm.

After your visit, continue walking eastward on Cheyne Walk. After crossing both Danvers Street and Church Street, if you detour a few buildings away from the river onto Old Church Street, you'll reach:

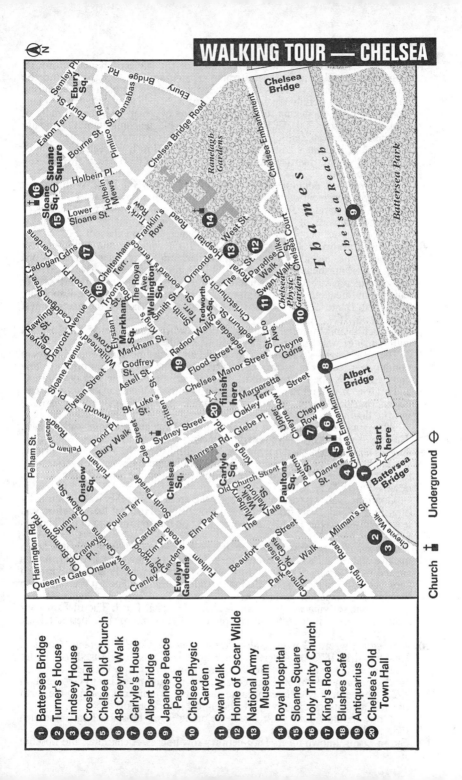

WALKING TOUR — CHELSEA

N

Chelsea Bridge

Battersea Park

T h a m e s

Chelsea Reach

Ranelagh Gardens

Chelsea Embankment

Royal Hospital Road

Albert Bridge

Battersea Bridge

start here

finish here

Sloane Square

Sloane Sq.

Ebury Sq.

Cadogan Gdns

Markham Sq.

Wellington Sq.

Carlyle Sq.

Chelsea Sq.

Onslow Sq.

Evelyn Gardens

1. Battersea Bridge
2. Turner's House
3. Lindsey House
4. Crosby Hall
5. Chelsea Old Church
6. 48 Cheyne Walk
7. Carlyle's House
8. Albert Bridge
9. Japanese Peace Pagoda
10. Chelsea Physic Garden
11. Swan Walk
12. Home of Oscar Wilde
13. National Army Museum
14. Royal Hospital
15. Sloane Square
16. Holy Trinity Church
17. King's Road
18. Blushes Café
19. Antiquarius
20. Chelsea's Old Town Hall

✝ Church   Ⓤ Underground

5. Chelsea Old Church, the parish church of the late Sir Thomas More. Its beauty is diminished only by the traffic outside and the fact that it and the neighborhood which contains it were heavily damaged by Nazi bombs during World War II. Gracefully repaired, it contains a chapel partly designed by Hans Holbein, an urn containing the earthly remains of a man who owned most of Chelsea during the 1700s, Sir Hans Sloane, and a plaque commemorating the life of American novelist Henry James, a longtime Chelsea resident who died nearby in 1916. The building's Lawrence Chapel is reputed to have been the scene of Henry VIII's secret marriage to Jane Seymour several days before their official marriage in 1536.

After your visit, continue walking eastward along Cheyne Walk. Within about a block, the pavement will branch to form a verdant copse of trees and lawn, behind which stand some of the most expensive and desirable town houses of Chelsea. Occupants of these elegantly proportioned buildings have included some very famous people, including Mick Jagger, who purchased:

6. No. 48 Cheyne Walk. Jagger lived here for a while, brushing elbows with neighbors who included guitarist Keith Richards, publishing magnate Lord Weidenfeld, and the grandson of the oil-industry giant, Paul Getty, Jr. Artistic denizens of an earlier age included George Eliot who lived for part of her flamboyant life (and later died) at no. 19. The star of the Pre-Raphaelite movement, Dante Gabriel Rossetti, lived in what is considered the street's finest building no. 16.

Branch inland from the Thames, heading north along Cheyne Row, where, within a short walk, at no. 5 Cheyne Row, stands:

7. ✪ Thomas Carlyle's House, considered one of the most interesting houses in London, particularly to literary enthusiasts. It is one of the neighborhood's few houses which is open to the public. The former home of "the sage of Chelsea" and his wife Jane, it offers a fascinating insight into the Victorian decors of its era. Notice the small gravestone in the garden marking the burial place of the author's favorite dog.

After your visit, retrace your steps to Cheyne Walk and continue walking east. The lacy iron bridge which looms into view is the:

8. Albert Bridge. Matched only by the Tower Bridge and the Westminster Bridge, this might be the most-photographed bridge in London. Created at the height of the Victorian fascination with the multiple possibilities of cast iron, it was designed in 1873 by R. M. Ordish.

Continue walking eastward beneath the trees of Cheyne Walk, eventually branching inland, away from the river, along Royal Hospital Road. Before you leave the banks of the Thames, however, look on the opposite end of the Thames for:

9. Japanese Peace Pagoda with its Buddhist-inspired form. Containing a massive statue of Buddha covered in gold leaf, and unveiled in 1985, it was crafted by 50 Japanese nuns and monks. Set at the riverside edge of Battersea Park, according to plans by the Buddhist leader Nichidatsu Fugii, it was offered to Britain by the Japanese government.

Continue walking northeast along Royal Hospital Road. The turf on your right (its entrance is at 66 Royal Hospital Road) belongs to the oldest surviving botanic garden in Britain, the:

10. Chelsea Physic Garden (also known as the Chelsea Botanic Garden). Established in 1673 on 4 acres of riverfront land which belonged to Charles Cheyne, it was founded by the Worshipful Society of Apothecaries, and later funded permanently by Sir Hans Sloane, botanist and physician to George II, in 1722. The germ of what later became international industries began in the earth of these gardens, greenhouses, and botanical laboratories.

Now, continue your walk northeast along Royal Hospital Road, but turn right at the first cross street:

11. Swan Lane, known for its 18th-century row houses. A charming and obscure part of Chelsea, walk down it, turning at the first left onto Dilke Street, and at its dead end, turn left onto Tite Street. (From here, your view of the Japanese Peace Pagoda on the opposite bank of the Thames might be even better than before.) At no. 34 Tite Street, you'll see a plaque commemorating:

12. **The Home of Oscar Wilde.** From here, Wilde wrote many of his most charming plays, including *The Importance of Being Earnest* and *Lady Windermere's Fan.* After Wilde was arrested and imprisoned during the most famous trial for homosexuality in British history, the house was sold to pay his debts. The plaque was presented in 1954, a century after Wilde's birthday. A few steps away on the same street lie houses which once belonged to two of America's most famous expatriates. No. 31 was the home of John Singer Sargent (and the studio where he painted many of his most famous portraits), and no. 35 was the home of James McNeill Whistler.

At the end of Tite Street, turn right onto Royal Hospital Road. Within a block, you'll reach the fortresslike premises of the:

13. **National Army Museum,** whose galleries are devoted to weapons, uniforms, and art, with dioramas of famous battles and such memorabilia as the skeleton of Napoléon's favorite horse.

Next door to the museum, a short distance to the northeast, is the building which contains the world's most famous horticultural exhibition, the Chelsea Flower Show, which is held every year amid the vast premises of:

14. **The Royal Hospital.** Designed in 1682 in the aftermath of the Great Fire of London by Sir Christopher Wren (and considered, after St. Paul's Cathedral, his masterpiece) it might have been built to compete with Louis XIV's construction of *Les Invalides* in Paris. Both were designed as a home for wounded or aging soldiers, and both are grandoise and immense.

Pass the Royal Hospital, eventually turning left (northeast) 4 blocks later at Chelsea Bridge Road. This street will change its name in about a block to Lower Sloane Street, which leads eventually to:

15. **Sloane Square,** considered the northernmost gateway to Chelsea, it was laid out in 1780 on land belonging to Sir Hans Sloane. His collection of minerals, fossils, and plant specimens were the core of what eventually became the British Museum. Detour ½ block north of Sloane Square (its entrance is on Sloane Street) to visit:

16. **Holy Trinity Church,** a church known as a triumph of the late 19th century's arts-and-crafts movement. Completed in 1890, it contains windows by William Morris following designs by Burne-Jones and embellishments in the Pre-Raphaelite style.

Exit from Sloane Square's southwestern corner, and stroll down:

17. ✪ **King's Road,** one of the most variegated and interesting commercial streets in London. Laden with antiques stores, booksellers, sophisticated and punk clothiers, restaurants, coffeehouses, tearooms, and diehard adherents of the "Sloane Ranger" mystique, it is a delight to observe the human comedy. Dozens of possibilities for food, sustenance, and companionship exist.

REFUELING STOP   18. Blushes Café, at 52 King's Road, S.W.3. (tel. 071/589-6640), serves wine by the glass, light snacks which include an array of well-made salads, such British-inspired dishes as game pie, and unusual and well-chosen wines.

After your refreshment (which can be repeated at any of the neighborhood's other pubs and cafés along the way), continue walking southwest along King's Road. Midway between Shawfield Street and Flood Street lies a warren of antiques sellers, all clustered together into a complex known as:

19. **Antiquarius,** at 131-141 King's Road, S.W.3. Browse at will, maybe you'll buy an almost-heirloom or perhaps something of lasting value.

As you continue down King's Road, oval-shaped blue and white plaques will identify buildings of particular interest. One which you should especially watch for is:

20. **Chelsea's Old Town Hall,** set on the south side of King's Road, midway between Chelsea Manor and Oakley Street. Its Georgian grandeur is the favorite hangout of everyone from punk rockers to soon-to-be-married couples applying for a marriage license. Many wedding parties are photographed in front of it.

   The energetic and/or still curious participants in this tour might transform the finale of this walking tour into a pub crawl, as the neighborhood is filled with many enticing choices.

WALKING TOUR 5 — Dickens's London

Start: Russell Square.
Finish: The Old Deanery.
Time: 2½ hours.
Best Time: Any daylight hours. Early Saturday or anytime on Sunday might have the least amount of traffic.

The writings of Charles Dickens have international appeal. Certain London neighborhoods are intimately linked to such works as *Little Dorrit,* the *Pickwick Papers,* and *David Copperfield.* Follow this walking tour for its insight into the overcrowded alleys, grimy buildings, and working conditions which were prevalent in the 19th century.

   Begin amid the regular symmetry of a neighborhood in the shadow of the British Museum. Start at:

1. **Russell Square,** where in addition to inspiring Dickens, its side streets were inhabited by other writers such as Ralph Waldo Emerson, an adolescent Edgar Allan Poe, and T. S. Eliot. Walk east along Guildford Street, where to the left, you'll see:

2. **Coram Fields,** the site where the Foundling Hospital (before it was moved to another part of London) stood in Victorian days, and the place where several of Dickens's characters—including the rebellious servant Tattycoram portrayed in *Little Dorrit*—was raised. Originally established around 1740, only the ornate gateway survives to remind passersby of the formerly influential organization which raised many of London's abandoned children.

   Turn right onto Doughty Street, but do not confuse this with Doughty Mews, which lies a block away. At no. 48 Doughty Street, you'll find:

3. ✪ **Dickens's House,** one of London's most potent homages to Dickens. The author rented it between 1837 and 1839, producing within its walls the manuscripts for *Oliver Twist,* the *Pickwick Papers,* and *Nicholas Nickleby.* Today, it's the headquarters of the Dickens's Fellowship, and contains a collection of Dickens memorabilia, one of his writing desks, and a re-creation in its cellar of a kitchen he described within the *Pickwick Papers.*

   Doughty Street soon changes its name to John Street. Continue south along it, until the end where you turn left at Theobald's Road. Two blocks later, turn right on Gray's Inn Road. On your right is:

4. **Gray's Inn,** the complex of buildings that, theoretically, was supposed to provide offices and residential flats for lawyers, and to admit applicants to the practice of law in England. A warren of offices, residences, and dark cubbyholes during the Victorian era, Dickens, in *The Uncommercial Traveller,* called it "one of the most depressing institutions in brick and mortar known to the children of men." This description was probably inspired by an unhappy experience, when Dickens was 15, working within no. 1 Gray's Inn, in 1827, as a clerk. Later, other addresses within Gray's Inn were used as settings in *David Copperfield* and served as inspiration for similarly depressing locales within others of his novels.

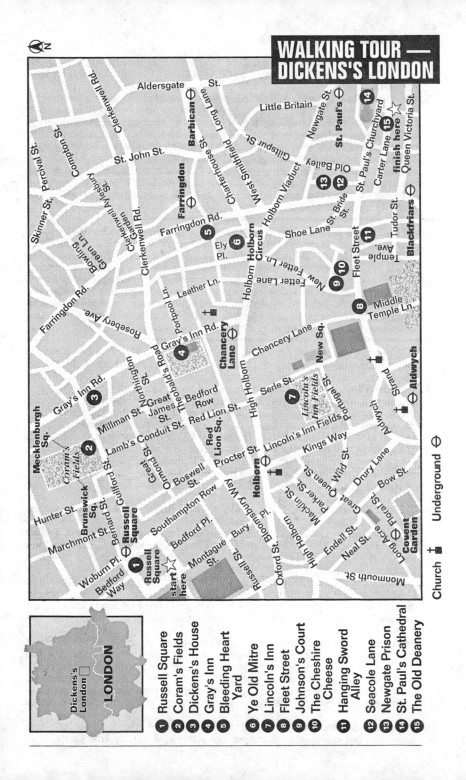

WALKING TOUR — DICKENS'S LONDON

1. Russell Square
2. Coram's Fields
3. Dickens's House
4. Gray's Inn
5. Bleeding Heart Yard
6. Ye Old Mitre
7. Lincoln's Inn
8. Fleet Street
9. Johnson's Court
10. The Cheshire Cheese
11. Hanging Sword Alley
12. Seacole Lane
13. Newgate Prison
14. St. Paul's Cathedral
15. The Old Deanery

Church ✝   Underground ⊖

LONDON

Dickens's London

From your position walking south on Gray's Inn, take the fifth left (Fox Court, which after about a block changes to Greville Street). Within 5 blocks, on your right, you'll see:

5. Bleeding Heart Yard, a dignified courtyard stained black by a century of industrial grime. This opening in the neighborhood's mass of masonry was made famous by Dickens in *Little Dorrit* as the locale of Doyce and Clennam's factory, and the grimy, underprivileged home of the Plornish family. The place's evocative name was attributed to a very old inn whose trademark was a brokenhearted Virgin, but the place was also associated with a certain Lady Hatton. She entered an alliance with the Devil, who—when the fun was over—came embodied as a dashing swain dressed entirely in black, to claim her. Spiriting her off to hell, he left only her bleeding heart beside the pump in a courtyard lane known as Bleeding Heart Yard.

REFUELING STOP Exit from the yard onto a narrow alley to its south known as Ely Place, where within a few blocks, you will come to **6. Ye Olde Mitre,** at Ely Court off Ely Place, E.C.1. (tel. 071/405-4751). An inn has stood beside the dingy brick-lined sides of this alleyway since 1547, but the incarnation you'll see today has dark-stained Victorian paneling and battered wooden floors, tables, and benches well-worn long ago by characters who might have filled the pages of Dickens. Filled today with a clientele of City financiers from the nearby jewelry district, the place serves simple food (place your order at the bar) and more mugs of Burton's ale than almost anywhere else in The City.

Continue south along Ely Place, then turn right into Holborn Circus, which will funnel into High Holborn Street. Proceed westward for 6 blocks to Chancery Lane. On the junction's southwest corner lies:

7. Lincoln's Inn, another group of weathered buildings, used a century ago as a complex of Victorian apartments and legal offices. Originally built during the 1400s, it's pervaded with associations of Dickens. Its Old Hall was the setting for the opening scene of *Bleak House*. A short distance to the west is an open space, Lincoln's Inn Fields where Betsey Trotwood of *David Copperfield* took lodgings in a building that flanked it. On the Fields' western border sits no. 58 Lincoln's Inn Fields, a town house which belonged to Dickens's friend John Forster, who entertained the author from time to time.

Retrace your steps eastward to Chancery Lane, then head south until you reach:

8. ✪ Fleet Street, the traditional headquarters of British publishing and journalism. Though its grip on British journalism is now a memory, many of Dickens's characters met or interacted with one another along Fleet Street. At no. 1 Fleet Street, you'll find The Williams and Glyn Bank, which in an earlier incarnation was Child's Bank which served as a model for "Tellson's Bank" in *A Tale of Two Cities*.

Fleet Street was crucially important to Dickens's career. In 1833, Chapman & Hall, the publishers of *Monthly Magazine,* published his first manuscript. To see the journalistic offices whose approval launched one of England's most important literary careers, turn north off Fleet Street into the postage-stamp-size confines of:

9. Johnson's Court. Farther along, from an entrance located at 145 Fleet Street (near the corner of Wine Office Court) is The Cheshire Cheese, a restaurant and pub familiar to Dickens which provided a setting for some of his scenes. If you want, you might order beer or coffee, but you'll have to wait until it reopens in 1993. Continue westward along Fleet Street. A very short block later, extending south of Fleet, is Whitefriars Street, which, if you'll enter, soon provides access to:

10. Hanging Sword Alley, where Dickens assigned the lodgings of Jerry Cruncher, one of the more gruesome characters in *A Tale of Two Cities*.

Fleet Street soon empties into a traffic circle known as Ludgate Circus. Continue your walk eastward, onto a street identified as Ludgate Hill. The first street on your left is:

11. Seacoal Lane where one of the Victorian era's most feared and loathed prisons once stood and where Mr. Pickwick was imprisoned for debt. Continue walking northeast on Seacoal Lane, which merges in about a block with Old Bailey, where you turn left. There, a grim-looking judicial building—the Central Criminal Court—occupies the site of:

12. Newgate Prison, an even more famous Victorian jail. Incarceration within one of its dank cells was perhaps the greatest fear of Fagin and his band of adolescent pickpockets in *Oliver Twist,* and its despair was later portrayed within sections of *Great Expectations.* Though Newgate was demolished in 1902, memories of it as one of the most truly horrible prisons of 19th-century Europe linger on within the neighborhood even today.

Turn south along Old Bailey for about a block, then go left (eastward) along Ludgate Hill until you come to:

13. ✪ St. Paul's Cathedral, a monument rich in connotations both for Dickens and for dozens of other writers. Dickens set some of the pivotal scenes of *David Copperfield* here, including episodes where Betsey Trotwood met secretly with a man whom readers later learned was her estranged husband. To the south of the cathedral, within a very short alleyway which signs will identify as Dean's Court, stands:

14. The Old Deanery, where Dickens worked for a brief period as a legal reporter in 1829.

WALKING TOUR 6 —— The British Museum

Start: Assyrian Transept.
Finish: Egyptian Galleries.
Time: 2 hours.
Best Time: Weekday when the museum opens at 10am.
Worst Time: Weekends when it's overcrowded.

As you enter the front hall of the British Museum, Great Russell Street, W.C.1 (tel. 071/636-1555), head first to the Assyrian Transept (Room 26) on the ground floor, where you'll find the:

1. Winged and human-headed bulls that once guarded the gateways to the palaces of Assyrian kings.
From here you can continue into the angular hall (Room 25) of Egyptian sculpture to see the:

2. ✪ Rosetta Stone, whose discovery led to the deciphering of the mysterious hieroglyphs, explained in a wall display behind the stone.
Immediately to your left (Room 19, in the Nimrud Gallery) is the:

3. Black Obelisk of Shalmaneser III (858–824 B.C.), a tribute from Jehu, king of Israel.
West of the Nimrud Gallery is the Duveen Gallery (Room 8), housing the:

4. ✪ Elgin Marbles, consisting of sculptures from the Parthenon. The frieze shows a ceremonial procession that took place in Athens every 4 years. Of the 91 metopes from the Parthenon, 15 are housed today in the British Museum. They depict the to-the-death struggle between the handsome Lapiths and the grotesque, drunken Centaurs. The head of the horse from the chariot of Selene, goddess of the moon, is one of the pediment sculptures.
Directly northeast of the Duveen Gallery is the:

5. Caryatid from the Erechtheum (Room of the Caryatid; Room 9), a temple started in 421 B.C. and dedicated to Athena and Poseidon. Displayed here, too, are sculptures from the Mausoleum at Halicarnassus (one of the Seven Wonders of the Ancient World), built for Mausolus, ruler of Caria, who died around 350 B.C.

In Room 14, to the east, the First Roman Room, is displayed:

6. **The Portland Vase,** considered the finest example of ancient cameo carving, having been made in the 1st century B.C. or A.D.

From here, cross the central Rotunda, the Reading Room, to enter the King's Library (Room 32), which holds such works as a copy of the:

7. **Gutenberg Bible,** the first book ever printed from movable type (1455). Other exhibits include Asian illuminated manuscripts, George III's Library, and early postage stamps, including the 1840 Great British Penny Black and the rare 1847 post office issues of Mauritius. The Diamond Sutra of 868 is the first dated example of printing.

Directly south of King's Library (Room 30) is the Grenville Library, repository of the:

8. **Magna Carta,** one of two surviving copies of King John's Magna Carta (1215), as well as the Lindisfarne Gospels (an outstanding example of the work of Northumbrian artists in the early period of English Christianity, written and illustrated about 698). Almost every major literary figure, including Shakespeare, is represented with signatures, including those of Dickens, Jane Austen, Charlotte Brontë, and Yeats. Also on display is Nelson's last letter to Lady Hamilton and the journals of Captain Cook. Other notable exhibitions in the library include the Benedictional (in Latin) of St. Ethelwold, Bishop of Winchester (963–984), the Luttrell Psalter, and the Harley Golden Gospels of about 800.

The Department of Medieval and Later Antiquities has its galleries on the first floor (second floor to Americans), reached by the main staircase. Of its exhibitions, one of the most important is in Room 41:

9. ✪ **The Sutton Hoo Anglo-Saxon burial ship,** discovered in Suffolk. It is, in the words of one expert, "the richest treasure ever dug from English soil," containing gold jewelry, armor, weapons, bronze bowls, and caldrons, silverware, and the inevitable drinking horn of Norse culture. No body was found, although the tomb was believed to be that of a king of East Anglia who died in the 7th century. You'll also see the bulging-eyed Lewis chessmen (12th century) in walrus ivory, Romanesque carvings in Scandinavian style of the 12th century, and the Ilbert collection of clocks and watches.

Featured attractions of the upper floor include the Egyptian galleries, especially the:

10. **Mummies,** resting in the upper Egyptian Galleries from Rooms 60–65. Egyptian Room 63 is extraordinary, with its cosmetics, domestic utensils, toys, tools, and other work. Some items of Sumerian art, unearthed from the Royal Cemetery at Ur (southern Iraq), also are contained within these galleries: a queen's bull-headed harp (the oldest ever discovered); a queen's sledge (the oldest known example of a land vehicle), a figure of a he-goat on hind legs (crafted about 2500 B.C.). In the Iranian section rests "The Treasure of the Oxus," a hoard of riches, perhaps a temple deposit, ranging in date from the 6th to the 3rd century B.C., containing a unique collection of goldsmith work, such as a nude youth, signet rings, a fish-shaped base, and votive plaques.

7. ORGANIZED TOURS

In addition to touring London by foot or tube, several bus tours will take you to see the sights, plus there are dozens of fascinating trips offered along the Thames.

THE EASIEST WAY TO SEE LONDON

For the first-timer, the quickest and most economical way to see the city is to take a 2-hour, 20-mile circular tour of the West End and the City of London on the guided

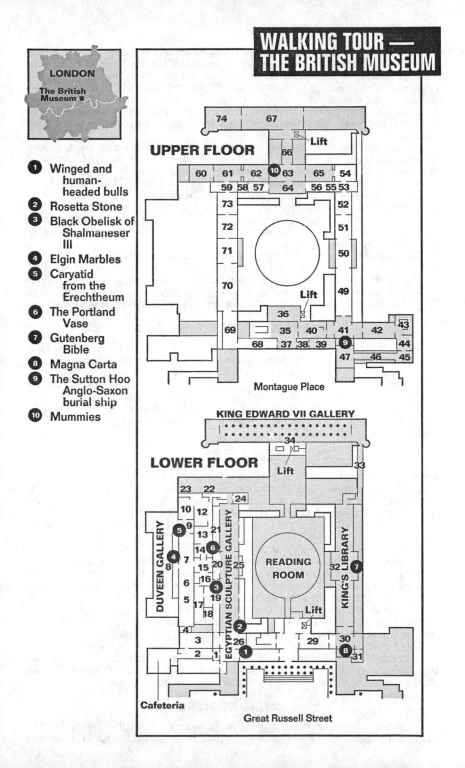

WALKING TOUR — THE BRITISH MUSEUM

LONDON

The British Museum ■

1. Winged and human-headed bulls
2. Rosetta Stone
3. Black Obelisk of Shalmaneser III
4. Elgin Marbles
5. Caryatid from the Erechtheum
6. The Portland Vase
7. Gutenberg Bible
8. Magna Carta
9. The Sutton Hoo Anglo-Saxon burial ship
10. Mummies

UPPER FLOOR

Montague Place

LOWER FLOOR

KING EDWARD VII GALLERY

DUVEEN GALLERY

EGYPTIAN SCULPTURE GALLERY

READING ROOM

KING'S LIBRARY

Cafeteria

Great Russell Street

Original London Transport Sightseeing Tour, which passes virtually all the major places of interest in central London. Operated by London Transport Tours, the journeys leave at frequent intervals daily from Victoria, Piccadilly Circus, Marble Arch, and Baker Street. Tickets cost £8 ($14.80) for adults and £4 ($7.40) for children and are available from the conductor. Tickets can also be purchased from London Regional Transport Travel Information Centres, where you can get a discount of £1 ($1.85) off each ticket. (See "Getting Around" in Chapter 3 for locations of the travel centers.)

London Transport also offers a 3-hour guided coach **West End tour,** passing Westminster Abbey (guided tour), Houses of Parliament, Horse Guards, Changing of the Guard at Buckingham Palace, Trafalgar Square, and Piccadilly Circus. Tickets for this tour cost £11.50 ($21.30) for adults and £9 ($16.65) for children under 14.

London Transport also has a popular **3-hour City tour** that includes guided trips to the Tower of London and St. Paul's Cathedral. The cost of this tour is £16 ($29.60) for adults, £13 ($24.05) for children under 14. The City tour leaves at 2pm Monday through Saturday from March to October. For about 3 months during the summer the tour also runs on Sunday.

These two tours are also combined to form the **London Day tour,** which costs £31.50 ($58.30) for adults and £28 ($51.80) for children under 14, including lunch.

The West End and City tours begin at London Transport's own Wilton Road coach station, alongside Victoria train station. To reserve seats or for information, call 071/227-3456, or go to a **London Transport Travel Information Centre.**

HARRODS SIGHTSEEING BUS

A double-decker bus in the discreet green-and-gold livery of **Harrods** takes sightseeing tours around London's attractions. The first departure from door 8 of Harrods on Brompton Road is at 10:30am and there are also tours at 1:30 and 4pm. Tea, coffee, and orange juice are served on board. The tour costs £14 ($25.90) for adults, £7 ($12.95) for children under 12. All-day excursion tours to Bath, Windsor, Stratford-upon-Avon, plus around all of London, are available. You can purchase tickets at Harrods, Sightseeing Department, lower ground floor (tel. 071/581-3603). **Tube:** Knightsbridge.

BOAT TRIPS

Touring boats operate on the Thames all year and can take you to various places within Greater London. Main embarkation points are Westminster Pier, Charing Cross Pier, and Tower Pier—a system that enables you, for instance, to take a "water taxi" from the Tower of London to Westminster Abbey. Not only are the boats energy-saving, but they allow you to sit back in comfort as you see London from the river.

Pleasure boats operate all year down the Thames from Westminster Pier to the Tower of London, Greenwich, and the Thames Barrier; they operate from 10am to 4pm and depart every 20 minutes in summer, and every 30 minutes in winter. It takes 20 minutes to reach the Tower and 40 minutes to arrive at Greenwich. In the summer, services operate upriver to Kew, Richmond, and Hampton Court from Westminster Pier. There are departures every 30 minutes from 10:30am to 4pm for the 1½-hour journey to Kew; and there are three departures daily for the 2½-hour Richmond trip and three departures daily for the 3- to 5-hour trip to Hampton Court.

The multitude of small companies operating boat services from Westminster Pier have organized themselves into the **Westminster Passenger Service Association,** Westminster Pier, Victoria Embankment (tel. 071/930-4097). Boats leave the pier for cruises of varying lengths throughout the day and evening.

CANAL CRUISES

The London canals were once major highways. Since the Festival of Britain in 1951, some of the traditional painted canal boats have been resurrected for Venetian-style trips through these waterways. One of them is the **Jason,** which takes you on a 90-minute trip from Blomfield Road through the long Maida Hill tunnel under Edgware Road, through Regent's Park, the Mosque, the Zoo, Lord Snowdon's Aviary, past the Pirate's Castle to Camden Lock, and returns to Little Venice.

The season begins Good Friday and lasts through September. During April, May, and September the boat runs at 10:30am, 12:30pm, and 2:30pm. In June, July, and August, there is an additional trip during the afternoon, but always call first. Refreshments are served on all trips. A Boatman's Basket salad lunch can be enjoyed on the 12:30 and 2:30pm trips, as well as a cream tea on the 4:30pm voyage. The return fare is £3.95 ($7.30) for adults, £2.75 ($5.10) for children. To inquire about bookings, contact Jason's Trip, opposite 60 Blomfield Road, Little Venice, W.9 (tel. 071/286-3428). Advance booking is essential in season.

Also offered are one-way trips to **Camden Lock** on Saturday and Sunday to enable passengers to view the flea market and craft shops. Passengers may finish the trip there or return to Little Venice on a later boat.

ON FOOT

John Wittich, of **J.W. Promotions,** 66 St. Michael's Street, W.2 (tel. 071/2620-9572), started walking tours of London in 1960. He is a Freeman of the City of London and a member of two of the ancient guilds of London, as well as the author of several books on London walks. The company concentrates on personal walking tours for families and groups who have booked in advance. John Wittich conducts all tours. The cost for 1½-hour walks is £10 ($18.50) minimum for one or two adults.

Discover hidden London. Walk in the footsteps of Jack the Ripper and Sherlock Holmes, journey through Shakespeare's and Dickens's London, inspect the haunts of ghosts, explore the Old Jewish Quarter, Theatreland, Lawyer's London, the Famous Square Mile, and the Square Mile (Soho) or savor Hampstead, vibrant Chelsea, or romantic Little Venice and take in some of London's historic old inns on a convivial pub walk. These and many other jaunts are included in the program of unusual and historical walks organized by London's oldest established walking-tour group, **The Original London Walks,** 31 Crediton Hill, London NW6 1HS (tel. 071/435-6413 or 071/794-1764). Walks take place every day all year. They cost £4 ($7.40) for adults, £2.50 ($4.65) for students. Children under 15 go free. No reservations are needed.

8. SPORTS & RECREATION

SPORTS

London can be as exciting for sports enthusiasts as for theater fans. That is, if they happen to be British sports enthusiasts.

Soccer is the national winter sport. The London teams that set British pulses racing are Arsenal, Chelsea, Tottenham Hotspurs.

In summer **cricket** is played at **Lord's** or **Oval Cricket Ground,** St. John's Wood Road, N.W.8 (tel. 071/289-1611). During the international test matches between Britain and Australia, the West Indies, or India (equivalent in importance to the World Series), the country goes into a state of collective trance, hanging glassy-eyed on every ball as described over the radio or on TV.

At the **All England Lawn Tennis & Croquet Club,** Church Road, Wimbledon, S.W.19 (tel. 081/946-2244), you can see some of the world's greatest **tennis** players in action. The annual championship Fortnight—the famous **Wimbledon**—is the last week in June and the first in July, with matches lasting from about 2pm till dark. (The gates open at 11:30am.) Although the British founded the All England Lawn Tennis & Croquet Club back in 1877, they now rarely manage to win against latecomers to the game from other countries. **Tube:** Southfields Station, then a special bus from there.

Within easy reach of central London, there are **horse-racing** tracks at **Kempton Park, Sandown Park,** and the most famous of them all, **Epsom,** where the **Derby** is the main feature of the meeting in early June. Racing takes place both midweek and on weekends, but not continuously. Sometimes during the summer there are evening races so phone **United Racecourses Ltd.,** Epsom, Surrey (tel. 0372/464348) for information. You can drive yourself or, if you want to travel by rail, call 071/928-5100 for details of train services.

Finally, we come to a spectacle for which it is difficult to find a comprehensive tag. The **Royal Tournament,** which takes place in mid-July for a 2½-week run. It is one of London's longest-running shows. It's a cross between a military and a sporting display put on by the three British services, plus foreign visiting displays.

The show includes the massed bands presenting stirring music, the Royal Navy field-gun competition, the Royal Air Force with their dogs, the Royal Marines in action, the King's Troop Royal Horse Artillery, the Household Cavalry, and many other spectacular acts.

There are two performances Tuesday to Saturday, at 2:30 and 7:30pm, at Earl's Court Exhibition Centre, Warwick Road, S.W.5. There are no performances on Sunday and no matinees on Monday. Seats cost from £6.50 ($12.05) to £20 ($37). For tickets and other information, write to the Royal Tournament Exhibition Centre, Warwick Road, London SW5 9TA (tel. 071/373-8141). For any other information, get in touch with the Royal Tournament, Horse Guards, Whitehall, London SW1 2AX (tel. 071/930-4288).

RECREATION

SWIMMING

Brittania Leisure Centre, 40 Hyde Road, N.1. (tel. 071/729-4485), has been called a "new style" leisure complex. Like a giant playground, its swimming pool has a wave machine, a towering flume, along with fountains and monstrous inflatables. Sports offered include badminton and volleyball. There are squash courts and a gym. Admission is 50p (90¢) for adults and 10p (20¢) for children. **Open:** Mon–Fri 9am–8:15pm, Sat–Sun 9am–4:45pm. **Tube:** Old Street.

HEALTH & FITNESS CENTERS

Jubilee Hall Sports Centre, 30 The Piazza, Covent Garden, W.C.2 (tel. 071/836-4835), is one of the best and most centrally located sports centers in London, charging an admission of £2.50 ($4.65) for nonmembers. It is known for its indoor "climbing wall." Activities include archery, badminton, basketball, aerobics, cricket, gymnastics, martial arts, self-defense training (for women), an indoor swimming pool, tennis, volleyball, and weight training. It is run by the City of Westminster. **Open:** Mon–Fri 7am–10pm, Sat–Sun 8am–10pm. **Tube:** Covent Garden.

9. EASY EXCURSIONS

It would be sad to leave England without having ventured into the countryside, at least for a day. From London, it's possible to take advantage of countless tours—either by conducted bus, boat, or via a do-it-yourself method on bus or train. On many trips, you can combine two or more methods of transportation; for example, you can go to Windsor by boat and return by coach or train.

I highly recommend the previously described Green Line Coaches, operated by London Country Bus Services Ltd. (see "Getting Around" in Chapter 2).

For longer tours, say, to Stratford-upon-Avon, trains are more convenient. (See "Getting Around" in Chapter 2 for the many bargain tickets available.) For further information about trains to a specific location, go to the British Rail offices on Lower Regent Street.

HAMPTON COURT PALACE

On the north side of the Thames, 13 miles west of London in East Molesey, Surrey (tel. 081/977-8441), this 16th-century palace of Cardinal Wolsey can teach us a lesson: Don't try to outdo your boss—particularly if he happens to be Henry VIII. The rich cardinal did just that, and he eventually lost his fortune, power, and prestige, and ended up giving his lavish palace to the Tudor monarch. Henry took over, even outdoing the Wolsey embellishments. The Tudor additions included the Anne Boleyn gateway, with its 16th-century astronomical clock that even tells the high-water mark at London Bridge. From Clock Court, you can see one of Henry's major contributions, the aptly named great hall, with its hammer-beam ceiling. Also added by Henry were the tiltyard, a tennis court, and kitchen.

To judge from the movie *A Man for All Seasons*, Hampton Court had quite a retinue to feed. Cooking was done in the great kitchens. Henry cavorted through the various apartments with his wives of the moment—everybody from Anne Boleyn to Catherine Parr (the latter reversed things and lived to bury her erstwhile spouse). Charles I was imprisoned here at one time and temporarily managed to escape his jailers.

Although the palace enjoyed prestige and pomp in Elizabethan days, it owes much of its present look to William and Mary—or rather to Sir Christopher Wren, who designed the Northern or Lion Gates, intended to be the main entrance to the new parts of the palace. The fine wrought-iron screen at the south end of the south gardens was made by Jean Tijou around 1694 for William and Mary. Today you can parade through the apartments that are filled with porcelain, furniture, paintings, and tapestries. The King's Dressing Room is graced with some of the best art. In Queen Mary's closet, you'll find Pieter Brueghel the Elder's macabre *Massacre of the Innocents*. Tintoretto and Titian deck the halls of the King's Drawing Room. Finally, be sure to inspect the royal chapel (Wolsey wouldn't recognize it). To confound yourself totally, you may want to get lost in the serpentine shrubbery maze in the garden, also the work of Sir Christopher Wren.

The gardens—including the Great Vine, King's Privy Garden, Great Fountain Gardens, Tudor and Elizabethan Knot Gardens, Board Walk, Tiltyard, and Wilderness—are open daily year round from 7am until dusk, but not later than 9pm, and can be visited free. The cloisters, courtyards, state apartments, great kitchen, cellars, Hampton Court exhibition, and Andrea Mantegna paintings gallery are open daily from 9:30am to 6pm mid-March to mid-October, and 9:30am to 4:30pm mid-October to mid-March. The Tudor tennis court and banqueting house are open the same hours as above, but only from mid-March to mid-October. Admission to all these attractions is £3.80 ($7.05) for adults, £2 ($3.70) for children (children under 5 free). The Maze is open daily the same times as the palace. A Maze-only ticket costs £1 ($1.85) for adults, 50p (90¢) for children. A garden café and restaurant is in the Tiltyard Gardens.

You can get to Hampton Court by bus, train, boat, or car. London Regional Transport buses no. 111, 131, 216, 267, and 461 make the trip, as do Green Line Coaches (ask at the nearest London Country Bus office for routes 715, 716, 718, and 726). Frequent trains from Waterloo Station (Network Southeast) go to Hampton Court Station. Boat service is offered to and from Kingston, Richmond, and Westminster.

KEW

Kew is 9 miles southwest of central London, near Richmond.

ROYAL BOTANIC GARDENS, KEW GARDENS, Kew, Surrey. Tel. 081/ 940-1171.

★ These are among the best-known gardens in Europe and contain thousands of varieties of plants. But Kew is no mere pleasure garden; it is essentially a vast scientific research center that happens to be beautiful. A pagoda, erected in 1761–62, represents the "flowering" of chinoiserie. The classical Orangery, near the main gate on Kew Green, houses an exhibit telling the story of Kew, as well as a bookshop where guides to the garden are available.

The gardens cover a 300-acre site encompassing lakes, greenhouses, walks, garden pavilions, and museums, together with fine examples of the architecture of Sir William Chambers. Whenever you visit Kew, there's always something to see: in spring, the daffodils and bluebells, through to the coldest months when the Heath Garden is at its best. Among the 50,000 plant species are notable collections of arum lilies, ferns, orchids, aquatic plants, cacti, mountain plants, palms, and tropical water lilies.

The least expensive and most convenient way to visit the gardens is to take the District Line tube to Kew Gardens on the south bank of the Thames. The most romantic way to come in summer is via a steamer from Westminster Bridge to Kew Pier.

Admission: £3 ($5.55) adults, £1 ($1.85) children.
Open: Mon–Sat 9:30am–4 to 6:30pm, Sun and public holidays 9:30am–8pm.
Closed: Jan 1 and Dec 25.

KEW PALACE, Kew Gardens, Kew, Surrey. Tel. 081/940-3321.

Much interest focuses on the red-brick palace (dubbed the Dutch House), a former residence of King George III and Queen Charlotte. Now a museum, it was built in 1631 and contains memorabilia of the reign of George III, along with a royal collection of furniture and paintings. It is reached by walking to the northern tip of the Broad Walk.

Admission: £1 ($1.85) adults, 50p (90¢) children.
Open: Apr–Sept daily 11am–5:30pm.

QUEEN CHARLOTTE'S COTTAGE, Kew Gardens, Kew, Surrey. Tel. 081/940-1171.

Built in 1771, this cottage is half-timbered and thatched; George III is believed to have been the architect. The house has been restored to its original splendor in great detail, including the original Hogarth prints that hung on the downstairs walls.

Admission: 60p ($1.10) adults, 40p (75¢) children.
Open: Apr–Sept Sat–Sun and bank holidays 11am–5:30pm.

KEW BRIDGE STEAM MUSEUM, Green Dragon Line, Brentford, Middlesex. Tel. 081/568-4757.

This museum houses what is probably the world's largest collection of steam-powered beam engines. These were used in the Victorian era and up to the 1940s to pump London's water, and one engine has a capacity of 700 gallons per stroke. There are six restored engines that are steamed on weekends, plus other unrestored engines, a steam railway, and a working forge. The museum has a tearoom, plus free parking.

The museum is north of Kew Bridge, under the tower, a 10-minute walk from Kew Gardens. You can reach it by a Southern Region British Rail train from Waterloo Station to Kew Bridge Station; by bus no. 27, 65, 237, or 267 (7 on Sunday); or by Gunnersbury or South Ealing tube and then by bus.

Admission: On steam days £2.10 ($3.90) adults, £1 ($1.85) children, £5.75 ($10.65) family; on other days £1.50 ($2.80) adults, 75p ($1.40) children, £3.75 ($7.40) family.
Open: In steam Sat–Sun and Mon—when it's a holiday—11am–5pm; static exhibition Mon–Fri 11am–5pm.

GREENWICH

Greenwich mean time, of course, is the basis of standard time throughout most of the world, the zero point used in the reckoning of terrestrial longitudes since 1884. But Greenwich is also home of the Royal Naval College, the National Maritime Museum, and the Old Royal Observatory. In drydock at Greenwich Pier is the clipper ship *Cutty Sark,* as well as Sir Francis Chichester's *Gipsy Moth IV.*

About 4 miles from The City, part of the fun of visiting Greenwich is getting there. Ideally, you'll arrive by boat, as Henry VIII preferred to do on one of his hunting expeditions. In summer, launches leave at regular intervals from the pier at Charing Cross, Tower Bridge, or Westminster. Boats leave daily for Greenwich about every half hour from 10am to 7pm (times are approximate, depending on the tides). Bus no. 1 runs from Trafalgar Square to Greenwich; bus no. 188 goes from Euston through Waterloo to Greenwich. From Charing Cross station, the British Rail train takes 15 minutes to reach Greenwich, and there is now the new Docklands Light Railway, running from Tower Gateway to Island Gardens on the Isle of Dogs. A short walk under the Thames through a foot tunnel brings you out in Greenwich opposite the *Cutty Sark.*

WHAT TO SEE & DO

On Saturday and Sunday in Greenwich, there are arts, crafts, and antiques markets. Ask at the **tourist information center** by the pier and *Cutty Sark* (tel. 081/858-6376), open Friday to Wednesday from 2:30 to 5pm.

CUTTY SARK, Cutty Sark Gardens, King William Walk, Greenwich Pier, S.E.10. Tel. 081/853-3589.

Unquestionably, the last of the great clippers holds the most interest and has been seen by millions. At the spot where the vessel is now berthed stood the 19th-century Ship Inn, where Victorians came for whitebait dinners. Ordered built by Capt. Jock Willis ("Old White Hat"), the clipper was launched in 1869 to sail the China tea-trade route. It was named after the Witch Nannie in Robert Burns's *Tam o' Shanter* (note the figurehead). Yielding to the more efficient steamers, the *Cutty Sark* later was converted to a wool-carrying clipper and plied the route between Australia and England. Before its retirement in 1954, it knew many owners, and even different names.

Admission: £2.50 ($4.70) adults, £1.25 ($2.30) children.

Open: Summer Mon–Sat 10am–6pm, Sun noon–6pm; winter Mon–Sat 10am–5pm, Sun noon–5pm.

GIPSY MOTH IV, Cutty Sark Gardens, King William Walk, Greenwich Pier, S.E.10. Tel. 081/853-3589.

Next to the clipper—and looking like a sardine beside a shark—lies the equally famous *Gipsy Moth IV.* This was the ridiculously tiny sailing craft in which Sir Francis Chichester circumnavigated the globe—solo! You can go on board and marvel at the minuteness of the vessel in which the gray-haired old sea dog made his incredible 119-day journey. His chief worry—or so he claimed—was running out of ale before he reached land.

Admission: 30p (55¢) adults, 20p (35¢) children under 16.

Open: Summer Mon–Sat 10am–6pm, Sun noon–6pm. **Closed:** Winter.

ROYAL NAVAL COLLEGE, King William Walk, Greenwich, S.E.10. Tel. 081/858-2154.

This college grew up on the site of the Tudor palace in Greenwich in which Henry VIII and Elizabeth I were born. William and Mary commissioned Wren to design the present buildings in 1695 to house naval pensioners, and these became the Royal Naval College in 1873. The buildings are baroque masterpieces, in which the Painted Hall (by Thornhill from 1708 to 1727) and the chapel are outstanding.

Admission: Free.

Open: Fri–Wed 2:30–5pm (last entrance 4:30pm). **Closed:** Some public holidays (check daily papers).

NATIONAL MARITIME MUSEUM, Romney Road, Greenwich, S.E.10. Tel. 081/858-4422.

Built around Inigo Jones's 17th-century Palladian Queen's House, this museum portrays Britain's maritime heritage. Actual craft, marine paintings, ship models, and scientific instruments are displayed, including the full-dress uniform coat that Lord Nelson wore at the Battle of Trafalgar. Other curiosities include the chronometer (or sea watch) used by Captain Cook when he made his Pacific explorations in the 1770s.

The Old Royal Observatory, Greenwich Park (tel. 081/8585-4422, ext. 221), part of the museum, is also worth exploring. Sir Christopher Wren was the architect; in fact, he was interested in astronomy even before he became famous. The observatory overlooks Greenwich and the Maritime Museum from a park laid out to the design of Le Nôtre, the French landscaper. Here you can stand at 0° longitude, as the Greenwich Meridian, or prime meridian, marks the first of the globe's vertical divisions. See also the big red time-ball used in olden days by ships sailing down the river from London to set their timepieces by.

Admission: £2.90 ($5.35) adults, £1.90 ($3.50) children 7–16.

Open: Apr–Sept Mon–Sat 10am–6pm, Sun 2–6pm; Oct–Mar Mon–Sat 10am–5pm, Sun 2–5pm. **Closed:** Jan 1, Good Friday, May bank holiday, and Dec 24–26.

WHERE TO EAT

CUTTY SARK FREE HOUSE, Ballast Quay, Lassell St., Greenwich, S.E.10. Tel. 081/858-3146.

Cuisine: ENGLISH. **Reservations:** Not needed. **Transportation:** BritRail's Greenwich train from Charing Cross Station to Maze Hill.

$ **Prices:** Restaurant appetizers £2.20–£4 ($4.05–$7.40); main courses £6–£9.50 ($11.10–$17.60); pub snacks £2.50–£4.50 ($4.65–$8.35). No credit cards.

Open: Restaurant daily lunch noon–3pm, dinner Wed–Sat 7–10pm; pub Mon–Sat 11am–11pm, Sun noon–3pm and 7–10:30pm.

With plenty of local color, this 1968 English riverside tavern is one of the most historic pubs in the environs of London. Today it's a preferred watering hole of a bevy of pop music stars who live in the area. There is sometimes live music on Tuesday night. Pub snacks are served in the bar. The restaurant offers lots of fish, including Tayside salmon in basil sauce, breaded escalope of veal, and trout in a Pernod and mushroom sauce.

TRAFALGAR TAVERN, Park Row, Greenwich, S.E.10. Tel. 081/858-2437.

Cuisine: ENGLISH. **Reservations:** Recommended for restaurant. **Transportation:** BritRail's Greenwich train from Charing Cross Station to Maze Hill.

$ **Prices:** Appetizers £2–£3.50 ($3.70–$6.45); main courses £9–£14 ($16.65–$25.90). AE, V.

Open: Restaurant lunch daily 11am–3pm, dinner Tues–Sun 7:30–10:30pm; pub Mon–Sat 11am–3pm and 6–11:30pm, Sun 7:30–10:30pm.

The Trafalgar Tavern, a 2-minute walk north of Greenwich Pier, overlooks the Thames at Greenwich and is surrounded by many attractions; directly opposite the tavern is the Royal Naval College. Ringed with nautical paintings and engravings, lots of heavy dark wood, and brass artifacts, the restaurant invites you to enjoy traditional English specialties that go well with the 18th-century naval memorabilia. Try the steak-and-kidney pie, one of the succulent steaks, perhaps chateaubriand. Pheasant and venison are also on the menu. You can also order daily specials, with freshly prepared vegetables. In the rear is a separate restaurant section specializing in fish. You can also visit the pub for snacks, served during pub opening hours, and priced from £3 to £5 ($5.55 to $9.25). Platters of roast beef are the specialty.

RUNNYMEDE

Two miles outside of Windsor is the 188-acre meadow on the south side of the Thames, in Surrey, where King John put his seal on the Great Charter. Today, Runnymede is also the site of the **John F. Kennedy Memorial,** an acre of English ground given to the United States by the people of Britain. The memorial, a large block of white stone, is hard to see from the road. The pagoda that you can see from the road was placed there by the American Bar Association to acknowledge the fact that American law stems from the English system.

The historic site, to which there is free access all year, lies on the Thames, ½ mile west of Runnymede Bridge on the south side of A308. If you're taking the M25, exit at Junction 13. The nearest rail connection is at Egham, ½ mile away. For bus information for the surrounding area, call 081/668-7261.

SYON PARK

Opened to the public in 1968, **Syon Park** lies in Brentford, Middlesex, 9 miles from Piccadilly Circus, on 5 acres of the duke of Northumberland's Thames-side estate. Called "The Showplace of the Nation in a Great English Garden," it is one of the most beautiful spots in all of Great Britain; there's always something in bloom. The park is also educational, showing amateurs how to get the most out of their small gardens. The vast flower- and plant-studded acreage betrays the influence of "Capability" Brown, who laid out the grounds in the 18th century.

Particular highlights include a 6-acre rose garden, a butterfly house, and the great conservatory, one of the earliest and most famous buildings of its type, built in 1822–29. There is a ¼-mile-long ornamental lake studded with waterlilies and silhouetted by cypresses and willows, even a gardening supermarket, and the Motor Museum, with the Heritage Collection of British cars. With some 90 vehicles, from the earliest 1895 Wolseley to the present day, it has the largest collection of British cars anywhere. Syon is also the site of the first botanical garden in England, created by the father of English botany, Dr. William Turner in 1548. Trees include a 200-year-old Chinese juniper, an Afghan ash, Indian bean trees, and liquidambars.

On the grounds is **Syon House,** built in 1431, the original structure incorporated into the duke of Northumberland's present home. The house was later remade to the specifications of the first duke of Northumberland in 1762–69. The battlemented facade is that of the original Tudor mansion, but the interior is from the 18th century, the design of Robert Adam. Basil Taylor said of the interior feeling: "You're almost in the middle of a jewel box." In the Middle Ages, Syon was a monastery, later suppressed by Henry VIII. Katherine Howard, the king's fifth wife, was imprisoned in the house before her scheduled beheading in 1542.

Admission to the gardens is £1.75 ($3.25) for adults and £1.25 ($2.30) for children. Admission to Syon House is £2 ($3.70) for adults, £1.50 ($2.80) for children. A combined ticket for house and gardens is £3.75 ($6.95) for adults, £2.75 ($5.10) for children. A separate ticket is required for entrance to the Motor Museum, costing £2.50 ($4.65) for adults, £1.75 ($3.25) for children.

The house is open from Easter to the end of September Sunday to Thursday from noon to 5pm. The gardens are open all year except for Christmas and Boxing Day. The gates open at 10am and close at dusk or 6pm. After October, the winter closing hour is 4pm. For more information, call 081/560-0882. Syon Park lies 2 miles west of Kew Bridge (the road is signposted from A315/310 at Busch Corner). By public transport, go to Waterloo Station in London and take British Rail to Kew Bridge Station. From there, catch bus no. 237 or 267 to the pedestrian entrance to Syon House. It's faster, however, to take the tube to Gunnersbury.

THORPE PARK

One of Europe's leading family leisure parks, **Thorpe Park,** Staines Road, Chertsey, Surrey (tel. 0932/569393), lies only 21 miles from central London on the A320 between Staines and Chertsey, with easy access from Junctions 11 and 13 on the M25. The entrance fee of £9.75 ($18.10) for adults and £8.25 ($15.25) for children under 14 includes all rides, shows, attractions, and exhibits. There are additional charges for roller-skate rental and coin-operated amusements. Some favorite rides and shows are Loggers Leap, Thunder River, Treasure Island, Magic Mill, Phantom Fantasia, the Family Tea Cup Ride, Cinema 180, and the Palladium Theatre. Newer attractions are the Flying Fish, an outdoor roller coaster, Carousel Kingdom, an undercover entertainment area, and A Drive in the Country, a vintage track ride, and the U.K.'s first four-lane water slide. Free transport is provided around the 500 acres by railway and waterbus.

Guests can picnic on the grounds or patronize one of the restaurants or fast-food areas, including Hamburger Palace, the French Café, Fish 'n' Chips, or the popular Mississippi Riverboat. The park is open daily from March 23 until October 27. From July 20 to September 8 it is open from 10am to 6pm. The nearest main-line station is Staines from Waterloo Station in London. Many bus services also operate directly from Victoria Coach Station in London to Thorpe Park.

WOBURN ABBEY

✪ Few tourists visiting Bedfordshire miss the Georgian mansion of Woburn Abbey, Woburn, Bedfordshire MK43 0TP, the seat of the dukes of Bedford for more than three centuries. It lies 44 miles north of London. The much-publicized 18th-century estate is signposted ½ mile from the village of Woburn, which lies 13 miles southwest of Bedford. Its state apartments are rich in furniture, porcelain, tapestries, silver, and a valuable art collection, including paintings by Van Dyck, Holbein, Rembrandt, Gainsborough, and Reynolds. A series of paintings by Canaletto, showing his continuing views of Venice, grace the walls of the Canaletto Room, an intimate dining room. Of all the paintings, one of the most notable from a historical point of view is the *Armada Portrait* of Elizabeth I. Her hand rests on the globe, as Philip's invincible armada perishes in the background.

Queen Victoria and Prince Albert visited Woburn Abbey in 1841; Victoria's Dressing Room contains a fine collection of 17th-century paintings from the Netherlands. Among the oddities and treasures at Woburn Abbey are a Grotto of Shells, a Sèvres dinner service (gift of Louis XV), and a chamber devoted to memorabilia of "The Flying Duchess." Wife of the 11th Duke of Bedford, she was a remarkable woman who disappeared on a solo flight in 1937 (the same year as Amelia Earhart). The duchess, however, was 72 years old at the time.

In the 1950s, the present duke of Bedford opened Woburn Abbey to the public to pay off millions of pounds in inheritance taxes. In 1974, he turned the estate over to his son and daughter-in-law, the marquess and marchioness of Tavistock, who reluctantly took on the business of running the 75-room mansion. And what a business it is, drawing hundreds of thousands of visitors a year and employing more than 300 people to staff the shops and grounds.

Today Woburn Abbey is surrounded by a 3,000-acre deer park that includes the famous Père David's deer herd, originally from China and saved from extinction at Woburn. The Woburn Wild Animal Kingdom contains lions, tigers, giraffe, camels, monkeys, Przewalski horses, bongos, elephants, and more.

The house and park are open only on Saturday and Sunday from January 1 to March 24. Visiting times for the house are from 11am to 4:45pm; for the park, 10:30am to 3:45pm. From March 25 to November 3, the abbey is open daily. The house can be visited Monday to Saturday from 11am to 5:45pm and on Sunday from 11am to 6:15pm. The park is open Monday to Saturday from 10am to 4:45pm and on Sunday from 10am to 5:45pm. Admission is £5 ($9.25) for adults and £2 ($3.70) for children.

Light meals are available at the Flying Duchess Pavilion Coffee Shop.

In summer, travel agents can book you on organized bus tours out of London. Otherwise, take the M1 (motorway) north to the junctions of 12 or 13 where Woburn Abbey directions are signposted.

HUGHENDEN MANOR

Outside High Wycombe, in Buckinghamshire, sits a country manor that not only gives insight into the Victorian age, but acquaints us with a remarkable man. In Benjamin Disraeli we meet one of the most enigmatic figures of 19th-century England. At age 21, Dizzy published anonymously his five-volume novel *Vivian Grey*. He married an older widow for her money, entered politics, and continued writing novels; his later ones met with more acclaim.

In 1848, Disraeli acquired Hughenden Manor, a country house that befitted his fast-rising political and social position. He served briefly as prime minister in 1868, but his political fame rests on his stewardship as prime minister from 1874 to 1880. He became Queen Victoria's friend—and in 1877 she paid him a rare honor by visiting him at Hughenden. In 1876, Disraeli became the earl of Beaconsfield: he had arrived, but his wife was dead, and he was to die in 1881. Instead of being buried at Westminster Abbey, he preferred the simple little graveyard of Hughenden Church.

Today Hughenden contains an odd assortment of memorabilia, including a lock of Disraeli's hair, letters from Victoria, autographed books, and a portrait of Lord Byron, known to Disraeli's father.

If you're driving to Hughenden Manor on the way to Oxford, continue north of High Wycombe on the A4128 for about 1½ miles. If relying on public transportation from London, take coach no. 711 to High Wycombe, then board a Beeline bus (High Wycombe–Aylesbury no. 323 or 324). The manor house and garden are open from April to October Wednesday to Saturday from 2 to 6pm, Sunday and bank holidays from noon to 6pm. It is open in early March Saturday and Sunday only from 2 to 6pm. It is closed from November to the end of March and on Good Friday. Admission is £2.80 ($5.20) for adults, £1.40 ($2.60) for children. For more information, call 0494/32580.

HATFIELD HOUSE

West of Hertford, Hatfield House, Hatfield, Hertfordshire AL9 5NQ (tel. 07107/262823), is one of the great English country houses. Only the banqueting hall of the original Tudor palace remains; the rest is Jacobean.

Hatfield was much a part of the lives of both Henry VIII and his daughter, Elizabeth I. In the old palace, built in the 15th century, Elizabeth played as a child. Although Henry was married to her mother, Anne Boleyn, at the time of Elizabeth's birth, the marriage was later nullified (Anne lost her head and Elizabeth her legitimacy). Henry also used to stash away his oldest daughter, Mary Tudor, at Hatfield. But when Mary became Queen of England, and set about earning the dubious distinction of "Bloody Mary," she found Elizabeth a problem. For a while she kept her in the Tower of London, but she eventually let her return to Hatfield. In 1558, while at Hatfield, Elizabeth learned of her ascension to the throne of England.

The Jacobean house that exists today contains antique furniture, tapestries, and paintings, as well as three often-reproduced portraits, including the ermine and rainbow portraits of Elizabeth I. The great hall is suitably medieval, complete with a minstrel's gallery. One of the rarest exhibits is a pair of silk stockings, said to have been worn by Elizabeth herself, the first lady in England to don such apparel. The park and the gardens are also worth exploring. Luncheons and teas are available from 11am to 5pm in the converted coach house in the old palace yard.

Hatfield is open from March 25 to the second Sunday in October Tuesday to Saturday from noon to 4:15pm, Sunday from 1:30 to 5pm, and on bank-holiday Mondays from 11am to 5pm; it's closed Good Friday. Admission is £3.90 ($7.20) for adults, £2.70 ($5) for children. The house is across from the station in Hatfield. From London, take Green Line coach no. 794 or 797, or the fast trains from King's Cross.

Elizabethan banquets are staged in the banqueting hall of Hatfield House Tuesday and Thursday to Saturday, with much gaiety and music. Guests are invited to drink in an anteroom, then join the long tables for a feast of five courses with continuous entertainment from a group of Elizabethan players, minstrels, and jesters. Wine is included in the cost of the meal, but you're expected to pay for your before-dinner drinks yourself. The best way to get there from London for the feast is to book a coach tour for an inclusive fee starting at £32 ($59.20). The Evan Evans agency has tours leaving from Russell Square or even from 41 Tottenham Court Road in London. The coach returns to London after midnight. If you get there under your own steam, the cost is £23 ($42.55) Tuesday and Thursday, £24 ($44.40) Friday, and £25 ($46.25) Saturday. For reservations, call 0707/262055.

LONDON SHOPPING & EVENING ENTERTAINMENT

When Prussian Field Marshal Blucher, Wellington's stout ally at Waterloo, first laid eyes on London, he allegedly slapped his thigh and exclaimed, "Herr Gott, what a city to plunder!"

He was gazing at what, for the early 19th century, was a phenomenal mass of shops and stores, overwhelming to Herr Blucher's unsophisticated eyes. Since those days, other cities have drawn level with London as shopping centers, but none has ever surpassed it.

And when nighttime falls, the pickings are equally rich, as London has one of the most diversified spectrums of after-dark diversions.

London establishments cover the entire social spectrum, from the sleekest haunts to the plainest proletarian strongholds, from overstuffed Victorian plush palaces to re-creations of the decor of the Edwardian era, often in formerly dilapidated buildings. The range of entertainment is equally wide: from graveyard silence to spastic rock bands, nude female performers, and even lunchtime and evening theater performances. Also popular in London are "drag" shows featuring female impersonators.

1. THE SHOPPING SCENE

In London, you can pick up bargains ranging from a still-functioning hurdy-gurdy to a replica of the crown jewels. For the best buys, search out new styles in clothing, as well as traditional and well-tailored men's and women's suits, small antiques and curios, woolens, tweeds, tartans, rare books, Liberty silks, Burberrys, English china, silver, even arms and armor, to name just a few.

London stores keep fairly uniform hours, usually shorter than their American equivalents. Most stores are open Monday to Saturday from 9am to 5:30pm with late shopping on Wednesday or Thursday to 7 or 8pm; however, many central shops close at around 1pm on Saturday. In the East End, around Aldgate and Whitechapel, many shops are open on Sunday from 9am to 2pm. There are a few all-night stores, mostly in the Bayswater section, and shops usually don't close for lunch. Bargains are everywhere, but are likely to be limited by the U.S. Customs regulations. According to the latest rules, you—and everyone traveling with you—are entitled to bring back

$400 worth of foreign-made merchandise without paying U.S. duty. This applies only to goods actually accompanying you. You can quite legitimately stretch that amount by mailing unsolicited gifts home; however, no gift can be worth more than $50, and you are not permitted to send more than one present per day to the same address.

Many London shops will help you beat the whopping purchase tax levied on much of England's merchandise. By presenting your passport, you can frequently purchase goods tax-free, but only on the following conditions: 1. You either have your purchase sent directly to your home address or 2. You have it delivered to the plane you're taking back.

The huge purchase taxes imposed on so-called luxury goods are responsible for the extremely high cost of items such as wines, spirits, tobacco, cigarettes, and gasoline.

SHOPPING AREAS

London's retail stores tend to cluster in certain areas, a holdover from the times when each guild or craft had its own street, so you can head in a certain direction to find a certain style of merchandise. The following is a rough outline of the main shopping districts (not including the "Specialty Shopping Districts," which I will detail below) to help get you started.

REGENT STREET

Curving down elegantly from Oxford Circus to Piccadilly Circus, this stylish thoroughfare is crammed with fashionable stores, selling everything from silks to silverware. It has both department stores and boutiques, but the accent is on the medium-size establishment in the upper-medium price range. **Tube:** Oxford Circus or Piccadilly Circus.

OXFORD STREET

The shopping drag of the metropolis, Oxford Street runs from St. Giles Circus to Marble Arch and is an endless, uninspiring, but utility-crammed band of stores, stores, and more stores. It contains six of London's major department stores, apart from just about every kind of retailing establishment under the sun. **Tube:** Oxford Circus or Bond Street.

PICCADILLY

Unlike the circus, Piccadilly Street is distinctly in the upper bracket, specializing in automobile showrooms, travel offices, art galleries, plus London's poshest grocery store, Fortnum & Mason. **Tube:** Piccadilly Circus.

BOND STREET

Divided into New and Old, Bond Street connects Piccadilly and Oxford Street and is synonymous with the luxury trade. Here are found the very finest—and most expensive—of tailors, hatters, milliners, cobblers, and antiques dealers. **Tube:** Bond Street.

KNIGHTSBRIDGE

Together with Kensington and Brompton roads, this forms an extremely svelte shopping district south of Hyde Park. It's patronized for furniture, antiques, jewelry, and Harrods department store. **Tube:** Knightsbridge.

THE STRAND

Stately, broad, and dignified, the Strand runs from Trafalgar Square into Fleet Street. It's lined with hotels, theaters, and specialty stores that you could spend a whole day peeking into. **Tube:** Charing Cross or Aldwych (weekdays only).

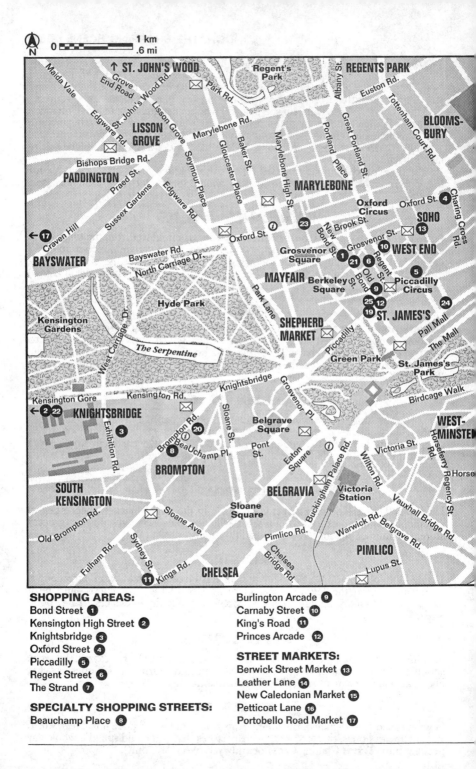

SHOPPING AREAS:
Bond Street ❶
Kensington High Street ❷
Knightsbridge ❸
Oxford Street ❹
Piccadilly ❺
Regent Street ❻
The Strand ❼

SPECIALTY SHOPPING STREETS:
Beauchamp Place ❽

Burlington Arcade ❾
Carnaby Street ❿
King's Road ⓫
Princes Arcade ⓬

STREET MARKETS:
Berwick Street Market ⓭
Leather Lane ⓮
New Caledonian Market ⓯
Petticoat Lane ⓰
Portobello Road Market ⓱

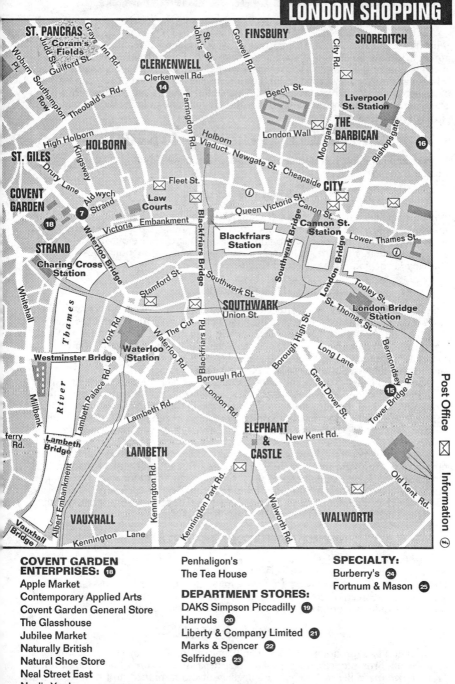

LONDON SHOPPING

ST. PANCRAS
Coram's Fields
Woburn Pl.
Judd St.
Guilford St.
Southampton Row
Grays Inn Rd.
Theobald's Rd.
High Holborn
Kingsway
Drury Lane
Aldwych
Strand

CLERKENWELL
Clerkenwell Rd.
14
Farringdon Rd.
Holborn Viaduct
Newgate St.
Holborn

FINSBURY
Goswell Rd.
St. John's St.
Beech St.
London Wall
Moorgate
Cheapside St.

SHOREDITCH
City Rd.
Liverpool St. Station
THE BARBICAN
Bishopsgate
16

HOLBORN
ST. GILES
COVENT GARDEN
18
7
STRAND
Charing Cross Station
Whitehall
Victoria Embankment
Waterloo Bridge

Fleet St.
Law Courts
Blackfriars Bridge
Blackfriars Station
Queen Victoria St.
Canon St.
Cannon St. Station
London Bridge
Lower Thames St.
Southwark Bridge
CITY

Thames
River
Westminster Bridge
Millbank
York Rd.
Lambeth Palace Rd.
Waterloo Station
The Cut
Waterloo Rd.
Stamford St.
Blackfriars Rd.
SOUTHWARK
Union St.
Southwark St.
Borough High St.
St. Thomas St.
Tooley St.
London Bridge Station
Bermondsey Rd.
Long Lane
Great Dover St.
Tower Bridge
15

ferry Rd.
Lambeth Bridge
Albert Embankment
VAUXHALL
Vauxhall Bridge
Kennington Lane
LAMBETH
Lambeth Rd.
Kennington Rd.
Borough Rd.
London Rd.
Kennington Park Rd.
ELEPHANT & CASTLE
New Kent Rd.
Walworth Rd.
WALWORTH
Old Kent Rd.

Post Office ✉

Information ⓘ

COVENT GARDEN ENTERPRISES: 18
Apple Market
Contemporary Applied Arts
Covent Garden General Store
The Glasshouse
Jubilee Market
Naturally British
Natural Shoe Store
Neal Street East
Neal's Yard

Penhaligon's
The Tea House

DEPARTMENT STORES:
DAKS Simpson Piccadilly 19
Harrods 20
Liberty & Company Limited 21
Marks & Spencer 22
Selfridges 23

SPECIALTY:
Burberry's 24
Fortnum & Mason 25

KENSINGTON HIGH STREET

This has been called "the Oxford Street of West London." Stretching for about 1½ miles, it includes many shops, such as the House of Fraser department store. You'll also find lots of stores on the side streets, such as Earl's Court Road, Abingdon Road, Thackeray Street, and Victoria Street. From Kensington High Street, you can walk up Kensington Church Street, which, like Portobello Road, is one of the city's main shopping avenues, selling everything from antique furniture to Impressionist paintings. **Tube:** High Street Kensington.

SPECIALTY SHOPPING STREETS

If you think London has unique department stores, wait until you see its equally unique shopping streets.

CARNABY STREET

Just off Regent, Carnaby Street is a legend. Alas, it no longer dominates the world of fashion as it did in the '60s, but it is still visited by the young, especially punkers. Some of its shops display lots of claptrap and quick-quid merchandise but for value, style, and imagination, the Chelsea (King's Road) and Kensington boutiques have left Carnaby far behind. **Tube:** Oxford Circus.

KING'S ROAD

The formerly villagelike main street of Chelsea starts at Sloane Square with Peter Jones's classy department store, and meanders on for a mile until it reaches a swank new shop-filled complex, Chelsea Harbour. Up until 1830, this was actually a king's private road, running from the palaces at Whitehall or St. James's to the country places at Hampton Court, Richmond, and Chelsea. (Queen Victoria ended that when she became the first sovereign to inhabit Buckingham Palace in 1837.)

The leap of King's Road to the "mod throne" in the late '60s came with the advent of designer Mary Quant (whose popularity seems to flourish mainly in Japan these days). But, back in the '60s, she scored a bull's-eye in the English fashion world with her then (and still) daring designs. Fashion boutiques, including the famous "Granny Takes a Trip" (it had half a motorcar crashing through its window), once lined the boulevard.

Today, the street is still crowded with young people and can still lay claim to being outrageous. More and more in the 1990s, King's Road is a lineup of markets and "multi-stores," large or small conglomerations of in- and outdoor stands, stalls, and booths fulfilling all sorts of functions within one building or enclosure. They spring up so fast that it's impossible to keep them tabulated, but few thorough shopping strolls in London can afford to ignore King's Road. **Tube:** Sloane Square.

SAINT CHRISTOPHER'S PLACE

One of London's most interesting and little-known (to the foreign visitor) shopping streets is Saint Christopher's Place, W.1. It lies just off Oxford Street—walk down Oxford from Selfridges toward Oxford Circus, ducking north along Gees Court across Barrett Street. There you will be surrounded by antiques markets and good shops for women's clothing and accessories. **Tube:** Bond Street.

BEAUCHAMP PLACE

Beauchamp Place (pronounced "*Bee*cham"), one of London's top shopping streets, is a block off Brompton Road, near Harrods department store. The *International Herald-Tribune* called it "a higgledy-piggledy of old-fashioned and trendy, quaint and with-it, expensive and cheap. It is deliciously unspecialized." Whatever you're looking for—from a pâté de marcassin to a carved pine mantelpiece—you are likely to find it here. Reject china, crystal, and pottery, secondhand silver, collages, custom-tailored men's shirts—whatever. It's pure fun, even if you don't buy anything. **Tube:** Knightsbridge.

PRINCES ARCADE

If you like "one-stop" shopping, you may be drawn to the restored Princes Arcade, which was opened by Edward VII in 1883, when he was Prince of Wales. Between Jermyn Street and Piccadilly, in the heart of London, the arcade has wrought-iron lamps that light your way as you search through some 20 bow-fronted shops, looking for that special curio—maybe a 16th-century nightcap or a pair of shoes made by people who have been satisfying royal tastes since 1847. Small signs hanging from metal rods indicate what kind of merchandise a particular store sells. **Tube:** Piccadilly Circus.

BURLINGTON ARCADE

Next door to the Royal Academy of Arts, the Burlington Arcade, W.1 (tel. 071/427-3568), is more than 150 years old; it was built in 1819 by Lord George Cavendish. The bawdy Londoners of those days threw rubbish over his garden wall, particularly oyster shells, so he built the arcade as a deterrent. Today, you can leisurely browse through the antiques and bric-a-brac in the 38 shops housed in this ancient monument, which is protected by Her Majesty.

The arcade has been popular with Londoners for years. Mary Ann Evans—alias George Eliot, the author of *The Mill on the Floss* and *Silas Marner*—met the journalist George Lewes in Jeff's Bookshop and they were lovers until he died in 1866. Even Charles Dickens commented on the arcade and its double row of shops, "like a Parisian passage," in his 1879 guide to London.

If you linger here until 5:30pm, you can watch the beadles (the last of London's top-hatted policemen and Britain's oldest police force) ceremoniously put in place the iron grilles that block off the arcade until 9am the next morning, when they just as ceremoniously remove them, marking the start of a new business day. Also at 5:30pm, a hand bell, called the Burlington Bell, is sounded, signaling the end of trading. **Tube:** Piccadilly Circus.

SHOPPING FOR KIDS

CHILDREN'S BOOK CENTRE, 237 Kensington High St., W.8. Tel. 071/937-7497.

This is the best place to go for children's books. Not only are there thousands of titles, but fiction books are arranged according to age, including a young adult section. **Open:** Mon–Sat 9:30am–6pm. **Tube:** High Street Kensington.

HAMLEYS OF REGENT STREET, 188-196 Regent St., W.1. Tel. 071/734-3161.

This is an Ali Baba's cave of toys and games, ranging from electronic games and Star Wars robots on the ground floor to different toys for all age groups on the other floors: table and card games, teddy bears, nursery animals, dolls, and outdoor games. **Open:** Mon–Wed and Fri–Sat 10am–6pm, Thurs 10am–8pm. **Tube:** Oxford Circus.

2. SHOPPING A TO Z

ANTIQUES

CHELSEA ANTIQUES MARKET, 245-253 King's Rd., S.W.3. Tel. 071/352-1720.

Sheltered in a rambling old building, this market offers endless browsing possibilities for the curio addict. You're likely to run across Staffordshire dogs, shaving mugs, Edwardian buckles and clasps, ivory-handled razors, old velours and lace gowns, wooden tea caddies, antique pocket watches, wormy Tudoresque chests, silver snuff boxes, grandfather clocks, and jewelry of all periods. **Open:** Mon–Sat 10am–6pm. **Tube:** Sloane Square.

GRAYS AND GRAYS, in the Mews Antiques Markets, 58 Davies St., and 1-7 Davies Mews, W.1. Tel. 071/629-7034.

Just south of Oxford Street and opposite the Bond Street tube station, these markets are in a triangle formed by Davies Street, South Molton Lane, and Davies Mews. The two old buildings have been converted into walk-in stands with independent dealers. The term "antique" here covers items from oil paintings to, say, the 1894 edition of *Encyclopaedia Britannica*. Also sold here are exquisite antique jewelry, silver, gold, maps and prints, bronzes and ivories, arms and armor, Victorian and Edwardian toys, furniture, antique luggage, antique lace, scientific instruments, crafting tools, and Chinese, Persian, and Islamic pottery, porcelain, miniatures, and antiquities. There is also a whole floor of repair workshops, an engraver, and a bureau de change. **Tube:** Bond Street.

ALFIES ANTIQUES MARKET, 13-25 Church St., N.W.8. Tel. 071/723-6066.

The biggest and one of the cheapest covered markets in London, this is where many dealers come to buy. Alfies is named after the father of Bennie Gray, the owner of Grays and Grays in the Mews Antiques Markets and the former owner of the Antiques Hypermarket Kensington and Antiquarius. The market contains more than 370 stalls, showrooms, and workshops on 35,000 square feet of floor, plus there's an enormous, 70-unit basement area. **Open:** Tues–Sat 10am–6pm. **Tube:** Edgware Road.

ANTIQUARIUS, 131-141 King's Rd., S.W.3. Tel. 071/351-5353.

Antiquarius echoes the artistic diversity of the street on which it is located. More than 150 stallholders offer specialized merchandise, such as period clothing, porcelain, silver, antique books, boxes, silver, clocks, prints, and paintings, with an occasional piece of antique furniture. You'll also find a lot of items dating from around 1950. **Open:** Mon–Sat 10am–6pm. **Tube:** Sloane Square.

CHENIL GALLERIES, 181-183 King's Rd., S.W.3. Tel. 071/351-5353.

These galleries seem to specialize in art nouveau and art deco objects, along with lots of jewelry. A permanent exhibition of an Epstein statue reflects the long association of the galleries with the arts. The merchandise includes Asian carpets, collector's dolls, teddy bears, as well as prints and maps, fine porcelain, chess sets, some period furniture, and 17th- and 18th-century paintings. **Tube:** Sloane Square.

MALL ANTIQUES ARCADE, at Camden Passage, Islington, N.1. No phone.

Here you'll find one of Britain's greatest concentrations of antiques businesses. Some 35 dealers specialize in fine furniture, porcelain, and silver and are housed in individual shop units. **Open:** Wed 7:30am–5pm; Tues, Thurs, and Fri 10am–5pm; Sat 9am–6pm. **Tube:** Angel.

ARTS & CRAFTS

On a Sunday morning along **Bayswater Road,** pictures, collages, and craft items are hung on the railings along the edge of Hyde Park and Kensington Gardens—for more than a mile. If the weather is right, start at Marble Arch. Along Piccadilly, you'll see much of the same thing by walking along the railings of **Green Park** on a Saturday afternoon.

CRAFTS COUNCIL, 12 Waterloo Place, S.W.1. Tel. 071/930-4811.

A public body that promotes crafts in England and Wales, this offers a broad program of changing crafts exhibitions from British domestic pottery to American traditional patchwork. Most exhibitions are free; concessions are available. Other facilities include a lively information center, which can direct you to craft events throughout Britain, a slide library, and a bookstall. (*Note:* The Crafts Council runs a quality craft shop at the Victoria and Albert Museum, South Kensington.) The galleries and information center keep the same hours. **Open:** Tues–Sat 10am–5pm, Sun 2–5pm. **Tube:** Piccadilly Circus.

BOOKS

W. & G. FOYLE LTD., 113-119 Charing Cross Rd., W.C.2. Tel. 071/439-8501.
Claiming to be the world's largest bookstore, this has an impressive array of hardcovers and paperbacks. The shop also sells travel maps, records, videotapes, and sheet music. **Tube:** Leicester Square.

HATCHARDS LTD., 187-188 Piccadilly, W.1. Tel. 071/439-9921.
An old-fashioned looking place on the south side of Piccadilly, Hatchards is stuffed with books ranging from popular fiction to specialized reference. There are shelves of guidebooks, atlases, cookbooks, paperbacks, and puzzle books. **Open:** Mon–Fri 9am–6pm, Sat 9am–5pm. **Tube:** Piccadilly Circus.

HISTORY BOOKSHOP, 2 Broadway, N.11. Tel. 081/368-8568.
This shop for history buffs stands at the corner of Friern Barnet Road and MacDonald Road. Behind its 1890s facade, this is one of the largest repositories of secondhand books in London and contains some 40,000 volumes scattered over three floors. It specializes in military history, and catalogs are issued at regular intervals. **Open:** Wed–Fri 10am–4pm. **Tube:** Arnos Grove.

STANFORDS, 12-14 Long Acre, W.C.2. Tel. 071/836-1321.
Established in 1852, this is not only the world's largest map shop, but it is also the best travel-book store in London. **Open:** Mon and Sat 10am–6pm; Tues, Wed, and Fri 9am–6pm; Thurs 9am–7pm. **Tube:** Leicester Square.

BRASS RUBBING

LONDON BRASS RUBBING CENTRE, at St. Martin-in-the-Fields Church, Trafalgar Square, W.C.2. Tel. 071/437-6023.
The center is in the big, brick-vaulted, 1730s crypt, alongside a brasserie restaurant, a bookshop, and a craft market. It has 85 exact copies of bronze portraits ready for use. Paper, rubbing materials, and instructions are furnished, and classical music is played as visitors work at the task. The charges range from 95p ($1.55) for a small copy to £10.50 ($19.45) for the largest, a life-size Crusader knight.
There is also a gift area, where you can buy brass-rubbing kits for children, budget-priced ready-made rubbings, and a wide variety of books, souvenirs, posters, and postcards. For those who wish to make brass rubbings in the countryside churches, the center offers instructions and sells guidebooks and the necessary materials. **Open:** Mon–Sat 10am–6pm, Sun noon–6pm. **Tube:** Charing Cross.

LONDON BRASS RUBBING CENTRE, at All Hallows Church by the Tower, Byward St., E.C.3. Tel. 071/481-2928.
The same company operates a brass-rubbing center at this fascinating church, next door to the Tower, which has a crypt museum, Roman remains, and traces of early London, including a Saxon wall predating the Tower. Samuel Pepys, the famed diarist, climbed to the spire of this church to watch the raging fire of London in 1666. Material and instruction are supplied, and the charges also range from 95p ($1.55) for a small copy to £10.50 ($19.45) for the largest. **Open:** Mon–Sat 10am–6pm, Sun noon–6pm; bookshop and restaurant Mon–Fri noon–2pm. **Tube:** Tower Hill.

BRITISH DESIGN

THE DESIGN CENTRE, 28 Haymarket, S.W.1. Tel. 071/839-8000.

The exhibitions here deal with topical design subjects of all kinds. The innovation center provides a showcase for new ideas and prototypes to attract potential manufacturers, and an information center offers advice and information. The Design Council Bookshop stocks a wide range of publications related to design, architecture, and crafts. In 1989, the Young Designers' Centre opened, providing the first permanent year-round national exhibition area dedicated to the work of design students and graduates. **Open:** Mon and Tues 10am–6pm, Wed–Sat 10am–8pm, Sun 1–6pm. **Tube:** Piccadilly Circus.

CHINA

LAWLEYS, 154 Regent St., W.1. Tel. 071/734-3184.
A wide range of English bone china, as well as crystal and giftware, is sold here. The firm specializes in Royal Doulton, Minton, Royal Crown Derby, Wedgwood, and Aynsley china; Royal Doulton, Stuart, Waterford, Swarovski, and Edinburgh crystal; Lladró figures; David Winter Cottages; Border Fine Arts; and other famous giftware ranges. They also sell cutlery. **Open:** Mon–Sat 9:30am–6pm (Thurs to 7pm). **Tube:** Piccadilly Circus or Oxford Circus.

WATERFORD-WEDGWOOD, 266-270 Regent St., W.1. Tel. 071/734-5656.
The staff at this large shop on the corner of Regent Street will explain their export plan to save you money on your souvenir buying. The store is like a miniature museum and is well worth a visit. Besides selling tableware and glassware, it offers a collection of china, jewelry, pendants, earrings, brooches, and inexpensive ashtrays. **Open:** Mon–Sat 9am–6pm (Thurs to 7pm). **Tube:** Oxford Circus.

THOMAS GOODE, 19 S. Audley St., Grosvenor Sq. W.1. Tel. 071/499-2823.
Established in 1827, 10 years before Queen Victoria came to the throne, this is perhaps the most famous china and glass shop in the world. Minton majolica elephants grace its front windows and the main entrance, which has its famous mechanical doors, leads you to the china, glass, and silverware displayed in the 14 showrooms. A Thomas Goode catalog is available. **Open:** Mon and Wed–Fri 9am–5pm; Tues 9:30am–5pm; Sat 9:30am–1pm. **Tube:** Hyde Park Corner.

CHOCOLATES

CHARBONNEL ET WALKER LTD., 1 Royal Arcade, 28 Old Bond St., W.1. Tel. 071/629-4396.
Here you'll find what may be the finest chocolates in the world. The staff of this bow-fronted shop, on the corner of the Royal Arcade off Old Bond Street, will send messages spelled out on the chocolates themselves. Prices are determined by weight. You can create your own box of candy or select one of their ready-made boxes. **Open:** Mon–Fri 9:30am–5:30pm, Sat 10am–4pm. **Tube:** Green Park.

PRESTAT, 14 Princes Arcade, S.W.1. Tel. 071/629-4838.
Prestat is chocolate-maker "to Her Majesty the Queen by appointment." Why not take home a box of assorted Napoléon truffles? Or, a wide assortment of other flavors may tempt you: coffee-flavored chocolate, mint-flavored chocolate, or chocolate-coated brandy cherries. All boxes are elegantly gift wrapped. **Open:** Mon–Fri 10am–6pm, Sat 9:30am–5:30pm. **Tube:** Bond Street.

CLOCKS

STRIKE ONE LIMITED, 51 Camden Passage, N.1. Tel. 071/226-9709.
In the heart of the Camden Passage Antiques Village in Islington, Strike One guarantees every clock for a year. A wide selection is displayed, ranging from Victorian dial clocks to early English long-cast timepieces. The shop clearly dates and prices each old clock, and they specialize in Act of Parliament clocks. Barometers are also for sale. The illustrated catalog is mailed internationally to all serious clock

collectors, and if a customer requests a clock that the shop does not have in stock, they will attempt to find it. **Open:** Wed and Sat 9am–5pm (other times by appointment). **Tube:** Angel.

CONTEMPORARY ART

CCA GALLERIES, 8 Dover St., W.1. Tel. 071/499-6701.
Originally established as a branch office of Christie's specializing in limited-edition prints, CCA broke away from its illustrious owner in 1987. Today, the gallery offers etchings, lithographs, and screen-prints by up-and-coming artists. It also offers major works, by such world masters as Moore, Miró, Chagall, and Matisse. **Open:** Mon–Fri 9:30am–5:30pm, Sat 10am–4pm. **Tube:** Green Park.

COVENT GARDEN ENTERPRISES

An impressive array of shops, pubs, and other attractions can be found in the Central Market Building at Covent Garden. For the shops listed below, take the tube to Covent Garden.

JUBILEE MARKET, Covent Garden Piazza, W.C.2.
At this small open-air general market, antiques are sold on Monday, crafts on Saturday, and various other items on other days by dozens of independent dealers who arrive early to set up their stalls. **Open:** Mon–Sat 9am–5pm.

APPLE MARKET, Covent Garden Piazza, W.C.3. Tel. 071/836-9136.
A fun, bustling place, the Apple Market almost qualifies as street entertainment. Much is what the English call "collectible nostalgia." You'll have to sift through some of the worthless items to find the genuinely worthy ones, such as brass door knockers. Be sure to keep your sales resistance up as you wander; some of the vendors are mighty persuasive.
On Monday, the antique section of Apple Market overflows into the Jubilee Market, Jubilee Hall, Covent Garden Piazza, W.C.2. Antiques are sold from 7am to 5pm (go early). **Open:** General market Tues–Fri 9am–5pm; crafts Sat–Sun 9am–5pm.

CONTEMPORARY APPLIED ARTS, 43 Earlham St., W.C.2. Tel. 071/ 836-6993.
This association of craftspeople encourages both traditional and progressive contemporary artwork. The galleries at the center house a diverse retail display that includes glass, rugs, lights, ceramics, fabric, clothing, paper, metalwork, and jewelry—all created by the most outstanding artisans currently in the country. There is also a program of special exhibitions that focuses on innovations in the crafts; these are lone or small-group shows from the membership. Many of Britain's best-established makers, as well as promising, lesser-known ones, are represented. **Open:** Mon–Sat 10am–5:30pm.

COVENT GARDEN GENERAL STORE, 111 Long Acre, W.C.2. Tel. 071/ 240-0331.
Thousands of gift ideas and souvenirs ranging in price from a few pence to several pounds are offered here. It is ideally situated in Covent Garden, and hours are extended: Monday to Saturday from 10am to 11:30pm, and Sunday from 11am to 7pm. The store also features the Covent Garden General Store Restaurant, which serves salads from a salad bar, jacket potatoes, chili con carne, and macaroni and cheese, among other items; the restaurant is downstairs. **Open:** Mon–Sat 10:30am–10pm, Sun noon–6pm.

NATURAL SHOE STORE, 21 Neal St., W.C.2. Tel. 071/836-5254.
Shoes for both men and women are stocked in this shop, which also does shoe repairs. The selection includes all comfort and quality footwear—from Birkenstock to the best of the British classics. **Open:** Mon–Tues and Sat 10am–6pm; Wed–Fri 10am–7pm.

THE TEA HOUSE, 15A Neal St., W.C.2. Tel. 071/240-7539.
Devoted to tea and "tea-phernalia," the Tea House boasts 69 different teas and more than 250 teapots. **Open:** Mon–Sat 10am–7pm.

THE GLASSHOUSE, 65 Long Acre, W.C.2. Tel. 071/836-9785.
Not only can you buy beautiful glass here, but you can also watch craftspeople produce glass works in the workshop. **Open:** Mon–Fri 10am–6pm, Sat 11am–4:30pm.

PENHALIGON'S, 41 Wellington St., W.C.2. Tel. 071/836-2150.
A Victorian perfumery established in 1870, Penhaligon's holds royal warrants to HRH Duke of Edinburgh and HRH Prince of Wales. It offers a large selection of perfumes, aftershaves, soaps, and bath oils for women and men. The antique silver perfume bottles make perfect gifts. **Open:** Mon–Fri 10am–6pm, Sat 10am–5:30pm.

NEAL STREET EAST, 5 Neal St., W.C.2. Tel. 071/240-0135.
In this vast shop devoted to Asian or Asian-inspired merchandise, you can find dried and silk flowers, pottery, baskets, chinoiserie, toys, calligraphy, modern and antique clothing, textiles, and ethnic jewelry. There is also an extensive cookware department and bookshop. **Open:** Mon–Sat 10am–7pm.

NATURALLY BRITISH, 13 New Row (by Covent Garden), W.C.2. Tel. 071/240-0551.
Naturally British aims to present the best of contemporary handmade crafts from many fields: pottery, jewelry, glass, clothes from Ireland, Wales, and Scotland, cosmetics, rocking horses, games, puzzles, painted firescreens, iron works, and soft toys. There is a wide range of prices. **Open:** Mon–Sat (and Sun in summer) 10:30am–6:45pm.

NEAL'S YARD, off Neal St., W.C.2. No phone.
Behind the warehouse off Neal Street runs a narrow road leading to Neal's Yard, a mews of warehouses that retain some of the old London atmosphere. The open warehouses display vegetables, health foods, fresh-baked breads, cakes, sandwiches, and, in an immaculate dairy, the largest variety of flavored cream cheeses you are ever likely to encounter.

DEPARTMENT STORES

HARRODS, 87-135 Brompton Rd., at Knightsbridge, S.W.1. Tel. 071/730-1234.
 As firmly entrenched in English life as Buckingham Palace, Harrods is an elaborate emporium, at times as fascinating as a museum. The store is undergoing refurbishing to restore it to the elegance and luxury of the '20s and '30s.

Aside from the fashion department (including high-level tailoring), you'll find such incongruous sections as a cathedral-ceilinged and arcaded meat market, even a funeral service. Harrods has everything: men's custom-tailored suits, tweed overcoats, cashmere or lambswool sweaters for both men and women, hand-stitched traveling bags, raincoats, mohair jackets, patterned ski sweaters, scarves of handwoven Irish wool, pewter reproductions, a perfumery department, "lifetime" leather suitcases, and pianos.

The fourth floor is devoted to leisure. Here, there is a Toy Kingdom with everything a child could want, from the latest video games to a large collection of traditional teddy bears. Other departments throughout the store include a men's grooming room, the first of its kind in Europe; an enormous jewelry department; a fantastic Sports and Leisure Complex, a huge complex combining equipment with fashionable clothing and accessories for dozens of different sports in one department; and the redesigned "Way In" Department for the younger customers.

There are 11 restaurants and bars to choose from. **Open:** Mon–Tues and Thur–Sat 9am–6pm, Wed 9am–8pm. **Tube:** Knightsbridge.

SELFRIDGES, Oxford St., W.1. Tel. 071/629-1234.

Much more economical, Selfridges is one of the biggest department stores in Europe, with more than 300 divisions, selling everything from artificial flowers to groceries. The specialty shops are particularly enticing, with good buys in Irish linen, Wedgwood, leather goods, silver-painted goblets, and cashmere and woolen scarves. There's also the Miss Selfridge Boutique, for the young. To help you travel light, the Export Bureau will air freight your purchases anywhere in the world, tax free. In the basement Services Arcade, the London Tourist Board will help you find your way around London with plenty of maps, tips, and advice. **Open:** Mon–Wed and Fri–Sat 9:30am–6pm, Thurs 10am–8pm. **Tube:** Oxford Street.

LIBERTY & COMPANY LIMITED, 210-220 Regent St., W.1. Tel. 071/734-1234.

Renowned worldwide for selling high-quality, stylish merchandise in charming surroundings, this chain has its flagship store on Regent Street, with six floors of fashion, fabrics, china, and home furnishings. The personal "corner shop" service is staffed with helpful and informed assistants. In addition to the famous Liberty Print fashion fabrics, furnishing fabrics, scarves, ties, luggage, and gifts, the shop sells well-designed high-quality merchandise from all over the world. The company also has outlets in Bath, Cambridge, Canterbury, Edinburgh, Glasgow, Manchester, Norwich, York, and Oxford. **Open:** Mon–Wed and Fri–Sat 9:30am–6pm, Thurs 9:30am–7:30pm. **Tube:** Oxford Street.

MARKS & SPENCER, 458 Oxford St., W.1. Tel. 071/935-7954.

Marks & Spencer attracts the thrifty British, who get fine buys here, especially in woolen goods. This chain has built a reputation for quality and value; it is said that 25% of the socks worn by men in Britain come from M&S. Prices are competitive. The main department store is 3 short blocks from Marble Arch. However, there are a number of branches in London as well as in most towns of any size in Britain. **Open:** Mon–Wed and Fri 7am–8pm, Thurs 9am–8pm, Sat 9am–6pm. **Tube:** Marble Arch.

DAKS SIMPSON PICCADILLY, 203 Piccadilly, W.1. Tel. 071/734-2002.

Simpson's, which opened in 1936 as the home of DAKS clothing, is known not only for men's wear, but also for women's fashions, perfume, jewelry, and lingerie. The high-quality clothes exude elegance and style, from casual weekend wear to a wide selection of evening dress. The store also has a good restaurant that offers traditional English food; an English breakfast, served from 9 to 11:30am, will cost £8 ($14.80) lunch, served from noon to 2:30pm, is likely to cost £15 ($27.75); and the afternoon tea, from 3:30 to 5:15pm, costs £5.50 ($10.20). **Open:** Mon–Wed and Fri–Sat 9am–5:30pm, Thurs 9am–7pm. **Tube:** Piccadilly Circus.

PETER JONES, Sloane Sq., S.W.1. Tel. 071/730-3434.

One of the finest department stores in Europe, this has an impressive array of home furnishings, kitchenware, household goods, china, glass, and antiques. The store is especially known for its Irish linens, a real value. The classy store also has an array of perfumes, fashions, and accessories for men and women. There are two restaurants and a coffee shop, and many women come just for the hair salon. **Open:** Mon–Tues, Thurs, and Sat 9am–5:30pm, Wed 9:30am–7pm. **Tube:** Sloane Square.

DESIGNER CLOTHING [SECONDHAND]

PANDORA, 16-22 Cheval Place, S.W.7. Tel. 071/589-5289.

A London institution since it was first established in the 1940s, Pandora is located in fashionable Knightsbridge, a stone's throw from Harrods. The store is known to carry the finest merchandise in London, including dozens of hand-me-down designer dresses. Several times a week, chauffeurs drive up with bundles from the anonymous gentry of England that are likely to include dresses, jackets, suits, and gowns. Identities of the owners are strictly guarded, but many buyers are thrilled with the thought of wearing a hand-me-down from royalty, perhaps Princess Di. Prices are generally one-third to one-half of their retail value. Chanel, Yves St. Laurent, and

Valentino are among the designers represented. **Open:** Mon–Sat 10am–5pm. **Tube:** Knightsbridge.

FASHIONS

AUSTIN REED, 113 Regent St., W.1. Tel. 071/734-6789.

Offering British and international designers, Austin Reed is known for quality clothing. The store always stocks top-notch but expensive cashmere jackets, along with well-made conventional clothes. Men can outfit themselves with everything from dressing gowns to overcoats. The third floor is devoted to women's clothing, with carefully selected suits, separates, coats, shirts, knitwear, and accessories. **Open:** Mon, Wed, and Fri–Sat 9am–5:30pm; Tues 9:30am–5:30pm; Thurs 9am–7pm. **Tube:** Piccadilly Circus.

MEN'S

The selection of menswear in England is perhaps the finest in the world and ranges from Savile Row (at celestial prices) to bargain-basement wear. Your best buys are in ready-to-wear, instead of the super-expensive tailored clothing (referred to as "bespoke").

AQUASCUTUM, 100 Regent St., W.1. Tel. 071/734-6090.

The popular *Time Out* said that this shop is "about as quintessentially British as you'll get this side of Savile Row, and it's a popular stop-off for American tourists wanting to look more British than the Brits." On a trio of floors, the classic shop sells only high quality British and imported clothing for men desiring the classic look. **Open:** Mon–Wed and Fri–Sat 9am–6pm, Thurs 9am–7pm. **Tube:** Piccadilly Circus.

GIEVES & HAWKES, 1 Savile Row, W.1. Tel. 071/434-2001.

Although this has a prestigious address on Savile Row and a list of clients that includes the Prince of Wales, prices are not the lethal tariffs of other stores along this street. It's expensive, but you get good quality, as befits its reputation as a supplier to the British Royal Navy since the days of Lord Nelson. Cotton shirts, silk ties, Shetland jumpers, and exceptional suits—both ready-to-wear and bespoke—are sold. **Open:** Mon–Sat 9am–5:30pm. **Tube:** Piccadilly Circus.

HARRODS, 87-135 Brompton Rd., Knightsbridge, S.W.1. Tel. 071/730-1234.

Harrods is a worthy choice for just about everything (see "Department Stores," above), but don't overlook its men's store, which has a huge array of high quality, ready-to-wear suits, and all the accessories, including shoes, knitwear, socks, shirts, and pajamas. **Tube:** Knightsbridge.

BURTON, 311 Oxford St., W.1. Tel. 071/491-0032.

Since tailor-made British suits tend to be too expensive, a much cheaper alternative is Burton's; there are 66 branches in the Greater London area alone. Ready-made suits, where a man selects first his jacket, then the trousers to match in his size, come in a number of economical price ranges. **Open:** Mon–Tues and Sat 9am–6pm; Wed and Fri 9:30am–7pm; Thurs 9:30am–8pm. **Tube:** Oxford Circus.

HILDITCH & KEY, 37 or 73 Jermyn St., S.W.1. Tel. 071/930-2329.

Perhaps the finest name in men's shirts, Hilditch & Key has been in business since 1899. There are two shops on this street, with no. 37 specializing in women's wear and no. 73 men's. Hilditch also has an outstanding tie collection. **Open:** Mon–Wed and Fri 9:30am–6pm, Thurs 9:30am–7pm, Sat 9:30am–5:30pm. **Tube:** Green Park or Piccadilly Circus.

THOMAS PINK, 35 Dover St., W.1. Tel. 071/493-6775.

These Dover Street shirtmakers, named after an 18th-century Mayfair tailor, gave the world the phrases "Hunting pink" and "In the pink." They have a prestigious reputation for making well-made cotton shirts, for both men and women. The shirts are made of the finest two-fold pure cotton poplin, coming in a wide range of patterns, plain colors, stripes, or checks. Some patterns are classic, others are more unusual. All are generously cut with extra-long tails and finished with a choice of double cuffs or single button cuffs. **Open:** Mon–Fri 9:30am–6pm; Sat 9:30am–5pm. **Tube:** Green Park.

WOMEN'S

For raincoats, see **Burberry's,** below, which other coats for women, along with scarves and handbags. For sporting wear, see **Lillywhites** under "Sporting Goods." **Daks Simpson Piccadilly** (see "Department Stores, above) used to be exclusively a men's store, but now offers a variety of fashions for women. And of course, you must preview the fashions at the world's most famous department store, **Harrods** (see "Department Stores," above).

The following are a few more suggestions, but know that there are hundreds of women's clothing stores in all parts of town.

BRADLEY'S, 85 Knightsbridge, S.W.1. Tel. 071/235-2902.
Bradley's is the best-known lingerie specialty store in London. Even some members of the royal family shop here. Bradley's fits "all sizes" in silk, cotton, lace, polycotton, whatever. You'll love the fluffy slippers and its satin or silk nightgowns. **Open:** Mon–Tues and Thurs–Sat 9:30am–6pm, Wed 9:30am–7pm. **Tube:** Knightsbridge.

THE CHANGING ROOM, 10A Gees Court, W.1. Tel. 071/408-1596.
This is a small shop but it displays the clothing of at least a dozen British designers giving it the special opportunity of "mixing and matching" the clothing and accessories of various designers. **Open:** Mon–Wed and Fri–Sat 10:30am–6:30pm, Thurs 10:30am–7:30pm. **Tube:** Bond Street.

FENWICK OF BOND STREET, 63 New Bond St., W.1. Tel. 071/629-9160.
Fenwick is a small department store that offers an excellent collection of women's wear, ranging from moderately priced ready-to-wear to designer fashions. A wide range of lingerie (in all price ranges) is also sold. The store dates from 1891, and no clerk will talk to you until you speak first—that's their policy. **Open:** Mon–Wed and Fri–Sat 9:30am–6pm, Thurs 9:30am–7:30pm. **Tube:** Bond Street.

HYPER-HYPER, 26-40 Kensington High St., W.8. Tel. 071/938-4343.
Showcasing young and talented British fashion designers since 1983, Hyper-Hyper displays the work of nearly 75 designers at all times. From sportswear to evening wear, with plenty of accessories thrown in, including shoes, Hyper-Hyper will thrill and intrigue. Menswear is also available. **Open:** Mon–Sat 10am–6pm. **Tube:** Kensington High Street.

LAURA ASHLEY, 256-258 Regent St., W.1. Tel. 071/427-9760.
This famous store will outfit you with flower print Victorian dresses and/or easy-to-wear jersey and knitwear. They also sell a wide range of accessories. **Open:** Mon–Tues 9:30am–6pm; Wed and Fri 9:30am–7pm; Thurs 9:30am–8pm; Sat 9am–6pm. **Tube:** Oxford Circus.

FOOD

FORTNUM & MASON LTD., 181 Piccadilly, W.1. Tel. 071/734-8040.
Fortnum and Mason is no mere grocery store—it has been a British tradition since 1707. Down the street from the Ritz, it draws the carriage trade, those from Mayfair or Belgravia who come seeking such tinned treasures as pâté de foie gras or a boar's head. Today this store exemplifies the elegance and style one would expect from an establishment with two royal warrants. Enter the doors and be transported to another world of deep-red carpets, crystal chandeliers, spiraling wooden staircases, and unobtrusive, tail-coated assistants.

The grocery department is renowned for its impressive selection of the finest foods from around the world—the best champagne, the most scrumptious Belgian chocolates, and succulent Scottish smoked salmon. You might choose one of their wicker baskets of exclusive foods to have shipped home, perhaps through their telephone and mail order service. Wander through the four floors and inspect the bone china and crystal cut glass, perhaps find the perfect present in the leather or stationery departments, or reflect on the changing history of furniture, paintings, and ornaments in the antiques department. Dining choices include Patio & Buttery, St. James's Restaurant, and the Fountain Restaurant. **Open:** Mon–Sat 9:30am–5:30pm. **Tube:** Piccadilly Circus or Green Park.

IRISH WARES

IRISH SHOP, 11 Duke St., W.1. Tel. 071/935-1366.

For 25 years this small family business has been selling a wide variety of articles shipped directly from Ireland. Choose from out-of-the-ordinary tweeds, traditional linens, hand-knit Aran fisherman's sweaters, and Celtic jewelry. Merchandise includes Belleek and Royal Tara china, tapes of Irish music, souvenirs, and gift items. Waterford crystal in all styles and types is a specialty. **Open:** Mon–Wed and Fri–Sat 9:30am–5:30pm, Thurs 9:30am–7pm. **Tube:** Bond Street.

JEWELRY

SANFORD BROTHERS LTD., 3 Holborn Bars, Old Elizabethan Houses, E.C.1. Tel. 071/405-2352.

This family firm has been in business since 1923. They sell anything in jewelry, both modern and Victorian, silver of all kinds, and a fine selection of clocks and watches. The Elizabethan buildings are one of the sights of old London. **Open:** Mon–Fri 10am–4:30pm. **Tube:** Chancery Lane.

LONDON DIAMOND CENTRE, 10 Hanover St., W.1. Tel. 071/629-5511.

Here you can take an organized tour of a permanent exhibition showing how diamonds are mined, cut, polished, and made into exclusive jewelry, as well as visit the showroom where unmounted diamonds and ready-to-wear diamond jewelry, plus other gem jewelry, can be purchased or ordered. The admission of £3.45 ($6.40) includes a souvenir brilliant-cut zirconium (not a diamond), which you can have mounted in a 9-karat gold setting of your choice at modest cost. **Open:** Mon–Fri 9:30am–5:30pm, Sat 9:30am–1:30pm. **Tube:** Oxford Circus.

MAPS & ENGRAVINGS

THE MAP HOUSE, 54 Beauchamp Place, S.W.3. Tel. 071/589-4325.

An ideal place to find an offbeat souvenir, the Map House sells antique maps and engravings and has a vast selection of old prints of London and England, including originals and reproductions. **Open:** Mon–Fri 9:45am–5:45pm, Sat 10:30am–5pm. **Tube:** Knightsbridge.

THE GREATER LONDON RECORD OFFICE AND HISTORY LIBRARY, 40 Northampton Rd., E.C.1. Tel. 071/633-6851.

Here you'll find archives, maps, books, and photographs on the history of London, and reproductions of old maps and prints of London are for sale. **Open:** Tues 9:30am–7:30pm, Wed–Fri 9:30am–4:45pm. **Tube:** Farringdon or Angel.

NOTIONS

FLORIS, 89 Jermyn St., S.W.1. Tel. 071/930-2885.

A variety of toilet articles and fragrances is found in the floor-to-ceiling mahogany cabinets that line Floris's walls, considered architectural curiosities in their own right. The walls were installed relatively late in the establishment's history (that is, 1851), long after the shop had received its royal warrants as suppliers of toilet articles to the king and queen. The business was established in 1730 by a

Minorcan entrepreneur, Juan Floris, who brought from his Mediterranean home a technique for extracting fragrances from local flowers. Today, you can buy essences of flowers grown in English gardens, including stephanotis, rose geranium, lily-of-the-valley, violet, white jasmine, and carnation. **Open:** Mon–Fri 9:30am–5:30pm, Sat 9:30am–4pm. **Tube:** Piccadilly Circus.

PHILATELY

NATIONAL POSTAL MUSEUM, King Edward Building, King Edward St., E.C.1. Tel. 071/239-5420.

Not only does the museum house a magnificent collection of postage stamps and allied material, but it also sells postcards illustrating the collection and has a distinctive Maltese Cross postmark first used on the Penny Black. A letter mailed from Heathrow Airport is franked at Hounslow with an attractive Concorde cancellation. In country areas, the post office provides a postbus service between many remote and otherwise isolated villages. Often passenger tickets are canceled with a special stamp of collector interest, and postcards depicting places of interest along the routes are issued and mailed from these buses. More specialized, many of the narrow-gauge and privately owned railroads in the country issue and cancel their own stamps. **Open:** Mon–Thurs 9:30am–4:30pm, Fri 9:30am–4pm. **Tube:** St. Paul's.

POSTERS

LONDON TRANSPORT MUSEUM SHOP, Covent Garden, W.C.2. Tel. 071/379-6344.

This unique shop carries a wide selection of posters, books, cards, T-shirts, and other souvenir items. London Underground maps can be purchased here, as well as massive pictorial posters as seen at tube stations (40 in. x 60 in.). **Open:** Daily 10am–5:45pm; closed Christmas Day and Boxing Day. **Tube:** Covent Garden.

RAINCOATS

BURBERRY'S, 18 Haymarket, S.W.1. Tel. 071/930-3343.

Where else but near the London offices of American Express? The word Burberry has been synonymous with raincoats ever since King Edward VII publicly ordered his valet to "bring my Burberry" when the skies threatened rain. Its circa-1912 Haymarket store connects three lavishly stocked floors to an oak-lined staircase upon which have trod some of the biggest names in politics, stage, and screen. There's also a collection of excellent men's shirts, sportswear, knitwear, and accessories. Women's raincoats are also available. Don't think you'll get anything cheap from such a world-famous retailer; you'll get prestige and quality. But sometimes there are sales. An impeccably trained staff will help you. **Open:** Mon–Wed and Fri–Sat 9am–5:30pm, Thurs 9am–7pm. **Tube:** Piccadilly Circus.

SHOES

London is called the footwear capital of the world, and somewhere in this city, you can find what you're looking for. In addition to the following, see "Natural Shoe Store" under "Covent Garden Enterprises," above if you like your shoes made from natural materials.

CHARLES JOURDAN, 39-43 Brompton Rd., S.W.1. Tel. 071/581-3333.

This store carries one of the largest range of women's shoes in London. Imelda Marcos would run wild here. **Open:** Mon–Tues and Thurs–Sat 10am–6:30pm, Wed 10am–7pm. **Tube:** Knightsbridge.

LILLEY & SKINNERS, 360 Oxford St., W.1. Tel. 071/629-6381.

The biggest shoe store in the world, Lilley & Skinners displays its merchandise across four floors and markets shoes with both its own label and designer labels. All sizes of feet are fitted here. Prices, likewise, are wide ranging. **Open:** Mon–Wed and Fri 9:30am–6:30pm, Thurs 9:30am–8pm, Sat 9am–6pm. **Tube:** Bone Street.

CHURCH'S, 143 Brompton Rd., S.W.3. Tel. 071/589-9136.
Top-quality shoes have been turned out by these famous shoemakers since 1873, when the company was founded at Northampton. A trio of brothers started what has become a tradition among well-outfitted English gents. Of course, the company has changed with the times and now offers more stylish selections along with their traditional footwear. There is also a fashionable selection of shoes for women. **Open:** Mon–Fri 9am–5:30pm, Sat 9am–5pm. **Tube:** Knightsbridge.

SILVER

LONDON SILVER VAULTS, Chancery Lane, W.C.2. Tel. 071/242-3844.
Established in Victoria's day (1882) these are the largest silver vaults in the world. You can actually shop in vault after vault for that special treasure. **Open:** Mon–Fri 9am–5:30pm, Sat 9am–12:30pm. **Tube:** Chancery Lane.

STANLEY LESLIE, 15 Beauchamp Place, S.W.3. Tel. 071/589-2333.
Here you'll find an array of high-quality Georgian, Victorian, and early 20th-century silver. It's just the place to spend hours ferreting around for a special present. **Open:** Mon–Fri 9am–5pm, Sat 9am–1pm. **Tube:** Knightsbridge.

SOUVENIRS

OLD CURIOSITY SHOP, 13-14 Portsmouth St., off Lincoln's Inn Fields, W.C.2. Tel. 071/405-9891.
One of the original Tudor buildings still remaining in London and built in 1567, this shop crams every nook and cranny with general knickknackery, and souvenirs, including Dickens first editions. A popular item is an unframed silhouette of a Dickens character. Horse brasses are also sold, as are Old Curiosity Shop bookmarks and ashtrays with Dickensian engravings. Upstairs is an exhibition relating the story of the Old Curiosity Shop, a series of letters from Charles Dickens, and other artifacts. **Open:** Apr–Oct Mon–Fri 9am–5:30pm, Sat–Sun 9:30am–5pm; Nov–Mar Mon–Fri 9:30am–5pm, Sat–Sun 9:30am–4:30pm. **Tube:** Holborn.

SPORTING GOODS

LILLYWHITES LTD., Piccadilly Circus, S.W.1. Tel. 071/930-3181.
Established in 1863, Lillywhites offers everything connected with sports, together with fashionable leisure wear for both men and women. This is Britain's biggest sports store and has floor after floor of sports clothing, equipment, and footwear. Special orders and the international departments offer a worldwide service. **Open:** Mon–Sat 9:30am–6pm, Thurs 9:30am–7pm. **Tube:** Piccadilly Circus.

STREET MARKETS

Street markets have played an important role in London, and I recommend them not only for bric-a-brac but also for a low-cost adventure. In fact, you don't have to buy a thing; but be warned—some of the stallkeepers are mighty convincing.

PORTOBELLO ROAD MARKET

A magnet for collectors of virtually everything, Portobello Market, Portobello Road, W.11, is mainly a Saturday happening from 8am (it's best to go early) to 5pm. The name came from Admiral Vernon's capture of a Caribbean city, Puerto Bello, in 1739. A farm once stood here, but by the 1860s a market grew. Once known mainly for fruit and vegetables (still sold throughout the week), Portobello in the past four decades became synonymous with antiques (but don't take the stallholder's word for it). You can also browse around for jewelry, weapons (modern and antique), toys, kitchenware, scientific instruments, china, books, movie posters, magazines long defunct, watches, pens, music boxes, whatever.

The market is divided among three major sections, including the most crowded, the southern antiques section running between Colville Road and Chepstow Villas. The greatest concentration of pickpockets is in this area, so be warned. The second sector (and the oldest part) is the "fruit and veg" market, which lies between Westway and Colville Road. In the third section, Londoners operate a flea market, selling bric-a-brac and lots of secondhand goods.

In addition to stalls, many permanent shops are found both on and off Portobello Road—mostly between Westway and Colville Road—and can be visited throughout the week. Many art galleries also operate in and around the area, such as on Kensington Park Road, Blenheim Crescent, and in the fruit and veg section of Portobello Road. **Open:** Sat 8am–5pm. **Tube:** Ladbroke Grove or Notting Hill Gate.

NEW CALEDONIAN MARKET

This is commonly known as the **Bermondsey Market,** because of its location at Bermondsey Square, S.E.1, at the corner of Long Lane and Bermondsey Street; the extreme east end of the market is at Tower Bridge Road. This is one of Europe's outstanding street markets in size and quality of goods offered. The stalls are well known, and many dealers come into London from the country. The market is held on Friday from 7am until noon. The most serious bargain hunters get here early; antiques plus other items are generally lower in price here than they are at Portobello Road and the other street markets, but bargains are gone by 9am. **Tube:** Elephant and Castle, then take bus no. 1 or 188.

PETTICOAT LANE

On Sunday between 9am and 2pm (go before noon), throngs of shoppers join the crowds on Petticoat Lane (also known as Middlesex Street, E.1), where you can buy clothing, food, antiques, and plenty of junk. The area is surrounded by a maze of lanes that begin at the Liverpool Street station on the Bishopgate side. **Open:** Sun 9am–2pm. **Tube:** Liverpool Street, Aldgate, or Aldgate East.

LEATHER LANE

At this lively market, you'll find a variety of items for sale: fruit, vegetables, books, and men's and women's clothing. There are no try-ons, so inspect the size of the clothing carefully. **Open:** Mon–Sat 11am–3pm. **Tube:** Chancery Lane.

BERWICK STREET MARKET

This may be the only street market in the world that is flanked by two rows of strip clubs, porno stores, and adult-movie dens; however, don't let that put you off. This array of stalls sells probably the best and cheapest fruit and vegetables in town, as well as ancient records that may turn out to be collector's items, tapes, books, and old magazines. **Open:** Mon–Sat 8am–5pm. **Tube:** Tottenham Court Road.

TRAVEL CENTER

BRITISH AIRWAYS FIRST, 156 Regent St., W.1. Tel. 071/434-4700.
The retail flagship of British Airways, housed on three floors, offers not only

worldwide travel and ticketing, but also a wide range of services and shops—including a travel clinic for immunization, a pharmacy, a bureau de change, a passport and visa service, as well as a theater-booking desk. The ground floor offers luggage and other quality goods, plus travel accessories. A coffee shop serves teas, coffee, and pastries. Other services include a change machine, photobooth, phones, toilets, public fax, and photocopying facilities. Passengers with hand baggage only can check in here for a BA flight. **Open:** Mon–Fri 9am–7pm, Sat 9am–5pm. **Tube:** Piccadilly Circus.

WOOLENS

SCOTCH HOUSE, 84 Regent St., S.W.1. Tel. 071/734-5966.

The Scotch House is renowned worldwide for its comprehensive selection of top-quality cashmere and wool knitwear for both men and women. Also available is a wide range of tartan garments and accessories, as well as Scottish tweed classics. The children's collection also offers excellent value and quality. **Open:** Mon–Sat 9am–6pm, Thurs 9am–7pm. **Tube:** Piccadilly Circus.

WESTAWAY & WESTAWAY, opposite the British Museum, 62-65 Great Russell St., W.C.1. Tel. 071/405-4479.

A visit here is a substitute for a shopping trip to Scotland. They stock an enormous range of kilts, scarves, waistcoats, capes, dressing gowns, and rugs in authentic clan tartans. What's more, they are knowledgeable on the subject of these minutely intricate clan symbols. They also sell superb—and untartaned—cashmere, camel-hair, and Shetland knitwear, along with Harris tweed jackets, Burberry raincoats, and cashmere overcoats for men. Another branch is at 92-93 Great Russell St., W.C.1. **Open:** Mon–Sat 9am–5:30pm. **Tube:** Tottenham Court Road.

BERK, 46 Burlington Arcade, W.1. Tel. 071/493-0028.

Berk, the cashmere specialist, is one of those irresistible "fancy shops" for which London is famous. To shelter your precious cashmere from the elements, the shop also carries Burberry's raincoats, golf jackets and caps, and rain hats. All this is displayed in the 150-year-old Burlington Arcade, an attraction in its own right. **Open:** Mon–Fri 9am–5:30pm, Sat 9am–5pm. **Tube:** Piccadilly Circus.

3. EVENING ENTERTAINMENT

Nowhere else will you find such a panorama of legitimate theaters, operas, concerts, gambling clubs, discos, vaudeville at Victorian music halls, striptease joints, jazz clubs, folk-music cafés, nightclubs, and ballrooms. Your choices are countless—from the dives of Soho to the elegant jazz clubs—and so much depends on your taste, pocketbook, and even the time of year. For more information, ask a newsstand dealer for a copy of *Time Out* or *What's On in London,* which both contain listings of restaurants, theaters, and nightclubs.

THE ENTERTAINMENT SCENE

Geographically, about 90% of the bright lights burn in the area roughly defined as the **West End.** The core of this region is **Piccadilly Circus** which, with Coventry Street running down to Leicester Square, resembles Broadway. To the north lies **Soho,** chockablock with entertainment. To the east is the theaterland of **Covent Garden,** to the south **Trafalgar Square,** and to the west the fashionable and expensive nightlife of **Mayfair.**

With a few widely scattered exceptions, this area encompasses all the nightlife of interest to visitors, most of the attractions within easy walking distance of each other. But there are a few peculiarities you should be warned about.

The midnight curtain falls over many of the nighttime pleasures. It prevents you,

LONDON THEATRES & CINEMA

0 — 200 m / 220 y

THEATERS:

Adelphi 40
Albert J. Garrick 32
Aldwych 17
Ambassadors 13
Apollo 26
Apollo Victoria 60
Arts Theatre Club/Unicorn Theatre 21
Cambridge Theatre 11
Cannon Planton Street 44
Comedy 45
Dominion 1
Duke of Yorks 39
Dutchess 22
Fortune 15
Globe 25
Her Majesty's 52
ICA 57
London Coliseum 43
London Palladium 7
New London 4
Lyric 28
Odeon Mezzanine 38
Palace 12
Phoenix 5
Piccadilly 33
Players Theatre 51
The Playhouse 53
Prince Edward 10
Prince of Wales 41
Queen's 24

Royal Opera House 14
Royalty 6
Shaftesbury 3
St. Martins 19
Strand 20
Theatre Royal Drury Lane 16
Theatre Royal Haymarket 50
Vaudeville 37
Victoria Palace 59
Westminster 58
Whitehall 55
Windhams 31

CINEMAS:

Cannon Haymarket 49
Cannon Oxford Street 2
Cannon Piccadilly 47
Cannon Shaftesbury Avenue 9
Curzon Phoenix 8
Curzon West End 18
Empire 30
ICA 56
Lumiere 35
Metro Cinema 23
National Film Theatre 54
Odeon 36 46
Odeon West End 42
Plaza 48
Premiere 34
Prince Charles 27
Warner West End 29

IMPRESSIONS

You know why the sun never sets on the British Empire, don't you?—It doesn't trust it.
—GILBERT HARDING, IN BRIAN MASTERS'S *DAILY TELEGRAPH* REVIEW, JANUARY, 1979

for instance, from just dropping into a place for a drink (you must have something to eat with a drink served after 11pm). It doesn't prevent you, after hours, from paying a cover charge (frequently disguised as a membership fee) and enjoying a stage show, taking a spin on a dance floor, trying your luck at a gambling table, eating a five-course meal, and drinking.

Many of the places I'll describe in this section have some kind of front-door mumbo jumbo that passes as membership enrollment. What it amounts to is a so-called temporary membership, which satisfies the letter (if not the spirit) of the law and enables you to get in without delay. In many cases the temporary membership fee is deducted from the cost of dinner. There is, however, no hard and fast rule. London's club world is full of "hostesses." Beware. Their purpose is to make you buy things—from drinks to dolls and cigarettes—and they can raise your tab considerably. However, London's recognized meeting spots, especially for the younger set, are the ballrooms and discos, neither of which employ hostesses.

THE PERFORMING ARTS

MAJOR PERFORMING ARTS COMPANIES

ROYAL SHAKESPEARE COMPANY [RSC], Barbican Centre, Silk St., Barbican, E.C.2. Tel. 071/638-8891 (box office).

One of the world's finest theater companies is based in Stratford-upon-Avon and here at the Barbican Centre. The central core of the company's work remains the plays of William Shakespeare, but it also presents a wide-ranging program of three different productions each week in the Barbican Theatre—the 1,200-seat main auditorium which has excellent sightlines throughout, thanks to a raked orchestra, and the Pit, the small studio space where much of the company's new writing is presented.

In recent years, the RSC has had great success in transferring its hit shows, such as *Les Misérables* and *Les Liaisons Dangereuses* (the basis of the film *Dangerous Liaisons*) to West End theaters, while continuing its diverse repertoire both in London and Stratford. **Tube:** Barbican or Moorgate.

Those wanting to experience Shakespeare on his home territory can take the **Shakespeare Connection,** a road/rail link from Euston/British Rail station to

---

THE MAJOR CONCERT & PERFORMANCE HALLS

The following is a quick-reference list of major performance spaces in London, with box office telephone numbers. Details are provided in the listings below.
Barbican Centre (tel. 071/638-8891)
London Coliseum (tel. 071/836-3161, or 240-5258)
National Theatre (tel. 071/928-2252)
Royal Albert Hall (tel. 071/589-8212)
Royal Court Theatre (tel. 071/730-1745)
Royal Opera House (tel. 071/240-1066)
South Bank Centre (including Royal Festival Hall) (tel. 071/928-8800)

Stratford-upon-Avon (bookings in advance at the station or by calling 0789/294466), which runs every day of the week, or the **Shakespeare Stopover,** a meal/theater ticket/accommodation package operated daily during the Stratford theater season, usually from early April to late January. For bookings, phone 0789/414999. In Stratford, the RSC plays in the 1,500-seat Royal Shakespeare Theatre and the 400-seat Swan Theatre. For bookings, call 0789/295623.

Tickets: £7–£18.50 ($12.95–$34.25) in Barbican Theatre, £7.50 ($13.90) matinees.

ENGLISH NATIONAL OPERA, London Coliseum, St. Martin's Lane, W.C.2. Tel. 071/836-3161 for reservations, 071/240-5258 for inquiries and credit-card booking.

The London Coliseum, built in 1904 as a variety theater and converted into an opera house in 1968, is London's largest and most splendid theater. The English National Opera is one of the two national opera companies and performs a wide range of works, from great classics to Gilbert and Sullivan to new and experimental works, staged with flair and imagination, and with every performance in English. A repertory of 18 to 20 productions is presented 5 or 6 nights a week for 11 months of the year. Although the balcony seats are cheaper, many visitors prefer the Upper Circle or Dress Circle. **Tube:** Charing Cross or Leicester Square.

Tickets: £2.50 ($4.65) balcony; £13–£37.50 ($24.05–$69.40) Upper Circle or Dress Circle; about 100 discount balcony tickets sold on day of performance from 10am during opera season (Aug–June).

MAJOR CONCERT HALLS & ALL-PURPOSE AUDITORIUMS

LONDON PALLADIUM, Argyle St., W.1. Tel. 071/437-7373.

It's hard to encapsulate the prestige of this show-business legend in a paragraph. The highlight of the season is the Royal Command Performance, held before the queen, which includes an introduction of the artists to Her Majesty.

In days of yore, the Palladium has starred Frank Sinatra, Shirley MacLaine, Andy Williams, Perry Como, Julie Andrews, Tom Jones, Sammy Davis, Jr., and so on. Today it is likely to present productions such as *The Pirates of Penzance,* while second-line program attractions are likely to include, say, "Los Paraguayos" and the Ukrainian Cossack Ensemble. The Palladium is usually closed on Sunday. **Tube:** Oxford Circus.

Tickets: £8–£20 ($14.80–$37).

ROYAL OPERA HOUSE, Bow St., W.C.2. (Box Office, 48 Floral St., W.C.2). Tel. 071/240-1200.

This classical building is on the northeast corner of Covent Garden, London's first square, laid out by Inigo Jones as a residential piazza. Until a few years ago, the whole area was a thriving fruit and vegetable market. In the 16th century, the section became fashionable to live in and was soon to become a center of London nightlife. The first theater was built on the present site in 1732. The existing opera house, one of the most beautiful theaters in Europe, was built in 1858 and is now the home of the **Royal Opera** and **Royal Ballet,** which are leading international companies. Check newspapers for details of performances. Open Monday to Saturday from 10am to 8pm. **Tube:** Covent Garden.

Tickets: £1.50–£49 ($2.80–$90.65) ballet, £3–£101 ($5.55–$186.85) opera.

SOUTH BANK CENTRE, at South Bank, S.E.1. Tel. 071/928-8800.

In recent years, the musical focal point in London has shifted to this superbly specialized complex of buildings on the South Bank side of Waterloo Bridge. It houses the Hayward Gallery, plus three of the most stylish, comfortable, and acoustically perfect concert structures in the world: the **Royal Festival Hall,** the **Queen Elizabeth Hall,** and the **Purcell Room.** Here, more than 1,200 performances a year are presented, including ballet and music concerts—classical, jazz, pop, and folk. The Royal Festival Hall is open from 10am every day and offers an extensive range of things to see and do. There are free exhibitions in the foyers and free lunchtime music from 12:30 to 2pm, plus guided tours of the building, and book, record, and gift shops. The Festival Buffet has a wide selection of food at reasonable prices, and there are a number of bars throughout the foyers. It is open daily from 10am to 9pm. **Tube:** Waterloo Station.

Tickets: £5–£25 ($9.25–$46.25).

BARBICAN CENTRE, Silk St., the Barbican, E.C.2. Tel. 071/638-4141.

Considered the largest art and exhibition center in Western Europe, the Barbican was created to make a perfect setting to enjoy good music and theater from comfortable, roomy seating. The theater is now the London home of the Royal Shakespeare Company (see above), and the Concert Hall is the permanent home of the **London Symphony Orchestra** and host to visiting orchestras and performers. **Tube:** Barbican.

Tickets: £5–£25 ($9.25–$46.25).

ROYAL ALBERT HALL, Kensington Gore, S.W.7. Tel. 071/589-8212.

Opened in 1871 and dedicated to the memory of Queen Victoria's consort, Prince Albert, this building encircles one of the world's largest and finest auditoriums with a seating capacity of 5,500. Home since 1941 to the **BBC Promenade Concerts,** the famous 8-week annual festival of classical music, it is also a popular venue for light music by stars such as Frank Sinatra plus the latest in rock and pop. In addition, sport and pageantry are popular events here, including boxing and covered court lawn tennis—with the Masters Doubles Championship being played here a month after the annual Royal British Legion Festival of Remembrance. **Tube:** South Kensington, High Street Kensington, or Knightsbridge.

Tickets: From £4.50 ($8.35) sold daily 9am–9pm.

WIGMORE HALL, 36 Wigmore St., W.1. Tel. 071/935-2141.

In this intimate auditorium, you'll hear excellent recitals and concerts—there are regular series, master concerts by chamber music groups and instrumentalists, song-recital series, and concerts featuring special composers or themes throughout the year. In addition to the nightly performances, there are Sunday Morning Coffee Concerts as well as Sunday performances at 4 and 7pm. A free list of the month's program is available from the hall. **Tube:** Bond Street or Oxford Circus.

Tickets: £4 ($7.40).

THEATER

In London, you'll have a chance to see the world-renowned English theater on its home ground. You may want to spend a classical evening at the National Theatre, catch up on that Broadway musical you missed in New York, or scout out a new play—perhaps next year's big Stateside hit.

If you want to see two shows in one day, you'll find that Wednesday, Thursday, and Saturday are always crammed with matinee performances. London theaters sometimes start and finish earlier than their American cousins: Evening performances begin between 7:30 and 8pm, midweek matinees start at 2:30 or 3pm. Some of the London theaters have licensed bars on the premises and serve hot coffee during intermission.

For full details on West End productions, pick up a free biweekly *London Theatre Guide* at the Booth or at any West End theater, tourist or travel information center, hotel, or library on your arrival in London.

RESERVATIONS You can either purchase your ticket from the theater's box office (most recommended), or from a ticket agent, such as the one at the reservations desk of American Express, which charges an agent's fee. In fact, all theater-booking agencies charge a fee, and once confirmed, the booking will be charged to your account even if you don't use the tickets. Incidentally, only cardholders can collect the tickets charged to their accounts. The agencies do come in handy, however, if you want to see specific shows, particularly hit ones, for they will enable you to reserve tickets well in advance.

Keith Prowse (tel. 071/793-1000) has an office in the United States that will reserve seats weeks or even months in advance; contact Keith Prowse, 234 West 44th Street, New York, NY 10036 (tel. 212/398-1430 or toll free 800/669-8687). Or, if you want to contact the agency when you're in London, look under "Keith" in the telephone book to find an office that is convenient for you.

British Airways operates one of the most sure-fire ticket-ordering agencies in Europe. Its box office service permits the telephone purchase of the best seats available for theater and musical productions in London, Stratford-upon-Avon, and the Edinburgh Festival. If, and only if, a passenger holds a ticket on BA, a phone call to the airline's telephone reservations service will prebook and reserve tickets, which may be charged to a credit card if reserved more than 7 days in advance. BA will issue a voucher, which will be exchanged in London for the actual tickets (seats preassigned). For reservations and information, call BA toll free at 800/AIRWAYS.

Many theaters will accept bookings by telephone if you give your name and credit-card number; then all you have to do is go to the theater before the performance to collect your tickets, which will be sold at the theater price. If you don't show up, they charge your account anyway. In a few theaters, you can even reserve seats in the gallery—the cheapest ones.

Under a British voluntary code, theater-ticket brokers must disclose the face value of a ticket as well as their fee. But since the requirement is voluntary, many brokers don't bother with this regulation. Their markup is at least 20% to 25%, but spot checks in London have revealed markups as high as 80%. Before you enter into such an agreement with a broker, it is wiser to call the theater directly to see if any tickets are available at the regular price. In the cases of hit shows, only brokers at certain times may be able to get you a seat, but you'll pay for the privilege.

DISCOUNT THEATER TICKETS   London theater prices are—by U.S. standards—quite reasonable. Matinees are on Wednesday (or Thursday at some theaters) and on Saturday. Prices for London shows can vary widely—usually from £7 to £25 ($12.95 to $46.25), depending on the seat. In some cases, the gallery seats—the cheapest ones—are sold only on the day of performance, so you'll have to buy your ticket early in the day and then return about an hour before the performance to queue up, as they're not reserved seats.

Discounted tickets are sometimes offered, but only to long-running plays on their last legs or to new "dogs," which you may not want to see anyway; also, reduced tickets are more likely to be available for matinees. A really hot musical in its early life will almost never offer discounted tickets.

Leicester Square Half-Price Ticket Booth, Leicester Square, W.C.2, sells theater tickets on the day of performance for half price (cash only) plus up to a £1.25 ($2.30) service charge. It's open Monday to Saturday from noon to 2pm for matinee performances and from 2:30 to 6:30pm for evening performances. A wide range of seats are available. There is a long queue, but it moves quickly. The shows for which tickets are available are displayed at the booth, so you can make up your mind on what to see as you wait in the queue. The booth is operated by The Society of West End Theatre.

Traveler's Advisory: Beware of scalpers who hang out in front of hit shows at London theaters. There are reports of scalpers selling forged tickets, and their prices are outrageous.

THE THEATERS   It is impossible to describe all of London's theaters in this space, so I'll mention just a few from the treasure trove.

NATIONAL THEATRE, South Bank, S.E.1. Tel. 071/928-2252.
This three-theater complex stands as a $32-million landmark beside the Waterloo Bridge on the south bank of the Thames. It was first suggested in 1848, and it took Parliament 101 years to pass a bill vowing government support. Flaring out like a fan, the most thrilling theater in this complex is the **Olivier,** named after Lord Laurence Olivier, its first director when the company was born in 1962. The Olivier Theatre bears a resemblance in miniature to an ancient Greek theater: It's an open-stage,

1,160-seat house. The **Cottesloe** is a simple box theater for 400 people that can be arranged in different ways. Finally, the 890-seat **Lyttelton** is a traditional proscenium-arch house that doesn't have one bad seat.

In the foyers, there are three bookshops, eight bars, two restaurants, and five self-service buffets (some open all day on Monday through Saturday), and many outside terraces with river views. A meal in the National Theatre Restaurant or one of the coffee bars will cost around £12 ($22.20); a snack will cost around £3.50 ($6.45). For everyone, with or without tickets for a play, there is free live foyer music before evening performances and Saturday matinees, plus free exhibitions. The foyers are open Monday to Saturday from 10am to 11pm. **Tube:** Waterloo Station.

Tickets: £7–£20 ($12.95–$37), midweek matinees cheaper.

THE OLD VIC, Waterloo Rd., S.E.1. Tel. 071/928-2651, or the box office at 071/928-7616.

The facade and much of the interior of this 170-year-old theater were restored in their original early 19th-century style, while much modernization occurred inside. The proscenium arch was moved back, and the stage trebled in size, and more seats and stage boxes added. The theater is air-conditioned and contains five bars. There are short seasons of plays by a variety of repertory theaters and other groups. **Tube:** Waterloo Station.

Tickets: Matinees £3–£16 ($5.55–$29.60), evening performances £4–£17.50 ($7.40–$32.40).

REGENT'S PARK, N.W.1. Tel. 071/486-2431.

This outdoor theater is right in the center of Regent's Park. The setting is idyllic, and the longest theater bar in London provides both drink and food. Presentations are mainly Shakespeare, usually in period costume, and both seating and acoustics are excellent. If it rains, you're given tickets for another performance. **Performances:** June to mid-Sept daily 7:45pm, plus Wed–Thurs and Sat 2:30pm. **Tube:** Baker Street.

Tickets: £5–£12 ($9.25–$22.20).

ROYAL COURT THEATRE, Sloane Sq., S.W.1. Tel. 071/730-1745.

The English Stage Company has operated this theater for more than 35 years; their emphasis is on new playwrights (John Osborne got his start here with the 1956 production of *Look Back in Anger*). Also on the premises is the Theatre Upstairs, a studio theater devoted to new and experimental works. Shows are Monday to Saturday at 8pm, plus Saturday at 4pm; in the upstairs theater, they're Monday to Saturday at 7:30pm, plus Saturday at 3:30pm. **Tube:** Sloane Square.

Tickets: Upstairs tickets all seats £5 ($9.25); downstairs tickets all seats Mon £5 ($9.25), Tues–Sat £6–£16 ($11.10–$29.60), Sat matinees £5–£13 ($9.25–$24.05).

SADLER'S WELLS, Rosebery Ave., E.C.1. Tel. 071/278-8916.

A theater has stood here since 1683, on the site of a well once known for the healing powers of its waters. Once the home of the famed Sadlers Wells Ballet which moved to Covent Garden to become the Royal Ballet, the theater today is a showcase for British and foreign modern ballet and modern dance companies and international opera. Performances usually begin at 7:30pm. **Tube:** Angel.

Tickets: £5–£28.50 ($9.25–$52.75).

THE YOUNG VIC, 66 the Cut, Waterloo, S.E.1. Tel. 071/928-6363.

This theater aims primarily at the 15-to-25 age group. The Young Vic's repertoire includes such authors as Shakespeare, Ben Jonson, Arthur Miller, and Harold Pinter, plus specially written new plays. Performances normally begin at 7:30pm. **Tube:** Waterloo Station.

Tickets: £9 ($16.65) adults, £5 ($9.25) students and children.

Dinner Theater

TALK OF LONDON, New London Theatre, Parker St., off Drury Lane, W.C.2. Tel. 071/408-1001.

A unique theater restaurant in a unique setting, that's the Talk of London. It is situated in the heart and soul of the city's theaterland. The restaurant is ingeniously designed so that every guest gets "the best seat in the house." Sitting in a circular layout on varying floor levels, everyone has an uninterrupted view of the show. The Talk of London offers a complete evening's entertainment: a four-course dinner of your choice, dancing to an orchestra, a top show band, and an international cabaret at 10:30pm. All this and coffee, service, and VAT are included in the price. Drinks are extra. Reservations are essential. **Open:** Four nights a week (different nights each week, so call) 8pm–midnight. **Tube:** Covent Garden.

Admission: £30 ($55.50) including dinner.

Gilbert & Sullivan Evenings

The English Heritage Singers present Gilbert and Sullivan programs at the **Mansion House at Grim's Dyke,** Old Redding, Harrow Weald, Middlesex HA3 6SH (tel. 081/954-4227), every other Sunday in winter and most Sundays the rest of the year. This is a dinner event, costing £32 ($59.20) per person. You arrive for cocktails in the Library Bar of the house where Gilbert once lived and where he and Sullivan worked on their charming operettas. A full Edwardian-style dinner is served at 8pm, with costumed performances of the most beloved of Gilbert and Sullivan songs both during and after the meal. You can request your favorite melodies from the Gilbert and Sullivan works—the singers know them all.

THE CLUB & MUSIC SCENE
NIGHTCLUBS/CABARETS

CAMDEN PALACE, 1A Camden High St., N.1. Tel. 071/387-0428.
Camden Palace is housed inside what was originally a theater. It draws an over-18 crowd who flock in various costumes and energy levels according to the night of the week. Since it offers a rotating style of music, it's best to phone in advance to see what's happening. Styles range from rhythm and blues to what young rock experts call "boilerhouse," "garage music," "acid funk," "hip-hop," and "twist and shout." A live band performs only on Tuesday. There's a restaurant if you get the munchies, and a pint of lager goes for £2 ($3.70). **Open:** Tues–Sat 9pm–2:30am. **Tube:** Camden Town or Mornington Crescent.

Admission: Tues–Thurs £4–£5 ($7.40–$9.25), Fri £8–£10 ($14.80–$18.50), Sat £6–£8 ($11.10–$14.80).

EVE, 189 Regent St., W.1. Tel. 071/734-0557.
Eve is London's longest-established late-night club. Doyen of London's nightlife, Jimmy O'Brien launched it in 1953. International variety acts (at 1am) have replaced the floor shows previously presented. Dancing is to relaxing music from the '40s to the '60s. Only one person in a party need be a member, and overseas visitors may be admitted on application without waiting the customary 48 hours. An à la carte menu is offered throughout the night. Liquor is served but not beer. Charming and attractive young women, many of whom speak more than one language, are available as dining or dancing partners for unaccompanied men. **Open:** Mon–Fri 10pm–3:30am. **Closed:** Last week of Aug, first week of Sept. **Tube:** Oxford Circus.

Admission: By membership only. £10 ($18.50) annual subscription, £2 ($3.70) 1-night membership, £10 ($18.50) entrance fee. Drinks from £7 ($12.95).

HENRY'S, 9 Young St., W.8. Tel. 071/937-9493.
Just off Kensington High Street, Henry's is a good place to go for a widely varied repertoire of music. Likewise, the patrons come from many different countries and backgrounds and span a wide age spectrum as well. **Open:** Tues–Thurs 10pm–2am, Fri–Sat 10pm–3am. **Tube:** Kensington High Street.

Admission: £3–£6 ($5.55–$11.10). **Prices:** Beer £2.50 ($4.65).

L'HIRONDELLE, 99-101 Regent St., W.1. Tel. 071/734-6666.
L'Hirondelle stands in the heart of the West End and puts on some of the most

lavishly gorgeous floor shows. What's more, it lets you dine, drink, and dance without the "temporary memberships." There's no entrance fee either. The shows are really full-scale revues and go on at 11pm and 1am. Dancing to the few live bands in London is from 9:30pm. Dancing-dining partners are available. The club offers a three-course dinner for £30 ($55.50) per person, including VAT and service charges, or you can choose from their very large à la carte menu. A bottle of wine costs from £23 ($43.55). **Open:** Mon–Sat 8:30pm–3:30am. **Tube:** Piccadilly Circus.

Admission: £10 ($18.50) cover charge for nondiners.

RHEINGOLD CLUB, Sedley Place, off 361 Oxford St., W.1. Tel. 071/629-5343.

The Rheingold, founded in 1959, is the oldest and most successful "singles club" in London, existing long before the term had been coined. It is a safe place for men to take their wives or girlfriends, and respectable single women are welcome and safe here.

This spot thrives in a century-old wine cellar and has a restaurant, two bars, and a good-size dance floor. The main attraction is a top-class band playing every evening except Sunday and bank holidays. There is also an occasional cabaret, usually with big-time guest stars.

The club offers a tasty German dish called champignon-schnitzel, a tender escallop of Dutch veal served with rice and peas in a cream-and-mushroom sauce, costing £7 ($12.95). It has a strong German draft beer at £1.20 ($2.20) for a half pint and excellent French and German wines from £8.50 ($15.75) for an *appellation contrôlée* or *qualitätswein* to £12.50 ($23.10) for château-bottled Bordeaux or a Moselle Spätlese. **Open:** Mon–Tues 7:30pm–1:30am, Wed–Thurs (cabaret nights) 7:30pm–2am, Fri–Sat 7:30pm–2:30am. **Tube:** Bond Street.

Admission: £5 ($9.25) temporary membership.

TIDDY DOLS, 55 Shepherd Market, Mayfair, W.1. Tel. 071/499-2357.

Housed in nine small atmospheric Georgian houses, circa 1741, this club is named for the famous gingerbread baker and eccentric. Guests come to Tiddy Dols to enjoy such dishes as jugged hare, game soup, plum pudding, and the original gingerbread of Tiddy Dol. While dining they are entertained with madrigals, Noël Coward, Gilbert and Sullivan, music hall songs, and a Town Crier. In the summer there is a large pavement café with parasols and a view of the "village" of Shepherd Market. During winter there are open fires. An à la carte dinner, costing from £30 ($55.50), is served nightly. Dancing is nowadays restricted to special evenings. **Open:** Daily 6pm–1am (11:30pm last arrivals). **Tube:** Green Park.

Admission: £1.55 ($2.85) cover charge. **Prices:** Drinks from £2.50 ($4.65).

COMEDY CLUBS

THE COMEDY STORE, 28A Leicester Sq., W.C.2. Tel. 0426/914433 outside London for program details (no local phone).

Set in the heart of the city's nighttime district, this is London's most visible showcase for rising comic talent. A prerecorded message will tell you the various comedians and musicians scheduled to appear during the upcoming week. Even if the names of the performers are unfamiliar to you (highly likely), you will still enjoy the live comedy performed before a live British audience. Visitors must be more than 18. There is no particular dress code at this place; many wear jeans. No reservations are accepted, and the club opens 1 hour before each show. **Open:** Wed and Sun from 7:30pm, Thurs from 8:30pm, Fri–Sat from 7pm. **Tube:** Leicester Square or Piccadilly Circus.

Admission: £6–£7 ($11.10–$12.95).

ROCK

GULLIVER'S, 15 Ganton St., W.1. Tel. 071/499-0760.

Established 20 years ago at another location, this well-rooted club now sits within a very modern black and gold-colored cellar off Carnaby Street. It specializes in

American and British soul music, although a highly appealing blend of other styles is presented at each of its opening nights. The venue ranges from "old soul" night (the Supremes, Otis Redding, et al.), to evenings which include Swing, Beat, and Rap music, with doses of Caribbean Calypso, reggae, and "soca music" (you heard right) thrown in. At the long expanse of bar, you can order a Budweiser for £2.50 ($4.65). **Open:** Wed and Thurs 10:30pm–3:30am, Fri and Sat 11pm–6am; Sun 9pm–1am. **Tube:** Oxford Circus.
   Admission: £6–£10 ($11.10–$18.50).

MARQUEE, 105 Charing Cross Rd., W.C.2. Tel. 071/437-6601.
   The Marquee is considered one of the best-known centers for rock in the world. Its reputation goes back to the 1950s, but it remains forever young. Famous groups such as the Stones played at the Marquee long before their names spread beyond the shores of England. Fortunately, you don't have to be a member—you just pay at the door. There's a coffee and a Coke bar for light snacks; those 18 or older can order hard drinks. Many well-known musicians frequent the place regularly on their nights off. The club occupies a building that was once a cinema. **Open:** daily 7pm–3am. **Tube:** Leicester Square or Tottenham Court Road.
   Admission: £5.50–£10 ($10.20–$18.50), depending on performer.

ROCK GARDEN RESTAURANT & ROCK MUSIC VENUE, 6-7 The Piazza, Covent Garden, W.C.2. Tel. 071/240-3961.
   This is the place where new bands are launched, where such renowned groups as Dire Straits, The Police, U2, and The Stanglers all played before becoming famous. In summer the restaurant offers outside seating in the heart of Covent Garden. A wide range of meals is offered, costing from £8 ($14.80). Both the restaurant and the Venue have licensed bars. **Open:** Restaurant, Mon–Thurs and Sun noon–midnight, Fri–Sat noon–1am; Venue Mon–Sat 7:30pm–3am, Sun 7:30pm–midnight. **Tube:** Covent Garden; night buses from neighboring Trafalgar Square.
   Admission: £5–£7 ($9.25–$12.95) at Venue. **Prices:** Drinks from £1.20 ($2.20).

JAZZ/BLUES

THE BASS CLEF/THE TENOR CLEF, 35 Coronet St./Hoxton Sq. Tel. 071/729-2476.
   Both of these jazz clubs are contained within the same sprawling brick-fronted building which was originally prominent as a hospital during the early 20th century. The Bass Clef (located within a cellar with an entrance on Coronet Street) specializes in free-form modern jazz, while the Tenor Clef (located one floor above street level with an entrance on Hoxton Square) presents somewhat more traditional jazz and a style labeled by its owners as "fusion jazz." Both are the kind of smoke-filled ambience-filled place beloved by London's jazz experts. Weeknights, a complicated series of stairs and hallways interconnects the two clubs, although on Friday and Saturday, each club is considered a fiscally separate entity. Both of them contain restaurants, where full meals cost around £12 ($22.20) each. **Open:** Nightly 7:30pm–2am, Sun 12:30–3pm. Live music begins at 9pm Mon–Sat, 1pm on Sun. **Tube:** Old Street.
   Admission: £4.50–£7 ($8.35–$12.95). **Prices:** Drinks from £2 ($3.70) each.

BULL'S HEAD, 373 Lonsdale Rd., Barnes, S.W.13. Tel. 081/876-5241.
   Bull's Head has presented live modern jazz concerts every night of the week for more than 30 years. One of the oldest hostelries in the area, it was a staging post in the mid-19th century where travelers on their way to Hampton Court and beyond could eat, drink, and rest while the coach horses were changed. Today the place is known for its jazz, performed by musicians from all over the world. Jazz concerts are presented on Sunday from 1pm to 2:30pm and 8:30 to 10:30pm. From Monday to Saturday, you can hear music from 8:30 to 11pm. You can order good food at the Carvery in the Saloon Bar daily and dine in the 17th-century Stable Restaurant. The restaurant, in the original, restored stables, specializes in steaks, fish, and other traditional fare.

Meals cost £6 ($11.10) and up. **Open:** Mon–Sat 11am–11pm, Sun noon–3pm and 7–10:30pm. **Tube:** Hammersmith, then bus no. 9 the rest of the way or else take the Hounslow Look Train from Waterloo Station and get off at Barnes Bridge Station, then walk 5 minutes to the club.

Admission: £3.50–£7 ($6.45–$12.95). **Prices:** Beer from £1.50 ($2.80).

100 CLUB, 100 Oxford St., W.1. Tel. 071/636-0933.

Although less plush and cheaper, the 100 Club is considered a serious rival of Bull's Head (see above) among many dedicated jazz gourmets. Its cavalcade of bands includes the best British jazz musicians, as well as many touring Americans. **Open:** Fri 8:30pm–3am, Sat 7:30pm–1am, Sun 7:30–11:30pm. **Tube:** Tottenham Court Road or Oxford Circus.

Admission: Fri £6 ($11.10); Sat £5 ($9.25) members, £7 ($12.95) nonmembers; Sun £4 ($7.40) members, £5 ($9.25) nonmembers. **Prices:** Drinks from £1.40 ($2.60).

RONNIE SCOTT'S, 47 Frith St., W.1. Tel. 071/439-0747.

⭐ Mention the word "jazz" in London and people immediately think of Ronnie Scott's, long the citadel of modern jazz in Europe where the best English and American groups are booked. Featured on almost every bill is an American band, often with a top-notch singer. It's in the heart of Soho, a 10-minute walk from Piccadilly Circus via Shaftesbury Avenue. Not only can you saturate yourself in the best of jazz, you get reasonably priced drinks and dinners as well. There are three separate areas: the Main Room, the Upstairs Room, and the Downstairs Bar. You don't have to be a member, although you can join if you wish. If you have a student ID you are granted entrance Monday to Thursday for £6 ($11.10). In the Main Room you can either stand at the bar to watch the show or sit at a table, where you can order dinner. The Downstairs Bar is more intimate, a quiet rendezvous where you can meet and talk with the regulars, often some of the world's most talented musicians. The Upstairs Room is separate and it has a disco called The Tango. **Open:** Main Room Mon–Sat 8:30pm–3am; Upstairs Room Mon–Sat 8:30pm–3am. **Tube:** Tottenham Court Road or Leicester Square.

Admission: From £12 ($22.25), depending on the performers. **Prices:** Drinks from £2.50 ($4.65); ½ pint beer £1.10 ($2.05).

DANCE CLUBS/DISCOS

BARBARELLA 2, 43 Thurloe St., S.W.7. Tel. 071/584-2000.

This place combines a first-class Italian restaurant with a carefully controlled disco. So that diners can converse in normal tones, the flashing lights and electronic music of the disco are separated from the dining area by thick sheets of glass. Full meals, costing from £20 ($37), include an array of Neapolitan-inspired dishes. Only clients of the restaurant are allowed into the disco, which prevents hordes of late-night revelers from cramming into the place when the regular pubs close. **Open:** Mon–Sat 7:30pm–3am (last food orders 12:45am). **Tube:** South Kensington.

Admission: Free. **Prices:** Drinks from £2.40 ($4.45); beer £1.60 ($2.95).

HIPPODROME, corner of Cranbourn St. and Charing Cross Rd., W.C.2. Tel. 071/437-4311.

⭐ Here you will find one of London's greatest discos, an enormous place where light and sound beam in on you from all directions. Revolving speakers even descend from the roof to deafen you in patches, and you can watch yourself on closed-circuit video. Golden Scan lights are a spectacular treat. There are six bars and a balcony restaurant. Lasers and a hydraulically controlled stage for visiting international performers are only part of the attraction. **Open:** Mon–Sat 9pm–3:30am. **Tube:** Leicester Square.

Admission: £8–£12 ($14.80–$22.20). **Prices:** Drinks from £2.50 ($4.65).

LONDON EMPIRE DISCOTHEQUE, Leicester Sq., W.C.2. Tel. 071/437-1446.

Europe's largest disco ballroom, this is in the heart of London's entertainment area. Top DJs and spectacular light shows are presented, along with live bands. **Open:** Mon–Thurs 8:30pm–2am, Fri–Sat 8:30pm–3:30am. **Tube:** Leicester Square.

Admission: Mon–Thurs £4–£6 ($7.40–$11.10), Fri–Sat £6–£8 ($11.10–$14.80). **Prices:** Drinks from £2.90 ($5.35); beer from £2.70 ($5).

ROYAL ROOF RESTAURANT, Royal Garden Hotel, 2-24 Kensington High St., W.8. Tel. 071/937-8000.

Situated on the top floor of the hotel, Royal Roof Restaurant is elegant and refined, and overlooks Kensington Gardens and Hyde Park. From your table you will see the lights of Kensington and Knightsbridge, with a view of London's West End skyline. In a romantic candlelit aura, you can dance to the resident band on Saturday and enjoy a five-course set dinner costing £33 ($61.05). On other nights there's a live pianist. Reservations are vital. **Open:** Mon–Sat 7pm–1am (last order 10:30pm Mon–Fri and 11:30pm Sat). **Tube:** Kensington High Street.

Admission: Free.

STRINGFELLOWS, 16-19 Upper St. Martin's Lane, W.C.2. Tel. 071/ 240-5534.

This is one of London's most elegant nighttime rendezvous spots. It is said to have £1 ($1.85) million worth of velvet and high-tech gloss and glitter. In theory, it's a members-only club, but—and only at the discretion of management—nonmembers may be admitted. It offers two lively bars and a first-class restaurant. Its disco has a stunning glass dance floor and a dazzling sound-and-light system. It's been called "an exquisite oasis of elegance," and its food "the best in London" (for a nightclub, that is). **Open:** Dinner Mon–Sat 8pm–3am, dancing 11pm–3am. **Tube:** Leicester Square.

Admission: Mon–Thurs from £8 ($14.80), Fri £12.50 ($23.15), Sat £15 ($27.75). **Prices:** Drinks £3.25 ($6); beer £2.25 ($4.16).

WAG CLUB, 35 Wardour St., W.1. Tel. 071/437-5534.

This popular dance club is set behind an innocuous-looking brick facade in one of the most congested neighborhoods of London's entertainment districts. Its two levels are decorated with unusual murals, some with themes from ancient Egypt. Clients all seem to love to dance, and hail from throughout Europe and the world. Live bands are sometimes presented on the street level, while the upstairs is reserved for highly danceable recorded music. **Open:** Mon–Wed 10:30pm–3:30am, Thurs 10:30pm–4am, Fri–Sat 10:30pm–6am. **Tube:** Piccadilly Circus or Leicester Square.

Admission: £5–£8 ($9.25–$14.80). **Prices:** Drinks £2 ($3.70).

GAY CLUBS

The most reliable source of information on gay clubs and activities is the **Lesbian and Gay Switchboard** (tel. 071/837-7324), open 24-hours.

HEAVEN, The Arches, Craven St., W.C.2. Tel. 071/839-3852.

Heaven is the biggest gay venue not only in Great Britain but perhaps in all of Europe. It also has a very sophisticated sound-and-laser system. A London landmark, set within the vaulted cellars of Charing Cross Railway Station and painted a universal black inside, Heaven is divided into at least four distinctly different areas, each connected by a labyrinth of catwalks, stairs, and hallways, allowing for different activities within the club at the same time. It features different theme nights. For example, Wednesday is for gay men and women; Saturday is men only; Thursday (at least partially) is straight night. **Open:** Tues–Sat 10:30pm–3:30am. **Tube:** Charing Cross/Embankment.

Admission: £5–£9 ($9.25–$16.65).

LONDON LESBIAN & GAY CENTRE, 67-69 Cowcross St., E.C.1. Tel. 071/608-1471.

This is the best place to meet and talk with like-minded individuals who are tired of the bar and disco scene. It always seems to stage some event of interest to the lesbian and gay community and does such in a relaxed, friendly atmosphere. Activities include cabarets, benefit discos, art exhibitions, comedy revues, and even counseling and legal advice. On Friday night there are mixed-theme discos, and on Saturday night a women-only disco. On the first floor is a women-only bar, The Orchid, with good drinks and bar snacks. Special entertainment evenings are featured here. **Open:** Mon–Thurs 5:30–11pm, Fri–Sat noon–2am, Sun noon–11pm. **Tube:** Farringdon.

    Admission: £3–£5 ($5.55–$9.25) 1-day membership. £3 ($5.55) entrance fee for the discos.

MADAME JO JO'S, 8 Brewer St., W.1. Tel. 071/734-2473.

    Set side by side with some of Soho's most explicit girlie shows, Madame Jo Jo also presents "girls," but they are in drag. This is London's most popular transvestite show, with revues staged nightly at 12:15am and 1:15am and a popular piano bar. **Open:** Mon–Sat 10pm–3am. **Tube:** Piccadilly Circus.

    Admission: £8–£10 ($14.80–$18.50). **Prices:** Drinks £2.75 ($5.10).

ROY'S, 206 Fulham Rd., S.W.10. Tel. 071/352-6828.

    Roy's is the leading gay restaurant of London. People come here not only for the good food but also for the entertaining and relaxing ambience. The set menu of freshly prepared ingredients is £15 ($27.75) at this basement restaurant. **Open:** Mon–Sat 7:30–11:30pm, Sun 1:30–3pm and 8–11:30pm. **Tube:** Earl's Court or South Kensington.

STEPH'S, 39 Dean St., W.1. Tel. 071/734-5976.

    Looking like a stage set for *Pink Flamingos,* Steph's is one of the most charming restaurants of Soho, near the exclusive Groucho Club. Its owner is Stephanie Cooke, a much-traveled former British schoolteacher. A theatrical mixed clientele, among others, is attracted here.

    You conceivably could go here just to have fun, but the food is worthy in its own right. Everything is cooked fresh; you can enjoy such specialties as Snuffy's chicken, beef-and-oyster pie, leek-and-pecan pancakes, or else selections from the charcoal grill, including lime chicken breast. Steph might even suggest her own "diet"—a plate of wild Scottish smoked salmon and a bottle of champagne. The ubiquitous burger also appears on the menu, as do salads and even a vegetarian club sandwich (how fashionable can you get?). Meals cost from £15 ($27.75). **Open:** Mon–Thurs noon–3pm and 5:30–11:30pm, Fri–Sat noon–3pm and 5:30–midnight. **Tube:** Piccadilly Circus.

THE BAR SCENE

PUBS, WINE BARS & BARS

AMERICAN BAR, in the Savoy Hotel, the Strand, W.C.2. Tel. 071/836-4343.

    The American Bar is still one of the most sophisticated places in London. The bartender is known for such special concoctions as Royal Silver and Savoy 90. From Monday to Saturday evenings, a pianist and singer entertain. The après-theater crowd flocks here (it's near many West End theaters) to listen to show tunes. Men should wear a jacket and tie. **Open:** Mon–Sat 11am–11pm, Sun noon–3pm and 7–10:30pm. **Tube:** Aldwych.

    Prices: Drinks from £6 ($11.10).

COCKTAIL BAR, Café Royal, 68 Regent St., W.1. Tel. 071/437-9090.

    In business since 1865, this bar was once patronized by Oscar Wilde, Whistler, and Aubrey Beardsley. Decorated in a 19th-century rococo style, it is one of the more glamorous places in London where one can order a drink. Café Royal cocktails, including Golden Cadillac and Royal Romance, begin at £4.50 ($8.35). Nonalcoholic drinks are also served, and you can order wine by the glass from the superb wine cellars. A traditional English tea, served between 3 and 5pm, costs £8.50 ($15.75). **Open:** Mon–Sat noon–11:30pm, Sun noon–10:30pm. **Tube:** Piccadilly Circus.

    Prices: Drinks from £2.20 ($4.05).

JULES, 85 Jermyn St., S.W.1. Tel. 071/930-4700.
For those who like bars instead of pubs, Jules is the best-known watering hole in St. James's. It was constructed originally as the Waterloo Hotel in 1830. After Jules Ribstein bought it in 1903, he turned it into a ground-floor restaurant, and in time it became a rendezvous for the "bucks and blades," the young dandies of the day. It's known mainly for its cocktails, some 50 in all, ranging from those made with champagne to a Hawaiian dream. "Godfather" is scotch and amaretto; "Godmother," vodka and amaretto. At the restaurant in back you can order smoked salmon, salmon and sole "as you like it," or perhaps one of a variety of steaks, with meals costing from £18 ($33.30). **Open:** Lunch Mon–Sat 11am–3pm; dinner Mon–Sat 5:30–11pm. **Tube:** Piccadilly Circus or Green Park.
Prices: Drinks from £2.90 ($5.35).

LILLIE LANGTRY BAR, in the Cadogan Hotel, Sloane St., S.W.1. Tel. 071/235-7141.
This spot epitomizes some of the charm and elegance of the Edwardian era. Lillie Langtry, actress and society beauty at the turn of the century (notorious as the mistress of Edward VII), used to live here. The bar, next to Langtry's Restaurant, exudes a 1920s aura. Oscar Wilde was arrested on charges of sodomy here, but that unfortunate event is long forgotten, and the playwright is honored on the drink menu with "Hock and Selzer," his favorite drink at the Cadogan, according to Sir John Betjeman's poem, "The Arrest of Oscar Wilde at the Cadogan Hotel." We'd call it a white wine spritzer today. One drink, a Green Carnation, honors the Cecil Graham character in Wilde's *Lady Windermere's Fan*. Still another drink—champagne, cognac, and strawberry liqueur—honors Queen Victoria. Cocktails are served from 11am to 11pm daily. **Tube:** Sloane Square.
Prices: Cocktails from £3.75 ($6.95).

RUMOURS, 33 Wellington St., W.C.2. Tel. 071/836-0038.
Rumours is the kind of place where you expect Tom Cruise to turn up as a bartender. Called the "granddaddy of modern American cocktail-style bars," it is a spacious, pillared bar, enveloped by mirrors. Once this was a flower market in the heyday of Covent Garden, but today it dispenses about 20 pages of cocktail suggestions; at least three dozen of these are considered originals and worthy of carrying a copyright. On Friday and Saturday nights, the place is packed. **Open:** Mon–Sat 5–11pm, Sun 7–10:30pm. **Tube:** Covent Garden.
Admission: Free. **Prices:** Cocktails with generous measures from £3.75 ($6.95).

SMOLLENSKY'S BALLOON, 1 Dover St., W.1. Tel. 071/491-1199.
A basement restaurant, this American eatery and drinking bar is packed during happy hour from 5:30 to 7pm with Mayfair office workers. The place has a 1930s piano-bar atmosphere, with polished wood and a mirrored ceiling. Steaks and french fries are its favorite fare, although you can also order well-prepared vegetarian dishes. Meals cost from £12 ($22.20). A pianist/singer entertains on Monday to Saturday evenings. **Open:** Mon–Sat noon–midnight, Sun noon–10:30pm. **Tube:** Green Park.
Admission: Free. **Prices:** House cocktails (good measures) from £2.65 ($4.90); beer £1.90 ($3.50).

SPECIALTY BARS
Bouzouki

ELYSÉE, 13 Percy St., W.1. Tel. 071/636-4804.
Elysée is for *Never on Sunday* devotees who like the reverberations of bouzouki and the smashing of plates. The domain of the Karegeorgis brothers—Michael, Ulysses, and the incomparable George—it offers hearty fun at moderate tabs. You can dance nightly to the music by Greek musicians. At two different intervals (last on at 1am) a cabaret is provided, highlighted by brother George's altogether amusing art of balancing wine glasses (I'd hate to pay his breakage bill). You can book a table on either the ground floor or the second floor, but the Roof Garden is a magnet in

summer. The food is good, too, including the house specialty, the classic moussaka, and the kebabs from the charcoal grill. **Open:** Mon–Sat 7pm–2:45am. **Tube:** Goodge Street or Tottenham Court Road.
   Admission: £3 ($5.55). **Prices:** Complete meal with wine £27.50 ($50.90).

Gay Bars

BRIEF ENCOUNTER, St. Martin's Lane, W.C.2. Tel. 071/240-2221.
   This aptly named place that stands across from the Duke of York's Theatre is in the very heart of West End theaterland. In fact, it's the most frequented West End gay pub. Bars are on two levels, but even so it's hard to find room to stand up, much less drink. The crowd's costumes vary; some men are in jeans and leather, others in business suits. **Open:** Mon–Sat 11am–11pm, Sun 7–10:30pm. **Tube:** Leicester Square or Charing Cross.
   Prices: Lager from £1.60 ($2.95).

COLEHERNE, 261 Old Brompton Rd., S.W.5. Tel. 071/373-8356.
   This leather-and-denim bar must have been featured in every guide to the gay scene in Europe ever written. As a consequence, it's often jammed. Lunch and afternoon tea are served upstairs. **Open:** Mon–Sat 11am–11pm, Sun noon–3pm and 7–10:30pm. **Tube:** Earl's Court.
   Prices: Lager from £1.60 ($2.95).

CABARET RIVER CRUISE

ROMANCE OF LONDON, Westminster Pier, Victoria Embankment, S.W.1. Tel. 071/620-0474.
   A 3½-hour long cabaret river cruise complete with commentary, Romance of London takes you all the way through the heart of London to the Thames Barrier. Shortly after boarding, you are served a superior four-course continental meal with wine, accompanied by entertainment at your table. Live cabaret and dancing are also featured. **Departures:** May–Sept Sun 7pm. **Tube:** Westminster.
   Admission: £31 ($57.35).

CASINOS

London was a gambling metropolis long before anyone had ever heard of Monte Carlo or Las Vegas.
   Queen Victoria's reign changed all that. For more than a century, games of chance were so rigorously outlawed that no bartender dared to keep a dice cup on the counter.
   However, according to the 1960 "Betting and Gaming Act," gambling was again permitted in "bona fide clubs" by members and their guests.
   There are at least 25 of them in the West End alone, with many more scattered throughout the suburbs. I cannot make specific recommendations. Under a new law, casinos aren't allowed to advertise, which in this context would mean appearing in a guidebook. It isn't illegal to gamble, only to advertise that you do. Most hall porters can tell you where you can gamble in London.
   You will be required to become a member of your chosen club, and in addition you must wait 24 hours before you can play at the tables . . . then strictly for cash. Most common games are roulette, blackjack, punto banco, and baccarat.

MOVIES

CANNON CINEMA, Panton St., off Leicester Sq., S.W.1. Tel. 071/930-0631.
   This streamlined, black-and-white block houses four superb theaters under one roof. They share one sleekly plush lobby, but each runs a separate program, always including at least one European film, along with the latest releases, often from the United States. **Tube:** Leicester Square.
   Tickets: £4–£7 ($7.40–$12.95).

ODEON LEICESTER SQUARE, Leicester Sq., S.W.1. Tel. 071/936-6111.
Odeon is another major London cinema with one screen, playing the latest international releases. **Tube:** Leicester Square.
Tickets: £4–£7 ($7.40–$12.95).

NATIONAL FILM THEATRE, South Bank, Waterloo, S.E.1. Tel. 071/928-3232.
This cinema is in the South Bank complex. More than 2,000 films a year from all over the world are shown here, including features, shorts, animation, and documentaries. **Tube:** Waterloo.
Admission: 40p (75¢) daily membership, £3.95 ($7.30) screenings with membership.

MOMI, the Museum of the Moving Image, underneath Waterloo Bridge, S.E.1. Tel. 071/401-2636.
MOMI is also part of the South Bank complex. Tracing the history of the development of cinema and television, it takes the visitor on an incredible journey from cinema's earliest experiments to modern animation, from Charlie Chaplin to the operation of a TV studio. There are artifacts to handle, buttons to push, and a cast of actors to tell visitors more. Allow 2 hours for a visit. **Open:** Daily 10am–6pm. **Tube:** Waterloo.
Admission: £4.95 ($9.15) adults, £3.50 ($6.45) children, £12 ($22.20) family ticket.

STRIP SHOWS

Soho has many strip shows, sometimes two in one building. Along Frith Street, Greek Street, Old Compton Street, Brewer Street, Windmill Street, Dean and Wardour streets, and the little courts and alleys in between, the disrobing establishments jostle cheek by jowl.

RAYMOND REVUEBAR, Walker's Court, Brewer St., W.1. Tel. 071/734-1593.
The Revuebar dates from 1958. Proprietor Paul Raymond is considered the doyen of strip society and his young, beautiful, hand-picked strippers are among the best in Europe. This strip theater occupies the much-restored premises of a Victorian dance hall, with a decor of flaming red velvet. There are two bars, which allow clients to take their drinks to their seats. Whisky costs £2.50 ($4.65) for a large measure. The club presents two shows nightly: at 8 and 10pm. **Open:** Mon–Sat 8pm and 10pm. **Tube:** Piccadilly Circus.
Admission: £15 ($27.75).

STORK CLUB, 99 Regent St., W.1. Tel. 071/734-3686.
This first-class nightclub incorporates good food, a Las Vegas-style cabaret with a lineup of attractive dancers who don't believe in overdressing, and an ambience noted for its good taste and theatrical flair. Located near the corner of Swallow Street in the upscale heart of Mayfair, it welcomes diners and drinkers to a recently renovated royal blue and peach–colored decor of art deco inspiration. Two shows are staged nightly, one at 11:30pm, another at 1am. Foreign visitors don't have to go through the tedium of obtaining membership. Clients who don't want dinner can sit at the bar and pay a £15 ($27.75) cover charge to see the show. **Open:** Mon–Sat 8:30pm–3:30am. **Tube:** Piccadilly Circus.
Admission: Three-course dinner £35 ($64.75). **Prices:** Drinks from £3 ($5.55).

CHAPTER 8

WINDSOR & OXFORD

1. **WINDSOR**
- **WHAT'S SPECIAL ABOUT WINDSOR & OXFORD**

2. **ASCOT**

3. **HENLEY-ON-THAMES**

4. **OXFORD**

5. **WOODSTOCK (BLENHEIM PALACE)**

The historical Thames Valley and Chiltern Hills lie so close to London that they can be easily reached by car, train, or Green Line bus. In fact, you can explore here during the day and return to London in time to see a West End show.

The most-visited historic site in England is Windsor Castle, 21 miles west of London, one of the most famous castles in Europe.

Certainly your principal reason for visiting Oxfordshire is to explore the university city of Oxford, about an hour's ride from London by car or train. But Oxford is not the only attraction in the county; the shire is a land of great mansions, old churches of widely varying architectural styles, and rolling farmland.

In a sense, Oxfordshire is a kind of buffer zone between the easy living in the southern towns and the industrialized cities of the heartland. Southeast are the chalky Chilterns, and in the west you'll be moving toward the wool towns of the Cotswolds. The Upper Thames winds its way across the southern parts of the country.

SEEING WINDSOR & OXFORD

A SUGGESTED ITINERARY

Day 1: Explore Windsor and its Castle and visit Eton College across the bridge.
Day 2: Either still based in London or else from a hotel in Oxford, explore the major colleges of this university city.

---

1. WINDSOR

21 miles W of London

GETTING THERE   By Train   From either Waterloo or Paddington Station a train takes 50 minutes.

By Bus   Green Line coaches no. 704 and 705 from Hyde Park Corner in London take about 1½ hours.

By Car   Take the M4 west from London.

WHAT'S SPECIAL ABOUT WINDSOR & OXFORD

Great Towns/Villages

☐ Oxford, one of the world's greatest universities—a seat of learning since the 12th century.

☐ Windsor, site of the castle founded by William the Conqueror (ca. 1070), the world's largest inhabited castle.

☐ Henley-on-Thames, a small town and resort at the foothills of the Chilterns, famed for its High Street and Royal Regatta.

Castles

☐ Windsor Castle, steeped in royal associations, is where the royal family spends Christmas.

☐ Blenheim Palace, majestic palace of the Duke of Marlborough at Woodstock, with decorative work by Grinling Gibbons.

Architectural Highlights

☐ St. George's Chapel, Windsor Castle—a notable example of Perpendicular architecture and rich vaulting, with several royal tombs.

☐ New College, Oxford, founded in 1379 by William of Wykcham. Its initial quadrangle formed the architectural design for the other colleges.

ESSENTIALS   The **area code** is 0753. A **Tourist Information Centre** is in the Central Station, Thames Street (tel. 0753/852010), in the railway station at the top of the hill, opposite the castle. There is also an information point in the tourist center at Windsor Coach Park.

Windsor, the site of England's greatest castle and its most famous boys' school, was called "Windlesore" by the ancient Britons who derived the name from winding shore—so noticeable as you walk along the Thames here.

WHAT TO SEE & DO

The bus will drop you near the Town Guildhall, to which Wren applied the finishing touches. It's only a short walk up Castle Hill to the top sights.

THE CASTLE SIGHTS

WINDSOR CASTLE, Castle Hill. Tel. 0753/868286 (ext. 252).

⭐ When William the Conqueror ordered a castle built on this spot, he began a legend and a link with English sovereignty that has known many vicissitudes: King John cooled his heels at Windsor while waiting to put his signature on the Magna Carta at nearby Runnymede; Charles I was imprisoned here before losing his head; Queen Bess did some renovations; Victoria mourned her beloved Albert, who died at the castle in 1861; the royal family rode out much of World War II behind its sheltering walls; and when Queen Elizabeth II is in residence, the royal standard flies.

The apartments contain many works of art, porcelain, armor, furniture, three Verrio ceilings, and several 17th-century Gibbons carvings. Several Rubens adorn the King's Drawing Room and in his relatively small dressing room is a Dürer, along with Rembrandt's portrait of his mother, and Van Dyck's triple portrait of Charles I. Of the apartments, the grand reception room, with its Gobelin tapestries, is the most spectacular.

The Windsor changing of the guard is a much more exciting experience, in my opinion, than the London exercises. In Windsor when the court is in residence, the guard marches through the town, stopping the traffic as it wheels into the castle to the tune of a full regimental band; when the queen is not there, a drum and pipe band is mustered. From May to August, the ceremony takes place Monday to Saturday at 11am. In winter, the guard is changed every 48 hours on Monday to Saturday, so call ahead to find out which days the ceremony will take place—you should also check what is open before visiting.

Admission: £2.80 ($5.20) adults, £1.20 ($2.20) children.

Open: Jan–Feb, early Mar, Nov, and early Dec Mon–Sat 10:30am–3pm; July–late Oct Mon–Sat 10:30am–5pm, Sun 1:30–5pm. Ticket sales cease about 30 minutes before closing; last admissions are 15 minutes before closing. **Closed:** About 6 weeks at Easter, June, 3 weeks in Dec.

QUEEN MARY'S DOLLHOUSE, Windsor Castle. Tel. 0753/868286.

Just about the greatest dollhouse in the world, this was presented to the late Queen Mary as a gift and was later used to raise money for charity. The dollhouse is a remarkable achievement and re-creation of what a great royal mansion of the 1920s looked like—complete with a fleet of cars, including a Rolls-Royce. All is done with the most exacting detail—even the champagne bottles in the wine cellar contain vintage wine of that era. In addition, you'll see a collection of dolls presented to the monarchy from nearly every nation of the Commonwealth. The dollhouse is open even when the state apartments are closed.

Admission: £1.20 ($2.20) adults, 50p (95¢) children.

Open: Same as Windsor Castle (see above).

ST. GEORGE'S CHAPEL, Windsor Castle. Tel. 0753/865538.

⭐ A gem of the Perpendicular style, this chapel shares the distinction with Westminster Abbey of being a pantheon of English monarchs (Victoria is a notable exception). The present St. George's was founded in the late 15th century by Edward IV on the site of the original Chapel of the Order of the Garter (Edward III, 1348). First enter the nave, which has fan vaulting (a remarkable achievement in English architecture) and contains the tomb of George V and Queen Mary, designed by Sir William Reid Dick. Off the nave is the Urswick Chapel, the Princess Charlotte memorial provides an ironic touch; if she had survived childbirth in 1817, she—and not her cousin, Victoria—would have ruled the British Empire. In the aisle are the tombs of George VI and Edward IV. The Edward IV "Quire," with its imaginatively carved 15th-century choir stalls (crowned by lacy canopies and Knights of the Garter banners), evokes the pomp and pageantry of medieval days. In the center is a flat tomb, containing the vault of the beheaded Charles I, along with Henry VIII and his third wife, Jane Seymour. Finally, inspect the Prince Albert Memorial Chapel, reflecting the opulent tastes of the Victorian era.

Admission: £2 ($3.70) adults, £1 ($1.85) children.

Open: Mon–Sat 10:45am–3:45 or 4pm, Sun 2–3:45 or 4pm. **Closed:** During services, Jan, and a few days in mid-June. Call first to check hours.

THE ROYAL MEWS, St. Albans St. Tel. 0753/868286.

The red-brick buildings of the Royal Mews and Burford House were built for Nell Gwynne in the 1670s and were named for King Charles II's natural son by her, the Earl of Burford. When the child was 14 years old, he was created Duke of St. Albans, from which the street outside takes its name.

Housed in the mews is the exhibition of the Queen's Presents and Royal Carriages. Displayed are pictures of several members of the royal family, including those of Queen Elizabeth II as Colonel-in-Chief of the Coldstream Guards riding in the grounds of Buckingham Palace, the Duke of Edinburgh driving his horses through a water obstacle at Windsor, and the Queen Mother with Prince Edward, Viscount Linley, and Lady Sarah Armstrong-Jones in the Scottish State Coach. There is also a full-size stable with model horses showing stable kit, harnesses, and riding equipment. A magnificent display of coaches and carriages kept in mint condition and in frequent use is in the coach house. The exhibition of the Queen's Presents includes unique items of interest given to Her Majesty and the Duke of Edinburgh throughout her reign. There is also a collection of pencil drawings of the queen and family with horses and dogs. The mews is just outside the entrance to the castle.

Admission: £1.20 ($2.20) adults, 50p (95¢) children.

Open: Nov–Mar Mon–Sat 10:30am–3pm; Apr–Oct Mon–Sat 10:30am–5pm (also May–Oct Sun 10:30am–3pm).

THE OTHER SIGHTS

The **town** of Windsor is largely Victorian, with lots of brick buildings and a few remnants of Georgian architecture. In and around the castle are two cobblestone streets, Church and Market, which have antique shops, silversmiths, and pubs. One shop on Church Street was supposedly occupied by Nell Gwynne, who needed to be within call of Charles II's chambers. After lunch or tea, stroll along the 3-mile, aptly named Long Walk.

On Sundays, there are often polo matches in **Windsor Great Park**—and at Ham Common—and you may see Prince Charles playing and Prince Philip serving as umpire. The queen often watches. For more information, telephone 0753/860633.

The famous company founded by Madame Tussaud in 1802 has taken over part of the Windsor and Eton Central Railway Station on Thames Street (tel. 0753/857837) to present an exhibition of **"Queen Victoria's Diamond Jubilee 1837– 1897."** At one of the station platforms is a replica of *The Queen,* the engine used to draw the royal coaches, disembarking the life-size wax figures of guests arriving at Windsor for the Jubilee celebration. Seated in the Royal Waiting Room are Queen Victoria and her family. In one of the carriages, the Day Saloon, are Grand Duke Serge and the Grand Duchess Elizabeth (the queen's granddaughter) of Russia. Waiting in the anteroom is the queen's faithful Indian servant, Hafiz Abdul Karim, the Munshi. Among the famous guests portrayed are the Prince and Princess of Wales (Edward VII and Alexandra), the Empress Frederick of Prussia (Queen Victoria's eldest daughter), and the prime minister, Lord Salisbury. The platform is busy with royal servants, a flower seller, a newsboy, an Italian with a barrel organ, and others who have come to see the arrival of the train. Drawn up on the ceremonial parade ground are the troops of the Coldstream Guards and the horse-drawn carriage that would take the party to the castle. With the sound of military bands in the background and the voices of officers commanding their troops, you really feel you are present for Her Majesty's arrival.

At the end of the walkway through the Victorian conservatory, you reach the 260-seat theater where a short audiovisual presentation with life-size animated models gives further glimpses of life during Victoria's reign. The entire visit takes about 45 minutes. The exhibition is open daily from 9:30am to 5:30pm (closed Christmas Day). Admission is £3.95 ($7.30) for adults, £2.95 ($5.45) for children.

TOURS

Guide Friday runs the best bus tours in Windsor, carefully tailored on a "come and go as you please" basis which is enormously appealing. Tours depart 7 days a week between 10:45am and 4:40pm from the Guide Friday office, which is set directly on the platform of Windsor's Central Railway Station, Station Approach (off High Street), midway between Eton and Windsor. For reservations and information, call 0753/855755. Note that the Central Railway Station is *not* to be confused with the Riverside Railway Station, which is smaller.

Tours cover a distance of 9 miles, and incorporate the best sights of Windsor, Eton, and Datchet (Datchet is a charming English village 4 miles east of Windsor). Tours are conducted in open-top buses and take about an hour. However, tours are designed to allow visitors to ascend, descend, whatever, at their whim, along any stage of the way, so some participants transform the tour into a ½-day outing.

Tours cost £4.50 ($8.35) for adults, £3.50 ($6.50) for senior citizens, £1 ($1.85) for children under 12; free for children under 5. No credit cards are accepted.

A 90-minute guided walking tour of Windsor and its castle leaves from the Tourist

Information Centre (tel. 0753/852010) in the Central Station. Tours usually include a look at the Long Walk, then the Guildhall, and Market Cross House, along with the Changing of the Guard, whenever possible. Within the castle precincts, you'll visit the cloisters and the Albert Memorial Chapel. No professional guides are allowed to give a commentary within the Castle's State Apartments, where tour participants walk through at their own pace. Subject to demand, tours leave daily at 2pm between April and September. The cost is £4 for adults ($7.40), and £3.50 ($6.50) for children.

Boat tours depart from an embarkation point on the Promenade, at Barry Avenue, for the 35-minute trip to Boveney Lock. You pass the Windsor Horse Racecourse and cruise past Eton College's boathouses and the Brocas Meadows. On the return, you'll have a perfect view of Windsor Castle. The cost is £1.60 ($2.95) for adults, 80p ($1.50) for children. However, you can also take a 2-hour trip through Boveney Lock and up past stately private riverside homes, the Bray Film Studios, Queens Eyot, and Monkey Island at a cost of £3.80 ($7.05) for adults, £1.90 ($3.50) for children. The boats carry light refreshments and have a licensed bar. There are toilets on board, and the decks are covered in case of an unexpected shower; however, your view of the river will be unimpaired. Tours are operated by **French Brothers Ltd.,** Clewer Boathouse, Mill Lane, Windsor, Berkshire SL4 5JH (tel. 0753/862933).

WHERE TO STAY

At the **Tourist Information Centre,** Central Station, Thames Street (tel. 0753/852010), you can book a bed ahead of time. This is a useful service, as many of the local guesthouses have no signs.

DOUBLES FOR LESS THAN £48 ($88.80)

ALMA HOUSE, 56 Alma Rd., Windsor, Berkshire SL4 3HA. Tel. 0753/862983. 4 rms (2 with shower). TV TEL
$ **Rates** (including English breakfast): £15 ($27.75) single without bath; £17 ($31.45) single with bath; £30 ($55.50) double without bath; £33 ($61.05) double with bath. No credit cards. **Parking:** Free.
This hotel (not to be confused with Alma Lodge on the same street) is a well-built Victorian structure. Many guests stay here and commute to Heathrow the following morning (depending on traffic, it's about a 20-minute ride). The hostess, Sally Shipp, is a wealth of information for travelers, and she sets aside one room for families. The hotel is a 5-minute walk south of the castle.

FAIRLIGHT LODGE, 41 Frances Rd., Windsor, Berkshire SL4 3AQ. Tel. 0753/861207. 10 rms (all with bath or shower). TV
$ **Rates** (including English breakfast): £30–£34 ($55.50–$62.90) single; £48–£52 ($88.80–$96.20) double; £65 ($120.25) family room for two adults and two children. AE, MC, V.
Built in 1885 as the home of the mayor of Windsor, this is a highly rated B&B. In a residential section only a few minutes' walk south from the heart of Windsor and the castle, it offers comfortable bedrooms with coffee-making facilities. One room has a large four-poster bed. There's a fully licensed Garden Restaurant, which serves meals from 7 to 9:30pm, costing from £8.50 ($15.75) for a three-courser. Parking is available.

TRINITY GUEST HOUSE, 18 Trinity Place, Windsor, Berkshire SL4 3AT. Tel. 0753/864186. 9 rms (4 with bath). TV
$ **Rates** (including English breakfast): £18 ($33.30) single without bath; £19 ($35.15) single with bath; £36 ($66.60) double without bath; £44 ($81.40) double with bath. MC, V.
 A 5-minute walk from the train station, this hotel offers one of the best values in town. All rooms have clock radios, hairdryers, and hot-beverage facilities. Some have private baths or showers. Breakfast is the only meal served. The guesthouse has ironing facilities.

WORTH THE EXTRA BUCKS

AURORA GARDEN, 14 Bolton Ave., Windsor, Berkshire SL4 3JF. Tel. 0753/868686. Fax 0753/831394. 14 rms (all with bath or shower). TV TEL
$ Rates (including English breakfast): £60.50–£65.50 ($111.95–$121.20) single; £72–£77 ($133.20–$142.45) double. AE, DC, MC, V.

This spacious Victorian house has been successfully converted and modernized. It charges more than your typical B&B in Windsor, but makes up for it in quality. The hotel's most notable feature is its water garden, and umbrella-shaded tables are placed outside in summer. Each well-furnished unit has an alarm clock radio. The location is in the vicinity of Long Walk and Windsor Great Park off Osborne Road (A332).

WHERE TO EAT

MEALS FOR LESS THAN £10 ($18.50)

ANGELO'S WINE BAR, 5 St. Leonards Rd. Tel. 857600.
    Cuisine: CONTINENTAL/ENGLISH. **Reservations:** Required. **Bus:** No. 407 or 412.
$ Prices: Appetizers £1.85–£4.85 ($3.40–$8.95); main courses £4.50–£12.95 ($8.35–$23.75); set menus £6.75 ($12.50) and £13.75 ($25.45). AE, DC, MC, V.
    Open: Lunch Mon–Sat noon–2:30pm; dinner Mon–Sat 5:30–11pm. **Closed:** Aug.

    Angelo's is the unbeatable choice for good Italian wine and the savory cuisine of the Mediterranean. Try the minestrone, then follow with an Italian or continental dish. It's a good value. English food is also served.

COUNTRY KITCHEN, 3 King Edward Court, Peascod St. Tel. 868681.
    Cuisine: CONTINENTAL. **Reservations:** Required for Sun carvery.
$ Prices: Appetizers £1.60–£2.50 ($2.95–$4.30); main courses £3.50–£3.85 ($6.50–$7.10); two-course Sun lunch £7 ($12.95). MC, V.
    Open: Mon–Sat 8am–5pm, Sun 11am–3pm.

Walk from the castle gateway down Peascod Street to King Edward Court for a good, home-cooked meal in this light, airy, self-service restaurant. They make their own soups, pâtés, quiches, scones, tea bread, flans, cheesecake, and desserts, and only good vegetable oils, honey, lemon juice, herbs, and spices are used in the preparation of the main dishes. There's always a vegetarian dish, some low-fat, low-calorie choices, and 14 different salads. Hot dishes include chicken curry, lasagne, and chili con carne, and you can choose from the display of scrumptious desserts, including passion cake. They offer five different teas and herbs—decaffeinated if you wish—and fine house wines by the carafe or glass. On Sunday, a special two-course carvery lunch is offered, with a selection from two or three roasts and five vegetables, or you can take the meat course and a selection of desserts. Everything is cooked on the premises.

THE COURT JESTER, Church Lane. Tel. 864257.
    Cuisine: ENGLISH. **Reservations:** None.
$ Prices: Bar snacks £2.75–£4 ($5.10–$7.40); pint of lager from £1.55 ($2.85). No credit cards.
    Open: Pub hours Mon–Fri 11am–11pm; Sun noon–3pm and 7–10:30pm; food service Nov–Mar 11:30am–3pm; Apr–Oct 11:30am–5pm.

This is one of the town's most popular pubs, especially with young people in the evening when loud music plays. No evening meals are offered, but the traditional pub snacks during the day include hot dishes during the winter and an extensive buffet in the summer. A wide range of English ales is served. It's located directly south from the fortification of Windsor Castle.

DOME, 5 Thames St. Tel. 864405.
    Cuisine: FRENCH. **Reservations:** Not needed.
$ Prices: Appetizers 95p–£3.95 ($1.75–$7.30); main courses £4.95–£7.50 ($9.15–$13.90). AE, MC, V.

Open: Mon–Sat 8am–10:30pm, Sun 9am–10:30pm.

Also across from the castle, this is one of the most popular cafés in town. Sometimes live music is featured, and its happy hour is perhaps the most engaging time of the day. The menu includes omelets, salmon mousse, salade niçoise, cassoulet, and fried squid. Look for the daily specials on a blackboard menu.

DRURY HOUSE RESTAURANT, 4 Church St. Tel. 863734.
    Cuisine: ENGLISH. **Reservations:** Required. **Bus:** No. 704.
$ Prices: Appetizers £1.35–£3 ($2.50–$5.55); main courses £4–£6 ($7.40–$11.10); set menu £6.50 ($12.05). No credit cards.
    Open: Tues–Sun 10am–5:30pm.

Owner Joan Hearne states with pride that all luncheons served in this wood-paneled, 17th-century restaurant, dating from the days of Charles II, are home-cooked "and very English." A visit here could be included in a tour of Windsor Castle, which is only a stone's throw away. A typical meal might include soup, meat, vegetables, and dessert. A refreshing tea is also served, with either homemade scones with jam and freshly whipped cream, or freshly made cream cakes.

HIDEAWAY BISTRO GRILL, 12 Thames St. Tel. 842186.
    Cuisine: ENGLISH. **Reservations:** Not needed.
$ Prices: Appetizers £2.25–£4.75 ($4.15–$8.80); main courses £5–£8 ($9.25–$14.80); two-course lunch £5 ($9.25); three-course set dinner £9.75 ($18.05). AE, DC, MC, V.
    Open: Lunch and afternoon tea Mon–Fri noon–6pm; Sat–Sun 11am–6pm; dinner daily 7–11pm.

 This bistro is operated by the prestigious Sir Christopher Wren's House Hotel and is very different from the hotel's more formal restaurant, The Orangerie, which lies within the hotel itself. The Hideaway, a short walk from the hotel and opposite the castle, offers morning coffee, pastries, cakes, a wine and salad bar, cream teas, and informal candlelit dinners. It also offers pre- and posttheater suppers. Try one of their fresh sandwiches (I'd suggest the Covent Garden). For dinner, begin with a pâté of duckling and follow with a grill, perhaps stir-fry vegetables.

WILLIAM IV HOTEL, Thames St., 100 yards from Eton Bridge. Tel. 851004.
    Cuisine: ENGLISH. **Reservations:** None.
$ Prices: Bar snacks £2–£5 ($3.70–$9.25). No credit cards.
    Open: Mon–Sat 11am–11pm, Sun noon–3pm and 7–10:30pm; food service Mon–Sat noon–7pm, Sun noon–3pm.

This is a lovely old place (ca. 1500) with its armor, beams, and log fire. Just outside is the chapter garden, where the Windsor martyrs were burned at the stake in 1544 for their religious beliefs; it was from this pub that they received their last cups of strong ale "in gratification of their last wish."

The house, built by Sir Christopher Wren for his own use, is opposite the William IV, and the great architect of St. Paul's was reputedly a regular visitor to the old taproom, as were diarists Evelyn and Pepys. Rub shoulders here with newspaper people and actors (nearby is the Theatre Royal), artists and river folk, and drink traditional ale. Food is home-cooked, and the portions are guaranteed to satisfy gargantuan appetites. You can sit at a sidewalk table in a pedestrian area by the Eton Bridge, gazing up at the castle while enjoying your lunch. At night, this is one of the busiest drinking spots in town. The William IV lies at the bottom of Windsor Hill on the approach road to the bridge, which is open to pedestrians only. (In spite of its name, this place doesn't rent rooms.)

EASY EXCURSIONS
ETON

To visit Eton, home of what is arguably the most famous public school in the world (Americans would call it a private school), you can take a train from Paddington

Station, drive, or take the Green Line bus to Windsor. If you drive, take the M4 motorway, leaving it at Exit 5 to Eton. However, parking is likely to be a problem, so I advise turning off the M4 at Exit 6 to Windsor; you can park there and take an easy stroll past Windsor Castle and across the Thames bridge. Follow Eton High Street to the college. (From Windsor Castle's ramparts, you can look down on the river and on the famous playing fields of Eton.)

Largest and best known of the public (private) schools of England, **Eton College,** Eton, Berkshire (tel. 0753/863593), was founded by a teenage boy himself, Henry VI, in 1440. Some of England's greatest men, notably the Duke of Wellington, have played on these fields. Twenty prime ministers were educated here, as well as such literary figures as George Orwell and Aldous Huxley. Even the late Ian Fleming, creator of James Bond, attended. If it's open, take a look at the Perpendicular chapel, with its 15th-century paintings and reconstructed fan vaulting.

The history of Eton College since its inception in 1440 is depicted in the **Museum of Eton Life,** Eton College (tel. 0753/863593), located in vaulted wine cellars, under College Hall, which were originally the storehouse for use of the college's masters. The displays, ranging from formal to extremely informal, include a turn-of-the-century boy's room, schoolbooks, sports trophies, canes used by senior boys to apply punishment they felt needful to their juniors, and birch sticks used by masters for the same purpose. Also to be seen are letters written home by students describing day-to-day life at the school, as well as samples of the numerous magazines produced by students over the centuries, known as ephemera because of the changing writers and ideas. Many of the items to be seen were provided by Old Etonians.

Admission to the school and museum, including guided tours, costs £2.80 ($5.20) for adults, £2.20 ($4.05) for children. The college is open from Easter to September daily from 2 to 4:30pm (during the summer holidays, from 10:30am to 5pm); guided tours are given at 2:15 and 3:15pm. Call the above number for the museum's hours—they're based on the school year and vary widely.

Where to Eat

ETON WINE BAR, 82-83 High St. Tel. 854921.
   Cuisine: FRENCH/ENGLISH/CONTINENTAL. **Reservations:** Recommended.
$ **Prices:** Appetizers £1.85–£3.15 ($3.40–$4.65); main courses £4.75–£6.50 ($8.80–$12.05). MC, V.
   Open: Lunch Mon–Fri noon–3pm, Sat–Sun noon–2pm; dinner Mon–Thurs 6–10:30pm, Fri 6–11pm, Sat–Sun 7–10pm.

Just across the bridge from Windsor, this charming place set among the antiques shops has pinewood tables and old church pews and chairs, and there is a small garden out back. Begin with one of the well-prepared soups, or mussels marinated in a Roquefort dressing. Main dishes include stuffed eggplant with a Provençal tomato sauce and rice, and there are always two daily specials. For dessert, try pineapple and almond flan or damson crunch. Wine can be ordered by the glass.

HOUSE ON THE BRIDGE, 71 High St. Tel. 860914.
   Cuisine: ENGLISH/INTERNATIONAL. **Reservations:** Recommended.
$ **Prices:** Appetizers £3–£22.95 ($5.55–$42.45); main courses £9.95–£16.95 ($18.40–$31.55). AE, DC, MC, V.
   Open: Lunch daily noon–2:30pm; dinner daily 6–11pm.

This restaurant is charmingly contained within a red-brick and terra-cotta Victorian house, set adjacent to the bridge, beside the river, at the edge of Eton. Near the handful of outdoor tables is an almost vertical garden whose plants cascade into the Thames. Some of the well-prepared main dishes are steak Diane, roast Aylesbury duckling, grilled Dover sole, and crêpes Suzette. Many of the most interesting dishes are prepared for two diners, so bring a friend.

SAVILL GARDEN

Savill Garden, Wick Lane, Englefield Green (tel. 0753/860222), is in Windsor Great Park and is signposted from Windsor, Egham, and Ascot. Started in 1932, the

35-acre garden is considered one of the finest of its type in the northern hemisphere. The display starts in spring with rhododendrons, camellias, and daffodils beneath the trees; then throughout the summer, there are spectacular displays of flowers and shrubs presented in a natural and wild state. It is open all year (except at Christmas) from 10am to 6 or 7pm; admission is £2.20 ($4.05) for adults, free for children under 14. It's located 5 miles from Windsor along the A30; turn off at Wick Road and follow the signs to the gardens. There is a licensed, self-service restaurant on the premises.

Adjoining the Savill Garden are the **Valley Gardens,** full of shrubs and trees in a series of wooded natural valleys running down to Virginia water. It's open daily, free, throughout the year.

WINDSOR SAFARI PARK

Britain's leading safari park offers an "African Adventure" for the whole family. You can come face to face with some of nature's most dangerous animals and marvel at the range of shows, including the Seaworld Show, which features dolphins and sea lions. Rides include the *African Queen* Riverboat Ride that journeys down the "Congo River" past tribal villages. Other facilities include free safari transport, restaurants, licensed bars, and refreshment kiosks. The park is on the B3022, just 3 miles from Windsor. Take Exit 6 on M4, Exit 3 on M3 and, Exit 13 on M25. By rail, go first to Windsor Station and catch Beeline or Green Line bus to the park. The all-inclusive admission price for entrance and all shows and attractions is £8.95 ($16.55) adults and £6.95 ($12.85) for children. For more information, call 0753/830886.

---

2. ASCOT

28 miles W of London

GETTING THERE   By Train   Rail service travels between Waterloo in London and Ascot Station, which is about 10 minutes from the racecourse. Service is about every 30 minutes during the day (and takes 30 minutes).

By Bus   Buses depart frequently throughout the day from Victoria Coach Station in London.

By Car   From Windsor, take the A332 for a 13-minute drive.

ESSENTIALS   The **area code** is 0344. The nearest tourist information office is at Windsor (see above).

While following the royal buckhounds through Windsor Forest, Queen Anne decided to have a racecourse on Ascot Heath. The first race meeting at Ascot, which is directly south of Windsor at the southern end of Windsor Great Park, was inaugurated in 1711. Since then, the Ascot Racecourse has been a symbol of high society as pictures of the royal family, including the queen and Prince Philip, have been flashed around the world. Nowadays instead of Queen Anne, you are likely to see Princess Anne, an avid horsewoman.

 **Ascot Racecourse,** High Street, Ascot, Berkshire SL5 7JN (tel. 0344/ 22211), the largest racecourse in the United Kingdom, is open from September to July. There are three enclosures: Tattersalls is the largest, Silver Ring the least expensive, and the third is the Members Enclosure. There are bars and restaurants to suit everybody's taste. Tickets cost £3 ($5.55) to £20 ($37) for adults, and children under 16 are admitted free if accompanied by an adult. The highlight of the Ascot social season—complete with fancy hats and white gloves—is Royal Week in late June, but there is excellent racing on the fourth Saturday in July and the last Saturday in September, with more than a million pounds in prize money.

Advance booking for the grandstand and paddock opens on January 1 every year. Write for tickets to the Secretary, Grandstand, Ascot Racecourse, Ascot, Berkshire,

SL5 7JN. For admission to the Royal Enclosure, write to Her Majesty's Representative, Ascot Office, St. James's Palace, London S.W.1 (tel. 071/930-9882). First-timers have a difficult time being admitted to the Royal Enclosure, as their application must be endorsed by someone who has been admitted to the Royal Enclosure at least eight times before.

WHERE TO STAY

HIGHCLERE HOUSE HOTEL, 19 Kings Rd., Sunninghill, Ascot, Berkshire SL5 9AD. Tel. 0344/25220. Fax 0344/872528. 11 rms (all with bath). TV TEL **$ Rates** (including English breakfast): Fri–Sun £48 ($88.80) single; £55 ($101.75) double; Mon–Thurs £55 ($101.75) single; £70 ($129.50) double. MC, V. **Parking:** Free.

This is a good, moderately priced hotel. Once an Edwardian private residence, the building has been refurbished and now has a cozy bar and licensed restaurant. All bedrooms have hot-beverage facilities. The hotel is only a 12-minute drive from Windsor Castle, a 2-minute drive south of Ascot.

EASY EXCURSIONS FROM ASCOT
MAPLEDURHAM HOUSE ON THE THAMES

The Elizabethan mansion home of the Blount family (tel. 0734/723350) lies beside the Thames in the unspoiled village of Mapledurham and can be reached by car from the A4074 Oxford-Reading road. A much more romantic view of the lovely old house can be reached by taking the boat that leaves the promenade next to Caversham Bridge at 2pm on Saturday, Sunday from Easter through September. The journey upstream takes about 40 minutes, and the boat leaves Mapledurham again at 5pm for the journey back to Caversham. This gives you plenty of time to walk through the house and see the Elizabethan ceilings and the great oak staircase, as well as the portraits of the two beautiful sisters with whom the poet Alexander Pope, a frequent visitor here, fell in love. The family chapel, built in 1789, is a fine example of modern Gothic. Cream teas with homemade cakes are available at the house. On the grounds, the last working watermill on the Thames still produces flour.

The house is open Easter to September on Saturday, Sunday, and public holidays from 2:30 to 5pm; entrance costs £3 ($5.55) for adults, £1.50 ($2.80) for children. The mill is open in summer on Saturday, Sunday, and public holidays from 1:30 to 5pm, and in winter on Sunday from 2 to 4pm; admission costs £2.50 ($4.65) adults, £1.25 ($2.30) for children.

The boat ride from Caversham costs £3 ($5.55) for adults, £2 ($3.70) for children for the round-trip. Further details about the boat can be obtained from **D & T Scenics Ltd.,** Pipers Island, Bridge Street, Caversham Bridge, Reading, Berkshire RG4 8AH (tel. 0734/481088).

THE WELLINGTON DUCAL ESTATE

This trip to **Stratfield Saye House,** Reading, Berkshire (tel. 0256/882882), 1 mile west of Reading on the A33 to Basingstoke, takes you a little farther afield. It has been the home of the dukes of Wellington since 1817, when the 17th-century house was bought for the Iron Duke to celebrate his victory over Napoléon at the Battle of Waterloo. Many memories of the first duke remain in the house, including his billiard table, battle spoils, and pictures. The funeral carriage that since 1860 had rested in St. Paul's Cathedral crypt is now in the ducal collection. In the gardens is the grave of Copenhagen, the charger ridden to battle at Waterloo by the first duke. There are also extensive pleasure grounds, a licensed restaurant, and a gift shop.

A short drive away is the **Wellington Country Park** (tel. 0734/326444) with a National Dairy Museum, where you can see relics of 150 years of dairying. Other attractions include a riding school, nature trails, and boating and sailing on the lake. In addition, there is a miniature steam railway, the Thames Valley Time Trail, and a deer park.

Stratfield Saye is open from May to the last Sunday in September Saturday to Thursday from 11:30am to 5pm. Admission is £3.25 ($6) for adults and £1.60 ($2.95) for children. Wellington Country Park is open from March to September daily from 10am to 5pm. Admission is £2.20 ($4.05) for adults, £1 ($1.85) for children. A combined ticket for the house and park costs £4 ($7.40) for adults, £2 ($3.70) for children.

---

3. HENLEY-ON-THAMES

35 miles from London

GETTING THERE By Train Trains depart from London's Paddington Station but require a change in the junction of Twyford. More than 20 trains make the journey daily, and take about 1 hour for the total trip.

By Bus About 10 buses depart daily from London's Victoria Coach Station. Although no transfers are required, bus travel is actually slower (about 1¾ hr.) than the train because of the multiple stops along the way.

By Car From London, take the M4 toward Reading, cutting northwest onto A423.

ESSENTIALS The **area code** is 0491. A summer-only **Tourist Information Centre** is at Town Hall, Market Place (tel. 0491/578034).

SPECIAL EVENTS The **Henley Royal Regatta** (June 28–July 2) is one of the premier racing events of England. For a closeup view from the Stewards' Enclosure, you'll need a guest badge, obtainable only through a member. Information is available from the Secretary, Henley Royal Regatta, Henley-on-Thames, Oxfordshire RG9 2LY (tel. 0491/572153).

At the eastern edge of Oxfordshire, Henley-on-Thames, a small town and resort on the river at the foothills of the Chilterns, is the headquarters of the Royal Regatta held annually in late June and early July. The regatta is the number-one event among European oarsmen and dates back to the first years of the reign of Victoria.

The Elizabethan buildings, the tearooms, and the inns along the town's High Street live up to one's conception of what an English country town should look like. Cardinal Wolsey is said to have ordered the building of the tower of the Perpendicular and Decorated parish church.

Henley-on-Thames makes for an excellent stopover en route to Oxford. However, readers on the most limited of budgets will find far less expensive lodgings in Oxford; the fashionable inns of Henley-on-Thames are not cheap.

WHERE TO STAY

During the Royal Regatta, rooms are difficult to secure unless you've made reservations months in advance.

FLOHR'S HOTEL AND RESTAURANT, 15 Northfield End, Henley-on-Thames, Oxfordshire RG9 2JG. Tel. 0491/573412. 9 rms (3 with shower). TV TEL
$ Rates (including English breakfast): £35 ($64.75) single without bath; £59 ($109.15) single with bath; £59 ($109.15) double without bath; £79 ($146.15) double with bath. AE, DC, MC, V. **Parking:** Free.
This 1750 Georgian mansion is at the edge of town, yet within walking distance of the center and the river. The owners personally manage Flohr's and offer modern comforts, but they have kept its original charm, with oak beams and some period

pieces. All rooms have hot-beverage facilities, and three have private showers and toilets. The restaurant boasts a creative continental menu, with many fish specialties; meals cost from £18 ($33.30).

WHERE TO EAT

THE FLOWER POT, Ferry Lane, Aston. Tel. 574721.
 Cuisine: ENGLISH. **Reservations:** Recommended for dinner.
 $ Prices: Appetizers £2–£4.50 ($3.70–$8.35); main courses £4–£8.50 ($7.40–$15.75). MC, V.
 Open: Lunch Mon–Sat 11am–3pm; Sun noon–3pm; dinner Mon–Sat 5:30–11pm; Sun 7–10:30pm.

The Flower Pot lies 2 miles southeast of Henley, off the A423 Henley-Maidenhead road. In the vicinity of the River Thames, it is a Victorian pub with plenty of atmosphere. The pub grub is far above standard, and all the dishes are well prepared with fine ingredients. The poultry is excellent. Also try poached salmon, fish pie, and pan-fried trout in a peach-flavored cream sauce. This is also a good place to visit just for a pint.

THE LITTLE ANGEL, Remenham Lane, Remenham. Tel. 574165.
 Cuisine: ENGLISH. **Reservations:** Not needed.
 $ Prices: Appetizers £2.50–£4 ($4.65–$7.40); main courses £6–£7.50 ($11.10–$13.90); bar meals from £8 ($14.80). AE, DC, MC, V.
 Open: Lunch daily 10am–2:30pm; dinner daily 6–11pm.

In this historic pub, right on the London-Henley highway, ¼ mile east of the center of Henley-on-Thames, you can enjoy meals in the pub or in the charming dining room. The pub serves ale brewed right in Henley and is also known for its fresh seafood. You can also order smoked salmon from Scotland, oysters and scallops, and many standard pub offerings. In fair weather, guests can enjoy sitting at outside tables, and in winter, they can retreat to an intimate alcove, enjoying softly flickering candlelight. The setting is warm and welcoming, with old beamed ceilings.

---

4. OXFORD

57 miles NE of London

GETTING THERE By Train Hourly trains from Paddington Station reach Oxford in 1¼ hours. A cheap day round-trip ticket costs £9.80 ($18.15).

By Bus Oxford City Link provides bus services from London's Victoria Coach Station to the Oxford Bus Station. Three buses per hour leave daily, taking 1½ hours with a day round-trip ticket costing £4 ($7.40).

By Car Take the M40 west from London.

ESSENTIALS The **area code** is 0865. **Oxford Information Centre** is at St. Aldate's Chambers, St. Aldate's, opposite the town hall, near Carfax (tel. 0865/726871).

A mug of cider in one of the old student pubs; the sound of a May Day dawn when choristers sing in Latin from Magdalen Tower; the Great Tom bell from Tom Tower, whose 101 peals traditionally signal the closing of the college gates; towers and spires rising majestically; the barges on the upper reaches of the Thames; nude swimming at Parson's Pleasure; the roar of a cannon launching the bumping races; a tiny, dusty bookstall where you can pick up a valuable first edition—all this is Oxford—home of one of the greatest universities in the world, and also an industrial center of a large automobile business.

Oxford is far less crowded, and therefore better for sightseeing, in summer, when the students are on vacation. However, at any time of the year, you can enjoy a tour of the colleges, many of which represent a peak in England's architectural kingdom, as well as a valley of Victorian contributions. The Oxford Information Centre (see above) offers guided walking tours daily throughout the year. Just don't mention the other place (Cambridge) and you shouldn't have any trouble.

The city predates the university—in fact, it was a Saxon town in the early part of the 10th century. By the 12th century, Oxford was growing in reputation as a seat of learning, at the expense of Paris, and the first colleges were founded in the 13th century. The story of Oxford is filled with conflicts too complex and detailed to elaborate here. Suffice it to say, the relationship between town and gown wasn't as peaceful as it is today. Riots often flared, and both sides were guilty of abuses.

Ultimately, the test of a great university lies in the caliber of the people it turns out. Oxford can name-drop a mouthful: Roger Bacon, Sir Walter Raleigh, John Donne, Sir Christopher Wren, Samuel Johnson, Edward Gibbon, William Penn, John Wesley, William Pitt, Matthew Arnold, Lewis Carroll, Arnold Toynbee, Harold Macmillan, Graham Greene, A. E. Housman, T. E. Lawrence, and many others.

Many Americans arriving in Oxford ask, "Where's the campus?" If a local shows amusement when answering, it's understandable: Oxford University is, in fact, made up of 35 colleges. To tour all of these would be a formidable task. Besides, a few are of such interest that they overshadow the rest.

ORIENTATION
PARK & RIDE

Traffic and parking are a disaster in Oxford, and not just during rush hours. However, there are three large car parks on the north, south, and west of the city's ring road, all well marked. Car parking is free at all times, but at any time from 9:30am on, and all day on Saturday, you pay 60p ($1.10) for a bus ride into the city, which drops you off at St. Aldates or Queen Street to see the city center. The buses run every 8 to 10 minutes in each direction. There is no service on Sunday. The car parks are on the Woodstock road near the Peartree roundabout, on the Botley road toward Faringdon, on the Abingdon road in the southeast, and on the A40 toward London.

TOURS & TOURIST SERVICES

The best way to see and learn about Oxford's sightseeing attractions is to go to the **Oxford Information Centre,** St. Aldate's Chambers, St. Aldate's, opposite the town hall, near Carfax (tel. 0865/726871). Two-hour walking tours through the city and the major colleges leave daily in the morning and afternoon and cost £3 ($5.55); the tours do not include New College or Christ Church. You can also get reservations for entertainment facilities, as well as for Stratford-upon-Avon and London West End theaters (tel. 0865/727855). The center sells a comprehensive range of maps, brochures, souvenir items, as well as the famous Oxford University T-shirt. It is open Monday through Saturday from 9:30am to 5pm; Sunday (May–Sept only) 10:30am to 1pm and 1:30 to 3:30pm.

A tourist reception center for Oxford is operated by **Guide Friday Ltd.,** Oxford Railway Station, Park End Street (tel. 0865/790522). Their office dispenses maps and brochures, operates tours, as well as a full range of tourist services, including accommodation references and car rental. In summer, the office is open daily from 9:30am to 6:30pm. In winter, hours are daily from 9:30am to 4pm. Guided tours of Oxford and the colleges leave daily from the railway station. In summer, aboard open-top, double-decker buses, departures are every 15 minutes. The tour can be a 60-minute panoramic ride, or you can get off at any of the stops in the city. The ticket is valid all day. The tour price is £4.25 ($7.85) adults, £3.50 ($6.50) children.

From mid-May until mid-September, **Salter's River Thames Services** run daily passenger boat services on many reaches of the River Thames. Trips are to or from Oxford, Abingdon, Reading, Henley, Marlow, Cookham, Maidenhead, Windsor, Runnymede, and Staines. Combined outings from London can be made in

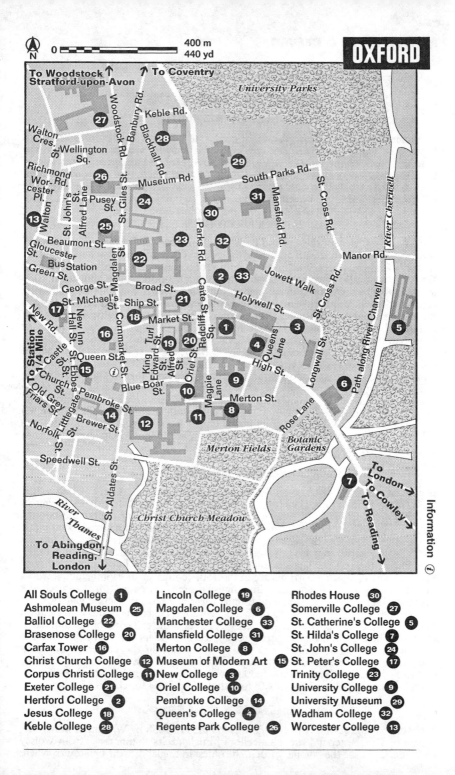

OXFORD

To Woodstock ↑ ↑ To Coventry
Stratford-upon-Avon

University Parks

Walton Cres.
Wellington Sq.
Richmond Wor-Rd.
cester Pl.
Walton
Beaumont St.
Gloucester St.
Green St.
Bus Station
George St.
St. Michael's St.
New Inn Hall St.
Castle St. St. Ebbes St.
Queen St.
Church St.
Old Grey Friars St.
Norfolk St.
Speedwell St.

Woodstock Rd.
Banbury Rd.
Keble Rd.
Blackhall Rd.
Museum Rd.
St. Giles St.
St. John's St.
Alfred Lane
Pusey St.
Magdalen St.
Broad St.
Ship St.
Market St.
Cornmarket St.
Turl St.
King Edward St.
Alfred St.
Oriel St.
Blue Boar St.
Pembroke St.
Brewer St.
Littlegate St.
St. Aldates St.

Parks Rd.
Castle St.
Magpie Lane

South Parks Rd.
Mansfield Rd.
St. Cross Rd.
Jowett Walk
Holywell St.
Queens Lane
High St.
Merton St.
Rose Lane
Longwall St.

Manor Rd.

River Cherwell

Path along River Charwell

Botanic Gardens

Merton Fields

Christ Church Meadow

River Thames

To Abingdon,
Reading,
London ↓

To Station
1/4 Mile ←
New Rd.

To London →
To Cowley →
To Reading →

Information ⓘ

College		College		College	
All Souls College	①	Lincoln College	⑲	Rhodes House	㉚
Ashmolean Museum	㉕	Magdalen College	⑥	Somerville College	㉗
Balliol College	㉒	Manchester College	㉝	St. Catherine's College	⑤
Brasenose College	⑳	Mansfield College	㉛	St. Hilda's College	⑦
Carfax Tower	⑯	Merton College	⑧	St. John's College	㉔
Christ Church College	⑫	Museum of Modern Art	⑮	St. Peter's College	⑰
Corpus Christi College	⑪	New College	③	Trinity College	㉓
Exeter College	㉑	Oriel College	⑩	University College	⑨
Hertford College	②	Pembroke College	⑭	University Museum	㉙
Jesus College	⑱	Queen's College	④	Wadham College	㉜
Keble College	㉘	Regents Park College	㉖	Worcester College	⑬

conjunction with train or bus services. Full details can be obtained from Salter Bros. Ltd., Folly Bridge, Oxford (tel. 0865/243421).

WHAT TO SEE & DO
A WORD OF WARNING

The main business of a university, is, of course, to educate—and unfortunately this function at Oxford has been severely interfered with by visitors who disturb the academic work of the university. Visiting is now restricted to certain hours and in small groups of six or fewer. In addition, there are areas where visitors are not allowed at all, but the tourist office will be happy to advise you when and where you may "take in" the sights of this great institution.

AN OVERVIEW

For a bird's-eye view of the city and colleges, climb **Carfax Tower.** This is the one with the clock and figures that strikes the hours. Carfax is the tower left from St. Martin's Church, where William Shakespeare once stood as godfather for William Davenant, who also became a playwright. A church stood on this spot from 1032 until 1896. The tower used to be higher, but after 1340 it was lowered, following complaints to Edward III that townspeople threw stones and fired arrows from it during town and gown disputes. Admission is 70p ($1.30) for adults; 30p (55¢) for children. The tower is open from late March to late October Monday to Saturday from 10am to 6pm, Sunday from 2 to 6pm. For information, call 0865/250239.

The **Oxford Story,** 6 Broad Street (tel. 0865/790055), will help you understand the complexities of Oxford University. Insight into the structure of the colleges and a look at some of the architectural and historical features that might otherwise be missed are highlighted. Visitors are also filled in on the general background of the colleges and the deeds of some of the famous people who have passed through its portals. The audiovisual presentation is given daily, with an admission of £3.75 ($6.95) for adults and £2.50 ($4.65) for children. Opening times from April to June are 9:30am to 5pm; July and August 9:30am to 7pm; September to October 9:30am to 5pm, and November to March 10am to 4pm.

CHRIST CHURCH

Begun by Cardinal Wolsey as Cardinal College in 1525, Christ Church (tel. 0865/276174), known as The House, was founded by Henry VIII in 1546. Facing St. Aldate's Street, Christ Church has the largest quadrangle of any college in Oxford. Tom Tower houses Great Tom, the 18,000-pound bell referred to earlier. It rings at 9:05 nightly, signaling the closing of the college gates. The 101 times it peals originally signified the number of students in residence at the time of the founding of the college. The student body number changed, but Oxford traditions live on. Some interesting portraits are in the 16th-century great hall, including works by Gainsborough and Reynolds. Prime ministers are pictured, as Christ Church was the training ground for 13 prime ministers. There is a separate picture gallery.

The cathedral was built over a period of centuries, beginning in the 12th century. (Incidentally, it's not only the college chapel, but also the cathedral of the diocese of Oxford.) The cathedral's most distinguishing features are its Norman pillars and the vaulting of the choir, dating from the 15th century. In the center of the great quadrangle is a statue of Mercury mounted in the center of a fish pond. The college and cathedral can be visited from 9:30am to 6pm in summer, 9:30am to 4:30pm in winter. Entrance fee is £1.50 ($2.80) for adults, 50p (95¢) for children.

MAGDALEN COLLEGE

Pronounced "*maud*-lin," this college was founded in 1458 by William of Waynflete, bishop of Winchester and later chancellor of England. Its alumni range from Wolsey to Wilde. Opposite the botanic garden, the oldest in England, is the bell tower, where the choristers sing in Latin at dawn on May Day. The reflection of the 15th-century tower is cast in the waters of the Cherwell below. On a not-so-happy day, Charles I—his days numbered—watched the oncoming Roundheads from the this tower. Visit the 15th-century chapel, in spite of many of its latter-day trappings. Ask when the hall and other places of special interest are open. The grounds of Magdalen are the most extensive of any Oxford college; there's even a deer park. You can visit Magdalen each day from 2 to 6:15pm.

MERTON COLLEGE

Founded in 1264, Merton College, Merton Street (tel. 0865/276310) is among the trio of the most ancient at the university. It stands near Corpus Christi College on Merton Street, the sole survivor of Oxford's medieval cobbled streets. Merton College is noted for its library, built between 1371 and 1379 and said to be the oldest college library in England. There was once a tradition of keeping some of its most valuable books chained. Now only one book is so secured, to show what the custom was like. One of the treasures of the library is an astrolabe (astronomical instrument used for measuring the altitude of the sun and stars), thought to have belonged to Chaucer. You pay only 30p (55¢) to visit the ancient library, as well as the Max Beerbohm Room (the satirical English caricaturist who died in 1956). The library and college are open Monday to Friday from 2 to 5pm and on Saturday and Sunday from 10am to 5pm.

A favorite pastime is to take **Addison's Walk** through the water meadows. The stroll is so named after a former alumnus, Joseph Addison, the 18th-century essayist and playwright noted for his contributions to *The Spectator* and *The Tatler*.

UNIVERSITY COLLEGE

University College, High Street (tel. 0865/276602), is the oldest one at Oxford and dates back to 1249, when money was donated by an ecclesiastic William of Durham. More fanciful is the old claim that the real founder was Alfred the Great. The original structures have all disappeared, and what remains today represents essentially the architecture of the 17th century, with subsequent additions in Victoria's day, as well as in more recent times. For example, the Goodhart Quadrangle was added as late as 1962. Its most famous alumnus, Shelley, was "sent down" for his part in collaborating on a pamphlet on atheism. However, all is forgiven today, as the romantic poet is honored by a memorial erected in 1894. The hall and chapel of University College can be visited daily during vacations from 2 to 4pm for a charge of £1 ($1.85) for adults, 40p (75¢) for children.

NEW COLLEGE

New College, off Queen's Lane (tel. 0865/279555), was founded in 1379 by William of Wykeham, bishop of Winchester and later lord chancellor of England. His college at Winchester supplied a constant stream of candidates. The first quadrangle, dating from before the end of the 14th century, was the initial quadrangle to be built in Oxford and formed the architectural design for the other colleges. In the antechapel is Sir Jacob Epstein's remarkable modern sculpture of *Lazarus* and a fine El Greco painting of St. James. One of the treasures of the college is a crosier (pastoral staff of a bishop) belonging to the founding father. In the garden, you can see the remains of the old city wall and the mound. The college (entered at New College Lane) can be visited from 11am to 5pm daily in summer. Admission is £1 ($1.85).

A LOCAL SPORT — PUNTING

At **Punt Station,** Cherwell Boathouse, Bardwell Road (tel. 0865/515978), you can rent a punt for £4.80 ($8.80) per hour, plus a £25 ($46.25) deposit. Similar charges are made on rentals at Magdalen Bridge Boathouse and at the Folly Bridge Boathouse. Hours are 10am to 10pm daily June to September.

SHOPPING

An arcade of first-class shops and boutiques, the **Golden Cross** lies between Cornmarket Street and the Covered Market (or between High Street and Market Street). Parts of the arcade date from the 12th century. Many buildings remain from the medieval era, along with some 15th- and 17th-century structures. The market also has a reputation as the Covent Garden of Oxford, where live entertainment takes place on Saturday mornings in summer. In the arcade shops you'll find a wide selection of merchandise, including handmade Belgian chocolates, specialty gifts, clothing for women and men, and luxury leather goods.

WHERE TO STAY

Accommodations in Oxford are limited, although the addition of motels on the outskirts has aided the plight of those who require modern amenities. Recently, some of the more stalwart candidates in the city center have been refurbished. In addition, motorists may want to consider country houses or small B&Bs on the outskirts of town, which offer the best living in Oxford if you don't mind commuting.

Oxford Information Centre, St. Aldate's Chambers, St. Aldate's (tel. 0865/726871), operates a year-round room-booking service for a fee of £2 ($3.70) and an 8% refundable deposit. If you'd like to seek lodgings on your own, the staff at the center will provide, for a fee, a list of accommodations, maps, and guidebooks.

DOUBLES WITHOUT BATH FOR LESS THAN £48 [$88.80]

ADAMS GUEST HOUSE, 302 Banbury Rd., Oxford, Oxfordshire OX2 7ED. Tel. 0865/56118. 6 rms (none with bath). TV **Bus:** No. 7, 20, 21, or 22.
$ Rates (including English breakfast): £18–£25 ($33.30–$46.25) single; £30–£34 ($55–$62.90) double. No credit cards.

In Summertown, 1¼ miles from Oxford, this is operated by John Strange and is one of the best B&Bs in the North Oxford area. The comfortable and cozy rooms have hot and cold running water, and some family rooms are available. Breakfast is served in a dining room decorated in an old-world style. Mr. Strange will provide touring tips. A bus runs every few minutes to the city center. Adams Guest House is located opposite the Midland Bank, and in its neighborhood are seven restaurants, shops, a post office, a swimming pool, a cycle-rental shop, and a launderette.

BELMONT GUEST HOUSE, 182 Woodstock Rd., Oxford, Oxfordshire OX2 7NG. Tel. 0865/53698. 4 rms (1 with shower). **Bus:** No. 60.
$ Rates (including English breakfast): £16–£18 ($29.60–$33.30) single; £32 ($59.20) double without bath, £36 ($66.60) double with shower. MC, V.
On a tree-lined avenue in the residential part of Oxford, this is about a mile from the city center. All rooms have central heating, hot and cold running water, and tea and coffee makers; only one has a private shower. Most rooms can be used as doubles, twins, or family rooms. The owners are Mr. and Mrs. J. Deadman.

BRAVALIA GUEST HOUSE, 242 Iffley Rd., Oxford, Oxfordshire OX4 1SE. Tel. 0865/241326. 5 rms (4 with bath or shower). TV **Bus:** No. 40, 41, 42, or 43.
$ Rates (including English breakfast): £20 ($37) single without bath; £30 ($55.50) single with bath; £30 ($55.50) double without bath; £40 ($74) double with bath. MC, V. **Parking:** Free.
About a mile from the heart of Oxford and about ½ mile from Magdalen College, this is small and well known, so reserve in advance in summer. Built in the late Victorian era, the house contains pleasantly furnished bedrooms, two of which are suitable for families. The Downes are your hosts.

BROWN'S GUEST HOUSE, 281 Iffley Rd., Oxford, Oxfordshire OX4 4AQ. Tel. 0865/246822. 6 rms (none with bath). TV **Bus:** No. 40, 41, 42, or 43.

$ Rates (including English breakfast): £18–£25 ($33.30–$46.25) single; £28–£30 ($51.80–$55.50) double. MC, V. **Parking:** Free.

This year-round guesthouse is run by the Brown family. The pleasantly furnished guest rooms have hot and cold running water, central heating, and hot-beverage facilities. There are adequate showers outside the rooms. Families are catered to, with special breakfasts if requested. The house is about a mile from the city center, with such nearby amenities as a post office, laundrette, grocery store, drugstore, and bike-rental shop.

COTSWOLD HOUSE, 363 Banbury Rd., Oxford, Oxfordshire OX2 7PL. Tel. 0865/310558. 6 rms (all with shower). TV **Bus:** No. 20, 21, or 22.

$ Rates (including English breakfast): £25–£30 ($46.25–$55.50) single; £44–£48 ($81.40–$88.80) double. No credit cards. **Parking:** Free.

Jim and Anne O'Kane operate this stone-built house that is one of the better B&Bs in the area. Bedrooms have refrigerators, coffee-making equipment, and hairdryers. Traditional and vegetarian breakfasts and fresh fruit are always available, all with generous Irish helpings. There is ample off-street parking. The O'Kanes help with maps and give good touring advice. Cotswold House is about 1½ miles from the center, but it is much easier for motorists to use the ring road. Buses pass by about every 5 minutes.

COURTFIELD PRIVATE HOTEL, 367 Iffley Rd., Oxford, Oxfordshire OX4 4DP. Tel. 0865/24291. 6 rms (4 with bath). **Bus:** No. 40, 41, 42, or 43.

$ Rates (including English breakfast): £20 ($37) single without bath; £25 ($46.25) single with bath; £38 ($70.30) double without bath; £44 ($81.40) double with bath AE, MC, V.

This is most suitable for motorists who don't want to face the congested center, because it stands on a tree-lined street close to the center of Iffley Village. If you're not driving, you will find adequate public transportation. The house has been modernized with triple-glazed windows in the bedrooms, most of which contain private baths or showers. Brian Tong, the owner, served with the city police force for 30 years and offers excellent advice to tourists.

GREEN GABLES, 326 Abingdon Rd., Oxford, Oxfordshire OX1 4TE. Tel. 0865/725870. 8 rms (6 with bath). TV

$ Rates (including English breakfast): £18 ($33.30) single without bath; £20 ($37) single with bath; £36 ($66.60) double without bath, £38–£42 ($70.30–$77.70) double with bath. MC, V. **Parking:** Free.

About a mile south of the university city, on the A4144, this was originally an Edwardian private residence. Mr. and Mrs. Jelfs rent comfortable bedrooms. Trees screen the house from the main road, and limited parking is available.

GALAXIE PRIVATE HOTEL, 180 Banbury Rd., Oxford, Oxfordshire OX2 7BT. Tel. 0865/515688. 34 rms (26 with bath). TV TEL **Bus:** No. 7, 20, 21, or 22.

$ Rates (including English breakfast): £29 ($53.65) single without bath; £39 ($72.15) single with bath; £46 ($85.10) double without bath; £56 ($103.60) double with bath. **Parking:** Free.

A bus service on Banbury Road will take you the 1½ miles from this small, owner-run hotel to the town center; the family hotel is in Summertown, a choice suburb. All of the spotlessly clean bedrooms are equipped with reading lights, electric shaving points, hot and cold running water, and central heating. Many of the units have showers and toilets, for which you'll pay more, of course. Parking is available.

HIGHFIELD WEST GUEST HOUSE, 188 Cumnor Hill, Oxford, Oxfordshire OX2 9PJ. Tel. 0865/863007. 5 rms (3 with bath). TV **Bus:** No. 42 or 43.

$ Rates (including English breakfast): £17 ($31.45) single without bath; £21 ($38.85) single with bath; £37 ($68.45) double without bath; £42 ($77.70) double with bath. No credit cards. **Parking:** Free.

Three miles from the heart of Oxford, this is on a good residential road, within easy access of the ring road surrounding Oxford. The little village of Cumnor, with its two country inns serving food and drink, is also within walking distance. Blenheim Palace is a few miles away, and a pleasant day can be spent in some of the Cotswold villages. Tina and Robin Barrett offer accommodations in single, double, twin, or family rooms, most with private baths. There is a lounge, and in season, visitors can enjoy the heated outdoor pool. A bus into Oxford stops just outside their front garden, and there is also a good local taxi service.

LAKESIDE GUEST HOUSE, 118 Abingdon Rd., Oxford, Oxfordshire OX1 4PZ. Tel. 0865/244725. 6 rms (3 with bath). TV **Bus:** 62 or 82.
$ Rates (including English breakfast): £28 ($51.80) single or double without bath; £40 ($74) single or double with bath. No credit cards. **Parking:** Free.
Proprietors Martin and Daniela Shirley run this Victorian house, which overlooks open fields and parklands that lead to the University Boat Houses. The house, which has been remodeled and updated, is about 5 minutes from Christ Church College, 1 mile south of the center (take A4144). There is hot and cold running water and hot-beverage facilities in all of the centrally heated rooms.

LONSDALE GUEST HOUSE, 312 Banbury Rd., Summertown, Oxford, Oxfordshire OX2 7ED. Tel. 0865/54872. 9 rms (6 with shower). **Bus:** No. 20, 21, or 22.
$ Rates (including English breakfast): £18 ($33.30) single without bath; £25 ($46.25) single with shower; £34 ($62.90) double without bath; £38 ($70.30) double with shower. No credit cards. **Parking:** Free.
 Another pleasant accommodation, this one is run by Roland and Christine Adams, who have established a gem of a little guesthouse. All of the comfortable units have twin beds, lounge chairs, occasionally antique chests of drawers, innerspring mattresses, soft down comforters, wall-to-wall carpeting, and central heating. If you arrive at term time, you may think you're in a fraternity house. A heated, indoor pool and several restaurants are about a 2-minute walk from the house. You will also find tennis courts and a launderette nearby.

NORHAM GUEST HOUSE, 16 Norham Rd., Oxford, Oxfordshire OX2 6SF. Tel. 0865/515352. 8 rms (none with bath). TV TEL **Bus:** No. 20, 21, or 22.
$ Rates (including English breakfast): £20 ($37) single; £38–£40 ($70.30–$74) double. No credit cards.
Owners Peter and Rosemary Welham provide one of the better B&Bs in the area, with well-kept bedrooms. In North Oxford, this late Victorian building enjoys a tranquil setting near parks. There is bus service to this district. Breakfast is the only meal served, and there is parking for four cars.

PINE CASTLE HOTEL, 290 Iffley Rd., Oxford, Oxfordshire OX4 1AE. Tel. 0865/241497. 6 rms (none with bath). **Bus:** No. 40, 41, 42, or 43.
$ Rates (including English breakfast): £19–£21 ($35.15–$38.85) single; £34–£38 ($62.90–$70.30) double. MC, V. **Parking:** Free.
 This comfortable Edwardian guesthouse is operated by Peter and Marilyn Morris and has a host of amenities to make your stay enjoyable. The hotel has central heating, hot beverage facilities, plus a TV lounge if you prefer to watch in company. The Morrises can supply you with shoe-cleaning equipment, an iron, a hairdryer, current adapters, and an alarm clock as needed, and there are laundry, dry-cleaning, and post office outlets across the street. Furniture for small children is available. They will also arrange tours of the city and university buildings. Their location is 1½ miles from the city center on a good bus route. Evening meals can be arranged if you'd like to stay in.

TILBURY LODGE PRIVATE HOTEL, 5 Tilbury Lane, Eynsham Rd., Botley Oxford, Oxfordshire OX2 9NB. Tel. 0865/862138. 9 rms (all with bath). TV TEL **Bus:** No. 40 or 41.

$ Rates (including English breakfast): £27–£30 ($49.95–$55.50) single; £45–£60 ($83.25–$111) double. MC, V. **Parking:** Free.

On a quiet country lane about 2 miles west of the center of Oxford, this is less than a mile from the railway station. Eddie and Eileen Trafford house guests in their well-furnished and comfortable rooms. Children over 6 are welcomed. If you don't come by car, Eddie will pick you up at the train station. A bus takes visitors to Botley, an area of Oxford.

WALTON GUEST HOUSE, 169 Walton St., Oxford, Oxfordshire OX1 2HD. Tel. 0865/52137. 17 rms (none with bath). **Bus:** No. 190.

$ Rates (including English breakfast): £17 ($31.45) single; £32 ($59.20) double. No credit cards.

Mr. and Mrs. R. J. Carter own this hotel, at the city end of Walton Street, 100 yards from the bus station, and ½ mile from the rail station. It overlooks the grounds of Worcester College. All the pleasantly furnished rooms have hot and cold running water, shaver points, central heating, and tea and coffee makers.

WILLOW REACHES HOTEL, 1 Whytham St., Oxford, Oxfordshire OX1 4SU. Tel. 0865/721545. Fax 0865/251139. 9 rms (all with bath). TV TEL **Bus:** 7, 9, or 21.

$ Rates (including English breakfast): £36–£39 ($66.60–$72.15) single; £48 ($88.80) double; £70 ($129.50) family room for 4. AE, DC, MC, V. **Parking:** Free.

This hotel is on a cul-de-sac about a mile south from the center of Oxford. All of the attractively furnished bedrooms contain private baths with showers. A three-course table d'hôte dinner of either English or Indian meals costs from £13 ($24.05) to £18 ($33.30) per person. Guests can relax in the garden or follow a special footpath to a nearby village for a pub meal or an early-morning walk.

WHERE TO EAT

MEALS FOR LESS THAN £11 ($20.35)

BLUE COYOTE, 36 St. Clements. Tel. 241431.

Cuisine: AMERICAN/ENGLISH. **Reservations:** Not needed. **Bus:** No. 52.

$ Prices: Appetizers £1.85–£3.45 ($3.40–$6.40); main courses £4.95–£10.95 ($9.15–$20.15). MC, V.

Open: Mon–Wed noon–11pm, Thurs–Sat noon–midnight, Sun 10am–11pm.

Homesick Americans will find solace here, enjoying a cuisine that might include everything from a T-bone steak to crabcakes Baltimore style. A zesty chili is also a popular order, and a limited selection of fish dishes is available. Against a backdrop of a blue coyote decor, the restaurant has simple wooden tables. Sunday is a good time to visit, especially if you want to enjoy an American brunch from 10am to noon. The restaurant is in the vicinity of Magdalen Bridge, on a highway leading out of Oxford, the A40.

BROWNS, 5-9 Woodstock Rd. Tel. 511995.

Cuisine: AMERICAN/CONTINENTAL. **Reservations:** Recommended. **Bus:** No. 52.

$ Prices: Side orders 85p–£1.45 ($1.55–$2.70); main courses £5.35–£7.65 ($10–$14.15). No credit cards.

Open: Mon–Sat 11am–11:30pm, Sun noon–11:30pm.

A big, bustling brasserie "à l'anglaise," this is popular with students who know of its quick snack meals. There is always a hamburger on the grill, and the staff will make you a hot pastrami on rye or perhaps a club sandwich. They also serve spaghetti with various sauces, salads, and fishermen's pie topped with Cheddar cheese pastry. Sometimes you'll see long lines of students waiting to get in, as this is the most popular dining place in Oxford.

CHERWELL BOATHOUSE RESTAURANT, Bardwell Rd. Tel. 52746.

Cuisine: FRENCH. **Reservations:** Recommended. **Bus:** No. 52.

$ Prices: Appetizers £2–£8 ($3.70–$14.80); main courses £8–£12 ($14.80–$22.20); fixed-price dinner from £15.75 ($29.15); Sun lunch £10.75 ($19.90). MC, V.

Open: Lunch Sun 12:30–2pm; dinner daily 6:30–10:30pm.

This virtual Oxford landmark, east of the center on River Cherwell, is owned by Tony Verdin, who has the help of a young crew. Two fixed menus are offered at each meal, and the cooks change the menu every 2 weeks to allow for the availability of fresh vegetables, fish, and meat. Appetizers include soups or fish or meat pâtés, followed by casseroles, pies, and hot pots. There is a very reasonable wine list. Children, if they don't order a full meal, are granted half price. In summer, the restaurant also serves on the terrace. Before dinner, you can try "punting" on the Cherwell; punts are rented on the other side of the boathouse for £6 ($11.10).

MUNCHY MUNCHY, 6 Park End St. Tel. 245710.
   Cuisine: SOUTHEAST ASIAN/INDONESIAN. **Reservations:** Required. **Bus:** No. 52.
$ Prices: Main courses £5.45–£7.50 ($10.10–$13.90). No credit cards.
   Open: Lunch Tues–Sat noon–2pm; dinner Tues–Sat 5:30–10pm. **Closed:** Jan, 3 weeks in Aug, 3 weeks in Dec.

Some Oxford students, who frequent this location near the station, claim that this restaurant offers the best food value in the city. Main dishes depend on what is available in the marketplace, and appetizers are not offered. Ethel Ow is adept at herbs and seasoning, and often uses fresh fruit inventively, as reflected by such dishes as scallops sautéed with ginger and lamb with passion-fruit sauce. Indonesian and Malaysian dishes are popular. The place is unlicensed, so bring your own bottle. Sometimes, especially on Friday and Saturday, long lines form at the door. Children under 6 are not allowed on Friday and Saturday evenings.

NOSEBAG, 6-8 St. Michael's St. Tel. 721033.
   Cuisine: ENGLISH. **Reservations:** None. **Bus:** No. 52.
$ Prices: Appetizers £1.50–£1.95 ($2.80–$3.60); main courses £2.25–£4.15 ($4.15–$7.70); set menu £5.50 ($10.20). No credit cards.
   Open: Mon 9:30am–5:30pm, Tues–Thurs 9:30am–10pm, Fri 9:30am–10:30pm, Sat 9:30am–10:30pm, Sun 9:30am–9pm.

One of the most popular places to eat with students is this self-service upstairs cafeteria on a side street off Cornmarket, opposite St. Michael's Church. At mealtimes, there's usually a line on the stairs. At lunch, you can get a homemade soup, followed by the dish of the day, perhaps a moussaka. Baked potato with a variety of fillings is a good accompaniment, as is the hot garlic bread. The menu increasingly leans to vegetarian dishes. Wine is available by the glass.

ST. ALDATE'S CHURCH COFFEE HOUSE, 94 St. Aldate's. Tel. 245952.
   Cuisine: ENGLISH. **Reservations:** Not needed. **Bus:** No. 52.
$ Prices: Appetizers all £1.55 ($2.85); main courses £2.45–£5 ($4.55–$9.25). No credit cards.
   Open: Mon–Sat 10am–5pm (hot lunches served noon–2pm).

Opened by the archbishop of Canterbury in 1963, this is almost opposite the entrance to Christ Church College, adjacent to St. Aldate's Church. An offbeat suggestion for eating, it is a bookshop/coffeehouse. Head for the back, where nonsmokers find a large restaurant with counter service, run by the church. All the food is homemade, including soups and salads made daily from fresh produce. Portions are generous.

GO DUTCH, 18 Park End St. Tel 240686.
   Cuisine: CONTINENTAL. **Reservations:** Not needed. **Bus:** No. 52.
$ Prices: Crêpes from £3.95 ($7.30). No credit cards.
   Open: Lunch daily noon–2:30pm; dinner daily 6–11pm.

Opposite the railway station, this restaurant evokes the Netherlands with crêpes served with savory fillings, such as bacon with apple or perhaps ham, corn, and green pepper. If you don't like the advertised stuffings, make up your own, perhaps with a few of the many sweet fillings. Try one of the crisp, fresh salads as a side dish. Go Dutch is licensed to sell beer and wine.

SWEENEY TODD'S, 6-12 George St. Tel. 723421.
   Cuisine: AMERICAN/CONTINENTAL. **Reservations:** Not needed. **Bus:** No. 2A or 2B.
   $ Prices: Appetizers £1.40–£3.40 ($2.60–$6.30); main courses £5–£9 ($9.25–$16.65). AE, DC, MC, V.
   Open: Daily noon–11pm.
If you saw the Broadway play, you'll agree that this is a rather controversial name to label a restaurant; nevertheless, it is one of the best family-type eateries in Oxford. The full array of standard fare includes hamburgers, barbecues, fresh salads, and pizzas. Meals are reasonable, and children are catered to as well. You can enjoy your meal either on the ground floor or in a two-level restaurant upstairs.

SPECIAL PUBS

BEAR INN, Alfred St. Tel. 244680.
   Cuisine: ENGLISH. **Reservations:** None. **Bus:** No. 2A or 2B.
   $ Prices: Snacks and bar meals £2–£4 ($3.70–$7.40). No credit cards.
   Open: Mon–Sat noon–11pm; Sun noon–3pm and 7–10:30pm.
A short block from The High, overlooking the north side of Christ Church College, this is the village pub and is an Oxford tradition. Its swinging inn sign depicts the bear and ragged staff, old insignia of the earls of Warwick, who were among the early patrons. Built in the 13th century, the inn has been known to many famous people who have lived and studied at Oxford. Over the years it's been mentioned time and time again in English literature.
   The Bear has served a useful purpose in breaking down social barriers, bringing a wide variety of people together in a relaxed way. You might talk with a raja from India, a university don, a titled gentleman—and the latest in a line of owners that goes back more than 700 years. Some former owners developed an astonishing habit: clipping neckties. Around the lounge bar you'll see thousands of the remains of ties, which have been labeled with their owners' names. For those of you who want to leave a bit of yourself, a thin strip of the bottom of your tie will be cut off (with your permission, of course). After this initiation, you may want to join in some of the informal songfests of the undergraduates.

TROUT INN, 195 Godstow Rd., Wolvercote. Tel. 54485.
   Cuisine: ENGLISH. **Reservations:** Not needed. **Bus:** No. 520 or 521 to Wolvercote, then walk.
   $ Prices: Appetizers £2.50–£7 ($4.65–$12.95); main courses £9–£13.50 ($16.65–$25); Sun barbecue grills £2.50–£4 ($4.65–$7.40) each; snacks £2–£5.50 ($3.70–$10.20). AE, DC, MC.
   Open: Restaurant lunch daily noon–2pm; dinner Mon–Sat 7–10pm; Sun barbecue 7–9:30pm; pub Mon–Fri 11am–3pm and 6–11pm; Sat 11am–11pm; Sun noon–3pm and 7–10:30pm.
Lying 2½ miles north of Oxford and hidden away from visitors and townspeople, the Trout is a private world where you can get ale and beer—and standard fare. Have your drink in one of the historic rooms, with their settles, brass, and old prints, or go out in sunny weather to sit on a stone wall. On the grounds are peacocks, ducks, swans, and herons that live in and around the river and an adjacent weir pool, who will join you if you're handing out crumbs. Take an arched stone bridge, stone terraces, architecture with wildly pitched roofs and gables, add the Thames River, and you have the Trout. The Stable Bar, the original 12th-century part, complements the inn's relatively new 16th-century bars. Daily specials are featured, and there is a cold snack bar. Hot

meals are served all day in the restaurant; salads are served in summer, and there are grills in winter. On your way there and back, look for the view of Oxford from the bridge.

THE TURF TAVERN, 4-5 Bath Place. Tel. 243235.
    Cuisine: ENGLISH. **Reservations:** None. **Bus:** No. 52.
  $ Prices: Buffet meals from £8 ($14.80); bar snacks from £3.50 ($6.95). No credit cards.
    Open: Mon–Sat 11am–11pm; Sun noon–3pm and 7–10:30pm.

This 13th-century tavern is on a very narrow passage in the area of the Bodleian Library, off New College Lane. Thomas Hardy used the place for the setting of *Jude the Obscure*. It was "the local" of Burton and Taylor when they were in Oxford many years ago making a film, and today's patrons might include Kris Kristofferson or John Hurt. At night, the old tower of New College and part of the old city wall are floodlit, and in warm weather, you can enjoy an al fresco evening in this historical setting. In winter, braziers are lighted in the courtyard and gardens.

Inside the low-beamed hospice, you can order traditional English pub food. More impressive, however, is a table about 8 feet long and 4 feet wide, covered with meats, fish, fowl, eggs, cheeses, bread puddings, sausages, cakes, and salads (all cold), and a selection of hors d'oeuvres, freshly prepared daily. Excellent local ales—try the Old Hooky—plus a range of country wines, are served all year, and a special punch is offered in winter from noon to 3pm and 7 to 10:30pm Sunday. The pub is reached via St. Helen's Passage between Holywell Street and New College Lane (you'll probably get lost, but any student worth his beer can direct you).

EASY EXCURSION

DIDCOT

A little town 10 miles south of Oxford near the Berkshire border, east of the A34, Didcot is served by trains from Paddington Station in London. Didcot Parkway is a principal intercity station, with good connections to Oxford, Bristol, Reading, and the south coast.

For the railway buff, the place is the home of the **Didcot Railway Centre,** Didcot, Oxfordshire (tel. 0235/817200). In the engine sheds are steam locomotives, and on "steaming days" you can roll along in a Great Western Railway train from Didcot Halt, a typical small country station. There is also a re-creation of Brunel's original, broad-gauge, Great Western track. In season various other preserved railways in the country send visiting locomotives. The center is open all year on Saturday and Sunday from 11am to 5pm and also from the end of May through August daily and bank holidays from 11am to 5pm. Admission charges are £2.30 ($4.25) to £4 ($7.40), depending on the event.

5. WOODSTOCK [BLENHEIM PALACE]

8 miles N of Oxford; 63 miles NW of London

GETTING THERE   By Train   Take the train to Oxford (see above).

By Bus   The Gloucester Green bus leaves Oxford about every 30 minutes during the day taking 36 minutes. Call 0865/722333 for more details.

By Car   Take the A34 from Oxford.

ESSENTIALS   The **area code** is 0993. The summer-only **information office** is at Hensington Road (tel. 0993/811038).

The small country town of Woodstock, the birthplace in 1330 of the Black Prince, ill-fated son of King Edward III, lies on the edge of the Cotswolds. Some of the stone houses here were constructed when Woodstock was the site of a royal palace, which had so suffered the ravages of time that its remains were demolished when Blenheim Palace was built. Woodstock was once the seat of a flourishing glove industry.

BLENHEIM PALACE

⭐ This extravagant baroque palace regards itself as England's answer to Versailles. Blenheim is the home of the 11th Duke of Marlborough, a descendant of John Churchill, the first duke, an on-again, off-again favorite of Queen Anne's. In his day (1650–1722), the first duke became the supreme military figure in Europe. Fighting on the Danube near a village named Blenheim, Churchill defeated the forces of Louis XIV, and the lavish palace of Blenheim was built for the duke as a gift from the queen. It was designed by Sir John Vanbrugh, who was also the architect of Castle Howard; landscaping was by Capability Brown.

The palace is loaded with riches: antiques, porcelain, oil paintings, tapestries, and chinoiserie. North Americans know Blenheim as the birthplace of Sir Winston Churchill. His birthroom forms part of the palace tour, as does the Churchill exhibition, four rooms of letters, books, photographs, and other relics. Today the former prime minister lies buried in Bladon Churchyard, near the palace.

Blenheim Palace (tel. 0993/811325) is open from mid-March to October daily from 10:30am to 5:30pm. The last admittance to the palace is at 4:30pm. Admission costs £4.90 ($9.05) for adults, £2.40 ($4.45) for children.

In the park is the Blenheim Butterfly and Garden Centre, which contains a Butterfly House with tropical moths and butterflies in free flight in a virtually natural habitat, an adventure play area, a garden café, a gift shop, and a shop for plants and gardening requirements.

WHERE TO STAY

THE LAURELS, 90 Hensington Rd., Woodstock, Oxfordshire OX7 1JL. Tel. 0993/812583. 3 rms (all with bath). **Directions:** At the Punch Bowl Public House, turn into Hensington Road and proceed for 250 yards.
$ **Rates** (including English breakfast): £25 ($46.25) single (in a double room); £36 ($66.60) double. No credit cards. **Parking:** Free.
Built in 1890 for the manager of the then flourishing glove factory in the area, this hotel has seen a lot of renovation. The decor is traditional, and Malcolm and Nikki Lloyd have furnished the house with Victorian and Edwardian pieces in keeping with the age of the Laurels. Rooms are attractively decorated in soft pastels and are well maintained. The location is just off the town center, but within a few minutes' walk of the heart of town and Blenheim Palace grounds.

KINGS ARMS HOTEL, 19 Market Place, Woodstock, Oxfordshire OX7 1ST. Tel. 0993/811412. Fax 0993/823353. 9 rms (all with bath). MINIBAR TV TEL **Bus:** Buses from Oxford stop 40 feet from door.
$ **Rates** (including English breakfast): £50–£55 ($92.50–$101.75) single; £65–£70 ($120.25–$129.50) double. AE, DC, MC, V.
Much like a country house hotel, this was one of the properties that Queen Elizabeth I gave to Woodstock when she came to the throne. The family-run hotel welcomes travelers on the A34 between Stratford-upon-Avon and the south. Go early to enjoy a drink in the bar, then later have a meal at Wheeler's St. James Restaurant, a branch of a well-known London seafood restaurant. Featuring the largest seafood menu in the area; they offer lunches for £10.50 ($6.95) and dinners for £16 ($29.60). The bedrooms are individually designed (one with a four-poster bed), each with a hairdryer and coffee-making facilities.

WHERE TO EAT

BROTHERONS BRASSERIE, 1 High St. Tel. 811114.
Cuisine: ENGLISH. **Reservations:** Not needed. **Bus:** No. 206.

$ Prices: Appetizers £2–£4.95 ($3.70–$9.15); main courses £5.95–£11 ($11–$20.35). AE, DC, MC, V.

Open: Lunch noon–2:30pm; dinner daily 6:30–10:30pm.

Right in the heart of town, this is your best bet. Carefully chosen fresh ingredients are one of the reasons for the success of this place. Potted plants, pine chairs and tables, and gas mantles make for a simple but effective decor. Meals are likely to feature a selection of crudités, smoked salmon, or game pie. There's always a vegetarian dish of the day, and families with small children are welcomed.

KENT & SURREY

L ying to the South and southeast of London are the shires (counties) of Kent and Surrey, both fascinating areas to explore and within easy commuting distance of the capital. Of all the tourist centers, Canterbury in Kent is of foremost interest.

Once the ancient Anglo-Saxon kingdom of Kent, this county is on the fringes of London yet far removed in spirit and scenery. Since the days of the Tudors, cherry blossoms have pinkened the fertile landscape. Not only orchards but hop fields abound, and the conically shaped oasthouses with kilns for drying the hops dot the rolling countryside. Both the hops and orchards have earned for Kent the title of the garden of England—and in England, the competition's rough.

SEEING KENT & SURREY

GETTING THERE

British Rail's Network Southeast offers frequent service to all the major towns and cities of Kent and Surrey through its Victoria or Charing Cross stations. National Express buses serve the region from Victoria's Coach Station (for specific bus routes in Surrey, call 071/5419365, and for information in Kent dial 0622/671411). Motorists take the A2/M2 connections east from London to Canterbury and Dover.

A SUGGESTED ITINERARY

Day 1: Head east for an overnight in Royal Tunbridge Wells, with stopover visits at Churchill's former home (Chartwell) and Knole. Before going to Canterbury the next morning, visit Penshurst Place and Hever Castle.

Day 2: Arrive in the late afternoon at Canterbury and visit its cathedral the following morning.

Day 3: Head for Dover to see its white cliffs and castle.

Day 4: Return to London via Maidstone for a visit to Leeds Castle.

Day 5: Continue west to Surrey visiting Dorking and overnighting at Guildford. One or two historic homes nearby can be included.

Kent suffered severe destruction in World War II, as it was the virtual alley over which the Luftwaffe flew in its blitz of London. But in spite of much devastation, it is still filled with interesting old towns, mansions, and castles. The country is also rich in

✓ WHAT'S SPECIAL ABOUT KENT & SURREY

Great Towns/Villages
- ☐ Canterbury, a cathedral city and the headquarters of the Anglican church—center of international pilgrimage.
- ☐ Dover, Britain's historic "gateway" to Continental Europe, famed for its white cliffs.

Castles
- ☐ Knole, one of the largest private houses of England—a great example of purely British Tudor architecture.
- ☐ Hever Castle, from the end of the 13th century, a gift from Henry VIII to the "great Flanders mare," Anne of Cleves.
- ☐ Penshurst Place, a magnificent English Gothic mansion, one of the outstanding country houses of Britain.

- ☐ Leeds Castle, near Maidstone—dating from A.D. 857—once called "the loveliest castle in the world."

Gardens
- ☐ Chilham Castle Gardens, landscaped by Capability Brown on former royal property 6 miles west of Canterbury.
- ☐ Sissinghurst Castle Garden, a garden for all seasons, built between the surviving parts of an Elizabethan mansion.

Historic Homes
- ☐ Chartwell House, former country home of Sir Winston Churchill with much memorabilia.

Dickensian associations—in fact, Kent is sometimes known as Dickens Country. His family once lived near the naval dockyard at Chatham.

Long before William the Conqueror marched his pillaging Normans across its chalky North Downs, Surrey was important to the Saxons. In fact, early Saxon kings were once crowned at what is now Kingston-on-Thames (their Coronation Stone is still preserved near the guildhall).

More recently, this tiny county has been in danger of being gobbled up by the growing boundaries of London. But Surrey still retains much unspoiled countryside, largely because its many heaths and commons form undesirable land for postwar suburban houses. Essentially, Surrey is a country of commuters (Alfred Lord Tennyson was among the first), since a worker in the city can travel to the remotest corner of Surrey from London in anywhere from 45 minutes to an hour.

A STOP EN ROUTE TO CANTERBURY FOR DICKENS FANS

In the cathedral city of Rochester, 30 miles from London, you can visit the **Charles Dickens Centre** (tel. 0634/843666), in Eastgate House, built in 1590, on High Street. The museum has tableaux depicting various scenes from Dickens's novels, including a Pickwickian Christmas scene, then the fever-ridden graveyard of *Bleak House*, scenes from *The Old Curiosity Shop* and *Great Expectations, Oliver Twist*, and *David Copperfield*.

Information is also available at the center on various other sights in Rochester associated with Dickens, including Eastgate House and, in the garden, the chalet transported from Gad's Hill Place, where Dickens died, as well as the Guildhall Museum, Rochester Cathedral, and the mysterious "6 Poor Travelers' House." Pick up a brochure that includes a map featuring the various places and the novels with which each is associated. Admission costs £1.70 ($3.15) for adults, £1.20 ($2.20) for children. It's open daily from 10am to 5pm.

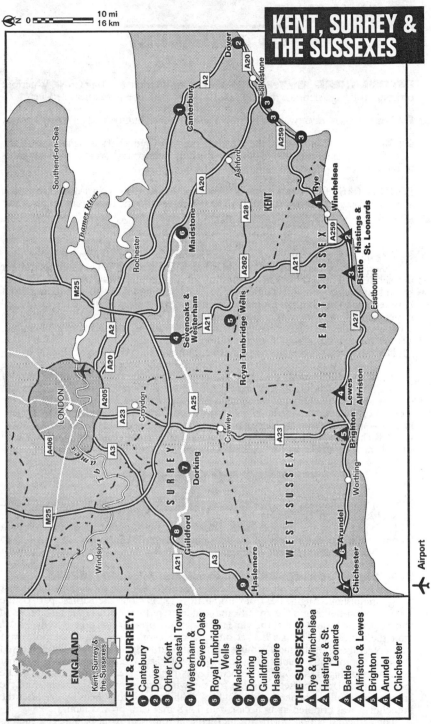

KENT, SURREY &
THE SUSSEXES

Southend-on-Sea

Thames River

Dover

Canterbury

Folkestone

Ashford

A2

A20

A20

A28

A262

A259

A259

Rye

Winchelsea

KENT

Maidstone

Rochester

M25

A2

A20

A205

A21

Sevenoaks & Westerham

Royal Tunbridge Wells

A21

A262

A21

EAST SUSSEX

Hastings & St. Leonards

Battle

Eastbourne

A27

LONDON

A406

Croydon

A23

A25

Crawley

A23

Lewes

Alfriston

Brighton

WEST SUSSEX

Dorking

A3

Worthing

M25

Guildford

A21

A3

Haslemere

Arundel

Chichester

Windsor

Airport

ENGLAND

Kent, Surrey & the Sussexes

KENT & SURREY:
1 Cantebury
2 Dover
3 Other Kent Coastal Towns
4 Westerham & Seven Oaks
5 Royal Tunbridge Wells
6 Maidstone
7 Dorking
8 Guildford
9 Haslemere

THE SUSSEXES:
1 Rye & Winchelsea
2 Hastings & St. Leonards
3 Battle
4 Alfriston & Lewes
5 Brighton
6 Arundel
7 Chichester

0 10 mi
   16 km

1. CANTERBURY

56 miles E of London

GETTING THERE **By Train** By train from Victoria, Charing Cross, Waterloo, or London Bridge stations, the trip takes 1½ hours. There is frequent service.

By Bus Buses leave twice daily from Victoria Coach Station and take 2 to 3 hours.

By Car From London take the A2, then the M2. Canterbury is signposted all the way. The city center is closed to cars, but it's only a short walk from several car parks to the cathedral.

ESSENTIALS The **area code** is 0227. The **Visitors' Information Centre** is at 34 St. Margaret's Street (tel. 0227/766567), a few doors away from St. Margaret Church.

Under the arch of the ancient West Gate journeyed Chaucer's knight, solicitor, nun, squire, parson, merchant, miller, and others—spinning tales. They were bound for the shrine of Thomas Becket, archbishop of Canterbury, who was slain by four knights of Henry II on December 29, 1170. (The king later walked barefoot from Harbledown to the tomb of his former friend, where he allowed himself to be flogged in penance.) The shrine was finally torn down in 1538 by Henry VIII, as part of his campaign to destroy the monasteries and graven images. Canterbury, by then, had already been an attraction of long standing.

The medieval Kentish city, on the River Stour, is the ecclesiastical capital of England. The city was once completely walled, and many traces of its old fortifications remain. Canterbury was known to have been inhabited centuries before the birth of Jesus Christ, and Julius Caesar arrived on the Kent coast in 54 B.C., but Roman occupation didn't begin until much later. Although its most famous incident was the murder of Becket, the medieval city witnessed other major moments in English history—including Bloody Mary's ordering of nearly 40 victims to be burned at the stake. Richard the Lion-Hearted came back this way from crusading, and Charles II passed through on the way to claim his crown.

WHAT TO SEE & DO

From April to October, daily guided tours of Canterbury are organized by the **Guild of Guides,** Arnett House, Hawks Lane (tel. 0227/459779), costing £2 ($3.70).

From just below the Weavers House, boats leave for ½-hour trips on the river with a commentary on the history of the buildings you pass. Umbrellas are provided to protect you against inclement weather.

CANTERBURY CATHEDRAL, The Precincts. Tel. 0227/762862.

The foundation of this splendid cathedral dates back to the coming of the first archbishop, Augustine, from Rome in A.D. 597 but the earliest part of the present building is the great Romanesque crypt built circa 1100. The monastic choir erected on top of this at the same time was destroyed by fire in 1174, only 4 years after the murder of Thomas Becket on a dark December evening in the northwest transept, still one of the most famous places of pilgrimage in Europe. The destroyed choir was immediately replaced by a magnificent early Gothic one, which was first used for worship in 1185. The cathedral was the first great Gothic church to be erected in England and set a fashion for the whole country. Its architects were the Frenchman, William of Sens, and "English" William who took Sens's place after the Frenchman was crippled in an accident in 1178 that later proved fatal.

The cathedral is noteworthy for its medieval tombs of royal personages, such as

King Henry IV and Edward the Black Prince, as well as numerous archbishops. To the later Middle Ages belongs the great 14th-century nave and the famous central "Bell Harry Tower." The cathedral stands in spacious precincts amid the remains of the buildings of the monastery—cloisters, chapter house, and Norman water tower, which have survived intact from the Dissolution in the time of King Henry VIII to the present day.

Becket's shrine was destroyed by the Tudor king, but the site of that tomb is in Trinity Chapel, near the high altar. The saint is said to have worked miracles, and the cathedral contains some rare stained glass depicting those feats. Perhaps the most miraculous event is that the windows escaped Henry VIII's agents of destruction as well as Hitler's bombs. The windows were removed as a precaution at the beginning of the war. During the war, a large area of Canterbury was flattened, but the main body of the church was unharmed. However, the cathedral library was damaged by a German air raid in 1942. The replacement windows of the cathedral were blown in, which proved the wisdom of having the medieval glass safely stored away. East of the Trinity Chapel is "Becket's Crown," in which is a chapel dedicated to "Martyrs and Saints of Our Own Time." St. Augustine's Chair, one of the symbols of the authority of the archbishop of Canterbury, stands behind the high altar.

Open: Summer daily 8:45am–7pm; winter daily 8:45am–5pm.

CANTERBURY TALES, St. Margaret's St. Tel. 0227/454888.
Pilgrim's Way re-creates the Thomas Becket pilgrimage of Chaucerian England. Visitors are taken on a tour through England's Middle Ages and meet some of Chaucer's pilgrims, including the Wife of Bath. Audiovisual techniques bring these characters to life, and stories of jealousy, pride, avarice, and love are recounted.

Admission: £2.50 ($4.65) adults; £1.50 ($1.95) children.
Open: Daily 9:30am–5:30pm. **Directions:** Off High Street near the cathedral.

WHERE TO STAY

Before you can begin any serious exploring, you'll need to find a room, and you have several possibilities within the city itself and on the outskirts.

DOUBLES WITHOUT BATH FOR LESS THAN £30 [$55.50]

ALEXANDRA HOUSE, 1 Roper Rd., Canterbury, Kent CT2 7EH. Tel. 0227/767011. 9 rms (all with shower). TV TEL
$ Rates: (including English breakfast): £16 ($29.60) single; £34 ($62.90) double with bath. No credit cards. **Parking:** Free.

 This guesthouse, off St. Dunstan's Street, is only a few minutes from the old city center and the cathedral. The house is centrally heated, and all rooms have hot-beverage facilities and hot- and cold-water basins in addition to showers.

ANN'S HOTEL, 63 London Rd., Canterbury, Kent CT2 8LR. Tel. 0227/768767. 19 rms (12 with bath). TV
$ Rates: (including English breakfast): £18 ($33.30) single without bath; £25 ($46.25) single with bath; £30 ($55.50) double without bath; £40 ($74) double with bath. AE, MC, V. **Parking:** Free.
This family-owned B&B stands on an artery leading out of town, a 10-minute walk from town center (follow signposts to M2 London). You enter into a Victorian hallway, where Lisa and Horatio Jones rent well-furnished and comfortable bedrooms, some with four-poster beds. Twelve of the rooms have color TVs and coffee-making facilities, and three rooms are on the ground floor. Parking is available.

KINGSBRIDGE VILLA, 15 Best Lane, Canterbury, Kent CT1 2BJ. Tel. 0227/766415. 11 rms (4 with bath). TV
$ Rates (including English breakfast): £16 ($29.60) single without bath; £18 ($33.30) single with bath; £30 ($33.30) double without bath; £40 ($74) double with bath. No credit cards. **Parking:** Free.
Located close to the cathedral, this is a bright, inviting guesthouse. It has comfortable

furnishings, and the bedrooms are well maintained. There's a small restaurant and bar in the basement, which is reached through the house or else by area steps past a medieval well, where they once found a coin dating from A.D. 163. Clay pipes adorn the red-brick walls, and there are comfortable settle seats around the bar.

**KINGSMEAD HOUSE, 68 St. Stephens Rd., Canterbury, Kent CT2 7JF.
Tel. 0227/760132.** 2 rms (both with bath).
$ Rates (including English breakfast): £36–£40 ($66.60–$74) double. No credit cards. **Parking:** Free.

Jan and John Clark, who own this lovely 17th-century house, are one of the most gracious and hospitable couples. The location of their timbered house is about 6 to 8 minutes from the heart of Canterbury off Kingsmead Road. They rent only one twin and one double, each well furnished with central heating.

**MAGNOLIA HOUSE, 36 St. Dunstan's Terrace, Canterbury, Kent CT2
8AX. Tel. 0227/765121.** 6 rms (all with bath). TV
$ Rates (including English breakfast): £20–£25 ($37–$46.25) single; £40–£48 ($74–$88.80) double. AE, MC, V. **Parking:** Free.

Owners Ann and John Davies run this quiet, pleasant Canterbury guesthouse off London Road, which has an interesting garden with a fish pond. The Georgian building stands within easy walking distance of the major sights, and there is limited off-street parking. A reservation is important to secure accommodation. Breakfasts are hearty.

**THE WHITE HOUSE, 6 St. Peter's Lane, Canterbury, Kent CT1 2SP. Tel.
0227/761836.** 5 rms (all with bath or shower). TV
$ Rates (including English breakfast): £35–£40 ($64.75–$74) double; £47 ($86.95) triple; £55 ($101.75) family room for four. No credit cards. **Parking:** £1.20 ($2.20) per night.

You'll find this Regency town house on a quiet lane within the old city walls off St. Peter's Street. The owner rents well-furnished bedrooms, but no singles are available. Breakfast is served around an eight-seat table. Before becoming a B&B, the house was owned by a church, and before that, it was supposedly occupied by the coach driver for Queen Victoria.

**ST. STEPHENS GUEST HOUSE, 100 St. Stephens Rd., Canterbury, Kent
CT2 7JL. Tel. 0227/767644.** 9 rms (4 with bath).
$ Rates (including English breakfast): £16 ($29.60) single, without bath; £30 ($55.50) double without bath; £36 ($66.60) double with bath. MC. **Parking:** Free.

This is in a quiet part of the city, yet is close to the main attractions. Set in well-kept gardens and lawns, St. Stephens is one of the most attractive buildings in Canterbury and is owned and managed by Robin and Valerie Quanstrom. While the character of the house has been retained, the accommodations are modern and include central heating, shaver points, and hot and cold water. The house can accommodate up to 16 guests. A fixed-price dinner is offered in summer for £6.50 ($12). Car parking is available at the rear. It's located off Kingsmead Road.

WORTH THE EXTRA BUCKS

**EBURY HOTEL, 65-67 New Dover Rd., Canterbury, Kent CT1 3DX. Tel.
0227/768433.** Fax 0227/459187. 15 rms (all with bath). TV TEL **Directions:**
Follow signs to A2 Dover Road.
$ Rates (including English breakfast): £35–£38 ($62.90–$70.30) single; £52–£58 ($96.20–$107.30) double. AE, MC, V. **Parking:** Free.

Acclaimed as one of the finest B&B hotels in Canterbury, this is a gabled Victorian house at the edge of the city. It is important to reserve here, as this owner-operated hotel is popular. Rooms are well furnished, roomy, and pleasantly decorated. The hotel has a heated, indoor swimming pool and spa, as well as a spacious lounge and licensed restaurant serving good food made with fresh vegetables.

ERSHAM LODGE, 12 New Dover Rd., Canterbury, Kent CT1 3AP. Tel. 0227/463174. Fax 0227/455482. 14 rms (all with shower). TV TEL
$ Rates (including English breakfast): £45 ($83.25) single; £48–£55 ($93.50–$101.75) double. AE, MC, V. **Parking:** Free.
Owners Mr. and Mrs. Pellay run this pleasant, redecorated lodge 500 yards outside the city walls on the road to Dover. The Tudor-style, 19th-century building is at the edge of town, set back from the road, in the midst of many shade trees, with a garden for children to play in. From the two-story living room, a winding staircase leads to the spacious and comfortably furnished corner bedrooms, which all have radios.

PILGRIMS HOTEL, 18 The Friars, Canterbury, Kent CT1 2AS. Tel. 0227/464531. 13 rms (all with bath). TV TEL
$ Rates (including English breakfast): £25–£27 ($46.25–$49.95) single; £47–£72 ($86.95–$133.20) double. AE, MC, V.
This hotel dates back in part more than 300 years and is just a short walk from the cathedral. Comfort is assured by such items as innerspring mattresses, and all rooms have hot-beverage facilities and a central-heating system. Directly opposite the hotel is the Marlowe Theatre, which has many international personalities with top shows and plays. The hotel has added a restaurant and bar, and there's an adjoining concrete car park, not owned by the hotel.

POINTERS, 1 London Rd., Canterbury, Kent CT2 8LR. Tel. 0227/456846. 14 rms (10 with bath or shower). TV TEL **Directions:** From the center, follow signposts to the M2/London Road.
$ Rates (including English breakfast): £28 ($51.80) single without bath; £35 ($64.75) single with bath; £40 ($74) double without bath; £50 ($92.50) double with bath. AE, DC, MC, V. **Parking:** Free.
One of the city's finest guesthouses, this Georgian building stands across from St. Dunstan's Church. Owner-operated, it offers clean, comfortable rooms, several for single travelers and couples (double- or twin-bedded accommodations), as well as some family units. Bedroom amenities include radios and beverage-making equipment. The location is about a 10-minute walk from the heart of Canterbury, and there is a private car park.

YORKE LODGE, 50 London Rd., Canterbury, Kent CT2 8LF. Tel. 0227/451243. Fax 0227/451243. 6 rms (all with bath). TV TEL **Directions:** Follow signposts to the M2/London Road.
$ Rates (including English breakfast): £22–£30 ($40.70–$55.50) single; £38–£40 ($70.30–$74) double. AE, MC, V. **Parking:** Free.
This spacious, elegant, Victorian guesthouse is close to the city center and the cathedral. The bedrooms for nonsmokers have hot-beverage facilities. There is a sitting room opening onto a walled garden, plus a library well stocked with information about the area. Breakfasts are large and offer variety. The aim of Robin Hall is to pamper his guests; for example, he serves sherry in the lounge to new arrivals. Off-street parking is available.

WHERE TO EAT

MEALS FOR LESS THAN £8.50 ($15.75)

ALBERRYS WINE AND FOOD BAR, 38 St. Margaret's St. Tel. 452378.
Cuisine: INTERNATIONAL. **Reservations:** Not needed.
$ Prices: Appetizers £1.75–£2.95 ($3.25–$5.45); main courses £3.50–£6 ($6.50–$11.10). MC, V.
Open: Mon–Thurs noon–3pm and 6pm–midnight, Fri–Sat noon–midnight.
The Victorian cartoons on Alberrys' wine list claim that "Tomorrow morning you'll be able to perform great feats of strength if you drink plenty of wine tonight." Today, you eat in the same area where slaves of the Romans once toiled (part of the exposed foundation was a section of a Roman amphitheater). Alberrys offers an inexpensive and frequently changing repertoire of well-prepared

food. A meal might include the soup of the day, baked potato filled with chili con carne, followed by Death by Chocolate. Pizzas and quiches are available. Beer and mixed drinks are served, and wine is available by the glass. This is a fun place located in the center near the bus station.

GEORGE'S BRASSERIE, 72 Castle St. Tel. 765658.

Cuisine: FRENCH. **Reservations:** Not needed.
$ Prices: Appetizers £2.60–£5.50 ($4.80–$10.20); main courses £4–£16 ($7.40–$29.60). AE, V.
Open: Mon–Thurs 10am–10pm, Fri–Sat 10am–10:30pm.

 This attractive establishment is run by a brother and sister, Simon Day and Beverly Holmes, who pride themselves on the cleanliness of their restaurant and the quality of their French food, made only of fresh ingredients. They serve everything from coffee and croissant to gourmet meals. On the à la carte listing, numerous appetizers are offered, including a fresh anchovy salad and George's terrines, all served with a basket of French bread. The selection of main dishes changes with the season, but it always includes fish and meat dishes and is served with new potatoes or french fries. The last order time is extended for theatergoers. The brasserie is located between Canterbury East Station and the Cathedral.

IL VATICANO, 35 St. Margaret St. Tel. 765333.

Cuisine: ITALIAN. **Reservations:** Not needed.
$ Prices: Appetizers £1.20–£4.95 ($2.20–$9.15); main courses £4.25–£6.95 ($8.80–$12.85). AE, DC, MC, V.
Open: Mon–Sat 11:30am–10:30pm, Sun noon–10pm.

This is the best-known pasta parlor in Canterbury. All pasta is made on the premises, and you get a choice of sauces, including bolognese, carbonara, or napolitana. Lasagne, cannelloni, and ravioli are also on the menu. The restaurant, decorated in a simple but sophisticated trattoria style, with bentwood chairs, small marble-topped tables, and exposed brick, lies off High Street in the commercial center of the city.

QUEEN ELIZABETH'S TEAROOM, 44-45 High St. Tel. 464080.

Cuisine: ENGLISH. **Reservations:** Not needed.
$ Prices: Appetizers all £1.50 ($2.80); main courses £3–£4 ($5.55–$7.40). No credit cards.
Open: Tues–Sat 10am–6pm.

The 16th-century interior, with its outstanding relief and wall paneling, recaptures the past admirably. Of special interest is the original room where Queen Elizabeth I entertained the Duke of Alençon while she was trying to decide whether to marry him. The food is fresh and home-cooked—from the rich-tasting soups, such as cream of vegetable, to the roast beef and vegetables, to the deep-dish apple pie with whipped cream for dessert. If you go early enough, select the seat next to the window so you can look down the High Street. English afternoon tea is a specialty. The restaurant is on Main Street; you can spot it easily by its gabled facade, which has plaster carving.

EASY EXCURSIONS FROM CANTERBURY

HOWLETTS ZOO PARK

At Bekesbourne, 3 miles southeast of Canterbury, the 55-acre Howletts Zoo Park (tel. 0227/721286), is John Aspinall's first zoo. Visitors can spy the lovely Sambar deer, the delicate blackbuck, and the Nilghai and hog deer. Around the perimeter, you will see the beautiful bongo, Siberian and Indian tigers, the four-horned Chousinga, gibbons, small cats, dhole, leopards, golden lion tamarins, and Javan Langurs, plus the first U.K.-born African elephants in a herd environment.

But Howletts is really famous for the world's largest gorilla colony. It is the aim of John Aspinall, who can often be seen playing with the gorillas on weekends, to return a family group back to the wilds of Africa.

Admission: £5.50 ($10.20) adults, £3.50 ($6.50) children 4–14.

Open: Daily 10am–5pm, or 1 hour before dusk. **Directions:** Signposted off the A2 southeast of Canterbury.

CHILHAM VILLAGE & CHILHAM CASTLE GARDENS

In Chilham Village, 6 miles west of Canterbury, Chilham Castle Gardens (tel. 0227/730319) were originally laid out by Tradescant and later landscaped by Lancelot "Capability" Brown. On a former royal property, the gardens are magnificent and look out over the Stour Valley. A Norman castle used as a hunting lodge once stood here and was frequented by more than one royal personage until King Henry VIII sold it. The Jacobean castle, built between 1603 and 1616 by Sir Dudley Digges (whose descendant was governor-general of Virginia), was reputedly designed by Inigo Jones and is one of the best examples extant of the architecture of its day; it's built around a hexagonal open-ended courtyard. Medieval banquets are held in the gothic hall throughout the year.

The castle is not open to the public—only the gardens. They are open from early April to mid-October daily from 11am to 6pm (last entry at 5pm). Admission is £2.50 ($4.65) for adults and £1.25 ($2.30) for children Tuesday, Wednesday, Thursday, Saturday, and Sunday; £2.20 ($4.05) for adults and £1.10 ($2.80) for children Monday and Friday. There are special events on some weekends in the season for which different admission prices are charged. Birds of prey are flown at 3:30pm on Tuesday through Thursday and Saturday and Sunday.

The little village of Chilham has a lively small square with a church at one end, the castle at the other, and a mass of half-timbered buildings interspersed with old, red-brick houses. It is on the A252 Canterbury-Maidstone road and the A28 Canterbury-Ashford road.

BROADSTAIRS

Northeast of Canterbury on the seacoast, Broadstairs was Dickens's favorite seaside resort, lying 78 miles east of London. The **Dickens House Museum,** on the main seafront (tel. 0843/62853) was once the home of Mary Pearson Strong, on whom Dickens based much of the character of Betsey Trotwood, David Copperfield's aunt. Admission is 60p ($1.10) adults; 35p (65¢) children. It's open April through October daily from 2:30 to 5:30pm. **Bleak House,** on Fort Road (tel. 0843/62224), a mansion high on the cliffs, was occupied by Dickens at the peak of his fame and inspired the title of one of his greatest works, *Bleak House.* Here he entertained many men famous in art and literature, and he wrote the greater part of *David Copperfield* during his sojourn here. The property also contains a Maritime Museum. An exhibit, "The Golden Age of Smuggling, 1780–1830," is in the cellar.

Admission: is £1.50 ($2.80) adults, 85p ($1.55) children under 12. It's open Easter through June daily from 10am to 6pm, Oct through Nov from 10am to 6pm, and July through September daily from 10am to 9pm.

2. DOVER

76 miles SE of London; 84 miles E of Brighton

GETTING THERE   By Train   Frequent trains run between Victoria Station or Charing Cross Station in London and Dover daily from 5am to 10pm. Arrivals in Dover are at Priory Station (tel. 0304/45-4411), off Folkestone Road. During the day two trains per hour depart Canterbury East Station heading for Dover.

By Bus   Frequent daily buses leave from London's Victoria Station bound for Dover. The local bus station is at Pencester Road (tel. 0304/240024). There is also frequent daily service between Canterbury and Dover.

By Car   From London, head first to Canterbury (see above), then continue along A2 southeast until you reach Dover on the coast.

ESSENTIALS The **area code** for Dover is 0304. The **Tourist Information Centre** is on Townwall Street (tel. 0304/205108).

One of the ancient Cinque Ports, Dover is famed for its white cliffs. In Victoria's day, it basked in popularity as a seaside resort, but today it is known as the port for major cross-channel car and passenger traffic between England and France (notably Calais). Dover was one of England's most vulnerable and easy-to-hit targets during World War II and suffered repeated bombings that destroyed much of its harbor.

WHAT TO SEE & DO

DOVER CASTLE, Castle Hill. Tel. 0304/201628.

Hovering nearly 400 feet above the port is one of the oldest and best known castles in England. Its keep was built at the command of Becket's fair-weather friend, Henry II, in the 12th century. The ancient castle was called back to active duty as late as World War II. The "Pharos" on the grounds is a lighthouse built by the Romans in the first half of the 1st century. The Romans first landed at nearby Deal in 54 B.C., but after 6 months they departed and did not return until nearly 100 years later, in A.D. 43, when they stayed and occupied the country for 400 years. The castle houses a military museum and a film center, and the restaurant is open all year.

Admission: £3 ($5.55) adults, £1.50 ($2.80) children.

Open: Apr–Sept daily 10am–6pm; off-season daily 10am–4pm. **Bus:** No. 90 bound for Deal.

HELLFIRE CORNER, Dover Castle, Castle Hill. Tel. 0304/201628.

Originally excavated to house cannons to counter the threat of an invasion by Napoléon, these secret tunnels were used during the evacuation from Dunkirk in 1940 and the Battle of Britain. Two hundred feet below ground, they were the headquarters of Operation Dynamo, which saw the evacuation of more than 300,000 troops from Dunkirk. For years, they were on the top-secret list, but now can be explored on a guided tour.

Admission: £1 ($1.85) adults, 50p (95¢) children.

Open: Same hours as castle (see above).

ROMAN PAINTED HOUSE, New St. Tel. 0304/203279.

This spectacular 1,800-year-old Roman mansion (hotel) has exceptionally well-preserved walls and an underfloor heating system. It is famous for its unique Bacchic murals and is the winner of four National Awards for presentation.

Admission: £1 ($1.85) adults, 50p (95¢) children.

Open: Apr–Oct Tues–Sun 10am–5pm. **Directions:** Off York Street near the bus station.

WHERE TO STAY

Because of the cross-channel traffic, Dover operates in a sellers' market, so hotel prices tend to run high; however, I've listed some bargains below.

DOUBLES WITH SHOWER FOR LESS THAN £39 [$72.15]

In Town

ARDMORE PRIVATE HOTEL, 18 Castle Hill Rd., Dover, Kent CT16 1QW. Tel. 0304/205895. 4 rms (all with bath). TV

$ Rates (including English breakfast): £19.50 ($36.10) single; £39 ($72.15) double. No credit cards.

The Morrisses operate this hotel and have done extensive redecoration of this 200-year-old building. There are four double or twin rooms and family rooms with hot-beverage facilities and double-glazed windows, and some rooms have views of the harbor. It stands next to Dover Castle.

BEULAH HOUSE, 94 Crabble Hill, London Rd., Dover, Kent CT17 0SA. Tel. 0304/824615. 20 rms (1 with shower).
$ Rates (including English breakfast): £18–£20 ($33.30–$37) single without bath; £34 ($62.90) double without bath, £36 ($66.60) double with shower. No credit cards. **Parking:** £2 ($3.70).

 This comfortably furnished house is run by its namesake, Beulah Abate, along with her husband, Donald. Each room has hot and cold running water, and the breakfasts are bountiful. What makes the house appealing is its gardens in back, which have sculptured yews and roses. The hotel is on the A256 (A2) road to London.

NUMBER ONE GUEST HOUSE, 1 Castle St., Dover, Kent CT16 1QH. Tel. 0304/202007. 5 rms (all with shower). TV
$ Rates (including English breakfast): £17 ($31.45) per person, double occupancy. No credit cards.
Built in 1800, this charming Georgian house overlooked by the castle is one of Dover's oldest remaining homes and is centrally located for the town and fort. John and Adeline Reidy offer comfortable twin, double, and family rooms, where you will find courtesy coffee and where you will be served breakfast. At the rear of this cozy, well-maintained house is a walled garden where one can relax on summer evenings. It's a 2-minute walk from Market Square.

ST. MARTINS GUEST HOUSE, 17 Castle Hill Rd., Dover, Kent CT16 1QW. Tel. 0304/205938. 9 rms (8 with shower). TV
$ Rates (including English breakfast): £20 ($37) single without bath, £25 ($46.25) single with shower; £35 ($64.75) double with shower. MC.
A few blocks from the cross-channel ferries and the hoverport, on the hillside leading to Dover Castle, this hotel is run by Mr. and Mrs. Morriss. The house is more than 150 years old and is maintained and furnished to high standards, with full central heating. The bedrooms with double-glazed windows have hot-beverage facilities, and most have private showers. The house has a guest lounge and a residential license. Ample parking is available.

WESTBANK GUEST HOUSE, 239 Folkestone Rd., Dover, Kent CT17 9LL. Tel. 0304/201061. 5 rms (2 with bath). TV
$ Rates (including English breakfast): £15 ($27.75) single without bath, £17 ($31.45) single with bath; £27 ($49.95) double without bath. No credit cards. **Parking:** Free.

 One of the best B&B houses in the area, this offers clean, comfortable, and well-appointed units, each with hot and cold running water and hot-beverage facilities. If they're given a few hour's notice, the hosts will provide an evening meal at £6.50 ($12.05) per person. It's located at the western outskirts along the A20.

On the Outskirts

FINGLESHAM GRANGE, Finglesham, near Deal, Kent CT14 0NQ. Tel. 0304/611314. 3 rms (all with bath or shower).
$ Rates (including English breakfast): £19.50 ($36.10) per person. No credit cards. **Parking:** Free.
On the coast about 8 miles northeast of Dover, 2 miles from Eastry village between A256 and A258, this stylish country house stands on 4½ acres of grounds. The house, run by Mr. and Mrs. R. W. Styles, is within easy reach of the channel ports, beaches, golf courses, and the Kentish countryside. Breakfast (plus morning and afternoon tea and a good-night drink) is offered to no more than six guests at a time, who stay in the

spacious double rooms. Guests can use the lounge with a TV and the billiard room, and evening meals can be served if arranged in advance. The Styleses are an accommodating and helpful couple.

WALLETT'S COURT, West Cliffe, St. Margaret-at-Cliffe, Dover, Kent CT15 6EW. Tel. 0304/852424. Fax 0304/853430. 7 rms (all with bath). TV TEL **Directions:** Take the B2058 to West Cliffe.

$ Rates (including English breakfast): £35–£53 ($64.75–$98.05) single; £42–£60 ($77.70–$111) double. MC, V. **Parking:** Free.

This hotel stands on about 3½ acres some 3 miles east of Dover. A building has stood on this site for nearly 1,000 years, and the present manor is a restored structure from the 17th century. Two of the accommodations are set aside for families. Thoughtful extras, such as fresh flowers in the rooms, make this an exceptional choice. A three-course dinner served from 7 to 8:30pm Monday to Friday costs £15 ($27.75), while a five-course repast on Saturday at 8:30pm costs £23 ($42.55).

WHERE TO EAT

Finding a good place to eat in Dover is not easy, but I have two recommendations. They're both in the town center.

BRITTANIA, 41 Townwall St. Tel. 203248.
   Cuisine: ENGLISH. **Reservations:** Recommended for restaurant.
   $ Prices: Appetizers £2–£4 ($3.70–$7.40); main courses £4–£10 ($7.40–$18.50). AE, MC, V.
   Open: Pub Mon–Sat 11am–11pm; Sun noon–3pm and 7–10:30pm; restaurant Mon–Sat noon–2pm and 3–9pm, Sun noon–9pm.

If you gravitate to typically English, pub-style meals, try this restaurant, near the seafront. It has a bow window, along with gilt and brass nautical accents on its ivory facade. A popular pub is on the ground floor, and the restaurant is one floor above street level. Try a prawn cocktail or a pâté for an appetizer, followed by rumpsteak or a mixed grill. Many different salads are offered, including one made with salmon, another with ham. Dover sole is a specialty.

RISTORANTE AL PORTO, 43 Townwall St. Tel. 204615.
   Cuisine: ITALIAN. **Reservations:** Required.
   $ Prices: Appetizers £1.10–£4.95 ($2.05–$9.15); main courses £5–£9.80 ($9.25–$18.15). AE, DC, MC, V.
   Open: Lunch Mon–Sat noon–2:30pm; dinner Mon–Sat 7–10:30pm.

One block from the landing dock of the ferry boats, this Italian-owned restaurant is decorated in a nautical style, with fishnets hanging from the ceiling. It offers one of the largest menus in town, featuring such specialties as steak in a black pepper, cream, and brandy sauce, along with cannelloni or succulent veal in a sauce of mushrooms, garlic, and tomatoes. Try the gelati misti (mixed ice cream) for dessert and a cup of espresso.

EASY EXCURSIONS

WALMER CASTLE AND GARDENS, Kingsdown Rd., Deal. Tel. 0304/364288.

Walmer Castle and Gardens, about 6 miles north of Dover, just south of Deal on the Strait of Dover, was one of some 20 coastal forts built by Henry VIII to protect England from invasion from the Continent. It is shaped like a Tudor rose, with a central three-story tower, and is surrounded by a moat, now dry. In the early 18th century, it became the official residence of the Lords Warden of the Cinque Ports, among them William Pitt the Younger and the Duke of Wellington, who died here in 1852. The duke's furnished rooms and possessions, including a uniform and his telescope, can be seen. Also preserved are rooms occupied by Queen Victoria and Prince Albert during visits. The magnificent formal gardens were laid out by Lady Hester Stanhope in 1805. A plaque at this location marks the spot where Julius Caesar is supposed to have landed in Britain in 54 B.C.

Admission: £2.20 ($4.05) adults, £1.10 ($2.05) children.
Open: Mid-Mar to mid-Oct Tues–Sat 9:30am–6:30pm, Sun 2–6:30pm; mid-Oct to mid-Mar Tues–Sat 9:30am–4pm, Sun 2–4pm.

DEAL CASTLE, on the seafront. Tel. 0304/372762.

Deal Castle is just a mile north of Walmer Castle and is a mile south of the Deal town center. A defensive fort built about 1540, it is the most spectacular example of the low, squat forts constructed by Henry VIII. Its 119 gun positions made it the most powerful of his defense forts. Centered around a circular keep surrounded by two rings of semicircular bastions, the castle was protected by an outer moat. The entrance was approached by a drawbridge with a portcullis. The castle was damaged by bombs during World War II but has been restored to its early form. An exhibition on coastal defenses is in the basement.

Admission: £1.15 ($2.15) adults, 60p ($1.10) children.
Open: Mid-Mar to mid-Oct Tues–Sat 9:30am–6:30pm, Sun 2–6:30pm, mid-Oct to mid-Mar Tues–Sat 9:30am–4pm, Sun 2–4pm.

3. OTHER KENT COASTAL TOWNS

Folkestone is a popular resort and major cross-channel port, lying 76 miles southeast of London and 8 miles directly west of Dover (reached along the A20). Hythe (see below) lies 6 miles directly west of Folkestone and is reached by continuing along the coastal road. From Hythe, continue along A259 to reach New Romney.

If you're rushed for time, it is best to have a rented car to explore the following attractions, as public transportation may be too cumbersome. You can, however, take a train from Charing Cross in London to Folkestone, where bus connections can be made to Hythe and New Romney.

FOLKESTONE-HYTHE
THREE NEARBY ATTRACTIONS

KENT BATTLE OF BRITAIN MUSEUM, Hawkings Airfield, Aerodrome Rd., Hawkings, near Folkestone. Tel. 030389/3140.

On a Battle of Britain airfield, this museum contains the most extensive collection of artifacts from this famous battle. Engines, parts of downed aircraft, photographs, equipment, and letters from RAF pilots are on display in the once-abandoned airfield buildings. The location is on A260 between Folkestone and Canterbury.

Admission: £2.50 ($4.65) adults, £1.50 ($2.80) children.
Open: Easter–Oct daily 10am–5pm.

LYMPNE CASTLE, near Hythe, Kent. Tel. 0303/267571.

Near Hythe stands the small, medieval Lympne Castle built in the 14th century on land that was given to the church at Lympne in the 18th century. There is mention of a Saxon abbey on the site in the *Domesday Book* of 1085. Right on the edge of a cliff, the castle has magnificent views over the channel and across Romney Marsh to Fairlight. An ideal lookout against invasion, it has a Norman tower in the east and a medieval one to the west, with turret stairways leading to the main rooms, including the great hall.

Besides the building and its furnishings, there are exhibits of toys and dolls and full-size reproductions of church brasses, as well as a small period costume display.

Admission: £1.50 ($2.80) adults, 50p (95¢) children 5–14.
Open: Easter–September daily 10:30am–6pm. **Directions:** The castle is 8 miles from Folkestone and 4 miles from Hythe off the B2067 Hythe-Aldington road and 2 miles from Junction 11 of the M20 motorway.

PORT LYMPNE ZOO PARK, MANSION, AND GARDENS, Lympne, near Hythe, Kent. Tel. 0303/264646.

John Aspinall's second zoo houses rare and endangered species in spacious enclosures in 300 acres of park and woodland. Visitors can take a 2-mile cross-country trek or shorter walks to see the animals in their natural settings. Included are Asian elephants, Siberian and Indian tigers, Barbary lions, and Przewalski horses (the latter two extinct in the wild), snow leopards, Canadian timber wolves, maned wolves, Cape hunting dogs, honey badgers, black and Sumatran rhinos, small cats, chimps, gibbons, and other rare animals.

You can also visit the historic mansion built in 1912 in Dutch Colonial style, called "the last historic house built in the United Kingdom this century." Features include a rare Rex Whistler Tent Room, the Moroccan patio, the hexagonal library where the Treaty of Paris was commenced after World War I, the newly commissioned and completed Spencer Roberts Southeast Asian Mural Room depicting more than 200 different species of animals and birds, a remarkable Trojan stairway with 125 steps from which you can see across Romney Marsh to France on a clear day, and the Conservatory Restaurant, with full bar facilities. The mansion is surrounded by 15 acres of terraced gardens.

Admission: £5 ($9.25) adults, £3 ($5.55) children 4–14.

Open: Daily 10am–5pm, or 1 hour before dusk. **Directions:** Lies 3 miles west of Hythe.

NEW ROMNEY

WHAT TO SEE & DO

The **Romney, Hythe & Dymchurch Light Railway Co.,** New Romney Station, New Romney (tel. 0679/62353), is the world's smallest public railway. The engines are mostly steam driven, and the carriages are covered so there's no fear of getting wet. The 13½-mile line runs from Hythe (Kent) to New Romney and Dungeness, and the trains are one-third-size miniature versions of the kind of trains that ran on English or North American main-line railways in the 1920s. The ride takes about an hour.

Fares depend on the distance traveled. An ordinary round-trip ticket from Hythe to Dungeness costs £6.60 ($12.25) for adults. It is valid on the date of issue for unlimited travel on the line. Children travel for half the adult fare. It operates from Easter to the end of September daily, with service in March and October on Saturday and Sunday only. Telephone for train times.

The terminal of the railway, Hythe, is near Folkestone, which can be reached by frequent trains from London. The railway is reached by road along the A259. Leave Canterbury on the Dover road; 5 miles out turn right and the town of Elham is 5 miles farther. A right turn and another 5 miles will take you to Hythe.

---

4. WESTERHAM & SEVEN OAKS

Near Westerham is one of the major attractions of Kent, Chartwell (Churchill's home) and in the vicinity are several more historic homes. All of these are more conveniently visited by car, but public transportation is available to some of them. From London's Victoria Station, trains run daily to Westerham, where taxis will be waiting to fan out to such places as Chartwell. If you're driving from London, head east along the M25, taking the exit to Westerham where the B2026 leads to Chartwell (road is signposted).

The town of Seven Oaks lies 26 miles east of London and there is frequent train service daily from London's Victoria Station. Seven Oaks has a certain charm but most visitors pass through here to visit one of the premier attractions of Southeast England, Knole, ancestral home of the Sackville family.

WESTERHAM

QUÉBEC HOUSE, Québec Square. Tel. 0959/62206.

An attraction for Canadian readers in particular is the square, red-brick, gabled house where James Wolfe, the English general who defeated the French in the battle for Québec, lived until he was 11 years old. A National Trust property, it contains an exhibition about the capture of Québec and memorabilia associated with the military hero, who was born in Westerham on January 2, 1727.

Admission: £1.70 ($3.15) adults, 90p ($1.65) children.

Open: Apr–Oct Sun–Wed and Fri 2–6pm. **Directions:** At the junction of the Edenbridge and Seven Oaks roads (the A25 and the B2026).

SQUERRYES COURT, just west of Westerham (signposted from the A25). Tel. 0959/62345.

This is a William and Mary–period manor house built in 1681 and owned by the Warde family for 250 years. Besides a fine collection of paintings, tapestries, and furniture, there is a collection of pictures and relics of the family of General Wolfe, who received his military commission in the grounds of the house at a spot marked by a cenotaph.

Admission: £2.40 ($4.45) adults, £1.40 ($2.60) children.

Open: House and grounds Mar Sun 2–6pm; Apr–Sept Wed, Sat–Sun, and bank holidays 2–6pm.

AN EXCURSION TO CHURCHILL'S HOME

For many years, Sir Winston lived at **Chartwell** (tel. 072/866368), which lies 2 miles south of Westerham in Kent, off the B2026, 26 miles east of London. Churchill, a descendant of the first Duke of Marlborough, was born in grand style at Blenheim Palace on November 30, 1874. Chartwell doesn't pretend to be as grand a place as Blenheim, but it's been preserved as a memorial. The rooms remain as Churchill left them, including maps, documents, photographs, pictures, and other personal mementos. In two rooms are displayed a selection of gifts that the prime minister received from people all over the world. There is also a selection of many of his well-known uniforms. Terraced gardens descend toward the lake, where you'll find black swans. Many of Churchill's paintings are in a garden studio.

Administered by the National Trust, Churchill's house, is open to the public April to October from noon to 5pm on Tuesday, Wednesday, and Thursday, and from 11am to 5pm on Saturday and Sunday. In March and November, it's open from 11am to 4pm on Wednesday, Saturday, and Sunday. The gardens and Churchill's studio are closed in March and November. Admission to the house only in March and November is £2.20 ($4.05); to the house and garden April to October, £3.70 ($6.85); to the garden only, £1.50 ($2.80); and to Churchill's studio only, 50p (95¢). Children enter for half price. A restaurant on the grounds serves from 10:30am to 5pm during days when the house is open.

A STOP EN ROUTE FROM LONDON

SEVEN OAKS

Down House, Luxted Road, Downe, Orpington (tel. 0689/859119), was the home of Charles Darwin from 1842 until his death in 1882. The drawing room and old study are restored to how they were when Darwin was working on his famous—and still controversial—book, *On the Origin of Species,* first published in 1859. The museum also includes collections and memorabilia from Darwin's voyage on the HMS *Beagle.* There is a room dedicated to his famous grandfather, Dr. Erasmus Darwin, and a modest exhibit on evolution is in the new study, the last room to be added to the house. An important feature of the museum is the garden, which retains original landscaping and a glass house, beyond which lies the Sand Walk or "Thinking Path," where Darwin took his daily solitary walk. The village of Downe is 5½ miles south of Bromley off A233. Admission is £1.50 ($2.80) adults, 50p (95¢) children. To get there from London's Victoria Station, take a daily train to Bromley South, then go by bus no. 146 to Downe. The bus does not run on Sunday. Downe House lies ¼ mile southeast of the village of Bromley along Luxted Road.

Two Nearby Attractions

KNOLE, at south end of town of Knole, east of A225, opposite St. Nicholas Church. Tel. 0732/450608.

✪ Begun in the mid-15th century by Thomas Bourchier, archbishop of Canterbury, Knole is one of the largest private houses in England and is considered one of the finest examples of purely British Tudor style architecture. It is set in a 1,000-acre deer park, 5 miles north of Tunbridge, at the Tunbridge end of the town of Seven Oaks. Virginia Woolf, often a guest of the Sackvilles, used Knole as the location for her novel *Orlando*.

Henry VIII liberated the former archbishop's palace from the church in 1537. He spent considerable sums of money on Knole, but there is little record of his spending much time here after extracting the place from the reluctant Archbishop Cranmer; history records one visit only, in 1541. It was then a royal palace until Queen Elizabeth I granted it to Thomas Sackville, first earl of Dorset, whose descendants have lived here ever since. The great hall and the Brown Gallery are Bourchier rooms, early 15th century, both much altered by the first earl, who made other additions in about 1603. The earl was also responsible for the Great Painted Staircase. The house covers 7 acres and has 365 rooms, 52 staircases, and seven courts. The elaborate paneling and plasterwork provide a background for the 17th- and 18th-century tapestries and rugs, Elizabethan and Jacobean furniture, and the collection of family portraits. The building was given to the National Trust in 1946.

Admission: To the house £3 ($5.55) adults, £1.50 ($2.80) children. On Fri (except Good Friday), extra rooms in Lord Sackville's private apartments are shown, costing £3.50 ($6.50) adults, £1.80 ($3.35) children for the more complete tour. Gardens only 60p ($1.10) adults, 30p (55¢) children.

Open: House Apr–Oct Wed–Sat and bank holidays 11am–5pm, Sun 2–5pm; closed Nov–Mar. Last admission is an hour before closing. Gardens May–Sept only on the first Wed of the month. Park open daily to pedestrians; cars are allowed to enter when the house is open.

Transportation: Frequent train service is available from London (about every 30 min.) to Seven Oaks, and then you can take a taxi or walk the remaining 1½ miles to Knole.

IGHTHAM MOTE, Ivy Hatch, Seven Oaks. Tel. 0732/810378.

A National Trust property, Ightham Mote is well worth a stop if you're in the area. It was extensively remodeled in the early 16th century, and the Tudor chapel with its painted ceiling, the timbered outer walls, and the ornate chimneys reflect that period. A stone bridge crosses the moat and leads into the central courtyard overlooked by the magnificent windows of the great hall. The rest of the house is built around the courtyard. From the great hall, a Jacobean staircase leads to the old chapel on the first floor, where you go through the solarium, with an oriel window, to the Tudor chapel.

Unlike many other ancient houses of England that have been lived in by the same family for centuries, Ightham Mote passed from owner to owner, each family leaving its mark on the place. When the last private owner, an American who was responsible for a lot of the restoration, died, he bequeathed the house to the National Trust.

Admission: £3 ($5.55) adults and £1.50 ($2.80) children weekdays; £3.50 ($6.50) adults, £1.80 ($3.35) children on Sun.

Open: Apr–October Mon, Thurs, and Fri noon–5:30pm, Sun 11am–5:30pm.

Directions: 2½ miles south of Ightham, off the A227, 6 miles east of Seven Oaks.

---

4. ROYAL TUNBRIDGE WELLS

36 miles SE of London; 33 miles NE of Brighton

GETTING THERE   By Train   Two to three trains per hour leave London's Charing Cross Station a day bound for Hastings but going via the town center of Royal Tunbridge Wells. The trip takes 50 minutes.

By Bus   There are no direct bus links with Gatwick Airport or London. However, there is hourly service during the day between Brighton and Royal Tunbridge Wells (call 0273/606605 for the bus schedule). You can purchase tickets aboard the bus.

By Car   After reaching the ring road around London, from whichever part of London you're in, continue east along the M25, cutting southeast at the exit for A21 to Hastings.

ESSENTIALS   The **area code** is 0892. The **Tourist Information Centre,** Monson House, Monson Way (tel. 0892/515675), will provide you with a full accommodation list and also offer a room reservations service.

Dudley Lord North, courtier to James I, is credited with the accidental discovery in 1606 of the mineral spring that led to the creation of a fashionable resort. Over the years the "Chalybeate Spring" became known for its curing properties and was considered the answer for everything from too many days of wine and roses to failing sexual prowess. It is still possible to "take the water" today.

The spa resort reached its peak in the mid-18th century under the foppish patronage of "Beau" Nash (1674–1761), a dandy and final arbiter on how to act, what to say, and even what to wear.

Tunbridge Wells continued to enjoy a prime spa reputation through to the reign of Queen Victoria, who used to holiday here as a child, and in 1909 Tunbridge Wells received its Royal status.

The most remarkable feature of Royal Tunbridge Wells is **"The Pantiles,"** a colonnaded walkway for shoppers, tea drinkers, and diners, built near the walls. The town boasts many other interesting and charming spots which can be viewed on a walk around the town, and a wide variety of entertainment is presented at the Assembly Hall and Trinity Arts Centre.

Canadians touring in the area may want to seek out the grave of the founder of their country's capital. Lt. Col. John By of the Royal Engineers (1779–1836) died at Shernfold Park in Frant, East Sussex, near Tunbridge Wells, and is buried in the churchyard there. His principal claim to fame is that he established what was later to be the capital of the Dominion of Canada, the city of Ottawa, and built the Rideau Canal.

Within easy touring distance from Royal Tunbridge Wells are a number of castles, gardens, and stately homes, all of with their own history and beauty; for example, Sissinghurst Castle, the home of novelist Vita Sackville-West, and Chartwell, former home of Sir Winston Churchill.

WHERE TO STAY

DOUBLES WITHOUT BATH FOR LESS THAN £32 ($59.20)

BANKSIDE, 6 Scotts Way, Royal Tunbridge Wells, Kent TN2 SRG. Tel. 0892/31776. 2 rms (none with bath).
$ Rates (including English breakfast): £23–£28 ($42.55–$51.80) double. No credit cards. **Parking:** Free.
For a real taste of English hospitality, try this guesthouse, located in a quiet neighborhood within walking distance of the restaurants, attractions, the train station. Mrs. Anne Kibbey offers pleasant, comfortable rooms, either double or twin (no singles). Her English breakfast will fortify you for the day.

CLARKEN GUEST HOUSE, 61 Frant Rd., Royal Tunbridge Wells, Kent TN2 5HL. Tel. 0892/33397. 9 rms (2 with bath). TV.
$ Rates (including English breakfast): £16–£24 ($29.60–$44.40) per person. No credit cards. **Parking:** Free.

This spacious, comfortable, 19th-century home is on the principal road between Eastbourne and Hastings. It lies about a 15-minute walk from the main train station, where rail connections are made into London. It is almost the same distance to the Pantiles. Two of the bedrooms are suitable for families.

GROSVENOR GUEST HOUSE, 215 Upper Grosvenor Rd., Royal Tunbridge Wells, Kent TN1 2EG. Tel. 0892/32601. 5 rms (none with bath). TV **Bus:** No. 218.

$ Rates (including English breakfast): £15 ($27.75) single; £30 ($55.50) double. No credit cards. **Parking:** Free.

One of the better B&B houses at the spa, this is owned by Paul and Jackie Tripley, who see that each guest is made comfortable. The house has full central heating, and the three double bedrooms and two family rooms have hot and cold running water. The Tripleys offer evening meals at moderate prices if arranged in advance, and the English breakfast is filling. There is parking for five cars.

HOUSE OF FLOWERS, 80 Ravenswood Ave., Royal Tunbridge Wells, Kent TN2 3SJ. Tel. 0892/523069. 3 rms (none with bath). TV

$ Rates (including English breakfast): £12 ($22.20) single; £24 ($44.40) double. No credit cards. **Parking:** Free.

This hotel takes its name not from the famous Broadway musical, but from a flower conservatory within the building, which is a 30-minute walk from the heart of the old spa, northeast of the center in the Sherwood residential district. A large English breakfast with homemade preserves is served. Joan Still is a welcoming hostess.

WHERE TO EAT

MEALS FOR LESS THAN £16 ($29.60)

CHEEVERS, 56 High St. Tel. 545524.
Cuisine: CONTINENTAL. **Reservations:** Required.
$ Prices: Appetizers £2.50–£4.50 ($4.65–$8.35); main courses £6.50–£12 ($12.05–$22.20). MC, V.
Open: Lunch Tues–Sat noon–2:30pm; dinner Tues–Sat 7–10:30pm. **Closed:** 1 week in Aug (dates vary).

This bustling little brasserie on the main street offers professional and polite service. The cookery is sound, as are the ingredients. The menu is wisely limited and is likely to include pheasant pot roast or a velvety mousse of crab wrapped in spinach. The wine list is reasonably priced.

EGLANTINE, 65 High St. Tel. 524957.
Cuisine: ENGLISH. **Reservations:** Required.
$ Prices: Appetizers £2.50–£4.50 ($4.65–$8.35); main dishes £6.50–£13 ($12.05–$24.05); set lunch £12 ($22.20); set dinner £19 ($35.15). AE, MC, V.
Open: Lunch Tues–Sat 12:15–1:45pm; dinner Mon–Fri 7:15–9:30pm, Sat 7:15–10pm.

The owner and chef of this charming little restaurant on the main street, Susan Richardson, offers a short but delectable menu. Her cooking is based on the freshest and best produce and ingredients available in every season. Food is beautifully presented and served. You might begin with a fruit-flavored poultry terrine, then follow with one of her fresh fish dishes, and end with a dessert prepared fresh daily, perhaps a gratin of strawberry.

EASY EXCURSIONS

PENSHURST PLACE, at Penshurst, near Tonbridge. Tel. 0892/870307.

A magnificent English Gothic mansion, this is one of the outstanding country houses in Britain. In 1338, Sir John de Pulteney, four times lord mayor of London, built the manor house whose great hall still forms the heart of Penshurst—after more than 600 years. The boy king, Edward VI, presented the house to Sir William Sidney, and it has remained in that family ever since. It was the birthplace in 1554 of Sir Philip Sidney, the soldier-poet. In the first half of the 17th century, Penshurst was known as a center of literature and attracted such personages as Ben Jonson, who was inspired by the estate to write one of his greatest poems. Today it is the home of William Philip Sidney, the Viscount De L'Isle. Lord De L'Isle was in Winston Churchill's cabinet in the 1950s and governor-general of Australia in the 1960s.

The Nether Gallery, below the Long Gallery, which contains a suite of ebony and ivory furniture from Goa, houses the Sidney family collection of armor. Visitors can also view the splendid state dining room. In the Stable Wing is an interesting toy museum.

Admission to the house and grounds is £3.50 ($6.50) for adults, £1.75 ($3.25) for children. It's open from April to the last Sunday in September Tuesday to Sunday—and it is open on Good Friday and all bank holidays. The gardens, home park, adventure playground, nature trail, and countryside exhibition are open from 12:30 to 6pm, the house from 1 to 5:30pm. The site is 6 miles west of Tonbridge.

HEVER CASTLE, Hever, near Edenbridge Tel. 0732/865224.

✪ Built at the end of the 13th century, Hever Castle was then just a fortified farmhouse surrounded by a moat. A dwelling house was added within the fortifications some 200 years later by the Bullen family. In 1506, the property was inherited by Sir Thomas Bullen, father of Anne Boleyn. It was here that Henry VIII courted Anne for 6 years before she became his second wife and later mother of Elizabeth, who became Queen Elizabeth I of England. In 1538, Hever Castle was acquired by Henry VIII, who granted it to his proxy (fourth) wife, Anne of Cleves, when he discovered that his mail-order bride did not live up to her Holbein portrait. This luckier Anne did not seem to mind, however. She owned this comfortable castle for 17 years, while supported by Henry with plenty of money.

In 1903, the castle was purchased by William Waldorf Astor, who spent 5 years restoring and redecorating it, as well as building the unique village of Tudor-style cottages connected to the castle, for use by his guests. Astor was responsible for the construction of the spectacular Italian gardens with fountains, classical statuary, maze, and an avenue of yew trees trimmed into fantastic shapes. He also had a 35-acre lake put in, through which the River Eden flows. The castle and its grounds have been used as locations for a number of motion pictures: The forecourt and the gardens were used in filming *Anne of a Thousand Days* in 1969; more recently, Hever Castle was used in the film *Lady Jane*. Two permanent exhibitions—"The Life and Times of Anne Boleyn" and "The Astors of Hever"—are on display.

Admission to both the castle and the gardens is £4.40 ($8.15) for adults, £2.20 ($4.05) for children. To visit the gardens only, adults pay £3 ($5.55), children £1.80 ($3.35). It's open from March 27 to November 4. The gardens can be entered daily from 11am to 6pm (last entry at 5pm). The castle opens at noon and closes at 6pm. For further information, call the Hever Castle Estate Office (tel. 0732/865224). The castle is a few miles northwest of Royal Tunbridge; 3 miles southeast of Edenbridge, midway between Seven Oaks and East Grinstead, 20 minutes from the M25 Junction 6.

SISSINGHURST CASTLE GARDEN, Sissinghurst. Tel. 0580/712850.

The writer, Vita Sackville-West, and her husband, Harold Nicolson, created the celebrated Sissinghurst Castle Garden, 2 miles northeast of Cranbrook, between the surviving parts of an Elizabethan mansion. The gardens are worth a visit at all seasons: There is a spring garden where bulb flowers flourish, a summer garden, and an autumn garden with flowering shrubs, as well as a large herb garden.

Admission is £4.50 ($8.35) for adults and £2.50 ($4.65) for children on Sunday, dropping to £4 ($7.40) for adults and £2 ($3.70) for children Tuesday to Saturday. Meals are available in the Granary Restaurant, open April to mid-October Tuesday to Friday from noon to 6pm, Saturday and Sunday from 10am to 6pm.

It's open April to mid-October Tuesday to Friday from 10am to 6:30pm, Saturday, Sunday, and Good Friday from 10am to 6:30pm. Sissinghurst Castle is 1 mile east of Sissinghurst on A262, 13 miles south of Maidstone. From Royal Tunbridge Wells, head east along A21 for 30 minutes.

---

6. MAIDSTONE

36 miles SW of London; 64 miles NE of Brighton

GETTING THERE By Train Frequent trains run from London's Victoria Station to Maidstone.

By Bus Daily buses run from London's Victoria Coach Station to Maidstone.

By Car From London's Ring Road continue east along the M26 and the M20.

ESSENTIALS The **area code** is 0622. The **Tourist Information Centre** is The Gatehouse, Old Palace Gardens, Mill Street (tel. 0622/673581).

The major attraction here is Leeds Castle. Maidstone itself, which lies on the rail line from London's Victoria Station, is a busy county town of Kent on the River Medway, 36 miles southeast of London.

LEEDS CASTLE

Once described by Lord Conway as the loveliest castle in the world, Leeds Castle, Maidstone, Kent ME17 1PL (tel. 0622/765400), dates from A.D. 857. Originally built of wood, it was rebuilt in 1119 in its present stone structure on two small islands in the middle of the lake, and it was an almost impregnable fortress before the importation of gunpowder. Henry VIII converted it to a royal palace.

The castle has strong links with America through the sixth Lord Fairfax who, as well as owning the castle, owned five million acres in Virginia and was a close friend and mentor of the young George Washington. The last private owner, the Hon. Lady Baillie, who restored the castle with a superb collection of fine art, furniture, and tapestries, bequeathed it to the Leeds Castle Foundation. Since then, royal apartments, known as "Les Chambres de la Reine" (the chambers of the queen), in the Gloriette, the oldest part of the castle, have been open to the public. The Gloriette, the last stronghold against attack, dates from Norman and Plantagenet times, with later additions by Henry VIII.

Within the surrounding parkland is a wildwood garden and duckery where rare swans, geese, and ducks can be seen. The redesigned aviaries contain a superb collection of birds, including parakeets and cockatoos. Dogs are not allowed here, but dog lovers will enjoy the Great Danes of the castle and the Dog Collar Museum at the gatehouse, with a unique collection of collars dating from the Middle Ages. A nine-hole golf course is open to the public. The Culpeper Garden is a delightful English country flower garden. Beyond are the castle greenhouses, the maze centered by a beautiful underground grotto, and the vineyard recorded in the *Domesday Book* and now again producing Leeds Castle English white wine.

In the summer, from April to October, Leeds Castle is open daily from 11am to 5pm. From November to March it is open Saturday and Sunday from 11am to 4pm. It is closed for annual open-air concerts June 29 and July 6. Admission to the castle and grounds is £5.60 ($10.35) for adults and £3.25 ($6) for children. If you want to visit only the grounds, the charge is £4.10 ($7.60) for adults, £2.40 ($4.45) for children. Car parking is free, with a free ride on a tractor-trailer available for persons who cannot manage the ½-mile or so walk from the car park to the castle.

Snacks, salads, cream teas, and hot meals are offered daily at a number of places on the estate, including Fairfax Hall, a restored 17th-century tithe barn with a self-service carvery restaurant and bar.

Kentish Evenings are presented in Fairfax Hall every Saturday throughout the year, starting at 7pm, with a sherry cocktail reception, then a guided tour of the castle.

Guests feast on Kentish pâté, followed by broth and roast beef carved at the table, plus seasonal vegetables. The meal is rounded off by dessert, cheese, and coffee. A half bottle of wine is included in the overall price of £31 ($57.35) per person. During the meal, musicians play a selection of music suitable to the surroundings and the occasion. Advance reservations are required, made by calling the castle. Kentish Evenings finish at 12:30am, and accommodation is available locally.

If you are not driving during your trip, British Rail and several London-based bus tour operators offer inclusive day excursions to Leeds Castle. The castle is 4 miles east of Maidstone at the junction of the A20 and the M20 London-Folkestone roads.

7. DORKING

26 miles S of London

GETTING THERE   By Train   It takes 35 minutes by frequent daily rail service from London's Victoria Station to reach Dorking.

By Bus   Green Line buses (take no. 714) leave from London's Victoria Coach Station daily, heading for Kingston with a stop at Dorking taking 1 hour.

By Car   Take A3 south from London.

ESSENTIALS   The **area code** is 0306. The nearest tourist information office is in Guildford (see below).

This town, birthplace of Laurence Olivier, lies on the Mole River, at the foot of the North Downs. Within easy reach are some of the most scenic spots in the shire, including Silent Pool, Box Hill, and Leith Hill.

Three miles to the northwest and 1½ miles south of Great Bookham, off the A246 Leatherhead-Guildford road, stands **Polesden Lacey** (tel. 0372/452048), a former Regency villa containing the Greville collection of antiques, paintings, and tapestries. In the early part of this century it was enlarged to become a comfortable Edwardian country house when it was the home of a celebrated hostess, who frequently entertained royalty. The estate consists of 1,000 acres, and the 18th-century garden is filled with herbaceous borders, a rose garden, and beech walks.

The house hours are April through October Wednesday to Sunday from 1:30 to 5:30pm, March and November Saturday and Sunday from 1:30 to 4:30pm. The charge to visit the house on Sunday and bank holiday Mondays is £3 ($5.55); on other days £2 ($3.70). To visit the garden from April until the end of October is £2 ($3.70). Children under 17 pay half price, and those under 5 are admitted free. A licensed restaurant on the grounds is open from 11am on the days the house can be visited.

WHERE TO STAY & EAT

STAR AND GARTER HOTEL, Station Approach, Dorking, Surrey RH4 ITF. Tel. 0306/882820. 12 rms (none with bath). TV
$ Rates (including English breakfast): £24 ($44.40) single; £38 ($70.30) double. AE, DC, MC, V. **Parking:** Free.

Bill and June Smith personally completed many of the renovations on what they call their "oldy worldly" establishment, which was originally built 150 years ago as the village's railroad inn. Today it is a popular pub and restaurant, serving such dishes as the traditional homemade steak-and-kidney pie. If you'd like such pub-type accommodations, you'll find spacious and comfortable bedrooms, all with hot beverage facilities. The snooker tables in the pub usually draw a lively crowd of onlookers. Lunch is served daily from noon to 2pm and dinner from 7 to 9pm, with meals ranging from £8 to £15 ($14.80 to $27.75). Everything tastes better when washed down with one of the inn's real ales. The Star and Garter lies 20 minutes from Gatwick Airport, and 35 minutes from Victoria.

ON THE OUTSKIRTS

ASHLEIGH HOUSE HOTEL, 39 Redstone Hill, Redhill, Surrey RH1 4BG. Tel. 0737/764763. 9 rms (4 with shower).
$ Rates (including English breakfast): £25 ($46.25) single without bath; £38 ($70.30) double without bath, £45 ($83.25) double with shower. No credit cards.
The Ashleigh House Hotel is about 8 miles east of Dorking, near Reingate, in the little town of Redhill, on the A25 to Seven Oaks. The hosts, Jill and Michael Warren, serve a good English breakfast in the dining room, which overlooks a garden. Some of the accommodations have private showers. There's a heated swimming pool for use of guests in summer, plus a TV lounge. The hotel is only about 15 minutes by car from Gatwick and 35 minutes by train from London.

LYNWOOD HOUSE, 50 London Rd., Redhill, Surrey RH1 1LN. Tel. 0737/766894. 10 rms (7 with bath). TV
$ Rates (including English breakfast): £20 ($37) single without bath, £25 ($46.25) single with bath; £35 ($65.70) double without bath, £40 ($74) double with bath. MC, V. **Parking:** Free.
A good B&B, this offers clean and comfortable accommodations, most with showers, all with hot and cold running water. Breakfast is generous and well prepared. The location, just under 15 minutes from Gatwick Airport by either car or train, is 200 yards from the Redhill Railway Station.

---

8. GUILDFORD

33 miles S of London

GETTING THERE By Train The train ride from London's Waterloo Station takes 40 minutes.

By Bus National Express operates buses from London's Victoria Coach Station daily, with a stopover at Guildford on its runs from London to Brighton. It's usually more convenient to take the train.

By Car From London, head south along A3.

ESSENTIALS The **area code** is 0483. The **Tourist Information Centre** is at Guildford House Gallery, 155 High Street (tel. 0483/444007).

The guildhall in this country town, which lies on the Wey River, has an ornamental projecting clock that dates from 1683, and Charles Dickens believed that the High Street, which slopes to the river, was one of the most beautiful in England.

Lying 2½ miles southwest of the city, **Loseley House,** Loseley Park, Guildford, Surrey GU3 1HS (tel. 0483/304440), a beautiful and historic Elizabethan mansion visited by Queen Elizabeth I, James I, and Queen Mary, has been featured on TV and in five films. Its works of art include paneling from Henry VIII's Nonsuch Palace, period furniture, a unique carved chalk chimney-piece, magnificent ceilings, and cushions made by the first Queen Elizabeth. The mansion is open from the end of May to the end of September on Wednesday, Thursday, Friday, and Saturday from 2 to 5pm, charging £3 ($5.55) for adults, £1.50 ($2.80) for children. Lunches and teas are served in the 17th-century tithe barn from 2 to 5pm, and you can tour the farm and visit the farm shop.

WHERE TO STAY

CARLTON HOTEL, 36-40 London Rd., Guildford, Surrey GU1 2AF. Tel. 0483/575158. Fax 0483/34669. 36 rms (19 with shower). TV TEL

$ **Rates** (including English breakfast): £26 ($48.10) single without shower, £36 ($66.60) single with shower; £40 ($74) double without shower, £46 ($85.10) double with shower. AE, MC, V.

This is just a 3-minute walk to the London Road Station on the London (Waterloo) to Guildford line via Cobham. Spend the day visiting the London museums or theater and come home here to have an evening meal. Bedrooms have central heating, hot and cold running water, radios, and intercoms; some have color TVs. For an evening's relaxation, a saloon bar beckons.

MRS. LINDA ATKINSON, 129 Stoke Rd., Guildford, Surrey GU1 1ET. Tel. 0483/38260. 4 rms (2 with bath or shower). TV
$ **Rates** (including English breakfast): £20 ($37) single without bath; £34 ($67.29) double without bath, £38 ($70.30) double with bath. No credit cards.

 This is the most reasonable B&B, considering the warmth of Mrs. Atkinson's welcome and the quality of her rooms. Three rooms have hot-beverage facilities, central heating, and TVs, and the use of ironing facilities is included in the rates. Her breakfasts are plentiful and well prepared. The house is a 10-minute walk to the town center, opposite the scenic park with tennis courts and swimming pool.

EASY EXCURSION

One of the great gardens of England, **Wisley Garden** (tel. 0483/224234) stands in Wisley near Ripley just off the M25 (Junction 10) on the A3 London-Portsmouth road. Every season of the year, this 250-acre garden has a profusion of flowers and shrubbery, ranging from the New Alpine House with its delicate blossoms in spring, to the walled garden with formal flowerbeds in summer, to the heather garden's colorful foliage in the fall, to a riot of exotic plants in the glasshouses in winter. This garden is the site of a laboratory where botanists, plant pathologists, and an entomologist experiment and assist amateur gardeners. There is a large gift shop with a wide range of gardening books and a licensed restaurant and cafeteria. Open all year Monday to Saturday from 10am to 7pm (or sunset if earlier). Admission is £3 ($5.55) for adults, and £1.20 ($2.20) for children ages 6 to 14.

9. HASLEMERE

42 miles S of London; 37 miles NW of Brighton

GETTING THERE   By Train   Haslemere is an hour's train ride from Waterloo Station in London.

By Bus   There is no bus service from London to Haslemere, because the train service is so excellent. Once in Haslemere, local buses connect the town to such nearby villages as Farnham and Grayshott.

By Car   From Guildford (see above) continue south on the A3100, going via Godalming and branching onto A286.

ESSENTIALS   The **area code** is 0428. The nearest tourist information office is in Guildford (see above).

In this quiet, sleepy town, early English musical instruments are made by hand, and an annual music festival (see below) is the town's main drawing card. Over the years, the Dolmetsch family has been responsible for the acclaim that has come to this otherwise unheralded little Surrey town, which lies in the midst of some of the shire's finest scenery.

THE FESTIVAL

⭐ It isn't often that one can hear such exquisite music played so skillfully on the harpsichord, the recorder, the lute, or any of the instruments from earlier centuries. Throughout the year, the Dolmetsch family makes and repairs these instruments and welcomes visitors to their place on the edge of Haslemere. They rehearse constantly, preparing for the concerts that are held in July and last nine days.

You can get specific information by writing to the **Haslemere Festival Office**, Jesses, Grayswood Road, Haslemere, Surrey GU27 2BS (or call 0428/642161 between 9am and 12:30pm daily). During the festival, matinees begin at 3:15pm, evening performances at 7:30pm. Balcony seats cost from £5 to £7 ($9.25 to $12.95), and stall seats cost from £3.25 to £6 ($6 to $11.10).

WHERE TO STAY

HOUNDLESS WATER, Bell Vale Lane, Haslemere, Surrey GU27 3DJ. Tel. 0428/642591. 3 rms (none with bath).
$ Rates (including English breakfast): £20 ($37) single; £36–£40 ($66.60–$74) double. No credit cards. **Parking:** Free.

This attractive period house dating back some 300 years is about 1¼ miles from the heart of town, lying off the A286. In one of the beauty spots of Surrey, this inn offers English country living in comfortable bedrooms. You can also arrange an evening meal for only £9.50 ($17.60), but you must order it by 10am that morning. Houndless Water lies only 50 minutes from Heathrow Airport and an hour from Gatwick Airport. Reservations as far in advance as possible are necessary because there are so few rooms.

WHERE TO EAT

THE RED LION PUB, The Green, Fernhurst. Tel. 643112.
Cuisine: ENGLISH. **Reservations:** Not needed.
$ Prices: Restaurant appetizers £2.95–£4.50 ($5.45–$8.35), main courses £6–£10.25 ($11.10–$18.95); pub snacks £2.50–£5 ($4.65–$9.25). MC, V.
Open: Restaurant lunch daily noon–2:30pm, dinner Mon–Sat 6–9:30pm; pub Mon–Sat 11am–2:30pm and 5:30–11pm, Sun 11am–2:30pm and 7–10:30pm.

This establishment—both a pub and a restaurant—sits directly on the village green within a 300-year-old sandstone-fronted building of great charm. Its *esprit de corps* seems strong and warm. Pub snacks are available during pub hours, and can be ordered across the bartop. À la carte meals, using fresh ingredients and good English produce, are served in the nearby dining room.

SHRIMPTONS RESTAURANT, 2 Grove Cottage, Kingsley Green. Tel. 643539.
Cuisine: ENGLISH/FRENCH. **Reservations:** Recommended.
$ Prices: Appetizers £3–£7.50 ($5.55–$13.90); main courses £12–£14 ($22.20–$25.90); four-course set dinner (Mon–Fri) £18.75 ($34.70); set lunch from £13.50 ($25). AE, DC, MC, V.
Open: Lunch Mon–Fri 12:30–1:45pm, when last food orders are taken; dinner Mon–Sat 6:30–9:45pm, when last food orders are taken.

⭐ If you're seeking more sophisticated dining, head for this restaurant, housed in a 17th-century building, where Beryl S. Keeley runs one of the foremost restaurants in the area, and certainly one of the oldest. It's on the A286 Haslemere to Midhurst Road, 1 mile outside Haslemere. The vegetables are served separately and in copious quantity, as indeed are all the dishes. Every dish is cooked to order and therefore available without the sauces—which are rich but still light and subtle—if requested. The restaurant is renowned for its fish, duck, guinea fowl, and game dishes. The menu may include breast of chicken filled with lobster, salmon escalope topped with spinach and mussels, or magret of duck with honey and cider. Vegetarian dishes are also offered.

CHAPTER 10

THE SUSSEXES

- **WHAT'S SPECIAL ABOUT THE SUSSEXES**
1. **RYE & WINCHELSEA**
2. **HASTINGS & ST. LEONARDS**
3. **BATTLE**
4. **ALFRISTON & LEWES**
5. **BRIGHTON**
6. **ARUNDEL**
7. **CHICHESTER**

SEEING THE SUSSEXES

GETTING THERE

If you're heading straight for the region, it's best to land at Gatwick Airport (tel. 0293/31299), which has convenient rail, bus, and road connections to all of the southeast. The airport is close to such major highways as A23 and M23. The area is also well served by British Rail's Network Southeast, with frequent departures from London's Victoria or Charing Cross Station for the east or Waterloo Station for West Sussex. National Express buses (tel. 071/730-0202) in London serve the region from London's Victoria Coach Station. A network of private bus companies also operate in the region. For East Sussex, phone 0273/481000 for bus information, and for West Sussex destinations, call 0243/777556.

A SUGGESTED ITINERARY

Day 1: Head for Rye and Winchelsea for the night.
Day 2: Explore Hastings in the morning, Battle Abbey in the afternoon, and overnight in the little village of Alfriston.
Day 3: Go west to Brighton for a day's fun and a visit to the Royal Pavilion.
Day 4: Explore Arundel Castle and overnight in the area, perhaps taking in a theatrical presentation in the evening at Chichester.

If King Harold hadn't loved Sussex so much, the course of English history might have been changed forever. Had the brave Saxon waited longer in the north, he could have marshaled more adequate reinforcements before striking south to meet the Normans. But Duke William's soldiers were ravaging the countryside he knew so well, and Harold rushed down to counter them.

Harold's enthusiasm for Sussex is understandable. The landscape rises and falls like waves. The county is known for its downlands and tree-thickened weald, from which came the timbers to build England's mighty fleet in days gone by. The shires lie south of London and Surrey, bordering Kent in the east, Hampshire in the west, and opening directly onto the sometimes sunny, seaside-town-dotted English Channel.

Sussex witnessed some of the biggest moments in the country's history. Apart from the Norman landings at Hastings, the most life-changing transformation occurred in the 19th century, as middle-class Victorians flocked to the seashore, pumping new spirit into Eastbourne, Worthing, Brighton, even old Hastings. The cult of the saltwater worshipers flourished, and has to this day. Although Eastbourne and Worthing are much frequented by the English, I'd place them several fathoms below Brighton and Hastings, which are much more suitable if you're seeking a holiday by the sea.

The old towns and villages of Sussex are far more intriguing than the seaside resorts, particularly Rye and Winchelsea, the ancient towns of the Cinque Port

☑ # WHAT'S SPECIAL ABOUT THE SUSSEXES

Great Towns/Villages
- [ ] Rye, former Cinque Port, now considered one of English's best-preserved medieval villages.
- [ ] Alfriston, ancient town in the Cuckmere Valley and a former smugglers' haunt.
- [ ] Brighton, first and largest seaside resort in the Southeast, with its famed Royal Pavilion.

Castles
- [ ] Arundel Castle, ancestral home of the dukes of Norfolk with an exceptional collection of paintings.
- [ ] Hastings Castle, first of the Norman castles to be built in England (ca. 1067).
- [ ] Battle Abbey, the setting for the Battle of Hastings in 1066.

Ace Attractions
- [ ] The Royal Pavilion at Brighton, a John Nash version of an Indian mogul's palace.
- [ ] The Hastings Embroidery, a commemorative needlework tracing 900 years of English history.

Literary Shrines
- [ ] Bateman's, northwest of Battle, home of Rudyard Kipling—filled with mementos of English days of empire in India.
- [ ] Monks House, outside Lewes, a National Trust property, home to Virginia and Leonard Woolf from 1919.

Confederation. No Sussex village is lovelier than Alfriston (and the innkeepers know it too); Arundel is noted for its castle; the cathedral city of Chichester is a mecca for theater buffs. Traditionally, and for purposes of government, Sussex is divided into East Sussex and West Sussex. I've adhered to that convenient dichotomy.

1. RYE & WINCHELSEA

62½ miles S of London

GETTING THERE By Train From London, the Southern Region Line offers trains south from Charing Cross to Cannon Street stations, with a change at Ashford, before continuing on to Rye. You can also go via Tunbridge Wells with a change in Hastings. Trains run every hour during the day, arriving at the Rye Train Station off Cinque Ports Street and taking 1½ to 2 hours.

By Bus You need to take the train to get to Rye but once you're there you'll find buses departing for many destinations, including Hastings. Schedules of the various bus companies are posted on signs in the parking lot. For bus connections information throughout the region, call 0797/223343.

By Car From London, take the M23, M26, and M20 east to Maidstone, going southeast along A20 to Ashford. At Ashford, continue south along the coast on A2070.

ESSENTIALS The **area code** is 0797. The **Tourist Information Center** is at 48 Cinque Ports Street (tel. 0797/222293).

"Nothing more recent than a Cavalier's Cloak, Hat and Ruffles should be seen in the streets of Rye," said Louis Jennings. This ancient town, formerly an island, flourished in the 13th century. Near the English Channel, Rye, and neighboring

Winchelsea, were once part of the "Antient" (with a "t") Cinque Port Confederation. Rye in its early days was a smuggling center, its denizens sneaking in contraband from the marshes to stash away in little nooks.

But the sea receded from Rye, leaving it perched like a giant whale out of water, 2 miles from the channel. Its narrow, cobblestone streets twist and turn like a labyrinth, with buildings jumbled along them whose sagging roofs and crooked chimneys indicate the town's medieval origins. The old town's entrance is **Land Gate,** where a single lane of traffic passes between massive, 40-foot-high stone towers. The parapet of the gate contains holes through which boiling oil used to be poured on unwelcome visitors, such as French raiding parties.

Attacked several times by French fleets, Rye was practically razed in 1377. But it rebuilt sufficiently, decking itself out in the Elizabethan style so that Queen Elizabeth I, during her visit in 1573, bestowed upon the town the distinction of Royal Rye. This has long been considered a special place and over the years has attracted the famous such as novelist Henry James.

Today the city has lots of sites of architectural interest, notably the mid-12th century **St. Mary's Parish Church,** Church Square (tel. 0797/222430), with its 16th-century clock flanked by two gilded cherubs, known as Quarter Boys from their striking of the bells on the quarter hour. If you're courageous, you can climb a set of wooden stairs and ladders to the bell tower of the church, from which there is an impressive view. Hours are daily 9am to 9pm June through September (10am to dusk off-season). Contributions are appreciated to enter the church. The tower costs £1 ($1.85) for adults and 50p (95¢) for children.

The neighbor Cinque Confederation port to Rye, **Winchelsea** has also witnessed the water's ebb. It traces its history back to Edward I and has experienced many dramatic moments, such as sacking by the French. The finest sight of this dignified residential town is a badly damaged 14th-century church, containing a number of remarkable tombs.

WHAT TO SEE & DO

LAMB HOUSE, West St. at the top of Mermaid St. Tel. 0797/224982.

Henry James lived in Lamb House from 1898 to 1916. Many of his mementos are in the house, which is set in walled gardens. Its owner rushed off to join the Gold Rush in North America but perished in the Klondike, and James was able to buy the freehold for a modest two thousand pounds. Some of his well-known books were written here.

Admission: £1.40 ($2.60).
Open: Apr–Oct Wed–Sat 2–5:30pm.

RYE MUSEUM, 4 Church Sq. Tel. 0797/223254.

Housed in the Ypres Tower, a fortification built about 1250 by order of Henry III as a defense against French raiders, this museum contains collections of military objects, shipping artifacts, toys, Cinque Ports relics, Victoriana, inn lore, and pottery.

Admission: £1.50 ($2.80) adults, 50p (95¢) children.
Open: Easter to mid-Oct Mon–Sat 10:30am–1pm and 2:15–5:30pm, Sun 11:30am–1pm and 2:15–5:30pm.

A NEARBY ATTRACTION

On the outskirts of Winchelsea, visit **Smallhythe Place,** at Tenterden in Kent (tel. 05806/2334), which for 30 years was the country house of Dame Ellen Terry. Ellen Terry was the English actress acclaimed for her Shakespearean roles who had a long theatrical association with Sir Henry Irving; she died in the house in 1928. This timber-framed house, known as a "continuous-jetty house," was built in the first half of the 16th century and is filled with Terry memorabilia. The house is on the B2082 near Tenterden, about 6 miles to the north of Rye, and is open April to October Saturday to Wednesday from 2 to 6pm. Adults pay £1.80 ($3.35) admission, children £1 ($1.85).

WHERE TO STAY

DOUBLES WITHOUT BATH FOR LESS THAN £36 [$66.60]

In Rye

In addition to the following, the Mermaid Inn (see "Where to Eat," below) also has rooms to rent.

CLIFF FARM, Military Rd., Iden Lock, Rye, East Sussex TN31 7NY. Tel. 07978/280331. 3 rms (none with bath).
$ Rates (including English breakfast): £12–£13 ($22.20–$24.05) double per person. No credit cards. **Parking:** Free. **Closed:** Dec–Feb.

Jeff and Pat Sullivin receive guests on their nearly 4½ acres of property. Because of the elevated position of the farm, you'll have good views of the area, particularly over Romney Marsh. There's a sitting room where a log fire blazes when the weather is cool. Farm produce means a generous country breakfast and you can see the farm animals as you stroll around. It's located 2 miles from Rye toward Iden Lock.

JEAKE'S HOUSE, Mermaid St., Rye, East Sussex TN32 7ET. Tel. 0797/228828. Fax 0797/222623. 12 rms (9 with bath or shower). TV TEL
$ Rates (including English breakfast): £22 ($40.70) single without bath; £36 ($66.60) double without bath, £48 ($88.80) double with bath. AE, MC, V. **Parking:** Free.

The premier B&B in Rye, this hidden treasure is on the same street as the famous Mermaid Inn (see "Where to Eat," below). The five-floor house near the rail station was originally constructed as a wool storehouse in 1689 for a Huguenot, Samuel Jeake II, for which it is named, and was then joined with a Quaker meetinghouse next door. The American writer Conrad Aiken, who wrote for *The New Yorker* under the *nom de plume* of Samuel Jeake, Jr., lived here for nearly a quarter of a century and was visited by such guests as T. S. Eliot, Henry James, the artist Paul Nash (who had a house nearby), and Radclyffe Hall (author of *The Well of Loneliness*). Today, the owners, Jenny and Francis Hadfield, lovingly take care of this house and are eager to share Aiken's collected letters and poems. The bedrooms, which have central heating and hot-drink trays, have been handsomely styled with Laura Ashley prints, and the bathrooms have hand-painted tiles made at a Sussex factory. Breakfast, traditional or vegetarian, is taken in a former galleried chapel, now elegantly converted.

LITTLE SALTCOTE, 22 Military Rd., Rye, East Sussex, TN31 7NY. Tel. 0797/223210. 5 rms (1 with bath). TV
$ Rates (including English breakfast): £17.50 ($32.40) single without bath; £30 ($55.50) double without bath, £34 ($62.90) double with bath. No credit cards. **Parking:** Free.
Owned by Sally and Terry Osborne, this attractive guesthouse is a 5-minute walk east from the town center, yet is in a peaceful rural setting. The well-appointed rooms have central heating, razor points, hot-beverage facilities, and hot and cold running water; one has a private bath. Guests are provided with forecourt parking and may wander freely in the large garden.

MIZPAH GUEST HOUSE, 89 Military Rd., Rye, East Sussex TN31 7NY. Tel. 0797/223657. 4 rms (all with shower). TV
$ Rates (including English breakfast): £14 ($25.90) per person. No credit cards. **Parking:** Free.
This reasonably priced accommodation is a 5-minute walk from the town center on the River Rother but there are only a few rooms, so you must reserve or call ahead. Two rooms are reserved for families. Rooms are large and contain hot and cold running water.

WORTH THE EXTRA BUCKS
In Rye

DURRANT HOUSE HOTEL, East St., Rye, East Sussex TN31 7LA. Tel. 0797/223182. 10 rms (all with bath). TV
$ Rates (including breakfast): £24–£40 ($44.40–$74) single; £34–£60 ($62.90–$111) double. DC, MC, V. **Parking:** Free.

⭐ This beautiful Georgian house is set on a quiet residential street, at the end of Market Street off High Street. The hotel possesses much charm and character and has a cozy lounge with an arched, brick fireplace and, across the hall, a residents' bar. Over the years, it has attracted many famous personages. In more recent times, the renowned artist Paul Nash lived next door until his death in 1946; in fact, his celebrated view, as seen in his painting, *View of the Rother,* can be enjoyed from the River Room of the hotel. The house is named for a previous owner, Sir William Durrant, a friend of the Duke of Wellington, who bought it in the 18th century. At one time, the house was used as a relay station for carrier pigeons; these birds brought news of the victory at Waterloo.

LITTLE ORCHARD HOUSE, 3 West St., Rye, East Sussex TN31 7ES. Tel. 0797/223831. 3 rms (all with bath). TV
$ Rates (including English breakfast): £35–£55 ($64.75–$101.75) single; £56–£70 ($103.60–$129.50) double. MC, V.

⭐ You'll find this to be among the most elegant and moderately priced accommodations in the old seaport. The 18th-century Georgian town house was originally the home of Rye's mayor, Thomas Proctor. Other prominent politicians (and/or smugglers) also lived here through the years, including Prime Minister David Lloyd George who lived here 70 years ago. The house is tastefully furnished with antiques and Georgian paneling. A large open fireplace in the lounge-study has a blazing fire when needed, a big bouquet of dried flowers otherwise. From this room and the intimate breakfast room, you can see the old-style walled garden, with espaliered fruit trees. The bedrooms all have hot-drink trays. The hotel is in the town center at the western end of High Street.

In Winchelsea

STRAND HOUSE, Winchelsea, East Sussex TN36 4JT. Tel. 0797/226276. 10 rms (all with bath). TV
$ Rates (including English breakfast): £22–£26 ($40.70–$48.10) single; £30–£42 ($55.50–$77.70) double. No credit cards. **Parking:** Free.

⭐ Sure to catch your eye is this weathered historic house and cottage set in a garden at the foot of a hill; sheep graze in the meadows that separate the hotel from the sea. The owners are conscious of comforts, and their high standard includes wall-to-wall carpeting, hot-beverage facilities, and central heating in all bedrooms. One of the rooms includes a four-poster bed. A private dining room with a huge inglenook fireplace is reserved for the guests, and there is ample parking within the hotel grounds.

The house is well over 500 years old and has irregular oak floors; the low, heavy oak ceiling beams came from ships. It is believed that a tunnel near the house leads up to Winchelsea Town and is a relic of the days when smuggling was one of the main industries of the area. In World War II, the wooded bank at the rear of the house was used to store rifles and ammunition in the event of a Nazi invasion (the meadow below was flooded to deter foot soldiers bent on invasion). The house is located just off A259.

THE COUNTRY HOUSE AT WINCHELSEA, Hastings Rd., Winchelsea, East Sussex TN36 4AD. Tel. 0797/226669. 4 rms (all with bath). TV
$ Rates (including English breakfast): £32–£38 ($59.20–$70.30) single or double. No credit cards. **Parking:** Free.

This 17th-century former Sussex farmhouse, now converted to receive guests, stands on 2 acres of grounds, with many species of bird and butterfly life. A building of charm and character, it offers comfortable bedrooms with complimentary hot-drinks trays. Rooms open onto views. Predinner drinks are served in a log-fired sitting room, followed by dinner in a candlelit room costing from £9.50 ($17.60) for three courses. The house is set back from the A259 on the Hastings side of Winchelsea, a 7-minute drive from Rye.

WHERE TO EAT

IN RYE

Meals For Less Than £5 [$9.25]

FLETCHER'S HOUSE, Lion St. (near St. Mary's Church). Tel. 223101.
   Cuisine: ENGLISH. **Reservations:** Not needed.
$ Prices: Appetizers 70p–£1.80 ($1.30–$3.35); main courses £2–£8 ($3.70–$14.80). MC, V.
   Open: Daily 10am–5pm.

In this ancient vicarage converted into a tearoom, you can enjoy morning coffee, hot or cold luncheons, and afternoon tea. Daily specials are always featured. The house, in the town center of High Street, is particularly noted for its Sussex cream teas—the scones for which are baked daily on the premises, and clotted cream is flown up from Devon weekly. John Fletcher, the Elizabethan dramatist and contemporary of Shakespeare, was born in the house in 1579, when his father was vicar of Rye. The house still retains many of its original architectural features, such as the old hidden-away front door with its design of York and Tudor roses and an impressive oaken room. Be sure to look at the clock on St. Mary's Church, which has animated figures.

SWISS PATISSERIE AND TEA ROOM, 50 Cinque Ports St. Tel. 222830.
   Cuisine: SWISS. **Reservations:** Not needed.
$ Prices: Pastries £1.50–£2.50 ($2.80–$4.65); cream tea £2.50 ($4.65). No credit cards.
   Open: Mon and Wed–Sat 8am–4:30pm, Tues 8am–12:30pm. **Closed:** 3 weeks in Jan (dates vary).

Here expatriate Swiss-born Claude Auberson concocts creamy Swiss cakes, cream meringues, buns, and pastries. Everything is good and fattening, and it's to be washed down in a tiny tearoom with coffee or Swiss-style hot chocolate. There is also a selection of hot savory snacks baked daily on the premises. It's located in the town center.

WORTH THE EXTRA BUCKS

DURRANT HOUSE RESTAURANT, East St. Tel. 223182.
   Cuisine: SEAFOOD. **Reservations:** Required.
$ Prices: Fixed-price five-course dinner £14.50 ($26.85); pub lunch from £4 ($7.40). DC, MC, V.
   Open: Restaurant dinner Fri–Tues 7–8:30pm; Wellington Bar lunch daily noon–2pm.

This restaurant is housed in a hotel of the same name (see above). Guests peruse a fixed-price menu for five freshly prepared courses. As befits a former seaport, the chef specializes in fresh fish, as well as fresh vegetables, and desserts and ice creams are homemade. While waiting for dinner, patrons can enjoy a view of the rear garden and can have a drink in the Wellington Bar, which not only serves real ale but also light pub lunches. The restaurant is in the town center at the eastern end of High Street.

MERMAID INN, Mermaid St. Tel. 223065.
   Cuisine: ENGLISH. **Reservations:** Recommended.
$ Prices: Appetizers £3–£6 ($5.55–$11.10); main courses £6–£12 ($11.10–$22.20); four-course set dinner from £15.75 ($29.15); set lunch £12 ($22.20). AE, DC, MC, V.

Open: Lunch daily 12:30pm; dinner daily 7:30–9:15pm.

⭐ This is the most famous of the old smugglers' inns of England—known to the band of cutthroats, the real-life Hawkhurst Gang, as well as to Russell Thorndike's fictional character, Dr. Syn. One of the present bedrooms, in fact, is called Dr. Syn's Bedchamber, and is connected by a staircase, set in the thickness of a wall, to the bar. The Mermaid had been open for 150 years when Elizabeth I visited Rye in 1573. The dining room has linenfold paneling, Caen-stone fireplaces, and an oak-beamed ceiling. In addition to serving good food, the most charming tavern in Rye also has 30 comfortable bedrooms to rent, three four-poster beds, and central heating. Even if you don't dine or stay at the Mermaid, drop in to the old Tudor pub, with its 16-foot-wide fireplace (look for a priest's hiding hole). It's located between West Street and the Strand.

2. HASTINGS & ST. LEONARDS

63 miles SE of London; 45 miles W of Dover

GETTING THERE   By Train   Daily trains run hourly from London's Victoria Station or Charing Cross to Hastings. The trip takes 1½ to 2 hours.

By Bus   Hastings is linked by bus to Maidstone, Folkestone, and Eastbourne which has direct service with departure hours. National Express operates regular daily service from London's Victoria Station.

By Car   From the M25 ring road around London, head southeast to the coast and Hastings on A21.

ESSENTIALS   The **area code** is 0424. The **Tourist Information Centre** is at 4 Robertson Terrace (tel. 0424/718888).

T he world has seen bigger battles, but few are as well remembered as the Battle of Hastings in 1066. When William, Duke of Normandy, landed on the Sussex coast and lured King Harold (already fighting Vikings in Yorkshire) southward to defeat, the destiny of the English-speaking people was changed forever. The actual battle occurred at what is now Battle Abbey (9 miles away), but the Norman duke used Hastings as his base of operation.

Linked by a 3-mile promenade along the sea, Hastings and St. Leonards were given a considerable boost in the 19th century by Queen Victoria, who visited several times. Both towns no longer enjoy such royal patronage; rather, they do a thriving business with Midlanders on vacation.

WHAT TO SEE & DO

HASTINGS CASTLE, Castle Hill Rd., West Hill. Tel. 0424/17963.
In ruins now, the first of the Norman castles to be built in England sprouted up on a western hill overlooking Hastings, circa 1067. Precious little is left to remind us of the days when proud knights, imbued with a spirit of pomp and spectacle, wore bonnets and girdles. The fortress was defortified by King John in 1216, and later served as a church. Owned by the Pelham dynasty from the latter 16th century to modern times, the ruins have been turned over to Hastings. There is now an audiovisual presentation of the castle's history, including the famous battle of 1066. From the mount, you'll have a good view of the coast and promenade.
    Admission: £2 ($3.70) adults, £1.25 ($2.30) children.
    Open: Easter–Oct daily 10am–5pm. **Transportation:** The West Cliff Railway from George Street takes you to the castle for 40p (75¢) adults, 25p (45¢) children.

THE HASTINGS EMBROIDERY, in the town hall, Queen's Rd. Tel. 0424/722026.

A commemorative work, the Hastings Embroidery is a remarkable achievement that traces 900 years of English history through needlework. First exhibited in 1966, the 27 panels, 243 feet in length, depict 81 historic scenes, including some of the nation's greatest moments and legends: the murder of Thomas Becket, King John signing the *Magna Carta*, the Black Plague, Chaucer's pilgrims going to Canterbury, the Battle of Agincourt with the victorious Henry V, the War of the Roses, the Little Princes in the Tower, Bloody Mary's reign, Drake's *Golden Hind*, the arrival of Philip's ill-fated Armada, Guy Fawkes's gunpowder plot, the sailing of the *Mayflower*, the disastrous plague of 1665, the great London fire of 1666, Nelson at Trafalgar, the Battle of Waterloo, the Battle of Britain, and the D-Day landings at Normandy. Also exhibited is a scale model of the battlefield at Battle, with William's inch-high men doing in Harold's minisoldiers. The exhibitions are in the town center near the Hastings Coach Station.

Admission: £1 ($1.85) adults, 50p (95¢) children.

Open: May–Sept Mon–Fri 10am–5pm; Oct–Apr Mon–Fri 11:30am–3:30pm; also Sat June–Sept 10am–5pm.

ST. CLEMENTS CAVES, West Hill. Tel. 0424/422964.

Here you can descend into underground haunts of smugglers in days of yore. The caves cover 4 acres of passages, caverns, and secret chambers below ground. You plunge 140 feet down the monk's walk, a candlelit passage into the depths of the caves, where you'll find an exhibition of costumes, weapons, artifacts, and "tools of the trade," which tell the story of smuggling in the 18th century. More than 50 life-size figures are displayed.

Admission: £3 ($5.55) adults, children £2 ($3.70).

Open: Mid-Mar to Oct daily 10am–6pm. **Transportation:** West Cliff Railway from George Street for 40p (75¢) adults, 25p (45¢) children.

WHERE TO STAY

DOUBLES WITHOUT BATH FOR LESS THAN £32 [$59.20]

ARGYLE, 32 Cambridge Gardens, Hastings, East Sussex TN34 1EN. Tel. 0424/421294. 8 rms (3 with shower).

$ Rates (including English breakfast): £16 ($29.60) single without bath, £17 ($31.45) single with bath; £28 ($51.80) double without bath, £32 ($59.20) double with bath. No credit cards.

Argyle, which enjoys a central location close to the oceanfront and the rail station, is one of the best B&Bs for value in the area. It offers comfortably furnished bedrooms; the three with showers are suitable for families. Breakfast is the only meal served.

EAGLE HOUSE HOTEL, 12 Pevensey Rd., St. Leonards, East Sussex TV38 0JZ. Tel. 0424/430535. Fax 0424/434338. 20 rms (all with bath). TV TEL

$ Rates: £27 ($49.95) single; £38–£45 ($70.30–$83.25) double. AE, DC, MC, V.
Parking: Free.

One of the best hotels in the area, this three-story mansion, originally built in 1860 as a palatial private home, lies in a residential section about a 10-minute walk from the beaches (it's adjacent to St. Leonards Shopping Centre). The well-furnished bedrooms have central heating and coffee-making facilities, and the hotel has a bar open in the evening.

GLASTONBURY GUEST HOUSE, 45 Eversfield Place, St. Leonards, East Sussex TN37 6DB. Tel. 0424/422280. Fax 0424/443297. 10 rms (2 with bath). TV **Directions:** Take A259 west of Hastings.

$ **Rates** (including English breakfast): £16–£18 ($29.60–$33.30) single without bath; £32 ($59.20) double without bath, £36 ($66.60) double with bath. No credit cards.

Right on the seafront, this is one of the better values in town. Two of the comfortable rooms have private baths and color TV, and all have hot-beverage facilities.

TAMAR GUEST HOUSE, 7 Devonshire Rd., Hastings, East Sussex TN34 1NE. Tel. 0424/434076. 5 rms (none with bath). TV

$ **Rates** (including English breakfast): £14–£15 ($25.90–$27.75) single; £22–£26 ($40.70–$48.10) double. No credit cards.

 A favorite of readers, this house opens onto the cricket ground of Hastings and has a good view of the castle. The hotel is centrally located and convenient to the train station, where connections are made to London. Bedrooms are comfortably furnished.

WHERE TO EAT

Because Hastings is a fishing center, it has a multitude of competitive small seafood restaurants along the street fronting the beach at the east side of the city (on the way to the old part of town). The second restaurant listed below is actually 5 miles outside of Hastings.

MILLIES, 45 High St., Old Town Hastings. Tel. 431896.
   Cuisine: VEGETARIAN. **Reservations:** Not needed.
$ **Prices:** Appetizers £1.50–£2 ($2.80–$3.70); main courses £2.50–£3.50 ($4.65–$6.45). No credit cards.
   Open: Thurs–Tues 10am–5pm, Wed 10am–2pm.

All the food served here is prepared and cooked on the premises. The menu lists a wide variety of salads, savory pies, and quiches, and homemade desserts include fruit pies and other rich confections. It is located on the main street.

CROSSWAYS, corner of Waites Lane, at Fairlight, near Hastings. Tel. 812536.
   Cuisine: ENGLISH. **Reservations:** Required.
$ **Prices:** Appetizers £1.95–£4.95 ($3.60–$9.15); main courses £5.75–£12.50 ($10.65–$23.15); lunch from £5 ($9.25); set three-course Sun lunch £6.50 ($12.05); set dinner £13.50 ($25). MC, V.
   Open: Lunch Tues–Sun 12:30–2pm; dinner daily 7–9:30pm.

 If you wish, you might leave Hastings and head east for this country village restaurant about 5 miles away. The Hastings/Rye bus passes by. It is known for its food, and many English residents in Sussex journey from miles around to enjoy the hospitality of Deirdre and Hartmut Seidler. Vegetarian dishes are available, and there is also a wide selection of homemade desserts. All the food is homecooked using fresh produce.

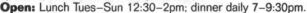

3. BATTLE

55 miles S of London; 34 miles NE of Brighton

GETTING THERE **By Train** The railway station at Battle is a stop on the London/Hastings rail link, with departures from both Charing Cross and Victoria stations in London. For more information, call 0424/429325. The trip takes 1 hour and 20 minutes.

By Bus It's best to go from London to Battle by train. However, if you're in Rye or Hastings in summer, you can take one of several frequent buses that run to Battle. For information and schedules, call 0424/431770.

By Car From M25 (the ring road around London), cut south to Seven Oaks and continue along A21 to Battle.

ESSENTIALS   The **area code** is 04246. The **Tourist Information Center** is at 88 High Street (tel. 04246/3721).

⭐ **S**even miles from Hastings, in the heart of the Sussex countryside, is the old market town of Battle, famed in history as the setting for the Battle of Hastings in 1066. King Harold, last of the Saxon kings, encircled by his housecarls, fought bravely, for his kingdom and his life; but he was killed by William, Duke of Normandy. To commemorate the victory, William the Conqueror founded **Battle Abbey** at the south end of Battle High Street (tel. 0426/63792), some of the stone for which was shipped from his own lands at Caen in northern France.

During the dissolution of the monasteries from 1538 to 1539 by King Henry VIII, the church of the abbey was largely destroyed. Some buildings and ruins, however, remain in what Tennyson called "O Garden, blossoming out of English blood." The principal building still standing is **Abbot's House,** which is leased to a private school for boys and girls and is only open to the general public during summer holidays. Of architectural interest is the **gatehouse,** which has octagonal towers and stands at the top of the Market Square. All of the north **Precinct Mall** is still standing, and one of the most interesting sights of the ruins is the ancient **Dorter Range,** where the monks once slept.

The town of Battle grew up around the abbey, but even though it has remained a medieval market town, many of the old half-timbered buildings regrettably have lost much of their original character because of stucco plastering carried on by past generations. The abbey is open mid-April through September daily from 10am to 6pm (closes at 4pm otherwise). Admission is £1.90 ($1.50) for adults and £1.50 ($2.80) for children. The Abbey lies a 5-minute walk from the rail station.

WHERE TO STAY

IN BATTLE

LA VIEILLE AUBERGE HOTEL AND RESTAURANT, 27 High St., Battle, East Sussex TN33 0EA. Tel. 04246/5171. Fax 04246/4015. 7 rms (5 with bath). TV TEL
$ Rates (including English breakfast): £29.50 ($54.60) single without bath, £35 ($64.75) single with bath; £45 ($83.25) double without bath, £55 ($101.75) double with bath. AE, DC, MC, V.

⭐ This hotel is housed in a structure rebuilt in 1688 using stones from the Battle Abbey kitchen, which was demolished in 1685. Each of the comfortable bedrooms has individually controlled central heating, a radio, hot-beverage facilities, a trouser press, and hot and cold running water. Most of the rooms contain private baths. It is located in the town center.

Mainly French cuisine is offered in the cozy restaurant, which has an inglenook fireplace, and the gourmet specialties are made with local products (fish, venison, and wild duck). The proprietors, Stephen and Kathy Dickey (Kathy is from Boston, Massachusetts), serve lunch daily from noon to 2pm and dinner from 7 to 10pm. The two-course dinner costs £14 ($25.90), and the three-courses £18 ($33.30). A set three-course lunch is £14.50 ($26.85). There is also a bar lounge.

NEARBY

KITCHENHAM FARM, Bodiam, near Robertsbridge, East Sussex TN32 5UN. Tel. 0580/850357. 2 rms (none with bath).
$ Rates (including English breakfast): £13 ($24.05) per person. No credit cards.
Parking: Free.
This 15th-century farmhouse is owned and operated as a farm by Mrs. Daws and her family. Their house is typical of East Sussex: weather-boarded, with an interior boasting old beams, a fireplace with an inglenook, and a well-kept garden. The farm was originally called St. Christopher, because it was a resting place for pilgrims en

route to Canterbury from Chichester. Try to call for a reservation before 6pm. Breakfast is prepared farm-style including bacon, grilled tomatoes, freshly laid eggs, and homemade jam.

The farm is on the Sussex border, ½ mile from Bodiam Castle, built in 1386, the last military castle in Britain. That's only 8 miles from Battle Abbey, the same distance from Rudyard Kipling's former home, and just 54 miles from London.

NETHERFIELD HALL, Netherfield, near Battle, East Sussex TN33 9PQ. Tel. 04246/4450. 4 rms (2 with bath). **Directions:** 3 miles west of Battle; take the A2100.

$ **Rates** (including English breakfast): £25 ($46.25) single without bath, £30 ($55.50) single with bath; £30 ($55.50) double without bath, £40 ($74) double with bath. No credit cards. **Parking:** Free.

 Three miles from Battle, this is a good base for exploring the countryside. Jean and Tony Blake offer well-furnished bedrooms, and guests are served tea on a wide covered veranda. There is a phone at the reception desk for guests, plus a TV lounge.

LITTLE HEMINGFOLD FARMHOUSE, Telham, Battle, East Sussex TN33 OTT. Tel. 04246/4338. 13 rms (11 with bath or shower). **Directions:** Take A2100 from Battle for 2 miles, turning off at signpost.

$ **Rates** (including English breakfast): £30 ($55.50) single without bath, £35 ($66.60) single with bath; £50 ($92.50) double without bath, £60 ($111) double with bath. MC, V. **Parking:** Free.

Little Hemingfold lies 1½ miles from Battle off A2100 and is reached by going down a steep road. It's a rustic white building that is part 17th century and part early Victorian. A little patio overlooks a lake, and guests often enjoy apéritifs on the lawn. A grass tennis court is available.

WHERE TO EAT

The following two recommendations are both in Battle.

THE GATEWAY RESTAURANT, 78 High St. Tel. 2856.
  Cuisine: ENGLISH. **Reservations:** Not needed.
$ **Prices:** Appetizers £1–£2.50 ($1.85–$4.65); main dishes £3.50–£4 ($6.45–$7.40); pastries 50p–£1.50 (95¢–$2.80); clotted cream tea £2.50 ($4.65). MC, V.
  Open: Sun–Fri 10am–5pm; lunch Sun–Fri noon–2:30pm; dinner Sat 7–10pm.

 A few paces from the entrance to Battle Abbey, this restaurant is the best place in town for afternoon tea, but it's also a good and reasonably priced restaurant. Contained within a low-beamed building from the 17th century, it was a forge for a blacksmith before its later transformation into a bakery. An avid gardener, the owner, Mrs. Ruth Reeve, along with her husband, Tony, maintain a rose garden with tables set beneath antique arbors. A wide variety of homemade pastries, including chocolate profiteroles, is displayed. In the afternoon, the clotted cream teas are a delight. Lunches include such classic English dishes as cottage pie, steak-and-kidney pie, chicken-and-leek pie, and beer-and-mushroom casserole. Dinner is served only on Saturday when reservations are necessary.

PILGRIMS REST RESTAURANT, Battle Village Green, High St. (adjacent to Battle Abbey). Tel. 2314.
  Cuisine: ENGLISH. **Reservations:** Not needed except on Sun.
$ **Prices:** Appetizers £1.65–£1.95 ($3.05–$3.60); main courses £3.25–£7.15 ($6–$13.25). No credit cards.
  Open: Daily 10am–6pm.

In an early 15th-century, black-and-white timbered house on the main street, this is a preferred place in town for morning coffee, lunch, or afternoon tea. You'll not only receive good portions of homemade food, but you'll also experience an authentic atmosphere. You may have your meal in the Long Room, the Great Hall, or in the garden, which has a view of the ancient stones of Battle Abbey Gateway, only 30 feet away. For afternoon tea, you can have a pot of tea, a Sussex cream tea, or something more substantial. The restaurant is licensed.

4. ALFRISTON & LEWES

60 miles S of London

GETTING THERE   By Train   Rail service is available from London's Victoria Station and London Bridge Station heading for Lewes. One train per hour makes the trip during the day taking 1¼ hours. Trains are more frequent during rush hours. There is no rail service to Alfriston.

By Bus   Buses run daily from London's Victoria Coach Station, although there are many stops along the way. The trip takes 3 hours; it's better to take the train. Once in Lewes, connect with a bus run by the Southdown Bus Company which will take you to Alfriston in 30 minutes. The bus station at Lewes is on East Street in the center of town.

By Car   Head east along M25 (the London ring road), cutting south along A26 via East Grinstead to Lewes. Once at Lewes, follow A27 east to the signposted turnoff for the village of Alfriston.

ESSENTIALS   The **area code for Alfriston** is 0323; the **area code for Lewes** is 0273. The **Tourist Information Centre** is in Lewes at Chapel Hill (tel. 0273/471600).

Nestled on the Cuckmere River, **Alfriston** is one of the most beautiful villages of England and has several old inns. Its High Street, with its old market cross, looks like one's fantasy of what an English village should be. Some of the old houses still have hidden chambers where smugglers stored their loot.

The village lies northeast of Seaford on the English Channel, in the vicinity of the resort of Eastbourne and the modern port of Newhaven. During the day, Alfriston is likely to be overrun by bus tours; it's that lovely, and that popular.

Only about a dozen miles along the A27 toward Brighton lies **Lewes,** an ancient Sussex town centered in the South Downs worth exploring. Since the home of the Glyndebourne Opera is only 5 miles to the east, accommodations are difficult to reserve during the Glyndebourne Opera festival. The town has many historical associations, listing such residents as Thomas Paine who lived at Bull House, High Street, now a restaurant.

WHAT TO SEE & DO

IN ALFRISTON

You can visit **Drusilla's Zoo Park** (tel. 0323/870656), off the A27, which has won awards. One mile outside Alfriston, it is not large, but is fascinating nonetheless with a flamingo lake, Japanese garden, and unusual breeds of some domestic animals, among other attractions. Children are especially delighted, as there is a playland covering more than one acre. The park is open from late March until October daily from 10am to 5pm (until dusk in winter), charging adults £3.95 ($7.30) and children £3.75 ($6.95).

IN LEWES

The half-timbered **Anne of Cleves House,** 52 Southover High Street (tel. 0273/474610), was part of Anne of Cleves's divorce settlement from Henry VIII, but Anne of Cleves never lived in the house, and there is no proof that she ever visited

Lewes. Today the house is a Museum of Local History and is cared for by the Sussex Archaeological Society. The museum has a furnished bedroom and kitchen and displays of furniture, local history of the Wealden iron industry, and other local crafts. Admission is £1.50 ($2.80) for adults, 75p ($1.40) for children. It's open April through October Monday through Saturday from 10am to 5pm, Sunday 2 to 5pm.

Lewes, of course, grew up around its Norman castle which today houses the **Museum of Sussex Archaeology,** at the junction of Castlegate and High Street (tel. 0273/474379). From the tower, you can enjoy a fine view of the countryside. A 20-minute audiovisual show is also presented. A joint admission ticket costs £2.50 ($4.65) for adults, £1.25 ($2.30) for children for castle, museum, and show. It's open Monday through Saturday from 10am to 5:30pm, Sunday 11am to 5:30pm.

EASY EXCURSION

KIPLING'S HOME IN SUSSEX

Rudyard Kipling, the British writer famous for his stories about the days of empire in India, lived his last 34 years—1902 to 1936—at **Bateman's,** a country house northwest of Battle half a mile south of Burwash, on the A265, the Lewes-Etchingham road (tel. 0435/882302). The sandstone house, built in 1634, was bequeathed, together with its 300 acres of land and its contents, to the National Trust by Kipling's widow. The interior is filled with Asian rugs, antique bronzes, and other mementos the writer collected in India and elsewhere. Kipling's library is among the points of interest to be visited. The house is open from April through October Saturday to Wednesday from 11am to 5:30pm. Admission to the house and garden is £3 ($5.55) for adults and £1.50 ($2.80) for children; on Saturday, Sunday, and bank holidays, it's £3.50 ($6.45) for adults and £1.80 ($3.35) for children.

WHERE TO STAY

IN ALFRISTON

The George Inn is also known for its good food.

PLEASANT RISE FARM, off B2108, Alfriston, near Polegate, East Sussex BN26 5TN. Tel. 0323/870545. 4 rms (1 with bath).
$ Rates (including English breakfast): £16–£18 ($29.60–$33.30) single without bath; £28 ($51.80) double without bath, £32 ($59.20) double with bath. No credit cards. **Parking:** Free.

This farmhouse is on 100 acres of farm land adjoining an old-world village off Seaford/Alfriston Road. Views are provided from the comfortable rooms, one with private bath. Indoor and outdoor tennis and badminton courts and country walks add to the pleasure. Mr. and Mrs. Savage will advise you on restaurants, sightseeing, and leisure activities.

GEORGE INN, High St., Alfriston, Polegate, East Sussex BN26 5SY. Tel. 0323/870319. Fax 0323/226995. 8 rms (6 with shower). TV TEL **Bus:** No. 727.
$ Rates (including English breakfast): £33 ($61.05) single without bath, £44 ($81.40) single with bath; £58 ($107.30) double without bath, £66–£90 ($122.10–$166.50) double with bath. AE, DC, MC, V.

First licensed as an inn in 1397, this long, low, and inviting inn was once a rendezvous for smugglers. The most expensive room is a historic four-poster bedroom. The George, however, is better known for its good food. If you're there for lunch, your meal will cost from £8 ($14.80). Food is served from noon to 2:15pm and 6:30 to 9:30pm daily. Dinner costs from £12 ($22.20) each. A garden is in back, but most guests head for the restaurant with its Windsor chairs and beamed ceiling.

IN LEWES

Accommodations are difficult during the Glyndebourne Opera Festival, but are adequate at other times.

CROWN HOTEL, 191 High St., Lewes, East Sussex BN7 2NA. Tel. 0273/480670. 12 rms (4 with bath). TV TEL
$ Rates: £25 ($46.25) single without bath; £35 ($64.75) single with bath; £35 ($64.75) double without bath, £42 ($77.70) double with bath. Breakfast £2 ($3.70) extra. MC, V.

This will not please everybody, and it's not grand in any way, but many readers like it. A bit creaky, it's one of the oldest bars in Lewes; in fact, this is really a Georgian pub. The hotel, run by Brian and Gillian Tolton, is considerably refurbished. All of the rooms have hot-beverage facilities. Opposite the war memorial, the hotel stands at a traffic circle on the main street. Pub lunches are available Monday to Saturday, and evening meals can be served on request Monday to Thursday only.

FELIX GALLERY, 2 Sun St. at Lancaster St., Lewes, East Sussex BN7 2QB. Tel. 0273/472668. 2 rms (none with bath). TV
$ Rates (including English breakfast): £17–£19 ($31.45–$35.15) single; £32–£36 ($59.20–$66.60) double. MC, V.

Completely up-to-date, this inviting cottage is one of the best buys in town. It lies in a tranquil location a short walk from the heart of town and the already-previewed Lewes Castle. Rooms have hot-beverage facilities, and public parking is available nearby.

WHERE TO EAT
IN LEWES

RONNIE'S WINE BAR, 197 High St. Tel. 477879.
Cuisine: CONTINENTAL. **Reservations:** Recommended. **Bus:** No. 127.
$ Prices: Appetizers £1.95–£2.15 ($3.60–$4); main courses £4–£8 ($7.40–$14.80). MC, V.
Open: Mon–Sat 10am–11pm, Sun 10am–3pm and 7–10:30pm.

A popular wine bar in the town center, this is attractively decorated in a café-bistro style, with dark-wood chairs and circular tables. Meals are likely to include special platters as vegetables, lasagne verde, roast beef salad, or chili con carne. Of the desserts, none is better than the hot chocolate fudge cake. Live music is sometimes featured in the evenings.

EASY EXCURSIONS
RODMELL

This small Downland village lies midway between Lewes and the port of Newhaven on the C7 road. The chief attraction is **Monks House,** a National Trust property that was bought by Virginia and Leonard Woolf in 1919 and was their home until his death in 1969. Virginia wrote of the profusion of fruit and vegetables produced by the garden and of the open water meadows looking out on the downs. Much of the house was furnished and decorated by Virginia's sister, Vanessa Bell, and the artist Duncan Grant. The house can be visited May through September Wednesday and Saturday from 2 to 6pm; April and October Wednesday and Saturday from 2 to 5pm. Last entry is half an hour before closing time. Admission is £1.70 ($3.15); children under 5 enter free.

Rodmell also has a 12th-century church, a working farm, and a tiny Victorian school still in use.

THE BLUEBELL RAILWAY

This railway is at Sheffield Park Station, near Uckfield in East Sussex (tel. 082572/2370 for Talking Timetable, 082572/3777 for information), on the A275 from Lewes to Danehill. It takes its name from the spring flowers that grow alongside the track, running from Sheffield Park to Horsted Keynes. A railway buff's delight, the steam locomotives date from 1872 to the 1950s and the end of steam in England. You can visit the locomotive sheds, plus a museum and a large buffet and bookshop. At Horsted Keynes, there's a carriage shed, and the Victorian room on the platform offers refreshments while you wait for your train. The journey from Sheffield Park, climbing out of the Ouse Valley through countryside, takes 15 minutes and costs adults £4 ($7.40) and children £2 ($3.70). There are several daily services from the end of May to the end of September. In spring and autumn, service is restricted mainly to Saturday and Sunday. In December, January, and February, trains operate on Sunday only.

5. BRIGHTON

52 miles S of London

GETTING THERE By Train Trains—41 a day—leave from Victoria or London Bridge Station taking 55 minutes.

By Bus Buses from Victoria Coach Station take around 2 hours.

By Car The M23 (signposted from Central London) leads to the A23 which will take you into Brighton.

ESSENTIALS The **area code** is 0273. At the **Tourist Information Centre,** Marlborough House, 54 Old Steine (tel. 0273/23755), by the Royal Albion Hotel and the bus terminal, you can make hotel reservations, reserve tickets for National Express buses, and pick up a list of current events.

Brighton was one of the first of the great seaside resorts of Europe. The village on the sea from which the present town grew was originally named Brighthelmstone. The original swinger who was to shape so much of its destiny arrived in 1783, after just turning voting age; he was the then Prince of Wales, whose presence and patronage gave immediate status to the seaside town.

Fashionable dandies from London, including Beau Brummell, turned up. The construction business boomed, as Brighton blossomed with charming and attractive town houses and well-planned squares and crescents. From the Prince Regent's title came the voguish word "Regency," which was to characterize an era, but more specifically refers to the period between 1811 and 1820. Under Victoria, and in spite of her cutting off the patronage of her presence, Brighton continued to flourish.

Alas, earlier in this century, as the English began to discover more glamorous spots on the continent, Brighton lost much of its old *joie de vivre*. It became more aptly tabbed as tatty, featuring the usual run of fun-fair-type English seaside amusements. However, that state of affairs has been changing, due largely to the huge numbers of Londoners moving in (some of whom have taken to commuting); the invasion is making Brighton increasingly light-hearted and sophisticated. For instance, a beach east of the town attracts nude bathers, Britain's first such venture.

The Lanes, a closely knit section of alleyways off North Street in Brighton (many of the present shops were formerly fisherman's cottages), were frequented in Victoria's day by style-setting curio and antiques collectors. Some are still there, although they now share space with boutiques.

WHAT TO SEE & DO
THE ROYAL PAVILION

Among the royal residences of Europe, the Royal Pavilion at Brighton (tel. 0273/603005), a John Nash version of an Indian mogul's palace, is unique. Ornate and exotic, it has been subjected over the years to the most devastating wit of English satirists and pundits; but today we can examine it more objectively as one of the outstanding examples of the orientalizing tendencies of the romantic movement in England.

The pavilion was originally built in 1787 by Henry Holland, but it no more resembled its present look than a caterpillar does a butterfly. By the time Nash had transformed it from a simple classical villa into an Oriental fantasy, the Prince Regent had become King George IV, and the king and one of his mistresses, Lady Conyngham, lived in the palace until 1827.

A decade passed before Victoria, then queen, arrived in Brighton. Although she was to bring Albert and the children on a number of occasions, the monarch and Brighton just didn't mix. The very air of the resort seemed too flippant for her. By 1845, Victoria began packing, and the royal furniture was carted off. Its tenants gone, the pavilion was in serious peril of being torn down, but by a narrow vote, Brightonians agreed to purchase it. Gradually, it was restored to its former splendor, enhanced in no small part by the return of much of its original furniture on loan by the present tenant at Buckingham Palace.

Of exceptional interest is the domed **Banqueting Hall,** with a chandelier of bronze dragons supporting lilylike glass globes. In the great kitchen, with its old revolving spits, is a collection of Wellington's pots and pans, his *batterie de cuisine,* from his town house at Hyde Park Corner. In the state apartments, particularly the domed salon, dragons wink at you, serpents entwine, lacquered doors shine. The music room, with its scalloped ceiling, is a salon of water lilies, flying dragons, sunflowers, reptilian paintings, bamboo, silk, and satin.

In the second-floor gallery, look for Nash's views of the pavilion in its elegant heyday. There is also an exhibition of pavilion history, illustrating the damage caused by rainwater, frequent alterations, and the impressive program of repair and reclamation in progress.

The pavilion is open October to May daily from 10am to 5pm, June to September to 6pm; it's closed Christmas and Boxing Day. Admission is £2.60 ($4.80) for adults, £1.30 ($2.40) for children 5 to 15. A family ticket for one adult and up to four children costs £3.90 ($7.20), for two adults and up to four children £6.50 ($12.05).

WHERE TO STAY

DOUBLES WITHOUT BATH FOR LESS THAN £50 [$92.50]

THE ADELAIDE HOTEL, 51 Regency Sq., Brighton, East Sussex BN1 2FF. Tel. 0273/205286. Fax 0273/220904. 12 rms (all with bath or shower). TV TEL **Bus:** No. 27
$ Rates (including English breakfast): £33–£60 ($61.05–$111) single; £52–£70 ($96.20–$129.50) double. MC, V. **Parking:** £6 ($11.10) per night.
The small hostelry is in a beautifully restored Regency building that has been tastefully modernized and decorated without losing its early 19th-century ambience. All units have hairdryers and hot-beverage facilities. The higher prices quoted above is for a room with a four-poster bed. The Adelaide is in the center of Brighton, just behind the West Pier.

AMBASSADOR, 22 New Steine, Marine Parade, Brighton, East Sussex BN2 1PD. Tel. 0273/676869. 9 rms (all with bath or shower). TV TEL
$ Rates (including English breakfast): £23–£25 ($42.55–$46.25) single; £44–£50 ($81.40–$92.50) double. Children under 12 can share room with two adults for half price. AE, DC, MC, V.
A family-run hotel lying on a waterfront square, this overlooks Palace Pier. All comfortably furnished bedrooms have hot beverage facilities. The front tearooms have a sea view, and there is also an attractive residents' lounge.

ASCOTT HOUSE HOTEL, 21 New Steine, Marine Parade, Brighton BN2 1PD. Tel. 0273/688085. 16 rms (10 with bath). TV TEL **Bus:** No. 27.
$ Rates (including English breakfast): £22 ($40.70) single without bath, £32

($59.20) single with bath; £42 ($77.70) double without bath, £60 ($111) double with bath. AE, DC, MC, V. **Parking:** Free.

 Michael and Avril Strong's establishment enjoys a location within a short walk of the Royal Pavilion. It's also near the pier and the famous Lanes, with their shops and boutiques. This popular licensed hotel has a reputation for comfort, cleanliness, and good breakfasts. The single, double, triple, and family bedrooms have radio/alarms, hairdryers, and hospitality trays, and most provide full private facilities. In addition, the front bedrooms have a sea view.

LE FLEMING'S HOTEL, 12A Regency Sq., Brighton, East Sussex BN1 2FG. Tel. 0273/27539. Fax 0273/27539. 9 rms (all with bath). TV TEL

$ Rates (including English breakfast): £25–£35 ($46.25–$64.75) single; £40–£50 ($74–$92.50) double. AE, DC, MC, V.

 One of the most highly acclaimed B&B hotels in the resort, this is only a short walk from the seafront and offers small, but handsomely furnished bedrooms. You'd better reserve in advance for this one—it's worth it.

MALVERN HOTEL, 33 Regent Sq., Brighton, East Sussex BN1 2GG. Tel. 0273/24302. 12 rms (all with shower). TV TEL **Bus:** No. 7 or 52.

$ Rates (including English breakfast): £32–£40 ($59.20–$74) single; £52–£60 ($96.20–$111) double. AE, DC, MC, V.

Only a stone's throw from the seafront, this 1820 Regency building is on an attractive square. Rooms are clean and brightly furnished and have hot-beverage facilities. There's a small lounge bar with a residential license to serve liquor only to hotel guests.

MARINA HOUSE HOTEL, 8 Charlotte St., Marine Parade, Brighton, East Sussex BN2 1AG. Tel. 0273/605349. Fax 0273/605349. 10 rms (7 with shower). TV TEL **Bus:** No. 7.

$ Rates: £13.50–£19 ($25–$35.15) single without bath; £29 ($53.65) double without bath, £39 ($72.15) double with bath. AE, DC, MC, V.

One of the best accommodations in its price range at Brighton, this white town house, built in the Regency style, sits about a block from the sea, near an interesting collection of antiques shops. Many accommodations have high ceilings and elaborate plasterwork; only double rooms have showers. Visitors have free use of the elegant front parlor, and evening meals are available upon request.

PASKINS HOTEL, 19 Charlotte St., Brighton, East Sussex BN2 1AG. Tel. 0273/601203. Fax 0273/621973. 18 rms (16 with bath). TV TEL **Bus:** No. 7 or 52.

$ Rates (including English breakfast): £25 ($46.25) single with bath; £50 ($92.50) double without bath, £52 ($96.20) double with bath. MC, V. **Parking:** Free.

This well-run, small hotel is owned by Michale Paskins and is only a short walk from the Palace Pier and Royal Pavilion. Tariffs depend on the plumbing and furnishings; the most expensive units are fitted with four-poster beds. The hotel is licensed and provides bar food most evenings, although it is surrounded by lots of restaurants.

ROWLAND HOUSE, 21 St. George's Terrace, Kemp Town, Brighton, East Sussex BN2 1JJ. Tel. 0273/603639. 10 rms (all with shower). TV **Bus:** No. 7 or 52.

$ Rates (including English breakfast): £16 ($29.60) single; £30–£32 ($55.50–$59.20) double. MC, V.

This well-furnished house has full central heating and units with room call and courtesy coffee. It is located just behind the Royal Crescent on Marine Parade, 250 yards from the beach. No rooms are higher than the second floor.

TROUVILLE PRIVATE HOTEL, 11 New Steine, Marine Parade, Brighton, East Sussex BN2 1PD. Tel. 0273/697384. 9 rms (2 with bath or shower). TV **Bus:** No. 7 or 52.

$ Rates (including English breakfast): £16–£18 ($29.60–$33.30) single without bath; £26 ($48.10) double without bath, £46 ($85.10) double with bath. AE, MC, V.

This period town house has been tastefully restored and is situated in a select square within walking distance of shops and restaurants. Double rooms have hot-beverage facilities. The most expensive double has a four-poster bed, balcony, and sea view.

WORTH THE EXTRA BUCKS

TOPPS HOTEL, 17 Regency Sq., Brighton, East Sussex BN1 2PG. Tel. 0273/729334. Fax 0273/203679. 12 rms (all with bath). A/C MINIBAR TV TEL **Bus:** No. 7 or 52.

$ Rates (including English breakfast): £40 ($74) single; £70–£90 ($129.50–$166.50) double. AE, DC, MC, V. **Closed:** Christmas and first week in Jan.

Flowerboxes fill the windows of this cream-colored town house, whose owners, Paul and Pauline Collins, have devoted years to upgrading it. The hotel enjoys a diagonal view of the sea from its position beside the sloping lawn of Regency Square. Each of the differently shaped and individually furnished accommodations has a radio and a trouser press. A small restaurant in the basement serves dinners to clients who reserve by giving the room number.

TWENTY-ONE HOTEL, 21 Charlotte St., Marine Parade, Brighton, East Sussex BN2 1AG. Tel. 0273/686450. 7 rms (5 with shower). TV TEL **Bus:** No. 7 or 52.

$ Rates (including English breakfast): £35 ($64.75) single without bath; £50 ($92.50) single with bath; £45 ($83.25) double without bath; £65 ($120.25) double with bath. AE, MC, V.

Perhaps the most sophisticated of the smaller hotels of Brighton, this early Victorian, white house is a block from the sea. Janet and David Power rent attractive and well-furnished bedrooms with radios and hot-beverage facilities. The basement-level garden suite opens directly onto an ivy-clad courtyard.

A menu (in French with an English translation) of four courses costs £22 ($40.70). Main courses are likely to include sliced breast of duck served pink with a lime sauce or wild poached salmon with fine strips of vegetables. Reservations are required.

In Hove

HOTEL BRUNSWICK, 69 Brunswick Place, Hove, East Sussex BN3 1NE. Tel. 0273/733326. 27 rms (6 with bath or shower). TV **Bus:** No. 52.

$ Rates (including English breakfast): £20 ($37) single without bath; £24 ($44.40) single with bath; £33 ($61.05) double without bath; £47 ($86.95) double with bath. AE, DC, MC, V.

Originally built 200 years ago in a gray-stone Regency design, this rises from a central position in the center of Hove. Some bedrooms are in a more modern wing originally built in the 1930s. Each unit contains coffee-making facilities.

CHATSWORTH PRIVATE HOTEL, 9 Salisbury Rd., Hove, East Sussex BN3 3AB. Tel. 0273/737360. 8 rms (none with bath). **Bus:** No. 52.

$ Rates (including English breakfast): £17.50 ($32.40) single; £35 ($64.75) double. No credit cards. **Parking:** Free.

This may be small, but it meets the tests of cleanliness, good food, comfortable beds, and a cozy lounge with television—not to mention the Swiss-style personal services of Francis Gerber. Bedrooms are large and suitably furnished, and there's a bathroom and toilet on every floor. It's located near the County Cricket Ground.

WHERE TO EAT

Of all towns in the south of England (excluding London, of course), Brighton has the best food and the widest choice of restaurants. My sampling represents the best of the budget establishments.

MEALS FOR LESS THAN £7.50 [$13.90]

ALLANJOHN'S, 8 Church St. Tel. 683087.
  Cuisine: SEAFOOD. **Reservations:** Not needed. **Bus:** No. 7 or 52.
$ **Prices:** Appetizers £1.50–£2.50 ($2.80–$4.65); main courses £3.50–£6.50 ($6.45–$12.05). No credit cards.
  Open: Mon–Thurs 10am–5:30pm, Fri 9:30am–6pm, Sat 9am–6pm, Sun 10:30am–3pm.
Here you'll find a fascinating display of fresh winkles, cockles, shrimp, crab, and lobster to be eaten with brown bread and butter, salt, and vinegar. Select a bowl of fresh crabmeat or a seafood plate with a salad. If you're lunching light, try the smoked salmon sandwich or the crab sandwich. Hot food includes cod and plaice filets, all served with salad and french fries.

BROWN'S RESTAURANT AND BAR, 3-4 Duke St. Tel. 23501.
  Cuisine: ENGLISH/CONTINENTAL. **Reservations:** None. **Bus:** No. 7 or 52.
$ **Prices:** Salads from £3 ($5.55); main courses £4–£10 ($7.40–$18.50). AE, MC, V.
  Open: Restaurant Mon–Sat 11am–11pm; Sun noon–11:30pm; bar Mon–Sat 11am–11pm, Sun 11am–3pm and 7–10:30pm.
On the western side of the Lanes, this 1930s place is actually two places—both a restaurant and bar. A shared kitchen interconnects the bar with the restaurant, although the entrance to the bar is technically at 34 Ship Street. In the bar, snacks are priced from £4 ($7.40), including a New York and Cajun–inspired menu. Specialties include spicy chicken wings, Dijon-laced chicken, and bagels with lox and cream cheese. The restaurant doesn't feature appetizers, although many diners begin with a salad. Try a club sandwich for lunch, or, for dinner, Brown's leg of lamb, a Scottish sirloin steak, or a steak, mushroom, and Guinness pie.

CRIPES, 7 Victoria Rd. Tel. 27878.
  Cuisine: CREPES. **Reservations:** Recommended. **Bus:** No. 49 or 52.
$ **Prices:** Crêpes £2.50–£3.75 ($4.65–$6.95). MC, V.
  Open: Lunch daily noon–2:30pm; dinner daily 6–11:30pm.
I think this should be named "Crêpes," because it specializes in those delectable and savory offerings from Brittany. A corner establishment, and rather cramped, this has an old-fashioned decor, with oak tables and bentwood chairs. The whole-meal, buckwheat crêpes—called galettes here—are made to order, and there are many fillings to choose from.

FOOD FOR FRIENDS, 17A Prince Albert St., the Lanes. Tel. 202310.
  Cuisine: VEGETARIAN. **Reservations:** None. **Bus:** No. 7 or 52.
$ **Prices:** Appetizers £1.10–£1.50 ($2.05–$2.80); main courses £2.50–£2.75 ($4.65–$5.10). No credit cards.
  Open: Mon–Thurs 9am–10pm, Fri–Sat 9am–11pm, Sun 11:30am–10pm.
 A standout on "Restaurant Row" in Brighton, this self-service restaurant seems to offer the freshest food and best value. There may be a wait, but most patrons don't mind. Of course, in a vegetarian restaurant you expect homemade soups, fresh salads, and the like, but here you get many exotic varieties of vegetarian cookery, including dishes from India, Bali, or Mexico, depending on the night.

PINOCCHIO PIZZERIA RISTORANTE, 22 New Rd. Tel. 677676.
  Cuisine: ITALIAN. **Reservations:** Recommended. **Bus:** No. 7 or 52.
$ **Prices:** Appetizers £1.45–£3.80 ($2.70–$7); main courses £3.55–£6.95 ($6.65–$12.85). AE, DC, MC, V.
  Open: Lunch daily noon–2:30pm; dinner daily 6–11:30pm.
In the center of the resort, this popular restaurant is near the Theatre Royal and is opposite the Royal Pavilion gardens. It offers a large selection of pastas and pizzas with specialty Italian desserts. Pinocchio's has a light, airy atmosphere together with a bright, efficient Italian staff.

POPGRADA, 125 King's Rd. Tel. 26302.
 Cuisine: ENGLISH/ITALIAN. **Reservations:** Recommended. **Bus:** No. 52.
$ **Prices:** Appetizers £1.50–£3.75 ($2.80–$6.95); main courses £3–£7.50 ($5.55–$13.90). AE, DC, MC, V.
 Open: Daily 11am–10pm.

This good value restaurant is in the semibasement of the Granville Hotel and under the same ownership. The little bistro has a patio overlooking the seafront. Depending on your taste, you can order such English dishes as roast lamb or steak-and-kidney pie, or go Italian with pasta and veal dishes.

---

6. ARUNDEL

58 miles S of London; 21 miles E of Brighton

GETTING THERE By Train Trains leave hourly during the day from London's Victoria Station taking 1¼ hours.

By Bus Most bus connections are through Littlehampton opening onto the English Channel, lying west of Brighton. From Littlehampton, leave the coastal road by taking bus no. 212 which runs between Littlehampton and Arundel hourly during the day.

By Car From London follow the signposts to Gatwick Airport and from there head south toward the coast along A29.

ESSENTIALS The **area code** is 0903. The **Tourist Information Centre** is at 61 High Street (tel. 0903/882268).

This small town in West Sussex nestles at the foot of one of England's most spectacular castles. The town was once an Arun River port, and its denizens enjoyed the prosperity of considerable trade and commerce. However, today the harbor traffic is replaced with buses filled with tourists.

WHAT TO SEE & DO

ARUNDEL CASTLE, Mill Road. Tel. 0903/883136.
 ⭐ The ancestral home of the dukes of Norfolk, this baronial estate off High Street is a much-restored mansion of considerable importance. Its legend is associated with some of the great families of England—the Fitzalans and the powerful Howards of Norfolk.

Arundel Castle has suffered destruction over the years, particularly during the Civil War, when Cromwell's troops stormed its walls, perhaps in retaliation for the 14th Earl of Arundel's (Thomas Howard) sizable contribution to Charles I. In the early 18th century, the castle virtually had to be rebuilt, and in late Victorian times, it was remodeled and extensively restored again. Today it is filled with a good collection of antiques, along with an assortment of paintings by old masters, such as Van Dyck and Gainsborough.

Surrounding the castle is a 1,100-acre park whose scenic highlight is Swanbourne lake.

 Admission £3.50 ($6.45) adults, £2.50 ($4.65) children 5-15.
 Open: Apr–last Fri in Oct Sun–Fri 1–5pm, but June–Aug daily and bank holidays noon–5pm. Last admission 4pm.

ARUNDEL TOY AND MILITARY MUSEUM, at "Doll's House," 23 High St. Tel. 0903/882908.
 In a Georgian cottage in the heart of historic Arundel, this museum displays an intriguing family collection spanning many generations of old toys and games, small militaria, dolls, dollhouses, tin toys, musical toys, famous stuffed bears, stuffed frogs, Britain's animals and soldiers, arks, boats, rocking horses, crested military models, an

eggcup collection, and other curiosities. The museum is opposite Treasure House Antiques and Collectors Market.

Admission: £1.25 ($2.30) adults, £1 ($1.85) children.
Open: Easter–Oct daily 10:45am–5pm.

ARUNDEL CATHEDRAL, London Rd. Tel. 0903/882297.

A Roman Catholic cathedral, the Cathedral of Our Lady and St. Philip Howard stands at the highest point in town. It was constructed for the 15th Duke of Norfolk by A. J. Hansom, who invented the Hansom taxi. However, it was not consecrated as a cathedral until 1965. The interior includes the shrine of St. Philip Howard, featuring Sussex wrought ironwork.

Admission: Free, but donations are appreciated.
Open: June–Sept daily 9am–6pm; off-season daily 9am–dusk. **Directions:** From center continue west from High Street.

WHERE TO STAY

DOUBLES WITHOUT BATH FOR LESS THAN £34 ($62.90)

ARDEN GUEST HOUSE, 4 Queens Lane, Arundel, West Sussex BW18 9JN Tel. 0903/882544. 8 rms (3 with bath or shower). TV **Bus:** No. 212.

$ Rates: (including English breakfast): £18 ($33.30) single without bath, £20 ($37) single with bath; £28 ($51.80) double without bath, £34 ($62.90) double with bath. No credit cards. **Parking:** Free.

Jeff and Carol Short, the proprietors, offer a warm welcome here. All of the comfortably furnished rooms have hot and cold running water and hot-beverage facilities. Single rooms are available only in winter.

ARUNDEL HOUSE, 11 High St., Arundel, West Sussex BN18 9AD. Tel. 0903/882136. 6 rms (4 with bath). TV **Bus:** No. 212.

$ Rates: (including English breakfast): £16 ($29.60) single without bath, £19 ($35.15) single with bath; £32 ($59.20) double without bath, £38 ($66.60) double with bath. MC, V.

 John and Christine Crowe are the resident owners of this 17th-century guesthouse and licensed restaurant. Only seconds away from the castle entrance, it offers clean, comfortable rooms with hot-beverage facilities. The house is open for morning coffee, hot meals, afternoon teas, and Sussex cream teas on Monday to Saturday from 10am to 2:30pm and 6:30 to 9pm, and Sunday from 10am to 7pm.

PORTREEVES ACRE, the Causeway, Arundel, West Sussex BN18 9JJ. Tel. 0903/883277. 3 rms (all with bath). TV **Bus:** No. 212.

$ Rates (including English breakfast): £22–£30 ($40.70–$55.50) single; £30–£38 ($55.50–$70.30) double. No credit cards. **Parking:** Free.

When this modern, two-story house was built by a local architect within a stone's throw of the ancient castle and rail station, it caused much local comment. Today the glass-and-brick edifice is the property of Charles and Pat Rogers. Double guest rooms are on the ground floor and have views of the flowering acre in back. The property is bordered on one side by the River Arun, near which rabbits and flowering trees flourish.

WORTH THE EXTRA BUCKS

DUKES, High St., Arundel, West Sussex BN18 9AD. Tel. 0903/883847. 5 rms (all with bath). TV **Bus:** No. 212.

$ Rates (including English breakfast and VAT): £30–£45 ($55.50–$83.25) single; £46–£62 ($85.10–$114.70) double. AE, MC, V.

The best of the small hotels in town is big on amenities, charm, and character. Mike and Valerie Moore are the guiding light behind this little gem, which has elegantly decorated rooms in the main building and two additional units in a Victorian cottage in the rear garden. The accommodations have TVs, coffee-making facilities, and modern baths, while a few still retain their Regency detailing and ornate plasterwork. The location is across a busy street from the crenellated fortifications surrounding the castle. The hotel's street-level restaurant is recommended below.

THE SWAN HOTEL, High St., Arundel, West Sussex BN18 9AG. Tel. 0903/882314. 11 rms (all with bath or shower). TV TEL **Bus:** No. 212.
$ Rates (including English breakfast): £47 ($86.95) single; £60 ($111) double. AE, DC, MC, V.

This Georgian inn on the River Arun provides one of the best moderately priced accommodations in Arundel. Ken and Diana Rowsell offer comfortably furnished bedrooms, most of which are twins or doubles, which all have equipment for making hot drinks. You can order drinks and snacks in the bar area, and the restaurant serves meals made with the freshest of ingredients. A fixed-price dinner costs £10.50 ($19.45), and the service is polite and attentive.

WHERE TO EAT

IN TOWN

DUKES, High St. Tel. 883847.
Cuisine: FRENCH. **Reservations:** Required. **Bus:** No. 212.
$ Prices: Appetizers £2.45–£4.95 ($4.55–$9.15); main courses £6.95–£10.95 ($12.85–$20.15); three-course set dinner £13.50 ($25). AE, MC, V.
Open: Dinner Sun–Thurs 6–9pm, Fri–Sat 6–10pm.

Already recommended as a hotel, Dukes is also one of the leading restaurant choices. Owners Valerie and Michael Moore invite guests into their elegant dining room, located on the street level. The restaurant is noted for its 17th-century, gilt-carved walnut ceiling, which was originally from a baroque Italian palace; part of this ceiling was once installed in the home of Douglas Fairbanks, Jr. Typical dishes include steak au poivre, trout with almonds, and sole meunière.

PARTNERS, 25A High St. Tel. 882018.
Cuisine: SANDWICHES. **Reservations:** None.
$ Prices: Salads £2.50–£3.25 ($4.65–$6); burgers and omelets £1.10–£1.60 ($2.05–$2.95); sandwiches 80p ($1.50). No credit cards.
Open: June–Sept daily 9am–5pm; off-season daily 9am–4pm.

The decor is that of a Formica-clad café whose modernity cannot conceal the beamed ceiling and the 200-year-old building containing it. Service is good natured, and the place is definitely mass market, appealing to those seeking fast food between visits to Arundel Castle. It has a take-out service if you'd like to go on a picnic along a country lane in West Sussex. It's located on the main street.

ON THE OUTSKIRTS

GEORGE & DRAGON, Houghton. Tel. 831559.
Cuisine: BRITISH/SEAFOOD. **Reservations:** None at lunch; required at dinner. **Directions:** Turn off the A284 at Bury Hill onto the B2139. **Bus:** No. 31.
$ Prices: Appetizers £3–£5 ($5.55–$9.25); main courses £5–£15 ($9.25–$27.75); pint of lager £1.45 ($2.70); pub snacks £2.50–£5 ($4.65–$9.25). MC, V.
Open: Restaurant dinner daily 6:30–9:30pm; pub Mon–Sat 11am–2:30pm and 6–11pm; Sun noon–3pm and 7–10:30pm.

Three miles north of Arundel is an old English pub known for excellent food. In 1651, Charles II, fleeing Cromwell's wrath after being crowned king at Scone in Scotland, stopped at the George & Dragon for food and drink before escaping to France. (He returned in 1660, after the death of Cromwell, to take the throne.) Originally a farmhouse, the inn is made up of two timber-and-flint cottages dating from the 13th century, with huge inglenook fireplaces and a shared chimney. An ancient spit in one of them was once used for preparing the roast joints of which the English are so fond. In winter, log fires blaze, making the pub toasty warm. The main bar and smaller apéritif bar, both with tapestry-covered seating and beamed ceilings, overlook the restaurant, where the cows dined back in the 17th century. In summer, you can eat in the pleasant garden or on the terrace.

Menu specialties include fresh fish, when available. In honor of a dish consumed, according to legend, by Charles II, spiced ox tongue is also served, along with homemade soups and pâtés, English cheese, and such traditional dishes as roast half duckling in a client's choice of orange, apple, port, or gooseberry sauce.

7. CHICHESTER

69 miles SW of London; 31 miles W of Brighton

GETTING THERE By Train Trains depart from London's Victoria Station every hour during the day taking 1½ hours. The last train back to London is at 9pm.

By Bus Buses leave from London's Victoria Coach Station at the rate of 4 per day.

By Car From London's ring road, head south along A3, turning onto A286 for the final approach to Chichester.

ESSENTIALS The **area code** is 0243. The **Tourist Information Centre** is at Peter's Market, West Street (tel. 0243/775888).

According to one newspaper, Chichester might have been just a market town if the Chichester Festival Theatre had not been established in its midst. One of the oldest Roman cities in England, Chichester draws a crowd from all over the world who come to see its theater's presentations.

Only a 5-minute walk from the Chichester Cathedral and the old Market Cross, the 1,400-seat theater, with its apron stage, stands on the edge of Oaklands Park. It opened in 1962 (first director: Lord Laurence Olivier), and its reputation has grown steadily, pumping new vigor and life into the former walled city.

CHICHESTER FESTIVAL THEATRE & MINERVA STUDIO THEATRE

The Chichester Festival Theatre offers plays and musicals with all-star casts during the summer season (May to September) and in the winter and spring months orchestras, jazz, opera, theater, ballet, and a Christmas show for all the family. Matinee performances begin at 2:30pm, evening performances at 7:30pm, except first nights, which begin at 7pm.

The Minerva is a studio theater which offers one of the most adventurous programs during the year in the south and houses a theater restaurant (tel. 0243/782219), society clubroom, and shop. Performances here begin at 2:45pm and 7:45pm.

Theater reservations made over the telephone will be held for a maximum of 4 days (call 0243/781312). It is better to mail inquiries and checks to the Box Office, Chichester Festival Theatre, Oaklands Park, Chichester, West Sussex PO19 4AP. MasterCard, VISA, and American Express are accepted.

WHERE TO STAY

DOUBLES WITHOUT BATH FOR LESS THAN £20 [$37]

WHYKE HOUSE, 13 Whyke Lane, Chichester, West Sussex PO19 2JR. Tel. 0243/788767. 4 rms (none with bath). TV
$ Rates (including continental breakfast): £10–15 ($18.50–$27.75) single; £20–£30 ($37–$55.50) double. No credit cards. **Parking:** Free.

A short distance from the heart of Chichester, the Whyke makes a good base for seeing a production at the theater and for exploring such attractions in the environs as Fishbourne Palace and old Bosham. It has a relaxed atmosphere, and rooms, one of which is suited for families, are tidily decorated, warm, and comfortable. Reservations are important. Smoking is not allowed.

WORTH THE EXTRA BUCKS

BEDFORD HOTEL, Southgate, Chichester, West Sussex PO19 1DP. Tel. 0243/785766. Fax 0243/533175. 3 rms (13 with bath). TV
$ Rates (including English breakfast): £32 ($59.20) single without bath, £42 ($77.70) single with bath; £48 ($88.80) double without bath, £60 ($111) double with bath. AE, DC, MC, V.

This is one of the best all-around moderately priced accommodations in Chichester; its origins are traced to the 18th century. The comfortable and quiet rooms contain hot and cold running water, and some also have private shower/baths and toilets. In summer, advance reservations are strongly advised. It's located in the town center.

WHERE TO EAT

MEALS FOR LESS THAN £8 ($14.80)

CLINCHS SALAD HOUSE, 14 Southgate. Tel. 788822.
 Cuisine: VEGETARIAN. **Reservations:** Not needed. **Bus:** No. 31.
$ Prices: Appetizers £1.40–£2.50 ($2.60–$4.65); all vegetarian dishes £2.40 ($4.45); pizzas £1.35 ($2.50). AE, DC, MC, V.
 Open: Mon–Sat 8am–5:30pm.

 The outstanding self-service vegetarian restaurant in the area is often frequented by health-conscious diners who aren't necessarily vegetarian. Salads are always freshly made of quality ingredients, and there are always several hot dishes of the day, usually "vegetable bakes." Wash it all down with an herbal tea. Children are especially welcomed, and the location is near the bus station.

NOBLE ROT BRASSERIE AND WINE BAR, Little London, off East St. Tel. 779922.
 Cuisine: CONTINENTAL. **Reservations:** Recommended. **Bus:** No. 31.
$ Prices: Appetizers £2.50–£4 ($4.65–$7.40); main courses £4–£7.50 ($7.40–$13.90); lunch buffet £6.50 ($12.05). MC, V.
 Open: Daily 11am–11pm.

Consisting of three 200-year-old wine cellars within the city walls, this has been converted into one of the most popular and lively before- and after-theater restaurants in West Sussex. The interior is covered with posters of famous theatrical productions from all over the world, and the atmosphere is decidedly continental. Meals might include roast duck in orange sauce, veal dijonnaise, or a variety of locally produced steaks. At lunchtime, a special inclusive buffet menu is available. To enter the establishment, you descend a flight of exterior steps from Little London.

ROUSSILLON COFFEE SHOP, Dolphin & Anchor, West St. Tel. 785121.
 Cuisine: ENGLISH. **Reservations:** Not needed. **Bus:** No. 31.
$ Prices: Appetizers £1.30–£2.90 ($2.40–$5.35); main courses £4.35–£7.50 ($5.60–$13.90). AE, DC, MC, V.
 Open: Daily 10am–6pm.

In one of Chichester's better-known hotels, this coffee shop attracts visitors throughout the day. It is decorated like an informal bistro, with bare wooden tables and big windows, occupying a white-fronted stone annex to the hotel. Dishes are typically English—nothing fancy, but everything fresh tasting and politely served. Try deep-fried mushrooms, sirloin steak, filet of plaice, or grilled ham.

NICODEMUS, 14 St. Pancras. Tel. 532372.
 Cuisine: ITALIAN. **Reservations:** Recommended. **Bus:** No. 31.
$ Prices: Appetizers £1.95–£4.35 ($3.60–$5.60); main courses £4.95–£7.60 ($9.15–$14.10). MC, V.
 Open: Dinner Tues–Sat 7–10:30pm.

This house, a 10-minute walk east of the town center, has an Old English decor with a partially beamed ceiling. Its building was originally a bakery 350 years ago. It offers what is reputed to be the best Italian cuisine in the area in the trattoria tradition. Try the cannelloni Nicodemus (with a minced lamb and spinach filling). You can also order various kinds of pasta with savory sauces. A house specialty is pork scallopine Nicodemus cooked in garlic butter with brandy and cream.

ON THE OUTSKIRTS

THE HUNTERS INN, Lavant, Chichester. Tel. 527329.
   Cuisine: ENGLISH. **Reservations:** Recommended.
$ Prices: Appetizers £2–£4 ($3.70–$7.40); main dishes £9.50–£12 ($17.60–$22.20); three-course Sunday lunch £8 ($14.80). AE, DC, MC, V.
   Open: Lunch daily noon–1:30pm; dinner daily 6:30–9:30pm.
This inn dates back to the early 16th century, but its present facade was added in the 18th century by the duke of Richmond. In the 1940s, it was the center for the Goodwood motor-racing fraternity, and now with extensive modernization it is an inn overlooking a garden.

The chef and patron, Allan Hope-Kirk, has two restaurants, a small à la carte dining room with an English and French cuisine, and the "Light Bite" bar, serving everything from sandwiches to steaks at reasonable prices, but still with waiter service. Fresh fish dishes are a specialty. The bars, both the public bar and the lounge bar, serve no fewer than 40 different beers and lagers. In winter, an open fireplace provides warmth. Try such appetizers as mussels marinara or duck liver pâté, followed by the catch of the day or lamb cutlets grilled pink with fresh rosemary and served with black currant coulis. Beef is prime Hampshire steer, and pheasant and saddle of venison are also featured. The restaurant is 1½ miles north of Chichester on the Midhurst Road (A286).

EASY EXCURSIONS

FISHBOURNE

A worthwhile sight that is only 1½ miles from Chichester is the remains of the **Roman Palace,** Salthill (tel. 0243/785859), the largest Roman residence yet discovered in Britain. Built around A.D. 75 in villa style, it has many mosaic-floored rooms and even an underfloor heating system. The gardens have been restored to their original 1st-century plan. The story of the site is told both by an audiovisual program and by text in the museum. There is a cafeteria.

The museum is open from March through November: March, April, and October daily 10am to 5pm; May to September daily 10am to 6pm; November daily 10am to 4pm; and December to February Sunday only from 10am to 4pm. Admission is £2.50 ($4.65) for adults, £1 ($1.85) for children. The museum is sited to the north of A259, off Salthill Road, and signposted from Fishbourne Village. Parking is free. Buses stop regularly at the bottom of Salthill Road, and the museum is within a 5-minute walk of British Rail's Fishbourne Station.

OLD BOSHAM

Bosham, a few miles west of Fishbourne, is one of the most charming villages in West Sussex and is principally a sailing resort, linked by good bus service to Chichester. It was the site of the first establishment of Christianity on the Sussex coast. The Danish King Canute made it one of the seats of his North Sea empire, and it was the site of a manor (now gone) of the last of England's Saxon kings, Harold, who sailed from here to France on a journey that finally culminated in the invasion of England by William the Conqueror in 1066.

Bosham's little church was depicted in the Bayeux Tapestry. Its graveyard overlooks the boats, and the church is filled with ship models and relics, showing the villagers' link to the sea. A daughter of King Canute is buried inside. Near the harbor, it is reached by a narrow lane.

Where to Stay

HATPINS, Bosham Lane, Bosham, near Chichester, West Sussex PO18 8HL. Tel. 0243/572644. 4 rms (2 with bath or shower). TV

$ Rates (including English breakfast): £25 ($46.25) single without bath; £40 ($74) double without bath, £50 ($92.50) double with bath. No credit cards. **Parking:** Free.

⭐ If you're seeking rooms, try one of the most delightful accommodations in the area. Run by Mr. and Mrs. Waller, it is far superior to your typical B&B, but there are only four bedrooms, so reservations are a must. Guests can enjoy breakfast in an attractive conservatory, or later an excellent English dinner. It's located off A259.

WEALD & DOWNLAND OPEN-AIR MUSEUM

In the beautiful Sussex countryside at Singleton, 6 miles north of Chichester on the A286 (London road), historic buildings that have been saved from destruction are being reconstructed on a 40-acre Downland site. The structures show the development of traditional building from medieval times to the 19th century in the weald and downland area of southeast England.

Exhibits include a Tudor market hall, a medieval farmstead and other houses dating from the 14th to 17th centuries, a working watermill producing stone-ground flour, a blacksmith's forge, plumbers' and carpenters' workshops, a toll cottage, a 17th-century treadwheel, agricultural buildings including thatched barns and an 18th-century granary, a charcoal burner's camp, and a 19th-century village school.

The museum is open April through October daily from 11am to 6pm. From November to March, it is open only on Wednesday and Sunday from 11am to 5pm. Admission is £3 ($5.55) for adults, £1.50 ($2.80) for children. For further information, call 024363/348.

HAMPSHIRE & DORSET

This countryside is reminiscent of scenes from Burke's *Landed Gentry*, from fireplaces where stacks of logs burn to wicker baskets of apples freshly brought in from the orchard. Old village houses, now hotels, have a charming quality. Beyond the pear trees, on the crest of a hill, you'll find the ruins of a Roman camp. A village pub, with two rows of kegs filled with varieties of cider, is where the hunt gathers.

You're in Hampshire and Dorset, two shires jealously guarded by the English, who protect their special rural treasures. Everybody knows of Southampton and Bournemouth, but less known is the hilly countryside farther inland. You can travel through endless lanes and discover tiny villages and thatched cottages untouched by the industrial invasion.

The area is rich in legend and in literary and historical associations. Here Jane Austen and Thomas Hardy wrote and set their novels. Here, too, King Arthur held court at the Round Table. And from here sailed such famous ships as the *Mayflower,* Lord Nelson's *Victory,* the D-Day invasion flotilla, and the *QE2.*

HAMPSHIRE

This is the county Jane Austen wrote of—firmly middle class, largely agricultural, its inhabitants doggedly convinced that Hampshire is the greatest place on earth. Austen wrote six novels, including *Pride and Prejudice* and *Sense and Sensibility,* that earned her a permanent place among the great 19th-century writers. Her books provide an insight into the manners and mores of the English who were to build up a powerful empire. Although the details of the life she described have now largely faded, much of the mood and spirit of the Hampshire depicted in her books remains.

Hampshire encompasses the South Downs, the Isle of Wight (Victoria's favorite retreat), and the naval city of Portsmouth. The more than 90,000 acres of the New Forest was preserved by William the Conqueror as a private hunting ground. William lost two of his sons in the New Forest—one killed by an animal, the other by an arrow. Today it is a vast woodland and heath, ideal for walking and exploring.

Although Hampshire is filled with many places of interest, for our purposes I've concentrated on two major areas: Southampton for convenience of transportation and accommodations and Winchester for history.

DORSET

This is Thomas Hardy country. Some of the towns and villages in Dorset, although altered considerably, are still recognizable from his descriptions. "The last of the great

WHAT'S SPECIAL ABOUT HAMPSHIRE & DORSET

Beaches

☐ Bournemouth, the premier seaside resort of Dorset, set among pines with sandy beaches and fine coastal views.

☐ Chesil Beach, a 20-mile-long wall-like bank of shingle running from Abbotsbury to the Isle of Portland. Great beachcombing.

Great Towns/Villages

☐ Winchester, ancient capital of England, with a cathedral built by William the Conqueror.

☐ Portsmouth, premier port of the south—the first dock built in 1194. Home to HMS *Victory*, Nelson's flagship.

☐ Lyme Regis, with its famed Cobb, a favorite of Jane Austen and a setting for *The French Lieutenant's Woman*.

Buildings

☐ Beaulieu Abbey, Lord Montagu's estate west of Southampton— sumptuous private home from 1538 and surrounded by gardens.

☐ Osborne House, Queen Victoria's most cherished residence, where she died on January 22, 1901.

☐ Broadlands, elegant Palladian house on the River Test, former home of the late Lord Mountbatten.

☐ Winchester Cathedral, dating from 1079, longest medieval cathedral in Britain.

Natural Spectacles

☐ The New Forest, 145 square miles of heath and woodland—once the hunting ground of Norman kings.

Literary Shrines

☐ Chawton Cottage, where novelist Jane Austen lived.

☐ Thomas Hardy's Cottage at Higher Bockhampton.

Victorians," as he was called, died in 1928 at the age of 88. His tomb is in a position of honor in Westminster Abbey.

One of England's smallest shires, Dorset encompasses the old seaport of Poole in the east and Lyme Regis in the west (known to Jane Austen). Dorset is a southwestern county and borders the English Channel. It's known for its cows, and Dorset butter is served at many an afternoon tea. This is mainly a land of farms and pastures, with plenty of sandy heaths and chalky downs.

The most prominent tourist center of Dorset is the Victorian seaside resort of Bournemouth. If you don't anchor there, you might also try a number of Dorset's other seaports, villages, and country towns; I mostly stick to the areas along the impressive coastline. Dorset, as the vacation-wise English might tell you, is a budget traveler's friend.

SEEING HAMPSHIRE & DORSET

GETTING THERE

The south is linked to London by excellent motorways, notably the M3 to Winchester, the M3 and A33 to Southampton, and the A3 to Portsmouth. British Rail serves the area frequently from London's Waterloo Station (call 071/928-5100 for specific schedules of London departures). It takes only 1 hour and 15 minutes to reach Southampton, 2 hours to Bournemouth, and 1 hour and 40 minutes to Portsmouth.

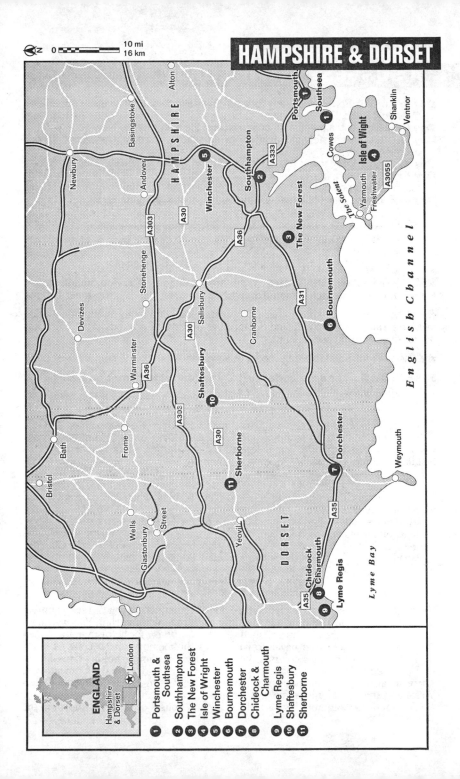

HAMPSHIRE & DORSET

10 mi
0
16 km

English Channel

HAMPSHIRE

DORSET

Lyme Bay

The Solent

Portsmouth
Southsea
Isle of Wight
Cowes
Shanklin
Ventnor
Yarmouth
Freshwater
A3055

Alton
Basingstoke
Newbury
Andover
Southampton
Winchester
A333
A36
A31
The New Forest
Bournemouth
A303
A30
Stonehenge
Salisbury
Cranborne
Devizes
Warminster
A36
Shaftesbury
A30
A303
Sherborne
A30
Dorchester
Weymouth
Bath
Frome
Bristol
Wells
Glastonbury
Street
Yeovil
Chideock
Charmouth
Lyme Regis
A35

ENGLAND
Hampshire
& Dorset
★ London

1 Portsmouth & Southsea
2 Southhampton
3 The New Forest
4 Isle of Wright
5 Winchester
6 Bournemouth
7 Dorchester
8 Chideock & Charmouth
9 Lyme Regis
10 Shaftesbury
11 Sherborne

A SUGGESTED ITINERARY

Day 1: Arrive in Portsmouth early for a full day's sightseeing of its many attractions. Overnight there.
Day 2: Using Southampton as a base, explore the sights of the New Forest.
Day 3: Visit Winchester and explore its attractions, including its cathedral, and overnight there.
Day 4: Devote 1 day to the Isle of Wight and visit Queen Victoria's Osborne House.
Day 5: Begin your tour of Dorset with an overnight stopover in the premier seaside resort of Bournemouth.
Day 6: End your tour of Dorset with an overnight stay at Lyme Regis.

1. PORTSMOUTH & SOUTHSEA

70 miles SE of London; 21 miles E of Southampton

GETTING THERE   By Train   Trains from London's Waterloo Station stop at Portsmouth and Southsea Station frequently throughout the day (trip time: 1½ hr.).

By Bus   National Express coaches operating out of London's Victoria Station make the run to Portsmouth and Southsea at the rate of one bus every 1½ hours during the day (trip time: 2½ hr.).

By Car   From London's ring road, cut south on A3.

ESSENTIALS   The **area code** is 0705. The **Tourist Information Centre** is at The Hard (without number; tel. 0705/826722).

Virginia, New Hampshire, even Ohio, may have their **Portsmouths,** but the forerunner of them all is the old port and naval base on the Hampshire coast. German bombers in World War II leveled the city, hitting about nine-tenths of its buildings. But the seaport has recovered admirably.

Its maritime associations are known around the world. From Sally Port, the most interesting district in the Old Town, countless naval heroes have embarked to fight England's battles. That was certainly true on June 6, 1944, when Allied troops set sail to invade occupied France.

Southsea, adjoining Portsmouth, is a popular seaside resort with fine sands, gardens, bright lights, and a host of vacation attractions. Many historic monuments can be seen along the stretches of open space, where you can walk on the Clarence Esplanade and look out on the Solent and view Portsmouth harbor.

WHAT TO SEE & DO

You might want to begin your tour on the Southsea front, where you can see a number of naval monuments. These include the big anchor from Nelson's ship, *Victory,* plus a commemoration of the officers and men of HMS *Shannon* for heroism in the Indian Mutiny. An obelisk with a naval crown honors the memory of the crew of HMS *Chesapeake,* and a massive column, the Royal Naval memorial, honors those lost at sea in the two world wars. A shaft is also dedicated to men killed in the Crimean War. There are also commemorations of persons who fell victim to yellow fever in Queen Victoria's service in Sierra Leone and Jamaica.

The Southsea Common, between the coast and houses of the area, known in the

13th century as Froddington Heath and used for army bivouacs, is a picnic and play area today.

THE *MARY ROSE* SHIP HALL AND EXHIBITION, College Rd. (without number), Portsmouth Naval Base. Tel. 0705/750521.

⭐ The *Mary Rose*, flagship of the fleet of wooden men-of-war of King Henry VIII, sank in the Solent in 1545 in full view of the king. In 1982, the heir to the throne, Charles, Prince of Wales, watched the *Mary Rose* break the water's surface after almost four centuries on the ocean floor, not exactly shipshape and Bristol fashion but surprisingly well preserved nonetheless. Now the remains are on view, but the hull must be kept permanently wet.

The hull and the more than 10,000 items brought up by divers constitute one of the major archeological discoveries in England in many years. Among the artifacts on permanent exhibit are the almost complete equipment of the ship's barber, with surgeon's cabin saws, knives, ointments, and plaster all ready for use; long bows and arrows, some still in shooting order; carpenters' tools; leather jackets; and some fine lace and silk. Close to the dock, near the hull, is the *Mary Rose* exhibition in boathouse 5, where artifacts rescued from the ship are stored. It features an audiovisual theater and a spectacular two-deck reconstruction of a segment of the ship, including the original guns. A display with sound effects recalls the sinking of the vessel.

For more information, write the *Mary Rose* Trust, College Road, HM Naval Base, Portsmouth, Hampshire PO1 3LX.

Admission: £3.50 ($6.45) adults, £2.25 ($4.15) children, £10 ($18.50) family (two adults and two children).

Open: Mar–Oct daily 10am–5:30pm; Nov–Feb daily 10:30am–5pm. **Closed:** Dec 25. **Directions:** Use entrance to Portsmouth Naval Base through Victory Gate (as for HMS *Victory*), and follow signs.

HMS *VICTORY,* No. 2 dry dock, in Portsmouth Naval Base. Tel. 0705/819604.

Of major interest is Lord Nelson's flagship, a 104-gun, first-rate ship. Although it first saw action in 1778, it earned its fame on October 21, 1805, in the Battle of Trafalgar when the English scored a victory over the combined Spanish and French fleets. It was in this battle that Lord Nelson lost his life. The flagship, after being taken to Gibraltar for repairs, returned to Portsmouth with Nelson's body on board (he was later buried at St. Paul's in London).

Admission: £3 ($5.55) adults, £1.60 ($2.95) children.

Open: Mar–Oct Mon–Sat 10:30am–5:30pm, Sun 1–5pm; Nov–Feb Mon–Sat 10:30am–5pm, Sun 1–5pm. **Closed:** Dec 25. **Directions:** use entrance to naval base through Victory Gate.

ROYAL NAVAL MUSEUM, in the dockyard, Portsmouth Naval Base. Tel. 0705/733060.

The museum is next to Nelson's flagship, HMS *Victory,* and the *Mary Rose* in the heart of Portsmouth's historic naval dockyard. The only museum in Britain devoted exclusively to the general history of the Royal Navy, it contains relics of Nelson and his associates, together with unique collections of ship models, naval ceramics, figureheads, medals, uniforms, weapons, and other naval memorabilia. Special displays feature "The Rise of the Royal Navy" and "H.M.S. *Victory* and the Campaign of Trafalgar." Other exhibits include the Victorian navy, the navy in the 20th century, the modern navy, and representations of the sailor in popular art and culture. The museum complex includes a buffet and souvenir shop.

Admission: 80p ($1.50) adults, 50p (95¢) students and children, £2.10 ($3.90) family of four.
Open: Daily 10:30am–5:30pm (last entrance at 5pm). **Closed:** Nov–Feb.

SOUTHSEA CASTLE, Clarence Esplanade, Southsea. Tel. 0705/827261.

A fortress built of stones from Beaulieu Abbey in 1545 as part of King Henry VIII's coastal defense plan, the castle is now a museum. Exhibits trace the development of Portsmouth as a military stronghold, as well as naval history and the archeology of the area. It's located in the center of Southsea near the D-Day Museum.

Admission: £1 ($1.85) adults, 60p ($1.10) children.
Open: Daily 10:30am–5:30pm. **Closed:** Dec 24–26.

THE D-DAY MUSEUM, Clarence Esplanade, Southsea. Tel. 0705/827261.

Right next door to Southsea Castle, the museum is devoted to the Normandy landings and contains the Overlord Embroidery, which shows the complete story of Operation Overlord. The appliquéd embroidery, believed to be the largest of its kind (272 feet long and 3 feet high), was designed by Sandra Lawrence and took 20 women of the Royal School of Needlework 5 years to complete. There is a special audiovisual program with displays, including reconstructions of various stages of the mission with models and maps. You'll see a Sherman tank in working order, Jeeps, field guns, and even a DUKW (popularly called a Duck), that incredibly useful amphibious truck that operated on land and sea.

Admission: £3 ($5.55) adults, £1.80 ($3.35) children, £7.80 ($14.45) family of four.
Open: Daily 10:30am–5:30pm. **Closed:** Dec 24–26.

PORTCHESTER CASTLE, near Farnham. Tel. 0705/378291.

On the northern side of Portsmouth Harbour on a spit of land are the remains of this castle, plus a Norman church. Built in the late 12th century by King Henry II, the castle is set inside the impressive walls of a 3rd-century Roman fort built as a defense against Saxon pirates, when this was the northwest frontier of the declining Roman Empire. By the end of the 14th century, Richard II had modernized the castle and had made it a secure small palace. Among the ruins are the hall, kitchen, and great chamber of this palace. Portchester was popular with medieval kings, who stayed here when they visited Portsmouth. The last official use of the castle was as a prison for French seamen during the Napoleonic wars.

Admission: £1.30 ($2.40) adults, 65p ($1.20) children.
Open: Apr–Sept Tues–Sun 10am–6pm; Oct–Mar Tues–Sun 10am–4pm. **Directions:** Lies west toward Southampton on M27.

ROYAL NAVY SUBMARINE MUSEUM, Haslar Jetty Rd., Gosport. Tel. 0705/529217.

Cross Portsmouth Harbour by one of the ferries that bustle back and forth all day to Gosport. Some departures go directly from the station pontoon to HMS *Alliance* for a visit to the submarine museum, which traces the history of underwater warfare and life from the earliest days to the present nuclear age and contains excellent models, dioramas, medals, and displays from all ages. There is also as much about submariners themselves as about the steel tubes in which they make their homes, and although the museum focuses on English boats, it includes much of international interest.

The principal exhibit is HMS *Alliance,* and after a brief audiovisual presentation, visitors are guided through the boat by ex-submariners. Midget submarines, not all of them English, including an X-craft, can be seen outside the museum. Also on display is HM *Torpedo Boat No. 1,* better known as *Holland I,* launched in 1901, which sank under tow to the breaker's yard in 1913 and was salvaged in 1982.

Admission: £2.60 ($4.80) adults, £1.60 ($2.95) children.
Open: Apr–Oct daily 10am–4:30pm; Nov–Mar daily 10am–3:30pm. **Transportation:** Ferry from The Hard in Portsmouth to Gosport or bus no. 9.

WHERE TO STAY
IN OLD PORTSMOUTH

FORTITUDE COTTAGE, 51 Broad St., Old Portsmouth, Hampshire PO1 2JD. Tel. 0705/823748. 3 rms (1 with bath). TV **Bus:** Old Portsmouth.

$ Rates (including English breakfast): £28 ($51.80) single without bath, £30 ($55.50) single with bath; £30 ($55.50) double without bath, £32 ($59.20) double with bath. No credit cards. **Parking:** Free.

 Carol Harbeck owns this charming small house on Camber inner harbor. It is a narrow, four-story structure, almost Dutch in style, with a steep outdoor staircase. Each bedroom has hot and cold running water, shaver points, and hot-beverage facilities.

MRS. F. E. FISHER, 9 Bath Sq., Old Portsmouth, Hampshire PO1 2JL. Tel. 0705/823748. 2 rms (none with bath). TV. **Bus:** Old Portsmouth.

$ Rates (including English breakfast): £30 ($55.50) single or double. No credit cards. **Parking:** Free.

The mother of Carol Harbeck of Fortitude Cottage (see above) also operates a B&B from this small house in the old part of town on a peninsula overlooking the harbor on both sides. Both of Mrs. Fisher's guest rooms—one double and one twin-bedded room—overlook the sea and contain tea- or coffee-making facilities. The bathroom is shared. Bedrooms are delightfully furnished, and the standard of service is high. Breakfast is served in an oak-paneled dining room.

IN SOUTHSEA

Southsea abounds with moderately priced small hotels or B&B houses.

BRISTOL HOTEL, 55 Clarence Parade, Southsea, Hampshire PO5 2HX. Tel. 0705/821815. 13 rms (11 with bath or shower). TV

$ Rates (including English breakfast): £16.50 ($30.55) single without bath, £32 ($59.20) single with bath; £35 ($64.75) double without bath, £42 ($77.70) double with bath. MC, V. **Parking:** Free.

One of the best of the Southsea establishments, this inviting family-run hotel occupies half of a twin-gabled Victorian house with views of a seaside park. It's run by Edward and Jean Fry (Edward spent 25 years in the Royal Navy). Bedrooms are modernized.

WHERE TO EAT

COUNTRY KITCHEN, 59 Marmion Rd., Southsea. Tel. 811425.

Cuisine: VEGETARIAN. **Reservations:** Not needed. **Bus:** No. 3 or 23.

$ Prices: Appetizers £1.35–£2.15 ($2.50–$4); main courses £2.35–£3.15 ($4.35–$5.85). No credit cards.

Open: Mon–Sat 9:30am–5pm.

 This self-service restaurant is a good place to eat. The fare includes homemade soups, fresh crisp salads, and special hot dishes of the day, followed by tea and cake. The kitchen is unlicensed. Only "free-range" eggs, vegetarian cheeses, and "ozone-friendly" packaging are used. The food, although vegetarian, and basically English, also has Indian influences. The brick-fronted corner building housing the restaurant is 500 years old, and the main restaurant is at street level, with additional seating one floor above.

ROSIE'S VINEYARD, 87 Elm Grove, Southsea. Tel. 755944.

Cuisine: CONTINENTAL. **Reservations:** Recommended. **Bus:** No. 3 or 23.

$ Prices: Appetizers £2 ($3.70); main courses £3–£8 ($5.55–$14.80). MC, V.

Open: Lunch Sun 12:30–2pm; dinner Mon–Sat 7–11pm, Sun 7–10:30pm.

 Rosie's is like a little place you might find on the Continent. In summer, guests prefer tables in the pergola garden. The cookery is accomplished and often imaginative, and the menu changes with the season. Look for the daily specials. Dishes include mussels marinara, lobster salad, and fried bream or plaice, with wines from around the world. This wine bar and bistro was originally a Victorian greengrocers, and its understated decor still includes some 19th-century stained-glass accents. Live jazz is heard on Friday at 8pm and at Sunday lunch (the only day lunch is offered), beginning at 12:30pm.

---

2. SOUTHAMPTON

87 miles SW of London; 161 miles E of Plymouth

GETTING THERE   By Plane   There is a small airport outside Southampton which is used mainly for flights to the Channel Islands. For information, call 0703/629600.

By Train   British Rail serves the south, with departures from London's Waterloo Station several times daily and taking 1¼ hours.

By Bus   National Express operates hourly departures from London's Victoria Station, heading for Southampton and taking 2½ hours.

By Car   Take M3 southwest from London.

ESSENTIALS   The **area code** is 0703. The **Tourist Information Centre** is at Above Bar Precinct (tel. 0703/221106).

To many North Americans, England's number-one passenger port, home base for the *Queen Elizabeth 2,* is the gateway to Britain. Southampton is a city of wide boulevards, parks, and shopping centers. In World War II, some 31½ million men set out from here (in World War I, more than twice that number passed through Southampton).

Its supremacy as a port dates from Saxon times, when the Danish conqueror, Canute, was proclaimed king here in 1017. Southampton was especially important to the Normans and helped them keep in touch with their homeland. Its denizens were responsible for bringing in the bubonic plague, which wiped out a quarter of the English population in the mid-14th century. On the Western Esplanade is a memorial tower to the Pilgrims, who set out on their voyage to the New World from Southampton on August 15, 1620. Both the *Mayflower* and the *Speedwell* sailed from here but were forced by storm damages to put in at Plymouth, where the *Speedwell* was abandoned. The memorial is a tall column with an iron basket on top—the type used as a beacon before lighthouses.

If you're waiting in Southampton between boats, you may want to explore some of the major sights of Hampshire on the periphery of the port—the New Forest, Winchester, the Isle of Wight, and Bournemouth in neighboring Dorset.

WHAT TO SEE & DO

In addition to the tours and museums listed below, **Ocean Village** and **town quay** on Southampton's waterfront are bustling with activity and are filled with shops, restaurants, and entertainment possibilities.

TOURS

Southampton has a long and varied history, as witnessed by the Roman settlement at Bitterne, the Saxon port of Hamvic, and the Norman town with town walls, some of which still stand. City tourist guides offer a wide range of free guided walks and regular city bus tours. Free guided walks of the medieval town are offered throughout the year on Sunday and Monday at 10:30am and in July, August, and September twice daily at 10:30am and 2:30pm. Tours start at Bargate. City bus tours run from mid-July to mid-September every Monday and Wednesday, and Friday in August. These tours depart at 2pm from outside the art gallery on the north side of the Civic Centre.

Charges are £2.50 ($4.65) for adults and £2 ($3.70) for children. Boat cruises around the docks and Solent run from Ocean Village most afternoons at 2:30pm. For more details, check with the tourist center (see above).

MUSEUMS

TUDOR HOUSE MUSEUM, St. Michael's Sq. Tel. 0703/832769.
The museum is housed in a late medieval timber-framed house with a banqueting hall furnished in a 16th-century style. It features exhibitions of Victorian and Edwardian domestic and social life and also sponsors temporary shows. Its garden, based on 16th-century texts and illustrations, is unique in southern England and has 50 species of herbs and flowers.
Admission: Free.
Open: Tues–Fri 10am–5pm, Sat 10am–4pm, Sun 2–5pm. **Bus:** No. 2, 6, 8, or 13.

MUSEUM OF ARCHEOLOGY, God's House Tower, Winkle St. Tel. 0703/220007.
Housed in part of the town's 15th-century defenses, the exhibitions here trace the history and portray the daily life of the Roman, Saxon, and medieval eras. The lives of the inhabitants are depicted in exhibitions.
Admission: Free.
Open: Tues–Fri 10am–5pm, Sat 10am–4pm, Sun 2–5pm. **Bus:** No. 2, 6, 8, or 13.

SOUTHAMPTON MARITIME MUSEUM, Town Quay. Tel. 0703/223941.
This museum features the history of the port of Southampton and has a model of the docks at their peak in the 1930s.
Admission: Free.
Open: Tues–Fri 10am–5pm, Sat 10am–4pm, Sun 2–5pm. **Bus:** No. 2, 6, 8, or 13.

AN EXCURSION TO BROADLANDS

Eight miles northwest of Southampton on the A31 stands **Broadlands** (tel. 0794/516878), home of the late Earl Mountbatten of Burma who was assassinated in 1979. Lord Mountbatten, who has been called "the last war hero," lent the house to his nephew, Prince Philip, and Princess Elizabeth as a honeymoon haven in 1947, and in 1981, Prince Charles and Princess Diana spent the first nights of their honeymoon here.

Broadlands is owned by Lord Romsey, Lord Mountbatten's eldest grandson, who has created a fine exhibition and audiovisual show that depicts the highlights of his grandfather's brilliant career as a sailor and statesman. The house, originally linked to Romsey Abbey, was purchased by Lord Palmerston in 1736 and was later transformed into an elegant Palladian mansion by Capability Brown and Henry Holland. Brown landscaped the parkland and grounds and made the river (the Test) the main object of pleasure. The house and the riverside lawns are open from mid-April to September daily from 10am to 4pm; it's closed Fridays except Good Friday until August 1. Admission is £4.50 ($8.35) for adults, £3 ($5.55) for children.

WHERE TO STAY

Finding an accommodation directly in Southampton isn't as important as it used to be. Few ships now arrive, and the places to stay just outside the city are just as good; if not better. For accommodations in the area, refer to the "New Forest" section below. However, I'll provide some budget accommodation listings for those who may want to stay within the city center.

DOUBLES WITHOUT BATH FOR LESS THAN £30 [$55.50]

BANISTER HOUSE HOTEL, 11 Brighton Rd., Southampton, Hampshire

SO1 2JJ. Tel. 0703/221279. 24 rms (14 with shower). TV TEL **Bus:** No. 11, 14, 15, or 20.

$ **Rates** (including English breakfast): £20.50 ($37.95) single without bath, £26.50 ($49.05) single with bath; £29.50 ($54.60) double without bath, £34 ($62.90) double with bath. AE, MC, V. **Parking:** Free.

This privately run hotel manages to be comfortable while charging bargain rates. You can eat in if you like, and enjoy the home-cooked meals costing from £10.50 ($19.45). The hotel has a licensed bar.

THE LINDEN, 51-53 The Polygon, Southampton, Hampshire SO1 2BP. Tel. 0703/225653. 13 rms (none with bath). TV **Bus:** No. 25 or 29.

$ **Rates** (including English breakfast): £13–£15 ($24.05–$27.75) single; £25–£28 ($46.25–$51.80) double. No credit cards.

This turn-of-the-century building, which has a green facade and an elaborate twin-gabled roof, is operated by Patricia and David Hutchins. Each room is equipped with hot and cold running water and coffee-making equipment. Only breakfast is served.

WORTH THE EXTRA BUCKS

HUNTERS LODGE HOTEL, 25 Landguard Rd., Shirley, Southampton, Hampshire SO1 5DL. Tel. 0703/227919. Fax 0703/230913. 20 rms (16 with bath or shower). TV TEL **Bus:** No. 25 or 29.

$ **Rates** (including English breakfast): £23 ($42.55) single without bath, £33 ($61.05) single with bath; £44 ($81.40) double without bath, £55 ($101.75) double with bath. AE, MC, V. **Parking:** Free.

One of the best of the small hotels of Southampton, this is only a short distance from the town center. The late Victorian building has outstanding gardens. An evening meal is served from 6:30pm, costing from £7.50 ($13.90).

ROSIDA GARDEN HOTEL, 25-27 Hill Lane, Southampton, Hampshire SO1 5AB. Tel. 0703/228501. Fax 0703/635501. 28 rms (all with bath). TV TEL **Bus:** No. 7, 9, or 10.

$ **Rates** (including English breakfast): £33–£43 ($61.05–$79.55) single; £45–£63 ($83.25–$116.55) double. AE, DC, MC, V.

In the heart of town this hotel respects the needs of travelers. It is equipped to accommodate visitors in a wheelchair and also has a heated outdoor swimming pool. Set in about 2 acres of grounds, including a small body of water, the hotel was renovated in the mid-1980s and is still well maintained. Guests enjoy a sun terrace in summer. You'll pay more here than in a typical B&B, but many feel it's worth it.

THE STAR HOTEL, 26 High St., Southampton, Hampshire SO9 4ZA. Tel. 0703/339939. Fax 0703/339939. 45 rms (39 with bath or shower). TV TEL **Bus:** No. 2, 6, 8, or 13.

$ **Rates** (including English breakfast): £30 ($55.50) single without bath, £52 ($96.20) single with bath; £60 ($111) double without bath, £70 ($129.50) double with bath. Discounts available for stays of 2 or more nights Fri–Sun, except in Sept–Oct. AE, DC, MC, V.

One of the better moderately priced inns in the town center, the Star was a fashionable meeting place in Georgian times. Its origins are uncertain (it may date from 1601). The public Victoria Room commemorates the visit of little Princess Victoria in 1831 at the age of 12. The Star has kept abreast of the times, and today it rents centrally heated bedrooms with radios and hot and cold running water. There's an informal but popular pub facing the street, plus an inexpensive restaurant on the premises.

WHERE TO EAT
MEALS FOR LESS THAN £10 ($18.50)

LA MARGHERITA, 4 Commercial Rd. Tel. 333390.
Cuisine: ITALIAN. **Reservations:** Not needed. **Bus:** No. 7, 9, or 10.

$ **Prices:** Appetizers 65p–£4.95 ($1.20–$9.15); main courses £4.90–£13.50 ($9.05–$25); set menus £10.50–£14.50 ($19.45–$26.85). AE, DC, MC, V.
Open: Lunch Mon–Sat noon–2pm; dinner Mon–Sat 6:30–11:15pm.

Popular with young people and families, this restaurant offers pizza and pasta, as well as veal, poultry, beef, and fish. Specialties include steak Diane and trout Mafiosa. You can order wine by the glass and end your meal with a strong espresso.

PEARL HARBOUR, 86A Above Bar St. Tel. 225248.
   Cuisine: CANTONESE. **Reservations:** Not needed. **Bus:** No. 5.
$ **Prices:** Appetizers £1.50–£2.50 ($2.80–$4.65); main courses £3.50–£7.50 ($6.45–$13.90); set dinner £10 ($18.50); set lunch £4 ($7.40). AE, DC, MC, V.
   Open: Daily noon–11:30am.

Here you can enjoy some of the best meals around, far superior to most Chinese restaurants on the southern coast. Concentrate on the fish specialties, such as braised lobster. The restaurant is on the second floor of a building right in the heart of town.

RED LION, High St. Tel. 333595.
   Cuisine: ENGLISH. **Reservations:** Not needed. **Bus:** No. 1, 2, 6, or 8.
$ **Prices:** Pub snacks from £2.50 ($4.65); lager from £1.32 ($2.45). No credit cards.
   Open: Mon–Sat 10am–11pm, Sun noon–3pm and 7–10:30pm.

One of the few architectural jewels to have survived World War II, this pub has its roots in the 13th century (as a Norman cellar), but its high-ceilinged and raftered Henry V Court Room is from Tudor times. The room was the scene of the trial of the earl of Cambridge and his accomplices, Thomas Grey and Lord Scrope, who were condemned to death for treason in plotting against the life of the king in 1415. Today, the Court Room is adorned with coats of arms of the noblemen who were peers of the condemned trio. The Red Lion is a fascinating place for a drink and a chat. Typical pub snacks are served.

---

3. THE NEW FOREST

95 miles SW of London; 10 miles W of Southampton

GETTING THERE   By Train   Go to Southampton (see above) where rail connections can be made to a few centers in the New Forest depending on where you are going. Where the train leaves off, bus connections are possible to all the towns and many villages.

By Bus   Southampton and Lymington have the best bus connections to New Forest villages.

By Car   Head west from Southampton along A35.

ESSENTIALS   The **area code** depends on the town or village (see individual places). The **information office** is at Appletree Court, Lyndhurst (tel. 0703/3121).

Stretching over about 92,000 acres, the New Forest is a large tract, 14 miles wide and 20 miles long. William the Conqueror laid out the limits of this then-private hunting preserve. Successful poachers faced the executioner if they were caught, and those who hunted but missed had their hands severed.

Henry VIII loved to hunt deer in the New Forest but he also saw an opportunity to build up the British naval fleet by supplying oak and other hard timbers to the boatyards at Buckler's Hard on the Beaulieu River. Today you can visit the old shipyards and the museum with its fine models of men-of-war, pictures of the old yard, and dioramas showing the building of these ships, their construction, and their launching. It took 2,000 trees to build one man-of-war.

Nowadays, a motorway cuts through the area, and the once thick forest has groves of oak trees separated by wide tracts of common land that is grazed by ponies and cows, hummocked with heather and gorse, and frequented by rabbits. But away from the main roads, where signs warn of wild ponies and deer, you'll find a private world of peace and quiet.

WHAT TO SEE & DO

BEAULIEU ABBEY—PALACE HOUSE, Beaulieu, on B3056 in the New Forest. Tel. 0590/612345.

The abbey and house, as well as the National Motor Museum, are on the property of Lord Montagu of Beaulieu (pronounced *"Bew*-ley"), at Beaulieu, 5 miles southeast of Lyndhurst and 14 miles west of Southampton. A Cistercian abbey was founded on this spot in 1204, and the ruins can be explored today. The Palace House was the great gatehouse of the abbey before it was converted into a private residence in 1538 and is surrounded by gardens.

On the grounds, the **National Motor Museum,** one of the best and most comprehensive motor museums in the world, with more than 250 vehicles, is open to the public. It traces the story of motoring from 1895 to the present. Famous autos include four land-speed record-holders, among them Donald Campbell's Bluebird. The collection was built around Lord Montagu's family collection of vintage cars. A special feature is called "Wheels." In a darkened environment, visitors can travel in specially designed "pods," each of which carries up to two adults and one child along a silent electric track. They move at a predetermined but variable speed, and each pod is capable of rotating almost 360°. This provides a means by which the visitor is introduced to a variety of displays spanning 100 years of motor development.

Sound and visual effects are integrated into individual displays. In one sequence, visitors experience the thrill of being involved in a Grand Prix race. For further information, contact the visitor reception manager, John Montagu Building, 590/612345.

Admission: £6 ($11.10) adults, £4 ($7.40) children.

Open: Easter–Sept daily 10am–6pm; Oct–Easter daily 10am–5pm. **Closed:** Dec 25. **Transportation:** Buses run from the Lymington bus station Mon–Sat. On Sun you'll need a taxi or private car.

THE MARITIME MUSEUM, Buckler's Hard. Tel. 0590/616203.

Buckler's Hard, an historic 18th-century village on the banks of the River Beaulieu, is where ships for Nelson's fleet were built, including the admiral's favorite, *Agamemnon,* as well as *Eurylus* and *Swiftsure.* The Maritime Museum reflects the shipbuilding history of the village. Its displays include shipbuilding at Buckler's Hard; Henry Adams, master shipbuilder; Nelson's favorite ship; Buckler's Hard and Trafalgar; and models of Sir Francis Chichester's yachts and items of his equipment. The cottage exhibits are a re-creation of 18th-century life in Buckler's Hard. Here you can stroll through the New Inn of 1793 and a shipwright's cottage of the same period, or look in on the family of a poor laborer at home. All displays include village residents and visitors of the late 18th century. The walk back to Beaulieu, 2½ miles along the riverbank, is well marked through the woodlands. During the summer, you can take a ½-hour cruise on the River Beaulieu in the present *Swiftsure,* an all-weather catamaran cruiser.

Admission: £2.20 ($4.05) adults, £1.30 ($2.40) children.

Open: Easter–May daily 10am–6pm; June–Sept daily 10am–9pm; Sept–Easter daily 10am–4:30pm.

WHERE TO STAY

DOUBLES WITHOUT BATH FOR LESS THAN £40 ($74)

BAY TREE HOUSE, 1 Clough Lane, Burley, near Ringwood, Hampshire BH24 4AE. Tel. 04253/3215. 2 rms (none with bath). TV **Directions:** From center of village green at Burley, follow signposts toward Ringwood.

$ **Rates** (including English breakfast): £14 ($25.90) per person. No credit cards. **Parking:** Free. **Closed:** Dec.

A single and a twin-bedded room are available for rent in this family home. Guests share the bathroom, and a cot is available for those with children. It's best to write to Annette Allen to reserve your room.

CATERS COTTAGE, Latchmoor, Brockenhurst, Hampshire SO42 7UP. Tel. 0590/23225. 4 rms (none with bath). TV **Directions:** Off Sway Road (B3055); call for specific details.

$ Rates (including English breakfast): £16 ($29.60) per person. No credit cards. **Parking:** Free.

Caters is among the more reasonably priced hotels and is in a village filled with thatched cottages and an array of expensive upmarket hotels. In its own patch of the forest, it's a cottage with a lot of character.

GROVE HOUSE, Newtown Minstead, near Lyndhurst, Hampshire SO43 7GG. Tel. 0703/813211. 1 rm (with bath). TV

$ Rates (including English breakfast): £30 ($55.50) single or double, £35 ($64.75) triple; £40 ($74) quad. No credit cards. **Parking:** Free.

Marlon Dixon offers accommodations in her own family's home. She has a comfortable guest room appropriate for families that faces south and west and can accommodate from one to four persons. This pleasant farmhouse is in a quiet rural location on the edge of the new forest village of Minstead. Rebuilt in 1920 after a fire on the foundation of an older house, Grove House is surrounded by an immaculate garden entwined with clematis, with a backdrop of horses and sheep grazing. An evening meal can be arranged from £9 ($16.65) per person.

THE VICARAGE, Church Corner, Burley, near Ringwood, Hampshire BA24 4AP. Tel. 04253/2303. Fax 04253/3453. 3 rms (none with bath).

$ Rates: £20–£25 ($37–$46.25) single; £26–£30 ($48.10–$55.50) double. No credit cards. **Parking:** Free.

 This house is set in an informal and secluded garden in a clearing in the New Forest, opposite the church in the village of Burley. The village lies between the A31 and the A35 main roads near Ringwood and is a good center for walking, riding, and enjoying the wild life of the forest. It is not far from the ancient cathedral cities of Salisbury and Winchester, the seacoast, and many other places of interest. The house is run by Mrs. Alan Clarkson, the vicar's wife, who can accommodate up to six people. Rooms are pleasant and comfortable, and a homey atmosphere prevails. Smoking is discouraged.

OLD WELL RESTAURANT AND GUESTHOUSE, Romsey Rd., Copythorne, Hampshire SO4 2PE. Tel. 0703/812321. 5 rms (none with bath).

$ Rates (including English breakfast): £20 ($37) per person. MC, V. **Parking:** Free.

On the A31 in the parish of Copythorne, 10 miles north of Southampton, is Pat and Laurie Martin's guesthouse. The Martin family used to own the village grocery store, and they are true forest folk renting simply furnished but comfortable rooms. In 1960, they bought the Old Well, which serves breakfast, morning coffee, and lunch in its restaurant, open Tuesday to Sunday from 11:30am to 2:30pm. A three-course lunch costs from £6 ($11.10). On Sunday they always have a traditional roast joint for lunch. Bar snacks are also available, and dinner is served from Tuesday to Sunday from 7 to 9:30pm.

WHITEMOOR HOUSE HOTEL, Southampton Rd., Lyndhurst, Hampshire SO43 7BU. Tel. 0703/282186. 5 rms (all with bath or shower). TV **Bus:** No. 56 from Lyndhurst.

$ Rates (including English breakfast): £26 ($48.10) single; £40 ($74) double. MC, V. **Parking:** Free.

On the A35 going out of Lyndhurst on the road to Southampton is the most desirable of Lyndhurst's inexpensively priced lodgings. It's small, so reservations are strongly recommended. Many of the bedrooms overlook New Forest moors. Each accommodation is immaculately kept and has plenty of room. Only breakfast is served, but the owners will direct you to dining places nearby. The house was built in the 1930s, and although the public rooms are comfortable the social center revolves around an outdoor patio sitting within sight of a pleasant garden and an ornamental pond stocked with fish.

WORTH THE EXTRA BUCKS

WHITLEY RIDGE, Beaulieu Rd., Brockenhurst, Hampshire SO42 7TA. Tel. 0590/22354. Fax 0590/228561. 12 rms (all with bath or shower). TV TEL **Transportation:** Take the train from Southampton to Brockenhurst; hotel is 1 mile away by taxi.

$ Rates (including English breakfast): £52–£60 ($96.20–$111) single; £72–£80 ($133.20–$148) double. AE, DC, MC, V. **Parking:** Free.

This Georgian country house was built as a royal hunting lodge around the 18th century. An extension was added in Victorian times to create a large and elegant home. It is set in nearly 5 acres of secluded grounds in the heart of the New Forest. All of the comfortable bedrooms include coffee-making equipment. The hotel, known for its food and wines, offers different meals ranging from imaginative dishes to classic cuisine. A fixed-price dinner, costing £15.50 ($25.60), is served from 7 to 8:30pm daily. An intimate bar is inviting, and there are two well-furnished lounges.

---

4. ISLE OF WIGHT

91 miles W of London; 4 miles W of Southampton

GETTING THERE   By Train   There is a direct train from London's Waterloo Station to Portsmouth, which deposits travelers directly at the pier for a ferryboat crossing to the Isle of Wight. Ferries are timed to meet train arrivals. Travel time from London to the arrival point of Ryde on the Isle of Wight (including ferry crossing time) is 2 hours. One train per hour departs daily from London to Portsmouth.

By Bus   Visitors can explore the Isle of Wight just for the day on **Around the Island Rover** bus trip. Tickets may be purchased on the bus, and you can board or leave the bus at any stop. The price of a Day Rover is £5.45 ($10.10) for adults per day and £2.75 ($5.10) for children. It also gives you passage on the island's only railway, which runs from the dock to Ryde to the center of Shanklin, a distance of 12 miles. For further information, call 0983/523821, the Newport Bus Station.

By Car   Drive to Southampton (see above) and take the ferry, or else leave Southampton and head west along A35, cutting south on A337 toward Lymington on the coast where the ferry crossing to Yarmouth (Isle of Wight) is shorter than at Southampton.

By Ferry   A car-ferry from Southampton goes to West Cowes (Isle of Wight). The price of the average car is £30 ($55.50) round-trip, the trip taking 32 to 40 minutes, depending on weather. A passenger-only high-speed ferryboat (a double-hulled catamaran) from Southampton to East Cowes costs £9.50 ($17.60) for adults and £4.75 ($8.80) for children round-trip and takes 20 minutes. A passenger-only ferry operates from Portsmouth ro Ryde, taking 20 minutes and costing £6.20 ($11.45) for adults and £3.10 ($5.75) for children round-trip. Departures during the day in summer are once every 30 minutes from Portsmouth or once an hour in winter. A high-speed Hovercraft from Southsea (Portsmouth's neighbor) also operates to Ryde, costing adults £7.20 ($13.30) and children £3.60 ($6.65) round-trip.

ESSENTIALS   The **area code** is 0983. The **information office** is at 67 High Street, Shankin (tel. 0983/862942).

The Isle of Wight is known for its sandy beaches and its ports. The island, which long attracted such literary figures as Alfred Lord Tennyson and Charles Dickens, is compact in size, measuring 23 miles from east to west, 13 miles from north to south. Ryde is the railhead for the island's communications system. Yarmouth is something else—a busy little harbor providing a mooring for yachts and also for one of the lifeboats in the Solent area.

Cowes is the premier port for yachting in Britain. Henry VIII ordered the castle built here, but it is now the headquarters of the Royal Yacht Squadron. The seafront, the Prince's Green, and the high cliff road are worth exploring. Hovercraft are built in the town, which is also the home and birthplace of the well-known maritime photographer, Beken of Cowes. It's almost *de rigueur* to wear oilskins and wellies, leaving a wet trail behind you.

Newport, a bustling market town in the heart of the island, is the capital and has long been a favorite of British royalty. Along the southeast coast are the twin resorts of Sandown, with its new pier complex and theater, and Shanklin, at the southern end of Sandown Bay, which has held the British annual sunshine record more times than any other resort. Keats once lived in Shanklin's Old Village. Farther along the coast, Ventnor is called the "Madeira of England," because it rises from the sea in a series of steep hills.

On the west coast are the many-colored sand cliffs of Alum Bay. The Needles, three giant chalk rocks, and the Needles Lighthouse, are other features of interest at this end of the island. If you want to stay at the western end of Wight, consider Freshwater Bay.

WHAT TO SEE & DO

OSBORNE HOUSE, 1 mile southeast of East Cowes. Tel. 0983/200022.

Queen Victoria's most-cherished residence, this house was built at her own expense. Prince Albert, with his characteristic thoroughness, contributed to the design of the Italian-inspired mansion, which stands in lush gardens, right outside the village of Whippingham. Rooms have remained as Victoria knew them, right down to the French piano she used to play and all the cozy clutter of her sitting room. Grief-stricken at the death of Albert in 1861, she asked that Osborne House be kept as it was, and so it has been. Even the turquoise scent bottles he gave her, decorated with cupids and cherubs, are still in place. It was in her bedroom at Osborne House that the queen died on January 22, 1901.

Admission: £4.30 ($7.95) adults, £2.20 ($4.05) children.

Open: Easter–Oct daily 10am–5pm. **Transportation:** "Around the Island Rover" bus.

CARISBROOKE CASTLE, 1¼ miles southwest of Newport. Tel. 0983/ 522107.

A different kind of attraction, this is where Charles I was imprisoned by the Roundheads in 1647. The fine medieval castle is in the center of the island. Everybody heads for the Well House, concealed inside a 16th-century stone building. Donkeys take turns treading a large wooden wheel connected to a rope that hauls up buckets of water.

Admission: £2.60 ($4.80) adults, £1.30 ($2.40) children.

Open: Mid-Mar to Oct Mon–Sat 10am–6pm; Nov to mid-Mar Mon–Sat 10am–4pm. **Transportation:** "Around the Island Rover" bus or bus no. 7, 1C, or 1B.

WHERE TO STAY

DOUBLES WITHOUT BATH FOR LESS THAN £33 [$61.05]

In Ryde

THE DORSET HOTEL, 31 Dover St., Ryde, Isle of Wight PO33 2BW. Tel. 0983/64327. 25 rms (12 with bath or shower). TV **Transportation:** "Around the Island Rover" bus.

$ Rates (including English breakfast): £16.50 ($30.50) single or double without bath per person; £19.50 ($36.05) single or double with bath per person. No credit cards. **Parking:** Free.

The Dorset was originally built in the late 19th century to accommodate government officials who accompanied Queen Victoria on her summer visits. An outdoor heated swimming pool is open throughout the year. Rooms are modernized and comfortable. It's a 5-minute walk from the ferry pier in Ryde.

HOLMSDALE GUEST HOUSE, 13 Dover St., Ryde, Isle of Wight PO33 2AQ. Tel. 0983/614805. 4 rms (all with bath or shower). TV **Transportation:** "Around the Island Rover" bus.

$ **Rates** (including English breakfast): £27–£36 ($49.95–$66.60) double. No credit cards. **Parking:** Free.

Ⓢ This guesthouse, owned by Ted and Jean Taylor, is within a 10-minute walk of the main shopping district, within a 5-minute walk of the ferryboat terminal, and within 200 yards of the beach. All but one room have toilets, and all have hot-beverage facilities. No singles are available.

SEAWARD GUEST HOUSE, 14-16 George St., Ryde, Isle of Wight PO33 2EW. Tel. 0983/63168. 6 rms (none with bath). **Transportation:** "Around the Island Rover" bus.

$ **Rates** (including English breakfast): £12.50 ($23.10) per person. No credit cards. **Parking:** Free.

A good anchor for the Isle of Wight is the Seaward, as Ryde is an ideal center for exploring the island; many tour buses leave from here, the ferry docks at Ryde, and the train stops nearby. Harold and Margaret Gath receive guests in their century-old home. Everything is well kept. Breakfast is four courses, and a four-course evening dinner will cost £6.50 ($12). Even if they can't accommodate you in their busy season, they'll have suggestions as to where you can find a room.

In Shanklin

APSE MANOR COUNTRY HOUSE, Apse Manor Rd., Shanklin, Isle of Wight, PO37 7PM. Tel. 0983/866651. 7 rms (all with bath). TV TEL **Transportation:** "Around the Island Rover" bus.

$ **Rates** (including English breakfast): £33 ($61.05) per person. No credit cards. **Parking:** Free.

This 16th-century manor house in an acre of secluded gardens is surrounded by woods and open country, but is still only 3 minutes from Shanklin's safe sandy beaches. All units have hot-beverage facilities and views of the grounds. There are no singles. Cooking is done under the personal supervision of Mrs. P. Boynton, proprietor, with a varied menu using fresh garden produce whenever possible.

In Totland Bay

LITTLEDENE LODGE HOTEL, Granville Rd., Totland Bay, Isle of Wight PO39 0AX. Tel. 0983/752411. 6 rms (all with bath). **Transportation:** "Around the Island Rover" bus.

$ **Rates** (including English breakfast): £17 ($31.45) single; £34 ($62.90) double. No credit cards.

Owned and managed by Mrs. Maureen Wright, this hotel is small enough so that you receive plenty of personal attention. There is a TV lounge, and the hotel is centrally heated. Maureen is proud of her reputation for serving good food in the spacious bar/dining room. Children are welcome.

WORTH THE EXTRA BUCKS
In Freshwater Bay

BLENHEIM HOUSE, Gate Lane, Freshwater Bay, Isle of Wight PO40 9QD. Tel. 0983/752858. 8 rms (all with shower). TV **Bus:** No. 1C or 7C.

$ **Rates** (including English breakfast): £19.50 ($36.10) single; £39 ($72.15) double. No credit cards. **Parking:** Free.

Some 300 yards from the beach and caves at Freshwater Bay is a twin-gabled, brick house with gingerbread trim, built in 1894 as a private house. Hazel and Jon Shakeshaft, the owners, rent centrally heated bedrooms, three of which are suitable for families. In back is a heated swimming pool. Good meals are served in the dining room, which has French windows that open onto the patio and lawn. Fresh local produce is used whenever possible.

In Ventnor

MADEIRA HALL, Trinity Rd., Ventnor, Isle of Wight PO38 1NS. Tel. 0983/852624. Fax 0983/854906. 8 rms (all with bath or shower). TV TEL **Transportation:** "Around the Island Rover" bus.
$ Rates (including half board): £39–£49 ($72.15–$90.65) single; £78–£98 ($144.30–$181.30) double. AE, MC, V. **Parking:** Free. **Closed:** Oct–Jan.

In an estate garden of lawns, tall trees, and flowering shrubs, this stone manor house has mullioned windows, gables, and bay windows. Among the interesting people who have stayed here is Lord Macauley, who wrote some of his well-known historical essays here. The hall is also associated with Miss Havisham in *Great Expectations* by Charles Dickens. On the grounds is a heated swimming pool and an 18-hole putting course. All the comfortably furnished bedrooms have hot-beverage facilities.

In Totland Bay

SENTRY MEAD HOTEL, Madeira Rd., Totland Bay, Isle of Wight PO39 0BJ. Tel. 0983/753212. 14 rms (all with bath). TV **Transportation:** "Around the Island Rover" bus.
$ Rates (including English breakfast): £26 ($48.10) single; £52 ($96.20) double. AE. **Parking:** Free.

Mike and Julie Hodgson run a year-round hotel in West Wight, 2½ miles from the ferry terminal at Yarmouth. The hotel, which was formerly a Victorian residence, is only a short walk from Alum Bay and Needles. In spacious grounds, it stands at the edge of Totland's Turf Walk and offers a view of the Solent. Bedrooms have hot and cold running water and radios. The breakfast included is four courses. Mrs. Hodgson, a master chef, prepares the international as well as British food served in both the dining room and the bar, where lunches are offered.

WHERE TO EAT

LUGLEYS, Staplers Rd., Wootten Common, Wootten, Isle of Wight PO33 4RW. Tel. 0983/882202.
Cuisine: ENGLISH. **Reservations:** Required. **Bus:** No. 1A.
$ Prices: Appetizers £2.55–£4.95 ($4.70–$9.15); main courses £11.95–£16.95 ($22.10–$31.35). No credit cards.
Open: Dinner Tues–Sat 7–9:30pm. **Closed:** 2 weeks Nov, 2 weeks Feb (dates vary).

One of the best restaurants on the island, worth a special trip, is on the main road running from Newport to Ryde, 4 miles from either town. There are only 16 table settings within the Victorian-inspired dining room of Angela Hewitt, who offers a variety of seasonal dishes throughout the year. Typical menu items include grilled spring lamb served with Welsh lava bread and orange sauce, seasonal local produce, and hormone-free, naturally raised beefsteak.

5. WINCHESTER

72 miles SW of London; 12 miles N of Southampton

GETTING THERE By Train From London's Waterloo Station there is frequent daily train service to Winchester taking 1 hour.

By Bus   National Express buses leaving from London's Victoria Coach Station depart every 2 hours for Winchester during the day and take 2 hours.

By Car   From Southampton, drive north along A335; from London take the M3 motorway west.

ESSENTIALS   The **area code** is 0962. The **Tourist Information Centre** is at the Winchester Guildhall, The Broadway (tel. 0962/840500).

The most historic city in all of Hampshire, Winchester is big on legends—it's even associated with King Arthur and the Knights of the Round Table. In the great hall, all that remains of Winchester Castle, a round oak table, with space for King Arthur and his 24 knights, is attached to the wall. But all that spells undocumented romantic history. What is known, however, is that when the Saxons ruled the ancient kingdom of Wessex, Winchester was the capital.

The city is also linked with King Alfred, who is honored today by a statue and is believed to have been crowned here. The Danish conqueror, Canute, came this way too, as did the king he ousted, Ethelred the Unready (Canute got his wife, Emma, in the bargain). The city is the seat of the well-known Winchester College, whose founding father was the bishop of Winchester, William of Wykeham. Established in 1382, it is reputed to be the oldest public (private) school in England.

Traditions are strong in Winchester. It is said (although I've never confirmed the assertion) that if you go to St. Cross Hospital, now an almshouse, dating from the 12th century, you'll get ye olde pilgrim's dole of ale and bread (and if there's no bread, you can eat cake!). Winchester is essentially a market town, on the Downs on the Itchen River.

WHAT TO SEE & DO

★ For centuries, **Winchester Cathedral,** The Square (tel. 0962/853137), has been one of the great churches of England. The present building, the longest medieval cathedral in Britain, dates from 1079, and its Norman heritage is still in evidence. When a Saxon church stood on this spot, St. Swithun, bishop of Winchester and tutor to young King Alfred, suggested modestly that he be buried outside. When he was later buried inside, it rained for 40 days. The legend lives on: Just ask a resident of Winchester what will happen if it rains on St. Swithun's Day, July 15, and you will get a prediction of rain for 40 days.

In the present building, the nave with its two aisles is most impressive, as are the chantries, the reredos (late 15th century), and the elaborately carved choir stalls. Of the chantries, that of William of Wykeham, founder of Winchester College, is perhaps the most visited (it's in the south aisle of the nave). The cathedral also contains a number of other tombs, notably those of Jane Austen and Izaak Walton (exponent of the merits of the pastoral life in *The Compleat Angler*). The latter's tomb is in the Prior Silkestede's Chapel in the South Transept. Jane Austen's grave is marked with a commemorative plaque. Winchester Cathedral contains in chests the bones of many of the Saxon kings and the remains of the Viking conqueror, Canute, and his wife, Emma, in the presbytery. The son of William the Conqueror, William Rufus (who reigned as William II), is also believed to have been buried at the cathedral. There are free guided tours from April through October, Monday to Saturday at 11am and 3pm.

The crypt is flooded for a large part of the year, and at such times it is closed to the public. When it's not flooded, there are two regular tours Monday to Saturday 10:30am and 2:30pm. The cathedral library and the Triforium Gallery are open during April to September on Monday from 2 to 4:30pm and on Tuesday to Saturday from 10:30am to 1pm and 2 to 4:30pm. From October to Easter visiting times are Saturday 10:30am to 4pm. The library comprises Bishop Morley's 17th-century book collection and an exhibition room containing the 12th-century Winchester Bible. The Triforium shows sculpture, woodwork, and metalwork from 11 centuries and affords magnificent views over the rest of the cathedral. Admission to the library and

Triforium Gallery is £1.50 ($2.80) for adults and 50p (95¢) for children. No admission fee is charged for the cathedral, but a donation of £1.50 ($2.80) is suggested.

WHERE TO STAY

DOUBLES WITHOUT BATH FOR LESS THAN £39 [$72.15]

ANN FARRELL, 5 Ranelagh Rd., St. Cross, Winchester, Hampshire SO23 9TA. Tel. 0962/869555. 5 rms (none with bath).
$ Rates (including English breakfast): £12.50–£13.50 ($23.15–$25) single; £25–£27 ($46.25–$49.95) double. No credit cards. **Parking:** Free.

Near the heart of the city, 800 yards south of town center on St. Cross Road, this Victorian house is furnished in period fashion but has modern comforts. Guest rooms have hot and cold running water and tea-making facilities.

AQUARIUS BED & BREAKFAST, 31 Hyde St., Winchester, Hampshire SO23 7DX. Tel. 0962/54729. 3 rms (none with bath). TV
$ Rates (including English breakfast): £16–£18 ($29.60–$33.30) per person. No credit cards.
The Aquarius is a stucco-covered Victorian town house within a 10-minute walk of the cathedral and a 5-minute walk from the train station. Rooms are simply furnished and comfortable. Baths with showers are next door to each room. Mrs. Maureen Hennessey serves a hearty five-course breakfast.

BRENTWOOD, 178 Stockbridge Rd., Winchester, Hampshire SO22 6RW. Tel. 0962/53536. 3 rms (none with bath). TV
$ Rates (including English breakfast): £18 ($33.30) single; £36 ($66.60) double. No credit cards. **Parking:** Free.
This turn-of-the-century, red-brick, semidetached house has a pleasant garden out back and is located on a main road between Winchester and Stockbridge, within a 10-minute walk of the cathedral and near the train station. Breakfast is the only meal served, but Mrs. Kathleen Jagger, the owner, will direct guests to the Roebuck Inn just across the road, where a meal costs from £8 ($14.80).

FLORUM HOUSE, 47 St. Cross Rd., Winchester, Hampshire SO23 9PS. Tel. 0962/840427. 10 rms (all with shower). TV
$ Rates (including English breakfast): £36 ($66.60) single; £46 ($85.10) double; £54 ($99.90) family unit for three persons. No credit cards. **Parking:** Free.
Originally built in 1887, this brick Victorian house is about a halfway between Winchester and village of St. Cross and is surrounded by private gardens. The comfortably furnished bedrooms have beverage-making equipment. A dinner can be ordered by 6pm on the night required. The house is licensed to serve alcohol to guests.

HARESTOCK LODGE, Harestock Rd., Winchester, Hampshire SO22 6NX. Tel. 0962/881870. 20 rms (9 with bath). TV TEL
$ Rates (including English breakfast): £31.50 ($58.30) single without bath, £37 ($68.45) single with bath; £39 ($72.15) double without bath, £47 ($86.95) double with bath. AE, MC, V. **Parking:** Free.

One of the best places to stay is this lovely country residence constructed in 1885 on the northern perimeter of the city between A32 Andover road and A272 Stockbridge highway. Rooms have radios, and the hotel has an outdoor swimming pool and an indoor spa pool. Good British cooking is featured in the restaurant, and there's plenty of parking.

WHERE TO EAT

MEALS FOR LESS THAN £8 [$14.80]

ANDERSON'S TEA ROOM, 12 The Square. Tel. 61736.
Cuisine: ENGLISH. **Reservations:** Not needed.
$ Prices: Light lunch £5 ($9.25); full cream tea £2.40 ($4.45). MC, V.

Open: Mon–Sat 10am–5pm.

Located above the Betjeman and Barton shop, this traditional English tearoom has been completely refurbished. It offers morning coffee with boiled eggs and pastries, plus light lunches including salads, toasted sandwiches, and a dish of the day. Afternoon teas are a particular feature, with 10 different kinds of tea. It's located near the bus station.

OLDE MARKET INN, 34 The Square, at Market St. Tel. 52585.
   Cuisine: ENGLISH. **Reservations:** Not needed.
$ **Prices:** Appetizers £1.20–£2.55 ($2.20–$4.70); main courses £3–£7 ($5.55–$12.95). No credit cards.
   Open: Mon–Sat 11am–11pm, Sun noon–3pm and 7–10:30pm.

In the oldest, most historic district of Winchester, this mellow old pub has timbered interiors, cozy nooks, and comfortable chairs. It's ideal for those who enjoy a local pub. A selection of hot and cold bar snacks is available at lunchtime, including home-cooked steak-and-kidney pie, cottage pie, and chicken-and-mushroom pie. Orders are placed over the bartops. It's located opposite the cathedral.

ROYAL OAK PUB, Royal Oak Passage. Tel. 61136.
   Cuisine: ENGLISH. **Reservations:** Not needed. **Bus:** No. 25.
$ **Prices:** Appetizers all £1.25 ($2.30); main courses £3–£4.50 ($5.55–$8.35); Sun lunch £8.50 ($15.75). MC, V.
   Open: Daily 11am–2:30pm and 6–11pm (lunch Mon–Sat noon–2pm, Sun noon–1:30pm).

A busy pub with plenty of atmosphere, this reputedly has the oldest bar in England. The cellar of this establishment was originally built in 947 to dispense drink to Winchester's pilgrims, and the present building was constructed in 1630 atop the much older foundation. Various hot dishes and snacks are available, and a traditional Sunday lunch is also served. The Royal Oak is found in a passageway next to the God Begot House in the High Street.

THE FORTE CREST HOTEL, Paternoster Row. Tel. 61611.
   Cuisine: ENGLISH. **Reservations:** Recommended. **Bus:** No. 25.
$ **Prices:** Appetizers £2–£3.50 ($3.70–$6.45) in coffee shop, £3.40–£4.50 ($6.30–$8.35) in Walton Restaurant; main courses £4–£8 ($7.40–$14.80) in coffee shop, £5–£10 ($9.25–$18.25) in Walton Restaurant; four-course dinner in Walton Restaurant £18 ($33.30); three-course lunch in Walton Restaurant £11.50 ($21.30). AE, DC, MC, V.
   Open: Coffee shop daily 7am–9pm; bar lunch daily noon–2pm; Walton Restaurant lunch daily 12:30–3pm, dinner daily 7–9:45pm.

Right by the cathedral, the Forte Crest has a bright coffee shop, with a separate entrance from the street, where hot and cold snacks are available all day. A typical meal includes soup, breaded plaice with fried potatoes, apple pie and cream, plus coffee. They also do a traditional afternoon tea. At lunchtime, the cocktail bar in the hotel has a table where you can help yourself to a selection of English cheeses and pâté, pickles, and salad ingredients; the chef's homemade soup and freshly baked rolls are also offered. You can have more formal meals in the elegant Walton Restaurant, which overlooks the cathedral.

AN EXCURSION TO CHAWTON

If you love Jane Austen, make a trip to **Chawton Cottage,** Jane Austen's House, Chawton, near Alton, Hampshire GU34 1SD, a mile southwest of Alton off A31 and B3006 (tel. 0420/83262). The location is 15 miles east of Winchester. The cottage is signposted at Chawton. Visitors can see the surroundings in which the novelist spent the last 7½ years of her life, her period of greatest accomplishment. In the unpretentious but pleasant cottage, sits the table on which Jane Austen penned new versions of three of her books and wrote three more, including *Emma*. Also see the rector's George III mahogany bookcase and a silhouette likeness of the Reverend

Austen presenting his son to the Knights. It was in this cottage that Jane Austen became ill in 1816 of what would have been diagnosed by the middle of the 19th century as Addison's disease.

There is an old bakehouse with Austen's donkey cart as well as an attractive garden where visitors are invited to have picnics. The home is open April to October daily from 11am to 4:30pm for £1 ($1.85) admission; children under 14, 50p (95¢). It is closed Monday and Tuesday in November, December and March; Monday to Friday in January and February; and Christmas Day and Boxing Day.

6. BOURNEMOUTH

104 miles SW of London; 15 miles W of the Isle of Wight

GETTING THERE **By Train** An express train from Waterloo Station takes 2 hours. There is frequent service throughout the day.

By Bus Buses leave London's Waterloo Station every 2 hours during the day, heading for Bournemouth, and take 2½ hours.

By Car Take the M3 southwest from London to Winchester, then A31 and A338 south to Bournemouth.

ESSENTIALS The **area code** is 0202. The **information office** is at Westover Road (tel. 0202/291715).

The south coast resort at the doorstep of the New Forest didn't just happen: It was carefully planned and executed, a true city in a garden. Flower-filled, park-dotted Bournemouth contains a great deal of architecture inherited from those arbiters of taste, Victoria and her son, Edward. (The resort was discovered back in Victoria's day, when sea-bathing became an institution.) Bournemouth's most distinguished feature is its chines (narrow, shrub-filled, steep-sided ravines) along the coastline.

It is estimated that of Bournemouth's nearly 12,000 acres, about one-sixth is made up of green parks and flowerbeds, such as the Pavilion Rock Garden, which amblers pass through day and night. The total effect, especially in spring, is striking and helps explain Bournemouth's continuing popularity with the garden-loving English.

Bournemouth, along with Poole and Christchurch, forms the largest urban area in the south of England. It makes a good base for exploring a historically rich part of England; on its outskirts are the New Forest, Salisbury, Winchester, and the Isle of Wight. It also has some 20,000 students attending the various schools or colleges, who explore, in their off-hours, places made famous by such poets and artists as Shelley, Beardsley, and Turner.

The resort's amusements are varied. At the Pavilion Theatre, for example, you can see West End–type productions from London. The Bournemouth Symphony Orchestra is justly famous in Europe. And there's the usual run of golf courses, band concerts, variety shows, and dancing. The real walkers might strike out at Hengistbury Head, and make their way past sandy beaches, the Boscombe and Bournemouth piers, all the way to Alum Chine, a distance of 6 miles.

WHERE TO STAY

DOUBLES WITHOUT BATH FOR LESS £46 [$85.10]

BELGRAVIA HOTEL, 56 Christchurch Rd., East Cliff, Bournemouth, Dorset BH1 3PF. Tel. 0202/290857. 24 rms (15 with bath or shower). TV **Bus:** No. 17 or 18.

$ Rates (including English breakfast): £16.50 ($30.55) single without bath, £18 ($33.30) single with bath; £30 ($55.50) double without bath, £36 ($66.60) double with bath. V. **Parking:** Free.

This gracious brick mansion in a posh section of the resort, set in a garden, is the pride of the owners. It was built a century ago with comfortable rooms. Breakfast is the only meal served. It's a 5-minute walk along a winding path from the Belgravia to the water, although the hotel has its own heated pool.

LAWNSWOOD HOTEL, 22A Studland Rd., Alum Chine, Bournemouth, Dorset BH4 8JA. Tel. 0202/761170. 8 rms (all with bath). TV **Bus:** No. 17 or 18.

$ Rates (including English breakfast): £14–£18 ($25.90–$33.30) per person. MC, V. **Parking:** Free.

Once the home of writer H. G. Wells, this privately run hotel has its own private access to the pines of the chine and is only a 2-minute walk to the beach and Promenade. Rooms are equipped with coffee-making equipment. If no double bookings are available, the owner, Thomas Mahoney, will rent to a single occupant. A four-course evening meal can be arranged in advance for £6 ($11.10).

SUNNYDENE, 11 Spencer Rd., Bournemouth, Dorset BH1 3TC. Tel. 0202/552281. 20 rms (none with bath). **Bus:** No. 121 or 124.

$ Rates (including English breakfast): £12.50–£18 ($33.30–$23.10) per person single or double. No credit cards. **Parking:** Free.

This turn-of-the-century private hotel is in a substantial gabled house on a tree-lined road between the Central Station and Bournemouth Bay. Recent additions include a cozy licensed bar, and the dining room has been expanded. Bedrooms are carpeted and centrally heated, with hot and cold running water. An excellent four-course dinner, with some choice of menu, will cost an extra £5 to £7 ($9.25 to $12.95) per person. You might want to reserve when it gets busy during July and August.

WESTCLIFF HOTEL, 27 Chine Crescent, West Cliff, Bournemouth, Dorset BH2 5LB. Tel. 0202/551062. 30 rms (all with bath or shower). TEL **Bus:** No. 25 or 34.

$ Rates (including English breakfast): £22–£30 ($40.70–$55.50) per person; half board £27–£37 ($49.95–$66.60) per person. V. **Parking:** Free.

This hotel, a 5-minute walk from the center, near Durley Chine was once the luxurious southern coast home of the duke of Westminster who had it built in 1876 in a "chine" (English for dried-out primeval riverbed). Now run by June and Victor Bennett, the hotel has many return customers. All rooms have hot-beverage facilities. You can order bar snacks or complete dinners at the hotel's Spanish-style restaurant. There's a large garden and a car park.

WEST CLIFF TOWERS HOTEL, 12 Priory Rd., Bournemouth, Dorset BH2 5DG. Tel. 0202/553319. 32 rms (all with bath or shower). TV TEL **Bus:** No. 25 or 34.

$ Rates (including English breakfast): £23–£32 ($42.55–$59.20) per person. AE, MC, V. **Parking:** Free.

Home of Pat and Dennis Perfect, the West Cliff is a longtime favorite with visitors to Bournemouth. It is 100 yards from the Bournemouth International Centre and is close to the pier, beach, shops, and gardens. Bedrooms have hot-beverage facilities. A wide choice of menus is available in the hotel's two restaurants, which use the fresh produce of the season.

WORTH THE EXTRA BUCKS

HINTON FIRS HOTEL, Manor Rd., East Cliff, Bournemouth, Dorset BH1 3HB. Tel. 0202/555409. Fax 0202/299607. 52 rms (all with bath or shower). TV TEL **Bus:** No. 17 or 18.

$ Rates (including English breakfast): £51 ($94.35) single; £84 ($155.40) double. MC, V. **Parking:** Free.

✪ In a tranquil environment near the sea is a turn-of-the-century country house set in a pine grove. The Waters family, owners of Hinton Firs for 40 years, have recently upgraded the house, and bedrooms now include modern furnishings and hot-beverage facilities. There's an array of tastefully decorated public rooms, including a bar, TV lounge, and a dining room, as well as a garden. An indoor swimming pool is complete with spa pool and underwater swim jet, and the outdoor swimming pool is heated seasonally. The hotel also has a sauna, a solarium, an elevator, and parking.

WHERE TO EAT

MEALS FOR LESS THAN £14 [$25.90]

CORIANDER, 14 Richmond Hill. Tel. 552202.
  Cuisine: MEXICAN. **Reservations:** Required on weekends. **Bus:** No. 17 or 18.
$ **Prices:** Appetizers 80p–£3.25 ($1.50–$6); main courses £4.50–£8.50 ($8.35–$15.75). MC, V.
  Open: Lunch Mon–Sat noon–2:30pm; dinner daily 5:30–10:30pm.
Coriander brings south-of-the-border flair to staid Bournemouth. The varied menu includes the usual range of Mexican specialties, plus some interesting vegetarian dishes. All the menu items are prepared with fresh ingredients. The coriander soup is a favorite, as is chicken Vesuvius. Try the spicy vegetable enchiladas.

LA MARGHERITA, 307 Wimbourne Rd., Winton, Bournemouth. Tel. 867212.
  Cuisine: ITALIAN. **Reservations:** Recommended. **Bus:** No. 2, 3, 4, or 5.
$ **Prices:** Appetizers £1.69–£3.95 ($3.15–$7.30); main courses £7.45–£9.15 ($13.80–$16.90). MC, V.
  Open: Lunch Tues–Sun noon–2pm; dinner Tues–Sun 6–11pm.
This is a favorite Italian restaurant, with a friendly staff and a bright, trattorialike decor. It's a family place, at the corner of Alma Road and Wimborne Road. Guests can select from an array of familiar Italian dishes, and pizza is a specialty.

OLD ENGLAND, 74 Poole Rd., Westbourne. Tel. 766475.
  Cuisine: ENGLISH. **Reservations:** Not needed. **Bus:** No. 101 or 104.
$ **Prices:** Appetizers £1.35–£3.95 ($2.50–$7.30); main courses £5.10–£10.25 ($9.45–$18.95); set dinner £10.95 ($20.25). MC, V.
  Open: Mar–Oct lunch daily 10:15–2:30pm, dinner daily 6–11pm; Nov–Feb lunch Tues–Sun 11:45am–2:30pm, dinner daily 6:30–10pm.
The food and atmosphere live up to the name, and the semiprivate booths are much in demand. Dishes include roast English beef, roast fresh Dorset chicken, and steak-and-kidney pie. For dessert, try a fruit pie with custard or cream.

EASY EXCURSIONS

KINGSTON LACY

An imposing 17th-century mansion, Kingston Lacy (tel. 0202/883402), at Wimborne Minster, on the B3082 Wimborne-Blandford road, 1½ miles west of Wimborne, was the home for more than 300 years of the Bankes family, who had as guests such distinguished persons as King Edward VII, Kaiser Wilhelm, Thomas Hardy, George V, and Wellington. The house contains a magnificent collection of artwork, tapestries, and furnishings brought from abroad by Sir Charles Barry (designer of the House of Commons) at the request of William Bankes, a friend of Lord Byron's.

The present house was built to replace Corfe Castle, the Bankes family's home that was destroyed in the Civil War. During her husband's absence in pursuit of duties as chief justice to King Charles I, Lady Bankes led the defense of the castle, withstanding two sieges before being forced to surrender to Cromwell's forces in 1646 through the actions of a treacherous follower. The keys of Corfe Castle hang in the library at Kingston Lacy.

The house, set in 250 acres of wooded park, is open from April to the end of October, Saturday to Wednesday from noon to 5:30pm. The park is open from 11:30am to 6pm. Admission to the house is £4.50 ($8.35) for adults, £2.20 ($4.05) for children. Admission to the garden is £1.40 ($3) for adults, 75p ($1.20) for children.

WAREHAM

This historic little town on the Frome River 2 miles west of Bournemouth is a good center for touring the South Dorset coast and the Purbeck Hills. It contains remains of early Anglo-Saxon and Roman town walls, plus the Saxon church of St. Martin with its effigy of T. E. Lawrence.

The district was known to T. E. Lawrence (Lawrence of Arabia), who died in a motorcycle crash in 1935. His former home, **Clouds Hill,** lies 7 miles west of Wareham (a mile north of Bovington Camp) and is extremely small. From April to October, it is open Wednesday, Thursday, Friday, and Sunday from 2 to 5pm; from November to March, it is open only on Sunday from 1 to 4pm. Admission is £2 ($3.70). No reduction for children.

WHERE TO STAY & EAT

THE OLD GRANARY, The Quay, Wareham, Dorset BH20 4LP. Tel. 0929/552010. 4 rms (2 with bath). TV

$ Rates (including English breakfast): £18 ($33.30) per person without bath; £24 ($44.40) per person with bath. AE, DC, MC, V.

A riverside country restaurant and inn, this is near a double-arched bridge on A351 between Poole and Swanage. You can dine either inside or on a terrace with a view of the boats and swans on the river. The charming dining room has an informal atmosphere, with bentwood chairs, a wine rack, a natural wood sideboard, and a collection of locally painted watercolors. The owners, Mr. and Mrs. Derek Sturton, try to stick to natural country foods, and their fine English cuisine is the secret to their success. Lunch is served daily from noon to 2pm and dinner is Sunday to Friday from 6:30 to 9pm and Saturday from 6:30 to 10pm. Meals cost from £15 ($27.75).

You can also spend the night in one of their four comfortably furnished guest rooms, all with TV. Two have private baths or showers. They do not allow children to stay overnight.

---

7. DORCHESTER

120 miles SW of London; 27 miles SW of Bournemouth

GETTING THERE   By Train   Hourly trains run from London's Waterloo Station during the day and take 2½ hours.

By Bus   Several National Express buses depart daily from London's Waterloo Station heading for Dorchester and taking 3 hours. In Dorchester, Bere Regis, 7 Bridgport Road (tel. 0305/62992), sells tickets for both National Express buses for London and local buses.

By Car   From London, take M3 motorway southwest, but near the end get onto the A30 in the direction of Salisbury, where you connect with the A354 to Dorchester.

ESSENTIALS   The **area code** is 0305. The **Tourist Information Centre** is at 7 Acland Road (tel. 0305/67992).

Thomas Hardy, in his 1886 novel *The Mayor of Casterbridge,* gave Dorchester literary fame. Actually, Dorchester was notable even in Roman times, when

Maumbury Rings, considered the best Roman amphitheater in Britain, was filled with the sounds of 12,000 spectators screaming for the blood of the gladiators. Dorchester, a county seat, was the setting of another bloodletting, the "Blody Assize" of 1685, when Judge Jeffreys condemned to death the supporters of the Duke of Monmouth's rebellion against James II.

WHAT TO SEE & DO
IN TOWN

DORSET COUNTY MUSEUM, High West St., next to St. Peter's Church. Tel. 0305/262735.

You may want to browse around this museum, which has a gallery devoted to memorabilia of Thomas Hardy's life. In addition, you'll find an archeological gallery with displays and finds from Maiden Castle, Britain's largest Iron Age hill fort, plus galleries on the geology, local history, and natural history of Dorset. The museum is on the main street.

Admission: £1.50 ($2.80) adults, 75p ($1.40) children 5–16; children under 5 free.

Open: Mon–Sat 10am–5pm.

NEARBY

HARDY'S COTTAGE, Higher Bockhampton. Tel. 0305/62366.

Thomas Hardy was born in 1840 at Higher Bockhampton, 3 miles northeast of Dorchester. His home, now a National Trust property, may be visited by appointment with the tenant. You approach the cottage on foot—it's a 10-minute walk after parking your vehicle in the space provided in the wood. Write in advance to Hardy's Cottage, Higher Bockhampton, Dorchester, Dorset, England OX10 7HH, or call the number above. It's 3 miles northeast of Dorchester, ½ mile south of Blandford Road (A35).

Admission: £2 ($3.70). No reduction for children.

Open: Mar–Oct daily 11am–6pm or dusk.

ATHELHAMPTON, on A35, 1 mile east of Puddletown. Tel. 0305/848363.

One of England's great medieval houses, this is considered to be the most beautiful and historic in the south. Thomas Hardy mentioned it in some of his writings, but called it Athelhall. It was begun in the reign of Edward IV on the legendary site of King Athelstan's palace. A family home for more than 500 years, this is noted for its 15th-century great hall, Tudor great chamber, state bedroom, and King's Room. The house is on 10 acres of formal and landscaped gardens, with a 15th-century dovecote, river gardens, fish ponds, fountains, and rare trees.

Admission: £3 ($5.55) adults, £1.50 ($2.80) children.

Open: Wed before Easter to Oct Wed–Thurs, Sun, and bank holidays (plus Mon–Tues in Aug) 2–6pm. **Directions:** Take the Dorchester-Bournemouth road (A35) east of Dorchester for 5 miles.

WHERE TO STAY
DOUBLES WITHOUT BATH FOR LESS THAN £38 [$70.30]
In Dorchester

WOLLASTON LODGE, Acland Rd., Dorchester, Dorset DT1 1EF. Tel. 0305/265952. 6 rms (one with bath).

$ Rates (including English breakfast): £13–£14 ($24.05–$25.90) per person in room without bath; £17–£20 ($31.45–$37) per person in room with bath. No credit cards. **Parking:** Free.

Ken and Gill Summers are your hosts in this Victorian town house, which retains its period character and has a collection of prints from the 1800s. The house has many

19th-century antiques. Rooms contain hot-beverage facilities. It's located in town near the tourist center.

WESTWOOD HOUSE HOTEL, 29 High West St., Dorchester, Dorset DT1 1UP. Tel. 0305/268018. 8 rms (5 with bath). MINIBAR TV TEL.

$ **Rates** (including English breakfast): £22 ($40.70) single without bath, £32 ($59.20) single with bath; £38 ($70.30) double without bath, £50 ($92.50) double with bath. MC, V. **Parking:** 50p (95¢).

A Georgian town house in the town center, this may have been built as a coaching house for Lord Ilchester. The hotel was recently restored, and the comfortably furnished rooms are equipped with hot-beverage facilities.

WORTH THE EXTRA BUCKS
In Dorchester

WESSEX ROYALE HOTEL, 32 High West St., Dorchester DT1 1UP. Tel. 0305/262660. Fax 0305/251941. 22 rms (all with bath or shower). TV TEL

$ **Rates** (including English breakfast): £30–£45 ($55.50–$83.25) single; £45–£59 ($83.25–$109.15) double. AE, DC, MC, V.

Built on medieval foundations, the Wessex is a Georgian structure that was once the home of Lord Ilchester. The public rooms contain much of the original wooden paneling, along with fireplaces and decorative work. The hotel has been modernized and considerably upgraded, each bedroom containing radio, hairdryer, trouser press, and beverage tray. Located in the town center, it has a busy licensed restaurant and a good wine list.

In Evershot

Several excellent accommodations are to be found in Evershot, 12 miles NW of Dorchester.

ACORN INN, 28 Fore St., Evershot, Dorset DT2 0JW. Tel. 093583/83228. 8 rms (all with bath or shower). TV TEL

$ **Rates** (including English breakfast): £26 ($48.10) single; £45 ($84.18) double. No credit cards. **Parking:** Free.

★ Thomas Hardy's historic 18th-century village inn is complete with log fires, a candlelit restaurant, and bars under ceiling beams. The inn has been carefully renovated and retains its original character. All of the well-furnished rooms have hairdryers and beverage-making equipment, some have four-poster beds, and one has a Jacuzzi. The owners are known for their good food, which is served either in the bars or in the more formal restaurant. Local produce is used in season. The inn is 1½ miles off the A37 Yeovil to Dorchester Road.

RECTORY HOUSE, Fore St., Evershot, Dorset DT2 0JW. Tel. 093583/273. 6 rms (all with bath or shower). TV

$ **Rates** (including English breakfast): £25–£50 ($46.25–$92.50) single; £46–£50 ($85.10–$92.50) double. No credit cards. **Parking:** Free.

This is a landmark 18th-century building which was once a rectory. Bedrooms are well furnished. All are doubles or twins, but singles are accepted on occasion. Meals are home-cooked with fresh produce. It's located 1½ miles off the A37 Yeovil to Dorchester Road.

WHERE TO EAT
IN DORCHESTER

THE HORSE WITH THE RED UMBRELLA, 10 High West St. Tel. 262019.
Cuisine: CONTINENTAL. **Reservations:** Not needed.

$ **Prices:** Appetizers 75p–£1.25 ($1.50–$2.30); main courses £2.70–£3.50 ($5–$6.45). No credit cards.
Open: Mon–Sat 8:30am–5:30pm.

The window of this shop/coffeehouse on the main street is filled with bakewell tarts and other baked goods, and inside you will find neat tables and chairs where you can watch the passing locals and enjoy quiche and various toasted snacks. In winter, they also offer stuffed baked potatoes. Pizzas, lasagne, omelets, and baked macaroni are featured.

JUDGE JEFFREYS' RESTAURANT, 6 High West St. Tel. 264369.
   Cuisine: INTERNATIONAL. **Reservations:** Recommended.
$ **Prices:** Appetizers £1.75–£3.25 ($3.25–$6); main courses £5.25–£9.75 ($9.70–$18.05); lunch from £3.50 ($6.45). AE, MC, V.
   Open: Mon–Sat 9:30am–5:30pm and 7–9pm.

 Opposite the County Museum, this restaurant is an attractive stopover on your cross-country jaunt. Built as a house in 1398, it had the dubious distinction of lodging that "cantankerous alcoholic," Judge Jeffreys, during the Bloody Assizes. The place has an Old English atmosphere of massive oak beams, a spiral staircase, stone-mullioned windows, and paneled rooms, along with Tudor fireplaces. It serves morning coffee, lunches, and traditional afternoon teas and offers an extensive à la carte menu in the evening. Try oven-baked trout or various chicken, pork, and steak dishes with choice of sauces.

---

8. BRIDPORT

150 miles SW of London; 16 miles W of Dorchester; 18 miles E of Exeter

GETTING THERE   By Train   The nearest rail connection is at Dorchester, where a bus or taxi will take you the rest of the way.

By Bus   A National Express Coach from London's Waterloo Station runs through Bridport. There are frequent buses throughout the day running west from Dorchester.

By Car   From Dorchester (see above), continue west along A35.

ESSENTIALS   The **area code** is 0308. The **Tourist Information Centre** is at 32 South Street (tel. 0308/24901).

In Thomas Hardy's fictional Wessex terrain, Bridport was Port Bredy. The town lies inland, although there is a harbor a mile away at the holiday resort of West Bay, near the end of Chesil Beach. Ropes and fishing nets are Bridport specialties. Many a man dangled from the end of a Bridport dagger—that is, a rope—especially when homegrown rebels were carted off to Dorchester to face Hanging Judge Jeffreys.

WHERE TO STAY & EAT

BRITMEAD HOUSE, 154 West Bay Rd., Bridport, Dorset DT6 4BG. Tel. 0308/22941. 7 rms (5 with bath). TV
$ **Rates:** £23 ($42.55) single without bath; £26 ($48.10) single with bath; £34 ($62.90) double without bath; £40 ($74) double with bath. AE, DC, MC, V. **Parking:** Free.

Located south of the A35 between Bridport and the harbor at West Bay, this hotel is one of your better bets. You'll get personal attention, as well as good, clean rooms. All are well equipped, with beverage-making facilities and hairdryers. Britmead House is renowned for its food, which often includes local seafood and produce.

BULL HOTEL, 34 East St., Bridport, Dorset DT6 3LF. Tel. 0308/22878. 22 rms (11 with bath). TV TEL
$ **Rates** (including English breakfast): £20 ($37) single without bath; £38 ($70.30) single with bath; £38 ($70.30) double without bath; £55 ($101.75) double with bath. MC, V. **Parking:** Free.

This 16th-century coaching inn in the town center still houses wayfarers. In 1939, George VI stopped here, and you may want to follow in his footsteps. Rooms are comfortable, neat, and clean. Nonresidents can patronize its restaurant, the Dorset Room, where fixed-price lunches cost £8 ($14.80) and are served daily from noon to 2pm. A fixed-price dinner is offered for £12.50 ($23.10) and is served from 7:15 to 9:15pm; you can also order à la carte. The menu includes steak au poivre, grilled salmon, and lobster thermidor.

EYPE'S MOUTH COUNTRY HOTEL, Eype, Bridport, Dorset DT6 6AL. Tel. 0308/23300. 18 rms (all with bath or shower). TV TEL
$ Rates (including English breakfast): £37.50–£48 ($69.40–$88.80) single; £52–£73 ($96.20–$135.05) double. MC, V. **Parking:** Free.
This gracious country house, about 1½ miles west of Bridport and a mile south of the A35 Bridport–Lyme Regis road, is a 5-minute walk from the beach. Bedrooms have hot-beverage facilities and are centrally heated. The hotel, owned by Mr. and Mrs. B. Rawlins, has a fine restaurant that welcomes nonresidents as well. The Jolly Smuggler is an old-world cellar bar, where you can order food from Easter to September. Outside, there's a pretty garden patio with views of the sea.

AN EXCURSION TO PARNHAM

An interesting jaunt from Bridport is a visit to Parnham at Beaminster (tel. 0308/862204). One of the loveliest houses in Dorset, it stands in a wooded valley beside the River Brit. Since Tudor times, it has been surrounded by sweeping lawns and magnificent trees, along with terraces and falling water. In 1976, John Makepeace, internationally famous designer and furniture maker, bought Parnham, made it his home, and set up his workshop in the former stables. Here his team of craftspeople work on commission and construct the unique furniture that Makepeace designs. The restored rooms of the great house display recently completed pieces from the workshop, and there are monthly exhibitions by Britain's leading contemporary artists, designers, and craftspeople. The ornate plastered ceilings, paneled walls, and stone fireplace creates a splendid setting for the best of 20th-century design and construction.

Light lunches and teas with homemade cakes and local clotted cream are served in the 17th-century licensed buttery. The house, gardens, exhibitions, and workshop are open April to October, Wednesday, Sunday, and bank holidays from 10am to 5pm. Admission is £3 ($5.55) for adults, £1.50 ($2.80) for children. Parnham is on the A3066, 5 miles north of Bridport.

9. CHIDEOCK & CHARMOUTH

157 miles SW of London; 1 mile W of Bridport

GETTING THERE By Train The nearest connection is through Dorchester (see above).

By Bus Buses run frequently throughout the day west from both Dorchester and Bridport.

By Car From Bridport, continue west along A35.

ESSENTIALS The **area code** for Chideock and Charmouth is 0297. For **tourist information,** ask at the center at Bridport (see above).

Chideock is a charming village hamlet of thatched houses, with a dairy farm in the center. About a mile from the coast, it's a gem for overnight stopovers, and even better for longer stays. The countryside, with its rolling hills, may tempt you to go exploring.

On Lyme Bay, Charmouth, like Chideock, is another winner. A village of Georgian houses and thatched cottages, Charmouth contains some of the most dramatic coastal scenery in West Dorset. The village is west of Golden Cap, which, according to the adventurers who measure such things, is the highest cliff along the coast of southern England.

WHERE TO STAY

IN CHIDEOCK

BETCHWORTH HOUSE, Main St., Chideock, Dorset DT6 6JW. Tel. 0297/89478. 6 rms (all with bath).
$ Rates (including English breakfast): £18 ($33.30) single; £40 ($74) double. No credit cards. **Parking:** Free.

At the edge of the village is a 17th-century guesthouse on the main road. The homelike accommodations are always kept immaculate. There's a large car park just opposite the house and a walled garden in back of the building.

CHIDEOCK HOUSE HOTEL, Main St., Chideock, Dorset DT6 6JN. Tel. 0297/89242. 9 rms (7 with bath).
$ Rates (including English breakfast): £30 ($55.50) single without bath; £36 ($66.60) single with bath; £44 ($81.40) double without bath; £50 ($92.50) double with bath. MC, V. **Parking:** Free.

In a village of winners, this 15th-century thatched house is perhaps the prettiest. The house quartered the Roundheads in 1645, and the ghosts of the village martyrs still haunt, as their trial was held at the hotel. Resident owners are Derek and Jenny Hammond. Set near the road on the main street with a protective stone wall, the house has a garden in back, and a driveway leads to a large car park. The beamed lounge has two fireplaces, one an Adam fireplace with a wood-burning blaze on cool days. Bedrooms have hot-beverage facilities. The cuisine is a local favorite with the best dessert table in town and offers a good table d'hôte or à la carte menu, served from 7 to 9pm daily.

IN CHARMOUTH

NEWLANDS HOUSE, Stonebarrow Lane, Charmouth, Dorset DT6 6RA. Tel. 0297/60212. 12 rms (11 with bath). TV
$ Rates (including English breakfast): £18.20 ($33.65) single without bath; £20.50 ($37.95) single with bath; £36.40 ($67.35) double without bath; £41 ($75.85) double with bath. MC. **Parking:** Free.

You'll find Newlands House on the periphery of the village off A35 and within walking distance of the beach. Originally a 16th-century farmhouse, it is set in 1½ acres of grounds at the foot of Stonebarrow Hill, which is part of the National Trust Golden Cup Estate. The hotel draws favorable reports from readers for its centrally heated bedrooms that are equipped with hot-beverage facilities. Children under 6 are not allowed.

QUEEN'S ARMES HOTEL, The Street, Charmouth, Dorset DT6 6QF. Tel. 0297/60339. 11 rms (10 with bath). TV
$ Rates (including English breakfast): £22 ($40.70) single without bath; £25 ($46.25) single with bath; £43 ($79.55) double without bath; £49 ($90.65) double with bath. MC, V. **Parking:** Free.

 Catherine of Aragón, the first of Henry VIII's six wives and the daughter of Ferdinand and Isabella of Spain, stayed at this hotel near the sea. A small medieval house, it also figured in the flight of the defeated King Charles with the Roundheads in hot pursuit. The Queen's Armes hidden virtues include a rear flower garden, oak-beamed interiors, a dining room with dark oak tables and Windsor chairs, and a living room with Regency armchairs and antiques. For an additional £12.50 ($23.15) per person, you can have dinner; the hotel specializes in well-prepared English and French fare. There's also a vegetarian menu.

WHERE TO EAT

IN CHIDEOCK

GEORGE INN, on the A35. Tel. 89419.
   Cuisine: ENGLISH. **Reservations:** Required.
   $ Prices: Appetizers £1–£2.30 ($1.85–$4.25); main courses £1.95–£9.50 ($3.60–$17.60). No credit cards.
   Open: Lunch daily noon–2pm; dinner daily 6:30–9:30pm.

Dating from 1685, this is the oldest hostelry in the village, 2 miles west of Bridport. The owners, Mike and Marilyn Tuck, offer food in either the bar or dining room and feature daily specials, such as venison in wine sauce, coq au vin, stuffed lemon sole, boeuf bourguignon, as well as stuffed omelets. The George Inn is fully licensed and has facilities for children, a game room, and a well-kept beer garden.

10. LYME REGIS

160 miles SW of London; 25 miles W of Dorchester

GETTING THERE   By Train   Take the London-Exeter train; get off at Axminster and continue the rest of the way by bus.

By Bus   Bus no. 31 runs hourly during the day from Axminster to Lyme Regis. There is also National Express bus service (no. 705) daily in summer at 9:50am from Exeter to Lyme Regis, the run taking 1¾ hours.

By Car   From Bridport, continue west along A35, cutting south to the coast at the junction with A3070.

ESSENTIALS   The **area code** for Lyme Regis is 0297. The **Tourist Information Centre** is in The Guildhall, Bridge Street (tel. 0297/442138).

On Lyme Bay near the Devonshire border, the resort of Lyme Regis is one of the most attractive centers along the south coast. For those who shun big, commercial holiday centers, such as Torquay or Bournemouth, Lyme Regis is ideal—it's the true English coastal town with a highly praised mild climate. Seagulls fly overhead; the streets are steep and winding; walks along Cobb Beach are brisk and stimulating; the views, particularly of the craft in the harbor, are photogenic. In addition to having been a major seaport (the duke of Monmouth landed here to begin his unsuccessful attempt to become king), Lyme Regis was also a small spa for a while and catered to such visitors as Jane Austen.

The town also boasts the world champion town crier. Richard Fox is just following a tradition of a thousand years when he announces the local news. He'll also take visitors on a 2-hour tour of the resort to see the Cobb, the harbor from which ships sailed to fight the Spanish Armada. Mr. Fox can be reached at Flat 2, 22A Broad Street (tel. 0297/443568). The walk heads up old Broad Street Tuesday at 3pm.

The surrounding area is a fascinating place for fossilism. Mary Anning discovered in 1810 at the age of 11 one of the first articulated ichthyosaur skeletons. She went on to become one of the first professional fossilists in the country. Books outlining walks in the area and the regions where fossils can be seen are available at the local information bureau, mentioned above.

WHERE TO STAY

DOUBLES WITHOUT BATH FOR LESS THAN £31 [$57.35]

NORMAN HOUSE, 29 Coombe St., Lyme Regis, Dorset DT7 3PP. Tel. 0297/443191. 5 rms (1 with bath). TV TEL

$ **Rates** (including English breakfast): £12 ($22.20) single without bath; £24 ($44.40) double without bath; £30 ($55.50) double with bath. No credit cards.

 Built in the 1500s, this is situated on a historic narrow street at the foot of Lyme Regis and a short walk from the sea wall which fronts the channel and the local museum. Steven and Jan Roberts will provide evening meals upon request.

THE WHITE HOUSE, 27 Silver St., Lyme Regis, Dorset DT7 3HR. Tel. 0297/443420. 7 rms (all with bath or shower). TV

$ **Rates** (including English breakfast): £31–£34 ($57.35–$62.90) double. No credit cards. **Parking:** Free.

John and Ann Edmondson run this small, centrally heated, well-maintained guest-house, which is only a few minutes' walk from the harbor and the town center. (It's on the A3070 Axminster–Lyme Regis Road.) The attractively furnished house has twin and double rooms, all with hot-beverage facilities and digital clock radios. Only one contains a bathtub; the rest have showers. A large lounge is set aside for residents. The White House is fully licensed and has a private car park.

WORTH THE EXTRA BUCKS

KERSBROOK HOTEL, Pound Rd., Lyme Regis, Dorset DT7 3HX. Tel. 0297/442596. 12 rms (all with bath or shower).

$ **Rates** (including half board): £47 ($86.95) single; £36–£38 ($66.60–$70.30) per person double. AE, MC, V. **Parking:** Free.

Built of stone in 1790 and crowned by a thatch roof, the Kersbrook sits on a ledge above the village, which provides a panoramic view of the coast, on 1½ acres of gardens redone according to the original 18th-century plans. Public rooms have been refurnished with antique furniture, re-creating old-world charm yet with all modern facilities. Mr. and Mrs. Eric Hall Stephenson are the resident proprietors.

The hotel is justifiably proud of its pink, candlelit restaurant, serving table d'hôte and à la carte meals daily from 7:30 to 9:30pm, with an extensive wine list.

WHERE TO EAT

PILOT BOAT, Bridge St. Tel. 443157.

Cuisine: ENGLISH. **Reservations:** Recommended.

$ **Prices:** Appetizers £1.50–£4.50 ($2.80–$8.35); main courses £2.95–£17.50 ($5.45–$32.40). No credit cards.

Open: Food daily noon–2pm and 7–9:30pm; pub Mon–Sat 11am–11pm; Sun noon–3pm and 7–10:30pm.

Once a hangout for smugglers, this is considered to be the best pub in Lyme Regis and has live entertainment on occasion. Its lounge bar has a nautical decor and views of the River Lym. Pub fare consists of fresh sandwiches made of locally caught crab, as well as a hot soup of the day. Hot main dishes are likely to include the ubiquitous steak-and-kidney pie or a mixed grill. The catch of the day is usually written on a blackboard menu, and the restaurant also offers a special children's menu. Desserts are in the old-fashioned English tradition.

---

11. SHAFTESBURY

115 miles SW of London; 29 miles N of Dorchester

GETTING THERE **By Train** There is no direct access. Take the Exeter train leaving from London's Waterloo Station to Gillingham in Dorset, where a 4-mile bus or taxi ride to Shaftesbury awaits you. Trains from London run hourly.

By Bus   Connections are possible from London's Victoria Coach Station once a day. There are also two or three daily connections from Bristol, Bath, and Bournemouth.

By Car   Head west from London along M3, continuing along A30 for the final approach.

ESSENTIALS   The **area code** is 0747. The **Tourist Information Centre** is at 8 Bell Street (tel. 0747/53514), and is open only from June to September.

The origins of this typical Dorsetshire market town date back to the 9th century when King Alfred founded the abbey and made his daughter the first abbess. King Edward the Martyr was buried there, and King Canute died in the abbey but was buried in Winchester. Little now remains of the abbey, but the ruins are beautifully laid out. The museum adjoining St. Peter's Church at the top of Gold Hill gives a good idea of what the ancient Saxon hilltop town was like.

Today, ancient cottages with thatched roofs and tiny paned windows line the steep cobbled streets, and modern stores compete with the outdoor market in the High Street and the cattle market off Christy's Lane. The town is an excellent center from which to visit Hardy Country (it appears as Shaston in *Jude the Obscure*), Stourhead Gardens, and Longleat House.

WHERE TO STAY

GULLIVERS FARM, East Orchard, near Shaftesbury, Dorset SP7 0LQ. Tel. 0747/811313. 2 rms (none with bath).
$ Rates (including English breakfast): £18.50 ($34.25) per person. No credit cards. **Parking:** Free.

 On the outskirts, 5 miles from Shaftesbury, this is a delightful house set on lovely grounds with a swimming pool. Commander and Mrs. Eoin Ashton-Johnson offer a twin and a single, both with hot and cold running water. Mrs. Ashton-Johnson is an excellent cook, so you may want to arrange to have dinner here, which will cost £14 ($25.90).

THE OLD RECTORY, St. James, Shaftesbury, Dorset SP7 8HG. Tel. 0747/52003. 3 rms (all with bath). **Directions:** ½ mile from Shaftesbury; from town center take B3091 in direction of Sturminster Newton.
$ Rates (including English breakfast): £25–£30 ($46.25–$55.50) single; £46–£50 ($85.10–$92.50) double. No credit cards. **Parking:** Free.
You can get one of the most moderately priced accommodations in the area about ½ mile from Shaftesbury. A Georgian building, it's on attractive grounds and offers well-furnished rooms. The hostess is a Cordon Bleu cook and serves excellent meals costing from £14 ($25.90) per person. Food service is from 7 to 9pm nightly.

VALE MOUNT, 17A Salisbury St., Shaftesbury, Dorset SP7 8EL. Tel. 0747/52991. 5 rms (none with bath).
$ Rates (including English breakfast): £13–£14 ($24.05–$25.90) single; £26–£28 ($48.10–$51.80) double. No credit cards. **Parking:** Free.

 About 2 minutes from the heart of town, this comfortable, pleasantly furnished house is a very good bargain. It is open all year. A free car park is nearby.

WHERE TO EAT NEARBY

MILESTONES TEA ROOM, Compton Abbas. Tel. 811360.
Cuisine: ENGLISH. **Reservations:** Not needed.
$ Prices: Homemade cakes 85p ($1.55) per portion; ploughman's lunch £2.65

($4.90); sandwiches £1.20 ($2.20); afternoon cream tea £2.70 ($5). No credit cards.

Open: Apr–Oct Sun–Wed, Fri–Sat 10am–5:30pm.

This 17th-century thatched cottage tearoom stands right next to the church, and has views over the Dorset hills. The spotless little place is presided over by Ann and Roy Smith who serve real farmhouse teas or a ploughman's lunch. Fresh sandwiches are also offered. This is really the ideal English tearoom, with a summer garden and a splashing fountain. You'll find it on the A350 Blandford road, 20 miles from Warminster, near Shaftesbury in Dorset.

EASY EXCURSION
OLD WARDOUR CASTLE

The ruined 14th-century English Heritage castle stands in a lakeside setting in the landscaped grounds of New Wardour Castle, a 1770 Palladian mansion that now houses a girls' school. Old Wardour Castle (tel. 0747/870487), built in 1392 by Lord Lovel, was acquired in 1547 by the Arundell family and modernized in 1578. After being besieged during the Civil War, however, it was abandoned. Today it houses displays on the war sieges and the landscape, as well as an architectural exhibition. It lies 1½ miles north of the A30 going west out of Salisbury, 2 miles southwest of Tisbury. Admission is 95p ($1.75) for adults, 45p (85¢) for children, and it's open March 24 to October 1 daily from 10am to 6pm; October 2 to March 23 Saturday and Sunday from 10am to 6pm.

12. SHERBORNE

128 miles SW of London; 19 miles N of Dorchester

GETTING THERE By Train Frequent trains throughout the day depart from London's Waterloo Station and take 2 hours.

By Bus There is one National Express Coach departure daily from London's Victoria Coach Station.

By Car Take the M3 motorway west from London, continuing southwest along A30.

ESSENTIALS The **area code** is 0935. The summer-only **Tourist Information Centre** is at Hound Street (tel. 0935/815341).

A little gem of a town, with well-preserved medieval, Tudor, Stuart, and Georgian buildings, Sherborne is in the heart of Dorset in a setting of wooded hills, valleys, and chalk downs. It was here that Sir Walter Raleigh lived before his fall from fortune.

WHAT TO SEE & DO

In addition to the attractions listed below, you can go to **Cerne Abbas,** a village south of Sherborne, to see the Pitchmarket, where Thomas and Maria Washington, uncle and aunt of America's George Washington, once lived.

SHERBORNE OLD CASTLE, ½ mile east of Sherborne. Tel. 0935/ 812730.

The castle was built in the early 12th century by the powerful Bishop Roger de Caen, but it was seized by the Crown at about the time of King Henry I's death in 1135 and Stephen's troubled accession to the throne. The castle was given to Sir Walter Raleigh by Queen Elizabeth I. The gallant knight built Sherborne Lodge in the deer park close by (now privately owned). The buildings were mostly destroyed in the Civil War, but you can still see a gatehouse, some graceful arcades, and decorative windows.

Admission: 85p ($1.55) adults, 40p (75¢) children.

Open: Apr–Sept daily 10am–6pm; Oct–Mar daily 10am–4pm. **Closed:** Jan 1 and Dec 24–26. **Directions:** Follow signposts east from center.

SHERBORNE CASTLE, Cheap St. Tel. 0935/813182.

Sir Walter Raleigh built this castle in 1594, when he decided that it would not be feasible to restore the old castle to suit his needs. This Elizabethan residence was a square mansion, to which later owners added four Jacobean wings to make it more palatial. After King James I had Raleigh imprisoned in the Tower of London, the monarch gave the castle to a favorite Scot, Robert Carr, and banished the Raleighs from their home. In 1617, it became the property of Sir John Digby, first earl of Bristol, and has been the Digby family home ever since. The mansion was enlarged by Sir John in 1625, and in the 18th century the formal Elizabethan gardens and fountains of the Raleighs were altered by Capability Brown, who created a serpentine lake between the two castles. The 20 acres of lawns and pleasure grounds around the 50-acre lake are open to the public. In the house are fine furniture, china, and paintings by Gainsborough, Lely, Reynolds, Kneller, and Van Dyck, among others. The castle is off New Road, a mile east of the town center.

Admission: Castle and grounds £3 ($5.55) adults, £1.50 ($2.80) children; grounds only £1.20 ($2.20) adults, 60p ($1.10) children.

Open: Easter–Sept Sat–Thurs, Sat–Sun, and bank holidays 2–5:30pm.

SHERBORNE ABBEY, Half Moon St. Tel. 093/812452.

The abbey is worth a visit to see the splendid fan vaulting of the roof, as well as the many monuments, including Purbeck marble effigies of medieval abbots and the Elizabethan four-poster beds and canopied Renaissance tombs. A baroque statue of the earl of Bristol standing between his two wives dates from 1698. A British public school operates out of the abbey's surviving medieval monastic buildings and was the setting of a novel by Alec Waugh, *The Loom of Youth,* and for MGM's film *Goodbye, Mr. Chips.* The abbey is in the town center.

Admission: £1.50 ($2.80) adults, £1.20 ($2.20) children.

Open: June–Sept daily 8am–6pm; winter daily 8am–4pm.

WHERE TO STAY

THE ANTELOPE HOTEL, Greenhill, Sherborne, Dorset DT9 4EP. Tel. 0935/812077. Fax 0935/816473. 19 rms (all with bath). TV TEL

$ Rates (including English breakfast): £30–£45 ($55.50–$83.25) single; £30–£59 ($55.50–$109.15) double. AE, DC, MC, V. **Parking:** Free.

This personally run, family-type hotel is in the historic district of Sherborne on the A30. It is a good base for touring the area and has comfortably furnished bedrooms. The hotel operates an "Olde Worlde" Bar and an Italian restaurant.

HALF MOON, Half Moon St., Sherborne, Dorset DT9 3LN. Tel. 0935/812017. 15 rms (all with bath). TV TEL

$ Rates (including English breakfast): £38–£48 ($70.30–$88.80) single; £48–£58 ($88.80–$107.30) double. AE, DC, MC, V. **Parking:** Free.

Centrally located in Sherborne, the Half Moon is in a red-brick, 17th-century building opposite the abbey. Guest rooms are well furnished and comfortable. The carvery restaurant, open daily from noon to 2pm and 6 to 10pm, offers one of the best food values in town at a cost of £8 ($14.80) for a meal.

NETHERCOOMBE HOUSE, Marston Rd., Sherborne, Dorset DT9 4BL. Tel. 0935/815427. 2 rms (none with bath). **Directions:** Head north on B3148.

$ Rates (including English breakfast): £13 ($24.05) per person. No credit cards. **Parking:** Free.

One of the best B&Bs in the area, this is about ½ mile from the city center. The guest accommodations are separate from the owners' quarters. The guests' sitting room has a TV, and each unit has beverage-making facilities.

DEVON

The great patchwork quilt area of southwest England, part of the "West Countree," abounds with cliffside farms, rolling hills, foreboding moors, semitropical plants, and fishing villages that provide some of the finest scenery in England. The British approach sunny Devon with the same kind of excitement one would normally reserve for hopping over to the continent. Especially along the coastline, the British Riviera, the names of the seaports, villages, and resorts have been synonymous with holidays in the sun: Torquay (Torbay), Clovelly, Lynton-Lynmouth.

It's easy to get involved in the West Country life. You can go pony trekking across moor and woodland, past streams and sheep-dotted fields or stop at local pubs to soak up atmosphere and ale.

Devon is a land of jagged coasts—the red cliffs in the south face the English Channel. In south Devon, the coast from which Drake and Raleigh set sail, the tranquil life prevails, and on the bay-studded coastline of north Devon, pirates and smugglers used to find haven. The heather-clad uplands of Exmoor, with its red deer, extend into north Devon from Somerset—a perfect setting for an English mystery. Much of the district is already known to those who have read Victorian novelist R. D. Blackmore's romance of the West Country, *Lorna Doone*. Aside from the shores, many of the scenic highlights are in the two national parks: Dartmoor in the south, Exmoor in the north.

Almost every hamlet is geared to accommodate tourists. However, many small towns and fishing villages do not allow cars to enter; these towns have car parks on their outskirts, but this can involve a long walk to reach the center of the harbor. From mid-July to mid-September the more popular villages get quite crowded, and one needs reservations in the limited number of hotels available. Chances are your oddly shaped bedroom will be in a barton (farm) mentioned in the *Domesday Book* or in a thatched cottage.

The two main bus companies of Devon and Cornwall combine to offer a Key West ticket, granting unlimited travel anywhere on the two networks for any 7 consecutive days at a cost of £19.80 ($36.65) for adults and £14.30 ($26.45) for children under 14. A family ticket—two adults and two children—costs £39.60 ($73.25). A 3-day ticket costs £12 ($22.20) for adults, £7.70 ($14.25) for children, or £33 ($62) for a family ticket. You can plan your journeys from the maps and timetables available at any Western National/Devon General offices when you purchase your ticket. Further information may be obtained from Devon General Ltd., Belgrave Road, Exeter, Devon EX1 2LB (tel. 0392/439333).

☑ WHAT'S SPECIAL ABOUT DEVON

Beaches

- ☐ The English Riviera, 22 miles of Devonshire coastline and 18 beaches, with Torquay at the center. There are even palm trees.

Great Towns/Villages

- ☐ Exeter, university city rebuilt after the 1940s bombings around its venerable cathedral. Notable waterfront buildings.
- ☐ Plymouth, largest city in Devon. From this major port and sea base, the Pilgrims set sail on the *Mayflower* for the New World.
- ☐ Torquay, Devon's premier seaside resort which grew from a small fishing village. Set against a backdrop of colorful cliffs and beaches.
- ☐ Clovelly, considered the most charming village in England by many. The village cascades down a mountainside.

Natural Spectacles

- ☐ Dartmoor, a national park northeast of Plymouth—a landscape of gorges and moors filled with gorse and purple heather. Home of the Dartmoor pony.

Buildings

- ☐ Exeter Cathedral, dating from Saxon times and built in the "Decorated" style of the 13th and 14th centuries.
- ☐ Buckland Abbey, near Yelverton— former home of the dashing Sir Francis Drake, hero to the English, "pirate" to the Spanish.

SEEING DEVON
GETTING THERE

There are airports at Plymouth and Exeter, but many visitors arrive by rail instead. British Rail runs trains to the area from London's Paddington Station, arriving in Exeter in 2¼ hours and in Plymouth in 3¼ hours. National Express coaches from London also service the area from London's Victoria Coach Station, arriving in Exeter in 3¾ hours and in Plymouth in 4½ hours. From London, the M4 and the M5 quickly connect you with Devon.

A SUGGESTED ITINERARY

Day 1: Visit Exeter and walk its old streets and see its cathedral.
Day 2: Spend a day touring the national park of Dartmoor, which is more sensibly done by car. Overnight in Moretonhampstead.
Day 3: Go to Torquay for a night at a major English seaside resort.
Day 4: Continue west to Plymouth, following in the footsteps of the Pilgrims.
Day 5: Head north from Plymouth for a luncheon stopover at Clovelly before continuing west to the twin resorts of Lynton-Lynmouth for the night.

1. EXETER

201 miles SW of London; 46 miles E of Plymouth

GETTING THERE   By Plane   The Exeter Airport (tel. 0392/67433) serves the southwest. It is also used for charter flights by the English heading south on a holiday. From Monday to Friday it offers flights on Brymon Airways to London's Gatwick

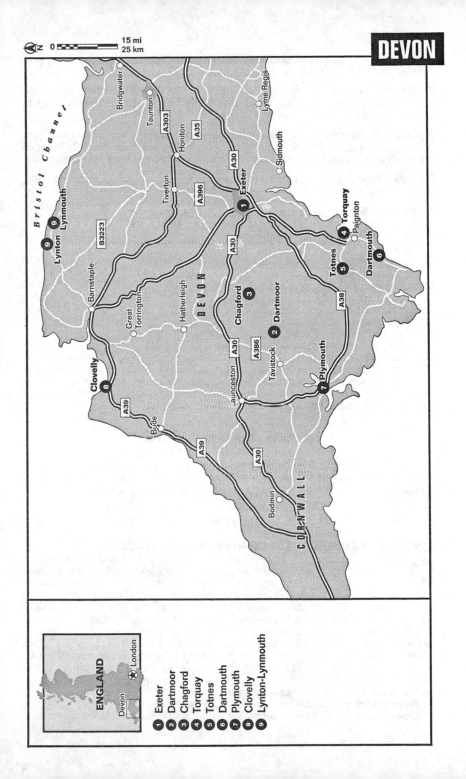

DEVON

Bristol Channel

Bridgwater
Taunton
A303
A35
Honiton
A30
Lyme Regis
Sidmouth
Tiverton
A396
Exeter **1**

Lynton Lynmouth **9**
9

Torquay
4 Paignton
Dartmouth **6**

B3223

Barnstaple

D E V O N

Chagford **3**
Dartmoor **2**

Totnes **5**

A38

Great Torrington
Hatherleigh

A30
A386
Tavistock

Plymouth **7**

Clovelly **8**

A39
Bude

Launceston

A39

A30

C O R N W A L L

Bodmin

ENGLAND
Devon
★ London

1 Exeter
2 Dartmoor
3 Chagford
4 Torquay
5 Totnes
6 Dartmouth
7 Plymouth
8 Clovelly
9 Lynton-Lynmouth

0   15 mi
    25 km

Airport where worldwide connections can be made. For reservations on Brymon Airways, call 0345/717383.

By Train   Trains from London's Paddington Station depart every hour during the day (trip time: 2½ hr.). Trains also run during the day between Exeter and Plymouth at the rate of one per hour (trip time: 1¼ hr.).

By Bus   A National Express coach departs from London's Victoria Station every 30 minutes during the day (trip time: 4 hr.). You can also take buses 38 or 39 between Plymouth and Exeter. During the day two coaches depart per hour (trip time: 1 hr.).

By Car   From London, take the M4 motorway west, cutting south to Exeter at the junction with M5.

ESSENTIALS   The **area code** is 0392. The **Tourist Information Centre** is at the Civic Centre, Paris Street (without number; tel. 0392/72434).

The county town of Devonshire, on the banks of the River Exe, Exeter was a Roman city founded in the 1st century A.D. Two centuries later, it was encircled by a mighty stone wall, traces of which remain today. Conquerors and would-be conquerors, especially the Vikings, stormed the fortress in the centuries to come; none was more notable than William the Conqueror. Irked at Exeter's refusal to capitulate (perhaps also because it sheltered Gytha, mother of the slain Harold), the Norman duke brought Exeter to its knees on short notice.

Under the Tudors, the city grew and prospered. Sir Walter Raleigh and Sir Francis Drake were two of the striking figures who strolled through Exeter's streets. In May 1942, the Germans bombed Exeter, destroying many of the city's architectural treasures. Exeter was rebuilt, but the new, impersonal-looking shops and offices couldn't replace the Georgian crescents and the black-and-white timbered buildings with their plastered walls. Fortunately, much was spared.

WHAT TO SEE & DO

Just off "The High," at the top of Castle Street stands an impressive Norman Gate House from William the Conqueror's Castle. Although only the house and walls survive, the view from here and the surrounding gardens is spectacular.

IN TOWN

EXETER CATHEDRAL, 1 The Cloisters. Tel. 0392/55573.
Owing its present look to the Decorated style of the 13th and 14th centuries, the Exeter Cathedral Church of St. Peter actually goes back to Saxon times. Even Canute, the Viking conqueror, got in on the act of rebuilding around 1017. The cathedral of Bishop Warelwast came into being in the early 12th century, and the north and south towers serve as reminders of the Norman period. The remarkable feature of the present Gothic building is the tierceron vaulting of the nave and quire, 300 feet long and unbroken by any central tower or spire. The cathedral did suffer damage in the 1942 German bombings, and lost its St. James's Chapel, which subsequently has been restored. But most of the treasures remained intact, including the rows of sculpture along the west front; the 14th-century minstrels' gallery, its angelic figures with Early English musical instruments in hand; and the carved oak 14th-century bishop's throne.
   Admission: Requested donation £1 ($1.85) adults.
   Open: Mon–Fri 7:15am–5:30pm, Sat–Sun 8:30am–6:30pm.

EXETER MARITIME MUSEUM, 60 Haven Rd. Tel. 0392/58075.

The maritime museum opposite the quay on the River Exe, has a collection of more than 200 small craft and it shelters the world's largest collection of English and foreign craft, from places ranging from the Congo to Corfu. The larger boats afloat in the canal basin can be boarded. There are canoes, proas, and boats that have been rowed across the Atlantic, and you can go aboard the oldest working steamboat or even picnic on a Hong Kong junk or an Arab dhow. This is an active museum, and the ISCA members who maintain the boats sail some of them during the summer months. Five colorful Portuguese chatas that carry a maximum of six passengers are available for rent at the museum from May to September; the boats are rowed along the 3 miles of navigable water on the historic canal at a charge of £3 ($5.55) per hour.

Admission: £3.25 ($6) adults, £1.90 ($3.80) children.
Open: Oct–June daily 10am–5pm; July–Sept daily 10am–6pm.

EXETER GUILDHALL, High St. (without number). Tel. 0392/265500.

This colonnaded building on the main street is regarded as the oldest municipal building in the kingdom; the earliest reference to the guildhall is contained in a deed of 1160. The Tudor front that straddles the pavement was added in 1593. Inside you'll find a fine display of silver, plus a number of paintings, including one of Henrietta Anne, daughter of Charles I (born Exeter, 1644). The ancient hall is paneled in oak.

Admission: Free.
Open: Tues–Sun 10am–4pm.

ROUGEMONT HOUSE MUSEUM, Castle St. (without number). Tel. 0392/265858.

Just by the gate house, in the center of town, is a charming Regency villa, adapted from an earlier house and now the home of Exeter's costume and lace. The museum features costumes displayed in period rooms (these change twice a year), along with one of the largest lace collections in Europe.

Admission: £1.50 ($2.80) adults, 75p ($1.40) children.
Open: Daily 10am–5:30pm.

ST. NICHOLAS PRIORY, The Mint, off Fore St. Tel. 0392/265858.

This is the guest wing of a Benedictine priory founded in 1070. You will see fine plaster ceilings and period furniture.

Admission: 70p ($1.20) adults, 35p (65¢) children.
Open: Tues–Sat 10am–5:30pm.

ON THE OUTSKIRTS

POWDERHAM CASTLE, Powderham. Tel. 0626/890243.

A castle was built here in the late 14th century by Sir Philip Courtenay, sixth son of the second earl of Devon, and his wife, Margaret, granddaughter of Edward I. Their magnificent tomb is in the south transept of Exeter Cathedral. The castle suffered damage during the Civil War and was restored and altered in the 18th and 19th centuries. The castle contains many family portraits and fine furniture, including a remarkable clock that plays full tunes at 4pm, 8pm, and midnight, some 17th-century tapestries, and a chair used by William III for his first council of state at Newton Abbot. The staircase hall contains some remarkable plasterwork set in bold relief against a turquoise background, more than 2 centuries old, as well as a detailed pedigree of the Courtenay family, a document more than 12 feet high. Powderham Castle is a private house lived in by Lord and Lady Courtenay and family. There is a tearoom for light refreshments.

Admission: £3.20 ($5.90) adults, £1 ($1.85) children 5–16.
Open: May–early Sept daily 2–5:30pm. **Directions:** Take the A379 Dawlish Rd. 8 miles south of Exeter. The castle is signposted.

WHERE TO STAY

DOUBLES WITH BATH FOR LESS THAN £32 [$59.20]

In Town

CLAREMONT, 36 Wonford Rd., Exeter, Devon EX2 4LD. Tel. 0392/ 74699. 3 rms (all with bath or shower). TV **Bus:** H.
$ Rates (including English breakfast): £20 ($37) single; £30 ($55.50) double. No credit cards. **Parking:** Free.

 This Regency-style 1840 town house, lies within a quiet residential part of the city, yet is within easy access to the heart. Bedrooms are well kept and have beverage-making equipment. Geoff and Jacqueline Self, who run the property, assist visitors in many ways, such as by storing luggage for them until they return. Nonsmokers are preferred.

LEA-DENE, 34 Alphington Rd. (A3777), St. Thomas, Exeter, Devon, EX2 8HN. Tel. 0392/57257. 8 rms (none with bath). TV TEL **Bus:** Blue minibus K from center.
$ Rates (including English breakfast): £18.50 ($34.25) single; £31 ($57.35) double; £37 ($68.45) triple. No credit cards. **Parking:** Free.
This hotel and the private house which abuts it were built of red brick before 1930. Set in a southern suburb of Exeter, a 5-minute walk from the town center, it contains many of the original accessories, a smallish garden, and a modern extension concealed around the establishment's back side. Rooms are carpeted and comfortably furnished. Mr. and Mrs. Colin Foster are the owners.

PARK VIEW HOTEL, 8 Howell Rd., Exeter, Devon EX4 4LG. Tel. 0392/ 7177. 16 rms (10 with bath or shower). TV TEL
$ Rates (including English breakfast): £17 ($31.45) single without bath, £28 ($51.80) single with bath; £32 ($59.20) double without bath, £45 ($83.25) double with bath. MC, V.
This hotel lies near the heart of town and the train terminal. A landmark Georgian house, it offers comfortably furnished bedrooms. Guests take their breakfast in a cozy room opening onto the hotel's garden. Breakfast is the only meal served, but the staff will prepare a packed lunch for touring.

TREES, 2 Queen's Crescent, York Rd., Exeter, Devon EX4 6AY. Tel. 0392/59531. 12 rms (1 with bath). TV
$ Rates (including English breakfast): £15 ($27.75) single without bath; £30 ($55.50) double without bath; £34 ($62.90) double with bath. No credit cards.
This "minihotel" is run by Valerie Daniel and is about a 5-minute walk from the city center and near the bus station. Bedrooms contain wash basins and shaver points. Valerie welcomes her guests with a pot of tea.

TRENANCE HOUSE HOTEL, 1 Queen's Crescent, York Rd., Exeter, Devon EX4 6AY. Tel. 0392/73277. 15 rms (8 with bath or shower). TV
$ Rates (including English breakfast): £18 ($33.30) single without bath; £24 ($44.40) single with bath; £28 ($51.80) double without bath; £34 ($62.90) double with bath. No credit cards. **Parking:** Free.
One of the best B&Bs in town, this lies just 3 minutes from the heart of town in the vicinity of the bus station. The resident owners, the Breading family, welcome guests to their comfortably furnished bedrooms.

WORTH THE EXTRA BUCKS

In Town

GIPSY HILL, Gipsy Hill Lane, via Pinn Lane, Pinhoe, Exeter, Devon EX1 3RN. Tel. 0392/65252. Fax 0392/64302. 40 rms (all with bath). TV TEL **Bus:** E.

$ Rates (including English breakfast): £47–£53 ($86.95–$98.05) single; £58–£65 ($107.30–$120.25) double. AE, MC, V. **Parking:** Free.

This late Victorian country house stands in beautiful gardens on the eastern edge of the city and is close to the airport (it is suitable for motorists and within easy reach of M5 Junction 30). Family operated, the house has been modernized and offers well-appointed bedrooms, some of which have four-poster beds. A restaurant on the premises serves both British and continental dishes.

LORD HALDON HOTEL, Kings Drive, Dunchideock, near Exeter, Devon EX6 7YF. Tel. 0392/832483. Fax 0392/33765. 20 rms (all with bath or shower). TV TEL

$ Rates (including English breakfast): £34.50–£47 ($63.85–$86.95) single; £49.50–£63 ($91.60–$116.55) double. MC, V. **Parking:** Free.

If you're driving, your best bet might be this hotel 4 miles SW of Exeter. Constructed in 1735 as the seat of the lords of Haldon, a major part of the original structure was destroyed in this century, but the remaining wing has been converted into a country-house hotel that still retains an archway created by 18th-century architect Sir Robert Adam. Most rooms have countryside views, and they all contain hot-beverage facilities. There are four rooms with four-poster beds. Fresh local produce is used for the traditional British dishes.

At Nearby Whimple

DOWN HOUSE, Whimple, Devon EX5 2QR. Tel. 0404/822860. 7 rms (2 with bath). TV **Directions:** Leave the A30, 7 miles east of Exeter and proceed down the lane to the village.

$ Rates: £25 ($46.25) single without bath; £32 ($59.20) single with bath; £32 ($59.20) double without bath; £38 ($70.30) double with bath. No credit cards.

Eight miles from Exeter and 9 miles from Sidmouth, which lies on the South Devon coast, Down House is an ideal base for touring in Devon. Alan and Vicky Jiggins welcome visitors to their gracious Edwardian farmhouse set in 5 acres of garden and paddocks. Guests can relax in the elegant lounge or on the terrace and enjoy the fine cuisine in which garden fruit and vegetables and local eggs are used. An evening meal is available for £8.50 ($15.75).

At Nearby Bickleigh

In the Exe Valley, 4 miles south of Tiverton and 9 miles north of Exeter, lies a hamlet with a river, an arched stone bridge, a mill pond, and thatch-roofed cottages—a cliché of English charm, one of the finest spots in all of Devon.

BICKLEIGH COTTAGE COUNTRY HOTEL, Bickleigh Bridge, Bickleigh, Devon EX16 8RJ. Tel. 08845/230. 9 rms (7 with bath). **Bus:** No. 354.

$ Rates (including English breakfast): £17 ($31.45) single without bath; £32 ($59.20) double without bath; £39 ($72.15) double with bath. MC, V. **Parking:** Free.

This is a thatched, 17th-century hotel with a riverside garden leading down to the much photographed Bickleigh Bridge. Add to this image swans and ducks gliding by. Inside, rooms are cozy, with oak beams and old fireplaces. Mr. and Mrs. Stuart Cochrane, the owners, provide good and nourishing meals. The raspberries and gooseberries come fresh from the garden and are topped with generous portions of Devonshire cream. Dinner is priced from £8.50 ($15.75).

THE TROUT INN, Bickleigh, near Tiverton, Devon EX16 8RJ. Tel. 08845/339. 4 rms (all with bath). TV **Bus:** No. 354. **Directions:** Take the main Tiverton-Exeter road, the A396, 4 miles south of Tiverton.

$ Rates (including English breakfast): £22.50 ($41.65) per person. DC, MC, V. **Parking:** Free.

Originally constructed in the early 1600s as a coaching inn and blacksmith shop, this charming inn is a short walk from the Bickleigh Bridge, whose idyllic setting supposedly inspired Simon & Garfunkel to write "Bridge Over Troubled

Water." Capped with a long and low thatch roof, and pierced with tiny leaded windows, the inn contains cozy bedrooms and a cozy antique-loaded pub and restaurant. Most visitors opt for lunch in the pub, and dinner in the somewhat more formal restaurant. The restaurant contains a fireplace which was built with stones gathered in the 17th century after the destruction of a medieval predecessor of today's bridge. At lunch, you can help yourself to the salad and cold buffet, where an all-you-can-eat meal costs £5.50 ($10.20). A la carte evening meals, served in the restaurant, cost from £12 ($22.20) each, and might include venison, chicken, steaks, and lamb cutlets. Dinner is served from 7 to 10pm daily, lunch daily from noon to 2pm.

WHERE TO EAT
MEALS FOR LESS THAN £8 [$14.80]

COOLINGS WINE BAR, 11 Gandy St. Tel. 434183.
  Cuisine: ENGLISH. **Reservations:** Not needed. **Bus:** N.
$ **Prices:** Soups £1.50 ($2.80); main courses £3–£4 ($5.55–$7.40). MC, V.
  Open: Mon–Sat lunch 11am–2:30pm; dinner Mon–Sat 5:30–11pm.
Set within a Victorian building on a short, cobble-covered street which intersects Exeter's High Street near the town center, this is a beckoning place with beams, checkered tablecloths, and tables which spill over into the cellar. Food is prepared on the premises and includes a plentiful selection of meats, pies, and quiches, as well as such changing specialties as chicken Waldorf and sugar-baked ham, each served with freshly prepared salads. Hot platters are chalked up on a blackboard, along with the featured wine of the day. Wine by the glass includes many dozens of vintages from throughout Europe.

PORT ROYAL INN, The Quay at Larkbeare Rd. Tel. 72360.
  Cuisine: ENGLISH. **Reservations:** Not needed. **Bus:** Blue minibus R, K, or S.
$ **Prices:** Appetizers £1.35–£3 ($2.50–$5.55); main courses £2.65–£10 ($4.90–$18.50). No credit cards.
  Open: Lunch daily noon–2pm; dinner daily 7–9:30pm.
Set close to the Maritime Museum, with a flowering patio at the edge of the River Exe, this charming antique pub was originally built 200 years ago as a boat repair shop. A recent winner of Exeter's "Flower in Bloom" award, it attracts drinkers and diners during warm weather to its outdoor patio, where a landing stage extends out into the river. This is a real ale house, also known for its ports and sherries. Salads are tempting, and you can order a ploughman's lunch or pâté and toast. Sandwiches made from granary bread are filled with meat or cheese. The two or three daily hot specials may include seafood, roast chicken, or roast lamb. There are also desserts and coffee with cream, and the pub serves real ales from various breweries. All food is ordered at the pub but will be delivered to your table by a waitress.

SHIP INN, St. Martin's Lane. Tel. 72040.
  Cuisine: ENGLISH. **Reservations:** Not needed.
$ **Prices:** Appetizers 75–£1.80 ($1.40–$3.35); main courses £3.95–£7.95 ($7.30–$14.70). AE, DC, MC, V.
  Open: Restaurant lunch daily noon–2pm; dinner Mon–Sat 6:30–10pm, Sun 7–9pm. Bar lunch Mon–Sat 11am–2:30pm, Sun noon–2pm; dinner Mon–Sat 5–11pm, Sun 7–10:30pm.
The Ship Inn was often visited by Sir Francis Drake, Sir Walter Raleigh, and Sir John Hawkins. Of it Drake wrote: "Next to mine own shippe, I do most love that old 'Shippe' in Exon, a tavern in Fyssh Street, as the people call it, or as the clergie will have it, St. Martin's Lane." The pub still provides tankards of real ales, lager, and stout and is still loved by both young and old. A large selection of snacks is offered in the bar every day, while the restaurant upstairs provides more substantial English fare. At either lunch or dinner, you can order from a wide selection including French onion soup, whole grilled lemon sole, and five different steaks. The price of the

main courses includes vegetables, a roll, and butter. Portions are large. It's in the town center.

---

2. DARTMOOR

213 miles SW of London; 13 miles W of Exeter

GETTING THERE   By Train   Take the train down from London to Exeter (see above), then depend on local buses to connect you with the various villages of Dartmoor.

By Bus   Transmoor Link, a public bus service, usually operates throughout the summer and is an ideal way to get onto the moor. Information on the Transmoor Link and on the bus link between various towns and villages on Dartmoor is available from the Transport Co-ordination Centre (tel. 0392/272123).

By Car   Exeter is the most easily reached "gateway" by highway. From Exeter continue west along B3212 to such centers of Dartmoor as Easton, Chagford, Moretonhampstead, or North Bovey. From these centers, tiny roads—often not really big enough for two cars—cut deeper into the moor.

ESSENTIALS   The **area code** is 0252. Accommodation information is offered by the **Dartmoor Tourist Association,** 8 Fitzford Cottages, Tavistock (tel. 0252/3501). Local information centers will also provide a list of accommodations.

This National Park lies northeast of Plymouth stretching from Tavistock and Okehampton on the west to Exeter in the east, a granite mass that sometimes rises to a height of 2,000 feet above sea level. The landscape offers vistas of gorges with rushing water, gorse and purple heather ranged over by Dartmoor ponies—a foreboding landscape for the experienced walker only.

Some 13 miles west from Exeter, the peaceful little town of **Moretonhampstead,** perched on the edge of Dartmoor, makes a good center. Moretonhampstead contains an old market cross and several 17th-century colonnaded almshouses.

The much visited Dartmoor village of **Widecombe-in-the-Moor** is only seven miles from Moretonhampstead. The fame of the village of Widecombe-in-the-Moor stems from an old folk song about Tom Pearce and his gray mare, listing the men who were supposed to be on their way to Widecombe Fair when they met with disaster: Bill Brewer, Jan Stewer, Peter Gurney, Peter Davy, Daniel Whiddon, Harry Hawke, and Old Uncle Tom Cobley. Widecombe also has a parish church worth visiting. Called the **Cathedral of the Moor,** with a roster of vicars beginning in 1253, the house of worship in a green valley is surrounded by legends. When the building was restored, a wall plate was found bearing the badge of Richard II (1377–99), the figure of a white hart.

In Dartmoor, you'll find 500 miles of footpaths and bridleways and more than 90,000 acres of common land with public access. The country is rough, and on the high moor you should make sure you have good maps, a compass, and suitable clothing and shoes. Don't be put off, because unless you are an experienced hiker, it is unlikely that you will go far from the well-trodden paths.

WHAT TO SEE & DO

Dartmoor National Park Authority (DNPA), runs guided walks of varying difficulty, ranging from 1½ to 6 hours for a trek of some 9 to 12 miles. All you have to do is turn up suitably clad at your selected starting point. Details are available from DNP information centers or from the **Dartmoor National Park Authority Headquarters,** Parke, Haytor Road, Bovey Tracey, Devon TQ13 9JQ (tel. 0626/832093). The charge for walks is £1 to £2 ($1.85 to $3.70).

✪ Throughout the area are stables where you can arrange for a day's trek across the moors. For horse riding on Dartmoor there are too many establishments to list. All are licensed, and you are accompanied by an experienced rider/guide. Prices are around £4.50 ($8.35) per hour, £12 ($22.20) for a half day, and £18 ($33.30) for a full day. Most riding stables are listed in a useful free publication, *The Dartmoor Visitor,* which also contains details of guided walks, places to go, accommodations, local events, and articles about the national park. *The Dartmoor Visitor* is obtainable from DNP information centers and tourist information centers or by post. Send an International Reply Coupon to the DNPA headquarters (address above).

The market town of Okehampton owes the existence of the **Museum of Dartmoor Life,** the Dartmoor Centre, West Street, Okehampton (tel. 0837/52295), to the Norman castle built by Baldwin de Bryonis, sheriff of Devon, under orders from his uncle, William the Conqueror, in 1068, just 2 years after the Conquest. The Courtenay family lived there for many generations until Henry VIII beheaded one of them and dismantled the castle in 1538. The museum is housed in an old mill with a water wheel and is part of the Dartmoor Centre, a group of attractions around an old courtyard. Also here are working craft studios, a Victorian Cottage Tea Room, and a Dartmoor National Park tourist information center. Museum displays cover all aspects of Dartmoor's history from prehistoric times, including geology, industries, living conditions, crafts, farm tools and machinery, and some old vehicles—a Devon box wagon of 1875, a 1922 Bullnose Morris motorcar, a 1937 motorcycle. There is a reconstructed cider press, a blacksmithy, and a tourist information center. The museum is open March to December Monday to Saturday from 10am to 5pm (Sunday in July and August). Admission is £1 ($1.85) for adults, 50p (95¢) for children.

WHERE TO STAY & EAT

Accommodation information is operated by the Dartmoor Tourist Association, 8 Fitzford Cottages, Tavistock (tel. 0252/3501). Local information centers will also provide a list of accommodations.

DOUBLES WITHOUT BATH FOR LESS THAN £40 [$74]

LEUSDON LODGE, Leusdon-Lower Town, Poundgate, Dartmoor, Devon TQ13 7PE. Tel. 03643/304. 9 rms (7 with bath). TV

$ Rates (including English breakfast): £18 ($33.30) single without bath, £24 ($44.40) single with bath; £36 ($66.60) double without bath, £48 ($88.80) double with bath; half board £30–£36 ($55.50–$66.60) per person. AE, DC, MC, V. **Parking:** Free.

 This is a 150-year-old granite country house set in Dartmoor National Park overlooking the Dart Valley. Most bedrooms have private baths, and there is a family room. Traditional English food and a hearty breakfast are served in the dining room, with hand-carved paneled walls and an ornate fireplace. A log fire burns in the lounge in winter. There is also a cozy bar. Leisure pursuits include horseback riding, canoeing, fishing, and walking the moors. The kitchen will prepare a picnic lunch for guests who participate in outdoor activities. Approaching from Exeter or Plymouth on A38, in the vicinity of Ashburton, don't enter the town but follow the blue signs for Princetown. The road is marked on some as either A384 or B3357 but has been declassified and carries no number at all. Continue on this road to Princetown for 5 miles, crossing two narrow bridges and negotiating some steep hills pass the village of Poundsgate. Turn right at the signpost pointing toward Leusdon, Ponsworthy, and Widecombe. In just less than ½ mile fork right at the Jubilee Stone toward Lower Town and at the next small junction keep right, going down a steep narrow hill past Leusdon Church to Leusdon Lodge on your right in about 300 yards.

LYDFORD HOUSE HOTEL, Lydford, near Okehampton, Devon EX20 4AU. Tel. 08282/347. Fax 082282/442. 13 rms (all with bath). TV TEL

$ Rates (including English breakfast): £26 ($48.10) single; £52 ($96.20) double. AE, V. **Parking:** Free.

This is a family-run, country-house hotel standing in some 8 acres of gardens and pastureland on the outskirts of Lydford, just on the edge of Dartmoor. It was built in 1880 for the Dartmoor artist William Widgery, and several of his paintings hang in the residents' lounge. All rooms have hot-beverage facilities. Owners Ron and Ann Boulter offer varied and interesting menus, all of which feature home cooking using local produce. A set dinner costs £10.50 ($19.45). The hotel is 7 miles south of Okehampton, just off the A386, and it's on your right as you approach the hamlet of Lydford. Lydford House has its own riding stables in the hotel grounds.

OLD WALLS FARM, Ponsworthy, near Widecombe-in-the-Moor and Newton Abbot, Devon TQ13 7PN. Tel. 03643/222. 3 rms (1 with bath).
$ Rates (including English breakfast): £19 ($35.15) single; £34 ($62.90) double. No credit cards. **Parking:** Free.

This country home is set on a working farm comfortably in the heart of the moors, and in the safe, knowing hands of owner Bill Fursdon, an expert on the area. He'll take you on a short walk around his farm and show you his cows, Jack Russell terriers, ducks, a pet goat, and a little river, which gives electric power to the house. He'll make handmade maps and pinpoint the places of interest within driving distance. Guests relax around a stone fireplace in the drawing room, or on a sunny day enjoy a crescent-shaped, all-glass sun room; from the latter, the view of the moorland is exceptional. The living room has an old grand piano, a Victorian card table, a soft sofa, and an armchair placed in a curving bay recess. Breakfast is a special event in the dining room, and you can eat as much as you want.

Old Walls Farm is reached from the A38 divided highway between Exeter and Plymouth. Turn right past Ashburton onto the B3357, then right at Poundsgate onto the Ponsworthy-Widecombe road. Go through the hamlet of Ponsworthy, passing the all-purpose post office and store, and look for the B&B sign on the left about 600 yards on.

RING OF BELLS, North Bovey, Devon TQ13 8RB. Tel. 0647/40375. 3 rms (all with bath). **Transportation:** Buses travel from Exeter and Torquay to the village of Moretonhampstead, 1½ miles away.
$ Rates (including English breakfast): £25 ($46.25) per person. No credit cards. **Parking:** Free.

Set beside the village green of a hamlet consisting almost entirely of thatched cottages, this family-run inn, restaurant, and pub was originally built during the 13th century. Today, it retains its thatch roof and cottage garden, though in back, part of the space has been transformed into an outdoor pool. The building's walls are as much as 3 feet thick, and some of the bedrooms contain four-poster beds. Beneath time-blackened beams, you can have meals in the establishment's pub, priced from £5 ($9.25) each. Tony and Brenda Rix, the live-in proprietors, also offer meals within their somewhat more formal restaurant, priced from £9 ($16.65) each. Golfers appreciate the proximity of the establishment to the Manor House Hotel, set a mile away, which contains an 18-hole golf course.

WORTH THE EXTRA BUCKS

WHITE HART HOTEL, The Square, Moretonhampstead, Newton Abbot, Devon TQ13 8NP. Tel. 0647/404406. Fax 0647/40565. 20 rms (all with bath). TV TEL
$ Rates (including English breakfast): £37.50–£40 ($69.40–$74) single; £57.50–£60 ($106.40–$111) double. AE, DC, MC, V. **Parking:** Free.

This 300-year-old inn is a Georgian posting house on the main street, with a white hart on the portico over the front door. Rooms vary in size, some have beamed ceilings, and all contain hot-beverage facilities and central heating. Meals are taken in the polished dining room graced by a carved sideboard, antique grandfather clock, and magnificent silver candelabra. You may enjoy a drink or snack in the cheerful oak-beamed bar, sharing the warmth of the log fire with the locals. A three-course meal will cost £13 ($24.05), or you can choose the tourist menu for £11 ($20.35). Dinner is served from 7 to 9pm daily. "Mine host" is Peter Morgan, hotelier in Devon for some three decades. Take the M5 (A38) to the Newton Abbot/Bovey Tracey/Moretonhampstead junction and join the A382 Bovey Tracey bypass, continuing 8 miles to Moretonhampstead.

---

3. CHAGFORD

218 miles SW of London;
20 miles N of Exeter, Torquay, and Plymouth; 6 miles NE of Postbridge

GETTING THERE   By Train   Go to Exeter, then take a local bus to Chagford.

By Bus   From Exeter take the Transmoor Link National Express bus No. 82.

By Car   From Exeter, take A30 west, then A382 south to Chagford.

ESSENTIALS   The **area code** is 0647. For tourist information contact the Dartmoor Tourist Association (see above).

Six hundred feet above sea level, Chagford is an ancient stannary town, and with the moors all around, it is a good base for your exploration of North Dartmoor. Chagford overlooks the Teign River in its deep valley and is itself overlooked by the high granite tors. There's good fishing in the Teign (ask at your hotel). From Chagford, the most popular excursion is to Postbridge, a village with a prehistoric clapper bridge.

WHAT TO SEE & DO

CASTLE DROGO, in the hamlet of Drewsteignton. Tel. 0647/433306.
     This massive granite castle was designed and built by Sir Edwin Lutyens and the castle's owner, Julius Drewe, in the early 20th century. It stands high above the River Teign, with views over the moors. The family can trace its origins back to the Norman Conquest. Drewe, who wanted to create a home worthy of his noble ancestors, found the bleak site high above the moors, and he and Lutyens created a splendid modern castle. The tour includes the elegant library, the drawing room, the dining room with fine paintings and mirrors, and a chapel, along with a vaulted-roof gun room and a garden. There is also a restaurant.
     Admission: Castle and grounds £3.80 ($7.05) adults, £1.90 ($3.50) children. Grounds only £1.60 ($2.95) adults, 80p ($1.50) children.
     Open: Castle Apr–Sept Sat–Thurs 11am–5:30pm; Oct Sat–Thurs 11am–4:30pm. Restaurant daily 11am–5:30pm. **Directions:** Lies 4 miles northeast of Chagford and 6 miles south of the Exeter to Okehampton Road (A30). Follow the signs from the A30.

SIR FRANCIS DRAKE'S HOUSE, Buckland Abbey, Yelverton. Tel. 0822/853607.
     Constructed in 1278, Sir Francis Drake's House was originally a Cistercian monastery. It was dissolved in 1539 and became the country seat of Sir Richard Grenville and later Sir Francis Drake (two great sailors). The house remained in the Drake family until 1946, when the abbey and grounds were given to the National Trust. The abbey is now a museum and houses exhibits including Drake's drum, banners, and other artifacts. (You probably won't get a chance to beat Drake's drum, but if you do, remember the words of Henry Newbold's poem: "Drake will quit the port of heaven and come to England's aid once more."). Light snacks are available.
     Admission: £3.60 ($6.65) adults, £1.80 ($3.35) children.

Open: Apr–Sept Fri–Wed 10:30am–5:30pm; Oct Fri–Wed 10:30–5pm; Nov–Mar Wed and Sat–Sun 2–5pm. **Directions:** Go 3 miles west of Yelverton off the A386.

WHERE TO STAY & EAT

DOUBLES WITHOUT BATH FOR LESS THAN £42 [$77.70]

In Chagford

BLY HOUSE, Chagford, Devon TQ13 8BW. Tel. 0647/432404. 6 rms (all with bath). TV **Directions:** Just walk past the Chagford car park.
$ **Rates** (including English breakfast): £26–£27 ($48.10–$49.95) single; £42–£44 ($77.70–$81.40) double. No credit cards. **Parking:** Free. **Closed:** Nov–Dec.

 Mr. and Mrs. G. B. Thompson welcome you to their country-house hotel converted from a former rectory. A short walk from the village of Chagford, it is set in 5 acres of grounds with sweeping lawns. The house is elegantly furnished with antiques, and some bedrooms have four-poster beds; all have hot-beverage facilities. Small children are not accepted. The hotel isn't licensed, but guests can bring their own liquor, perhaps enjoying it in front of the log fire in the comfortable lounge when the weather is cool, although the house is centrally heated. Breakfast is the only meal served, but there are six good pub restaurants in the village.

GLENDARAH HOUSE, Lower Street, Chagford, Devon TQ13 8BZ. Tel. 0647/433270. 7 rms (none with bath), 1 suite.
$ **Rates** (including English breakfast): £16.50 ($30.55) single without bath; £33 ($61.05) double without bath; £45 ($83.25) suite with bath. No credit cards. **Parking:** Free.

 This is a clean, comfortable guesthouse run by Edward and Marian Willett located at the edge of town. The house makes a good base for exploring Dartmoor National Park. The Willetts offer good accommodations, with color TV in the residents' lounge and a licensed bar featuring a range of local wines. The two baths in the house contain showers. There is also a cottage suite with a four-poster bed, a complete bath, exposed oak beams, and color TV; it is in converted stables, only a short distance from the house. Mrs. Willett provides ample breakfasts and an excellent four-course dinner every night.

TORR HOUSE, Thorn, Chagford, Devon TQ13 8DX. Tel. 0647/432228. 5 rms (3 with bath or shower).
$ **Rates** (including English breakfast): £23 ($42.55) single without bath, £28.50 ($52.75) single with bath; £38 ($70.30) double without bath, £45 ($83.25) double with bath. AE, MC, V. **Parking:** Free.
This is a family-managed, Georgian house standing in 1½ acres of gardens on the periphery of Dartmoor. Over the years, this old house had played many roles—ranging from an army headquarters to a rest home for the invalid. Today, it is a welcoming hotel run by Hazel and John Cork who rent well-kept and comfortable rooms. Guests meet each other for conversation in the lounge. One feature of this house, which is licensed, is its good home-cooked English food. Dinner, if arranged in advance, is served nightly at 7pm. Vegetarian meals can also be arranged. There is parking for eight cars. The hotel lies 1½ miles from Chagford. Take the Fernworthy signs from Chagford Square and the Kestor sign at Waye Cross. Torr House is in the next hamlet of Thorn. Turn a sharp right off the main lane between the thatched cottages down a private road, and the house will be 100 yards on your right.

THREE CROWNS HOTEL, High St., Chagford, Devon TQ13 8AJ. Tel. 0647/433444. Fax 0647/433117. 21 rms (16 with bath or shower). TV
$ **Rates** (including English breakfast): £21 ($38.85) single without bath, £29.50 ($54.60) single with bath; £42 ($77.70) double without bath, £59 ($109.15) double with bath. AE, MC, V. **Parking:** Free.

This is a 13th-century granite inn built to withstand the rigors of the climate, with open fireplaces, roaring log fires, and old oak beams. Much of the furniture is of the period. The old manor house has modern conveniences and central heating.

The bar snacks are very good and are served both at lunch and in the evening. Some specialty dishes include coq au vin and escalope of Devon veal. There are desserts and a good selection of cheese assortments. The fixed-price dinner costs from £15 ($27.75) with lunches going for £6.25 ($11.55). The hotel is located on the main street.

At Postbridge

LYDGATE HOUSE HOTEL, Postbridge, Devon PL2O 6TJ. Tel. 0822/ 88209. 8 rms (6 with bath). TV **Directions:** From Exeter, take the A38 Plymouth Road to Peartree Cross (signposted Ashburton to Dartmoor), follow the B3357 to Two Bridges, and turn right onto the B3212.

$ Rates (including English breakfast): £22 ($40.70) single without bath, £28 ($51.80) single with bath; £40 ($74) double without bath, £48 ($88.80) double with bath. MC, V. **Parking:** Free.

Near the heart of Postbridge, this hotel began life as a squatter's cottage in the early 1700s. What you'll see today is a Victorian enlargement. The Dart River runs through the grounds, covering 38 acres. The owners provide log fires on cold nights, and big windows open onto view of the river. Rooms are simply but comfortably furnished. In the snug bar, drinks are served, followed by a three-course set dinner for £10.50 ($19.45).

---

4. TORQUAY

223 miles SW of London; 23 miles S of Exeter

GETTING THERE   By Plane   The nearest connection is Exeter Airport (see above), 40 minutes away.

By Train   Frequent trains run throughout the day from London's Paddington Station to Torquay and take 2 hours and 30 minutes.

By Bus   National Express bus links from London's Victoria Station leave every 2 hours during the day for Torquay.

By Car   From Exeter (see above) head west along A38, veering south at the junction with A380.

ESSENTIALS   The **area code** for Torquay is 0803. The **Tourist Information Centre** is at Vaughan Parade (tel. 0803/297428).

In 1968, the towns of Torquay, Paignton, and Brixham joined to form "The English Riviera" as part of a plan to turn the area into one of the super three-in-one resorts of Europe. The area today—the birthplace of mystery writer Agatha Christie—opens onto 22 miles of coastline and 18 beaches.

To follow up on the Riviera label, Torquay would definitely be the Cannes section, whereas Paignton invites family fun (long, safe beaches), and Brixham is a busy fishing port.

Torquay is set against a backdrop of the red cliffs of Devon, with many sheltered pebbly coves. With its parks and gardens, including numerous subtropical plants and palm trees, it is often compared to the Mediterranean, a setting you hardly expect in England. At night, concerts, productions from the West End (the D'Oyly Carte Opera appears occasionally at the Princess Theatre), vaudeville shows, and ballroom dancing keep the holiday makers—and many honeymooners—entertained.

WHERE TO STAY

In addition to the following the Mulberry Room (see "Where to Eat," below) also rents rooms.

DOUBLES WITHOUT BATH FOR LESS THAN £44 [$81.40]

COLINDALE, 20 Rathmore Rd., Torquay, Devon TQ2 6NY. Tel. 0803/ 293947. 9 rms (3 with bath).
$ Rates (including English breakfast): £14–£16 ($25.90–$29.60) per person. No credit cards. **Parking:** Free.
This hotel is a good choice, and it's about as central as you'd want. Opening onto King's Garden, it lies within a 5-minute walk of Corbyn Beach and a 3-minute walk from the railway station. The hotel has a cocktail bar and a residents' lounge and dining room offering a set dinner for £6.50 ($12.05). Colindale is one of a row of attached brick Victorian houses, with gables and chimneys. It's set back from the road, with a parking court in front.

CRAIG COURT HOTEL, 10 Ash Hill Rd., Castle Circus, Torquay, Devon TQ1 3HZ. Tel. 0803/294400. 10 rms (4 with bath). **Directions:** Take St. Marychurch Rd. (signposted St. Marychurch, Babbacombe) from Castle Circus (town hall); make first right onto Ash Hill Rd.; go 200 yards and hotel is on right.
$ Rates (including English breakfast): £18 ($33.30) single without bath; £36 ($66.60) double without bath, £41 ($75.85) double with bath; half board £20– £27.50 ($37–$50.90) per person. No credit cards. **Parking:** Free. **Closed:** Oct–Easter.
This hotel is in a large Victorian mansion with a southern exposure and lies a short walk from the heart of town. The owners, Joyce and David Anning, offer excellent value with discreetly modernized bedrooms, many with private facilities. In addition to enjoying the good, wholesome food served here, guests can also make use of a well-appointed lounge or an intimate bar opening onto the grounds (there is a model railway in the garden).

CRANBORNE HOTEL, 58 Belgrave Rd., Torquay, Devon TQ2 5HY. Tel. 0803/294100. 12 rms (10 with bath). TV
$ Rates (including English breakfast): £15–£16 ($27.75–$29.60) single without bath; £32 ($59.20) double without bath, £36 ($66.60) double with bath. MC, V. **Parking:** £1 ($1.85).
 This is a small, family-run enterprise where guests get a personal welcome from Mr. and Mrs. Dawkins, who rent comfortably furnished bedrooms, with hot-beverage facilities. Guests mix informally either in a lounge reserved for them or on the patio. The hotel lies off Torbay Road near English Riviera Centre.

CRESTA HOTEL, St. Agnes Lane, Torquay, Devon TQ2 6QD. Tel. 0803/ 607241. 10 rms (all with bath).
$ Rates (including English breakfast): £20 ($37) per person; half board £24 ($44.40) per person. No credit cards. **Parking:** Free.
 This is a family hotel full of character overlooking the sea in a secluded position close to the train terminal. The hosts, John and Lucy Macmillan, are helpful and offer comfortably furnished rooms, some with sea views. Free TV and hot-beverage facilities are available on request. Half board includes a traditional roast for a four-course evening meal with tea or coffee in addition to bed and breakfast.

FAIRMOUNT HOUSE HOTEL, Herbert Rd., Chelston, Torquay, Devon TQ4 6RW. Tel. 0803/605446. 8 rms (all with bath or shower). TV **Directions:** Follow the signs to Cockington Village.
$ Rates (including English breakfast): £22–£24 ($40.70–$44.40) single; £44–£48 ($81.40–$88.80) double. **Closed:** Mid-Nov to mid-Feb. AE, MC, V. **Parking:** Free.

This Victorian building has been well preserved with stained glass, marble fireplaces, and other adornments of that grand age, and lies in a tranquil residential area of the resort, about a mile from the harbor. Guest rooms are comfortably furnished, and good, sound British cooking can be ordered. After a meal, guests can relax in the public rooms, including a conservatory bar lounge where bar lunches are available at noon.

GLENORLEIGH, 26 Cleveland Rd., Torquay, Devon TQ2 5BE. Tel. 0803/ 292135. 16 rms (9 with bath or shower). **Directions:** When you reach the traffic lights at Torre Station, bear right into Avenue Rd. (A379). Cleveland Rd. is the first turning on the left.

$ Rates (including English breakfast): £20 ($37) single without bath, £30 ($55.50) single without bath; £40 ($74) double without bath, £56 ($103.60) double with bath. No credit cards. **Parking:** £6–£10 ($11.10–$18.50) per night based on size of car.

Known in many circles as the "best B&B in Torquay," this is a worthy choice. Bedrooms have been tastefully modernized and are well maintained. In summer, many guests are booked in for the week, so you'll have to call and see if they have space. The hotel has a solarium and a heated swimming pool.

KELVIN HOUSE, 46 Bampfyld Rd., Torquay, Devon TQ2 5AY. Tel. 0803/297313. 10 rms (6 with shower). **Directions:** From Torbay Rd. on the water take The Kings Drive north cutting onto Falkland Rd.

$ Rates (including English breakfast): £12 ($22.20) single without bath, £15 ($27.75) single with bath; £24 ($44.40) double without bath, £30 ($55.50) double with bath. MC, V. **Parking:** Free.

This Victorian villa is within walking distance of the sea, the English Riviera Leisure and Conference Centre, and the town center. Rooms are extra clean and sufficiently comfortable. There's no skimping, since the bedrooms have innerspring mattresses and basins with hot and cold running water, plus some have TVs. In addition, the resident owners, Mr. and Mrs. Geoff Kirkby, have provided a lounge with a television and a pleasant bar for that after-dinner English pint. Dinners cost from £5.50 ($10.20).

WORTH THE EXTRA BUCKS

BLUE HAZE HOTEL, Seaway Lane, Torquay, Devon TQ2 6PS. Tel. 0803/607186. 10 rms (all with bath). MINIBAR TV **Directions:** 300 yards up the hill behind Torquay Rail Station.

$ Rates (including English breakfast): £60–£62 ($111–$114.70) double. MC, V. **Parking:** Free. **Closed:** Nov to mid-Mar.

This is an elegant Victorian house with a large garden, set in a residential area 500 yards from the beaches. The spacious bedrooms contain refrigerators, tea and coffee makers, and hairdryers. There are no singles. The hosts, Doug and Hazel Newton, serve four-course, home-cooked meals in their licensed hotel, and there is a large private car park.

WHERE TO EAT

MEALS FOR LESS THAN £17.50 [$32.40]

CAPERS RESTAURANT, 7 Lisburne Sq. Tel. 291177.
Cuisine: SEAFOOD. **Reservations:** Recommended. **Bus:** No. 32 or 85.
$ Prices: Appetizers £4–£5 ($7.40–$9.25); main courses £12–£14 ($22.20–$25.90); lunches from £7.50 ($13.90). MC, V.
Open: Mon–Sat noon–1:30pm and 7–9:30pm.

In this attractive, cozy restaurant on Lisburne Square, lying slightly outside the heart of Torquay, the chef-owner, Ian Cawley, makes everything himself (except the wines), using herbs and many vegetables grown under his supervision. Capers specializes in fish, although there are always two or three meat dishes on the menu. "The menu is just ideas," Mr. Cawley says. "I can always cook things in different ways because it is all cooked to order."

MULBERRY ROOM, 1 Scarborough Rd., Torquay, Devon TQ2 5UJ. Tel. 213639.
 Cuisine: ENGLISH. **Reservations:** Required for dinner. **Directions:** From seafront, turn up Belgrave Rd., then first right onto Scarborough Rd.
$ **Prices:** Appetizers: £1.85–£2.75 ($3.40–$5.10); main courses £4.50–£8.50 ($8.35–$15.75); set dinner £8.50–£15.50 ($15.75–$28.70); set lunch £6.50–£7.50 ($12.05–$13.90). No credit cards.
 Open: Lunch Wed–Sun 12:15–2:30pm; dinner Sat 7:30–9pm.

Lesley Cooper is an inspired cook and will feed you well in her little dining room which seats some two dozen diners at midday. The restaurant is situated in the dining area of one of Torquay's Victorian villas and faces onto a patio of plants and flowers, with outside tables for summer lunches and afternoon teas. The vegetarian will find selections here and other diners can feast on her baked lamb or honey-roasted chicken, among other dishes. Traditional roasts draw the Sunday crowds. The choice is wisely limited so that everything served will be fresh. You can even stay here in one of the three bedrooms, each simply but comfortably furnished and well kept. B&B charges range from £12.50 to £16.50 ($23.15 to $30.55) per person daily, making it one of the bargains of the resort.

OLD VIENNA, 6 Lisburne Sq. Tel. 295861.
 Cuisine: AUSTRIAN. **Reservations:** Recommended. **Bus:** No. 32 or 85.
$ **Prices:** Three-course set menu £17.50 ($32.40). AE, MC, V.
 Open: Lunch Mon–Fri noon–2pm; dinner Tues–Sun 7–10:30pm.
This restaurant, owned by Linz-born Werner Rott, offers a modernized, stylized, Austrian-inspired cuisine adapted for British tastes. It is housed within an early Victorian town house with an open fireplace and pinewood paneling. Ample portions and a free glass of schnapps complete any meal. The menu changes three times a year, but it is likely to offer Paprikaschnitzel and Tafelspitz, the famed boiled beef dish of Old Vienna. Although the menu is fixed price, the choice under each category is vast.

5. TOTNES

224 miles SW of London; 12 miles N of Dartmouth

GETTING THERE   By Train   Totnes is on the main London (Paddington Station)/Plymouth line. Trains leave London frequently throughout the day.

By Bus   Totnes is served locally by the Western National and Devon General bus companies (tel. 0803/63226 in Torquay for information about individual routings).

By Boat   Many visitors approach Totnes by river steamer from Dartmouth. Contact Dart Pleasure Craft, River Link (tel. 0803/2277 for information).

By Car   From Torquay, head west along B3210.

ESSENTIALS   The **area code** is 0803. The summer-only **Tourist Information Centre** is at The Plains (tel. 0803/863168).

One of the oldest towns in the West Country, the ancient borough of Totnes rests quietly in the past, seemingly content to let the Torbay area remain in the vanguard of the building boom. On the River Dart, upstream from Dartmouth, Totnes is so totally removed in character from Torquay that the two towns could be in different countries. Totnes has several old historic buildings, notably the ruins of a Norman castle, an ancient guildhall, and the 15th-century church of St. Mary, made of red sandstone. In the Middle Ages, the old cloth town was encircled by walls, and the North Gate serves as a reminder of that period.

WHERE TO STAY

IN TOWN

OLD FORGE, Seymour Place, Totnes, Devon TQ9 5AY. Tel. 0803/ 862174. 10 rms (6 with bath). TV **Directions:** From the monument at the foot of Shopping St., cross the bridge over the river and take the second turning on the right.
$ Rates (including English breakfast): £30 ($55.50) single without bath, £40 ($74) single with bath; £35 ($64.75) double without bath, £55 ($101.75) double with bath. MC, V. **Parking:** Free.
This is a restored former blacksmith's and wheelwright's workshop dating back six centuries. The owner of Old Forge, Peter Allnutt and his wife, Jeannie, still carry on this ancient tradition. Part of the present-day Old Forge is said to have incorporated the Totnes jail. Near the River Dart, B&B accommodations are provided in attractively decorated bedrooms, four of which are ideal for families.

ON THE OUTSKIRTS

BROOMBOROUGH HOUSE FARM, Broomborough Dr., Higher Plymouth Rd., Totnes, Devon TQ9 5LU. Tel. 0803/863134. 3 rms (none with bath). TV
$ Rates (including English breakfast): £17 ($31.45) single; £33 ($61.05) double. AE. **Parking:** Free.
In a secluded valley with magnificent views of Dartmoor National Park, this house is an elegant gabled mansion. It was designed by Sir George Gilbert Scott, who also designed the Albert Memorial and other structures of architectural heritage in London. The house has central heating, spacious lounges, and the bedrooms have hot beverage facilities and electric blankets. Bob and Joan Veale operate the house along with their 600-acre farm and will give good advice. The house is a 10-minute walk from the town center; many country inns and restaurants are nearby.

FORD FARM HOUSE, Harberton, near Totnes, Devon TQ9 7SJ. Tel. 0803/863539. 3 rms (1 with shower). **Directions:** Take the A381 Totnes-Kingsbridge road for 2½ miles. Farm is signposted at the village of Harberton.
$ Rates (including English breakfast): £18 ($33.30) single without bath; £35 ($64.75) double without bath, £36–£39 ($66.60–$72.15) double with bath. No credit cards. **Parking:** Free.
This is a 17th-century house in a rural village of South Devon. Near the moors, the house is capably managed by Mike and Sheila Edwards, who rent a single and a twin-bedded room with hot- and cold-water basins, plus a double with a private shower and toilet.

WHERE TO EAT

IN TOWN

WILLOW VEGETARIAN RESTAURANT, 87 High St. Tel. 862605.
Cuisine: VEGETARIAN. **Reservations:** Required for dinner.

$ Prices: Appetizers 80p–£2.20 ($1.50–$4.05); main courses £1–£5.50 ($1.85–$10.20). No credit cards.
Open: Lunch Mon–Sat 10am–5pm; dinner Tues–Sat 6:30–10pm.

Right in the town center, this is a vegetarian whole-food restaurant, offering live music on Friday and an Indian menu on Wednesday. Otherwise, it serves "real English food," including main dishes, cakes, and salads that are made on the premises from fresh, natural, high-quality ingredients. Organic ingredients are used as much as possible, and microwaves don't exist as far as the kitchen is concerned. It's self-service during the day, with table service in the evening. There is also an organic wine list.

AN EXCURSION TO DARTINGTON

For such a small hamlet, Dartington attracts a surprising share of international visitors, mainly because of the **Dartington Hall Estate** (tel. 0803/862271). After 1925, a Yorkshire man and his American-born wife (one of the Whitneys), Leonard and Dorothy Elmhirst, poured energy, courage, imagination, and money into the theory that a rural economy could become self-sufficient. They restored the late 14th-century historic Dartington Hall. And in the surrounding acres of undulating hills and streams, several village industries were created: housing construction, advanced farming, milling of cloth, and an experimental school. One famous activity here is the College of Arts, in which students live and work in a series of modern buildings erected since the formation of the college in 1961. The Summer School of Music spends the month of August here, occupying the college buildings and giving numerous concerts. During the day, visitors are welcome to make purchases at the **Cider Press Centre,** a complex designed to provide a showcase for the work of leading British craftspeople. You'll find a craft gallery and shop, print gallery, souvenir shop, toy shop, and Cranks health-food restaurant. One of the shops sells Dartington glass seconds along with many interesting souvenirs. The center is open Monday to Saturday from 9:30am to 5:30pm (also on Sunday in summer).

WHERE TO STAY

COTT INN, Dartington, near Totnes, Devon TQ9 6HE. Tel. 0803/863777. Fax 0803/866629. 6 rms (5 with bath). TV TEL **Transportation:** Bus No. X80 travels from Totnes to Dartington, but most hire a taxi for the 1½-mile journey.
$ Rates (including English or continental breakfast): £57.50 ($106.40) single; £62.50 ($115.65) double. AE, MC, V. **Parking:** Free.
Built in 1320, this hotel is the second-oldest inn in England. It is a low, rambling two-story building of stone, cob, and plaster, with a thatched roof and walls 3 feet thick, on the old Ashburton-Totnes turnpike. Steve and Gill Culverhouse rent low-ceilinged, double rooms upstairs, with modern conveniences, including hot and cold running water. The inn is a gathering place for the people of Dartington, and you'll feel the pulse of English country life. In winter, log fires keep the lounge and bar snug. You'll surely be intrigued with the tavern, where you can also order a meal. A buffet is laid out at lunchtime, priced according to your choice of dish. The à la carte dinners feature local produce prepared in interesting ways; scallops, duck, steak, or fresh salmon may be available. Even if you're not staying over, at least drop in at the pub (seven beers are on draft). Pub hours are Monday to Saturday from 11am to 2:30pm and 6 to 11pm, and Sunday from noon to 2:30pm and 7 to 10:30pm.

WHERE TO EAT

CRANKS HEALTH FOOD RESTAURANT, Dartington Cider Press Centre, Shinners Bridge. Tel. 862388.

Cuisine: VEGETARIAN. **Reservations:** None. **Transportation:** Bus no. X80 travels to Dartington from Plymouth and Torquay.

$ **Prices:** Appetizers £1.50 ($2.80), pizzas, quiches, and burgers £1.75 ($3.25), cream teas £1.80 ($3.35), main courses £3 ($5.55). No credit cards.

Open: Daily 10am–5pm. **Closed:** Sun in winter.

Affiliated with Crank's restaurant chain, whose other branches all lie within London, this is the region's leading health-food restaurant. Contained within the crafts center of Dartington (actually part of an old Devonshire farmstead), ringed with whitewashed stone walls and furnished with ashwood tables, it serves only compost-grown vegetables, live-culture yogurts, and freshly extracted fruit juices. The place is very busy, and strictly self-service, with an ample buffet containing salads. The Devonshire cream teas served include whole-meal scones, whole-fruit jams, and freshly clotted local cream. There's additional seating available within the pleasant garden.

6. DARTMOUTH

236 miles SW of London; 35 miles S of Exeter

GETTING THERE By Train Dartmouth is not easily reached by public transport. British Rail trains run to Totnes (see above) and Paignton.

By Bus There is one bus a day from Totnes to Dartmouth.

By Car From Exeter, take A38 southwest, cutting southeast toward Totnes along A381. Follow A381 to the junction with B3207,

By Boat There are river boats making the 10-mile run from Totnes to Dartmouth, but these are dependent on tide and operated only during Easter to the end of October. Check at the Totnes tourist office (see above) for details about possible boat schedules.

ESSENTIALS The **area code** is 0803. The **Tourist Information Centre** is at 11 Duke Street. (tel. 0803/4224).

At the mouth of the Dart River, this ancient seaport is the home of the Royal Naval College. Traditionally linked to England's maritime greatness, Dartmouth sent out the young midshipmen who saw to it that "Britannia ruled the waves." You can take a river steamer up the Dart to Totnes (book at the kiosk at the harbor); the scenery along the way is breathtaking, as the Dart is Devon's most beautiful river.

Dartmouth's 15th-century castle was built during the reign of Edward IV. The town's most noted architectural feature is the Butterwalk, which lies below Tudor houses. The Flemish influence in some of the houses is pronounced.

WHERE TO STAY
DOUBLES WITH BATH £45 ($83.25)

BORINGDON HOUSE, 1 Church Rd., Dartmouth, Devon TQ6 9HQ. Tel. 0803/832235. 3 rms (all with bath or shower). TV **Directions:** From Dartmouth, head up College Way, take first left into Townstal Rd., then first right onto Church Rd.

$ **Rates** (including English breakfast): £34–£40 ($62.90–$74) single or double. No credit cards. **Parking:** Free.

This is an exceptional upmarket B&B for the area. Pamela and Geoffrey Goodwin receive guests in their spacious Georgian house, which stands in a garden overlooking the town and harbor. They rent attractively furnished

bedrooms, each one a double. Since space is limited, and demand, especially in summer, is great. Reservations are needed.

CAPTAIN'S HOUSE, 18 Clarence St., Dartmouth, Devon TQ6 9NW. Tel. 0803/832133. 5 rms (all with bath). TV
$ Rates (including English breakfast): £25–£27 ($46.25–$49.95) single; £38–£40 ($70.30–$74) double. No credit cards.

Run by Ann and Nigel Jestico, this hotel is a 200-year-old Georgian house near the waterfront. The well-run, clean, and inviting house has central heating, and all bedrooms have radios and tea and coffee makers. You get excellent hospitality and good beds.

FORD HOUSE, 44 Victoria Rd., Dartmouth, Devon TQ6 9DX. Tel. 0803/834047. 3 rms (all with bath). TV
$ Rates (including English breakfast): £39 ($72.15) single; £45 ($83.25) double. Reductions for stays of 3 days or more. MC, V. **Parking:** Free.

Sheltered within its own walled garden, this pale pink Regency house, originally built in 1820, is maintained by Richard and Henrietta Turner. Graced with an iron balcony entwined with flowering vines and a view of the garden, the house is filled with the Victorian furnishings which the owners acquired over many years at nearby auctions. Located a short walk west of the center of town (and named after a spot where, during the Middle Ages, a ford was used to cross a tributary of the River Dart) the house is charming and comfortable, a refreshing place for the well-prepared evening meals which are served upon request in the dining room. The cost of dinner is £17 ($31.45). A local "hoppa" bus stops regularly on its route up and down Victoria Road.

VICTORIA HOTEL, 27-29 Victoria Rd., Dartmouth, Devon TQ6 9RT. Tel. 0803/832572. 10 rms (4 with bath). TV **Transportation:** Take the "hoppa" bus.
$ Rates (including English breakfast): £16.50 ($30.55) single without bath, £20 ($37) single with bath; £33 ($61.05) double without bath, £48 ($88.80) double with bath. MC, V. **Parking:** Free.

 This family-run hotel is in the center of Dartmouth, only 150 yards from the harbor. The characteristic cottage-style bedrooms are tastefully furnished. Bar snacks are available from the spacious bar/lounge area, and an evening meal can be ordered in the restaurant.

WHERE TO EAT
MEALS FOR LESS THAN £9 ($16.65)

BILLY BUDD'S, 7 Foss St. Tel. 834842.
Cuisine: ENGLISH. **Reservations:** Required. **Bus:** No. 93.
$ Prices: Lunch pastas, omelets, salads, and hot dishes £4–£4.50 ($7.40–$8.35); set-dinner menus £16.50 ($30.55) for two courses, £18.50 ($34.25) for three courses. MC, V.
Open: Lunch Tues–Sat noon–2pm; dinner Tues–Sat 7:30–10pm.

Although this might suggest a Herman Melville story to most American visitors, the owners insist that the inspiration for its name was the opera by British composer Benjamin Britten. At this simply decorated local favorite, you'll be treated to "cheap and cheerful" lunch dishes which might include omelets, pastas, salads, and such platters of the day as ragoût of chicken. Dinners are more formal and elaborate, and include locally fattened lamb, salmon from the Dart River, very fresh fish, and desserts made with thick cream from Devonshire cows. Dishes are imaginative, but served with a refreshing lack of pretense.

SCARLET GERANIUM, 10 Fairfax Place. Tel. 832491.
Cuisine: ENGLISH. **Reservations:** Not needed.
$ Prices: Appetizers £1.35–£3.50 ($2.50–$6.45); main courses £4.25–£9.95 ($7.85–$18.40); three-course set lunch £6.50 ($12.05). No credit cards.
Open: Lunch daily noon–2:30pm; dinner daily 7–9:30pm.

Built originally in 1333, this charming old restaurant in the town center off The Quay was once known as the Albion Inn. Try it for morning coffee or dinner, which features roast leg of lamb or baked Wiltshire ham. When available, you can order the locally caught and dressed crab or fresh-caught salmon. A licensed bar is on the premises.

7. PLYMOUTH

242 miles SW of London; 161 miles E of Southampton

GETTING THERE **By Plane** Plymouth Airport lies 4 miles from the center of the city. Brymon Airways has direct service from both London airports at Heathrow and Gatwick to Plymouth. For service, call Brymon (tel. 0752/707023).

By Train Frequent trains run from London's Paddington Station to Plymouth in 3 to 3½ hours, depending on the train.

By Bus National Express has frequent daily bus service between London's Victoria Coach Station and Plymouth taking 4½ hours.

By Car From London take the M4 motorway west to the junction of M5 going south to Exeter. From Exeter head southwest on A38 to Plymouth.

Essentials The **area code** is 0752. **Tourist Information Centre** is at Civic Centre, Royal Parade (tel. 0752/264849).

The historic seaport of Plymouth is more romantic in legend than in reality. But this was not always so. In World War II, the blitzed area of greater Plymouth lost at least 75,000 buildings. The heart of present-day Plymouth, including the municipal civic center on the Royal Parade, has been entirely rebuilt—the way that it was done the subject of much controversy.

For the old you must go to the Elizabethan section, known as the **Barbican,** and walk along the quay in the footsteps of Sir Francis Drake (once the mayor of Plymouth) and other Elizabethan seafarers, such as Sir John Hawkins, English naval commander and slave trader. It was from here in 1577 that Drake set sail on his round-the-world voyage. An even more famous sailing took place in 1620, when the Pilgrims left their final port in England for the New World.

Legend has it that while playing bowls on Plymouth Hoe (Celtic for "high place"), Drake was told that the Spanish Armada had entered the sound and, in a masterful display of confidence, finished the game before going into battle. A local historian questions the location of the bowls game, if indeed it happened, starring Sir Francis. I am told that the Hoe in the 16th century was only gorse-covered scrubland outside tiny Plymouth and that it is more likely that the officers of the Royal Navy would have been bowling (then played on a shorter green than today) while awaiting the armada arrival at the Minerva Inn, Looe Street, 20 yards from the house where Sir Francis lived, about 2 minutes' walk from the Barbican. My informant says that other captains, knowing that it would take about 20 minutes to ready their ships to sail against the Spanish, may have sent their executive officers to prepare while they finished their drinks and game. Doubt is cast on Drake's display of such insouciance, however, the feeling being that "5 feet 2 inches of red-haired impetuosity as he was, he'd have been off like a flash!"

Of special interest to visitors from the United States is the final departure point of the Pilgrims in 1620, the already-mentioned Barbican. The two ships, *Mayflower* and *Speedwell,* that sailed from Southampton in August of that year put into Plymouth after they suffered storm damage. Here the *Speedwell* was abandoned as unseaworthy, and the *Mayflower* made the trip to the New World alone. The Memorial Gateway to the Waterside on the Barbican marks the place, tradition says, whence the Pilgrims' ship sailed.

WHAT TO SEE & DO

The Barbican is a mass of narrow streets, old houses, and quayside shops selling antiques, brasswork, old prints, and books. Fishing boats still unload their catch at the wharves, and passenger-carrying ferryboats run short harbor cruises. A trip includes a visit to Drake's Island in the sound, the dockyards, and naval vessels, plus a view of the Hoe from the water. A cruise of Plymouth Harbour costs £2.50 ($4.65) for adults and £1.25 ($2.30) for children. Departures are from February to November, with cruises leaving every half hour from 10am to 4pm daily. These **Plymouth Boat Cruises** are booked at the Phoenix Wharf, the Barbican (tel. 0752/822797).

BARBICAN CRAFT CENTRE, White Lane. Tel. 0752/662338.

Contained within its premises are the workshops and showrooms of about a half dozen artisans. These include potters, wood-carvers, leather workers, and weavers. You can buy their products at reasonable prices, and even commission your own design if the craftsperson agrees. The center is located about a 5-minute walk southeast of Plymouth's center.

Admission: Free.
Open: Mon–Sat 9am–5:30pm. **Bus:** No. 39.

BLACK FRIARS REFECTORY ROOM, Plymouth Gin Distillery, Southside St. Tel. 0752/667062.

Considered an important national monument, this historic room is contained within one of Plymouth's oldest surviving buildings. It was within its precincts that the Pilgrims met prior to setting sail for the New World. The building is owned by the Plymouth Gin Distillery, which includes a visit to its interior as part of their tours of their distillery. Free tours depart every 45 minutes, Monday to Saturday from 10:30am to 4pm from Easter to September. Tours should be reserved by calling first. Bus: No. 54.

PRYSTEN HOUSE, Finewell St. Tel. 0752/661414.

Built in 1490 as a town house close to St. Andrew's Church, it is now a church house and working museum. Rebuilt in the 1930s with American help, it contains a model of Plymouth in 1620 and tapestries depicting the colonization of America. At the entrance is the gravestone of the captain of the U.S. brig *Argus,* who died on August 15, 1813, after a battle in the English Channel. It is located in the town center.

Admission: 70p ($1.30) adults, 30p (55¢) children.
Open: Apr–Oct Mon–Sat 10am–4pm.

WHERE TO STAY

Present-day pilgrims from the New World who didn't strike it rich are advised to head for the Hoe, where there are a number of inexpensive B&B houses on a peaceful street near the water.

DOUBLES WITHOUT BATH FOR LESS THAN £38 ($70.30]

CAMELOT HOTEL, 5 Elliot St., The Hoe, Plymouth, Devon PL1 2PP. Tel. 0752/221255. Fax 0752/603660. 17 rms (all with bath). TV TEL **Bus:** No. 54.
$ Rates (including English breakfast): £34 ($64.75) single; £48 ($88.80) double. AE, DC, MC, V.

This neat, tall hotel stands on a small road just off the grassy expanse of the Hoe. There is a lounge with color TV and video, or you can watch from your own set in your comfortably furnished bedroom. Guests frequent the pleasant small bar and restaurant, with set-menu meals and a short à la carte menu in the evening. Laundry and dry-cleaning facilities are nearby.

GEORGIAN HOUSE, 51 Citadel Rd., The Hoe, Plymouth, Devon PL1 3AU. Tel. 0752/663237. 10 rms (all with bath or shower). TV TEL **Bus:** No. 54.

$ Rates (including English breakfast): £26–£28 ($48.10–$51.80) single; £36–£38 ($66.60–$70.30) double. AE, DC, MC, V. **Parking:** Free.

⑤ One of the finest guesthouses in Plymouth, this Georgian town house also includes the fully licensed Fourposter Restaurant. Each of the rooms is well maintained and comfortably furnished and contains beverage-making equipment, a trouser press, and a hairdryer. British and international dishes are served in the candlelit restaurant, costing from £12 ($22.20) for a meal. You might precede your meal with a drink in the cocktail bar. The restaurant is open Monday to Saturday from 6:30 to 9:30pm. The location is on the Hoe about 5 minutes from the ferry terminal.

HOE GUEST HOUSE, 20 Grand Parade, West Hoe, Plymouth, Devon PL1 3DF. Tel. 0752/665274. 6 rms (3 with bath). TV **Bus:** No. 19.

$ Rates (including English breakfast): £22 ($40.70) single without bath, £28 ($51.80) single with bath; £32 ($59.20) double without bath, £40 ($74) double with bath. No credit cards. **Parking:** Free.

Originally built in 1904, this small and charming stone-fronted guesthouse benefits from its ownership by Anne Grindon, and has a sweeping view of Plymouth Sound and Drake's Island. Each unit is comfortably appointed and well maintained. You can walk to the Barbican and the center of Plymouth. Only breakfast is served.

IMPERIAL HOTEL, 3 Windsor Villas, Lockyer St., The Hoe, Plymouth, Devon PL1 2OD. Tel. 0752/227311. 22 rms (15 with bath). TV TEL **Bus:** No. 54.

$ Rates (including English breakfast): £28 ($51.80) single without bath, £38 ($70.30) single with bath; £38 ($70.30) double without bath, £48 ($88.80) double with bath. AE, DC, MC, V. **Parking:** Free.

Owned by Alan and Prue Jones, this attractive and tastefully decorated Victorian hotel on Plymouth Hoe (off Notte Street) offers a homelike atmosphere. Alan was in the merchant navy for 13 years and is a former chairman of the Personal Service Hotel Group and a director of the Marketing Bureau in Plymouth. With their experience, Alan and Prue are more than able to help and advise overseas visitors with limited time on where to go and what to see. Ground-floor rooms are available, and there is ample parking space on the premises.

INVICTA HOTEL, 11-12 Osborne Place, Lockyer St., The Hoe, Plymouth, Devon PL1 2PU. Tel. 0752/664997. Fax 0751/664994. 23 rms (20 with bath or shower). TV TEL **Bus:** No. 54.

$ Rates (including English breakfast): £26 ($48.10) single without bath, £38 ($70.30) single with bath; £38 ($70.30) double without bath, £50 ($92.50) double with bath. MC, V. **Parking:** Free.

This Victorian building stands at the entrance to Plymouth Hoe. Family operated, it is convenient not only to the heart of Plymouth but also to the ferries departing for Brittany on the French coast. The modernized hotel offers comfortably and pleasantly furnished bedrooms with hot and cold running water and beverage-making equipment. The Invicta also has a restaurant serving grills, for the most part.

OSMOND GUEST HOUSE, 42 Pier St., Plymouth, Devon PL1 3BT. Tel. 0752/229705. 6 rms (2 with bath). TV **Bus:** No. 54.

$ Rates (including English breakfast): £13 ($24.05) per person single or double without bath; £17 ($31.45) per person single or double with bath. No credit cards. **Parking:** Free.

Contained within a gray-fronted, three-story house originally built in 1898, this hotel is well known and popular. Inside, the original high plaster ceilings have been carefully preserved. Each room has tea- and coffee-making equipment. The owner, Mrs. Carol Richards, will agree to pick passengers up at the bus or train stations if they arrange it in advance.

ST. RITA HOTEL, 76-78 Alma Rd., Plymouth, Devon PL3 4HD. Tel. 0752/667024. 14 rms (one with bath). TV **Bus:** No. 14 or 76.

$ **Rates** (including English breakfast): £14.50–£16.50 ($26.85–$30.55) single without bath; £29 ($53.65) double without bath, £33 ($61.05) double with bath. No credit cards. **Parking:** Free.

 This is close to the Plymouth train station in a row of blue Victorian houses on the main bus route to the city center, which is approximately a mile away. Rooms are clean and comfortable with hot and cold running water and coffee-making equipment. The accommodations at the back are quieter. Evening meals are offered only from October to May. There is parking in the rear.

WILTUN, 39 Grand Parade, West Hoe, Plymouth, Devon PL1 3DQ. Tel. 0752/667072. 9 rms (none with bath). TV **Directions:** Follow signs to the Hoe, western end of city. **Bus:** No. 54.

$ **Rates** (including English breakfast): £17.50 ($32.40) single; £30–£35 ($55.50–$64.75) double. MC, V.

The Wiltun is set on Plymouth's historic foreshore overlooking Drake's Island and Plymouth Sound. This Victorian house has many modern facilities, but it retains several of the architectural features of the 1850s. Some rooms are suitable for families. There's a private lawn to relax on and watch the ships go by. The well-prepared evening meal goes for £8 ($14.80).

WHERE TO EAT

MEALS FOR LESS THAN £9.45 ($17.50)

THE GANGES, 146 Vauxhall St. Tel. 220907.
   Cuisine: INDIAN. **Reservations:** Not needed. **Bus:** No. 54.

$ **Prices:** Appetizers £2.50–£3.50 ($4.65–$6.45); main courses £4–£7.50 ($7.40–$13.90). MC, V.

   Open: Daily 5:30–11:45pm.

This Indian tandoori restaurant, provides a good change of pace from English cookery. Part of a chain that has other locations in the West Country, it is decorated with touches of the East. You can dine in air-conditioned, candlelit comfort, while enjoying an array of spicy dishes. One of the chef's specialties is a whole tandoori chicken superbly spiced and flavored. You can also order the usual array of curries and biryanis. Vegetarians will find sustenance here as well.

GREEN LANTERNS, 31 New St., the Barbican. Tel. 660852.
   Cuisine: ENGLISH. **Reservations:** Recommended for dinner. **Bus:** No. 54.

$ **Prices:** Appetizers £1.50–£3.40 ($2.80–$6.30); main courses £3.50–£7.50 ($6.45–$13.90). MC, V.

   Open: Lunch Mon–Sat 11:45am–2:15pm; dinner Mon–Sat 6:30–10:45pm.

A 16th-century eating house on a Tudor street, the Green Lanterns lies 200 yards from the Mayflower Steps. The lunch menu offers a selection of grills, chicken, and fish—all served with vegetables. The kitchen also features blackboard specials such as Lancashire hot pot. Some unusual dishes are on the dinner menu such as goose breasts in breadcrumbs, wild duck (teal), and venison in red wine. Chicken, beef, turkey, plaice, and mackerel are also available—all served with vegetables. Family owned, the Green Lanterns is run by Sally M. Russell and Kenneth Pappin, who are fully aware that voyaging strangers like the Elizabethan atmosphere, traditional English fare, and personal service. The restaurant is near the municipally owned Elizabethan House.

QUEEN ANNE EATING HOUSE, 2 White Lane, the Barbican. Tel. 262101.
   Cuisine: ENGLISH. **Reservations:** Not needed. **Bus:** No. 54.

$ **Prices:** Appetizers 80p–£2.40 ($1.50–$4.45), main dishes £5.25–£9.95 ($9.70–$18.40); cream teas £2 ($3.70); children's menus from £1.50 ($2.80). No credit cards.

   Open: Sun–Thurs 10:30am–9:30pm (till 5pm in midwinter), Fri–Sat year-round 10:30am–10:30pm.

Set next to the Barbican Craft Centre, this bow-fronted, white-painted establishment is a friendly and nautically inspired place where you can order everything from coffee and tea to full-blown meals. Food is plentiful and wholesome, and includes such English-inspired fare as roast beef and Yorkshire pudding, steak-and-kidney pie, roast fresh fish from the local markets, fish-and-chips, and other hot meals. Service is fast and polite, and the furniture is solid and oaken. If you're not looking for a full meal, try a Devonshire cream tea, which is served any time of the day, with homemade scones baked with half white and half whole-wheat flour.

THE SHIP, the Barbican. Tel. 667604.
   Cuisine: ENGLISH. **Reservations:** Recommended. **Bus:** No. 54.
$ **Prices:** Carvery £9.45 ($17.50) adults; children under 11 eat free. AE, DC, MC, V.
   Open: Lunch daily noon–2pm; dinner daily 6:30–10:30pm.

 This stone building faces the marina, and its tables are placed to offer a view over the harbor. You pass through a pub and take a flight of stairs one floor above street level, where a well-stocked salad bar and a carvery await you. The carvery presents at least three roast joints, and you're allowed to eat as much as you want; the first course is from a help-yourself buffet, and a chef carves your selection of meats for your second course. Desserts cost extra. This is one of the best food values in Plymouth.

---

8. CLOVELLY

240 miles W of London; 11 miles W of Bideford

GETTING THERE   By Train   From London's Paddington Station, trains depart for Exeter frequently. At Exeter, passengers transfer to a train headed for the end destination of Barnstable. Travel time from Exeter to Barnstable is 1¼ hours. From Barnstable, passengers transfer to Clovelly by bus.

By Bus   Hourly buses from Barnstable, maintained by either the Red Bus Company or the Filers Bus Company, require about 40 minutes to reach Bideford. At Bideford, connecting buses (with no more than a 10-minute wait between arrival and departure) continue on for the 30-minute drive to Clovelly. Two Land Rovers make continuous round-trips to the Red Lion Inn from the top of the hill, costing 40p (75¢) per person each way.

By Car   From London, head west along the M4 motorway, cutting south at the junction of the M5 motorway. At the junction near Bridgwater, continue west along A39 in the direction of Lynton. The A39 runs all the way to the signposted turnoff for Clovelly.

ESSENTIALS   The **area code** is 0237. Clovelly doesn't have a tourist office, but information about the area is available at the summer-only **Tourist Information Centre** at The Quay (tel. 02372/477676), in nearby Bideford.

This is the most charming of all Devon villages and is one of the main attractions of the West Country. Starting at a great height, the village cascades down the mountainside, with its narrow, cobblestone High that makes travel by car impossible—you park your car at the top and make the trip by foot, and supplies are carried down by donkeys. Every yard of the way provides views of tiny cottages, with their terraces of flowers lining the main street. The village fleet is sheltered at the stone quay at the bottom.
   Tips: To avoid the flock of tourists, stay out of Clovelly from around 11 in the morning until teatime. After tea, settle in your room and have dinner. The next morning after breakfast, walk around the village or go for a swim in the harbor, then visit the nearby villages during the middle of the day when the congestion sets in. Also,

to avoid the climb back up the slippery incline, go to the rear of the Red Lion inn and queue up for a Land Rover. In summer, the line is often long, but considering the alternative, it's worth the wait.

WHERE TO STAY

IN TOWN

RED LION, The Quay, Clovelly, near Bideford, Devon EX39 5TF. Tel. 0237/431237. 12 rms (all with bath). TV
$ Rates (including English breakfast): £30 ($55.50) single; £50 ($92.50) double. MC, V. **Parking:** Free.

At the bottom of the steep cobbled street, right on the stone seawall of the little harbor, the Red Lion may well occupy the jewel position of the village. Rising three stories with gables and a courtyard, it is actually an unspoiled country inn, where life centers around an antique pub and village inhabitants, including sea captains. Most bedrooms look directly onto the sea, and all contain hot and cold running water and adequate furnishings. Dinner is available in the seaview dining room for £8 ($14.80), with a choice of four main dishes, two of which are always fresh local fish, then a selection from the dessert trolley. The manager suggests that the Red Lion is not suitable for children under 7 years of age.

IN HIGHER CLOVELLY

Overflow lodgings in summer are available in the tiny hamlet of Higher Clovelly, which lies above the main village. Although Higher Clovelly has none of the charm of Clovelly, you don't have to face the problem of carting luggage down that steep cobblestone street.

THE FOUR POSTER, 5 Underdown, Clovelly, Bideford, Devon EX39 5TA. Tel. 0237/431748. 6 rms (none with bath).
$ Rates (including English breakfast): £11 ($20.35) per person. No credit cards. **Parking:** Free.

This is the most romantically named accommodation in the upper or lower villages. It's also one of the most reasonable in price, which includes a wake-up pot of tea and "crackers" (biscuits) served early in the morning. Mr. and Mrs. T. W. L. Clark are among the most accommodating hosts in Clovelly. Mr. Clark, a retired military man, is a fount of information on local, regional, and nationwide attractions. He also makes all his own wine, beer, and cider. The immaculately kept stone house adjacent to Clovelly main car park, was built originally for use of the Coast Guard. A four-course evening meal with wine is available for £11 ($20.35), if you order before 5pm.

9. LYNTON-LYNMOUTH

206 miles W of London; 59 miles N of Exeter

GETTING THERE   By Train   The resort is remote, and it's recommended that you rent a car. However, local daily trains from Exeter arrive at Barnstaple.

By Bus   From Barnstaple, bus service is provided to Lynton every 2 hours.

By Car   Take the M4 west from London to the junction of M5, then head south to junction of A39. Continue west on A39 to Lynton-Lynmouth.

ESSENTIALS   The **area code** for Lynton-Lynmouth is 0598. The **Tourist Information Centre** is at Lee Road (tel. 0598/52225).

The north coast of Devon is set off dramatically in Lynton, a village some 500 feet high, which is a good center for exploring the Doone Valley and that part of

Exmoor that overflows into the shire from neighboring Somerset. The Valley of Rocks, west of Lynton, offers the most spectacular scenery.

The town is joined by a cliff railway to Lynmouth, about 500 feet lower. The length of the track is 862 feet with a gradient of 1 inch which gives a vertical height of approximately 500 feet. The two passenger cars are linked together with two steel cables, and the operation of the lift is on the counterbalance system, which is simply explained as a pair of scales where one side, when weighted by water ballast, pulls the other up.

The East Lyn and West Lyn rivers meet in Lynmouth, a popular resort with the British. For a panoramic view of the rugged coastline, you can walk on a path halfway between the towns that runs along the cliff. From Lynton, or rather from Hollerday Hill, you can look out onto Lynmouth Bay, Countisbury Foreland, and Woody Bays in the west.

WHERE TO STAY

DOUBLES WITHOUT BATH FOR LESS THAN £37 [$68.45]

BONNICOTT HOTEL, 10 Watersmeet Rd., Lynmouth, Lynton, Devon EX35 6EP. Tel. 0598/53346. 9 rms (5 with bath). TV. **Bus** No. 310 from Barnstable.

$ Rates (including English breakfast): £18–£20 ($33.30–$37) per person without bath; £23.50 ($43.50) per person with bath. AE, MC, V. **Parking:** Free overnight, £1.50 ($2.80) during the day.

Built 170 years ago as a stone-sided, slate-roofed rectory, this is now owned and run by John and Brenda Farrow, who are most helpful. Bedrooms are attractively decorated, most with views over Lynmouth Bay or the Lyn Valley. On cooler days, a log fire burns in the lounge and bar. John and Brenda, who used to own a pub in London, offer good food, such as local fish and Scottish steak, served in the Bonnicott Grill; special diets and vegetarian meals can also be provided. A four-course set evening meal costs £10.50 ($19.45) per person. During sunny weather, guests congregate on the terraced patio, where miniature fish ponds and artificial waterfalls add a welcome diversion.

THE DENES GUEST HOUSE, Longmead, Lynton, Devon EX35 6DQ. Tel. 0598/53573. 7 rms (none with bath).

$ Rates (including English breakfast): £17 per person. No credit cards.

Ⓢ Built during the 1920s, in a style popularized by the Victorians, this slate-roofed gabled house sits at the end of a small terrace on a quiet residential street, nestled in a valley at the western edge of town. The tastefully decorated accommodations are maintained by Dennis and Jean Gay, who accept only nonsmokers. The clean bedrooms are spacious, and each contains hot and cold running water. For an additional £8 ($14.80), dinner is provided; the tasty and filling meals are served in cheerful dining room. The hotel sits at the edge of a local geological oddity known as the Valley of Rocks, whose striations give unusual insight into the glacial activities of the Ice Age.

GORDON HOUSE HOTEL, 31 Lee Rd., Lynton, Devon EX35 6BS. Tel. 0598/53203. 6 rms (all with bath and shower). TV

$ Rates (including English breakfast): £22–£27 ($40.70–$49.95) single; £34–£44 ($70.30) double. MC, V. **Parking:** Free. **Closed:** Dec–Feb.

An old hotel with much warmth and character, this has comfortably furnished and well-maintained bedrooms. The hotel was built in Victoria's day and has been rejuvenated in keeping with its antique charm. Since the small hotel is noted for its good, wholesome food, you may also request an evening meal, provided you don't mind dining by 7 or 7:30pm. An evening meal costs £8 ($14.80). It is located west of Church Hill.

HAZELDENE, 27 Lee Rd., Lynton, Devon EX35 6BP. Tel. 0598/52364. 9 rms (all with bath or shower). TV

$ Rates (including English breakfast): £20–£25 ($37–$46.25) single; £35–£38 ($64.75–$70.30) double. AE, MC, V. **Parking:** Free. **Closed:** Christmas holidays.

 Hazeldene is a Victorian home with a good deal of charm; many consider it among the best of the small B&Bs in the area. Bedrooms, which have beverage-making equipment, are kept sparkling clean and are a pleasure to return to after a day of walking along the coast. You can enjoy a drink in a cozy bar and later a meal in the candlelit dining room. It's located west of Church Hill.

SANDROCK, Longmead, Lynton, Devon EX35 6DH. Tel. 0598/53307. 9 rms (7 with bath). TV TEL

$ Rates (including English breakfast): £17.50 ($32.40) single without bath, £20 ($37) single with bath; £37 ($68.45) double without bath, £44 ($81.40) double with bath. AE, MC, V. **Parking:** Free.

 This substantial, three-story house on the road that leads from Lynton to Valley of the Rocks, is one of the best economy oases in North Devon. The house is on the lower part of a hill beside the road, with most of its bedrooms opening onto views of the beginning peaks of the Valley of Rocks. Fortunately, the hotel has many windows, and the rooms are sunny and bright. The bedrooms, generally quite large, are interestingly shaped and have water basins. The third floor has dormer windows, which make the rooms even cozier. Beds have innerspring mattresses, and there are adequate shared bathrooms. Owners Mr. and Mrs. Harrison take a personal interest in the welfare of their guests. Their baked goods are a delight, especially the deep-dish apple and rhubarb pies, which are tasty, tart, and sweet at the same time. In the Anglers' Bar, foreign visitors meet the Lynton locals after dinner, which costs from £10.50 ($19.45).

WHERE TO EAT

GREENHOUSE RESTAURANT, 6 Lee Rd., Lynton. Tel. 53358.
Cuisine: ENGLISH/INDIAN. **Reservations:** Not needed. **Bus:** No. 310 from Barnstable stops outside.

$ Prices: Appetizers £1.10–£2.85 ($2.05–$5.30), main dishes £4–£11.25 ($7.40–$20.80). MC, V.

Open: Daily 10:30am–10pm. Lunch daily noon–3pm; dinner daily 6–9pm.

Originally a conservatory built in 1890 for the oldest hotel in Lynton, this airy building (despite the replacement of many of its windows and skylights with solid walls and ceilings) still retains the look of a Victorian greenhouse. Homemade dishes include trout, duck, Cornish pasties, and roasts. These are supplemented on weekends with Indian food prepared by its Anglo-Indian owners. Know in advance that anything identified as "Madras" is extra-hot and spicy. Snacks are served outside lunch and dinner hours.

CORNWALL

The ancient duchy of Cornwall is the extreme southwestern part of England, often called "the toe." This peninsula is a virtual island—spiritually if not geographically. Encircled by coastline, it abounds with rugged cliffs, hidden bays, fishing villages, sandy beaches, and sheltered coves where smuggling was once rampant. Although many of the little seaports with hillside cottages resemble towns along the Mediterranean, Cornwall retains its own distinctive flavor. The ancient land had its own language up until about 250 years ago, and some of the old words ("pol" for pool, "tre" for house) still survive.

The Celtic-Iberian origin of the Cornish people is apparent in superstition, folklore, and fairy tales. King Arthur, of course, is the most vital legend of all. When Cornish people speak of King Arthur and his Knights of the Round Table, they're not just handing out a line to tourists. To them, Arthur and his knights really existed, roaming around Tintagel Castle, now in ruins—Norman ruins, that is—300 feet above the sea, 19 miles from Bude.

Berth at one of the smaller fishing villages, such as East and West Looe, Polperro, Mousehole, or Portloe—where you'll experience the true charm of the duchy. Many of the villages, such as St. Ives, are artists' colonies. Except for St. Ives and Port Isaac, some of the most interesting places lie on the southern coast, often called the Cornish Riviera. However, the north coast also has its own charm.

SEEING CORNWALL

GETTING THERE

If you're driving, the fastest way there is to take the M4 and M5 motorways. Eventually, the M5 will link up with the A30 which will take you all the way to Land's End at the tip of Cornwall. British Rail offers frequent service to the southwest from London's Paddington Station, arriving at Penzance and the end of the line in 5 hours. National Express buses also service the region from London's Victoria Coach Station, but it will take 8 hours to reach Penzance.

A SUGGESTED ITINERARY

Day 1: Explore both Looe and Polperro, overnighting in either resort.
Day 2: Head for Penzance along the southern coast, and visit St. Michael's Mount.

WHAT'S SPECIAL ABOUT CORNWALL

Beaches
- A majestic coastline—both north and south—studded with fishing villages and hidden coves for swimming.

Great Towns/Villages
- Penzance, granite-built resort and fishing port on Mount's Bay, with a Victorian promenade.
- St. Ives, old fishing port and artists' colony, with a good surfing beach.
- Mousehole, considered the most charming old fishing port in Cornwall, filled with twisting lanes and granite cottages.

Natural Spectacles
- The Isles of Scilly, 27 miles off the Cornish coast—with five islands inhabited out of 100.

- Land's End, where England comes to an end—lying 9 miles west of Penzance.

Castles
- Tintagel Castle, on a wild stretch of the Atlantic coast—legendary castle of King Arthur, Lancelot, and Merlin.
- St. Michael's Mount, off the coast of Penzance, rising 250 feet from the area—part medieval, part 17th century.

Gardens
- The Abbey Gardens of Tresco on the Isles of Scilly—735 acres with 5,000 species of plants from some 100 countries.

Day 3: After leaving Penzance, spend a leisurely day exploring little fishing villages and Land's End before journeying to St. Ives for the night.

Day 4: After a look at St. Ives in the morning, drive along the north Cornish coast to Port Isaac for lunch, overnighting in Tintagel after a visit to King Arthur's legendary castle.

1. LOOE

20 miles W of Plymouth; 264 miles SW of London

GETTING THERE   By Train   Daily trains run from Plymouth, and rail connections can also be made from Exeter (Devon) and Bristol (Avon).

By Bus   Local bus companies have various routings from Plymouth into Looe. Ask at the tourist office in Plymouth for a schedule (see Chapter 12).

By Car   From Plymouth, take the A38 west, then the B3253.

ESSENTIALS   The **area code** is 0503. The **Tourist Information Centre** (summer only) is at The Guildhall, Fore Street (tel. 0503/2072).

The ancient twin towns of East and West Looe are connected by a seven-arched stone bridge that spans the river. Houses on the hills are stacked one on top of the other in terrace fashion. In both fishing villages you can find good accommodations. Fishing and sailing are two of the major sports, and the sandy coves, as well as East Looe Beach, are spots for seabathing. Beyond the towns are cliff paths and downs worth a ramble. Looe is noted for its shark fishing, but you may prefer simply walking the narrow, crooked medieval streets of East Looe, with its old harbor and 17th-century guildhall.

WHERE TO STAY

Space and prices are at a premium in July and August. Some hotels are so heavily booked that they can demand Saturday-to-Saturday clients only.

DOUBLES WITHOUT BATH FOR LESS THAN £36 [$66.60]

In West Looe

JESMOND GUEST HOUSE, Hannafore Rd., Looe, Cornwall PL13 2DQ. Tel. 0503/4156. 6 rms (2 with shower). TV
$ **Rates** (including English breakfast): £18 ($33.30) single without bath; £36 ($66.60) double without bath, £44 ($81.40) double with bath. No credit cards. **Parking:** Free. **Closed:** Nov–Mar.

This is in one of the best locations in town, since it's only 3 minutes from the water and in the town center. Run by Carol and Christopher Webb, it provides good views and a homelike atmosphere in its comfortable bedrooms. Jesmond is licensed to serve drinks.

KANTARA GUEST HOUSE, 7 Trelawney Terrace, West Looe, Cornwall PL13 2AG. Tel. 0503/2093. 6 rms (none with bath).
$ **Rates** (including English breakfast): £10–£14 ($18.50–$25.90) single; £20–£28 ($37–$51.80) double. AE, MC, V. **Parking:** Free.

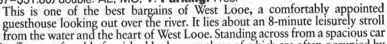

This is one of the best bargains of West Looe, a comfortably appointed guesthouse looking out over the river. It lies about an 8-minute leisurely stroll from the water and the heart of West Looe. Standing across from a spacious car park, it offers comfortably furnished bedrooms, three of which are often occupied by families. There's a color TV in the lounge. After crossing the bridge into Looe, Kantara is on the left-hand side up the hill.

PANORAMA HOTEL, Hannafore Rd., West Looe, Cornwall PL13 2DE. Tel. 0503/2123. 10 rms (all with bath). TV
$ **Rates** (including English breakfast): £20–£25 ($37–$46.25) single; £40–£51 ($74–$94.35) double. MC, V. **Parking:** Free.

From this immaculate hotel in the town center you can enjoy the scenic vistas of the surrounding area. You always get a polite welcome and personal service at this Cornish outpost, and bedrooms are comfortable.

In East Looe

OSBORNE HOUSE HOTEL AND RESTAURANT, Lower Chapel St., East Looe, Cornwall PL13 1AT. Tel. 0503/2970. 4 rms (all with bath). TV
$ **Rates** (including English breakfast): £22.50–£24.50 ($41.65–$45.35) single; £35–£39 ($64.75–$72.15) double. MC, V. **Parking:** Free.

This small Jacobean inn is on one of the tiny streets in the town center, about a minute's walk from the sea. All rooms have hot-beverage facilities. Even if you're not staying here, there is a cheerful bar patronized by locals, plus a dining room bright with gleaming brass. The owners, Wilma and Richard Hatcher, offer a varied salad lunch menu at £4.50 ($8.35) per head along with afternoon teas featuring home baking. A full à la carte evening menu averages £16 ($29.60), and the wide selection includes fresh fish and lobster, as well as a fine wine list.

PIXIES HOLT HOTEL, Shutta, East Looe, Cornwall PL13 1JD. Tel. 0503/262726. 7 rms (3 with bath). **Directions:** Turn into the road beside The Globe Public House and proceed straight ahead for 500 feet.
$ **Rates** (including English breakfast): £15 ($27.75) single without bath, £19 ($35.15) single with bath; £30 ($55.50) double without bath, £37.50 ($69.40) double with bath. AE, MC, V. **Parking:** Free. **Closed:** Late Oct–Mar.

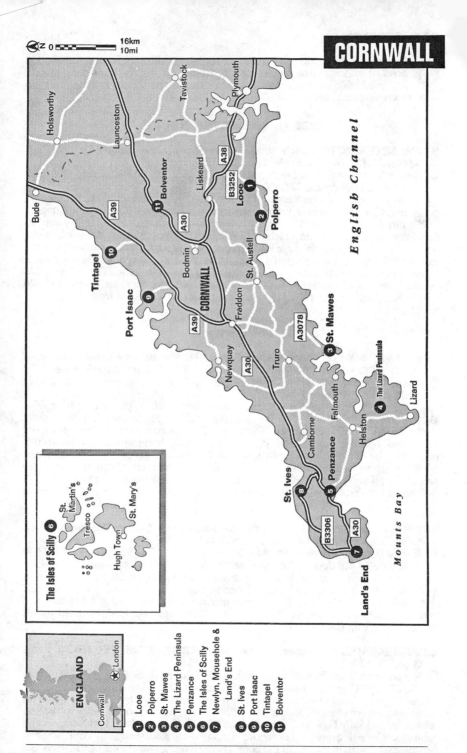

CORNWALL

16km
10mi

English Channel

Mounts Bay

Holsworthy
Launceston
Tavistock
Plymouth
Bolventor
Liskeard
Looe
Polperro
Bude
Tintagel
Bodmin
CORNWALL
St. Austell
Port Isaac
Fraddon
Newquay
Truro
St. Mawes
The Lizard Peninsula
Lizard
Falmouth
Helston
Camborne
Penzance
St. Ives
Land's End

A38
B3252
A39
A30
A39
A3078
A30
B3306
A30

The Isles of Scilly 6
St. Martin's
Tresco
St. Mary's
Hugh Town

ENGLAND
London
Cornwall

1 Looe
2 Polperro
3 St. Mawes
4 The Lizard Peninsula
5 Penzance
6 The Isles of Scilly
7 Newlyn, Mousehole &
   Land's End
8 St. Ives
9 Port Isaac
10 Tintagel
11 Bolventor

One of the most acclaimed little guesthouses in the area is set on about 1½ acres of land with panoramic views. Bedrooms are well kept and comfortable, and the breakfast is substantial. The cooking is reliable, so you may want to have an evening meal here.

WORTH THE EXTRA BUCKS

KLYMIARVEN HOTEL, Barbican Hill, East Looe, Cornwall PL13 1BH. Tel. 0503/2333. 14 rms (all with bath). TV TEL
$ **Rates** (including English breakfast): £30–£34 ($55.50–$62.90) single, £60–£68 ($111–$125.80) double. MC, V.

Set on 2 acres of woodland and terraced gardens with views of the harbor, this hotel is one of the best accommodations in the area. It has an elegant lounge, a sun lounge bar, and a terrace overlooking a heated swimming pool. Its tastefully furnished bedrooms include beverage-making equipment. It is run by Greg and Rosemary Symons, who have built a reputation for a relaxed atmosphere, and the excellent British cuisine prepared with fresh produce served in their candlelit restaurant, which offers both a fixed-price and an à la carte menu. The 400-year-old cellars have lots of character, with a smugglers' passage, flagstone floors, and old timber beams. Klymiarven is best approached from Barbican Road from the village of St. Martin.

Nearby

THE SLATE HOUSE, Bucklawren Farm, St. Martins-by-Looe, Cornwall PL13 1NZ. Tel. 05043/481. Fax (same as phone). 3 rms (none with bath). TV
$ **Rates** (including English breakfast): £13.50 ($25) per person, single or double. No credit cards. **Parking:** Free.

Rambling, country-elegant, and surrounded with a pleasant garden, this converted farmhouse is the largest and probably the oldest building of a hamlet originally mentioned in *The Domesday Book.* Constructed of honey-colored stone and outfitted with floral chintzes and antique furniture, it's beautifully maintained by John and Bettyanne Baynes-Reid. If you arrive on a cool day, you'll find a log fire burning in the oversized inglenook fireplace. Four-course evening meals are prepared and served in the dining room, at a per-person cost of £8.50 ($15.75). Bedrooms are comfortable and charming. It's located 4 miles east of Looe beside A387.

TREGOAD FARM HOTEL, St. Martins-by-Looe, Looe, Cornwall PL13 1PB. Tel. 0503/2718. 6 rms (none with bath). TV
$ **Rates** (including English breakfast): £15–£20 ($27.75–$37) single; £26–£36 ($48.10–$66.60) double. No credit cards. **Parking:** Free. **Closed:** Nov–Mar.

Just 1½ miles east of Looe is this lovely old Georgian farmhouse. Set on a hilltop, the house overlooks the sea; you can sit in bed and watch the Looe fisherman in the bay. The owners produce large, nourishing breakfasts and lunches, as well as five-course dinners. There are hot-beverage facilities in the rooms and a color TV in the residents' lounge.

COOMBE FARM, Widegates, Cornwall PL13 1QN. Tel. 0503/233. 8 rms (1 with bath).
$ **Rates** (including English breakfast): £16.65–£18.50 ($30.80–$34.25) single; £30.30–£37 ($56.05–$68.45) double. No credit cards. **Parking:** Free.

About 3½ miles from Looe is this country house, surrounded by 10½ acres of lawns, meadows, woods, streams, and ponds, with views down a wooded valley to the sea. Alexander and Sally Low have furnished the centrally heated house with antiques and paintings. Open log fires blaze in the dining room and lounge in cool weather. Bedrooms, all with fine views of the countryside, have hot- and cold-water basins. Six contain TV. Dinner, served in the candlelit dining room with views of the sea, include traditional English and Cornish dishes. Guests may use the heated outdoor swimming pool in the summer. Coombe Farm lies on the B3253 road just south of Widegates Village between Hessenford (1 mile) and Looe (3½ miles).

WHERE TO EAT

Looe's culinary selection is not great but there are a few exceptions.

MEALS FOR LESS THAN £16 [$29.60]

THE TALLAND BAY HOTEL, Talland Bay, Talland-by-Looe. Tel. 72667.
  Cuisine: ENGLISH/CONTINENTAL. **Reservations:** Required.
$ **Prices:** Fixed-price meals £16 ($29.60). AE, DC, MC, V.
  Open: Lunch daily 12:30–2pm; dinner daily 7:30–9pm.

This old country house set on 2½ acres of land serves the best food in the area. Lunch is a cold but enticing buffet, and the traditional Sunday roast beef lunch also proved delicious. Cornish seafood is the most desirable bill of fare, especially the locally caught crab and scallops. A cold buffet is served at lunch, a set dinner in the evening. Lobster from the tank carries a supplement. The restaurant is 3 miles southwest of Looe by A387.

THE WATER RAIL, Lower Market St., East Looe. Tel. 2314.
  Cuisine: SEAFOOD. **Reservations:** Required in summer only.
$ **Prices:** Appetizers £1.40–£4.25 ($2.60–$7.85); main courses £5.25–£12.50 ($9.70–$23.15). AE, DC, MC, V.
  Open: Dinner daily 6:30–10pm. **Closed:** Last 3 weeks in Jan.

This restaurant, housed in a 14th-century structure near the quay, has won the praise of many a diner. It lies a 2-minute walk from the river and the beach. The kitchen specializes in the fresh fish from the area, including, on occasion, sardines. Daily offerings are based on seasonal availability of produce, and the menu is an interesting mix of dishes. Wine is available by the glass.

2. POLPERRO

271 miles SW of London; 6 miles SW of Looe; 26 miles W of Plymouth

GETTING THERE By Train The nearest main line station is at Liskeard, less than 4 hours from London's Paddington Station, with a branch line to Looe (see above). Taxis meet incoming trains to take visitors to the various little villages in the area.

By Bus Local bus services are possible from Liskeard or Looe.

By Car Take the A387 southwest from Looe.

ESSENTIALS The **area code** is 0503. There is no local information office. Ask at Looe (see above) but in summer only.

This ancient fishing village is reached by a steep descent from the top of a hill from the main road leading to Polperro. You can take the 4½-mile cliff walk from Looe to Polperro, but the less adventurous will want to drive. Motorists in July and August are forbidden to take cars into town unless they are booked in a hotel, in order to avoid traffic bottlenecks. There's a large car park, which charges according to the length of your stay. For those unable to walk, a horse-drawn bus carries visitors to the town center.

Polperro is one of the handsomest villages in Cornwall, and it looks in parts as if it were still in the 17th century. The village is surrounded by cliffs, and a stream called the Pol, runs through it. The heart of the village is its much photographed, much painted fishing harbor, where the pilchard boats, loaded to the gunwales, used to dock. At one time it was estimated that nearly every man, woman, and child in the village spent time salting down pilchards for the winter or smuggling. Today, tourist trade has replaced contraband.

WHERE TO STAY

In and around Polperro, you'll find a number of colorful cottages and houses that receive paying guests.

DOUBLES WITHOUT BATH FOR LESS THAN £35 ($64.75)

LANDAVIDDY MANOR, Landaviddy Lane, Polperro, Cornwall PL13 2RT. Tel. 0503/72210. 9 rms (5 with shower). TV **Directions:** Turn right at the main village car park (by the Crumplehorn Inn) and follow the lane until you reach a T-junction. Landaviddy Manor is then signposted to the left.
$ **Rates** (including English breakfast): £25 ($46.25) single without bath; £35 ($64.75) double without bath, £56 ($103.60) double with bath. DC, MC, V. **Parking:** Free.

This 200-year-old manor house built of gray Cornish stone sits on a secluded hill above the village on the west side of Polperro, and has a view of Polperro Bay. It adjoins National Trust land and is near the cliff paths and coves along the coast; the Cornish moors and Dartmoor are also easily accessible, as are numerous beaches nearby. Landaviddy, which is run by Sylvia and Derek Richards, may have a period feel to it, but all its bedrooms have hot and cold running water and innerspring mattresses. The more expensive rooms have four-poster beds, and sea and country views. There is central heating as well, plus a comfortable lounge with TV, a cozy bar, and a licensed dining room, where dinner of three courses and coffee is £13.50 ($25) per person. Reservations are required for dinner.

NEW HOUSE, Talland Hill, Polperro, Cornwall PL13 2RX. Tel. 0503/72206. 4 rms (1 with bath). **Directions:** From A38 take the first turn to Looe, then turn right over the bridge onto Polperro Rd. and continue for 4 miles. On the left at a telephone kiosk and bus shelter, fork left and continue 200 yards and turn right, going down a steep hill. New House is on the left.
$ **Rates** (including English breakfast): £26 ($48.10) double without bath; £32 ($59.20) double with bath. No credit cards. **Parking:** Free.

This guesthouse is in a dramatic location, overlooking the harbor and out toward the Eddystone light. Ken and Polly Perkins welcome guests warmly to their immaculate house. Rooms—all doubles—are comfortable and well maintained. Among the attractions are a garden and a lounge with color TV. Reservations are required.

WORTH THE EXTRA BUCKS

ALLHAYS COUNTRY HOUSE HOTEL, Talland Bay, Looe, Cornwall PL13 2JB. Tel. 0503/72434. 8 rms (7 with bath or shower). TV TEL **Directions:** Follow A387 from Looe to Polperro.
$ **Rates** (including English breakfast): £24–£33 ($44.40–$61.05) per person. MC, V. **Parking:** Free.
At the edge of a narrow lane on the outskirts of Polperro, this hotel is surrounded by nearly 2 acres of gardens and grounds, and has a greenhouse with flowers and grapes. The large country house has a lot of character, with its white stucco walls, cozy nooks, comfortable furniture, and imposing stone fireplaces. Lynda and Brian Spring, urban refugees from London, purchased the place in 1985 and have upgraded the 1930s house considerably. The rooms, many of which have views of the channel, include the master bedroom with a brass four-poster bed, and the carriage house,

recently converted to a luxury bedroom with a Victorian-style bath. Good English food is served in an Edwardian conservatory. Dishes are likely to include duck with orange and lemon sauce or chicken in cider and honey. The hotel lies 2½ miles east of Looe, 2½ miles west of Polperro.

WHERE TO EAT

MEALS FOR LESS THAN £10.95 [$20.25]

THE CAPTAIN'S CABIN, Lansallos St. Tel. 72292.

Cuisine: SEAFOOD. **Reservations:** Recommended.
$ **Prices:** Appetizers £1.20–£8.90 ($2.20–$16.45); main courses £3.95–£12 ($7.30–$22.20); three-course dinner £10.95 ($20.25); four-course dinner £14.50 ($26.85). AE, DC, MC, V.
Open: Lunch Sun–Fri 11am–4pm; dinner daily 7–10:30pm.

You can dine among antiques and brass in the low-ceilinged dining room of this 16th-century fisherman's cottage in the town center. The owner, Lesley Jacobs, and her staff offer a diverse cuisine. The wide variety of fresh local fish is brought in daily by the fishers of Polperro. The chef has a fine reputation for his seafood dishes, such as crab mornay, lobster thermidor, or grilled lemon sole. You can also get special snacks and sandwiches, such as fresh crab and salad, and there's a chef's special daily.

CRUMP'S BISTRO, Crumplehorn. Tel. 72312.

Cuisine: ENGLISH. **Reservations:** Recommended for dinner; not needed at lunchtime.
$ **Prices:** Lunch main courses £2.20–£4.25 ($4.05–$7.85); dinner appetizers 60p–£2.85 ($1.10–$5.30), dinner main courses £3.75–£9.25 ($6.95–$17.10). MC, V.
Open: Lunch daily 11am–5pm; dinner daily 7–9:30pm.

Considered inexpensive, this unpretentious bistro is contained within a pair of stone and slate farmer's cottages (originally built around 1620) which were architecturally united long ago. Operated by the mother-daughter team of Hilda (hostess) and Susan (the chef) Brown, it serves lunchtime sandwiches, portions of chili or chicken curry, and ploughman's lunches, and more formal evening fare which might include pepper steak or roasted ham with pineapple. The restaurant is a 10-minute walk north of the town's harbor, beside the road to Looe.

NELSONS RESTAURANT, Saxon Bridge. Tel. 72366.

Cuisine: ENGLISH/FRENCH. **Reservations:** Recommended.
$ **Prices:** Appetizers £1.75–£8 ($3.25–$14.80); main courses £9.50–£17.50 ($17.60–$32.40); three-course dinner £10.95–£18.50 ($20.25–$34.25) DC, MV, V.
Open: Lunch Sun and Tues–Fri noon–2pm; dinner Tues–Sat 7–10pm. **Closed:** Mid-Jan to mid-Feb.

This restaurant is owned and run by Peter, Betty, and their son Tony Nelson—Peter and Tony do the cooking, and Betty takes care of everything up front. They always have at least three homemade soups, which may include fish, crab, lobster, meat, or vegetables. You can also order ham or beef, served with a vegetable and salad. For dessert, try one of their homemade ice creams using fresh fruit. They also offer many classic flans and pies. The place is richly decorated in reds with nautical trappings. It's located in the town center.

THE THREE PILCHARDS, The Quay. Tel. 72233.

Cuisine: ENGLISH. **Reservations:** Not needed.
$ **Prices:** Pub snacks £1–£4 ($1.85–$7.40). No credit cards.
Open: Mon–Sat 11am–11pm, Sun noon–3pm and 7–10:30pm.

Locals and sophisticates alike come to this pub near the harbor. It's a large L-shaped room with a black oak interior and a fireplace that burns brightly at night. You can sit in the windowseat and listen to the talk of the villagers, although you may not be able to understand a word of their Cornish dialect. Food items include everything from

Polperro Farmhouse casserole to fishermen's pie. Bar snacks and plates of food are served during regular hours. From the main car park, it's a 10-minute walk.

WORTH THE EXTRA BUCKS

THE KITCHEN, Fish na Bridge. Tel. 72780.
    Cuisine: ENGLISH. **Reservations:** Required.
$ **Prices:** Set dinners £16–£24 ($29.60–$44.40). MC, V.
    Open: Summer dinner daily 7–9:30pm; winter dinner Fri–Sat 7–9:30pm.
    Closed: Jan.

⭐ Good English cookery is available at this pink cottage about halfway down to the harbor from the car park. Housed in what was once a wagon builder's shop, the restaurant is run by Vanessa and Ian Bateson—Ian is the chef, and Vanessa makes all the homemade desserts and breads. The menu changes seasonally and is based mainly on local fresh fish. Typical dishes include crab in phyllo pastry and seafood Provençal, and there are separate menus for vegetarian and lobster dinners.

---

3. ST. MAWES

300 miles SW of London; 2 miles E of Falmouth; 18 miles S of Truro

GETTING THERE   **By Train**   Trains leave from London's Paddington Station for Truro several times a day, taking 4½ hours. Passengers interested in taking the train descend at Truro to catch one of two buses which make the 45-minute bus trip from Truro to St. Mawes. Much easier and better is to hire a taxi from either Truro or, even better, from the village of St. Austell, which is the train stop *before* Truro.

By Ferryboat   There is a ferryboat traveling to St. Mawes from both Falmouth and Truro, but schedules are erratic, and vary with the tides and the weather conditions.

By Bus   Buses depart from London's Victoria Coach Station several times a day for Truro, requiring 6 hours for the transit. Most prefer the train.

By Car   To reach St. Mawes, fork left off the A390, the main road along the southern coast of Cornwall, at a junction 4 miles past St. Austell on to the Tregony road which will take you into St. Mawes.

ESSENTIALS   The **area code** is 0326.

Overlooking the mouth of the Fal River, St. Mawes is often compared to a port on the French Riviera—it's sheltered from northern winds, so subtropical plants can grow here. From the town quay, you can take a boat to Frenchman's Creek, Helford River, as well as other places. St. Mawes is noted for its sailing, boating, fishing, and yachting, and half a dozen sandy coves lie within 15 minutes by car from the port. The town, built on the Roseland Peninsula, makes for interesting walks, with its colorful cottages and sheltered harbor. On Castle Point, Henry VIII ordered the construction of St. Mawes Castle.

WHERE TO STAY & EAT

DOUBLES WITHOUT BATH FOR LESS THAN £38 [$70.30]

BRAGANZA, 4 Grove Hill, St. Mawes, Cornwall TR2 5BJ. Tel. 0326/ 270281. 6 rms (4 with bath or shower).
$ **Rates** (including English breakfast): £19 ($35.15) single without bath, £25 ($46.25) single with bath; £38 ($70.30) double without bath, £40 ($74) double with bath. No credit cards. **Parking:** Free.

Opposite the Catholic Church is a Regency house with a beautiful staircase, furnished with antiques and furniture of the period. The house has a lounge with TV, and bedrooms have hot-beverage facilities and are centrally heated. The house, operated by the owner, Mrs. Zofia Moseley, has an extensive garden overlooking the harbor of St. Mawes, where yacht racing takes place twice a week in the summer. Lord Byron, who stayed in Falmouth in 1809, is believed to have visited this house, for he mentions its name in one of his poems. It's said that his limping step can be heard at the Braganza on windy nights.

GREEN LANTERNS, Marine Parade, St. Mawes, Cornwall TR2 5DW. Tel. 0326/270502. 10 rms (all with bath or shower). TV
$ Rates (including English breakfast): £21–£25 ($38.85–$46.25) single; £33–£42 ($61.05–$77.70) double. AE, DC, MC, V.
Originally built in 1900, the stone exterior is now painted white. The hotel is one of the better guesthouses in the area, and each accommodation has beverage-making equipment. Dinner is offered to both residents and nonresidents daily from 7 to 9:30pm, costing from £13.50 to £15 ($25 to $27.75). It's located in the town center on the water.

ST. MAWES HOTEL, The Seafront, St. Mawes, Cornwall TR2 5DW. Tel. 0326/270266. 7 rms (all with bath). TV
$ Rates (including half board): £33–£40 ($61.05–$74) per person. MC, V.
Parking: £1.20 ($2.20). **Closed:** Dec–Jan.
This little gem along the waterfront was built as a hotel in the 17th century in an architectural style known as William and Mary; several historians have mentioned the hotel in accounts of long ago. Clifford and Juliet Burrows run the kind of place that people in the cold north dream of for their holiday on the Cornish Riviera. In spite of the antiquity of the place, everything is kept up-to-date. Reservations are essential, especially during July and August. Even if you don't stay here, you can visit their restaurant for British and continental dishes, with dinners costing £17.50 ($32.40). The kitchen specializes in fresh fish, including lobster and crab.

---

4. THE LIZARD PENINSULA

323 miles SW of London; 21 miles S of Falmouth

GETTING THERE By Train The nearest railway station is 23 miles from Lizard peninsula in the town of Redruth, which is on the direct London to Penzance line. Trains leave London for Paddington Station.

By Bus No bus service is available.

By Car From Falmouth, take the A394 west to the junction with A3083, which you can take south to Lizard Point.

ESSENTIALS The **area code** is 0326.

The most southerly point of England is Lizard, a remarkable spot with jagged rocks reaching out into the sea where cormorants and gulls fish. Lizard is the lesser known of Cornwall's two peninsulas, most are more familiar with Lands End. The Lizard is characterized by its beaches, small villages, coastal walks, and craft studios. Some of the best beaches are at the coves, Poldhu and Kynance. The seagoing people of Lizard have long known of the often furious nature of the coastline, and have given certain places epithets like "the Devil's Frying Pan." Rare flora and fauna can be found at Goonhilly Downs. Many shipwreck victims were buried in the cemetery at the Church of St. Keverne in the village of the same name, and British TeleCom's

Goonhilly Satellite Earth Station can be seen from most parts of the peninsula—it beams TV pictures across the Atlantic, and is the country's largest radio-receiving and space-tracking station.

There are those who claim that Lizard is "the most Cornish place" in Cornwall, and it was the last place where the Cornish language was spoken before the language underwent a modernization.

There are no big resorts here, just scattered small hotels and B&B houses (some of which close in the winter, as this is essentially a summer place). Most of the accommodations and places to eat are at the village of Mullion.

WHAT TO SEE & DO

Right on the point, beneath the lighthouse, is the workshop of a man who must surely have the most perfect one-man cottage industry in the country. Mr. Casley runs **Lizard Point Serpentine Works** (tel. 0326/290706) in one of the small shacks by the car park. He turns and polishes the serpentine stone found only in this part of the country, fashioning it into pots, vases, ashtrays, and dishes as well as costly ornamental barometers and clocks. The veins in the stone can be green, gray, or sometimes red. His two sons assist with the quarrying of the stone, which comes from under Goonhilly Downs close by.

WHERE TO STAY & EAT

DOUBLES WITH BATH FOR LESS THAN £40 [$74]

HOUSEL BAY HOTEL, Housel Cove, Lizard, Cornwall TR12 7PG. Tel. 0326/290417. 23 rms (all with bath or shower). TV TEL **Directions:** Take the A30 to Redruth, then follow signs to Helston and the Lizard.

$ **Rates** (including English breakfast): £20–£26 ($37–$48.10) single; £40–£84 ($74–$155.40) double. AE, MC, V. **Parking:** Free. **Closed:** Jan.

This is considered Britain's most southerly hotel, and owners Derek and Freda Oswald are proud of their old-fashioned, Cornish hospitality. The Victorian building offers multifaceted views of the surrounding area. Housel Bay is one of the best places in the area for food, and offers British and international dishes, with lunches going for £7.50 ($13.90) and dinner for £19 ($35.15) and up. Dinner is served until 9pm.

MOUNT'S BAY HOUSE HOTEL, Penmenner Rd., Lizard, Cornwall, TR12 7NP. Tel. 0326/290305. 7 rms (all with bath or shower). **Directions:** From the market town of Helston, take B3083 to Lizard Village. Penmenner Road is the first right after the village green.

$ **Rates** (including English breakfast): £16–£20.25 ($29.60–$37.45) single; £32–£40.50 ($59.20–$74.95) double. MC, V. **Parking:** Free. **Closed:** Nov.

This informal place, operated by Sam and Grace Crossley, is in a cul-de-sac at the termination of the point, overlooking Kynance Cove. It is definitely for tranquility-seekers. Although the Victorian structure has been renovated several times, many of the original architectural elements are still intact. An evening meal can be arranged at 7:30pm.

MRS. INGRID SOWDEN'S HOUSE, Villa Clare, Lizard Point near Helston, Cornwall TR12 7NU. Tel. 0326/290300. 3 rms (none with bath). TV **Directions:** From Lizard, follow road signs to "the most southerly point."

$ **Rates** (including English breakfast): £12–£15 ($22.20–$27.75) single; £22–£24 ($40.70–$44.40) double. No credit cards. **Parking:** Free. **Closed:** Dec 24–Jan 2.

 This home is definitely the most southerly house in the country, built on solid granite with a terraced garden. It provides fantastic views over the sea and the cliff edge from the garden fence some 170 feet above sea level. Despite the height, the house is frequently showered by spray from the breakers below during storms. Mrs. Sowden will recommend one of her friends in the village if she can't take you in. If given advance notice, she will also prepare a four-course evening meal for £7 ($12.95).

PENMENNER HOUSE HOTEL, Penmenner Rd., Lizard, Cornwall TR12 7NR. Tel. 0326/290370. 8 rms (5 with bath). TV **Directions:** Take the A30 to Redruth, then follow signs to Helston and Lizard.

$ **Rates** (including English breakfast): £21 ($38.85) single without bath, £23 ($42.55) single with bath; £38 ($70.30) double without bath, £42 ($77.70) double with bath. MC, V. **Parking:** Free.

Behind a simple facade is one of the most appealing guesthouses in the area. Guests receive Cornish hospitality and cozy, comfortable accommodations. It is strongly recommended that you reserve your room here. Dinner here starts at £11.50 ($21.25).

5. PENZANCE

280 miles SW of London; 77 miles SW of Plymouth

GETTING THERE **By Train** British Rail runs 10 daily express trains from Paddington Station in London to Penzance taking 5 hours and costing £40 ($74) one-way.

By Bus The Rapide, run by National Express from Victoria Coach Station, 172 Buckingham Palace Road, London, S.W.1. (tel. 071/730-0202), costs £26 ($48.10) for the one-way trip from London, about 8 hours. The buses have toilets and reclining seats and a hostess dispenses coffee, tea, and sandwiches.

By Car Continue southwest across Cornwall on the A30 all the way to Penzance.

ESSENTIALS The **area code** is 0736. The **Tourist Information Centre** is on Station Road (tel. 0736/62207).

This little harbor town, which Gilbert and Sullivan made famous, is at the end of the Cornish Riviera. It is noted for its equable climate (it's one of the first towns in England to blossom with spring flowers), and summer throngs descend for fishing, sailing, and swimming. Overlooking Mount's Bay, Penzance is graced in places with subtropical plants, as well as palm trees.

Those pirates in *The Pirates of Penzance* were not entirely fictional. The town was raided by Barbary pirates, destroyed in part by Cromwell's troops, sacked and burnt by the Spaniards, and bombed by the Germans. In spite of its turbulent past, it offers tranquil resort living today.

The most westerly town in England, Penzance makes a good base for exploring Land's End, the Lizard peninsula, St. Michael's Mount, the old fishing ports and artists' colonies of St. Ives, Newlyn, and Mousehole—even the Isles of Scilly.

WHAT TO SEE & DO

CASTLE, on St. Michael's Mount, Mount's Bay. Tel. 0736/710507.

Rising about 250 feet from the sea, St. Michael's Mount is topped by a partially medieval, partially 17th-century castle; it's 3 miles east of Penzance, and is reached at low tide by a causeway. At high tide the mount becomes an island, reached only by motor launch from Marazion. A Benedictine monastery, the gift of Edward the Confessor, stood on this spot in the 11th century. The castle, with its collections of armor and antique furniture, is open, weather and tide permitting, from 10:30am to 4:45pm Monday to Friday from the end of March to the end of October. In winter, you can only go over when the causeway is dry. There is a tea garden on the island, as well as a National Trust restaurant, both of which are open in summer. The steps up to the castle are steep and rough, so wear sturdy shoes. To avoid disappointment, it is a good idea to call first to learn the state of the tides, especially during the cooler months.

Admission: £2.80 ($5.20) adults, £1.40 ($2.60) children.

Open: Apr–Oct Mon–Fri 10:30am–4:45pm; Nov–Mar Mon, Wed, and Fri by conducted tour only leaving at 11am, noon, 2pm, and 3pm. **Bus:** Penzance, take bus no. 20, 21, or 22, and get off at Marazion, the town opposite St. Michael's Mount.

THE MINACK THEATRE, Porthcurno. Tel. 0736/810694.

Located 9 miles from Penzance, this unique theater can hold 750 people in the amphitheater, from which the rocky coast can be seen beyond the stage. There's also an exhibition hall that houses a permanent record of the life and work of Rowena Cade, creator of the theater, and gives you the opportunity to visit the theater outside of performance times.

Tour: £1.30 ($2.40) daily 10am–5:30pm. **Prices:** Seats: £4 ($7.40).

Open: Exhibition hall Easter–Oct; performance season end of May to mid-Sept. Matinees at 12:45pm, evening shows 6:45pm. **Directions:** Leave Penzance on the A30 heading toward Land's End. After 3 miles, bear left onto the B3283 and follow signposts to Porthcurno.

WHERE TO STAY

DOUBLES WITHOUT BATH FOR LESS THAN £32 [$59.20]

In Penzance

CARNSON HOUSE HOTEL, East Terrace, Penzance, Cornwall TR18 2TD. Tel. 0736/65589. 8 rms (2 with bath or shower). TV

$ Rates (including English breakfast): £15–£16 ($27.75–$29.60) single without bath; £30 ($55.50) double without bath, £32.50 ($60.15) double with bath. AE, DC, MC, V. **Parking:** 60p ($1.10).

 Carnson House is personally run by the two helpful owners, Trisha and Richard Hilder. Close to the harbor, town center, train station, and beach, their 250-year-old house is a convenient location for most. All bedrooms have automatic hot-beverage facilities. There is a comfortable lounge with TV. The Hilders also provide a tourist information service on local things to do and will help to arrange for car rentals, local bus and coach tours, as well as for the steamer service to the Isles of Scilly. The house is licensed to serve alcoholic beverages. An excellent three-course dinner is served for £7.50 ($13.90).

KIMBERLEY HOUSE, 10 Morrab Rd., Penzance, Cornwall TR18 4EZ. Tel. 0736/62727. 9 rms (none with bath). TV

$ Rates (including English breakfast): £14 ($25.90) single; £26–£28 ($48.10–$51.80) double. MC, V. **Parking:** Free.

This B&B lies in a Victorian house of character between the Promenade and the town center, opposite Penlee Park and near the Morrab Gardens. Avril and Rex Mudway have run this house since his retirement after a long seagoing career. They are gracious to their guests, providing good food and accommodations and also offering tips about what to see in the area. A rather large dinner of home-cooked English food here goes for £8 ($12.95).

MINCARLO, 45 Chapel St., Penzance, Cornwall TR18 4AE. Tel. 0736/62848. 3 rms (none with bath).

$ Rates (including English breakfast): £11.50 ($21.35) per person double. No credit cards.

The owner, Mrs. Welsh, tends to this large house herself, and serves hearty breakfasts in her dining room, which is filled with antiques. One guest room includes a four-poster bed. Mincarlo is near the Admiral Benbow restaurant in the town center connecting with Western Promenade.

RICHMOND LODGE, 61 Morrab Rd., Penzance, Cornwall TR18 4EP. Tel. 0736/65560. 7 rms (3 with bath). TV

$ Rates (including English breakfast): £13 ($24.05) single without bath; £25 ($46.25) double without bath, £29 ($53.65) double with bath. No credit cards. **Parking:** 50p (95¢).

This comfortable early Victorian house with a nautical flavor is a few steps from Market Jew Street (the main street) and within an easy walk of the promenade along the sea wall; the Morrab Gardens are across the street. The owner, Mrs. Jean Eady, is courteous and down-to-earth. Mrs. Eady provides faultless service in this homelike place, with full central heating and a fully licensed bar. The slightly higher rates will get you rooms with four-poster beds. Dinner can be ordered daily at £7 ($12.95).

SEA & HORSES HOTEL, Alexandra Terrace, Penzance, Cornwall TR18 4NX. Tel. 0736/61961. 11 rms (all with bath or shower). TV TEL
$ Rates (including English breakfast): £16–£18 ($29.60–$33.30) single; £32–£38 ($59.20–$70.30) double. MC, V. **Parking:** Free. **Closed:** Mid-Nov to mid-Feb.

Originally built in 1830 as a "gentleman's private house," this structure with a solid granite exterior is only 150 yards from the sea. You'll find it on the western outskirts of town, within easy walking distance of the town center and overlooking Bolitho Gardens. Alec Mansfield, the owner, rents comfortable bedrooms with beverage-making equipment. Four-course, fixed-price dinners can also be ordered here for £9.50 ($17.60).

TREMONT HOTEL, Alexandra Rd., Penzance, Cornwall TR18 4LZ. Tel. 0736/62614. 9 rms (6 with showers). TV
$ Rates (including English breakfast): £12 ($22.20) single without bath; £24 ($44.40) double without bath, £28 ($51.80) double with bath. No credit cards. **Parking:** Free on street.

This stone house is on a tree-lined street just up from Mount's Bay off The Promenade and the seafront. Mrs. Maureen Pengelly runs this guesthouse with its scrupulously clean, centrally heated bedrooms and comfortable furnishings. Some rooms are suitable for families. Single rooms have no private baths. A well-prepared dinner will run about £7 ($12.95), and you should arrange for it in advance.

WORTH THE EXTRA BUCKS

ALEXANDRA HOTEL, Alexandra Terrace, Seafront, Penzance, Cornwall TR18 4NX. Tel. 0736/62644. 32 rms (30 with bath or shower). TV
$ Rates (including English breakfast): £23 ($42.55) per person without bath; £25 ($46.25) per person with bath. AE, MC, V. **Parking:** Free.

Situated on a private terrace overlooking the seafront and Bolitho Gardens, the Alexandra is one of the best bets for accommodations. All rooms have radios and beverage-making equipment, and 20 have phones as well. Originally built in 1850 for retired sea captains, the hotel is only a 10-minute walk from the town center. The lounge and bar have views of the sea, as do some of the bedrooms. A four-course dinner is £9 ($16.65) per person, and the hotel is licensed to serve drinks at the bar.

Nearby

ENNYS, Trewhella Lane, St. Hilary, Penzance, Cornwall TR20 9BZ. Tel. 0736/740262. 5 rms (all with shower). TV **Directions:** From St. Hilary, head toward the village of Relubbus (farm is signposted).
$ Rates (including English breakfast): £17.50–£20 ($32.45–$37) per person; £55 ($101.75) family suite. No credit cards. **Parking:** Free.

 Ennys is a farmhouse Cornish manor in a woodland setting 5 miles from Penzance. Two family suites are available in a converted barn, called either the Hayloft or Nippers Stable. Sue and John White, your hosts, are part of a farming family and warmly accept travelers with children. Bedrooms are furnished in an old-fashioned farmhouse style with patchwork quilts. All have beverage-making equipment, and the preferred accommodation has a four-poster bed. Guests have use of a laundry room.

Food is home-cooked, using homegrown and local produce when available, as well as freshly caught Newlyn fish. Since the inn doesn't have a license, guests are invited to bring their own bottle of wine for dinner, which costs £11 ($20.35). Breakfast in fair weather can be served on a patio overlooking a walled garden. The nearest beach, Prussia Cove, is about a 10-minute drive from the farm.

LESCEAVE CLIFF HOTEL, Praa Sands, near Penzance, Cornwall TR20 9TX. Tel. 0736/762325. Fax 0736/763607. 17 rms (9 with bath or shower). TV TEL

$ Rates (including half board): £29 ($53.65) per person without bath; £35–£37.50 ($64.75–$69.45) per person with bath. MC, V. **Parking:** Free.

The hotel is on 3½ acres of grounds at the eastern end of Praa Sands. It overlooks the entire Mount's Bay from the Lizard peninsula in the east to Mousehole in the west. Fifty yards away from the main building, a lodge has additional bedrooms with private baths or showers. Most lodge rooms have sea views. Both English and continental cuisine are offered. The hotel welcomes children and is near a mile-long sandy beach. Riding stables are a short drive from the hotel, as are three golf courses. It's located 9 miles from Penzance in the direction of Helston (A394) and 2 miles from the coastal road (hotel is signposted).

WHERE TO EAT

MEALS FOR LESS THAN £7.50 ($13.90)

ENZO'S, Newbridge. Tel. 63777.
   Cuisine: ITALIAN. **Reservations:** Recommended. **Bus:** No. 10B.
$ Prices: Appetizers £1.40–£4 ($2.60–$7.40); pastas £2.60–£5.85 ($4.80–10.85); main dishes £5.50–£9 ($10.20–$16.65) AE, DC, MC, V.
   Open: Dinner daily 7–9:30pm. **Closed:** Thurs in winter.

Located 2 miles west of Penzance, on the road to St. Just, this establishment serves the best Italian food in the area. It's owned by two Scottish-born immigrants to Cornwall, Anne and Bill Blows. You can have a predinner drink in the bar before selecting a seat in either an old-fashioned dining room or within a glass-walled conservatory reserved exclusively for nonsmokers. Within the conservatory, diners enjoy a "cuisine as theater" view of the family preparing pastas and grilled fish. Specialties include spaghetti with clam sauce, pollo Vesuviano (chicken with tomatoes, mozzarella, and herbs), and an array of veal and beef dishes.

OLIVE BRANCH VEGETARIAN RESTAURANT, 3A The Terrace, Market Jew St. Tel. 62438.
   Cuisine: VEGETARIAN. **Reservations:** Not needed.
$ Prices: Appetizers £1–£2.50 ($1.85–$4.65); main courses £2.50–£4 ($4.65–$7.40). No credit cards.
   Open: Lunch Mon–Sat 10am–2:30pm, Easter–Sept dinner Mon–Sat 5–8pm.

S This second-floor dining room is over a store in the town center. Try for a view overlooking St. Michael's Mount. You might begin with a homemade vegetable soup, then follow with a "bean burger" or else parsnip-and-cashew patties. Snacks or sandwiches are made to order.

TURK'S HEAD, Chapel St. Tel. 63093.
   Cuisine: ENGLISH. **Reservations:** Not needed. **Directions:** From the rail station, turn left just past Lloyd's Bank.
$ Prices: Appetizers £1.10–£3.50 ($2.05–$6.45); main courses £3.75–£9.50 ($6.95–$11.55); bar snacks £1.50 ($2.80). No credit cards.
   Open: Lunch Mon–Sat 11am–2:30pm, Sun noon–2:30pm; dinner Mon–Sat 5:30–10pm, Sun 7–10pm. Bar June–Sept Mon–Sat 11am–11pm, Sun noon–3pm and 7–10:30pm; winter Mon–Fri 11am–3pm, Sat 11am–11pm, Sun noon–3pm and 7–10:30pm.

Dating from 1233, this inn is reputed to be the oldest in Penzance. It serves the finest food of any pub in town, far superior to its chief rival, the nearby Admiral Benbow. In summer, drinkers overflow into the garden. Inside, the inn is decorated in a mellow style, as befits its age, with flatirons and other artifacts hanging from its time-worn beams. Meals include fishermen's pie, T-bone steaks, and chicken curry.

6. THE ISLES OF SCILLY

27 miles WSW of Land's End

GETTING THERE   By Plane   British International Helicopters, at the Penzance Heliport (tel. 0736/63871), operates a year-round helicopter service from Penzance to St. Mary's and Tresco. Flight time is 20 minutes. The standard fare from Penzance to the islands is £37 ($68.45) each way. Flights start at 7:50am July to September, and at 8:45am the rest of the year. They continue regularly throughout the day, with the last flight back to Penzance at 6:15pm in summer, 3:40pm otherwise. A bus runs to the heliport from Penzance railway station: the fare is £1 ($1.85).

By Rail   The rail lines ends in Penzance (see above).

By Ship   You can travel via the Isles of Scilly Steamship Company Ltd., Quay Street, Penzance (tel. 0736/62009), with daily departures from April to October. The trip from Penzance to Hugh Town, St. Mary's, takes 2½ hours. Steamships leave Penzance daily at 9:15am and return from Scilly at 4:45pm. In winter, there is a restricted service. A same-day, round-trip ticket costs £29 ($53.65) for adults, £15 ($27.75) for children. You can buy an onward ticket for Tresco, including the ferry and landing charges at £4 ($7.40).

ESSENTIALS   The **area code** is 0720. For information about Tresco's boat schedules, possible changes in hours and prices at the Abbey Gardens, and other matters, call 0720/22849. St. Mary's **Tourist Information Office** is at Porthcressa Bank, St. Mary's (tel. 0720/22536).

It's only a short trip from Penzance to the Isles of Scilly, which lie off the Cornish coast. There are five inhabited and more than 100 uninhabited islands in the group. Some consist of only a few square miles, while others, such as the largest, St. Mary's encompass some 30 square miles. Three of these islands attract tourists, Tresco, St. Mary's, and St. Agnes.

The isles of Scilly were known to the early Greeks and the Romans, and in Celtic legend they were inhabited entirely by holy men. There are more ancient burial mounds on these islands than anywhere else in southern England, and artifacts have clearly established that people lived here more than 4,000 years ago. Today there is little left of this long history for the visitor to see.

St. Mary's is the capital, with about seven-eighths of the total population of all the islands, and it is here that the ship from the mainland docks at Hugh Town. However, if you wish to make this a day visit, I recommend the helicopter flight from Penzance to Tresco, the neighboring island, where you can enjoy a day's walk through the 735 acres, mostly occupied by the Abbey Gardens.

TRESCO

No cars or motorbikes are allowed on Tresco, but bikes can be rented by the day; the hotels use a special wagon towed by a farm tractor to transport guests and luggage from the harbor.

⭐ **The Abbey Gardens** are the most outstanding features of Tresco, started by Augustus Smith in the mid-1830s. When he began his work, the area was a barren hillside, a fact visitors now find hard to believe.

The gardens are a nature-lover's dream, with more than 5,000 species of plants from some 100 different countries. The old abbey, or priory, is a ruin said to have been founded by Benedictine monks in the 11th century, although some historians date it from A.D. 964. Of special interest in the gardens is **Valhalla,** a collection of nearly 60 figureheads from ships wrecked around the islands; these gaily painted figures from the past have a rather eerie quality, each one a ghost with a different story to tell. Hours are 10am to 4pm daily. Admission is £2.50 ($4.65) adults; £1.50 ($2.80) children.

After a visit to the gardens, take a walk through the fields, along paths, and across dunes thick with heather. Flowers, birds, shells, and fish are abundant. Birds are so unafraid that they land within a foot or so of you and feed happily. You can call 0720/22849 for information about the abbey.

WHERE TO STAY & EAT

NEW INN, Tresco, Isles of Scilly, Cornwall TR24 0PU. Tel. 0720/ 22844. 12 rms (all with bath). TEL
$ Rates (including half board): £32–£49 ($59.20–$90.65) per person. No credit cards. **Parking:** Free.
Built of stone, this good pub hotel is on the island's main road, with an outdoor area for those who wish to eat and drink. Inside, the bar is a meeting place for locals and visitors alike. Lunch snacks are available, and a bar meal costs £6 ($11.10) for two courses. Dinners are £16.50 ($30.55) and are served nightly at two sittings—7pm and 8:30pm. The pictures in the bar show many of the ships that sank or foundered around the islands in the past, as well as some of the gigs used in pilotage, rescue, smuggling, and pillage. The inn has a heated, outdoor swimming pool.

ST. MARY'S

GETTING AROUND

Cars are available but hardly necessary. The **Island Bus Service** has a basic charge of 70p ($1.30) from one island point to another. However, sightseers can circumnavigate the island for £1 ($1.85). Children are charged half fare.

Bicycles are one of the most practical means of transport. **Buccabu Bicycle Rentals,** The Strand, St. Mary's (tel. 0720/22289), is the major rental agency. The cost, depending on the bicycle, ranges from £5 to £20 ($9.25 to $37) per day, the latter being the price for a tandem bike.

WHAT TO SEE & DO

Isles of Scilly Museum, Church Street, on St. Mary's (tel. 0720/22337), is open daily June to September from 10am to noon, 1:30 to 4:30pm, and 7 to 9pm. Off-season hours are from 2 to 4pm only on Wednesday. Admission is 50p (95¢) for adults, 10p (20¢) for children. The museum shows the history of the islands from A.D. 1500 with artifacts from wrecked ships, drawings, and relics discovered in the Scillies.

WHERE TO STAY ON ST. MARY'S

Doubles Without Bath for Less than £44 ($81.40)

CREBINICK HOUSE, Church St., Hugh Town, St. Mary's, Isles of Scilly, Cornwall TR21 0JT. Tel. 0720/22968. 6 rms (none with bath).
$ Rates (including half board): £30.10 ($55.70) per person. No credit cards. **Open:** Mar–Oct.
Named after one of the massive offshore rocks that in the 19th century caused a major shipwreck, this house is owned and operated by two refugees from the urban landscape of London, Lesley and Phillip Jones. Originally built of granite blocks in 1760, modern additions have significantly expanded it in the rear. A "listed" building, its facade can't be altered. The house lies in the village center. There are no sea views,

but the water is reachable in two directions after a 50-yard walk. The Jones couple rents prettily furnished bedrooms filled with floral-patterned fabrics. Dinners for residents only are prepared by Lesley.

EVERGREEN COTTAGE GUEST HOUSE, The Parade, Hugh Town, St. Mary's, Isles of Scilly, Cornwall TR21 0LP. Tel. 0720/22711. 5 rms (none with bath).
$ Rates (including English breakfast): £15–£18 ($27.75–$33.30) double per person. No credit cards.
One of the island's oldest cottages, Evergreen was originally the home of sea captains and was at one time a smithy. It has a lot of character, with its maritime artifacts and one of the rarest, long-case clocks in Britain. The guesthouse has been modernized to provide adequate facilities for guests, and the resident proprietors will provide an evening meal for £6.50 ($12.05). It is located in the town center.

LYONNESSE GUEST HOUSE, The Strand, Hugh Town, St. Mary's, Isles of Scilly, Cornwall TR21 0PS. Tel. 0720/22458. 9 rms (none with bath).
$ Rates (including half board): £25 ($46.25) per person.
This is a large family home in the quieter part of Hugh Town, but close to shops and the harbor. Derek and Melanie Woodcock are both young islanders who take pride in telling their guests about the Scillies. There is a large lounge, and the house is well appointed, the front rooms and lounge having views of the harbor and islands. All units have heating, hot- and cold-water basins, and shaver points. It's located in the center opening onto Town Beach.

MINCARLO GUEST HOUSE, The Strand, Hugh Town, St. Mary's, Isles of Scilly, Cornwall TR21 0PT. Tel. 0720/22513. 13 rms (4 with shower).
$ Rates (including English breakfast): £18.40–£19.60 ($34.05–$36.25) single without bath; £37 ($68.45) double without bath, £46 ($85.10) double with bath. No credit cards. **Closed:** Nov–Feb.
The Duncan family has owned this lovely house right on the edge of the harbor for 40 years. Colin and Jill Duncan offer a variety of accommodations, many of them overlooking the harbor, which is only a 5-minute walk away. Colin prepares and cooks the evening meal, featuring a selection of local produce, fish, and shellfish.

TREMELLYN GUEST HOUSE, Church Rd., St. Mary's, Isles of Scilly, Cornwall TR21 0NA. Tel. 0720/22656. 4 rms (2 with bath).
$ Rates (including English breakfast): £23 ($42.55) single without bath; £44 ($81.40) double without bath, £50 ($92.50) double with bath. No credit cards. **Closed:** Nov–Mar.
This Victorian house on a hill behind Hugh Town, 5 minutes from the town center, has sheltered gardens and a beautiful view of the islands. Colin and Liz Ridsdale run a trim ship, offering comfortable rooms with hot and cold water, and hot-beverage facilities. A five-course English dinner is around £11 ($20.35). The hotel caters to special diets. Boating, sailing, cycling, golf, tennis, and squash can be arranged.

Worth the Extra Bucks

ATLANTIC HOTEL, Hugh Town, St. Mary's, Isles of Scilly, Cornwall TR21 0P. Tel. 0720/22417. Fax 0720/23009. 23 rms (all with bath). TV TEL
$ Rates (including English breakfast): £53.50–£56.50 ($99–$104.55) single; £48–£61 ($88.80–$112.85) double. MC, V. **Closed:** Nov–Mar.

This is the only hotel in the islands that is actually set at the water's edge; from your seat in the restaurant, you feel you're in the midst of the fishing boats bobbing about. The inn is old and rambling, and many bedrooms have water views. The Shipwreck Bar and Cocktail Bar lead directly onto a patio from which you can climb down to the beach at low tide. At the restaurant, you can get a four-course, fixed-price dinner with such main dishes as grilled Cornish mackerel or freshly caught John Dory, a local fish.

EASY EXCURSIONS TO ST. AGNES

One of the Isles of Scilly, St. Agnes is a small farming community relatively undiscovered. The island is known for its snorkeling and diving, and its crystal-clear waters. Little traffic moves on the single-track lanes crossing the island, and the curving sandbar between St. Agnes and the neighbor island of Gugh is considered one of the best beaches in the archipelago. Much of the area is preserved by the Nature Conservancy Council.

GETTING THERE

There are about three boats, departing in each direction, every day between St. Mary's and the much less densely populated island of St. Agnes. Something called a "tripper boat" will depart from the quay at St. Mary's every morning at 10:15am, requiring a 15- to 20-minute transfer to St. Agnes, for a round-trip of about £3 ($5.55). Boats return on a schedule determined by the tides, usually at 2:15 and again at 3pm. The particular boat information is chalked on a blackboard on the quay at St. Mary's every day. Schedules allow for easy "day-tripping" from St. Mary's.

WHERE TO STAY & EAT

COASTGUARDS, St. Agnes, Isles of Scilly, Cornwall TR22 0PL. Tel. 0720/22373. 2 rms (none with bath).
$ Rates (including half board): £18.50–£21 ($34.25–$38.85) per person. No credit cards. **Closed:** Nov–Mar.

When you visit St. Agnes, it is worth considering a stay at the home of Danny and Wendy Hick, which has excellent sea views. One of their double rooms has two beds, and there are hot-beverage facilities in the rooms. There is no choice on the daily menu, but special diets are catered to if advance notice is given. The price of half board depends on whether you order a two-course or a four-course evening meal. Mr. Hick is a model-ship maker who sells his fine works through agents in London and New England, as well as doing work on private commissions. The house is near St. Warna's Cove.

THE TURKS HEAD, The Harbourfront, St. Agnes. Tel. 22434.
Cuisine: English. **Reservations:** Not needed.
$ Prices: Appetizers: £1.10–£2.40 ($2.05–$4.45); main courses £3–£7 ($5.55–$12.95). No credit cards.
Open: Lunch daily noon–2:30pm; dinner daily 7–9:30; pub hours daily 11am–4:30pm and 7–10:30pm.
Contained within a solid-looking building which was originally built about a century ago as a boathouse, this is the only pub on the island. Prominently located a few steps from the pier, it's run by John and Pauline Dart, who serve pub snacks and also more solid fare which includes steaks and platters of local fish. The pub is the second building after the arrival point of the ferryboats from St. Mary's.

7. NEWLYN, MOUSEHOLE & LAND'S END

Newlyn: 1 mile S of Penzance
Mousehole: 3 miles S of Penzance, 2 miles S of Newlyn
Land's End: 9 miles W of Penzance

GETTING THERE   By Train   From London, travel first to Penzance (see above), then rely on local buses for the rest of the journey.

By Bus   From Penzance, take bus A to Mousehole and bus no. 1 to Land's End. There is frequent service throughout the day.

By Car   After reaching Penzance, cut south along B3315.

ESSENTIALS   The **area code** is 0736. The nearest tourist information office is in Penzance (see above).

NEWLYN

From Penzance, a promenade leads to Newlyn, another fishing village of infinite charm on Mount's Bay. In fact, its much-painted harbor seems to have more fishing craft than that of Penzance. Stanhope Forbes, now dead, founded an art school in Newlyn, and in the past few years the village has gained an increasing reputation for its artists' colony, attracting both the serious painter and the Sunday sketcher. From Penzance, the old fishermen's cottages and crooked lanes of Newlyn are reached by bus.

WHERE TO STAY & EAT

PANORAMA PRIVATE HOTEL, Chywoone Hill, Newlyn, Cornwall TR18 5AR. Tel. 0736/68498. 8 rms (4 with bath). TV **Directions:** From Penzance rail station, follow the sea road across the Promenade to Newlyn and look for a signpost pointing the direction up the hill to the small hotel's large car park.
$ Rates (including English breakfast): £17–£20 ($31.45–$37) single without bath; £34 ($62.90) double without bath, £40 ($74) double with bath. AE, DC, MC, V. **Parking:** Free.

Harry and Teresa Shead extend a warm welcome to their guests. All rooms have central heating, hot-beverage facilities, and hot and cold running water. Four units contain private baths and have sea views. Dinner costs about £10 ($18.50). The hotel is licensed to serve drinks, and outside guests can have dinner but must make reservations.

SMUGGLERS HOTEL AND RESTAURANT, Fore St., Newlyn, Cornwall TR18 5JR. Tel. 0736/64207. 14 rms (5 with bath). TV TEL
$ Rates (including English or continental breakfast): £20 ($37) single without bath, £24 ($44.40) single with bath; £34 ($62.90) double without bath, £38 ($70.30) double with bath. AE, MC, V.

Smugglers was understandably chosen by the British Tourist Board to represent the "best of Cornish accommodation" in one of their campaigns. It has a crooked beamed front, irregular windows, and an uneven roof. Most of the accommodations have views of the fishing boats in the harbor and across Mount's Bay, and all have hot and cold running water. The Cellar Bar epitomizes the old inn's atmosphere. The restaurant enjoys a good local reputation, and you can sample some of the inn's specialties, including duck à l'orange, pork marsala, or beef bourguignon. Dinners, served nightly from 7 to 10:30pm, cost from £12 ($22.20).

MOUSEHOLE

The Cornish fishing village of Mousehole attracts hordes of tourists. But the cottages still sit close to the harbor wall, the fishermen still bring in the day's catch, the salts sit around smoking tobacco, talking about the good old days, and the lanes are as narrow as ever. About the most exciting thing to happen here was the arrival in the late 16th century of the Spanish galleons, whose ungallant sailors sacked and burned the village. In a sheltered cove off Mount's Bay, Mousehole (pronounced *mou*-sel) today has developed the nucleus of an artists' colony.

WHERE TO STAY

DOLPHINS, The Parade, Mousehole, Cornwall TR19 6PT. Tel. 0736/ 731828. 4 rms (3 with bath or shower).

$ **Rates** (including breakfast): £17 ($31.45) single without bath; £40 ($74) double with bath. No credit cards. **Parking:** Free.

At the end of the steep drive up to this house you will be rewarded with peace and quiet, plus a view of Mount's Bay with the harbor and fishing boats below. Guests can relax and sunbathe in the garden, later enjoying the comfortable lounge before retreating to one of the well-furnished bedrooms. Hot-beverage facilities are in all the units, and the two bedrooms overlooking the sea have color TVs. Dolphins is run by Yvonne Lodge, who for many years was a naval nursing officer. On entering Mousehole from Newlyn, there is a public car park on the left side (sea side). Opposite this is Dolphins Drive, leading to the house on the top.

RENOVELLE, 6 The Parade, Mousehole, Cornwall TR19 6PN. Tel. 0736/ 731258. 3 rms (all with shower).

$ **Rates** (including English breakfast): £12–£12.50 ($22.20–$23.15) per person. No credit cards. **Parking:** Free.

At the edge of the village just past the large car park is a pretty blue-and-white villa. It's on a cliff right beside the sea. Mrs. Stella Bartlett, the owner, has made the inn so charming and comfortable that her guests keep returning. Each bedroom is comfortable, with good views of the sea. It's a pleasure to have breakfast set before you in the sunny little dining room.

WHERE TO EAT

PAM'S PANTRY, Mill Lane. Tel. 731532.
  Cuisine: SEAFOOD. **Reservations:** Not needed.
$ **Prices:** Appetizers £1.10–£1.50 ($2.05–$2.80); main courses £2–£6 ($3.70–$11.10). AE.
  Open: Daily 8:30am–9pm.

 Some of the dishes at this small and cheerful café on the main rod feature fish caught locally. You can order crab salad, a summer favorite, or smoked mackerel. To complete the meal, a homemade apple pie with clotted cream is served.

LAND'S END

Craggy Land's End is where England comes to an end. America's coast is 3,291 miles away to the west of the rugged rocks that tumble into the sea beneath Land's End.

WHAT TO SEE & DO

Publicity says that "everyone should stand here, at least once." This is based on the romantic conception that this is the piece of England closest to America and the most distant point you can go on mainland England. It still retains some of its mystique even if shoddy commercial entertainments and souvenir stands have opened. If these do not interest you, you can simply enjoy the cliff walks and spectacular views.

WHERE TO STAY & EAT

OLD SUCCESS INN, Sennen Cove, Land's End, Cornwall TR19 7DG. Tel. 0736/871232. 11 rms (8 with bath). TV **Bus:** No. 1.
$ **Rates** (including half board): £35–£42 ($64.75–$77.70) double per person. MC, V. **Parking:** Free.

To reach this inn, turn right and follow the road down to Sennen Cove just before you reach Land's End. The Old Success is at the bottom, facing the sea and wide sandy beaches. Surfing rollers come in from the Atlantic almost to the foot of the sea wall beneath this 17th-century fishermen's inn. Over the years it has been extended and modernized, and now offers bright, clean rooms with radios, hot-beverage facilities, electric heaters, and washbasins. Downstairs, the inn has a lounge with color TV and panoramic views of the Atlantic, a cozy lounge bar, and Charlie's Bar where the locals and fishers join the residents of the evening. The staff provides a varied dinner menu in the Seine Room, the house restaurant, for £10 ($18.50) and up. It's open daily from 11am to 2:30pm and 6:30 to 11pm.

8. ST. IVES

319 miles SW of London; 21 miles NE of Land's End; 10 miles N of Penzance

GETTING THERE **By Train** There is frequent service throughout the day between London's Paddington Station and the rail terminal at St. Ives. The trip takes 5½ hours.

By Bus Several coaches a day run from London's Victoria Coach Station to St. Ives taking 7 hours.

By Car Take the A30 across Cornwall, cutting northwest at the junction of B3306, leading to St. Ives on the coast. During the summer months, many of the streets in the center of town are closed to vehicles. You may want to leave your car in the Lelant Saltings Car Park, 3 miles from St. Ives on the A3074, and take the regular train service into town, an 11-minute journey. Departures are every half hour. It's free to all car passengers and drivers, and the car-park charge is £3.50 ($6.45) per day. You can also use the large Trenwith Car Park, close to the town center, for 35p (65¢) and then walk down to the shops and harbor or take a bus costing 30p (55¢) for adults and 15p (30¢) for children.

ESSENTIALS The **area code** is 0736. The Tourist Information Centre is at The Guildhall, Street-an-Pol (tel. 0736/796297).

This north coast fishing village, with its sandy beaches, is England's most famous artists' colony. It is a village of narrow streets and well-kept cottages.

The artist's colony has been established long enough to have developed several schools or "splits," and they almost never overlap—except in a pub where the artists hang out, or where classes are held. The old battle continues between the followers of the representational and the devotees of the abstract in art, with each group recruiting young artists all the time. In addition, there are the potters, weavers, and other craftspeople—all working, exhibiting, and selling in this area.

A word of warning: St. Ives becomes virtually impossible to visit in August, when you're likely to be trampled underfoot by busloads of tourists, mostly the English themselves. However, in spring and early fall, the pace is much more relaxed, and a visitor can have the true experience of the art colony.

WHAT TO SEE & DO

At **Trewyn Studio and Garden,** on Barnoon Hill (tel. 0736/796226), the former home of Dame Barbara Hepworth contains a museum of sculpture by the artist from 1929 until her death in 1975, together with photographs, letters, and other papers documenting her life and background. The garden, too, contains sculpture and is well worth a visit. The museum is open Monday to Saturday from 10am to 5:30pm in summer, to 4:30pm in winter. Admission is 50p (95¢) for adults, 25p (45¢) for children. There is limited parking some 200 yards away.

WHERE TO STAY

Avoid the snug suburban houses built on the edge of St. Ives and go instead to the end of the peninsula, or "island" as it's called (it isn't actually). In these winding streets, you'll find the studios of the working artists, the fishers, and the unusual places set aside to show and sell works of art. And you'll also find a number of B&B guesthouses and cottages. For the most part, they are easy to find; simply look for B&B signs as you walk along the narrow streets.

DOUBLES WITHOUT BATH FOR LESS THAN £34 [$62.90]

CRAIGMEOR, Beach Rd., St. Ives, Cornwall TR26 1JY. Tel. 0736/ 796611. 3 rms (none with bath).
$ **Rates** (including English or health-conscious breakfast): £14 ($25.90) per person. No credit cards. **Parking:** Free.
Open: Apr–Sept.
This semidetached building was constructed a few months after World War II, and affords a good view of the coastal footpath which skirts the beaches of Cornwall. Each room has fitted carpets, patterned curtains, and hot and cold running water. The owner, Mrs. Ada Taylor, prides herself on her low-cholesterol breakfasts and maintains a rigid ban against smokers on her premises. Each room contains tea- and coffee-making facilities. The hotel is a 5-minute walk west of the center, beside Porthmeor Beach.

HOBBLERS GUEST HOUSE AND RESTAURANT, The Wharf, St. Ives, Cornwall TR26 1LR. Tel. 0736/796439. 3 rms (none with bath).
$ **Rates** (including English breakfast): £15 ($27.75) single; £28 ($51.80) double. AE, DC, MC, V. **Closed:** Nov–2 weeks before Easter.
This black-and-white building is right on the harborside, next to a shellfish shop. The house, currently owned and run by Paul Folkes, was built in the 17th century as a pilot's house. Paul's main interest is in his restaurant (see below). Because it's bull's-eye center, you may have a hard time getting a room here in high season.

HOLLIES HOTEL, 4 Talland Rd., St. Ives, Cornwall TR26 2DF. Tel. 0736/796605. 10 rms (all with bath or shower). TV
$ **Rates** (including English breakfast): £17–£22 ($31.45–$40.70) single; £34–£44 ($62.90–$81.40) double. No credit cards. **Parking:** Free.
Much of this hotel's charm is due to its owners, an Anglo-American couple, John and Beverly Dowland, who seem to enjoy what they are doing. Only a 5-minute walk from Porthminster Beach, the house is built of gray granite with a slate roof and lies in a row of about a dozen similar semidetached homes, each constructed a century ago. A fixed-price three-course meal goes for £7 ($12.95). The hotel is fully licensed to serve dishes to its residents and members of the community.

THE OLD VICARAGE HOTEL, Parc-an-Creet, St. Ives, Cornwall TR26 2ET. Tel. 0736/796124. 8 rms (4 with bath or shower). TV
$ **Rates** (including English breakfast): £17.50 ($32.40) single without bath, £20 ($37) single with shower; £31 ($57.35) double without bath, £41 ($75.85) double with bath. AE, MC, V. **Parking:** Free.
This Victorian house is one of the most desirable of the B&Bs in the area. It's located about ½ mile from the heart of the resort and beach area off St. Ives/Land's End Road, away from the bustling tourist activity along the harbor. It also has plenty of parking space, unlike St. Ives center. The house is known locally for its home-cooked food. Guests meet for drinks in the Victorian bar or else enjoy one of the books from the hotel library.

PONDAROSA, 10 Porthminster Terrace, St. Ives, Cornwall TR26 2DQ. Tel. 0736/795875. 9 rms (2 with bath). TV
$ **Rates** (including English breakfast): £13–£16 ($24.05–$29.60) single without bath; £28 ($51.80) double without bath, £36 ($66.60) double with bath. No credit cards. **Parking:** Free.

This Edwardian house offers good value for the money and is in a prominent location near the harbor and Porthminster Beach. All rooms have hot and cold running water, beverage-making equipment, and central heating. Sylvia Richards, the owner, will prepare an evening meal of good quality if notified in advance. There's a private car park adjoining the house.

WOODCOTE HOTEL, The Saltings, Lelant, St. Ives, Cornwall TR26 3DL. Tel. 0736/753147. 7 rms (2 with bath). TV

$ Rates (including half board): £20 ($37) without bath per person; £25 ($46.25) with bath per person. No credit cards. **Parking:** Free.

The Woodcote was originally built in 1920 on a peninsula jutting out from the Cornish coast. Constructed in the mock-Tudor style, it became the first vegetarian hotel/restaurant in Britain. Still going strong under the ownership of John and Pamela Barrett, it has a small copse of trees in back and sweeping views of the tidal estuary of the Hayle. The hotel lies 3½ miles south of St. Ives in the hamlet of Lelant. The local scenic train to St. Ives stops nearby. The beach is about a 10-minute walk from the hotel. If there is space, nonresidents can dine here (see "Where to Eat," below).

WORTH THE EXTRA BUCKS

BLUE HAYES GUEST HOUSE, Trelyon Ave., St. Ives, Cornwall TR26 2AD. Tel. 0736/797129. 9 rms (5 with bath or shower). TV

$ Rates (including English breakfast): £24.50 ($45.35) per person without bath; £28 ($51.80) per person with bath. MC, V. **Parking:** Free. **Closed:** Late Oct–Easter.

Set within a garden on land that rolls down to the sea, with a sweeping view over Porthminster Point, this solid, Edwardian-style home was originally constructed in 1922. The warm and cozy house has a gray stucco facade and a gray slate roof. The charming hosts, Jan and John Shearn, prepare a three-course evening meal for residents only at a cost of £9.50 ($17.60). The guesthouse lies within a 10-minute walk east of both the beach and the heart of St. Ives. Hayes, incidentally, is the old Devonshire word for "fields."

PRIMROSE VALLEY HOTEL, Primrose Valley Hill, St. Ives, Cornwall TR26 7ED. Tel. 0736/794939. 11 rms (6 with bath or shower). TV

Directions: Approach the hotel from the A3074 and turn right down Primrose Valley Hill.

$ Rates (including English breakfast): £22.50 ($41.65) single without bath; £45 ($83.25) double without bath, £51–£56 ($94.25–$103.60) double with bath. No credit cards. **Parking:** Free.

Located on a private road in the vicinity of Porthminster Beach, this is a most desirable accommodation that offers well-furnished and comfortable bedrooms. Children are welcome, and the food is good. The hotel is a 5-minute walk from the town center.

WHERE TO EAT

MEALS FOR LESS THAN £10 ($18.50)

HOBBLERS RESTAURANT, The Wharf. Tel. 796439.

Cuisine: SEAFOOD. **Reservations:** Not needed.

$ Prices: Appetizers £1.25–£2.95 ($2.30–$5.45); main courses £5–£10 ($9.25–$18.50). AE, DC, MC, V.

Open: Daily 6–11pm. **Closed:** Jan–Mar.

At this previously recommended guesthouse, you can get some of the finest seafood in St. Ives. Dishes are likely to include scallops, halibut, scampi, and plaice, along with mussels and a cream-of-lobster bisque to start with. If you don't want fish, you might enjoy the chicken Kiev or a filet steak. Of course, the dishes come with "chips" and peas. The paneled rooms are decorated with pictures of ships and seascapes. It's cramped, nautical, and intimate. It's located in the harbor.

THE SLOOP INN, The Wharf. Tel. 796584.

Cuisine: ENGLISH. **Reservations:** Not needed.

$ Prices: Bar snacks £1–£3 ($1.85–$5.55). No credit cards.

Open: Pub Mon–Sat 11am–11pm, Sun noon–3pm and 7–10:30pm; lunch Mon–Sat noon–2:30pm, dinner Mon–Sat (summer only) 5:30–8:30pm.

Built upon a foundation dating from the early 14th century, this stone and slate building contains one of the most popular pubs—perhaps the most popular—in St. Ives. Most come to drink amid comfortably battered furnishings. Food orders are placed at the bar, and include only bar snacks such as platters of chicken, sausage, scampi, chili, sandwiches, and lasagne. It's located on the harborfront in the town center.

WOODCOTE HOTEL, The Saltings, Lelant. Tel. 753147.
   Cuisine: VEGETARIAN. **Reservations:** Required. **Transportation:** "Hoppa bus" makes frequent trips from St. Ives, or else take local scenic rail line.
   $ Prices: Four-course set dinner £9.50 ($17.60). No credit cards.
   Open: Daily dinner 6:30–7:30pm.

Previously recommended as the first vegetarian hotel ever built in Britain, and set 3 miles from St. Ives at the edge of a bird sanctuary and saltwater estuary, the Woodcote accepts fill-in bookings from nonresidents if there is space available. Typical dishes include leek-and-potato soup, savory pancakes filled with mushrooms, spinach, and cheese sauce, and fresh bilberries with coconut for dessert. The kitchen uses eggs but no fish. This is an unusual choice for St. Ives if such fare appeals to you.

9. PORT ISAAC

266 miles SW of London; 14 miles SW of Tintagel; 9 miles N of Wadebridge

GETTING THERE   **By Train**   Bodmin is the nearest railway station. It lies on the main line from London (Paddington) to Penzance (about a 4- or 4½-hour trip). From Bodmin, many hotels will send a car to pick up guests. If you insist on taking a bus from Bodmin, transfer at Wadebridge (connections are not good). Driving time from Bodmin to Port Isaac is 40 minutes. Taxis charge £20 ($37) but most hoteliers can arrange to have you picked up for £15 ($27.75).

By Bus   A bus to Wadebridge goes to Port Isaac about six times a day. It is maintained by the Prout Brothers Bus Co. (tel. 0208/880208). Wadebridge is a local bus junction to many other places within the rest of England.

By Car   From London, take the M4 west, then cut south onto the junction with M5. Head west again at the junction of A39, continuing to the junction with B3267 which you follow until you reach the signposted cutoff for Port Isaac.

ESSENTIALS   The **area code** is 0208. The nearest **Tourist Information Center** is at Newquay, Cliff Road (tel. 0637/871345).

The most unspoiled fishing village on the north Cornish coastline, this coastal resort retains its original character, in spite of the intrusion of large numbers of summer visitors. Wander through its winding, narrow lanes, gazing at the whitewashed fishers' cottages with their rainbow trims.

WHERE TO STAY

DOUBLES WITHOUT BATH FOR LESS THAN £34 [$62.90]

THE OLD SCHOOL, Port Isaac, Cornwall PL29 3RB. Tel. 0208/880721.
   8 rms (all with bath or shower), 5 suites. TV TEL
   $ Rates (including English breakfast): £17 ($31.45) single; £34 ($62.90) double; suite from £62 ($114.70). MC, V. **Parking:** Free.

Dating from 1875, this guesthouse on a clifftop overlooks a pier built in the reign of Henry VIII, and has views of the harbor and sea. Sports enthusiasts are drawn to the hotel, which offers shark and deep-sea fishing, sailing, windsurfing, and waterskiing. Others just enjoy the harbor view and a day or two's rest in the comfortable rooms. Some of the suites have half-tester beds. Breakfast is eaten in the refectory, a long room with tall windows and tables with settle benches. A three- or four-course dinner costs from £11.50 ($21.30). Owner Mike Warner goes out of his way to make guests comfortable.

ROGUES RETREAT, 8 Roscarrock Hill, Port Isaac, Cornwall PL29 3RG.
Tel. 0208/880566. 7 rms (2 with shower).
$ Rates (including English breakfast): £15.50 ($28.70) single without bath; £25 ($46.25) double without bath, £29 ($53.65) double with shower. No credit cards.
Parking: Free.

 This is a licensed guesthouse run by Frank and Jill Gadman, who are marvelous hosts, often drawing repeat business. Their comfortable bedrooms have hot and cold running water and hot-beverage facilities. Rooms—all doubles—are sometimes rented as singles when vacancies occur. The guesthouse has scenic views of the fishing village and harbor, and is adjacent to a National Trust footpath where walkers can enjoy the scenery of the coast and deserted coves. An evening meal with a selection of fine wines is served from 7pm in a cozy dining room with color-coordinated table settings in royal blue and white. An evening meal costs £7 ($12.95). They have private parking, unusual for Port Isaac.

WORTH THE EXTRA BUCKS

CASTLE ROCK HOTEL, 4 New Rd., Port Isaac, Cornwall PL29 3SB. Tel. 0208/880300. 19 rms (16 with bath). TV TEL
$ Rates (including English breakfast): £24 ($44.40) per person without bath, £26 ($48.10) per person with bath; July–Aug supplement £2–£4 ($3.70–$7.40) per person. MC, V. **Closed:** Jan–Feb. **Parking:** Free.
Considered the most desirable accommodation in Port Isaac, this carefully cared for pink house, originally built in the 1920s, has a magnificent view of the Cornish coast to as far away as Tintagel. Guests meet each other at the well-stocked bar before going into the dining room. The proprietors, Geoffrey and Christine Wells, arrange home-cooked meals priced at £12 ($22.20). They use local produce whenever possible. The good food served here—most of which is personally prepared by Geoffrey—is part of the Castle Rock's attraction. The hotel is adjacent to the town's main car park, a short walk northwest of the town center.

WHERE TO EAT
MEALS FOR LESS THAN £8 ($14.80)

GOLDEN LION, Fore St. Tel. 880336.
Cuisine: ENGLISH. **Reservations:** Recommended for the bistro.
$ Prices: Pub snacks £1.50–£3.75 ($2.80–$6.95); appetizers £1.45–£4 ($2.70–$7.40); main courses £3.75–£12 ($6.95–$22.20). MC, V.
Open: Pub June–Sept Mon–Sat 11am–11pm, Sun 11am–3pm and 7–10:30pm; off-season Mon–Sat 11am–3pm and 7–11pm, Sun 11am–3pm and 7–10:30pm. Bistro daily 6:30–10pm.
Set a few steps from the harbor's edge, this establishment has contained some kind of eating house or pub since it was originally built in the 17th century. Behind stone walls which are, in places, 5 feet thick, you'll find a street-level bar (whose windows open out over the water), and a basement-level bistro. You can always order chili, lasagne, or sandwiches at the bar, or head to the bistro for more formal meals which might include steaks, shellfish, fresh crab in butter sauce, and crayfish with garlic butter on a bed of mushrooms and rice.

HARBOUR SEAFOOD RESTAURANT, 1-3 Fore St. Tel. 880237.
Cuisine: SEAFOOD. **Reservations:** Recommended for dinner.
$ Prices: Appetizers £2–£4 ($3.70–$7.40); main courses £4.50–£8 ($8.35–$14.80). No credit cards.
Open: Apr–Oct. Hours vary according to the whim of the owner, but food is usually served daily 10:30am–2pm and 4–9:30pm.
Catering to a clientele containing equal numbers of local residents and temporary visitors, this gruff and unpretentious place enjoys a special fame since it was featured several times on British television and once in scenes from a Sherlock Holmes thriller, *The Devil's Foot*. It's designated as a building of architectural and historic interest and

is one of several on this treacherous stretch of coast that used the timber of wrecked ships in its construction. Meals are likely to include locally caught fish, crab, and lobster.

---

10. TINTAGEL

264 miles SW of London; 49 miles W of Plymouth

GETTING THERE By Train   The nearest railway station is in Bodmin, which lies on the main rail lines from London to Penzance. From Bodmin, take a taxi or car ride of 30 minutes to get to Tintagel, costing around £15 to £18 ($27.75 to $33.30). There is no bus service from Bodmin to Tintagel.

By Bus   If you insist on taking the bus, passengers usually travel from London to Plymouth by bus or train. In Plymouth, the bus and rail stations lie almost adjacent to one another. There is a bus traveling from Plymouth to Tintagel, departing once a day, at 4:20pm, but it takes twice the time (2 hours) that is required for a private car, which only takes about 50 minutes. The bus stops at dozens of small hamlets along the way.

By Car   From Exeter, head across Cornwall on A30, continuing west at the junction of A395. From this highway, various secondary roads (all signposted) lead to Tintagel.

ESSENTIALS   The **area code** is 0840.

On a wild stretch of the Atlantic coast, Tintagel is forever linked with the legends of King Arthur, Lancelot, and Merlin. If you become excited by tales of Knights of the Round Table, you can go to **Camelford,** 5 miles inland from Tintagel. The market hall there dates from 1790, but more interestingly, the town has claims to being Camelot.

WHAT TO SEE & DO

TINTAGEL CASTLE, ½ mile NW of Tintagel. Tel. 0840/770328.
The 13th-century ruins of what is popularly known as King Arthur's Castle stand 300 feet above the sea on a rocky promontory, a ½ mile northwest of Tintagel. The colorful writing of Lord Tennyson in *Idylls of the King* has greatly increased interest in Tintagel, as have the works of Geoffrey of Monmouth. The ruins, which date from Geoffrey's time, are what remains of a castle built on the foundations of a Celtic monastery from the 6th century. They are also a long, steep, tortuous walk from the car park. In summer, many make the ascent to **Arthur's lair,** up 100 rock-cut steps. You can also visit **Merlin's Cave.**
   Admission: £1.60 ($2.95) adults, 80p ($1.50) children.
   Open: Good Friday–Sept Tues–Sun 10am–6pm; Oct–Good Friday Tues–Sun 10am–4pm.

THE OLD POST OFFICE, 3-4 Tintagel Center. Tel. 0208/4281.
   This National Trust property in the village center was once a 14th-century manor, but since the 19th century it has had connections with the post office. It has a genuine Victorian post room.
   Admission: £1.60 ($2.95) adults, 80p ($1.50) children.
   Open: Apr–Sept daily 11am–5:30pm; Oct daily 11am–4:45pm.

WHERE TO STAY

BELVOIR HOUSE, Tregatta, Tintagel, Cornwall PL34 0DY. Tel. 0840/ 770265. 7 rms (6 with bath). TV
$ Rates (including English breakfast): £13.50 ($25) single without bath; £28 ($51.80) double with bath. No credit cards. **Parking:** Free.

Belvoir House was formed by combining two Cornish cottages with an old smithy, which is my favorite section. Other rooms are comfortably and tastefully furnished. Guests enjoy both a sun lounge and a TV lounge, and the hotel has a residential license. For £7 ($12.95) per person, an evening dinner can be arranged with the owner, Joyce Martin. In chilly weather, a log fire burns in the lounge. The house is on the B3263 approach road into Tintagel from Camelford.

PENNALLICK HOTEL, Treknow, near Tintagel, Cornwall PL34 0EJ. Tel. 0840/770296. 8 rms (5 with bath or shower). TV
$ Rates (including half board): July–Sept £30 ($55.50) per person; off-season £27.50 ($50.90) per person. No credit cards. **Parking:** Free.
This is another small, family-run hotel, where the living is relaxed and homelike. Edna and Jim Russell welcome you to their house overlooking spectacular cliffs and coastline, with cliff walks to secluded beaches and coves. The hotel is only 1 mile from historic Tintagel off B3263 Camelford Road. Bedrooms all have hot and cold running water, and doubles have showers, TVs, and hot-beverage facilities. The hotel has a lounge and a small licensed bar.

---

11. BOLVENTOR

260 miles SW of London; 20 miles E of Newquay

GETTING THERE   By Train   Trains with a final destination of Penzance leave London's Paddington Station, pass through Plymouth, then (several stations later) stop first at both Liskeard and then at Bodmin. Either of these stations lie close enough to Bolventor to take a taxi for a 20-minute ride on to Bolventor.

By Bus   There are no buses to Bolventor.

By Car   Take the A30 across Cornwall to Launceston and follow the signs.

ESSENTIALS   The **area code** is 0566.

This village in central Cornwall near Launceston which is east of Tintagel, is visited by the fans of Daphne du Maurier, as it was the setting for her novel *Jamaica Inn* (see below). The inn is named for the Caribbean island where the one-time owner of the inn had become prosperous from sugar on his plantation there. Opposite the inn, a small road leads to Dozmary Pool where the "waves wap and the winds wan" into which Sir Bedivere threw Excalibur at King Arthur's behest.

WHERE TO STAY & EAT

JAMAICA INN, Bolventor, Launceston, Cornwall, PL15 7TS. Tel. 0566/ 86250. 6 rms (all with bath). TV
$ Rates (including English breakfast): £27.50–£30 ($50.90–$55.50) single; £45–£65 ($83.25–$120.25) double. MC, V. **Parking:** Free.
This is a long, low building beside the main A30 road across Bodmin Moor. Built in 1547 as a coaching inn, it today has a room dedicated to the memory of Daphne du Maurier and her novel, *Jamaica Inn*, mentioned above. One bedroom includes a four-poster bed. The hotel has a bar, a grill restaurant, and waitress service (open only in the evening), and a bar open daily all year. If you're passing through, snacks are available daily from 9:30am to 10pm.

CHAPTER 14

WILTSHIRE, SOMERSET & AVON

For our final look at the "West Countree," we move now into Wiltshire, Somerset, and Avon, the most antiquity-rich shires of England.

WILTSHIRE

When you cross into Wiltshire, you'll be entering a county of chalky, grassy uplands and rolling plains. Much of the shire is agricultural, and a large part is devoted to pastureland. Wiltshire produces an abundance of England's dairy products and is noted for its sheep raising. You'll traverse the Salisbury Plain, the Vale of Pewsey, and the Marlborough Downs (the latter making up the greater part of the land mass), along with Stonehenge, England's oldest prehistoric monument.

SOMERSET

The western shire of Somerset is composed of some of the most beautiful scenery in England. The undulating limestone hills of Mendip and the irresistible Quantocks are especially lovely in spring and fall. Somerset opens onto the Bristol Channel, with Minehead being the chief resort.

Somerset is rich in legend and history, with particularly fanciful associations with King Arthur and Queen Guinevere, Camelot, and Alfred the Great. Its villages are noted for the tall towers of their parish churches.

You may end up in a vine-covered old inn, or you'll find a large estate in the woods surrounded by bridle paths and sheep walks (Somerset was once a great wool center); or maybe you'll settle down in a 16th-century thatched stone farmhouse set in the midst of orchards in a vale. By the way, Somerset is reputed to have the best cider anywhere.

AVON

Avon is the name that has been given to the area around the old port of Bristol, and area that used to be in Somerset. In addition to Bristol's seaports, the old Roman city of Bath is the main point of interest.

WHAT'S SPECIAL ABOUT WILTSHIRE, SOMERSET & AVON

Great Towns/Villages
☐ Bath, a Georgian spa city beside the River Avon, known for its abbey and spa waters.
☐ Glastonbury, with its famed abbey, a country town with many religious and historical links—associated with the legends of King Arthur.

Ancient Monuments
☐ Stonehenge, a huge circle of lintels and megalithic pillars, some 3,500 to 5,000 years old—the most important prehistoric monument in Britain.
☐ Old Sarum, outside Salisbury, the remains of an Iron Age fortification.

Buildings
☐ Glastonbury Abbey, the oldest Christian foundation and once the most important abbey in England.

☐ Wells Cathedral, one of the best examples of the Early English style of architecture—known for the medieval sculpture of its west front.
☐ Salisbury Cathedral—just as John Constable painted it, with its 404-foot pinnacle, the tallest in England.

Natural Spectacles
☐ Exmoor National Park, once the English royal hunting preserve, stretching for 265 square miles on the north coast of Devon and Somerset.

Palaces
☐ Wilton House, at Wilton—magnificent home of the earl of Pembroke with 17th-century state rooms by Inigo Jones.

SEEING WILTSHIRE, SOMERSET & AVON

GETTING THERE

The M4 from London provides fast access to the region. British Rail offers frequent service from London's Paddington Station, taking 70 to 90 minutes to reach Bath, for example. National Express coaches from London's Victoria Coach Station also service the area conveniently, taking 2½ hours, for example, to reach Bath.

A SUGGESTED ITINERARY

Day 1: From London, head first for Salisbury to see its cathedral and spend the afternoon exploring Stonehenge.
Day 2: Head west in the morning for a visit to the abbey at Glastonbury, journeying to Wells in the north to see its cathedral. Overnight in Wells.
Day 3: Transfer to Bath for a full day of sightseeing.
Day 4: Head west for Bristol to see its attractions and spend the night.

1. SALISBURY

91 miles SW of London; 53 miles SE of Bristol

GETTING THERE By Train A Network Express train departs hourly from Waterloo Station in London bound for Salisbury taking 2 hours, and British Rail's Sprinter trains make a speedy journey from Portsmouth, Bristol, and South Wales, also departing hourly. There is also direct rail service from Exeter, Plymouth, Brighton, and Reading.

By Bus   National Express runs five buses daily from London Monday to Friday. On Saturday and Sunday four buses depart Victoria Coach Station heading for Salisbury. Trip time is 2½ hours.

By Car   From London, head west on the M3 to the end of the run continuing the rest of the way along A30.

ESSENTIALS   The **area code** is 0722. The **Tourist Information Centre** is at Fish Row (tel. 0722/334956).

Long before you've even entered Salisbury, the spire of Salisbury Cathedral comes into view—just as John Constable painted it so many times. The 404-foot pinnacle of the Early English and Gothic cathedral is the tallest in England.

Salisbury, or New Sarum, lies in the valley of the Avon River, and is a fine base for touring such sights as Stonehenge. Filled with Tudor inns and tearooms, it is known to readers of Thomas Hardy as Melchester and to the Victorian fans of Anthony Trollope as Barchester.

WHAT TO SEE & DO

SALISBURY CATHEDRAL, The Close. Tel. 0722/328726.

You can search all of England, but you'll find no better example of the Early English than Salisbury Cathedral. Construction began as early as 1220 and took 38 years to complete, which was fast in those days (it was customary for cathedral-building to take three centuries at least). The soaring spire was completed at the end of the 13th century. Despite an ill-conceived attempt at renovation in the 18th century, the architectural integrity of the cathedral has been retained.

The cathedral's 13th century octagonal chapter house (note the fine sculpture) is especially attractive, and contains one of the four surviving original texts of *Magna Carta*, along with treasures from the diocese of Salisbury and manuscripts and artifacts belonging to the cathedral. The cloisters enhance the beauty of the cathedral, and the exceptionally large close, with at least 75 buildings in its compound (some from the early 18th century and others predating that), sets off the cathedral most effectively. The cathedral is between West Walk and North Walk.

Admission: Cathedral £1 ($1.85); chapter house 50p (95¢).
Open: May–Aug daily 8:30am–8:30pm; off-season daily 8:30am–6:30pm.

BRASS RUBBING CENTRE, at the cathedral. Tel. 0722/328726.

Here you can choose from a selection of exact replicas molded perfectly from the original brasses. The small charge made for each rubbing includes the cost of materials and a donation to the church from which it comes. You can also purchase ready-made rubbings. The center is at The Close.

Admission: Free.
Open: Mon–Sat 10am–5pm, Sun 2–5pm.

MOMPESSON HOUSE, in The Close. Tel. 0722/335659.

This is one of the most distinguished houses in the area. Built by Charles Mompesson in 1701, while he was Member of Parliament for Old Sarum, it is an outstandingly beautiful example of the Queen Anne style, well known for its fine plasterwork ceilings and paneling. There is also a magnificent collection of 18th-century drinking glasses.

Admission: £2 ($3.70) adults, £1 ($1.85) children.
Open: Apr–Oct Sat–Wed noon–5:30pm or dusk.

**REGIMENTAL MUSEUM OF THE DUKE OF EDINBURGH'S ROYAL REGI-
MENT, The Wardrobe, 58 The Close. Tel. 0722/433683, ext. 2683.**
This elegant house originally dates from 1254. Now one of the finest military

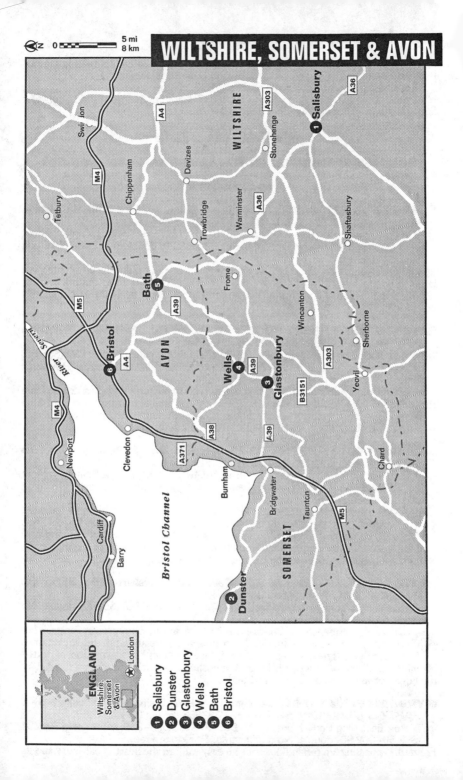

WILTSHIRE, SOMERSET & AVON

0 | 5 mi
8 km

WILTSHIRE

Swindon
A4
Devizes
Chippenham
Stonehenge
1 Salisbury
A303
A36
A36
Warminster
Shaftesbury
Trowbridge
M4
Tetbury
A36
Frome
Bath **5**
A39
M5
Wincanton
River Severn
6 Bristol
A4
A39
Sherborne
AVON
Wells **4**
A39
A303
3 Glastonbury
Yeovil
B3151
Newport
M4
Clevedon
A371
A38
A39
Chard
Cardiff
Burnham
Barry
Bridgwater
Taunton
M5
Bristol Channel
SOMERSET
2 Dunster

ENGLAND
Wiltshire, Somerset & Avon
★ London

1 Salisbury
2 Dunster
3 Glastonbury
4 Wells
5 Bath
6 Bristol

museums in the country, it has exhibits covering nearly 250 years of this famous regiment, including uniforms, pictures, weapons, and other militaria.

Admission: £1.30 ($2.40) adults, 70p ($1.30) children.

Open: Feb–Mar and Nov Mon–Fri 10am–4:30pm; Apr–June and Sept–Oct Sun–Fri 10am–4:30pm; July–Aug daily 10am–4:30pm.

WHERE TO STAY

DOUBLES WITHOUT BATH FOR LESS THAN £30 [$55.50]

In Salisbury

GLEN LYN GUEST HOUSE, 6 Bellamy Lane, Milfort Hill, Salisbury, Wiltshire SP1 2SP. Tel. 0722/327880. 7 rms (4 with bath). TV
$ Rates (including English breakfast): £15–£17 ($27.75–$31.45) single without bath; £30 ($55.50) double without bath; £32 ($59.20) double with bath. No credit cards. **Parking:** Free.
In a quiet cul-de-sac off Churchill Way, a few minutes' walk from the city center, is a large Victorian house, run by Tony and Jean Poat. All units have central heating, hot-beverage facilities, and shaver points. Parking is easy. The house is completely no-smoking.

HAYBURN WYKE GUEST HOUSE, 72 Castle Rd., Salisbury, Wiltshire SP1 3RL. Tel. 0722/412627. 6 rms (2 with shower). TV
$ Rates (including English breakfast): £20 ($37) single without bath; £30 ($55.50) double without bath, £35 ($64.75) double with bath. No credit cards. **Parking:** Free.
At this handsomely decorated Victorian house, next to Victoria Park and ½ mile from the cathedral and Old Sarum, you will receive a warm welcome from Dawn and Alan Curnow. They offer bedrooms with hot and cold running water and hot-beverage facilities. The house is on A345, ½ mile from the city center.

RICHBURN GUEST HOUSE, 23-25 Estcourt Rd., Salisbury, Wiltshire SP1 3AP. Tel. 0722/325189. 10 rms (2 with bath).
$ Rates (including English breakfast): £16–£18 ($29.60–$33.30) single without bath; £28 ($51.80) double without bath, £34 ($62.90) double with bath. No credit cards. **Parking:** Free.
 One of the better bargains in Salisbury, this spacious Victorian home has been converted to receive paying guests and is run by Sandra and David Loader. Two family rooms and a large TV lounge are available. Bedrooms have hot and cold running water and beverage-making equipment. The location, close to St. Mark's Roundabout, is convenient to the town center and parking is available.

WHITE LODGE, 68 London Rd., Salisbury, Wiltshire SP1 3ES. Tel. 0722/327991. 7 rms (none with bath). TV
$ Rates (including English breakfast): £17 ($31.45) single; £28 ($52.73) double. No credit cards. **Parking:** Free.
 This is the residence of Canada-born Barbara Smith, who receives guests in her attractive brick-gabled house. Bedrooms are pleasant and the breakfast is personalized. The entrance to White Lodge is a greenhouse, with lots of potted geraniums and trailing vines. It is located opposite St. Mark's Church, on the A30 at the edge of the city coming in from London.

WYNDHAM PARK LODGE, 51 Wyndham Rd., Salisbury, Wiltshire SP1 3AB. Tel. 0722/328851. Fax 0722/338683. 3 rms (all with bath).
$ Rates (including English breakfast): £15–£19 ($27.75–$35.15) single; £30–£34 ($55.50–$62.90) double. No credit cards. **Parking:** Free.
From this appealing Victorian house, it's an easy walk to the heart of Salisbury and its

magnificent cathedral. It's about a 5-minute walk from a swimming pool and the bus station. Reservations are needed.

WORTH THE EXTRA BUCKS
In Salisbury

STRATFORD LODGE, 4 Park Lane, Castle Rd., Salisbury, Wiltshire SP1 3NP. Tel. 0722/325177. Fax 0722/412699. 8 rms (all with bath or shower). TV

$ Rates (including English breakfast): £20–£30 ($37–$55.50) single; £40–£50 ($74–$92.50) double. No credit cards. **Parking:** Free.

Run by Jill Bayly, this lodge stands in a residential area across from Victoria Park off Castle Road (A345). The house is furnished with pictures and antiques. Whenever possible, home produce is offered, and the cookery is so good that you should stay for dinner at £13 ($24.05) per person.

On the Outskirts

HOLMHURST, Downtown Rd., Salisbury, Wiltshire SP2 8AR. Tel. 0722/ 323164. 8 rms (5 with shower). **Bus:** No. 3.

$ Rates (including English breakfast): £18 ($33.30) single without bath, £25 ($46.25) single with bath; £28 ($51.80) double without bath, £32 ($59.20) double with bath. No credit cards. **Parking:** Free.

You'll find Holmhurst on the A338 Ringwood-Bournemouth road. Mr. and Mrs. Curley invite you to share their home, and offer you a good, clean, well-furnished accommodation.

MILL HOUSE, Berwick St., St. James, Salisbury, Wiltshire SP3 4TS. Tel. 0722/790331. 5 rms (1 with bath). TV **Directions:** Head a short distance northwest of Salisbury on the A36, turn right onto the B3083.

$ Rates (including English breakfast): £25 ($46.25) single without bath; £40 ($74) double without bath, £50 ($92.50) double with bath. No credit cards. **Parking:** Free.

Built in 1785, this house was expanded and modernized in 1960, and five of the bedrooms have hot- and cold-water basins. Standing in a garden through which the River Till runs, the house is the pride of Mrs. Diana Gifford-Mead. You must walk over a bridge from the barns and garage to the house. The old mill with two large wheels is about 100 yards up the river from the bridge, and pumps water for the farm. The mill is in the midst of a 12-acre nature reserve where you can see birds and wildflowers that have been destroyed elsewhere. The pretty village of Berwick St. James, near Salisbury, has a population of about 150, a church, a pub, and a village shop.

NUHOLME, Ashfield Rd., Salisbury, Wiltshire SP2 7EW. Tel. 0722/ 336592. 3 rms (none with bath).

$ Rates (including English breakfast): £11 ($20.35) per person. No credit cards. **Parking:** Free.

In a large row house just a few minutes from the train station you'll find this fine B&B. The warm and hospitable proprietor, Mrs. G. Spiller, will serve a good, home-cooked breakfast. From Salisbury, follow the A30 road until you run into Wilton Road (still the A30); Ashfield Road turns off opposite the Horse and Groom Inn.

WHERE TO EAT
MEALS FOR LESS THAN £13.50 ($25)

HARPER'S RESTAURANT, 7-9 Ox Row, Market Sq. Tel. 333118.
Cuisine: ENGLISH/INTERNATIONAL. **Reservations:** Recommended.

$ Prices: Appetizers £1.50–£4.50 ($2.80–$8.35); main courses £3.50–£11 ($6.45–$20.35); set dinner £13.50 ($25); set lunch £6.70 ($12.40). DC, MC, V.
Open: Lunch Mon–Sat noon–2pm; dinner Mon–Sat 6:30–10pm.

Its chef-patron, Adrian Harper, prides himself on specializing in "real food," homemade and wholesome. His wife, Ann, welcomes guests into the dining room. The restaurant offers such à la carte selections as Harper's pâté with whole-meal toast, and smoked, peppered filet of mackerel, Sicilian fish soup. Main dishes include breast of chicken cooked in fresh tarragon, brandy, and cream, and grilled lamb steak tikka with tandoori-style mint sauce and vegetarian food. Luscious desserts complete the menu. Kids enjoy fish sticks, beefburgers, or sausage, all with french fries, beans, and ice cream. It's located in the town center at Market Square.

MAINLY SALADS, 18 Fisherton St. Tel. 322134.
   Cuisine: VEGETARIAN. **Reservations:** Not needed.
$ **Prices:** Soup 68p ($1.25); main courses £1.20–£2 ($2.20–$3.70). No credit cards.
   Open: Mon–Sat 10am–5pm.
What makes this self-service restaurant in the town center interesting is its imaginative salad combinations. Fresh, crisp salads, including slices of red pepper with peanuts, or leek, lentil, and mushrooms, are on display on a long counter. Try their curried nut loaf and for dessert, if featured, a Dutch apple pie. The unlicensed restaurant can get exceptionally busy during the lunch break. You might also try it for morning coffee or afternoon tea.

MICHAEL J. R. SNELL, 8 St. Thomas's Sq. Tel. 336037.
   Cuisine: TEA/PASTRIES. **Reservations:** Not needed.
$ **Prices:** Appetizers 75p–£2.45 ($1.40–$4.55); main courses £4.50–£6 ($8.35–$11.10). No credit cards.
   Open: Mon–Sat 9am–5:30pm; lunch Mon–Sat noon–2:30pm.
The best all-around tearoom and pâtisserie in Salisbury, this place specializes in tea, coffee, and handmade chocolates. In fair weather, umbrella-shaded tables are set out on the square where you can enjoy a Wiltshire clotted cream tea with scones. Among the dessert specialties, try the *forêt noire gateau,* a Black Forest cake. Try also the black cherry cheesecake. A reasonable luncheon menu, which is likely to include everything from local smoked trout to pizza flan, is offered from noon to 2:30pm. Each main dish is served with a choice of salads. Coffee is roasted on the premises, and you can see the coffee-roasting room by the river. Children's portions are also available. The pâtisserie is in the city center next to St. Thomas's Church.

MO'S, 62 Milford St. between High St. and Churchill Way. Tel. 331377.
   Cuisine: AMERICAN/ENGLISH. **Reservations:** Required.
$ **Prices:** Appetizers £1.90–£2.75 ($3.50–$5.10); main courses £3.95–£9.75 ($7.30–$18.05). MC, V.
   Open: Lunch daily noon–2pm; dinner Mon–Thurs 6–11pm, Fri–Sat 6pm–midnight, Sun 6–10:30pm.

 One of the most popular low-cost spots in Salisbury, Mo's is at its busiest in the evening. It serves familiar food—steaks, barbecue spareribs, chili con carne, and American burgers (try the one with mozzarella on a sesame bun). Of course, British food isn't neglected either; you'll find steak-and-kidney pie and other such fare on the menu. Vegetarian selections are also offered.

THE NEW INN, 41-43 New St., Salisbury, Wiltshire SP1 2PH. Tel. 0722/327679.
   Cuisine: ENGLISH. **Reservations:** Recommended.
$ **Prices:** Appetizers £1.95–£2.95 ($3.60–$5.45); main dishes £3–£9 ($5.55–$16.65); three-course set dinner £11.50 ($21.30). AE, DC, MC, V.
The inn isn't all that new; in the oldest part of the city, it has a richly half-timbered Elizabethan facade surrounded with a walled garden adjoining the Cathedral Close. Originally established in the 15th century, it enjoys a good reputation for the quality and excellence of its traditional English ales, fine wines, and freshly prepared food, personally created and well presented by J. F. Spicer and his partners. Food items include vegetarian pies, lasagne, ham steak, and other informal fare.

The inn also rents seven tastefully restored bedrooms to nonsmokers only. Ea
has an individual bathroom, although three of these (while reserved only for tr
occupants of any particular room) must walk across a hallway. Bedrooms are cozy
heavily beamed, and richly evocative of an earlier century. Each contains TV and
tea-making facilities. With a buffet breakfast included, singles range from £29 to £35
($53.65 to $64.75), doubles £45 to £65 ($83.25 to $120.25). The inn is in the middle
of town, adjacent to the cathedral.

OLD HOUSE RESTAURANT, 47 New St. Tel. 334651.
Cuisine: ENGLISH. **Reservations:** Not needed.
$ Prices: Appetizers £1.35–£2.85 ($2.50–$5.30); main courses £3.25–£10.50
($6–$19.45). AE, MC, V.
Open: Lunch daily noon–2pm; dinner Tues–Sat 7–9:30pm.

In this early 15th-century building near the cathedral, you can get light lunches, teas,
and grills. A home-cooked all-day breakfast is featured, including sausages, egg,
bacon, chips, baked beans, mushrooms, and tomatoes. Deep fried whitebait comes
with a salad bowl, and various sandwiches are featured, as is a homemade soup of the
day.

RED LION HOTEL, Milford St. Tel. 323334.
Cuisine: ENGLISH. **Reservations:** Not needed.
$ Prices: Appetizers £1.75–£6.50 ($3.25–$12.05); main courses £7.50–£12.75
($13.90–$23.60); set dinner £13.25 ($24.50). AE, DC, MC, V.
Open: Lunch daily 12:30–1:45pm; dinner daily 7–9pm.

Since the 1300s, the Red Lion has been putting up wayfarers who rumbled in
stagecoaches from London across the Salisbury Plain to the West Countree. You walk
under an arch into a courtyard with a hanging and much-photographed creeper, a red
lion, and a half-timbered facade, and you'll be transplanted back to the good old days.
The dinner is recommended, and house specialties include jugged hare with red
currant jelly, roast venison, steak-and-kidney pie, and roast beef with horseradish
sauce. The hotel is in the town center off the Market Square.

EASY EXCURSIONS FROM SALISBURY

OLD SARUM

⭐ About 2 miles north of Salisbury off the A345 is Old Sarum (tel. 0722/335398),
the remains of what is believed to have been an Iron Age fortification. The
earthworks were known to the Romans as Sorbiodunum, and later to the
Saxons. The Normans, in fact, built a cathedral and a castle in what was then a walled
town of the Middle Ages. Parts of the old cathedral were disassembled to erect the
cathedral at New Sarum. Admission is 85p ($1.60) for adults, 65p ($1.20) for children.
It's open from Good Friday through September, Tuesday to Sunday 10am to 6pm;
other times, Tuesday to Sunday 10am to 4pm. Bus no. 5 runs every 15 minutes during
the day from the Salisbury bus station.

WILTON HOUSE

⭐ In the town of Wilton, 2½ miles west of Salisbury, is one of England's great
country estates, the home of the earls of Pembroke. Wilton House in Wilton
(tel. 0722/743115), dates from the 16th century, but has undergone numerous
alterations, most recently in Victoria's day. It is noted for its 17th-century state rooms
by the celebrated architect Inigo Jones. Many famous personages have either lived at
or visited Wilton. It is also believed that Shakespeare's troupe entertained here. Plans
for the D-Day landings at Normandy were laid out here by Eisenhower and his
advisors, with only the silent Van Dycks in the Double Cube room as witnesses.

The house is filled with beautifully maintained furnishings and displays some of
the finest paintings in England, including works by Rembrandt, Rubens, and
Reynolds. There are exhibitions of 7,000 model soldiers; the Pembroke Palace
dollhouse; a historic tableau of dolls and toys through the ages, together with a unique

...lection of tiny dolls' clothes; and a 400-foot-square model railway with models of ...lisbury Cathedral and Wilton House. There is also a huge adventure playground for ...hildren.

Growing on the 20-acre estate are giant cedars of Lebanon, the oldest of which were planted in 1630. The Palladian Bridge was built in 1737 by the ninth earl of Pembroke and Roger Morris. You can walk through with guides in attendance; however, guided tours are by appointment only. An inclusive ticket to the house, grounds, and exhibitions is £4.20 ($7.75) for adults, £3 ($5.55) for children under 16. A ticket to the grounds only is £1.60 ($2.95) for adults, £1.10 ($2.05) for children. Wilton House is open Easter to mid-October, Tuesday to Saturday and bank holidays from 11am to 6pm, and Sunday from 1 to 6pm. Last admission is 5:15pm. To get here from Salisbury, take bus 60 or 61.

STONEHENGE

Two miles west of Amesbury, and about 9 miles north of Salisbury at the junction of the A303 and the A344/A360, is the renowned Stonehenge, Stone Circle (tel. 0272/7344727), believed to be anywhere from 3,500 to 5,000 years old. This circle of lintels and megalithic pillars is the most important prehistoric monument in Britain.

Some Americans have expressed their disappointment after seeing the concentric circles of stones. Admittedly, they are not the pyramids, and some imagination must be brought to bear on them. They do represent an amazing engineering feat; many of the boulders, the bluestones in particular, were moved many miles (perhaps from southern Wales) to this site by the ancients.

The widely held view of the 18th- and 19th-century romantics that Stonehenge was the work of the Druids is without foundation. The boulders, many weighing several tons, are believed to have predated the arrival in Britain of that Celtic cult. Recent excavations continue to bring new evidence to bear on the origin and purpose of Stonehenge. Controversy surrounds the prehistoric site especially since the publication of *Stonehenge Decoded* by Gerald S. Hawkins and John B. White, which maintains that Stonehenge was an astronomical observatory—that is, a neolithic "computing machine" capable of predicting eclipses.

Others who discount this theory adopt Henry James's approach to Stonehenge, which regards it as "lonely in history," its origins and purposes (sunworshiping site? burial ground? human sacrificial temple?) the secret of the silent, mysterious Salisbury Plain.

Your ticket permits you to go inside the fence surrounding the site to protect the stones from vandals and souvenir hunters. You can go all the way up to a short rope barrier about 50 feet from the stones. If you don't have a car, take a bus from the Salisbury train station. The first bus—marked Stonehenge—leaves Salisbury at 8:40am. The last bus back from Stonehenge is 4:15pm. Trip time is 40 minutes. There are also organized bus tours out of Salisbury. Admission is £1.70 ($3.15) for adults, 85p ($1.60) for children. Stonehenge is open April 1 through September daily from 10am to 6pm. From October through March it's open daily from 10am to 4pm.

NETHER WALLOP

On a country road between the A343 and the A30 east of Salisbury is the little village of Nether Wallop (not to be confused with Over Wallop or Middle Wallop in the same vicinity). Aficionados of television's "Mystery" series about Agatha Christie's Miss Marple will be interested in this village, used as Miss Christie's fictitious St. Mary Mead, home of Miss Marple.

The village is about 12 miles from Stonehenge, 8 miles from Salisbury, and 10 miles from Winchester.

Where to Stay

BROADGATE FARM, off B3084, Nether Wallop, Stockbridge, Hamp-shire SO20 8HA. Tel. 0264/781439. 3 rms (none with bath).

$ Rates (including English breakfast): £18–£20 ($33.30–$37) single; £30–£ ($55.50–$59.20) double. No credit cards. **Parking:** Free.

You will enjoy a stay at this beautiful Georgian farmhouse with a walled garden, right in the center of Nether Wallop and next door to the village pub. Susan and Richard Osmond offer spacious bedrooms with full central heating, a dining room, and a well-furnished lounge. Richard's family has farmed in Nether Wallop since 1622, and the Osmonds still run the farm, with grain crops, sheep, and a pedigree herd of Friesian cows.

---

2. DUNSTER

3 miles SE of Minehead; 184 miles W of London

GETTING THERE By Train The best rail link is to Minehead via Taunton, which is easily reached on the main London/Penzance line from Paddington Station in London. From Minehead you have to reach Dunster either by taxi or coach.

By Bus At Taunton, take the Southern National coach (no. 28), leaving hourly, seven times a day, Monday to Saturday. There is only one bus on Sunday. Trip time is 1 hour and 10 minutes. Buses (no. 38 and no. 39) from Minehead stop in Dunster Village once an hour but only from June to September. Off-season visitors have to take a taxi.

By Car From London, head west along M4, cutting south at the junction with M5 until you reach the junction with A39 going west to Minehead. Before your final approach to Minehead, cut south to Dunster along A396.

ESSENTIALS The **area code** is 0643. Dunster doesn't have an official tourist office, but an **Exmoor National Park Information Centre** is found at Dunster Steep Car Park (tel. 0643/821499), 2 miles east of Minehead. It is open from March to mid-November from 10am to 5pm.

The village of Dunster in Somerset is near the eastern edge of Exmoor National Park (see below). It grew up around the original Dunster Castle, constructed as a fortress for the de Mohun family, whose progenitor came to England with William the Conqueror. The village, about 4 miles from the Cistercian monastery at Cleeve, has an ancient priory church and dovecote, a 17th-century gabled yarn market, and little cobbled streets dotted with whitewashed cottages.

WHAT TO SEE & DO

DUNSTER CASTLE, on A396, just off A39 in Dunster. Tel. 0643/ 821314.

The castle is on a tor (high hill), from which you can see the Bristol Channel, and it stands on the site of a Norman castle granted to William de Mohun of Normandy by William the Conqueror shortly after the conquest of England. The 13th-century gateway built by the de Mohuns is all that remains of the original fortress. In 1376 the castle and its lands were bought by Lady Elizabeth Luttrell and belonged to her family until given to the National Trust in 1976, together with 30 acres of surrounding parkland. The first castle was largely demolished during the Civil War, and the present Dunster Castle is a Jacobean house built in the lower ward of the original fortifications in 1620, then rebuilt in 1870 to look like a castle. From the terraced walks and gardens, you'll have good views of Exmoor and the Quantock Hills.

Some of the outstanding artifacts within are the 17th-century panels of embossed painted and gilded leather depicting the story of Antony and Cleopatra, and a remarkable allegorical 16th-century portrait of Sir John Luttrell shown wading naked through the sea with a female figure of peace and a wrecked ship in the background.

...e 17th-century plasterwork ceilings of the dining room, and the finely carved ...aircase balustrade of cavorting huntsmen, hounds, and stags are also noteworthy.

Admission: Castle and grounds £4 ($7.40) adults, £2 ($3.70) children; grounds only £1.90 ($3.50) adults, 80p ($1.50) children.

Open: Mar 25–Sept Sat–Wed 11am–5pm; Oct–Nov 3 noon–4pm. **Bus:** No. 38 or 39 from Minehead.

WHERE TO STAY & EAT

BILBROOK LAWNS, Bilbrook, near Minehead, Somerset TA24 6HE. Tel. 0984/40331. 7 rms (4 with bath). TV TEL

$ Rates (including English breakfast): £22 ($40.70) single without bath, £27 ($49.95) single with bath; £34 ($62.90) double without bath, £44 ($81.40) double with bath. AE. **Parking:** Free. **Closed:** Nov–Easter.

The Whymark family's white Georgian house is 1½ miles east of the center of Dunster and about a mile from the sea (on the north side of A39). A brook runs through the extensive garden, and the building has a large veranda where you can spend your summer nights reading a book or chatting. A fixed-price, three-course dinner can be arranged for £10.50 ($19.45) per person; last orders for dinner are taken at 7:30pm.

DOLLONS HOUSE, 10 Church St., Dunster, near Minehead, Somerset TA24 6SH. Tel. 0643/821880. 3 rms (all with bath or shower). TV

$ Rates (including English breakfast): £30 ($55.50) single; £38–£42 ($70.30–$77.70) double. AE, MC, V. **Closed:** Jan–Feb.

A landmark building stands in the heart of this ancient village, located below the historic hilltop castle. Dinner—good, wholesome English food—is served nightly from 7:30pm. The cost is £8.50 ($15.75). Reservations should be made well in advance, especially during the busy summer months. Rooms are comfortable but no singles are available, although singles are accepted at a special rate. The house is completely non-smoking.

EASY EXCURSIONS

COMBE SYDENHAM HALL, Monksilver. Tel. 0984/56284.

This hall was the home of Elizabeth Sydenham, wife of Sir Francis Drake, and it stands on the ruins of monastic buildings that were associated with nearby Cleeve Abbey. Here you can see a cannon ball that legend says halted the wedding of Lady Elizabeth to a rival suitor in 1585. The gardens include Lady Elizabeth's Walk, which circles ponds originally laid out when the knight was courting his bride-to-be. The valley ponds are fed by springwater full of rainbow trout (ask about getting fly-fishing instruction). Woodland walks are possible to Long Meadow with its host of wildflowers. Also to be seen are a deserted hamlet whose population reputedly was wiped out by the Black Death, and a historic corn mill. In the hall's tearoom, smoked trout and pâté are produced on oak chips, as in days of yore, and there are a shop and car park. Combe Sydenham is 5 miles south of Watchet on the B3188 road between Monksilver and Elsworthy.

Incidentally, it was from Watchet, a few miles east of Minehead along the coast, that Coleridge's Ancient Mariner sailed.

Admission: £2.50 ($4.65) adults, £1.80 ($3.35) children.

Open: Hall July–Sept Mon–Fri 11am–4pm; Apr–June, Oct 11am–3pm. Country park July–Sept Mon–Fri 11am–6pm; Apr–June, Oct 11am–5pm.

COLERIDGE COTTAGE, Nether Stowey, near Bridgwater. Tel. 0278/ 732662.

The hamlet of Nether Stowey is on the A39, north of Taunton across the Quantock Hills to the east of Exmoor. Here you can visit the home of Samuel Taylor Coleridge when he wrote *The Rime of the Ancient Mariner*. The parlor and reading

room of this National Trust property are open to visitors. The cottage is at the w
end of Nether Stowey on the south side of the A39 and 8 miles west of Bridgwater.
Admission: £1.20 ($2.20) adults, 60p ($1.10) children.
Open: Apr–Sept Tues–Thurs, Sun 2–5pm.

EXMOOR NATIONAL PARK

The far west of Somerset forms most of the Exmoor National Park, a wooded
area abounding in red deer and wild ponies, with much of its moorland 1,200
feet above sea level. In addition to the heather covered moor, the park includes
the wooded valleys of the Rivers Exe and Barle, the Brendon Hills, and the sweeping
stretch of coast from Minehead to the boundary of Devon. This is more of the land of
Blackmore's *Lorna Doone.* You can walk up Badgworthy Water from Malmsmead to
Doone Valley, divided by the Somerset-Devon line. The moors, which rise to 1,707
feet at Dunkery Beacon, are inviting to walkers and pony trekkers, with ponies and
wild deer roaming freely.

Visit England's smallest complete church at Culbone and the centuries-old clapper
bridge over the River Barle at **Tarr Steps.** Some of England's prettiest villages are
within the national park, and some lie along its borders. Selworthy, an idyllic little
town, is in Exmoor, as is Allerford, with its packhorse bridge and its walnut tree, both
of them owned and preserved by the National Trust.

Minehead, a fine resort, is just outside the park's northeastern boundary, but in
some ways the little villages that have that town as a focal point have more charm. Bus
service in and around the park is erratic; it is better to explore by car. Buses run by
Southern National (tel. 0823/272033) are the most reliable means of transport. More
information is available at the Dunster Steep Car Park (see above).

3. GLASTONBURY

136 miles SW of London; 26 miles S of Bristol; 6 miles SW of Wells

GETTING THERE   By Train   Go to Taunton which is on the London/
Penzance line leaving frequently from London's Paddington Station. At Taunton
proceed the rest of the way by bus, or else leave London's Paddington Station for
Bristol Temple Meads, then go the rest of the way by Badgerline bus. no. 376.

By Bus   From Taunton, take the Southern National bus (no. 17) to Glastonbury
Monday to Saturday. There are from one to three departures per day. Trip time is 1
hour. A Badgerline bus (no. 376) runs from Bristol via Wells to Glastonbury every
hour from Monday to Saturday. On Sunday, the bus runs every 2 hours. Trip time is
1½ hours. For information about bus schedules of Badgerline, call 0749/73084; for
data about Southern National, call 0823/272033. National Express coaches run one
bus a day (no. 602), leaving London's Victoria Coach Station at 5:30pm and arriving in
Glastonbury at 9:40pm.

By Car   Take the M4 west from London, then cut south on the A4 going via Bath
to Glastonbury.

ESSENTIALS   The **area code** is 0458. The **Tourist Information Centre** is at
1 Marchant's Buildings, Northland Street (tel. 0458/32954). It is open only from June
to September.

Glastonbury may be one of the oldest inhabited sites in Britain. Excavations have
revealed Iron Age lakeside villages on its periphery, and some of the discoveries

viewed in a little museum in the High Street. After the destruction of bbey, the town lost prestige; today it is a market town. The ancient to the abbey is a museum, and its principal exhibit is a scale model of its community buildings as they stood in 1539, at the time of the

WHAT TO SEE & DO

GLASTONBURY ABBEY, Abbey Gatehouse. Tel. 0458/32267.

⭐ Once one of the wealthiest and most prestigious monasteries in England it is no more than a ruined sanctuary today; but it provides Glastonbury's claim to historical greatness, an assertion augmented by legendary links to such figures as Joseph of Arimathea, King Arthur, Queen Guinevere, and St. Patrick.

It is said that Joseph of Arimathea journeyed to what was then the Isle of Avalon, with the Holy Grail in his possession. According to tradition, he buried the chalice at the foot of the conically shaped Glastonbury Tor, and a stream of blood burst forth. You can scale this more than 500-foot-high hill today, on which rests a 15th-century tower.

Joseph, so it goes, erected a church of wattle in Glastonbury. (The town, in fact, may have had the oldest church in England, as excavations have shown.) And at one point, the saint is said to have leaned against his staff, which immediately was transformed into a fully blossoming tree; a cutting alleged to have survived from the Holy Thorn can be seen on the abbey grounds today—it blooms at Christmastime. Some historians have traced this particular story back to Tudor times.

The most famous link—popularized for Arthurian fans in the Victorian era by Tennyson—concerns the burial of King Arthur and Queen Guinevere on the abbey grounds. In 1191, the monks dug up the skeletons of two bodies on the south side of the lady chapel, said to be those of the king and queen. In 1278, in the presence of Edward I, the bodies were removed and transferred to a black marble tomb in the choir. Both the burial spot and the shrine are marked today.

A large Benedictine Abbey of St. Mary grew out of the early wattle church. St. Dunstan, who was born nearby, was the abbot in the 10th century and later became archbishop of Canterbury. Edmund, Edgar, and Edmund "Ironside," three early English kings, were buried at the abbey.

In 1184, a fire destroyed most of the abbey and its vast treasures. It was eventually rebuilt after much difficulty, only to be dissolved by Henry VIII. Its last abbot, Richard Whiting, was hanged at Glastonbury Tor. Like the Roman forum, the abbey for years was used as a stone quarry.

Today you can visit the ruins of the chapel, linked by an Early English "Galilee" to the nave of the abbey. The best-preserved building on the grounds is a 14th-century octagonal Abbot's Kitchen, where oxen were once roasted whole to feed the wealthier of the pilgrims.

Admission: £1.50 ($2.80) adults, £1 ($1.85) children under 16.
Open: Daily 9:30am–6pm or dusk.

SOMERSET RURAL LIFE MUSEUM, Chilkwell St., Glastonbury. Tel. 0458/31197.

The history of the Somerset countryside since the early 19th century is illustrated in this museum based in the abbey farm. The centerpiece of the museum, the abbey barn, was built around 1370. The magnificent timbered room, stone tiles, and sculptural details (including the head of Edward III), make it special. There is also a Victorian farmhouse comprising exhibits illustrating farming in Somerset during the "horse age" and domestic and social life in Victorian times. In summer, there are demonstrations of buttermaking, weaving, basketwork, and many other traditional craft and farming activities, which are rapidly disappearing. There is a museum shop and tearoom.

Admission: £1 ($1.85) adults, 25p (45¢) children.
Open: Apr–Oct Mon–Fri 10am–5pm, Sat–Sun 2–4pm; winter daily 2:30–5pm.

WHERE TO STAY

In case the rooms listed are taken, there's a nonprofit tourist information center (tel. 0458/32954) that can help you. Enter from Northload Street; look for a narrow passage at the end of which is a terrace of flower-bedecked old brick cottages (the tourist office is in the first cottage). It is open Easter to late October Monday to Saturday from 9:30am to 5pm, plus 10am to 4pm Sunday in summer.

DOUBLES WITHOUT BATH FOR LESS THAN £30 ($55.50)

In Glastonbury

BEREWALL FARM COUNTRY GUEST HOUSE, Cinnamon Lane, Glastonbury, Somerset BA6 8LL. Tel. 0458/31451. 9 rms (all with bath). TV **Directions:** Follow the main Shepton Mallet road out of Glastonbury past the 30 m.p.h. sign. After ½ mile (Edgarley School on your right), turn into Cinnamon Lane.
$ Rates (including English or continental breakfast): £21 ($38.85) single; £37 ($68.45) double. No credit cards. **Parking:** Free.
Operated by Mrs. Nurse on the periphery of Glastonbury, this place offers country living on 30 acres and panoramic views of Glastonbury Tor. Family rooms are available. Because of the good hearty farmhouse cooking, stick around for dinner.

LITTLE ORCHARD, Ashwell Lane, Glastonbury, Somerset BA6 8BG. Tel. 0458/31620. 10 rms (none with bath).
$ Rates (including English breakfast): £11–£12 ($20.35–$22.20) single; £20–£23 ($37–$42.55) double. No credit cards. **Parking:** Free.

On the A361 Glastonbury-Shepton Mallet road, 2 miles from the center, is a Tyrolean-type brick structure at the foot of Glastonbury Tor, which has striking views of the Vale of Avalon. Rodney and Dinah Gifford rent centrally heated bedrooms with hot- and cold-water basins. There is a color TV lounge. In summer, guests can enjoy the sun patio and large garden. Note the stained-glass window in the staircase.

MARKET HOUSE INN, 21 Magdalene St., Glastonbury, Somerset BA6 9EW. Tel. 0458/32220. 5 rms (none with bath). TV. **Bus:** No. 29.
$ Rates (including English breakfast): £17.50 ($32.40) single; £29 ($53.65) double. MC, V. **Parking:** Free.

This two-story, red-brick 18th-century building has Georgian detailing, a long history, and a superb location across from the ruined abbey. Though most of the town's residents appreciate it as a popular pub, it also contains a handful of upstairs bedrooms, each of which tends to fill up quickly in summertime. Advance reservations are important.

ST. EDMUNDS HOUSE, 26 Wells Rd., Glastonbury, Somerset BA6 9BS. Tel. 0458/33862. 2 rms (none with bath). **Directions:** From High St. head north on Wells Rd.
$ Rates (including English breakfast): £24–£30 ($44.40–$55.50) double. No credit cards. **Parking:** Free.
This spacious Victorian house with an enclosed garden is an easy walk from the ruins of Glastonbury Abbey and High Street. Doreen and Trevor Butler offer two doubles, that are simply but comfortably furnished. Each contains hot and cold running water and tea-making equipment.

TOR DOWN, Ashwell Lane, Glastonbury, Somerset BA6 4BG. Tel. 0458/32287. 6 rms (none with bath). TV
$ Rates (including English or vegetarian breakfast): £15 ($27.75) single; £23–£25 ($42.55–$46.25) double. No credit cards. **Parking:** Free.

Bucolic and charming, this is a late Victorian red-brick house "just beneath the tor." A brisk 15-minute downhill walk is required to reach the center of Glastonbury. Ms. Parfitt or her sister will welcome you into their home, which is well cared for and centrally heated. There's an expansive view from the tor of the Isle of Avalon. Guests gather in the parlor in the evening for tea and biscuits, and Ms. Parfitt will pack lunches if asked.

WOODLANDS, 52 Bove Town, Glastonbury, Somerset BA6 8JE. Tel. 0458/32119. 3 rms (none with bath).

$ Rates (including English or continental breakfast): £15–£18.50 ($27.75–$34.25) per person. No credit cards. **Parking:** Free.

 Considered by local architects as an extremely interesting house, its oldest section was built in 1720, with subsequent additions added on as the need arose. Interiors range from high-ceilinged Regency to low-beamed and cozy. Two of the three bedrooms have timbered ceilings, and the back of the house—the side opening onto the 1½-acre garden facing Chalice Hill and the Glastonbury Tor—is early Victorian. Mrs. Yvonne Early, resident of the house for many years, is the owner. The house sits on a road which intersects with Glastonbury's High Street, a 5-minute walk east of the center.

ACCOMMODATIONS NEARBY

CRADLEBRIDGE FARM, Cradlebridge, Glastonbury, Somerset BA16 9SD. Tel. 0458/31827. 4 rms (all with bath or shower). TV

$ Rates (including English breakfast): £16–£17.50 ($29.60–$32.40) double per person; single person in double room £18.50 ($34.25). No credit cards. **Parking:** Free.

This secluded farmhouse is about 2 miles from Glastonbury. Mr. and Mrs. Henry Tinney will go out of their way to make you comfortable and will prepare a traditional farmhouse breakfast. Some units have TVs and hot-beverage facilities. You reach the farm by taking the A39 road from Glastonbury; turn at the second right after passing the Morlands Shoe Factory, then take the first left, and Cradlebridge Farm will be at the end of the road.

HAYVATT MANOR GUEST HOUSE, Hayvatt, Somerset BA6 8LF. Tel. 0458/32330. 4 rms (none with bath). TV

$ Rates (including English breakfast): £15 ($27.75) single; £25 ($46.25) double. No credit cards. **Parking:** Free.

A stone house set back from the road, this has English gardens, plus a hothouse where grapes are grown for making wine. The manor house is 3 miles from Glastonbury via the Shepton Mallet road, close to the foot of Glastonbury Tor and the abbey ruins. All rooms have beverage-making equipment. The owners, Mr. and Mrs. E. N. Collins, quickly become Norman and Molly, they are so hospitable, and will tell you where to eat dinner nearby.

THE VICARAGE, Compton Dundon, Somerset TA11 6PE. Tel. 0458/72324. 2 rms (with bath). **Directions:** From Glastonbury, take the B3151 road south toward Somerton. After 5 miles you reach Compton Dunden village. After passing a garage, turn right into Ham Lane and go ½ mile to the crossroads where you should turn left up a hill. At the top of the hill make a sharp right up the lane.

$ Rates (including English breakfast): £16 ($29.60) single without bath; £26 ($48.10) double without bath, £29 ($53.65) double with bath. No credit cards.

For a deeply rural setting, head 5 miles south of Glastonbury. Run by Joy Adams, the Vicarage was built of local stone in 1867 on the site of a medieval manor and next to a medieval church. A well in the vicarage cellar is part of the ancient house. Each room has beverage-making equipment, can accommodate two people, and has views of the unspoiled hills where deer can sometimes be seen. The house is furnished with some interesting antiques, including a grandfather clock and a Welsh dresser. In addition to full central heating, log fires burn on cooler days. The 2-acre garden surrounding the property includes a Somerset orchard.

WHERE TO EAT

MEALS FOR LESS THAN £8 [$14.80]

MARKET HOUSE INN, 21 Magdalene St., Glastonbury, Somerset. Tel. 32220.

Cuisine: ENGLISH. **Reservations:** Not needed. **Bus:** No. 358 or 158.

$ **Prices:** Appetizers £2–£3.50 ($3.70–$6.45); main courses £4.50–£6.50 ($8.35–$12.05); pub platters and snacks £2.50–£4 ($4.65–$7.40). MC, V.

Open: Restaurant lunch daily noon–2pm, dinner daily 7–9pm; pub Mon–Sat 11am–11pm, Sun noon–3pm and 7–10:30pm.

In this previously recommended 18th-century inn (see above) you can enjoy restaurant meals on an à la carte menu or bar food. The food is home cooked, and prices are reasonable. Roast English meals are featured in the restaurant. Platters and snacks are offered in the pub, including lasagne, chili, or sandwiches.

RAINBOW'S END CAFE, 17A High St. Tel. 33896.

Cuisine: VEGETARIAN. **Reservations:** None. **Bus:** No. 358 or 158.

$ **Prices:** Soups 95p ($1.75); salads, quiches, and hot platters £1–£2 ($1.85–$3.70). No credit cards.

Open: Mon–Sat 10am–4:30pm.

You will be satisfied with the ratatouilles, cheese and pasta bakes, vegetable casseroles, quiches, and salads served at this café, where changing exhibitions of works by local artists are part of the ambience. In summer food is served on a patio in the garden. Daily specials are posted on a blackboard. Laura Ashley prints and stripped pinewood furniture make up the decor.

---

4. WELLS

21 miles SW of Bath; 123 miles SW of London

GETTING THERE **By Train** Take the train to Bath (see below) and continue the rest of the way by bus.

By Bus Bus no. 175 links Wells with Bath. Departures are every hour Monday to Saturday and every 2 hours on Sunday. Both no. 376 and 378 buses run between Bristol and Glastonbury every hour Monday to Saturday and every 2 hours on Sunday.

By Car Take the M4 west from London, cutting south on the A4 toward Bath and continuing along A39 into Wells.

ESSENTIALS The **area code** is 0749. The **Tourist Information Centre** is at Town Hall, Market Place (tel. 0749/72552).

To the south of the Mendip Hills, the cathedral town of Wells is a medieval gem. Wells was a vital link in the Saxon kingdom of Wessex—that is to say, it was important in England long before the arrival of William the Conqueror. Once the seat of a bishopric, it was eventually toppled from its ecclesiastical hegemony by the rival city of Bath. But the subsequent loss of prestige has paid off handsomely in Wells today: After experiencing the pinnacle of prestige, it fell into a slumber—hence, much of its old look remains. Wells was named after wells in the town, which were often visited by pilgrims to Glastonbury in the hope that their gout could be eased by its supposedly curative waters.

WHAT TO SEE & DO

Begun in the 12th century, **Wells Cathedral** (tel. 0749/74483), in the town center, is a well-preserved example of the Early English style of architecture. The medieval sculpture (six tiers of hundreds of statues recently restored) of its west front is without equal. The western facade was completed in the mid-13th century. The landmark central tower was erected in the 14th century, with the fan vaulting attached later. The inverted arches were added to strengthen the top-heavy structure.

Much of the stained glass dates from the 14th century. The fan-vaulted lady chapel, also from the 14th century, is in the Decorated style. To the north is the vaulted chapter house, built in the 13th century. Look also for a medieval astronomical clock in the north transept. There is no charge to enter the cathedral; however, visitors are asked to make voluntary donations of £1.50 ($2.80) for adults, 75p ($1.40) for students and children. The Cloister Restaurant and Cathedral Shop are adjacent to the cathedral.

After a visit to the cathedral, walk along its cloisters to the moated **Bishop's Palace.** The great hall, built in the 13th century, is in ruins. Finally, the street known as the Vicars' Close is one of the most beautifully preserved streets in Europe. The cathedral is usually open from 7:15am to 6pm or until dusk in summer.

WHERE TO STAY

You may want to stay in Wells, as its budget establishments are more reasonably priced than equivalent lodgings at Bath.

DOUBLES WITHOUT BATH FOR LESS THAN £36 [$66.60]

In Wells

BEKYNTON HOUSE, 7 St. Thomas St., Wells, Somerset, BA5 2UU. Tel. 0749/672222. 9 rms (3 with shower). TV **Directions:** Follow signs to Shepton Mallet and Radstock; St. Thomas St. is the B3139 to Radstock behind the cathedral. By bus from Bath, get off at the bottom of St. Thomas St. just opposite Bekynton House.

$ Rates (including English breakfast): £18–£19 ($33.30–$35.15) single without bath; £32 ($59.20) double without bath, £39 ($72.15) double with bath. MC, V. **Parking:** Free.

You might want to consider staying at this family-run guesthouse, rather than at the higher-priced inns in the center of Wells, about a 5-minute walk away. Rooms are clean and comfortable, and some are for families. Evening meals can be arranged in the dining room, although there are several good restaurants nearby. The Bekynton has a car park where guests can leave their cars and walk to sights in Wells, where parking space is scarce.

THE COACH HOUSE, Stoberry Park, Wells, Somerset BA5 3AA. Tel. 0749/676535. 3 rms (all with bath or shower). TV **Directions:** See below.

$ Rates (including English breakfast): £36 ($66.60) double. No credit cards. **Parking:** Free.

About a 15-minute walk from Wells center, this house stands in 6 acres of secluded grounds on the southern slope of the Mendip Hills, on the northern outskirts of Wells. From College Road, off A39, you follow a ¼-mile drive through parkland dotted with ancient trees to the spacious, immaculate guesthouse run by Ian and Fay Poynter. Each of the comfortable rooms is a double. From this pastoral setting, you can enjoy views of the city of Wells and the cathedral as well as Glastonbury in the distance.

SHERSTON INN, Priory Rd., Wells, Somerset BA5 1SU. Tel. 0749/ 673743. 4 rms (none with bath).

$ Rates (including English breakfast): £15 ($27.75) single; £26 ($48.10) double. MC, V. **Parking:** Free.

 This is a pub on the edge of town on the road (A39) to Glastonbury, with a car park and beer garden. Part of the building is from the 17th century. Margaret Brittan rents modest but clean bedrooms, some with TV. Bar meals are served in the cozy Moat Bar or the more spacious Knights Bar, and dishes include chicken cooked with Cheddar cheese and chestnut filling in a cider and cream sauce. Daily home-cooked specials and the Sunday roast beef lunch are especially popular. Meals are served daily from noon to 3pm and 7 to 10pm, and cost from £6.50 ($12.05).

TOR GUEST HOUSE, 20 Tor St., Wells, Somerset BA5 2US. Tel. 0749/ 72322. 9 rms (2 with bath). **Bus:** No. 173 (Badgerline).

$ Rates (including English breakfast): £16 ($29.60) single without bath; £36 ($66.60) double without bath, £40 ($74) double with bath. V. **Parking:** Free.

Adrian and Letitia Trowell welcome you to their 1610 home. From the front rooms, there is a view of the Bishop's Palace and the east face of the cathedral, which are reached by a 3-minute walk along the palace moat. Tor House has a Queen Anne shell front porch, and in the front garden is a 300-year-old magnolia tree said to be the oldest in Europe. Rooms are centrally heated. The house has its own large car park and is open all year.

WORTH THE EXTRA BUCKS
In Wells

ANCIENT GATE HOUSE HOTEL, 12 Sadler St., Wells, Somerset BA5 2RR. Tel. 0749/672029. 9 rms (5 with bath or shower). TV

$ Rates (including English breakfast): £30 ($55.50) single without bath, £35 ($64.75) single with bath; £50 ($92.50) double without bath, £60 ($111) double with bath. AE, DC, MC, V.

 Run by Francesco Rossi, this hotel faces Sadler Street, and the back has views of the cathedral and the open lawn in front of the cathedral's west door. Six rooms have four-poster beds. Each room is comfortable and well furnished.

Franco also runs the Rugantino Restaurant attached to the hotel, where pastas and Italian dishes are a specialty. Popular dishes are *scaloppine rustica* (breadcrumbed veal escalope topped with tomato sauce and grated cheese and glazed) and *tournedo au champignons* (filet steak, shallow-fried with button mushrooms, shallots, brandy, and espagnole sauce). There's also a list of interesting appetizers. Vegetarian dishes and fresh vegetables are offered, including some imported items. A set dinner costs around £12.50 ($23.15).

On the Outskirts

BURCOTT MILL, Burcott, near Wells, Somerset BA5 1NJ. Tel. 0749/ 673118. 5 rms (2 with bath).

$ Rates (including English breakfast): £16.50–£17.50 ($30.55–$32.40) single or double per person. No credit cards. **Parking:** Free.

This hotel was originally built in the 18th century as a stone-sided flour mill. It is set on the outskirts of the village of Wookey (on B3139), beside the River Axe about 2 miles from Wells. Bedrooms are country comfortable. Opposite is an English pub serving meals.

EASTWATER COTTAGE, Wells Rd., Priddy, near Wells, Somerset BA5 3AZ. Tel. 0749/676252. 7 rms (none with bath). **Directions:** From Bath or Bristol, follow signs to Wells (A39). Shortly before Wells, pass crossroads at Green Ore (B3135 Cheddar Road). After ½ mile, turn right to Priddy (it's signposted). Take this road for 1 mile. Continue past another crossroads noting Hunters Lodge Inn on your left. Eastwater Cottage is a mile farther on right.

$ Rates (including English breakfast): £15 ($27.75) single; £25 ($46.25) double. No credit cards. **Parking:** Free.

The cottage lies 4 miles from Wells in the Mendip Hills, an area of natural beauty; Cheddar Gorge is just 4 miles away. The house, operated by Mrs. J. M. Clements, is a 250-year-old Somerset farmhouse, with large flagstone floors and whitewashed walls. Mrs. Clements will provide an evening meal, although there are four good local inns nearby.

MANOR FARM, Old Bristol Rd., Upper Milton, near Wells, Somerset BA5 3AH. Tel. 0749/673394. 3 rms (none with bath). **Directions:** Take

A39 north out of Wells and turn left at second turning after mini-traffic circle at edge of the city; then turn right up Old Bristol Road.
$ Rates (including English breakfast): £15 ($27.75) single; £25 ($46.25) double. No credit cards. **Parking:** Free.

On the slopes of the Mendips lies a stone Elizabethan manor house, which is supported by the proceeds of 130 acres of farmland. The owner, Mrs. Janet Gould, has renovated three corner rooms with the best views ("clear to the Bristol Channel on a day that's not misty"), has made them suitable for B&B guests, and transformed the attic into a bathroom. The full breakfast includes about five choices as a main course. Summer days and evenings are often spent on a flagstoned terrace, enjoying views of the meadow and of the pale roses that climb over the stone walls. The manor lies about a mile from Wells.

WHERE TO EAT

MEALS FOR LESS THAN £10.95 ($20.25)

THE CITY ARMS, 69 High St. Tel. 73916.
  Cuisine: ENGLISH. **Reservations:** Recommended.
$ Prices: Appetizers £1.75–£3.25 ($3.25–$6); main dishes £4.15–£10 ($7.70–$18.50). MC, V.
  Open: Lunch Mon–Sat noon–2pm; dinner Mon–Sat 7–10pm. Pub daily 10:30am–4pm and 6–11pm.

The former city jail is now a pub with an open courtyard furnished with tables, chairs, and umbrellas. In summer, it's a mass of flowers, and there is an old vine growing in the corner. Full meals are likely to include a homemade soup of the day, fresh salmon, steaks, lamb in burgundy sauce, stuffed quail in a Cointreau sauce, and Somerset Stroganoff (pork filet with white wine, cider, and sour cream). The restaurant is in the center, 2 blocks from the bus station.

CROWN HOTEL RESTAURANT, Crown Hotel, Market Place. Tel. 73457.
  Cuisine: INTERNATIONAL. **Reservations:** Recommended. **Bus:** No. 17.
$ Prices: Appetizers £1.25–£4 ($2.30–$7.40); main courses £3.50–£12 ($6.50–$22.20); three-course set meal £10.95 ($20.25). AE, DC, MC, V.
  Open: Daily 10am–9pm.

Originally established as a coaching inn, this hotel bears a sign saying that William Penn, founder of Pennsylvania, preached to a vast congregation from a window of this inn in 1685. The establishment's restaurant is justly famous for its food. Within a cozy setting of ceiling beams, rustic artifacts, and a small cocktail bar, you can order such dishes as lemon sole *bonne femme,* escalope of salmon or trout, English lamb, Scottish steaks, and a changing array of chef's specials.

EASY EXCURSION TO THE CAVES OF MENDIP

Easily reached by heading west out of Wells, The Caves of Mendip are two exciting natural sightseeing attractions in Somerset—the great caves of Cheddar and Wookey Hole.

What to See & Do

WOOKEY HOLE CAVES & MILL, Wookey Hole, near Wells. Tel. 0749/72243.
  Just 2 miles from Wells, you'll first come to the source of the Axe River. In the first chamber of the caves, as legend has it, is the Witch of Wookey turned to stone. These caves are believed to have been inhabited by prehistoric people at least 60,000 years ago. A tunnel, opened in 1975, leads to the chambers unknown in early times and previously accessible only to divers.
  Leaving the caves, follow a canal path to the mill, where paper has been made by hand since the 17th century. You can watch the best quality paper being made by

skilled workers according to the traditions of their ancient craft. Also in the mill is a "Fairground Memories" exhibition, a colorful assembly of relics from the world's fairgrounds, and an Edwardian Penny Pier Arcade where new pennies can be exchanged for old ones with which to play the original machines. There is also a museum covering the history of the caves from prehistoric times to modern cave-diving expeditions, as well as a giant working water wheel.

Free parking and a self-service restaurant and picnic area are provided.

Admission: Two-hour tour £4.50 ($8.35) adults, £2.95 ($5.45) children under 17.

Open: June–Sept daily 9:30am–5:30pm; off-season daily 10:30am–4:30pm.

Closed: Week before Christmas. **Directions:** Follow signs from the center of Wells for 2 miles.

CHEDDAR SHOW CAVES, Cheddar Gorge. Tel. 0934/742343.

A short distance from Bath, Bristol, and Wells, is the village of Cheddar, home of Cheddar cheese. It lies at the foot of Cheddar Gorge, within which are the Cheddar Caves, underground caverns with impressive formations. There is a museum displaying prehistoric artifacts dating from when the caves were the home of Cheddar Man, whose 9,000-year-old skeleton is also on display. A climb up the 274 steps of Jacob's Ladder offers views over Somerset, and on a clear day you may even see Wales. Adults and children over 12 can also go adventure caving, taking tours of a subterranean world beyond the showcaves. Overalls, helmets, and lamps are provided.

Admission: £4 ($7.40) adults, £2.50 ($4.65) children.

Open: Easter–Sept daily 10am–5:30pm; Oct–Easter daily 10:30am–4:30pm.

Closed: Dec 24–25. **Directions:** From the A38 cut onto the A371 to Cheddar village.

CHEWTON CHEESE DAIRY, Priory Farm, Chewton Mendip. Tel. 076121/666.

The dairy is owned by Lord Chewton, and visitors are welcome to watch through the viewing window in the restaurant as the traditional cheese-making process is carried out most mornings. The best time to visit the dairy is between noon and 2:30pm. Although the dairy is open on Sunday and Thursday, there is no cheese-making demonstration then. Purchase a "truckle" (or wheel) of mature Cheddar to send home. The restaurant offers coffee, snacks, farmhouse lunches, and cream teas. The dairy is 6 miles north of Wells along A39 Bristol/Wells Road.

Admission: Free.

Open: Daily 8:30am–5pm.

---

5. BATH

115 miles W of London; 13 miles E of Bristol

GETTING THERE   By Train Trains leave London's Paddington Station for Bath every hour during the day and take 70 to 90 minutes.

By Bus National Express coaches leave London's Victoria Coach Station every 2 hours during the day and take 2½ hours. Coaches also leave from Bristol bound for Bath taking 50 minutes.

By Car Head west along the M4 motorway to the junction of A4 at which you continue west to Bath.

ESSENTIALS The **area code** is 0225. **Bath Tourist Information** is at the Colonnades Shopping Centre, Bath Street (tel. 0225/462831), opposite the Roman Baths. It's open in summer Monday to Saturday from 9:30am to 7pm, Sunday from 10am to 6pm; in winter Monday to Saturday from 9:30am to 5pm.

Avon is the name that has been given to the area around the old port of Bristol, an area that used to be in Somerset. In 1702, Queen Anne made the trek from London mineral springs of Bath, thereby launching a fad that was to make the city the celebrated spa in England.

The most famous personage connected with Bath's popularity was the 18th-century dandy, Beau Nash. He was the final arbiter of taste and manners (he made dueling déclassé). While dispensing (at a price) trinkets to the courtiers and aspirant gentlemen of his day, Beau was carted around in a sedan chair. The 18th-century architects John Wood the Elder and his son provided a proper backdrop for his considerable social talents. These architects designed a city of stone from the nearby hills, a feat so substantial and lasting that Bath today is the most harmoniously laid-out city in England.

The Georgian city on a bend of the Avon River was to attract a following among leading political and literary figures—Dickens, Thackeray, Nelson, Pitt. Canadians may already know that General Wolfe lived on Trim Street, and Australians may want to visit the house at 19 Bennett Street where their founding father, Admiral Philip, lived. Even Henry Fielding came this way, observing in *Tom Jones* that the ladies of Bath "endeavour to appear as ugly as possible in the morning, in order to set off that beauty which they intend to show you in the evening."

Bath has had two lives. Long before its Queen Anne, Georgian, and Victorian popularity, it was known to the Romans as Aquae Sulis. The foreign legions founded their baths here (which may be visited today), so they might ease rheumatism in the curative mineral springs.

Remarkable restoration and careful planning have ensured that Bath retains its handsome look today. The city suffered devastating destruction from the infamous Baedeker air raids of 1942, when Luftwaffe pilots seemed more intent on bombing historical buildings than in hitting any military target.

SPECIAL EVENTS

Bath's graceful Georgian architecture provides the setting for one of Europe's most prestigious international festivals of music and the arts. For 17 days in late May and early June each year the city is filled with more than 1,000 performers. The **Bath International Festival** focuses on classical music, jazz, and the contemporary visual arts, with orchestras, soloists, and artists from all over the world. In addition to the main music and art program, there is all the best in talks and tours. Full details can be obtained from **Bath Festival,** 1 Pierrepont Place, Bath BA1 1JY (tel. 0225/462231). In the United States, full details and tickets are available from **Keith Prowse,** 234 West 44th Street, New York, NY 10036 (tel. 212/398-1430).

WHAT TO SEE & DO

In addition to the following, you may want to visit some of the buildings, crescents, and squares in town. The **North Parade,** where Goldsmith lived, and the **South Parade,** where Frances Burney (English novelist and diarist) once resided, represent harmony, the work of John Wood the Elder. The younger Wood, on the other hand, designed the **Royal Crescent,** an elegant half-moon row of town houses copied by Astor architects for their colonnade in New York City in the 1830s. **Queen Square** is one of the most beautiful (Jane Austen and Wordsworth used to live here, though not together), showing off quite well the work of Wood the Elder. And don't miss his **Circus,** built in 1754, as well as the shop-lined **Pulteney Bridge,** designed by Robert Adam and compared to the Ponte Vecchio of Florence.

BATH ABBEY, Orange Grove. Tel. 0225/330289.

Built on the site of a much larger Norman cathedral, the present-day abbey is a fine example of the late Perpendicular style. When Queen Elizabeth I came to Bath in 1574, she ordered that a national fund be set up to restore the abbey. The west front is the sculptural embodiment of a Jacob's Ladder dream of a 15th-century bishop. When you go inside and see its many windows, you'll understand why the abbey is called the "Lantern of the West." Note the superb fan vaulting, with its scalloped effect. Beau Nash was buried in the nave and is honored by a simple monument totally out of keeping with his flamboyant character. The abbey is in the town center near Parade Gardens.

Admission: Donation 50p (95¢) adults, 20p (35¢) children.

Open: Apr–Oct Mon–Sat 9am–6pm, Nov–Mar 9am–4:30pm, Sun year-round 1–2:30pm and 4:30–5:30pm.

PUMP ROOM AND ROMAN BATHS, Abbey Churchyard. Tel. 0225/461111, ext. 327.

Founded in A.D. 75 by the Romans and dedicated to the goddess Sulis Minerva the baths, in their day, were an engineering feat. Even today they are considered among the finest Roman remains in the country, and are still fed by Britain's most famous hot springwater. After centuries of decay, the original baths were rediscovered in Victoria's reign. The site of the Temple of Sulis Minerva has been excavated and is now open to view. The museum contains many interesting objects from Victorian and recent digs (look for the head of Minerva). Coffee, lunch, and tea, usually with music from the Pump Room Trio, can be enjoyed in the 18th-century pump room, overlooking the hot springs. There's also a drinking fountain with hot mineral water.

Admission: £3.25 ($6) adults, £1.50 ($2.80) children.

Open: July–Aug daily 9am–7pm; Mar–Oct daily 9am–6pm; Nov–Feb Mon–Sat 9am–5pm, Sun 10am–5pm.

THE THEATRE ROYAL, Sawclose at Barton St. Tel. 0225/448844.

The Theatre Royal has been restored and refurbished with plush red-velvet seats, red carpets, and a painted proscenium arch and ceiling, and is now thought to be the most beautiful theater in Britain. It is a 1,000-seat theater with a small pit and grand circles rising to the upper circle. Beneath the theater, reached from the back of the stalls or by a side door, are the theater vaults. There you will find a bar in one of the curved vaults with stone walls. In the next vault is the brasserie, and a Japanese restaurant is beside the stage door.

The theater advertises a list of forthcoming events with a repertoire that includes, among other offerings, West End shows.

Admission: Tickets £4–£20 ($7.40–$37); matinees £4.50–£6 ($8.35–$11.10).

Open: Box office Mon–Sat 9:30am–8pm. Shows Mon–Wed 7:30pm; Thurs–Sat 8pm; Wed matinee 2:30pm, Sat matinee 4:30pm. For credit card bookings, call 0225/448861.

NO. 1 ROYAL CRESCENT, 1 Royal Crescent. Tel. 0225/428126.

The inside of this Bath town house has been redecorated and furnished by the Bath Preservation Trust to appear as it might have looked toward the end of the 18th century. The house is positioned at one end of Bath's most magnificent crescent, west of The Circus.

Admission: £2.50 ($4.65) adults, £1.50 ($2.80) children.

Open: Mar–Oct Tues–Sat 11am–5pm, Sun 2–5pm; Nov–Christmas Tues–Sat 11am–3pm. Last admission 30 minutes before closing.

THE AMERICAN MUSEUM, Bathwick Hill. Tel. 0225/460503.

Some 2½ miles outside Bath, you can get a glimpse of life as it was lived by a diversified segment of American settlers until Lincoln's day. It was the first American museum established outside the United States. In a Greek Revival house, designed by a Georgian architect, Claverton Manor, the museum sits proudly on extensive grounds high above the Avon valley. Among the authentic exhibits—shipped over from the States—are a New Mexico room, a Conestoga wagon, an early American beehive oven (try gingerbread baked from the recipe of George Washington's mother), the dining room of a New York town house of the early 19th century, and (on the grounds) a copy of Washington's flower garden at Mount Vernon. There is a permanent exhibition in the New Gallery of The Dallas Pratt Collection of Historical Maps, and there is an American arboretum on the grounds.

Admission: £4 ($7.40) adults, £2.50 ($4.65) children.

Open: Late Mar–late Oct Tues–Sun 2–5pm. **Bus:** No. 18.

WHERE TO STAY

DOUBLES WITHOUT BATH FOR LESS THAN £44 [$81.40]

GROVE LODGE GUEST HOUSE, 11 Lambridge, London Rd., Bath, Avon BA1 6BJ. Tel. 0225/310860. 8 rms (none with bath). TV. **Bus:** No. 3, 13, 23, 33.

$ Rates (including English breakfast): £20 ($37) single; £35–£40 ($64.75–$74) double. Discounts available with three or more persons. No credit cards. **Parking:** Free.

This typical Georgian home dates from 1787, and has well-furnished and spacious rooms, most with large windows overlooking a stone terrace, a garden, and the surrounding wooded hills. A warm welcome and personal attention are guaranteed by the owners, Roy and Rosalie Burridge. There are large family rooms available, which can sleep three or four people, and all units are equipped with hot and cold running water. Drinks of all kinds are served until 10:30pm. Near the city center, the lodge is serviced by frequent buses at the front gate.

HARINGTON'S HOTEL AND RESTAURANT, 8-10 Queen St., Bath, Avon BA2 1HE. Tel. 0225/461728. 12 rms (8 with shower). TV

$ Rates (including English breakfast): £24 ($44.40) single without bath; £34 ($62.90) double without bath; £40 ($74) single or double with bath. AE, V.

Harington's is known primarily as a place to eat, but the proprietors, Anthony and Sally Dodge, also offer overnight accommodations in rooms with water basins, radios, intercoms, and hot-beverage facilities. Harington's consists of several 19th-century buildings on the corner of Harington Place and Queen Street, on land owned by the Harington family after the dissolution of the monasteries. Sir John Harington was a godson of Queen Elizabeth I, and his main claim to fame is his invention of the water closet (flush toilet). Harington's is on a cobbled street in the center of the city and is within easy walking distance of the shops and the Theatre Royal.

OLDFIELDS, 102 Wells Rd., Bath, Avon BA2 3AL. Tel. 0225/317984. 14 rms (8 with shower). TV **Bus:** No. 3, 13, 23, 15, 16.

$ Rates (including English breakfast): £25 ($46.25) single without bath, £40 ($74) single with bath; £35 ($64.75) double without bath, £50 ($92.50) double with bath. MC, V. **Parking:** Free.

This traditional bed-and-breakfast accommodation occupies two semidetached Victorian houses dating from 1875. Anthony and Nicole O'Flaherty joined their family home to the one next door and restored the facilities, so that now they offer nicely appointed rooms with hot-beverage facilities. The house has a spacious lounge with decorated plaster ceilings and tall windows with lace curtains. Fine views of the hills and the city are part of the attraction. Parking is available at Oldfield, about a 12-minute walk from the heart of Bath.

PARADISE HOUSE HOTEL, 88 Holloway, Bath, Avon BA2 4PX. Tel. 0225/317723. 9 rms (7 with bath). TV TEL **Directions:** From the railway station, follow the one-way system round to the Churchill Bridge across the Avon. Continue under the railway viaduct and round the traffic circle, taking the A367 exit leading up the hill. Continue up the hill, the Wellsway, about ¾ mile and turn left at a small shopping center. Continue left down the hill into the cul-de-sac.

$ Rates (including English breakfast): £37 ($68.45) single without bath, £53 ($98.05) single with bath; £44 ($81.40) double without bath, £60 ($111) double with bath. AE, MC, V. **Parking:** Free.

In a ½-acre garden on a quiet cul-de-sac, the hotel is within a 10-minute walk of the city center. It was built around 1730 of blocks of local beige stone, and each well-decorated accommodation contains a radio and beverage-making equipment.

TASBURGH HOTEL, Warminster Rd., Bathampton, Bath, Avon, BA2 6SH. Tel. 0225/425096. 13 rms (10 with bath). TV. **Bus:** No. 4.

$ **Rates** (including English breakfast): £31 ($57.35) single without bath, £38 ($70.30) single with bath; £43 ($79.55) double without bath, £55 ($101.75) double with bath. MC, V. **Parking:** Free.

Set about a mile east of Bath center, amid 7 acres of parks and gardens, this spacious Victorian country house was built in 1890 and was once occupied by one of the royal family's official photographers. The red-brick structure contains a lounge, a glassed-in conservatory, and individually decorated bedrooms which usually have sweeping panoramic views. Each contains hot-beverage facilities. The Avon and Kennet Canal runs along the rear of the property, and guests enjoy summer walks along the adjacent towpath.

DOUBLES WITH BATH FOR LESS THAN £50 ($92.50)

BAILBROOK LODGE HOTEL, 35-37 London Rd. West, Bath, Avon BA1 7HZ. Tel. 0225/659090. 14 rms (all with bath or shower). TV
$ **Rates** (including English breakfast): £30 ($55.50) single; £45–£65 ($83.25–$120.25) double. AE, DC, MC, V. **Parking:** Free.
Four of the accommodations in this restored Georgian town house contain four-poster beds, and all rooms offer outstanding views of the Avon Valley. You can order a traditional "English recipe" dinner for £10.50 ($19.45). The hotel adjoins A4 1 mile east of Bath.

BROMPTON HOUSE HOTEL, St. John's Rd., Bathwick, Bath, Avon BA2 6PT. Tel. 0225/420972. 12 rms (all with bath or shower). TV TEL **Directions:** From M4 motorway, take Exit 18 and proceed along A46 to Bath. At the approach to the city, turn left at the traffic light (signposted to city center). Over the Cleveland Bridge take an immediate right.
$ **Rates** (including English breakfast): £30–£35 ($55.50–$64.75) single; £50–£55 ($92.50–$101.75) double. MC, V. **Parking:** Free.
This elegant Georgian rectory is set in tranquil grounds within an easy commute of the heart of the city. Formerly the old rectory of St. Mary's Church back in the days when Bathwick was merely a village, it was constructed in 1777 and built on the site of a manor farm from the 16th century. Its Victorian owners added a wing. Today, the hotel is well run, and its owners, Edward and Ida Mills, are helpful. Each room has beverage-making equipment and a radio, and instead of the English breakfast, you can have a whole-food breakfast.

CHERITON HOUSE, 9 Upper Oldfield Park, Bath, Avon BA2 3JZ. Tel. 0225/429862. 9 rms (all with bath or shower). TV **Bus:** No. 3, 6, 13, 14, 17, or 23.
$ **Rates** (including English breakfast): £32–£36 ($59.20–$66.60) single; £45–£55 ($83.25–$101.75) double. MC, V. **Parking:** Free.
This is an elegant late-Victorian home that still has the many of the architectural adornments, including the original fireplaces. Mike and Jo Babbage work hard to make their guests comfortable, and their large house is spotlessly clean. This is really a house for adults, not young children. Only breakfast is served.

DORIAN HOUSE, Upper Oldfield Park, Bath, Avon BA2 3JK. Tel. 0225/426336. 7 rms (all with bath or shower). TV **Bus:** No. 3, 6, 13, 14, 17, or 23.
$ **Rates** (including English breakfast): £30 ($55.50) single; £45 ($83.25) double. MC, V. **Parking:** Free.
This is a restored 100-year-old Victorian residence owned by Ian and Doreen Bennetts, who are always on hand to suggest what to see in Bath. On the southern slopes, the house is only a 10-minute walk to the city center, and is furnished with antiques and many period pieces. Bedrooms have good views and hot-beverage facilities, and some have canopied beds.

FERN COTTAGE HOTEL, 9 Northend, Batheaston, near Bath, Avon BA1

7EE. Tel. 0225/858190. 6 rms (all with bath or shower). TV **Directions:** Take A4 from Bath toward Chippenham. In Batheaston, take the second left. Fern Cottage is about 400 yards after the turn, on the left opposite School Lane.

$ Rates (including English breakfast): £25–£40 ($46.25–$74) single; £45–£55 ($83.15–$101.75) double. No credit cards. **Parking:** Free.

The hotel is in a quiet spot with plenty of parking space, at the end of St. Catherines, the most southerly of the Cotswold valleys. It has modern amenities, but its furnishings and decor are in keeping with the period in which it was built, some 250 years ago. All rooms have facilities for making tea or coffee. The hotel has a TV lounge, a dining room where evening meals are available, and a bar lit with the original gaslights installed in Fern Cottage around 1890. Some 3 miles southeast of Bath, the establishment is at the foot of Little Solsbury Iron Age Hill Fort (the location of Bath before the Romans).

HAYDON HOUSE, 9 Bloomfield Park, Bath, Avon BA2 2BY. Tel. 0225/ 444919. Fax 0225/469020. 4 rms (all with bath). TV TEL. **Bus:** No. 14 or 15.

$ Rates (including English breakfast): £35–£38 ($64.75–$70.30) single; £48–£55 ($88.80–$101.75) double. MC, V. **Parking:** Free.

Originally built of honey-colored stone at the beginning of the Edwardian age, this house lies in a garden a mile south of the city center. Today it is the domain of Gordon and Magdalene Ashman (he is a former commander in the Royal Navy). They are justifiably known for their "Bloomfield Breakfasts," which incorporate such fare as whisky or rum porridge, scrambled eggs with smoked salmon, and other country-inspired recipes. Platters of fresh fruit and health-conscious regimes are also available. Guests meet one another in the chintz- and antique-filled lounge, beside a fireplace that was removed from a house in Bath where African leader Haile Selassie, emperor of Ethiopia, was sheltered from World War II's Italian invasion of Ethiopia; when the house was demolished, Haydon House got the mantelpiece.

HIGHWAYS HOUSE, 143 Wells Rd., Bath, Avon BA2 3AL. Tel. 0225/ 421238. 7 rms (all with shower). TV **Bus:** No. 3, 13, or 14.

$ Rates (including English breakfast): £32–£34 ($59.20–$62.90) single; £48–£52 ($88.80–$96.20) double. No credit cards. **Parking:** Free.

This elegant Victorian family home is within minutes of the historic center. There is private, off-street parking for guests, a rare facility in a city which was built when the sedan chair and coach and horses reigned supreme. Highways is the home of David and Davina James and their family. All rooms have hot-beverage facilities, and ice is always available. The ironing facilities may come in handy in an emergency, and drinks and snacks can be arranged. The hosts know a lot about Bath and its environs and will help guests in their planning. A local minibus service passes the door every few minutes.

LEIGHTON HOUSE, 139 Wells Rd., Bath, Avon BA2 3AL. Tel. 0225/ 314769. 7 rms (all with bath or shower). TV TEL **Directions:** On approaching Bath, follow A367 Exeter signs but ignore "light vehicles only" sign. Turn left onto A367 (the Wells Road). Follow black railings uphill (500 yd.). When railings end, turn left into Hayesfield Park, and Leighton House will be on right.

$ Rates (including English breakfast): £40–£46 ($74–$85.10) single; £50–£56 ($92.50–$103.60) double. MC, V. **Parking:** Free.

 David and Kathleen Slape offer one of the best value accommodations in the area. Their house is a Victorian residence from the 1870s, with parking space at the southern side of the city on the A367 road to Exeter (Devon). It's about a 10-minute walk from the center of Bath, and minibuses pass by frequently. Bedrooms are refurbished.

SOMERSET HOTEL, 35 Bathwick Hill, Bath, Avon BA2 6DL. Tel. 0225/ 466451. 9 rms (all with bath). TEL

$ Rates (including half board): £44 ($81.40) per person. AE, MC, V. **Parking:** Free.

This Georgian stone house was constructed as a private home in 1827, and is really a lot like a big country home in the middle of the city: It's in the district of Bathwick, residential neighborhood within a 12-minute walk of the center of Bath. Within its garden grows one of the oldest and largest Judas trees in Britain—it's probably 350 years old. The house has its own walled garden, but many of the vegetables served at Somerset are grown by its owner, Malcolm Seymour, and his wife, Jean.

Food is served in what was originally built as a butler's pantry. Nonresidents who call in advance are welcome. Somerset House is fully licensed. Meals cost from £15.50 ($28.70). Specialties are inspired by the West Country and tend to use a lot of pork (usually cooked with apples and cider). Many dishes also rely on the use of brandy and liqueur. Vegetarian food is served. The hotel is on Bathwick Hill, the road that leads to Bath University on the southeast side of Bath.

WORTH THE EXTRA BUCKS

HOLLY LODGE, 8 Upper Oldfield Park, Bath, Avon BA2 3JZ. Tel. 0225/ 424042. Fax 0225/481138. 6 rms (all with bath). TV TEL **Bus:** No. 3, 6, 13, 14, 17, or 23.
$ **Rates** (including English breakfast): £40 ($74) single; £58–£65 ($107.30–$120.25) double. AE, MC, V. **Parking:** Free.

One of Bath's most upmarket B&Bs is a real delight, as well as a choice piece of real estate. In 1880, a big landowner built a mansion on a hilltop near the center of his acreage. But a century later, it had decayed into a derelict hovel inhabited by squatters. In 1986, partners Carrolle Sellick and George Hall restored the beige stone exterior made of Bath Ashler stone and turned the remaining acre into a park and garden. Capped with a turret offering wide-scope views of the surrounding landscape, the establishment is within a 10-minute walk from the town center. Inside, you'll find the original Victorian marble fireplaces, clusters of antiques, richly detailed cove moldings, and 15-foot-high ceilings. Bedrooms are carefully decorated, sometimes with brass beds and Laura Ashley fabrics, and they are well worth the splurge. Each accommodation contains beverage-making equipment and is for nonsmokers only. Breakfast is served in a room filled with white wicker chairs with French doors and a view of Bath.

ORCHARD HOUSE, Warminster Rd., Bathampton, Bath, Avon BA2 6XG. Tel. 0225/466115. 14 rms (all with bath or shower). TV TEL **Directions:** Take A36 to Bathampton for 5 minutes.
$ **Rates** (including English breakfast): £45 ($83.25) single; £57–£60 ($105.45–$111) double. AE, DC, MC, V. **Parking:** Free.
All rooms here have hot-beverage facilities, radios, central heating, and double glazing on the windows to keep out noise. Built in 1984, the hotel has an à la carte restaurant, as well as a sauna and solarium in a special health facility. Owners Keith and Barbara Reynolds make guests feel welcome, and this tranquil place is in semirural surroundings. There is off-street parking.

WHERE TO EAT

MEALS FOR LESS THAN £14 [$25.90]

CLARETS RESTAURANT & WINE BAR, 7A Kingsmead Sq. Tel. 466688.
Cuisine: ENGLISH. **Reservations:** Not needed.
$ **Prices:** Appetizers £2.95–£3.50 ($5.45–$6.45); main courses £7.95–£10.95 ($14.70–$20.25); bar snacks £2.95–£4.50 ($5.45–$8.35). AE, V.
Open: Lunch Mon–Sat noon–2pm; dinner Mon–Thurs 5:30–10:30pm, Fri–Sat 5:30–11pm.

This is a stylish, modern English restaurant in four vaults (one a strictly no-smoking area) under a Georgian terrace. The imaginative food is an excellent value, and the menu provides a wide choice, including fish and vegetarian dishes. Some of the specialties are "marvellous mushrooms"—mushrooms sautéed with smoked bacon, onions, and chives; salmon combined with cream cheese in phyllo pastry; and a whole-meal choux bun filled with onion, celery, mushroom, nd served with a Stilton sauce. For desserts, try such treats as treacle tart, l-butter pudding, or chocolate extravaganza. Clarets is near the Theatre th's three cinemas and is ideal for pre- and postshow dinner and or nmer, tables and chairs are placed in Kingsmead Square for al fresco dining or drinking.

CRYSTAL PALACE, Abbey Green. Tel. 423944.

Cuisine: ENGLISH. **Reservations:** Not needed.

$ **Prices:** Appetizers £1.50 ($2.80); main courses £3.50–£4 ($6.50–$7.40). No credit cards.

Open: Mon–Fri 11am–3pm and 6–11pm, Sat 11am–11pm; Sun noon–3 and 7–10:30pm. Food service stops at 8:30pm.

Set on a small square in the oldest part of town, this is one of the few places in England where you can order Thomas Hardy ale, a densely caloric drink with the highest alcoholic content (12%) of any beer brewed in England. In summer, guests can drink and dine near a grape arbor outside, and in cooler weather, they can enjoy the dark beams, the paneling, and the fireplace inside. Food items include sandwiches, baked stuffed potatoes, ploughman's lunches, and steak-and-kidney pie. Crystal Palace is in the town center, around the corner from Bath Abbey.

EVANS FISH RESTAURANT, 7-8 Abbeygate St. Tel. 463981.

Cuisine: SEAFOOD. **Reservations:** Not needed.

$ **Prices:** Appetizers 50p–55p (95¢–$1.05); main courses £3.15–£4.20 ($5.85–$7.75). AE, MC, V.

Open: Lunch Mon–Sat 11:30am–2:30pm; dinner (summer only) Mon–Sat 6–8:30pm. Self-service and take-out Mon–Sat 11:30am–6pm year round.

Only a 3-minute walk from the abbey and train station, this family restaurant was created by Mrs. Harriet Evans in 1908, and features superb fish dinners at moderate prices. Today Mr. Webster carries on the tradition established by the Evans family. A meal might include the soup of the day, fried filet of fish with chips, and a choice of desserts. Only the freshest of fish is served. The lower floor has a self-service section, and on the second floor is an Abbey Room catering to families. The preferred dining spot is the Georgian Room—so named after its arched windows and fireplace. From the take-out section, you can order a number of crisply fried fish specialties, such as deep-fried scampi with chips.

HARINGTON'S HOTEL AND RESTAURANT, 8-10 Queen St. Tel. 461728.

Cuisine: ENGLISH/FRENCH. **Reservations:** Recommended.

$ **Prices:** Appetizers £1.80–£3.95 ($3.35–$7.30); main courses £6.95–£11 ($12.85–$20.35). AE, MC, V.

Open: Lunch daily noon–2pm; dinner daily 6:30–10pm.

This hotel restaurant is an excellent choice for lunch or dinner, one of the most discreetly popular choices among locals for years. (See "Where to Stay," above, for the hotel recommendation.) Sheltered behind a honey-colored facade of Bath stone originally built in 1752, it's hidden from the casual visitor on a narrow cobble-covered street in the heart of Bath. The protruding bay window lets in the sun, and offers wide-angled views of the passing parade. Fully licensed, the restaurant serves such dishes as Harington's Dover sole, chateaubriand, seafood crêpes, grilled trout, steaks, and smoked haddock *en papillote*.

THE PUMP ROOM RESTAURANT, Roman Baths. Tel. 444477.

Cuisine: ENGLISH. **Reservations:** Not needed.

$ **Prices:** Appetizers 95p–£6.50 ($1.75–$12.05); main courses £3.50–£8.50 ($6.50–$15.75). V.

Open: June–Sept daily 10am–6:30pm; off-season daily 10am–4:30pm. Hot dishes served 11:30am–2:30pm.

Now run by Milburns Restaurants, this is a tradition in Bath (see "What to See & Do," above). The Pump Room has been a meeting place since the 18th century, and the newest Pump Room Restaurant opened in 1988. Guests often enjoy music from the Pump Room Trio or from the resident pianist while they drink or eat. Typical dishes served during coffee are Cobbs Original Bath Bun or plain scones served with clotted cream and strawberry jam. Hot dishes include steak-kidney-and-oyster pudding or lobster pots with anchovy straws. The famous Pump Room tea is a favorite, even among the locals who enjoy their Earl Grey, Darjeeling, or whatever, along with sandwiches, scones, cakes, and pastries for £5.50 ($10.20).

SALLY LUNN'S HOUSE, 4 North Parade Passage. Tel. 461634.
   Cuisine: ENGLISH. **Reservations:** Required for dinner.
$ **Prices:** Set dinner £8.50 ($15.75), £10.50 ($19.45), and £12.50 ($23.15); snacks from £1.85 ($3.40). AE, MC, V (for dinner only).
   Open: Mon–Sat 10am–6pm, Sun noon–6pm; dinner Tues–Sun 6–9pm.
This is a tiny gabled licensed coffeehouse and restaurant, with a Georgian bow window set in the "new" stone facade put up around 1720. Original Tudor fireplaces and secret cupboards are inside. The house is a landmark in Bath—the present wood-frame building dates from about 1482 and is the oldest in the city. It was built on the site of the monastery kitchen that dated from around 1150, which itself was constructed on the site of a Roman mansion erected in about A.D. 200. Visitors to Bath have been eating here for more than 1,700 years. The restaurant is a 1-minute walk from the Abbey Church and Roman Baths.

Sally Lunn, who may have been a fictional character, is a legend in Bath. She supposedly came from France during the 1680s, and her baking became so popular and her buns, based on the French brioche, so well known, that locals and visitors named the house and the bun after her. Today the cellar bakery where she worked and recent excavations showing the earlier buildings are a museum open Monday to Saturday.

On the ground and first floors, the Sally Lunn buns are served sweet or savory, fresh from the modern bakery on the third floor. Excellent coffee and toasted buns with "lashings" of butter, whole fruit strawberry jam, and real clotted cream is everybody's favorite. You can have a bun served with various salads, chili, curry, traditional Welsh rarebit (a cooked cheese dish), or many other ways. The all-day menu is great for travelers. Candlelit dinners are likely to include duck in a honey and lemon sauce or venison with juniper and red wine.

THEATER VAULTS RESTAURANT, Sawclose at Barton St. Tel. 465074.
   Cuisine: INTERNATIONAL. **Reservations:** Not needed.
$ **Prices:** Appetizers £2–£4 ($3.70–$7.40); main courses £7.50–£10 ($13.90–$18.50); two-course dinner from £8 ($14.80). AE, DC, MC, V.
   Open: Coffee Mon–Sat 10am–12:30pm; lunch Mon–Sat 12:30–2:30pm; dinner Mon–Sat 6–11pm.
It took an imaginative entrepreneur to convert the stone vaults beneath the Theatre Royal into an engagingly decorated brasserie. Its late closing makes it a favorite of an after-theater crowd. However, daytime people can drop in to enjoy morning coffee, drinks, or lunch. Menu specialties include homemade game terrines and soups, fresh fish of the day, juicy steaks, and regional dishes prepared by the French chef.

THE WALRUS AND THE CARPENTER, 28 Barton St. Tel. 314864.
   Cuisine: ANGLO-AMERICAN/VEGETARIAN. **Reservations:** None.
$ **Prices:** Appetizers £2.30 ($4.25), burgers and main nonvegetarian courses £5.70–£6.20 ($10.55–$11.45), full vegetarian lunches £5 ($9.25). MC, V.
Named after a Lewis Carroll poem, and decorated like a whimsical and very hip version of a French bistro, this poster-plastered establishment defines itself as Bath's "bohemian hangout for everybody." Waitresses invariably wear leggings or smocks, and serve food with humor and flair usually inspired by the establishment's flamboyant manager, Jane Martinez. Specialties include steaks and burgers, and such vegetarian dishes as mushroom moussaka with pita bread and salad, spinach lasagne, and an array of salads usually considered meals in themselves. The building which contains it, incidentally, is a Georgian building of historical interest. It's in the town center, near the Theatre Royal.

EASY EXCURSIONS FROM BATH

LONGLEAT HOUSE

⭐ Between Bath and Salisbury, Longleat House, Warminster in Wiltshire (tel. 0985/844551), owned by the sixth marquess of Bath, lies 4 miles southwest of Warminster, 4½ miles southeast of Frome on the A362. The first view of this magnificent Elizabethan house, built in the early Renaissance style, is romantic enough, but the wealth of paintings and furnishings within its lofty rooms is enough to dazzle.

From the Elizabethan great hall, through the library, the state rooms, and the grand staircase, the house is filled with variety. The state dining room is full of silver and plate, and fine tapestries and paintings adorn the walls in profusion. The library represents the finest private collection in the country. The Victorian kitchens are open during the summer months, offering a glimpse of life below the stairs in a well-ordered country home. Various exhibitions are mounted in the stable yard. Events are staged frequently in the grounds, and the safari park contains a vast array of animals in open parklands, including Britain's only white tiger.

A maze, believed to be the largest in the world, was added to the attractions by Lord Weymouth, son of the marquess. It has more than 1½ miles of paths. The first part is comparatively easy, but the second part is very complicated.

Admission to Longleat House is £3.50 ($6.45) for adults, £1.50 ($2.80) for children. Admission to the safari park £4.50 ($8.35) for adults, £3.50 ($6.45) for children. Special exhibitions and rides require separate admission tickets. It's open Easter through September, daily from 10am to 6pm, and October to Easter daily from 10am to 4pm. The safari park is open mid-March to early November from 10am to 6pm (last cars are admitted at 5:30pm or sunset).

STOURHEAD

After Longleat, you can drive 6 miles down Route 3092 to Stourton, a village just off the B3092, 3 miles northwest of Mere (A303). A Palladian house, Stourhead at Stourton, near Warminster (tel. 0747/840348), was built in the 18th century by the banking family of Hoare. The magnificent gardens became known as *le jardin anglais* in that they blended art and nature. Set around an artificial lake, the grounds are decorated with temples, bridges, islands, and grottoes, as well as statuary.

Admission to the house, open from March 25 to November 3, Saturday to Wednesday from noon to 5:30pm, is £3.50 ($6.45) for adults, £1.70 ($3.15) for children. Admission to the gardens from April to October is £3.50 ($6.45) for adults, £1.70 ($3.15) for children; from November to February, £2.30 ($4.25) for adults, £1.20 ($2.20) for children. The gardens are open daily all year 8am to 7pm, or sunset if earlier.

AVEBURY

One of the largest prehistoric sites in Europe, Avebury lies on the Kennet River, 7 miles west of Marlborough. Unlike at Stonehenge, visitors can walk the 28-acre site at Avebury, winding in and out of the circle of more than 100 stones, some weighing up to 50 tons. The stones are made of sarsen, a sandstone found in Wiltshire. Inside this large circle are two smaller ones, each with about 30 stones standing upright. Native Neolithic tribes are believed to have built these circles.

Avebury is on the A361 between Swindon and Devizes and 1 mile from the A4 London/Bath Road. The closest rail station is at Swindon, some 12 miles away, which is served from the main rail line from London to Bath. Limited bus service runs from Swindon to Devizes through Avebury.

AVEBURY MUSEUM, Avebury. Tel. 06723/250.

Founded by Alexander Keiller, this museum houses one of Britain's most

important archeological collections. It began with Keiller's material from excavations at Windmill Hill and Avebury, and now includes artifacts from other prehistoric digs at West Kennet, Long Barrow, Silbury Hill, West Kennet Avenue, and the Sanctuary.
Admission: 85p ($1.55) adults, 45p (85¢) children.
Open: Good Friday–Sept daily 10am–6pm; Oct–Good Friday 10am–4pm.

THE GREAT BARN MUSEUM OF WILTSHIRE RURAL LIFE, Avebury. Tel. 06723/555.
Housed in a 17th-century thatched barn is a center for the display and interpretation of Wiltshire life during the last three centuries. There are displays on cheesemaking, blacksmithing, thatching, sheep and shepherds, the wheelwrighting and other rural crafts, as well as local geology and domestic life.
Admission: 95p ($1.75) adults, 50p (95¢) children.
Open: Mid-March to Oct daily 10am–5:30pm; Nov to mid-Mar, Sat 1–4:30pm, Sun 11am–4:30pm.

Where to Eat in Avebury

STONES RESTAURANT, High St. Tel. 514.
Cuisine: INTERNATIONAL. **Reservations:** None.
$ **Prices:** Appetizers £1.75–£2 ($3.25–$3.70); main courses £4.25–£5.50 ($7.85–$10.20); afternoon cream teas £2.80 ($5.20). No credit cards.
Open: Apr–Oct daily 10am–6pm. Hot food 12–2:30pm.
This restaurant has made an impact since its opening in 1984 by two trained archeologists, Dr. Hilary Howard and her husband, Michael Pitts. They specialize in freshly made food grown organically without artificial additives, which are prepared in original ways and sold at reasonable prices. Pastries, coffee, fruit juices, bottled beer, cold quiche, snacks, and an array of Welsh and English cheeses are available throughout the day. (Especially attractive is the midafternoon cream teas served with whole-wheat scones and clotted cream imported from Cornwall.) The owners make it a point to travel abroad every winter, bringing back the culinary inspirations they accumulated during their trips. The restaurant is adjacent to the Great Barn museum of Wiltshire folk life.

---

6. BRISTOL

13 miles W of Bath; 121 miles W of London

GETTING THERE   By Plane   The Bristol Airport (tel. 0272/027587) is conveniently situated beside the main A38 road, just over 7 miles from the city center. Flights arrive during the day from London.

By Train   Rail services to and from the area are among the fastest and most efficient in Britain. British Rail runs hourly services from London's Paddington Station to each of Bristol's two main stations: Temple Meads in the center of Bristol, or Parkway on the city's northern outskirts. Trip time is 1½ hours.

By Bus   National Express buses depart every hour during the day from London's Victoria Coach Station. Trip time is 2½ hours.

By Car   Head west from London along M4.

ESSENTIALS   The **area code** is 0272. The **Tourist Information Centre** is at 14 Narrow Quay (tel. 0272/260767).

Bristol, the largest city in the West Country, is just across the Bristol Channel from Wales and is a good center for touring western Britain. This historic inland port is linked to the sea by 7 miles of the navigable Avon River. Bristol has long been rich in seafaring traditions and has many links with the early colonization of America. In fact, some claim that the new continent was named after a Bristol town clerk, Richard

Ameryke. In 1497, John Cabot sailed from Bristol, which led to the discovery of the northern half of the New World.

WHAT TO SEE & DO

Guided walking tours are conducted in summer and last about 1½ hours. The tour departs from Neptune's Statue Saturday at 2:30pm and Thursday at 7pm. Guided tours are also conducted through Clifton, a suburb of Bristol, which has more Georgian houses than Bath.

SS *GREAT BRITAIN*, City Docks, entrance via the Maritime Heritage Centre. Tel. 0272/260680.

In Bristol, the world's first iron steamship and luxury liner has been restored to its 1840 glory. This "floating palace" weighs 3,443 tons and was created by Isambard Brunel, a Victorian engineer.

Incidentally, at the age of 25 in 1831, Brunel began a Bristol landmark, a suspension bridge over the 250-foot-deep Avon Gorge at Clifton.

Admission: £2.50 ($4.65) adults, £1.70 ($3.15) children.

Open: June–Sept daily 10am–6pm; winter daily 10am–5pm. **Bus:** No. 511 from city center.

BRISTOL CATHEDRAL, College Green. Tel. 0272/250692.

Construction on the cathedral, once an Augustinian abbey, was begun in the 12th century, and the central tower was added in 1466. The chapter house and gatehouse are good examples of late Norman architecture, and the choir is magnificent. The cathedral's interior was singled out for praise by Sir John Betjeman, the late poet laureate.

Admission: A donation of £2 ($3.70) per visitor is requested.

Open: Daily 8am–6pm.

ST. MARY REDCLIFFE, 10 Redcliffe Parade West. Tel. 0272/291487.

This church was called "the fairest, the goodliest, and most famous parish church in England" by none other than Elizabeth I. Built in the 14th century, it has been carefully restored. One of the chapels is called "The American Chapel," where the kneelers show the emblems of all the states of the U.S.A. The tomb and armor of Admiral Sir William Penn, father of the founder of Pennsylvania, are in the church. The location is 400 yards from the Temple Meads Station.

Admission: Free.

Open: Oct–May daily 8am–6pm; June–Sept daily 8am–8pm.

THEATRE ROYAL, King St. off Queen Sq. Tel. 0272/250250 (box office), or 0272/277466 (administration).

Built in 1776, this is now the oldest working playhouse in the United Kingdom. It is the home of the Bristol Old Vic. Backstage tours leave from the foyer.

Tours: Fri–Sat noon.

Admission: £1.50 ($2.80) adults; £1 ($1.85) children and students under 19.

Open: Call the box office for the current schedule.

WHERE TO STAY

DOUBLES WITHOUT BATH FOR LESS THAN £42 ($77.70)

ALANDALE HOTEL, 4 Tyndall's Park Rd., Clifton, Bristol, Avon BS8 1PG. Tel. 0272/735407. 17 rms (15 with bath). TV TEL **Bus:** No. 8 or 9.

$ Rates (including English breakfast): £28 ($51.80) single without bath, £33 ($61.05) single with bath; £38 ($70.30) double without bath, £46 ($85.10) double with bath. MC, V. **Parking:** Free.

This elegant early Victorian house retains many of its original features, including a marble fireplace and ornate plasterwork. Note the fine staircase in the imposing entrance hall. The hotel is under the supervision of Mr. Burgess, who still observes the old traditions of personal service; for example, afternoon tea is served, as are sandwiches, drinks, and snacks in the lounge (up to 11:15pm). A continental breakfast is available in your bedroom until 10am, unless you'd prefer the full English breakfast in the dining room. All bedrooms have hot-beverage facilities.

CLIFTON HOTEL, St. Paul's Rd., Clifton, Bristol, Avon BS8 1LX. Tel. 0272/736882. Fax 0272/741082. 63 rms (45 with bath or shower). TV TEL **Bus:** No. 8 or 9.
$ **Rates:** £24 ($44.40) single without bath, £42 ($77.70) single with bath; £36 ($66.60) double without bath, £60 ($111) double with bath. AE, DC, MC, V. **Parking:** Free.
On a peaceful street near the University of Bristol, the Clifton has been improved greatly. Rooms contain hot-beverage facilities. The hotel has a wine bar converted from the old cellars and a fully licensed restaurant with an excellent chef.

DOWNLANDS GUEST HOUSE, 33 Henleaze Gardens, Henleaze, Bristol, Avon BS9 4HH. Tel. 0272/621639. 10 rms (2 with bath or shower). TV **Bus:** No. 1.
$ **Rates** (including English breakfast): £19–£20 ($35.15–$37) single without bath; £34 ($62.90) double without bath, £36 ($66.60) double with bath. No credit cards.
This is a well-appointed Victorian home lying on a tree-lined road on the periphery of the Durdham Downs. About 2 miles from the center of Bristol, it lies on a bus route in a residential suburb. The Newman family receives guests all year, and will provide a 6pm meal if arranged in advance.

OAKFIELD HOTEL, Oakfield Rd., Clifton, Bristol, Avon BS8 2BG. Tel. 0272/735556. 27 rms (none with bath). TV **Bus:** No. 8 or 9.
$ **Rates** (including English breakfast): £24–£26 ($44.40–$48.10) single; £34–£36 ($62.90–$66.60) double. No credit cards. **Parking:** Free.
Instead of finding lodgings in the center of Bristol, many visitors prefer to seek out accommodations in the leafy Georgian suburb of Clifton, near the famous suspension bridge. This impressive guesthouse with an Italian facade would be called a town house in New York. It's on a quiet street, and everything is kept spick-and-span under the watchful eye of Mrs. D. L. Hurley. Each bedroom has hot and cold running water and central heating. For another £6.50 ($12.05), you can enjoy a good dinner.

ORCHARD HOUSE, Bristol Rd., Chew Stoke, Avon BS18 8UB. Tel. 0272/333143. 5 rms (3 with shower). **Directions:** From Bristol, take the A38 south for 4 miles to B3130 at Barrow Gurney. Turn left and continue for 2½ miles. At crossroads ½ mile before Chew Magna, turn right and go into Chew Stoke. Orchard House is on the main street nearly opposite the post office.
$ **Rates** (including English breakfast): £14.50–£16 ($26.85–$29.60) single without bath; £29 ($53.65) double without bath, £32 ($59.20) double with shower. No credit cards. **Parking:** Free.
This 200-year-old Georgian house with stucco-covered stonework is about 8 miles south of Bristol and is run by Ann and Derek Hollomon, who offer comfortable and immaculately clean bedrooms. Evening meals with the family cost from £6 to £8 ($11.10 to $14.80) per person, but notice must be given in advance. Local produce is used, and house wines are served. Chew Stoke is a good center for touring the area, and there is a nearby lake for trout fishing.

WASHINGTON HOTEL, 11-15 St. Paul's Rd., Clifton, Bristol, Avon BS8 1LX. Tel. 0272/733980. Fax 0272/741082. 46 rms (35 with bath). TV TEL **Bus:** No. 8 or 9.
$ **Rates:** £26 ($48.10) single without bath, £42 ($77.70) single with bath; £42 ($77.70) double without bath, £56 ($103.60) double with bath. AE, DC, MC, V. **Parking:** Free.
On a quiet street just north of the city center, this hotel has its own parking space. All bedrooms contain radios, hot-beverage facilities, and hairdryers, and have been refurbished to a high standard.

WORTH THE EXTRA BUCKS

GLENROY HOTEL, 30 Victoria Sq., Clifton, Bristol, Avon BS8 4EW. Tel. 0272/739058. Fax 0272/739058. 50 rms (all with bath or shower). TV TEL **Bus:** No. 8 or 99.
$ **Rates** (including English breakfast): £40 ($74) single; £52–£60 ($96.20–$111) double. MC, V.

⭐ Across from a park in a Regency neighborhood, you'll find one of the finest moderately priced hotels in Clifton. The Glenroy, built of honey-colored limestone, with lawns and flowering shrubs, has a big bow-windowed breakfast room, along with an adjacent bar lounge. You can still see many of the elaborate ceiling and cove moldings from the house's original construction. Each accommodation has a radio and coffee-making equipment. In Clifton, the hotel is within walking distance of the suspension bridge. Jean and Mike Winyard are the owners. The hotel has a Carvery Restaurant and a bar.

WHERE TO EAT

MEALS FOR LESS THAN £11.95 ($22.10)

CHERRIES VEGETARIAN BISTRO, 12 St. Michael's Hill. Tel. 293675.
Cuisine: VEGETARIAN. **Reservations:** Recommended. **Bus:** No. 508 or 509.
$ **Prices:** Appetizers £2.65 ($4.90); main courses £7.45 ($13.80); three-course menu Mon–Thurs £11.95 ($22.10). MC, V.
Open: Dinner Mon–Sat 7–11:30pm.

⭐ Cherries is an informal bistro that serves the finest vegetarian dishes in town; look for the blackboard specials. The tasty, flavorsome dishes are made with fresh, wholesome ingredients. Vegetables are concocted into a different soup every day, followed by crêpes stuffed with vegetables, then a wide range of succulent desserts, including perhaps a chocolate mousse. Drinks include herbal teas, domestic and imported beers, and some excellent reasonably priced wines, including those made with organically grown grapes.

51 PARK STREET RESTAURANT, 51 Park St. Tel. 214616.
Cuisine: INTERNATIONAL. **Reservations:** Recommended for dinner, not needed at lunch. **Bus:** No. 1, 2, 3, 8, 9, 40, 41, or 54.
$ **Prices:** Appetizers £2–£3 ($3.70–$5.55); main courses £5–£8.25 ($9.25–$15.25). AE, DC, MC, V.
Open: daily noon–11pm.

⭐ Breezy, stylish, and sophisticated, this simply decorated restaurant was established by Texas-born Terry Timmons within a Georgian-era building on the main shopping street of town. Most remember it for its enormous (8 by 12 ft.) plate-glass window overlooking the sidewalk. The variety of food is such that you can have a snack or a three-course meal, depending on your needs, at any time. A full bar serves margaritas and American martinis, while diners enjoy such broadly international dishes as salads niçoise, an American club sandwich, or poached salmon on a bed of spinach with vermouth sauce.

FLIPPER, 6 St. James Barton. Tel. 290262.
Cuisine: FISH & CHIPS. **Reservations:** None. **Bus:** No. 20, 22, or 75.
$ **Prices:** £2.50–£3 ($4.65–$5.55) per portion of fish-and-chips, 60p ($1.10) extra for salad. No credit cards.
Open: Daily 7:30am–6:30pm.

Ⓢ Set a short distance from the bus station, in the center of the city's biggest cluster of stores, Flipper is said to serve the best fish 'n' chips in Bristol. Good tasting codfish (and slightly more expensive plaice or halibut) is served from a fast food countertop on the street level. An upstairs wood-paneled dining room offers waitress service.

CHAPTER 15

THE COTSWOLDS

- **WHAT'S SPECIAL ABOUT THE COTSWOLDS**
1. **TETBURY**
2. **CIRENCESTER & PAINSWICK**
3. **CHELTENHAM**
4. **BIBURY**
5. **BURFORD**
6. **BOURTON-ON-THE-WATER**
7. **STOW-ON-THE-WOLD**
8. **MORETON-IN-MARSH**
9. **BROADWAY**
10. **CHIPPING CAMPDEN**

The Cotswolds, a stretch of limestone hills sometimes covered by grass, often barren plateaus known as wolds, is a pastoral land dotted by ancient villages and deep wooded ravines. This bucolic scene in the middle of southwest England, about a 2-hour drive from London, is found mainly in Gloucestershire, with portions in Oxfordshire, Wiltshire, and Worcestershire. The wolds or plateaus led to this area's being given the name Cotswold, Old English for "God's high open land."

Cotswold lambs used to produce so much wool that they made their owners very rich—wealth they invested in some of the finest domestic architecture in Europe, made out of honey-brown Cotswold stone. The wool-rich gentry didn't neglect their church contributions either. Often the simplest of villages will have a church that in style and architectural detail seems far beyond the means of the hamlet.

If possible, explore the area by car. That way, you can survey the land of winding goat paths, rolling hills, and sleepy hamlets, with names such as Stow-on-the-Wold, Wotton-under-Edge, Moreton-in-Marsh, Old Sodbury, Chipping Campden, Shipton-under-Wychwood, Upper and Lower Swell, and Upper and Lower Slaughter, often called "the Slaughters."

SEEING THE COTSWOLDS

GETTING THERE

Motorists take the M4 from London to Gloucestershire for a tour of the Cotswolds. At Exit 20, take M5 north to enter the area, perhaps beginning in or around Cheltenham. You can also take Exit 15 along the M4, then A361 to enter the Cotswolds. British Rail serves the western part of the region from London's Paddington Station. For example, it takes only 1 hour and 50 minutes to reach Moreton-in-Marsh from London. However, the train does not connect with the most beautiful and charming villages. Once you arrive at a station, you'll have to take a connecting bus to reach a particular village. National Express coaches from London's Victoria Coach Station service the major cities of the region, such as Cheltenham. Trip time is 2 hours and 40 minutes. Once at one of the major centers you'll have to rely on local bus services with somewhat erratic schedules to explore some of the more remote villages.

A SUGGESTED ITINERARY

Day 1: From London, visit Cheltenham for an overnight, strolling its Promenade and tasting its spa waters.

☑ WHAT'S SPECIAL ABOUT THE COTSWOLDS

Great Towns/Villages

☐ Broadway, called "the show village of England," with 16th-century stone houses and cottages.

☐ Painswick, considered by some the prettiest village in England, with a 15th-century parish church.

☐ Bibury, vying with Painswick for the title of England's prettiest village. Noted for its 15th-century Arlington Row of cottages.

☐ Stow-on-the-Wold, attractive Cotswold wool town with large market place and fine old houses.

Museums

☐ Corinium Museum, Cirencester, one of the finest collections of Roman antiquities in Britain.

Cool for Kids

☐ Birdland, Bourton-on-the-Water, a garden set on 8½ acres with some 1,200 birds of 361 different species.

Architectural Highlights

☐ The High Street of Broadway, representing some of the finest domestic architecture in Britain.

☐ The High Street of Chipping Campden—the historian G. M. Trevelyan called it "the most beautiful village street now left in the land."

Spa Retreats

☐ Cheltenham, one of England's most fashionable spas, with Regency architecture of ironwork, balconies, and verandas.

Day 2: Detour south from Cheltenham to Painswick for a morning visit and a luncheon stopover, followed by an overnight in Cirencester after a walk to the Corinium Museum.

Day 3: From Cirencester, head west for Bibury—perhaps a luncheon stopover—followed by an overnight stop in Burford.

Day 4: From Burford, visit Bourton-on-the-Water in the northwest, then continue northeast to Stow-on-the-Wold for an overnight stop.

Day 5: From Stow-on-the-Wold head north to Moreton-in-Marsh for a luncheon stopover, followed by a walk along the High Street in Chipping Campden, with an overnight in Broadway.

1. TETBURY

113 miles W of London; 27 miles NE of Bristol

GETTING THERE By Train   There is no direct service from London. Frequent daily trains run from London's Paddington Station to Kemble, 7 miles east of Tetbury. There is adequate bus service between Kemble and Tetbury.

By Bus   National Express buses leave from London's Victoria Coach Station with direct service to Cirencester, 10 miles northeast of Tetbury. From Cirencester, several buses a day run to Tetbury.

By Car   From London, take the M40 northwest to Oxford, continuing along A40 to the junction with A429. Cut south to Cirencester where you connect with the A433 southwest into Tetbury.

ESSENTIALS   The **area code** is 0666. The **Tourist Information Centre** is The Old Court House, 63 Long Street (tel. 0666/53552). It is open June to September only.

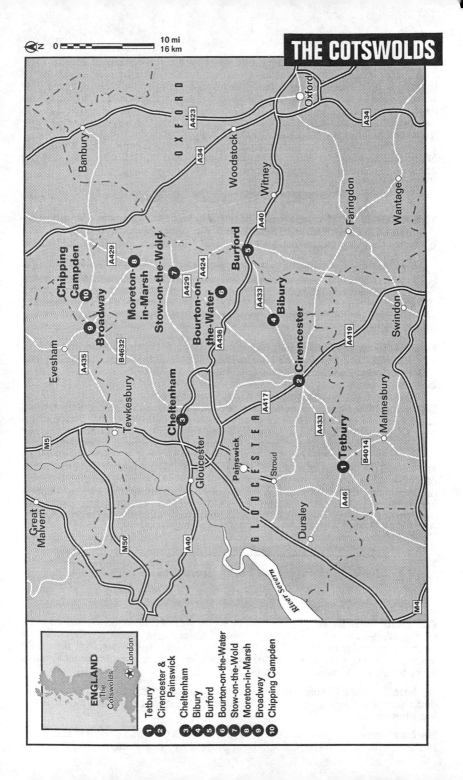

THE COTSWOLDS

0 |====| 10 mi
16 km

Oxford

A423

Banbury

A34

OXFORD

Woodstock

Witney

A34

A40

Faringdon

Wantage

A34

Chipping Campden ⑩

A429

Moreton-in-Marsh ⑧

Stow-on-the-Wold ⑦

Burford ⑤

A424

A429

Broadway ⑨

Evesham

A435

B4632

Bourton-on-the-Water ⑥

A433

Bibury ④

A436

Swindon

Tewkesbury

Cheltenham ③

A419

A419

Gloucester

Painswick

A417

Cirencester ②

A433

Malmesbury

GLOUCESTER

Stroud

A433

Tetbury ①

B4014

Great Malvern

M5

M50

A40

Dursley

A46

M4

River Severn

ENGLAND
The Cotswolds

★ London

① Tetbury
② Cirencester & Painswick
③ Cheltenham
④ Bibury
⑤ Burford
⑥ Bourton-on-the-Water
⑦ Stow-on-the-Wold
⑧ Moreton-in-Marsh
⑨ Broadway
⑩ Chipping Campden

In the rolling Cotswolds, Tetbury was never in the mainstream of tourism like Oxford or Stratford-upon-Avon; however, ever since an attractive man and his lovely bride took up residence in the Macmillan place, a Georgian building on nearly 350 acres, it is now drawing crowds from all over the world. Charles and Diana may one day be king and queen of England. Their nine-bedroom mansion, Highgrove, lies just outside the town on the way to Westonbirt Arboretum. The house cannot be seen from the road, but you might see Princess Di shopping in the village.

The town has a 17th-century market hall and a lot of antique shops, along with boutiques. Its inns, even before the royal couple moved in, were not cheap, and the prices certainly have not dropped since that time.

WHERE TO STAY & EAT

THE CROWN INN, Gumstool Hill off Market Pl., Tetbury, Gloucestershire GL8 8DG. Tel. 0666/502469. 4 rms (none with bath). TV

$ Rates (including English breakfast): £19 ($35.15) single; £32 ($59.20) double. AE, DC, MC, V.

One of the best bargains in this expensive Cotswold town is a stone structure with three gables. A downstairs pub serves wines and good beer and ale, which can be enjoyed in a garden in fair weather. Bar snacks are available, and you can also order full dinners costing from £9 ($16.65). Rooms are small but comfortable, often with beamed ceilings. Units contain hot and cold running water, and there is central heating.

THE HARE & HOUNDS HOTEL, Westonbirt, Tetbury, Gloucestershire, GL8 8QL. Tel. 0666/88233. Fax 0666/88241. 29 rms (all with bath). TV TEL
Directions: 2½ miles southwest of Tetbury on A433.

$ Rates (including English breakfast): £53–£61 ($98.05–$112.85) single; £74–£82 ($136.90–$151.70) double. AE, MC, V. **Parking:** Free.

One of the more substantial buildings in the area, this has stone-mullioned windows and gables and is set on 10 acres of private grounds with two hard-surface tennis courts. Originally a farmhouse in the 19th century, the Hare & Hounds was turned into a Victorian inn, and the lounge and country bars remain from those days. However, the main hotel building was added in 1928, but it was constructed so faithfully in the original stone that it looks much older. This traditional country hotel, often favored as a conference place, is run by the Price brothers. They do a good job of entertaining their guests, and make the place a worthy splurge choice. Under a hammerbeam ceiling, the restaurant serves a combination of British and continental dishes, with seasonal specialties. A four-course fixed-price dinner goes for £16.50 ($30.55) with lunches costing from £10.50 ($19.45).

---

2. CIRENCESTER & PAINSWICK

89 miles W of London; 16 miles S of Cheltenham;
17 miles SE of Gloucester; 36 miles W of Oxford

GETTING THERE   By Train   Because Cirencester has no railway station of its own, passengers usually descend at Kemble, 4 miles to the southwest. Trains depart several times a day from London's Paddington Station, to Kemble. Trip time is 80 minutes. Passengers are sometimes asked to transfer trains at Swindon. From Kemble, a bus travels to Cirencester four to five times a day.

By Bus   National Express buses leave from London's Victoria Coach station with direct service to Cirencester. From Cirencester, you can visit Painswick by one of the local bus services.

By Car   From London, take the M40 northwest to Oxford, continuing along A40 to the junction with A429. Cut south on the A429 to Cirencester.

Don't worry about how to pronounce the name of the town. Even the English are in disagreement. Just say "*siren*-cess-ter" and you won't be too far off.

Cirencester is often considered the unofficial capital of the Cotswolds, probably a throwback to its reputation in the Middle Ages, when it flourished as the center of the great Cotswold wool industry. In Roman Britain, five roads converged on Cirencester, which was called Corinium in those days. In size, it ranked second only to London. Today it is chiefly a market town, and a good base for touring.

WHAT TO SEE & DO

CORINIUM MUSEUM, Park St. Tel. 0285/655611.

The museum houses one of the finest collections of archeological remains from the Roman occupation, all found locally in and around Cirencester. Mosaic pavements found here on Dyer Street in 1849 and other mosaics are the most important exhibits. Provincial Roman sculpture, such as figures of Minerva and Mercury, pottery, and artifacts salvaged from long-decayed buildings provide a link with the remote civilization that once flourished here. The museum has been completely modernized to include full-scale reconstructions and special exhibitions on local history and conservation. It is located in the center near Thomas Street and Coxwell Street.

Admission: £1 ($1.85) adults, 50p (95¢) children.
Open: Mon–Sat 10am–5:30pm, Sun 2–5:30pm.

CIRENCESTER PARISH CHURCH, Market Place. Tel. 0285/653142.

Dating back to Norman times and Henry I is the Church of John the Baptist, overlooking Market Place. (Actually, a church may have stood on this spot in Saxon times.) In size, the Cirencester church appears to be a cathedral—not a mere parish church. The present building represents a variety of styles, largely Perpendicular, as in the early 15th-century tower. Among the treasures inside are a 15th-century pulpit and a silver-gilt cup given to Queen Anne Boleyn 2 years before her execution.

Admission: Free. Donations invited.
Open: Mon–Fri 9:30am–5pm; Sun 12:30–6pm.

WHERE TO STAY

DOUBLES WITHOUT BATH FOR LESS THAN £40 ($74)

RAYDON HOUSE HOTEL, 3 The Avenue, Cirencester, Gloucestershire GH7 1EH. Tel. 0285/653482. 15 rms (7 with bath or shower). TV TEL
Directions: From Market Place, drive along Cricklade St. and Watermoor Rd., turning left on The Avenue.
$ Rates (including English breakfast): £25 ($46.25) single without bath, £35 ($64.75) single with bath, £40 ($74) double without bath, £55 ($101.75) double with bath. AE, MC, V. **Parking:** Free.

This Victorian mansion is only 5 minutes from the town center in a peaceful residential area next to a garden complex. All units have hot-beverage facilities. The hotel has an excellent restaurant and bar. Parking space is available.

WARWICK COTTAGE GUEST HOUSE, 75 Victoria Rd., Cirencester, Gloucestershire GL7 1ES. Tel. 0285/656279. 4 rms (all with shower). TV
$ Rates (including English breakfast): £13.50–£16 ($25–$29.60) per person. No credit cards. **Parking:** Free.

This attractive Victorian town house with full central heating is owned and run by Pat and Dave Gutsell, and is within easy walking distance of the town center and Cirencester Parish Church. Bedrooms have hot and cold running water, radios, and hot-beverage facilities. Evening meals are available and range from £6.50 to £8 ($12.05 to $14.80). Pat and Dave can also provide services such as baby-sitting, hairdressing, and transportation to and from bus and rail stations. Car parking is available at the rear of the house.

WIMBORNE HOUSE, 91 Victoria Rd., Cirencester, Gloucestershire GL7 1ES. Tel. 0285/653890. 5 rms (all with bath). TV
$ Rates (including English breakfast): £20–£25 ($37–$46.25) single; £25–£32 ($46.25–$59.20) double. No credit cards. **Parking:** Free.

This Cotswold stone house built in the Victorian era (1886) is a 5-minute walk from the town center and Market Place, which is dominated by the parish church. Cirencester Park, with 3,000 acres of beautifully wooded parkland, the abbey grounds, and the Corinium Museum are nearby. A welcoming atmosphere is provided by the owners, Dianne and Marshall Clarke. All the centrally heated bedrooms have hot-beverage facilities and clock radio-alarms. An evening meal will cost £8 ($14.80).

WORTH THE EXTRA BUCKS

LA RONDE HOTEL, 52-54 Ashcroft Rd. off Cricklade St., Cirencester, Gloucestershire GL7 1QX. Tel. 0285/654611. 10 rms (all with bath or shower). TV
$ Rates (including English breakfast): £20–£39.50 ($37–$73.10) single; £45 ($83.25) double; £50 ($92.50) family room. MC, V. **Parking:** Free.
The Shales family runs this licensed small hotel, which stands in the town center within walking distance of Cirencester Park, the abbey grounds, Corinium Museum, and the parish church. The accommodations are centrally heated, with hot-beverage facilities. There is a cozy bar and an intimate restaurant with an open fire, where you can choose from a varied menu and a good wine list. Dinners cost from £10 ($18.50) per person. Bar lunches are available on request. La Ronde serves as a touring base for the Cotswolds, and the Shales family can provide a printed leaflet detailing 14 different tours of the surrounding area.

WHERE TO EAT

MEALS FOR LESS THAN £8 ($14.80)

COTTAGE OF CONTENT, 117 Cricklade St. Tel. 652071.
Cuisine: ENGLISH. **Reservations:** Recommended.
$ Prices: Appetizers 75p–£2.80 ($1.40–$5.20) main courses £4.50–£11 ($8.35–$20.35). No credit cards.
Open: Dinner Tues–Fri 7:30–9:30pm, Sat 7:30–10:30pm. **Closed:** Bank holidays.
This delightful little restaurant is owned and run by Mr. and Mrs. Pugh, who cook, serve, and even do the washing up. Serving only in the evening, they have a variety of succulent T-bone steaks, all served with fresh vegetables, salads in season, and a dessert. It's located in the center near Cirencester Parish Church.

SHEPHERD'S BISTRO AND WINE BAR, Fleece Hotel, Market Place. Tel. 658507.
Cuisine: ENGLISH. **Reservations:** Not needed.
$ Prices: Appetizers £1.50–£2.50 ($2.80–$4.65); main courses £2.50–£7 ($4.65–$12.95); afternoon cream teas £2.25 ($4.15); glass of house wine from £1.35 ($2.50). AE, DC, MC, V.
Open: Lunch daily noon–2:30pm; dinner daily 7–10pm, snacks and drinks daily 11am–11pm.

This unpretentious bistro in the town center is the less expensive of two restaurants which are each contained within a hotel whose half-timbered facade hints at its origins as an Elizabethan coaching inn. Inside, a pair of open fireplaces warm a beamed interior which lies across a courtyard from the hotel. Local residents shuffle through a layer of sawdust to order reliable but frequently changing daily specials. Any of these might be concluded with a portion of English cheese. Wine is sold by the glass or the bottle.

SLUG AND LETTUCE, 17 West Market Place. Tel. 653206.
   Cuisine: ENGLISH. **Reservations:** Not needed.
$ **Prices:** Appetizers £2.75–£3.65 ($5.10–$6.75); main courses £3.70–£5.60 ($6.85–$10.35). MC, V.
   Open: Pub Mon–Sat 11:30am–11pm, Sun noon–3pm and 7–10:30pm. Meals Mon–Sat noon–10pm, Sun noon–3pm and 7–10pm.

This is the best-loved and most popular pub in town, with a flower- and vine-ringed beer garden in back which adds to the ambience. A coaching inn since the 14th century, it stands opposite the parish church. Many of its original architectural features have been preserved. The setting is one of log fires, country chairs, cushioned pews, and plain stonework. The Crown serves pub food that is far better than the usual. Daily specials are written on a blackboard and might include homemade eggplant casserole, grilled sausages, and black pudding with scrambled eggs.

PAINSWICK

4 miles NE of Stroud; 107 miles W of London; 10 miles S of Cheltenham

GETTING THERE By Train The nearest railway station is at Stroud, 3 miles away. Trains depart from London's Paddington Station several times a day, sometimes requiring a change of train at Swindon. Trip time is 90 to 120 minutes depending on the train. From Stroud, buses run to Painswick, once every hour. There are also many taxis waiting at the Stroud railway station.

By Bus Buses depart from Bath in the directions of Cheltenham twice a day, stopping in Painswick along the way. The train is more convenient.

By Car From Cirencester (see above), continue west along A419 to Stroud, then head north along B4073.

ESSENTIALS The **area code** is 0452. The **Tourist Information Centre** is at the Painswick Library, Stroud Road (tel. 0452/813552).

The sleepy little town of Painswick is considered a model village. All its houses, although erected at different periods, blend harmoniously because the former villagers used only Cotswold stone as their building material. The one distinctive feature on the Painswick skyline is the spire of its 15th-century parish church. It's also known for its annual **Clipping Feast** (when the congregation joins hands and circles around the church as if it were a maypole, singing hymns as they do). Ancient tombstones dot the churchyard.

WHERE TO STAY

FALCON HOTEL, New St., Painswick, Gloucestershire GL6 6YB. Tel. 0452/812189. 12 rms (all with bath or shower). TV TEL
$ **Rates** (including English breakfast): £32 ($59.20) single; £45 ($83.25) double. AE, MC, V. **Parking:** 50p (95¢).

Across from the village churchyard, this limestone Georgian-era building was originally built in 1554, and was later renovated in 1711. The hotel is now owned by the Kimber family. Guests enjoy use of a cocktail lounge (very English with flowery wallpaper), and twin limestone fireplaces illuminate the dining room. Even if you're not staying at the hotel, you may want to consider a meal here at a cost of £12 ($22.20). Dishes include tournedos Rossini, roast lamb with mint sauce, and cuts from the Kimbers' own Aberdeen Angus beef. Meals are served daily from noon to 2pm and 7:15 to 10pm. The dining room is closed on Sunday night.

WHERE TO EAT

PAINSWICK HOTEL, Kemps Lane. Tel. 812160.
  Cuisine: ENGLISH/FRENCH. **Reservations:** Recommended.
$ **Prices:** Set two-course lunch £7 ($12.95), set four-course dinner £21 ($22.20). Special set Sunday lunch £14.50 ($26.85). AE, MC, V.
  Open: Lunch Mon–Sat noon–2pm; dinner Mon–Sat 7:30–9:30pm.

⭐ The hotel that contains this restaurant is the most prestigious place to stay in this most delightful of English villages. Although its accommodations are over our budget for this guidebook, it nevertheless offers one of the finest and most reasonably priced lunches (and some of the most elegant dinners) in the area. Lunches are served one flight above street level, within the establishment's antique pub. The more formal evening meals are served within the street-level oak-paneled dining room. Typical menu items might include terrine of chicken and lobster served with a French bean and tomato salad, poached filets of lemon sole with a spinach mousse glazed under a white wine sabayon, and a pastry tartlet of veal kidneys served on a bed of spinach with a grain mustard sauce. The hotel sits immediately behind the village church.

3. CHELTENHAM

99 miles NW of London; 9 miles E of Gloucester; 43 miles W of Oxford

GETTING THERE By Train Twenty-one trains from London's Paddington Station arrive every hour taking 2 hours and 15 minutes and often involving a change of trains at either Bristol or Swindon. Trains between Cheltenham and Bristol take only an hour, with continuing service to Bath.

By Bus National Express offers nine buses daily from London's Victoria Coach Station to Cheltenham. Trip time is 2 hours and 35 minutes.

By Car From London, head northwest along M40 to Oxford, continuing along A40 to Cheltenham.

ESSENTIALS The **area code** is 0242. The **Tourist Information Centre** is at 77 Promenade (tel. 0242/522878).

SPECIAL EVENTS The **International Festival of Music** and the **Festival of Literature** take place each year in July and October, respectively, and attract internationally acclaimed performers and orchestras.

In a sheltered area between the Cotswolds and the Severn Vale, a mineral spring was discovered by chance. Legend has it that the Cheltenham villagers noticed pigeons drinking from a spring and observed how healthy they were—which is why the pigeon has been incorporated into the town's crest.
    Always seeking a new spa, George III arrived in 1788 and launched the town. The Duke of Wellington came to ease his liver disorder. Even Lord Byron came this way, proposing marriage to Miss Millbanke.
    Cheltenham is one of England's most fashionable spas. It is also the winner of a contest, "Beautiful Britain in Bloom," and many visitors come here just to see its gardens from spring to autumn.

The architecture is mainly Regency, with lots of ironwork, balconies, and verandas. Attractive parks and open spaces of greenery make the town especially inviting. The main street, the Promenade, has been called "the most beautiful thoroughfare in Britain." Rather similar are such thoroughfares as Lansdowne Place and Montpelier Parade. The design for the dome of the Rotunda was based on the Pantheon in Rome. Montpelier Walk, with its shops separated by caryatids, is one of the most interesting shopping centers in England.

WHAT TO SEE & DO

Escorted coach tours of the Cotswolds take place every Tuesday, Thursday, and Sunday from June through December; for details, call the information center listed above.

PITTVILLE PUMP ROOM, W. Approach Dr., Pittville Park. Tel. 0242/ 512470.

Cheltenham Waters are the only natural, consumable alkaline waters in Great Britain, and are still taken from one of the spa's finest Regency buildings. Every Sunday from the end of May until the end of September, the Pittville Pump Room is open for a host of activities, including Sunday brunch, afternoon cream teas, live classical music, landau carriage rides around the city, and brass bands playing in Pittville Park—it's real traditional England. The Gallery of Fashion is also situated in the pump room, and depicts the social history of Cheltenham Spa. Memorabilia include photographs and prints of when the U.S. Army was stationed at Pittville in the 1940s. To reach the pump room from the center, take Portland Street and Evesham Road.

Admission: Pump room free; gallery 55p ($1).

Open: Pump room year-round Tues–Sat 10:30am–5pm; gallery Apr–Oct Tues–Sun 10:30am–5pm.

CHELTENHAM ART GALLERY & MUSEUM, Clarence St. Tel. 0242/ 237431.

The gallery houses one of the foremost collections of the arts and crafts movement, notably the fine furniture of William Morris and his followers. One section is devoted to Edward Wilson, Cheltenham's native son who died with Captain Scott on the Antarctic Expedition of 1913. The gallery is near Royal Crescent and Coach Station.

Admission: Free.

Open: Mon–Sat 10am–5:20pm; Apr–Sept Sun 2–5:20pm.

EVERYMAN THEATRE, Regent St. Tel. 0242/572573.

Cheltenham is the cultural center of the Cotswolds, and this restored theater is the only professional repertory theater in Gloucestershire. It offers a mixed program of musicals, dramas, comedies, and classics. It's located in the center near the Imperial Gardens.

Prices: Depends on the event, but tickets generally £5–£14 ($9.25–$25.90). Pick up a free copy of the monthly *What's On* from the tourist office (see above).

Open: Box office Mon–Sat 10am–8pm.

WHERE TO STAY

DOUBLES WITHOUT BATH FOR LESS THAN £38 ($70.30)

BEAUMONT HOUSE HOTEL, 56 Shurdington Rd., Cheltenham, Gloucestershire GL53 OJE. Tel. 0242/245986. 18 rms (17 with bath or shower). TV TEL **Transportation:** "Metro" bus.

$ Rates (including English breakfast): £16 ($29.60) single without bath, £30 ($55.50) single with bath; £38 ($70.30) double without bath, £46 ($85.10) double with bath. AE, MC, V. **Parking:** Free.

This detached Victorian-era building with gardens offers a tranquil environment, only minutes from the town center. The house has been tastefully converted to receive paying guests, and the amenities include beverage-making equipment. Good British and French fare is also served in the dining room, where you may want to reserve for dinner.

CENTRAL HOTEL, 7-9 Portland St., Cheltenham, Gloucestershire GL52 4NZ. Tel. 0242/582172. 17 rms (8 with bath or shower). TV

$ Rates (including English breakfast): £21 ($38.85) single without bath, £29 ($53.65) single with bath; £38 ($70.30) double without bath, £45 ($83.25) double with bath. AE, DC, MC, V. **Parking:** Free.

Centrally situated just off the inner ring road on the way to the racecourse and near Cheltenham's range of attractions and theaters, this is a family-run hotel, in a preserved Regency building. Fully licensed, the hotel serves lunches and evening meals daily. A car park is available.

LAWN HOTEL, 5 Pittville Lawn, Cheltenham, Gloucestershire GL52 2BE. Tel. 0242/526638. 9 rms (none with bath). TV

$ Rates (including English or health-conscious breakfast): £17.50 ($32.40) single; £35 ($64.75) double. No credit cards. **Parking:** Free.

 Built 175 years ago with a brick exterior long ago sheathed with a protective layer of stucco, this Regency-era house lies within the iron gates leading to the Pittville Gardens and Pump Room. The house is one of about 300 town houses constructed at about the same time, and one of the few within the neighborhood that are still maintained as single units. Owned by the Armitage family, it offers simply decorated rooms with tea-making facilities and hot and cold running water. Evening meals can be arranged beginning at around £6.50 ($12.05) each, as well as afternoon teas. The hotel is at the northern edge of town, midway between the town's racetrack and its historic core, a 5-minute walk from either.

NORTH HALL HOTEL, Pittville Circus Rd. off All Saints Rd., Cheltenham, Gloucestershire GL52 2PZ. Tel. 0242/520589. Fax 0242/261953. 20 rms (12 with bath). TV TEL

$ Rates: £19.75 ($36.55) single without bath, £29.75 ($55.05) single with bath; £33 ($61.05) double without bath, £46 ($85.10) double with bath. Discounts available for children. MC, V.

Parking: Free.

This substantial and attractive house lies close to the town center as well as the racecourse and Pittville Park. The house is nicely appointed and has full central heating. The well-furnished and comfortable rooms have beverage-making facilities, hot and cold running water, and razor plugs. There's a lounge and a dining room that serves good but simple English-style food, such as roast chicken with savory stuffing or roast beef with horseradish sauce; a complete meal costs from £10.50 ($19.45).

WHERE TO EAT

MEALS FOR LESS THAN £12 ($22.20)

BELOW STAIRS RESTAURANT, 103 Promenade. Tel. 234599.
Cuisine: CONTINENTAL. **Reservations:** Not needed.
$ Prices: Appetizers £1.50–£4.50 ($2.80–$8.35); main courses £6.25–£15.25 ($11.55–$28.10). DC, MC, V.
Open: Lunch Mon–Sat noon–3pm; dinner Thurs–Sat 6pm–midnight.

In the heart of the spa, this restaurant is indeed below street level; you enter from the Promenade through a basement doorway. But this is no dank, Dickensian cellar: It's one of the best and most rewarding places for food and drink in Cheltenham. The menu caters to local and foreign tastes alike. You may choose, for example, a bowl of mussels marinara or a fresh crab crêpe with a mixed salad. Fish comes up from Cornwall three times a week, and oysters and mussels arrive from Cherbourg (France) every Wednesday. Meat is obtained from a beef specialist in Scotland, and fresh vegetables are delivered daily. Game is a seasonal feature.

THE RETREAT, 10-11 Suffolk Parade. Tel. 235436.
   Cuisine: INTERNATIONAL/VEGETARIAN. **Reservations:** Recommended.
$ **Prices:** Appetizers £1.95–£3 ($3.60–$5.55); main courses £2.70–£9 ($
   $16.65); glass of house wine from £1.10 ($2.05). AE, DC, MC, V.
   Open: Wine bar Mon–Sat noon–11pm; hot food Mon–Sat noon–2:30pm.

 Contained within a red-brick building at least a century old, this is probably the most popular pub/wine bar in town. Its most distinctive feature is its plant-filled courtyard, which is filled with chattering diners during fine weather. Only lunch is served—the rest of the day the place is devoted to drinking. Place your order at a specially designated food counter, whereupon at least part of it will be carried to your table by a waitress. Meals are likely to include an array of fresh salads, with health-conscious ingredients blended into a medley of imaginative combinations. A typical daily special might include spinach-with-cream-cheese strudel covered with a fresh tomato and basil sauce, served with a choice of two different salads. Wines, from throughout Europe, are sold by the bottle or glass. The Retreat is a 5-minute walk south of the village center.

4. BIBURY

86 miles W of London; 30 miles W of Oxford; 26 miles E of Gloucester

GETTING THERE   By Train   About five trains per day depart from London's Paddington Station for Kemble. Trip time is 1 hour and 10 minutes. Some of these will require a rapid change of train in Swindon (just across the tracks to another waiting train). From Kemble, 13 miles south of Bibury, there are no buses, but most hoteliers will arrange for a car to meet guests if you make arrangements in advance.

By Bus   From London's Victoria Coach Station, you can take one of the five daily buses which depart for Cirencester, 7 miles from Bibury. There are no buses into Bibury but local hotels will send a car and there are many taxis.

By Car   Take the M4 from London, getting off at Exit 15 toward Cirencester. Then, take the A33 (which on some maps is still designated as the B4425) to Bibury.

ESSENTIALS   The **area code** is 028574. The nearest tourist information office is in Cheltenham (see above).

On the road from Burford to Cirencester, Bibury is one of the loveliest spots in the Cotswolds. In fact, the utopian romancer of Victoria's day, poet William Morris, called it England's most beautiful village. On the banks of the tiny Coln River, Bibury is noted for **Arlington Row,** a gabled group of 15th-century cottages, its biggest and most-photographed attraction, which is protected by the National Trust.

   Dating from the 17th century, the **Arlington Mill Museum** (tel. 028574/268) was in use as a mill until 1914. Mill machinery, agricultural implements, cobbler's and blacksmith's equipment, printing and weaving devices, and Victorian costumes and wedding finery are on display. There are William Morris and John Keble rooms, and you can see arts-and-crafts exhibits, including furniture. There is pottery for sale. The museum is on the Cirencester to Burford Road (A433).

   Admission is £2 ($3.70) for adults, £1.25 ($2.30) for children. The museum is open mid-March to October daily from 10:30am to 7pm (or dusk); from November through February Saturday and Sunday from 10:30am to dusk.

WHERE TO STAY

**BIBURY COURT HOTEL, Bibury, Gloucestershire GL7 5NT. Tel. 028574/
   337.** Fax 028574/660. 18 rms (all with bath). TV TEL
$ **Rates** (including English breakfast): £40–£50 ($74–$92.50) single; £60–£66
   ($111–$122.10) double. AE, DC, MC, V. **Parking:** Free.

This Jacobean manor house in the village center was built by Sir Thomas Sackville in 1633 (parts of it date from Tudor times). You enter the 8 acres of grounds through a large gateway, and the lawn extends to the Coln River. The house was privately owned until it was turned into a hotel in 1968. The structure is built of Cotswold stone, with many gables, huge chimneys, leaded-glass stone-mullioned windows, and a formal graveled entryway. Inside, there are many country-manor furnishings and antiques, as well as an open stone log-burning fireplace. Many of the rooms have four-poster beds, original oak paneling, and antiques. Meals are an event in the Coach House Restaurant where dinners are priced from £18 ($33.30). Lunchtime bar meals cost from £5 ($9.25). After tea and biscuits in the drawing room, walk across the lawn along the river where you'll find a little church.

5. BURFORD

76 miles NW of London; 20 miles W of Oxford

GETTING THERE By Train The nearest station is at Oxford (see Chapter 8). Many trains depart from London to Oxford every day and take 45 minutes. From Oxford, passengers walk a very short distance to the entrance of The Taylor Institute, from which buses, about three or four per day, make the 30-minute run to Burford.

By Bus A National Express Coach runs from London's Victoria Coach Station to Burford several times a day, with many stops along the way. Trip time is 2 hours.

By Car From Oxford, head west along A40 to Burford.

ESSENTIALS The **area code** is 099382 for 4-figure phone numbers or 0993 for 6-figure numbers. The **Tourist Information Centre** is at Sheep Street (tel. 099382/3558).

In Oxfordshire, Burford is an unspoiled medieval town built of Cotswold stone that serves as a gateway to the Cotswolds and is largely famous for its early Norman church (c. 1116) and its High Street lined with coaching inns. Oliver Cromwell passed this way, as (in a happier day) did Charles II and his mistress, Nell Gwynne. Burford was one of the last of the great wool centers, the industry bleating out its last breath as late as Victoria's day. You may want to photograph the bridge across the Windrush River where Queen Elizabeth I once stood. Burford is definitely equipped for tourists, as the antiques shops along the High will testify.

Minster Lovell is visited because of **Minster Lovell Hall** (tel. 0993/775315), which lies in ruins and dates from the 1400s. The medieval dovecote with nesting boxes survives. An early Lovell is said to have hidden in the moated manor house and subsequently starved to death after a battle in the area. The legend of the mistletoe bough originated in the village by the Windrush River. Minster Lovell is mainly built of Cotswold stone, with thatch or stone-slate roofs. It's a pity that there is a forest of TV antennas, but the place is still attractive to photographers. Admission is 95p ($1.75) for adults, 45p (85¢) for children. It's open Good Friday through September from 10am to 6pm. Minster Lovell lies 2½ miles west of Witney. To reach Minster Lovell from Burford, take the A40 to Oxford, cutting northeast along the secondary road signposted to Minster Lovell.

WHERE TO STAY & EAT

DOUBLES WITHOUT BATH FOR LESS THAN £40 ($74)

ANDREWS HOTEL, 99 High St., Burford, Oxfordshire OX8 4RJ. Tel. 099382/3151. Fax 099382/3240. 10 rms (all with bath). TV
$ Rates (including English breakfast): £28.75–£48.75 ($53.20–$90.20) single; £48.75–£68.75 ($90.20–$127.20) double. AE, DC.

This 15th-century, Cotswold stone-and-timber village residence is one of the best B&Bs in town. The units are attractive and comfortable. There is no restaurant, but the hotel has a tea garden.

THE BOLTONS, 9 Windrush Close, Burford, Oxfordshire OX8 4SL. Tel. 099382/2051. 3 rms (all with bath). TV **Directions:** From High Street, head east on Swan Lane.
$ Rates (including English breakfast): £24 ($44.40) double. No credit cards.
Parking: Free.

 Mrs. E. Barrett's guesthouse is made of Cotswold stone with a natural slate roof. From many of the windows, you can look out over gardens, green fields, hills, and sheep. The units—all doubles—are kept clean and neat. Mrs. Barrett is a warm hostess; she maintains a "home away from home" atmosphere. Send an International Reply Coupon when requesting reservations.

THE BULL, 105 High St., Burford, Oxfordshire OX8 4RH. Tel. 099382/2220. 14 rms (10 with bath). TV TEL
$ Rates (including English breakfast): £27.50 ($50.90) single without bath; £40 ($74) double without bath, £45 ($83.25) double with bath. AE, DC, MC, V.
Parking: Free.

This three-star hotel on the main street is the oldest in Burford, with a very long history. Its core dates from at least 1475, although it could possibly be much older than that. The establishment of a rest house for Burford Priory was authorized by papal bull (hence the name) sometime before 1403. The priory was given by Henry VIII to his barber-surgeon in 1544 after the monasteries were dissolved, and from 1603, when John Silvester became inn holder, the history of the Bull can be traced. The inn has had such visitors as the king's troops in the battle with Cromwell's Parliament Dragoons, Cromwell himself, and later King Charles II and Nell Gwynne. During the 18th century, the Bull was an important stop on the road, with 40 coaches passing through Burford each day. The hotel is distinguished by its brick-and-stone front dating from 1658, when additions increased the size of the hostelry. Today, old-world charm blends with modern comfort. All bedrooms have central heating. Even if you don't stay here, drop in for a drink at the establishment's pub or for a good meal. Pub snacks, priced from £3 to £5 ($5.55 to $9.25) each, are served daily from noon to 10:30am, and more formal fixed-price evening meals—priced at £10 ($18.50) for four courses—are served in the dining room every night between 6 and 10:30pm.

THE WINTERS TALE HOTEL, Oxford Rd., Burford, Oxfordshire OX8 4PH. Tel. 099382/3176. Fax 0993/842924. 22 rms (5 with bath or shower). TV TEL
$ Rates (including English breakfast): £28 ($51.80) single without bath; £38 ($70.30) double without bath, £46 ($85.10) double with bath. AE, MC, V.
Parking: Free.
You might be attracted to this hotel by its literary name alone. It is an early 19th-century, stone-built inn at the edge of Burford next to Burford Golf Club. Clients get to meet each other in the cozy bar, and in winter, log fires burn. The hotel also serves English and international meals, with lunches costing from £7 ($12.95) and dinners from £12 ($22.20).

---

6. BOURTON-ON-THE-WATER

85 miles NW of London; 36 miles NW of Oxford

GETTING THERE   By Train   Trains go from Paddington Station in London to nearby Moreton-in-the-Marsh. Trip time is 2 hours. From Moreton-in-the-Marsh, Pulhams bus company runs buses for the 15-minute (6-mile) journey on to Bourton-on-the-Water. Other cities which also have train service into London include

Cheltenham or Kingham, and each of those, while somewhat more distant, also has bus connections into Bourton-on-the-Water.

By Bus   National Coach Services, from Victoria Coach Station in London, travels to both Cheltenham or Stow-on-the-Wold. From either of those towns, Pulhams Bus Company operates about four buses a day into Bourton-on-the-Water.

By Car   From Oxford, head west along A40, until you reach the junction with A429 (Fosse Way). Take it northeast to Bourton-on-the-Water.

ESSENTIALS   The **area code** is 0451. The nearest tourist information office is in Stow-on-the-Wold (see below).

In this scenic Cotswold village, you may feel like Gulliver, voyaging to Lilliput. Bourton-on-the-Water lies on the banks of the tiny Windrush River. Its mellow stone houses, its village greens on the banks of the water, and its bridges have earned it the title of the Venice of the Cotswolds. But that label tends to obscure its true charm.

WHAT TO SEE & DO
IN TOWN

OLD NEW INN, High St. Tel. 0451/20467.
To see Lilliput, you have to visit this inn on the main street. In the garden is a near-perfect and most realistic model village.
Admission: £1.10 ($2.05) adults, 80p ($1.50) children.
Open: Daily 9:30am–6pm or dusk.

BIRDLAND, Rissington Rd. Tel. 0451/20689.
Birdland, directly east of the center, is a handsomely designed garden set on about 8½ acres, that contains some 1,200 birds of 361 different species. Included is the largest and most varied collection of penguins in any zoo, with places for underwater viewing. Hummingbirds are in the tropical house, and many of the birds are on view in captivity for the first time.
Admission: £3 ($5.55) adults, £2 ($3.70) children 14 and under.
Open: Mar–Nov 10am–6pm; Dec–Feb 10am–4pm.

NEARBY ATTRACTIONS

COTSWOLD COUNTRYSIDE COLLECTION, Fosse Way, Northleach, Cheltenham (Cotswold District Council). Tel. 0451/60715.
Opened in 1981, this is a museum of rural-life displays. You can see the Lloyd-Baker collection of agricultural history, including wagons, horse-drawn implements, and tools, as well as a seasons-of-the-year display. A Cotswold gallery records the social history of the area. Below Stairs is an exhibition of laundry, dairy, and kitchen implements. The museum was once a house of correction, and its history is displayed in the reconstructed cellblock and courtroom. It's located off the A40 between Burford and Cheltenham.
Admission: £1 ($1.85) adults, 50p (95¢) children.
Open: Apr–Oct Mon–Sat 10am–5:30pm, Sun 2–5:30pm.

WHERE TO STAY
DOUBLES WITHOUT BATH FOR LESS THAN £32 [$59.20]

BROADLANDS GUEST HOUSE, Clapton Row, Bourton-on-the-Water, Cheltenham, Gloucestershire GL54 2DN. Tel. 0451/22002. 11 rms (all with bath).
$ Rates (including English breakfast): £28 ($51.80) single; £35 ($64.75) double. No credit cards. **Parking:** Free.
One of the more distinctive B&B's in the area is in a renovated Victorian building

which retains many of its original features, including a glassed-in conservatory arrangements are made in advance, dinner can be ordered. One of the bedroor contains a four-poster bed. The hotel sits in a pleasantly isolated spot, somewha removed from the congestion of the village itself but only 5-minutes away.

DUKE OF WELLINGTON, Sherbourne St., Bourton-on-the-Water, Cheltenham, Gloucestershire GL54 2BY. Tel. 0451/20539. 4 rms (none with bath). TV.
$ Rates (including English breakfast): £20.50 ($37.95) single; £31 ($57.35) double. No credit cards. **Parking:** Free.

Most of the town's residents define this place as a pub rather than as a hotel, but it does offer a handful of limited but cozy accommodations. It was constructed as an inn in 1588, and has remained one throughout most of its long life. Each room has tea-making facilities and hot and cold running water. Even if you don't stay in one of the upper bedrooms, you might consider dropping in for a drink or informal meal within its antique premises. Its pub is divided into three different bar areas, each of which is among the most consistently popular drinking places in the village; it's open Sunday to Friday from 11am to 2:30pm and 6 to 11pm, and Saturday from 11am to 11pm. Order your drinks and food at the bar, and waitresses will carry it to your table. Platters, priced at £3.25 to £7.50 ($6 to $13.90), include steaks, jacket potatoes stuffed with various fillings, trout, ham, shepherd's pie, and steaks. The house is near the river in the heart of town.

FARNCOMBE, Clapton, Bourton-on-the-Water, Cheltenham, Gloucestershire GL54 2LG. Tel. 0451/20120. 3 rms (1 with shower). TV **Directions:** Take A429 toward Cirencester.
$ Rates (including English breakfast): £27 ($49.95) double; single use of double £16 ($29.60). No credit cards. **Parking:** Free.

 On the outskirts, Farncombe lies 2½ miles from Bourton-on-the-Water. The little hamlet of some 20 houses is an address known only to the discerning English who stay here when the more popular and more famous place is overrun with tourists. Mrs. J. M. Wright receives guests all year. Her house makes a good base for touring the Cotswolds. The property opens onto views of the Windrush Valley.

LITTLE RISSINGTON MANOR, Little Rissington Rd., near Bourton-on-the-Water, Cheltenham, Gloucestershire GL54 2NB. Tel. 0451/21078. 6 rms (3 with bath). **Directions:** Leave Bourton-on-the-Water on Little Rissington Rd.; pass Great Rissington, turn and continue 400 yards uphill; turn right through white gates next to lodge and follow gravel drive.
$ Rates (including English breakfast): £16–£20 ($29.60–$37) single without bath; £32 ($59.20) double without bath, £40 ($74) double with bath. No credit cards. **Parking:** Free. **Closed:** Oct–Feb.

This 19th-century Victorian manor house is set on 11 acres of grounds, which include a tennis court, croquet lawn, and swimming pool. Mrs. Annabel Kirkpatrick will welcome you to one of her comfortably furnished bedrooms. She can accommodate only a few guests, so you should reserve.

WHERE TO EAT

MEALS FOR LESS THAN £14.95 ($27.65)

CHESTER HOUSE RESTAURANT, Chester House Hotel and Motel, Victoria St. Tel. 21522.
Cuisine: ENGLISH/CONTINENTAL. **Reservations:** Required.
$ Prices: Appetizers £3–£7 ($5.55–$12.95); main courses £8.50–£14.50 ($15.75–$8.35); set dinner from £14.95 ($27.65); lunch from £8.50 ($15.75). AE, DC, MC, V.
Open: Lunch Feb–Nov daily noon–2pm; dinner year-round daily 7–9:30pm.

Part of this popular motel in the village center was constructed around what was once

...able for horses. Good-tasting food is served in the dining room, where the chef ...es on quality ingredients. Try the rack of lamb with a port and red-currant sauce, ...epper steak, or a casserole of wood pigeon. Traditional English soups are served as appetizers.

OLD NEW INN, High St. Tel. 20467.
  Cuisine: ENGLISH. **Reservations:** Not needed.
  $ **Prices:** Appetizers £1–£2.50 ($1.85–$4.65); main courses £5–£8 ($9.25–$14.80); set dinner £13 ($24.05); set lunch £10 ($18.50); bar snacks from £2.50 ($4.65). MC, V.
  Open: Lunch daily 12:30–1:45pm; dinner daily 7:30–8:45pm.
With its popular wine garden, this is one of the best places for food in Bourton-on-the-Water. At lunchtime, guests not only enjoy the snacks but can also play darts or chat with the villagers. The local residents know of its good, fresh, and reasonably priced bar snacks (which can easily be turned into a full meal), and you can also partake of more formal dinners in the evening, enjoying good English cookery.

EN ROUTE TO STOW-ON-THE-WOLD

Midway between Bourton-on-the-Water and Stow-on-the-Wold are the twin villages of **Upper and Lower Slaughter.** Don't be put off by the names, because these are two of the prettiest villages in the Cotswolds. Actually the name "Slaughter" was a corruption of "de Sclotre," the name of the original Norman landowner.

The houses are constructed of honey-colored Cotswold stone, and a stream meanders right through the street, providing a home for the ducks that wander freely about. From Bourton-on-the Water head directly north for 5 minutes.

7. STOW-ON-THE-WOLD

9 miles SE of Broadway; 10 miles S of Chipping Campden;
4 miles S of Moreton-in-March; 21 miles S of Stratford-upon-Avon

GETTING THERE   By Train   From London, take a train to Moreton-in-Marsh (see below) from London's Paddington Station, a service possible several times a day. From Moreton-in-Marsh, continue by a Pulhams Coach for the 10-minute ride to Stow-on-the-Wold.

By Bus   National Express Coaches also run daily from London's Victoria Coach Station to Moreton-in-Marsh, where a Pulhams Coach goes the rest of the way to Stow-on-the-Wold. Several Pulhams Coaches also run to Stow-on-the-Wold daily from Cheltenham.

By Car   From Oxford, take the A40 west to the junction near Burford with A424. Head northwest along A424 to Stow-on-the-Wold.

ESSENTIALS   The **area code** is 0451. The **Tourist Information Centre** is at Talbot Court (tel. 0451/31082).

Stow-on-the-Wold is an unspoiled Cotswold market town, in spite of the busloads of tourists who stop off en route to Broadway and Chipping Campden. The town is the loftiest in the Cotswolds, built on a wold (rolling hills) about 800 feet above sea level. In its open market square, you can still see the stocks where offenders in days gone by were jeered at and punished by the townspeople, who threw rotten eggs at the accused. The final battle between the Roundheads and the Royalists took place in

Stow-on-the-Wold. The town, which is really like a village, is used by many as a base for exploring the Cotswold wool towns, as well as Stratford-upon-Avon.

WHERE TO STAY

DOUBLES WITHOUT BATH FOR LESS THAN £30 [$55.50]

THE LIMES, Tewkesbury Rd., Stow-on-the-Wold, Gloucestershire GL54 1EN. Tel. 0451/30034. 4 rms (2 with shower).
$ Rates (including English breakfast): £27 ($49.95) double without bath, £35 ($64.75) double with shower. No credit cards. **Parking:** Free.

This Georgian building of character is along A424 (Evesham Road), about a 4-minute walk from the heart of this famed Cotswold village. It has a lovely garden, and in chilly weather log fires make it warm and inviting. Bedrooms—all doubles—have washbasins and hot and cold running water, and one has a four-poster bed. The owners, Mr. and Mrs. Keyte, personally supervise the operation of The Limes, and cater to vegetarians.

SOUTH HILL FARM HOUSE, Fosse Way, Stow-on-the-Wold, Gloucestershire GL54 1JU. Tel. 0451/31219. Fax 0451/658031. 4 rms (1 with bath or shower).
$ Rates (including English breakfast): £15 ($27.75) per person without bath; £18 ($33.30) per person with bath. V. **Parking:** Free.

This Victorian farmhouse built in Cotswold stone lies ¼ mile from Stow along A429, and is set in large grounds with plenty of parking. Shaun and Gaye Kenneally offer a high standard of traditional B&B accommodation and service. All rooms are centrally heated, and there is a lounge and TV area.

WEST VIEW, Fosse Way, Stow-on-the-Wold, Gloucestershire GL54 1DW. Tel. 0451/30492. 3 rms (none with bath).
$ Rates (including English breakfast): £11.50–£12 ($21.30–$22.20) per person. No credit cards. **Parking:** Free.
Nancy White, a gracious hostess, has furnished the place attractively, in part with antiques. The shared bathroom has a shower with plenty of hot and cold running water. The location is about a 3-minute walk from the center of Stow.

WORTH THE EXTRA BUCKS

THE OLD STOCKS HOTEL, The Square, Stow-on-the-Wold, Gloucestershire GL54 1AF. Tel. 0451/30666. Fax 0451/870014. 17 rms (all with bath). TV TEL
$ Rates (including English breakfast): £30 ($55.50) single; £60–£70 ($111–$129.50) double. MC, V.

In spite of its ominous name, this is one of the most inviting inns of Stow-on-the-Wold. Alan and Caroline Rose run the mellow inn which overlooks the marketplace. The hotel is made up of a trio of buildings from the 1500s and 1600s, which were constructed in part with natural stone and oak timbers from sailing vessels. In winter, you can warm yourself by a log fire, while in summer, you can retreat to a walled garden.
Even if you're not staying here, you may want to order a three-course meal for £9 ($16.65) or a fixed-price dinner costing £15 ($27.75).

THE WHITE HOUSE, The Square, Stow-on-the-Wold, Gloucestershire GL54 1AF. Tel. 0451/30674. 7 rms (3 with bath). TV
$ Rates (including English breakfast): £25.50 ($47.20) single without bath; £41.50 ($76.80) double without bath, £54.50 ($100.85) double with bath. With half board

£34.50 ($63.85) single, £56–£67 ($103.60–$123.95) double. AE, DC, MC, V.
Parking: Free.

This limestone-fronted building is on the main square of town. You register at the bar of the street-level pub, which is laden with brass accents and open fireplaces. Since 1698, this has been a thriving coaching inn, welcoming wayfarers from all over the world. There is a healthy respect for the traditional around here, and the place has a mellow period atmosphere, with its uneven floors and low doorways. All guest rooms have coffee-making equipment. The food, such as steak-and-kidney pie and grilled local trout, and especially the steak, is good.

WHERE TO EAT

MEALS FOR LESS THAN £6 [$11.10]

PRINCE OF INDIA, 5 Park St. Tel. 31198.
  Cuisine: INDIAN. **Reservations:** Recommended.
$ Prices: Appetizers £1.75–£2.50 ($3.25–$4.65); main courses £3–£4 ($5.55–$7.40). AE, MC, V.
  Open: Lunch daily noon–2:30pm; dinner daily 6–11:30pm.

The cuisine here features spices skillfully used in a wide range of dishes. If you have an indestructable palate, try the meat vindaloo, but you can also order less tongue-wilting fare, including tandoori chicken or hot and sour prawns Madras. Leavened bread is served, and there are many vegetarian dishes. A savory beginning is the lentil soup. The restaurant is a short walk from the town center, near the bus stop.

ST. EDWARDS, The Square. Tel. 30351.
  Cuisine: ENGLISH. **Reservations:** Not needed.
$ Prices: Three-course lunch £7 ($12.95); fixed-price tea £3.50 ($6.45). No credit cards.
  Open: June–Sept daily 9am–6pm; off-season daily 9am–5:30pm.

This little tearoom is easy to spot, as it opens onto the market square. It has a formal facade with fluted stone pilasters. Inside, you can have morning coffee, lunch, or afternoon tea, while sitting on Windsor chairs in front of an open fireplace. A typical lunch might include homemade soup, a steak "pastie," apple pie with fresh cream, and coffee. The afternoon tea includes freshly baked muffins and cake.

---

8. MORETON-IN-MARSH

83 miles NW of London; 8 miles N of Bourton-on-the-Water;
4 miles N of Stow-on-the-Wold; 8 miles W of Broadway; 7 miles S of Chipping Campden; 17 miles S of Stratford-upon-Avon

GETTING THERE   By Train   From London's Paddington Station, British Rail provides daily service to Moreton-in-Marsh. Trip time is 1 hour, 50 minutes.

By Bus   National Express coaches run from London's Victoria Coach Station to Moreton-in-Marsh daily.

By Car   From Stow-in-the-Wold (see above), take the A429 4 miles north.

ESSENTIALS   The area code is 0608. The nearest tourist office is in Stow-on-the-Wold (see above).

M oreton-in-Marsh is an important center for British Rail passengers headed for the Cotswolds because it is near many villages of interest. Incidentally, don't take the

name "Moreton-in-Marsh" too literally. "Marsh" derives from an old word
"border." Look for the 17th-century market hall and the old curfew tower, a
walk down the High (the main street), where Roman legions trudged centurie
The town once lay on the ancient Fosse Way.

WHERE TO STAY

DOUBLES WITHOUT BATH FOR LESS THAN £34 ($62.90)

In Moreton-in-Marsh

**BLUE CEDAR HOUSE, Stow Rd., Moreton-in-Marsh, Gloucestershire
GL56 0DW. Tel. 0608/50299.** 5 rms (2 with shower).
$ Rates (including English breakfast): £26 ($48.10) double without bath, £36
($66.60) double with bath. No credit cards. **Parking:** Free.

 Named after an enormous tree growing in the front yard, this brown-brick
house was erected in 1952 on the edge of the village center along the A429. It is
owned and operated by Sandra and Graham Billinger, who offer comfortable
bedrooms—all doubles—plus a TV lounge. The house stands on a ½ acre of land
with a fish pond, and it is within a 10-minute walk from the rail station.

**TREETOPS, London Rd., Moreton-in-Marsh, Gloucestershire GL56 0HE.
Tel. 0608/51036.** 7 rms (4 with bath). TV
$ Rates (including English breakfast): £16 ($29.60) single without bath, £25
($46.25) single with bath; £26 ($48.10) double without bath, £34 ($62.90) double
with bath. No credit cards. **Parking:** Free.

Treetops dates from 1983, when Brian and Elizabeth Dean realized their dream
of designing and building their own house. They assembled most of the house
themselves, including the honey-colored facade of Cotswold stone blocks.
Their house stands amid fir and beech trees in almost an acre of garden, about a
5-minute stroll from the heart of Moreton-in-Marsh. Its driveway is identified with a
sign visible from the main A44 highway. Each accommodation contains tea-making
facilities.

**MORETON HOUSE, High St., Moreton-in-Marsh, Gloucestershire GL56
0LQ. Tel. 0608/50747.** 12 rms (5 with bath or shower). TV
$ Rates (including English breakfast): £18.50 ($34.25) single without bath; £34
($62.90) double without bath, £44 ($81.40) double with bath. MC, V. **Parking:**
Free.
Set on the main street in town, this is perhaps the most desirable budget accommodation in the center of this popular Cotswold village. A mellow old house with a Tudor
facade of honey-colored sandstone, it has a very correct and attractive tearoom on
street level, where you register at a small reception desk. Evening meals are served
nightly from 6:30 to 8:30pm. The house is at the junction of A429 and A44.

Nearby

**NEW FARM, Dorn, Moreton-in-Marsh, Gloucestershire GL56 9NS. Tel.
0608/50782.** 3 rms (2 with bath).
$ Rates (including English breakfast): £15 ($27.75) single without bath; £26
($48.10) double without bath, £30 ($55.50) double with bath. No credit cards.
Parking: Free.
Catherine Righton accepts guests at this B&B, which is a mile north of Moreton-in-
Marsh, just off the A429. The farmhouse, built about 300 years ago of Cotswold
stone, is a dairy farm of about 250 acres and 90 Friesian milk cows. Two bedrooms
have a private bath and one is big enough for a family. The full breakfast includes
fresh hot bread.

WHERE TO EAT

MARKET HOUSE, 4 High St. Tel. 50767.
Cuisine: ENGLISH. **Reservations:** Recommended.

COTSWOLDS

s: Appetizers £1.25–£2.60 ($2.30–$4.80); main courses £1.75–£8.50
.5–$15.75). No credit cards.
en: June–Sept Mon–Sat 9am–7:30pm, Sun 10am–6pm; off-season Mon–
at 9am–5pm, Sun 11am–4:30pm.

behind a prominent bow window and a facade of Cotswold stone, this
..ablishment provides a tearoom-style setting which is ideal for morning coffee, a
.avorful lunch, or a reasonably priced early supper. You can enjoy dishes which
include prawn cocktails or soups, steaks or grilled lamb and mutton, or chicken Kiev,
fried plaice, haddock, or cod, followed by a piece of moist cake or some other dessert.
Sandwiches and fresh salads are also served. Market House is on the town's main
street, a few paces from Town Hall.

9. BROADWAY

15 miles SW of Stratford-upon-Avon; 93 miles NW of London;
15 miles NE of Cheltenham

GETTING THERE By Train The nearest railway stations are at Cheltenham or
Stratford (each 10 miles away) or at Evesham (5 miles away). From any of these, local
buses come into Broadway, but many visitors prefer to hire a taxi.

By Bus From London's Victoria Coach Station, one or two National Express
Buses depart for Broadway taking 2½ hours. Bus and train connections are really best
through Stratford (see Chapter 16), which is extremely convenient. From Stratford, a
local bus (Barry's Coaches) connects Stratford to Evesham, and then continues on
after a change of equipment to Broadway.

By Car From Oxford, head west along A40 until you reach Cheltenham and the
junction of A46 going northeast to Broadway.

ESSENTIALS The area code is 0386. The **Tourist Information Centre** is 1
Cotswold Court (tel. 0386/852937), open June to September only.

Many of the prime attractions of the Cotswolds as well as the Shakespeare Country
lie within easy reach of Broadway, which is near Evesham at the southern tip of
Hereford and Worcester. The best-known Cotswold village, Broadway has a wide and
beautiful High Street flanked with honey-colored stone buildings, remarkable for
their harmony of style and design. Overlooking the Vale of Evesham, it is a major
stopover for bus tours and is mobbed in summer; however, it manages to retain its
charm in spite of the invasion.

WHERE TO STAY

For lodgings, Broadway has the dubious distinction of having some of the most
expensive inns in the Cotswolds. The guesthouses can also command a good
price—and get it.

DOUBLES WITHOUT BATH FOR LESS THAN £35 [$64.75]

**THE CROWN AND TRUMPET, Church St., Broadway, Hereford and
Worcester WR12 7AE. Tel. 0386/853202.** 5 rms (none with bath). TV
$ Rates (including English breakfast): £22 ($40.70) single; £35 ($64.75) double. No
credit cards. **Parking:** Free.
Better known within Broadway as a public house than as a hotel, this 16th-century inn
nonetheless offers a handful of simple upstairs bedrooms to visitors passing through.
Set behind a facade of honey-colored Cotswold stone, it serves bar snacks throughout

the day priced at from £3.50 to £7 ($6.50 to $12.95) each. The pub is open Sunday to Friday from 11am to 3pm and 6 to 11pm, and Saturday from 11am to 11pm, serving food and drink. It is located just behind the town's village green.

EAST BANK, Station Drive, Broadway, Hereford and Worcester WR12 7DF. Tel. 0386/852659. 6 rms (all with bath). TV
$ **Rates** (including English breakfast): £40–£50 ($74–$92.50) double; £56 ($103.60) family room. No credit cards. **Parking:** Free.

The stone house where Anne and Ken Evans receive B&B guests is a bargain for Broadway, and is in a tranquil location off the A44, about a 12-minute walk from the village center. There's unlimited parking on the grounds of the house and on the approach drive. The house is centrally heated, but in addition a log fire blazes in the guest lounge during cooler weather. With prior notice, a selection of evening meals can be provided, each costing £11.50 to £15.50 ($21.30 to $28.70).

OLIVE BRANCH GUEST HOUSE, 78-80 High St., Broadway, Hereford and Worcester WR12 7AJ. Tel. 0386/853440. 9 rms (6 with bath). TV
$ **Rates** (including English breakfast): £17–£18.50 ($31.45–$34.25) single without bath; £33 ($61.05) double without bath, £37 ($68.45) double with bath. AE. **Parking:** Free.
In the heart of an expensive village, this budget oasis is managed by Andrew Riley. The house, dating back to the 17th century, retains its old Cotswold architectural features. Behind the house is a large walled English garden and car park. Guests are given a discount in the owners' attached antiques shop.

PATHLOW HOUSE, 82 High St., Broadway, Hereford and Worcester WR12 7AJ. Tel. 0386/853444. 5 rms (2 with bath). TV
$ **Rates** (including English breakfast): £35 ($64.75) double without bath, £38 ($70.30) double with bath. No credit cards. **Parking:** Free.
The rates are quite reasonable considering the location, right in the heart of the village. From spring through autumn, guests from around the world are received here. Rooms available in the house as well as in a small cottage in the courtyard. Each unit is a double. The house, run by Des and Iris Porter, is centrally heated and all bedrooms have hot-beverage facilities. There is parking in the rear.

PENNYLANDS, Evesham Rd., Broadway, Hereford and Worcester WR12 7DG. Tel. 0386/858437. 3 rms (all with bath or shower). TV
$ **Rates** (including English breakfast): £29–£31 ($53.65–$57.35) double. No credit cards. **Parking:** Free.
This is a former private home, built in Edwardian times, but now receiving B&B guests in its comfortably furnished rooms, all doubles. It lies on the outskirts of Broadway, 1 mile from the center, and can be a base for touring the historic village and also the Cotswolds.

SOUTHWOLD HOUSE, Station Rd., Broadway, Hereford and Worcester WR12 7DE. Tel. 0386/853681. Fax 0386/858653. 8 rms (5 with bath or shower). TV
$ **Rates** (including English breakfast): £18 ($33.30) single without bath; £31 ($57.35) double without bath, £37 ($68.45) double with bath. MC, V. **Parking:** Free.
Built as a private home in Edwardian times, now it welcomes B&B guests all year. The location is about 5 minutes from the heart of the village along A44, and there is limited parking. An evening meal will be served if arranged in advance.

WHITEACRES, Station Rd., Broadway, Hereford and Worcester WR12 7DE. Tel. 0386/852320. 6 rms (all with bath). TV
$ **Rates** (including English breakfast): £25 ($46.25) single; £38–£40 ($70.30–$74) double. No credit cards. **Parking:** Free. **Open:** Mar–Oct.

One of the best and most charming B&Bs in this high-priced town, it occupies an unpretentious Victorian house on the southern extension of High Street, a 5-minute walk from the center. Owned and operated by Helen and Alan

Richardson, its bedrooms are pretty and very comfortable. Its public rooms are cozy, with white walls adorned with porcelain either collected or inherited by the congenial owners.

MILESTONE HOUSE, 122 Upper High St., Broadway, Hereford and Worcester WR12 7AJ. Tel. 0386/853432. 4 rms (all with bath). TV
$ Rates (including English breakfast): £39.50–£49.50 ($73.10–$91.60) double. AE, MC, V.

This is the kind of place found only in England. Luigi and Pauline Bellorini have created a homelike atmosphere in the private small hotel, once an inn known as the Fox & Dog. The immaculately kept rooms have soft, downy beds, central heating, and plenty of hot and cold running water. Each room is a double.

Dinner is served daily in an old beamed dining room from 7:30 to 9:30pm. The menu is a mix of traditional English and Italian, as you might guess, since Luigi is Italian and Pauline is English. The owners have added a conservatory of glass and Cotswold stone, which is an extension to the dining room. In summer, this seems to bring the garden into the house. There is also a small bar.

WHERE TO EAT

GOBLETS WINE BAR, High St. Tel. 852255.
Cuisine: ENGLISH. **Reservations:** Not needed.
$ Prices: Appetizers £1.75–£3.10 ($3.25–$5.75); main courses £4–£5 ($7.40–$9.25). AE, DC, MC, V.
Open: Lunch daily noon–2pm; dinner daily 7–9:30pm.

⑤ With black-and-white timbered walls, this 17th-century inn built of Cotswold stone and filled with antiques is frequented by Broadway locals and tourists. Additions to the menu, which is changed every 6 weeks, are marked on the blackboard, and orders should be placed at the bar. The limited but tasty menu begins with such appetizers as taramosalata and goes on to such daily specials as chicken Marengo or duckling in orange sauce. About four desserts appear daily, including, for example, a hot gingerbread pudding. The coffee is good, and the atmosphere is warm. The inn is next to the Lygon Arms.

10. CHIPPING CAMPDEN

36 miles NW of Oxford; 12 miles S of Stratford-upon-Avon;
93 miles NW of London

GETTING THERE By Train Trains depart from London's Paddington Station for Moreton-in-the-Marsh, requiring about 90 to 120 minutes for the transit. At Moreton-in-the-Marsh, a bus—operated by Barry's Coaches—travels the 7 miles to Chipping Camden only 2 days a week. Most visitors get a taxi at Moreton-in-the-Marsh for the continuation on to Chipping Campden, for a cost of about £7 ($12.95) each way.

By Bus The largest nearby bus depot is Cheltenham, which receives service several times a day from London's Victoria Coach Station. From Cheltenham, however, bus service (again by Barry's Coaches) is infrequent and uncertain, departing at the most only three times per week.

By Car From Oxford, take the A40 west to the junction of A424 which you take northwest, passing by Stow-on-the-Wold. The route becomes A44 until you reach the junction of B4081 which you take northeast to Chipping Campden.

ESSENTIALS The **area code** is 0386. The summer-only **Tourist Information Centre** is at Woolstaplers Hall Museum, High Street (tel. 0386/840289).

The English, regardless of how often they visit the Cotswolds, are attrac town, once a great wool center. It's neither too large nor too small. Of road, it's easily accessible to major points of interest, and double-dec frequently run through here on their way to Oxford or Stratford-upon-Av

On the northern edge of the Cotswolds above the Vale of Evesham, Campden, a Saxon settlement, was recorded in the *Domesday Book*. In medieval times, rich merchants built homes of Cotswold stone along its model High Street, described by the historian G. M. Trevelyan as "the most beautiful village street now left in the island." The houses have been so well preserved that Chipping Campden to this day remains a gem of the Middle Ages. Its church dates from the 15th century, and its old market hall is the loveliest in the Cotswolds. Look also for its almshouses, which, along with the market hall, were built by a great wool merchant, Sir Baptist Hicks, whose tomb is in the church.

WHERE TO STAY

DOUBLES WITHOUT BATH FOR LESS THAN £31 ($57.35)

DRAGON HOUSE, High St., Chipping Campden, Gloucestershire GL55 6AG. Tel. 0386/840734. 2 rms (none with bath).
$ Rates (including English breakfast): £26–£32 ($48.10–$59.20) double. No credit cards. **Parking:** Free.
Close to the marketplace, Dragon House is run by a Yorkshire proprietor, Mrs. Valerie James, who serves you tea in the evening as well as an excellent and plentiful breakfast the next morning. Rooms—all doubles—are attractively decorated and quite comfortable. No evening meals are served.

HOLLY MOUNT, High St., Mickleton, Chipping Campden, Gloucestershire GL55 6SL. Tel. 0386/438243. Fax 0386/438858. 3 rms (all with shower). TV
$ Rates (including English breakfast): £19 ($35.15) per person. No credit cards. **Parking:** Free.
On the outskirts, Holly Mount lies 3 miles north of Chipping Campden in a village called "the northern gateway to the Cotswolds." Patrick and Jennifer Green have taken a former farmhouse dating from the early 19th century and have converted it to provide three double rooms, each with beverage-making equipment. There are queen-size beds in the "Pink or Peach Room" and king- or twin-size in the "Blue Room." All rooms are tastefully decorated in the early 19th-century style. For your evening meal you will be directed to two local pubs within walking distance of Holly Mount, but breakfast is served on the premises in the Victorian Conservatory. Holly Mount is between Stratford-upon-Avon and Broadway on B4632.

SANDALWOOD HOUSE, Back-Ends, Chipping Campden, Gloucestershire GL55 6AU. Tel. 0386/840091. 2 rms (none with bath). **Directions:** Turn right off High Street at the Roman Catholic Church.
$ Rates (including English breakfast): £20 ($37) single; £31–£35 ($57.35–$64.75) double. No credit cards. **Parking:** Free.
Peacefully situated in a garden with safe parking in its own driveway, the house is a 5-minute walk from the town center. The two rooms are spotless, large, and airy, with comfortable beds, washbasins, and hot-beverage facilities. The bathroom has a tub and shower. Diana Bendall, the hostess, has two dining rooms where you have a choice of dishes from a breakfast menu. There is a cozy lounge where Di serves hot drinks every evening at 9:30pm. Sandalwood House accepts nonsmokers only.

SPARLINGS, Leysbourne, Chipping Campden, Gloucestershire GL55 6HL. Tel. 0386/840505. 2 rms (both with bath).
$ Rates (including English breakfast): £37–£39 ($68.45–$72.15) double. Double room occupied as a single £22 ($40.70). No credit cards. **Parking:** Free.

Sparlings, at the far north end of Chipping Campden's High Street, is a restored 18th-century Cotswold-stone town house, named after two well-known women who used to live there. Owned by Graeme Black, the house has exposed beams, stone walls, and some flagstone floors. Unrestricted parking for cars is available on a service road, and bikes are secure at the rear of the property.

WORTH THE EXTRA BUCKS

THE MALT HOUSE, Broad Campden, Chipping Campden, Gloucestershire GL55 6 UU. Tel. 0386/840295. Fax 0386/841334. 6 rms (4 with bath). TV
$ Rates (including English breakfast): £20 ($37) single without bath; £60 ($111) double without bath, £80 ($148) double with bath. MC, V.

This is in the satellite hamlet of Broad Campden, a mile west of Chipping Campden. It was purchased by Ms. Pat Robinson, who transformed it into a B&B with oak beams, diamond-patterned leaded windows, and stone mullions. It was originally built 400 to 500 years ago as a cottage within 4½ acres of gardens. Bedrooms are tastefully furnished and well maintained. If you order it at breakfast, a four-course dinner can be prepared for £9 ($16.65) per person.

SEYMOUR HOUSE HOTEL & RESTAURANT, High St., Chipping Campden, Gloucestershire GL55 6AH. Tel. 0386/840429. Fax 0386/ 840369. 15 rms (all with bath). TV TEL
$ Rates: £60 ($111) single; £80–£125 ($148–$231.25) double. AE, MC, V.

This well-established hotel is composed of four interconnected buildings, two of which date from the 15th century. The decor today, including the facade, is basically Georgian. A fireplace is likely to be burning in the lobby if the day is cold. The hotel is owned and operated by the same company that caters to the Royal Shakespeare Theatre in Stratford-upon-Avon. The units that overlook the hotel's walled garden in back are quieter. The hotel welcomes nonresidents to its Italian-style restaurant (see below).

WHERE TO EAT

MEALS FOR LESS THAN £13.95 ($25.80)

BANTAM TEA ROOMS, High St. Tel. 840386.
   Cuisine: ENGLISH. **Reservations:** Not needed.
$ Prices: Appetizers £1.40–£2.75 ($2.60–$5.10); main courses £3–£5.50 ($5.55–$10.20); cream tea £2.25 ($4.15).
   Open: Tea Mon–Sat 9:30am–5pm, Sun 3–5pm. Meals daily noon–2:30pm.
   Closed: Mon mid–Sept to Apr.

Opposite the historic market hall, is a bow-windowed, 17th-century stone house where old-fashioned English afternoon teas are served. Tea can be just a pot of the brew and a tea cake, or you can indulge in homemade scones, crumpets, sandwiches, and homemade pastries and cakes. Lunches are served, with a selection of local ham and salad, chicken pie, pâtés, omelets, and salads.

BADGER BISTRO AND WINE BAR, High St. Tel. 840529.
   Cuisine: CONTINENTAL. **Reservations:** Required.
$ Prices: Appetizers £1.60–£3.25 ($2.95–$6); main courses £3.95–£7.95 ($7.30–$14.70). MC, V.
   Open: Lunch Fri–Wed noon–2:30pm; dinner Fri–Wed 6:30–10:30pm.

This is a very attractive little Cotswold shop with a bar and tables all made of pinewood. A comfortable, cheerful place, it offers such items as grilled local trout, chicken fricassee hunter style, and whole-food lasagne and salad. In fair weather, tables are placed in the garden. Colin and Diane Clarke run the Badger.

GREENSTOCKS ALL-DAY EATERIE, Cotswold House Hotel, The Square. Tel. 840330.

Cuisine: ENGLISH. **Reservations:** Not needed.
$ **Prices:** Appetizers £2.25–£3.75 ($4.15–$6.95); main courses £4.95–£13.20 ($9.15–$24.40). AE, DC, MC, V. Minimum charge £20 ($37).
Open: Coffee, pastries daily 9:30am–noon; lunch daily noon–2pm; dinner Sun–Thurs 6:30–9:30pm, Fri–Sat 6:30–10pm.

⭐ Conceivably, you can eat everything from breakfast to a late dinner here, thus avoiding the sometimes draconian English opening and closing hours. Mr. and Mrs. Greenstock, who own and run Chipping Campden's most elegant hostelry, oversee a staff that will serve you dishes such as jugged beef with orange, or even a sirloin steak. They are noted for their desserts, which the English call "pudding." Try the treacle tart.

KINGS ARMS, The Square. Tel. 840256.
Cuisine: ENGLISH/CONTINENTAL. **Reservations:** Not needed.
$ **Prices:** Appetizers £1.40–£3 ($2.60–$5.55); main courses £3–£5.50 ($5.55–$10.20); set lunch £9.25 ($17.10); set dinner £12.50 ($23.10). AE, MC, V.
Open: Lunch daily noon–2pm; dinner daily 6–10:30pm.

A full restaurant and pub are in the King's Arms, one of the town's leading inns whose rooms are over our budget. Even if you don't stay here, try to visit for the best bar snacks in Chipping Campden. You're likely to be tempted with artichokes and Stilton dressing, baked eggs, crab with Gruyère cheese and cream, fresh filet of mackerel with a mustard cream sauce, and taramosalata with hot toast, plus the more prosaic soups and pâtés. Main dishes include such continental fare as roast duck in a piquant orange sauce, beef Stroganoff, and filet of pork Calvados.

SEYMOUR HOUSE HOTEL & RESTAURANT, High St. Tel. 840429.
Cuisine: ITALIAN. **Reservations:** Required.
$ **Prices:** Appetizers £2.50–£8.50 ($4.65–$15.75); main courses £7.95–£12.75 ($14.70–$23.60); set dinner £13.95 ($25.80). AE, MC, V.
Open: Lunch daily 12:30–2pm; dinner daily 7:30–9:30pm.

⭐ This previously recommended hotel (see above) is also a good choice for Italian dining. A single large vine twines itself among the rafters beneath a room pierced with skylights. The appetizers are the best in the village, including carpaccio with wild mushrooms, followed by such main dishes as osso buco with saffron rice or a half guinea fowl roasted with herbs and served with a sauce of passion fruit. A selection of fresh seasonal vegetables accompanies the main course. For dessert, try zuccotto, half mousse, half ice cream (laced with Strega liqueur). Always ask about the day's special.

CHAPTER 16
STRATFORD-UPON-AVON & WARWICK

- **1. STRATFORD-UPON-AVON**
- • **WHAT'S SPECIAL ABOUT STRATFORD & WARWICK**
- **2. WARWICK**
- **3. KENILWORTH**

Shakespeare Country in the heart of England is the district most visited by North Americans, second only to London. Many who don't recognize the county name, Warwickshire, know its foremost tourist town, Stratford-upon-Avon, birthplace of England's greatest writer.

The county and its neighboring shires form a land of industrial cities, green fields; and market towns dotted with buildings, some of which have changed little since Shakespeare's time. Here are many of the places that attract overseas visitors, not only Stratford-upon-Avon, but also Warwick and Kenilworth castles, as well as Coventry Cathedral.

SEEING STRATFORD-UPON-AVON & WARWICK
GETTING THERE

Motorists from London take M40 toward Oxford, continuing along A34 to reach Stratford. British Rail has services to Stratford-upon-Avon, involving changes at Oxford and Leamington Spa. Service to Coventry is from London's Euston Station. At Coventry, connections are made in Stratford. National Express coaches leaving from London's Victoria Coach Station also service both Stratford and Warwick.

A SUGGESTED ITINERARY

Days 1 & 2: Explore Stratford, taking in the literary pilgrimage centers. Visit Ragley Hall and George Washington's Sulgrave Manor. Go to the theater.

Days 3 & 4: Overnight in Warwick. Visit Warwick Castle in the morning, and explore the ruins of Kenilworth Castle in the early afternoon before a late afternoon visit to Coventry Cathedral.

1. STRATFORD-UPON-AVON
91 miles NW of London; 40 miles NW of Oxford; 8 miles S of Warwick

GETTING THERE   By Train   The train from London's Paddington Station takes you here in 2½ hours. There is frequent service during the day.

By Bus   National Express coaches from Victoria Station in London run daily to Stratford-upon-Avon. Eight coaches a day leave from London taking 2¾ hours. A single day round-trip ticket costs £9.60 ($17.75).

WHAT'S SPECIAL ABOUT
STRATFORD & WARWICK

Great Towns/Villages

☐ Stratford-upon-Avon, famous as Shakespeare's home town. Great for theater and literary shrines.

☐ Warwick, known for its castle rising above the River Avon.

Castles

☐ Warwick Castle, between Stratford and Coventry, regarded as England's finest medieval castle.

☐ Kenilworth Castle, in magnificent ruins—setting of Sir Walter Scott's romance, *Kenilworth.*

Buildings

☐ Ragley Hall, built in 1680 outside Stratford, home of the marquess of Hertford.

☐ Coventry Cathedral, designed by Sir Basil Spence and consecrated in 1962 in a modern style that sent traditional architectural devotees protesting.

Literary Shrines

☐ Shakespeare's Birthplace, Stratford where the Bard was born on April 23, 1564.

☐ Anne Hathaway's Cottage, 1 mile from Stratford, a wattle-and-daub cottage where Anne Hathaway lived before marrying Shakespeare.

Theatrical Events

☐ Attending a performance at the Royal Shakespeare Theatre on the River Avon in Stratford.

By Car Take the M40 toward Oxford and continue to Stratford-upon-Avon on the A34.

ESSENTIALS The **area code** is 0789. The **Tourist Information Centre,** Bridgefoot (tel. 0789/293127), has all the details about the Shakespeare properties. It's open March to October, Monday to Saturday from 9am to 5:30pm and Sunday from 2 to 5pm. From November to February, it's open Monday to Saturday from 10:30am to 4pm. A tourist reception center operated by **Guide Friday Ltd.,** the Civic Hall, 14 Rother Street (tel. 0789/294466), dispenses free maps and brochures on the town and area and operates tours. Also available here is a full range of tourist services, including accommodation booking, car rental, and theater tickets. In summer, the center is open daily from 9am to 7pm. In winter, hours are from 9am to 5:30pm Monday to Friday, from 9am to 4pm Saturday, and from 9:30am to 4pm Sunday.

To contact the **Shakespeare Birthplace Trust,** which runs many of the attractions, send a self-addressed envelope and International Reply Coupon to the Director, the Shakespeare Centre, Henley Street, Stratford-upon-Avon, Warwickshire CV37 6QW (tel. 0789/204016).

Tourism is responsible for the magnitude of traffic to this market town on the Avon River. Actor David Garrick really launched the shrine in 1769, when he organized the first of the Bard's commemorative birthday celebrations. William Shakespeare, of course, was born in Stratford-upon-Avon, but his biographers concede how little is known about his early life. Perhaps because documentation is so poor, much useless conjecture has arisen about the authorship of Shakespeare's work. But the view that Francis Bacon (or for that matter, Elizabeth I) wrote the plays would certainly stir up a tempest if suggested seriously to the innkeepers of Stratford-upon-Avon. Admittedly, however, some of the stories and legends connected with Shakespeare's days in Stratford are largely fanciful, invented to amuse and entertain the vast number of literary fans who make the pilgrimage.

Another magnet for tourists today is the Royal Shakespeare Theatre, where Britain's foremost actors perform during a long season that lasts from Easter until late January. Stratford-upon-Avon is also a good center for trips to Warwick Castle, Kenilworth Castle, Sulgrave Manor (ancestral home of George Washington), and Coventry Cathedral.

THE "ROAD & RAIL LINK"

The Shakespeare Connection **"Road and Rail Link"** is a sure way to attend the Royal Shakespeare Theatre and return to London on the same day. It leaves from London's Euston Station Monday to Friday at 8:40, 10:10, and 10:40am and 5:10pm; Saturday at 8:30 and 10:30am and 5pm; and Sunday at 9:40am and 6:10pm. If you only want to attend the evening performance at the theater, trains leave London at 5:10pm Monday to Friday. Returns to London are timed to fit theater performances, with departure at 11:15pm from either the Guide Friday Ltd. office at the Civic Hall, 14 Rother Street, or just opposite the theater. Journey time from London to Stratford averages 2 hours. It is operated by **British Rail** and **Guide Friday** (tel. 0789/294466). Prices are £20 ($33) for a one-way fare, £24.50 ($45.35) for a round-trip ticket valid for 3 months. Ask for a Shakespeare Connection ticket at London's Euston Station or at any British Rail London Travel Centre. BritRail pass holders using the service simply pay the bus fare to Stratford-upon-Avon from Coventry, £5 ($9.25) one-way, £7 ($12.95) for a round-trip ticket.

WHAT TO SEE & DO

THE THEATER

⭐ The **Royal Shakespeare Company** has a major showcase in Stratford-upon-Avon, the Royal Shakespeare Theatre, Waterside (tel. 0789/295623). Built on the banks of the Avon and seating 1,500 patrons, the theater has a season that runs from early April to late January. The company has some of the finest actors on the British stage. In an average season, five Shakespearean plays are staged.

Usually, you'll need reservations. There are two successive booking periods, each opening about 2 months in advance. You can pick these up from a North American or an English travel agent. If you wait until your arrival in Stratford, it may be too late to get a good seat. Tickets can be booked through New York agents Edwards and Edwards or Keith Prowse, or directly with the theater box office with payment by major credit card. Call the box office at the number listed above. The box office is open Monday to Saturday 9:30am to 8pm. The price of seats generally ranges from £5 to £35 ($9.25 to $64.75). A small number of tickets are always held for sale on the day of a performance. You can make a credit-card reservation and pick up your ticket on the day it is to be used, but you can't cancel once your reservation is made.

The **Swan Theatre** (same address and phone as Royal Shakespeare Theatre) opening in 1986. It seats 430, and stages many plays by Shakespeare and later writers. The interior of the Swan Theatre is in the style of an Elizabethan playhouse. It was erected after the Victorian-style Memorial Theatre, dating from 1879, was destroyed by fire in 1926. The original art gallery, library, and the collections escaped the fire, and now the Swan has displays on stagecraft from medieval mummers to the present day, as well as costumes, props, and photographs from Royal Shakespeare Company productions. The Swan Theatre, presents a repertoire of five plays each season, with tickets ranging from £8 to £21 ($14.80 to $38.85).

The RSC Collection is open all year, except Christmas and Boxing Day, Monday to Saturday from 9:15am to 8pm and Sunday from noon to 5pm (November to March, Sunday from 11am to 4pm). Admission is £2.50 ($2.80) for adults, £1 ($1.85) for children. Theater tours of the Royal Shakespeare and Swan theatres are at 1:30pm and 5:30pm (excluding matinee days) and four times on Sunday, production schedules permitting. Prices of tours for adults is $3.50 ($6.45) for children £2.50 ($4.65).

For information on the RSC Collection and Theatre Tours, call 0789/296655, extension 421.

THE SIGHTS

Besides the attractions on the periphery of Stratford, there are many Elizabethan and Jacobean buildings in this colorful town—many of them administered by the Shakespeare Birthplace Trust. One ticket—costing £6 ($11.10) for adults, £2.50 ($4.65) for children 16 or under—will permit you to visit the five most important sights. You should pick up the ticket if you're planning to do much sightseeing (obtainable at your first stopover at any one of the Trust properties).

SHAKESPEARE'S BIRTHPLACE, Henley St. Tel. 0789/204016.

The son of a glover and whittawer (saddler), the Bard was born on St. George's day (April 23) in 1564, and died 52 years later on the same day. Filled with Shakespeare memorabilia, including a portrait, and furnishings of the writer's time, the Trust property is a half-timbered structure, dating from the first part of the 16th century. The house was bought by public donors in 1847 and preserved as a national shrine. You can visit the oak-beamed living room, the bedroom where Shakespeare was born, a fully equipped kitchen of the period (look for the "babyminder"), and a Shakespeare Museum, illustrating his life and times. Later, you can walk through the garden. It is estimated that some 660,000 visitors pass through the house annually. It is located in the center near Union Street. Next door to the birthplace is the modern Shakespeare Centre, built to commemorate the 400th anniversary of the Bard's birth. It serves both as the administrative headquarters of the Birthplace Trust and as a library and study center. An extension to the original center, which opened in 1981, includes a visitors' center which acts as a reception area for all those coming to the birthplace.

Admission: £2.20 ($4.05) adults, 90p ($1.65) children.

Open: Mar–Oct Mon–Sat 9am–5:30pm, Sun 10am–5:30pm; Nov–Feb Mon–Sat 9:30–4pm, Sun 1:30–4pm. **Closed:** Jan 1, Good Friday, and Dec 24–26.

ANNE HATHAWAY'S COTTAGE, Shottery. Tel. 0789/204016.

In the hamlet of Shottery 1 mile from Stratford-upon-Avon, is the thatched, wattle-and-daub cottage where Anne Hathaway lived before her marriage to the poet. It is the most interesting and seemingly the most photographed of the Trust properties. The Hathaways were yeoman farmers, and the cottage provides a rare insight into the life of a family of Shakespeare's day. Many of the original furnishings, including the courting settle and utensils, are preserved inside the house, which was occupied by descendants of Shakespeare's wife's family until 1892. After a visit to the house, relax in the garden and orchard.

Admission: £1.80 ($3.35) adults, 80p ($1.50) children.

Open: Mar–Oct Mon–Sat 9am–5:30pm, Sun 10am–5:30pm; Nov–Feb Mon–Sat 9:30am–4pm, Sun 1:30–4pm. **Closed:** Jan 1, Good Friday, and Dec 24–26.

Directions: Walk across the meadow to Shottery from Evesham Place in Stratford (pathway marked), or take a bus from Bridge Street.

NEW PLACE/NASH'S HOUSE, Chapel St. Tel. 0789/204016.

This site is where Shakespeare retired in 1610, a prosperous man to judge from the standards of his day. He died there 6 years later, at the age of 52. Regrettably, only the site of his former home remains today, as the house was torn down. You enter the gardens through Nash's House (Thomas Nash married Elizabeth Hall, a granddaughter of the poet). Nash's House has 16th-century period rooms and an exhibition illustrating the history of Stratford. The popular Knott Garden adjoins the site, and represents the style of a fashionable Elizabethan garden. New Place has its own great garden, which once belonged to Shakespeare. Here, the Bard planted a mulberry tree, so popular with latter-day visitors to Stratford that the cantankerous owner of the garden chopped it down. The mulberry tree that grows there today is said to have been planted from a cutting of the original tree.

Admission: £1.50 ($2.80) adults, 60p ($1.10) children. The house is on Chapel Street, a continuation of High Street heading west.

Open: Mar–Oct Mon–Sat 9am–5:30pm, Sun 10am–5:30pm; Nov–Feb Mon–Sat 9:30am–4pm. **Closed:** Jan 1, Good Friday, and Dec 24–26.

MARY ARDEN'S HOUSE AND THE SHAKESPEARE COUNTRYSIDE MUSEUM, Wilmcote. Tel. 0789/298574.

This Tudor farmstead, with its old stone dovecote and various outbuildings, was the girlhood home of Shakespeare's mother. The house contains rare pieces of country furniture and domestic utensils. Within the barns, stable, cowshed, and farmyard you'll find an extensive collection of farming implements illustrating life and work in the local countryside from Shakespeare's time to the present.

Visitors also see the neighboring Glebe Farm whose interior evokes farm life in late Victorian and Edwardian times. A working smithy and displays of country crafts are added attractions. Light refreshments are available, and there is a picnic area.

Admission: £2.50 ($4.65) adults, £1 ($1.85) children.

Open: Mar–Oct Mon–Sat 9am–5:30pm, Sun 10am–5:30pm; Nov–Feb Mon–Sat 9:30am–4pm. **Closed:** Jan 1, Good Friday, and Dec 24–26. **Directions:** Take the A34 (Birmingham) road for 3½ miles.

HALLS'S CROFT, Old Town. Tel. 0789/297848.

Not far from the parish church, Holy Trinity, this house was where Shakespeare's daughter Susanna lived with her husband, Dr. John Hall. It's an outstanding Tudor house with a beautiful walled garden, furnished in the style of a middle-class home of the time. Dr. Hall was widely respected and built up a large medical practice in the area. Exhibits illustrating the theory and practice of medicine in Dr. Hall's time are on view. Visitors are welcome to use the adjoining Hall's Croft Club, which serves morning coffee, lunch, and afternoon tea.

Admission: £1.50 ($2.80) adults, 60p ($1.10) children.

Open: Mar–Oct Mon–Sat 9am–5:30pm, Sun 10am–5:30pm; Nov–Feb Mon–Sat 9:30am–4pm. **Closed:** Jan 1, Good Friday, and Dec 24–26. **Directions:** Walk west from High Street which becomes Chapel Street and Church Street. At the intersection with Old Town, go left.

HOLY TRINITY CHURCH, Trinity St. Tel. 0789/266316.

In an attractive setting near the Avon river, the parish church of Stratford-upon-Avon is distinguished mainly because Shakespeare was buried in the chancel ("and curst be he who moves my bones"). The Parish Register records his baptism and burial (copies of the original, of course). The church has been described as one of the most beautiful parish churches in the world.

Admission: Church free; Shakespeare's tomb 40p (75¢) adults, 25p (45¢) students.

Open: Apr–Oct Mon–Sat 8:30am–6pm, Sun 2–5pm; Nov–Mar Mon–Sat 8:30am–4pm, Sun 2–5pm. **Directions:** Continue past the Royal Shakespeare Theatre with the river on your left. You'll reach the church after a 4-minute walk.

HARVARD HOUSE, High St. Tel. 0789/204507.

Harvard House is a fine example of an Elizabethan town house. Rebuilt in 1596, it was once the home of Katherine Rogers, mother of John Harvard, founder of Harvard University. In 1909 the house was purchased by a Chicago millionaire, Edward Morris, who presented it as a gift to the American university. It is the most ornate house in Stratford. The rooms are filled with period furniture, and floors are made of the local flagstone. Look for the Bible Chair, used for hiding the Bible during the days of Tudor persecution.

Admission: £1 ($1.85) adults, 50p (95¢) students and children.

Open: Apr–Sept Mon–Sat 9am–1pm and 2–6pm, Sun 2–6pm.

THE ROYAL SHAKESPEARE THEATRE SUMMER HOUSE, Avonbank Gardens. Tel. 0789/297671.

This is actually a brass-rubbing center, where medieval and Tudor brasses illustrate the knights and ladies, scholars, merchants, and priests of a bygone era. The Stratford collection contains a large assortment of exact replicas of brasses. The charge made for the rubbings includes the special paper and wax, and any instruction you might need. The house is directly east of Royal Shakespeare Theatre.

Admission: Free.
Open: Apr–Sept daily 10am–6pm; Oct daily 11am–4pm.

TOURS

Guided tours of Stratford-upon-Avon leave the **Guide Friday Tourism Centre** daily. In summer, aboard open-top double-decker buses, departures are every 15 minutes from 9:30am to 5:30pm. You can take a 1-hour ride without stops, or you can get off at any or all of the Shakespeare's Birthplace Trust properties. Anne Hathaway's Cottage and Mary Arden's House are the two logical stops to make outside the town. Tour tickets are valid all day so you can hop on and off the buses. The price for these tours is £4 ($7.40) adults, £1.50 ($2.80) children.

NEARBY ATTRACTIONS

RAGLEY HALL, Alcester. Tel. 0789/762090.
   A magnificent, 115-room Palladian country house, **Ragley Hall,** built in 1680, is the home of the marquess and marchioness of Hertford and their family. It's located in Alcester, 9 miles from Stratford-upon-Avon. The house has been restored and appears much as it did during the early 1700s. Great pains have been taken to duplicate colors, and in some cases the original wallpaper patterns. The pictures, furniture, and works of art that fill the vast and spacious rooms represent 10 generations of collecting by the Seymour family. Ragley Hall may be a private home but it has a museumlike quality, and many of its artifacts have great historical importance.
   Perhaps the most spectacular attraction is the lavishly painted south staircase hall. The present marquess commissioned muralist Graham Rust to paint the modern tromp l'oeil work on the subject of the Temptation, but this religious theme stops with the lavishly evil Devil offering a gold circlet to Christ in the central ceiling medallion.
   The house is open Easter to September Tuesday to Thursday and Saturday and Sunday from noon to 5pm. Gardens are open 10am to 6pm. Admission to the house, garden, and park is £4 ($7.40) for adults, £3 ($5.55) for children. For the park and gardens only adults pay £3 ($5.55) and children £2 ($3.70). There is no suitable bus service so visitors arrive by car. The location is on the A435 road to Evesham, about 1½ miles west of the town of Alcester. There is easy access from the main motorway network, including the M40 from London, some 100 miles away.

COVENTRY

Coventry, **19 miles** north of Stratford-upon-Avon, has long been noted in legend as the ancient market town through which Lady Godiva took her famous ride, giving birth to a new name in English: Peeping Tom. The accuracy of the Lady Godiva story is hard to ascertain. It has been suggested that the good lady never appeared in the nude, but was the victim of scandalmongers who unknowingly immortalized her. Coventry today is a Midlands industrial city.
   ★ The main attraction of the city is **Coventry Cathedral,** Priory Row (tel. 0203/24323). Sir Basel Spence's controversial cathedral was consecrated in 1962. Though the city was partially destroyed during the blitz in the early '40s, the restoration is miraculous. The cathedral is on the same site as the 14th-century Perpendicular building, and you can visit the original tower.
   Outside is Sir Jacob Epstein's bronze masterpiece, *St. Michael Slaying the Devil.* Inside, the outstanding feature is the 70-foot-high altar tapestry by Graham Sutherland, said to be the largest in the world. The floor-to-ceiling abstract stained-glass windows are the work of the Royal College of Art. The West Window is most interesting, with its engraved glass depicting rows of stylized saints and prophets with angels flying between them.
   In the undercroft of the cathedral is a visitor center, the **Spirit of Coventry.** There you can see the Walkway of Holograms, three-dimensional images created with laser light, depicting the Stations of the Cross. It is an exciting walk through sound,

light, and special effects, including a bombed house. The treasures of the cathedral are on show. An audiovisual on the city and church includes the fact that 450 aircraft dropped 40,000 firebombs on the city in 1 day.

After visiting the cathedral, have tea in Fraters Restaurant nearby.

Admission: Tower £1 ($1.85) adults, 80p (95¢) children; visitor center £1.25 ($2.30) adults, 75p ($1.40) children 6–16.

Open: June–Sept daily 9:30am–7pm; off-season daily 9:30am–5:30pm. **Directions:** Local buses from Stratford-upon-Avon run north to Coventry every 20 minutes during the day, a round-trip fare costing £2.90 ($5.35).

SULGRAVE MANOR, Manor Rd., Sulgrave, Banbury, Oxfordshire OX17 25D. Tel. 0295/76205.

⭐ American visitors will be especially interested in this small mid-16th-century Tudor manor. As part of Henry VIII's plan to dissolve the monasteries he sold the priory-owned manor in 1539 to Lawrence Washington, who had been mayor of Northampton; George Washington was a direct descendant of Lawrence (seven generations removed). The Washington family occupied Sulgrave for more than a century, and in 1656, Col. John Washington left for the New World.

In 1914, the manor was purchased by a group of English people in honor of the friendship between Britain and America. Over the years, major restoration has taken place, with an eye toward returning it as much as possible to its original state. The Colonial Dames have been largely responsible for raising the money. From both sides of the Atlantic, the appropriate furnishings were donated, including a number of portraits—even a Gilbert Stuart original of the first president. On the main doorway is the Washington family coat of arms—two bars and a trio of mullets—which is believed to have been the inspiration for the "Stars and Stripes."

Admission: £2.50 ($4.65) adults, £1.25 ($2.30) children.

Open: Mar and Oct–Dec Thurs–Tues 10:30am–1pm and 2–4pm; Apr–Sept Thurs–Tues 10:30am–1pm and 2–5:30pm. **Closed:** Jan–Feb. **Directions:** From Stratford-upon-Avon, take the A422 via Banbury (whose famous cross entered nursery-rhyme fame) and continue to Brackley. Six miles from Brackley leave the A422 and join B4525, which goes to the tiny village of Sulgrave. Follow signs to Sulgrave Manor.

WHERE TO STAY

During the long theater season, it's best to have a reservation. However, you can go to the tourist information center (tel. 0789/293127) daily from 9am to 5:30pm from April to the end of October; from November to the end of March, Monday to Saturday from 10:30am to 4:30pm. They will help find an accommodation for you in the price range you are seeking. The fee for room reservations made is 10% of the first night's stay (bed-and-breakfast rate only) deductible from the visitor's final bill.

It is also possible to reserve accommodations if you write well in advance to the **Tourist Information Centre** (tel. 0789/293127), Bridgefoot, Stratford-upon-Avon, Warwickshire, CV37 6AU. Be sure to specify the price range and the number of beds required. For this postal "book-a-bed-ahead" service, the charge is £2.90 ($5.35), payable in pounds sterling only.

DOUBLES WITHOUT BATH FOR LESS THAN £35 [$64.75]

AIDAN GUEST HOUSE, 11 Evesham Place, Stratford-upon-Avon, Warwickshire CV37 6HT. Tel. 0789/292824. 6 rms (1 with shower). **Directions:** From the center at the police station on Rother St., walk west.

$ Rates (including English breakfast): £28 ($51.80) double without bath, £38 ($70.30) double with bath. AE. **Parking:** Free.

This is a large Victorian family house belonging to Kari and Barry Coupe. Close to the town center, the house is a 5-minute walk from the theater and railway station. All rooms—each a double—have central heating, hot and cold running water, and hot-beverage facilities. The place is particularly recommended for those with small children, as baby-sitting can be arranged. Children's cots are also available. The Coupes keep their place impeccably clean and have furnished it tastefully.

ASHBURTON HOUSE, 27 Evesham Place, Stratford-upon-Avon, War-wickshire CV37 6HT. Tel. 0789/292444. 4 rms (2 with shower). TV
Directions: From the center at the police station on Rother St., walk west.
$ **Rates** (including English breakfast): £14.50–£15 ($26.85–$27.75) single without bath; £28 ($51.80) double without bath, £30 ($55.50) double with bath. AE, MC, V. **Parking:** Free.

This guesthouse is one of the better selections in Stratford. Rooms are handsomely furnished and equipped with hot-beverage facilities. The establishment is centrally heated, and hot water is available for baths and showers at all times. Hosts Steve and Bridget Downer are delighted to receive foreign visitors. They also have a restaurant license and will serve dinner if booked 48 hours in advance, charging £12 ($22.20) for the four-course pretheater repast served at 6pm. Then you can make the 8-minute walk to the Royal Shakespeare Theatre. Advance reservations by letter with a £5 ($9.25) per person deposit are strongly recommended.

COURTLAND HOTEL, 12 Guild St., Stratford-upon-Avon, Warwickshire CV37 6RE. Tel. 0789/292401. 7 rms (2 with bath). TV
$ **Rates** (including English or continental breakfast): £15 ($27.75) single without bath; £28 ($51.80) double without bath, £40 ($74) double with bath; £36–£46 ($66.60–$85.10) family room. AE. **Parking:** Free.

The hotel is in a large Georgian house with antique furniture. The rooms have hot and cold running water, and the owner, Mrs. Bridget Johnson, gives them her personal attention. She will also pick up guests from the station upon request. The location is in the town center, a minute from the bus station, a 5-minute walk from the rail station, and 3 minutes from the theater. The preserves served with breakfast are homemade, and special diets will be catered to upon request.

CRAIG CLEEVE HOUSE, 67-69 Shipston Rd., Stratford-upon-Avon, War-wickshire CV37 7LW. Tel. 0789/296573. Fax 0789/299452. 16 rms (9 with shower). TV
$ **Rates** (including English breakfast): £17.50–£20.50 ($32.40–$37.95) single without bath; £35 ($64.75) double without bath, £45 ($83.25) double with bath. AE, DC, MC, V. **Parking:** Free.

This family-run place is owned by Terry and Margarita Palmer. There is a comfortable guest lounge with TV. The house is off the A34 Oxford Road, is just across the old Clopton Bridge from Stratford, a span which was there in Shakespeare's time. The theater is no more than 10 minutes' walk from the guesthouse if you use the old tramway bridge across the river.

THE CROFT, 49 Shipston Rd., Stratford-upon-Avon, Warwickshire CV37 7LN. Tel. 0789/293419. 9 rms (6 with bath). TV
$ **Rates** (including English breakfast): £17 ($31.45) single without bath; £26 ($48.10) double without bath, £43 ($79.55) double with bath. Family rates available for 3 to 5 persons. **Parking:** Free.

Kevin and Jeanne Hallworth run this traditional guesthouse, which has been in business many years and is kept up-to-date. The Croft stands on the A34 only 5 minutes from the town center and the Royal Shakespeare Theatre. Fully modernized, the house has central heating and hot-beverage facilities in all rooms. A pretheater evening meal can be arranged at £8.50 ($15.75). Gardens lead to the River Avon.

THE HOLLIES, 16 Evesham Place, Stratford-upon-Avon, Warwickshire CV37 6HQ. Tel. 0789/266857. 6 rms (1 with bath). TV. **Directions:** From the center at the police station on Rother Street, walk west.
$ **Rates:** £30 ($55.50) double without bath; £37 ($68.45) double with bath. No credit cards. **Parking:** Free.

This establishment is run by a mother and daughter, Mrs. Mavis Morgan and Mrs. L. Burton. Their guesthouse is in a renovated three-story building that was once a school, although it looks like a stately old home. Bedrooms—all doubles—are large with plenty of wardrobe space, and beds have good, firm mattresses. They serve a plentiful breakfast in a sunny dining room decorated with hand-cut crystal. Baby-sitting can be arranged.

HUNTERS MOON, 150 Alcester Rd., Stratford-upon-Avon, Warwickshire CV39 9DR. Tel. 0789/292888. 7 rms (all with shower). TV
$ Rates (including English breakfast): £17.50–£20 ($32.40–$37) single; £33–£40 ($61.05–$74) double. No credit cards. **Parking:** Free.
On the fringe of Stratford near Anne Hathaway's Cottage is this guesthouse, owned and operated by John Monk for more than 35 years. The house has been completely modernized and refurbished. All rooms have dual-voltage shaver points, fitted hairdryers, and beverage-making facilities. It's 1½ miles from Stratford on the A422 Stratford-Worcester road.

LEMARQUAND, 186 Evesham Rd., Stratford-upon-Avon, Warwickshire CV37 9BS. Tel. 0789/204164. 3 rms (2 with bath or shower). **Directions:** From the center at the police station on Rother St., walk west.
$ Rates (including English breakfast): £13–£15 ($24.05–$27.75) double per person. No credit cards.
Bedrooms here are comfortably equipped and contain hot and cold running water. Each unit is a double. Anne Cross gives good service, and the location is close to the theater and town center.

PARKFIELD GUEST HOUSE, 3 Broad Walk, Stratford-upon-Avon, Warwickshire CV37 6HS. Tel. 0789/293313. 7 rms (4 with shower). TV
$ Rates (including English breakfast): £15 ($27.75) single without bath; £30 ($55.50) double without bath, £36 ($66.60) double with bath. MC, V. **Parking:** Free.

Pauline Rush is the hostess with the mostest, having gotten more reader recommendations than any other place in Stratford-upon-Avon. Rooms at this conveniently located guesthouse have hot-beverage facilities. Breakfast is superb, better than the usual. Mrs. Rush, if possible, will help guests obtain theater tickets. The house is just off A439 (Evesham Road), a 5-minute walk from Royal Shakespeare Theatre.

RAVENHURST HOTEL, 2 Broad Walk, Stratford-upon-Avon, Warwickshire CV37 6HS. Tel. 0789/292515. 7 rms (3 with bath). TV
$ Rates (including English breakfast): £32 ($59.20) double without bath, £40 ($74) double with bath. AE, DC, MC, V. **Parking:** Free.
In a quiet street near the town center is a Victorian townhouse within easy reach of the historic district. Richard and Brenda Workman invite guests to enjoy the comfortable rooms, all of which have beverage-making facilities. Each unit is a double. The Workmans' extensive knowledge of the area can be a big help. The house is directly west of the center, just off the A439 Evesham Rd.

SALAMANDER GUEST HOUSE, 40 Grove Rd., Stratford-upon-Avon, Warwickshire CV37 6PB. Tel. 0789/205728. 8 rms (3 with bath). **Bus:** X16.
$ Rates (including English breakfast): £12.50–£15 ($23.15–$27.75) single without bath; £25 ($46.25) double without bath, £30 ($55.50) double with bath. No credit cards. **Parking:** Free.
One of the better guesthouses of Stratford-upon-Avon is well maintained and homelike, fronting a woodsy park. Maurice and Ninon Croft rent comfortably furnished rooms, including one for families, and the two bathrooms are shared. Four units contain TV. Evening meals, prepared by Maurice, who is a qualified chef, can be ordered, costing from £7 ($12.95) for three courses. Serving is timed so patrons can get to the theater for the evening performances. The house is about a 5-minute walk from the town center.

SEQUOIA HOUSE, 51-53 Shipston Rd., Stratford-upon-Avon, Warwick-

shire CV37 7LN. Tel. 0789/68852. Fax 0789/414559. 25 rms (20 with bath or shower). TV TEL
$ Rates (including English breakfast): £28 ($51.80) single without bath, £42 ($77.70) single with bath; £33 ($61.05) double without bath, £55 ($101.75) double with bath. AE, DC, MC, V. **Parking:** Free.

 This privately run hotel has its own beautiful garden on ¾ acre, and it is conveniently located for visiting the major Shakespeare properties of the National Trust. It is also within easy walking distance of the theater. In fact, the hotel is just across the Avon River opposite the theater. Renovation has vastly improved the house, which was created from two late Victorian buildings. Today it offers rooms with beverage-making equipment and hot and cold running water. Guests gather in a lounge that has a licensed bar and an open Victorian fireplace. The hotel also has a private car park.

TWELFTH NIGHT, Evesham Place, Stratford-upon-Avon, Warwickshire CV37 6HT. Tel. 0789/414595. 7 rms (6 with shower), TV **Directions:** From the center at the police station on Rother St., head west.
$ Rates (including English breakfast): £18 ($33.30) single without bath; £36 ($66.60) double with shower. No credit cards. **Parking:** Free.
The place is aptly named; for a quarter of a century it has accommodated actors from the Royal Shakespeare Theatre Company, many of whom have appeared in productions of *Twelfth Night*. This restored Victorian house is today rated one of the finest guest accommodations in Stratford. Only nonsmokers are accepted.

THE MARLYN HOTEL, 3 Chestnut Walk, Stratford-upon-Avon, Warwickshire CV37 6HG. Tel. 0789/293752. 8 rms (none with bath).
$ Rates (including English breakfast): £16–£17 ($27.60–$31.45) single; £30–£32 ($55.50–$59.20) double. MC, V. **Parking:** Free.
This Victorian house has been welcoming guests since 1890. It is conveniently situated near Hall's Croft, the former home of Shakespeare's daughter, and is within a 5-minute walk of the town center and the Royal Shakespeare Theatre. The hotel is centrally heated, and each bedroom contains tea- and coffee-making facilities. There is also a small lounge with TV. If you don't want to pack your Shakespeare, don't worry. A copy of the complete works of the Bard is available for reference in every bedroom. The Marlyn has been owned and managed since 1973 by the Allen family, and Mrs. Mary Allen endeavors to make guests comfortable throughout their stay.

MIDWAY GUEST HOUSE, 182 Evesham Rd., Stratford-upon-Avon, Warwickshire CV37 9BS. Tel. 0789/204154. 4 rms (all with bath or shower). **Directions:** From the center at the police station on Rother St., head west.
$ Rates (including English breakfast): £17–£22 ($31.45–$40.70) single; £34–£44 ($62.90–$81.40) double. No credit cards. **Parking:** Free.
This is the domain of Janet and Keith Cornwell. All bedrooms have carpeting and up-to-date furnishings and amenities such as beverage-making equipment, hairdryers (on request), and alarm-clock radios.

MOONRAKER HOUSE, 40 Alcester Rd., Stratford-upon-Avon, Warwickshire CV37 9DB. Tel. 0789/267115. Fax 0789/295504. 15 rms (all with shower), 3 suites (all with bath). TV
$ Rates (including English breakfast): £25 ($46.25) single; £34–£38 ($62.90–$70.30) double; £55 ($101.75) suite. AE, MC, V. **Parking:** Free.
The hardworking owners Mike and Maureen Spencer receive guests in rooms with hairdryers and hot-beverage facilities. A luxury suite is available with a bedroom, lounge, and kitchenette, plus two more suites, each with two rooms. Among amenities are four-poster beds, a no-smoking lounge area, and garden patios. The house is 2 minutes by car from the heart of town on the A422.

NEWLANDS, 7 Broad Walk, Stratford-upon-Avon, Warwickshire CV37 6HS. Tel. 0789/298449. 3 rms (1 with bath). TV

$ Rates (including English breakfast): £14–£15 ($25.90–$27.75) single without bath; £28 ($51.80) double without bath, £34 ($62.90) double with bath. No credit cards. **Parking:** Free.

Sue and Rex Boston welcome guests, especially fellow theatergoers, to their centrally heated rooms, all with hot and cold water basins, and hot-beverage facilities. Each room is comfortably furnished and well maintained. The owners are aware of the sightseeing possibilities in the area, and are happy to help visitors. The house is just off the A430 (Evesham Road), a 10-minute walk from the Royal Shakespeare Theatre.

NEARBY ACCOMMODATIONS

BROOM HALL INN, Broom, near Alcester, Warwickshire B50 4HE. Tel. 0789/773757. 12 rms (all with bath). TV **Directions:** Head west from Stratford along A439 to Bideford-on-Avon and take the turning signposted to Broom. Broom Hall is ½ mile on the left-hand side.

$ Rates (including English breakfast): £32.50–£35 ($60.15–$64.75) single; £45–£50 ($83.25–$92.50) double. AE, DC, MC, V. **Parking:** Free.

A privately owned 16th-century inn, it stands in the little hamlet of Broom on the River Alne, right near the Avon. It's near Bideford-on-Avon, about 6 miles from Stratford-upon-Avon and 10 miles from Broadway in the Cotswolds. The building is a black-and-white timbered Elizabethan structure in a rural area away from main roads. Steve Tavener, who owns and manages the inn, also operates a carvery restaurant serving a number of à la carte specialties. Meals cost from £8 ($14.80). A special Sunday lunch menu is also offered.

CHURCH FARM, Long Marston, Stratford-upon-Avon, Warwickshire CV37 8RH. Tel. 0789/720275. 2 rms (none with shower). TV **Directions:** From Stratford, take A34 south, forking right onto B4632. Go for about 3 miles and after passing an airfield on your right, turn right (signposted Long Marston). At the T-junction, turn right again into the village. Church Farm is on your left.

$ Rates (including English breakfast): £18–£22 ($33.30–$40.70) single; £25–£30 ($46.25–$55.50) double. No credit cards. **Parking:** Free.

This 17th-century farmstead in a secluded garden is about 6 miles from Stratford. The owner, Mrs. Wiggy Taylor, enjoys meeting people from other countries and welcomes children (she can provide baby-sitting services). You can rent a large room, with hot and cold running water and beverage-making equipment.

KING'S LODGE, Long Marston, Stratford-upon-Avon, Warwickshire CV37 8RL. Tel. 0789/720705. 3 rms (1 with bath); 3 apartments. **Directions:** From Stratford, take the A34 Oxford road; on the outskirts of town, fork right on to the B4632 Cheltenham road and continue for 4½ miles. Turn right at the signpost to Long Marston and proceed to a "T" junction, turning right.

$ Rates (including English breakfast): £16.50 ($30.55) single without bath; £155 ($286.75) weekly apartment. No credit cards. **Parking:** Free. **Closed:** Dec–Jan.

This place is 6 miles southwest of Stratford-upon-Avon, built on the site of a manor house where Charles II hid out as a manservant after the Battle of Worcester. George and Angela Jenkins welcome guests to three comfortably furnished and centrally heated bedrooms with hot and cold water basins. One bedroom features a traditional four-poster bed hewn from timber grown on the estate. Besides the bedrooms in the lodge, there are self-service apartments on the grounds, but when the other accommodations are full, the Jenkinses will rent any unoccupied apartments on a B&B basis. For £8 ($14.80) you can enjoy a three-course dinner with coffee at an oak table in what was once part of the manor's great hall. The restored room is dominated by a large stone inglenook fireplace. Mullioned windows frame vistas of green lawns and stately trees.

LOXLEY FARM, Stratford Rd., Loxley, Warwickshire CV35 9JN. Tel. 0789/840265. 3 rms (all with bath). **Directions:** Take the small Loxley Rd. southeast of the center.

$ Rates (including English breakfast): £25 ($46.25) single; £34–£37 ($62.90–$68.45) double. No credit cards. **Parking:** Free.

The nearby village of Loxley, just 3½ miles from Stratford-upon-Avon, is an ancient community, boasting one of the oldest Saxon churches in England, the parish church of St. Nicholas. This quiet country village, said to be the original home of Robin Hood (Sir Robin of Loxley), is a quiet little place with a delightful old pub.

Roderick and Anne Horton live in a real dream of a thatched cottage with creeper climbing up the old walls. The garden is full of apple blossoms, roses, and sweet-scented flowers. A stone path leads across the grass and into the flagstone hall, with nice old rugs and a roaring fire. Accommodations are in the main house and in the 17th-century half-timbered thatched barn in the orchard. Two rooms contain TV. The barn has been remodeled to include a sitting room and kitchen.

PEAR TREE COTTAGE, Church Rd., Wilmcote, Stratford-upon-Avon, Warwickshire CV37 9XJ. Tel. 0789/205889. 7 rms (all with bath). TV
$ Rates (including English breakfast): £26 ($48.10) single; £36 ($66.60) double. No credit cards. **Parking:** Free.

In the home village of Shakespeare's mother, Mary Arden, is this late 16th-century farmhouse (with later additions). Exposed beams and antique furniture give the house a period charm, while such things as modern plumbing and central heating add 20th-century comfort. No longer a farmhouse, the cottage stands in nearly an acre of lawn and gardens. Mr. and Mrs. Mander can accommodate up to 15 guests. A sitting room has color TV and comfortable chairs. Mary Arden's birthplace is visible across the field from the house. The cottage is 3½ miles northwest of Stratford-upon-Avon in the direction of Wilmcote (1 mile off the A3400 road to Birmingham).

WHERE TO EAT

MEALS FOR LESS THAN £10 [$18.50]

Restaurants

BOBBY BROWN'S, 12 Sheep St. Tel. 292554.
Cuisine: ENGLISH/FRENCH. **Reservations:** Not needed.
$ Prices: Appetizers £1.95–£3.95 ($3.60–$7.30); main courses £3.95–£9.95 ($7.30–$18.40); pretheater dinner £9.50 ($17.60); snack lunch £3 ($5.55). AE, DC, MC, V.
Open: Lunch Mon–Fri noon–2:30pm, Sun noon–5pm; dinner Mon–Fri 6–11pm, Sun 7–10pm; Sat noon–11pm.

This is a black-and-white timbered building with a high gabled wing dating from the early 16th century. On the second floor, a maze of three rooms is filled with antique oak tables, Windsor chairs, and settles. The whole place has a certain medieval charm. You can enjoy steaks, lasagne, meat pies such as beef Guiness, and the like.

THE COTTAGE TEA GARDEN, Cottage Lane, Shottery. Tel. 293122.
Cuisine: LIGHT LUNCHES/TEA. **Reservations:** Not needed.
Transportation: Stratford's "blue minibus" passes nearby every 10 minutes throughout the day.
$ Prices: Sandwiches £1.20–£1.50 ($2.20–$2.80); countryman platters £2.95 ($5.45); cream teas £2.50 ($4.65); pot of tea 60p ($1.10). No credit cards.
Open: Mar–Sept daily 10am–5pm.

This tea garden is set within its own rose garden a few paces from Anne Hathaway's Cottage, on a country lane 1½ miles from Stratford-upon-Avon. It is almost hidden by the entrance to a large parking lot. The tearoom offers a verdant and refreshing place for respite from the whirlwind of sightseeing. Though most visitors prefer a chair on the outdoor patio, a glassed-in conservatory offers indoor seating for 25. Available throughout the day are at least five kinds of countryman's platters, which include salads, raw vegetables, and cheese (a ploughman's lunch); ham (a huntsman's lunch); tuna (a fisherman's lunch); cold roast beef (a cowman's lunch); and Cornish pasties (a

Cornishman's lunch). Only one kind of tea is offered, presumably a locally popular blend.

HATHAWAY TEA ROOMS, 19 High St. Tel. 292404.
  Cuisine: ENGLISH. **Reservations:** Not needed.
$ **Prices:** Appetizers £1.50 ($2.80); main courses £3.85–£4.50 ($7.15–$8.35); high teas £4.20 ($7.75); cream teas £2.75 ($5.10). No credit cards.
  Open: Mon–Sat 9am–5:30pm, Sun 11am–5:30pm.

    Housed in a mellowed building almost 400 years old, it's as timbered and rickety as its across-the-street neighbor, Harvard House. It's also near the landmark Holy Trinity Church. You pass through a bakery shop and climb to the second floor, into a forest of oaken beams. Sitting at the English tables and chairs, you can order wholesome food which might include a vegetarian dish of the day, Welsh rarebit, quiches and salads, and the traditional favorite of steak-and-kidney pie. A classic steaming fruit pie might round off your meal. You can also visit for high tea, which is a cream tea enhanced with sandwiches.

LORD'S BISTRO, 6 Union St. Tel. 269106.
  Cuisine: CONTINENTAL. **Reservations:** Recommended, especially Fri–Sat night.
$ **Prices:** Appetizers £1.99–£3.99 ($3.70–$7.40); main courses £4.95–£10 ($9.15–$18.50). AE, MC, V.
  Open: Daily noon–11pm.

The bistro is next to Slug & Lettuce, north of Bridge Street in the town center. Its mood is informal, and it is decorated with Iberian wood paneling. The chefs turn out a selection of dishes such as lemon sole or beef Wellington. Vegetarian lasagne and charcoal-grilled beef and lamb are also served. Watch for the ever-changing daily specials. Finish with "death by chocolate."

THE RIVER TERRACE RESTAURANT, Royal Shakespeare Theatre, Waterside. Tel. 293226.
  Cuisine: ENGLISH. **Reservations:** None.
$ **Prices:** Appetizers £1.25–£3.50 ($2.30–$6.45); main courses £3.50–£4.80 ($6.45–$8.90). No credit cards.
  Open: Mon–Sat 10:30am–9:30pm, Sun 10:30am–5:30pm.

    Also in the theater overlooking the Avon, this coffee shop and licensed restaurant is open to the general public as well as to theatergoers. This self-service establishment offers typical English and pasta dishes, as well as morning coffee and afternoon teas. Try baked ham, carbonade of beef, or lasagne.

SLUG & LETTUCE, 38 Guild St. Tel. 299700.
  Cuisine: ENGLISH. **Reservations:** Recommended.
$ **Prices:** Bar snacks £4.50–£5.25 ($8.35–$9.70); appetizers £2–£3.75 ($3.70–$6.95); main courses £7.50–£12 ($13.90–$22.20). MC, V.
  Open: Drinks and pub snacks Mon–Sat 11am–11pm; Sun noon–3pm and 7–10:30pm; lunch daily noon–2:30pm; dinner Mon–Sat 5:30–9:30pm, Sun 7–9:30pm.

This brick-fronted establishment was created in the early 1980s when a pair of much older pubs was interconnected to form a larger whole. Popular both with locals and tourists, the pub is rustic and cozy, with good food and ale. In fair weather, tables are set up on the sidewalk outside. The menu is robustly prepared with fresh ingredients, and might include pork chops cooked with apples and flavored with Calvados, fresh mussels in garlic butter, and Cumberland sausage served in a mushroom and mustard sauce. The restaurant is a 5-minute walk north of the center, on a busy street eventually designated the A38 leading to Birmingham.

VINTNER WINE BAR, 5 Sheep St. Tel. 297259.
  Cuisine: CONTINENTAL. **Reservations:** Recommended. **Bus:** X16 or X18.
$ **Prices:** Appetizers £1.75–£3 ($3.25–$5.55); main courses £3.75–£7.25 ($6.95–$13.40); glass of house wine £1.40 ($2.60). DC, MC, V.

Open: Daily 10:30am–11pm.

The Vintner demonstrates why wine-bar dining is all the rage in England. The Elizabethan decor is fitting in the town of Shakespeare, and the name comes from a wine merchant, John Smith, who occupied this address early in the 17th century. Around the corner from the Shakespeare Hotel, a short walk from the Royal Shakespeare Theatre, this popular drinking and dining spot has daily specials posted on the blackboard. Many guests prefer one of the tempting cold plates at lunch. You can also order a vegetable dish of the day, a grilled sirloin, or a salmon steak.

A Restaurant Complex

Marlowe's Restaurant, Marlowe's Alley, 17-18 High Street (tel. 204999), is made up of the Elizabethan Room, a 16th-century oak-paneled dining room, and Georgies, once the hayloft of this ancient house. Meals in the Elizabethan Room start from around £11 ($20.30). The garden patio overflows with flowers, and the owners, George and Judy Kruszynskyj, invite you to have a drink or even an al fresco meal here. Hours are from pretheater to 10:30pm Monday to Friday, and to 11pm Saturday. A traditional Sunday lunch of roast beef and Yorkshire pudding is served from noon to 2:30pm, and it is also open Sunday evening from 7 to 9:30pm.

Georgies, in the former hayloft, serves meals starting at £5 ($9.25), specializing in lunch snacks and evening bistro-style dining. Hours are from 6 to 10pm Monday to Saturday.

Pubs

THE BLACK SWAN, Waterside. Tel. 297312.

Cuisine: ENGLISH. **Reservations:** Not needed.

$ **Prices:** Appetizers £2–£3.50 ($3.70–$6.45); main courses $4.50–£6.50 ($8.35–$12.05); pint of ale £1.33 ($2.45). No credit cards.

Open: Lunch Mon–Sat 11am–4pm, Sun noon–2pm; dinner Mon–Sat 5:30–11pm.

Affectionately known as the Dirty Duck, this has been a popular hangout for Stratford players since the 18th century. The wall is lined with autographed photos of its patrons, such as Lord Olivier. The front lounge and bar crackles with intense conversation. In the spring and fall an open fire blazes. In the Dirty Duck Grill Room, typical English grills, among other dishes, are featured. You'll be faced with a choice of a dozen appetizers, most of which would make a meal in themselves. Main dishes include braised kidneys or oxtails or honey-roasted duck. In fair weather, you can have drinks in the front garden and watch the swans on the Avon glide by. The pub overlooks Avon between the Royal Shakespeare Theatre and Holy Trinity Church.

THE GARRICK INN, 25 High St. Tel. 292186.

Cuisine: ENGLISH. **Reservations:** Recommended.

$ **Prices:** Appetizers £1.10–£1.95 ($2.05–$3.60); main courses £3–£7 ($5.55–$12.95). MC, V.

Open: Pub Mon–Sat 11am–11pm, Sun noon–3pm and 7–10:30pm. Lunch daily noon–3pm; dinner Mon–Sat 5–7:30pm.

This black-and-white timbered Elizabethan pub has an unpretentious charm. It is named after David Garrick, one of England's greatest actors. The front bar is decorated with tapestry-covered settles, an old oak refectory table, and an open fireplace where the locals gravitate. The black bar has a circular fireplace with a copper hood and mementos on the triumphs of the English stage. Menu choices include curried vegetarian crêpes known as a *samosas,* a mixed farmhouse grill, grilled lamb chops, or a succulent version of rumpsteak. The pub is in the center of Stratford's main street, close to the Harvard House.

WHITE SWAN, Rother St. Tel. 297022.

Cuisine: ENGLISH. **Reservations:** Not needed.

$ **Prices:** Appetizers £2.50–£3.50 ($4.65–$6.50); main courses £3.50–£7 ($6.45–$12.95); lunches £6 ($11.10); pint of ale £1.33 ($2.45). AE, DC, MC, V.

Open: Lunch Mon–Sat 10:30am–2:30pm, Sun noon–3pm; dinner Mon–Sat 6–11pm, Sun 7–10:30pm.

This is one of the most atmospheric pubs in Stratford-upon-Avon. Once you step inside, you're drawn into a world of cushioned leather armchairs, old oak settles, oak paneling, and fireplaces. It is believed that Shakespeare may have come here to drink back when it was called Kings Head. At lunch you can partake of the hot dishes of the day along with fresh salads and sandwiches. The pub is in the center near the police station.

WORTH THE EXTRA BUCKS

THE BOX TREE RESTAURANT, Royal Shakespeare Theatre, Waterside. Tel. 293226.

Cuisine: FRENCH/ITALIAN/ENGLISH. **Reservations:** Required.

$ **Prices:** Dinner (fixed-price) Mon–Thurs £20.25 ($37.45); Fri–Sat £21.25 ($39.30); Mon–Sat matinee lunch (fixed-price) £13.50 ($25). AE, MC, V.

Open: Lunch matinees Mon–Sat noon–2:30pm; dinner Mon–Sat 5:45–10pm.

This place is in the best location in town, right in the theater itself, with walls of glass providing an unobstructed view of the Avon and its swans. During intermission, there is a snack feast of smoked salmon and champagne. After each evening's performance you can dine by flickering candlelight. There's a special phone for reservations in the theater lobby.

---

2. WARWICK

92 miles NW of London; 8 miles N of Stratford-upon-Avon

GETTING THERE By Train Trains run frequently between Stratford-upon-Avon and Warwick.

By Bus A Midland Red bus from Stratford-upon-Avon (no. 18 or X16) departs Stratford-upon-Avon during the day every hour. Trip time is 15 to 20 minutes.

By Car You can reach Warwick via the A46 from Stratford-upon-Avon.

ESSENTIALS The **area code** is 0926. The **Tourist Information Centre** is at The Court House, Jury Street (tel. 0926/494316).

Visitors seem to come to this town on the Avon just to see Warwick Castle. Then they're off, usually to the ruins of Kenilworth Castle. But the historic center of medieval Warwick has a lot more to offer, and deserves greater respect.

In 1694, a fire swept through the heart of Warwick, destroying large parts of the town, but a number of Elizabethan and medieval buildings still survive, along with some fine Georgian structures from a later date. (Very few traces of the town walls remain, except the East and West gates.) Warwick cites Ethelfleda, daughter of Alfred the Great, as its founder. But most of its history is associated with the earls of Warwick, a title created by the son of William the Conqueror in 1088. The story of those earls—the Beaumonts, the Beauchamps (such figures as "Kingmaker" Richard Neville)—makes for an exciting episode in English history but is too complicated to go into here.

WHAT TO SEE & DO

WARWICK CASTLE, Castle Hill. Tel. 0926/495421.

Perched on a rocky cliff above the Avon, this stately late 17th-century style mansion is surrounded by a magnificent 14th-century fortress. The first significant fortifications at Warwick were built by Ethelfleda, daughter of Alfred the Great, in A.D. 915. In 1068, 2 years after the Norman Conquest, William the Conqueror ordered the construction of a motte and baily (timber and plaster) castle.

The castle mound is all that remains today of the Norman castle, as this was sacked by Simon de Montfort in the Barons' War of 1264.

The Beauchamp family, the most illustrious medieval earls of Warwick, are responsible for the way the castle looks today, and much of the external structure remains unchanged from the mid-14th century. When the castle was granted to Sir Fulke Greville by James I in 1604, he spent £20,000 (an enormous sum in those days) converting the existing castle buildings into a luxurious mansion. The Grevilles have held the earl of Warwick title since 1759, when it passed from the Rich family.

The state rooms and great hall house fine collections of paintings, furniture, arms, and armor. The armory, dungeon, torture chamber, ghost tower, clock tower, and Guy's tower create a vivid picture of the castle's turbulent past and its important role in the history of England.

The private apartments of Lord Brooke and his family, who in recent years sold the castle to Madame Tussaud's waxworks company, are open to visitors. They house a display of a carefully reconstructed Royal Weekend House Party of 1898. The major rooms contain wax models of important figures of the time; young Winston Churchill, the duchess of Devonshire, Winston's widowed mother, Jennie, and Clara Butt, the celebrated singer, along with the earl and countess of Warwick and their family. In the Kenilworth bedroom, the Prince of Wales, later to become King Edward VII, reads a letter, and in the red bedroom, the duchess of Marlborough prepares for her bath. Surrounded by gardens, lawns, and woodland, where peacocks roam freely, and skirted by the Avon, Warwick Castle was described by Sir Walter Scott in 1828 as "that fairest monument of ancient and chivalrous splendor which yet remains uninjured by time."

Don't miss the Victorian rose garden, a re-creation of an original design from 1868 by Robert Marnock. The original garden had fallen into disrepair, and a tennis court had been built on the site. In 1980 it was decided to restore the garden, and as luck would have it, Marnock's original plans were discovered in the county records office. Close by the rose garden is a Victorian alpine rockery and water garden. The romantic castle is host to various colorful pageants. There are regular appearances of the magnificent Red Knight on his splendid warhorse, and traditional Morris Dancers perform on the lawns. Some form of live entertainment is presented almost every day on the grounds in summer.

Admission: £5.50 ($10.20) adults, £3.50 ($6.50) children.

Open: Mar–Oct daily 10am–5:30pm; Nov–Feb daily 10am–4:30pm. **Closed:** Christmas Day.

ST. MARY'S CHURCH, Warwick Parish Office, Old Square. Tel. 0926/400771.

Destroyed in part by the fire of 1694, this church with its rebuilt battlemented tower and nave is considered among the finest examples of late 17th- and early 18th-century architecture. The Beauchamp Chapel, spared from the flames, encases the Purbeck marble tomb of Richard Beauchamp, a well-known earl of Warwick who died in 1439 and is commemorated by a gilded bronze effigy. The most powerful man in the kingdom, not excepting Henry V, Beauchamp has a tomb considered one of the finest remaining examples of Perpendicular-Gothic style from the mid-15th century. The tomb of Robert Dudley, earl of Leicester, a favorite of Elizabeth I, is against the north wall. The Perpendicular-Gothic choir dates from the 14th century, as do the Norman crypt and the chapter house.

Admission: Free (donations only).

Open: June–Sept 9am–6pm; off-season 9am–4pm. **Transportation:** All buses to Warwick stop at Old Square.

LORD LEYCESTER HOSPITAL, High St. Tel. 0926/491422.

At the West Gate, this group of half-timbered almshouses was also spared from the great fire. The buildings were erected in about 1400, and the hospital was founded in 1571 by Robert Dudley, the earl of Leicester, as a home for old soldiers. It is still in use by ex-servicemen and their wives today. On top of the West Gate is the attractive little chapel of St. James, dating from the 12th century but renovated many times since.

Admission: £1.80 ($3.30) adults, 50p (95¢) children.
Open: June–Sept Mon–Sat 10am–5:30pm; off-season 10am–4pm. Last admission 15 minutes before closing.

WARWICK DOLL MUSEUM, Oken's House, Castle St. Tel. 0926/ 495546.
In one of the most charming Elizabethan buildings in Warwick is this doll museum, located near St. Mary's Church off Jury Street in the center. Its seven rooms contain an extensive collection of dolls in wood, wax, and porcelain. The house once belonged to Thomas Oken, a great benefactor of Warwick.
Admission: 75p ($1.40) adults, 50p (95¢) children.
Open: Easter–Sept Mon–Sat 10am–5pm; Sun 2–5pm.

WARWICKSHIRE MUSEUM, The Market Place. Tel. 0926/412500.
This museum was established in 1836 to house a collection of geological remains, fossils, and an exhibit of amphibians from the Triassic period. There are also displays illustrating the history, archeology, and natural history of the county, including the famous Sheldon tapestry map.
Admission: Free.
Open: May–Sept Mon–Sat 10am–5:30pm, Sun 2:30–5pm. **Directions:** From Jury Street in the center, take a right onto Swan Street which leads to the museum.

ST. JOHN'S HOUSE, St. John's. Tel. 0926/412132.
At Coten End, not far from the castle gates, is this early 17th-century house with exhibits on Victorian domestic life. A schoolroom is furnished with original 19th-century school furniture and equipment. During the school term, Warwickshire children, dressed in period costumes, can be seen enjoying Victorian-style lessons. A study room is available where you can see objects from the reserve collections. The costume collection is a particularly fine one, and visitors can study the drawings and photos that make up the costume catalog. These facilities are available by appointment only. Upstairs is a military museum, tracing the history of the Royal Warwickshire Regiment from 1674 to the present day. For more information and for appointments in the study room, call the Keeper of Social History at the number listed above. The house is at the crossroads of the main Warwick/Leamington road (A425/A429), and the Coventry road (A429).
Admission: Free.
Open: Oct–Apr, Tues–Sat 10am–12:30pm and 1:30–5:30pm; May–Sept Sun 2:30–5pm.

WHERE TO STAY

Many prefer to seek lodgings in Warwick, then commute to Stratford-upon-Avon. The area is full of pubs and restaurants that serve good English food at reasonable prices.

DOUBLES WITHOUT BATH FOR LESS THAN £35 [$64.75]

CAMBRIDGE VILLA, 20A Emscote Rd., Warwick, Warwickshire CV34 4FL. Tel. 0926/491169. 16 rms (6 with bath). TV **Directions:** From St. John's, continue along Coten End to Emscote Rd. in the direction of Leamington Spa.
$ **Rates** (including English breakfast): £17.50 ($32.40) single without bath, £26 ($48.10) single with bath; £35 ($64.75) double without bath, £45 ($83.25) double with bath. MC, V. **Parking:** Free.
This place lies within a 4-minute walk west of Warwick Castle, but you can also take an even more pleasant walk through St. Nicholas Park to reach it. Bedrooms are decorated in a comfortable modern style. The hotel has a good Italian restaurant.

THE OLD RECTORY, Vicarage Lane, Stratford Rd., Sherbourne, near Warwick, Warwickshire CV35 8AB. Tel. 0926/624562. 14 rms (all with bath or shower).
$ **Rates** (including English breakfast): £25–£30 ($46.25–$55.50) single; £34–£42

($62.90–$77.70) double; £45 ($83.25) family room. No credit cards. **Parking:** Free.

This 300-year-old farmhouse has been restored and decorated with antiques by the owners, Sheila and Martin Greenwood. There are rooms in the main house, as well as a converted carriage house suitable for a family. Several bedrooms have antique brass beds. It's just off the A46 between Warwick and Stratford-upon-Avon, less than 3 miles southwest of Warwick.

PENDERRICK, 36 Coten End, Warwick, Warwickshire CV34 4NP. Tel. 0926/499399. 7 rms (all with bath or shower). TV

$ Rates (including English breakfast): £25.50 ($47.20) single; £39.50–£43 ($73.10–$79.55) double; £45 ($83.25) family room. AE, DC, MC, V. **Parking:** Free.

This place was originally built in 1838. The architect carefully positioned it so it would not harm the enormous copper beech in the front yard. It was constructed of a blue-toned stone quarried near Birmingham, which had been procured from the ruins of a nearby prison. Today the Blackband family receives guests, and the beech tree is bigger than ever. There's a long and narrow garden in back (the hotel actually occupies only half of the original house), and visitors can walk in St. Nicholas Park, whose entrance is just 50 yards from Penderrick. A fixed-price, three-course dinner can be served at £10 ($18.50) to guests who request it in advance. The house is a 5-minute walk from castle toward Leamington Spa Road.

WESTHAM GUEST HOUSE, 76 Emscote Rd., Warwick, Warwickshire CV34 5QC. Tel. 0926/491756. 7 rms (2 with bath). TV **Directions:** From St. John's, continue along Coten End leading to Emscote Rd. in the directions of Leamington Spa.

$ Rates (including English breakfast): £14–£15 ($25.90–$27.75) single without bath; £28 ($51.80) double without bath, £32 ($59.20) double with bath. No credit cards. **Parking:** Free.

Lying within a residential section of town along a busy road, this canopied building with a garden is managed by the Donald family. It's about a 5-minute walk from Warwick center. The guest house is licensed to serve drinks to guests and has an extensive bar menu served nightly from 7 to 9pm. The guesthouse lies on the A445, the main road leading to Leamington Spa. If approaching from London, you can come in from the M1, then follow signs for Coventry on to the A46, leading into Warwick.

WARWICK LODGE GUEST HOUSE, 82 Emscote Rd., Warwick, Warwickshire CV34 5QJ. Tel. 0926/492927. 7 rms (none with bath). TV **Directions:** From St. John's, continue along Coten End to Emscote Rd. in the direction of Leamington Spa.

$ Rates (including English breakfast): £14–£16 ($25.90–$29.60) single; £26–£28 ($48.10–$51.80) double. MC, V. **Parking:** Free.

Run by Grace and Bernard Smith, this informal place is close enough to Stratford-upon-Avon to be a base for touring Shakespeare Country. All rooms have hot-beverage facilities, central heating, hot and cold running water, and comfortable beds. The location is ½ mile from Warwick.

WORTH THE EXTRA BUCKS

TUDOR-HOUSE INN & RESTAURANT, 90-92 West St., Warwick, Warwickshire CV34 6AW. Tel. 0926/495447. Fax 0926/492948. 11 rms (8 with bath or shower). TV TEL

$ Rates: (including English breakfast): £24 ($44.40) single without bath, £40 ($74) single with bath; £54 ($99.90) double without bath, £60 ($111) double with bath. AE, DC, MC, V. **Parking:** Free.

 At the edge of town on the A429 road to Stratford, is a black-and-white timbered inn built in 1472. It is one of the few buildings to escape the fire that destroyed High Street in 1694. Off the central hall are two large rooms, each of which could be the setting for an Elizabethan play. All bedrooms have washbasins, and two have doors only 4 feet high. In the corner of the lounge is an open turning staircase. A regular meal in the restaurant and steak bar costs from £10 ($18.50). Tudor House is on the main road from Stratford-upon-Avon leading to Warwick Castle.

WHERE TO EAT

MEALS FOR LESS THAN £12 ($22.20)

BAR ROUSSEL, 62A Market Place. Tel. 491983.
　　Cuisine: INTERNATIONAL. **Reservations:** Not needed. **Directions:** From Jury St. in the center, take a right turn into Swan St.
$　Prices: Appetizers £1.50–£2 ($2.80–$3.70); main courses £3.40–£3.90 ($6.30–$7.20). MC, V.
　　Open: Lunch Mon–Sat noon–2:30pm; dinner daily 6–9:45pm.

This bistro and wine bar offers a choice of 53 wines, beers, and "spirits." Every day there is a freshly made soup followed by a homemade dish of the day, a hot casserole or a meat pie. The cheese board features nine different selections with crackers and bread. Vegetarian dishes are featured, as are occasional Mexican and Indian dishes.

NICOLINIS BISTRO, 18 Jury St. Tel. 495817.
　　Cuisine: ITALIAN. **Reservations:** Recommended.
$　Prices: Appetizers £1.60–£8.50 ($2.95–$15.75); main courses £6.50–£8 ($12.05–$14.80). No credit cards.
　　Open: Tues–Sun 9:30am–10:30pm.
This is a touch of Italy in staid Warwick. Lynne and Nicky, as they are known, welcome you to their attractive restaurant, which is decorated with greenery. Check out the crisp salads and luscious Italian desserts at the enclosed counter. You're faced with an array of appetizers, pizzas, pastas, salads, and desserts, not to mention the main courses. Pizzas come in sizes of 6½ to 9 inches, and Nicolinis Choice includes "everything." For a main course you can order chicken Kiev with potatoes, although the lasagne would be more typical. The restaurant is in the town center at the castle.

PICCOLINO'S, 31 Smith St. between Jury St. and Coten End. Tel. 491020.
　　Cuisine: ITALIAN. **Reservations:** Not needed.
$　Prices: Appetizers £1.55–£3.20 ($2.85–$5.90); main courses £3.55–£7.95 ($6.55–$14.70). MC, V.
　　Open: Lunch noon–2:30pm; dinner 5–10:30 or 11:30pm.
The pasta and pizza joint of Warwick has beamed ceilings, pictures and miniature spotlights. This Italian restaurant is informal and fun, serving a wide selection of pizzas, including a "red hot Mamma" with a zesty chili flavor. You can also order such filling pasta dishes as tortellini à la crema and tagliatelle carbonara. Italian wine may be ordered by the glass.

---

3. KENILWORTH

5 miles N of Warwick; 13 miles N of Stratford-upon-Avon;
102 miles NW of London

GETTING THERE　By Train　From London (both Paddington and Euston) InterCity train lines make frequent and fast connections to either Coventry or Stratford-upon-Avon, from which the Midland Red Line buses make regular connections into Kenilworth.

By Bus　Midland Red Line buses run frequently from either Stratford-upon-Avon or Coventry.

By Car From Warwick (see above), drive to Kenilworth along A46 on the road to Coventry.

ESSENTIALS The **area code** is 0926. The **Tourist Information Centre** is at the Kenilworth Library, 11 Smalley Place (tel. 0926/52595).

The major attraction here is **Kenilworth Castle,** Kenilworth (tel. 0926/52078), now in magnificent ruins. It once had walls that enclosed an area of 7 acres. It is the subject of Sir Walter Scott's romance, *Kenilworth*. In 1957 Lord Kenilworth presented the decaying castle to England, and limited restoration has since been carried out.

The castle was built by Geoffrey de Clinton, a lieutenant of Henry I. Caesar's Tower, with its 16-foot thick walls, is all that remains of the original castle. Edward II was forced to abdicate at Kenilworth in 1327, before being carried off to Berkeley Castle in Gloucestershire, where he was undoubtedly murdered. In 1563 Elizabeth I gave the castle to her favorite, Robert Dudley, earl of Leicester. The earl built the gatehouse, which the queen visited on several occasions. After the Civil War, the Roundheads were responsible for breaching the outer walls and towers, and blowing up the north wall of the keep. This was the only damage caused following the earl of Monmouth's plea that it be "Slighted with as little spoil to the dwellinghouse as might be."

Admission is £1.15 ($2.15) for adults, 60p ($1.10) for children under 16. From Good Friday to the end of September, the castle is open daily from 10am to 6pm. In other months, hours are Tuesday to Sunday from 10am to 4pm. The castle is closed December 24 to December 26 and January 1.

WHERE TO STAY

DOUBLES WITHOUT BATH FOR LESS THAN £30 [$55.50]

ABBEY, 41 Station Rd., Kenilworth, Warwickshire CV8 1JD. Tel. 0926/ 512707. 7 rms (3 with bath or shower). TV
$ Rates (including English breakfast): £25 ($46.25) single without bath; £30 ($55.50) double without bath, £36 ($66.60) double with bath. No credit cards. **Parking:** Free.
One of the preferred guesthouses in the area near the train station, it has a certain old-fashioned Victorian quality. A good English dinner is served punctually at 7pm. Limited parking is available.

ENDERLEY GUEST HOUSE, 20 Queens Rd., Kenilworth, Warwickshire CV8 1JQ. Tel. 0926/55388. 5 rms (all with bath or shower).
$ Rates (including English breakfast): £23–£29 ($42.55–$53.65) single; £34–£40 ($62.90–$74) double. No credit cards.

This family-operated place off Warwick Road offers bedrooms which are well kept and inviting. The guesthouse is within an easy reach of the heart of Kenilworth. In fact, you might choose to stay here and let the summer crowds fight it out in Stratford-upon-Avon.

THE PRIORY GUEST HOUSE, 58 Priory Rd., Kenilworth, Warwickshire CV8 1LQ.Tel. 0926/56173. 5 rms (2 with bath). TV
$ Rates (including English breakfast): £16–£22 ($29.60–$40.70) single without bath; £30 ($55.50) double without bath, £35 ($64.75) double with bath. No credit cards. **Parking:** Free.
This small Victorian guesthouse in Kenilworth center is the home of Nina and Richard Haynes. They offer rooms with coffee-making equipment and hot and cold running water. Many guests use this house as a base for exploring the countryside, including Stratford-upon-Avon and the Cotswolds.

WHERE TO EAT

MEALS FOR LESS THAN £12 [$22.20]

ANA'S BISTRO, 121-123 Warwick Rd. Tel. 53763.
Cuisine: ENGLISH/FRENCH. **Reservations:** Recommended weekdays; required Fri–Sat.
$ Prices: Appetizers £1.60–£2.95 ($2.95–$5.45); main courses £5.85–£8.20 ($10.80–$15.15).
Open: Dinner Tues–Sat 7–10:30pm. **Closed:** Aug 1–21.
Ana's is located downstairs, under the Restaurant Diment (which some consider is the finest in Kenilworth for those willing to spend the extra money). However, at Ana's you get food that is well prepared and based on the availability of fresh produce. Try grilled whole plaice, homemade lasagne, or sirloin steak in red wine sauce. It's located south of town toward Warwick.

GEORGE RAFTERS, 41 Castle Hill. Tel. 52074.
Cuisine: ENGLISH/CONTINENTAL. **Reservations:** Recommended.
$ Prices: Appetizers £1.95–£3.45 ($3.60–$6.40); main courses £4.45–£8.95 ($8.25–$16.55); fixed-price three-course Sun lunch £9 ($16.65) per person. AE, DC, MC, V.
Open: Lunch daily noon–2pm; dinner daily 7–10:30pm.
Containing room for only about 40 diners, this is an intimate and charming choice for lunch or dinner. Set only a few steps from the castle within a room filled with English knickknacks and oil paintings, it prepares original and unusual dishes. Examples include mushrooms in a cider-and-cream sauce, deviled and fried herring roe served with a piquant sauce, scampi served in a basil and shallot-butter sauce, and steak served either with lobster butter, hollandaise, or bordelaise sauce.

CHAPTER 17

EAST ANGLIA: CAMBRIDGE, ESSEX, SUFFOLK & NORFOLK

- **WHAT'S SPECIAL ABOUT EAST ANGLIA**
1. **CAMBRIDGE**
2. **ELY**
3. **SAFFRON WALDEN/THAXTED**
4. **DEDHAM**
5. **NEWMARKET**
6. **LONG MELFORD**
7. **LAVENHAM**
8. **WOODBRIDGE & ALDEBURGH**
9. **NORWICH**

The four counties of East Anglia—Essex, Suffolk, Norfolk, and Cambridgeshire—are essentially bucolic. East Anglia was an ancient Anglo-Saxon kingdom under domination of the Danes. Beginning in the 12th century, its cloth industry brought it prosperity, which is apparent today in the impressive spires of some of its churches. In part, it is a land of heaths, fens, marshes, and "broads" in Norfolk. Cambridge is the most-visited city in East Anglia, but don't neglect to pass through Suffolk and Essex, the Constable country, containing some of the finest landscapes in England. Norwich, the seat of the dukes of Norfolk, is less popular, but the few who go that far toward the North Sea will be rewarded.

CAMBRIDGESHIRE

Most visitors gravitate to Cambridge, the center of Cambridgeshire, but those with more time may want to visit some of the county itself, especially the cathedral city of Ely. Cambridgeshire is in large part an agricultural region, with some distinct geographic features, including the peat black soil of the Fens, a district crisscrossed by dykes and drainage ditches. Many old villages and market towns abound, including Peterborough which sits on the divide between the flat Fens and the "wolds" of the East Midlands. Birdwatchers, fishermen, walkers, and cyclists are all drawn to the area.

Many famous figures in English history came from this land, including Oliver Cromwell (1699–1758), the Lord Protector during the English Civil War.

ESSEX

Even though it is close to London and industrialized in places, Essex is a land of rolling fields that contains unspoiled rural areas and villages. Most motorists pass through it on the way to Cambridge. In the east there are many seaside towns and villages, because Essex borders on the North Sea.

The major city is Colchester, in the east, known for its oysters and roses. Fifty miles

✔️

WHAT'S SPECIAL ABOUT EAST ANGLIA

Great Towns/Villages

☐ Cambridge, one of the world's oldest and greatest universities, on the River Cam with 31 colleges.

☐ Thaxted, a "classic" East Anglia small town with outstanding buildings—dominated by a hilltop medieval church.

☐ Long Melford, one of Suffolk's loveliest villages, remarkable for the length of its High Street.

☐ Lavenham, the showplace of Suffolk small towns—a symphony of color-washed buildings.

Castles

☐ Sandringham, the country home of British monarchs since the days of King Edward VII.

Architectural Highlights

☐ King's College Chapel, Cambridge, founded by the teenage Henry VI in 1441.

Cathedrals

☐ Ely Cathedral, dating from 1081, a handsome example of the Perpendicular style.

☐ Norwich Cathedral, dating from 1096, with two-story cloisters—the only one of its type in England.

Buildings

☐ Audley End House, outside Saffron Walden, a Jacobean mansion, considered the finest in East Anglia.

---

from London, it was the first Roman city in Britain, the oldest recorded town in the kingdom. Parts of its Roman fortifications remain. A Norman castle has been turned into a museum, housing a fine collection of Roman-British artifacts. Among the former residents of Colchester were King Cole, subject of the nursery rhyme, and Cunobelinus, the warrior king, known to Shakespearean scholars as Cymbeline.

However, Colchester is not the pathway of most visitors—so I have concentrated instead on tiny villages in the western part of Essex, including Saffron Walden and Thaxted, which represent the best part of the shire. You can explore all of East Anglia quite easily on your way to Cambridge or on your return trip to London. It lies roughly from 25 to 30 miles south of Cambridge.

SUFFOLK

The easternmost county of England, Suffolk is a refuge for artists, just as it was in the day of its famous native sons, Constable and Gainsborough. Through them, many of the Suffolk landscapes have ended up in museums on canvas.

A fast train can make it from London to East Suffolk in approximately 1½ hours. Still, its fishing villages, dozens of flint churches, historic homes, and national monuments remain far removed from mainstream tourism.

The major towns of Suffolk are Bury St. Edmunds, the capital of West Suffolk, and Ipswich in the east, a port city on the Orwell River. But to capture the true charm of Suffolk, explore its little market towns and villages. Beginning at the Essex border, we'll head toward the North Sea, highlighting the most scenic villages as we move eastward across the shire.

NORFOLK

Bounded by the North Sea, Norfolk is the biggest of the East Anglian counties. It's a low-lying area, with fens, heaths, and salt marshes. An occasional dike or windmill makes you think you're in the Netherlands. One of the features of Norfolk is its network of Broads—miles and miles of lagoons, shallow in parts, connected by streams. Summer sports people flock to Norfolk to hire boats for sailing or fishing.

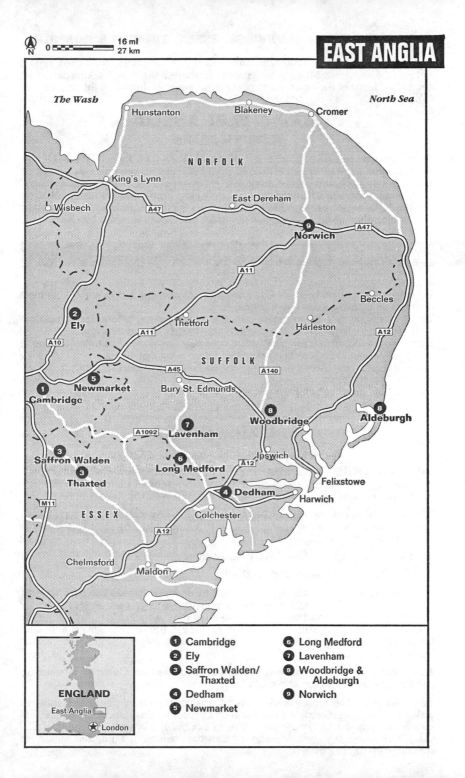

EAST ANGLIA

0 ___ 16 ml
___ 27 km

The Wash

North Sea

Hunstanton

Blakeney

Cromer

NORFOLK

King's Lynn

Wisbech

A47

East Dereham

❾ Norwich

A47

A11

Beccles

❷ Ely

A10

A11

Thetford

Harleston

A12

SUFFOLK

A45

A140

❺ Newmarket

Bury St. Edmunds

❽ Woodbridge

❽ Aldeburgh

❶ Cambridge

A1092

❼ Lavenham

Ipswich

❸ Saffron Walden

❻ Long Medford

A12

Felixstowe

M11

❸ Thaxted

❹ Dedham

Harwich

ESSEX

Colchester

Chelmsford

A12

Maldon

ENGLAND

East Anglia ⬚

★ London

❶ Cambridge
❷ Ely
❸ Saffron Walden/ Thaxted
❹ Dedham
❺ Newmarket
❻ Long Medford
❼ Lavenham
❽ Woodbridge & Aldeburgh
❾ Norwich

From Norwich itself, Wroxham, capital of the Broads, is easily reached, only 8 miles to the northeast. Motorboats regularly leave from this resort, taking parties on short trips. Some of the best scenery of the Broads is to be found on the periphery of Wroxham.

SEEING EAST ANGLIA
GETTING THERE

From London, motorists head north along M11 to Cambridge. The M11 also connects with the A11 to Norwich. A12 from London goes through East Suffolk via Colchester, Ipswich, and Great Yarmouth to reach some of the charming little villages. British Rail runs trains to Cambridge and East Anglia from London's Liverpool Street Station. National Express coaches from London's Victoria Coach Station service the area, taking about 2 hours to reach Cambridge or 3 hours to reach Norwich.

A SUGGESTED ROUTE

Day 1: From London, head for Cambridge for an overnight stopover. Visit its most interesting colleges and overnight there.

Day 2: Head north to Ely to see its cathedral in the morning before dipping south to explore the villages of Saffron Walden and Thaxted. Spend the night.

Day 3: From Thaxted or Saffron Walden, head east, enjoying a luncheon stopover in Long Melford, before visiting Lavenham for an overnight stopover.

Day 4: From Lavenham head northeast to Norwich, capital of Norfolk, for an overnight stopover.

Day 5: Visit Sandringham Castle, north of Norwich.

1. CAMBRIDGE

55 miles NE of London; 80 miles NE of Oxford

GETTING THERE   By Train   There is frequent rail service, with trains departing from Liverpool Street Station and King's Cross Station in London. Trip time is 1 hour. The round-trip ticket on a day return is £9.80 ($18.15).

By Bus   National Express coaches run hourly between London's Victoria Coach Station, arriving at Drummer Street Station in Cambridge. Trip time is 2 hours. A single or day return costs £7.75 ($14.35).

By Car   Head north on the M11 from London.

ESSENTIALS   The **area code** is 0223.

Orientation   The center of Cambridge is made for pedestrians, so park your car at one of the many car parks (they get more expensive as you get nearer to the city center), and take the opportunity to visit some of the colleges spread throughout the city. Follow the courtyards through to the "Backs" (the college lawns) and walk through to Trinity (where Prince Charles studied) and St. John's colleges, including the Bridge of Sighs.

Information   The **Cambridge Tourist Information Centre,** Wheeler St. (tel. 0223/322640), is behind the guildhall.

Fast Facts   The most popular way of getting around in Cambridge, next to walking, is bicycling. **Geoff's Bike Hire,** 65 Devonshire Road (tel. 0223/65629), has bicycles for rent for £5 ($9.25) per day or £12 ($22.20) per week. A deposit of £20 ($37) is required. It's open Monday to Saturday 9am to 5:30pm, and Sunday in summer 9am to 5:30pm.

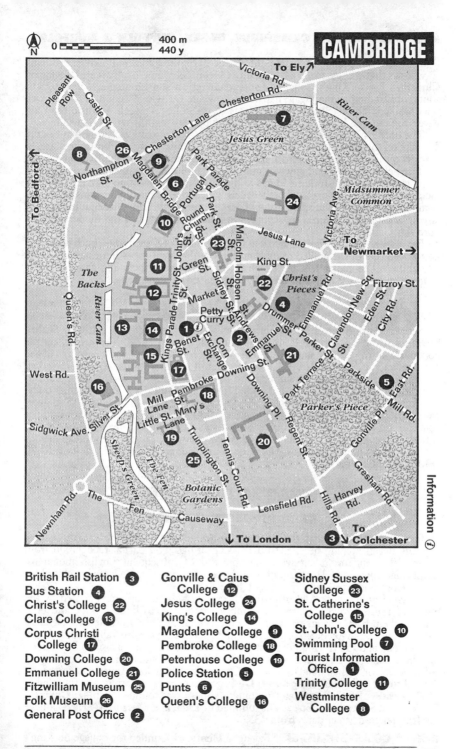

CAMBRIDGE

0 ——— 400 m / 440 y

N

Information ⓘ

- British Rail Station ❸
- Bus Station ❹
- Christ's College ㉒
- Clare College ⑬
- Corpus Christi College ⑰
- Downing College ⑳
- Emmanuel College ㉑
- Fitzwilliam Museum ㉕
- Folk Museum ㉖
- General Post Office ❷
- Gonville & Caius College ⑫
- Jesus College ㉔
- King's College ⑭
- Magdalene College ❾
- Pembroke College ⑱
- Peterhouse College ⑲
- Police Station ❺
- Punts ❻
- Queen's College ⑯
- Sidney Sussex College ㉓
- St. Catherine's College ⑮
- St. John's College ⑩
- Swimming Pool ❼
- Tourist Information Office ❶
- Trinity College ⑪
- Westminster College ❽

Cambridge is a collage of images: the Bridge of Sighs; spires and turrets; drooping willows that witness much punting; dusty secondhand bookshops; carol singing on Christmas Eve in King's College Chapel; dancing till sunrise at the May balls; the sound of Elizabethan madrigals; narrow lanes where Darwin, Newton, and Cromwell once walked; The Backs, where the lawns of the colleges sweep down to the Cam River; the tattered black robe of a hurrying upperclassman flying in the wind.

The university city of Cambridge is one of the ancient seats of learning in Britain. The city on the banks of the Cam River is also the county town of Cambridgeshire. In many ways, the stories of Oxford and Cambridge are similar—particularly the age-old conflict between town and gown (rent-gouging landlords vs. impoverished scholars).

There are many historic buildings in the city center, all within walking distance, including Great St. Mary's Church (from which the original Westminster chimes come), St. Bene't's Church, the Round Church, the Fitzwilliam Museum (one of the largest and finest provincial museums), the Folk Museum, and the modern Kettles Yard Art Gallery.

For a more detailed insight into the life and times of Cambridge, both town and gown, join one of the guided tours from the Cambridge Tourist Information Centre (see above). The center has a wide range of information, including data on public transportation in the area and on different sightseeing attractions.

TOURIST SERVICES

A tourist reception center for Cambridge and Cambridgeshire is operated by **Guide Friday Ltd.** at Cambridge Railway Station (tel. 0223/62444). The center, on the concourse of the railway station, dispenses maps for 10p (20¢) and brochures of the city area and operates tours. Also available is a full range of tourist services, including accommodation booking. In summer the tourist center is open daily from 9am to 6:30pm, closing at 4pm in winter. Guided tours of Cambridge leave the center daily. In summer, aboard open-top, double-decker buses, departures are every 15 minutes from 9am to 6pm. In winter, departures are hourly. The tour can be a 1-hour ride or you can get off at any of the many stops, such as King's College Chapel or the American Cemetery, then rejoin the tour when you wish. Tickets are valid all day for you to hop on and off the buses. The price of this tour is £4.20 ($7.75) adults or £1.70 ($3.15) for children.

WHAT TO SEE & DO

CAMBRIDGE UNIVERSITY

Oxford University predates the one at Cambridge. But in the early 13th century scholars began coming here. Eventually, Cambridge won partial recognition from Henry III, rising or falling with the approval of subsequent English monarchs. Cambridge consists of 31 colleges for both men and women. Colleges are closed for exams from mid-April until the end of June.

A Word of Warning: Unfortunately, because of the disturbances caused by the influx of tourists to the university, Cambridge has had to limit visitors, and even exclude them from various parts of the university altogether. In some cases, a small entry fee will be charged. Small groups of up to six people are generally admitted with no problem, and you can inquire from the local tourist office about visiting hours here.

These listings are only a representative selection of some of the more interesting colleges. If you're planning to stop in Cambridge for a long time, you might get around to the following. **Magdalen College** on Magdalen Street was founded in 1542; **Pembroke College** on Trumpington Street was founded in 1347; **Christ's College** on St. Andrew's Street was founded in 1505; and **Corpus Christi** College on Trumpington Street dates from 1352.

KING'S COLLEGE CHAPEL Teenaged Henry VI founded the college on King's Parade in 1441. Most of its buildings today are from the 19th century. The

Perpendicular Chapel, dating from the Middle Ages, is its crowning glory, and one of the architectural gems of England. The chapel, owing to the chaotic vicissitudes of English kings, wasn't completed until the early years of the 16th century.

⭐ Its most characteristic features are the magnificent fan vaulting—all of stone—and the great windows, most of which were fashioned by Flemish artisans between 1517 and 1531 (the west window, however, dates from the late Victorian period). The stained glass, in hues of red, blue, and amber, portrays biblical scenes. The long range of the windows, from the first on the north side at the west end, all the way around the chapel back to the first on the south side, depicts the Birth of the Virgin, the Annunciation, the Birth of Christ, the Life, Ministry, and Death of Christ, the Resurrection, the Ascension, the Acts of the Apostles, and the Assumption. The upper range contains Old Testament parallels to these New Testament stories. The chapel also houses *The Adoration of the Magi* by Rubens. The rood screen is from the early 16th century. Henry James called King's College Chapel "the most beautiful in England."

It is open during vacation time Monday to Saturday, 9:30am to 5:45pm, and on Sunday from 10:30am to 5:45pm. During term time the public is welcome to join choral services, which are at 5:30pm Monday to Saturday (service on Monday), and at 10:30am and 3:30pm Sunday. In term the chapel is open to visitors daily from 9:30am to 3:45pm, from 2 to 3pm and from 4:30 to 5:45pm Sunday; closed December 26 to January 1. It may be closed at other times for recording sessions.

There is an exhibition in the seven northern side chapels showing why and how the chapel was built. Admission to the exhibition is £1 ($1.85) for adults, 50p (95¢) for children.

PETERHOUSE   This college on Trumpington Street is visited largely because it is the oldest Cambridge college, founded in 1284. The founder was Hugh de Balsham, the bishop of Ely. Of the original buildings, only the hall remains, but this was restored in the 19th century and now contains stained-glass windows by William Morris. Old Court was constructed in the 15th century, but renovated in 1754, and the chapel dates from 1632. Ask permission to enter at the porter's desk.

TRINITY COLLEGE   On Trinity Street, Trinity College (not to be confused with Trinity Hall) is the largest in Cambridge. It was founded in 1546 by Henry VIII, who consolidated a number of smaller colleges that had existed on the site. The courtyard is the most spacious in Cambridge, built when Thomas Nevile was master. Sir Christopher Wren designed the library. For admission to the college, apply at the porter's lodge, or call 0223/338400 for information.

EMMANUEL COLLEGE   On St. Andrew's Street, Emmanuel (tel. 0223/334200) was founded in 1584 by Sir Walter Mildmay, a chancellor of the exchequer to Elizabeth I. It is of interest to Harvard students, since John Harvard, founder of that university, studied here. Take a stroll around its attractive gardens and visit the chapel designed by Sir Christopher Wren and consecrated in 1677. Both the chapel and college are open daily from 9:30am to 12:15pm and 2 to 6pm.

⭐ **QUEENS' COLLEGE**   On Queens' Lane, Queens' College (tel. 0223/335511) is thought by some to be the loveliest in the architectural galaxy. Dating back to 1448, it was founded at different times by two English queens, one the wife of Henry VI, the other the wife of Edward IV. Its second cloister is the most interesting, flanked by the early 16th century, half-timbered President's Lodge. The college may be visited during the day from mid-March to mid-October. Admission is 50p (95¢) and a short printed guide is issued. Normally, individual visitors are admitted daily from 1:45 to 4:30pm, but during July, August, and September, the college is also open to visitors daily from 10:15am to 12:45pm. Entry and exit is by the old porters' lodge in Queens' Lane only. The old hall and chapel are usually open to the public when not in use.

ST. JOHN'S COLLEGE   On St. John's Street, the college was founded in 1511 by Lady Margaret Beaufort, mother of Henry VII. A few years earlier she had founded

Christ's College. Before her intervention, an old monk-run hospital had stood on the site of St. John's. The impressive gateway bears the Tudor coat-of-arms, and Second Court is a fine example of late Tudor brickwork. But its best-known feature is the Bridge of Sighs crossing the Cam, built in the 19th century, patterned after the bridge in Venice. It connects the older part of the college with New Court, a Gothic revival on the opposite bank from which there is an outstanding view of the famous "backs." The Bridge of Sighs is closed to visitors but can be viewed from the neighboring Kitchen Bridge. Wordsworth was an alumnus of St. John's College. The chapel is open Monday to Friday from 9am to 4pm, and on Saturday from 9am to noon. On Sunday, the chapel is open to visitors attending the choral service.

OTHER SIGHTS

Colleges aren't the only thing to see in Cambridge, as you'll assuredly agree if you explore the following attractions.

THE FITZWILLIAM MUSEUM, Trumpington St. (near Peterhouse). Tel. 0221/332900.

This museum was the gift of the Viscount Fitzwilliam, who in 1816 gave Cambridge University his paintings and rare books—along with £100,000 to build the house in which to display them. Other gifts have since been bequeathed to the museum, and now it is one of the finest in England. It is noted for its porcelain, old prints, archeological relics, and oils (17th-century Italian, including Titian, Veronese, and Tintoretto; Rubens; Van Dyck; French impressionists; and a superb collection of 18th- and 19th-century British paintings). It is a 10-minute walk down from King's College.

Admission: Free.

Open: Tues–Sat 10am–5pm, Sun 2:15–5pm. **Closed:** Good Friday, Dec 24–31, and New Year's Day.

GREAT ST. MARY'S, King's Parade. Tel. 0223/350914.

The university church is built on the site of an 11th-century church, but the present building dates largely from 1478. It was closely associated with events of the Reformation. The cloth that covered the hearse of King Henry VII is on display in the church. A fine view of Cambridge may be obtained from the top of the tower. It lies opposite King's College Chapel.

Admission: 50p (95¢) adults, 20p (35¢) children.

Open: Daily 9am–5pm.

TOURS

If you're in the Cambridge area Mrs. Isobel Bryant, operates **Heritage Tours** (tel. 0638/741440) from her 200-year-old home, Manor Cottage, Swaffham Prior. A highly qualified expert on the region, she will arrange tours starting from your hotel or Cambridge railway station to Lavenham with its thatched and timbered houses, to the fine medieval churches of the Suffolk villages, to Ely Cathedral, or to one of the grand mansions nearby with their many treasures. The charge of £35 to £70 ($64.75 to $129.50) for the day covers up to three passengers and all travel expenses, including the service of the driver/guide. Lunch in a village pub and admission fees add £5 ($9.25) per person.

There are also walking tours around the colleges of Cambridge given by Mrs. Bryant costing £25 ($46.25) for a family-size party, lasting about 2 hours. There is a tour of Newmarket, headquarter of the horseracing industry. That tour includes getting to watch training gallops, a visit to the racing museum or a stud stable, seeing the bloodstock-sales center, and being shown the jockey club. For a group of 12 or more persons, a whole-day tour costs £15 ($27.75) per person, a ½-day tour going for £8 ($14.80) per person. A shorter tour can be arranged for individuals or a family group. If you want lunch at a private manor house with Cordon Bleu cooking, the cost will be £10 ($18.50) per person, with wine included, for groups of 12 or more. All prices include VAT.

BOATING

Punting on the Cam (nothing to do with football) is a traditional pursuit of students and visitors in Cambridge, but there are other types of boating available if you don't trust yourself to stand up and pole a punt under and around the weeping willow trees. Upriver, you can go a distance of about 2 miles to Grantchester, which was immortalized by the poet Rupert Brooke. Downstream, you pass along the Backs behind the colleges of the university.

Scudamore's Boatyards, Granta Place (tel. 0223/359750), by the Anchor Pub, has been in business since 1910. All craft rent for £6 ($11.10) per hour, including punts, canoes, and rowboats. A £30 ($55.50) deposit, payable with cash or credit card, is required. There is a maximum of six persons per punt.

WHERE TO STAY

During vacation periods, there are a few rooms available for tourists that are used by students in term time. The tourist office (tel. 0223/322640), on Wheeler Street, opposite the Arts Theatre and in the rear of the guildhall on Market Place, will give you information on available accommodations through their booking service, charging £1 ($1.85) per person for finding a room in or around Cambridge. If you have no reservation and want to try it on your own, check your luggage at the train station and go to the beginning of Chesterton Road, knocking on front doors displaying a B&B sign.

DOUBLES FOR LESS THAN £32 ($59.20)

ASHTREES GUEST HOUSE, 128 Perne Rd., Cambridge, Cambridgeshire CH1 3RR. Tel. 0223/411233. 7 rms (2 with bath). TV
$ Rates (including English breakfast): £16–£19 ($29.60–$35.15) single without bath; £28 ($51.80) double without bath, £35 ($64.75) double with bath. MC, V. **Parking:** Free.
This family-run guesthouse is within an easy commute of the heart of historic Cambridge. It's 1½ miles from city center off A1134, near the Addenbrookes Hospital and the rail terminal. Parking is provided. The little guesthouse will also provide an evening meal between 5 and 6:30pm.

AVIEMORE GUEST HOUSE, 310 Cherryhinton Rd., Cambridge, Cambridgeshire CB1 4AU. Tel. 0223/410956. Fax 0223/212119. 4 rms (1 with bath). TV **Bus:** No. 4 or 5.
$ Rates (including English breakfast): £16–£20 ($29.60–$37) single without bath; £29 ($53.65) double without bath, £36 ($66.60) double with bath. MC, V. **Parking:** Free.
This place is about 1½ miles from the heart of Cambridge, near Addenbrookes Hospital. One of the more recently inaugurated guesthouses of Cambridge, it offers a good standard of B&B accommodation, but reservations are important. Accommodations contain beverage-making equipment and hot and cold running water. Parking is available, or you can depend on reliable public transportation to go back and forth (many visitors prefer to walk the distance).

DRESDEN VILLA GUEST HOUSE, 34 Cherryhinton Rd., Cambridge, Cambridgeshire CB1 4AA. Tel. 0223/247539. 10 rms (7 with shower). TV **Bus:** No. 4 or 5.
$ Rates (including English breakfast): £18–£21 ($33.30–$38.85) single without bath; £32 ($59.20) double without bath, £36 ($66.60) double with shower. No credit cards. **Parking:** Free.
This guesthouse has an Edwardian-era painted facade with a quartet of sunny bay windows. Within a 10-minute walk of the Cambridge Railway Station, it is owned by

the Ruggiero family, who came here many years ago from a village near Sorrento, Italy. English or Italian fixed-price meals can be arranged in the evening for £8.50 ($15.75) per person. The location is about 1¼ miles south of the Market Place in Cambridge.

DYKELANDS GUEST HOUSE, 157 Mowbray Rd., Cambridge, Cambridgeshire CB1 4SP. Tel. 0223/244300. 8 rms (6 with bath). TV. **Bus:** No. 4, 44, or 197.
$ **Rates** (including English breakfast): £18.50 ($34.25) single without bath, £22.50 ($41.65) single with bath; £32 ($59.20) double without bath, £36 ($66.60) double with bath. MC, V. **Parking:** Free.
Built of red brick between the two world wars, this family-run guesthouse lies about 2 miles south of the city center in the suburb of Adkins Corner. Mrs. Glenys Denton, the owner, prepares evening meals for £8 ($14.80) for guests who reserve in advance.

HAMILTON LODGE HOTEL, 156 Chesterton Rd., Cambridge, Cambridgeshire CB4 1DA. Tel. 0223/65664. Fax 0223/314866. 5 rms (10 with bath or shower). TV TEL **Bus:** No. 3 or 3A.
$ **Rates** (including English breakfast): £18 ($33.30) single without bath, £25 ($46.25) single with bath; £30 ($55.50) double without bath, £45 ($83.25) double with bath. MC, V. **Parking:** Free.
One of the better and more reasonably priced of the small hotels of Cambridge, it lies about a mile from the heart of Cambridge, close to the River Cam. A well-run hotel, it stands on a busy highway but there is car parking out back. Bedrooms contain beverage-making equipment. The hotel has a licensed bar, offering pub food and snacks.

FAIRWAYS, 141-143 Cherryhinton Rd., Cambridge, Cambridgeshire CB1 4BX. Tel. 0223/246063. Fax 0223/212093. 14 rms (6 with bath). TV **Bus:** No. 4 or 5.
$ **Rates:** £18.50 ($34.25) single without bath, £25 ($46.25) single with bath; £32 ($59.20) double without bath, £37 ($68.45) double with bath. MC, V. **Parking:** Free.
About 1½ miles south of Cambridge center, this is a handsomely restored red-brick Victorian-era house whose upper floors are rented out to visitors. Rooms are simple but comfortable, each with tea-making equipment. The hotel contains a bar/lounge which serves drinks and bar snacks to residents and their guests.

NUMBER ELEVEN, 11 Gibson Rd., Cambridge, Cambridgeshire CB1 2HA. Tel. 0223/461142. 5 rms (3 with bath). TV
$ **Rates** (including English breakfast): £32 ($59.20) double without bath, £38 ($70.30) double with bath. No credit cards. **Parking:** Free.
Small but choice, this 19th-century town house near the heart of Cambridge and the train station offers upmarket, well-decorated bedrooms that normally are found only in better hotels. Each unit is a double. One room is available for families.

DOUBLES WITH BATH FOR LESS THAN £49 ($90.65)

ASHLEY HOTEL, 74 Chesterton Rd., Cambridge, Cambridgeshire CB4 1ER. Tel. 0223/350059. 16 rms (14 with bath). TV TEL **Bus:** No. 3 or 3A.
$ **Rates** (including English breakfast): £24 ($44.40) single without bath, £38 ($70.30) single with bath; £43 ($79.55) double with bath. MC, V. **Parking:** Free.
This is one of the best B&Bs in Cambridge, but you should reserve early if you decide to stay here. Set within a gray stone Edwardian building originally constructed as a private home, it lies near the River Cam and Jesus Green, a verdant 5-minute walk from the town center. Each accommodation contains a radio and tea-making facilities, and there's a rose garden in back. Although only breakfast is served, guests are welcome to use the dining and drinking facilities of this establishment's companion hotel, the Arundel House Hotel, at 53 Chesterton Road.

THE BRIDGE GUEST HOUSE, 151-153 Hills Rd., Cambridge, Cambridgeshire CB2 2RJ. Tel. 0223/247942. 18 rms (all with bath or shower). TEL **Bus:** No. 5 or 6.

$ Rates (including English breakfast): £25–£30 ($46.25–$55.50) single; £38–£42 ($70.30–$77.70) double. AE, DC, MC, V. **Parking:** Free.

Standing a mile south of the city center, it is composed of a pair of adjacent houses with a modern extension in the back. A fixed-price dinner is offered for £11.50 ($21.30) at this fully licensed house.

THE LENSFIELD HOTEL, 53 Lensfield Rd., Cambridge, Cambridgeshire CB2 1EN. Tel. 0223/312022. 36 rms (26 with bath). TV TEL **Directions:** From the center take Tennis Court Rd. south.

$ Rates (including English breakfast): £30 ($55.50) single without bath, £40 ($74) single with bath; £48–£60 ($89–$111) double with bath. AE, DC, MC, V. **Parking:** Free.

Set within easy reach of the colleges and the Cam River, this small hotel has many of the amenities of a well-run, small-town hotel. Rooms include radios and tea-making facilities. The hotel also has a good restaurant and a cozy bar.

PARKSIDE GUEST HOUSE, 25 Parkside, Cambridge, Cambridgeshire CB1 1JE. Tel. 0223/311212. Fax 0223/356926. 11 rms (6 with bath). TV TEL **Bus:** No. 78 or 79.

$ Rates (including English breakfast): £27 ($49.95) single without bath, £29 ($53.65) single with bath; £47 ($86.95) double without bath, £49 ($90.65) double with bath. No credit cards. **Parking:** Free.

Originally built in the 1850s as a residence for lecturers at Peterhouse College, it was transformed during World War II into the headquarters for the Peterhouse Jewish Association, and sheltered Jewish academics from other parts of Europe. Later, the organist from St. John's College lived here and, after a brief period when it was owned by another college (Robinson College) within Cambridge University, it was sold to Mr. John Sutcliffe, who operates it today as a hotel. Located very close to the town center, it's considered one of the city's better B&Bs. The establishment contains a tiny laundry, a bar and lounge, a collection of reference books about the city and university, and an amazing variety of breakfast cereals for those who don't care for bacon and eggs.

THE SUFFOLK HOUSE HOTEL, 69 Milton Rd., Cambridge, Cambridgeshire CB4 1XA. Tel. 0223/352016. 8 rms (all with shower). TV **Directions:** Guests using the M11 motorway or the A45 Cambridge bypass should exit at junction A10 (Ely) entering Cambridge on the A1309 which is Milton Road.

$ Rates (including English breakfast): £40–£50 ($74–$92.50) single; £50–£60 ($92.50–$111) double. MC, V. **Parking:** Free.

Once the home of a well-known local doctor, it has long since been turned into one of the more winning B&Bs in Cambridge. This privately run licensed hotel is a bit on the outskirts, but it is only about a 15-minute stroll to the colleges. In the back of this detached house there is a garden, and the location is peaceful. Guests may reserve a table for the well-prepared dinners served each night. Only nonsmokers are accepted.

WORTH THE EXTRA BUCKS

CENTENNIAL HOTEL, 63-71 Hills Rd., Cambridge, Cambridgeshire CB2 1PG. Tel. 0223/314652. Fax 0223/315443. 39 rms (all with bath or shower). TV TEL **Bus:** No. 5 or 6.

$ Rates (including English breakfast): £44 ($81.40) single; £58–£65 ($107.30–$120.25) double; £75 ($138.75) family room for three. AE, DC, MC, V. **Parking:** Free.

This family-type hotel attracts business travelers, but in summer becomes a tourist favorite. It provides a number of facilities, such as a fully licensed restaurant, featuring both a fixed-price menu and an à la carte selection from 6:30 to 9:30pm. It's only a short walk from the railway station at Cambridge. If you're driving, there is parking behind the hotel. You pay more here than in a typical B&B house, but many consider the extra amenities worth it.

HELEN HOTEL, 167-169 Hills Rd., Cambridge, Cambridgeshire CB2 2RJ. Tel. 0223/246465. Fax 0223/214406. 29 rms (25 with bath). TV TEL. **Bus:** No. 5 or 6.

$ **Rates** (including English or continental breakfast): £30 ($55.50) single without bath, £33 ($61.05) single with bath; £48 ($88.80) double with bath, £67.50 ($124.90) triple with bath. MC, V. **Parking:** Free.

This white-fronted Victorian hotel, set about a mile from the town center, is a charming Mediterranean-inspired refuge maintained by Gino and Helen Agodino. Born in San Remo and Naples, respectively, they prepare some of the best Italian dinners in Cambridge (featuring homemade raviolis and pastas) for guests who reserve in advance. The cost of a four-course dinner is £13 ($24.05). The hotel is much bigger than many other hotels within this guidebook's section, and benefits from gardens laid out with boxwood in a symmetrical and formal Italian style. The hotel contains a lounge and cocktail bar, and each bedroom has tea-making facilities, a hairdryer, and a radio. An extra bed can be set up in any bedroom for £6 ($11.10) per night.

WHERE TO EAT

MEALS FOR LESS THAN £10 [$18.50]

Restaurants

THE ANCHOR, Silver St. Tel. 353554.
   Cuisine: ENGLISH. **Reservations:** Not needed.
$ **Prices:** Bar snacks and main courses £3.60–£4.25 ($6.65–$7.90). MC, V.
   Open: Pub Mon–Sat 11am–11pm, Sun noon–3pm and 7–10:30pm. Food served daily in pub noon–2:30pm and in café Mon–Sat 11am–5:30pm.

Set a few steps from the Cam, beside the Silver Street Bridge, this verdant and time-tested establishment in the center has a bar and terrace where punters will agree to row up to four visitors up and down the river, giving a running commentary *en route*. The price for an oarsman/guide and up to four passengers is £20 ($37) per hour. You'll have a choice of sitting within either the Riverview Saloon Bar or the Café Bar. Drinks and hand-pulled ales are available in either, as well as such simple food items as lasagne with salad, roast beef platters, scampi, chicken nuggets, hot pots, and steak-and-ale pies.

BROWNS, 23 Trumpington St. Tel. 511995.
   Cuisine: ENGLISH/CONTINENTAL. **Reservations:** Not needed. **Bus:** No. 2.
$ **Prices:** Appetizers £1.75–£5.95 ($3.25–$11); main courses £4.35–£8.95 ($8.05–$16.55). No credit cards.
   Open: Mon–Sat 11am–11:30pm, Sun noon–11:30pm.

Long a favorite at Oxford, it also became a sensation at Cambridge some time ago. With a neoclassical colonnade in front, it has all the grandeur of the Edwardian era. It was actually built in 1914 as the outpatient department of a hospital dedicated to Edward VII. Today it is the most lighthearted place for dining in the city, with wicker chairs, high ceilings, pre–World War I woodwork, and a long bar covered with bottles of wine. The extensive bill of fare includes various renditions of spaghetti, fresh salads (even Mrs. Brown's a vegetarian), several selections of meat and fish (from charcoal-grilled leg of lamb with rosemary to fresh fish in season), hot sandwiches, and the chef's daily specials posted on a blackboard. If you drop by in the afternoon, you can also order thick milk shakes or natural fruit juices.

FREE PRESS, 7-9 Prospect Row. Tel. 68337.
   Cuisine: ENGLISH. **Reservations:** None.
$ **Prices:** Bar snacks £3.50–£4.25 ($6.50–$7.85). No credit cards.
   Open: Daily noon–2:30pm, Mon–Sat 6–11pm, Sun 7–10:30pm.

This is a small, noisy, crowded, and convivial pub in the center behind the police station that offers flavorful grub and a crowd which sometimes tunes in enthusiastically to local soccer matches. Food items include freshly made soups, meat pies, moussaka, vegetarian platters, and hot chef's specials of the day. There are a very limited number of outdoor tables, which are much in demand during warm weather.

HOBBS PAVILION, Park Terrace of Regent St. Tel. 67480.
  Cuisine: CREPES. **Reservations:** Not needed.
  $ **Prices:** Crêpes £2.95–£6.10 ($5.45–$11.30); set two-course lunch £4.85 ($8.95); set three-course dinner £6.75 ($12.50). No credit cards.
  Open: Lunch Tues–Sat noon–2:30pm; dinner Tues–Wed and Fri–Sat 7–10pm, Thurs 8:30–10pm. **Closed:** Mid-Aug to mid-Sept.

In the vicinity of the University Arms Hotel is this delightful and deservedly popular place. It is called "a crêperie with a difference" and is located in the historic, brick-built Cricket Pavilion. You get a choice of nearly four dozen crêpes, both for a main course and as a dessert. Stuffings range from spicy ratatouille to black pudding and mustard. This savory list is backed up by a selection of freshly prepared soups and salads.

MARTIN'S COFFEE HOUSE, 4 Trumpington St. Tel. 61757.
  Cuisine: TEA/SANDWICHES/PASTRIES. **Reservations:** None. **Bus:** No. 4 or 5.
  $ **Prices:** Sandwiches 80p–90p ($1.50–$1.60), pot of tea 40p (75¢), pastries 70p–£1 ($1.30–$1.85); English breakfast £2.50 ($4.65). No credit cards.
  Open: Mon–Sat 8:30am–5pm, Sun 9:30am–5pm.
Near the Fitzwilliam Museum is a small, simple, and modern coffeehouse with high standards, decorated in tones of peach. It offers a pleasing array of sandwiches and pastries, along with English breakfast. Whole-meal rolls are filled with turkey, ham, beef, salad, cheese, and eggs. Homemade cakes, scones, and doughnuts are also sold, usually to accompany the endless pots of tea which emerge, steaming from a modern samovar.

VARSITY RESTAURANT, 35 St. Andrew's St. between Sidney and Regent Sts. Tel. 356060.
  Cuisine: GREEK/CONTINENTAL. **Reservations:** Not needed.
  $ **Prices:** Appetizers 80p–£2 ($1.50–$3.70); main courses £3.50–£7 ($6.45–$12.95). AE, MC, V.
  Open: Lunch daily 11:30am–3pm; dinner daily 5–11pm.
In a bare whitewashed room with black beams and pictures of boats and islands on the walls, you can dine on Greek specialties. Kebabs are served with rice and salad, and there are some continental dishes for less adventurous palates. Meals include a glass of wine and coffee.

SHAO TAO, 72 Regent St. Tel. 353942.
  Cuisine: CHINESE. **Reservations:** Recommended Fri–Sat. **Bus:** No. 1, 4, or 5.
  $ **Prices:** Appetizers £3–£3.50 ($5.55–$6.45); main courses £4–£6 ($7.40–$11.10); four-course set menu, with wine, for two £35 ($64.75). AE, DC, MC, V.
  Open: Lunch daily noon–2:30pm; dinner daily 6pm–11pm.
Set on a busy commercial street in the town center, this pastel-colored restaurant specializes in Hunan, Szechuan, and Peking cuisine. The menu offers such dishes as aromatic crispy duck, crispy shredded beef with chilis and carrots, "three kinds of meat" soup, and a host of other dishes. If you're confused, order the "leave it to us" feast, and are likely to be happily surprised.

Pubs

CAMBRIDGE ARMS, 4 King St. Tel. 359650.
  Cuisine: ENGLISH. **Reservations:** None.
  $ **Prices:** Bar snacks £3.95 ($7.30) each. No credit cards.
  Open: Mon–Sat 11am–11pm, Sun noon–3pm and 7–10:30pm. Food service Mon–Sat noon–7pm, Sun noon–3pm.
This bustling, no-nonsense pub in the center of town's busiest commercial district,

has plenty of atmosphere, and dispenses endless platters of food to clients who order it over the bar's countertop. Menu possibilities include chef's daily specials, grilled steaks, lasagne, and an array of both hot and cold dishes

THE GREEN MAN, 59 High St., Grantchester. Tel. 841178.
  Cuisine: ENGLISH. **Reservations:** Not needed. **Bus:** No. 118 from Cambridge.
$ **Prices:** Appetizers: £1.50–£3 ($2.80–$5.55); main courses £3.95–£7.25 ($7.30–$13.40); fixed-price four-course Sun lunch £10 ($18.50). AE, DC, MC, V.
  Open: Lunch daily 11am–3pm; dinner Mon–Sat 6–11pm, Sun 7–10:30pm.

Named in honor of Robin Hood, whose depiction hangs outside, this 400-year-old inn is perhaps the most popular pub outing from Cambridge. It's set beside the A603, 2 miles south of Cambridge in the hamlet of Grantchester. The village was made famous by Rupert Brooke, the famed Edwardian-era poet best known for his sonnet, "The Soldier." Grantchester is considered one of the shire's most beautiful villages, with an old church and gardens leading down to a series of peaceful meadows. Even if you've never heard of Brooke, you might enjoy spending a late afternoon here, wandering through the old church and then heading, as everybody does, to the Green Man. In winter, you'll be welcomed with a crackling fire, but in summer, you might want to retreat to the beer garden in back. From there, stroll to the edge of the River Cam. Place your food order at the counter, after which an employee will carry it to your table. Menu choices include steak and kidney pie, shepherd's pie, lasagne, fresh salads, English cheeses, and pâtés.

EVENING ENTERTAINMENT

An outstanding attraction in Cambridge is the **Arts Theatre,** 6 St. Edward's Passage, adjacent to the city center and the tourist information office and fitted into a maze of lodging houses and shops. It provides Cambridge and the surrounding area with its most important theatrical events. Almost all of the leading stars of the British stage have performed here at one time or another. Call 0223/352000 to find out what's playing. Seats for most productions are £8 to £12 ($14.80 to $22.20).

2. ELY

70 miles NE of London; 16 miles N of Cambridge

GETTING THERE   By Train   Ely is a major railway junction served by express trains to Cambridge. Service is frequent from London's Liverpool Street Station.

By Bus   Frequent buses run between Cambridge and Ely.

By Car   From Cambridge, take the A10 north.

ESSENTIALS   The **area code** is 0353. The **Tourist Information Centre** is at Oliver Cromwell's House, 29 St. Mary's Street (tel. 0353/662062).

The top attraction in the fen country, outside of Cambridge, is Ely Cathedral. Ely used to be known as the Isle of Ely, until the surrounding marshes and meres were drained. The last stronghold of Saxon England, Ely was defended by Hereward the Wake, until his capitulation to the Normans in 1071.

WHAT TO SEE & DO

ELY CATHEDRAL, Minster Place. Tel. 0353/667735.

The near-legendary founder of the cathedral was Etheldreda, the wife of a Northumbrian king who established a monastery on the spot in 673. The present structure dates from 1081. Visible for miles around, the landmark, octagonal lantern is the crowning glory of the cathedral. It was erected in 1322, following the collapse of the old tower, and represents a remarkable engineering achievement. Four hundred tons of lead and wood hang in space, held there by timbers reaching to the eight pillars.

Enter the cathedral through the Galilee West Door, a good example of the Early English style of architecture. The lantern tower and the Octagon are the most notable features inside, but visit the lady chapel. Although its decor has deteriorated over the centuries, it's still a handsome example of the Perpendicular style, having been completed in the mid-14th century. The entry fee goes to help preserve the castle. **Admission:** £2.40 ($4.45) adults; £1.75 ($3.25) children 12–16; free under 12. **Open:** June–Sept daily 7am–7pm; off-season Mon–Sat 7:30am–6pm, Sun 7:30am–5pm.

ELY MUSEUM, 28C High St. Tel. 0353/66655.

Artifacts from the area are displayed there, including a rare collection of 17th-century Ely trade tokens. A gallery presents old films of Ely and the surrounding fenland. **Admission:** 80p ($1.50) adults, 40p (75¢) children 6–16. **Open:** Tues–Sat 10:30am–1pm and 2:15–5pm, Sun 1:15–5pm.

NEARBY ATTRACTIONS

GRIME'S GRAVES, 2¾ miles northeast of Brandon, Norfolkshire. Tel. 0842/810656.

On the B1108, off the main A1065 road from Swaffham to Mildenhall east of Ely, and 2¾ miles northeast of Brandon (Norfolkshire), visit the largest group of neolithic flint mines in the country. This is sparsely populated, fir-wooded country, and it's easy to imagine yourself transported back to ancient times. The mines are well signposted, and you'll soon find yourself at a small parking lot presided over by a custodian who will open up one or several of the shafts, allowing you to enter a remnant of ancient Britain, from a time even before that of the Anglo-Saxons. Restoration has been carried out, and it is now possible to see where work took place. If you're lucky, you may find a worked flint of your own to present to the custodian. It's best to have a flashlight handy. The steep climb down is only for the vigorous.

The mines are close to the air force bases so well known to countless American air crews during World War II. **Admission:** 95p ($1.75) adults, 45p (85¢) children. **Open:** Good Friday–Sept, Tues–Sun 10am–6pm; Oct–Good Friday 10am–4pm.

IMPERIAL WAR MUSEUM, Newmarket Rd., Duxford Airfield at Junction 10 of the M11. Tel. 0223/833963.

It was a former Battle of Britain station and the U.S. Eighth Air Force base in World War II. In hangars that date from World War I, you'll find a huge collection of historic civil and military aircraft from both world wars, including the only B-29 Superfortress in Europe. Other exhibits include midget submarines, tanks, and a variety of field artillery pieces, as well as a special historical display on the U.S. Eighth Air Force. Special charges are made for special events. Parking is free. The museum is on the A505 Royston to Newmarket road, 8 miles south of Cambridge, right next to Junction 10 of the M11 motorway. Cambus (no. 103) operates between Drummer Street Station in Cambridge and Duxford Airfield. **Admission:** £4.50 ($8.35) adults, £2.25 ($4.15) children. **Open:** Mar 10–Oct daily 10am–6pm; off-season daily 10am–4pm. **Closed:** Christmas and New Year's Day.

WHERE TO STAY

THE NYTON, 7 Barton Rd., Ely, Cambridgeshire CB7 4HZ. Tel. 0353/662459. 13 rms (all with bath or shower). TV
$ Rates (including English breakfast): £30–£35 ($55.50–$64.75) single; £50–£55 ($92.50–$101.75) double. AE, DC, MC, V. **Parking:** Free.

In a quiet residential section of Ely is a licensed family-run hotel surrounded by a

2-acre flower garden with lawns and trees. It's also right next to an 18-hole golf course. You'll have views of a wide area of fenland and of the cathedral. Each bedroom has beverage-making equipment. Bar snacks are available from noon to 2pm, and dinner is offered nightly from 6:30 to 8:30pm. Barton Road is accessible from the cathedral and railway station, lying on the A142 Ely-Newmarket road off the A10 Ely-Cambridge road.

WHERE TO EAT

THE OLD FIRE ENGINE HOUSE, St. Mary's St. Tel. 662582.
    Cuisine: ENGLISH. **Reservations:** Recommended. **Bus:** No. 109.
$ Prices: Appetizers £2.20–£4.95 ($4.05–$9.15); main courses £9.80–£12 ($18.15–$22.20). No credit cards.
    Open: Lunch daily 12:30–2pm; dinner Mon–Sat 7:30–9pm.

Opposite St. Mary's Church is one of the finer restaurants in East Anglia. It's worth making a detour to this converted fire station in a walled garden, in a complex of buildings that includes an art gallery. Soups are served in huge bowls, accompanied by coarse-grained crusty bread. Main dishes include duck with orange sauce, jugged hare, steak-and-kidney pie, baked stuffed pike, casserole of rabbit, and pigeon with bacon and black olives. Desserts include fruit pie and cream, although I'd recommend the syllabub, made with cream and liquor. In summer you can dine outside in the garden, even order a cream tea. It is owned and in large part run by Ann Ford, who still finds time to talk to customers.

3. SAFFRON WALDEN/THAXTED

43 miles N of London; 15 miles SE of Cambridge

GETTING THERE   **By Train**   Trains leave London's Liverpool Street Station to Cambridge several times a day. Two or three stations before Cambridge, passengers should descend in the hamlet of **Audley End,** which lies 8 miles north of Thaxted and a mile from Saffron Walden. There is a circumvoluted bus from Audley End, but it meanders so wildly that most visitors opt for a taxi instead. Taxi fare from Audley End to Thaxted costs about £7 ($12.95) each way, or about £2 ($3.70) to Saffron Walden.

By Bus   Cambus (no. 122) leaves Cambridge Monday to Saturday at 12:15pm, 2:40pm, and 5:35pm, heading for Saffron Walden. Cambus (no. 9) departs on Sunday every 1½ hours between 10am to 6pm. The last bus back on Sunday departs Saffron Walden at 7:10pm. National Express Buses leave London's Victoria Coach Station several times a day and stop at Saffron Walden, 6 miles north of Thaxted. From there, there are about 3 (at the most) buses heading on to Thaxted. Most opt instead for a taxi, which is easier.

By Car   From Cambridge, take the A1301 southeast, connecting with the B184 (also southeast) into Saffron Walden. The B184 also leads to the adjoining village of Thaxted.

ESSENTIALS   The **area code** is 0799 for Saffron Walden and 0371 for Thaxted. The **Tourist Information Centre** is at 1 Market Place, Market Square (tel. 0799/24282), in Saffron Walden.

SAFFRON WALDEN

In the northern corner of Essex, a short drive from Thaxted, is the ancient market town of Walden, renamed Saffron Walden because of the fields of autumn crocus that used to grow around it. In spite of its proximity to London, it isn't disturbed by heavy tourist traffic. Residents of Cambridge escape to this old borough for their weekends.

Many of the houses in Saffron Walden are distinctive in England, in that the 16th- and 17th-century builders faced their houses with parget—a kind of plaster-work (sometimes made with cow dung), used for ornamental facades. There are many 15th- and 16th-century, timber-framed houses with pargeting, as well as the 14th-century Sun Inn, and the Perpendicular-style church of Saffron Walden, the largest in Essex. Saffron Walden is one of the few market towns in England which still has its original medieval street pattern.

WHAT TO SEE & DO

One mile west of Saffron Walden (on the B1383) is **Audley End House** (tel. 0799/22399), considered one of the finest mansions in East Anglia. This Jacobean house was begun by Sir Thomas Howard, treasurer to the king, in 1605, built on the foundation of a monastery. James I is reported to have said, "Audley End too large for a king, though it might do for a lord treasurer." Among the house's outstanding features is an impressive great hall with an early 17th century screen at the north end, considered one of the most beautiful ornamental screens in England. Rooms decorated by Robert Adam contain fine furniture and works of art. A "Gothick" chapel and a charming Victorian ladies' sitting room are among the attractions. The park surrounding the house was landscaped by Capability Brown. It has a lovely rose garden, a river and cascade, and a picnic area. In the stables, built at the same time as the mansion, is a collection of agricultural machinery, as well as a Victorian coach, old wagons, and the estate fire wagon. It's all open daily from 1 to 6pm from April 1 to the end of September. The grounds are open from noon to 5pm. Admission to the house is £4 ($7.40) for adults, £2 ($3.70) for children.

The location is 1¼ miles from Audley End Station where trains arrive from Cambridge. It's a 20-minute walk from the station.

WHERE TO STAY & EAT

CROSS KEYS HOTEL, 32 High St., Saffron Walden, Essex CB10 1AZ. Tel. 0799/26550. 6 rms (3 with bath). TV
$ Rates (including English breakfast): £36 ($66.60) single with or without bath; £45–£55 ($83.25–$101.75) double with or without bath; £55 ($101.75) triple with bath. MC, V. **Parking:** Free.

Considered as famous for its pub as it is for its rooms, this fine example of Elizabethan architecture was built in 1449 and retains its black-and-white half-timbered facade. Bedrooms are cozily arranged beside crooked upstairs hallways, and each has comfortable furnishings and vaguely modernized charm. Even if you don't stay here, consider dropping into the pub for a pint of lager beside the huge inglenook fireplace where fleeing priests used to hide within what was known as a priest's hole. Meals, chosen from a large menu which is supplemented with daily specials, are served Monday to Saturday from 10:30am to 11pm, and Sunday from noon to 4pm and 7 to 10:30pm. Meals cost from £8 ($14.80) and include such items as soups, prawn cocktails, mixed grills, ham steak, and the chef's daily specials. The hotel is opposite the post office, at the northern end of the town's main street.

EIGHT BELLS, 18 Bridge St. Tel. 22790.
Cuisine: INTERNATIONAL. **Reservations:** Recommended in restaurant.
$ Prices: Bar snacks £4–£10.50 ($7.40–$19.45); three-course set menus £12– £20 ($22.20–$37). AE, MC, V.
Open: Mon–Sat 11am–3pm and 6–11pm, Sun noon–3pm and 7–10:30pm. Lunch daily noon–2:30pm; dinner Mon–Sat 6:30–9:30pm, Sun 7–9:30pm.

Set behind an Elizabethan-era black and white half-timbered facade, this is the most popular restaurant and pub in town, a favorite of students visiting from Cambridge.

Bar snacks include such dishes as saffron-glazed chicken breasts stuffed with shrimp, and either prawn or mushrooms thermidor. The more formal restaurant—a timbered hall with oaken beams and furniture—serves set menus with a wide choice of selections which usually include very fresh meats and vegetables. Eight Bells lies beside the main road leading to Cambridge, a 5-minute walk from the center.

QUEEN'S HEAD INN, High St., Littlebury, near Saffron Walden, Essex CB11 4TD. Tel. 0799/22251. 6 rms (all with bath or shower). TV TEL
$ Rates (including English breakfast): £35 ($64.75) single; £45 ($83.25) double. MC, V. **Parking:** Free.

In the environs, the Queen's Head is on the B1383, 5 minutes from Junction 9 (M11). The hotel and licensed restaurant rents comfortably furnished bedrooms, all with beverage-making equipment. The inn dates from the 16th century, and it is only minutes from the heart of Saffron Walden by car. Queens Head provides a large car park, and it also has a good restaurant, serving English and classic French food.

THAXTED

The Saxon town of Thaxted sits on a hill crest. It houses the most beautiful small church in England, whose graceful spire can be seen for miles around. Its bells are heard throughout the day, in an area where church life is very important. Dating back to 1340, the church is a near-perfect example of religious architecture. Thaxted also has a number of well-preserved Elizabethan houses and a wooden-pillared Jacobean guildhall.

This little village of **Finchingfield,** only a short drive east of Thaxted, is in many ways an archetypal English village. It's an idyllic place, surrounded by the quiet life of the countryside. If you're staying in either Saffron Walden or Thaxted, you might want to drive here.

WHERE TO STAY

FOUR SEASONS HOTEL, Walden Rd., Thaxted, Essex CM6 2RE. Tel. 0371/830129. Fax 0371/830835. 9 rms (all with bath). TV TEL
$ Rates (including English breakfast): £50–£60 ($92.50–$111) single; £65 ($120.25) double. AE, MC, V. **Parking:** Free.

Set within an acre of lawns and gardens (one of whose attractions is a natural pond), this modernized tile-roofed hotel stands on a 16th-century foundation. Well known for its busy restaurant, it also contains one of the region's most popular brass knickknacks, exposed beams, and a selection of bar snacks served throughout the day. Full meals in the more formal restaurant cost from around £13 ($24.05) each, and might include grilled lamb cutlets with mint sauce, grilled Dover sole, beef Stroganoff, steak Diane, and steak au poivre. The restaurant is open Monday to Thursday from noon to 2pm and 7 to 10pm, from 7 to 10:30pm Friday and Saturday. It's located ½ mile northwest of the village center, beside the B184 highway.

WHERE TO EAT

RECORDER'S HOUSE RESTAURANT, 17 Town St. Tel. 830438.
Cuisine: CONTINENTAL. **Reservations:** Recommended.
$ Prices: Appetizers £2.75–£5.95 ($5.10–$11); main courses £8.50–£12.50 ($15.75–$23.15); fixed-price lunch £12.50 ($23.15). MC, V.
Open: Lunch Wed–Sun noon–2pm; dinner Wed–Sat 7–10pm.

Near the guildhall in the village center, Recorder's was built in 1450 and is believed to have once incorporated part of the medieval Thaxted Manor House. It is named after the recorder who used to live here, collecting taxes for the crown. Apparently, there were objections to these taxes, as the winding staircase was built with steps that pitch outward, so that an attacking swordsman would be thrown off balance. In front of an inglenook fireplace, you'll dine in a room with the same linenfold paneling, wide oak floors, and candlelight atmosphere as Edward IV enjoyed when he honeymooned here with his queen. The cuisine is the best in the area, and dinner includes a choice of five different steaks and seafood cooked on the charcoal broiler. Specials could include roast haunch of venison.

4. DEDHAM

63 miles N of London; 8 miles NE of Colchester

GETTING THERE By Train Trains depart every 20 minutes from London's Liverpool Street Station for the 50-minute ride to Colchester. From Colchester, it is possible to take a taxi from the railway station to the bus station, then board a bus run by the Eastern National Bus Company for the 5-mile trip to Dedham. (Buses leave about once an hour). Most people opt for taking a taxi from Colchester directly to Dedham, for a one-way price of about £6 ($11.10).

By Bus National Express buses depart from London's Victoria Coach Station for Colchester, where you then make the connection described above. Again, many opt for a taxi.

By Car From the London ring road, branch northeast along A12 to Colchester, turning off at East Bergholt onto a small secondary road leading east to Dedham.

ESSENTIALS The **area code** is 0206. The Tourist Information Centre is at 1 Queen Street at Colchester (tel. 0206/712920).

Remember Constable's *Vale of Dedham?* In this little Essex village on the Stour River, you're in the heart of Constable country. Flatford Mill is only a mile farther down the river. The village, with its Tudor, Georgian, and Regency houses, is set in the midst of the water meadows of the Stour. Constable painted its church and tower. Dedham is right on the Essex-Suffolk border and makes a good center for exploring both North Essex and the Suffolk border country.

About ¾ mile from the village center is **Castle House,** East Lane, Dedham (tel. 0206/322127), home of Sir Alfred Munnings, the president of the Royal Academy (1944–49) and painter extraordinaire of racehorses and animals. The house and studio contain sketches and other works, and are open early May to early October on Sunday, Wednesday, and bank holidays, as well as on Thursday and Saturday in August. Hours are 2 to 5pm. Admission is £2 ($3.70) for adults, 25p (45¢) for children.

The English landscape painter John Constable (1776–1837) was born at East Bergholt, directly north of Dedham. Near the village is **Flatford Mill,** East Bergholt, Colchester CO7 6UL (tel. 0206/298283), subject of one of his most renowned works. The mill, in a scenic setting, was given to the National Trust in 1943, and since has been leased to the Field Studies Council for use as a residential college.

Weekly courses are offered on all aspects of the countryside and the environment. None of the buildings has exhibits, nor are they open to the general public, but students of all ages are welcome to attend the courses. The fee for 1 week is inclusive of accommodation, meals, and tuition. Details may be obtained from Director of Studies, Field Studies Council, Flatford Mill Field Centre, East Bergholt, Colchester, Essex CO7 6UL.

WHERE TO STAY

DEDHAM HALL, Brook St., Dedham, Essex CO7 6AD Tel. 0206/ 323027. 13 rms (9 with bath).
$ Rates (including English breakfast): £26 ($48.10) single without bath, £34 ($62.90) single with bath; £39 ($72.15) double without bath, £57 ($105.45) double with bath. MC, V. **Parking:** Free.
Originally built in 1380, today this is a rambling Elizabethan farmhouse, with a pink stucco exterior and a partially half-timbered interior. Set upon 6 acres of park, garden, and field, it's the domain of Jim and Wendy Sarton, who raise sheep and geese, and

run a small evening restaurant on the premises. From the front windows of much of the house, you can see a privately owned pond and the steeple of the village church. There's a resident's bar near the dining room, and a trio of sitting rooms for extended conversations. Fresh-cooked three-course meals with a wide choice of dishes are served at dinnertime Tuesday through Saturday for a set price of £16.50 ($30.55). Lunch is served only on Sunday, three courses costing £14.50 ($26.85). Meals might include breast of chicken in a cider and cream sauce, or fillet of beef with a cream and mushroom sauce, and at least one vegetarian dish of the day. Advance reservations for nonresidents are recommended. Dedham Hall is a 10-minute walk east of the town center.

WHERE TO EAT

MARLBOROUGH HEAD, Mill Lane. Tel. 0206/323124.
  Cuisine: ENGLISH. **Reservations:** None.
$ Prices: Appetizers £1.50–£4.50 ($2.80–$8.35); main courses £3.50–£7 ($6.50–$12.95); sandwiches £1.50–£4.50 ($2.80–$8.35). MC, V.
  Open: Drinks Mon–Sat 11am–2:30pm and 6–11pm, Sun noon–2pm and 6–10:30pm. Food daily noon–2pm and 6–10:30pm.

This is considered the most historic and popular pub in the area, and a place which also rents a trio of upstairs bedrooms to passersby. Set opposite Constable's old school, and known for its stone and frame construction, it contains sections which date from the 1400s. During warm weather, the crowd moves onto an outdoor patio near a small garden. Children are welcome and you're likely to see more than one family dining together. Place your food order at the bar counter and an employee will bring it to your table. Food items include an array of pâtés, quiches, beef, fish, poultry, and offal (such as kidney and liver) dishes, each prepared in solidly conservative English ways.

The inn's three bedrooms each contain plaster walls and wooden floors engagingly skewed and sloped because of their age. Each contains a shower, toilet, and sink, and each has a TV. For B&B, rates are £30 ($55.50) for a single, and £47.50 ($87.90) for a double.

5. NEWMARKET

62 miles NE of London; 13 miles NE of Cambridge

GETTING THERE   By Train   Trains depart from London's Liverpool Street Station every 45 to 60 minutes for Cambridge. In Cambridge, change trains and head in the direction of Mildenhall. Three stops later is Newmarket.

By Bus   About eight National Express Buses depart from London's Victoria Coach Station for Norwich every day, stopping at Stratford, Stansted, and (finally) Newmarket along the way.

By Car   From Cambridge, head east along A133.

ESSENTIALS   The **area code** is 0638. The address of the **Tourist Information Centre** is Atheneum, Angel Hill in Bury Street, Edmunds (tel. 0284/757082).

This old Suffolk town has been famous as a racing center since the time of King James I. Visitors can see Nell Gwynne's House, but mainly they come to visit Britain's first and only equestrian museum.

WHAT TO SEE & DO

NATIONAL HORSERACING MUSEUM, 99 High St. Tel. 0638/667333.
  The museum is housed in the old subscription rooms, early 19th-century rooms used for placing and settling bets. Visitors will be able to see the history of horseracing over a 300-year period. There are fine paintings of famous horses, pictures on loan

from Queen Elizabeth II, and copies of old Parliamentary Acts governing races. There is also a replica of a weighing-in room, plus explanations of the signs used by the ticktack men who keep the on-course bookies informed of changes in the price of bets. A continuous 53-minute audiovisual presentation shows races and racehorses.

The museum also offers popular tours of this historic town. You will be able to watch morning gallops on the heath, see bronzes of stallions from the past, and other points of interest. An optional tour of a famous training establishment is offered, plus a visit to the Jockey Club Rooms, known for a fine collection of paintings. Reservations are necessary, but the tour, which lasts a whole morning, is conducted April to October. Equine tours are available. The museum is closed from December to March, but those with a special interest in seeing it during those months can telephone.

Admission: £2 ($3.70) adults, 50p (95¢) children.
Open: Tues–Sat 10am–5pm, Sun 2–5pm. **Closed:** Dec–Mar; Mon except bank holidays in Aug.

THE NATIONAL STUD, July Race Course. Tel. 0638/663464.
Next to Newmarket's July Race Course, 2 miles southwest of the town, is the place to see some of the world's finest horseflesh, as well as watch a working thoroughbred breeding stud in operation. A tour lasting about 1¼ hours lets you see many mares and foals, plus horses in training for racing. Reservations for tours must be made at The National Stud office or by phoning the number given above.
Admission: £3 ($5.55) adults, £2 ($3.70) children.

WHERE TO STAY

RUTLAND ARMS HOTEL, High St., Newmarket, Suffolk CB8 8NB. Tel. 0638/664251. Fax 0638/666298. 45 rms (all with bath). TV TEL
$ Rates (including English breakfast): £52–£60 ($96.20–$111) single; £62–£72 ($114.70–$133.20) double. AE, DC, MC, V. **Parking:** Free.
At the clock end of High Street is an imposing Georgian coaching inn dating in part from the reign of Charles II. No two rooms are the same. Each has been restored to preserve the original character. A good three-course lunch, costing £9.50 ($17.60), is served from 12:30 to 2pm, and a fixed-price dinner for £12 ($22.20) is available from 7 to 9:30pm.

WHITE HART HOTEL, High St., Newmarket, Suffolk CB8 8JP. Tel. 0638/663051. Fax 0638/667284. 21 rms (all with bath). TV TEL
$ Rates (including English breakfast): £46 single ($85.10); £62 ($114.70) double. AE, DC, MC, V. **Parking:** Free.
This gabled historic inn rises three stories in the town center, opposite the Horseracing Museum. It was constructed on the site of an inn dating from the 1600s. The hotel rooms and the bars are decorated with racing pictures and prints. All accommodations are tastefully furnished (you might even get a four-poster bed), and each has a hairdryer, trouser press, and hot-beverage facilities. Bar snacks are available daily from noon to 2pm and 7 to 9pm, with various hot and cold dishes. The restaurant offers both à la carte and fixed-price menus. A fixed-price lunch goes for £6 ($11.10), while a fixed-price dinner costs £10.25 ($18.95). Lunch is served daily from noon to 2pm, and dinner is served Monday to Thursday from 7 to 9pm; Friday and Saturday from 7 to 9:30pm, and Sunday from 7 to 8:30pm.

---

6. LONG MELFORD

61 miles S of London; 34 miles E of Cambridge

GETTING THERE **By Train** From Cambridge, take a train in the direction of Ipswich and descend at Sudbury. From Sudbury, take a taxi the 3-mile ride to Long Melford.

By Bus   From Cambridge, take a bus (maintained by Chambers Bus Company) to **Bury,** then change buses for the final ride into Long Melford. Chambers runs these circumvoluted routes about once an hour throughout the day and early evening.

By Car   From Newmarket (see above), continue east along A45 to Bury St. Edmunds, but cut south along A134 (direction: Sudbury) to Long Melford.

ESSENTIALS   The **area code** is 0787.

Long Melford has been famous since the days of the early clothmakers. Like Lavenham, it grew in prestige and importance in the Middle Ages. Of the old buildings remaining, the village church is often called "one of the glories of the shire." Along its 3-mile-long High Street—said to boast the highest concentration of antiques shops in Europe—are many private homes erected by wealthy wool merchants of yore. Of special interest are Long Melford's two stately homes.

WHAT TO SEE & DO

MELFORD HALL, Long Melford (east side of A134), Sudbury, Suffolk CO10 9AA. Tel. 0787/880286.
   Standing in Long Melford, 3 miles north of Sudbury, was the ancestral home of Beatrix Potter, who often visited. Her Jemima Puddleduck still occupies a chair in one of the bedrooms upstairs, and other of her figures are on display. The house, built between 1554 and 1578, contains paintings, fine furniture, and Chinese porcelain. Melford Hall is a National Trust property.
   Admission: £2.40 ($4.45) adults, £1.20 ($2.20) children.
   Open: May–Sept Wed–Thurs, Sat–Sun and bank holidays 2–6pm; Apr–Oct Sat–Sun 2–6pm.

KENTWELL HALL, on the A134 between Sudbury and Bury St. Edmunds. Tel. 0787/310207.
   At the end of an avenue of linden trees, the red-brick Tudor mansion surrounded by a broad moat has been restored by its owners, the barrister Patrick Phillips and his wife. A 15th-century moat house, interconnecting gardens, a brick-paved maze, and a costume display are of interest, and there are also rare-breed farm animals to be seen. The hall hosts regular re-creations of Tudor domestic life including the well-known annual events for the weeks June 24 to July 15, and small events over holiday weekends. The entrance is north of the green in Long Melford on the west side of the A134, about ½ mile north of Melford Hall.
   Admission: £3 ($5.55) adults, £1.75 ($3.25) children.
   Open: Easter weekend, mid-Apr to mid-June Sun 2–6pm; mid-July to Sept Wed–Sat 2–6pm; bank holidays 11am–6pm.

WHERE TO STAY & EAT

CROWN INN, Hall St., Long Melford, Suffolk CO10 9JL. Tel. 0787/ 77666. Fax 0787/881883. 11 rms (all with bath). TV TEL
$ **Rates** (including English breakfast): £39.50 ($73.10) single; £50–£55 ($92.50–$101.75) double. MC, V. **Parking:** Free.
This attractive Suffolk inn has a small garden partially hidden from the road by a high stone wall and a country-cottage flavor. Its comfortable interior contains a sitting room for guests that is filled with armchairs. Many fine wines are stored in the Pre-Tudor cellars. Lunch is served daily from noon to 2:30pm, costing from £8 ($14.80). Dinner is served daily from 7pm to 9 and costs from £14 ($25.90). Of special interest in the lounge is a stained-glass panel depicting a scene from Shakespeare's

A *Midsummer Night's Dream*. The inn is on the village's main street, near the center.

BULL HOTEL, Hall St. Tel. 78494.
   Cuisine: ENGLISH/CONTINENTAL. **Reservations:** Recommended.
$ **Prices:** Appetizers £2.50–£4 ($4.65–$7.40); main courses £5.50–£9.50 ($10.20–$17.60); fixed-price lunch £12.95 ($23.95). AE, DC, MC, V.
   Open: Lunch daily noon–2:30pm; dinner daily 7–9:30pm.

⭐ If you're passing through, try to visit one of the old (1540) inns of East Anglia. Built by a wool merchant, it is considered Long Melford's finest and best-preserved building. Incorporated into the general inn is a medieval weavers' gallery and an open hearth with Elizabethan brickwork. The dining room is the Bull's outstanding feature, with its high-beamed ceilings, trestle tables, settles, and handmade chairs, as well as a 10-foot fireplace. On the dinner menu, you can expect a changing array of English and Continental dishes.

THE COUNTRYMEN RESTAURANT, Black Lion, The Green. Tel. 312356.
   Cuisine: ENGLISH/CONTINENTAL. **Reservations:** Recommended.
$ **Prices:** Fixed-price lunch £10–£15 ($18.50–$27.75); set dinner £17–£25 ($31.45–$46.25). MC, V.
   Open: Lunch daily noon–1:30pm; dinner Mon–Fri 7–9pm, Sat 7–9:30pm.

⭐ The restaurant operates out of a fully restored 17th-century coaching inn overlooking one of Suffolk's loveliest village greens near Holy Trinity Church. At night the dining room is warmed by candlelight, and during the day there are views of a Victorian walled garden. Fixed-price meals are available for both lunch and dinner, with menus changing monthly. Dinner is expensive, but well worth the splurge. Prices include unlimited coffee. The kitchen is likely to turn out such dishes as a delicate poached filet of sole, sirloin steak with a piquant sauce, or deep-fried whitebait. Roast prime English beef is a Sunday feature.

---

7. LAVENHAM

66 miles N of London; 7 miles N of Sudbury; 11 miles
SE of Bury St. Edmunds; 35 miles SE of Cambridge

GETTING THERE   By Train   Board a train at London's North Street Station to Colchester. These depart at least once an hour. There, connect to the town of Sudbury. Connections are good. At Sudbury, there are about 9 daily buses making the short run to Lavenham. These buses are maintained by Beeston's Coaches, Ltd. Total trip time from London is between 2 and 2½ hours.

By Bus   A National Express Coach departs from Victoria Coach Station for Lavenham, but it doesn't arrive in Lavenham till 15 hours later, stopping at every hamlet in East Anglia along the way. Take the train.

By Car   From Bury St. Edmunds continue south on the A134 toward Long Melford (see above), but at the junction with A1141 cut southeast to Lavenham.

ESSENTIALS   The **area code** is 0787. The **Tourist Information Centre** is at Market Place (tel. 0787/248207).

ⓘ nce a great wool center, Lavenham is considered a typical East Anglian village. It is filled with a number of half-timbered Tudor houses, washed in the characteristic Suffolk pink. The prosperity of the town in the days of wool manufacture is apparent in the guildhall, on the triangular main "square," built from wool-trading profits. Inside are exhibits on the textile industry of Lavenham, showing how yarn was spun, then "dyed in the wool" with woad (the plant used by the ancient Picts to dye themselves blue), and following on to the weaving process. There is also a display showing how half-timbered houses were constructed.

The Church of St. Peter and St. Paul, at the edge of Lavenham, contains interesting carvings on the misericords and the channel screen, as well as ornate tombs. This is one of the "wool churches" of the area, built by pious merchants in the Perpendicular style with a landmark tower.

WHERE TO STAY

ANGEL HOTEL, Market Place, Lavenham, Suffolk CO10 9QZ. Tel. 0787/ 247388. 7 rms (all with bath). TV TEL
$ **Rates** (including English breakfast): £25–£30 ($46.25–$55.50) single; £40–£50 ($74–$92.50) double. MC, V. **Parking:** Free.

★ Children are welcome at the Angel Hotel, which may be the best little B&B in town. Rooms are well furnished, comfortable, and beautifully maintained. It's possible to order a three-course dinner from the inn's à la carte menu, paying from £8 ($14.80).

WHERE TO EAT

IN TOWN

TIMBERS RESTAURANT, High St. Tel. 247218.
 Cuisine: ENGLISH. **Reservations:** Required.
$ **Prices:** Appetizers £1.95–£7.50 ($3.60–$13.90); main courses £4.95–£11.95 ($9.15–$22.10); set dinner £8.95 ($16.55); lunch £3.50–£5.25 ($6.45–$9.70). MC, V.
 Open: Lunch Tues–Sat noon–2pm; dinner Tues–Sat 7:30–9:30pm. **Closed:** First 3 weeks Oct, first 3 weeks Feb.
Popular with villagers and visitors alike, the Timbers provides traditional English meals in a 15th-century building of low ceilings and oak tables. You can order such classic dishes as rack of English lamb flavored with rosemary, steak-and-kidney pie, or beef Wellington. Desserts are rich and tempting.

NEARBY

THE BELL INN, The Street, Kersey, near Ipswich, Suffolk IP7 6DY. Tel. 823229.
 Cuisine: ENGLISH. **Reservations:** Recommended.
$ **Prices:** Appetizers £2.50–£4 ($4.65–$7.40); main courses £5.50–£7.50 ($10.20–$13.90). DC, MC, V.
 Open: Lunch daily 11:30am–2pm; dinner daily 6:30–10pm.
Off the A1141/B1115 road from Lavenham to Hadleigh, and 15 minutes from the main A12 trunk road, the Bell Inn lies in what has been called "the prettiest village in the world," with a "watersplash" fountain right in the middle of the main street. The inn, dating from the 13th-century, has a blazing fireplace and ceiling beams. The Bell offers good snacks in a timbered bar with glinting horse brasses. In the Pink Room, the main restaurant, lunches and dinners include the finest lamb, duck, sole, and fish dishes, even some vegetarian specialties.

The inn also rents 11 comfortably furnished bedrooms with private bath or shower, costing from £25 ($46.25) in a single or £45 ($83.25) in a double of B&B.

8. WOODBRIDGE & ALDEBURGH

Woodbridge: 81 miles NE of London; 47 miles N of Norwich
Aldeburgh: 97 miles NE of London; 41 miles SE of Norwich

GETTING THERE   By Train   Aldeburgh doesn't have a rail station. Trains leave either London's Victoria Station or London's Liverpool Street Station (depending on the schedule) about six per day in the direction of the line's last stop, **Lowestoft.** Six stops after Ipswich, the train will stop in the hamlet of Saxmundham. From

Saxmundham, there are about a half dozen buses traveling the 6 miles to Aldeburgh. These tend to be daytime buses. Many visitors hire a taxi at Saxmundham instead for the transit on to Aldeburgh. Woodbridge, larger and busier than Aldeburgh, has a railway station. The same line described above stops at Woodbridge, which lies two stops after Ipswich on the line whose final destination is Lowestoft.

By Bus A National Express coach departs once per day from London's Victoria Coach Station for Great Yarmouth, and passes through Aldeburgh (and also through Woodbridge) along the way. Travel time to Aldeburgh is woefully slow (4¼ hours) because it visits every country town along the way. Note that Aldeburgh and Woodbridge lie 15 miles from one another, and are interconnected frequently with bus no. 80/81, which is maintained by the Eastern Counties Bus Company. Buses between the towns are frequent. Many visitors reach both towns with the buses which come from Ipswich. Bus connections for Ipswich to both Woodbridge and Aldeburgh are about a half dozen per day, and are maintained by the Eastern Counties Bus Company.

By Car From London's ring road, the A12 runs northeast to Ipswich. From Ipswich, continue northeast on A12 to Woodbridge or else stay on the road until you reach the junction of A1094, at which point head east to the North Sea and Aldeburgh.

ESSENTIALS The **area code** for Aldeburgh is 072885 for 4-figure numbers or 0728 for 6 figure-numbers. The summer-only **Tourist Information Centre** is at The Cinema, High Street (tel. 0728/453637) in Aldeburgh. The area code for Woodbridge is 03943 for 4-figure numbers or 0394 for 6-figure numbers. There is no tourist office.

The market town of Woodbridge is also a yachting center, situated on the Deben River. Its most famous resident was Edward Fitzgerald, the Victorian poet and translator of *The Rubaiyat of Omar Khayyam*. The poet died in 1883 and was buried nearly 4 miles away at Boulge.

Woodbridge is a good base for exploring the East Suffolk coastline, particularly the small resort of Aldeburgh, noted for its moot hall.

Bordering on the North Sea, Aldeburgh is a favorite resort of the educated traveler, even attracting the Dutch who make the sea crossing via Harwich and Felixstowe, now major entry ports for traffic from the Continent. It was the home of Benjamin Britten (1913–76), the renowned composer of the operas *Peter Grimes* and *Billy Budd*, as well as many orchestral works. Many of his compositions were first performed at the **Aldeburgh Festival,** which he founded in 1946. The festival takes place in June, featuring internationally known performers. There are other concerts and events throughout the year. The **Snape Maltings Concert Hall** nearby is generally regarded as one of the more successful of the smaller British concert halls, and it also contains the Britten-Pears School of Advanced Musical Studies, established in 1973.

The town dates from Roman times, and has long been known as a small port for North Sea fisheries. There are two golf courses, one at Aldeburgh and another at Thorpeness, 2 miles away. A yacht club is set on the River Alde 9 miles from the river's mouth. Two bird sanctuaries are also nearby, Minsmere and Havergate Island. Both are famous for their water fowl, and they are managed by the Royal Society for the Protection of Birds.

Constructed on a shelf of land at the level of the sea, the High, or main street, runs parallel to the often-turbulent waterfront. A cliff face rises some 55 feet above the main street. A major attraction is the 16th-century **Moot Hall Museum** (tel. 072885/2158). The hall dates from the time of Henry VIII, but its tall, twin chimneys are later additions. The timber-frame structure contains old maps and prints. It's open July to September daily from 10am to 4pm; Easter to June it's open only Saturday and Sunday from 2:30 to 5pm. Admission is 50p (95¢) for adults, free for children.

Aldeburgh also contains the nation's northernmost martello tower, erected to protect the coast from a feared invasion by Napoléon.

WHERE TO STAY

NEAR WOODBRIDGE

THE KING'S HEAD INN, Front St., Oxford, near Woodbridge, Suffolk IP12 2LW. Tel. 0394/450271. 6 rms (none with bath). TV **Directions:** Take the B1084. Orford is signposted on the outskirts of Woodbridge.
$ **Rates** (including English breakfast): £34–£36 ($62.90–$66.60) double. DC. **Parking:** Free.
At this ancient town, known for the ruins of its 12th-century castle, you can stay at the King's Head, a 13th-century inn reputed to have a smuggling history, lying in the shadow of St. Bartholomew's Church. Bedrooms—all doubles—are comfortably furnished and well maintained. A wealth of old beams and a candlelit dining room add to the ambience of the inn, which is owned and run by Joy and Alistair Shaw. Alistair, who is also the chef, prepares tasty meals, using fresh produce from the sea and locally caught game. Lunchtime bar snacks are available. Boat trips can be booked in advance. If you'd like to visit just to eat, hours are from noon to 2pm and 7 to 9pm daily.

IN ALDEBURGH

COTMANDENE GUEST HOUSE, 6 Park Lane between Lee and Fawcett Rds., Aldeburgh, Suffolk IP15 5HL. Tel. 072885/3775. 7 rms (5 with bath or shower). TV
$ **Rates** (including English breakfast): £15–£22 ($27.75–$40.70) single without bath; £35 ($64.75) double with bath. MC, V. **Parking:** Free.
This is considered the best guesthouse in the area (as opposed to the more expensive hotels). A Victorian, double-fronted structure, it stands in a tranquil neighborhood. If you go for a walk, you will undoubtedly be following not only in Britten's footsteps, but those of frequent visitor E. M. Forster. Amenities include hairdryers, shoe cleaning, and ironing facilities. Wholesome English cookery is served.

UPLANDS HOTEL, Victoria Rd., Aldeburgh, Suffolk IP15 5DX. Tel. 0728/452420. 20 rms (17 with bath), 7 chalets. TV TEL
$ **Rates** (including English breakfast): £25 ($46.25) single without bath, £40 ($74) single with bath; £55 ($101.75) double with bath. AE, DC, MC, V. **Parking:** Free.
This 18th-century inn is more like a private home that takes in paying guests. At one time it was the childhood home of Elizabeth Garrett Anderson, the first woman doctor in England. Once inside the living room, you'll sense its informality and charm. There are twin-bedded chalets in the garden, each with private bath and TV. The chef, who has won many cooking awards, offers an à la carte dinner for £15 ($27.75) and up. A typical meal might include escalope de veau "uplands" or roast Aylesbury duck. You can have coffee in front of the fireplace or, in fair weather, in the garden. The hotel is opposite the parish church on the main road into Aldeburgh.

WHERE TO EAT

IN WOODBRIDGE

CAPTAIN'S TABLE, 3 Quay St. Tel. 383145.
Cuisine: SEAFOOD. **Reservations:** Recommended.
$ **Prices:** Appetizers £2–£3.50 ($3.70–$6.45); main courses £4.50–£8 ($8.35–$14.80); bar lunch £7.50 ($13.90). MC, V.
Open: Lunch Tues–Sat noon–2pm; dinner Tues–Sat 6:30–9:30pm.

This a good choice for intimate dining near the railway station. The food is well prepared, the atmosphere near the wharf is colorful. The licensed restaurant serves a number of specialties, including Dover sole, and scallops cooked in butter with bacon and garlic. Vegetables are extra, and desserts are rich and good tasting. The day's specials are written on a blackboard, including oysters, sea salmon, and turbot in lobster sauce.

LANE O'GORMAN WINE BAR, 17 Thoro'fare. Tel. 2557.
   Cuisine: CONTINENTAL. **Reservations:** Not needed.
$ **Prices:** Appetizers £2.20–£3 ($4.05–$5.55); main courses £5–£7.50 ($9.25–$13.90). No credit cards.
   Open: Lunch Tues–Sat noon–2:30pm; dinner Tues–Sat 7–11pm.
This is a popular dining spot in the town center offering reasonably priced food. Food is home-cooked and based on seasonal produce. Many guests come just for a glass of wine (18 available by the glass) or a beer. You might begin with a tartlet of minty cream cheese topped with cucumber and poppy seeds or buckwheat blinis with smoked salmon, smoked halibut, and a ceviche of salmon marinated in lime juice and served with a horseradish cream sauce. Main courses include lamb loin noisettes with a sauce of rosemary and garlic sitting on a bed of braised spinach. You might also try pork tenderloin noisettes in a ginger and coriander sauce with a bacon and potato cake. Desserts are sumptuous, including a caramelized brazilnut and orange tart or else a whisky-and-honey parfait served with praline.

IN ALDEBURGH

ALDEBURGH FISH AND CHIP SHOP, 226 High St. Tel. 452250.
   Cuisine: FISH-AND-CHIPS. **Reservations:** Not needed.
$ **Prices:** Main courses £1.60–£2.25 ($2.95–$4.15). No credit cards.
   Open: Lunch Tues–Sat 11:45am–1:45pm; dinner Tues–Sat 5–9pm.
The composer Benjamin Britten and his longtime friend Peter Pears used to bring visitors from London or America to sample locally caught fish, notably plaice and cod. Many guests pick up their treat here and picnic on the seawall. The shop smokes its own salmon. It's located on the main street.

YE OLD CROSS KEYS, Crabbe St. Tel. 452637.
   Cuisine: ENGLISH/SEAFOOD. **Reservations:** None.
$ **Prices:** Appetizers £1.60–£5.90 ($2.95–$10.90); main courses £2.50–£9 ($4.65–$16.65). No credit cards.
   Open: Lunch daily noon–2pm; dinner daily 7–9pm. Pub Mon–Sat 11am–2:30pm and 5:30–11pm, Sun noon–2:30pm and 7–10:30pm.
Set a few paces from the sea in the town center, this is a genuine 16th-century pub with the atmosphere of a Suffolk local. In the summer, drinkers take their mugs of real English ale or lager out and sit on the seawall and watch the pounding waves, always within the sightlines of the many flowering baskets which hang from the building's eaves. The pub is favored by local artists, who during the cooler months sit beside an old brick fireplace and eat platters of oysters and smoked salmon. Place your food order at a special counter, and someone will usually bring lunch or dinner directly to where you are sitting.

9. NORWICH

109 miles NE of London; 20 miles W of the
North Sea; 120 miles E of Nottingham

GETTING THERE   By Train   There is hourly service from London's Liverpool Street Station. Trip time is 1 hour and 50 minutes.

By Bus   National Express buses depart London's Victoria Coach Station every hour. Trip time is 3 hours.

By Car From London's ring road, head north to Cambridge on M11, but turn northeast at the junction of A11 which will take you to Norwich.

ESSENTIALS The **area code** is 0603. There is a **tourist information center** at the guildhall, Gaol Hill (tel. 0603/666071).

Norfolk still holds its claim as the capital city of East Anglia. The county town of Norfolk, Norwich is a charming and historic city, despite its partial industrialization. It is the most important shopping center in East Anglia and has a lot to offer in the way of hotels and entertainment. In addition to its cathedral, it has more than 30 medieval parish churches built of flint.

There are many interesting hotels in the narrow streets and alleyways, and a big open-air market, busy every weekday, where fruit, flowers, vegetables, and other goods are sold from stalls with colored canvas roofs.

WHAT TO SEE & DO

IN TOWN

NORWICH CATHEDRAL, 62 The Close off Palace St. Tel. 0603/626290.

⭐ Principally of Norman design, the cathedral dates from 1096. It is noted primarily for its long nave, with its lofty columns. Its spire, built in the late Perpendicular style, rises 315 feet, and shares distinction with the keep of the castle as the significant landmarks on the Norwich skyline. On the vaulted ceiling are more than 300 bosses (knoblike ornamental projections) depicting biblical scenes. The impressive choir stalls with the handsome misericords date from the 15th century. Edith Cavell—"Patriotism is not enough"—the English nurse executed by the Germans in World War I, was buried on the cathedral's Life's Green. The quadrangular cloisters go back to the 13th century, and are among the most spacious in England.

The cathedral visitor's center includes a refreshment area and an exhibition and film room with tape/slide shows about the cathedral. A short walk from the cathedral will take you to Tombland, one of the most interesting old squares in Norwich.

Admission: Free. Treasury 50p (95¢).

Open: Oct–May daily 7:30am–6pm; June–Sept daily 7:30am–7pm.

NORWICH CASTLE (Norfolk Museums Service), Castle Meadow. Tel. 0603/222222, ext. 71224.

In the center of Norwich, on a partly artificial mound, sits the castle, formerly the county gaol (jail). Its huge 12th-century Norman keep and the later prison buildings are used as a civic museum and headquarters of the countywide Norfolk Museums Service.

The museum's art exhibits include an impressive collection of pictures by artists of the Norwich School, the most distinguished of which were John Crome, born 1768, and John Sell Cotman, born 1782. The castle museum also contains the best collection of British ceramic teapots in the world and unrivaled collections of Lowestoft porcelain and Norwich silver. Rare prehistoric gold jewelry and other archeological finds help to illustrate Norfolk's wealth and importance and the life of its people. A set of dioramas shows Norfolk wildlife in its natural setting. You can also visit a geology gallery and a permanent exhibition, Norfolk in Europe. There's a cafeteria open Monday to Saturday from 10am to 4:30pm, as well as a bar serving from 10:30am to 2:30pm.

Admission: £1 ($1.85) adults, 20p (35¢) children.

Open: Museum Mon–Sat 10am–5pm, Sun 2–5pm.

SAINSBURY CENTRE FOR VISUAL ARTS, University of East Anglia, Earlham Rd. Tel. 0603/506060.

The center was the gift in 1973 of Sir Robert and Lady Sainsbury, who contributed their private collection to the University of East Anglia, 3 miles west of

Norwich on Earlham Road. Along with their son, David, they gave an endowment to provide a building to house the collection. Designed by Foster Associates, the center was opened in 1978, and since then the building has won many national and international awards. Features of the structure are its flexibility, allowing solid and glass areas to be interchanged, and the superb quality of light, which allows optimum viewing of works of art.

The Sainsbury Collection is one of the foremost in the country, including modern, ancient, classical, and ethnographic art. It is especially strong in works by Francis Bacon, Alberto Giacometti, and Henry Moore. Other displays include the Anderson collection of art nouveau and the university aggregation of 20th-century abstract art and design. There is also a regular program of special exhibitions. The restaurant on the premises offers a self-service buffet Monday to Friday from 10:30am to 2pm and a carvery service from 12:30 to 2pm. A conservatory coffee bar serves light lunches and refreshments Tuesday to Sunday from noon to 4:30pm.

Admission: 75p ($1.40) adults, 40p (75¢) children.
Open: Tues–Sun noon–5pm. **Bus:** No. 526 or 527 from Castle Meadow.

THE MUSTARD SHOP, 3 Bridewell Alley. Tel. 0603/627889.

The Victorian-style Mustard Shop in the center near the Castle is a wealth of mahogany and shining brass. There is an old cash register to record your purchase, and the standard of service and pace of life also reflect the personality of a bygone age. In the Mustard Museum is a series of displays illustrating the history of the Colman Company and the making of mustard, its properties and origins. There are old advertisements, as well as packages and "tins." You can browse in the shop, selecting whichever mustards you prefer. Really hot, English-type mustards are sold, as well as the continental blends. Besides mustards, the shop sells aprons, tea towels, chopping boards, pottery mustard pots, and mugs.

Admission: Free.
Open: Mon–Sat 9am–5:30pm.

U.S. ARMY MEMORIAL ROOM (at the central library), Bethel St. off Giles St. Tel. 0603/222222, ext. 52.

A memorial room honoring the Second Air Division of the Eighth United States Army Air Force is part of the central library. A memorial fountain also honoring the United States airmen who were based in Norfolk and Suffolk in World War II, many losing their lives in the line of duty, is in the library courtyard. The fountain incorporates the insignia of the Second Air Division and a stone from each state of the United States. Books, audiovisual materials, and records of the various bomb groups are in the library.

Admission: By donation.
Open: Daily 10am–5pm.

WHERE TO STAY

Norwich is better equipped than most East Anglian cities to handle guests who arrive without reservations. The Norwich City **Tourist Information Centre** maintains an office at the guildhall, Gaol Hill, opposite the market (tel. 0603/666071). Each year a new listing of accommodations is drawn up, including both licensed and unlicensed hotels, B&B houses, and even living arrangements on the outskirts.

DOUBLES WITHOUT BATH FOR LESS THAN £36 ($66.60)

CROFTERS HOTEL, 2 Earlham Rd., Norwich, Norfolk NR2 3DA. Tel. 0603/613287. 15 rms (9 with bath). TV

$ Rates: £22.50 ($41.65) single without bath, £31 ($57.35) single with bath; £36 ($66.60) double without bath, £44 ($81.40) double with bath. No credit cards.
Parking: Free.

Originally built in 1840 of yellow brick which long ago turned gray, it was originally intended as a gentlemen's private residence. Located in the vicinity of St. John's Cathedral, it is today the personal domain of Jonathan and Dawn Cumby, who maintain a separate TV lounge for their guests, and serve (if notified in advance) three-course evening meals for £8 ($14.80) per person. Families are welcome, and on weekends, an evening salad buffet is provided free.

MARLBOROUGH HOUSE HOTEL, 22 Stracey Rd., Norwich, Norfolk NR1 1EZ. Tel. 0603/628005. 11 rms (5 with shower). TV

$ Rates (including English breakfast): £15 ($27.75) single without bath; £35 ($64.75) double with bath; £42 ($77.70) family room with bath. No credit cards. **Parking:** Free.

This centrally heated hotel offers bedrooms with hot-beverage facilities. Evening meals with home-style cooking, costing £6.50 ($12.05) and up, are served daily from 5:30 to 7pm. There is a comfortable TV lounge and a licensed bar. The hotel has a small car park as well as adequate parking facilities outside. It is centrally situated close to the railway station, Riverside Walk, the cathedral, and the central library.

SANTA LUCIA HOTEL, 38-40 Yarmouth Rd., Norwich, Norfolk NR7 0EQ. Tel. 0603/33207. 30 rms (12 with bath). TV **Bus:** No. 12.

$ Rates (including English breakfast): £11.50 ($21.30) single without bath; £23 ($42.55) double without bath, £28 ($51.80) double with bath. No credit cards. **Parking:** Free.

 For value, this is the best of the hotels outside Norwich. Only 1½ miles from the center, the hotel offers inexpensive accommodations, an inviting atmosphere, and an attractive setting by the river. Each room has running water and a clock radio. There are sun terraces for relaxing, modern bathrooms and showers, and plenty of parking space. Two buses pass by the door heading for the city center.

WEDGEWOOD GUEST HOUSE, 42-44 St. Stephens Rd. off King's Rd., Norwich, Norfolk NR1 3RE. Tel. 0603/625730. 11 rms (8 with bath). TV

$ Rates (including English breakfast): £15.50–£16.50 ($28.70–$30.55) single without bath; £32 ($59.20) double without bath, £34 ($62.90) double with bath. AE, MC, V. **Parking:** Free.

Close to the bus station, the Wedgewood is not only convenient for exploring many of Norwich's attractions, it offers good rooms at a fair price. Keys are provided so guests can come and go as they wish. An iron and ironing board are available.

WORTH THE EXTRA BUCKS

THE BEECHES HOTEL, 4-6 Earlham Rd., Norwich, Norfolk NR2 3DB. Tel. 0603/621167. 32 rms (12 with bath or shower). TV TEL

$ Rates (including English breakfast): £25 ($48.10) single without bath, £40 ($74) single with bath; £55 ($101.75) double without bath, £65 ($120.25) double with bath. MC, V. **Parking:** Free.

The hotel was created by combining two private homes in Victoria's day. Some accommodations are rented exclusively to nonsmokers. The hotel is in the center of the historic district, just a short distance from the city center, near Plantation Garden, 3 acres of pleasure grounds in the heart of the city.

WHERE TO EAT

MEALS FOR LESS THAN £10 [$18.50]

ASSEMBLY HOUSE, Theatre St. Tel. 626402.

Cuisine: ENGLISH. **Reservations:** Required. **Transportation:** 10 city buses run nearby.

$ Prices: Appetizers £1–£1.75 ($1.85–$3.25); main courses £2.70–£3.95 ($5–$7.30). No credit cards.

Open: Coffee Mon–Sat 10am–noon; lunch Mon–Sat noon–2pm; tea Mon–Sat 2–5pm; dinner Mon–Sat 5–7:30pm.

 This house is a good example of Georgian architecture. You enter the building through a large front courtyard, which leads to the central hall with its columns, fine paneling, and crystal chandelier. The restaurant is administered

by H. J. Sexton Norwich Arts Trust. On your left is a high-ceilinged room with paneling, fine paintings, and a long buffet table for self-service. After making your selection, take your plate to any one of the many tables. Often you'll share—perhaps with an artist. There is an unusually varied selection of hors d'oeuvres. A big bowl of homemade soup might get you started. Hot main courses are made with fresh ingredients. After dining, stroll through the rest of the building. Art exhibits are usually held regularly in the Ivory and Hobart rooms, open from 10am to 5:30pm. Concerts are sponsored in the Music Room, with its chandeliers and sconces. There's even a little cinema.

BRITON ARMS COFFEE HOUSE, Elm Hill. Tel. 623367.

Cuisine: ENGLISH. **Reservations:** Not needed.

$ **Prices:** Appetizers 65p–£1.10 ($1.20–$2.05); main courses £2.50–£3.50 ($4.65–$6.45). No credit cards.

Open: Mon–Sat 9:30am–5pm; lunch Mon–Sat 12:15–2:30pm.

In the heart of the old city near the train station, the Briton Arms overlooks the most beautiful cobbled street in Norwich. Tracing its history back to the days of Edward III, it's now one of the least expensive eating places in Norwich. It's certainly one of the most intimate and informal, with old beamed ceilings and Tudor benches. The coffeehouse has several rooms, including one in back with an inglenook. The procedure here is to go to the little counter, where you purchase your lunch and bring it to the table of your choice. Everything I've tried was homemade and well prepared. Try lamb casserole and white wine and juniperberries or seafood gratin. Every day a different kind of soup is offered. It's a good place to stop after you tour the cathedral, only a block away.

CAFE LA TIENDA, 10 St. Gregory's Alley off Charing Cross St. Tel. 629122.

Cuisine: CONTINENTAL/VEGETARIAN. **Reservations:** Not needed.

$ **Prices:** Appetizers £1.50–£2 ($2.80–$3.70); main courses £2.50–£3.50 ($4.05–$6.45). No credit cards.

Open: Mon–Sat 10am–4pm.

This informal, two-story restaurant is in an ethnic part of the city. Its devotees are drawn to its fresh, natural foods and low prices. Meals include such dishes as mushroom Stroganoff and pita bread with various stuffings.

EASY EXCURSIONS FROM NORWICH

BLICKLING HALL, Blickling, near Aylsham, Norfolk NR11 6NF. Tel. 0263/733084.

A long drive, bordered by massive yew hedges which frame your first view of this old house, leads you to Blickling Hall. A great Jacobean house built in the early 17th-century, it is one of the finest examples of such architecture in the country. The long gallery has an elaborate 17th-century ceiling, and the Peter the Great Room, decorated later, has a fine tapestry on the wall. The house is set in ornamental parkland with a formal garden and an orangery. Meals and snacks are available. Blickling Hall lies 14 miles north of the city of Norwich; 1½ miles west of Aylsham on the B1354 road. It is signposted off the A140 Cromer Road.

Admission: House and gardens £4 ($7.40) adults, £2 ($3.70) children; gardens £2 ($3.70) adults, £1 ($1.85) children.

Open: Apr–Oct Tues–Wed, Fri–Sun 1–5pm (gardens, shop, and restaurant noon–5pm).

SANDRINGHAM, Sandringham, 8 miles NE of King's Lynn (off A149). Tel. 0553/772675.

Some 110 miles northeast of London, Sandringham has been the country home of four generations of British monarchs, ever since the Prince of Wales (later King Edward VII) purchased it in 1861. The son of Queen Victoria, along with his Danish wife, Princess Alexandra, rebuilt the house, standing on 7,000 acres of grounds, and in time it became a popular meeting place for British society. The red-brick, Victorian-Tudor mansion consists of more than 200 rooms, and in recent times some rooms have been opened to the public, including two drawing rooms and a dining room. Sandringham joins Windsor Castle and the Palace of Holyroodhouse in Edinburgh as the only British royal residences that can be examined by the public. Guests can also visit a lofty saloon with a minstrels' gallery.

A group of former coach houses has been converted into a museum of big-game trophies, plus a collection of cars, including the first vehicle purchased by a member of the royal family, a 1900 Daimler Tonneau that belonged to Edward VII. The house and grounds are open, except when the queen or members of the royal family are there. The 70-acre gardens are richly planted with azaleas, rhododendrons, hydrangeas, and camellias.

Admission: House and grounds £2.20 ($4.05) adults, £1.40 ($2.60) children; grounds only £1.70 ($3.15) adults, £1 ($1.85) children.

Open: House Mon–Sat 11am–4:45pm, Sun noon–4:45pm; grounds Mon–Sat 10:30am–5pm, Sun 11:30am–5pm. **Closed:** House and grounds Apr 29–Sept Sun–Thurs; house third week in July–first week in Aug. **Transportation/ Directions:** Sandringham lies 50 miles east of Norwich and 8 miles northeast of King's Lynn (off the A149). King's Lynn is the end of the main train route from London's Liverpool Street Station that goes via Cambridge and Ely. Trains to King's Lynn arrive from London every two hours. Trip time is 2½ hours. From Cambridge, the train ride takes 1 hour. Buses from both Cambridge and Norwich run to King's Lynn, from which you can catch bus no. 411 to take you to Sandringham.

THE NORTHWEST

Industrialization has cast so much darkness over England's northwest that the area has been relatively neglected by the foreign visitor. At best, Americans rush through it heading for the Lake District and Scotland.

However, the northwest, in spite of its bleak commercial areas, has much beauty for those willing to find it. Manchester, Lancaster, Morecambe, and Southport—to name only a few—are all interesting cities, and much of the countryside is beautiful, filled with inns, restaurants, and pubs, along with many sightseeing attractions.

I will concentrate on two of the more popular cities—Chester and Liverpool, followed by the most interesting towns of the Lake District, such as Windermere.

Cheshire, the county in which Chester lies, is world renowned for its cheese. This lowlying northwestern county is largely agricultural. It borders Wales, accounting for its turbulent history, and forms a good base for touring North Wales, the most beautiful part of that little country. Chester, the capital of Cheshire, has a wealth of accommodations, and Nantwich, an easy excursion from Chester, is an old salt town.

Liverpool, home of the Beatles, has done much in recent years to revitalize its tourist industry, especially since the restoration of its waterfront, which today contains many museums and exhibitions. An extension of London's Tate Gallery also opened there in 1988, with its display of modern art. Yet many visit just to follow in the footsteps of the Beatles.

One of England's most popular summer retreats in Queen Victoria's day was the Lake District. In its time the district has lured such writers as Samuel Taylor Coleridge, Charlotte Brontë, Charles Lamb, Percy Bysshe Shelley, John Keats, Alfred Lord Tennyson, and Matthew Arnold.

The Lake District is a miniature Switzerland condensed into about 32 miles, principally in Cumbria, although it begins in the northern part of Lancashire.

The best activity in the wilds of this northwestern shire is walking. Don't go out without a warning, however. There is a great deal of rain and heavy mist. When the mist starts to fall, drop in at a pub, and warm yourself beside an open fireplace.

The far northwestern part of the shire, bordering Scotland, used to be called Cumberland. Now part of Cumbria, it is generally divided geographically into a trio of segments: the Pennines, dominating the eastern sector (loftiest point at Cross Fell, nearly 3,000 feet high); the Valley of Eden; and the lakes and secluded valleys of the west, by far the most interesting. The area, so beautifully described by the romantic Lake Poets, enjoys many literary associations.

The largest town is Carlisle in the north—a possible base for explorations to

WHAT'S SPECIAL ABOUT THE NORTHWEST

Great Towns/Villages

☐ Chester, a Roman and medieval walled city, famed for its Rows (galleried arcades reached by steps from the street).

☐ Liverpool, the home of the Beatles, a major 18th-century port.

☐ Windermere, major center for England's most beautiful lake.

Natural Spectacles

☐ Scafell Pike, rising to a height of 3,210 feet—the tallest peak in England.

☐ Lake Windermere, the grandest of lakes, a recreational center in summer.

Literary Shrines

☐ Rydal Mount, outside Ambleside, home of William Wordsworth from 1813 until his death in 1850.

☐ Brantwood, home of John Ruskin, the poet, artist, and towering figure of the Victorian age.

Cathedrals

☐ Cathedral Church of Christ, Liverpool, the last Gothic-style cathedral erected on earth. The fifth largest cathedral in the world.

Museums

☐ Tate Gallery, Liverpool, the great collection of 20th-century art in the north of England.

Hadrian's Wall. Built in the second century A.D. by the Romans, the 75-mile wall stretches from Wallsend in the east to Bowness on the Solway. Brockhole National Park Centre, between Ambleside and Windermere, is well worth a visit.

SEEING THE NORTHWEST
GETTING THERE

From London, the M1 and the M6 motorways head north; Chester and Liverpool are easily reached. The M6 continues north, with cut offs to various villages and towns in the Lake District. British Rail serves the region from London's Euston Station. Change at the Oxenholme Lake District Station for branch lines into Windermere. It takes about 4½ hours to reach the Lake District from London. National Express coaches also service the region from London's Victoria Coach Station, arriving in Windermere in about 7½ hours.

A SUGGESTED ROUTE

Day 1: Explore the walled city of Chester and spend the night.

Day 2: See the attractions of Liverpool, including the Tate Gallery and the restored waterfront. Spend the night.

Day 3 & 4: Spend time in the Lake District, exploring literary shrines, while based in Windermere. Or, use one of the neighboring villages as a center, perhaps Ambleside, Hawkshead, or Grasmere.

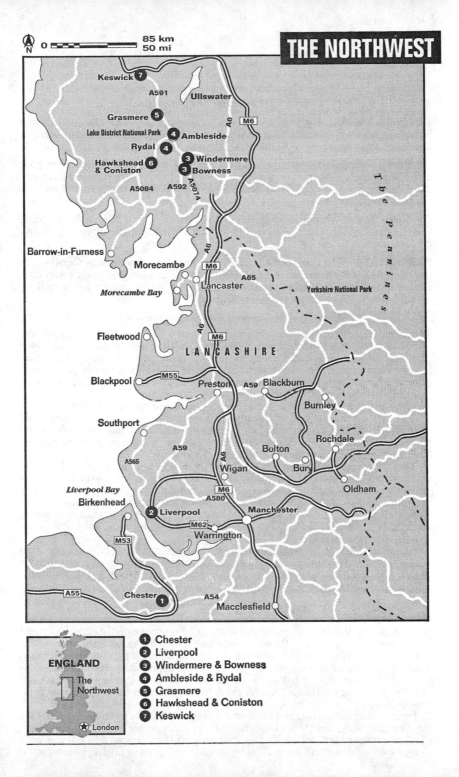

THE NORTHWEST

0 ━━━━ 85 km
       50 mi

Keswick ❼

A591

Ullswater

Grasmere ❺

Lake District National Park Ambleside ❹

Rydal ❹

Hawkshead ❻ & Coniston Windermere ❸

Bowness ❸

A5084 A592 A5074

A6 M6

Barrow-in-Furness

Morecambe

M6

Lancaster

A65

Yorkshire National Park

Morecambe Bay

The Pennines

Fleetwood

A6

M6

LANCASHIRE

Blackpool

M55

Preston

A59 Blackburn

Burnley

Southport

A59

Bolton

Rochdale

A565

A6

Wigan

Bury

Oldham

Liverpool Bay

M6

Birkenhead

A580

❷ Liverpool

Manchester

M62

M53

Warrington

A55

Chester ❶

A54

Macclesfield

ENGLAND

The Northwest

★ London

❶ Chester
❷ Liverpool
❸ Windermere & Bowness
❹ Ambleside & Rydal
❺ Grasmere
❻ Hawkshead & Coniston
❼ Keswick

1. CHESTER

207 miles NW of London; 19 miles S of
Liverpool; 91 miles NW of Birmingham

GETTING THERE By Train   About 21 trains per day from London's Euston Station depart every hour for Chester. Trip time is 3 hours. Trains also run between Liverpool and Chester every 30 minutes. Trip time is 45 minutes.

By Bus   National Express buses run between Birmingham and Chester every hour daily. Trip time is 2 hours. The same bus line also offers service between Liverpool and Chester. It's also possible to catch a National Express coach from London's Victoria Station to Chester.

By Car   From London, head north on M1, crossing onto M6 at the junction. Continue northwest which leads to M54. Near the end of the motorway (M54), continue northwest on A41.

ESSENTIALS   The **area code** is 0244. The **Tourist Information Centre** is at the town hall, Northgate Street (tel. 0244/313126), and offers a hotel reservation service and information. Arrangements can also be made for coach tours or walking tours of Chester (including a ghost-hunter tour).

Chester is ancient, having been founded by a Roman legion on the Dee River in the first century A.D. It reached its pinnacle as a bustling port in the 13th and 14th centuries but then declined following the gradual silting up of the river. The upstart Liverpudlians captured the sea-trafficking business. While other walls of medieval cities of England were either torn down or badly fragmented, Chester still retains 2 miles of fortified city walls intact.

The main entrance into Chester is Eastgate, which dates back to only the 18th century. Within the walls are half-timbered houses and shops; of course not all of them came from the days of the Tudors. Chester has unusual architecture in that some of its builders kept to the black-and-white timbered facades even when erecting buildings during the Georgian and Victorian periods.

The Rows are double-decker layers of shops, one tier on the street level, the others stacked on top and connected by a footway. The upper tier is like a continuous galleried balcony—rain is never a problem. Shopping upstairs is much more adventurous than down on the street. Thriving establishments operate in this traffic-free paradise: tobacco shops, restaurants, department stores, china shops, jewelers, and antiques dealers. For the most representative look, take a walk on arcaded Watergate Street.

At the junction of Watergate, Northgate, and Bridge streets, at noon and 3pm Tuesday to Saturday, April to September, at the City Cross, the town crier issues his news to the accompaniment of a hand bell. Eastgate Street is now a pedestrian way, and musicians often play beside St. Peter's Church and the Town Cross.

WHAT TO SEE & DO

In a big Victorian building opposite the Roman amphitheater, the largest uncovered in Britain, **Chester Visitor Centre,** Vicars Lane (tel. 0244/351609), offers a number of services to visitors. A visit to a life-size Victorian street complete with sounds and smells helps your appreciation and orientation to Chester. The center has a gift shop, a licensed restaurant serving meals and snacks all day, and a currency exchange. Admission is free, and the center is open daily from 9am to 9pm, to 7pm in winter.

For a view of the town, take a walk on the **city wall.** In the town center, you'll see the Eastgate clock, the most photographed timepiece in the world after Big Ben. Climb the stairs near it, which lead up to the top of the city wall, and you can walk along it looking down on Chester. Passing through centuries of English history, you'll go by a cricket field, see the River Dee, which was formerly a major trade artery, and get a look at many old buildings of the 18th century. The wall also goes past some Roman ruins, and it is possible to leave the walkway to explore them. The walk is free.

CHESTER CATHEDRAL, St. Werburgh St. Tel. 0244/324756.

The present building founded in 1092 as a Benedictine abbey was created as a cathedral church in 1541. Considerable architectural restorations were carried out in the 19th century, but older parts have been preserved. Notable features include the fine range of monastic buildings, particularly the cloisters and refectory, the chapter house, and the superb medieval wood carving in the quire (especially the misericords). Also worth seeing are the long south transept with its various chapels, the consistory court, and the medieval roof bosses in the lady chapel. A freestanding bell tower, the first to be built in England since the Reformation, was completed in 1975 and may be seen southeast of the main building. Facilities include a refectory, a bookshop, and an audiovisual presentation. The cathedral is in the center near Town Hall Square.

Admission: Free.
Open: Daily 7am–6:30pm.

CHESTER ZOO, off A41, north of Center. Tel. 0244/380280.

Just off the A41 on the outskirts of Chester, 2 miles from the city center, the Chester Zoo is world-famous for its wide collection of mammals, birds, reptiles, and fish. Many rare and endangered species breed freely in spacious enclosures, and the zoo is particularly renowned for the most successful group of chimpanzees and orangutans in Europe. The 110 acres of gardens are worth seeing in any season, with 160,000 plants in the spring and summer bedding displays alone. The waterbus, a popular summer feature, allows you to observe the hundreds of waterbirds who make their home here. The zoo has several facilities if you get hungry or thirsty during your visit: the licensed Oakfield Restaurant, the Jubilee self-service cafeteria, the Oasis snack bar, and the Rainbow kiosk for either meals or snacks and drinks.

Admission: £4.60 ($8.50) adults, £2.30 ($4.25) children 3–15.
Open: Daily 10am–dusk. **Closed:** Christmas Day. **Directions:** From the center head north along Liverpool Rd.

WHERE TO STAY

DOUBLES WITHOUT BATH FOR LESS THAN £38 ($70.30)

DERRY RAGHAN GUEST HOUSE, 54 Hoole Rd., Chester, Cheshire CH2 3NL Tel. 0244/318740. 2 rms (2 with bath). **Directions:** Take A56 north from the city center.
$ Rates (including English breakfast): £14–£15 ($25.90–$27.75) per person. No credit cards. **Parking:** Free.

This guesthouse lies about a mile from the heart of Chester and some 3 miles from the zoo. Bill and Doris Millar welcome guests to their pleasantly furnished rooms, complete with hot-beverage facilities. Parking is available.

EVERSLEY HOTEL, 9 Eversley Park, Chester, Cheshire CH2 2AJ. Tel. 0244/373744. 11 rms (9 with bath). TV TEL **Directions:** Head north from the center in the direction of the zoo.
$ Rates (including English breakfast): £20–£22 ($37–$40.70) single without bath; £38 ($70.30) double without bath, £42 ($77.70) double with bath. No credit cards. **Parking:** Free.

The Eversley lies off Liverpool Road, about a mile from the heart of old Chester in a residential section. The owners have fully modernized the hotel with hot-beverage facilities, hot and cold water basins, razor sockets, radios, and intercoms. Evening meals are available in the candlelit dining room, and you can enjoy snacks in the Deva Bar.

RIVERSIDE HOTEL AND RECORDER HOTEL, 22 City Walls Rd., Chester, Cheshire CH1 1SB. Tel. 0244/326580. Fax 0244/311567. 23 rms (all with bath or shower). TV TEL **Directions:** From the center take St. Martin's Way to the intersection with City Walk Rd.

$ **Rates** (including English breakfast): £35 ($64.75) single; £36–£60 ($66.60–$111) double. AE, MC, V. **Parking:** Free.

This hotel is actually two hotels off Lower Bridge Street. Most of it has been recently modernized and enjoys an enviable location—on the old Roman Wall, within easy walking distance of the main attractions in the town center. Some of the comfortably furnished accommodations open onto views of the River Dee, and the licensed hotel also has a garden in front. A car park is in the rear. It also has a restaurant.

WORTH THE EXTRA BUCKS

CAVENDISH HOTEL, 44 Hough Green, Chester, Cheshire CH4 8JQ. Tel. 0244/675100. Fax 0244/679942. 20 rms (all with bath). TV TEL **Bus:** No. 28.

$ **Rates** (including English breakfast): £39.50 ($58.33) single; £49.50 ($73.10) double. AE, MC, V. **Parking:** Free.

Set on the A549 coastal road, about a mile west of the city center on a verdantly tree-filled street, this hotel was originally built by the Victorians around 1840 and later adapted by the Edwardians at the turn of the century. The lounge contains a scattering of early 20th-century antiques and a small residents' bar. The hotel is owned by Scotland-born Bill White and his partner Monica Varey, who prepare sophisticated evening meals for around £11 ($20.35) each. In all, the hotel has a lot of cozy charm.

REDLAND HOTEL, 64 Hough Green, Chester, Cheshire CH4 8JY. Tel. 0244/671024. 12 rms (all with bath), 2 suites. TV TEL

$ **Rates** (including English breakfast): £35–£40 ($64.75–$74) single; £45–£55 ($83.25–$101.75) double; £55 ($101.75) honeymoon suite. No credit cards. **Parking:** Free.

Many judges have rated this the finest small hotel in Chester. It is a Victorian town house of character and charm, with oak paneling and stained-glass windows. Open year round, it lies but a mile from the center of Chester opposite Chester Golf Course in the direction of the Welsh border, and many guests use it as a base for exploring North Wales. Mrs. T. M. White has added such amenities to the hotel as a sauna and solarium. There is a residential license for serving alcohol.

YE OLDE KING'S HEAD HOTEL, 48-50 Lower Bridge St., Chester, Cheshire CH1 1RS. Tel. 0244/324855. Fax 0244/315693. 8 rms (all with bath). TV TEL

$ **Rates** (including English breakfast): £40 ($74) single; £50 ($92.50) double. AE, DC, MC, V. **Parking:** Free.

This hotel is a 16th-century museum piece of black-and-white architecture. From 1598 to 1707, it was occupied by the well-known Randle Holme family of Chester, noted heraldic painters and genealogists (some of their manuscripts have made it to the British Museum). Since 1717, the King's Head has been a licensed inn. The host rents handsome bedrooms with hot-beverage facilities and central heating. Many of the walls and ceilings are sloped and highly pitched, with exposed beams. The dining room, Mrs. B's Restaurant, has a country farmhouse theme and serves wholesome dishes, including prime English roast, steak, or chicken. Meals cost from £12 ($22.20) each, and are served daily from noon to 2:30pm and 7:30 to 10pm. The hotel is a 5-minute walk south of Chester's Town Hall.

WHERE TO EAT

Two of the following listings, the Bear and Billet and the Boot Inn, are popular pubs in Chester.

MEALS FOR LESS THAN £10 [$18.50]

ABBEY GREEN RESTAURANT/GARDEN HOUSE RESTAURANT, 1 Rufus Court, Northgate St. Tel. 313251.
Cuisine: VEGETARIAN/INTERNATIONAL. **Reservations:** Recommended.
$ **Prices:** Appetizers £3–£5 ($5.55–$9.25); main dishes £6.50–£8.50 ($12.05–$15.75); teatime pastries £1–£1.50 ($1.85–$2.80). DC, MC, V.
Open: Lunch Mon–Sat noon–2:30pm, Sun 11am–4pm; dinner Tues–Sun 6:30–10:30pm, afternoon tea and pastries Mon–Sat 2:30–6pm; Morning coffee Mon–Sat 9am–11:30am.

⭐ This is the newest headquarters of a restaurant which has repeatedly won many of Chester's civic and gastronomic awards. Contained within a complex of Georgian buildings originally constructed as an archbishop's palace (and later occupied by the city's hangman), it's near a handful of boutiques, other restaurants, and either of the town's bus stations. Its street level is devoted to the Abbey Green Vegetarian restaurant, where chef Julia Dunning, and her brother, Duncan Lochhead, prepare dishes inspired by her travels in the Middle East, Central America, and Australia. (Examples include hummus with pita bread, Mexican tostados, and the imagined cuisine of some South Sea island.) Upstairs, at the top of a sweeping Georgian staircase, amid oil portraits and silver chandeliers, is a more formal gourmet (nonvegetarian) restaurant, where dishes might include smoked pigeon salad in a horseradish cream sauce, terrine of duck flavored with juniperberries and red-wine jelly, and rack of Welsh lamb in a honey-rosemary sauce. Both areas are open for morning coffee and afternoon tea. These are sometimes consumed within the large outdoor garden, where pieces of sculpture are placed amid the shrubberies.

BEAR AND BILLET, 94 Lower Bridge St. Tel. 321272.
Cuisine: ENGLISH. **Reservations:** Not needed. **Directions:** From the center take Bridge Street to Lower Bridge Street near Old Dee Bridge. **Bus:** No. 6 or 16.
$ **Prices:** Appetizers 95p–£2.75 ($1.85–$3.10); main courses £4.15–£7.50 ($7.75–$13.95); bar snacks £2.50 ($4.65). DC, MC, V.
Open: Restaurant lunch daily noon–2:30pm; dinner daily 7–9pm. Pub Mon–Sat 11am–11pm, Sun noon–3pm and 7–10:30pm.
One of the most famous pubs in Chester, this was the former town house of the earls of Shrewsbury and built in 1644. Full meals are served in the upstairs dining room, and bar snacks are served at the street-level pub throughout the day. Because of its intricately timbered and highly decorative facade, this is one of the most photographed buildings in Chester.

BOOT INN, Eastgate Row. Tel. 324540.
Cuisine: ENGLISH. **Reservations:** None. **Bus:** No. 10 or 16.
$ **Prices:** Bar snacks £3–£5 ($5.55–$9.25). No credit cards.
Open: Mon–Thurs 11am–3:30pm and 5:30–11pm, Fri–Sat 11am–11pm, Sun noon–3pm and 7–10:30pm.
Established in 1643 on a street immediately adjacent to the back of the cathedral, this is the smallest and most unspoiled pub in Chester. It has low ceilings, high-backed benches, and a multitude of the publican's mementos cluttering the walls. It's reached by entering a narrow covered passageway which is accessible via the pedestrian walkway of Eastgate Row. Food items include such informal fare as a ploughman's lunch, quiche with salad, and "giant's Yorkshire pudding," made by treating a leaf of "pud" like a crêpe and stuffing it with steak-and-kidney stew or a ragoût of chicken with mushrooms.

CLAVERTON'S CONTINENTAL WINE BAR, 14 Lower Bridge St. Tel. 319760.
Cuisine: ENGLISH. **Reservations:** Recommended. **Bus:** No. 6 or 16.
$ **Prices:** Appetizers £1.20–£1.80 ($2.20–$3.35); main courses £3–£6 ($5.55–$11.10); glass of wine from £1 ($1.85). No credit cards.
Open: Mon–Fri 11am–11pm, Sat 11am–4:30pm and 6–11pm, Sun noon–3pm

and 7–10:30pm. Food served Mon–Fri 11am–5:30pm, Sat 11am–4:30pm, Sun noon–3pm.

Very popular with the locals in the evening, Claverton's is a good way to see—if not to meet—the people of Chester. The imposing building which Claverton's occupies began as a private residence in 1715 and became the Albion Hotel in 1818. Since then, the building has seen many changes. The wine bar is attractively decorated, and the food, served throughout the day, is good and reasonable. However, many diners consider the best value to be from 12:30 to 2:30pm, when a £6 ($11.10) buffet is served. You can begin with a soup, perhaps leek-and-potato, followed by a selection from the cold buffet. A popular dish is fish mousse. A good dish is the fresh trout stuffed with celery and nuts. Chicken roulade is a specialty. In addition to the regular mixed drinks, wines are available by the glass, as are "mocktails" for drivers. In summer, tables are set outside.

FRANCS RESTAURANT, 14 Cuppin St. Tel. 317952.
   Cuisine: FRENCH. **Reservations:** Required. **Transportation:** All buses into the center.
$ **Prices:** Appetizers £1.60–£4.80 ($2.90–$8.90); main courses £3.45–£8.95 ($6.45–$16.65); set dinner from £12.85 ($23.85); Sun set lunch from £6.95 ($12.85). AE, MC, V.
   Open: Lunch daily noon–3pm; dinner daily 6–10pm.

This restaurant serves what many consider the finest food—for the price—in Chester. Within the city walls, it is housed in a building constructed with oak beams in the 1600s. Inside, the cuisine is French—the way they cook in the countryside—and you can order an array of dishes including homemade sausages, good-tasting casseroles, and plats du jour, which might be your best bet. The wine list is reasonably priced, and the atmosphere is informal and convivial. The location is adjacent to the police station in the vicinity of the main North Wales traffic circle.

GALLERY RESTAURANT, 24 Paddock Row, Grosvenor Precinct. Tel. 347202.
   Cuisine: ENGLISH/FRENCH. **Reservations:** Recommended.
$ **Prices:** Appetizers £1–£2.95 ($1.85–$5.45); main courses £3.50–£6.50 ($6.55–$12.05). MC, V.
   Open: Mon–Sat 10am–5pm.

Walking in this restaurant is a little like going into an indoor garden—it's festooned with masses of green plants. A varied continental menu is offered including seafood medley, steak-and-kidney pie, and crêpes. It's located in the town center.

JAY-JAY'S CAFÉ BAR, 19 Frodsham St. Tel. 311836.
   Cuisine: ENGLISH. **Reservations:** Recommended.
$ **Prices:** Appetizers £1.45–£4.75 ($2.70–$8.80); main courses £2.95–£10 ($5.45–$18.50), pizzas £5–£7 ($9.25–$12.95), morning coffee or afternoon tea 95p ($1.75). AE, DC, MC, V.
   Open: Mon–Sat 9am–10:30pm, Sun noon–10:30pm.

Decorated with an old-world charm with a beamed ceiling, this restaurant remains open most of the day for morning coffee, afternoon teas, and full meals anytime in between. Order one of seven different kinds of pizzas, barbecued spareribs, or chicken dishes prepared either in the style of Cheshire or India. The café is a short walk from the Anglican cathedral, on one of Chester's busiest commercial streets.

EASY EXCURSIONS
NANTWICH

Fifteen miles southeast of Chester, this old market town on the Weaver River is particularly outstanding because of its black-and-white timbered houses. It can easily be tied in with a visit to Chester.

WHERE TO EAT

CHURCHE'S MANSION RESTAURANT, 150 Hospital St. Tel. 0270/
625933.

Cuisine: ENGLISH. **Reservations:** Recommended.

$ **Prices:** Appetizers £2–£4 ($3.70–$7.40); main courses £6.50–£11.50
($12.05–$ 21.30); three-course fixed-price lunch £10 ($18.50); four-course fixed-
price dinner £20 ($37). MC, V.

Open: Morning coffee daily 10am–11:45; lunch daily noon–2pm; dinner daily
7–9:30pm.

The most enchanting restaurant in Chesire, Churche's Mansion lies in
Nantwich at the junction of Newcastle Road and the Chester bypass (A52 and
A534), a ½ mile east of the center. Many years ago, the late Dr. and Mrs. E. C.
Myott learned that this historic home had been advertised for sale in America and
asked the town council to step in and save it. Outbidding the American syndicate who
wanted to transport it to the United States, they sought out the mysteries of the house:
a window in the side wall, inlaid initials, a Tudor well in the garden, and a long-ago
love knot with a central heart (a token of Richard Churche's affection for his young
wife). Today the house is widely known and recommended for its quality preparations
of English lamb, beef, chicken, and fish.

2. LIVERPOOL

219 miles NW of London; 103 miles NW of
Birmingham; 35 miles S of Manchester

GETTING THERE By Plane Liverpool has its own airport, Spoke (tel.
051/486-8877), which has frequent daily flights from many parts of the United
Kingdom, including London, Isle of Man, and Ireland.

By Train Express trains from London's Euston Station arrive frequently into
Liverpool. Trip time is 2¼ hours. There is also frequent service from Manchester. Trip
time is 1 hour.

By Bus National Express buses from London's Victoria Coach Station depart
every 2 hours. Trip time is 4¼ hours. Buses also arrive every hour from Manchester.
Trip time is 1 hour.

By Car From London, head northwest on M1, until it links with M6. Continue
northwest on M6 until the junction with M62 heading west to Liverpool.

ESSENTIALS The **area code** is 051. The **Tourist Information Centre** is at
29 Lime Street (tel. 051/7093631).

Liverpool, with its famous waterfront on the River Mersey, is a great shipping port
and industrial center that gave the world such famous figures as the fictional Fannie
Hill and the Beatles. King John launched it on its road to glory when he granted it a
charter in 1207. Before that, it had been a tiny 12th-century fishing village, but it
quickly became a port for shipping men and materials to Ireland. In the 18th century,
its port grew to prominence as a result of the sugar, spice, and tobacco trade with the
Americans. By the time Victoria came to the throne, Liverpool had become Britain's
biggest commercial seaport. Recent refurbishing of the Albert Docks, establishment
of a Maritime Museum, and the converting of warehouses into little stores similar to
those in Ghirardelli Square in San Francisco, have made this an up-and-coming area
once again.

Liverpudlians are proud of their city, with its new hotels, two cathedrals, shopping
and entertainment complexes, and parks and open spaces (2,400 acres in and around
the city). Liverpool's main shopping street, Church, is traffic-free.

WHAT TO SEE & DO

Liverpool has a wealth of things for the visitor to see and enjoy—major cathedrals, waterfront glories restored, cultural centers, even the places where the Beatles began their meteoric rise to fame.

TOURS

For £4.50 ($8.30), Beatles fans can take a 2-hour guided tour of famous locations, such as Penny Lane and Strawberry Fields. For those who prefer to do it themselves, a Beatles map can be purchased for £1 ($1.85). For more information, contact one of the Merseyside Tourism Board's two information centers at the Clayton Square Shopping Centre (tel. 051/709-3631), opposite the main railway station, and the Albert Dock (tel. 051/708-8854). Both centers are open daily.

THE CATHEDRALS

CATHEDRAL CHURCH OF CHRIST, Saint James Mount. Tel. 051/709-6271.

⭐ The great new Anglican edifice was begun in 1903 and was largely completed 74 years later. On a rocky eminence overlooking the River Mersey, this might possibly be the last Gothic-style cathedral to be built. Dedicated in the presence of Queen Elizabeth II in 1978, it is the largest church in the country and is the fifth largest in the world: Its vaulting under the tower is 175 feet high, the highest in the world, and its length of 619 feet makes it one of the longest cathedrals in the world. The organ contains nearly 10,000 pipes, the biggest found in any church. The tower houses the highest (219 feet) and the heaviest (31 tons) ringing peals of bells in the world, and the Gothic arches are the highest ever built. From the tower, you can see into North Wales.

The architect, Giles Scott, won a competition in 1903 for the building's design and went on to rebuild the House of Commons, gutted by bombs, after World War II. He personally laid the last stone on the highest tower pinnacle.

In 1984, a Visitor Centre and Refectory was opened, and its dominant feature is an aerial sculpture of 12 huge sails, with a ship's bell, clock, and light that change color on an hourly basis. Full meals may be taken in the charming refectory. To reach the cathedral from the center, head out Duke Street.

Admission: Tower £1.50 ($2.80) adults, 50p (95¢) children; cathedral Free.
Open: Daily 9am–6pm.

ROMAN CATHOLIC METROPOLITAN CATHEDRAL OF CHRIST THE KING, Mount Pleasant. Tel. 051/709-9222.

⭐ A half mile away from the Anglican cathedral stands the Roman Catholic Cathedral—the two are joined by a road called Hope Street. The sectarian strife of earlier generations has ended, and a change in attitude, called by some the "Mersey Miracle," was illustrated clearly in 1982 when Pope John Paul II drove along Hope Street to pray in both cathedrals. The Metropolitan Cathedral is so-called because Liverpool is, in Catholic terms, the mother city, the "metropolis" of the north of England.

Designed by Sir Edwin Lutyens, the construction of the cathedral was started in 1930, but when World War II halted progress in 1939, not even the granite and brick vaulting of the crypt was complete. At the end of the war, it was estimated that the cost of completing the structure as Lutyens had designed it would be some £27 million. Architects throughout the world were invited to compete to design a more realistic project to cost about £1 million and to be completed in 5 years. Sir Frederick Gibberd won the competition and was commissioned to oversee the construction of the circular cathedral in concrete and glass, pitched like a tent at one end of the piazza that covered all the original site, crypt included.

Between 1962 and 1967, the construction was completed, and today the cathedral provides seating for a congregation of more than 2,000, all within 50 feet of the

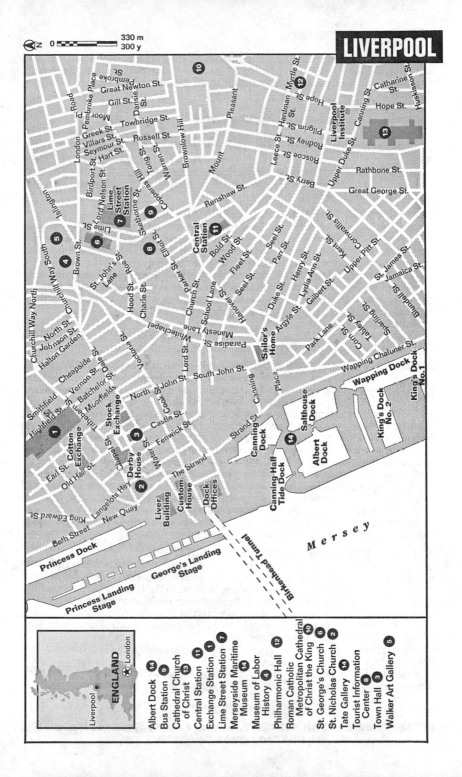

central altar. Above the altar rises a multicolored glass lantern weighing 2,000 tons and rising to a height of 290 feet. Called a "space age" cathedral, this has a bookshop, a tearoom, and tour guides. The cathedral is off Bronnlow Hill, west of University Precinct.

Admission: Free.

Open: June–Sept daily 8am–6pm; off-season daily 8am–5pm.

SIGHTS ON THE WATERFRONT

A fun thing to do is to take the famous Mersey Ferry that travels from the Pier Head to both Woodside and Seacombe. Services operate daily from early morning to early evening throughout the year. For more information, contact the **Mersey Ferries,** Victoria Place, Seacombe, Wallasey (tel. 051/630-1030).

ALBERT DOCK, Albert Dock Co. Ltd. Tel. 051/708-7334.

Built of brick, stone, and cast iron, this showpiece development on Liverpool's waterfront opened in 1846, saw a long period of decline, and has been renovated and refurbished so that it is now England's largest Grade 1 Listed Building, a designation for landmark buildings. The dockland warehouses now contain quality shops, restaurants, cafés, an English pub, and a cellar wine bar. One pavilion houses the main building of the Merseyside Maritime Museum (see below) and another is the home of the Tate Gallery Liverpool, the National Collection of modern art in the north of England (see below). Car parking is available.

Admission: Free.

Open: Shops daily 10am–6pm. Bars and restaurants daily 10am–11pm. **Bus:** Take the Albert Dock Shuttle linking the waterfront with city center.

MERSEYSIDE MARITIME MUSEUM, Albert Dock. Tel. 051/207-0001.

Set in the historic heart of Liverpool's magnificent waterfront, this large museum provides a unique blend of floating exhibits, craft demonstrations, working displays, and special events. In addition to restored waterfront buildings, exhibitions show the story of mass emigration through Liverpool in the last century, shipbuilding on Merseyside, and many other aspects of Liverpool's maritime heritage. One exhibition traces the story of the Beatles. You can see a restored piermaster's house and a working cooperage, and you can take a steamboat trip around the historic Albert Dock complex. A smörgåsbord restaurant, a coffee shop, a waterfront café, gift shops (open 7 days a week), and ample parking space are among the facilities. There is wheelchair access to all floors of the main museum building and most areas of the Maritime Park, and disabled visitors are welcome.

Admission: £1.50 ($2.80) adults, 75p ($1.45) children.

Open: Daily 10:30am–5:30pm (last admission at 4:30pm). **Transportation:** Take the Albert Dock Shuttle from city center.

TATE GALLERY, Albert Dock. Tel. 051/709-3223.

Opened in 1988, this gallery houses the National Collection of 20th century art in the north of England. Lack of space in London made it impossible to show the entire collection of London's Tate Gallery, so the board of directors made a decision to move 85% of its modern collection from vaults to this gallery, the "Tate Gallery of the North." Some of the world's greatest modern artists, such as Picasso, Dali, Magritte, and Rothko, are likely to be on display at any time, along with changing temporary exhibitions and events.

Admission: Free except for special exhibitions when it's £1 ($1.85) adults, 50p (95¢) children.

Open: June–Sept Tues–Sun 11am–7pm; off-season Tues–Sun 11am–6pm.

Transportation: Take the Albert Dock Shuttle from city center.

MORE SIGHTS

MUSEUM OF LABOUR HISTORY, former County Sessions House, William Brown St. Tel. 051/207-0001, ext. 279.

This museum traces what it was like to live and work in Merseyside over the la.
150 years. Exhibits cover people struggling for legal and political rights, establishing
trade unions, and improving working conditions. It is located near the rail station.
   Admission: Free.
   Open: Mon–Sat 10am–5pm, Sun 2–5pm. **Closed:** Jan 1, Good Friday, and Dec
24–26.

WALKER ART GALLERY, William Brown St. Tel. 051/207-0001.
   This gallery has one of the finest collections of paintings outside London and is
known for its European pictures and sculptures from 1300 to the present. It is located
near the rail station.
   Admission: Free.
   Open: Mon–Sat 10am–5pm, Sun 2–5pm. **Closed:** Jan 1, Good Friday, and Dec
24–26.

WHERE THE BEATLES BEGAN

Whether or not they're Beatles fans, most visitors who come to Liverpool want to take
a look at where Beatlemania began in the Swinging Sixties. Mathew Street is the heart
of Beatleland, and **Cavern Walks** (tel. 051/236-9082) is a shopping development
and tour service built on the site of the former Cavern Club, where the Beatles
performed almost 300 times. John Doubleday's statue of the group is in the central
piazza of the Cavern complex, surrounded by shops and restaurants. The outside of
Cavern Walks was decorated by Cynthia Lennon, John's first wife. Another statue of
John, Paul, George, and Ringo, this one by Liverpool sculptor Arthur Dooley, is
opposite the building facade.
   Farther along Mathew Street is the **John Lennon Memorial Club** and **The
Beatles Shop,** 31 Mathew Street (tel. 051/236-8066), open Monday to Saturday
from 9:30am to 5:30pm, plus Sunday from April through December from 10:30am to
4pm. Around the corner on Stanley Street is a statue of Eleanor Rigby, seated on a
bench.

WHERE TO STAY

DOUBLES WITHOUT BATH FOR LESS THAN £32 [$59.20]

**APLIN HOUSE HOTEL, 35 Clarendon Rd., Garston, Liverpool,
Merseyside L19 6PJ. Tel. 051/427-5047.** 5 rms (1 with shower).
   $ Rates (including English breakfast): £19–£22 ($35.15–$40.70) single without
   bath; £32 ($59.20) double without bath; £37 ($68.45) double with shower. No
   credit cards. **Parking:** Free.
This well-kept Victorian residence facing the park is run by Mr. and Mrs. Atherton.
Rooms are comfortable and three contain a TV. Mrs. Atherton makes breakfast "as
you want it." Evening meals are offered and cost from £8 ($14.80). The hotel is about
10 minutes by train from the city center, 2 miles from Liverpool airport, and 20
minutes by car from the Irish ferries. It is off A561, close to Garston Railway Station.

**AACHEN HOTEL, 89-91 Mount Pleasant, Liverpool, Merseyside L3 5TB.
Tel. 051/709-3477.** Fax 051/709-3477. 18 rms (12 with bath). TV TEL
   $ Rates (including English breakfast): £18 ($33.30) single without bath; £26
   ($48.10) single with shower; £32 ($59.20) double without bath; £40 ($74) double
   with bath. AE, DC, MC, V. **Parking:** £2 ($3.70).
Each of the modernized bedrooms here has hot and cold running water, a hairdryer,
in-house movies, a radio alarm, beverage-making facilities, and a trouser press. The
hotel has a bar. The location is about 5 minutes from the city center, near the Roman
Catholic Metropolitan Cathedral.

**BRADFORD HOTEL, Tithebarne St., Liverpool, Merseyside L2 2EW. Tel.
051/236-8782.** Fax 051/236-2679. 43 rms (32 with bath) TV TEL **Bus:**
Liverpool's Circular Bus.

Rates (including English breakfast): £25 ($46.25) single without bath, £40 ($74) single with bath; £30–£40 ($55.50–$74) double without bath, £47.50 ($87.90) double with bath. AE, MC, V. **Parking:** £3 ($5.55).

 Located in the commercial heart of the city, near the docklands, the railway, and ferryboat stations, this is the oldest (built around 1820) and one of the most reasonably priced hotels in Liverpool. Set behind an elaborate facade of brown brickwork, it contains comfortably unpretentious bedrooms, a cocktail lounge, and a restaurant where fixed-price meals at lunch and dinner cost £8 ($14.80) for three courses. Each room contains a radio and tea-making facilities.

NEW MANX HOTEL, 39 Catharine St. near Lime St., Liverpool, Merseyside L8 7NE. Tel. 051/708-6171. 12 rms (3 with shower). TV
$ Rates (including English breakfast): £12.50 ($23.15) single without bath; £25 ($46.25) double without bath, £28 ($51.80) double with bath. No credit cards. **Parking:** Free.

A small, unlicensed hotel, this seems to delight visitors. Families with children are especially welcomed, as James Gilmour's avocation is writing stories for them; he is known for his Santa Claus letter service. About a 5-minute run from the center, the hotel has comfortably furnished and well-maintained rooms. Only breakfast is offered, and it's a generous meal.

WHERE TO EAT

MEALS FOR LESS THAN £12.50 [$23.15]

EVERYMAN BISTRO, 9 Hope St. Tel. 708-9545.
  Cuisine: INTERNATIONAL. **Reservations:** Not needed.
$ Prices: Appetizers 75p–£1.50 ($1.45–$2.80); main courses £2.50–£4.50 ($4.65–$8.35). No credit cards.
  Open: Mon–Sat 10am–midnight.

Everyman Bistro is informal, crowded on weekends, fun, and reasonably priced. It is part of the Everyman Theatre complex. A buffet is offered with a wide range of pâtés, quiches, pizzas, soups, meat and vegetarian main courses, seasonal salads, cheeses, desserts, and pastries. The menu is changed twice daily and is influenced by the season, with only fresh produce used. A typical three-course meal might consist of carrot soup with French bread, chicken pie with new potatoes and green salad, strawberries in white wine with cream, and coffee. It is on the street connecting the Catholic and Anglican cathedrals.

KISMET RESTAURANT, 105 Bold St. Tel. 709-8469.
  Cuisine: INDIAN/ENGLISH. **Reservations:** Not needed.
$ Prices: Appetizers 90p–£2.95 ($1.65–$5.45); main courses £5–£11 ($9.25–$20.35). AE, V.
  Open: Lunch daily 11:30am–2:30pm; dinner daily 5:30pm–2am.
A well-patronized restaurant, this has some of the best Indian food in Liverpool and specializes in tandoori dishes. Among these are their *tandoori masala* (lamb, chicken, or king prawns cooked in special gravy in the clay ovens). The Kismet special is a mild curry with prawns, chicken, meat, and pineapple with an omelet garnished with tomato, raisins, and coconut. *Rogan josh* (lamb spiced with herbs and cashew nuts) and *sag gosht* (beef cooked with fresh leaf spinach) are tasty selections. They also prepare English dishes. It's located near Lime Street Central Station.

LA GRANDE BOUFFE, 48a Castle St. Tel. 236-3375.
  Cuisine: INTERNATIONAL. **Reservations:** Recommended. **Bus:** No. 20, 21, or 80.
$ Prices: Appetizers £2.50–£4.45 ($4.65–$8.25); main courses £8.75–£11.95 ($16.20–$22.10); three-course fixed-price lunch £9.50 ($17.60). AE, MC, V.
  Open: Lunch Mon–Fri noon–2pm; dinner Mon–Sat 6–10:30pm.

S A French-inspired cellar bistro in the center of the city's commercial heartland, it offers satisfyingly sophisticated food at reasonable prices, including a set lunch that is one of the best values in Liverpool. The menu changes often, but the chefs use fresh ingredients and handle them deftly. Dinners tend to be more relaxed than meals served to the lunchtime crowds. Menu choices might include a terrine of duckmeat with pistachios, smoked filet of halibut served with aromatic Chinese pickles and cabbage, suprême of chicken in a fresh tarragon sauce, and filet of pork with raisins, pine nuts, and balsamic vinegar.

MAYFLOWER, 48 Duke St. Tel. 709-6339.
   Cuisine: CHINESE. **Reservations:** Required. **Bus:** No. 5, 6, 26, or 27.
$ Prices: Appetizers £1.30–£7.50 ($2.40–$13.90); main courses £5.50–£9.50 ($10.20–$17.60); set dinner £11.50 ($21.30); set lunch £4.20 ($7.75). AE, DC, MC, V.
   Open: Mon–Fri noon–4am, Sat–Sun 6pm–4am.

S This is one of the finest Chinese dining rooms in town. It offers excellent Cantonese fare, classic food from Beijing, plus fiery hot Szechuan dishes. Dozens and dozens of selections await your decision. Its good-value set lunches and dinners are among the best in the city. Vegetarians will also find solace here.

THE PEACOCK RESTAURANT, in the Feathers Hotel, 119-125 Mount Pleasant, Liverpool, Merseyside L3 5TF. Tel. 709-9655.
   Cuisine: ENGLISH. **Reservations:** Required.
$ Prices: Appetizers 90p–£3 ($1.65–$5.55); main courses £4.50–£11 ($8.30–$20.35); set menu £7.95 ($14.70). AE, DC, MC, V.
   Open: Dinner daily 6:30–8:30pm.
For some really good old-English cooking, this is a long-standing favorite that is moderately priced. Here you can sample the famous Lancashire hot pot, a casserole where the lamb chops are layered with onions and potatoes; it's traditionally eaten with pickled red cabbage. The restaurant is near Lime Street Station.

PHILHARMONIC HOTEL, 36 Hope St. Tel. 709-1163.
   Cuisine: ENGLISH. **Reservations:** Not needed. **Bus:** No. 86, 87, or H25.
$ Prices: Appetizers £1.25–£1.50 ($2.30–$2.80); main courses £2.20–£3.20 ($4.05–$5.90). No credit cards.
   Open: Mon–Sat 11:30am–11pm, Sun noon–3pm and 7–10:30pm.

★ This favorite pub has splendid turn-of-the-century architectural features, such as stained glass, carving, and plasterwork. You pass through wrought-iron gates into a selection of several bars, some named after famous composers. The heart of the pub is the Horseshoe Bar, which has a mosaic floor and stained glass—fine Edwardian flamboyance. The atmosphere is like that within a private club, and almost any regular will advise a stranger what kind of local ale is good. The habitués refer to it as "The Phil." (Phil also happens to be the name of the manager, who is assisted by his wife, Carol Ross.) Attracting art, drama, and music students as well as actors, it serves pub snacks which are usually carried to your table by a waitress.

ST. GEORGE'S CARVERY, St. George's Hotel, St. John's Precinct, Lime St. Tel. 709-7090.
   Cuisine: ENGLISH. **Reservations:** Recommended. **Bus:** No. 12 or 13.
$ Prices: Three-course carvery lunch or dinner £12.50 ($23.15) AE, DC, MC, V.
   Open: Lunch daily noon–2pm; dinner daily 7–10pm.

 Set within the very modern premises of one of Liverpool's busiest commercial hotels, this might be one of the best food values in Liverpool. A uniformed assistant will help you carve portions of honey-baked ham, turkey, beef, leg of lamb, and pork, and you'll serve yourself from steaming dishes of vegetables and seasonal specialties. Children aged 5 to 14 pay half price, and children under 5 dine for free.

3. WINDERMERE & BOWNESS

274 miles NW of London; 10 miles NW of Kendal

GETTING THERE By Train Trains to Windermere meet with the main line at Oxenholme for connections north to Scotland or south to London. For information about rail services in the area call the Oxenholme Railway Station at 05394/720397. Frequent connections are possible throughout the day.

By Bus The National Express bus link, originating at London's Victoria Coach Station, services Windermere, with good connections also to Preston, Manchester, and Birmingham. Local buses to various villages and towns in the Lake District (see below) are operated mainly by Cumberland Motor Services (CMS) which goes to Kendal, Ambleside, Grasmere, and Keswick. Information on various routings within the Lake District can be obtained by calling the Windermere Bus Station at 05394/6499.

By Car Head north from London, as if going toward Liverpool (see above), but stay on the M6 until you reach the A685 junction heading west to Kendal. From Kendal, A591 continues west to Windermere.

By Ferry There are boat cruises from Bowness, 1½ miles from Windermere, in summer. These are operated by the Bowness Bay Boating Company (tel. 05394/3360 for information). There is also a ferry service from Bowness across the lake to the western shore costing £1 ($1.85) for cars and 10p (20¢) for pedestrians.

ESSENTIALS The **area code** for Windermere and Bowness is 05394. The **Tourist Information Centre** at Windermere is on Victoria Street (tel. 05394/6499), and the **Tourist Information Centre** at Bowness is a summer-only office at The Glebe (tel. 05394/2895).

The largest lake in England is Windermere, whose shores wash up against the town of Bowness, with Windermere in close reach. Both of these resorts lie on the eastern shore of the lake. A ferry service connects Hawkshead and Bowness. Windermere, the resort, is the end of the railway line.

From either town, you can climb **Orrest Head** in less than an hour for a panoramic view of England's lakeland. From that vantage point, you can even see **Scafell Pike,** rising to a height of 3,210 feet—the peak pinnacle in all of England.

The twin resorts of Windermere and Bowness are separated by 1½ miles. The rail station is at Windermere. To go to Bowness and its pier (from which you can catch a ferry across the lake), turn left from the rail terminal and traverse the center of Windermere until you reach New Road. This eventually changes its name to Lake Road before it approaches the outskirts of Bowness. It's about a 20-minute walk downhill. The CMS Lakeland Experience bus also runs from the Windermere Station to Bowness every 20 minutes.

WHAT TO SEE & DO

Windermere Steamboat Museum, Rayrigg Road, Windermere (tel. 05394/5565), was founded and developed by George Pattinson, who discovered the fascination of steam many years ago and now has probably the best and most comprehensive collection of steamboats in the country. The wet boatsheds house some dozen boats, including the veteran *Dolly*, probably the oldest mechanically powered boat in the world, dating from around 1850. It was raised from the lake bed in the early 1960s and run for several years with the original boiler and steambox.

Also displayed is the *Espérance,* an iron steam yacht registered with Lloyds in 1869, as well as many elegant Victorian and Edwardian steam launches. Attached to the boathouses is the speedboat *Jane,* dating from 1938, the first glider-plane to take off from the water in 1943, and the hydroplane racer *Cookie.* Boats that have been added to the collection include the steam launch *Kittiwake,* the motorboat *Lady Hamilton,* and the fast speedboat *Miss Windermere IV.*

The museum is open from Easter to October, charging an admission of £2.20 ($4.05) for adults and £1.40 ($2.60) for children. The *Osprey* is regularly in steam, and visitors can make a 45-minute trip on the lake at £3 ($5.55) for adults and £2 ($3.70) children.

It's also possible to make trips on Ullswater and on Coniston, and there is regular steamer service around Windermere, the largest of the lakes, which serves the outlying villages as well as operating for visitors in summer.

ORGANIZED TOURS

Windermere is the center of many interesting tours in the Lake District. To provide a true appreciation of the Lake District and its many attractions, try **Mountain Goat Holidays,** Victoria Street, Windermere (tel. 05394/5161). Begun in 1972 by Chris Taylor, it has become firmly established in the Lake District for touring or walking holidays. Mountain Goat also runs daily minibus tours that take you to many of the otherwise inaccessible spots of the area.

These tours include trips to the Northern Lakes, Grasmere, Keswick, Buttermere, and Honister Pass, with a visit to Wordsworth's home in Grasmere, Rydal Mount. Cost is £18 ($33.30) per person.

An interesting day out is the tour up Hardknott and Wrynose passes to Eskdale, following the old Roman route to Hardknott Roman fort. A pub lunch can be had in Eskdale. You can take a ride on the miniature Ravenglass-Eskdale railway before having tea at Ravenglass and returning over the fells to Duddon Bridge, Coniston, and Windermere. The cost is £18 ($33.30) per person. Other tours visit Hawkshead and the home of Beatrix Potter for £9 ($16.65) for a half day.

Also, there is a ½-day tour, the Duddon Valley Picnic, for £13 ($24.05). Mountain Goat also runs a regular bus service to York on Monday, Wednesday, Friday, and Saturday, for £15 ($27.75) round-trip.

Mountain Goat Holidays run for a week (from Saturday to Saturday) or for a 2-night short break. Based in Windermere or Keswick, they include dinner, bed, and breakfast in a hotel of your choice. All holidays in this category start at £292 ($540.20) per person, for 7 nights. For £65 ($120.25) for 2 nights you get bed and breakfast, plus the tour.

WHERE TO STAY

DOUBLES WITHOUT BATH FOR LESS THAN £30 ($55.50)

BRENDAN CHASE, College Rd., Windermere, Cumbria LA23 1BU. Tel. 05394/5638. 8 rms (4 with shower). **Directions:** Take High Street.
$ **Rates** (including English breakfast): £12.50 ($23.15) single without bath, £20 ($37) single with shower; £25 ($46.25) double without bath, £38 ($70.30) double with shower. No credit cards. **Parking:** Free.

Mr. and Mrs. Graham are pleased to welcome guests to their long-established Edwardian home 150 yards off A591 leading into town. In the center of the Lakeland resort, the guesthouse is nevertheless in a tranquil location yet convenient to the attractions. Each comfortably furnished room has beverage-making equipment. Families are also welcomed and quoted special rates. The Grahams have proved helpful and courteous to their many visitors, who gather at night in the large color TV lounge. There is adequate parking adjacent to the guesthouse.

KENILWORTH GUESTHHOUSE, Holly Rd., Windermere, Cumbria LA23 2AF. Tel. 05394/4004. 6 rms (1 with bath). TV
$ **Rates** (including English breakfast): £13–£15 ($24.05–$27.75) single without

bath; £26–£30 ($48.10–$55.50) double without bath, £31–£36 ($57.35–$66.60) double with bath; £32–£36 ($59.20–$66.60) family room. No credit cards. **Parking:** Free.

⑤ This is a house known for its cleanliness and comfort. Brian and Jean Gosling offer a good bargain in the centrally heated, pleasant bedrooms, each with hot and cold running water. Guests are received from March to October. An informal atmosphere prevails. It's located near Broad Street in the town center.

ROCKSIDE GUEST HOUSE, Ambleside Rd., Windermere, Cumbria LA23 1AQ. Tel. 05394/5343. 15 rms (10 with bath). TV TEL
$ Rates (including English breakfast): £14 ($25.90) single without bath, £20.50 ($37.95) single with bath; £30 ($55.50) double without bath, £42 ($77.70) double with bath MC, V. **Parking:** Free.

This guesthouse near the train station is run by Neville and Mavis Fowles, who came to live in this area with their two daughters several years ago, thus achieving their ambition to live in "the most beautiful corner of England." They have since made Rockside one of the best B&B establishments in the area. Standard rooms have hot and cold running water basins, while those listed as "top choice" contain private showers and toilets, beverage-making facilities, and hairdryers. Guests can choose from among six breakfasts big enough to start the day well whether you are walking or driving around the area. At the rear of the house is a car park for 12 vehicles, but Rockside is only 2 minutes' walk from the bus, train, or village of Windermere.

DOUBLES WITH BATH FOR LESS THAN £44 [$81.40]

FIR TREES, Lake Rd., Windermere, Cumbria LA23 2EQ. Tel. 05394/ 2272. 7 rms (all with bath or shower). TV
$ Rates (including English breakfast): £22.50–£26.50 ($41.65–$49.05) single; £35–£43 ($64.75–$79.55) double. AE, V. **Parking:** Free.

★ This is by most accounts the finest guesthouse in Windermere, a place where the competition is keen. At this well-run place, you get hotellike standards at B&B tariffs. Allene and Ira Fishman, the proprietors, offer a warm welcome and a guarantee of a relaxing family hotel by the lakes. They rent well-furnished and beautifully maintained bedrooms, each with beverage-making equipment, and other thoughtful amenities. Fir Trees is opposite St. John's Church between Windermere and Bowness.

HAWKSMOOR, Lake Rd. between Windermere and Bowness, Windermere, Cumbria LA23 2EQ. Tel. 05394/2110. 10 rms (all with shower). TV
$ Rates (including English breakfast): £22–£25 ($40.70–$46.25) single; £40–£50 ($74–$92.50) double. No credit cards. **Parking:** Free.

★ Robert and Barbara Tyson have restored this old Lake District home, which must be at least a century old. However, guests must stay in a room at least 2 nights. Some family-style rooms are also available. Mrs. Tyson reveals her decorating flair in her warm, inviting dining room, which is of a standard far superior to your typical B&B. Here you can order a four-course evening meal costing from £9 ($16.65) per head. Always call or write in advance. Chances are, you'll be glad you did.

WILLOWSMERE HOTEL, Ambleside Rd., Windermere, Cumbria LA23 1ES. Tel. 05394/3575. 13 rms (all with bath or shower).
$ Rates (including English breakfast): £22.50–£23.50 ($41.65–$43.50) single; £44–£47 ($81.40–$86.95) double. AE, DC, MC, V. **Parking:** Free.
This is a handsome Edwardian stone hotel along the A591, a ½ mile from the center. Willowsmere is owned by David F. Scott, who is assisted by his daughter, Heather, the fifth generation of the Scott family to be catering in the Lake District. Heather's husband, Alan Cook, also helps run the business. Regular guests say that it is most appropriate that Heather's married name is now Cook, as her father receives many glowing compliments on her culinary abilities. The best way to stay here is to request

the dinner and B&B rate of £37 ($68.45) per person nightly. The evening meal is a well-prepared six-courses. Bedrooms contain toilets, shaving points, tea and coffee makers, and unmetered heat. Guests gather at night to socialize and watch the "telly." If you want to go on a lakeside ramble the next day, Heather will pack you a lunch.

WORTH THE EXTRA BUCKS

HIDEAWAY HOTEL, Phoenix Way, Windermere, Cumbria LA23 1DB. Tel. 05394/3070. 15 rms (all with bath or shower). **Directions:** On entering Windermere, pass the Windermere Hotel on your right; 100 yards farther on you will see a small hotel on your left called the Ravensworth. Phoenix Way, a small lane, runs right by the hotel's front door.
$ **Rates** (including English breakfast): £30–£35 ($55.50–$64.75) single; £60–£70 ($111–$129.50) double; half board £45 ($83.25) per person. No credit cards.
Parking: Free.

Tim and Jackie Harper own this renovated 1850 Lakeland house, surrounded by neat lawns where tea is served on balmy summer evenings. The house is solid and comfortable, with a bar, open fire, and oak settles, along with a sitting room and an attractive dining room. Bedrooms come with beverage-making equipment. The hotel has a Switzerland-trained chef and has received awards for its cuisine, which includes roast meats, game pies, local trout, homemade soups, and good desserts.

WHERE TO EAT

MEALS FOR LESS THAN £10 ($18.50)

MILLER HOWE KAFF, Lakeland Plastics, Station Precinct. Tel. 2255.
Cuisine: INTERNATIONAL. **Reservations:** None.
$ **Prices:** Appetizers £1.50–£3 ($2.80–$5.55); main courses £5–£7 ($9.25–$12.95). MC, V.
Open: Restaurant Mon–Sat 9am–5pm. Shop Mon–Fri 8am–6pm, Sat 9–5pm.

⭐ This restaurant was opened by former actor John Tovey, the celebrated owner of Miller Howe Hotel, a prestigious lakeside inn known for fine dining. That place is not for those on a budget. However, in an off-moment Mr. Tovey created this charming little place, which is now owned by the head chef (Ian Dutton) at Tovey's famous hotel.

The restaurant lies at the back of a shop which is known as the largest distributor of plastic kitchenware in the Lake District. Within a brightly colored (navy blue and red) and very modern decor, clients place their food orders at a countertop, then wait until the dishes are brought to their tables by waitresses. Cuisine draws upon culinary traditions from around the world, and includes such dishes as diced and curried beef in a very spicy sauce, filet of salmon with a fresh garden herb sauce, macaroni baked with heavy cream and red Cheddar cheese, and breast of chicken served in a red-wine gravy. Naturally, no one will object if you decide to stock up on kitchenware after your meal. The restaurant is adjacent to the town's railway station.

MILLERS RESTAURANT, 31-33 Crescent Rd. Tel. 3877.
Cuisine: ENGLISH. **Reservations:** None.
$ **Prices:** Appetizers £1.35–£3.95 ($2.50–$7.30); main courses £5.50–£11 ($10.20–$20.35); tea with scones, clotted cream, and jam £2 ($3.70). MC, V.
Open: Daily 11am–2:30pm and 5:30–10:30pm.

Located in a prominent position along the town's main commercial street, this restaurant is contained within a stone-sided 19th-century house and has a simple tearoom decor. Offering solid and conservative food (steak pies, lasagne, T-bone steaks), it's a refreshing spot for a meal or a pot of tea. Brian English is the proprietor. The town's only bus (it's green and open-topped) stops nearby in summer.

VILLAGE PIZZA AND STEAK RESTAURANT, Victoria St. Tel. 3429.
Cuisine: PIZZA/STEAK. **Reservations:** Not needed.

$ Prices: Appetizers £1.20–£3.20 ($2.20–$5.90); main courses £2.60–£9.60 ($4.80–$17.75). MC, V.
Open: Dinner Fri–Wed 6–9:30pm. **Closed:** Mid-Nov to mid-Feb.

Near the railway station at the junction of Victoria and Cross streets, this restaurant has an inviting decor. Fresh natural flavors are the hallmark of the kitchen. You are also likely to be tempted by such selections as sautéed chicken chasseur, lasagne, and moussaka. There is a small selection of vegetarian dishes also.

EASY EXCURSION TO BOWNESS-ON-WINDERMERE

A short way south of Windermere on Bowness Bay of the lake, the attractive town of Bowness has some interesting old architecture. This has been an important center for boating and fishing for a long time, and you can rent boats of all descriptions to explore the lake.

WHERE TO STAY

BELSFIELD GUEST HOUSE, 4 Belsfield Terrace, Kendal Rd., Bowness-on-Windermere, Cumbria LA23 3EQ. Tel. 05394/5823. 9 rms (all with shower). TV
$ Rates (including English breakfast): £22–£27 ($40.70–$49.95) single; £39–£45 ($72.15–$83.25) double. No credit cards. **Parking:** Free.

This is a small, family-style guesthouse in the center near the lake. It's owned by Peter and Anne Godfrey, who have modernized the house. Their welcome is personalized, and they provide cleanliness and an inviting atmosphere. The Godfreys offer family rooms, doubles, and twins.

LINDETH FELL HOTEL, Lyth Valley Rd., Bowness-on-Windermere, Cumbria LA23 3JP. Tel. 05394/3286. 14 rms (all with bath or shower). TV TEL **Directions:** Take the A5074 1 mile south of Bowness.
$ Rates (including half board): £44 ($81.40) single; £82.50–£95 ($152.65–$175.75) double. MC, V. **Parking:** Free.

⭐ High above the town and the lake, is a traditional large Lakeland house built of stone and brick in 1907, with many of its rooms overlooking the handsome gardens and the lake. The owners, the Kennedys, run the place more like a country house than a hotel, achieving an atmosphere of comfort in pleasingly furnished surroundings. The cooking is under the supervision of Diana Kennedy and a resident chef, with local produce used when possible to prepare a variety of Lakeland and traditional English dishes. In pursuit of the country-house atmosphere, the Kennedys offer tennis, croquet, and putting on the lawn, as well as a private tarn for fishing. All bedrooms have beverage-making facilities. It is open from March 15 to mid-November.

LINDETH HOWE, Longtail Hill, Storrs Park, Bowness-on-Windermere, Cumbria LA23 3JF. Tel. 05394/5759. 13 rms (all with bath or shower). TV
$ Rates (including English or continental breakfast): £28.50–£31 ($52.75–$57.35) per person. MC, V. **Parking:** Free.

⭐ This is a country house in a scenic position above Lake Windermere, standing on 6 acres of grounds. The house, part stone and part red brick with a roof of green Westmorland slate, was built for a wealthy mill-owner in 1879, but its most famous owner was Beatrix Potter, who installed her mother here while she lived across the lake at Sawrey. The present owners, Eileen and Clive Baxter, have furnished it in elegant style and offer bedrooms, most of which have lake views. They are comfortably furnished, with in-house movies, beverage-making facilities, and central heating. Two of the rooms have handsome four-poster beds. There are no singles. The dining room has two deep bay windows overlooking the lake. The lounge contains a brick fireplace with a solid oak mantel set in an oak-framed inglenook. The hotel has a sauna and solarium. It's located south of the village on B5284.

4. AMBLESIDE & RYDAL

278 miles NW of London; 14 miles NW of Kendal; 4 miles N of Windermere

GETTING THERE   By Train   Go to Windermere (see above), then continue by bus.

By Bus   Cumberland Motor Services (CMS) has hourly bus service from Grasmere and Keswick (see below) and from Windermere. All these buses into Ambleside are labeled either no. 555 or 557.

By Car   From Windermere (see above), continue northwest along A591.

ESSENTIALS   The **area code** is 05394. The summer-only **Tourist Information Centre** is at Old Courthouse, Church Street (tel. 05394/32582).

An idyllic retreat, Ambleside is one of the major centers of the Lake District, attracting pony trekkers, fell hikers, and rock scalers. The charms are here all year, even in late autumn, when it's fashionable to sport a mackintosh. Ambleside is perched at the top of Lake Windermere. It's just a small village without many attractions, but is used primarily as a refueling stop or overnight stopover for those exploring the lake district.

Between Ambleside (at the top of Lake Windermere) and Wordsworth's former retreat at Grasmere is **Rydal**, a small village on one of the smallest lakes, Rydal Water. The village of Rydal is noted for its sheep-dog trails at the end of summer. The location is 1½ miles north of Ambleside on A591.

WHAT TO SEE & DO

Rydal Mount, off A591, 1½ miles north of Ambleside (tel. 05394/33002), was the home of William Wordsworth from 1813 until his death in 1850. Part of the house was built as a farmer's lake cottage around 1575. A descendant of Wordsworth's still owns the property, now a museum containing many portraits, furniture, and family possessions as well as mementos and books of the poet. The 3½-acre garden was landscaped by Wordsworth and contains rare trees, shrubs, and other features of interest. The house is open daily from 9:30am to 5pm from March to October; 10am to 4pm from November to February; closed Tuesday in winter. Admission is £2 ($3.70) for adults, 80p ($1.50) for children 5 to 16.

WHERE TO STAY

AT AMBLESIDE

CROW HOW HOTEL, Rydal Rd., Ambleside, Cumbria LA22 9PN. Tel. 05394/32193. 9 rms (all with bath). TV
$ Rates (including English breakfast): £21–£23 ($38.85–$42.55) single; £50–£55 ($92.50–$101.75) double. No credit cards. **Parking:** Free.
Along a private drive off the A591 north of Ambleside, the Crow How is only a few minutes' walk from Rydal Water. This was originally a large farmhouse of Lakeland stone. The proprietors, Mark and Glenise Heywood, charge a 10% surcharge for a single-night booking. Bedrooms have beverage-making facilities, and controllable heaters, while public rooms are centrally heated. The hotel has a large guest lounge, a

small but well-stocked bar, and 2 acres of gardens. Dinner is optional at £10 ($18.50) per person.

QUEENS HOTEL, Market Place, Ambleside, Cumbria LA22 9BU. Tel. 05394/32206. Fax 05394/32721. 28 rms (23 with bath). TV TEL
$ Rates (including English breakfast): £25 ($46.25) single without bath, £35 ($64.75) single with bath; £50 ($92.50) double without bath, £70 ($129.50) double with bath. AE, DC, MC, V.

In the heart of the resort area, is Queens, an old-fashioned and long-established family-run hotel where guests are housed and fed well. Since the hotel has two fully licensed bars and restaurants, you may want to dine here. The food is good and hearty. Locals and tourists alike gravitate to the Steadman Bar, dedicated to the famous Cumberland wrestler. Bar meals are served throughout the day. An evening dinner at the restaurants cost £12 ($22.20). The Queens is centrally heated in winter.

ROTHAY GARTH HOTEL, Rothay Rd., Ambleside, Cumbria LA22 0EE. Tel. 05394/32217. Fax 05394/34400. 16 rms (14 with bath). TV TEL
$ Rates (including half board): £35 ($64.75) per person without bath; £58 ($107.30) per person with bath. AE, MC, V. **Parking:** Free.

On the southern edge of Ambleside along the A591 from Kendal, is an elegant, century-old country house set in beautiful gardens. Bedrooms are tastefully decorated, warm, and comfortable, with hairdryers, and tea and coffee makers. A varied cuisine is served in the restaurant, and reduced half-board rates are quoted for 2 nights or more. Prices depend on the season. Fresh flowers are arranged throughout the hotel daily, and guests can enjoy a sunny garden room or the cozy lounge with its seasonal log fires. A wide choice of connoisseur bar lunches are served all year in the Loughrigg Bar. The special ploughman's lunch has received much praise. Yachts, canoes, and sailboards can be rented. Tennis courts, a pitch-and-putt golf area, and a croquet lawn are adjacent to the hotel. Laundry and ironing facilities are available.

AT RYDAL

FOXGHYLL, Under Loughrigg, Rydal, near Ambleside, Cumbria LA22 9LL. Tel. 05394/33292. 3 rms (all with bath). TV
$ Rates (including English breakfast): £18–£20 ($33.30–$37) single; £36–£40 ($66.60–$74) double. No credit cards. **Parking:** Free.

You may need good directions to find Foxghyll but if you succeed, you will have arrived at one of the best-value small B&Bs in the Rydal and Ambleside district. You are welcomed by Timothy and Marjorie Mann, who are happy to share this handsomely restored house that was once occupied by the writer Thomas (*Confessions of an English Opium Eater*) De Quincey. Each room contains a radio, hairdryer, and a comfortable chair or settee for reading. One room has a Jacuzzi-style tub and another has a four-poster bed. Each is decorated as if in an affluent private home. The Manns can only accept about six paying guests a night, so reservations are important. Much of the house a a decorative overlay familiar to Queen Victoria, but parts of the building are said to date from the 1600s. The house stands on extensive grounds, which you can explore at leisure. It's about a 1-mile walk north of town.

NAB COTTAGE, Rydal, Ambleside, Cumbria LA22 9SD. Tel. 05394/ 35311. 6 rms (2 with shower).
$ Rates (including English breakfast): £16.50–£18.50 ($30.55–$34.25) per person. No credit cards. **Parking:** Free.

This is a 300-year-old cottage whose architectural facade is protected by the local building commission. That pleases Tim and Liz Melling, who own the cottage, dating from 1702, which was once the residence of Hartley Coleridge, son of the famous poet, Samuel Taylor Coleridge. The writer Thomas de Quincey was also a resident. The cottage is well situated on the shore of Rydal Water about 2 miles outside of Grasmere and Ambleside on the A591, with views of the lake from many of the bedroom windows. Dinner costs an additional £11 ($20.35). Much of the original character remains in the in-house pub, where a log fire wards off the cold-weather chill.

RYDAL LODGE, Rydal, Ambleside, Cumbria LA22 9LR. Tel. 05394/ 33208. 8 rms (2 with bath).
$ **Rates** (including English breakfast): £21 ($38.85) single with or without bath; £34 ($62.90) double with or without bath. DC, MC, V. **Parking:** Free.

Well managed by the Haughan and Owen families (who are interrelated through marriage), this hotel is contained within a historically important building originally built as an inn in 1655. Set beside the roadway leading between Ambleside and Grasmere, it lies within about an acre of garden and parkland, and contains secluded gardens which skirt the edges of both the Rothay River and the lake known as Rydal Water. Many guests include a five-course dinner—priced at £12.50 ($23.15) per person—as a part of their experience here. Meals are cooked with fresh ingredients (some of which come from the family's garden) and are accompanied with wine from the well-stocked cellars. Each bedroom contains electric blankets and a handful of comfortable extras. Rydal Lodge, during earlier eras, hosted such famous 19th-century educators and authors as Matthew Arnold and Harriet Martineau, and is today an appropriate base for walking and touring the whole of the Lake District. The lodge lies opposite the entrance to the driveway of Wordsworth's ancestral home, Rydal Mount.

AT ELTERWATER

BRITANNIA INN, Elterwater, Ambleside, Cumbria LA22 9HP. Tel. 09667/210. Fax 09667/311. 9 rms (6 with shower). TV TEL **Directions:** Take A593 from Ambleside to Coniston for 2½ miles, then right onto B5343 to Elterwater.
$ **Rates** (including English breakfast): £47 ($86.95) double without bath, £53 ($98.05) double with bath. MC, V. **Parking:** Free.

Just off the B5343 west of Ambleside, is a 400-year-old traditional village inn adjoining the green in the unspoiled village of Elterwater. Views from the inn are over the meadows to the three tarns making up Elterwater ("lake of the swan") and the fells beyond. Bar meals are served in the cozy bar where a log fire blazes in cool weather. David Fry, the innkeeper, rents well-appointed double bedrooms all with tea and coffee maker and hairdryers. Evening meals at £13 ($24.05) are served in a Victorian dining room. The inn receives guests all year, except Christmas.

WHERE TO EAT

AT AMBLESIDE

APPLE PIE EATING HOUSE, Rydal Rd. Tel. 33679.
Cuisine: ENGLISH. **Reservations:** None.
$ **Prices:** Appetizers £1.80–£2 ($3.35–$3.70); main dishes £4 ($7.40); "filled rolls" (sandwiches) 85p–£1.15 ($1.60–$2.15); slice of apple pie 50p (95¢). No credit cards.
Open: Mon–Sat 9am–5:30pm, Sun 10am–5:30pm.

The most visible aspect of this bustling restaurant is its animated take-out counter. Lines form for the pastries, sandwiches, and take-out salads, stuffed "jacket potatoes," and soups which are dispensed by a hardworking battalion of waitresses. A closer inspection, however, reveals a self-service cafeteria line where quiches, pastries, meat pies, sandwiches, and snacks are dispensed to dozens of hungry daytime diners. Whether you decide to buy "takeaway food" or eat at one of the simple tables, you might opt for a slice of the establishment's trademark pastry, a cinnamon-laced chunk of apple pie. The restaurant is beside Ambleside's main car park, in the town center.

HARVEST WHOLEFOOD VEGETARIAN RESTAURANT, Compston Rd. Tel. 33151.

Cuisine: VEGETARIAN. **Reservations:** None. **Bus:** No. 555.

$ **Prices:** Appetizers £1.50–£2.50 ($2.80–$4.65); all main courses £5.60 ($10.35). No credit cards.

Open: Lunch mid-June to early Sept daily noon–2:30pm; dinner daily year-round 5–9pm.

Set on the town's main street, within a stone-fronted building accented with very large windows, this restaurant has a pleasingly wholesome decor of pastel colors and well-scrubbed pinewood tables. Smoking is not permitted, special diets are catered, and cuisine is pure, simple, and wholesome. The all-vegetarian homemade fare includes vegetable lasagne, vegetarian casseroles (when I was there, the stewpot of the day included squash, peppers, eggplant, cauliflower, mushrooms, and fresh herbs), and vegetable curries. Wine and beer are served.

SHEILA'S COTTAGE COUNTRY RESTAURANT AND TEA ROOM, The Slack. Tel. 33079.

Cuisine: INTERNATIONAL. **Reservations:** Recommended for dinner.

$ **Prices:** Lunch salads and platters £3–£7 ($5.55–$12.95); dinner appetizers £4–£6 ($7.40–£11.10); dinner main courses £9–£12 ($16.65–$22.20); three-course Sun set lunch £11.25 ($20.80); afternoon cream tea £5.50 ($10.20). No credit cards.

Open: Mon–Sat morning coffee 11am–noon; lunch noon–2:30pm; afternoon tea 2:45–5pm; dinner 7–9:30pm; Sun lunch noon–2pm.

Established many years ago by a since-departed woman named Sheila, this charming restaurant is contained within a 250-year-old stone-sided Lake District cottage in the town center near the post office. Lunches are relatively informal, featuring side dishes which might include a salad made with tiny shrimp from nearby brackish estuaries, and Swiss-inspired *Rösti* made from shredded potatoes laced with cream and leeks. Dinners are more elaborate, with such dishes as a tartare of marinated Argyll salmon, smoked filet of Lakeland trout with fresh asparagus and chive vinaigrette, a seafood ragoût from Scotland's Kyle of Lochalsh, and roast loin of lamb with an herb crust covered with a fricassee of sweetbreads. Stewart Greaves is the owner.

ZEFFIRELLIS, Compston Rd. Tel. 33845.

Cuisine: WHOLE-FOOD VEGETARIAN. **Reservations:** Not needed. **Bus:** No. 555.

$ **Prices:** Appetizers £1.60–£3 ($2.95–$5.55); main dishes £3.50–£6 ($6.50–$11.10). MC, V.

Open: Garden Room Café daily 10am–5:30pm; pizzeria and restaurant lunch Sat–Sun noon–2pm; dinner daily 5–9:45pm.

Contained within the town's only movie theater, these restaurants are tucked away into simply decorated corners. At least some of the diners come as part of an evening on the town, incorporating a movie into their dinner schedule. The theater itself is an old-fashioned, small-scale, and charming piece of architecture with a Japanese-inspired art deco theme. Food is completely vegetarian and organically grown, and includes pastas, pizzas, salads, quiches, and platters of fresh vegetables covered, perhaps, in a sauce of Stilton cheese. Wine and beer are sold, too. The presentation of films within the theater is always postponed in favor of performances by local theater companies and local musicians.

5. GRASMERE

282 miles NW of London; 18 miles NW of Kendal; 43 miles S of Carlisle

GETTING THERE   By Train   Go to Windermere (see above) and continue by bus.

By Bus   Cumberland Motor Services (CMS) runs hourly bus service to Grasmere from Keswick (see below) and Windermere (see above). Buses running in either direction are marked either 555 or 557.

By Car   From Windermere (see above), continue along A591 northwest.

ESSENTIALS   The **area code** is 09665. The summer only **Tourist Information Centre** is at Red Bank Road (tel. 09665/245).

On a lake that bears its name, Grasmere was the home of Wordsworth from 1799 to 1808. He called this area "the loveliest spot that man hath ever known." The nature poet lived with his sister, Dorothy (the writer and diarist), at **Dove Cottage,** which is now a museum administered by the Wordsworth Trust. Wordsworth, who followed Southey as poet laureate, died in the spring of 1850, and was buried in the graveyard of the village church at Grasmere. Another tenant of Dove Cottage was Thomas De Quincey (*Confessions of an English Opium Eater*). For a combined ticket costing £3.50 ($6.45) for adults, £1.60 ($2.95) for children, you can visit both **Dove Cottage** and the adjoining **Wordsworth Museum.** The location of these attractions is on A591 directly south of the village of Grasmere on the road to Kendal. The Wordsworth Museum houses, manuscripts, paintings, and memorabilia. There are also various special exhibitions throughout the year, exploring the art and literature of English Romanticism. The property is open daily from 9:30am to 5:30pm; closed from mid-January to mid-February. For further information, call 09665/544; 09665/268 for Dove Cottage Restaurant information.

WHERE TO STAY

DOUBLES WITH BATH FOR LESS THAN £44 [$81.40]

CRAIGSIDE HOUSE, Grasmere, Cumbria LA22 9SG. Tel. 09665/292.
Fax 09665/619. 3 rms (all with bath). TV
$ Rates (including English breakfast): £44–£52 ($81.40–$96.20) single or double. No credit cards. **Parking:** Free.

⭐ This house is set in 1½ acres of garden, with views over the lake to the hills beyond. It's just above Wordsworth's Dove Cottage. It was he who pointed out this site to the people who agreed with him that this was an ideal location for a house and built Craigside back in 1839. Ken and Shirley Wood, who operate the Moss Grove Hotel (see below), run this guesthouse as well. One of the rooms has a Hepplewhite four-poster bed.

HOW FOOT LODGE, Town End, Grasmere, Cumbria LA22 9SQ. Tel. 09665/366. 6 rms (all with bath). TV
$ Rates (including English breakfast): £30–£40 ($55.50–$74) single; £44–£50 ($81.40–$92.50) double. MC, V. **Parking:** Free.

⭐ This Victorian house that once belonged to Wordsworth's friends, lies directly south along A591, the road from Dove Cottage and Rydal Mount. The bedrooms, which are elegant, all have radios, and tea and coffee makers. No meals other than breakfast are served. The hotel is owned by the Wordsworth Trust, which plans eventually to turn the property into a Wordsworth library, so this may be your last chance to stay here. The place prides itself on a slowly rotating series of paintings on loan from the Wordsworth Collection. Several paintings are by Percy Horton, who was director of the Royal Academy of Fine Arts in World War II and was responsible for evacuating many British masterpieces out of London during the blitz bombings. The managers will direct you to the Dove Cottage Restaurant for meals. It, too, is owned by the Wordsworth Trust.

ROTHAY LODGE GUEST HOUSE, White Bridge, Grasmere, Cumbria LA22 9RH. Tel. 09665/341. 6 rms (4 with bath or shower). TV
$ Rates (including English breakfast): £20–£22.50 ($37–$41.65) single without bath; £34 ($62.90) double without bath, £39 ($72.15) double with bath. No credit cards. **Parking:** Free.

This is a traditional 19th-century Lakeland house built of stone and standing in landscaped grounds by the Rothay River at White Bridge. It is about a 5-minute walk from Grasmere center. The house is known for its commanding views of the countryside. From March to November, guests are received in tastefully decorated rooms furnished with antiques. An evening meal can be arranged for £9 ($16.65).

WORTH THE EXTRA BUCKS

GRASMERE HOTEL, Broadgate, Grasmere, Cumbria LA22 9TA. Tel. 09665/277. 12 rms (all with bath). TV TEL
$ Rates (including English breakfast): £40–£45 ($74–$83.25) single; £76–£98 ($140.60–$181.30) double. MC, V. **Parking:** Free.
The main feature of this Lakeland Victorian country house is the large, modern dining room at the rear where Ian and Annette Mansie provide mouth-watering evening meals for their guests. Prettily decorated tables cluster around the central buffet on which desserts are displayed, along with a huge slate cheeseboard. Both Ian and Annette do the cooking, and their green-and-white kitchen is almost as popular a meeting place for guests as is the sitting room and bar. The four-course meals include such delectable dishes as lamb stuffed with apricots, celery, and walnuts. Rooms are named after local poets, writers, or characters. The hotel is in the town center.

MOSS GROVE HOTEL, Grasmere, Cumbria LA22 9SW. Tel. 09665/251. 16 rms (15 with bath). TV TEL
$ Rates (including English breakfast): £23.50 ($43.50) single without bath, £33.50 ($62) single with bath; £53 ($98.05) double without bath, £67 ($123.95) double with bath. MC, V. **Parking:** Free.
This old Lakeland house in the town center, just past the Grasmere Church, is owned and run by Ken and Shirley Wood. The hotel is warm and well furnished (some of the accommodations contain four-poster beds). There are two lounges, one with TV, the other with a small bar. Dinner is a well-cooked meal, usually with a roast joint or poultry along with fresh vegetables. Facilities include a sauna, and there is free use of a nearby swimming pool. The hotel is open from February to December.

WHERE TO EAT

MEALS FOR LESS THAN £10 [$18.50]

BALDRY'S, Red Lion Sq. Tel. 301.
Cuisine: ENGLISH. **Reservations:** Not needed.
$ Prices: All appetizers £1.45 ($2.70); main dishes £2.15–£4.50 ($4–$7.40). No credit cards.
Open: Sept–June daily 9:30am–5:30pm; July–Aug daily 9:30am–8pm.
This family-run establishment serves wholesome homemade food at prices which most diners find appetizing. Within a stone-sided Lake District house, whose walls are adorned with framed newspaper clippings and mementos of the district's history, Elaine and Paul Nelson have created a cozy refuge. Many dishes are vegetarian (there's always a meatless dish of the day) such as whole-meal pasta in a mushroom and cream sauce, as well as such light fare as meat pies, salads, pastries, tea, and scones.

COFFEE BEAN, Red Lion Sq. Tel. 234.
Cuisine: ENGLISH. **Reservations:** Not needed.
$ Prices: Appetizers £1.50–£2 ($2.80–$3.70); main courses £3.50–£4.50 ($6.45–$8.35). No credit cards.
Open: Mid-March to Nov daily 9am–5:30pm; Nov to mid-March Sat–Sun 10am–4pm.
Located right in the center of Grasmere, the Coffee Bean offers soups, sandwiches (toasted or not), coffee, tea, chocolate, pastries, pies, and cookies, among other items. Food can be eaten here or taken out. They will fill flasks of hot tea or coffee for you. Everything is freshly made and much is home-baked.

TRAVELLER'S REST, Dunmail Raise, Hwy. A591. Tel. 09665/378.
  Cuisine: ENGLISH. **Reservations:** None.
$ **Prices:** Platters £3.50–£8 ($6.50–$14.80). No credit cards.
  Open: Pub Mon–Sat 11am–11pm, Sun noon–3pm and 7–10:30pm; lunch daily noon–3pm; dinner Mon–Sat 6–10pm, Sun 7–10pm.

Set within a carefully interconnected trio of late 16th-century stone cottages, this is a much-patronized pub that attracts locals as well as summer visitors and Lakeland hikers. Place your order for one of the platters at the bar, and carry it to a table in either the pub itself or to a seat in the adjacent dining room. Typical dishes include steak-and-kidney pie, hamburgers, ploughman's lunches, or lasagne. Most visitors wash everything down with lager or ale, sometimes from a seat on the panoramic patio.

   The pub also contains six unpretentious bedrooms on the upper floors, none of which has a private bathroom. With an English breakfast included, singles rent for £23.50 ($43.50), doubles for £39 ($72.15). The pub is ½ mile north of Grasmere beside the highway.

---

6. HAWKSHEAD & CONISTON

263 miles NW of London; 52 miles S of Carlisle; 19 miles NW of Kendal

GETTING THERE   By Train   Go first to Windermere (see above) and proceed by bus.

By Bus   Cumberland Motor Services (CMS) runs buses from Windermere to Hawkshead and Coniston three times a day Monday to Saturday or twice a day on Sunday. Take bus no. 505 or 515 from Windermere.

By Car   From Windermere proceed north along A591 to Ambleside, cutting southwest on B5285 to Hawkshead.

By Ferry   The Bowness Bay Boating Company (tel. 09662/3360 for information) in summer operates a ferry service from Bowness, directly south of Windermere, to Hawkshead, costing £1 ($1.85) for cars or 10p (20¢) for pedestrians. It reduces driving time considerably.

ESSENTIALS   The **area code** for Hawkshead is 09666, and the area code for Coniston is 05394. The **Tourist Information Centre** is at Hawkshead at the Main Car Park (tel. 09666/525). It is open only in summer.

Discover the village of Hawkshead, with its 15th-century grammar school where Wordsworth went to school for 8 years (he carved his name on a desk that still remains). Near Hawkshead, in the vicinity of Esthwaite Water, is the 17th-century Hill Top Farm, former home of Beatrix Potter, the author of the *Peter Rabbit* books, who died during World War II.

   At Coniston, 4 miles west of Hawkshead, visit the village famously associated with John Ruskin. Coniston is a good base for rock climbing. The Coniston "Old Man" towers in the background at 2,633 feet, giving mountain climbers one of the finest views of the Lake District.

WHAT TO SEE & DO

BRANTWOOD, Coniston. Tel. 05394/42396.
   John Ruskin, poet, artist, and critic, was one of the great figures of the Victorian age and a prophet of social reform, inspiring such diverse men as Proust, Frank Lloyd Wright, and Gandhi. He moved to his home, Brantwood, on the east side of Coniston Water, in 1872 and lived there until his death in 1900. The house today is open for visitors to view much Ruskiniana, including some 200 pictures

by him. Also displayed are his coach and boat, the *Jumping Jenny*. A video program tells the story of Ruskin's life and work.

An exhibition illustrating the work of W. J. Linton is laid out in his old printing room. Linton was born in England in 1812 and died at New Haven, Connecticut, in 1897. Well known as a wood engraver and for his private press, he lived at Brantwood, where he set up his printing business in 1853. He published *The English Republic*, a newspaper and review, before immigrating to America in 1866, where he set up his printing press in 1870. The house is owned and managed by the Education Trust, a self-supporting registered charity. Part of the 250-acre estate is open as a nature trail.

The Brantwood stables, designed by Ruskin, have been converted into a tearoom and restaurant, the Jumping Jenny. Also in the stable building is the Lakeland Guild Craft Gallery, which follows the Ruskin tradition in encouraging contemporary craft work of the finest quality.

Literary fans may want to pay a pilgrimage to the graveyard of the village church, where Ruskin was buried; his family turned down the invitation to have him interred at Westminster Abbey.

Admission: £2.40 ($4.45) adults, £1.25 ($2.30) children, £6.25 ($11.55) family; nature walk 50p (95¢) adults, 25p (45¢) children.

Open: Mid-March to mid-Nov daily 11am–5:30pm; winter Wed–Sun 11am–5:30pm.

JOHN RUSKIN MUSEUM, Yewdale Rd., Coniston Village. Tel. 05394/ 41387.

At this institute you can see Ruskin's personal possessions and relics, sketchbooks, letters, and a collection of mineral rocks he collected. It's located in the village center.

Admission: 50p (95¢).

Open: Easter–Oct daily 10am–5:30pm.

WHERE TO STAY

In addition to the following listings, Queen's Head under "Where to Eat" also has sleeping accommodations.

DOUBLES WITHOUT BATH FOR LESS THAN £38 [$70.30]

IVY HOUSE HOTEL, Main St., Hawkshead, near Ambleside, Cumbria LA22 0NS. Tel. 09666/204. 11 rms (6 with bath).

$ Rates (including English breakfast): £19–£22 ($35.15–$40.70) single without bath; £38 ($70.30) double without bath, £44 ($81.40) double with bath. No credit cards. **Parking:** Free.

Located in the center of Hawkshead, this is an ideal headquarters from which to branch out for visits on Lake Windermere. Bedrooms are centrally heated and have hot and cold running water. A modern, motel-type annex handles overflow guests. Log fires blaze in the lounge in early and late season. The hospitable proprietors, David and Jane Vaughan, are used to welcoming overseas visitors. Because of their charming house and situation, they are heavily booked, so it's wise to reserve in advance. They also provide good English cooking. The house is open from March to November only.

KINGS ARMS, The Square, Hawkshead, near Ambleside, Cumbria LA22 0NZ. Tel. 09666/372. 9 rms (4 with bath).

$ Rates (including English breakfast): £22.50 ($41.63) single without bath, £25 ($46.25) single with bath; £36 ($66.60) double without bath, £45 ($83.25) double with bath. AE, MC, V. **Parking:** Free.

This is a crooked-fronted old coaching inn in the middle of the village near the police station, with leaded windows and sloping roofs. Inside, low beams and whitewashed walls complete the picture, along with a friendly bar patronized by the locals. There is also a neat buttery, and in the rear a room for bar games. The inn offers grills and steaks at mealtimes, and also experiments on the locals with national evenings, including Indian, Far Eastern, or Greek fare. Dinners start at £11 ($20.35).

WORTH THE EXTRA BUCKS

FIELD HEAD HOUSE, Outgate, Hawkshead, Cumbria LA22 0PY. Tel. 09666/240. 8 rms (all with bath or shower). TV **Directions:** From Hawkshead, take the Ambleside Rd. (B5286), then take the second turning on the left, a mile from Hawkshead (signposted Field Head). After about ¼ mile, Field Head is on your right.
$ **Rates** (including half board): £55.50 ($102.80) single; £95–£115 ($175.75–$212.75) double. No credit cards. **Parking:** Free. **Closed:** Jan.

★ This is a bit hard to find but worth the search. Once there, you will be welcomed by the Dutch-born owners, Eeke and Bob van Gulik, to this marvelous old Lake District home whose origins go back to the 1600s, when it was built as a hunting lodge for a duke. A friend of William Wordsworth, the artist John Harden lived in this house for about a decade from 1834. Field Head House is located on its own 6 acres of wooded grounds and gardens.

Even if you can't stay here, call and see if you can have dinner; their food is considered the best in the area. From 7:30, a superb five-course dinner is served for £20 ($37). The menu changes nightly, but a typical meal might include a pear-and-Stilton savory, mushroom soup, roast shoulder of venison with five different fresh vegetables (often from their own garden), English cheese, and peaches and cream, followed by coffee. No dinner is served on Tuesday. It is imperative to make a reservation.

NEARBY ACCOMMODATIONS

In Coniston

CONISTON SUN HOTEL, Coniston, Cumbria LA21 8HQ. Tel. 05394/41248. 11 rms (9 with bath). TV TEL
$ **Rates** (including English breakfast): £30 ($55.50) single without bath; £53 ($98.05) double without bath, £66 ($122.10) double with bath. MC, V. **Parking:** Free.
This is the most popular, traditional, and attractive pub, restaurant, and hotel in this Lakeland village. In reality it is a country-house hotel of much character, dating from 1902, although the inn attached to it is from the 16th century. Standing on its own beautiful grounds above the village, it lies at the foot of the Coniston "Old Man." Donald Campbell made this place his headquarters during his attempt on the world water-speed record. Each bedroom is decorated with style and flair, and two of them contain four-poster beds. Fresh local produce is used whenever possible in the candlelit restaurant. Log fires take the chill off a winter evening, and guests relax informally in the lounge, which is like a library. Many sports can be arranged. The hotel is near the village center off A593.

At Far Sawrey

SAWREY HOTEL, Hawkshead Rd., Far Sawrey, near Ambleside, Cumbria LA22 0LQ. Tel. 09662/3425. 17 rms (13 with bath or shower). TV
$ **Rates** (including breakfast and dinner): £19.50 ($36.10) single without bath, £24.50 ($45.35) single with bath; £39 ($72.15) double without bath, £49 ($90.65) double with bath. No credit cards. **Parking:** Free.
This hotel is in the village where Beatrix Potter lived the happiest years of her life. The inn was built of stone and "pebble-dash" (a form of stucco) as a coaching inn in the early 18th century. Nonresidents are welcome to come and dine on bar snacks at lunch 11:30am to 2:30pm, and on a five-course fixed-price dinner costing £12.50 ($23.15) everyday from 7 to 8:45pm. David Brayshaw is the host. The hotel is 1 mile from Windermere car-ferry on B5285.

WHERE TO EAT

In addition to the following listing, the Field Head House (see "Where to Stay" above) also has an excellent restaurant.

QUEEN'S HEAD, Main St., Hawkshead, near Ambleside, Cumbria LA22 ONS. Tel. 09666/271.
Cuisine: ENGLISH. **Reservations:** Recommended.
$ Prices: Appetizers £1.75–£4.25 ($3.25–$7.85); main courses £7.50–£11.25 ($13.90–$20.80); three-course set lunch £4.95 ($9.15). AE, MC, V.
Open: Lunch daily noon–2:15pm; dinner daily 6:45–9pm.

This is the most famous pub in the town center. It's really more an inn than a pub, as it also rents 10 bedrooms. Behind a mock black-and-white timbered facade, it is a 17th-century structure of character, serving Hartley's Ulverston and Robinson's of Stockport from the wood. Try a sizzling sirloin steak, grilled rainbow trout, or perhaps pheasant in casserole. The comfortably old-fashioned bedrooms, half of which contain private baths or showers, cost from £24 to £31 ($44.40 to $57.35) daily in a single, from £40 to £47 ($74 to $86.95) in a double. Breakfast is included.

7. KESWICK

22 miles NW of Windermere; 294 miles NW of London; 31 miles S of Kendal

GETTING THERE By Train Go first to Windermere (see above) and proceed the rest of the way by bus.

By Bus Cumberland Motor Services (CMS) has hourly service from Windermere and Grasmere (bus no. 555 or 557).

By Car From Windermere, proceed northwest along A591.

ESSENTIALS The **area code** is 07687. The **Tourist Information Centre** is at Moot Hall, Market Square (tel. 07687/72645).

Keswick opens onto Derwentwater, one of the loveliest lakes in the district. It makes a good center for exploring the northern half of the Lake District National Park. The small town has two landscaped parks, and above the town is a historic Stone Circle thought to be some 4,000 years old.

St. Kentigern's Church dates from A.D. 553, and a weekly market held in the center of Keswick descends from a charter granted in the 13th century. It's but a short walk to the classic view point of Friar's Crag on Derwentwater. The walk also takes you past boat landings with launches operating regularly on tours around the lake.

Around Derwentwater are many places with literary associations, evoking memories of Wordsworth, Robert Southey (poet laureate), Coleridge, and Hugh Walpole. Several of Beatrix Potter's legendary stories were based at Keswick. The town also has a professional repertory theater offering shows in summer. There is a modern leisure swimming pool, plus an 18-hole golf course at the foot of the mountains 4 miles away.

Close by are villages and lakes, including Borrowdale, Buttermere, and Bassenthwaite, while the open country of "John Peel" fame is to the north of the 3,053-foot Skiddaw.

WHERE TO STAY

DOUBLES WITHOUT BATH FOR LESS THAN £36.50 [$67.55]

ALLERDALE HOUSE, 1 Eskin St., Keswick, Cumbria CA12 4DH. Tel. 07687/73891. 6 rms (all with bath or shower). TV TEL
$ Rates: £35 ($64.75) double. No credit cards. **Parking:** Free.

This is a large Victorian-era home close to the town center that might be ideal lodgings for your base near Derwentwater. Here you get real Lakeland hospitality, a warm welcome, and comfortable bedrooms, each a double. Rooms are pleasantly furnished and well maintained. Guests are accepted year round (except in December), and they can also arrange to have a home-cooked dinner in the evening.

GEORGE HOTEL, St. John St., Keswick, Cumbria CA12 5AZ. Tel. 07687/72076. 17 rms (none with bath).
$ Rates: £18 ($33.30) single; £36 ($66.60) double. MC, V. **Parking:** Free.
Known to Southey and Coleridge, the George Hotel is a 400-year-old coaching inn, the oldest inn in town, once known as the George & Dragon. Still offering unvarnished charm, it lies in the middle of town near the market square, which comes alive on Saturday morning. An additional £12 ($22.20) provides dinner. The inn, particularly the two old-world bars, offers a relaxed atmosphere. Bar snacks and pub grub are served every day at lunchtime only from noon to 2pm. Platters average about £3.50 ($6.50) each.

THE KING'S ARMS HOTEL, Main St., Keswick, Cumbria CA12 5BL. Tel. 07687/72083. 13 rms (all with bath). TV
$ Rates: £23 ($42.55) per person. MC, V.
This is a coaching inn dating back more than 200 years to the time of George III. In the middle of town, it offers comfortably furnished bedrooms, all doubles with in-house videos, and tea and coffee makers. The Restaurant offers an extensive à la carte menu, and snacks are served at lunchtime in a charming oak-beamed bar and lounge. If you prefer, there is the Loose Box Pizzeria in the courtyard, which was the original stables. The Casablanca Video Bar offers occasional live music.

LINNETT HILL HOTEL, 4 Penrith Rd., Keswick, Cumbria CA12 4HF. Tel. 07687/3109. 10 rms (all with bath or shower). TV
$ Rates (including English breakfast): £20.25 ($37.45) single without bath; £36.50 ($67.55) double without bath, £38.50 ($71.25) double with bath. MC, V. **Parking:** Free.
Linnett Hill has been thoroughly modernized, yet it retains oak beams and other typical characteristics. This private town house dates from 1812, and its decorations are Victorian. Sylvia and Richard Harland offer bedrooms with electric shaver points, and central heating. They charge another £9 ($16.65) to £12 ($22.20) for an evening dinner. Meals are not only large, they're beautifully prepared and served. The hotel has a comfortable lounge, a small private bar, and a private car park. It is situated opposite the River Greta and Fitz Park, with open views of Skiddaw Range and Latrigg, 5 minutes' walk to the lakeshore.

NEARBY ACCOMMODATIONS

COLEDALE INN, near Keswick, Cumbria CA12 5TN. Tel. 059682/272. 8 rms (all with shower). TV TEL
$ Rates (including English breakfast): £16–£19 ($29.60–$35.15) single; £38–£44 ($70.30–$81.40) double. MC, V. **Parking:** Free.
At the foot of Whinlatter Pass, 1½ miles west of Keswick on A66 in the village of Braithwaite, stands the Coledale Inn a typical Victorian Lakeland country inn that started life as a woollen mill. It has a busy Georgian bar, circa 1824, a large lounge bar, a comfortable residents' lounge, and a restaurant. It is full of attractive Victorian prints and antique furnishings. A full bistro menu is available daily, including local specialties such as Flookburgh shrimp, Borrowdale trout, Cumberland sausage, and Cumbrian farmhouse cheese. Traditional English desserts with custard are also a treat. Upstairs, all the spacious rooms have mountain views.

COTTAGE IN THE WOOD, Whinlatter Pass, Keswick, Cumbria CA12 5TW. Tel. 059682/409. 7 rms (all with bath or shower). **Directions:** Take B5292 west from Keswick.
$ Rates (including English breakfast): £25.50–£28.50 ($47.20–$52.75) per person. No credit cards. **Parking:** Free. **Closed:** Dec–Feb.
This place is in the heart of Thornthwaite Forest close to the top of Whinlatter Pass which was once an old coaching inn providing a staging post for coaches and wagons traveling to and from the Cumbrian coast. Now it is a welcoming small country hotel with full central heating and cozy lounges containing deep armchairs and a warming fire. The bedrooms, each a double, are decorated and furnished in cottage style. All

have hot-beverage facilities. Lunches are from £3 ($5.55), and evening meals from £12.50 ($23.15). The emphasis is on traditional English cooking, with Lakeland specialties featured.

WHERE TO EAT

DOG & GUN, 2 Lake Rd. Tel. 73463.
 Cuisine: ENGLISH. **Reservations:** Not needed.
$ Prices: Appetizers £1–£2.35 ($1.85–$4.35); main courses £1.70–£4.95 ($3.15–$9.15). No credit cards.
 Open: Lunch Mon–Sat 11:30am–2pm, Sun noon–2pm; dinner Mon–Sat 6–9:30pm, Sun 7–9:30pm.

This is the most famous pub in Keswick. Inside, there's warmth and character, along with tasty bar snacks or full-size meals. A tavern with two rooms, it offers an atmosphere of low beams and open fires in winter. Meals include such hearty fare as Hungarian goulash, curries, and roast chicken.

CHAPTER 19

THE NORTHEAST

- **WHAT'S SPECIAL ABOUT THE NORTHEAST**
1. **LINCOLN**
2. **YORK**
3. **NORTH YORK MOORS NATIONAL PARK**
4. **HAWORTH**
5. **HEXHAM & HADRIAN'S WALL**

The northeast of England is rich in attractions. Its most visited cities, Lincoln and York, lie on the "cathedral circuit."

Lincoln is the largest city of Lincolnshire, bordered on one side by the North Sea. Of all England's counties (or shires) of the East Midlands, Lincolnshire is the most interesting to visit. Within Lincolnshire, other than the cathedral city of Lincoln, the most interesting section is Holland.

Located in the southeast, Holland is known for its fields of tulips, marshes and fens, and windmills reminiscent of the Netherlands. Tourists, particularly North Americans, generally pass by the busy port of Boston before swinging north to Lincoln.

Yorkshire, known to readers of *Wuthering Heights* and *All Creatures Great and Small*, embraces both the moors of North Yorkshire and the Dales. With the radical changing of the old county boundaries, the shire is now divided into North Yorkshire (the most interesting from the tourist's point of view), West Yorkshire, South Yorkshire, and Humberside.

Away from the cities and towns that still carry the taint of the Industrial Revolution, the beauty is wild and remote, and is characterized by limestone crags, caverns along the Pennines, mountainous uplands, rolling hills, chalkland wolds, heather-covered moorlands, broad vales, and tumbling streams.

Yorkshire offers not only the beauty of its inland scenery, but its 100 miles of shoreline, with its rocky headlands, cliffs, sandy bays, rock pools, sheltered coves, fishing villages, bird sanctuaries, former smugglers' dens, and yachting havens, is definitely worth a visit.

Across this vast region came the Romans, the Anglo-Saxons, the Vikings, the monks of the Middle Ages, kings of England, lords of the manor, craftspeople, hill farmers, and wool growers, all leaving their own mark. You can still see Roman roads and pavements, great abbeys and castles, stately homes, open-air museums, and craft centers, along with parish churches, old villages, and cathedrals. In fact, Yorkshire's battle-scarred castles, Gothic abbeys, and great country manor houses (from all periods) are unrivaled anywhere in Britain.

Northumbria is made up of the counties of Northumberland, Cleveland, and Durham. Tyne and Wear is a small county with Newcastle upon Tyne as its center. The whole area evokes ancient battles and bloody border raids. Space limitations prevent a proper exploration of this area, which is often overlooked by the rushed North American visitor. However, you should venture into the area at least to see Hadrian's Wall, a Roman wall that was considered one of the wonders of the Western world. The finest stretch of the wall lies within the Northumberland National Park, between the stony North Tyne River and the county boundary at Gilsland.

SEEING THE NORTHEAST
GETTING THERE

Although one of the more remote parts of England, the northeast is relatively easy to reach from London or points in the south. Motorists take the M1 from London; British Rail trains reach Lincoln in about 2 hours and York in about 2 hours, too. York is farther away but Lincoln takes the same amount of time because of a change of

WHAT'S SPECIAL ABOUT THE NORTHEAST

Great Towns/Villages
☐ Lincoln, ancient city dominated by its towering 11th century cathedral with triple towers.
☐ York, Roman walled city nearly 2,000 years old—containing many well-preserved medieval buildings.

Cathedrals
☐ York Cathedral, with a history spanning some 800 years. Noted for its 100 stained-glass windows.
☐ Lincoln Cathedral, dating from the 12th century with a tower rising 271 feet, the second tallest in England.

Ancient Monuments
☐ Hadrian's Wall, built by conquering Romans—once considered one of the wonders of the Western world.

Natural Spectacles
☐ Yorkshire Dales, some 700 square miles of water-carved wonderland preserved as a national park.
☐ Yorkshire Moors, heather-covered moorland. The 553-square-mile parkland borders the North Sea.

Literary Shrines
☐ Haworth, where the novelist sisters, the Brontës, wrote their classic works such as Emily's *Wuthering Heights* or Charlotte's *Jane Eyre*.

Buildings
☐ Castle Howard, near Malton in North Yorkshire—lakes, fountains, extensive gardens. Main location for "Brideshead Revisited" TV series.

trains. National Express buses also cover the area from London's Victoria Coach Station, reaching York, for example, in about 4 hours.

A SUGGESTED ITINERARY

Day 1: Head for Lincoln for a day of sightseeing and a visit to its cathedral.

Days 2 & 4: Continue to York and base there for 3 nights, using it as a center for its own attractions and for some sights in its environs, including Castle Howard and the Yorkshire Dales.

Day 5: Call on the literary shrines of the Brontës at Haworth in West Yorkshire and overnight there.

Day 6: Visit Thirsk of *All Creatures Great and Small* fame and spend the rest of the time exploring the Yorkshire moors.

1. LINCOLN

140 miles N of London; 94 miles N of Cambridge; 82 miles S of York

GETTING THERE   By Train   Trains arrive every hour during the day from London's King's Cross Station. Trip time is 2 hours. These trains usually involve a change of trains at Newark. Trains also arrive from Cambridge, also involving a change at Newark.

By Bus   National Express buses from London's Victoria Coach Station service Lincoln. Trip time is about 3 hours. Once at Lincoln, local and regional buses service the county from the City Bus Station, off St. Mary's Street, opposite the rail station.

By Car   From London, take the motorway (M1) north until you reach the junction with A57 heading east to Lincoln.

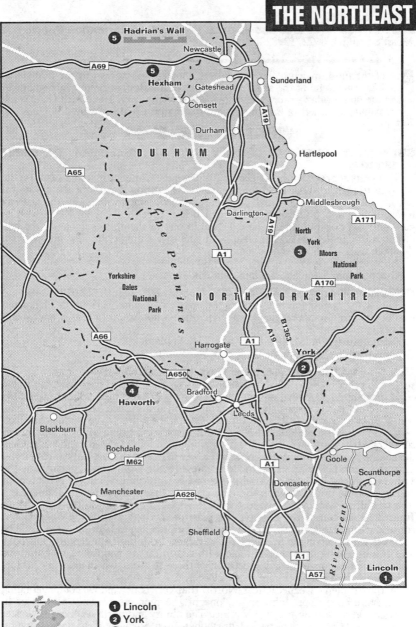

THE NORTHEAST

Hadrian's Wall ⑤

Newcastle

A69

⑤ Hexham

Gateshead
Consett

Sunderland

A19

Durham

D U R H A M

Hartlepool

A65

Middlesbrough

Darlington

A19

A171

North
York
③ Moors
National
Park

The Pennines

A170

Yorkshire
Dales
National
Park

N O R T H   Y O R K S H I R E

A66

A1

Harrogate

A1

A19

B1363

York
②

A650

④
Haworth

Bradford

Leeds

Blackburn

Rochdale

M62

A1

Goole

Scunthorpe

Manchester

A628

Doncaster

River Trent

Sheffield

A1

A57

Lincoln
①

ENGLAND
★ London

① Lincoln
② York
③ North York Moors National Park
④ Haworth
⑤ Hexham & Hadrian's Wall

ESSENTIALS The **area code** is 0522. The **Tourist Information Centre** is at 9 Castle Hill (tel. 0522/529828).

One of the most ancient cities of England, Lincoln was known to the Romans as Lindum and some of the architectural glory of the Roman Empire still stands to charm the present-day visitor. The renowned Newport Arch (the North Gate) is the last remaining arch left in Britain that still spans a principal highway.

WHAT TO SEE & DO

GREYFRIARS CITY AND COUNTY MUSEUM, Broadgate. Tel. 0522/530401.

Two years after the Battle of Hastings, William the Conqueror built a castle on the site of a Roman fortress. Used for administrative purposes, parts of the castle still remain, including the walls, the 12th-century keep, and fragments of the gateway tower. In addition, you can visit the High Bridge over the Witham River, with its half-timbered houses (you can have a meal in one of them); this is one of the few medieval bridges left in England that has buildings nestling on it. The museum is a 3-minute walk north of the bus station.

Admission: 50p (95¢) adults, 25p (45¢) children.

Open: Mon–Sat 10am–5:30pm, Sun 2:30–5pm.

MUSEUM OF LINCOLNSHIRE LIFE, Burton Rd. Tel. 0522/528448.

This is the largest folk museum in the area, a 5-minute walk north of Lincoln Castle, and has displays ranging from a Victorian schoolroom to locally built steam engines.

Admission: 80p ($1.50) adults, 40p (75¢) children.

Open: Mon–Sat 10am–5:30pm, Sun 2–5:30pm.

LINCOLN CATHEDRAL, Minster Yard. Tel. 0522/544544.

No other English cathedral dominates its surroundings as does Lincoln. Visible from up to 30 miles away, the central tower is 271 feet high, which makes it the second tallest in England. Lincoln's central tower once carried a huge spire, which, prior to heavy gale damage in 1549, made it the tallest in the world at 525 feet.

Construction on the original Norman cathedral was begun in 1072, and it was consecrated 20 years later. It sustained a major fire and, in 1185, an earthquake. Only the central portion of the West Front and lower halves of the western towers survive from this period. The present cathedral represents the Gothic style, particularly the early English and Decorated periods. The nave is 13th century, but the black font of Tournai marble originates from the 12th century. In the Great North Transept is a rose medallion window known as the Dean's Eye. Opposite it, in the Great South Transept, is its cousin, the Bishop's Eye. East of the high altar is the Angel Choir, consecrated in 1280, and so called after the sculpted angels high on the walls. The exquisite wood carving in St. Hugh's Choir dates from the 14th century. Lincoln's roof bosses, dating from the 13th and 14th centuries, are handsome, and a mirror trolley assists visitors in their appreciation of these features, which are some 70 feet above the floor. Oak bosses are in the cloister.

In the Seamen's Chapel (Great North Transept) is a window commemorating Lincolnshire-born Capt. John Smith, one of the pioneers of early settlement in America and the first governor of Virginia. The library and north walk of the cloister were built in 1674 to designs by Sir Christopher Wren. Viewing of the fine restoration work, newly completed in the Wren Library, is available by appointment. An extensive range of gifts, including facsimiles of the Lincoln Magna Carta, are available in the two minster gift shops, and refreshments are served in the cloister coffee shop. In the Treasury, there is fine silver plate from the churches of the diocese.

Admission: Suggested donation £1.50 ($2.80).

Open: Treasury daily 11am–3pm. Cathedral Nov–Mar daily 7:15am–5pm; Apr–Oct daily 7:15am–8pm.

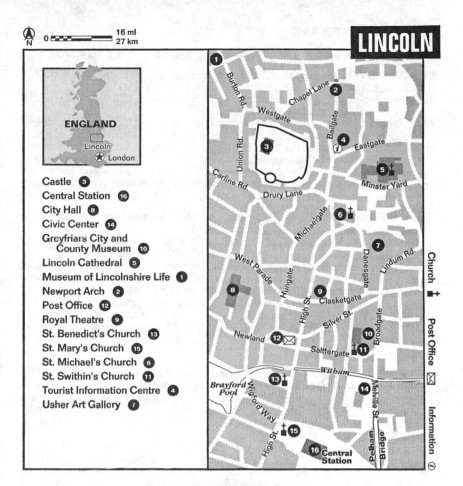

LINCOLN

0 — 16 ml
27 km
N

ENGLAND
Lincoln
★ London

Castle ③
Central Station ⑯
City Hall ⑧
Civic Center ⑭
Greyfriars City and
County Museum ⑩
Lincoln Cathedral ⑤
Museum of Lincolnshire Life ①
Newport Arch ②
Post Office ⑫
Royal Theatre ⑨
St. Benedict's Church ⑬
St. Mary's Church ⑮
St. Michael's Church ⑥
St. Swithin's Church ⑪
Tourist Information Centre ④
Usher Art Gallery ⑦

Church ✠
Post Office ⊠
Information ⑦

WHERE TO STAY

DOUBLES WITHOUT BATH FOR LESS THAN £35 ($64.75)

CARLINE, 3 Carline Rd., Lincoln, Lincolnshire LN1 1HN. Tel. 0522/ 530422. 12 rms (10 with bath or shower). TV

$ Rates (including English breakfast): £13 ($24.05) single without bath, £25 ($46.25) single with bath; £26 ($48.10) double without bath, £31 ($57.35) double with bath. MC. **Parking:** Free.

 This is considered among the finest B&Bs in this city. Lying about a leisurely 6-minute stroll from the cathedral, it has well-furnished and comfortable bedrooms. There is limited parking. No dinner is provided, but Lincoln has several dining possibilities at night. From the cathedral, Drury Lane leads to Carline Road.

HOLLIES HOTEL, Carholme Rd., Lincoln, Lincolnshire LN1 1RT. Tel. 0522/522419. 11 rms (4 with bath). TV

$ Rates (including English breakfast): £22 ($40.70) single without bath; £35 ($64.75) double without bath; £44 ($81.40) double with bath. MC, V. **Parking:** Free.

Owned by the Colston family, this hotel provides clean, comfortable accommodations at fair prices. Each room is centrally heated, with hot and cold running water and a radio. Bar meals are served until 9pm. It is located on A57 below West Parade.

DOUBLES WITH BATH FOR LESS THAN £55 ($101.75)

CASTLE HOTEL, Westgate, Lincoln, Lincolnshire LN1 3AS. Tel. 0522/ 538801. Fax 0522/510291. 20 rms (all with bath). TV TEL
$ Rates (including English breakfast): £45 ($83.25) single; £55 ($101.75) double. AE, DC, MC, V. **Parking:** Free.

The red-brick Castle Hotel rises three stories high and lies within a 3-minute walk of the cathedral in old Lincoln. When it was built around 1858, it was the North District National School, but it has been successfully converted into a hotel of character and comfort. A bar laden with Chesterfield-style leather sofas is located a few steps from the reception desk. Good English-style cooking is served in the Westgate Restaurant, open daily from noon to 2pm and 7 to 9pm, where lunches cost from £8 ($14.80) and dinners cost from £12 ($22.20).

DUKE WILLIAM HOTEL, 44 Bailgate, Lincoln, Lincolnshire LN1 3AP. Tel. 0522/533351. 11 rms (all with bath) TV TEL
$ Rates: Mon–Thurs £42 ($77.70) single, £52 ($96.20) double; Fri–Sun £32 ($59.20) single, £46 ($85.10) double. AE, DC, MC, V. **Parking:** Free.

This is located in the heart of historic Lincoln near the Roman arch, within walking distance of the cathedral. Although the structure has seen many architectural changes since its establishment in 1791, care has been taken to preserve the atmosphere of an 18th-century inn; many of the bedrooms still have their original heavy timbers. The hotel has both a good restaurant and a cozy bar. A tasty luncheon, costing from £6 ($11.10) is served every day from noon to 1:45pm. Dinners are more elaborate, are served daily from 7:30 to 9:30pm, and cost £9 ($16.65) for a four-course table d'hôte meal.

HILLCREST HOTEL, 15 Lindum Terrace, Lincoln, Lincolnshire LN2 5RT. Tel. 0522/510182. 17 rms (all with bath or shower). TV TEL **Directions:** From Wragby Rd., connect with Upper Lindum St. Continue to the bottom of this street and make a left onto Lindum Terrace. The hotel is 200 yards on the right.
$ Rates (including English breakfast): £36.50 ($67.55) single; £49.50 ($91.60) double. AE, MC, V. **Parking:** Free.

This fine, red-brick house was built in 1871 as the private home of a local vicar, and although it has been converted into a comfortable, small licensed hotel, it retains many of the features of its original use. The Hillcrest is suitable for those who appreciate a cozy atmosphere where personal tastes can be accommodated. It is on a quiet, tree-lined road overlooking 26 acres of parkland, in the old high town and within easy walking distance of Lincoln Cathedral and the Roman remains. All bedrooms have radios. The Terrace Restaurant offers a wide variety of French and English dishes cooked to order, with special menus for vegetarians and children.

TENNYSON, 7 S. Park Ave., Lincoln, Lincolnshire LN5 8EN. Tel. 0522/ 521624. 8 rms (all with bath or shower). TV
$ Rates (including English breakfast): £25–£27.50 ($46.25–$50.90) single; £39– £42 ($72.15–$77.70) double. AE, MC, V.

Also a leading B&B, this is really more of a small hotel than a typical bed-and-breakfast. Lying 1½ miles from the cathedral precincts in the vicinity of South Park Common, near the A15 and A1435 junction, Tennyson makes a good base for exploring the area, especially if you have a car. Their food is good, and they serve dinner nightly from 6:30 to 8pm.

WHERE TO EAT

MEALS FOR LESS THAN £10 ($18.50)

BROWN'S PIE SHOP, 33 Steep Hill. Tel. 527330.
Cuisine: ENGLISH. **Reservations:** Not needed.

$ Prices: £1.50–£3.50 ($2.80–$6.45); main courses £3.95–£10.95 ($7.30–$20.25). AE, MC, V.

Open: Lunch Mon–Sat 11:30am–5:30pm; dinner Mon–Sat 5:30–9:30pm.

This restaurant, housed in a building dating from 1527, was previously a hotel and sheltered Lawrence of Arabia several times. Near the cathedral, it is today a beamed and rustic English dining room. Pies, as its name suggests, are the specialty, and they come in many varieties, including fish pies, vegetarian pies, steak-and-kidney pies, chicken-and-chestnut pies, and more. Don't like pies? Try the Cumberland lamb steak.

CRUST, 46 Broadgate. Tel. 540322.

Cuisine: ENGLISH. **Reservations:** Recommended.

$ Prices: Appetizers 80p–£3.30 ($1.50–$5.90); main courses £4.95–£11.25 ($9.15–$20.80); fixed-price lunch £4–£7 ($7.40–£12.95). No credit cards.

Open: Coffee and cake Tues–Sun 10am–2:30pm; lunch Tues–Sat 11:30am–2:30pm, Sun noon–1:45pm; dinner Tues–Thurs 7–10:15pm, Fri–Sat 7–11:15pm.

In a century-old building, this old-world-style restaurant occupies a site on the old Roman Road. Assisted by his wife, Sylvia, the chef-patron, Malta-born Victor Vella, has won a number of gold and silver medals for his cookery. The à la carte dinner menu is elaborate and includes escalope of veal maréchale and coq au vin. The three-course fixed-price lunch for £4 ($7.40) is one of the best bargains in Lincoln, and the Sunday lunch consists of the traditional roast beef and Yorkshire pudding. Sandwiches and bar snacks are served in the coffee lounge. Crust is located in the center near Monks Road and Silver Street.

GRAND HOTEL, St. Mary's St. Tel. 524211.

Cuisine: ENGLISH. **Reservations:** Recommended.

$ Prices: Appetizers £1.20–£5.25 ($2.20–$9.70); main courses £7.50–£9.75 ($13.90–$18.05); four-course fixed-price dinner £9.75 ($18.05); three-course lunch £7.25 ($13.40). AE, DC, MC, V.

Open: Lunch daily noon–2pm; dinner daily 7–9pm. Buttery daily 10:30am–10pm.

 The food here is not only typically English, but the portions are ample. The first course usually consists of a bowl of soup. Then comes the meat, poultry, or fish course, perhaps grilled rainbow trout with almonds or chicken chasseur. Desserts can be selected from the trolley. But that's not all: Even cheese and biscuits (crackers) are included in the fixed-price dinner. The hotel is nearly opposite the rail station.

STOKES HIGH BRIDGE CAFE, 207 High St. Tel. 513825.

Cuisine: ENGLISH. **Reservations:** Not needed.

$ Prices: Appetizers 45p–£1.50 (85¢–$2.80); main courses £3–£4 ($5.55–$7.40); set lunch £3–£4 ($5.55–$7.40). No credit cards.

Open: Daily 9:30am–5:30pm; lunch daily 11:30am–2pm.

 This 16th-century tearoom, built over the medieval bridge spanning the River Witham, is one of the nicest sightseeing attractions of Lincoln. If you're seeking only tea and coffee, R. W. Stokes & Sons are specialists, and food here is a bargain. From the room on the top floor there is a view of the river and bridge. Try a complete luncheon of roast beef with Yorkshire pudding, vegetables, and a dessert (perhaps steamed blackberry and apple pudding). You reach the tearoom by going through a little shop on the bridge level.

TROFF'S BISTRO-DINER, 35 Steep Hill. Tel. 510333.

Cuisine: CONTINENTAL. **Reservations:** Not needed.

$ Prices: Appetizers £1.95–£2.95 ($3.60–$5.45); main courses £4.45–£6.95 ($8.25–$12.85). MC, V.

Open: Mon–Fri 5–10:30pm, Sat–Sun 11am–11pm.

 This is operated by the town's finest restaurant, Harvey's, as a tag-along bistro to its more glamorous (and more expensive) parent. It sits upstairs from Harvey's, at the corner of a medieval street named Exchequergate, within a

200-year-old building offering views over Lincoln Cathedral. It's located between the cathedral and the castle in the heart of Old Lincoln, a 2-minute walk from either. Within a modern decor whose late 20th-century lithographs and art posters are in deliberate contrast to the historic building which contains them, you can enjoy freshly ground rumpsteak burgers, and such bistro-inspired food as *cassoulet* (a succulent stew made with beans) in the style of Toulouse, strips of chicken breast cooked with mushrooms and cream and served with Swiss-inspired *Rösti*, seafood lasagne, and steaks.

WORTH THE EXTRA BUCKS

WIG & MITRE, 29 Steep Hill. Tel. 535190.

Cuisine: ENGLISH. **Reservations:** Not needed.

$ Prices: Appetizers £4.50–£9.95 ($8.35–$18.40); main courses £9.95–£13.50 ($18.40–$25). No credit cards.

Open: Daily 8am–midnight.

Run by Michael and Valerie Hope, this is not only one of the best pubs in old Lincoln, but it also serves a bill of fare better than that found in most restaurants. Sitting on the aptly named Steep Hill near the cathedral, decorated in an Old English atmosphere, the place operates somewhat like a café-brasserie. The main restaurant, behind the drinking section on the second floor, has oak timbers, Victorian armchairs, and settees. This 14th-century pub, which has been much restored over the years, also has a summer beer garden. If the restaurant is full, all dishes can be served in the bar downstairs. Blackboard specials change daily, and you are likely to be offered roast rack of lamb resting on onion and sage purée, fricassee of guinea fowl, and roast duck suprême garnished with pink grapefruit. A favorite dessert is chocolate roulade.

2. YORK

203 miles N of London; 26 miles NE of Leeds; 88 miles N of Nottingham

GETTING THERE   By Plane   British Midland flights arrive at Leeds/Bradford Airport, a 50-minute flight from London's Heathrow Airport. Connecting buses at the airport take you east to York.

By Train   From London's King's Cross Station, York-bound trains leave every 10 minutes. Trip time is 2 hours.

By Bus   National Express buses from London's Victoria Coach Station depart 4 times a day. Trip time is 4½ hours.

By Car   From London, head north along the motorway (M1), cutting northeast below Leeds at the junction of A64 heading east to York.

ESSENTIALS   The **area code** is 0904. The **Tourist Information Centre** is at De Grey Rooms, Exhibition Square (tel. 0904/621756).

Few cities in England are as rich in history as York. It is still encircled by its 13th- and 14th-century city walls—about 2½ miles long—with four gates. One of these, Micklegate, once grimly greeted visitors coming up from the south with the heads of traitors. To this day, you can walk on the footpath of the medieval walls.

The crowning achievement of York is its minster, or cathedral, which makes the city an ecclesiastical center equaled only by Canterbury. In spite of this, York is one of the most overlooked cities on the cathedral circuit. Perhaps foreign visitors are intimidated by the feeling that the great city of northeastern England is too far north. Actually, it lies about 203 miles north of London on the Ouse River and can easily be tied in with a drive to Edinburgh. Or, after visiting Cambridge, make a swing through a too-often-neglected cathedral circuit: Ely, Lincoln, York, and Ripon.

There was a Roman York (Hadrian came this way), then a Saxon York, a Danish

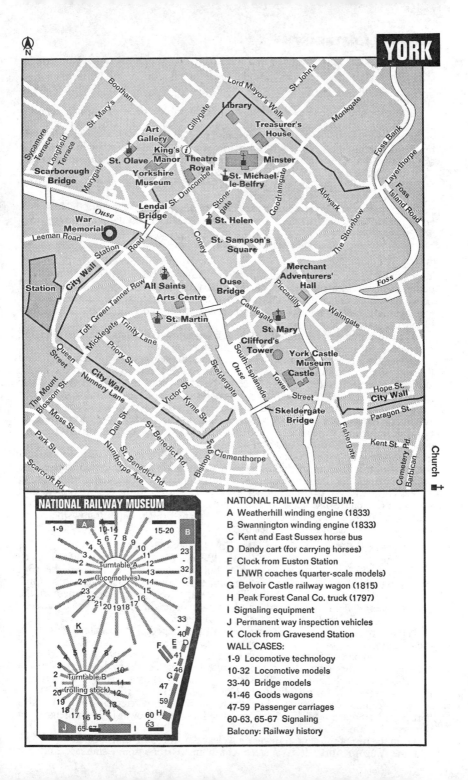

YORK

NATIONAL RAILWAY MUSEUM:

A Weatherhill winding engine (1833)
B Swannington winding engine (1833)
C Kent and East Sussex horse bus
D Dandy cart (for carrying horses)
E Clock from Euston Station
F LNWR coaches (quarter-scale models)
G Belvoir Castle railway wagon (1815)
H Peak Forest Canal Co. truck (1797)
I Signaling equipment
J Permanent way inspection vehicles
K Clock from Gravesend Station

WALL CASES:

1-9 Locomotive technology
10-32 Locomotive models
33-40 Bridge models
41-46 Goods wagons
47-59 Passenger carriages
60-63, 65-67 Signaling
Balcony: Railway history

York, a Norman York (William the Conqueror slept here), a medieval York, a Georgian York, and a Victorian York (the center of a flourishing rail business). Today, a large amount of 18th-century York remains, including Richard Boyle's restored Assembly Rooms.

At some point in your exploration, visit the Shambles, once the meat-butchering center of York that dates back before the Norman Conquest. This messy business has given way, but the ancient street survives and is filled with jewelry stores, cafés, and buildings that huddle so closely together that you can practically stand in the middle of the pavement, arms outstretched, and touch the houses on both sides of the street.

Recently, special interest has been focused on discoveries of the Viking era, from 867 to 1066, when the city was known as Jorvik, the Viking capital and a major Scandinavian trade center (see below).

Incidentally, the suffix "gate" used for streets and sites in York is from the Scandinavian word for "street," a holdover from the era when Vikings held sway here.

WHAT TO SEE & DO

To get to know York I suggest you start from York Minster and walk down past Youngs Hotel, the reputed birthplace of Guy Fawkes. Turn right into Stonegate, a pedestrian area with old shops, a 12th-century house on the right, and some old coffeehouses. Continue across Davygate into St. Helen's Square to see the guildhall and Mansion House, then go left onto Coney Street and take a right into Lower Ousegate.

At the beginning of Ouse Bridge, take the steps down to Kings Staithe, with a pub on the left for refreshment, before you continue on into South Esplanade and St. George's Gardens beside the river. At the bridge, join the road again and turn left, and in front of you stand the Castle Museum, the Assize Courts, and Clifford's Tower. Walk up Tower Street and Clifford Street to Nessgate. Turn right into High Ousegate and continue across Parliament Street to the beginning of the Shambles on the left.

Walk up the Shambles past the attractive shops and ancient buildings to Kings Square, then bear right into Goodramgate. Walk down Goodramgate and, at the end, cross Deangate into College Street with St. William's College on the right. At the end, a narrow road leads to the Treasurer's House.

You're now behind the east end of the minster. Walk around to the west end and then up Bootham Bar, through the city gate, and turn left into Exhibition Square. The art gallery is on the right, the tourist information center to the left, and beside it, York's Theatre Royal. Continue down St. Leonard's Street to the crossroads and turn right into Museum Street. Cross the river and go right to join part of the old medieval wall, which you follow all the way to Skeldergate Bridge. Then follow the river's course upstream again to the center of York.

YORK MINSTER, High Petergate. Tel. 0904/624426.

⭐ One of the great cathedrals of the world, York Minster traces its origins back to the early 7th century; the present building, however, dates from the 13th century. Like the cathedral at Lincoln, York Minster is characterized by three towers built in the 15th century. The central tower is lantern shaped in the Perpendicular style, the cathedral stands at the converging point of several streets: Deangate, Duncombe Place, Minster Yard, and Petergate.

Perhaps the distinguishing characteristic of the cathedral is its stained glass from the Middle Ages—in glorious Angelico blues, ruby reds, forest greens, and honey ambers. See in particular the large east window, the work of a 15th-century Coventry glass painter. In the north transept is an architectural gem of the mid-13th century, the "Five Sisters," which has lancets. The late 15th-century choir screen has an impressive line-up—everybody from William the Conqueror to the overthrown Henry VI.

At a reception desk near the entrance to the minster, parties can be put in touch with a guide, if one is available, for a conducted tour. Gifts toward the maintenance of the cathedral are requested.

From the top of the central tower on a clear day, there are unrivaled views of York and the Vale of York. It is a steep climb up a stone spiral staircase and not recommended for the very elderly, very young, or anyone with a heart condition or breathing difficulties.

Admission: Chapter house 60p ($1.10) adults, 30p (55¢) children; crypt 60p ($1.10), 30p (55¢) children; refurbished foundations £1.50 ($2.80) adults, 60p ($1.10) children; tower £1.50 ($2.80) adults, 70p ($1.30) children.

Open: Chapter house Mon–Sat 10am–5pm, Sun 1–5pm; crypt Mon–Sat 10am–5pm, Sun 1–5pm; refurbished foundations Mon–Sat 10am–5pm, Sun 1–5pm.

TREASURER'S HOUSE, Minster Yard. Tel. 0904/624247.

The treasurer's House stands on a site where there's been a building since Roman times. The main part of the house was rebuilt in 1620 and was lived in as a private home until 1930. It has a magnificent series of rooms with fine furniture, glass, and china of the 17th and 18th centuries. An audiovisual program describes the work of the medieval treasurers and some of the personalities with which this York house is associated. The house has an attractive small garden. On some evenings in summer, you can enjoy coffee by candlelight in the great hall. An attractive shop and licensed restaurant, where Yorkshire specialties are served, are open the same hours as the house.

Admission: £2.30 ($4.25) adults, £1 ($1.85) children.

Open: Apr–Oct daily 10:30am–5pm (last entry at 4:30pm); summer nightly 7:30–9:30pm.

YORK CASTLE MUSEUM, Eye of York off Tower St. Tel. 0904/653611.

On the site of York's Castle this is one of the finest folk museums in the country. Its unique feature is a re-creation of a Victorian cobbled street, "Kirkgate," named for the museum's founder, Dr. John Kirk. He acquired his large collection while visiting his patients in rural Yorkshire at the beginning of this century. Period rooms range from a neoclassical Georgian dining room through an overstuffed and heavily adorned Victorian parlor, to the 1953 sitting room with a brand-new television set purchased to watch the coronation of Elizabeth II. In the Debtors' Prison, former prison cells display craft workshops. There is also a superb collection of arms and armor. In the Costume Gallery, displays are changed regularly to reflect the collection's variety. Half Moon Court is an Edwardian street, with a gypsy caravan and a pub (sorry, the bar's closed!). During the summer, visit a watermill on the bank of the River Foss. It is recommended that you allow at least two hours for a visit to this museum. It's located South of the center near St. Georges Field.

Admission: £3 ($5.55) adults, £1.50 ($2.80) children.

Open: Apr–Oct Mon–Sat 9:30am–6:30pm, Sun 10am–6:30pm; Nov–Mar Mon–Sat 9:30am–5pm, Sun 10am–5pm (last admission 1 hour before closing).

NATIONAL RAILWAY MUSEUM, Leeman Rd. Tel. 0904/621261.

This was the first national museum to be built away from London, and it has attracted millions of visitors since it opened in 1975. Adapted from an original steam locomotive depot, the museum gives visitors a chance to see how Queen Victoria traveled in luxury and to look under and inside steam locomotives. In addition, there's a full-size collection of railway memorabilia, including an early 19th-century clock and penny machines for purchasing tickets on the railway platform. More than 20 full-size locomotives are on display. One, the *Agenoria,* dates from 1829 and is a contemporary of Stephenson's well-known *Rocket.* It's almost identical to the first American locomotive, the *Stourbridge Lion,* sent to the United States from England in 1828. Exhibitions change from time to time, but there is always a fine selection of the beautifully colored, British steam locomotives on display. *Mallard,* the fastest steam locomotive in the world, is in the museum when it's not at work on the railroad. Of several royal coaches, the most interesting is the century-old Royal Saloon, in which Queen Victoria rode until her death; it's like a small hotel, with polished wood, silk, brocade, and silver accessories. The museum is appropriately located near the train station.

Admission: £3 ($5.55) adults, £1.50 ($2.80) children.

Open: Mon–Sat 10am–6pm, Sun 11am–6pm.

JORVIK VIKING CENTRE, Coppergate between Piccadilly and Castlegate. Tel. 0904/643211.

This Viking city was discovered many feet below the present ground level and was reconstructed exactly as it stood in A.D. 948. In a "time car," you can travel back through the ages to 1067 when Normans sacked the city and then ride slowly through the street market peopled by faithfully modeled Vikings. You also go through a house where a family lived and down to the river to see the ship chandlers at work and a Norwegian cargo ship unloading. At the end of the ride, you pass through the Finds Hut, where thousands of artifacts are displayed. Departures on the time train are at regular intervals.

Admission: £3 ($5.55) adults, £1.50 ($2.80) children.
Open: Apr–Oct daily 9am–7pm; Nov–Mar daily 9am–5:30pm.

THEATRE ROYAL, St. Leonard's Place. Tel. 0904/623568.

This old, traditional theater building has modern additions to house the box office, bars, and restaurant. It is worth inquiring about the current production as the Royal Shakespeare Company includes York in its tours; the Arts Council presents dance, drama, and opera; and visiting celebrities appear in classics. There is also an excellent resident repertory company.

Admission: Gallery seats £4.50 ($8.35), dress circle seats £9.50 ($17.60).
Open: Shows daily at 7:30pm or 8pm.

AN ORGANIZED WALKING TOUR

The best way to see York is to go to the tourist information center, De Grey Rooms, Exhibition Square (tel. 0904/621756), where you'll be met by a volunteer guide who will take you on a free 1½-hour walking tour of the city. You'll learn about history and lore through numerous intriguing stories. Tours are given from April through October daily at 10:15am and 2:15pm, plus at 7pm from June to August; from November to March, a daily tour is given at 10:15am.

WHERE TO STAY

DOUBLES WITHOUT BATH FOR LESS THAN £34 ($62.50)

ABERFORD HOUSE HOTEL, 35-36 East Mount Rd., York, North Yorkshire YO2 2BD. Tel. 0904/622694. 12 rms (4 with bath or shower). TV
$ Rates (including English breakfast): £17–£22 ($31.45–$40.70) single without bath; £32 ($59.20) double without bath, £50 ($92.50) double with bath. AE, MC, V.
Parking: Free.

Situated just 5 minutes from the railway station off A64, this family-run hotel is on a quiet road close to the great southern city gateway. Rooms have wash basins, shaver points, and hot-beverage facilities. The dining room has a good breakfast menu, and a three-course dinner with coffee is served at 7pm, if it is ordered in advance. The hotel has a well-stocked cellar bar and a private car park.

ARNOT HOUSE, 17 Grosvenor Terrace, Bootham, York, North Yorkshire YO3 7AG. Tel. 0904/641966. 6 rms (none with bath). TV **Bus:** No. 9.
$ Rates (including English breakfast): £14 ($25.90) single; £28 ($51.80) twin or double. No credit cards. **Parking:** Free.

Like other houses on the terrace, the Arnot House has views over Bootham Park, and in the distance you can see the minster. The owners welcome guests to this Victorian house, which has its original fireplaces, cornices, and a fine old staircase. The atmosphere is warm and comfortable, and the bedrooms have hot- and cold-water basins and hot-beverage facilities. A four-course set dinner is served in the candlelit dining room and costs from £8.50 ($15.75). The house is licensed. Grosvenor Terrace is a 15- to 20-minute walk from the train station, off Bootham (A19), 400 yards outside the city walls at Bootham Bar.

BARRINGTON HOUSE, 15 Nunthorpe Ave. off Scarcroft Rd., York,

North Yorkshire YO2 1PF. Tel. 0904/634539. 5 rms (all with bath or shower). TV **Bus:** No. 18.
$ Rates (including English breakfast): £14–£17 ($25.90–$31.45) per person. No credit cards. **Parking:** Free.
The small, family-run guesthouse is operated by Jeff and Pauline Topham. They have a guest lounge, and each of their bedrooms, all doubles, have shaver points and hot-beverage facilities. Evening meals can be served if arranged in advance. Jeff is a local tour guide, so he can be especially helpful to guests.

CLIFTON GREEN HOTEL, 8 Clifton Green, York, North Yorkshire YO3 6LN. Tel. 0904/623523. 8 rms (3 with bath). TV **Bus:** No. 9. **Directions:** Take the A19 road toward Thirsk.
$ Rates (including English breakfast): £16 ($29.60) single without bath; £30 ($55.50) double without bath, £32 ($59.20) double with bath. No credit cards.
About a 10-minute walk from Bootham Bar, the north gate of old York, this is an immaculate small hotel fronting on a green. The bedrooms, rented by Ben and Gloria Braithwaite, are carpeted and have central heating, hot- and cold-water basins, hot-beverage facilities, bed lights, wardrobes with hangers, dressing tables, nightstands, filled tissue dispensers, and other amenities to make a stay here rewarding. The hotel offers private parking, some in covered spaces, and the bus comes almost to the door.

CRAIG-Y-DON, 3 Grosvenor Terrace, Bootham, York, North Yorkshire YO3 7AG. Tel. 0904/637186. 8 rms (1 with bath). TV **Bus:** No. 9.
$ Rates (including English breakfast): £13–£15 ($24.05–$27.75) single without bath; £26 ($48.10) double without bath, £34 ($62.90) double with bath. MC, V. **Parking:** Free.
Mr. and Mrs. Oliver are two of the most hospitable hosts in the heart of York. They run an immaculately kept and most inviting home and serve a large Yorkshire breakfast. Mrs. Oliver also welcomes children.

DAIRY WHOLEFOOD GUEST HOUSE, 3 Scarcroft Rd., York, North Yorkshire YO2 1ND. Tel. 0904/639367. 5 rms (2 with bath or shower). TV **Bus:** No. 18.
$ Rates (including English breakfast): £22 ($40.70) single without bath; £28 ($51.80) double without bath, £36 ($66.60) double with bath. No credit cards.
You'll find this lovely house decorated throughout with ideas and furnishings in the "Habitat, Sanderson, Laura Ashley" style, with emphasis on pine and plants and an enclosed courtyard. It lies only 200 yards south of the medieval city walls, within easy access of car parking. Breakfast choices range from traditional English to whole-food vegetarian. Bedrooms have hot-beverage facilities.

FARTHINGS HOTEL, 5 Nunthorpe Ave., York, North Yorkshire YO2 1PF. Tel. 0904/653545. 7 rms (1 with bath). **Bus:** No. 18.
$ Rates (including English breakfast): £28–£34 ($51.80–$62.90) double. No credit cards.
A handsomely rejuvenated Victorian-era private home has been turned into a small hotel lying in a cul-de-sac, about a 10-minute stroll from the heart of the historic district. Audrey and Robert Reid welcome guests to their pleasantly furnished bedrooms, each a double. Guests meet in the lounge in the evening. There is a residential liquor license.

FEVERSHAM LODGE, 1 Feversham Crescent, York, North Yorkshire YO3 7HQ. Tel. 0904/623882. 10 rms (7 with showers). **Bus:** No. 18. **Directions:** From Bootham Bar, proceed north along Gillygate. Feversham Crescent is a left turn.
$ Rates (including English breakfast): £14–£16 ($25.90–$29.60) single without bath; £34 ($62.90) double without bath, £36 ($66.60) double with bath. No credit cards. **Parking:** Free.
This lodge is a 19th-century Methodist manse converted to receive guests. It still

retains its lofty dining room, and there is a TV lounge. Bob and Jill Peacock have neatly kept bedrooms, all of which have central heating. There is space to park your car.

GLENEAGLES LODGE GUEST HOUSE, 27 Nunthorpe Ave., York, North Yorkshire YO2 1PF. Tel. 0904/637000. 6 rms (3 with bath). **Bus:** No. 18.
$ Rates (including English breakfast): £14–£16 ($25.90–$29.60) single without bath; £25 ($46.25) double without bath, £30 ($55.50) double with bath. No credit cards.

 This well-maintained, comfortable guesthouse is handsomely decorated and furnished. On a quiet street, it is within walking distance of all York's historical attractions and is also near the train station and a number of restaurants serving good, reasonably priced food. The success of Gleneagles has everything to do with the hospitality of Michael and Wendy Cager, who are kind and gracious. Don't be surprised if coffee and fresh scones are brought in to greet you on arrival.

HAZELWOOD, 24-25 Portland St., Gillygate, York, North Yorkshire YO3 7EH. Tel. 0904/626548. Fax 0904/628032. 15 rms (11 with bath or shower). TV **Bus:** No. 18.
$ Rates (including English breakfast): £17–£19 ($31.45–$35.15) single without bath; £32 ($59.20) double without bath, £46 ($85.10) double with bath. MC, V. **Parking:** Free.
An easy walk from York Minster, Hazelwood is the domain of Joy and Peter Cox. Their place is immaculately kept and well furnished, and they are always willing to answer your questions about touring in York and the surrounding moors and dales. Their breakfast is large and well prepared.

LINDEN LODGE HOTEL, 6 Nunthorpe Ave. off Scarcroft Rd., York, North Yorkshire YO2 1PF. Tel. 0904/620107. 12 rms (3 with showers). **Bus:** No. 18.
$ Rates (including English breakfast): £15 ($27.75) single without bath, £22 ($40.70) single with shower; £27 ($49.95) double without bath, £44 ($81.40) double with shower. MC, V.
Run by Joan and Bill Wharton, this hotel has up-to-date bedrooms with hot and cold running water. The TV lounge is adjacent to the dining room and licensed bar. Three rooms contain TV.

MINSTER VIEW, 2 Grosvenor Terrace, Bootham, York, North Yorkshire YO3 7AG. Tel. 0904/655034. 89 rms (4 with bath). TV **Bus:** No. 9.
$ Rates (including English breakfast): £12.50–£15 ($23.15–$27.75) single without bath; £25 ($46.25) double without bath, £36 ($66.60) double with bath. No credit cards. **Parking:** Free.

 This is a brick Victorian guesthouse with warm, comfortable bedrooms with hot- and cold-water basins and hot-beverage facilities are rented in this brick Victorian guesthouse. The excellent dinner menu, which costs £9 ($16.65), and wine list will add to your pleasure of visiting York. The house has private parking and is about a 15-minute walk from the city center.

SYCAMORE HOTEL, 19 Sycamore Place, Bootham, York, North Yorkshire YO3 7DW. Tel. 0904/624712. 7 rms (3 with bath). TV
$ Rates (including English breakfast): £15–£16 ($27.75–$29.60) single without bath; £32 ($59.20) double without bath, £36 ($66.60) double with bath. No credit cards. **Parking:** Free.
Built as a private dwelling in 1902, this has been carefully converted to maintain much of its original splendor. Now it's a family-owned and -run hotel and offers a high level of accommodation. Rooms have hot and cold running water, central heating, and hot-beverage facilities. The location is close to the city center off A19 to Thirsk (a 10-minute walk to the minster, a 15-minute walk to the rail station), yet it occupies a position in a quiet cul-de-sac. Keys are provided to each guest, and car parking is available.

WORTH THE EXTRA BUCKS

FRESHNEY'S, 54 Low Petergate, York, North Yorkshire YO1 2HZ. Tel. 0904/622478. 11 rms (5 with bath). TV TEL

$ Rates (including English breakfast): £20–£25 ($37–$46.25) single without bath; £44 ($81.40) double without bath; £58 ($107.30) double with bath. MC, V. **Parking:** £1.50 ($2.80).

 Located in a Georgian brick building, Freshney's has cellars containing some beams believed to date back to the 13th century, as well as a beautiful Adam fireplace and three priest holes. It is owned by Mike and Janis Freshney (Janis used to work as a personal secretary to the prime minister at No. 10 Downing Street). Some bedrooms have views of the Rose Window of the minster, and four-poster or half-tester beds, and all have hot-beverage facilities. Lunch and dinner are offered in the restaurant, and the lodge has a cocktail bar. The hotel is in a centrally located base, in the center near Stonegate and Petergate, and it is within easy reach of the railway station.

GRASMEAD HOUSE HOTEL, 1 Scarcroft Hill, York, North Yorkshire YO2 1DF. Tel. 0904/629996. 6 rms (all with bath). TV **Bus:** No. 18.

$ Rates (including English breakfast): £48 ($88.80) double. MC, V. **Parking:** Free.

One American guest departing from Grasmead was overheard remarking, "This hotel is just like an *Alice in Wonderland* place—so super inside." It doesn't have any white rabbits or mad hatters, but it does boast four-poster beds in all the rooms, each a double. It's been refurbished with excellent fabrics and made comfortable with good mattresses. The resident owners provide a real welcome and personal service. Their small family-run hotel lies within easy walking distance of the center, close to the castle museum. While only some rooms look out toward the city walls and minster, they all have easy chairs and hot-beverage facilities.

PRIORY HOTEL, 126 Fulford Rd., York, North Yorkshire YO1 4BE. Tel. 0904/625280. 20 rms (all with shower). **Bus:** No. 8.

$ Rates (including English breakfast): £25 ($46.25) single; £44–£50 ($81.40–$92.50) double. AE, DC, MC, V. **Parking:** Free.

The Priory Hotel stands on the main route into York from the south, on the A19. Lying in a residential area, it has many double- and twin-bedded rooms. Breakfast is served in the elegant period dining room. A riverside walk will take you to the heart of "monumental" York. Resident proprietors George and Barbara Jackson can offer helpful advice to the visitor.

WHERE TO EAT

MEALS FOR LESS THAN £10 [$18.50]

BETTY'S CAFE & TEA ROOMS, St. Helens Square. Tel. 659142.
Cuisine: ENGLISH. **Reservations:** None.

$ Prices: Appetizers £2–£4 ($3.70–$7.40); main courses £5–£6 ($9.25–$11.10); cream tea £4 ($7.40); pastries £1–£3 ($1.85–$5.55). MC, V.
Open: Daily 9am–9pm.

Originally established in 1919, and now one of the most visible tearoom chains in Yorkshire, Betty's invites you to drop in for a quick coffee and pastry or treat yourself to a full English breakfast, a Yorkshire cheese lunch, or a Yorkshire rarebit. Genteel afternoon teas with scones as well as fish-and-chips high teas are favorites, and selections of healthy salads and whole-food quiches are also available. Betty's is famous for its cream cakes. The light suppers and wide variety of cooked and cold meals make this a good place to stop in the evening, and you can order a fine Alsatian wine to complete your meal. A café concert (usually a pianist) entertains customers some evenings as they dine, usually between 6 and 9pm. Families with children are made especially welcome. Betty's is located within a pedestrian zone a 2-minute walk from the cathedral.

BLACK SWAN, Peaseholme Green, York YO1 2PR. Tel. 0904/625236.
Cuisine: ENGLISH. **Reservations:** Not needed.

$ Prices: All appetizers £1.50 ($2.80); main courses £2.50–£3 ($4.65–$5.55); beer from £1 ($1.85). No credit cards.
Open: Mon–Sat 11am–11pm, Sun noon–3pm and 7–10:30pm.

The Black Swan is a fine, timbered, frame house that was once the home of the lord mayor of York in 1417; the mother of Gen. James Wolfe of Québec also lived here. One of the oldest inns in the city, it offers pub meals, which can be enjoyed in front of a log fire in a brick inglenook. Food consists of sandwiches, homemade soups, and Yorkshire puddings filled with beef stew. You can also stay here, as the pub rents three double bedrooms, each with private bath or shower, for £35 ($64.75). It's located 200 yards east of York Shopping Centre.

COCKATOO CREPERIE, 34 Fossgate. Tel. 635351.
Cuisine: CREPES. **Reservations:** Not needed. **Transportation:** All buses to city center.
$ Prices: Salads 70p ($1.30); crêpes £2.75–£4 ($5.10–$7.40). MC, V.
Open: Lunch Tues–Sat (plus Mon June–Oct) noon–2:30pm; dinner Tues–Sun (plus Mon June–Oct) 6–11pm.

In the center of York, Cockatoo Crêperie is an ideal place and has a casual but smart decor. Lausanne-trained André and Daphne Herrenschmidt feature buckwheat and wheat-flour crêpes served with many different stuffings—perhaps turkey and mushrooms in a tarragon sauce—plus fresh green salads. Dessert crêpes are a special feature, and include one made with passion-fruit coulis and sorbet.

KINGS ARMS PUBLIC HOUSE, King's Staithe. Tel. 659435.
Cuisine: ENGLISH. **Reservations:** None.
$ Prices: Appetizers £1.50 ($2.80); main courses £2.50–£3.50 ($4.65–$6.50); sandwiches 80p–£1.25 ($1.50–$2.30). No credit cards.
Open: Lunch daily noon–2pm; dinner daily 5:30–8pm; pub Mon–Sat 11am–11pm, Sun noon–3pm and 7–10:30pm.

Set at the base of the Ouse Bridge, a few steps from the edge of the river, near the foundation of York's most famous bridge, this 16th century pub is roisterous, bawdy, and fun. Considered a historic monument in its own right, it's filled with charm and character, and has the ceiling beams, paneling, and weathered brickwork you'd expect. A board records various disastrous flood levels, the most recent of which inundated the place in 1990. In summer, rows of outdoor tables are placed beside the river. Your hosts serve a full range of draft and bottled beers, the most popular of which (Samuel Smith's) is still brewed in Tadcaster, only 10 miles away. Place your food order at the counter for bar snacks which could include burgers, homemade curries, soups, and steak-and-kidney pie.

KOOKS BISTRO, 108 Fishergate. Tel. 637553.
Cuisine: INTERNATIONAL. **Reservations:** Recommended.
$ Prices: Appetizers £1.50–£2.95 ($2.80–$5.45); main courses £3.50–£8.95 ($6.45–$16.55). MC, V.
Open: Dinner Tues–Sun 7–10:30pm.

This informal, relaxed eating place is run by the owner, Angie Cowl. Decorated in dark green with individually painted flamingos and a collection of memorabilia on the same theme given by customers, it features a varied and unusual menu of English, American, Mexican, French, and vegetarian food, with several dishes distinctive to Kooks. Most main courses include in the price a choice of baked potato, french fries, or side salad. Meats range from burgers to beef Stroganoff. The service is prompt and the atmosphere relaxed, with varied background music and handmade jigsaws and other puzzles and games on every table. Kooks is fully licensed. It's within walking distance of the city center, along A19 out of York.

LEW'S PLACE, Kings Staithe. Tel. 628167.
Cuisine: INTERNATIONAL. **Reservations:** Not needed.
$ Prices: Appetizers £1.25–£3.50 ($2.30–$6.45); main courses £4.50–£8.25 ($8.35–$15.25). MC, V.

Open: Lunch Mon–Sat noon–2pm; dinner Mon–Sat 6:30–10pm.

The owners of this old wharfside gathering place, on the left bank of the Ouse River, try to cater for most tastes. Even some of their rival restaurant and café owners drop in whenever they're free—it's that relaxed. The food is good too, and is certainly hearty. The menu changes daily, but the fare is likely to include homemade moussaka, a lamb steak (marinated in red wine, herbs, and garlic), even chili con carne. Usually a soup is offered for an appetizer.

RUSSELL'S RESTAURANT, 34 Stonegate. Tel. 641432.
   Cuisine: ENGLISH. **Reservations:** Recommended.
 $ **Prices:** Appetizers £1.65–£3.15 ($3.05–$5.85); main courses £6–£8 ($11.10–$14.80); three-course fixed-price lunch or dinner £9.95 ($18.40). MC, V.
   Open: Lunch daily noon–2:30pm; dinner daily 6–10:30pm (slightly earlier in winter if lack of business justifies an earlier closing.)

With another branch in York at 26 Coppergate (tel. 644330), Russell's restaurants are, in the words of one observer, "probably the only true British restaurants in York." Although this point may be arguable, Russell's does offer fresh food of a high standard. Many of its recipes are considered "just like mother used to make"—that is, if your mother came from northeast England. Fare includes roast beef with Yorkshire pudding, along with roast potatoes and seasonal vegetables. A good range of appetizers is also offered, and the desserts are very English and very good, especially bread-and-butter pudding. Wine is available by the glass or bottle, and the kitchen always has a good selection of English cheese. The restaurant sits beside York's most ancient street, a 1-minute walk from the cathedral.

RESTAURANT BARI, 15 The Shambles. Tel. 633807.
   Cuisine: ITALIAN. **Reservations:** Not needed. **Transportation:** All buses to city center.
 $ **Prices:** Appetizers £1.30–£3.65 ($2.40–$67.55); main courses £3.90–£10.95 ($72.15–$20.25). MC, V.
   Open: Lunch daily 11:30am–2:30pm; dinner daily 6–11pm.

This restaurant stands in one of York's oldest and most colorful streets, originally the street of the butchers, mentioned in the *Domesday Book*. In a continental atmosphere, you can enjoy a quick single course or a full leisurely meal. Ten different pizzas are offered, and the lasagne and cannelloni are superb. A main-dish specialty is veal topped with ham and cheese.

ST. WILLIAMS RESTAURANT, 3 College St. Tel. 634830.
   Cuisine: ENGLISH. **Reservations:** Not needed. **Directions:** All buses to city center.
 $ **Prices:** Appetizers £1.05–£1.80 ($1.95–$3.35); main courses £1.70–£2.60 ($3.15–$4.80). No credit cards.
   Open: Breakfast daily 10am–noon; lunch daily noon–2:30pm; afternoon tea daily 2:30–5pm.

St. Williams lies within the shadow of the great East Window of the minster. With its half-timbering and leaded-glass windows, it is a medieval and oak-beamed setting, where you can order some of the best of the low-cost food of York. Selections include much "olde English fayre," including roast rib of beef or one of the "raised pies," such as pork-and-apricot. A self-service cafeteria, this draws many young people to its precincts, as they know they get good value here.

YE OLDE STARRE INNE, 40 Stonegate. Tel. 623063.
   Cuisine: ENGLISH. **Reservations:** None.
 $ **Prices:** Appetizers £1.50 ($2.80); main courses £2.25–£3.60 ($4.15–$6.65). AE, DC, MC, V.
   Open: Pub Mon–Thurs 11am–11pm, Fri–Sat 11am–3:30pm and 7–11pm, Sun noon–3pm and 7–10:30pm; lunch Mon–Sat 11:30am–3pm, Sun noon–2:30pm, dinner Mon–Thurs 5:30–8pm.

On a pedestrian street in the heart of Old York, a 2-minute walk from the cathedral, this dates back to 1644 and is York's oldest licensed pub. Some inn of one kind or another may have stood on this spot since A.D. 900. In a pub said to be haunted by an old lady, a little girl, and a cat, you enter into an atmosphere of cast-iron tables, an open fireplace, oak Victorian settles, and time-blackened beams. In addition to standard alcoholic beverages, the pub offers an array of such English staples as steak-and-kidney pie, several different versions of hot pots, lasagne, and platters of roast beef with Yorkshire pudding. A recent addition to the nationwide Chef & Brewer chain of pubs and restaurants, the establishment offers a duet of outdoor courtyards which guests enjoy during fine weather.

EASY EXCURSIONS

CASTLE HOWARD

In its dramatic setting of lakes, fountains, and extensive gardens, Castle Howard, at Malton in North Yorkshire (tel. 065384/333), the 18th-century palace designed by Sir John Vanbrugh, is undoubtedly the finest private residence in Yorkshire. Principal location for the TV series "Brideshead Revisited," this was the first major achievement of the architect who later created the lavish Blenheim Palace near Oxford. The Yorkshire palace was begun in 1699 for the third earl of Carlisle, Charles Howard. The striking facade is topped by a painted and gilded dome, which reaches more than 80 feet into the air. The interior boasts a 192-foot long gallery, as well as a chapel with magnificent stained-glass windows by the 19th-century artist Sir Edward Burne-Jones. Besides the collections of antique furniture, porcelains, and sculpture, the castle contains a number of important paintings, including a portrait of Henry VIII by Holbein, and works by Rubens, Reynolds, and Gainsborough.

The seemingly endless grounds around the palace also offer some memorable sights, including the domed Temple of the Four Winds, by Vanbrugh, and the richly designed family mausoleum by Hawksmoor. There are two rose gardens, one with old-fashioned roses, the other featuring modern creations. The stable court houses the Costume Galleries, the largest private collection of 18th- to 20th-century costumes in Britain. Authentically dressed mannequins are exhibited in period settings.

Castle Howard is open to the public daily from March 20 to October 31. The grounds are open from 10am, the cafeteria, house, and Costume Galleries from 11am. It closes at 5pm, with last admission to the house and galleries at 4:30pm. Admission is £5 ($9.25) for adults, £2 ($3.70) for children. You can enjoy sandwiches, hot dishes, and good wines in the self-service cafeteria. It lies 15 miles northeast of York, 3 miles off the A64. Reynard Pullman in York (tel. 0904/622992 for reservations) conducts an afternoon tour to Castle Howard on Monday, Wednesday, and Friday, costing £3.50 ($6.45) for the transportation.

HAREWOOD HOUSE & BIRD GARDEN

At the junction of the A61/A659, midway between Leeds and Harrogate, stands **Harewood House,** Harewood, West Yorkshire (tel. 0532/886225), the home of the earl and countess of Harewood, one of England's great 18th-century houses which has always been owned by the Lascelles family. The fine Adam interior has superb ceilings and plasterwork, and furniture made especially for Harewood by Chippendale. There are also important collections of English and Italian paintings and Sèvres and Chinese porcelain.

The gardens designed by Capability Brown include terraces, lakeside and wood-land walks, and a 4½-acre bird garden which contains exotic species from all over the world, including penguins, macaws, flamingos, and snowy owls, as well as a tropical rain-forest exhibit. Other facilities include shops, a restaurant, and a cafeteria. Parking is free, and there is a picnic area, plus an adventure playground for the children. Admission to Harewood costs £2 ($3.70) for adults and £1 ($1.85) for children. The house, bird garden, and adventure playground are open Easter to October daily from 10am to 5pm. The location is 7 miles south of Harrogate; 8 miles north of Leeds on the Leeds/Harrogate Road (junction A61/A659) at Harewood Village; 5 miles from the A1 at Wetherby, and 22 miles west of York. From York, head west along B1224 in the direction of Wetherby and follow the signposts to Harewood from there.

FOUNTAINS ABBEY & STUDLEY ROYAL

 At Fountains, 4 miles southwest of Ripon off the B6265, stands Fountains Abbey and Studley Royal, Fountains (tel. 076586/333), on the banks of the Silver Skell. The abbey was founded by Cistercian monks in 1132 and is the largest monastic ruin in Britain. In 1987, it was awarded world heritage status. The ruins provide the focal point of the 18th-century landscape garden at Studley Royal, one of the few surviving examples of a Georgian green garden. It is known for its water gardens, ornamental temples, follies, and vistas. The garden is bounded at its northern edge by a lake and 400 acres of deer park.

Admission is £2.70 ($5) adults and £1.20 ($2.20) children. A family ticket costs £6.60 ($12.20) for four. The site is open January to March daily 10am to 5pm (or dusk); April to June and September daily 10am to 7pm; July to August daily 10am to 8pm; October daily 10am to 6pm (to dusk); November to December Saturday to Thursday 10am to 5pm (or dusk). It's closed December 24 and 25.

It's best to visit the sight by private car, although it can be reached from York by public transportation. From York, take bus no. 143 leaving from the York Hall Station to Ripon, 23 miles to the northwest (the A59, A1, and B6265 lead to Ripon). From Ripon, take a taxi 4 miles to the southwest, although some prefer to go on foot, as it is a scenic walk.

HAWES

About 65 miles northwest of York on the A684, Hawes is the natural center of Yorkshire Dales National Park. On the Pennine Way, it's England's highest market town and the capital of Wensleydale, which is famous for its cheese. There are rail connections from York taking you to Garsdale, which is 5 miles from Hawes. From Garsdale, bus connections will take you into Hawes.

The **Upper Dales Folk Museum,** Station Yard (the old train station) (tel. 0969/494), traces folk life in the area of the Upper Dales. Peat cutting and cheesemaking, among other occupations, are depicted. The museum hours are March 20 through July and in September Monday to Saturday from 11am–5pm and Sunday from 2 to 5pm; in August, hours are Monday to Saturday and Sunday from 2 to 5pm; in October, it is open daily from noon to 5pm. The museum is closed in winter. Admission is 75p ($1.40).

Hawes is a good center for exploring the Yorkshire Dales National Park, some 700 square miles of water-carved country that have been designated as a national park.

Before you visit England, you can write for information about the park from the Yorkshire & Humberside Tourist Board, 312 Tadcaster Road, York, North Yorkshire YO2 2HF, England (tel. 0904/707961).

Once in Hawes, you can also visit the **National Park Information Centre,** Station yard (tel. 0969/667450). State your interests and the amount of time you have, and the staff will help you plan a trip. The center is open in July and August from 9:30am to 4:30pm and in April to June and September to October from 10am to 4pm.

In the dales you'll find dramatic white limestone crags, roads and fields bordered by drystone walls, fast-running rivers, isolated sheep farms, and clusters of sandstone cottages—all hallmarks of the impressive Yorkshire Dales.

Malhamdale receives more visitors annually than any dale in Yorkshire. Two of the most interesting historic attractions are the 12th-century ruins of Bolton Priory and the 14th-century Castle Bolton, to the north in Wensleydale.

Richmond, the most frequently copied town name in the world, stands at the head of the Dales and like Hawes, makes a good center for touring the surrounding countryside.

Where to Stay at Hawes

COCKETT'S HOTEL, Market Place, Hawes, North Yorkshire DL8 3RD. Tel. 0969667/312. 8 rms (6 with bath or shower). TV TEL
$ Rates (including English breakfast): £25 ($46.25) single without bath; £32 ($59.20) double without bath, £50 ($92.50) double with bath. MC, V. **Parking:** Free.

 You can not only stay at this little gem, but you can also have some of the best food in Hawes. Jackie Bryan and John Oddi are your hosts, and they welcome guests from all over the world who walk under their door, dated from 1668. Each room is individually decorated, and two of them contain four-poster beds. A four-course dinner is served nightly for £14.95 ($27.65). The hotel is in the town center.

ROOKHURST GEORGIAN COUNTRY HOUSE, West End, Gayle, near Hawes, North Yorkshire DL8 3RT. Tel. 0969667/454. 6 rms (5 with bath). MINIBAR TV
$ Rates (including English breakfast): £32 ($59.20) single without bath; £60 ($111) double without bath, £75 ($138.75) double with bath. MC, V. **Parking:** Free.

Mrs. Iris VenDerSteen owns this handsome stone hotel fronting the Pennine Way, located on the outskirts of the village of Gayle, about 5 minutes' walk from Hawes. The bedrooms with views over the surrounding fells are individually furnished, all with unusual or antique beds, including a brass four-poster bed and a large mahogany four-poster bed. The Georgian rooms in part of the house, which was once named "West End" and was originally built in 1734 as a farmhouse, are heavily oak beamed; those in the Victorian wing added in 1869 are larger and elegant. A four-course dinner is served daily in the Mullion Restaurant for £12 ($22.20), coffee included, for residents only. Afternoon cream teas are offered on the patio in good weather.

3. NORTH YORK MOORS NATIONAL PARK

The moors, on the other side of the Vale of York, have a wild beauty all their own, quite different from that of the dales. This rather barren moorland blossoms in summer with purple heather. Bounded on the east by the North Sea, it embraces a 553-square-mile area which England has turned into a national park. For information before you go, especially for good maps, write to the **Yorkshire & Humberside Tourist Board,** 312 Tadcaster Road, York, North Yorkshire, YO2 2HF, England (tel. 0904/707961).

Bounded by the Cleveland and Hambleton hills the moors are dotted with early burial grounds and ancient stone crosses. At Kilburn a white horse can be seen hewn out of the hillside.

Pickering and Northallerton, both market towns, serve as gateways to the moors. The most popular trek is the Lyke Wake Walk a 40-mile hike over bog, heather, and stream from Mount Grace Priory to Ravenscar on the seacoast.

The isolation and the beauty of the landscape attracted the founders of three great abbeys: the Cistercians who established Rievaulx near Helmsley, and Byland Abbey near the village of Wass; and the Benedictines who founded Ampleforth Abbey near Coxwold, one of the most attractive villages in the Moors. Rievaulx and Byland abbeys are in ruins, but Ampleforth still functions as a monastery and well-known Roman Catholic boys' school. Although many of its buildings date from the 19th and 20th century, they do contain earlier artifacts.

Along the eastern boundary of the park North Yorkshire's 45-mile coastline shelters such traditional seaside resorts as Filey, Whitby, and Scarborough, the latter claiming to be the oldest seaside spa in Britain located supposedly on the site of a Roman signaling station. The spa was founded in 1622, when mineral springs with medicinal properties were discovered. In the 19th century, its Grand Hotel, a Victorian structure, was acclaimed as the best in Europe. The Norman castle on big cliffs overlooks the twin bays.

You can drive through the moorland while still based in York, but if you'd like to be closer to the moors, there are many centers where you can base, notably Thirsk (see below).

THIRSK

This old market town in the Vale of Mowbray 24 miles north of York on A19 is on the western fringe of the park. It has a fine parish church, but what makes it such a popular stopover is its association with James Herriot, author of *All Creatures Great and Small*. Mr. Herriot still practices veterinary medicine in Thirsk, and visitors can photograph his office and perhaps get a picture of his partner standing in the door.

WHERE TO STAY

BROOK HOUSE, Ingramgate, Thirsk, North Yorkshire YO7 1DD. Tel. 0845/22240. 3 rms (all with bath). TV

$ Rates (including English breakfast): £25 ($46.25) per person. Discounts available for children. No credit cards. **Parking:** Free.

This large Victorian house is set in 2 acres of land, some of which is filled with flowerbeds, and overlooks the open countryside; however, the Market Square is only a 3-minute walk away. Mrs. Margaret McLauchlan, the owner, is charming and kind, and has even been known to do a batch of washing for guests at no extra cost (but, I can't promise that). She serves a good Yorkshire breakfast, hearty and filling, plus an English tea in the afternoon. Tea-making facilities are also available for the guests, and a spacious and comfortable living room has color TV. The house is centrally heated, and in the guests' drawing room there is an open log fire in cool weather. There is ample parking for cars.

ST. JAMES HOUSE, 36 The Green, Thirsk, North Yorkshire YO7 1AQ. Tel. 0845/22676. 4 rms (2 with bath or shower). TV

$ Rates (including English breakfast): £30 ($55.50) double without bath, £37 ($68.45) double with bath. No credit cards. **Parking:** Free. **Closed:** Nov–Mar.

A lovely, three-story, 18th-century, Georgian, brick house on the village green, it's located near the former maternity home where James Herriot's children were born. The guesthouse, operated by Mrs. Liz Ogleby, is tastefully furnished, with some Regency antiques. (Mr. Ogleby is an antique dealer.) The attractive bedrooms, each a double, have such touches as good bone china to use with the hot-beverage facilities.

---

4. HAWORTH

45 miles W of York; 21 miles W of Leeds

GETTING THERE By Train   To reach Haworth by rail, catch the train from Leeds to Keighley. Leeds has rail connections to York. At Keighley board a privately run train, the Keighley and Worth Valley Railway, for the trip to Haworth. Some five to seven trains per day run between Keighley and Haworth in July and August. From March to June and in September and October, seven trains per day make the trip. For information, call 0535/43629.

By Bus   Yorkshire Rider offers bus service between Hebden Bridge (which has rail links to Leeds and York) and Haworth. Bus no. 500 makes the trip between Hebden Bridge and Haworth June to September only, Sunday to Friday, four times a day or once on Saturday. For information, call 0274/732237.

By Car From York, head west for Leeds along A64. After traversing the Leeds industrial area, continue west along A650 to Keighley, dipping south on B6143 to Haworth.

ESSENTIALS The **area code** is 0535. The **Tourist Information Centre,** 2-4 West Lane in Haworth (tel. 0535/42329), is open April through October daily from 9:30am to 5:30pm, November to March daily from 9:30am to 5pm.

Famous as the home of the Brontë sisters, this village is in West Yorkshire, a county that might easily be overlooked otherwise. On the high moors of the Pennines, it is the most visited literary shrine in England after Stratford-upon-Avon because it was the home of Charlotte, Emily, and Anne Brontë, who all distinguished themselves as novelists. Anne wrote two novels, *The Tenant of Wildfell Hall* and *Agnes Grey*. Charlotte wrote two masterpieces *Jane Eyre* and *Villette* which depicted her experiences as a teacher; *Jane Eyre* enjoyed enormous popular success in its day and is now considered a classic of British fiction. But it is Emily's fierce and tragic *Wuthering Heights* that is best loved; a novel of passion and haunting melancholy, it has come to be appreciated by later generations far more than those for whom she'd written it. Charlotte and Emily are buried in the family vault under the church of St. Michael's, and the parsonage where they lived has been preserved as the **Brontë Parsonage Museum,** Main Street (tel. 0535/42323), which houses their furniture, personal treasures, pictures, books, and manuscripts. It may be visited April to September daily from 11am to 5pm, October to March daily from 11am to 4:30pm. It is closed from January 22 to February 9 and at Christmas. Admission is £2.50 ($4.65) for adults and 50p (95¢) for children.

From Haworth, you can walk to Withens, the "Wuthering Heights" of the novel.

WHERE TO STAY

IN TOWN

FERNCLIFFE, Hebden Rd. Haworth, Keighley, West Yorkshire BD22 8RS. Tel. 0535/643405. 6 rms (all with shower).
$ Rates (including English breakfast): £19.50 ($36.10) single; £36–£39 ($66.60–$72.15) double. V. **Parking:** Free.

✪ Ferncliffe offers one of the most outstanding accommodations in the area; be sure to reserve in advance as far as possible. Modern and comfortable, the hotel and restaurant open onto views of the "Wuthering Heights" countryside. The hosts are gracious and give guests their personal attention, and each bedroom is comfortably and attractively furnished. The hotel also serves good Yorkshire cooking, and evening meals costing £8.75 ($16.20) can be arranged beginning at 7pm, but warn the staff that morning of your intention to eat in as all the food is freshly prepared that day. It's located just outside the village on A6033 road to Hebden Bridge.

MOORFIELD GUEST HOUSE, 80 West Lane, Haworth, Keighley, West Yorkshire BD22 8EN. Tel. 0535/643689. 6 rms (5 with shower). TV
$ Rates (including English breakfast): £15 ($27.75) single without bath; £50 ($92.50) double without bath, £62 ($114.70) double with bath. MC, V. **Parking:** Free.
In a rural setting on the edge of town overlooking the moors, Moorfield is only a 3-minute walk to the center of Haworth and the Brontë Parsonage. The owners of this Victorian house rent well-furnished and comfortable bedrooms. A four-course evening meal can also be arranged.

NEARBY ACCOMMODATIONS

PONDEN HALL, Stanbury, near Keighley, West Yorkshire BD22 0HR. Tel. 0535/644154. 3 rms (1 with bath).

$ Rates (including English breakfast): £13.50 ($25) per person. No credit cards.

About 3 miles from Haworth, this 400-year-old farmhouse, a Brontë landmark, lies about ⅓ mile from the main road between Ponden Reservoir and the moors. The wide, rough track that is a part of the Pennine Way long-distance footpath leads to this Elizabethan farmhouse with traditional hospitality to tourists, children, and pets. The hall was extended in 1801 and is reputedly the model for Thrushcross Grange, Catherine's home after her marriage to Edgar Linton in Emily Brontë's *Wuthering Heights*. Today it provides spacious and homelike farmhouse accommodation. The dining hall has an open fire, traditional flagstone floor, original oak beams, timbered ceilings, and mullioned windows. A home-cooked dinner is offered at £7 ($12.95), and vegetarian and special diets are catered to.

WHERE TO EAT

WEAVER'S RESTAURANT, 15 West Lane. Tel. 43822.
  Cuisine: ENGLISH. **Reservations:** Required. **Directions:** Follow the signs for the Brontë Parsonage Museum.
$ Prices: Appetizers £2–£5 ($3.70–$9.25); main courses £6–£12 ($11.10–$22.20); set lunch or dinner £11.50 ($21.30). AE, DC, MC, V.
  Open: Lunch Nov–Feb Tues–Sun 12:30–1:30pm; dinner (year round) Tues–Sat 7–9:30pm.

Once a group of cottages for weavers, this has been turned into the best restaurant in the Brontë hometown. British to the core, it not only has an inviting and informal atmosphere, but it also serves excellent food made with fresh ingredients. Jane and Colin Rushworth have a great talent in the kitchen; try one of the classics such as Yorkshire pudding with gravy, or, if featured, one of the Gressingham ducks, which are widely praised in Britain for the quality of their meat. For dessert, you might select a Yorkshire cheese or one of the superb homemade desserts. The restaurant is likely to be closed for a certain time each summer for vacation, so call in advance to check.

5. HEXHAM & HADRIAN'S WALL

304 miles N of London; 37 miles E of Carlisle;
21 miles W of Newcastle upon Tyne

GETTING THERE   By Train   Take one of the many daily trains from London's Kings Cross Station to Newcastle upon Tyne. At Newcastle, change trains and take one in the direction of Carlisle. The fifth or sixth (depending on the schedule) stop after Newcastle will be Hexham. Hexham lies 14 miles southeast of Hadrian's Wall.

Visitors interested in the wall rather than in Hexham should get off the Carlisle-bound train at the second stop (Bardon Mill) or at the third stop (Haltwhistle), which lie 4 miles and 2½ miles, respectively, from the wall. At either of these hamlets, take a taxi on to whichever part of the wall you care to visit. Taxis line up freely at the railway station in Hexham, less frequently at the hamlets. If you get off in one of the above-mentioned hamlets and don't see a taxi, call 0434/344272 for the local taxis, and they will come to get you. Many visitors request their taxi to return at a prearranged time to pick them up after their excursion on the windy ridges near the mall.

By Bus   Bus passengers headed for Hexham from both York and London will need to transfer at Newcastle upon Tyne onto a bus which heads for Carlisle every hour or so throughout the day. The bus company is the Northumbria Bus Lines (tel. 91/261-6077). The bus follows the same route as the above-mentioned train line, stopping in the hamlets mentioned above (and also in Hexham).

By Car   From Newcastle upon Tyne, head west along A69, until you see the cutoff south to Hexham.

ESSENTIALS The **area code** is 0434. The **Tourist Information Centre** is at The Manor Office, Hallgate (tel. 0434/605225).

Above the Tyne River, this historic old market town has narrow streets, an old market square, a fine abbey church, and a moot hall. It makes a good base for exploring Hadrian's Wall (see below) and the Roman supply base of Corstopitum at Corbridge-on-Tyne, the ancient capital of Northumberland. The tourist office (see above), has masses of information on the wall for walkers, drivers, campers, and picnickers.

The **Abbey Church of St. Wilfrid** is full of ancient relics. The Saxon font, the misericord carvings on the choir stalls, Acca's Cross, and St. Wilfrid's chair are well worth seeing.

WHERE TO STAY

BEAUMONT HOTEL, Beaumont St., Hexham, Northumberland NE46 3LT. Tel. 0434/602331. Fax 0434/602331. 23 rms (all with bath or shower). TV TEL
$ Rates (including English breakfast): £42 ($77.70) single; £66 ($122.20) double. AE, DC, MC, V.
In the town center overlooking the abbey and a park, the Beaumont offers excellent facilities, including two comfortable bars, an elevator, and a delightful restaurant. Martin and Linda Owens have completely refurbished their bedrooms. Dinner from an extensive à la carte menu costs from £12 ($22.20).

ROYAL HOTEL, Priestpopple, Hexham, Northumberland NE46 1PQ. Tel. 0434/602270. 24 rms (all with bath). TV TEL
$ Rates (including English breakfast): £38 ($70.30) single; £58 ($107.30) double. AE, DC, MC, V. **Parking:** Free.
The Royal Hotel stands just off the market place with its "shambles" and moot hall. Two buildings are linked together by a central square tower and dome, and the car park is entered through the original coaching arch. The bedrooms are comfortable and well appointed, and all have hot-beverage facilities. Dinner in the restaurant costs from £12 ($22.20), and a salad buffet is presented each day in the lounge bar.

WEST CLOSE HOUSE, Hextol Terrace, Hexham, Northumberland NE46 2AD. Tel. 0434/603307. 4 rms (none with bath). **Directions:** Take first left off the Allendale road, the B6305.
$ Rates (including English or continental breakfast): £15–£16 ($27.75–$29.60) single; £32–£34 ($59.20–$62.90) double. No credit cards. **Parking:** Free.
A detached 1920s residence tastefully refurbished, this is set in prize-winning secluded gardens in a quiet cul-de-sac with private parking, ½ mile from Hexham. Patricia Graham-Tomlinson welcomes guests into relaxed surroundings, where comfortable accommodations consist of bedrooms with washbasins, heating, and hot-beverage facilities. There's a bathroom with a separate shower, and guests can watch color TV in the dining room/lounge. Packed lunches and light suppers are available on order.

HADRIAN'S WALL & ITS FORTRESSES

This wall, which extends for 73 miles across the north of England, from the North Sea to the Irish Sea, is particularly interesting for a stretch of 10 miles west of Housesteads, which lies 2¾ miles northeast of Bardon Mill on the B6318. Only the lower courses of the wall are preserved intact; the rest were reconstructed in the 19th century using the original stones. From the wall, there are incomparable views north to the Cheviot Hills along the Scottish border and south to the Durham moors.

The wall was built after the visit of the Emperor Hadrian in A.D. 122 who was inspecting far frontiers of the Roman Empire and wished to construct a dramatic line between the empire and the barbarians. Legionnaires were ordered to build a wall across the width of the island of Britain, stretching for 73½ miles, beginning at the North Sea and ending at the Irish Sea.

The wall is a major Roman attraction in Europe ranking with Rome's Colosseum. The western end can be reached from Carlisle, which also has a good museum of Roman artifacts; the eastern end can be reached from Newcastle upon Tyne (where some remains can be seen on the city outskirts; there's also a good museum at the university).

Along the wall are several Roman forts. The one at Housesteads was built about A.D. 130 to house an infantry of 1,000 men. The fort was called Vercovicium. Admission is £1.60 ($2.95) for adults, 70p ($1.30) for children. The site is open April through September daily from 10am to 6pm and October through March daily from 10am to 4pm. For information call 0434/344363.

Just west of Housesteads, Vindolanda (tel. 0434/344277) is another very well-preserved fort south of the wall. It lies on a minor road 1¼ miles southeast of Twice Brewed off B6318. There is also an excavated civilian settlement outside the fort with an interesting museum of artifacts of everyday Roman life. Admission is £2 ($3.70) for adults, £1 ($1.85) for children. It's open daily from 10am to 5pm (or dusk).

Near Vindolanda at the garrison fort at Carvoran, near the village of Greenhead, the **Roman Army Museum** (tel. 06972/485) traces the growth and influence of Rome from its early beginnings to the development and expansion of the empire, with special emphasis on the role of the Roman army and the garrisons of Hadrian's Wall. A barracks room shows basic army living conditions. Realistic life-size figures make this a striking visual museum experience. Admission is £1.50 ($2.80) for adults; £1.10 ($2.05) for children. It is open April to September daily from 10am to 5:30pm and from March to October daily from 10am to 5pm. The location is at the junction of A69 and B6318, 18 miles west of Hexham.

Within easy walking distance of the Roman Army Museum lies one of the most imposing and high-standing sections of Hadrian's Wall, Walltown Crags, where the height of the wall and magnificent views to north and south are impressive.

VISITING THE WALL   From July 20 to September 1, the town council of Hexham maintains four buses which depart daily from a point near the railway station in Hexham at 10am, noon, 2pm, and 4pm. They visit every important site along the wall, then turn around in the village of Haltwhistle and return to Hexham. The cost is £4 ($7.40) for an all-day ticket, which is by far the most popular. Many visitors take one bus out, and return on the subsequent bus 2, 4, or 6 hours later. Also, very rarely, a well-interested local scholar will lead Sunday walking tours of the wall, lasting 2 hours, and arrangeable through the Hexham Tourist Information Centre (see above).

INDEX

GENERAL INFORMATION

DESTINATIONS

KEY TO ABBREVIATIONS: *W* = Worth the Extra Bucks; *$* = Special Savings; * = Author's Favorite

NOW, SAVE MONEY ON ALL YOUR TRAVELS!
Join Frommer's™ Dollarwise® Travel Club

Saving money while traveling is never easy, which is why the **Dollarwise Travel Club** was formed 32 years ago to provide cost-cutting travel strategies, up-to-date travel information, and a sense of community for value-conscious travelers from all over the world.

In keeping with the money-saving concept, the annual membership fee is low—$20 for U.S. residents and $25 for residents of Canada, Mexico, and other countries—and is immediately exceeded by the value of your benefits, which include:

1. Any TWO books listed on the following pages;
2. Plus any ONE Frommer's City Guide;
3. A subscription to our quarterly newspaper, *The Dollarwise Traveler;*
4. A membership card that entitles you to purchase through the Club all Frommer's publications for 33% to 40% off their retail price.

The eight-page *Dollarwise Traveler* tells you about the latest developments in good-value travel worldwide and includes the following columns: **Hospitality Exchange** (for those offering and seeking hospitality in cities all over the world); and **Share-a-Trip** (for those looking for travel companions to share costs).

Aside from the various Frommer's Guides, the Gault Millau Guides, and the Real Guides you can also choose from our Special Editions, which include such titles as *Caribbean Hideaways* (the 100 most romantic places to stay in the Islands); and *Marilyn Wood's Wonderful Weekends* (a selection of the best mini-vacations within a 200-mile radius of New York City).

To join this Club, send the appropriate membership fee with your name and address to: Frommer's Dollarwise Travel Club, 15 Columbus Circle, New York, NY 10023. Remember to specify which single city guide and which two other guides you wish to receive in your initial package of member's benefits. Or tear out the pages, check off your choices, and send them to us with your membership fee.

FROMMER BOOKS
PRENTICE HALL TRAVEL   Date_____
15 COLUMBUS CIRCLE
NEW YORK, NY 10023

Friends: Please send me the books checked below.

FROMMER'S™ COMPREHENSIVE GUIDES
(Guides listing facilities from budget to deluxe, with emphasis on the medium-priced)

☐ Alaska $14.95	☐ Italy. $19.00
☐ Australia $14.95	☐ Japan & Hong Kong $17.00
☐ Austria & Hungary $14.95	☐ Morocco $18.00
☐ Belgium, Holland & Luxembourg $14.95	☐ Nepal. $18.00
☐ Bermuda & The Bahamas. $17.00	☐ New England. $17.00
☐ Brazil $14.95	☐ New Mexico $13.95
☐ California $18.00	☐ New York State $19.00
☐ Canada $16.00	☐ Northwest $16.95
☐ Caribbean. $17.00	☐ Puerta Vallarta (avail. Feb. '92). $14.00
☐ Carolinas & Georgia $17.00	☐ Portugal, Madeira & the Azores $14.95
☐ Colorado (avail. Jan '92) $14.00	☐ Scandinavia $18.95
☐ Cruises (incl. Alaska, Carib, Mex, Hawaii,	☐ Scotland (avail. Feb. '92) $17.00
Panama, Canada & US) $16.00	☐ South Pacific $20.00
☐ Delaware, Maryland, Pennsylvania &	☐ Southeast Asia $14.95
the New Jersey Shore (avail. Jan. '92) . .$19.00	☐ Switzerland & Liechtenstein $19.00
☐ Egypt. $14.95	☐ Thailand. $20.00
☐ England $17.00	☐ Virginia (avail. Feb. '92). $14.00
☐ Florida $17.00	☐ Virgin Islands $13.00
☐ France $15.95	☐ USA. $16.95
☐ Germany $18.00	

0891492

FROMMER'S CITY GUIDES

(Pocket-size guides to sightseeing and tourist accommodations and facilities in all price ranges)

☐ Amsterdam/Holland $8.95	☐ Minneapolis/St. Paul $8.95
☐ Athens. $8.95	☐ Montréal/Québec City. $8.95
☐ Atlanta $8.95	☐ New Orleans. $8.95
☐ Atlantic City/Cape May $8.95	☐ New York $12.00
☐ Bangkok. $12.00	☐ Orlando $12.00
☐ Barcelona. $12.00	☐ Paris $8.95
☐ Belgium $7.95	☐ Philadelphia $11.00
☐ Berlin. $10.00	☐ Rio $8.95
☐ Boston. $8.95	☐ Rome. $8.95
☐ Cancún/Cozumel/Yucatán. $8.95	☐ Salt Lake City $8.95
☐ Chicago. $9.95	☐ San Diego. $8.95
☐ Denver/Boulder/Colorado Springs. . . .$8.95	☐ San Francisco $12.00
☐ Dublin/Ireland. $10.00	☐ Santa Fe/Taos/Albuquerque. $10.95
☐ Hawaii $12.00	☐ Seattle/Portland $12.00
☐ Hong Kong. $7.95	☐ St. Louis/Kansas City. $9.95
☐ Las Vegas. $8.95	☐ Sydney. $8.95
☐ Lisbon/Madrid/Costa del Sol $8.95	☐ Tampa/St. Petersburg $8.95
☐ London $12.00	☐ Tokyo. $8.95
☐ Los Angeles $8.95	☐ Toronto $8.95
☐ Mexico City/Acapulco. $8.95	☐ Vancouver/Victoria. $7.95
☐ Miami $8.95	☐ Washington, D.C. $12.00

FROMMER'S $-A-DAY® GUIDES

(Guides to low-cost tourist accommodations and facilities)

☐ Australia on $40 a Day $13.95	☐ Israel on $40 a Day. $13.95
☐ Costa Rica, Guatemala & Belize	☐ Mexico on $45 a Day $18.00
on $35 a Day. $15.95	☐ New York on $65 a Day. $15.00
☐ Eastern Europe on $25 a Day $16.95	☐ New Zealand on $45 a Day $16.00
☐ England on $50 a Day. $17.00	☐ Scotland & Wales on $40 a Day $18.00
☐ Europe on $45 a Day $19.00	☐ South America on $40 a Day $15.95
☐ Greece on $35 a Day $14.95	☐ Spain on $50 a Day $15.95
☐ Hawaii on $70 a Day. $18.00	☐ Turkey on $40 a Day. $22.00
☐ India on $40 a Day. $20.00	☐ Washington, D.C., on $45 a Day. $17.00
☐ Ireland on $40 a Day. $17.00	

FROMMER'S CITY $-A-DAY GUIDES

☐ Berlin on $40 a Day $12.00	☐ Madrid on $50 a Day (avail. Jan '92) . . .$13.00
☐ Copenhagen on $50 a Day $12.00	☐ Paris on $45 a Day $12.00
☐ London on $45 a Day $12.00	☐ Stockholm on $50 a Day (avail. Dec. '91)$13.00

FROMMER'S FAMILY GUIDES

☐ California with Kids $16.95	☐ San Francisco with Kids. $17.00
☐ Los Angeles with Kids $17.00	☐ Washington, D.C., with Kids (avail. Jan
☐ New York City with Kids (avail. Jan '92) $18.00	'92). $17.00

SPECIAL EDITIONS

☐ Beat the High Cost of Travel. $6.95	☐ Marilyn Wood's Wonderful Weekends
☐ Bed & Breakfast—N. America $14.95	(CT, DE, MA, NH, NJ, NY, PA, RI, VT) . .$11.95
☐ Caribbean Hideaways. $16.00	☐ Motorist's Phrase Book (Fr/Ger/Sp) . . .$4.95
☐ Honeymoon Destinations (US, Mex &	☐ The New World of Travel (annual by
Carib). $14.95	Arthur Frommer for savvy travelers) . . .$16.95

(TURN PAGE FOR ADDITONAL BOOKS AND ORDER FORM)

0891492

| ☐ Paris Rendez-Vous . . . .$10.95 | ☐ Travel Diary and Record Book . . . .$5.95 |
| ☐ Swap and Go (Home Exchanging) . . . . .$10.95 | ☐ Where to Stay USA (from $3 to $30 a night) . . . .$13.95 |

FROMMER'S TOURING GUIDES

(Color illustrated guides that include walking tours, cultural and historic sites, and practical information)

☐ Amsterdam $10.95	☐ New York $10.95
☐ Australia $12.95	☐ Paris $8.95
☐ Brazil $10.95	☐ Rome $10.95
☐ Egypt $8.95	☐ Scotland $9.95
☐ Florence $8.95	☐ Thailand $12.95
☐ Hong Kong $10.95	☐ Turkey $10.95
☐ London $12.95	☐ Venice $8.95

GAULT MILLAU

(The only guides that distinguish the truly superlative from the merely overrated)

☐ The Best of Chicago $15.95	☐ The Best of Los Angeles $16.95
☐ The Best of Florida $17.00	☐ The Best of New England $15.95
☐ The Best of France $16.95	☐ The Best of New Orleans $16.95
☐ The Best of Germany $18.00	☐ The Best of New York $16.95
☐ The Best of Hawaii $16.95	☐ The Best of Paris $16.95
☐ The Best of Hong Kong $16.95	☐ The Best of San Francisco $16.95
☐ The Best of Italy $16.95	☐ The Best of Thailand $17.95
☐ The Best of London $16.95	☐ The Best of Toronto $17.00

☐ The Best of Washington, D.C. $16.95

THE REAL GUIDES

(Opinionated, politically aware guides for youthful budget-minded travelers)

☐ Amsterdam $9.95	☐ Mexico $11.95
☐ Berlin $11.95	☐ Morocco $12.95
☐ Brazil $13.95	☐ New York $9.95
☐ California & the West Coast $11.95	☐ Paris $9.95
☐ Czechoslovakia $13.95	☐ Peru $12.95
☐ France $12.95	☐ Poland $13.95
☐ Germany $13.95	☐ Portugal $10.95
☐ Greece $13.95	☐ San Francisco $11.95
☐ Guatemala $13.95	☐ Scandinavia $14.95
☐ Hong Kong $11.95	☐ Spain $12.95
☐ Hungary $12.95	☐ Turkey $12.95
☐ Ireland $12.95	☐ Venice $11.95
☐ Italy $13.95	☐ Women Travel $12.95
☐ Kenya $12.95	☐ Yugoslavia $12.95

ORDER NOW!

In U.S. include $2 shipping UPS for 1st book; $1 ea. add'l book. Outside U.S. $3 and $1, respectively.

Allow four to six weeks for delivery in U.S., longer outside U.S. We discourage rush order service, but orders arriving with shipping fees plus a $15 surcharge will be handled as rush orders.

Enclosed is my check or money order for $_____

NAME _____

ADDRESS _____

CITY _____ STATE _____ ZIP _____

0891492